Dictionary Catalog of the

G. ROBERT VINCENT
VOICE LIBRARY

at Michigan State University

EAST LANSING, MICHIGAN

Editors:
Leonard E. Cluley
Pamela N. Engelbrecht

G. K. HALL & CO., 70 LINCOLN STREET, BOSTON, MASS.
1975

ISBN 0-8161-1149-9

For Richard E. Chapin, who conceived of this book,
and the Cataloging Department, who gave it reality.

PREFACE

The *Dictionary Catalog of the G. Robert Vincent Voice Library at Michigan State University* represents a unique collection of taped recordings of the voices of famous people. Originally the private library of G. Robert Vincent, the collection particularly emphasizes the recorded voices of well-known personalities in politics, the arts, academia, show business and popular culture.

Recordings document the people and events of the twentieth century with strengths in the history of radio, the First and Second World Wars, American isolationism, the Nuremburg trials, the United Nations and American politics up to and including the Watergate affair.

The collection ranges from the recorded voices of Theodore Roosevelt, Jane Addams, William Jennings Bryan and Florence Nightingale, to those of Sarah Bernhardt, Admiral Peary, Kaiser Wilhelm, General Pershing, P. T. Barnum, Ellen Terry, Rudolph Valentino, Woodrow Wilson and Mahatma Gandhi. In a recording made in 1890, the only surviving trumpeter of the Charge of the Light Brigade repeats the "Charge" using a bugle from the Battle of Waterloo loaned by the British Museum for the occasion.

These acquisitions were primarily the labor of G. Robert Vincent, who worked in Edison's laboratory, established his own sound and recording studio in the 1920s, served in the Armed Forces Radio Service, operated the multilingual interpreting system at the Nuremburg War Crimes Trials and was Chief Sound and Recording officer for the United Nations. The Library, from which Mr. Vincent retired in 1973, is in a constant state of growth, taking voices from broadcasts, live presentations and interviews, receiving donations and making trades of tapes with other collections.

The Voice Library has the capacity to reproduce any of its holdings onto either reels or cassettes, and will make copies for educational purposes of all materials not under copyright or other limitations. The Library is a service of Michigan State University which is its sole source of support. Specific inquiries should be addressed to The Voice Library, Library Building, Michigan State University, East Lansing, Michigan, 48824; or may be telephoned to (517) 355-5122.

MAURICE A. CRANE
Director
PAMELA N. ENGELBRECHT
Librarian

CATALOGING of the COLLECTION

Cataloging of the material for this volume was based largely on the information provided by G. Robert Vincent along with the original collection presented to Michigan State University Library. The operating premise is that a speaker on a tape equates with an author of a book.

Miss Mary Black edited Mr. Vincent's copy to make it conform to Michigan State University Libraries' system. Additional added entries and subject headings were supplied by Pamela Engelbrecht and Leonard Cluley. New material added to the collection subsequent to the retirement of Mr. Vincent, including the more than 400 entries for the Michael Whorf Kaleidoscope series, was cataloged by Leonard Cluley.

The catalog is arranged in dictionary form: entry, added entry, subject, title. The major exception to the dictionary form is that for any given speaker items are arranged in chronological order, paralleling the speaker's career.

As many cross references to the speakers have been provided as the size of this book allows.

Voice Lib.
M1726　Aaron, Hank, 1934–
bd.3　　　Interviewed on Hank Aaron Day in New York
City, by Curt Gowdy, Joe Garagiola, Tom
Brokaw, and Gene Shalitt.　NBC, June 18,
1974.
　　　　10 min.　phonotape (1 r.　7 1/2 i.p.s.)

　　　　1. Aaron, Hank, 1934–　　2. Baseball.
I. Gowdy, Curt. II. Garagiola, Joe.
III. Brokaw, Tom.　IV. Shalitt, Gene.

ABORTION
Voice Lib.
M1686　Wald, George
　　　Address at Michigan State University.
WKAR, March 4, 1970.
　　　50 min.　phonotape (1 r.　7 1/2 i.p.s.)

　　　1. Science - Addresses, essays, lectures.
2. Abortion.

Voice Lib.
M760　Aberbach, Jean
bd.7　　　Excerpt from "What All the Screaming's
About" (Program 1); the real reason for the
success of Elvis Presley and the Beatles.
Westinghouse Broadcasting Corporation, 1964.
　　　1 min.　phonotape (1 r.　7 1/2 i.p.s.)
(The music goes round and round)

　　　1. Music, Popular (Songs, etc.) - U.S.
2. Presley, Elvis Aron, 1955–　3. The
Beatles.　I. Title: What all the screaming's
about. II. Series.

C1
S74　Whorf, Michael, 1933–
　　　Abracadabra.
　　　1 tape cassette.　(The visual sounds of
Mike Whorf.　Social, S74)
　　　Originally presented on his radio program, Kaleidoscope,
WJR, Detroit.
　　　Duration: 37 min.
　　　Magic! Throughout civilization magic has brought men's
curiosity to a head. Every culture has had its superstitions, its
sorcerers. Throughout mankind's history magic has been studied,
has been practiced.
　　　1. Magic.　I. Title.

Voice Lib.
M760　Aberbach, Jean
bd.10　　　Excerpt from "The big beat" (Program 2);
comments on decline in band business after
World War II; coming to popularity of Negro
blues records.　Westinghouse Broadcasting
Corporation, 1964.
　　　1 min., 10 sec.　phonotape (1 r.
7 1/2 i.p.s.)　(The music goes round and
round)
　　　1. Blues (Songs, etc.) - U.S.　I. Title:
The big beat.　II. Series.

Voice Lib.
M1619　Stone, Chuck
bd.2　　　Perspectives in Black, with Roz Abrahms,
Cheri Mazingo, and J. Markisha Johnson.
WKAR, 1974.
　　　27 min.　phonotape (1 r.　7 1/2 i.p.s.)

　　　1. Race discrimination - U.S.　2. Watergate
Affair, 1972–　I. Abrahms, Roz.
II. Mazingo, Cheri.　III. Johnson, J.
Markisha.

Voice Lib.
M743　Abernathy, Ralph David, 1926–
　　　Civil rights march on Montgomery, Alabama.
Announcer's description of scene as
marchers arrive in Montgomery; entertainment by Harry Belafonte and others; A.F.L.
speaker; Dr. Ralph Abernathy presiding.
CBS, March 25, 1965.
　　　38 min.　phonotape (1 r.　7 1/2 i.p.s.)

　　　1. Negroes - Civil rights.　I. Belafonte,
Harold, 1927–　II. Abernathy, Ralph
David, 1926–

C1
R25　Whorf, Michael, 1933–
　　　The accusative - John Calvin.
　　　1 tape cassette.　(The visual sounds of
Mike Whorf.　Religion, R25)

　　　Originally presented on his radio program, Kaleidoscope,
WJR, Detroit.
　　　Duration: 30 min.
　　　Born of an affluent family in France, John Calvin turned from the
study of law to the scriptures as his religious convictions deepened.
His work and his life illustrate the burning fires of reformation which
raged through Europe.

　　　1. Calvin, Jean, 1509-1564.　I. Title.

Voice Lib.
M1687　Abernathy, Ralph David, 1926–
　　　Address at Michigan State University.
WKAR, 1972.
　　　50 min.　phonotape (1 r.　7 1/2 i.p.s.)

　　　1. Negroes.　2. U.S. - Social conditions.

Voice Lib.
M854　Acheson, Dean Gooderham, 1893–
bd.1　　　Address from Washington, D.C. speaking
on various topics: conditions in European
and other countries at end of World War II;
U.S. aid to foreign countries; explanation
of U.N.R.R.A. and eligibility of countries
for relief.　NBC, December 8, 1946.
　　　1 reel (7 in.)　7 1/2 in. per sec.
phonotape.

Voice Lib.
353 Acheson, Dean Gooderham, 1893-1971
bd.19 Russia and the bomb, discussed by various
       personalities. NBC, September 25, 1949.
       1 reel (7 in.) 7 1/2 in. per sec.
       phonotape.

       Participants: Harrison Brown, Harold Urey,
       Samuel Allison, Thornton Hugness, Brien McMahon,
       Paul Douglas, John Foster Dulles, Leslie Groves,
       Winston Churchill, Dean Acheson, James Fleming.

       I. Brown, Harrison Scott, 1917-   II.
       Urey, Harold Clayton, 1893-   III. Allison,
                           (Continued on next card)

Voice Lib.
M1057 ACTING
bd.1 Forbes-Robertson, Sir Johnston, 1854-1937.
       Discussing Shakespearean acting and
       narrating some famous excerpts of his
       plays. HMV, 1931.
       1 reel (7 in.) 7 1/2 i.p.s.   phonotape.

       1. Acting.

Voice Lib.
353 Acheson, Dean Gooderham, 1893-1971.
bd.19 Russia and the bomb... 1949. (Card 2)

       Samuel King, 1900-   IV. Hugness, Thornton.
       V. McMahon, James O'Brien, 1903-1952. VI.
       Douglas, Paul Howard, 1892-   VII. Dulles,
       John Foster, 1888-1959. VIII. Groves, Leslie
       R   1896-1970. IX. Churchill, Winston
       Leonard Spencer, 1874-1965. X. Acheson, Dean
       Gooderham, 1893-1971. XI. Fleming, James,
       1915-

ACTING AS A PROFESSION
Voice Lib.
M1280 Olivier, Sir Laurence Kerr, 1907-
       A conversation at Expo 67, Montreal, with
       Sir Laurence Olivier discussing the National
       Theatre of Great Britain, his interpretation
       of Othello and of the techniques of acting.
       NET, July 30, 1967.
       1 reel (7 in.) 7 1/2 in. per sec.
       phonotape.

Voice Lib.
353 Acheson, Dean Gooderham, 1893-1971.
bd.1 Outbreak of the Korean conflict; events
       in State Department on the day the conflict
       began, action of Pres. Truman, U.S. military
       action. NBC, July, 1950.
       1 reel (7 in.) 7 1/2 in. per sec.
       phonotape.

       Original disc off-speed.

       1. Korean War, 1950-1953

C1
FA22 ADAMS, BROOKS, 1848-1927
       Whorf, Michael, 1933-
         Brooks Adams.
         1 tape cassette. (The visual sounds of
       Mike Whorf. The forgotten America, FA22)

         Originally presented on his radio program, Kaleidoscope,
       WJR, Detroit.
         Duration: 12 min., 47 sec.
         A philosopher of history, he stood alone preaching simplicity,
       responsibility, honor, and service.

         I. Adams, Brooks, 1848-1927. I. Title.

"Acres of Diamonds"
Voice Lib.
M757 Conwell, Russell Herman, 1843-1925.
bd.1 "Acres of Diamonds"; a lecture by Dr. Conwell.
       Rodeheaver Record Co., 1916.
       1 reel (7 in.) 7 1/2 in. per sec.
       phonotape.

       I. Title.

C1
FA3 ADAMS, CHARLES FRANCIS, 1835-1915
       Whorf, Michael, 1933-
         Charles A. Adams. [sic]
         1 tape cassette. (The visual sounds of
       Mike Whorf. The forgotten American, FA3)

         Originally presented on his radio program, Kaleidoscope,
       WJR, Detroit.
         Duration: 11 min., 30 sec.
         Scion of a famous family, Adams was appointed by Lincoln
       as minister to England. His actions there help to prevent England
       from recognizing the Confederacy.

         I. Adams, Charles Francis, 1835-1915. I. Title.

ACTING
Voice Lib.
352 Carradine, John, 1906-
bd.6 On why actors and actresses attempt to
       succeed on the American stage. NBC, 1949.
       1 reel (7 in.) 7 1/2 in. per sec.
       phonotape.

Adams, Franklin Pierce, 1881-1960
Voice Lib.
M932 Information, please (radio program)
       Panel of experts questioned by Clifton
       Fadiman; panel includes Christopher Morley,
       John Kieran, Franklin P. Adams, Col. Eagan.
       Lloyd Grosse, 1943.
       1 reel (7 in.) 7 1/2 in. per sec.
       phonotape.

       I. Fadiman, Clifton, 1904-   II. Morley,
       Christopher Darlington, 1890-   III. Kieran,
       John, 1892-   IV. Adams, Franklin Pierce,
       1881-1960. V. Eagan, Col.

Adams, John G

Voice Lib.
M1022   U.S. Congress. Senate. Committee on Government Operations.
bd.1   Permanent Subcommittee on Investigations.
             Proceedings of the [8 th session] of Senate Army-McCarthy
         hearings, May 3, 1954. Participants: Secretary of the Army
         Stevens and Senator McCarthy discussing the case of Major
         Peress; controversy between Army counsel Adams and
         McCarthy; McCarthy questioning creditability of Secretary
         Stevens. WJR, May 3, 1954.
             1 reel (7 in.) 7 1/2 in. per sec. phonotape.

             L. McCarthy-Army controversy, 1954. L. Stevens, Robert
         Ten Broeck, 1899-   II. McCarthy, Joseph Raymond, 1909-
         1957. III. Adams, John G

Adams, Rich

Voice Lib.
M1744   Allende Gossens, Salvador, 1908-1973.
bd.4   Interview with John Wallach. WKAR,
         August, 1973.
             2 min., 40 sec. phonotape (1 r.   7 1/2
         i.p.s.)

             Wallach in turn was interviewed by Rich Adams.

             1. Chile - Pol & govt. 2. Socialism in
         Chile. 3. Allende Gossens, Salvador, 1908-
         1973. I. Wallach, John. II. Adams, Rich.

Adams, John G
Voice Lib.
M1296   U.S. Congress. Senate. Committee on Government Operations.
bd.2   Permanent Subcommittee on Investigations.
             Proceedings of the 15th session of Senate Army-McCarthy
         hearings, Part I, May 12, 1954. Army counsel Adams describes
         resentment of McCarthy counsel Roy Cohn at being restricted
         in certain areas at Ft. Monmouth, N.J. Also, complaints by
         Adams at being abused by Cohn regarding Private David Schine.
         CBS-TV, May 12, 1954.
             1 reel (7 in.) 7 1/2 in. per sec. phonotape.

             L. McCarthy-Army controversy, 1954. L. Adams, John G

Voice Lib.
209   Adams, Sherman, 1899-
bd.3   Speech announcing resignation as assistant
         to President. Source (?), September 22,
         1958.
             1 reel (7 in.)   7 1/2 in. per sec.
         phonotape.

Adams, John G
Voice Lib.
M1299   U.S. Congress. Senate. Committee on Government Operations.
bd.2   Permanent Subcommittee on Investigations.
             Proceedings of the 15th session of Senate Army-McCarthy
         hearings, Part II, May 12, 1954. Army Counsel Adams
         describes luncheon with McCarthy, Cohn and himself; further
         abuse and pressure to station Private David Schine; Cohn's
         threat, "We'll wreck the army if Schine is sent overseas".
         CBS-TV, May 12, 1954.
             1 reel (7 in.) 7 1/2 in. per sec. phonotape.

             L. McCarthy-Army controversy, 1954. L. Adams, John G

Voice Lib.
M1723   Adams, Walter, 1922-
bd.1   Speech at Martin Luther King Memorial
         Service at Michigan State University.
         WKAR, April 4, 1969.
             10 min. phonotape (1 r.   7 1/2 i.p.s.)

             1. King, Martin Luther, 1929-1968.

Voice Lib. Adams, John G
M1319   U.S. Congress. Senate. Committee on Government Operations.
             Permanent Subcommittee on Investigations.
             Proceedings of the 16th session of Senate Army-McCarthy
         hearings, May 13, 1954. Ray Jenkins questioning John Adams
         about actions of Sec. Stevens. Was Sec. Stevens afraid to ship
         Private Schine overseas due to pressure by Roy Cohn and Sen.
         McCarthy? Was discussion of Mr. Adams private law practice?
         CBS-TV, May 13, 1954.
             1 reel (7 in.) 7 1/2 in. per sec. phonotape.

             L. McCarthy-Army controversy, 1954. L. Jenkins, Ray
         Howard, 1897-   II. Adams, John G

Adams, Walter, 1922-
Voice Lib.
M1380   Plimpton, Calvin H
bd.1   Commencement address at Michigan State
         University on "Musings about the contemporary
         college scene". Introduced by Acting President
         Walter Adams. On-campus recording, June 8,
         1969.
             1 reel (7 in.)   7 1/2 in. per sec.
         phonotape.

             I. Adams, Walter, 1922-

Voice Lib. Adams, John G
M1320   U.S. Congress. Senate. Committee on Government Operations.
             Permanent Subcommittee on Investigations.
             Proceedings of the 17th session of Senate Army-McCarthy
         hearings, May 14, 1954. Sen. Mundt questioning Mr. Adams
         about high-level meeting dealing with United Nations. Exchanges
         between Senator Mundt and Army Counsel Welch. Senator
         McCarthy examining Sen. Dirksen. Discussion of purgery charges
         against Carr. Cohn and Adams speak about private dinner party.
         CBS TV, May 14, 1954.
             1 reel (7 in.) 7 1/2 in. per sec. phonotape.

             L. McCarthy-Army controversy, 1954. I. Mundt, Karl Earl,
         1900-   II. Welch, Joseph Nye, 1890-1960. III. McCarthy,
         Joseph Raymond, 1909-1957. IV. Dirksen, Everett McKinley, 1896-
         1969. V. Cohn, Roy M   1927-   VI. Adams, John G

Voice Lib.
540   Addams, Jane, 1860-1935.
bd.20   Signatures obtained from public on
         disarmament. Fox Movietone, 1932.
             1 reel (7 in.) 7 1/2 in. per sec.
         phonotape.

             1. Disarmament.

Voice Lib.
M1065   Addams, Jane, 1860-1935.
bd.2   Excerpt of remarks at World Conference on
Disarmament, regarding women's fight for
universal disarmament. Fox Movietone,
1933.
     1 reel (7 in.)   7 1/2 in. per sec.
phonotape.

     1. Disarmament.

Voice Lib.
M714   Adenauer, Konrad, 1876-1967.
bd.4   Interview with West German Chancellor
pertaining to origin of Nazi regime,
Rhineland occupation, Hitler, etc., by
Daniel Schorr. CBS.
     5 min., 42 sec.   phonotape (1 r.
7 1/2 i.p.s.)

     I. Schorr, Daniel Louis, 1916-

Voice Lib.
M350   Adenauer, Konrad, 1876-1967.
bd.1   Tribute to Eisenhower on assuming the
Presidency. CBS, January, 1953.
     1 reel (7 in.)   7 1/2 i.p.s.   phonotape.

     1. Eisenhower, Dwight David, Pres. U.S.,
1890-1969.

C1
H36   The admiral - John Paul Jones
Whorf, Michael, 1933-
     The admiral - John Paul Jones.
     1 tape cassette. (The visual sounds of
Mike Whorf. History and heritage, H36)
     Originally presented on his radio program, Kaleidoscope,
WJR, Detroit.
     Duration 38 min., 30 sec.
     He was a revolutionary - from his trials and hardships as a
young Scotsman to his days as the admiral of a brave, young,
inexperienced navy.

     I. Jones, John Paul, 1747-1792. I. Title.

C1
.PWM13   The adolescent years
Whorf, Michael, 1933-
     The adolescent years.
     1 tape cassette. (The visual sounds of
Mike Whorf. Panorama; a world of music, PWM-13)
     Originally presented on his radio program, Kaleidoscope,
WJR, Detroit.
     Duration: 23 min.
     A discussion with examples of the music of the gay
nineties.

     I. Music, Popular (Songs, etc.) - U.S. I. Title.

C1
S20   The adolescent years
Whorf, Michael, 1933-
     The adolescent years.
     1 tape cassette. (The visual sounds of
Mike Whorf. Social, S20)
     Originally presented on his radio program, Kaleidoscope,
WJR, Detroit.
     Duration: 43 min.
     With rich harmonies of those wonderful gay-ninety songs, with
memoires of band concerts, of tree-lined streets of which travelled
the horseless carriage, comes this delightful musical narrative
depicting life when the world was young.

     I. U.S. - Social life and customs. I. Title.

         AERONAUTICS - ACCIDENTS
Voice Lib.
M714   Air collision disaster, worst aircrash in
bd.1   history; TransWorld Airlines and United
Airlines in New York. Description by
CBS newscasters on-the-spot and various
witnesses to the tragedy. December 16,
1960.
     7 min., 18 sec.   phonotape (7 in.   7 1/2
i.p.s.)

     1. Aeronautics - Accidents.

         AERONAUTICS, COMMERCIAL
Voice Lib.
587   Musick, Edwin K
bd.3   Air transportation in 1935; acknowledges
NBC salute to Pan-American Airways for
China Clipper flights in 1935. NBC,
January 1, 1936.
     1 reel (7 in.)   7 1/2 in. per sec.
phonotape.

         AFRICA - RELATIONS (GENERAL) WITH THE U.S.
Voice Lib.
M1679   Williams, G   Mennen, 1911-
     The United States and Africa. WKAR,
May 18, 1970.
     45 min.   phonotape (1 r.   7 1/2 i.p.s.)

     1. U.S. - Relations (General) with Africa.
     2. Africa - Relations (General) with the U.S.

Voice Lib.
M826   Africa and the arts; discussion of Africa
and the arts. KPFK, July 23, 1964.
     35 min., 15 sec.   phonotape (1 r.
7 1/2 i.p.s.)

     1. Art, African.

AGASSIZ, LOUIS, 1807-1873

C1
A36
Whorf, Michael, 1933-
An imposing symposium.
1 tape cassette. (The visual sounds of Mike Whorf.
Art, music and letters, A36)
Originally presented on his radio program, Kaleidoscope,
WJR, Detroit.
Duration: 38 min., 30 sec.
Longfellow, Agassiz, Emerson, Dana, these were the kings of
the world of literature in the nineteenth century. Every Saturday
night they met at a private club to discuss the current events of
their day.
1. Longfellow, Henry Wadsworth, 1807-1882. 2. Agassiz,
Louis, 1807-1873. 3. Emerson, Ralph Waldo, 1803-1882.
4. Dana, Richard Henry, 1815-1882. I. Title.

C1
S8
Age of anxiety
Whorf, Michael, 1933-
Age of anxiety.
1 tape cassette. (The visual sounds of
Mike Whorf. Social, S8)
Originally presented on his radio program, Kaleidoscope,
WJR, Detroit.
Duration: 48 min., 45 sec.
A man standing up for an ideal, acting to improve the lot
of others, striking out against injustice; such was the life of
Robert F. Kennedy.
1. Kennedy, Robert Francis, 1925-1968. I. Title.

Voice Lib.
M1473   Agnew, Spiro T   1918-
Speech on TV network newscasts delivered
to Midwest Regional Republican Committee in
Des Moines, Iowa. NBC, November 13, 1969.
1 reel (7 in.)   7 1/2 i.p.s.   phonotape.

1. Television broadcasting of news.

AGNEW, SPIRO T., 1918-
Voice Lib.
M1562   Kiker, Douglas
bd.1   Announcement of the resignation of Vice
President Spiro Agnew; special news report.
NBC, September 26, 1973.
3 min.   phonotape (1 r.   7 1/2 i.p.s.)

1. Agnew, Spiro T., 1918-

AGNEW, SPIRO T   1918-
Voice Lib.
M1405   Sixty minutes (Television program)
Agnew TV controversy: CBS TV program
devoted entirely to defending the
television newscasters' points of view
regarding the criticism of the media by
Vice-President Spiro T. Agnew.   CBS-TV,
November 25, 1969.
1 reel (7 in.)   7 1/2 in. per sec.
phonotape.

1. Agnew, Spiro T   1918-

AGNEW, SPIRO T   1918-
Voice Lib.
M1455   Sixty minutes (Television program)
bd.1   Semi-monthly CBS documentary with a
biography of Vice-President Spiro Agnew.
CBS TV, 1970.
1 reel (7 in.)   7 1/2 in. per sec.
phonotape.

1. Agnew, Spiro T   1918-

AGRICULTURAL ASSISTANCE, AMERICAN
Voice Lib.
M1701   Brown, Lester Russell, 1934-
International agricultural development.
WKAR, October 31, 1968.
90 min.   phonotape (1 r.   7 1/2 i.p.s.)

1. Agricultural assistance, American.

Agronski, Martin
Voice Lib.
M311   National Broadcasting Company, inc.
bd.1   Assassination: excerpts from the three
hour "Today" show; comments about Lyndon
B. Johnson, reading of New York Times
editorial. NBC, November 23, 1963.
1 reel (7 in.)   7 1/2 in. per sec.
phonotape.

1. Kennedy, John Fitzgerald, Pres. U.S.,
1917-1963 - Assassination.   I. Agronski, Martin

Ain't Misbehavin'
Voice Lib.
262   Robinson, Bill, 1878-1949.
bd.4   "Ain't Misbehavin'."   Brunswick,
1923.
1 reel (7 in.)   7 1/2 in. per sec.
phonotape.

I. Title.

Ain't you coming out, Melinda?
Voice Lib.
611   Van and Schenck
bd.10-   Comedy team singing "Ain't You Coming
11   Out, Melinda?" and "Wang Wang Blues".
Columbia Graphophone Company, 1920, 1922.
1 reel (7 in.)   7 1/2 in. per sec.
phonotape.

I. Title: Ain't you coming out, Melinda?
II. Title: Wang Wang blues.

Voice Lib.
M714   Air collision disaster, worst aircrash in
bd.1   history; TransWorld Airlines and United
          Airlines in New York. Description by
          CBS newscasters on-the-spot and various
          witnesses to the tragedy.   December 16,
          1960.
          7 min., 18 sec.   phonotape (7 in.   7 1/2
          i.p.s.)

          1. Aeronautics - Accidents.

C1   ALAMO - SIEGE, 1836
H15   Whorf, Michael, 1933-
          Remember the Alamo.
          1 tape cassette.   (The visual sounds of
Mike Whorf. History and heritage, H15)
          Originally presented on his radio program, Kaleidoscope,
WJR, Detroit.
          Duration: 39 min.
          Travis, Crockett, Bowie - these were the heroes of the Alamo,
where a handful of Texans took on the forces of Santa Anna's Mexican
army.

          I. Alamo - Siege, 1836. I. Title.

Voice Lib.
M738   Air raid sirens and bombing over London
bd.4   during Blitzkrieg.   CBS, 1940.
          55 sec. phonotape (1 r.   7 1/2 i.p.s.)

          1. World War, 1939-1945 - Gt. Brit.

C1   ALASKA - HISTORY - TO 1867
H16   Whorf, Michael, 1933-
          Seward's big deal - purchase of Alaska.
          1 tape cassette.   (The visual sounds of
Mike Whorf. History and heritage, H116)
          Originally presented on his radio program, Kaleidoscope,
WJR, Detroit.
          Duration: 36 min., 10 sec.
          They called it Seward's ice box or Seward's folly - this big deal
made by William Seward. This program tells the story of Seward,
the man, the man responsible for the purchase of Alaska.

          I. Seward, William Henry, 1801-1872. 2. Alaska - History -
To 1867. I. Title.

          AIR-SHIPS
Voice Lib.
M1464   Eckener, Hugo, 1868-1954.
bd.5   Giving his ideas on dirigibles, their
          future, and the airship "Graf Zeppelin".
          Peteler, 1932.
          1 reel (7 in.)   7 1/2 in. per sec.
          phonotape.

Voice Lib.
M737   Albert I, King of the Belgians, 1875-1934.
bd.3   Address at Antwerp exposition.   H.M.V.,
          1930.
          1 reel (7 in.)   7 1/2 in. per sec.
          phonotape.

          AIR TRAVEL
Voice Lib.
M1227   Chamberlain, Clarence
bd.8   Experiences during his first trans-
          Atlantic flight from New York to Germany,
          from West to East, and his reception in
          Berlin. Peteler, June 6, 1927.
          1 reel (7 in.)   7 1/2 i.p.s.   phonotape.

          1. Air travel.

Voice Lib.
M1800   Alch, Gerald
WG   Testimony before the Senate Committee
0523.03 investigating the Watergate Affair.
          Pacifica, May 23, 1973.
          109 min.   phonotape (2 r.   3 3/4 i.p.s.)
          (Watergate gavel to gavel, phase 1)

          1. Watergate Affair, 1972-

          Alabamy bound
Voice Lib.
M1034   Jolson, Al, 1886-1950.
bd.10   Excerpt of Kraft Music Hall radio program;
          singing "Alabamy Bound". TV & R, 1937.
          1 reel (7 in.)   7 1/2 in. per sec.
          phonotape.

          I. Title: Alabamy bound.

Voice Lib.
M1800   Alch, Gerald
WG   Testimony before the Senate Committee
0524.01 investigating the Watergate Affair.
          Pacifica, May 24, 1973.
          188 min.   phonotape (3 r.   3 3/4 i.p.s.)
          (Watergate gavel to gavel, phase 1)

          1. Watergate Affair, 1972-

C1
SC3-
SC4

ALCOHOLICS

Whorf, Michael, 1933-
   The man in the glass box.
   2 tape cassettes.   (The visual sounds of
Mike Whorf. Science, SC3-SC4)
     Originally presented on his radio program, Kaleidoscope,
WJR, Detroit.
     Duration: 39 min., 46 min.
     Two documentary programs on one of today's greatest
medical and social problems ... alcoholism.

     L Alcoholics. L Title.

C1
A6

ALCOTT, LOUISA MAY, 1832-1888

Whorf, Michael, 1933-
   The little woman.
   1 tape cassette.   (The visual sounds of
Mike Whorf. Art, music, and letters, A6)

     Originally presented on his radio program, Kaleidoscope,
WJR, Detroit.
     Duration: 34 min., 45 sec.
     Louisa May Alcott's story is found in her work "Little women,"
but there is another view of her life.

     L Alcott, Louisa May, 1832-1888. L Title.

Voice Lib.
M1732   Aldridge, John W
     Address at Michigan State University.
   Introduction by Russel B. Nye.   WKAR,
   October 28, 1968.
     50 min.   phonotape (1 r.   7 1/2 i.p.s.)

     1. Literature, Modern - 20th century - Hist.
& crit. 2. Fiction - 20th century - Hist. &
crit. I. Nye, Russel Blaine, 1913-

Aldrin, Buzz
   see
Aldrin, Edwin E   1930-

Voice Lib.
M1384   Aldrin, Edwin E   1930-
bd.1   Apollo 11 (space flight): launch day, July 16,
   1969. Description of astronauts going up
   the elevator; conversation between Walter
   Cronkite and Walter Schirra at approximately
   2 hours before launch.   CBS TV, July 16, 1969.
     1 reel (7 in.)   7 1/2 in. per sec.
   phonotape.
     L Project Apollo. 2. Space flight to the moon. 3. Aldrin,
Edwin E   1930-   4. Collins, Michael, 1930-   5. Armstrong,
Neil, 1930-   L Aldrin, Edwin E   1930-   II. Collins,
Michael, 1930-   III. Armstrong, Neil, 1930-   IV. Cronkite,
Walter Leland, 1916-   V. Schirra, Walter Marty, 1923-

Voice Lib.
M1384   Aldrin, Edwin E   1930-
bd.2   Apollo 11 (space flight): biographical sketches
   of the three astronauts, Edwin Aldrin,
   Michael Collins, and Neil Armstrong, by Chet
   Huntley, at approximately 78 minutes before
   launch time.   NBC TV, July 16, 1969.
     1 reel (7 in.)   7 1/2 in. per sec.
   phonotape.
     L Project Apollo. 2. Space flight to the moon. 3. Aldrin,
Edwin E   1930-   4. Collins, Michael, 1930-   5. Armstrong,
Neil, 1930-   L Aldrin, Edwin E   1930-   II. Collins,
Michael, 1930-   III. Armstrong, Neil, 1930-   IV. Huntley,
Chet, 1911-1974.

Voice Lib.
M1384   Aldrin, Edwin E   1930-
bd.3   Apollo 11 (space flight): Frank McGee giving
   an itinerary of space ships, dates, times,
   etc. NBC TV, July 16, 1969.
     1 reel (7 in.)   7 1/2 in. per sec.
   phonotape.
     1. Project Apollo. 2. Space flight to the
moon. 3. Aldrin, Edwin E   1930-   4.
Collins, Michael, 1930-   5. Armstrong, Neil,
1930-   I. Aldrin, Edwin E   1930-   II.
Collins, Michael, 1930-   III. Armstrong, Neil,
1930-   IV. McGee, Frank, 1921-1974.

Voice Lib.
M1384   Aldrin, Edwin E   1930-
bd.6   Apollo 11 (space flight): launch day progress
   of countdown by Apollo 11 control at 4
   minutes 15 seconds to actual take-off.
   Houston takes over and describes progress
   up to 1,000 miles downrange and successful
   orbit.   NBC TV, July 16, 1969.
     1 reel (7 in.)   7 1/2 in. per sec.
   phonotape.
     L Project Apollo. 2. Space flight to the moon. 3. Aldrin,
Edwin E   1930-   4. Collins, Michael, 1930-   5. Armstrong,
Neil, 1930-   L Aldrin, Edwin E   1930-   II. Collins,
Michael, 1930-   III. Armstrong, Neil, 1930-

Voice Lib.
M1385   Aldrin, Edwin E   1930-
bd.1   Apollo 11 (space flight): Frank McGee speaking
   about communications between "Eagle" and
   ground. Conversation between Houston and
   astronauts. Message of "Go for PDI"; "The
   Eagle has landed" (102 hours, 45 minutes,
   40 seconds) Description of rocks and
   boulders on moon.   NBC TV, July 20, 1969.
     1 reel (7 in.) 7 1/2 in. per sec. phonotape.
     L Project Apollo. 2. Space flight to the moon. 3. Aldrin,
Edwin E   1930-   4. Collins, Michael, 1930-   5.
Armstrong, Neil, 1930-   L Aldrin, Edwin E   1930-
II. Collins, Michael, 1930-   III. Armstrong, Neil, 1930-
IV. McGee, Frank. 1921-1974.

Voice Lib.
M1385   Aldrin, Edwin E   1930-
bd.2   Apollo 11 (space flight): Neil Armstrong
   requesting everyone everywhere to pause and
   give thanks. Preparing to open hatch and
   walk on the moon. Armstrong backing out
   from hatch, describing lunar surface. "One
   small step for man, one giant step for mankind" (109 hours, 24 minutes, 20 seconds.)
   Bringing down cameras.   CBS TV, July 20, 1969.
     1 reel (7 in.) 7 1/2 in. per sec. phonotape.
     L Project Apollo. 2. Space flight to the moon. 3. Aldrin,
Edwin E   1930-   4. Collins, Michael, 1930-   5. Armstrong,
Neil, 1930-   L Aldrin, Edwin E   1930-   II. Collins, Michael,
1930-   III. Armstrong, Neil, 1930-

Aldrin, Edwin E   1930-
Voice Lib.
M1386   Apollo 11 (space flight): conversation with
bd.1   broadcasters Walter Cronkite and Wally
          Schirra. Including Armstrong's activities
          on moon alone; pictures, rock descriptions,
          then Aldrin coming down ladder; rock boxes
          put to use. TV cameras put at 30' panoramic
          position. Reading inscription of plaque
          with U.S. flag and setting it up. Telephone
          call from Washington to astronauts and their
          acknowledgement. CBS TV, July 20, 1969.
          1 reel (7 in.)   7 1/2 in. per sec.
          phonotape.
                                    (Continued on next card)

Voice Lib.   Aldrin, Edwin E   1930-
M1386   Apollo 11 (space flight): blessing by Pope
bd.2   Paul VI from the Vatican to Apollo 11
          astronauts. CBS TV, July 20, 1969.
          1 reel (7 in.)   7 1/2 in. per sec.
          phonotape.

          1. Project Apollo. 2. Space flight to the
          moon. 3. Aldrin, Edwin E   1930-   4.
          Collins, Michael, 1930-   5. Armstrong, Neil,
          1930-   I. Aldrin, Edwin E   1930-   II.
          Collins, Michael, 1930-   III. Armstrong, Neil,
          1930-   IV. Paulus VI, Pope, 1897-

Voice Lib.   Aldrin, Edwin E   1930-
M1386   Apollo 11 (space flight): excerpts of old
bd.3   Mercury Theatre "War of the Worlds" of
          1938; an interview with Orson Welles by
          Mike Wallace. CBS TV, July 20, 1969.
          1 reel (7 in.)   7 1/2 in. per sec.
          phonotape.
          1. Project Apollo. 2. Space flight to the moon. 3. Aldrin,
          Edwin E   1930-   4. Collins, Michael, 1930-
          5. Armstrong, Neil, 1930-   I. Aldrin, Edwin E   1930-
          II. Collins, Michael, 1930-   III. Armstrong, Neil, 1930-
          IV. Welles, Orson, 1915-   V. Wallace, Mike, 1918-

Aldrin, Edwin E   1930-
Voice Lib.
M1387   Apollo 11 (space flight): description of
bd.1   ascent from moon by Frank McGee. Count-
          down, ignition, and lift-off. Meeting the
          command module "Columbia"; docking; trans-
          fer of gear from "Eagle" to "Columbia".
          Recap by ABC's Jules Bergman and Frank
          Reynolds. NBC and ABC TV, July 21, 1969.
          1 reel (7 in.)   7 1/2 in. per sec.   phonotape.
          1. Project Apollo. 2. Space flight to the moon. 3. Aldrin,
          Edwin E   1930-   4. Collins, Michael, 1930-   5.
          Armstrong, Neil, 1930-   I. Aldrin, Edwin E   1930-   II.
          Collins, Michael, 1930-   III. Armstrong, Neil, 1930-   IV.
          McGee, Frank, 1921-1974.   V. Bergman, Jules   VI. Reynolds,
          Frank.

Voice Lib.   Aldrin, Edwin E   1930-
M1387   Apollo 11 (space flight): recovery. Walter Cronkite and Wally
bd.2   Schirra announce proceedings from aircraft carrier "Hornet";
          trying to track spacecraft coming down; chutes opening at
          10,500 feet; voice contact with spacecraft; visual of chutes;
          splashdown 9 miles from "Hornet", upside-down. Collar
          attached to spacecraft. NBC and ABC TV, July 24, 1969.
          1 reel (7 in.)   7 1/2 in. per sec.   phonotape.

          1. Project Apollo. 2. Space flight to the moon. 3. Aldrin,
          Edwin E   1930-   4. Collins, Michael, 1930-   5.
          Armstrong, Neil, 1930-   I. Aldrin, Edwin E   1930-   II.
          Collins, Michael, 1930-   III. Armstrong, Neil, 1930-
          IV. Cronkite, Walter Leland, 1916-   V. Schirra, Walter Marty,
          1923-

Aldrin, Edwin E   1930-
Voice Lib.
M1388   Apollo 11 (space flight): Walter Cronkite and Wally Schirra
bd.1   describing recovery. Maneuvers by frogmen and helicopters
          at splashdown spot; "air boss" describes close-up scene;
          decontamination process; helicopter landing on "Hornet" with
          astronauts; reception. Description of proceedings on "Hornet"
          by CBS newscasters. CBS TV, July 24, 1969.
          1 reel (7 in.)   7 1/2 in. per sec.   phonotape.

          L. Project Apollo. 2. Space flight to the moon. 3. Aldrin,
          Edwin E   1930-   4. Collins, Michael, 1930-   5. Armstrong,
          Neil, 1930-   L. Aldrin, Edwin E   1930-   II. Collins,
          Michael, 1930-   III. Armstrong, Neil, 1930-   IV. Cronkite,
          Walter Leland, 1916-   V. Schirra, Walter Marty, 1923-

Voice Lib.   Aldrin, Edwin E   1930-
M1388   Apollo 11 (space flight): personal greeting
bd.2   by President Nixon to the astronauts on
          the "Hornet" and their replies. Chaplain's
          prayer. Nixon taking off. CBS and NBC TV,
          July 24, 1969.
          1 reel (7 in.)   7 1/2 in. per sec.
          phonotape.
          L. Project Apollo. 2. Space flight to the moon. 3. Aldrin,
          Edwin E   1930-   4. Collins, Michael, 1930-   5.
          Armstrong, Neil, 1930-   L. Aldrin, Edwin E   1930-
          II. Collins, Michael, 1930-   III. Armstrong, Neil, 1930-
          IV. Nixon, Richard Milhous, Pres. U.S., 1913-

Voice Lib.   Aldrin, Edwin E   1930-
M1389   Apollo 11 (space flight): excerpt of press
bd.1   conference with Apollo 11 astronauts in
          Houston. CBS TV, August 12, 1969.
          1 reel (7 in.)   7 1/2 in. per sec.
          phonotape.

          1. Project Apollo. 2. Space flight to the
          moon. 3. Aldrin, Edwin E   1930-   4.
          Collins, Michael, 1930-   5. Armstrong, Neil,
          1930-   I. Aldrin, Edwin E   1930-   II.
          Collins, Michael, 1930-   III. Armstrong,
          Neil, 1930-

Voice Lib.   Aldrin, Edwin E   1930-
M1389   Apollo 11 (space flight): welcome to Apollo 11 astronauts on their
bd.2   arrival at Kennedy Airport at New York; ferried by Marine
          helicopter to Wall Street; boat whistles harbor greeting.
          Flashbacks to former important New York parades (Frank McGee)
          Walter Cronkite, CBS, describing beginning of motorcade
          and parade to city hall. CBS [and NBC] TV, August 13, 1969.
          1 reel (7 in.)   7 1/2 in. per sec.   phonotape.

          L. Project Apollo. 2. Space flight to the moon. 3. Aldrin,
          Edwin E   1930-   4. Collins, Michael, 1930-   5.
          Armstrong, Neil, 1930-   L. Aldrin, Edwin E   1930-
          II. Collins, Michael, 1930-   III. Armstrong, Neil, 1930-
          IV. McGee, Frank, 1921-1974.   V. Cronkite, Walter Leland, 1916-

Voice Lib.   Aldrin, Edwin E   1930-
M1390   Apollo 11 (space flight): reception for
          Apollo 11 astronauts in New York. Descrip-
          tion of approach and ceremony at city hall.
          Cardinal Cooke's invocation. Introduction
          by Mayor Lindsay. Presentation of Medal of
          Honor. Reply by all astronauts. Benediction.
          NBC TV, August 13, 1969.
          1 reel (7 in.)   7 1/2 in. per sec.   phonotape.
          L. Project Apollo. 2. Space flight to the moon. 3. Aldrin,
          Edwin E   1930-   4. Collins, Michael, 1930-   5.
          Armstrong, Neil, 1930-   L. Aldrin, Edwin E   1930-   II.
          Collins, Michael, 1930-   III. Armstrong, Neil, 1930-   IV.
          Cooke, Terence James, cardinal, 1921-   V. Lindsay, John Vliet,
          1921-

Aldrin, Edwin E   1930–

Voice Lib.
M1391 Apollo 11 (space flight): reception of Apollo 11 astronauts at
bd.1   United Nations Plaza. Statement by U. N. Secretary-
          General U Thant. Reply by Neil Armstrong. Presentation
          of tokens of appreciation to all three astronauts and their
          wives and Dr. Thomas Paine. Presentation of duplicate of
          plaque left on moon to U Thant. NBC TV, August 13, 1969.
          1 reel (7 in.) 7 1/2 in. per sec. phonotape.

          1. Project Apollo. 2. Space flight to the moon. 3. Aldrin,
          Edwin E   1930–   4. Collins, Michael, 1930–   5.
          Armstrong, Neil, 1930–   I. Aldrin, Edwin E   1930–
          II. Collins, Michael, 1930–   III. Armstrong, Neil, 1930–
          IV. Thant, U, 1909–   V. Paine, Thomas Otten, 1921–

Ali, Muhammad
   see
Muhammad Ali, 1942–

Aldrin, Edwin E   1930–

Voice Lib.
M1391 Apollo 11 (space flight): reception of
bd.2   Apollo 11 astronauts in Chicago. Descrip-
          tion of motorcade on way to Civic Center
          Plaza and ceremonies there. Cardinal Cody's
          invocation. JFK flashback predicting moon
          landing before decade is out. Mayor Daley
          and Alderman Klene resolution making August
          13 "Astronauts' Day". Senator Percy and
          Governor Ogilvie of Illinois. Presentation
          of honorary citizenship to astronauts.
          [Source?] August 13, 1969.

          (Continued on next card)

Voice Lib.
M1718 Alinsky, Saul David, 1909–
          Address at Michigan State University's
          University College Colloquium on the Plight
          of the Cities. WKAR, January 27, 1969.
          50 min. phonotape (1 r. 7 1/2 i.p.s.)

          1. Cities and towns. I. Colloquium on
          the Plight of the Cities, Michigan State
          University, 1969.

Aldrin, Edwin E   1930–

Voice Lib.
M1391 Apollo 11 (space flight): reception of Apollo
bd.2   11 astronauts ... 1969. (Card 2)

          1 reel (7 in.) 7 1/2 in. per sec.
          phonotape.

          1. Project Apollo. 2. Space flight to the moon. 3. Aldrin,
          Edwin E   1930–   4. Collins, Michael, 1930–   5. Armstrong,
          Neil, 1930–   I. Aldrin, Edwin E   1930–   II. Collins,
          Michael, 1930–   III. Armstrong, Neil, 1930–   IV. Cody,
          John Patrick, cardinal, 1907–   V. Kennedy, John Fitzgerald,
          Pres. U.S., 1917–1963. VI. Daley, Richard J   1902– VII.
          Percy, Charles Harting, 1919– VIII. Ogilvie, Richard Buell,
          1923–

All the world's a stage
C1
A22
       Whorf, Michael, 1933–
          All the world's a stage, Shakespeare.
          1 tape cassette. (The visual sounds of
       Mike Whorf. Art, music, and letters, A22)

          Originally presented on his radio program, Kaleidoscope,
       WJR, Detroit.
          Duration: 44 min., 10 sec.
          William Shakespeare is considered the father of literature, for
       this prolific author composed plays, stories, sonnets and poems that
       are as popular today as when he first wrote them.

          1. Shakespeare, William, 1564–1616. I. Title.

Voice Lib.
M763 Alexander, Willard
bd.3   Excerpt from "The Scope of Jazz" (Program 6);
          comments on Goodman's success, disappearance
          of swing bands. Westinghouse Broadcasting
          Company, 1964.
          1 reel (7 in.) 7 1/2 in. per sec.
          phonotape. (The Music Goes Round and Round)

          1. Jazz music. I. Title: The scope of jazz.
          II. Series.

Voice Lib.
M1463 Alleged BBC broadcast in German about
bd.1   Prime Minister Chamberlain's peace
          mission to Germany. Peteler, September 27,
          1938.
          1 reel (7 in.) 7 1/2 i.p.s. phonotape.

          1. Chamberlain, Neville, 1869–1940.

ALEXANDER THE GREAT, 356–323 B.C.
C1
B65
       Whorf, Michael, 1933–
          Apostles of destruction; Caesar, Alexander,
       Ghenghis Khan, Hitler.
          1 tape cassette. (The visual sounds of Mike Whorf.
       History and heritage, H65)

          Originally presented on his radio program, Kaleidoscope,
       WJR, Detroit.
          Duration: 39 min.
          Here are graphically related the tales of the despots of the ages –
       for though many would strive for goodness and the best in man – a
       few were blindly corrupt and evil, and in their time attempted to
       bring the world to ruin.
          1. Caesar, C. Julius. 2. Alexander the Great, 356–323 B.C.
       3. Jenghis Khan, 1162–122? 4. Hitler, Adolf, 1889–1945.
       I. Title.

ALLEN, ETHAN, 1738–1789
C1
H61
       Whorf, Michael, 1933–
          Portrait of a patriot – Ethan Allen.
          1 tape cassette. (The visual sounds of
       Mike Whorf. History and heritage, H61)
          Originally presented on his radio program, Kaleidoscope,
       WJR, Detroit.
          Duration: 40 min.
          Ethan Allen's small band of Green Mountain boys captured the
       heavily- fortified garrison at Fort Ticonderoga in a daring attack
       at dawn, and gave the struggling Continental Congress a much-
       needed victory.

          1. Allen, Ethan, 1738–1789. I. Title.

Voice Lib.
192   Allen, Fred, 1894-1956.
     Excerpts of songs and skits from Golden
Age of Radio; other radio celebrities
included. Nation Vocarium, 1920's
to 1930's.
     1 reel (7 in.)   7 1/2 in. per sec.
phonotape.

Voice Lib.
157   Allen, Fred, 1894-1956.
bd.2   Starring in "My Client Curley".   CBS
Workshop, 1930's.
     1 reel (7 in.)   7 1/2 in. per sec.
phonotape.

Voice Lib.
M706   Allen, Fred, 1894-1956.
bd.1   "Command performance"; variety show of
Armed Forces Radio Service.   Melchior
collection, December 2, 1943.
     1 reel (7 in.)   7 1/2 in. per sec.
phonotape.

Voice Lib.
M707   Allen, Fred, 1894-1956.
bd.1   "Fred Allen Show"; excerpts, radio variety
show.   Melchior collection, December 16,
1945.
     1 reel (7 in.)   7 1/2 in. per sec.
phonotape.

Voice Lib.
M705   Allen, Fred, 1894-1956.
bd.1   Variety show (radio), "The Fred Allen
Show".   Melchior collection, February 2,
1947.
     1 reel (7 in.)   7 1/2 in. per sec.
phonotape.

Voice Lib.
M719   Allen, Fred, 1894-1956.
bd.1   "The Big Show", with Tallulah Bankhead
and Laurits Melchior and all star cast.
December 2, 1951.
     10 min., 56 sec.   phonotape (1 r.
7 1/2 i.p.s.)

     I. Bankhead, Tallulah, 1902-1968. II.
Melchior, Laurits Lebrecht Hommel, 1890-
1973. III. Title.

Voice Lib.
321   Allen, Fred, 1894-1956.
     Biography in sound: excerpts from various
Allen programs, comments by many famous
persons. NBC, 1956.
     1 reel (7 in.)   7 1/2 in. per sec.
phonotape.

     1. Allen, Fred, 1894-1956

           Allen, Fred, 1894-1956
Voice Lib.
M618   Radio in the 1930's (Part I): a series of
bd.1-   excerpts from important broadcasts of the
14   1930's; a sample of radio of the period.
NVL, April, 1964.
1 reel (7 in.)   7 1/2 in. per sec.   phonotape.
I. Shaw, George Bernard, 1856-1950. II. Crosby, Bing, 1901-
III. Barkley, Alban William, 1877-1956. IV. Roosevelt, Franklin
Delano, Pres. U.S., 1882-1945. V. Hoover, Herbert Clark, Pres.
U.S., 1874-1964. VI. Long, Huey Pierce, 1893-1935. VII. Townsend, Francis Everett, 1867-1960. VIII. Coughlin, Charles Edward,
1891-   IX. Rogers, Will, 1879-1935. X. Pius XII, Pope, 1876-
1958. XI. Edward VIII, king of Great Britain, 1894-1972. XII.
Barrymore, John, 1882-1942. XIII. Woollcott, Alexander, 1887-
1943. XIV. Allen, Fred, 1894-1956. XV. Benchley, Robert Charles,
1889-1945.

           Allen, Fred, 1894-1956
Voice Lib.
M619   Radio in the 1930's (Part II): a series of
bd.1-   excerpts of the 1930's; a sample of radio
14   of the period. NVL, April, 1964.
1 reel (7 in.)   7 1/2 in. per sec.   phonotape.
I. Allen, Fred, 1894-1956. II. Delmar, Kenny   III. Donald,
Peter   IV. Pious, Minerva   V. Fennelly, Parker   VI.
Boyer, Charles, 1899-   VII. Dunne, Irene, 1904-   VIII.
DeMille, Cecil Blount, 1881-1959. IX. West, Mae, 1893-   X.
Dafoe, Allan Ray, 1883-1943. XI. Dionne quintuplets. XII. Ortega,
Santos   XIII. War of the worlds (radio program)   XIV. Ives, Burl,
1909-   XV. Robinson, Earl, 1910-   XVI. Temple, Shirley,
1928-   XVII. Earhart, Amelia, 1898-1937. XVIII. Lawrence,
Gertrude, 1901-1952. XIX. Cohan, George Michael, 1878-1942.
XX. Shaw, George Bernard, 1856-1950. XXI. Hitler, Adolf, 1889-
1945. XXII. Chamberlain, Neville, 1869-1940. XXIII. Roosevelt,
Franklin Delano, Pres. U.S., 1882-1945.

Voice Lib.
M1049   Allen, Fred, 1894-1956.
     Chase and Sanborn 101st anniversary radio
show with Edgar Bergen as emcee, featuring
various Fred Allen skits from his famous
radio programs. NBC, November 14, 1965.
     1 reel (7 in.)   7 1/2 in. per sec.
phonotape.

     I. Bergen, Edgar, 1903-

Allen, Fred, 1894-1956
Voice Lib.
M322   Biography in sound (radio program)
       W.C. Fields, the magnificent rogue.
       NBC, 1955.
         1 reel (7 in.)   7 1/2 in. per sec.   phonotape.
       I. Fields, W.C., 1879-1946.   I. Fields, W.C., 1879-1946.
       II. Allen, Fred, 1894-1956. III. LaBaron, William   IV.
       Taylor, Robert Lewis, 1912-   V. McCarey, Thomas Leo, 1898-
       1969. VI. Harkins, James   . VII. Chevalier, Maurice,
       1889-1972. VIII. Kuromoto, Mrs. George   IX. Flynn,
       Errol Leslie, 1909-1959. X. Wynn, Ed, 1886-1966. XI. Dowling,
       Ray Dooley   XII. Sennett, Mack   XIII. Overacher,
       Ronald Leroy   XIV. Bergen, Edgar, 1903-   XV. Taurog,
       Norman, 1899-   XVI. Runnell, Ann   XVII. Cowen,
       Lester

Allen, Fred, 1894-1956
Voice Lib.
M709   Texaco Star Theater.
bd.3   Radio variety show. Speaker: Fred Allen.
       Melchior collection, CBS, December 10, 1943.
         25 min., 50 sec.   phonotape (1 r.
       7 1/2 i.p.s.)

       I. Allen, Fred, 1894-1956.

Voice Lib. ALLEN, FRED, 1894-1956
580-   Downs, Hugh Malcolm, 1921-
581   "Today" show tribute to Fred Allen. Hosts
       show, talks with various personalities, reads
       series of jokes written by Fred Allen, reads
       quote from James Thurber. Excerpt from NBC-TV
       production "The Jazz Age" which Allen narrates,
       recorded shortly before his death on March 17,
       1956. NBC, March 18, 1964.
         2 reels (7 in.)   7 1/2 in. per sec.
       phonotape.
         1. Allen, Fred, 1894-1956.

Voice Lib.
M894   Allen, Frederick Lewis, 1890-
bd.4   Reviewing books "Middletown" and
       "Middletown in Transition", by Robert S.
       Lynd and Helen Merrell Lynd. WQXR,
       January 19, 1938.
         1 reel (7 in.)   7 1/2 in. per sec.
       phonotape.

         I. Lynd, Robert Staughton, 1892-   /
       Middletown. II. Lynd, Robert Staughton,
       1892-   /Middletown in transition.

Allen, Gracie, 1906-
Voice Lib.
M1047 Old-time radio excerpts of the 1930's and
       1940's, including: Rudy Vallee singing
       "Linger a little longer"; Will Rogers on
       panaceas for the Depression; Bing Crosby
       singing "Sweet Georgia Brown"; Eddie Cantor;
       Jimmy Durante singing "Inka-dinka-do";
       musical skit by Clayton, Jackson and Durante;
       wit by Harry Hershfield; musical selection
       "Thinking of you" by Kay Kyser; Kate Smith
       singing theme song, "When the moon comes over
       the mountain"; W.C. Fields' temperance

       (Continued on next card)

Allen, Gracie, 1906-
Voice Lib.
M1047 Old-time radio excerpts of the 1930's and
       1940's... (Card 2)

       lecture; Al Jolson singing "Rocka-by-your
       baby"; and George Burns and Gracie Allen
       skit. TV&R, 1930's and 1940's.
         1 reel (7 in.)   7 1/2 in. per sec.
       I. Vallee, Rudy, 1901-   II. Rogers, Will, 1879-1935. III.
       Crosby, Bing, 1901-   IV. Cantor, Eddie, 1893-1964. V. Durante,
       Jimmy, 1893-   VI. Clayton, Patti   VII. Jackson,
       Eddie   VIII. Hershfield, Harry, 1885-   IX. Kyser, Kay,
       1906-   X. Smith, Kate, 1909-   XI. Fields, W.C., 1879-
       1946. XII. Jolson, Al, 1886-1950. XIII. Burns, George, 1896-
       XIV. Allen, Gracie, 1906-

Allen, Gracie, 1905-
Voice Lib.
M1034 Burns, George, 1896-
bd.9   With Gracie Allen in radio comedy skit.
       TV&R, 1935.
         1 reel (7 in.)   7 1/2 in. per sec.
       phonotape.

         I. Allen, Gracie, 1905-

Voice Lib.
M1681 Allen, Samuel W
bd.4   Richard Wright and Black America.
       WKAR, December 3, 1968.
         25 min.   phonotape (1 r.   7 1/2 i.p.s.)

         1. Wright, Richard, 1908-1960.

Allen, Viola
Voice Lib.   Packard, Frederick
M225   Styles in Shakespearean acting, 1890-1950.
           Creative Associates, 1963?
             1 reel (7 in.)   7 1/2 l.p.s.   phonotape.

           I. Sothern, Edward Askew, 1826-1881. II. Marlowe,
         Julia, 1865-1950. III. Booth, Edwin, 1833-1893. IV. Gielgud,
         John, 1904-   V. Robeson, Paul Bustill, 1898-   VI. Terry,
         Dame Ellen, 1848-1928. VII. Allen, Viola. VIII. Welles,
         Orson, 1915-   IX. Skinner, Otis, 1858-1942. X. Barrymore,
         John, 1882-1942. XI. Olivier, Sir Laurence Kerr, 1907-
         XII. Forbes-Robertson, Sir Johnston, 1853-   XIII. Evans,
         Maurice. XIV. Thorndike, Dame Sybil, 1882-   XV. Robson,
         Flora. XVI. LeGallienne, Eva, 1899-   XVII. Anderson,
         Judith. XVIII. Duncan, Augustin. XIX. Hampden, Walter.
         XX. Speaight, Robert, 1904-   XXI. Jones, Daniel.

Voice Lib.
M1744 Allende Gossens, Salvador, 1908-1973.
bd.4   Interview with John Wallach. WKAR,
       August, 1973.
         2 min., 40 sec.   phonotape (1 r.   7 1/2
       i.p.s.)

         Wallach in turn was interviewed by Rich Adams.

         1. Chile - Pol & govt. 2. Socialism in
       Chile. 3. Allende Gossens, Salvador, 1908-
       1973. I. Wallach. John. II. Adams, Rich.

Voice Lib.
M1100   Allilueva, Svetlana, 1925-
bd.1   Press conference held at Hotel Plaza in
New York, answering written questions by
correspondents pertaining to her recent
defection from the Soviet Union, her present
beliefs and plans. CBS-TV, April 26, 1967.
        1 reel (7 in.)   7 1/2 in. per sec.
phonotape.

            Allison, Samuel King, 1900-
Voice Lib.
353   Russia and the bomb, discussed by various
bd.19   personalities. NBC, September 25, 1949.
        1 reel (7 in.)   7 1/2 in. per sec.
phonotape.

        Participants: Harrison Brown, Harold Urey,
Samuel Allison, Thornton Hugness, Brien McMahon,
Paul Douglas, John Foster Dulles, Leslie Groves,
Winston Churchill, Dean Acheson, James Fleming.

        I. Brown, Harrison Scott, 1917-   II.
Urey, Harold Clayton, 1893-   III. Allison,
                            (Continued on next card)

            Allison, Samuel King, 1900-
Voice Lib.
353   Russia and the bomb... 1949. (Card 2)
bd.19

Samuel King, 1900-   IV. Hugness, Thornton.
V. McMahon, James O'Brien, 1903-1952. VI.
Douglas, Paul Howard, 1892-   VII. Dulles,
John Foster, 1888-1959. VIII. Groves, Leslie
B   1896-1970. IX. Churchill, Winston .
Leonard Spencer, 1874-1965. X. Acheson, Dean
Gooderham, 1893-1971. XI. Fleming, James,
1915-

            Alpert, Herb, 1935(?)-
Voice Lib.
M1263   Armstrong, Louis, 1900-1971.
        Kraft Music Hall with Herb Alpert and
Tijuana Brass, with guest stars Jackie
Vernon and Robin Wilson. NBC-TV,
August 13, 1967.
        1 reel (7 in.)   7 1/2 in. per sec.
phonotape.

        I. Alpert, Herb, 1935(?)-   II. Vernon,
Jackie   III. Wilson, Robin

Voice Lib.
M1634   Alsop, Stewart, 1914-
bd.4   Interviewed about his terminal leukemia,
by Barbara Newman. WKAR, April 15, 1974.
        15 min.   phonotape (1 r.   7 1/2 i.p.s.)

        1. Alsop, Stewart, 1914-   2. Leukemia -
Personal narratives. I. Newman, Barbara.

            The amazing Mr. Frost
C1
A19   Whorf, Michael, 1933-
        The amazing Mr. Frost.
        1 tape cassette. (The visual sounds of
Mike Whorf. Art, music, and letters, A19)
        Originally presented on his radio program, Kaleidoscope,
WJR, Detroit.
        Duration: 43 min., 45 sec.
        Actual recordings of Frost reading his own works make up the
body of this program, yet the narrator brings in important aspects
of his life that made Robert Frost the man he was.

        I. Frost, Robert, 1874-1963.   I. Frost, Robert, 1874-1963.
II. Title.

            AMERICA - DISCOVERY AND EXPLORATION - NORSE
C1
H28   Whorf, Michael, 1933-
        The men before Columbus.
        1 tape cassette. (The visual sounds of
Mike Whorf. History and heritage, H28)
        Originally presented on his radio program, Kaleidoscope,
WJR, Detroit.
        Duration: 40 min., 15 sec.
        1000 years before Columbus' exploration of San Salvador came
the Vikings whose culture and life style made little impression on the
world, but their knowledge of sailing and their spirit of adventure
would inspire others to undertake the role of discoverer.

        1. Vikings. 2. America - Discovery and exploration - Norse.
I. Title.

            AMERICA - DISCOVERY AND EXPLORATION - SPANISH
C1
H48   Whorf, Michael, 1933-
        The conquistadors.
        1 tape cassette. (The visual sounds of
Mike Whorf. History and heritage, H48)
        Originally presented on his radio program, Kaleidoscope,
WJR, Detroit.
        Duration: 44 min., 15 sec.
        Sent from Spain to settle and civilize the new world, they
plundered, killed, stole, and vanquished the Indian nations of the
Southwest, Central America, and Mexico.

        1. America - Discovery and exploration - Spanish. I. Title.

Voice Lib.
M534-   "America first" anti-war rally in Madison
536   Square Garden, New York City. GRV,
October, 1941.
        3 reels (7 in.)   7 1/2 i.p.s.   phonotape.

        1. U.S. - Foreign relations.

            "America, Here's My Boy"
Voice Lib.
603   Peerless Quartet.
bd.7   "America, Here's My Boy", World War I song.
Victor Talking Machine Company, 1917.
        1 reel (7 in.)   7 1/2 in. per sec.
phonotape.

        I. Title.

America, the beautiful

Voice Lib.
M718   Price, Leontyne, 1929-
bd.1   Singing "America, the Beautiful".
        Presidential Inaugural ceremonies.
        January 20, 1965.
          1 reel (7 in.)   7 1/2 in. per sec.
        phonotape..

            I. Title: America, the beautiful.

America the beautiful

C1
S38   Whorf, Michael, 1933-
        America the beautiful; pollution, part 2.
          1 tape cassette.   (The visual sounds of
        Mike Whorf. Social, S38)
          Originally presented on his radio program, Kaleidoscope,
        WJR, Detroit.
          Duration: 54 min.
          This second narration looks at the types of pollution which have
        engulfed the globe. Here are the acts of water and air poisoning
        which man has slowly but deliberately committed, and the results
        of his carelessness and negligence.

            I. Pollution. 2. Nature - Influence of man on. I. Title.

Voice Lib.
M310   American Broadcasting Company.
        Tribute to President John Fitzgerald Kennedy
        from the arts. Fredric March emcees; Jerome
        Hines sings "Worship of God and Nature" by
        Beethoven; Florence Eldridge recites "When
        lilacs last in the door-yard bloom'd" by Walt
        Whitman; Marian Anderson in two songs. Includes
        Charlton Heston, Sidney Blackmer, Isaac Stern,
        Nathan Milstein, Christopher Plummer, Albert
        Finney. ABC, November 24, 1963.
          35 min. phonotape (7 in.   7 1/2 i.p.s.)

            (Continued on next card)

Voice Lib.
M310   American Broadcasting Company.   Tribute to
        President John Fitzgerald Kennedy...
        1963.   (Card 2)
          I. Kennedy, John Fitzgerald, Pres. U.S., 1917-1963. I.
        March, Fredric, 1897-   II. Hines, Jerome, 1921-   III.
        Beethoven, Ludwig van, 1770-1827. / Worship of God and Nature.
        IV. Eldridge, Florence, 1901-   V. Whitman, Walt, 1819-1892. /
        When lilacs last in the door-yard bloom'd. VI. Anderson, Marian,
        1902-   VII. Heston, Charlton, 1924-   VIII. Blackmer,
        Sidney, 1895-1973. IX. Stern, Isaac, 1920-   X. Milstein,
        Nathan, 1904-   XI. Plummer, Christopher, 1929-   XII.
        Finney, Albert, 1936-

Voice Lib.
M313   American Broadcasting Company.
bd.2   Descriptions of preparations of transfer
        of Oswald from Municipal Jail in Dallas.
        ABC, November 24, 1963.
          1 reel (7 in.)   7 1/2 in. per sec.
        phonotape.

            1. Oswald, Lee Harvey, 1939-1963. 2.
        Kennedy, John Fitzgerald, Pres. U.S., 1917-
        1963 - Assassination.

Voice Lib.
M313   American Broadcasting Company.
bd.3   Transfer and shooting of Oswald in
        basement of police station; interviews
        with spectators and Policeman Dean in
        Dallas. ABC, November 24, 1963.
          1 reel (7 in.)   7 1/2 in. per sec.
        phonotape.

            1. Oswald, Lee Harvey, 1939-1963. 2.
        Kennedy, John Fitzgerald, Pres. U.S., 1917-
        1963 - Assassination.

Voice Lib.
M314   American Broadcasting Company.
bd.1   Assassination: on death of Oswald.   Dallas,
        WFAA-TV (ABC), November 24, 1963.
          1 reel (7 in.)   7 1/2 i.p.s.   phonotape.

            1. Oswald, Lee Harvey, 1939-1963.

Voice Lib.
M314   American Broadcasting Company.
bd.2   Comments about Kennedy's assassination;
        on new arrivals in Washington at Dulles
        Airport. ABC, November 24, 1963.
          1 reel (7 in.)   7 1/2 in. per sec.
        phonotape.

            1. Kennedy, John Fitzgerald, Pres. U.S.,
        1917-1963 - Assassination.

Voice Lib.
M314   American Broadcasting Company.
bd.4   Assassination: proceedings at the Capitol
        Rotunda in Washington. ABC, November 24,
        1963.
          1 reel (7 in.)   7 1/2 in. per sec.
        phonotape.

            1. Kennedy, John Fitzgerald, Pres. U.S.,
        1917-1963 - Assassination.

The American dance craze

C1
PWM16   Whorf, Michael, 1933-
        The American dance craze.
          1 tape cassette.   (The visual sounds of
        Mike Whorf. Panorama; a world of music,
        PWM-16)
          Originally presented on his radio program, Kaleidoscope,
        WJR, Detroit.
          Duration: 25 min.
          A discussion of dancing in the United States, with examples
        of dance music.

            1. Dancing. 2. Dance music, American. I. Title.

C1
M53

The American dance craze

Whorf, Michael, 1933-
The American dance craze.
1 tape cassette. (The visual sounds of
Mike Whorf. Miscellaneous, M53)

Originally presented on his radio program, Kaleidoscope,
WJR, Detroit.
Duration:
For those that are musically inclined here is a program
concerning the famous dances of the American people.
Along with the music are capsule anecdotes about the life and
times of those who are swept up in the American dance craze.

L Dancing - U.S.   L Title.

Voice Lib.
M878- American mood series (Radio program)
879   Conversation on a party line... 1963.
bd.1   (Card 2)

2 reels (7 in.)   7 1/2 in. per sec.
phonotape.

1. U.S. - Social life & customs - 20th cent.
I. Hamilton, John David   II. Project
'64.

Voice Lib.   AMERICAN DRAMA - HISTORY AND CRITICISM
M609   Koch, Frederick Henry, 1877-1944.
bd.9   Carolina playmakers; description of origin
and history of American folk plays.
G.R.Vincent, January 3, 1942.
1 reel (7 in.)   7 1/2 i.p.s.   phonotape.

1. American drama - History and criticism.

Voice Lib.
M879   American mood series (Radio program)
bd.2-   The real American revolution. California,
881   the real American revolution. Opinions on
bd.1   liberalism and also opinions by John Birch
Society members and conservatives. Discussion
by magazine editor; San Diego resident talking
about John Birch Society and a discussion
about Barry Goldwater. Discussion of life and
culture in Southern California; cause for the
influx of people; lack of family roots and
analysis of social contacts; broad discussion
of L.A. social prob` e. Discussions of
(Continued on next card)

Voice Lib.
M874   American mood series (Radio program)
bd.2-   Appalachia: first program in a series of
M875   documentaries by John David Hamilton recording
on-the-spot candid sounds and interviews, in
1963. White evangelists' sermons; statements
by teachers and sociologists and natives in
the mountain regions of North Carolina, Tenn-
essee and Kentucky, which include feuding,
square dancing, moon-shining, etc. Native
women recollecting life in the past in Appalachia; origin of feuds; discussion of moon-
shining; native folk songs, including the TVA
(Continued on next card)

Voice Lib.
M879   American mood series (Radio program) The
bd.2-   real American revolution... 1963.
881   (Card 2)
bd.1

uprising of college students and a general
discussion of Southern California compared to
Canada. CBC Radio, 1963.
2 reels (7 in.)   7 1/2 in. per sec.
phonotape.

1. California - Soc. condit.   I. Hamilton,
John David   II. Project '64.

Voice Lib.
M874   American mood series (Radio program)
bd.2-   Appalachia... 1963.   (Card 2)
M875

song; church service excerpts; the Texas
scene, fundamentalism, philosophy, humor,
songs, etc. CBC, 1963.
2 reels (7 in.)   7 1/2 in. per sec.
phonotape.

1. Appalachian Mountains, Southern - Social
Life and customs.   I. Hamilton, John David
II. Project '64.

Voice Lib.
M881,   American mood series (Radio program)
bd.2-   Reverberations from the think tanks. Future of America being
882   discussed by outstanding thinkers. Final documentary in the
American mood series wherein John David Hamilton visits the
Rand Corp. in Santa Monica, discussing its objectives, type of
work and long-range military strategy. Speakers are: James F.
Digby, Robert D. Specht, Bernard Brody, of the Rand Corporation.
Also interviews with: W. H. Ferry, Walter Millis, and Dr. Robert
Hutchins at the Center for Democratic Institutions in Santa Barbara,
Calif.; the Aspen Institute in Aspen, Colo. Speakers are: business
executives, Robert O. Anderson and William Gomberg discussing
social and economic problems from a business executive's viewpoint;
roles of the individual; distinct optimism. CBC Radio, 1964.
2 reels (7 in.)   7 1/2 L.p.s. phonotape.

I. Hamilton, John David   II. Project '64.

Voice Lib.
M878- American mood series (Radio program)
879   Conversation on a party line: John David
bd.1   Hamilton talking to people in North Carolina,
Connecticut, New York, Texas, Colorado, New
Mexico, all intellectuals and numerous school
teachers. "Little Boxes" (the conformity song);
description of American life and its meaning;
definition of socialism; discussing Americans'
international ideas; discussion of Texas
University students and attitudes; Berkeley
professor attitudes; discussion on how to make
money; advocating the study of medicine.
CBC, 1963.

Voice Lib.
M876- American mood series (Radio program)
877   The Southern moderate: the South as seen
through the eyes of a Canadian, John David
Hamilton. The case of the white moderate;
statements by moderate whites about the racial
situation; sentiments about Negroes by Atlanta,
Georgia newspapermen; appreciation of South-
erners' way of life. New Orleans historian's
appraisal of economic conditions in Louisiana.
Mississippi Chamber of Commerce manager eval-
uating situation in Mississippi. Oldtime
justice described by South Carolina citizen.
(Continued on next card)

Voice Lib.
M876- American mood series (Radio program) The
877   Southern moderate... 1963. (Card 2)
        Mississippi's concealed weapons law; opinions
        on violence; discussion of white supremacy
        in intellect and education; protests about
        taxes to aid colored relief; pro and con
        opinions about Negroes' rights from Louisianans
        and Georgians. CBC Radio, 1963.
          2 reels (7 in.) 7 1/2 in. per sec.
        phonotape.
          1. Southern states - Civilization. I.
        Hamilton, John Davi⟨ ⟩ II. Project '64.

C1
M21   The American troubador
          Whorf, Michael, 1933-
            The American troubador.
            1 tape cassette. (The visual sounds of
          Mike Whorf. Miscellaneous, M21)
            Originally presented on his radio program, Kaleidoscope,
          WJR, Detroit.
            Duration: 40 min.
            This narrative deals with the life and trials of the gifted, but
          melancholy Stephen Foster.
            L. Foster, Stephen Collins, 1826-1864. L. Title.

Voice Lib.
603   American Quartet.
bd.5   "Keep Your Head Down, Fritzie Boy",
        Lieutenant Gitz Rice's World War I song.
        Victor Talking Machine Co., 1918.
          1 reel (7 in.) 7 1/2 in. per sec.
        phonotape.

          I. Title.

C1
H82   America's first citizen, the President
          Whorf, Michael, 1933-
            America's first citizen, the President.
            1 tape cassette. (The visual sounds of
          Mike Whorf. History and heritage, H82)
            Originally presented on his radio program, Kaleidoscope,
          WJR, Detroit.
            Duration: 37 min., 30 sec.
            Here are the ins and outs, the political aspects and
          attributes of the election of a president.
            L. Presidents - U.S. - Election. L. Title.

Voice Lib.
603   American Quartet.
bd.6   "Let's All Be Americans Now", Irving
        Berlin's World War I song. Victor Talking
        Machine Co., 1917.
          1 reel (7 in.) 7 1/2 in. per sec.
        phonotape.

          I. Title.

C1
H19   America's first modern
          Whorf, Michael, 1933-
            America's first modern.
            1 tape cassette. (The visual sounds of
          Mike Whorf. History and heritage, H19)
            Originally presented on his radio program, Kaleidoscope,
          WJR, Detroit.
            Duration: 40 min., 15 sec.
            The leader whose ideas shocked, alienated, and eventually
          reformed the early Pilgrim settlements, Roger Williams turned
          his back on the intolerance of the Puritans in Massachusetts
          and his face toward true freedom in his own colony.
            L. Williams, Roger, 1604?-1683. L. Title.

Voice Lib.
M611   American Quartet.
bd.7   World War I song "You're a grand old flag".
        Victor Talking Machine Co., 1918.
          1 reel (7 in.) 7 1/2 i.p.s. phonotape.

          1. European War, 1914-1918 - Songs and
        music. I. Title: You're a grand old flag.

C1
H100   America's grand old man - Benjamin Franklin
          Whorf, Michael, 1933-
            America's grand old man - Benjamin Franklin.
            1 tape cassette. (The visual sounds of
          Mike Whorf. History and heritage, H100)
            Originally presented on his radio program, Kaleidoscope,
          WJR, Detroit.
            Duration: 36 min.
            The wise man of America has become one of the most quoted,
          most remembered men of the American Revolution. His life revolved
          around his country, his countrymen. His books, his studies, and his
          maxims echo to us throughout history.
            L. Franklin, Benjamin, 1706-1790. L. Title.

C1
H101   An American story, as we have forgotten it -
          Joseph Warren
          Whorf, Michael, 1933-
            An American story, as we have forgotten it -
          Joseph Warren.
            1 tape cassette. (The visual sounds of Mike Whorf. History
          and heritage, H101)
            Originally presented on his radio program, Kaleidoscope,
          WJR, Detroit.
            Duration: 35 min., 10 sec.
            A young American doctor, active in Revolutionary politics,
          Joseph Warren eagerly participated in many rebel militia activities.
          Constantly fighting for the American cause Dr. Warren helped
          create independence.
            L. Warren, Joseph,   1741-1775. L. Title.

C1
S77   America's tarnished Robinhood - John Dillinger
          Whorf, Michael, 1933-
            America's tarnished Robinhood - John Dillinger.
            1 tape cassette. (The visual sounds of
          Mike Whorf. Social, S77)
            Originally presented on his radio program, Kaleidoscope,
          WJR, Detroit.
            Duration: 37 min.
            1934, with the country climbing out of depression, John
          Dillinger arrived upon the scene. The clever criminal's
          escapades are fully described as we learn about the tarnished
          Robin Hood.
            L. Dillinger, John, 1903-1934. L. Title.

Amos 'n' Andy
see
Correll, Charles J., 1890-1972
and
Gosden, Freeman Fisher, 1899-

Voice Lib.
M1083 Analysis and criticism of President Kennedy's
bd.2 administration after a year and a half of
its incumbency, by Howard K. Smith, Leon
Keyserling, Roy Wilkins, Theodore Sorensen,
and various economists, mostly adverse
opinions; comparison to Wilson and FDR
administrations. Bergman, July 25, 1962.
1 reel (7 in.) 7 1/2 in. per sec. phonotape.
I. Kennedy, John Fitzgerald, Pres. U.S., 1917-1963. I.
Smith, Howard Kingsbury, 1914- II. Keyserling, Leon Hersch,
1908- III. Wilkins, Roy, 1901- IV. Sorensen, Theodore
Chaikin, 1928-

The Anatomy of a Hit
Voice Lib.
M765 Campana, Frank
bd.2 Excerpt from "The Anatomy of a Hit"
(Program 9); comments on the role of the
promotion man, also the album business.
Westinghouse Broadcasting Corporation, 1964.
1 reel (7 in.) 7 1/2 in. per sec.
phonotape. (The Music Goes Round and Round)

I. Title: The Anatomy of a Hit. II. Series.

Voice Lib. The anatomy of a hit
M765 Goldmark, Goldie
bd.4 Excerpt from "The anatomy of a hit"
(Program 9); gives advice on how to get
a new record on a popular music station.
Westinghouse Broadcasting Corporation, 1964.
1 min., 41 sec. phonotape (1 r. 7 1/2
i.p.s.) (The music goes round and round)
1. Music, Popular (Songs, etc.)
2. Phonorecords. I. Title: The anatomy of
a hit. II. Series.

The anatomy of a hit
Voice Lib.
M765 Kapp, Mickey
bd.6 Excerpt from "The Anatomy of a Hit" (Program
9); relates his experience with the record
"Hello, Dolly", including the song as sung
by Louis Armstrong. Westinghouse Broadcasting
Corporation, 1964.
1 reel (7 in.) 7 1/2 in. per sec.
phonotape. (The Music Goes Round and Round)

I. Title: The anatomy of a hit. II. Series.

The anatomy of a hit
Voice Lib.
M765 Levy, Leonard
bd.8 Excerpt from "The Anatomy of a Hit"
(Program 9); answers the question, "What
does a company do when one of its artists
is no longer selling?" Westinghouse
Broadcasting Corporation, 1964.
1 reel (7 in.) 7 1/2 in. per sec.
phonotape. (The Music Goes Round and Round)

I. Title: The anatomy of a hit. II. Series.

The anatomy of a hit
Voice Lib.
M765 Sholes, Steven H 1911-1968.
bd.1 Excerpt from "The Anatomy of a Hit"
(Program 9); comments on why the A&R man
is the most important person in the production
of a hit record; the changing attitude of
the juke box operator. Westinghouse
Broadcasting Corporation, 1964.
1 reel (7 in.) 7 1/2 in. per sec.
phonotape. (The Music Goes Round and Round)

I. Title: The anatomy of a hit. II. Series.

The anatomy of a hit
Voice Lib.
M765 Spector, Phil
bd.7 Excerpt from "The Anatomy of a Hit"
(Program 9); answers the questions, Was
the popularity of "Hello, Dolly" a freak?
Could it happen again and how did it happen
in the first place? Westinghouse Broadcasting Corporation, 1964.
1 reel (7 in.) 7 1/2 in. per sec.
phonotape. (The Music Goes Round and Round)

I. Title: The anatomy of a hit. II. Series.

The anatomy of a hit
Voice Lib.
M765 Steinberg, Dick
bd.5 Excerpt from "The Anatomy of a Hit" (Program
9); comments on the difficulty of compiling
sheet list of the top records in the country.
Westinghouse Broadcasting Corporation, 1964.
1 reel (7 in.) 7 1/2 in. per sec.
phonotape. (The Music Goes Round and Round)

I. Title: The anatomy of a hit. II. Series.

The anatomy of a hit
Voice Lib.
M765 Wax, Morty
bd.3 Excerpt from "The anatomy of a hit"
(Program 9); comments on his role as an
independent record promoter; also answers
question whether or not the songs we are
hearing day after day are being given to us
against our will. Westinghouse Broadcasting
Corporation, 1964.
2 min., 55 sec. phonotape (1 r. 7 1/2 i.p.s.)
(The music goes round and round)
1. Music, Popular (Songs, etc.) - Writing & publishing.
2. Phonorecords. I. Title: The anatomy of a hit.
II. Series.

C1
M25
     And the band played on
     Whorf, Michael, 1933-
       And the band played on.
       1 tape cassette.   (The visual sounds of
     Mike Whorf. Miscellaneous, M25)

       Originally presented on his radio program, Kaleidoscope,
WJR, Detroit.
       Duration: 55 min., 30 sec.
       A highly successful and original work, depicting musically
what the instruments are, what they do and sound like.

       L Bands (Music) L Title.

      Anders, William Alison, 1933-
Voice Lib.
M1351 Apollo 8 (space flight): interview with
bd.1   astronauts William Anders, James Lovell,
     and Frank Borman on CBS TV program "Face
     the nation".   CBS TV, January 12, 1969.
     1 reel (7 in.) 7 1/2 in. per sec.
phonotape.

     1. Project Apollo. 2. Anders, William
Alison, 1933-   3. Lovell, James Arthur, 1928-
4. Borman, Frank, 1928-   I. Anders, William
Alison, 1933-   II. Lovell, James Arthur,
1928-   III. Borman, Frank, 1928-

C1
M40
     And the days grow short when you reach
       September
     Whorf, Michael, 1933-
       And the days grow short when you reach
     September.
       1 tape cassette.   (The visual sounds of
Mike Whorf. Miscellaneous, M40)
       Originally presented on his radio program, Kaleidoscope,
WJR, Detroit.
       Duration: 36 min., 25 sec.
       Here in an evocative word-portrait of autumn, is brought to life
the bittersweet qualities of this special season. As the leaves turn
to brilliant scarlets, yellows and oranges and the nip of frost steals
into the evenings, your mind's eye will conjure up visions and
memories.
       L Autumn. L Title.

      ANDERSEN, HANS CHRISTIAN, 1805-1875
Voice Lib.
M1005 Hans Christian Andersen (Television program)
     TV adaptation of film of same title, with
     Danny Kaye and Victor Borge.   ABC-TV, Nov. 3,
     1966.
     1 reel (7 in.) 7 1/2 in. per sec.
phonotape.

     1. Andersen, Hans Christian, 1805-1875.
I. Kaye, Danny, 1913-   II. Borge,
Victor, 1909-

C1
SC27
     And then came the light - Copernicus, Galileo
     Whorf, Michael, 1933-
       And then came the light - Copernicus, Galileo.
       1 tape cassette.   (The visual sounds of
Mike Whorf. Science, SC27)
       Originally presented on his radio program, Kaleidoscope,
WJR, Detroit.
       Duration: 39 min., 15 sec.
       For the true stargazer here is an accurate account of the great
astronomers. Included are brief accounts of the lives of Copernicus,
Galileo, and others who have contributed to the science of
astronomy.

       L Copernicus, Nicolaus, 1473-1543. 2. Galilei, Galileo,
1564-1642. L Title.

Voice Lib.
131   Anderson, Clinton Presba, 1895-
bd.4   Address at Michigan State University,
     with introduction by President John A.
     Hannah. WKAR, 1961.
     1 reel (7 in.) 7 1/2 in. per sec.
phonotape.

     I. Hannah, John Alfred, 1902-

Voice Lib. Anders, William Alison, 1933-
M1347- Apollo 8 (space flight): recovery. CBS TV
1348,   description of recovery of astronauts and
bd.1   their reception on aircraft carrier "York-
     town". CBS TV, December 27, 1968.
     2 reels (7 in.) 7 1/2 in. per sec.
phonotape.

     1. Project Apollo. 2. Anders, William
Alison, 1933-   3. Lovell, James Arthur, 1928-
4. Borman, Frank, 1928-   I. Anders, William
Alison, 1933-   II. Lovell, James Arthur,
1928-   III. Borman, Frank, 1928-

Voice Lib.
M1495 Anderson, Donald
     Series of poems, narrated by the author,
     handicapped college student Donald Anderson,
     compiled on Christmas, 1971.
     1 reel (7 in.) 7 1/2 in. per sec.
phonotape.

Voice Lib. Anders, William Alison, 1933-
M1348 Apollo 8 (space flight): reception of Apollo
bd.2   8 astronauts at Joint Session of Congress,
     including addresses by the astronauts.
     CBS TV, January 1, 1969.
     1 reel (7 in.) 7 1/2 in. per sec.
phonotape.
     1. Project Apollo. 2. Anders, William
Alison, 1933-   3. Lovell, James Arthur, 1928-
4. Borman, Frank, 1928-   I. Anders, William
Alison, 1933-   II. Lovell, James Arthur,
1928-   III. Borman, Frank, 1928-   IV.
McCormack, John William, 1891-

Voice Lib. Anderson, Judith
M225   Packard, Frederick
       Styles in Shakespearean acting, 1890-1950.
     Creative Associates, 1963?
       1 reel (7 in.) 7 1/2 i.p.s. phonotape.

       L Sothern, Edward Askew, 1826-1881. II. Marlowe,
Julia, 1865-1950. III. Booth, Edwin, 1833-1893. IV. Gielgud,
John, 1904- V. Robeson, Paul Bustill, 1898- VI. Terry,
Dame Ellen, 1848-1928. VII. Allen, Viola. VIII. Welles,
Orson, 1915- IX. Skinner, Otis, 1858-1942. X. Barrymore,
John, 1882-1942. XI. Olivier, Sir Laurence Kerr, 1907-
XII. Forbes-Robertson, Sir Johnston, 1853- XIII. Evans,
Maurice. XIV. Thorndike, Dame Sybil, 1882- XV. Robson,
Flora. XVI. LeGallienne, Eva, 1899- XVII. Anderson,
Judith. XVIII. Duncan, Augustin. XIX. Hampden, Walter,
XX. Speaight, Robert, 190?- XXL Jones, Daniel.

Voice Lib.
191   Anderson, Marian, 1902-
       Singing spirituals. RCA Victor, 1958.
       1 reel (7 in.)   7 1/2 in. per sec.
       phonotape.

              Anderson, Marian, 1902-
Voice Lib.
M310   American Broadcasting Company.
       Tribute to President John Fitzgerald Kennedy
       from the arts. Fredric March emcees; Jerome
       Hines sings "Worship of God and Nature" by
       Beethoven; Florence Eldridge recites "When
       lilacs last in the door-yard bloom'd" by Walt
       Whitman; Marian Anderson in two songs. Includes
       Charlton Heston, Sidney Blackmer, Isaac Stern,
       Nathan Milstein, Christopher Plummer, Albert
       Finney. ABC, November 24, 1963.
       55 min. phonotape (7 in.   7 1/2 i.p.s.)
                                    (Continued on next card)

              Anderson, Robert Bernerd, 1910-
Voice Lib.
M1368 Some friends of General Eisenhower (TV program)
       CBS-TV special recalling anecdotes about
       General Eisenhower by some of his friends:
       Bob Hope, Kevin McCann, General Omar Bradley,
       Robert B. Anderson, General Alfred Gruenther,
       with Walter Cronkite acting as emcee. CBS-TV,
       March 29, 1969.
       1 reel (7 in.) 7 1/2 in. per sec.
       I. Eisenhower, Dwight David, Pres. U.S., 1890-1969. I.
       Hope, Bob, 1903-   II. McCann, Kevin   III. Bradley, Omar
       Nelson, 1893-   IV. Anderson, Robert Bernerd, 1910-   V.
       Gruenther, Alfred Maximilian, 1899-   VI. Cronkite, Walter
       Leland, 1916-

Voice Lib.
652   Anderson, William Robert, 1921-
bd.9   Voice taped aboard the "Nautilus", four
       to ten miles from the North Pole under the
       ice cap; addressed to crew on this historic
       occasion. CBS, August 8, 1958.
       1 reel (7 in.)   7 1/2 in. per sec.
       phonotape.

       1. Underwater exploration.

Voice Lib.
M1706 Andrews, Julie, 1935-
bd.2   Discusses her career and her two books
       and her family on the Today Show with
       Barbara Walters. NBC, June 5, 1974.
       10 min. phonotape (1 r.   7 1/2 i.p.s.)

       1. Andrews, Julie, 1935-   I. Walters,
       Barbara, 1931-

Voice Lib. Andrews, Julie, 1935-
126   Lerner, Alan Jay, 1918-
       Lerner and Loewe; condensed NBC-TV special
       with Julie Andrews, Richard Burton, Robert
       Goulet, Alan Lerner and Frederick Loewe.
       NBC, February 2, 1962.
       1 reel (7 in.)   7 1/2 in. per sec.
       phonotape.
       I. Andrews, Julie, 1935-   II. Burton,
       Richard, 1925-   III. Goulet, Robert
       Gerard, 1933-   IV. Loewe, Frederick, 1904-

              Another day in June - D-Day
C1
H50   Whorf, Michael, 1933-
       Another day in June - D-Day.
       1 tape cassette. (The visual sounds of
       Mike Whorf. History and heritage, H50)
       Originally presented on his radio program, Kaleidoscope,
       WJR, Detroit.
       Duration: 42 min.. 30 sec.
       June 6, 1944 - D-Day. Here is an unusual account of the
       greatest armada to ever set sail in the Allies' attempt to turn
       the tide of battle in their favor.
       1. World War, 1939-1945 - Campaigns - Normandy.
       I. Title.

              ANTI-COMMUNIST MOVEMENTS
Voice Lib.
M1912 Freedom house; special TV program. Filmed
       documentary about men and their methods in
       the fight to combat communist tyranny;
       featuring the Murrow-McCarthy debates from
       "See It Now" TV programs; also excerpts
       from Army-McCarthy Senate hearings, state-
       ments by Gen. Eisenhower and Bishop Sheil.
       CBS, 1954.
       1 reel (7 in.)   7 1/2 i.p.s. phonotape.
       1. Anti-communist movements. 2. McCarthy-
       Army controversy, 1954.

              ANTI-NAZI MOVEMENT
Voice Lib.
M1228 Gaulle, Charles de, Pres. France, 1890-
bd.4   1970.
       Radio appeal made over the BBC about
       resistance to the German occupation after
       the surrender of France and the founding
       of the Free French Forces. Peteler.
       June 23, 1940.
       1 reel (7 in.)   7 1/2 in. per sec.
       phonotape.

              ANTINEOPLASTIC AGENTS
Voice Lib.
M1434 Rosenberg, Barnett
       MSU professor of biophysics, Dr. Barnett
       Rosenberg, in lecture pertaining to new
       anti-tumor agent. MSU Information Services,
       April 24, 1969.
       1 reel (7 in.)   7 1/2 i.p.s. phonotape.

       1. Antineoplastic agents.

Voice Lib.
M1328   Apollo 7 (space flight): description of
od.2   launching of Apollo 7 spacecraft, morning
           of October 11, 1968, and comments by various
           broadcasters,including Walter Cronkite.
           Description includes countdown and take-off;
           remarks by astronauts.   CBS TV, October 11,
           1968.
              1 reel (7 in.)   7 1/2 in. per sec.   phonotape.
              1. Project Apollo. 2. Eisele, Donn F   1930-   3. Cunning-
           ham, R   Walter, 1932-   4. Schirra, Walter Marty, 1923-
           I. Eisele, Donn F   1930-   II. Cunningham, R   Walter,
           1932-   III. Schirra, Walter Marty, 1923-   IV. Cronkite,
           Walter Leland, 1916-

Voice Lib.
M1364   Apollo 9 (space flight): splashdown, part 1.
           CBS correspondents with anchorman Walter
           Cronkite describe recovery of Apollo 9
           from the time astronauts are over Australia
           to the opening of the hatch.   CBS TV,
           March 13, 1969.
              1 reel (7 in.)   7 1/2 in. per sec.
           phonotape.
              1. Project Apollo. 2. McDivitt, James Alton, 1929-   3.
           Scott, David Randolph, 1932-   4. Schweickart, Russell L
           1936-   I. McDivitt, James Alton, 1929-   II. Scott, David
           Randolph, 1932-   III. Schweickart, Russell L   1936-
           IV. Cronkite, Walter Leland, 1916-

Voice Lib.
M1347- Apollo 8 (space flight): recovery.   CBS TV
1348,   description of recovery of astronauts and
bd.1   their reception on aircraft carrier "York-
           town".   CBS TV, December 27, 1968.
              2 reels (7 in.)   7 1/2 in. per sec.
           phonotape.
              1. Project Apollo. 2. Anders, William
           Alison, 1933-   3. Lovell, James Arthur, 1928-
           4. Borman, Frank, 1928-   I. Anders, William
           Alison, 1933-   II. Lovell, James Arthur,
           1928-   III. Borman, Frank, 1928-

Voice Lib.
M1365   Apollo 9 (space flight): splashdown, part 2.
           CBS TV description of retrieval of Apollo 9
           astronauts, starting with the opening of the
           hatch to their examination in sick bay on
           the recovery ship.   Includes telegram by
           President Nixon and brief remarks by the
           astronauts.   CBS TV, March 13, 1969.
              1 reel (7 in.)   7 1/2 in. per sec.
           phonotape.
              1. Project Apollo. 2. McDivitt, James Alton, 1929-   3.
           Scott, David Randolph, 1932-   4. Schweickart, Russell L
           1936-   I. McDivitt, James Alton, 1929-   II. Scott, David
           Randolph, 1932-   III. Schweickart, Russell L   1936-

Voice Lib.
M1348   Apollo 8 (space flight): reception of Apollo
bd.2   8 astronauts at Joint Session of Congress,
           including addresses by the astronauts.
           CBS TV, January 1, 1969.
              1 reel (7 in.)   7 1/2 in. per sec.
           phonotape.
              1. Project Apollo. 2. Anders, William
           Alison, 1933-   3. Lovell, James Arthur, 1928-
           4. Borman, Frank, 1928-   I. Anders, William
           Alison, 1933-   II. Lovell, James Arthur,
           1928-   III. Borman, Frank, 1928-   IV.
           McCormack, John William, 1891-

Voice Lib.
M1377   Apollo 10 (space flight): lift-off.   Commentary
bd.1   by NBC TV news; countdown, lift-off.   Astro-
           nauts Tom Stafford, John Young, Eugene Cernan.
           NBC TV, May 18, 1969.
              1 reel (7 in.)   7 1/2 in. per sec.
           phonotape.
              1. Project Apollo. 2. Space flight to the
           moon. 3. Stafford, Thomas F   1931-   4.
           Young, John Watts, 1930-   5. Cernan, Eugene
           Andrew, 1934-   I. Stafford, Thomas F   1931-
           II. Young, John Watts, 1930-   III. Cernan,
           Eugene Andrew, 1934-

Voice Lib.
M1351   Apollo 8 (space flight): interview with
bd.1   astronauts William Anders, James Lovell,
           and Frank Borman on CBS TV program "Face
           the nation".   CBS TV, January 12, 1969.
              1 reel (7 in.)   7 1/2 in. per sec.
           phonotape.
              1. Project Apollo. 2. Anders, William
           Alison, 1933-   3. Lovell, James Arthur, 1928-
           4. Borman, Frank, 1928-   I. Anders, William
           Alison, 1933-   II. Lovell, James Arthur,
           1928-   III. Borman, Frank, 1928-

Voice Lib.
M1377   Apollo 10 (space flight): television pictures.
bd.2   Commentary from astronauts, NBC TV, on
           initial separation and docking of Lunar
           Landing Module, first live color television
           pictures from space, and pictures of the
           earth from 6,500 nautical miles out.   NBC
           TV, May, 1969.
              1 reel (7 in.)   7 1/2 in. per sec.   phonotape.
              1. Project Apollo. 2. Space flight to the moon. 3. Stafford,
           Thomas P   1931-   4. Young, John Watts, 1930-   5.
           Cernan, Eugene Andrew, 1934-   I. Stafford, Thomas P
           1931-   II. Young, John Watts, 1930-   III. Cernan, Eugene
           Andrew, 1934-

Voice Lib.
M1355   Apollo 9 (space flight): lift-off of Apollo 9
bd.3   space flight at 11 a.m., March 3, 1969.
           Description by CBS-TV commentators, Mission
           Control, and astronauts.   CBS TV, March 3,
           1969.
              1 reel (7 in.)   7 1/2 in. per sec.
           phonotape.
              1. Project Apollo. 2. McDivitt, James Alton, 1929-   3.
           Scott, David Randolph, 1932-   4. Schweickart, Russell L
           1936-   I. McDivitt, James Alton, 1929-   II. Scott, David
           Randolph, 1932-   III. Schweickart, Russell L   1936-

Voice Lib.
M1377   Apollo 10 (space flight): splashdown and
bd.3   recovery of Apollo 10; astronauts' first
           words after returning to earth; from the
           recovery ship U.S.S. "Princeton".   CBS TV,
           May 26, 1969.
              1 reel (7 in.)   7 1/2 in. per sec.
           phonotape.
              1. Project Apollo. 2. Space flight to the moon. 3. Stafford,
           Thomas P   1931-   4. Young, John Watts, 1930-   5.
           Cernan, Eugene Andrew, 1934-   I. Stafford, Thomas P
           1931-   II. Young, John Watts, 1930-   III. Cernan, Eugene
           Andrew, 1934-

Voice Lib.
M1384   Apollo 11 (space flight): launch day, July 16,
bd.1   1969. Description of astronauts going up
           the elevator; conversation between Walter
           Cronkite and Walter Schirra at approximately
           2 hours before launch. CBS TV, July 16, 1969.
           1 reel (7 in.)   7 1/2 in. per sec.
           phonotape.
           1. Project Apollo. 2. Space flight to the moon. 3. Aldrin,
           Edwin E   1930-   4. Collins, Michael, 1930-   5. Armstrong,
           Neil, 1930-   I. Aldrin, Edwin E   1930-   II. Collins,
           Michael, 1930-   III. Armstrong, Neil, 1930-   IV. Cronkite,
           Walter Leland, 1916-   V. Schirra, Walter Marty, 1923-

Voice Lib.
M1385   Apollo 11 (space flight): Frank McGee speaking
bd.1   about communications between "Eagle" and
           ground. Conversation between Houston and
           astronauts. Message of "Go for PDI"; "The
           Eagle has landed" (102 hours, 45 minutes,
           40 seconds)   Description of rocks and
           boulders on moon. NBC TV, July 20, 1969.
           1 reel (7 in.) 7 1/2 in. per sec. phonotape.
           1. Project Apollo. 2. Space flight to the moon. 3. Aldrin,
           Edwin E   1930-   4. Collins, Michael, 1930-   5.
           Armstrong, Neil, 1930-   I. Aldrin, Edwin E   1930-
           II. Collins, Michael, 1930-   III. Armstrong, Neil, 1930-
           IV. McGee, Frank, 1921-1974.

Voice Lib.
M1384   Apollo 11 (space flight): biographical sketches
bd.2   of the three astronauts, Edwin Aldrin,
           Michael Collins, and Neil Armstrong, by Chet
           Huntley, at approximately 78 minutes before
           launch time. NBC TV, July 16, 1969.
           1 reel (7 in.)   7 1/2 in. per sec.
           phonotape.
           1. Project Apollo. 2. Space flight to the moon. 3. Aldrin,
           Edwin E   1930-   4. Collins, Michael, 1930-   5. Armstrong,
           Neil, 1930-   I. Aldrin, Edwin E   1930-   II. Collins,
           Michael, 1930-   III. Armstrong, Neil, 1930-   IV. Huntley,
           Chet, 1911-1974.

Voice Lib.
M1385   Apollo 11 (space flight): Neil Armstrong
bd.2   requesting everyone everywhere to pause and
           give thanks. Preparing to open hatch and
           walk on the moon. Armstrong backing out
           from hatch, describing lunar surface. "One
           small step for man, one giant step for man-
           kind" (109 hours, 24 minutes, 20 seconds.)
           Bringing down cameras. CBS TV, July 20, 1969.
           1 reel (7 in.) 7 1/2 in. per sec. phonotape.
           1. Project Apollo. 2. Space flight to the moon. 3. Aldrin,
           Edwin E   1930-   4. Collins, Michael, 1930-   5. Armstrong,
           Neil, 1930-   I. Aldrin, Edwin E   1930-   II. Collins, Michael,
           1930-   III. Armstrong, Neil, 1930-

Voice Lib.
M1384   Apollo 11 (space flight): Frank McGee giving
bd.3   an itinerary of space ships, dates, times,
           etc. NBC TV, July 16, 1969.
           1 reel (7 in.)   7 1/2 in. per sec.
           phonotape.
           1. Project Apollo. 2. Space flight to the
           moon. 3. Aldrin, Edwin E   1930-   4.
           Collins, Michael, 1930-   5. Armstrong, Neil,
           1930-   I. Aldrin, Edwin E   1930-   II.
           Collins, Michael, 1930-   III. Armstrong, Neil,
           1930-   IV. McGee, Frank, 1921-1974.

Voice Lib.
M1386   Apollo 11 (space flight): conversation with
bd.1   broadcasters Walter Cronkite and Wally
           Schirra. Including Armstrong's activities
           on moon alone; pictures, rock descriptions,
           then Aldrin coming down ladder; rock boxes
           put to use. TV cameras put at 30' panoramic
           position. Reading inscription of plaque
           with U.S. flag and setting it up. Telephone
           call from Washington to astronauts and their
           acknowledgement. CBS TV, July 20, 1969.
           1 reel (7 in.)   7 1/2 in. per sec.
           phonotape.
                          (Continued on next card)

Voice Lib.
M1384   Apollo 11 (space flight): interviews between
bd.4   Frank McGee and Neil Armstrong previous to
           the flight of Apollo 11. NBC TV, July 16,
           1969.
           1 reel (7 in.)   7 1/2 in. per sec.
           phonotape.
           1. Project Apollo. I. McGee, Frank, 1921-
           1974. II. Armstrong, Neil, 1930-

Voice Lib.
M1386   Apollo 11 (space flight): conversation with
bd.1   broadcasters... July 20, 1969. (Card 2)

           1. Project Apollo. 2. Space flight to the
           moon. 3. Aldrin, Edwin E   1930-   4.
           Collins, Michael, 1930-   5. Armstrong,
           Neil, 1930-   I. Aldrin, Edwin E   1930-
           II. Collins, Michael, 1930-   III. Armstrong,
           Neil, 1930-   IV. Cronkite, Walter Leland,
           1916-   V. Schirra, Walter Marty, 1923-
           VI. Nixon, Richard Milhous, Pres. U.S., 1913-

Voice Lib.
M1384   Apollo 11 (space flight): launch day progress
bd.6   of countdown by Apollo 11 control at 4
           minutes 15 seconds to actual take-off.
           Houston takes over and describes progress
           up to 1,000 miles downrange and successful
           orbit. NBC TV, July 16, 1969.
           1 reel (7 in.)   7 1/2 in. per sec.
           phonotape.
           1. Project Apollo. 2. Space flight to the moon. 3. Aldrin,
           Edwin E   1930-   4. Collins, Michael, 1930-   5. Armstrong,
           Neil, 1930-   I. Aldrin, Edwin E   1930-   II. Collins,
           Michael, 1930-   III. Armstrong, Neil, 1930-

Voice Lib.
M1386   Apollo 11 (space flight): blessing by Pope
bd.2   Paul VI from the Vatican to Apollo 11
           astronauts. CBS TV, July 20, 1969.
           1 reel (7 in.)   7 1/2 in. per sec.
           phonotape.
           1. Project Apollo. 2. Space flight to the
           moon. 3. Aldrin, Edwin E   1930-   4.
           Collins, Michael, 1930-   5. Armstrong, Neil,
           1930-   I. Aldrin, Edwin E   1930-   II.
           Collins, Michael, 1930-   III. Armstrong, Neil,
           1930-   IV. Paulus VI, Pope, 1897-

Voice Lib.
M1386 Apollo 11 (space flight): excerpts of old
bd.3   Mercury Theatre "War of the Worlds" of
        1938; an interview with Orson Welles by
        Mike Wallace. CBS TV, July 20, 1969.
        1 reel (7 in.)   7 1/2 in. per sec.
        phonotape.
        L. Project Apollo. 2. Space flight to the moon. 3. Aldrin,
        Edwin E   1930-   4. Collins, Michael, 1930-
        5. Armstrong, Neil, 1930-   L. Aldrin, Edwin E   1930-
        II. Collins, Michael, 1930-   III. Armstrong, Neil, 1930-
        IV. Welles, Orson, 1915-   V. Wallace, Mike, 1918-

Voice Lib.
M1386 Apollo 11 (space flight): excerpts of
bd.4   interview between Walter Cronkite and
        Lyndon B. Johnson two weeks before the
        moon flight regarding development of American
        space effort. CBS TV, July 20, 1969.
        1 reel (7 in.)   7 1/2 in. per sec.
        phonotape.
        1. Project Apollo. 2. Space flight to the
        moon. I. Cronkite, Walter Leland, 1916-
        II. Johnson, Lyndon Baines, Pres. U.S., 1908-
        1973.

Voice Lib.
M1587 Apollo 11 (space flight): description of
bd.1   ascent from moon by Frank McGee. Count-
        down, ignition, and lift-off. Meeting the
        command module "Columbia"; docking; trans-
        fer of gear from "Eagle" to "Columbia".
        Recap by ABC's Jules Bergman and Frank
        Reynolds. NBC and ABC TV, July 21, 1969.
        1 reel (7 in.)   7 1/2 in. per sec.   phonotape.
        L. Project Apollo. 2. Space flight to the moon. 3. Aldrin,
        Edwin E   1930-   4. Collins, Michael, 1930-   5.
        Armstrong, Neil, 1930-   L. Aldrin, Edwin E   1930-   II.
        Collins, Michael, 1930-   III. Armstrong, Neil, 1930-   IV.
        McGee, Frank, 1921-1974. V. Bergman, Jules VI. Reynolds,
        Frank

Voice Lib.
M1387 Apollo 11 (space flight): recovery. Walter Cronkite and Wally
bd.2   Schirra announce proceedings from aircraft carrier "Hornet";
        trying to track spacecraft coming down: chutes opening at
        10,500 feet; voice contact with spacecraft; visual of chutes;
        splashdown 9 miles from "Hornet", upside-down. Collar
        attached to spacecraft. NBC and ABC TV, July 24, 1969.
        1 reel (7 in.)   7 1/2 in. per sec.   phonotape.
        L. Project Apollo. 2. Space flight to the moon. 3. Aldrin,
        Edwin E   1930-   4. Collins, Michael, 1930-   5.
        Armstrong, Neil, 1930-   L. Aldrin, Edwin E   1930-
        II. Collins, Michael, 1930-   III. Armstrong, Neil, 1930-
        IV. Cronkite, Walter Leland, 1916-   V. Schirra, Walter Marty,
        1923-

Voice Lib.
M1388 Apollo 11 (space flight): Walter Cronkite and Wally Schirra
bd.1   describing recovery. Maneuvers by frogmen and helicopters
        at splashdown spot; "air boss" describes close-up scene;
        decontamination process; helicopter landing on "Hornet" with
        astronauts; reception. Description of proceedings on "Hornet"
        by CBS newscasters. CBS TV, July 24, 1969.
        1 reel (7 in.)   7 1/2 in. per sec.   phonotape.
        L. Project Apollo. 2. Space flight to the moon. 3. Aldrin,
        Edwin E   1930-   4. Collins, Michael, 1930-   5. Armstrong,
        Neil, 1930-   L. Aldrin, Edwin E   1930-   II. Collins,
        Michael, 1930-   III. Armstrong, Neil, 1930-   IV. Cronkite,
        Walter Leland, 1916-   V. Schirra, Walter Marty, 1923-

Voice Lib.
M1388 Apollo 11 (space flight): personal greeting
bd.2   by President Nixon to the astronauts on
        the "Hornet" and their replies. Chaplain's
        prayer. Nixon taking off. CBS and NBC TV,
        July 24, 1969.
        1 reel (7 in.)   7 1/2 in. per sec.
        phonotape.
        L. Project Apollo. 2. Space flight to the moon. 3. Aldrin,
        Edwin E   1930-   4. Collins, Michael, 1930-   5.
        Armstrong, Neil, 1930-   L. Aldrin, Edwin E   1930-
        II. Collins, Michael, 1930-   III. Armstrong, Neil, 1930-
        IV. Nixon, Richard Milhous, Pres. U.S., 1913-

Voice Lib.
M1389 Apollo 11 (space flight): excerpt of press
bd.1   conference with Apollo 11 astronauts in
        Houston. CBS TV, August 12, 1969.
        1 reel (7 in.)   7 1/2 in. per sec.
        phonotape.
        1. Project Apollo. 2. Space flight to the
        moon. 3. Aldrin, Edwin E   1930-   4.
        Collins, Michael, 1930-   5. Armstrong, Neil,
        1930-   I. Aldrin, Edwin E   1930-   II.
        Collins, Michael, 1930-   III. Armstrong,
        Neil, 1930-

Voice Lib.
M1389 Apollo 11 (space flight): welcome to Apollo 11 astronauts on their
bd.2   arrival at Kennedy Airport at New York; ferried by Marine
        helicopter to Wall Street; boat whistles harbor greeting.
        Flashbacks to former important New York parades (Frank McGee)
        Walter Cronkite, CBS, describing beginning of motorcade
        and parade to city hall. CBS [and NBC] TV, August 13, 1969.
        1 reel (7 in.)   7 1/2 in. per sec.   phonotape.
        L. Project Apollo. 2. Space flight to the moon. 3. Aldrin,
        Edwin E   1930-   4. Collins, Michael, 1930-   5.
        Armstrong, Neil, 1930-   L. Aldrin, Edwin E   1930-
        II. Collins, Michael, 1930-   III. Armstrong, Neil, 1930-
        IV. McGee, Frank, 1921-1974. V. Cronkite, Walter Leland, 1916-

Voice Lib.
M1390 Apollo 11 (space flight): reception for
        Apollo 11 astronauts in New York. Descrip-
        tion of approach and ceremony at city hall.
        Cardinal Cooke's invocation. Introduction
        by Mayor Lindsay. Presentation of Medal of
        Honor. Reply by all astronauts. Benediction.
        NBC TV, August 13, 1969.
        1 reel (7 in.)   7 1/2 in. per sec.   phonotape.
        L. Project Apollo. 2. Space flight to the moon. 3. Aldrin,
        Edwin E   1930-   4. Collins, Michael, 1930-   5.
        Armstrong, Neil, 1930-   L. Aldrin, Edwin E   1930-   II.
        Collins, Michael, 1930-   III. Armstrong, Neil, 1930-   IV.
        Cooke, Terence James, cardinal, 1921-   V. Lindsay, John Vliet,
        1921-

Voice Lib.
M1391 Apollo 11 (space flight): reception of Apollo 11 astronauts at
bd.1   United Nations Plaza. Statement by U.N. Secretary-
        General U Thant. Reply by Neil Armstrong. Presentation
        of tokens of appreciation to all three astronauts and their
        wives and Dr. Thomas Paine. Presentation of duplicate of
        plaque left on moon to U Thant. NBC TV, August 13, 1969.
        1 reel (7 in.)   7 1/2 in. per sec.   phonotape.
        L. Project Apollo. 2. Space flight to the moon. 3. Aldrin,
        Edwin E   1930-   4. Collins, Michael, 1930-   5.
        Armstrong, Neil, 1930-   L. Aldrin, Edwin E   1930-
        II. Collins, Michael, 1930-   III. Armstrong, Neil, 1930-
        IV. Thant, U, 1909-   V. Paine, Thomas Otten, 1921-

Voice Lib.
M1391   Apollo 11 (space flight): reception of
bd.2   Apollo 11 astronauts in Chicago. Descrip-
        tion of motorcade on way to Civic Center
        Plaza and ceremonies there. Cardinal Cody's
        invocation. JFK flashback predicting moon
        landing before decade is out. Mayor Daley
        and Alderman Klene resolution making August
        13 "Astronauts' Day". Senator Percy and
        Governor Ogilvie of Illinois. Presentation
        of honorary citizenship to astronauts.
        [Source?] August 13, 1969.
                        (Continued on next card)

Voice Lib.
M1391   Apollo 11 (space flight): reception of Apollo
bd.2   11 astronauts ... 1969. (Card 2)
        1 reel (7 in.)   7 1/2 in. per sec.
        phonotape.
        1. Project Apollo. 2. Space flight to the moon. 3. Aldrin,
        Edwin E   1930- 4. Collins, Michael, 1930- 5. Armstrong,
        Neil, 1930-   I. Aldrin, Edwin E   1930- II. Collins,
        Michael, 1930-   III. Armstrong, Neil, 1930- IV. Cody,
        John Patrick, cardinal, 1907-   V. Kennedy, John Fitzgerald,
        Pres. U.S., 1917-1963. VI. Daley, Richard J   1902- VII.
        Percy, Charles Harting, 1919- VIII. Ogilvie, Richard Buell,
        1923-

Voice Lib.
M1403   Apollo 12 (space flight): lift-off of Apollo
bd.1   12; the electrical "glitch" and instructions
        and corrections; Dr. Paine and President
        Nixon speaking from VIP section. CBS TV,
        November 19, 1969.
        1 reel (7 in.)   7 1/2 in. per sec.
        phonotape.
        1. Project Apollo. 2. Space flight to the moon. 3. Conrad,
        Charles, 1930- 4. Bean, Alan L   1932- 5. Gordon,
        Richard F   1929-   I. Conrad, Charles, 1930- II. Bean,
        Alan L   1932- III. Gordon, Richard F   1929- IV.
        Paine, Thomas Otten, 1921-   V. Nixon, Richard Milhous, Pres.
        U.S., 1913-

Voice Lib.
M1403   Apollo 12 (space flight): landing on the
bd.2   moon; conversations of Frank McGee and
        mission control; dialogue of Pete Conrad
        preparing to step out on moon; coached on
        going down ladder; Conrad singing from the
        moon; trouble with TV camera. NBC TV,
        November 19, 1969.
        1 reel (7 in.) 7 1/2 in. per sec. phonotape.
        1. Project Apollo. 2. Space flight to the moon. 3. Conrad,
        Charles, 1930- 4. Bean, Alan L   1932- 5. Gordon,
        Richard F   1929-   I. Conrad, Charles, 1930- II. Bean,
        Alan L   1932- III. Gordon, Richard F   1929- IV.
        McGee, Frank, 1921-1974.

Voice Lib.
M1404   Apollo 12 (space flight): description of
bd.1   last minutes on the moon of Apollo 12
        crew; countdown, lift-off from the moon.
        CBS TV, November 20, 1969.
        1 reel (7 in.)   7 1/2 in. per sec.
        phonotape.
        1. Project Apollo. 2. Space flight to the
        moon. 3. Conrad, Charles, 1930- 4. Bean,
        Alan L   1932- 5. Gordon, Richard F
        1929-   I. Conrad, Charles, 1930- II.
        Bean, Alan L   1932- III. Gordon, Richard
        F   1929-

Voice Lib.
M1404   Apollo 12 (space flight): description of
bd.2   splashdown of Apollo 12 and proceeding
        to aircraft carrier "Hornet". CBS TV,
        November 24, 1969.
        1 reel (7 in.)   7 1/2 in. per sec.
        phonotape.
        1. Project Apollo. 2. Space flight to the
        moon. 3. Conrad, Charles, 1930- 4. Bean,
        Alan L   1932- 5. Gordon, Richard F
        1929-   I. Conrad, Charles, 1930- II.
        Bean, Alan L   1932- III. Gordon, Richard
        F   1929-

Voice Lib.
M1423   Apollo 13 (space flight): resumé of flight
        of Apollo 13, including lift-off, mal-
        function, and splashdown, and interviews
        on future of space program. NBC TV,
        April, 1970.
        1 reel (7 in.)   7 1/2 in. per sec.
        phonotape.
        1. Project Apollo. 2. Space flight to the moon. 3. Haise,
        Fred W   1934- 4. Lovell, James Arthur, 1928- 5.
        Swigert, John L   1932-   I. Haise, Fred W   1934-
        II. Lovell, James Arthur, 1928- III. Swigert, John L   1932-

Voice Lib.
M1424   Apollo 13 (space flight): oxygen malfunction
        on Apollo 13 described by NASA, astronauts,
        and Howard K. Smith. ABC TV, April 14, 1970.
        1 reel (7 in.)   7 1/2 in. per sec.
        phonotape.
        1. Project Apollo. 2. Space flight to the
        moon. 3. Haise, Fred W   1934- 4.
        Lovell, James Arthur, 1928- 5. Swigert,
        John L   1932-   I. Haise, Fred W   1934-
        II. Lovell, James Arthur, 1928- III. Swigert,
        John L   1932- IV. Smith, Howard Kingsbury,
        1914-

Voice Lib.
M1438   Apollo 14 (space flight): take-off from Cape
bd.1   Kennedy, including countdown. CBS,
        January 31, 1971.
        1 reel (7 in.)   7 1/2 in. per sec.
        phonotape.
        1. Project Apollo. 2. Space flight to the
        moon. 3. Shepard, Alan Bartlett, 1923- 4.
        Mitchell, Edgar D   1931- 5. Roosa,
        Stuart A   1934-   I. Shepard, Alan Bartlett,
        1923- II. Mitchell, Edgar D   1931- III.
        Roosa, Stuart A   1934-

Voice Lib.
M1438   Apollo 14 (space flight): lunar landed on the
bd.2   moon and moon walk. CBS, February 5, 1971.
        1 reel (7 in.)   7 1/2 in. per sec.
        phonotape.
        1. Project Apollo. 2. Space flight to the
        moon. 3. Shepard, Alan Bartlett, 1923- 4.
        Mitchell, Edgar D   1931- 5. Roosa, Stuart
        A   1934-   I. Shepard, Alan Bartlett,
        1923- II. Mitchell, Edgar D   1931- III.
        Roosa, Stuart A   1934-

Voice Lib.
M1438 Apollo 14 (space flight): Apollo 14 splash-
bd.3-   down and reception on aircraft carrier.
M1439   CBS, February 9, 1971.
bd.1   2 reels(7 in.) 7 1/2 in. per sec.
          phonotape.

          1. Project Apollo. 2. Space flight to the
     moon. 3. Shepard, Alan Bartlett, 1923- 4.
     Mitchell, Edgar D 1931-   5. Roosa,
     Stuart A   1934-   I. Shepard, Alan Bartlett,
     1923- II. Mitchell, Edgar D 1931- III.
     Roosa, Stuart A   1934-

Voice Lib.
M1480 Apollo 15 (space flight): lift-off.
bd.1   CBS TV, July 26, 1971.
         1 reel (7 in.) 7 1/2 in. per sec.
         phonotape.

         1. Project Apollo. 2. Space flight to the
     moon. 3. Scott, David Randolph, 1932- 4.
     Irwin, James B   1932- 5. Worden, Alfred
     M   1930-   I. Scott, David Randolph,
     1932- II. Irwin, James B   1932- III.
     Worden, Alfred M   1930-

Voice Lib.
M1480 Apollo 15 (space flight): beginning of power
bd.2   descent to moon. NBC TV, July 31, 1971.
         1 reel (7 in.) 7 1/2 in. per sec.
         phonotape.

         1. Project Apollo. 2. Space flight to the
     moon. 3. Scott, David Randolph, 1932- 4.
     Irwin, James B   1932- 5. Worden, Alfred
     M   1930-   I. Scott, David Randolph,
     1932-   II. Irwin, James B   1932- III.
     Worden, Alfred M   1930-

Voice Lib.
M1480 Apollo 15 (space flight): walk in deep space
bd.3   by Al Worden to retrieve film packages.
         Commentary of Gene Cernan, who walked in
         space during Gemini 9 flight. NBC TV,
         August, 1971.
         1 reel (7 in.) 7 1/2 in. per sec.
         phonotape.

         1. Project Apollo. 2. Space flight to the moon. 3. Scott,
     David Randolph, 1932- 4. Irwin, James B   1932- 5.
     Worden, Alfred M   1930-   L. Scott, David Randolph, 1932-
     II. Irwin, James B   1932- III. Worden, Alfred M   1930-
     IV. Cernan, Eugene Andrew, 1934-

Voice Lib.
M1480 Apollo 15 (space flight): splashdown
bd.4   commentary, speeches. NBC TV, August 7,
         1971.
         1 reel (7 in.) 7 1/2 in. per sec.
         phonotape.

         1. Project Apollo. 2. Space flight to the
     moon. 3. Scott, David Randolph, 1932- 4.
     Irwin, James B   1932- 5. Worden, Alfred
     M   1930-   I. Scott, David Randolph,
     1932-   II. Irwin, James B   1932- III.
     Worden, Alfred M   1930-

C1
R3   The apostle
     Whorf, Michael, 1933-
          The apostle.
          1 tape cassette. (The visual sounds of
     Mike Whorf. Religion, R3)
          Originally presented on his radio program, Kaleidoscope,
     WJR, Detroit.
          Duration: 35 min., 30 sec.
          Paul of Tarsus was a man who persecuted and tormented the early
     believers of the Christian following. Yet he would one day become
     one of them and bring organization and firmness to the early church.

          L. Paul, Saint, apostle. L. Title.

C1
H77   The apostle of the strenuous life, Theodore Roosevelt
     Whorf, Michael, 1933-
          The apostle of the strenuous life, Theodore
     Roosevelt.
          1 tape cassette. (The visual sounds of
     Mike Whorf. History and heritage, H77)
          Originally presented on his radio program, Kaleidoscope,
     WJR, Detroit.
          Duration: 38 min., 45 sec.
          America's favorite hero is the underdog, the frail, ninety-
     seven pound weakling who rises to accept no threat from any
     adversary. One such man was Theodore Roosevelt, a weak and
     frail youth who builds his body and character, and one day reaches
     the highest office in the land.
          L. Roosevelt, Theodore   Pres., U.S., 1858-1919. L. Title.

C1
R5   APOSTLES
     Whorf, Michael, 1933-
          Miracle of the twelve.
          1 tape cassette. (The visual sounds of
     Mike Whorf. Religion, R5)
          Originally presented on his radio program, Kaleidoscope,
     WJR, Detroit.
          Duration: 35 min., 40 sec.
          Grouped together as a determined force carrying the word of the
     Messiah, were twelve men selected by the Christ to bring to the
     world a philosophy which mankind has never improved on.

          L. Apostles. L. Title.

C1
H65   Apostles of destruction
     Whorf, Michael, 1933-
          Apostles of destruction; Caesar, Alexander,
     Ghenghis Khan, Hitler,
          1 tape cassette.. (The visual sounds of Mike Whorf.
     History and heritage, H65)
          Originally presented on his radio program, Kaleidoscope,
     WJR, Detroit.
          Duration: 39 min.
          Here are graphically related the tales of the despots of the ages -
     for though many would strive for goodness and the best in man - a
     few were blindly corrupt and evil, and in their time attempted to
     bring the world to ruin.
          L. Caesar, C. Julius. 2. Alexander the Great, 356-323 B.C.
     3. Jenghis Khan, 1162-1227 4. Hitler, Adolf, 1889-1945.
     L. Title.

          APPALACHIAN MOUNTAINS, SOUTHERN - SOCIAL LIFE
Voice Lib.   AND CUSTOMS
M874   American mood series (Radio program)
bd.2- Appalachia: first program in a series of
M 875   documentaries by John David Hamilton recording
         on-the-spot candid sounds and interviews, in
         1963. White evangelists' sermons; statements
         by teachers and sociologists and natives in
         the mountain regions of North Carolina, Tenn-
         essee and Kentucky, which include feuding,
         square dancing, moon-shining, etc. Native
         women recollecting life in the past in Appala-
         chia; origin of feuds; discussion of moon-
         shining; native folk songs, including the TVA
(Continued on next card)

APPALACHIAN MOUNTAINS, SOUTHERN - SOCIAL LIFE
AND CUSTOMS
Voice Lib.
M874   American mood series (Radio program)
 bd.2-   Appalachia... 1963. (Card 2)
M875
        song; church service excerpts; the Texas
        scene, fundamentalism, philosophy, humor,
        songs, etc. CBC, 1963.
        2 reels (7 in.) 7 1/2 in. per sec.
        phonotape.

        1. Appalachian Mountains, Southern - Social
        life and customs. I. Hamilton, John David
        TT. Project '64.

        The Arabian prophet - Mahomet
C1
R28   Whorf, Michael, 1933-
        The Arabian prophet - Mahomet.
        1 tape cassette. (The visual sounds of
        Mike Whorf. Religion, R28)
            Originally presented on his radio program, Kaleidoscope,
        WJR, Detroit.
            Duration: 38 min., 15 sec.
            He was the founder of Islam and became its prophet. Today
        millions of people the world over revere his teachings, and follow
        the precepts which he ordained.

            L Muhammad, the prophet. L Title.

        ARAB COUNTRIES - FOREIGN RELATIONS - ISRAEL
Voice Lib.
M1728   Dinitz, Simcha, 1929-
        Speech delivered to National Press Club
        on Arab-Israeli relations, with Ken Scheibel.
        WKAR, June 13, 1974.
        40 min.   phonotape (1 r.   7 1/2 i.p.s.)

        1. Israel - For. rel. - Arab countries.
        2. Arab countries - For. rel. - Israel.
        I. Scheibel, Ken.

        ARCTIC REGIONS
Voice Lib.
654   Cook, Frederick Albert, 1865-1940.
 bd.2   "How I Reached the North Pole".
        Description of Dr. Cook's preparations
        and journey on Arctic expedition, 1909.
        Source(?), [n.d.]
        1 reel (7 in.)   7 1/2 in. per sec.
        phonotape.

        1. Arctic regions. 2. Peary, Robert Edwin,
        1856-1920.

        ARAB COUNTRIES - FOREIGN RELATIONS -
        ISRAEL
Voice Lib.
M1641   Hussein, King of Jordan, 1935-
        Peace in the Middle East; National Press
        Club Address. WKAR-AM, March 15, 1974.
        45 min. phonotape (1 r.   7 1/2 i.p.s.)

        Includes question and answer period.

        1. Arab countries - Foreign relations -
        Israel. 2. Israel - Foreign relations -
        Arab countries.

Voice Lib.
M1585   Ardrey, Robert
 bd.2   Property, status, and self-respect.
        WKAR-TV, February 23, 1974.
        15 min.   phonotape (1 r.   7 1/2 in. per sec.)

        1. Territoriality (Zoology) 2. Communism.
        3. Cities & towns - Planning.   I. Halverson,
        Craig.

        ARAB COUNTRIES - FOREIGN RELATIONS - ISRAEL
Voice Lib.
M1241   Reynolds, Frank
        ABC-TV documentary, including reports from
        Cairo and Tel Aviv and a review of the
        Arab-Israeli conflicts past and present.
        ABC-TV, May 25, 1967.
        1 reel (7 in.) 7 1/2 i.p.s.   phonotape.

        1. Israel - Foreign relations - Arab
        countries. 2. Arab countries - Foreign
        relations - Israel.

        Are you happy?
Voice Lib.
M1056 McPherson, Aimee Semple, 1890-1944.
 bd.7   Religious dialogue. "Are You Happy?".
        Salter, 1931.
        1 reel (7 in.)   7 1/2 in. per sec.
        phonotape.

        I. Title: Are you happy?

        ARAB COUNTRIES - RELATIONS (GENERAL) WITH
        ISRAEL
Voice Lib.
M1683   Sayegh, Fayez Abdullah, 1922-
        Interviewed by William Buckley on Firing
        Line. WKAR-TV, May 21, 1974.
        45 min.   phonotape (1 r. 7 1/2 i.p.s.)

        1. Arab countries - Relations (general)
        with Israel. 2. Israel - Relations (general)
        with Arab countries.   I. Buckley, William
        Frank, 1925-

        ARISTOTELES
C1
S68   Whorf, Michael, 1933-
        Statesmen and sages; Demosthenes, Aristotle,
        Socrates, Cicero.
        1 tape cassette. (The visual sounds of Mike Whorf. Social, S68)

            Originally presented on his radio program, Kaleidoscope,
        WJR, Detroit.
            Duration: 36 min.
            As ancient Greece and Rome served as the cradle of our modern
        democracy, so do their citizens serve as shining examples of wisdom
        and statecraft for us today.

            L Demosthenes. 2. Aristoteles. 3. Socrates. 4. Cicero,
        Marcus Tullius. L Title.

Voice Lib.
M1055 Arliss, George, 1868-1946.
bd.2   Speech about preparedness and national
service upon outbreak of war in England.
BBC, 1939.
   1 reel (7 in.)   7 1/2 in. per sec.
phonotape.

Voice Lib.
M840   Armstrong, Louis, 1900-1971.
bd.7   "Mop, Mop"; musical selection from jam
session at Metropolitan Opera House, New
York.   V-discs, April 4, 1944.
   1 reel (7 in.)   7 1/2 in. per sec.
phonotape.

C1
H52   Whorf, Michael, 1933-
   ARMISTICE DAY
   Known but to God - Armistice Day.
   1 tape cassette.   (The visual sounds of
Mike Whorf. History and heritage, H52)

   Originally presented on his radio program, Kaleidoscope,
WJR, Detroit.
   Duration: 38 min., 45 sec.
   A solemn approach to America's fallen - a tribute to the
unknown soldier - a brief biographical sketch of Sergeant Alvin
York is the content of this Armistice Day program.

   1. Armistice Day. 2. York, Alvin Cullum, 1887-
1. Title.

Voice Lib.
372   Armstrong, Louis, 1900-1971.
bd.2   "Satchmo the great;" Paris interview
with Edward R. Murrow.   CBS, 1956.
   1 reel (7 in.)   7 1/2 in. per sec.
phonotape.

   I. Murrow, Edward Roscoe, 1908-1965.

C1
H103   Whorf, Michael, 1933-
   ARMORED VESSELS
   The Valentine's Day ironclad (Galena,
Monitor, Merrimac)
   1 tape cassette.   (The visual sounds of Mike Whorf.
History and heritage, H103)
   Originally presented on his radio program, Kaleidoscope,
WJR, Detroit.
   Duration: 38 min., 10 sec.
   The birth of the ironclads during the Civil War was on the
tongue of every citizen. Although the Monitor and the Merrimac
were household words, the ship Galena was nearly unknown. Our
story tells of the American ironclads, their rise, their fall.
   1. Armored vessels. 1. Title.

Armstrong, Louis, 1900-1971
Voice Lib.
M621   Radio in the 1940's (Part II): a series of
bd.1-   excerpts from important broadcasts of the
12   1940's; a sample of radio of the period.
NVL, April, 1964.
   1 reel (7 in.)   7 1/2 in. per sec.   phonotape.
   1. Daly, John Charles, 1914-   II. Hall, Josef Washington,
1894-   III. Shirer, William Lawrence, 1904-   IV. Roosevelt,
Eleanor (Roosevelt) 1884-1962. V. Roosevelt, Franklin Delano,
Pres. U.S., 1882-1945. VI. Churchill, Winston Leonard Spencer,
1874-1965. VII. Wainwright, Jonathan Mayhew, 1883-1953. VIII.
Cantor, Eddie, 1893-1964. IX. Sinatra, Francis Albert, 1917-
X. Hope, Bob, 1903-   XI. Crosby, Bing, 1901-   XII. Shore,
Dinah, 1917(?)-   XIII. Bergen, Edgar, 1903-   XIV. Armstrong,
Louis, 1900-1971. XV. Eldridge, Roy, 1911-

Voice Lib.
M1562 Armstrong, Anne
bd.2   Speech to National Press Club, Washington,
D.C.   Introduced by Sam Fogg.   February 14,
1974.
   25 min.   phonotape (1 r.   7 1/2 i.p.s.)

   1. U.S. - Centennial celebrations, etc.
I. Fogg, Sam.

Voice Lib.
M1263 Armstrong, Louis, 1900-1971.
   Kraft Music Hall with Herb Alpert and
Tijuana Brass, with guest stars Jackie
Vernon and Robin Wilson.   NBC-TV,
August 13, 1967.
   1 reel (7 in.)   7 1/2 in. per sec.
phonotape.

   I. Alpert, Herb, 1935(?)-   II. Vernon,
Jackie   III. Wilson, Robin

Armstrong, Hamilton Fish, 1893-1973
Voice Lib.
235-   Tito, Josip Broz, Pres. Yugoslavia, 1892-
237   Interview by Edward R. Murrow, with comments
bd.1   and analysis by Richard C. Hottelet, Clare
Boothe Luce, William H. Lawrence, and Hamilton
F. Armstrong, CBS, June 30, 1957.
   3 reels (7 in.)   7 1/2 in. per sec.
phonotape.

   I. Hottelet, Richard Curt   II. Luce,
Clare (Boothe) 1903-   III. Lawrence,
William H   IV. Armstrong, Hamilton Fish,
1893-1973.

Voice Lib.
M1481 Armstrong, Louis, 1900-1971.
bd.1   Tribute after his death by David Frost.
Replay of last number performed by Louis
Armstrong on The David Frost Show: "The
Boy from New Orleans".   Group-W News,
August 5, 1971.
   1 reel (7 in.)   7 1/2 in. per sec.
phonotape.

   1. Armstrong, Louis, 1900-1971.
I. Frost, David Paradine, 1939-

Voice Lib.   Armstrong, Neil, 1930-
M950- Gemini 8 (space flight): press conference at
951   Houston, Texas, Space Center regarding
     astronauts' space flight on Gemini 8. NBC
     TV, March 26, 1966.
     2 reels (7 in.) 7 1/2 in. per sec.
     phonotape.

       1. Project Gemini. 2. Armstrong, Neil, 1930-
     3. Scott, David Randolph, 1932-   I. Armstrong,
     Neil, 1930-   II. Scott, David Randolph,
     1932-

Voice Lib.   Armstrong, Neil, 1930-
M1384 Apollo 11 (space flight): launch day, July 16,
bd.1   1969. Description of astronauts going up
     the elevator; conversation between Walter
     Cronkite and Walter Schirra at approximately
     2 hours before launch. CBS TV, July 16, 1969.
     1 reel (7 in.) 7 1/2 in. per sec.
     phonotape.
       1. Project Apollo. 2. Space flight to the moon. 3. Aldrin,
     Edwin E 1930- 4. Collins, Michael, 1930- 5. Armstrong,
     Neil, 1930-   I. Aldrin, Edwin E 1930- II. Collins,
     Michael, 1930-   III. Armstrong, Neil, 1930- IV. Cronkite,
     Walter Leland, 1916-   V. Schirra, Walter Marty, 1923-

Voice Lib.   Armstrong, Neil, 1930-
M1384 Apollo 11 (space flight): biographical sketches
bd.2   of the three astronauts, Edwin Aldrin,
     Michael Collins, and Neil Armstrong, by Chet
     Huntley, at approximately 78 minutes before
     launch time. NBC TV, July 16, 1969.
     1 reel (7 in.) 7 1/2 in. per sec.
     phonotape.
       1. Project Apollo. 2. Space flight to the moon. 3. Aldrin,
     Edwin E 1930- 4. Collins, Michael, 1930- 5. Armstrong,
     Neil, 1930-   I. Aldrin, Edwin E 1930- II. Collins,
     Michael, 1930-   III. Armstrong, Neil, 1930- IV. Huntley,
     Chet, 1911-1974.

Voice Lib.   Armstrong, Neil, 1930-
M1384 Apollo 11 (space flight): Frank McGee giving
bd.3   an itinerary of space ships, dates, times,
     etc. NBC TV, July 16, 1969.
     1 reel (7 in.) 7 1/2 in. per sec.
     phonotape.

       1. Project Apollo. 2. Space flight to the
     moon. 3. Aldrin, Edwin E   1930-   4.
     Collins, Michael, 1930- 5. Armstrong, Neil,
     1930-   I. Aldrin, Edwin E   1930- II.
     Collins, Michael, 1930-   III. Armstrong, Neil,
     1930- IV. McGee, Frank, 1921-1974.

Voice Lib.   Armstrong, Neil, 1930-
M1384 Apollo 11 (space flight): interviews between
bd.4   Frank McGee and Neil Armstrong previous to
     the flight of Apollo 11. NBC TV, July 16,
     1969.
     1 reel (7 in.) 7 1/2 in. per sec.
     phonotape.

       1. Project Apollo. I. McGee, Frank, 1921-
     1974. II. Armstrong, Neil, 1930-

Voice Lib.   Armstrong, Neil, 1930-
M1384 Apollo 11 (space flight): launch day progress
bd.6   of countdown by Apollo 11 control at 4
     minutes 15 seconds to actual take-off.
     Houston takes over and describes progress
     up to 1,000 miles downrange and successful
     orbit. NBC TV, July 16, 1969.
     1 reel (7 in.) 7 1/2 in. per sec.
     phonotape.
       1. Project Apollo. 2. Space flight to the moon. 3. Aldrin,
     Edwin E 1930- 4. Collins, Michael, 1930- 5. Armstrong,
     Neil, 1930-   I. Aldrin, Edwin E 1930- II. Collins,
     Michael, 1930-   III. Armstrong, Neil, 1930-

Voice Lib.   Armstrong, Neil, 1930-
M1385 Apollo 11 (space flight): Frank McGee speaking
bd.1   about communications between "Eagle" and
     ground. Conversation between Houston and
     astronauts. Message of "Go for PDI"; "The
     Eagle has landed" (102 hours, 45 minutes,
     40 seconds) Description of rocks and
     boulders on moon. NBC TV, July 20, 1969.
     1 reel (7 in.) 7 1/2 in. per sec. phonotape.
       1. Project Apollo. 2. Space flight to the moon. 3. Aldrin,
     Edwin E 1930- 4. Collins, Michael, 1930- 5.
     Armstrong, Neil, 1930-   I. Aldrin, Edwin E   1930-
     II. Collins, Michael, 1930-   III. Armstrong, Neil, 1930-
     IV. McGee, Frank, 1921-1974.

Voice Lib.   Armstrong, Neil, 1930-
M1385 Apollo 11 (space flight): Neil Armstrong
bd.2   requesting everyone everywhere to pause and
     give thanks. Preparing to open hatch and
     walk on the moon. Armstrong backing out
     from hatch, describing lunar surface. "One
     small step for man, one giant step for man-
     kind" (109 hours, 24 minutes, 20 seconds.)
     Bringing down cameras. CBS TV, July 20, 1969.
     1 reel (7 in.) 7 1/2 in. per sec. phonotape.
       1. Project Apollo. 2. Space flight to the moon. 3. Aldrin,
     Edwin E   1930- 4. Collins, Michael, 1930- 5. Armstrong,
     Neil, 1930- I. Aldrin, Edwin E   1930- II. Collins, Michael,
     1930- III. Armstrong, Neil, 1930-

Voice Lib.   Armstrong, Neil, 1930-
M1386 Apollo 11 (space flight): conversation with
bd.1   broadcasters Walter Cronkite and Wally
     Schirra. Including Armstrong's activities
     on moon alone; pictures, rock descriptions,
     then Aldrin coming down ladder; rock boxes
     put to use. TV cameras put at 30' panoramic
     position. Reading inscription of plaque
     with U.S. flag and setting it up. Telephone
     call from Washington to astronauts and their
     acknowledgement. CBS TV, July 20, 1969.
     1 reel (7 in.) 7 1/2 in. per sec.
     phonotape.
        (Continued on next card)

Voice Lib.   Armstrong, Neil, 1930-
M1386 Apollo 11 (space flight): blessing by Pope
bd.2   Paul VI from the Vatican to Apollo 11
     astronauts. CBS TV, July 20, 1969.
     1 reel (7 in.) 7 1/2 in. per sec.
     phonotape.

       1. Project Apollo. 2. Space flight to the
     moon. 3. Aldrin, Edwin E   1930-   4.
     Collins, Michael, 1930-   5. Armstrong, Neil,
     1930-   I. Aldrin, Edwin E   1930- II.
     Collins, Michael, 1930-   III. Armstrong, Neil,
     1930-   IV. Paulus VI, Pope, 1897-

Armstrong, Neil, 1930-
Voice Lib.
M1386   Apollo 11 (space flight): excerpts of old
bd.3   Mercury Theatre "War of the Worlds" of
          1938; an interview with Orson Welles by
          Mike Wallace.   CBS TV, July 20, 1969.
          1 reel (7 in.)   7 1/2 in. per sec.
        phonotape.
          L Project Apollo. 2. Space flight to the moon. 3. Aldrin,
        Edwin E   1930-   4. Collins, Michael, 1930-
        5. Armstrong, Neil, 1930-   L Aldrin, Edwin E   1930-
        II. Collins, Michael, 1930-   III. Armstrong, Neil, 1930-
        IV. Welles, Orson, 1915-   V. Wallace, Mike, 1918-

Armstrong, Neil, 1930-
Voice Lib.
M1389   Apollo 11 (space flight): excerpt of press
bd.1   conference with Apollo 11 astronauts in
          Houston.   CBS TV, August 12, 1969.
          1 reel (7 in.)   7 1/2 in. per sec.
        phonotape.

          1. Project Apollo. 2. Space flight to the
        moon. 3. Aldrin, Edwin E   1930-   4.
        Collins, Michael, 1930-   5. Armstrong, Neil,
        1930-   I. Aldrin, Edwin E   1930-   II.
        Collins, Michael, 1930-   III. Armstrong,
        Neil, 1930-

Armstrong, Neil, 1930-
Voice Lib.
M1387   Apollo 11 (space flight): description of
bd.1   ascent from moon by Frank McGee. Count-
          down, ignition, and lift-off. Meeting the
          command module "Columbia"; docking; trans-
          fer of gear from "Eagle" to "Columbia".
          Recap by ABC's Jules Bergman and Frank
          Reynolds.   NBC and ABC TV, July 21, 1969.
          1 reel (7 in.)   7 1/2 in. per sec.   phonotape.
          L Project Apollo. 2. Space flight to the moon. 3. Aldrin,
        Edwin E   1930-   4. Collins, Michael, 1930-   5.
        Armstrong, Neil, 1930-   L Aldrin, Edwin E   1930-   II.
        Collins, Michael, 1930-   III. Armstrong, Neil, 1930-   IV.
        McGee, Frank, 1921-1974.   V. Bergman, Jules   VI. Reynolds,
        Frank

Armstrong, Neil, 1930-
Voice Lib.
M1389   Apollo 11 (space flight): welcome to Apollo 11 astronauts on their
bd.2   arrival at Kennedy Airport at New York; ferried by Marine
          helicopter to Wall Street; boat whistles harbor greeting.
          Flashbacks to former important New York parades (Frank McGee)
          Walter Cronkite, CBS, describing beginning of motorcade
          and parade to city hall.   CBS [and NBC] TV, August 13, 1969.
          1 reel (7 in.)   7 1/2 in. per sec. phonotape.

          L Project Apollo. 2. Space flight to the moon. 3. Aldrin,
        Edwin E   1930-   4. Collins, Michael, 1930-   5.
        Armstrong, Neil, 1930-   L Aldrin, Edwin E   1930-
        II. Collins, Michael, 1930-   III. Armstrong, Neil, 1930-
        IV. McGee, Frank, 1921-1974.   V. Cronkite, Walter Leland, 1916-

---

Armstrong, Neil, 1930-
Voice Lib.
M1387   Apollo 11 (space flight): recovery. Walter Cronkite and Wally
bd.2   Schirra announce proceedings from aircraft carrier "Hornet";
          trying to track spacecraft coming down; chutes opening at
          10,500 feet; voice contact with spacecraft; visual of chutes;
          splashdown 9 miles from "Hornet", upside-down. Collar
          attached to spacecraft. NBC and ABC TV, July 24, 1969.
          1 reel (7 in.)   7 1/2 in. per sec.   phonotape.

          L Project Apollo. 2. Space flight to the moon. 3. Aldrin,
        Edwin E   1930-   4. Collins, Michael, 1930-   5.
        Armstrong, Neil, 1930-   L Aldrin, Edwin E   1930-
        II. Collins, Michael, 1930-   III. Armstrong, Neil, 1930-
        IV. Cronkite, Walter Leland, 1916-   V. Schirra, Walter Marty,
        1923-

Armstrong, Neil, 1930-
Voice Lib.
M1390   Apollo 11 (space flight): reception for
          Apollo 11 astronauts in New York. Descrip-
          tion of approach and ceremony at city hall.
          Cardinal Cooke's invocation. Introduction
          by Mayor Lindsay. Presentation of Medal of
          Honor. Reply by all astronauts. Benediction.
          NBC TV, August 13, 1969.
          1 reel (7 in.)   7 1/2 in. per sec.   phonotape.
          L Project Apollo. 2. Space flight to the moon. 3. Aldrin,
        Edwin E   1930-   4. Collins, Michael, 1930-   5.
        Armstrong, Neil, 1930-   L Aldrin, Edwin E   1930-   II.
        Collins, Michael, 1930-   III. Armstrong, Neil, 1930-   IV.
        Cooke, Terence James, cardinal, 1921-   V. Lindsay, John Vliet,
        1921-

Armstrong, Neil, 1930-
Voice Lib.
M1388   Apollo 11 (space flight): Walter Cronkite and Wally Schirra
bd.1   describing recovery. Maneuvers by frogmen and helicopters
          at splashdown spot; "air boss" describes close-up scene;
          decontamination process; helicopter landing on "Hornet" with
          astronauts; reception. Description of proceedings on "Hornet"
          by CBS newscasters. CBS TV, July 24, 1969.
          1 reel (7 in.)   7 1/2 in. per sec.   phonotape.

          L Project Apollo. 2. Space flight to the moon. 3. Aldrin,
        Edwin E   1930-   4. Collins, Michael, 1930-   5. Armstrong,
        Neil, 1930-   L Aldrin, Edwin E   1930-   II. Collins,
        Michael, 1930-   III. Armstrong, Neil, 1930-   IV. Cronkite,
        Walter Leland, 1916-   V. Schirra, Walter Marty, 1923-

---

Armstrong, Neil, 1930-
Voice Lib.
M1391   Apollo 11 (space flight): reception of Apollo 11 astronauts at
bd.1   United Nations Plaza. U. N. Secretary-
          General U Thant. Reply by Neil Armstrong. Presentation
          of tokens of appreciation to all three astronauts and their
          wives and Dr. Thomas Paine. Presentation of duplicate of
          plaque left on moon to U Thant. NBC TV, August 13, 1969.
          1 reel (7 in.)   7 1/2 in. per sec.   phonotape.

          L Project Apollo. 2. Space flight to the moon. 3. Aldrin,
        Edwin E   1930-   4. Collins, Michael, 1930-   5.
        Armstrong, Neil, 1930-   L Aldrin, Edwin E   1930-
        II. Collins, Michael, 1930-   III. Armstrong, Neil, 1930-
        IV. Thant, U, 1909-   V. Paine, Thomas Otten, 1921-

Armstrong, Neil, 1930-
Voice Lib.
M1388   Apollo 11 (space flight): personal greeting
bd.2   by President Nixon to the astronauts on
          the "Hornet" and their replies. Chaplain's
          prayer. Nixon taking off.   CBS and NBC TV,
          July 24, 1969.
          1 reel (7 in.)   7 1/2 in. per sec.
        phonotape.
          L Project Apollo. 2. Space flight to the moon. 3. Aldrin,
        Edwin E   1930-   4. Collins, Michael, 1930-   5.
        Armstrong, Neil, 1930-   L Aldrin, Edwin E   1930-
        II. Collins, Michael, 1930-   III. Armstrong, Neil, 1930-
        IV. Nixon, Richard Milhous, Pres. U.S., 1913-

Armstrong, Neil, 1930-
Voice Lib.
M1391   Apollo 11 (space flight): reception of
bd.2   Apollo 11 astronauts in Chicago. Descrip-
          tion of motorcade on way to Civic Center
          Plaza and ceremonies there. Cardinal Cody's
          invocation. JFK flashback predicting moon
          landing before decade is out. Mayor Daley
          and Alderman Klene resolution making August
          13 "Astronauts' Day". Senator Percy and
          Governor Ogilvie of Illinois. Presentation
          of honorary citizenship to astronauts.
          [Source?] August 13, 1969.

                                    (Continued on next card)

Voice Lib.
M1391   Armstrong, Neil, 1930-
bd.2   Apollo 11 (space flight): reception of Apollo
         11 astronauts ... 1969. (Card 2)
         1 reel (7 in.) 7 1/2 in. per sec.
         phonotape.
         L. Project Apollo. 2. Space flight to the moon. 3. Aldrin,
         Edwin E   1930- 4. Collins, Michael, 1930- 5. Armstrong,
         Neil, 1930- L. Aldrin, Edwin E   1930- IL. Collins,
         Michael, 1930- III. Armstrong, Neil, 1930- IV. Cody,
         John Patrick, cardinal, 1907-   V. Kennedy, John Fitzgerald,
         Pres. U.S., 1917-1963. VL. Daley, Richard J   1902- VIL.
         Percy, Charles Harting, 1919-   VIII. Ogilvie, Richard Buell,
         1923-

ARMY-MCCARTHY CONTROVERSY, 1954
see
MCCARTHY-ARMY CONTROVERSY, 1954

VOICE LIBRARY

Voice Lib.
M1206   Arrival of British troops in France;
bd.4   British descriptive war scenes of troops
         cheering, singing, talking. Br. Col.,
         1916.
         1 reel (7 in.) 7 1/2 i.p.s.   phonotape.

         1. European War, 1914-1918.

ART, AFRICAN
Voice Lib.
M826   Africa and the arts; discussion of Africa
         and the arts. KPFK, July 23, 1964.
         35 min., 15 sec. phonotape (1 r.
         7 1/2 i.p.s.)

         1. Art, African.

ART AND MORALS
Voice Lib.
M819-   Rexroth, Kenneth, 1905-
820,   The artist and his social and personal
bd.1   morals; a discussion about Picasso, Brecht,
         Dostoevsky and other artists. KPFK,
         July 11, 1964.
         58 min., 30 sec. phonotape (2 r.
         7 1/2 i.p.s.)

         1. Art and morals. 2. Artists.

ART AND STATE
Voice Lib.
M1750   Berman, Richard
         Government and the arts; on "Firing Line"
         with William F. Buckley. WKAR, June 28,
         1974.
         45 min. phonotape (1 r. 7 1/2 i.p.s.)

         1. The Arts - U. S. 2. Art and State. 3.
         State encourgement of science, literature,
         and art - U. S.   I. Buckley, William Frank,
         1925-

C1   ARTHUR, KING
H85
         Whorf, Michael, 1933-
         In days of old when knights were bold -
         knighthood.
         1 tape cassette.   (The visual sounds of
         Mike Whorf. History and heritage, H85)
         Originally presented on his radio program, Kaleidoscope,
         WJR, Detroit.
         Duration: 36 min., 50 sec.
         The romance and the glories of knighthood are a heritage of
         chivalry, but with a misty background in the Arthurian legends.

         L. Knights and knighthood. 2. Arthur, King. L. Title.

ARTIFICIAL SATELLITES
Voice Lib.
N715   Sputnick: first earth satellite to orbit
bd.12   the globe announced over Moscow radio by
         U.S.S.R., followed by sound signals from
         satellite. October 4, 1957.
         1 reel (7 in.) 7 1/2 in. per sec.
         phonotape.

         1. Artificial satellites.

ARTISTS
Voice Lib.
M819-   Rexroth, Kenneth, 1905-
820,   The artist and his social and personal
bd.1   morals; a discussion about Picasso, Brecht,
         Dostoevsky and other artists. KPFK,
         July 11, 1964.
         58 min., 30 sec. phonotape (2 r.
         7 1/2 i.p.s.)

         1. Art and morals. 2. Artists.

THE ARTS - U.S.
Voice Lib.
M1750   Berman, Richard
         Government and the arts; on "Firing Line"
         with William F. Buckley. WKAR, June 28,
         1974.
         45 min. phonotape (1 r. 7 1/2 i.p.s.)

         1. The Arts - U. S. 2. Art and State. 3.
         State encourgement of science, literature,
         and art - U. S.   I. Buckley, William Frank,
         1925-

Voice Lib.
M724   Arvey, Jack
bd.5   Speaking about his ideas regarding the
          picking of winning political tickets.
             1 reel (7 in.)   7 1/2 in. per sec.
          phonotape.

                    ASCORBIC ACID
Voice Lib.
M1734   Pauling, Linus Carl, 1901-
           Orthomolecular medicine; address given at
         Michigan State University.   WKAR, April 19,
         1972.
             50 min.   phonotape (1 r.   7 1/2 i.p.s.)

             1. Ascorbic acid.   2. Diet.   3. Human
         genetics.

          Arvey, Jacob
Voice Lib.
M273-   Biography in sound (radio program)
274   Franklin Delano Roosevelt: the friends and
bd.1   former associates of Franklin Roosevelt on
        the tenth anniversary of the President's death.
        NBC Radio, April, 1955.
             2 reels (7 in.)   7 1/2 in. per sec.
        phonotape.
           L. Roosevelt, Franklin Delano, Pres. U.S., 1882-1945. L.
        McIntire, Ross T   II. Mellett, Lowell, 1884-1960.
        III. Tully, Grace   IV. Henderson, Leon, 1895-
        V. Roosevelt, Eleanor (Roosevelt) 1884-1962. VI. DeGraaf, Albert
        VII. Lehman, Herbert Henry, 1878-1963. VIII. Rosenman, Samuel
        Irving, 1896-   IX. Arvey, Jacob   X. Moley, Raymond,
        1886-   XI. Farley, James Aloysius, 1888-   XII. Roosevelt,
                    (Continued on next card)

                    ASCORBIC ACID
Voice Lib.
M1671   Pauling, Linus Carl, 1901-
           Vitamin C and the common cold; controversy
         and harassment.   WKAR, April 20, 1972.
             50 min.   phonotape (1 r.   7 1/2 i.p.s.)

             1. Cold (Disease)   2. Ascorbic acid.

          As big as all outdoors
C1
864   Whorf, Michael, 1933-
          As big as all outdoors; the story of Canada.
       1 tape cassette.   (The visual sounds of
       Mike Whorf. Social, S64)
          Originally presented on his radio program, Kaleidoscope,
       WJR, Detroit.
          Duration: 37 min., 30 sec.
          As big as all outdoors is the story of America's great neighbor
       to the north - Canada. A country of riches - wealthy in people,
       land, beauty, and raw material, yet a country that has not
       reached its destiny.

          L. Canada.   L. Title.

Voice Lib.
M1244-Ashby, Sir Eric, 1904-
1245   Lecture at MSU pertaining to the influence
bd.1   of students on a university, their opinions,
        and associated topics.   MSU Information
        Services, 1965.
             2 reels (7 in.)   7 1/2 in. per sec.
        phonotape.

Voice Lib.
M915-   As we knew him; words of reminiscence of
916   friends and relatives about the life of
        J.F. Kennedy. Narration by Charles Kuralt;
        participants: Charles Bartlett, Lemayne
        Billings, Robert Kennedy, Rose Kennedy,
        James Reed, Adlai Stevenson, Gen. Chester B.
        Clifton, etc.   Columbia Records Inc., 1965.
             2 reels (7 in.)   7 1/2 in. per sec.
        phonotape.
             1. Kennedy, John Fitzgerald, Pres. U.S.,
        1917-1963. I. Kuralt, Charles, 1934-
                          (Continued on next card)

          Ashley, Barbara
Voice Lib.
M1037   Biography in sound (radio program)
bd.1   "The Actor", narrated by Morgan Beatty.
        Cast includes Tallulah Bankhead, Hy Gardner,
        Rocky Graziano, Arthur Miller, Uta Hagen,
        Jackie Cooper, Sir Laurence Olivier, Gad
        Gayther, Barbara Ashley, Hortense Powdermaker,
        Peter Ustinov, Alfred Hitchcock, Leonard Lyons,
        John Guston, Helen Hayes, Dick Mayne, Ralph
        Bellamy, Lionel Barrymore, Sir Ralph Richardson,
        José Ferrer, and Walter Kerr.   NBC Radio, 1950's.
             1 reel (7 in.)   7 1/2 in. per sec.
        phonotape.   (Continued on next card)

Voice Lib.
M915-   As we knew him... 1965.   (Card 2)
916
           II. Bartlett, Charles   III. Billings,
        Lemayne   IV. Kennedy, Robert Francis,
        1925-1968. V. Kennedy, Rose Fitzgerald, 1890-
        VI. Reed, James   VII. Stevenson, Adlai
        Ewing, 1900-1965. VIII. Clifton, Chester B

Voice Lib.
M1075   Ashmore, Harry Scott, 1916-
bd.2   Discussion among three well-known book
        publishers about authors of the past, the job
        of book editors, the publishing business, book
        reviewers, etc. Held in the Library at the
        Center for the Study of Democratic Institutions
        at Santa Barbara, California.   CSDI, 1960.
             1 reel (7 in.)   7 1/2 in. per sec.
        phonotape.

           L. Publishers and publishing. L. Knopf, Alfred A., 1892-
        II. Ferry, W. H.

Voice Lib.
382   Ashurst, Henry Fountain, 1874-1962.
bd.4   Philosophical outlook in 1938.   CBS, [1938]
        1 reel (7 in.)   7 1/2 in. per sec.
        phonotape.

Voice Lib.
M309   Assassination: comments by visitors in
bd.8   Washington.   NBC, November 23, 1963.
        1 reel (7 in.)   7 1/2 in. per sec.
        phonotape.

        1. Kennedy, John Fitzgerald, Pres. U.S.,
      1917-1963. - Assassination

Voice Lib.
M1587- Asimov, Isaac, 1920-
1588   Utopian change; excerpts.   WKAR-AM,
        March 3, 1974.
        60 min.   phonotape (2 r.   7 1/2 in. per
        sec.)

            1. Science fiction.   2. Atomic weapons.

              ASTOR, JOHN JACOB, 1763-1848
C1
H78   Whorf, Michael, 1933-
        The fur trader - John Jacob Astor.
        1 tape cassette.   (The visual sounds of
      Mike Whorf.   History and heritage, H78)
        Originally presented on his radio program, Kaleidoscope,
      WJR, Detroit.
        Duration: 37 min., 50 sec.
        This depicts the life and style of John Jacob Astor, a German
      immigrant who literally turned the sidewalks into gold and paved
      the streets with silver.

        1. Astor, John Jacob, 1763-1848.   L. Title.

Voice Lib.   Askew, Reubin O'D
M1707   Milliken, William G   1922-
bd.   Governors Milliken, Lucey and Askew at
        the Governors' Conference in Seattle on the
        new financing morality.   Richard Threlkeld,
        reporting.   CBS, June 5, 1974.
        3 min.   phonotape (1 r.   7 1/2 i.p.s.)

            1. Watergate Affair, 1972-   I. Lucey,
        Patrick Joseph, 1918-   II. Askew,
        Reubin O'D.   III. Threlkeld, Richard.

              Astrology
C1
S28   Whorf, Michael, 1933-
        Astrology.
        1 tape cassette.   (The visual sounds of
      Mike Whorf.   Social, S28)
        Originally presented on his radio program, Kaleidoscope,
      WJR, Detroit.
        Duration: 56 min., 45 sec.
        Here are a few pro and con observations on one of mankind's
      oldest interests, astrology.

        1. Astrology.   I. Title.

Voice Lib.
M1698   Aspin, Les, 1938-
bd.2   Interviewed on Firing Line by William
        Buckley.   WKAR-TV, May 28, 1974.
        15 min.   phonotape (1 r.   7 1/2 i.p.s.)

            1. Industry and state - U.S.   2. U.S. -
        Military policy.   I. Buckley, William
        Frank, 1925-

              ASTROLOGY
C1
S28   Whorf, Michael, 1933-
        Astrology.
        1 tape cassette.   (The visual sounds of
      Mike Whorf.   Social, S28)
        Originally presented on his radio program, Kaleidoscope,
      WJR, Detroit.
        Duration: 56 min., 45 sec.
        Here are a few pro and con observations on one of mankind's
      oldest interests, astrology.

        1. Astrology.   I. Title.

        The assassin
C1
H16   Whorf, Michael, 1933-
        The assassin.
        1 tape cassette.   (The visual sounds of
      Mike Whorf.   History and heritage, H16)
        Originally presented on his radio program, Kaleidoscope,
      WJR, Detroit.
        Duration: 37 min.
        Violence stalked the land in the person of John Wilkes Booth,
      a bitter man, a resentful man, a man full of hate whose deed was
      the ultimate act of tragedy.

        1. Booth, John Wilkes, 1838-1865.   I. Title.

              ASTRONAUTS
Voice Lib.
M1747   Bean, Alan L   1932-
        Address at Michigan State University,
        discussing the training of Astronauts before
        the first lunar landing, and training for
        survival in case of accident.   WKAR,
        196-?
        40 min.   phonotape (1 r.   7 1/2 i.p.s.)

            1. Astronauts.

ATLANTA

Voice Lib.
M1551-   Young, Andrew, 1932-
.1552   A lecture series by the College of Urban
          Affairs, Michigan State University, with
          Prof. Robert Green and Asst. Prof. Barnes
          McConnell.   MSU Dept. of Information
          Services, January 17, 1974.
             90 min.   phonotape (2 r.   7 1/2 i.p.s.)

          1. Local transit. 2. Atlanta.   I. Green,
       Robert Lee.   II. McConnell, Barnes.

ATOMIC BOMB

Voice Lib.
M1025 Radio news special report regarding first
bd.2   use of atomic bomb on Japan, August 7, 1945;
         description by pilot of actual detonation.
         CBS Radio, August 7, 1945.
            1 reel (7 in.)   7 1/2 in. per sec.
         phonotape.

ATOMIC BOMB

Voice Lib.
M717   Atomic bomb test at Bikini Atoll. Description
bd.3   by on-the-spot witnesses and remarks by
         Vice-Admiral Blandy, U.S.N., on board
         U.S.S. Mt. McKinley.   July 24, 1946.
         1 min., 38 sec.   phonotape (1 r.
         7 1/2 i.p.s.)

          1. Atomic bomb.   I. Blandy, William
       Henry Purnell, 1890-1954.

ATOMIC BOMB

Voice Lib.
353   Russia and the bomb, discussed by various
bd.19   personalities.   NBC, September 25, 1949.
           1 reel (7 in.)   7 1/2 in. per sec.
         phonotape.

           Participants: Harrison Brown, Harold Urey,
         Samuel Allison, Thornton Hugness, Brien McMahon,
         Paul Douglas, John Foster Dulles, Leslie Groves,
         Winston Churchill, Dean Acheson, James Fleming.

           I. Brown, Harrison Scott, 1917-   II.
         Urey, Harold Clayton, 1893-   III. Allison,

                               (Continued on next card)

ATOMIC BOMB

Voice Lib.
353   Russia and the bomb...   1949.   (Card 2)
bd.19

          Samuel King, 1900-   IV. Hugness, Thornton.
       V. McMahon, James O'Brien, 1903-1952. VI.
       Douglas, Paul Howard, 1892-   VII. Dulles,
       John Foster, 1888-1959. VIII. Groves, Leslie
       R   1896-1970. IX. Churchill, Winston
       Leonard Spencer, 1874-1965. X. Acheson, Dean
       Gooderham, 1893-1971. XI. Fleming, James,
       1915-

ATOMIC BOMB - RUSSIA

Voice Lib.
197   Bradley, Omar Nelson, 1893-
bd.2   Russian atomic bomb development, a speech
         before American Forestry Association.
         Detroit, WJR, October 12, 1949.
            1 reel (7 in.)   7 1/2 in. per sec.
         phonotape.

          1. Atomic bomb - Russia.

Voice Lib.
M717   Atomic bomb test at Bikini Atoll. Description
bd.3   by on-the-spot witnesses and remarks by
         Vice-Admiral Blandy, U.S.N., on board
         U.S.S. Mt. McKinley.   July 24, 1946.
         1 min., 38 sec.   phonotape (1 r.
         7 1/2 i.p.s.)

          1. Atomic bomb.   I. Blandy, William
       Henry Purnell, 1890-1954.

ATOMIC ENERGY

Voice Lib.
M1742 Kaul, Triloki Nath
bd.3   Discussion on capacity for nuclear war
         in Egypt and Israel, by Triloki Nath Kaul and
         Herbert F. York on the "Today Show". WKAR,
         June 21, 1974.
            10 min.   phonotape (1 r.   7 1/2 i.p.s.)

          1. Atomic energy. 2. Jewish-Arab relations.
       I. York, Herbert Frank, 1921-

ATOMIC ENERGY

Voice Lib.
M1096 Roosevelt, Eleanor (Roosevelt) 1884-1962.
bd.1   Weekly panel of guests on live television
         program entitled, "Today with Mrs. Roosevelt",
         discussing the future of atomic energy and
         the hydrogen bomb. NBC-TV, February 12,
         1950.
            1 reel (7 in.)   7 1/2 i.p.s.   phonotape.

          1. Atomic energy.   I. Title: Today with
       Mrs. Roosevelt.

ATOMIC POWER

Voice Lib.
M846   Truman, Harry S, Pres. U.S., 1884-1972.
bd.1   Navy Day address by President Truman in
         Central Park, New York City, stating postwar
         U.S. foreign policy and the outlook for uses of
         atomic power. NBC, October 27, 1945.
            1 reel (7 in.)   7 1/2 in. per sec.
         phonotape.

          1. U.S.- Foreign policy. 2. Atomic power.

ATOMIC POWER - INTERNATIONAL CONTROL
Voice Lib.
M344   Dean, Arthur Hobson, 1898-
bd.3   Discusses the resumption of nuclear
test ban talks in news conference. CBS,
November 24, 1961.
1 reel (7 in.)   7 1/2 in. per sec.
phonotape.

1. Atomic power - International control.

ATOMIC POWER - INTERNATIONAL CONTROL
Voice Lib.
M243   Dulles, John Foster, 1888-1959.
bd.11   On air and ground inspection. CBS,
August 6, 1957.
1 reel (7 in.)   7 1/2 in. per sec.
phonotape.

1. Atomic power - International control.

ATOMIC POWER - INTERNATIONAL CONTROL
Voice Lib.
M345   Dulles, John Foster, 1888-1959.
bd.13   Statement on suspension of nuclear
tests; excerpt from press conference.
CBS, April 1, 1958.
1 reel (7 in.)   7 1/2 in. per sec.
phonotape.

1. Atomic power - International Control.

ATOMIC POWER - INTERNATIONAL CONTROL
Voice Lib.
M258   White, Lincoln
bd.16   Press conference at the White House on the
recall of the chief U.S. negotiator from
the test ban talks in Geneva. New York,
CBS, June 20, 1961.
1 reel (7 in.)   7 1/2 in. per sec.
phonotape.

Voice Lib.   ATOMIC WEAPONS
M1587- Asimov, Isaac, 1920-
1588   Utopian change; excerpts. WKAR-AM,
March 3, 1974.
60 min.   phonotape (2 r.   7 1/2 in. per
sec.)

1. Science fiction. 2. Atomic weapons.

Voice Lib. ATOMIC WEAPONS
M389   Bush, Vannevar, 1890-
bd.3   Development of nuclear weapons; problems
of outlawing the atomic bomb. Hearst
Metrotone News, 1963.
1 reel (7 in.)   7 1/2 in. per sec.
phonotape.

ATOMIC WEAPONS
Voice Lib.
M389   Einstein, Albert, 1879-1955.
bd.5   Development of nuclear weapons; describes
armament race between U.S. and Russia.
Hearst Metrotone News, 1963.
1 reel (7 in.)   7 1/2 in. per sec.
phonotape.

ATOMIC WEAPONS
Voice Lib.
M389   Oppenheimer, Julius Robert, 1904-1967.
bd.2   Development of nuclear weapons; describes
effect atomic bombs could have on U.S.,
describes inability to develop a deterrent
force. Hearst Metrotone News, 1963.
1 reel (7 in.)   7 1/2 in. per sec.
phonotape.

ATOMIC WEAPONS
Voice Lib.
M389   Pauling, Linus Carl, 1901-
bd.6   Development of nuclear weapons; foresees
future for world if atomic testing continues,
tells of his suit against the nations of the
world. Hearst Metrotone News, 1963.
1 reel (7 in.)   7 1/2 in. per sec.
phonotape.

ATOMIC WEAPONS
Voice Lib.
M730   Russell, Bertrand Russell, 3rd earl,
bd.2   1872-1970.
Forum address. Conference pertaining to
the statement about the significance of
nuclear warfare issued by various scientists.
BBC, 1955.
1 reel (7 in.)   7 1/2 in. per sec.
phonotape.

Voice Lib. ATOMIC WEAPONS
M389   Teller, Edward, 1908-
bd.7   Development of nuclear weapons; describes
    effects atomic energy through fallout could
    have on future generations, on peaceful world.
    Hearst Metrotone News, 1963.
       1 reel (7 in.)   7 1/2 in. per sec.
    phonotape.

              Attlee, Clement Richard Attlee, 1st earl,
Voice Lib.   1883-1967
573   I can hear it now (radio program)
bd.2-   1945-1949. CBS, 1950?
574   2 reels (7 in.) 7 1/2 in. per sec.
bd.1 phonotape.
      I. Murrow, Edward Roscoe, 1908-1965. II. Nehru, Jawaharlal,
1889-1964. III. Philip, duke of Edinburgh, 1921- IV. Elizabeth II,
Queen of Great Britain, 1926- V. Ferguson, Homer, 1889- VI.
Hughes, Howard Robard, 1905- VII. Marshall, George Catlett,
1880- VIII. Ruth, George Herman, 1895-1948. IX. Lilienthal,
David Eli, 1899- X. Trout, Robert, 1908- XI. Gage, Arthur.
XII. Jackson, Robert Houghwout, 1892-1954. XIII. Gromyko, Anatolii Andreevich, 1908- XIV. Baruch, Bernard Mannes, 1870-
1965. XV. Churchill, Winston Leonard Spencer, 1874-1965. XVI.
Winchell, Walter, 1897-1 XVII. Davis, Elmer Holmes, 1890-
                  (Continued on next card)

Voice Lib. ATOMIC WEAPONS
M389   Urey, Harold Clayton, 1893-
bd.4   Development of nuclear weapons; calls for
    development of hydrogen bomb and winning of
    arms race. Hearst Metrotone News, 1963.
       1 reel (7 in.)   7 1/2 in. per sec.
    phonotape.

C1   AUDUBON, JOHN JAMES, 1788-1851
A24
       Whorf, Michael, 1933-
       Romance of the Audubons--John and Lucy.
       1 tape cassette. (The visual sounds of
    Mike Whorf. Art, music, and letters, A24)
      Originally presented on his radio program, Kaleidoscope,
WJR, Detroit.
    Duration: 46 min.
    From the reaches of time is drawn this story of romance, of
the love of John Audubon and his wife, Lucy, who survived the
struggles and hardships of the wilderness so that her gifted husband
would achieve his ambition and dreams.

      I. Audubon, John James, 1788-1851. 2. Audubon, Lucy
(Bakewell) I. Title.

       ATOMIC WEAPONS - TESTING
Voice Lib.
M121   Kennedy, John Fitzgerald, Pres. U.S., 1917-1963.
    Nuclear testing, resumption of. NBC,
March 2, 1965.
       1 reel (7 in.)   7 1/2 i.p.s.   phonotape.

    1. Atomic weapons - Testing.

C1   AUDUBON, LUCY (BAKEWELL)
A24
       Whorf, Michael, 1933-
       Romance of the Audubons--John and Lucy.
       1 tape cassette. (The visual sounds of
    Mike Whorf. Art, music, and letters, A24)
      Originally presented on his radio program, Kaleidoscope,
WJR, Detroit.
    Duration: 46 min.
    From the reaches of time is drawn this story of romance, of
the love of John Audubon and his wife, Lucy, who survived the
struggles and hardships of the wilderness so that her gifted husband
would achieve his ambition and dreams.

      I. Audubon, John James, 1788-1851. 2. Audubon, Lucy
(Bakewell) I. Title.

Voice Lib.
M742   Attlee, Clement Richard Attlee, 1st earl,
bd.6   1883-1967.
       Speaking during British election campaign.
BBC, September 29, 1959.
       1 reel (7 in.)   7 1/2 in. per sec.
    phonotape.

C1   Augustine, the saint
R30
       Whorf, Michael, 1933-
       Augustine, the saint.
       1 tape cassette. (The visual sounds of
    Mike Whorf. Religion, R30)
      Originally presented on his radio program, Kaleidoscope,
WJR, Detroit.
    Duration: 36 min., 30 sec.
    In the history of the Christian Church, few stories are as
inspiring as that of Saint Augustine. Here is presented the
account of his life and of his devotion to God.

      I. Augustinus, Aurelius, Saint, bp. of Hippo. I. Title.

Voice Lib.   Attlee, Clement Richard Attlee, 1st earl,
           1883-1967
M384   I can hear it now (radio program)
bd.2   CBS, February 2, 1951.
       1 reel (7 in.)   7 1/2 in. per sec.
    phonotape.

      I. Taft, Robert Alphonso, 1889-1953. II.
Rayburn, Samuel Taliaferro, 1882-1961. III.
Barkley, Alban William, 1877-1956. IV. Rabaut,
Louis Charles, 1886-1961. V. Attlee, Clement
Richard Attlee, 1st earl, 1883-1967. VI.
Kelly, Capt., U.S.A.

C1   AUGUSTINUS, AURELIUS, SAINT, BP OF HIPPO
R30
       Whorf, Michael, 1933-
       Augustine, the saint.
       1 tape cassette. (The visual sounds of
    Mike Whorf. Religion, R30)
      Originally presented on his radio program, Kaleidoscope,
WJR, Detroit.
    Duration: 36 min., 30 sec.
    In the history of the Christian Church, few stories are as
inspiring as that of Saint Augustine. Here is presented the
account of his life and of his devotion to God.

      I. Augustinus, Aurelius, Saint, bp. of Hippo. I. Title.

Voice Lib.
M763   Austin, Bob
bd.6   Excerpt from "The Scope of Jazz" (Program
6); his reasons for demise of big bands.
Westinghouse Broadcasting Corporation, 1964.
1 reel (7 in.)   7 1/2 in. per sec.
phonotape.   (The Music Goes Round and Round)

I. Title: The scope of jazz. II. Series.
1. Jazz music

Voice Lib.   Austin, Warren Robinson, 1877-1962
385   I can hear it now (radio program)
CBS, February 2, 1951.
1 reel (7 in.)   7 1/2 in. per sec.
phonotape.

I. Austin, Warren Robinson, 1877-1962. II.
Pandit, Vijaya Lakshmi (Nehru) 1900-   III.
Roosevelt, Eleanor (Roosevelt) 1884-1962. IV.
Morse, Wayne Lyman, 1900-   V. Chandler,
Albert Benjamin, 1898-   VI. Taylor, Telford,
1908-   VII. Whi( )Jack.

    AUTHORS - CORRESPONDENCE, REMINISCENCES,
       ETC.
Voice Lib.
M1721   Stout, Rex, 1886-
bd.4   Interviewed on Book Beat by Robert Cromie.
WKAR-TV, June 12, 1974.
20 min.   phonotape (1 r.   7 1/2 i.p.s.)

1. Authors - Correspondence, reminiscences,
etc.   I. Cromie, Robert.

    AUTHORS - CORRESPONDENCE, REMINISCENCES,
       ETC.
Voice Lib.
M1548   Sullivan, Frank, 1892-
     Interviewed on Bob Crombie's "Book Beat"
program.   WKAR, February 13, 1974.
28 min.   phonotape (1 r.   7 1/2 i.p.s.)

1. Authors - Correspondence, reminiscences,
etc.   I. Crombie, Robert.

    Autocrat of the breakfast table - O. W. Holmes,
      Sr.
C1
A40   Whorf, Michael, 1933-
     Autocrat of the breakfast table - O. W. Holmes,
Sr.
1 tape cassette.   (The visual sounds of
Mike Whorf. Art, music and letters, A40)
    Originally presented on his radio program, Kaleidoscope,
WJR, Detroit.
    Duration: 36 min., 30 sec.
    Oliver Wendell Holmes, Sr., was a poet and philosopher, and
here mixed with his works is the story of his life.

    1. Holmes, Oliver Wendell, 1809-1894. I. Title.

        AUTOMOBILES
C1
SC14-   Whorf, Michael, 1933-
SC15   Four wheel American dream - the automobile.
2 tape cassettes.   (The visual sounds of
Mike Whorf. Science, SC14-SC15)
    Originally presented on his radio program, Kaleidoscope,
WJR, Detroit.
    Duration: 54 min., 20 sec.; 50 min., 5 sec.
    Two narratives dealing with the automobile industry. The
saga of its invention and a technical approach explaining the
car as a machine.

    1. Automobiles. I. Title.

        AUTUMN
C1
M40   Whorf, Michael, 1933-
     And the days grow short when you reach
September.
1 tape cassette.   (The visual sounds of
Mike Whorf. Miscellaneous, M40)
    Originally presented on his radio program, Kaleidoscope,
WJR, Detroit.
    Duration: 36 min., 25 sec.
    Here in an evocative word-portrait of autumn, is brought to life
the bittersweet qualities of this special season. As the leaves turn
to brilliant scarlets, yellows and oranges and the nip of frost steals
into the evenings, your mind's eye will conjure up visions and
memories.
    1. Autumn. I. Title.

Voice Lib.
M1674   The Avenger (radio program)
bd.2   The tunnel of disaster.   Golden Age
Radio Records, 1941.
20 min.   phonotape (1 r.   7 1/2 i.p.s.)

        Ayen, Woody
Voice Lib.
M1579   Gentile, Eric Anton, 1943-
bd.3   Reading Woody Ayen's State News editorial
(November 15, 1973) calling for action from
and/or resignation of MSU Planning Director
Milton Baron.   MSU Voice Library, February
13, 1974.
3 min.   phonotape (1 r.   7 1/2 i/p.s.)

1. Physically handicapped. 2. Baron,
Milton.   I. Ayen, Woody.

      BACH, JOHANN SEBASTIAN, 1685-1750
C1
A11   Whorf, Michael, 1933-
     Music for the heavens.
1 tape cassette.   (The visual sounds of
Mike Whorf. Art, music, and letters, A11)
    Originally presented on his radio program, Kaleidoscope,
WJR, Detroit.
    Duration: 36 min., 45 sec.
    Was Johann Sebastian Bach the most creative and brilliant
musical artist on the European scene? Those aspects and attitudes
can conceivably be confirmed as one delves into his life and times.

    1. Bach, Johann Sebastian, 1685-1750. I. Title.

Back to the blankets

C1
S11
Whorf, Michael, 1933-
Back to the blankets.
1 tape cassette. (The visual sounds of
Mike Whorf. Social, S11)
Originally presented on his radio program, Kaleidoscope,
WJR, Detroit.
Duration: 52 min., 45 sec.
The Indian's world for the past 100 years has been on the
reservation, yet he has frequently been induced to compete in the
outside world. What have been and what are the results?

L. Indians of North America. L. Title.

Voice Lib.
M975   Baden-Powell, Sir Robert Stephenson Smyth
bd.6   Baden-Powell, 1857-1941.
Address about Wolf Cub Boy Scouts.
Rococo-Can., 1910.
1 reel (7 in.)   7 1/2 in. per sec.
phonotape.

1. Boy Scouts

Voice Lib.
M1257 Baden-Powell, Sir Robert Stephenson Smyth Baden-
bd.4   Powell, 1857-1944.
Remarks by Lord Baden-Powell addressed to
Queen Wilhelmina of Holland on the occasion
of the 5th World Scout Jamboree, held at
Vogelenzang (near Bloemendaal) Holland.
Shortwave radio, July 31, 1937.
1 reel (7 in.)   7 1/2 in. per sec.
phonotape.

1. Boy Scouts.

Voice Lib.
610   Baden-Powell, Sir Robert Stephenson Smyth
bd.2   Baden-Powell, 1857-1941.
Speech opening Fifth World Scouting
Jamboree, Holland. NBC, 1936.
1 reel (7 in.)   7 1/2 in. per sec.
phonotape.

1. Boy Scouts

BADEN-POWELL, SIR ROBERT STEPHENSON SMYTH-
BADEN-POWELL, 1857-1944
C1
S73
Whorf, Michael, 1933-
The birth of the Boy Scouts.
1 tape cassette. (The visual sounds of
Mike Whorf. Social, S73)
Originally presented on his radio program, Kaleidoscope,
WJR, Detroit.
Duration: 36 min., 35 sec.
A historic narration of Lord Baden-Powell's life work of
creating boys into young adults. The history of the Boy Scouts
from its initiation to the present day world-wide organization is
presented.

L. Boy Scouts. 2. Baden-Powell, Sir Robert Stephenson
Smyth-Baden-Powell, 1857-1944. L. Title.

Badenweiler Marsch
Voice Lib.
M1301 Nazi march music (instrumental): "Badenweiler
bd.1   Marsch". Peteler, 1941.
1 reel (7 in.)   7 1/2 in. per sec.
phonotape.

I. Title: Badenweiler Marsch.

Voice Lib.
M1042 Baez, Joan, 1941-
Film interview with Joan Baez made in 1965
at her home in Carmel Valley, California;
outlining her political beliefs and discussing
her school, the Institute for the Study of
Non-Violence; includes several of her musical
selections. NET-TV, February 1., 1965.
1 reel (7 in.)   7 1/2 in. per sec.
phonotape.

1. Baez, Joan, 1941-

Voice Lib. Bailey, Francis Lee, 1933-
M1269 Dirksen, Everett McKinley, 1896-1969.
bd.1   Excerpt of conversation with Senator
Dirksen and his wife at their home in
Washington, D.C., with F. Lee Bailey from
TV program "Good Company." Discussion of
public speaking, forty years of marriage,
recording ventures, advice to youth, plans
for another term as senator. NBC-TV,
September 14, 1967.
1 reel (7 in.)   7 1/2 in. per sec.   phonotape.
L. Dirksen, Louella Carver, 1899-   II. Bailey, Francis
Lee, 1933-   III. Good Company (Television program)

Voice Lib.
M1586 Baker, Howard H., 1925-
The lessons of Watergate. WKAR,
February 28, 1974.
30 min. phonotape (1 r.   7 1/2 in. per
sec.)

1. Watergate Affair, 1972. 2. Campaign
funds.

Voice Lib.
M1702 Baker, Howard H., 1925-
On Watergate, with Clyde Lamont, of the
National Press Club. WKAR, May 30, 1974.
50 min. phonotape (1 r.   7 1/2 i.p.s.)

1. Watergate Affair, 1972.   2. U.S. -
Politics and government. I. Lamont, Clyde

Voice Lib.
M1800

Baker, Howard H., 1925-
U.S. Congress. Senate. Select Committee on Presidential
Campaign Activities.
Watergate gavel to gavel, phase I: May 17 - August 7, 1973.
Pacifica, May 17 - August 7, 1973.
172 reels (5 in.) 3 3/4 i.p.s. phonotape.

"These tapes include commentaries by Pacifica's Washington
correspondents and interviews with members of the Senate Committee
taped during recesses of the hearings."

I. Presidents - U.S. - Elections - 1972. 2. Watergate Affair,
1972- I. Ervin, Samuel James, 1896- II. Talmadge,
Herman Eugene, 1913- III. Inouye, Daniel Ken, 1924-
IV. Baker, Howard H., 1925- V. Gurney, Edward John, 1914-
VI. Weicker, Lowell P., 19   VII. Title.

Voice Lib.
M653
bd.8

Baker, Newton Diehl, 1871-
Choice and opportunity.   Predictions
of post-World War I world.   Nation's
Forum, 1918.
1 reel (7 in.)   7 1/2 i.p.s.   phonotape.

Voice Lib.
M1698

BAKER, ROBERT GENE, 1928-
Ervin, Samuel James, 1896-
The lesson of Watergate; address at the
National Press Club. WKAR, May 29, 1974.
45 min. phonotape (1 r.   7 1/2 i.p.s.)

1. Constitutional law. 2. Baker, Robert
Gene, 1928-   3. Sirica, John Joseph, 1904-

Voice Lib.
M1800
WG
0524.03

Baldwin, Alfred
Testimony before the Senate Committee
investigating the Watergate Affair.
Pacifica, May 24, 1973.
84 min. phonotape (1 r.   3 3/4 i.p.s.)
(Watergate gavel to gavel, phase 1)

1. Watergate Affair, 1972-

Voice Lib.
M1082-
1083,
bd.1

Baldwin, James, 1924-
An interview with James Baldwin by Studs
Turkel about "The Black man in America".
Credo Records, 1963.
2 reels (7 in.)   7 1/2 in. per sec.
phonotape.

1. Negroes - U.S.   I. Turkel, Studs.

Voice Lib.
344
bd.16

Ball, George Wildman, 1909-
Speech in Los Angeles on objectives of
U.N. in the Congo.   CBS, December 19,
1961.
1 reel (7in.)   7 1/2 in. per sec.
phonotape.

1. Congo question. 2. United Nations.

Voice Lib.
M746
bd.2

Bancroft, Griffin
U.S. Congress. Senate. Committee on Government Operations.
Permanent Subcommittee on Investigations.
Proceedings of the [1st session] of Senate Army-McCarthy
hearings, April 22, 1954. Testimony by various witnesses
regarding pressure put on the Army to obtain a commission for
Private David Schine. Some of the people speaking are:
Griffin Bancroft, CBS announcer, describing the scenes at the
hearings; Joseph N. Welch, counsel for the Army; Ray Jenkins,
counsel for the subcommittee; Army Secretary Robert Stevens;
General Reber and Senator McClellan of Arkansas.   CBS Radio,
April 22, 1954.
1 reel (7 in.)   7 1/2 in. per sec.   phonotape.
I. McCarthy-Army controversy, 1954. I. Bancroft, Griffin
II. Welch, Joseph Nye, 1890-1960. III. Jenkins, Ray Howard,
1897-   IV. Stevens, Robert Ten Broeck, 1899-   V.
Reber, Miles   VI. McClellan, John Little, 1896-

Voice Lib.
M1281

Bancroft, Griffin
U.S. Congress. Senate. Committee on Government Operations.
Permanent Subcommittee on Investigations.
Proceedings of the 11th session of Senate Army-McCarthy
hearings, May 6, 1954. Sen. McCarthy on witness stand, pertaining
to missing letter from J. Edgar Hoover regarding possible spies at
Ft. Monmouth, N.J. Other speakers: Roy Cohn, Committee Counsel
Jenkins, Robert A. Collier.   Summary by CBS' Griffin Bancroft.
CBS Radio, May 6, 1954.
1 reel (7 in.)   7 1/2 in. per sec.   phonotape.

I. McCarthy-Army controversy, 1954. I. McCarthy,
Joseph Raymond, 1909-1957. II. Cohn, Roy M   1927-
III. Jenkins, Ray Howard, 1897-   IV. Collier, Robert A
V. Bancroft, Griffin

Voice Lib.
M766
bd.7

Banda, Antonio
Excerpt from "Popular Music of Europe"
(Program 11); comments on the popular music
in Spain, including musical number "Chin chin".
Westinghouse Broadcasting Corporation, 1964.
3 min., 3 sec. phonotape (1 r.   7 1/2
i.p.s.)   (The music goes round and round)

1. Music, Popular (Songs, etc.) - Spain.
I. Title: Popular music of Europe.
II. Series.

C1
M25

BANDS (MUSIC)

Whorf, Michael, 1933-
And the band played on.
1 tape cassette.   (The visual sounds of
Mike Whorf. Miscellaneous, M25)

Originally presented on his radio program, Kaleidoscope,
WJR, Detroit.
Duration: 55 min., 30 sec.
A highly successful and original work, depicting musically
what the instruments are, what they do and sound like.

I. Bands (Music) I. Title.

Banghardt, Kenneth
Voice Lib.
M275- Biography in sound (radio program)
276 Alexander Woollcott. N.B.C., date?
bd.1 2 reels (7 in.) 7 1/2 in. per sec.
phonotape.
 L. Woollcott, Alexander, 1887-1943. L. Woollcott, Alexander,
1887-1943. IL. Banghardt, Kenneth III. Hecht, Ben, 1893-
1964. IV. Roosevelt, Eleanor (Roosevelt) 1884-1962. V. Walker,
Danton VI. Brackett, Charles, 1892-1969. VII. Grant,
Jane VIII. Rude, Robert Barnes IX. West,
Rebecca, pseud. X. Henessy, Joseph XI. Letterer,
Charles XII. Welles, Orson, 1915-

BANKS AND BANKING - U.S.
Voice Lib.
M714 Roosevelt, Franklin Delano, Pres. U.S.,
bd.3 1882-1945.
 First fireside chat, on banking situation
in the U.S. (opening and closing statements
of this broadcast). March 12, 1933.
 2 min., 9 sec. phonotape (1 r. 7 1/2
i.p.s.)
 1. U.S. - Economic conditions. 2. Banks
& banking - U.S.

Voice Lib.
M1800 Barker, Bernard, 1917?-
WG Testimony before the Senate Committee
0524.02 investigating the Watergate Affair.
Pacifica, May 24, 1973.
 117 min. phonotape (2 r. 3 3/4 i.p.s.)
(Watergate gavel to gavel, phase 1)

 1. Watergate Affair, 1972-

Barker, Robert W.
Voice Lib.
M1800 Stans, Maurice Hubert, 1908-
WG Testimony before the Senate Committee
0612.02 investigating the Watergate Affair.
Includes statement by Robert W. Barker,
counsel. Pacifica, June 12, 1973.
 46 min. phonotape (1 r. 3 3/4 i.p.s.)
(Watergate gavel to gavel, phase 1)

 1. Watergate Affair, 1972-
 I. Barker, Robert

Voice Lib.
M1034 Barkley, Alben William, 1877-1956.
bd.5 Excerpt of nominating speech for Franklin D.
Roosevelt at 1932 Democratic National
Convention. CBS, 1932.
 1 reel (7 in.) 7 1/2 in. per sec.
phonotape.

 1. Roosevelt, Franklin Delano, Pres. U.S.,
1882-1945

Voice Lib.
M717 Barkley, Alben William, 1877-1956
bd.5 Excerpts of proceedings at Democratic
National Convention. Chicago, CBS, 1932.
 1 reel (7 in.) 7 1/2 in. per sec.
phonotape.

Voice Lib.
M724 Barkley, Alben William, 1877-1956.
bd.3 Alben Barkley and James Farley at
Democratic convention of 1940, speaking for
nomination of Franklin D. Roosevelt for
third term. 1940.
 1 min., 40 sec. phonotape (1 r. 7 1/2
i.p.s.)

 L. Roosevelt, Franklin Delano, Pres. U.S., 1882-1945.
2. Presidents - U.S. - Election - 1940. L. Farley, James
Aloysius, 1888-

Voice Lib.
M724 Barkley, Alben William, 1877-1956.
bd.5 Introducing President Roosevelt to
the convention in 1940. 1940.
 1 reel (7 in.) 7 1/2 in. per sec.
phonotape.

 1. Roosevelt, Franklin Delano, Pres. U.S.,
1882-1945

Voice Lib.
652 Barkley, Alben William, 1877-1956.
bd.6 Campaign wind-up speech. CBS, November 1,
1948.
 1 reel (7 in.) 7 1/2 in. per sec.
phonotape.

Voice Lib.
184 Barkley, Alben William, 1877-1956.
bd.3 End of address at convention as Barkley
collapses. WJR, May 4, 1956.
 1 reel (7 in.) 7 1/2 in. per sec.
phonotape.

Voice Lib.
M740 Barkley, Alben William, 1877-1956.
bd.1   Excerpt from address reviewing his career,
reflecting that he was U.S. Vice-President
and is now junior Senator from Kentucky;
then he collapses and is carried from
platform. CBS, May 4, 1956.
1 reel (7 in.) 7 1/2 in. per sec.
phonotape.

C1   BARLOW, JOEL, 1754-1812
FA4   Whorf, Michael, 1933-
Joel Barlow.
1 tape cassette. (The visual sounds of
Mike Whorf. The forgotten American, FA4)
Originally presented on his radio program, Kaleidoscope,
WJR, Detroit.
Duration: 13 min., 50 sec.
Appointed minister to France by President Madison during the
time of the War of 1812. Barlow worked for a trade treaty with
Napoleon.
I. Barlow, Joel, 1754-1812. I. Title.

Barkley, Alben William, 1877-1956
Voice Lib.
M618 Radio in the 1930's (Part I): a series of
bd.1-   excerpts from important broadcasts of the
14   1930's; a sample of radio of the period.
NVL, April, 1964.
1 reel (7 in.) 7 1/2 in. per sec. phonotape.
I. Shaw, George Bernard, 1856-1950. II. Crosby, Bing, 1901-
III. Barkley, Alban William, 1877-1956. IV. Roosevelt, Franklin
Delano, Pres. U.S., 1882-1945. V. Hoover, Herbert Clark, Pres.
U.S., 1874-1964. VI. Long, Huey Pierce, 1893-1935. VII. Townsend, Francis Everett, 1867-1960. VIII. Coughlin, Charles Edward,
1891- IX. Rogers, Will, 1879-1935. X. Pius XII, Pope, 1876-
1958. XI. Edward VIII, king of Great Britain, 1894-1972. XII.
Barrymore, John, 1882-1942. XIII. Woollcott, Alexander, 1887-
1943. XIV. Allen, Fred, 1894-1956. XV. Benchley, Robert Charles,
1889-1945.

Voice Li..
M1294 Barnard, Christiaan Neethling, 1923-
One hour NBC special TV program, recorded and
filmed on location at Capetown, South Africa.
Interviews with Dr. Christiaan Barnard, his
brother, his wife, and former teachers. Descriptions of his youth and studies and two
famous heart surgery cases. NBC-TV, January 6,
1968.
1 reel (7 in.) 7 1/2 in. per sec. phonotape.
1. Barnard, Christiaan Neethling, 1923-

Barkley, Alben William, 1877-1956
Voice Lib.
M384   I can hear it now (radio program)
bd.2   CBS, February 2, 1951.
1 reel (7 in.) 7 1/2 in. per sec.
phonotape.
I. Taft, Robert Alphonso, 1889-1953. II.
Rayburn, Samuel Taliaferro, 1882-1961. III.
Barkley, Alban William, 1877-1956. IV. Rabaut,
Louis Charles, 1886-1961. V. Attlee, Clement
Richard Attlee, 1st earl, 1883-1967. VI.
Kelly, Capt., U.S.A.

Voice Lib.
610   Barnes, Alma
bd.1   Imitates popular entertainers of motion
pictures and radio of the thirties in song
routine. G.R. Vincent, 1935.
1 reel (7 in.) 7 1/2 in. per sec.
phonotape.

Barkley, Alben William, 1877-1956
Voice Lib.
M384   I can hear it now (radio program)
bd.1   Biography of a pint of blood. CBS,
February, 1951.
1 reel (7 in.) 7 1/2 in. per sec.
phonotape.
1. Blood. I. McIntire, Ross T., 1899-
II. Hope, Bob, 1903- III. Ridgway,
Matthew Bunker, 1895- IV. Barkley,
Alban William, 1877-1956.

Barney Google
Voice Lib.
M617   Radio in the 1920's: a series of excerpts
bd.1-   from important broadcasts of the 1920's,
bd.25   with brief prologue and epilogue; a sample
of radio of the period. NVL, April, 1964.
1 reel (7 in.) 7 1/2 in. per sec.
phonotape.
I. Radio programs. I. Marconi, Guglielmo, marchese, 1874-
1937. II. Kendall, H G III. Coolidge, Calvin, Pres. U.S.,
1872-1933. IV. Wilson, Woodrow, Pres. U.S., 1856-1924. V.
Roosevelt, Franklin Delano, Pres. U.S., 1882-1945. VI. Lodge,
Henry Cabot, 1850-1924. VII. LaGuardia, Fiorello Henry, 1882-1947.
VIII. The Happiness Boys (Radio program) IX. Gallagher and Sheen.
X. Barney Google. XI. Vallee, Rudy, 1901- XII. The two
(Continued on next card)

Barkley, Alben William, 1877-1956
Voice Lib.
573   I can hear it now (radio program)
bd.2-   1945-1949. CBS, 1950?
574   2 reels (7 in.) 7 1/2 in. per sec.
bd.1 phonotape.
I. Murrow, Edward Roscoe, 1908-1965. II. Nehru, Jawaharlal,
1889-1964. III. Philip, duke of Edinburgh, 1921- IV. Elizabeth II,
Queen of Great Britain, 1926- V. Ferguson, Homer, 1889- VI.
Hughes, Howard Robard, 1905- VII. Marshall, Georg. Catlett,
1880- VIII. Ruth, George Herman, 1895-1948. IX. Lilienthal,
David Eli, 1899- X. Trout, Robert, 1908- XI. Gage, Arthur.
XII. Jackson, Robert Houghwout, 1892-1954. XIII. Gromyko, Ana-
tolii Andreevich, 1908- XIV. Baruch, Bernard Mannes, 1870-
1965. XV. Churchill, Winston Leonard Spencer, 1874-1965. XVI.
Winchell, Walter, 1897- XVII. Davis, Elmer Holmes, 1890-
(Continued on next card)

C1   BARNUM, BAILEY AND RINGLING NORTH
M7   Whorf, Michael, 1933-
The big top.
1 tape cassette. (The visual sounds of Mike Whorf.
Miscellaneous, M7)
Originally presented on his radio program, Kaleidoscope,
WJR, Detroit.
Duration: 40 min., 45 sec.
Here is a fascinating look at the three-ringed world wherein
lies the greatest show on earth, the animals, the clowns, the
aerialist, the animal trainer, the marvelous magic of Barnum,
Bailey and Ringling North.
1. Circus - U.S. 2. Barnum, Bailey and Ringling North.
I. Title.

Voice Lib.
BARON, MILTON
M1579   Gentile, Eric Anton, 1943-
bd.3   Reading Woody Ayen's State News editorial
        (November 15, 1973) calling for action from
        and/or resignation of MSU Planning Director
        Milton Baron.   MSU Voice Library, February
        13, 1974.
        . 3 min.   phonotape (1 r.   7 1/2 i/p.s.)

        1. Physically handicapped. 2. Baron,
Milton. I. Ayen, Woody.

Voice Lib.
M299   Barrymore, Ethel, 1879-1959.
bd.1   "Today" Show Memorial on the death of
        Ethel Barrymore (6-18-59).   Voice of
        America-NBC-TV, June 19, 1959 (recorded,
        1941).
        1 reel (7 in.)   7 1/2 in. per sec.
        phonotape.

        1. Barrymore, Ethel, 1879-1959.

Voice Lib.
616   Barrymore, John, 1882-1942.
bd.4   "Hamlet's Soliloquy" (excerpt); speaks
        informally, narrates excerpt. Famous
        Record Company, 1925.
        1 reel (7 in.)   7 1/2 in. per sec.
        phonotape.

        I. Title.

Voice Lib.
M301   Barrymore, John, 1882-1942.
bd.1   Excerpts from Shakespeare's Richard III.
        Voice of America - NBC, 1937 (rebroadcast
        1950).
        1 reel (7 in.)   7 1/2 in. per sec.
        phonotape.

        I. Shakespeare, William, 1564-1616./
Richard III.

Voice Lib.
M299   Barrymore, John, 1882-1942.
bd.2   Excerpts from Shakespeare's Twelfth Night.
        Voice of America - NBC (rebroadcast 1950),
        1937.
        1 reel (7 in.)   7 1/2 in. per sec.
        phonotape.

        I. Shakespeare, William, 1564-1616./
Twelfth night.

Voice Lib.
M1494   Barrymore, John, 1882-1942.
        Excerpts of "Hamlet" acted by John Barrymore,
        with his own narration as bridges.
        Shakespeare Society, 1947.
        1 reel (7 in.)   7 1/2 in. per sec.
        phonotape.

        I. Shakespeare, William, 1564-1616./Hamlet.

Barrymore, John, 1882-1942
Voice Lib.
M618   Radio in the 1930's (Part I): a series of
bd.1-   excerpts from important broadcasts of the
14   1930's; a sample of radio of the period.
        NVL, April, 1964.
        1 reel (7 in.)   7 1/2 in. per sec.   phonotape.
        L. Shaw, George Bernard, 1856-1950. II. Crosby, Bing, 1901-
        III. Barkley, Alban William, 1877-1956. IV. Roosevelt, Franklin
        Delano, Pres. U.S., 1882-1945. V. Hoover, Herbert Clark, Pres.
        U.S., 1874-1964. VI. Long, Huey Pierce, 1893-1935. VII. Town-
        send, Francis Everett, 1867-1960. VIII. Coughlin, Charles Edward,
        1891-   IX. Rogers, Will, 1879-1935. X. Pius XII, Pope, 1876-
        1958. XI. Edward VIII, king of Great Britain, 1894-1972. XII.
        Barrymore, John, 1882-1942. XIII. Woollcott, Alexander, 1887-
        1943. XIV. Allen, Fred, 1894-1956. XV. Benchley, Robert Charles,
        1889-1945.

Barrymore, John, 1882-1942
Voice Lib.
M225   Packard, Frederick
        Styles in Shakespearean acting, 1890-1950.
        Creative Associates, 1963?
        1 reel (7 in.)   7 1/2 i.p.s.   phonotape.

        L. Sothern, Edward Askew, 1826-188L. II. Marlowe,
        Julia, 1865-1950. III. Booth, Edwin, 1833-1893. IV. Gielgud,
        John, 1904-   V. Robeson, Paul Bustill, 1898-   VI. Terry,
        Dame Ellen, 1848-1928. VII. Allen, Viola. VIII. Welles,
        Orson, 1915-   IX. Skinner, Otis, 1858-1942. X. Barrymore,
        John, 1882-1942. XI. Olivier, Sir Laurence Kerr, 1907-
        XII. Forbes-Robertson, Sir Johnston, 1853-   XIII. Evans,
        Maurice. XIV. Thorndike, Dame Sybil, 1882-   XV. Robson,
        Flora. XVI. LeGallienne, Eva, 1899-   XVII. Anderson,
        Judith. XVIII. Duncan, Augustin. XIX. Hampden, Walter.
        XX. Speaight, Robert, 1904-   XXI. Jones, Daniel.

Barrymore, Lionel, 1878-1954
Voice Lib.
M1037   Biography in sound (radio program)
bd.1   "The Actor", narrated by Morgan Beatty.
        Cast includes Tallulah Bankhead, Hy Gardner,
        Rocky Graziano, Arthur Miller, Uta Hagen,
        Jackie Cooper, Sir Laurence Olivier, Gad
        Gayther, Barbara Ashley, Hortense Powdermaker,
        Peter Ustinov, Alfred Hitchcock, Leonard Lyons,
        John Guston, Helen Hayes, Dick Mayne, Ralph
        Bellamy, Lionel Barrymore, Sir Ralph Richardson,
        José Ferrer, and Walter Kerr.   NBC Radio, 1950's.
        1 reel (7 in.)   7 1/2 in. per sec.
        phonotape.
                                 (Continued on next card)

Barrymore, Lionel, 1878-1954
Voice Lib.
134   Dickens, Charles, 1812-1870.
        Christmas Carol, dramatized by an all-star
        cast led by Lionel Barrymore and Rudy Vallee.
        NBC, 1941.
        1 reel (7 in.)   7 1/2 in. per sec.
        phonotape.

        I. Barrymore, Lionel, 1878-1954. II.
        Vallee, Rudy, 1901-   III. Title.

Voice Lib.   Bartlett, Charles
M915-   As we knew him; words of reminiscence of
916   friends and relatives about the life of
     J.F. Kennedy. Narration by Charles Kuralt;
     participants: Charles Bartlett, Lemayne
     Billings, Robert Kennedy, Rose Kennedy,
     James Reed, Adlai Stevenson, Gen. Chester B.
     Clifton, etc. Columbia Records Inc., 1965.
     2 reels (7 in.) 7 1/2 in. per sec.
   phonotape.
     1. Kennedy, John Fitzgerald, Pres. U.S.,
1917-1963. I. Kuralt, Charles, 1934-

(Continued on next card)

Voice Lib.
541   Bartlett, Robert Abram, 1875-1946
bd.1 Peary, Robert Edwin, 1856-1920.
     Address to Peary Arctic Club in New York;
     log of voyage of S.S. "Roosevelt" and adventures
     in discovery of the North Pole; introductory
     remarks by Robert Bartlett. Edison, 1909.
     1 reel (7 in.) 7 1/2 in. per sec.
   phonotape.

     I. Bartlett, Robert Abram, 1875-1946.

C1
SC20   BARTON, CLARA HARLOWE, 1821-1912
   Whorf, Michael, 1933-
     Daughter of mercy - Clara Barton.
     1 tape cassette. (The visual sounds of
Mike Whorf. Science, SC20)
    Originally presented on his radio program, Kaleidoscope,
WJR, Detroit.
    Duration: 48 min., 55 sec.
    This narrative concerns the crusading Clara Barton, the "angel
of the battlefield," and the founder of the Red Cross in America.

    I. Barton, Clara Harlowe, 1821-1912. I. Title.

C1
FA6   BARTRAM, WILLIAM, 1739-1823
   Whorf, Michael, 1933-
     William Bartram.
     1 tape cassette. (The visual sounds of
Mike Whorf. Forgotten American, FA6)
    Originally presented on his radio program, Kaleidoscope,
WJR, Detroit.
    Duration: 10 min., 10 sec.
    One of the first notable American ornithologists, he wrote his
Travels, which is so rich in colorful details, Coleridge and Words-
worth used is as a source for some of their poems.

    I. Bartram, William, 1739-1823. I. Title.

Voice Lib.
M1439 Baruch, Andre
bd.3   Narrated description of General Patton's
     speech to U.S. troops in England before
     invasion of Europe (D-Day), by Major Andre
     Baruch. AFRS, 1944.
     1 reel (7 in.) 7 1/2 in. per sec.
   phonotape..

     1. World War, 1939-1945 - Campaigns -
Normandy.

Voice Lib.
M739 Baruch, Bernard Mannes, 1870-1965.
bd.6   Speaking on mobilization for Korean war
     effort. CBS, 1951.
     1 reel (7 in.) 7 1/2 in. per sec.
   phonotape.

Voice Lib.
652   Baruch, Bernard Mannes, 1870-1965.
bd.10 On recession and danger of inflation.
     CBS, April 1, 1958.
     1 reel (7 in.) 7 1/2 in. per sec.
   phonotape.

     1. U.S. - Economic conditions.

Voice Lib.
345   Baruch, Bernard Mannes, 1870-1965.
bd. 14 Statement on recession and dangers of
     inflation. CBS, April 1, 1958.
     1 reel (7in.) 7 1/2 in. per sec.
   phonotape.

     1. Inflation (finance).

    Baruch, Bernard Mannes, 1870-1965
Voice Lib.
573   I can hear it now (radio program)
bd.2- 1945-1949. CBS, 1950?
574   2 reels (7 in.) 7 1/2 in. per sec.
bd.1 phonotape.
    I. Murrow, Edward Roscoe, 1908-1965. II. Nehru, Jawaharlal,
1889-1964. III. Philip, duke of Edinburgh, 1921- IV. Elizabeth II,
Queen of Great Britain, 1926- V. Ferguson, Homer, 1889- VI.
Hughes, Howard Robard, 1905- VII. Marshall, George Catlett,
1880- VIII. Ruth, George Herman, 1895-1948. IX. Lilienthal,
David Eli, 1899- X. Trout, Robert, 1908- XI. Gage, Arthur.
XII. Jackson, Robert Houghwout, 1892-1954. XIII. Gromyko, Anatolii Andreevich, 1908- XIV. Baruch, Bernard Mannes, 1870-
1965. XV. Churchill, Winston Leonard Spencer, 1874-1965. XVI.
Winchell, Walter, 1897-19 XVII. Davis, Elmer Holmes, 1890-
(Continued on next card)

     BASEBALL
Voice Lib.
M1726 Aaron, Hank, 1934-
bd.3   Interviewed on Hank Aaron Day in New York
     City, by Curt Gowdy, Joe Garagiola, Tom
     Brokaw, and Gene Shalitt. NBC, June 18,
     1974.
     10 min. phonotape (1 r. 7 1/2 i.p.s.)

     1. Aaron, Hank, 1934-   2. Baseball.
I. Gowdy, Curt. II. Garagiola, Joe.
III. Brokaw, Tom. , Shalitt, Gene.

Voice Lib. BASEBALL
M1248 Baseball fifty years ago; interviews with four
famous old time baseball players, on NBC
"Today" show, by host Hugh Downs, supported by
sportcaster Joe Garagiola and Dr. Lawrence
Ritter, author of new book. NBC-TV, June 9,
1967.
1 reel (7 in.) 7 1/2 in. per sec. phonotape.
I. Baseball. I. Downs, Hugh Malcolm, 1921- II. Garagiola,
Joe. III. Ritter, Lawrence S. / The glory of their times. IV. Roush,
Edd, 1893- V. Marquart, Rube, 1890- VI. O'Doul, Lefty,
1897- VII. Meyers, John, 1880-

BASEBALL
Voice Lib.
376 Rickey, Branch (Wesley), 1881-1965.
bd.1 "Baseball: the Game"; on origin of, as a
national past-time; his youth and sports;
college sports and professionalism; eligibility
in college sports; professional sports; career
for college graduates; review of career in
World War I; development of modern farm system.
WOED, 1958.
1 reel (7 in.) 7 1/2 in. per sec.
phonotape.

Voice Lib. BASEBALL
M1064 Cobb, Tyrus Raymond, 1886-1961.
bd.8 Interview with Ty Cobb in Georgia after
his retirement from baseball. Fox Movietone.
1929.
1 reel (7 in.) 7 1/2 in. per sec.
phonotape.

BASEBALL
Voice Lib.
M757 Ruth, George Herman, 1894-1948.
bd.7 Babe Ruth's home run story; monologue.
Humorous recitation. Actuelle (Pathes
Frères), 1923.
1 reel (7 in.) 7 1/2 in. per sec.
phonotape.

BASEBALL
Voice Lib.
540 Cobb, Tyrus Raymond, 1886-1961.
bd.16 Baseball. Fox Movietone, 1933.
1 reel (7 in.) 7 1/2 in. per sec.
phonotape.

1. Baseball.

BASEBALL
Voice Lib.
M948 Ruth, George Herman, 1894-1948.
bd.7 In a comedy skit with Lou Gehrig. 1938.
1 reel (7 in.) 7 1/2 in. per sec.
phonotape.

I. Gehrig, Lou, 1903-1941.

BASEBALL
Voice Lib.
209 Di Maggio, Joseph Paul, 1914-
bd.2 Joe Di Maggio's farewell to baseball.
Source (?), December 11, 1951.
1 reel (7 in.) 7 1/2 in. per sec.
phonotape.

BASEBALL
Voice Lib.
M948 Ruth, George Herman, 1894-1948.
bd.6 Pep talk to American boys about baseball.
1948.
1 reel (7 in.) 7 1/2 in. per sec.
phonotape.

BASEBALL
Voice Lib.
M730 Rickey, Branch (Wesley), 1881-1965.
bd.7 Speaking on mobilization for Korean War
as it affects baseball. CBS, 1951.
1 reel (7 in.) 7 1/2 in. per sec.
phonotape.

BASEBALL
Voice Lib.
M263- U.S. Congress. Senate. Special Committee to
265 investigate organized crime in interstate
bd.1 commerce.
Committee anti-trust hearing on baseball;
interrogation and testimony of Casey Stengel.
CBS, July 9, 1958.
3 reels (7 in.) 7 1/2 in. per sec.
phonotape.

1. Baseball. I. Stengel, Casey

C1
M31
BASEBALL

Whorf, Michael, 1933-
    The great American pastime - baseball.
    1 tape cassette.   (The visual sounds of
Mike Whorf. Miscellaneous, M31)
    Originally presented on his radio program, Kaleidoscope,
WJR, Detroit.
    Duration: 39 min.
    "Whoever would understand the heart and mind of America had
better learn the game of baseball ..." As this quotation sums up
our attitude toward the national pastime, so our program illuminates
the origin and the history of the great game of baseball.

    I. Baseball. I. Title.

C1
M11
BASEBALL

Whorf, Michael, 1933-
    The man in the iron mask.
    1 tape cassette.   (The visual sounds of
Mike Whorf. Miscellaneous, M11)

    Originally presented on his radio program, Kaleidoscope,
WJR, Detroit.
    Duration: 42 min., 10 sec.
    An account of the thoughts and ideas of a big league catcher.
The emphasis is on baseball, but a ball player thinks of other
things as well.

    I. Freehan, Bill, 1941-   2. Baseball. I. Title.

Voice Lib.
M1248 Baseball fifty years ago; interviews with four
    famous old time baseball players, on NBC
    "Today" show, by host Hugh Downs, supported by
    sportcaster Joe Garagiola and Dr. Lawrence
    Ritter, author of new book. NBC-TV, June 9,
    1967.
    1 reel (7 in.)   7 1/2 in. per sec. phonotape.

    I. Baseball. I. Downs, Hugh Malcolm, 1921-   II. Garagiola,
Joe. III. Ritter, Lawrence S./The glory of their times. IV. Roush,
Edd, 1893-   V. Marquart, Rube, 1890-   VI. O'Doul, Lefty,
1897-   VII. Meyers, John, 1880-

Voice Lib.
M1486
Batchellor, John

Nixon, Richard Milhous, Pres. U.S., 1913-
    One hour documentary describing an entire
    day in the life of Pres. Richard M. Nixon
    in the White House, with NBC's John Batchellor,
    including visit of Canadian Prime Minister
    Pierre Trudeau. NBC-TV, December 6, 1971.
    1 reel (7 in.)   7 1/2 in. per sec.
    phonotape.

    I. Batchellor, John.

C1
M18
BATES, KATHERINE LEE, 1859-1929

Whorf, Michael, 1933-
    The splendid Americans.
    1 tape cassette.   (The visual sounds of
Mike Whorf. Miscellaneous, M18)

    Originally presented on his radio program, Kaleidoscope,
WJR, Detroit.
    Duration: 54 min., 30 sec.
    This is the story of those who wrote the songs of a nation and
a people, songs which gave a different kind of courage to the
people.

    I. Bates, Katherine Lee, 1859-1929. 2. Key, Francis Scott,
1779-1929. 3. Patriotic music, American. I. Title.

Voice Lib.
M708
bd.1
The battle hymn of the republic

Traubel, Helen, 1903-1972.
    Helen Traubel sings "The Battle Hymn of
    the Republic": excerpts from NBC's VE-day
    program. Melchior collection, May 8, 1945.
    1 reel (7 in.)   7 1/2 in. per sec.
    phonotape.

Voice Lib.
M1029
bd.2
Baukhage, Hilmar Robert

Kaltenborn, Hans von, 1878-1965.
    "A Tribute to Hans von Kaltenborn".
    Excerpts of various radio news braodcasts by
    Mr. Kaltenborn, and comments by his colleagues
    upon his death. Speakers: Morgan Beatty,
    narrator; Mary Margaret McBride; H. R. Baukhage;
    Harry S Truman. MSU Dept. of TV and Radio, 1965.
    1 reel (7 in.)   7 1/2 in. per sec.
    phonotape.

    I. Kaltenborn, Hans von, 1878-1965. I. Beatty, Morgan.
II. McBride, Mary Margaret, 1899-   III. Baukhage, Hilmar
Robert IV. Truman, Harry S, Pres. U.S., 1884-1972.

Voice Lib.
M830
Baukhage, Hilmar Robert

Roosevelt, Franklin Delano, Pres. U.S., 1882-1945.
    Description of proceedings at Joint Session of Congress on
December 8, 1941, prior to President's address asking for
declaration of war; including news flashes by NBC correspondents
Carlton Smith, Morgan Beatty, and Baukhage. NBC, December 8,
1941.
    32 min. phonotape (1 r.   7 1/2 i.p.s.)

    I. World War, 1939-1945 - U.S. I. Smith, Carlton.
II. Beatty, Morgan. III. Baukhage, Hilmar Robert.

Voice Lib.
603
bd.1

Bayes, Nora
    "Over There"; sings original recording of
George M. Cohan's World War I song.   Victor
Talking Machine Co., 1917.
    1 reel (7 in.)   7 1/2 in. per sec.
    phonotape.

    I. Title.

C1
H59
BEACONSFIELD, BENJAMIN DISRAELI, 1ST EARL OF,
    1804-1881

Whorf, Michael, 1933-
    To live with honor, Disraeli.
    1 tape cassette.   (The visual sounds of
Mike Whorf. History and heritage, H59)
    Originally presented on his radio program, Kaleidoscope,
WJR, Detroit.
    Duration: 41 min., 15 sec.
    Rising above the discrimination against his Judaic heritage,
Disraeli was an accomplished linguist, a writer of gay and brilliant
satire, possessed of a phenomenal memory, and schooled in the
social graces.

    I. Beaconsfield, Benjamin Disraeli, 1st Earl of, 1804-1881.
I. Title.

Voice Lib.
M1747   Bean, Alan L   1932-
      Address at Michigan State University,
discussing the training of Astronauts before
the first lunar landing, and training for
survival in case of accident. WKAR,
196-?
      40 min. phonotape (1 r. 7 1/2 i.p.s.)

      1. Astronauts.

Voice Lib.
518   Beard, Daniel Carter, 1850-1941.
bd.2   On formation of the Boy Scouts of
America. GRV, June 21, 1939.
      1 reel (7in.) 7 1/2 in. per sec.
phonotape.

      1. Boy Scouts.

      Bean, Alan L   1932-
Voice Lib.
M1403 Apollo 12 (space flight): lift-off of Apollo
bd.1   12; the electrical "glitch" and instructions
and corrections; Dr. Paine and President
Nixon speaking from VIP section. CBS TV,
November 19, 1969.
      1 reel (7 in.) 7 1/2 in. per sec.
phonotape.
      1. Project Apollo. 2. Space flight to the moon. 3. Conrad,
Charles, 1930- 4. Bean, Alan L 1932- 5. Gordon,
Richard F 1929- I. Conrad, Charles, 1930- II. Bean,
Alan L 1932- III. Gordon, Richard F 1929- IV.
Paine, Thomas Otten, 1921- V. Nixon, Richard Milhous, Pres.
U.S., 1913-

Voice Lib.
M1498 Beard, Dita Davis, 1918-
bd.1   Interview with Mrs. Dita Beard, ITT
lobbyist, with Mike Wallace on CBS "60
Minutes" regarding the famous memo about a
$400,000 contribution to the Republican
convention of 1972, and Mrs. Beard's personal
association with Attorney General Mitchell
pertaining to the Hartford Fire Insurance
anti-trust case. CBS-TV, April 2, 1972.
      1 reel (7 in.) 7 1/2 in. per sec.
phonotape.
      I. Wallace, Mike, 1918-

      Bean, Alan L   1932-
Voice Lib.
M1403 Apollo 12 (space flight): landing on the
bd.2   moon; conversations of Frank McGee and
mission control; dialogue of Pete Conrad
preparing to step out on moon; coached on
going down ladder; Conrad singing from the
moon; trouble with TV camera. NBC TV,
November 19, 1969.
      1 reel (7 in.) 7 1/2 in. per sec. phonotape.
      1. Project Apollo. 2. Space flight to the moon. 3. Conrad,
Charles, 1930- 4. Bean, Alan L 1932- 5. Gordon,
Richard F 1929- I. Conrad, Charles, 1930- II. Bean,
Alan L 1932- III. Gordon, Richard F 1929- IV.
McGee, Frank, 1921-1974.

      THE BEATLES
Voice Lib.
M760 Aberbach, Jean
bd.7   Excerpt from "What All the Screaming's
About" (Program 1); the real reason for the
success of Elvis Presley and the Beatles.
Westinghouse Broadcasting Corporation, 1964.
      1 min. phonotape (1 r. 7 1/2 i.p.s.)
(The music goes round and round)

      1. Music, Popular (Songs, etc.) - U.S.
2. Presley, Elvis Aron, 1935- 3. The
Beatles. I. Title: What all the screaming's
about. II. Series.

      Bean, Alan L   1932-
Voice Lib.
M1404 Apollo 12 (space flight): description of
bd.1   last minutes on the moon of Apollo 12
crew; countdown, lift-off from the moon.
CBS TV, November 20, 1969.
      1 reel (7 in.) 7 1/2 in. per sec.
phonotape.
      1. Project Apollo. 2. Space flight to the
moon. 3. Conrad, Charles, 1930- 4. Bean,
Alan L 1932- 5. Gordon, Richard F
1929- I. Conrad, Charles, 1930- II.
Bean, Alan L 1932- III. Gordon, Richard
F 1929-

      THE BEATLES
Voice Lib.
M760 Kellem, Manny
bd.4   Excerpt from "What All the Screaming's
About" (Program 1); promotion of the Beatles,
including remarks by teenaged girls of their
feelings toward the new singing group called
the Beatles. Westinghouse Broadcasting
Corporation, 1964.
      1 reel (7 in.) 7 1/2 in. per sec.
phonotape. (The Music Goes Round and Round)

      I. Title: What all the screaming's about.
II. Series.

      Bean, Alan L   1932-
Voice Lib.
M1404 Apollo 12 (space flight): description of
bd.2   splashdown of Apollo 12 and proceeding
to aircraft carrier "Hornet". CBS TV,
November 24, 1969.
      1 reel (7 in.) 7 1/2 in. per sec.
phonotape.
      1. Project Apollo. 2. Space flight to the
moon. 3. Conrad, Charles, 1930- 4. Bean,
Alan L 1932- 5. Gordon, Richard F
1929- I. Conrad, Charles, 1930- II.
Bean, Alan L 1932- III. Gordon, Richard
F 1929-

      THE BEATLES
Voice Lib.
M760 Mann, Arthur
bd.3   Excerpt from "What All The Screaming's
About" (Program 1); English-based music
of Beatles; what serious musicians find
interesting about the music of the Beatles.
Westinghouse Broadcasting Corporation, 1964.
      1 reel (7 in.) 7 1/2 in. per sec.
phonotape. (The Music Goes Round and Round)

      1. The Beatles. I. Title: What all the
screaming's about. II. Series.

THE BEATLES

Voice Lib.
M760 Schimmel, John L
bd.5   Excerpt from "What All the Screaming's
    About" (Program 1); psychiatrist's approach
    to Beatlemania and its effects on teenage
    girls. Westinghouse Broadcasting Corporation,
    1964.
      1 reel (7 in.) 7 1/2 in. per sec.
    phonotape. (The Music Goes Round and Round)

      I. Title: What all the screaming's about.
    II. Series.

Voice Lib.
M822 The Beatles; interview with the Beatles by
bd.2   the BBC, and samples of their performances.
    KPFK, July 23, 1964.
      1 reel (7 in.) 7 1/2 in. per sec.
    phonotape.

Beatrice Lillie sings

Voice Lib.
M955 Lillie, Beatrice, 1898-
bd.1-   Singing selections from album "Beatrice
10   Lillie Sings". JJC Records, 1939.
      1 reel (7 in.) 7 1/2 in. per sec.
    phonotape.
      CONTENTS. -bd.1. "Mad about the boy" (school girl version)-
    bd.2. "Mad about the boy" (Cockney maid version)-bd.3. "Three
    white feathers". -bd.4. "Weary of it all". -bd.5. "I went to a
    marvelous party". -bd.6. "Get yourself a geisha". -bd.7. "Paree". -
    bd.8. "Mother told me so". -bd.9. "The gutter song". -bd.10. "I
    hate spring".
      I. Title: Beatrice Lillie sings.

Beatty, Morgan

Voice Lib.
M1037 Biography in sound (radio program)
bd.1   "The Actor", narrated by Morgan Beatty.
    Cast includes Tallulah Bankhead, Hy Gardner,
    Rocky Graziano, Arthur Miller, Uta Hagen,
    Jackie Cooper, Sir Laurence Olivier, Gad
    Gayther, Barbara Ashley, Hortense Powdermaker,
    Peter Ustinov, Alfred Hitchcock, Leonard Lyons,
    John Guston, Helen Hayes, Dick Mayne, Ralph
    Bellamy, Lionel Barrymore, Sir Ralph Richardson,
    José Ferrer, and Walter Kerr. NBC Radio, 1950's.
      1 reel (7 in.) 7 1/2 in. per sec.
    phonotape.
    (Continued on next card)

Beatty, Morgan

Voice Lib.
M1029 Kaltenborn, Hans von, 1878-1965.
bd.2   "A Tribute to Hans von Kaltenborn".
    Excerpts of various radio news braodcasts by
    Mr. Kaltenborn, and comments by his colleagues
    upon his death. Speakers: Morgan Beatty,
    narrator; Mary Margaret McBride; H. R. Baukhage;
    Harry S Truman. MSU Dept. of TV and Radio, 1965.
      1 reel (7 in.) 7 1/2 in. per sec.
    phonotape.
      I. Kaltenborn, Hans von, 1878-1965. L Beatty, Morgan
    II. McBride, Mary Margaret, 1899-   III. Baukhage, Hilmar
    Robert   IV. Truman, Harry S, Pres. U.S., 1884-1972.

Beatty, Morgan
Voice Lib.
M830 Roosevelt, Franklin Delano, Pres. U.S., 1882-1945.
    Description of proceedings at Joint Session of Congress on
    December 8, 1941, prior to President's address asking for
    declaration of war; including news flashes by NBC correspondents
    Carlton Smith, Morgan Beatty, and Baukhage. NBC, December 8,
    1941.
      32 min. phonotape (1 r. 7 1/2 L.p. s.)

      L World War, 1939-1945 - U.S. L Smith, Carlton.
    II. Beatty, Morgan. III. Baukhage, Hilmar Robert.

Beck, Dave, 1894-

Voice Lib.
229 Reuther, Walter Philip, 1907-1970.
bd.1   The Dave Beck story. Source (?),
    March 28, 1957.
      1 reel (7 in.) 7 1/2 in. per sec.
    phonotape.

      I. Beck, Dave, 1894-

Voice Lib.
M836 Beecham, Sir Thomas, bart., 1879-1961.
bd.2   Interviewing with Sir Osbert Sitwell on
    the occasion of Sir Thomas' 70th birthday.
    RCA, 1949.
      1 reel (7 in.) 7 1/2 in. per sec.
    phonotape.

      I. Sitwell, Sir Osbert, bart., 1892-1969.

Beemer, Brace, 1903-1965

Voice Lib.
M741 WJR (radio station) Detroit.
bd.1   Memorial program for the late Brace
    Beemer, including former members of Lone
    Ranger radio cast and Mr. Beemer himself
    in reminiscences. WJR, March 4, 1965.
      37 min. phonotape (1 r. 7 1/2 i.p.s.)

      1. Beemer, Brace, 1903-1965. I. Beemer,
    Brace, 1903-1965.

Beethoven, Ludwig van, 1770-1827.
Voice Lib. Worship of God and Nature
M310 American Broadcasting Company.
    Tribute to President John Fitzgerald Kennedy
    from the arts. Fredric March emcees; Jerome
    Hines sings "Worship of God and Nature" by
    Beethoven; Florence Eldridge recites "When
    lilacs last in the door-yard bloom'd" by Walt
    Whitman; Marian Anderson in two songs. Includes
    Charlton Heston, Sidney Blackmer, Isaac Stern,
    Nathan Milstein, Christopher Plummer, Albert
    Finney. ABC, November 24, 1963.
      35 min. phonotape (7 in. 7 1/2 i.p.s.)
    (Continued on next card)

C1
PWM1
BEETHOVEN, LUDWIG VAN, 1770-1827

Whorf, Michael, 1933-
Beethoven.
1 tape cassette. (The visual sounds of
Mike Whorf. Panorama; a world of music, PWM-1)
Originally presented on his radio program, Kaleidoscope,
WJR, Detroit.
Duration: 25 min.
The life and times of Beethoven, including excerpts of
his music.

1. Beethoven, Ludwig van, 1770-1827. I. Title.

C1
A10
BEETHOVEN, LUDWIG VAN, 1770-1827

Whorf, Michael, 1933-
Beethoven, the incredible.
1 tape cassette. (The visual sounds of
Mike Whorf. Art, music, and letters, A10)
Originally presented on his radio program, Kaleidoscope,
WJR, Detroit.
Duration: 37 min., 30 sec.
Dealing not with symphonies and serenades, but rather with
emotions and feelings, this is the story of perhaps the greatest
musical genius who ever lived, Beethoven.

1. Beethoven, Ludwig van, 1770-1827. I. Title.

C1
PWM1
Beethoven

Whorf, Michael, 1933-
Beethoven.
1 tape cassette. (The visual sounds of
Mike Whorf. Panorama; a world of music, PWM-1)
Originally presented on his radio program, Kaleidoscope,
WJR, Detroit.
Duration: 25 min.
The life and times of Beethoven, including excerpts of
his music.

1. Beethoven, Ludwig van, 1770-1827. I. Title.

C1
A10
Beethoven, the incredible

Whorf, Michael, 1933-
Beethoven, the incredible.
1 tape cassette. (The visual sounds of
Mike Whorf. Art, music, and letters, A10)
Originally presented on his radio program, Kaleidoscope,
WJR, Detroit.
Duration: 37 min., 30 sec.
Dealing not with symphonies and serenades, but rather with
emotions and feelings, this is the story of perhaps the greatest
musical genius who ever lived, Beethoven.

1. Beethoven, Ludwig van, 1770-1827. I. Title.

C1
S16
The beginning of man

Whorf, Michael, 1933-
The beginning of man.
1 tape cassette. (The visual sounds of
Mike Whorf. Social, S16)
Originally presented on his radio program, Kaleidoscope,
WJR, Detroit.
Duration: 40 min., 35 sec.
This program takes an open-minded look in a narrative
which concerns itself with the possibility of evolution and
how man began.

1. Evolution. 2. Man - Origin. I. Title.

Voice Lib.
M1041
bd.2
Behind the scenes in the CBS newsroom; CBS
radio news with Elmer Davis, Edward R.
Murrow and Paul White, describing the
operations of radio news broadcasting.
CBS Radio, June 1, 1941.
1 reel (7 in.) 7 1/2 i.p.s. phonotape.

1. Radio journalism. I. Davis, Elmer
Holmes, 1890-1958. II. Murrow, Edward
Roscoe, 1908-1965. III. White, Paul Welrose,
1902-1955.

Voice Lib.
M743
Belafonte, Harold, 1927-
Civil rights march on Montgomery, Alabama.
Announcer's description of scene as
marchers arrive in Montgomery; entertain-
ment by Harry Belafonte and others; A.F.L.
speaker; Dr. Ralph Abernathy presiding.
CBS, March 25, 1965.
38 min. phonotape (1 r. 7 1/2 i.p.s.)

1. Negroes - Civil rights. I. Belafonte,
Harold, 1927- II. Abernathy, Ralph
David, 1926-

Voice Lib.
M1369
bd. 2
Bell, Jack
"The men who covered Ike". CBS-TV Face the Nation program,
discussing the late General Dwight David Eisenhower, by the
newspaper and TV correspondents. UPI, Merriman Smith;
Newsweek, Kenneth Crawford; Chicago Daily News, Peter
Lisager; AP, Jack Bell; CBS, George Herman, acting as emcee.
CBS-TV, March 30, 1969.
1 reel (7 in.) 7 1/2 i.p.s. phonotape.

1. Eisenhower, Dwight David, Pres. U.S., 1890-1969.
I. Smith, Merriman. II. Crawford, Kenneth. III. Lisager,
Peter. IV. Bell, Jack. V. Herman, George.

Voice Lib.
M553
bd.3
Bell Telephone Laboratories, inc.
Synthesized speech created by digital
computer recites soliloquy from "Hamlet",
sings "Bicycle built for two". Explanation
of computer's operation. American Telephone
and Telegraph Co., 1963.
1 reel (7 in.) 7 1/2 i.p.s. phonotape.

1. Computer sound processing. I. Shakespeare, William, 1564-1616./Hamlet. II.
Title: Bicycle built for two.

Voice Lib.
M1037
bd.1
Bellamy, Ralph, 1904-
Biography in sound (radio program)
"The Actor", narrated by Morgan Beatty.
Cast includes Tallulah Bankhead, Hy Gardner,
Rocky Graziano, Arthur Miller, Uta Hagen,
Jackie Cooper, Sir Laurence Olivier, Gad
Gayther, Barbara Ashley, Hortense Powdermaker,
Peter Ustinov, Alfred Hitchcock, Leonard Lyons,
John Guston, Helen Hayes, Dick Mayne, Ralph
Bellamy, Lionel Barrymore, Sir Ralph Richardson,
José Ferrer, and Walter Kerr. NBC Radio, 1950's.
1 reel (7 in.) 7 1/2 in. per sec.
phonotape.
(Continued on next card)

Voice Lib.
352   Benchley, Robert Charles, 1889-1945.
bd.9   On camping in Canadian north.   NBC,
         date unknown.
           1 reel (7 in.)   7 1/2 in. per sec.
         phonotape.

Voice Lib.
352   Benchley, Robert Charles, 1889-1945.
bd.8   Various personalities recall Benchley.
         NBC, 1949.
           1 reel (7 in.)   7 1/2 in. per sec.
         phonotape.

Voice Lib.   Benchley, Robert Charles, 1889-1945
M618   Radio in the 1930's (Part I): a series of
bd.1-   excerpts from important broadcasts of the
14   1930's; a sample of radio of the period.
         NVL, April, 1964.
           1 reel (7 in.) 7 1/2 in. per sec. phonotape.
         L. Shaw, George Bernard, 1856-1950. IL. Crosby, Bing, 1901-
         III. Barkley, Alban William, 1877-1956. IV. Roosevelt, Franklin
         Delano, Pres. U.S., 1882-1945. V. Hoover, Herbert Clark, Pres.
         U.S., 1874-1964. VI. Long, Huey Pierce, 1893-1935. VII. Town-
         send, Francis Everett, 1867-1960. VIII. Coughlin, Charles Edward,
         1891-   IX. Rogers, Will, 1879-1935. X. Pius XII, Pope, 1876-
         1958. XI. Edward VIII, king of Great Britain, 1894-1972. XII.
         Barrymore, John, 1882-1942. XIII. Woollcott, Alexander, 1887-
         1943. XIV. Allen, Fred, 1894-1956. XV. Benchley, Robert Charles,
         1889-1945.

Voice Lib.
M506   Benes, Edvard, Pres. Czechoslovak Republic, 1884-1948.
           Postwar plans for small countries. Responsibilities and
         plans for small European countries, treaty of Versailles,
         aggression in East, review of Hitler aggressions and dealing with
         him, need for true democracy in Europe, advantages of small
         nations, modern technological developments and their
         influence on politics of Europe, political profile of post-World War
         II Europe, politics of post-war Czechoslovakia, need for plans to
         form efficient international organization, describes roles of major
         post-war countries (Britain, France, USSR), maintenance of U. N.
         allies, preparation for future defense of freedom. Speech
         delivered in Chicago. CBS, May 22, 1943.
           1 reel (7 in.) 7 1/2 i.p.s. phonotape.

         L. Europe - Politics - 20th century.

Voice Lib.   Bennett, Richard Dyer
M622   Radio in the 1940's (Part III): a series of
bd.1-   excerpts from important broadcasts of the 1940's; a sample
bd.15   of radio of the period. NVL, April, 1964.
           1 reel (7 in.) 7 1/2 in. per sec. phonotape.
         L. Radio programs. L. Miller, Alton Glenn, 1909(?)-1944. IL.
         Diles, Ken   III. Wilson, Donald Harlow, 1900-   IV.
         Livingstone, Mary   V. Benny, Jack, 1894-   VI. Harris,
         Phil   VII. Merman, Ethel, 1909-   VIII. Smith, "Wonderful"
         IX. Bennett, Richard Dyer   X. Louis, Joe, 1914-   XI.
         Eisenhower, Dwight David, Pres. U. S., 1890-1969. XII. MacArthur,
         Douglas, 1880-1964. XIII. Romulo, Carlos Pena, 1899-   XIV.
         Welles, Orson, 1915-   XV. Jackson, Robert Houghwout, 1892-1954.
         XVI. LaGuardia, Fiorello Henry, 1882-1945. XVII. Nehru, Jawa-
         harlal, 1889-1964. XVIII. Gandhi, Mohandas Karamchand, 1869-1948.

Voice Lib.   Benny, Jack, 1894-
M622   Radio in the 1940's (Part III): a series of
bd.1-   excerpts from important broadcasts of the 1940's; a sample
bd.15   of radio of the period. NVL, April, 1964.
           1 reel (7 in.) 7 1/2 in. per sec. phonotape.
         L. Radio programs. L. Miller, Alton Glenn, 1909(?)-1944. IL.
         Diles, Ken   III. Wilson, Donald Harlow, 1900-   IV.
         Livingstone, Mary   V. Benny, Jack, 1894-   VI. Harris,
         Phil   VII. Merman, Ethel, 1909-   VIII. Smith, "Wonderful"
         IX. Bennett, Richard Dyer   X. Louis, Joe, 1914-   XI.
         Eisenhower, Dwight David, Pres. U.S., 1890-1969. XII. MacArthur,
         Douglas, 1880-1964. XIII. Romulo, Carlos Pena, 1899-   XIV.
         Welles, Orson, 1915-   XV. Jackson, Robert Houghwout, 1892-1954.
         XVI. LaGuardia, Fiorello Henry, 1882-1945. XVII. Nehru, Jawa-
         harlal, 1889-1964. XVIII. Gandhi, Mohandas Karamchand, 1869-1948.

Voice Lib.
M1499   Benny, Jack, 1894-
bd.2   Portion of TV program "Playhouse New York"
         with excerpts of old Jack Benny radio
         programs, including current commentary
         by Benny about them. NET, May 6, 1972.
           1 reel (7 in.)   7 1/2 in. per sec.
         phonotape.

Voice Lib.
132   Benson, Ezra Taft, 1899-
bd.1   Address at Michigan State University,
         with introduction by President John A.
         Hannah. WKAR, 1961.
           1 reel (7 in.)   7 1/2 in. per sec.
         phonotape.

         I. Hannah, John Alfred, 1902-

                 BENSON, EZRA TAFT, 1899-
Voice Lib.
M345   Eisenhower, Dwight David, Pres. U.S., 1890-1969.
bd.2   Excerpt from news conference: Secretary
         Benson and the farm problem. CBS,
         February 26, 1958.
           1 reel (7 in.)   7 1/2 i.p.s.   phonotape.

         1. Benson, Ezra Taft, 1899-

Voice Lib.   Benton, Nelson
M1549-   Nixon, Richard Milhous, Pres. U.S., 1913-
1550,   News conference recorded over CBS
bd.1   television network. CBS, October 26, 1973.
           35 min.   phonotape (2 r.   7 1/2 i.p.s.)

         Includes question and answer session, including Nelson
         Benton.

         L. U.S. - Politics and government - 1969-
         2. Watergate Affair, 1972. 3. Power resources - U.S.
         L. Benton, Nelson

Voice Lib.　Benton, William Burnett, 1900-1973
383　　I can hear it now (radio program)
　　　　CBS, February 9, 1951.
　　　　1 reel (7 in.)　7 1/2 in. per sec.
　　　　phonotape.
　　　　　L. Wilson, Charles Edward, 1886-1972. IL Gabrielson, Guy
　　　　George, 1891-　　III. Taft, Robert Alphonso, 1889-1953. IV.
　　　　Martin, Joseph William, 1884-1965. V. McCarthy, Joseph
　　　　Raymond, 1909-1957. VI. Benton, William Burnett, 1900-1973.
　　　　VII. Malone, George Wilson, 1890-1961. VIII. Capehart, Homer
　　　　Earl, 1897-　IX. Eisenhower, Dwight David, Pres. U.S., 1890-
　　　　1969.　X. Lee, J　V　XI. Hodge, John Reed, 1893-
　　　　1963. XII. Overton, Watkins　XIII. DiSalle, Michael
　　　　Vincent, 1908-　XIV. Boyce, Eddy　XV. Conklin, Ed
　　　　XVI. Collins, Joseph Lawton, 1896-

Voice Lib.
M707　Bergen, Edgar, 1903-
bd.3　　"Chase and Sanborn Hour"; radio variety
　　　　show.　Melchior collection, May 5, 1945.
　　　　1 reel (7 in.)　7 1/2 in. per sec.
　　　　phonotape.

Voice Lib.
M710　Bergen, Edgar, 1903-
bd.2　　"Chase and Sanborn Hour"; radio variety
　　　　program.　Melchior collection, May 18, 1947.
　　　　1 reel (7 in.)　7 1/2 in. per sec.
　　　　phonotape.

Voice Lib.　Bergen, Edgar, 1903-
M621　Radio in the 1940's (Part II): a series of
bd.1-　　excerpts from important broadcasts of the
12　　　1940's; a sample of radio of the period.
　　　　NVI, April, 1964.
　　　　1 reel (7 in.)　7 1/2 in. per sec.　phonotape.
　　　　　L. Daly, John Charles, 1914-　II. Hall, Josef Washington,
　　　　1894-　III. Shirer, William Lawrence, 1904-　IV. Roosevelt,
　　　　Eleanor (Roosevelt) 1884-1962. V. Roosevelt, Franklin Delano,
　　　　Pres. U.S., 1882-1945. VI. Churchill, Winston Leonard Spencer,
　　　　1874-1965. VII. Wainwright, Jonathan Mayhew, 1883-1953. VIII.
　　　　Cantor, Eddie, 1893-1964. IX. Sinatra, Francis Albert, 1917-
　　　　X. Hope, Bob, 1903-　XI. Crosby, Bing, 1901-　XII. Shore,
　　　　Dinah, 1917(?)-　XIII. Bergen, Edgar, 1903-　XIV. Armstrong,
　　　　Louis, 1900-1971. XV. Eldridge, Roy, 1911-

Voice Lib.　Bergen, Edgar, 1901-
M1049　Allen, Fred, 1894-1956.
　　　　Chase and Sanborn 101st anniversary radio
　　　　show with Edgar Bergen as emcee, featuring
　　　　various Fred Allen skits from his famous
　　　　radio programs.　NBC, November 14, 1965.
　　　　1 reel (7 in.)　7 1/2 in. per sec.
　　　　phonotape.

　　　　I. Bergen, Edgar, 1903-

Voice Lib.　Bergen, Edgar, 1903-
M322　Biography in sound (radio program)
　　　　W.C. Fields, the magnificent rogue.
　　　　NBC, 1955.
　　　　1 reel (7 in.)　7 1/2 in. per sec.　phonotape.
　　　　　L. Fields, W.C., 1879-1946. L. Fields, W.C., 1879-1946.
　　　　II. Allen, Fred, 1894-1956. III. LaBaron, William　IV.
　　　　Taylor, Robert Lewis, 1912-　V. McCarey, Thomas Leo, 1898-
　　　　1969. VI. Harkins, James　- VII. Chevalier, Maurice,
　　　　1889-1972. VIII. Kuromoto, Mrs. George　IX. Flynn,
　　　　Errol Leslie, 1909-1959. X. Wynn, Ed, 1886-1966. XI. Dowling,
　　　　Ray Dooley　XII. Sennett, Mack　XIII. Overacher,
　　　　Ronald Leroy　XIV. Bergen, Edgar, 1903-　XV. Taurog,
　　　　Norman, 1899-　XVI. Runnell, Ann　XVII. Cowen,
　　　　Lester

Voice Lib.　Bergman, Ingrid, 1917-
M1028　Lux presents Hollywood: montage of excerpts
bd.7　　from various Lux radio shows. George Raft,
　　　　Virginia Mayo, Cedric Hardwicke, and
　　　　Ingrid Bergman.　Michigan State University,
　　　　Department of Television and Radio, 1940's.
　　　　1 reel (7 in.)　7 1/2 in. per sec.
　　　　phonotape.

　　　　I. Raft, George　　II. Mayo, Virginia
　　　　III. Hardwicke, Sir Cedric, 1893-1964. IV.
　　　　Bergman, Ingrid, 1917-

Voice Lib.
M1291　Bergman, Ingrid, 1917-
bd.2　　Conversation conducted by Cecil Smith,
　　　　drama critic of Los Angeles Times, about
　　　　her entire career and present activities.
　　　　NET, December 3, 1967.
　　　　1 reel (7 in.)　7 1/2 in. per sec.
　　　　phonotape.

　　　　I. Smith, Cecil Michener, 1906-

Voice Lib.　Bergman, Jules
M1587　Apollo 11 (space flight): description of
bd.1　　ascent from moon by Frank McGee.　Count-
　　　　down, ignition, and lift-off.　Meeting the
　　　　command module "Columbia"; docking; trans-
　　　　fer of gear from "Eagle" to "Columbia".
　　　　Recap by ABC's Jules Bergman and Frank
　　　　Reynolds.　NBC and ABC TV, July 21, 1969.
　　　　1 reel (7 in.)　7 1/2 in. per sec.　phonotape.
　　　　　L. Project Apollo.　2. Space flight to the moon.　3. Aldrin,
　　　　Edwin E　1930-　4. Collins, Michael, 1930-　5.
　　　　Armstrong, Neil, 1930-　I. Aldrin, Edwin E　1930-　II.
　　　　Collins, Michael, 1930-　III. Armstrong, Neil, 1930-　IV.
　　　　McGee, Frank, 1921-1974.　V. Bergman, Jules　VI. Reynolds,
　　　　Frank

Voice Lib.
M1066　Berle, Adolph Augustus, 1895-1971.
　　　　Address in New York at 10th anniversary
　　　　of founding of "Fund for the Republic",
　　　　entitled "The challenge to democracy in
　　　　the next decade"; dealing with corporate
　　　　power and the American economy.　CSDI,
　　　　1962.
　　　　1 reel (7 in.)　7 1/2 in. per sec.
　　　　phonotape.

　　　　I. Title: The challenge to democracy in the
　　　　next decade.

Voice Lib.
M658-   Berle, Adolph Augustus, 1895-1971
659   Dialogues in depth: the LaGuardia years
bd.1   (TV program from the New York World's Fair).
          Anecdotes and reminiscences about the late
          New York mayor, Fiorello LaGuardia.
          July 22, 1964.
          2 reels (7 in.)   7 1/2 i.p.s.   phonotape.

          L. LaGuardia, Fiorello Henry, 1882-1947. L. Canudo,
          Eugene R. II. Berle, Adolph Augustus, 1895-1971.
          III. Van Arsdale, Harry, 1905-   IV. Delany, Hubert T.
          V. Morris, Newbold, 1902-1966.

Voice Lib.
M952   Berliner, Emile, 1851-1929.
bd.2   Message of greetings by Dr. Berliner in
          Philadelphia, Pennsylvania to Mrs. Hahn in
          Hannover, Germany on her 70th birthday.
          H.E. Scholz, November 18, 1890.
          1 reel (7 in.)   7 1/2 in. per sec.
          phonotape.

          1. Phonorecords - History

Voice Lib.
331   Berlin, Irving, 1888-
bd.2   Music appreciation dinner: receives
          award for writing "God bless America"
          and tells how the composition came to be
          written. G. R. Vincent private recording,
          1939.
          1 reel (7in.)   7 1/2 in. per sec.
          phonotape.

Voice Lib.
M952   Berliner, Emile, 1851-1929.
bd.3   Dr. Berliner discussing his experiments
          on recording and playing back cylinder
          phonograph records. H.E. Scholz, 1900.
          1 reel (7 in.)   7 1/2 i.p.s.   phonotape.

          1. Phonorecords - History.

Voice Lib.   BERLIN - BLOCKADE, 1948-1949
228   Hottelet, Richard Curt
bd.2   Richard C. Hottelet and others on the
          Berlin Airlift and its cessation. CBS,
          May 12, 1949.
          1 reel (7 in.)   7 1/2 in. per sec.
          phonotape.

          1. Berlin - Blockade, 1948-1949.

Voice Lib.
M1750   Berman, Richard
          Government and the arts; on "Firing Line"
          with William F. Buckley. WKAR, June 28,
          1974.
          45 min.   phonotape (1 r.   7 1/2 i.p.s.]

          1. The Arts - U. S. 2. Art and State. 3.
          State encouragement of science, literature,
          and art - U. S. I. Buckley, William Frank,
          1925-

Voice Lib.   BERLIN WALL (1961-
M344   Brandt, Willy, 1913-
bd.19   Comments made to CBS after his news
          conference on Berlin and the wall.
          CBS, December 29, 1961.
          1 reel (7 in.)   7 1/2 i.p.s.   phonotape.

          1. Berlin Wall (1961-

Voice Lib.
M982   Bernard, Al
bd.7   Comedy song selection "The Preacher and
          the Bear". Perfect Records, 1912.
          1 reel (7 in.)   7 1/2 in. per sec.
          phonotape.

          I. Title: The preacher and the bear.

Voice Lib.
M952   Berliner, Emile, 1851-1929.
bd.1   First phonograph recording made in
          Germany by Dr. Emile Berliner; march
          music. H. C. Scholz, 1892.
          1 reel (7 in.)   7 1/2 i.p.s.   phonotape.

          1. Phonorecords - History.

Voice Lib.
M795   Bernhardt, Sarah, 1844-1923.
bd.3   Excerpt from Victor Hugo play "Un peu de
          Musique". Paris, 1902.
          1 reel (7 in.)   7 1/2 in. per sec.
          phonotape.

          I. Hugo, Victor Marie, comte, 1802-1885./
          Un peu de musique.

Voice Lib.
M795   Bernhardt, Sarah, 1844-1923.
bd.2   Excerpt from Racine play "Phèdre".
        G&T, 1903.
            1 reel (7 in.)   7 1/2 in. per sec.
        phonotape.

            I. Racine, Jean Baptiste, 1639-1699./
        Phèdre.

Voice Lib.
M1034   Bernie, Ben, 1891?-1943.
bd.7   Excerpt of closing sequence on radio
        program. TV&R, 1934.
            1 reel (7 in.)   7 1/2 in. per sec.
        phonotape.

Voice Lib.
M795   Bernhardt, Sarah, 1844-1923.
bd.1   Excerpt from Rostand play "La Samaritaine".
        G&T, 1903.
            1 reel (7 in.)   7 1/2 in. per sec.
        phonotape.

            I. Rostand, Edmond, 1868-1918./La Samari-
        taine.

            Bernstein, Carl
Voice Lib.
M1704   Woodward, Robert
            Woodward and Bernstein, exposers of
        Watergate, at the National Press Club,
        talking to other reporters. Includes
        Clark Mollenhoff. WKAR, June 6, 1974.
            50 min.   phonotape (1 r.   7 1/2 i.p.s.)

            1. Watergate Affair, 1972-
        I. Bernstein, Carl. II. Mollenhoff, Clark
        Raymond, 1921-

Voice Lib.
272   Bernhardt, Sarah, 1844-1923.
bd.3   L'Aiglon (excerpt).   National Voice
        Library, 1904.
            1 reel (7 in.)   7 1/2 in. per sec.
        phonotape.

Voice Lib.
M1457   Berrigan, Daniel, 1921-
bd.2-   Biographical documentary, narrated partly
1458   by Fr. Dan Berrigan and his brother Fr. Phil
bd.1   Berrigan, about their burning of draft files.
        NET, April 9, 1970.
            2 reels (7 in.)   7 1/2 in. per sec.
        phonotape.

            I. Berrigan, Philip, 1923-

Voice Lib.
M1056   Bernhardt, Sarah, 1844-1923.
bd.1   Various dramatic scenes in French, recorded
        from cylinder records: "L'Aiglon"; "Phèdre";
        "Les Bouffons". Edison Labs, 1904.
            1 reel (7 in.)   7 1/2 in. per sec.
        phonotape.

            Berrigan, Philip, 1923-
Voice Lib.
M1457   Berrigan, Daniel, 1921-
bd.2-   Biographical documentary, narrated partly
1458   by Fr. Dan Berrigan and his brother Fr. Phil
bd.1   Berrigan, about their burning of draft files.
        NET, April 9, 1970.
            2 reels (7 in.)   7 1/2 in. per sec.
        phonotape.

            I. Berrigan, Philip, 1923-

Voice Lib.
M1040   Bernie, Ben, 1891?-1943.
bd.3   Radio program of Ben Bernie Orchestra in
        selection "Au Revoir"; with closing remarks
        by Ben Bernie. TV&R, 1930's.
            1 reel (7 in.)   7 1/2 in. per sec.
        phonotape.

Voice Lib.
M1678   Berryman, John, 1914-1972.
            Reading from "The dream songs" at
        Michigan State University. WKAR, June 17,
        1969.
            45 min.   phonotape (1 r.   7 1/2 i.p.s.)

            I. Title: The dream songs.

C1
R29
The best that is in me - William Bradford

Whorf, Michael, 1933-
      The best that is in me - William Bradford.
      1 tape cassette. (The visual sounds of
Mike Whorf. Religion, R29)
      Originally presented on his radio program, Kaleidoscope,
WJR, Detroit.
      Duration: 35 min., 45 sec.
      In the story of the hardships and the struggles of the Pilgrims'
journey to the New World, William Bradford stands out as a pillar
of strength. Instrumental in the success of the venture, at all
times he gave his best.

      L Bradford, William, 1588-1657.   L Title.

Voice Lib.
M1464   Beyerlein, Alfred
bd.3   Narrating Victor Hugo's speech on
          Voltaire in German translation. Peteler,
          1932.
              1 reel (7 in.)   7 1/2 i.p.s.   phonotape.

          1. Voltaire, François Marie Arouet de,
          1694-1778.   I. Hugo, Victor Marie, comte,
          1802-1885.

Voice Lib.
M1466   Bethmann-Holweg, Theobold Von, 1856-1921.
bd.3   Excerpt of speech before the German
          Reichstag. Peteler, September, 1914.
              1 reel (7 in.)   7 1/2 in. per sec.
          phonotape.

C1
R24
BIBLE

Whorf, Michael, 1933-
      The greatest book ever written.
      1 tape cassette. (The visual sounds of
Mike Whorf. Religion, R24)
      Originally presented on his radio program, Kaleidoscope,
WJR, Detroit.
      Duration: 38 min.
      Few stories shed such fascinating sidelights on the history
of man as the heritage of the body of literature which we now
know as the Bible.

      L Bible. L Title.

Voice Lib.
M952   Bethmann-Hollweg, Theobold von, 1856-1921.
bd.7   Statement by the German Reich Chancellor.
          H. E. Scholz, February 27, 1917.
              1 reel (7 in.)   7 1/2 in. per sec.
          phonotape.

Bicycle built for two

Voice Lib.
M553   Bell Telephone Laboratories, inc.
bd.3   Synthesized speech created by digital
          computer recites soliloquy from "Hamlet",
          sings "Bicycle built for two". Explanation
          of computer's operation. American Telephone
          and Telegraph Co., 1963.
              1 reel (7 in.)   7 1/2 i.p.s.   phonotape.

              1. Computer sound processing. I. Shake-
          speare, William, 1564-1616./Hamlet. II.
          Title: Bicycle built for two.

Voice Lib.
M952   Bethmann-Hollweg, Theobold Von, 1856-1921.
bd.17   Address at the German Reichstag.
          F. Peteler, February 27, 1917.
              1 reel (7 in.)   7 1/2 in. per sec.
          phonotape.

The big beat

Voice Lib.
M760   Aberbach, Jean
bd.10   Excerpt from "The big beat" (Program 2);
          comments on decline in band business after
          World War II; coming to popularity of Negro
          blues records. Westinghouse Broadcasting
          Corporation, 1964.
              1 min., 10 sec.   phonotape (1 r.
          7 1/2 i.p.s.)   (The music goes round and
          round)

              1. Blues (Songs, etc.) - U.S.   I. Title:
          The big beat.   II. Series.

Bevan, Aneurin, 1897-1960

Voice Lib.
381-   I can hear it now (radio program)
382   CBS, April 26, 1951.
bd.1   2 reels (7 in.)   7 1/2 in. per sec.   phonotape.
          L Radio Free Europe. 2. Strategic Air Command. L
Ridgway, Matthew Bunker, 1895- IL Churchill, Winston Leonard
Spencer, 1874-1965. III. Bevan, Aneurin, 1897-1960. IV. Nixon,
Richard Milhous, Pres. U.S., 1913-   V. Kerr, Robert Samuel, 1896-
1963. VI. Brewster, Ralph Owen, 1888-1962. VII. Wherry, Kenneth
Spicer, 1892-1951. VIII. Capehart, Homer Earl, 1897-   IX.
Lehman, Herbert Henry, 1878-1963. X. Taft, Robert Alphonso,
1889-1953. XL Moody, Arthur Edson Blair, 1902-1954. XII.
Martin, Joseph William, 1884-1968. XIII. McMahon, James O'Brien,
1903-1952. XIV. MacArthur, Douglas, 1880-1964. XVII. Wilson,
Charles Edward, 1886-1972.   XVIII. Irvine, Clarence T

The big beat

Voice Lib.
M760   Burton, Robert J
bd.14   Excerpt from "The Big Beat" (Program 2);
          comments on the content of the audience of
          popular music. Westinghouse Broadcasting
          Corporation, 1964.
              1 reel (7 in.)   7 1/2 in. per sec.
          phonotape. (The Music Goes Round and Round)

              I. Title: The big beat. II. Series.

The big beat

Voice Lib.
N760   Levy, Leonard
bd.16   Excerpt from "The Big Beat" (Program 2);
        comments on the many artists who are only
        one-shot record artists and the ones who
        have true talent; including song by Bobby
        Vinton, "Blue Velvet". Westinghouse
        Broadcasting Company, 1964.
           1 reel (7 in.)   7 1/2 in. per sec.
        phonotape. (The Music Goes Round and Round)

           I. Title: The big beat. II. Series.

Voice Lib.
M943   Big Ben; first sound effect record made
bd.5   by technicians at Edison House, London,
        of Big Ben striking 10:30, 10:45 and 11:00.
        G. R. Vincent re-recording.   July 16, 1890.
           1 reel (7 in.)   7 1/2 in. per sec.
        phonotape.

           1. Phonorecords - History.

The big beat

Voice Lib.
N762   Lieber, Jerry
bd.12   Excerpt from "The Big Beat" (Program 2);
        changes in the market for rock-and-roll
        records; including the song "Surfin' Bird".
        Westinghouse Broadcasting Corporation, 1964.
           1 reel (7 in.)   7 1/2 in. per sec.
        phonotape. (The Music Goes Round and Round)

           I. Title: Surfin' bird. II. Title: The
        big beat. III. Series.

C1   The big broadcast
M19   Whorf, Michael, 1933-
           The big broadcast.
           1 tape cassette. (The visual sounds of
        Mike Whorf. Miscellaneous, M19)

           Originally presented on his radio program, Kaleidoscope,
        WJR, Detroit.
           Duration: 53 min.
           The history and the personalities who made the radio a
        fixture in the household.

           1. Radio broadcasting. L. Title.

The big beat

Voice Lib.
N760   Miller, Mitch, 1911-
bd.15   Excerpt from "The Big Beat" (Program 2);
        criticizing rock-and-roll; feels like people
        who like it are lowering themselves.
        Westinghouse Broadcasting Corporation, 1964.
           1 reel (7 in.)   7 1/2 in. per sec.
        phonotape. (The Music Goes Round and Round)

           I. Title: The big beat. II. Series.

Voice Lib.   "The Big Show"
N719   Allen, Fred, 1894-1956.
bd.1   "The Big Show", with Tallulah Bankhead
        and Lauritz Melchior and all star cast.
        December 2, 1951.
           10 min., 56 sec.   phonotape (1 r.
        7 1/2 i.p.s.)

           I. Bankhead, Tallulah, 1902-1968. II.
        Melchior, Lauritz Lebrecht Hommel, 1890-
        1973. III. Title.

The big beat

Voice Lib.
N760   Sholes, Steven H   1911-1968.
bd.11   Excerpt from "The Big Beat" (Program 2);
        formation of popular music, including a
        song by Eddie Arnold, "There's a Star-
        Spangled Banner Waving Somewhere". Westing-
        house Broadcasting Corporation, 1964.
           1 reel (7 in.)   7 1/2 in. per sec.
        phonotape. (The Music Goes Round and Round)

           I. Title: The big beat. II. Series.

The big stick blues

Voice Lib.
M946   Handy, William Christopher, 1873-1958.
bd.9   Singing his own composition "The Big
        Stick Blues". GRV private recording, 1953.
           1 reel (7 in.)   7 1/2 in. per sec.
        phonotape.

           I. Title: The big stick blues.

The big beat

Voice Lib.
N760   Stoller, Mike
bd.13   Excerpt from "The Big Beat" (Program 2);
        comments on how the musical tastes of people
        change and have changed. Westinghouse
        Broadcasting Corporation, 1964.
           1 reel (7 in.)   7 1/2 in. per sec.
        phonotape. (The Music Goes Round and Round)

           I. Title: The big beat. II. Series.

C1   The big top
N7   Whorf, Michael, 1933-
           The big top.
           1 tape cassette. (The visual sounds of Mike Whorf.
        Miscellaneous, M7)

           Originally presented on his radio program, Kaleidoscope,
        WJR, Detroit.
           Duration: 40 min., 45 sec.
           Here is a fascinating look at the three-ringed world wherein
        lies the greatest show on earth, the animals, the clowns, the
        aerialist, the animal trainer, the marvelous magic of Barnum,
        Bailey and Ringling North.

           1. Circus - U.S. 2. Barnum, Bailey and Ringling North.
        L. Title.

Voice Lib.   Billings, Lemayne
M915- As we knew him; words of reminiscence of
916   friends and relatives about the life of
    J.F. Kennedy. Narration by Charles Kuralt;
    participants: Charles Bartlett, Lemayne
    Billings, Robert Kennedy, Rose Kennedy,
    James Reed, Adlai Stevenson, Gen. Chester B.
    Clifton, etc. Columbia Records Inc., 1965.
    2 reels (7 in.)   7 1/2 in. per sec.
    phonotape.

    1. Kennedy, John Fitzgerald, Pres. U.S.,
1917-1963. I. Kuralt, Charles, 1934-

(Continued on next card)

Voice Lib.
M1037 Biography in sound (radio program)
bd.1   "The Actor", narrated by Morgan Beatty.
    Cast includes Tallulah Bankhead, Hy Gardner,
    Rocky Graziano, Arthur Miller, Uta Hagen,
    Jackie Cooper, Sir Laurence Olivier, Gad
    Gayther, Barbara Ashley, Hortense Powdermaker,
    Peter Ustinov, Alfred Hitchcock, Leonard Lyons,
    John Guston, Helen Hayes, Dick Mayne, Ralph
    Bellamy, Lionel Barrymore, Sir Ralph Richardson,
    José Ferrer, and Walter Kerr. NBC Radio, 1950's.
    1 reel (7 in.) 7 1/2 in. per sec.
    phonotape.

(Continued on next card)

Voice Lib.
M1037 Biography in sound (radio program) "The
bd.1   Actor"... 1950's. (Card 2)

    L. Beatty, Morgan   II. Bankhead, Tallulah, 1903-1968.
III. Gardner, Hy, 1904-   IV. Graziano, Rocky, 1921- V.
Miller, Arthur, 1915-   VI. Hagen, Uta Thyra, 1919- VII.
Cooper, Jackie, 1922-   VIII. Olivier, Sir Laurence Kerr, 1907-
IX. Gayther, Gad   X. Ashley, Barbara   XI.
Powdermaker, Hortense, 1903-1970. XII. Ustinov, Peter Alexander,
1921-   XIII. Hitchcock, Alfred Joseph, 1899- XIV. Lyons,
Leonard   XV. Guston, John   XVI. Hayes, Helen, 1900-
XVII. Mayne, Dick   XVIII. Bellamy, Ralph, 1904-
XIX. Barrymore, Lionel, 1878-1954. XX. Richardson, Sir Ralph
David, 1902-   XXI. Ferrer, José, 1912-   XXII. Kerr,
Walter, 1913-

Voice Lib.
324   Biography in sound (radio program)
    Albert Schweitzer: at Aspen, Colorado;
    Goethe Conference (in French, translation
    by Emery Ross); excerpt from Schweitzer
    film; Schweitzer at piano, speaks in German
    on Bach. NBC, 1954.
    1 reel (7 in.) 7 1/2 in. per sec.
    phonotape.

    1. Schweitzer, Albert, 1875-1965. I.
Schweitzer, Albert. 1875-1965.

Voice Lib.
M275- Biography in sound (radio program)
276   Alexander Woollcott. N.B.C., date?
bd.1   2 reels (7 in.) 7 1/2 in. per sec.
    phonotape.

    L. Woollcott, Alexander, 1887-1943. L. Woollcott, Alexander,
1887-1943. II. Banghardt, Kenneth   III. Hecht, Ben, 1893-
1964. IV. Roosevelt, Eleanor (Roosevelt) 1884-1962. V. Walker,
Danton   VI. Brackett, Charles, 1892-1969. VII. Grant,
Jane   VIII. Rude, Robert Barnes   IX. West,
Rebecca, pseud. X. Henessy, Joseph   XI. Letterer,
Charles   XII. Welles, Orson, 1915-

Voice Lib.
M273- Biography in sound (radio program)
274   Franklin Delano Roosevelt: the friends and
bd.1   former associates of Franklin Roosevelt on
    the tenth anniversary of the President's death.
    NBC Radio, April, 1955.
    2 reels (7 in.) 7 1/2 in. per sec.
    phonotape.

    L. Roosevelt, Franklin Delano, Pres. U. S., 1882-1945. L.
McIntire, Ross T 1899- II. Mellett, Lowell, 1884-1960.
III. Tully, Grace   IV. Henderson, Leon, 1895-
V. Roosevelt, Eleanor (Roosevelt) 1884-1962. VI. DeGraaf, Albert
VII. Lehman, Herbert Henry, 1878-1963. VIII. Rosenman, Samuel
Irving, 1896-   IX. Arvey, Jacob   X. Moley, Raymond,
1886-   XI. Farley, James Aloysius, 1888-   XII. Roosevelt,
(Continued on next card)

Voice Lib.
M273- Biography in sound (radio program) Franklin
274   Delano Roosevelt... 1955. (Card 2)
bd.1
    Franklin Delano, Pres. U. S., 1882-1945. XIII. Sherwood, Robert
Emmet, 1896-1955. XIV. Perkins, Frances, 1882-1965. XV.
Wallace, Henry Agard, 1888-1965. XVI. Cohen, Benjamin
Victor, 1894-   XVII. Harkness, Richard   XVIII.
Godwin, Earl   XIX. Palmer, George   XX. Hassett,
William D 1880-   XXI. Bowles, Chester Bliss, 1901-
XXII. Elsie, George   XXIII. Churchill, Winston Leonard
Spencer, 1874-1965. XXIV. Cunningham, Paul   XXV.
Landon, Alfred Mossman, 1887-

Voice Lib.
M272 Biography in sound (radio program)
bd.1   Heywood Broun. NBC, date?
    1 reel (7 in.) 7 1/2 in. per sec.
    phonotape.

    L. Broun, Heywood Campbell, 1888-1939. L. Broun,
Heywood Campbell, 1888-1939. II. Swope, Herbert Bayard,
1882-1958. III. Wilson, Mattie   IV. Jackson, Gardner
V. Meany, Thomas   VI. Waldron, Beatrice   VII.
Gordon, Max   VIII. Madison, Connie   IX. Gannett,
Lewis Stiles, 1891-1966. X. Collins, Joseph, 1866-1950. XI.
Brown, Earl Louis, 1900-   XII. Levy, Newman, 1888-
XIII. Growth, John   XIV. Bye, George   XV.
Roosevelt, Franklin Delano, Pres. U. S., 1882-1945. XVI.
Reynolds, Quentin James, 1902-1965.

Voice Lib.
M322 Biography in sound (radio program)
    W.C. Fields, the magnificent rogue.
    NBC, 1955.
    1 reel (7 in.) 7 1/2 in. per sec. phonotape.
    L. Fields, W.C., 1879-1946. L. Fields, W.C., 1879-1946.
II. Allen, Fred, 1894-1956. III. LaBaron, William   IV.
Taylor, Robert Lewis, 1912-   V. McCarey, Thomas Leo, 1898-
1969. VI. Harkins, James   VII. Chevalier, Maurice,
1889-1972. VIII. Kuromoto, Mrs. George   IX. Flynn,
Errol Leslie, 1909-1959. X. Wynn, Ed, 1886-1966. XI. Dowling,
Ray Dooley   XII. Sennett, Mack   XIII. Overacher,
Ronald Leroy   XIV. Bergen, Edgar, 1903-   XV. Taurog,
Norman, 1899-   XVI. Runhell, Ann   XVII. Cowen,
Lester

Voice Lib.
M323 Biography in sound (radio program)
    Will Rogers of Oklahoma. "All I know ...",
    singing "In the blue of the night", marriage
    is a poker game, on acting, excerpt from radio
    program (Rogers' Lottery Plan), excerpt
    closing broadcast with his famous alarm
    clock. NBC, 1955.
    1 reel (7 in.) 7 1/2 in. per sec.
    phonotape.

    L. Rogers, Will, 1879-1935. L. Rogers, Will, 1879-1935.

Voice Lib.
M947   Birkett, Norman Birkett, baron, 1883-
bd.2   Remarks at celebration of Shakespeare's
        birthday, held at Stratford-on-Avon.
        British Decca, April 23, 1938.
           1 reel (7 in.)   7 1/2 in. per sec.
        phonotape.

Voice Lib.
M948   Birkett, Norman Birkett, baron, 1883-
bd.1   Address made at dinner in honor of Alec
        Bedser at the Dorchester Hotel entitled
        "Cricketers everywhere".   British Decca,
        September 22, 1960.
           1 reel (7 in.)   7 1/2 in. per sec.
        phonotape.

Voice Lib.
M947   Birkett, Norman Birkett, baron, 1883-
bd.1   "The art of advocacy"; talking about
        ethics of an advocate and examples of their
        techniques.   British Decca, May 28, 1961.
           1 reel (7 in.)   7 1/2 in. per sec.
        phonotape.

BIRMINGHAM, ALA.
Voice Lib.
M362-   Birmingham: a testament of non-violence.   In six parts.
372,   WRVR, May 1963.
bd.1   11 reels (7 in.)   7 1/2 l.p.s.   phonotape.
           CONTENTS. -pt. 1. "A happy day in Birmingham". -pt. 2.
        "The Klan, two bombs, and a riot"; Alabama crowd, bombing
        of a home and motel, rioting that followed, interviews with
        citizens of Birmingham. -pt. 3. "Mother's Day, 1963". -pt. 4.
        "Back to school in Birmingham"; students in non-violence
        movement, methods of organization. -pt. 5. "Keep Birmingham
        southern"; unidentified 78-year old Birmingham citizen, white,
        analyzes integration problem; Birmingham Medical College
        faculty member analyzes situation; Birmingham College white
        student gives ideas od integration; white Birmingham mothers
        chatting about integration problem; Birmingham insurance
                                    (Continued on next card)

BIRMINGHAM, ALA.
Voice Lib.
M362-   Birmingham: a testament of non-violence.   1963.
372,   (Card 2)
bd.1
           CONTENTS (Cont'd) executive's opinion on situation. -
        pt. 6. "Blacks and whites together".

           1. Birmingham, Ala. 2. Race discrimination - U.S.

Voice Lib.
M362-   Birmingham: a testament of non-violence.   In six parts.
372,   WRVR, May 1963.
bd.1   11 reels (7 in.) 7 1/2 l.p.s.   phonotape.
           CONTENTS. -pt. 1. "A happy day in Birmingham". -pt. 2.
        "The Klan, two bombs, and a riot"; Alabama crowd, bombing
        of a home and motel, rioting that followed, interviews with
        citizens of Birmingham. -pt. 3. "Mother's Day, 1963". -pt. 4.
        "Back to school in Birmingham"; students in non-violence
        movement, methods of organization. -pt. 5. "Keep Birmingham
        southern"; unidentified 78-year old Birmingham citizen, white,
        analyzes integration problem; Birmingham Medical College
        faculty member analyzes situation; Birmingham College white
        student gives ideas od integration; white Birmingham mothers
        chatting about integration problem; Birmingham insurance
                                    (Continued on next card)

Voice Lib.
M362-   Birmingham: a testament of non-violence.   1963.
372,   (Card 2)
bd.1
           CONTENTS (Cont'd) executive's opinion on situation. -
        pt. 6. "Blacks and whites together".

           1. Birmingham, Ala. 2. Race discrimination - U.S.

C1   Birth of a nation
H22   Whorf, Michael, 1933-
           Birth of a nation; Columbus, the adventurer.
           1 tape cassette.   (The visual sounds of
        Mike Whorf. History and heritage, H22)
           Originally presented on his radio program, Kaleidoscope,
        WJR, Detroit.
           Duration: 38 min., 10 sec.
           A generous mixture of poetry and seldom-presented historical
        fact is blended to tell this greatest of all nautical tales. Aboard
        three ships, they sailed into the unknown. "Sail on, sail on and
        on," commanded the admiral and sail they did, into high adventure,
        the like of which the world had never known.

           1. Colombo, Cristoforo.   1. Title.

C1   The birth of the Boy Scouts
S73   Whorf, Michael, 1933-
           The birth of the Boy Scouts.
           1 tape cassette.   (The visual sounds of
        Mike Whorf. Social, S73)
           Originally presented on his radio program, Kaleidoscope,
        WJR, Detroit.
           Duration: 36 min., 35 sec.
           A historic narration of Lord Baden-Powell's life work of
        creating boys into young adults. The history of the Boy Scouts
        from its initiation to the present day world-wide organization is
        presented.

           1. Boy Scouts. 2. Baden-Powell, Sir Robert Stephenson
        Smyth-Baden-Powell, 1857-1944. 1. Title.

C1   BISMARCK (BATTLESHIP)
M15   Whorf, Michael, 1933-
           The sinking of the Bismarck.
           1 tape cassette.   (The visual sounds of
        Mike Whorf. Miscellaneous, M15)
           Originally presented on his radio program, Kaleidoscope,
        WJR, Detroit.
           Duration: 25 min.
           During the early years of World War II, the German ship
        Bismarck, was the terror of the high seas. Challenged by the
        ships of the English fleet, it was a day of retribution and one
        that changed the course of battle in the north Atlantic.

           1. Bismarck (Battleship) 2. World War, 1939-1945 - Naval
        operations, British.   1. Title.

C1
H42
    BISON, AMERICAN
    Whorf, Michael, 1933-
       The great American buffalo.
       1 tape cassette. (The visual sounds of
    Mike Whorf. History and heritage, H42)
       Originally presented on his radio program, Kaleidoscope,
WJR, Detroit.
       Duration: 40 min., 45 sec.
       The bison supplied every need for the sustenance of the Indian;
yet, later he would be wantonly slain for the rugs and coats of the
American Caucasian. He was a beautiful, gigantic beast, who
nearly became extinct, but today survives in ever-growing numbers.

       I. Bison, American.   I. Title.

BLACK NATIONALISM
Voice Lib.
M1672   McKissick, Floyd, 1922-
       Black power and white response.
       WKAR, January 27, 1969.
       45 min. phonotape (1 r.   7 1/2 i.p.s.)

       1. Black nationalism.

C1
S14
    The black cowboy
    Whorf, Michael, 1933-
       The black cowboy.
       1 tape cassette. (The visual sounds of
    Mike Whorf. Social, S14)
       Originally presented on his radio program, Kaleidoscope,
WJR, Detroit.
       Duration: 30 min.
       Along with the rustlers, wranglers, badmen and heroes, were
Black men who rode the same trails and equalled the exploits
of Earp, Bass, Bonney and Hickok.

       I. Negroes as cowboys. I. Title.

Voice Lib. Blackmer, Sidney, 1895-1973
M310   American Broadcasting Company.
       Tribute to President John Fitzgerald Kennedy
    from the arts. Fredric March emcees; Jerome
    Hines sings "Worship of God and Nature" by
    Beethoven; Florence Eldridge recites "When
    lilacs last in the door-yard bloom'd" by Walt
    Whitman; Marian Anderson in two songs. Includes
    Charlton Heston, Sidney Blackmer, Isaac Stern,
    Nathan Milstein, Christopher Plummer, Albert
    Finney. ABC, November 24, 1963.
       35 min. phonotape (7 in.   7 1/2 i.p.s.)

(Continued on next card)

    Black magic
C1
M12
    Whorf, Michael, 1933-
       Black magic.
       1 tape cassette. (The visual sounds of
    Mike Whorf. Miscellaneous, M12)
       Originally presented on his radio program, Kaleidoscope,
WJR, Detroit.
       Duration: 30 min.
       Considered by many to be one of the greatest comics who
ever lived, Bert Williams was idolized by millions and adored
by those who knew him.

       I. Williams, Bert. I. Title.

Voice Lib.
M1456- Blake, Eubie
1457   Composer and pianist recalls his early
bd.1   career in ragtime music and plays various
       selections. NET, 1970.
       2 reels (7 in.) 7 1/2 in. per sec.
    phonotape.

       1. Jazz music

    BLACK MUSLIMS
Voice Lib.
M1087 Little, Malcolm, 1925-1965.
bd.1   Speaking at MSU press conference about
    race problem and aim of Black Muslims;
    Meredith case and Mississippi; followed
    by various takes of interview for MSU film.
    Location recording, June 22, 1963.
       1 reel (7 in.) 7 1/2 i.p.s. phonotape.

       1. Black Muslims. 2. Race discrimination -
U.S.

Voice Lib. Blandy, William Henry Purnell, 1890-1954
M717   Atomic bomb test at Bikini Atoll. Description
bd.3   by on-the-spot witnesses and remarks by
    Vice-Admiral Blandy, U.S.N., on board
    U.S.S. Mt. McKinley. July 24, 1946.
       1 min., 38 sec. phonotape (1 r.
    7 1/2 i.p.s.)

       1. Atomic bomb. I. Blandy, William
Henry Purnell, 1890-1954.

    BLACK MUSLIMS
Voice Lib.
M1690 Muhammad Ali, 1942-
       Integration, separation, politics, and
    violence. WKAR, February 27, 1970.
       50 min. phonotape (1 r. 7 1/2 i.p.s.)

       1. Muhammad Ali, 1942-   2. Frazier,
Joe, 1944-   3. Black Muslims.

C1
M22
    A blare of bugles and a ruffle of drums
    Whorf, Michael, 1933-
       A blare of bugles and a ruffle of drums.
       1 tape cassette. (The visual sounds of
    Mike Whorf. Miscellaneous, M22)
       Originally presented on his radio program, Kaleidoscope,
WJR, Detroit.
       Duration: 39 min., 30 sec.
       He was called the "march king" and indeed he was, for
John Philip Sousa gave the world hundreds of stirring melodies.

       I. Sousa, John Philip, 1854-1932. I. Title.

C1
PWM20   Blare of bugles, ruffle of drums
    Whorf, Michael, 1933–
      Blare of bugles, ruffle of drums.
    1 tape cassette.   (The visual sounds of
Mike Whorf. Panorama; a world of music,
PWM-20)

    Originally presented on his radio program, Kaleidoscope,
WJR, Detroit.
    Duration: 28 min.
    The life and times of John Philip Sousa, with excerpts of
his music.

    I. Sousa, John Philip, 1854-1932. I. Title.

BLOOD
Voice Lib.
M384   I can hear it now (radio program)
bd.1   Biography of a pint of blood.   CBS,
February, 1951.
    1 reel (7 in.)   7 1/2 in. per sec.
phonotape.

    1. Blood.   I. McIntire, Ross T., 1899–
II. Hope, Bob, 1903–   III. Ridgway,
Matthew Bunker, 1895–   IV. Barkley,
Alban William, 1877-1956.

Voice Lib.   Bley, Wulf, 1890–
M981   Nazi news report of a torchlight parade in
bd.3   Berlin on the assumption of power by Nazi
Party. Reports by Wulf Bley and Heinz
von Lichberg.   Peteler, January 30, 1933.
    1 reel (7 in.)   7 1/2 in. per sec.
phonotape.

    I. Bley, Wulf, 1890–   II. Lichberg,
Heinz von

C1
H69   The blue and the gray
    Whorf, Michael, 1933–
      The blue and the gray; Civil War, part 2.
    1 tape cassette.   (The visual sounds of
Mike Whorf. History and heritage, H69)
    Originally presented on his radio program, Kaleidoscope,
WJR, Detroit.
    Duration: 37 min., 35 sec.
    This program concerns itself with the stories of the northern
soldier and the southern yeoman, their convictions emblazoned
in history. The north and the south, the blue and the gray, brave
men fighting for ideals - not for right or wrong - but fighting for
what they believed was their sacred duty.

    I. U.S - History - Civil War, 1861-1865. I. Title.

BLIND
Voice Lib.
M1579   Osgood, Charles
bd.4   Interviewing Sy Leaderman, blind man, who
bowls 247 in a league where all others have
sight.   CBS Morning News, February 21, 1974.
    2 min., 15 sec.   phonotape (1 r.   7 1/2
i.p.s.)

    1. Blind. 2. Physically handicapped.
I. Leaderman, Sy.

Voice Lib.
M1675   The blue beetle (radio program)
bd.3   The blue beetle.   Golden Age Radio
Records, 1943.
    15 min.   phonotape (1 r.   7 1/2 i.p.s.)

BLIND
Voice Lib.
M1741   Walker, Ed
bd.3   The blindness of the sighted.   WKAR,
June 17, 1974.
    25 min.   phonotape (1 r.   7 1/2 i.p.s.)

    1. Blind.

BLUES (SONGS, ETC.) - U.S.
Voice Lib.
M760   Aberbach, Jean
bd.10   Excerpt from "The big beat" (Program 2);
comments on decline in band business after
World War II; coming to popularity of Negro
blues records.   Westinghouse Broadcasting
Corporation, 1964.
    1 min., 10 sec.   phonotape (1 r.
7 1/2 i.p.s.)   (The music goes round and
round)

    1. Blues (Songs, etc.) - U.S.   I. Title:
The big beat.   II. Series.

Voice Lib.
576,   Blitzkrieg; report on beginning of World War
bd.2–   II, with voices of the actual participants.
577,   Columbia Records, Inc., 1953.
bd.1   2 reels (7 in.)   7 1/2 in. per sec.
phonotape.

    1. World War, 1939-1945

Voice Lib.
M828   Blythe, Samuel George, 1868–
bd.1   Witty introductory remarks at Chicago
political rally of Mr. Irvin S. Cobb.
Blue Network, November 1, 1940.
    1 reel (7 in.)   7 1/2 in. per sec.
phonotape.

Voice Lib.
M1097 Bogart, Humphrey, 1899-1957.
A biographical documentary program about the
career of Humphrey Bogart by Flaum-Grinberg
Productions, including various sequences from
his motion pictures and comments by his former
associates, co-ordinated by Charlton Heston.
ABC-TV, April 23, 1967.
1 reel (7 in.)   7 1/2 in. per sec.
phonotape.
1. Bogart, Humphrey, 1899-1957. 1. Heston, Charlton, 1924-

C1   The bold buccaneers - Kidd, Teach, Lafitte
H32
Whorf, Michael, 1933-
The bold buccaneers - Kidd, Teach, Lafitte.
1 tape cassette.   (The visual sounds of
Mike Whorf. History and heritage, H32)

Originally presented on his radio program, Kaleidoscope,
WJR, Detroit.
Duration: 55 min., 20 sec.
William Kidd, Edward Teach, Jean Lafitte were bold captains
who sailed the bounding main in search of rich prizes. Who were
they and why did they sail under the Jolly Roger? Here is the
picturesque account of the bold buccaneers.

1. Pirates. 1. Title.

Voice Lib.
M1471 Boldt, Gerhard, of Lübeck.
bd.1-A   Musical lead-in followed by description
about the surroundings in the "Fuehrerbunker"
in Berlin at the beginning of February, 1945.
1965.
1 reel (7 in.)   7 1/2 in. per sec.
phonotape.

1. Germany - Politics and government -
1933-1945.

Voice Lib.
M1471   Boldt, Gerhard, of Lübeck
bd.1-B   Description of the last conferences in
the "Fuehrerbunker" in Berlin, approximately
April 22, 1945 to April 29, 1945.   1965.
1 reel (7 in.)   7 i.p.s.   phonotape.

1. Germany - Politics and government -
1933-1945.

C1   BOLIVAR, SIMON, 1783-1830
H86
Whorf, Michael, 1933-
The liberator - Simon Bolivar.
1 tape cassette.   (The visual sounds of
Mike Whorf. History and heritage, H86)

Originally presented on his radio program, Kaleidoscope,
WJR, Detroit.
Duration: 34 min., 15 sec.
He was called the Washington of South America and it was a
title richly deserved. Bolivar struck a blow for freedom against the
misrule of Spain, and led his countrymen in the battles that changed
the map of a continent and the future of a people.

1. Bolivar, Simon, 1783-1830. 1. Title.

Voice Lib.
M1571   Bolling, Richard, 1916-
bd.2   Speaking at the National Press Club on
the need for reorganizing Congress.
WKAR, April 18, 1974.
20 min.   phonotape (1 r.   7 1/2 i.p.s.)

1. U.S. Congress.

Voice Lib.
M1640   Bond, Julian, 1940-
Politics and Black progress, on "Firing
Line" with William F. Buckley and John
Lewis. WKAR-FM, March 17, 1974.
45 min.   phonotape (1 r.   7 1/2 i.p.s.)

1. Negroes - Politics and suffrage.
I. Buckley, William Frank, 1925-
II. Lewis, John.

        Bond, Julian, 1940-
Voice Lib.
M1323- Democratic Party. National Convention,
M1328,   Chicago, 1968.
bd.1   Hubert Humphrey, Democratic presidential nom ..,
announcing his selection of Sen. Muskie as his running mate;
convention floor reports; interview with Mrs. Humphrey. Mayor
Daley of Chicago defending police action. Interviews with Senator McGovern and Jesse Unruh of California. Remote address by
Sen. Edward Kennedy introducing a memorial motion picture on
the late Sen. Robert F. Kennedy. Various reports on riots and
general confusion, reluctance of delegates to come to order.
Nominations for Vice-President; seconding speeches for Sen.
Muskie and nominating speech by Wisconsin delegation of Julian
Bond of Georgia. Interview with Julian Bond, who declined
nomination of the vice-presidency. Story told by chairman of
the New Hampshire delegation regarding his arrest. Interview
(Continued on next card)

        Bond, Julian, 1940-
Voice Lib.
M1323- Democratic Party. National Convention,
M1328,   Chicago, 1968...   (Card 2)
bd.1   with Paul O'Dwyer of the New York delegation regarding the
nomination of Richard Daley for Vice-President. General
confusion. Nomination of Sen. Edmund Muskie as Vice-President
and resulting confusion with the Oregon delegation. Followed by
Sen. Muskie's acceptance speech. NBC-TV, August 29, 1968.
6 reels (7 in.) 7 1/2 in. per sec.   phonotape.
1. Humphrey, Hubert Horatio, 1911- II. Humphrey, Muriel Fay
(Buck) 1912-   III. Daley, Richard J   1902-   IV. McGovern,
George Stanley, 1922-   V. Unruh, Jesse Marvin, 1922-   VI.
Kennedy, Edward Moore, 1932-   VII. Bond, Julian, 1940-   VIII.
O'Dwyer, Paul, 1907-   IX. Muskie, Edmund S   1914-

        The bonny land of Scotland
C1
M42
Whorf, Michael, 1933-
The bonny land of Scotland.
1 tape cassette.   (The visual sounds of
Mike Whorf. Miscellaneous, M42)

Originally presented on his radio program, Kaleidoscope,
WJR, Detroit.
Duration: 36 min., 10 sec.
An ancient land with a proud people, Scotland is a heritage
for its descendants, and a state of mind for all.

1. Scotland. 1. Title.

Voice Lib.
M540   Boole, Ella Alexander, 1858-1952.
bd.7   Prohibition; advantages of prohibition for
       all Americans. Fox Movietone, 1932.
          1 reel (7 in.) 7 1/2 in. per sec.
       phonotape.

          1. Prohibition.

BOOTH, JOHN WILKES, 1838-1865

C1
H16   Whorf, Michael, 1933-
          The assassin.
          1 tape cassette. (The visual sounds of
       Mike Whorf. History and heritage, H16)
          Originally presented on his radio program, Kaleidoscope,
       WJR, Detroit.
          Duration: 37 min.
          Violence stalked the land in the person of John Wilkes Booth,
       a bitter man, a resentful man, a man full of hate whose deed was
       the ultimate act of tragedy.

          L Booth, John Wilkes, 1838-1865. L Title.

Voice Lib.   Boom boom surf
M766   Stampa, Fred
bd.5   Excerpt from "Popular Music of Europe"
       (Program 11); comments on style of singing
       of Dominco Modugno, including song "Boom
       boom surf" by Peppino Di Capri and the
       Hollerers.   Westinghouse Broadcasting
       Corporation, 1964.
          1 min., 44 sec. phonotape (1 r.   7 1/2 L.p. s.)
       (The music goes round and round)

          L Modugno, Dominco. L Title: Boom boom surf.
       IL Title: Popular music of Europe. III. Series.

Voice Lib.
M756   Booth, William, 1829-1912.
bd.6   "Don't forget"; an address by the late
       General Booth, founder of the Salvation
       Army. VTM, 1910.
          1 reel (7 in.) 7 1/2 in. per sec.
       phonotape.

          1. Salvation Army

BOONE, DANIEL, 1734-1820

C1
H10   Whorf, Michael, 1933-
          Life and times of Daniel Boone.
          1 tape cassette. (The visual sounds of
       Mike Whorf. History and heritage, H10)
          Originally presented on his radio program, Kaleidoscope,
       WJR, Detroit.
          Duration: 84 min.
          He was our nation's most illustrious pioneer, a man of action,
       a man of determination. Boone was a legend in his own time and a
       hero among the many who explored the wilderness of early
       America.

          L Boone, Daniel, 1734-1820. L Title.

Voice Lib.
M756   Booth, William, 1829-1912.
bd.9   "Please, sir, save me !" An address by
       the late General William Booth, founder of
       the Salvation Army. VTM, 1910.
          1 reel (7 in.) 7 1/2 in. per sec.
       phonotape.

          1. Salvation Army

Voice Lib.   Booth, Edwin, 1833-1893
M225   Packard, Frederick
          Styles in Shakespearean acting, 1890-1950.
       Creative Associates, 1963?
          1 reel (7 in.) 7 1/2 in. per sec. phonotape.

          L Sothern, Edward Askew, 1826-1881. IL Marlowe,
       Julia, 1865-1950. III. Booth, Edwin, 1833-1893. IV. Gielgud,
       John, 1904-   V. Robeson, Paul Bustill, 1898-   VL Terry,
       Dame Ellen, 1848-1928. VII. Allen, Viola. VIII. Welles,
       Orson, 1915-   IX. Skinner, Otis, 1858-1942. X. Barrymore,
       John, 1882-1942. XL Olivier, Sir Laurence Kerr, 1907-
       XII. Forbes-Robertson, Sir Johnston, 1853-   XIII. Evans,
       Maurice. XIV. Thorndike, Dame Sybil, 1882-   XV. Robson,
       Flora. XVL LeGallienne, Eva, 1899-   XVII. Anderson,
       Judith. XVIII. Duncan, Augustin. XIX. Hampden, Walter.
       XX. Speaight, Robert, 1904-   XXL Jones, Daniel.

Voice Lib.
M756   Booth, William, 1829-1912.
bd.7   "Rope wanted"; an address by the late
       General Booth, founder of the Salvation
       Army. VTM, 1910.
          1 reel (7 in.) 7 1/2 in. per sec.
       phonotape.

          1. Salvation Army

BOOTH, EDWIN, 1833-1893

C1
H53   Whorf, Michael, 1933-
          In the shadow of tragedy - Edwin Booth.
          1 tape cassette. (The visual sounds of
       Mike Whorf. History and heritage, H53)

          Originally presented on his radio program, Kaleidoscope,
       WJR, Detroit.
          Duration: 37 min., 45 sec.
          A splendid tragedian, fate would deal with him cruelly.
       Despite talent, creative genius and a warm friendly personality,
       Edwin Booth would never overcome the blows that destiny dealt him.

          L Booth, Edwin, 1833-1893. L Title.

Voice Lib.
M756   Booth, William, 1829-1912.
bd.8   "Through Jordan"; an address in verse
       by the late General Booth, founder of the
       Salvation Army. VTM, 1910.
          1 reel (7 in.) 7 1/2 in. per sec.
       phonotape.

          1. Salvation Army. I. Title.

BOOTH, WILLIAM, 1829-1912

C1
S15   Whorf, Michael, 1933-
     Marching as to war.
     1 tape cassette.   (The visual sounds of
Mike Whorf.   Social, S15)
    Originally presented on his radio program, Kaleidoscope,
WJR, Detroit.
    Duration: 42 min.
    Outlined against the background of the 19th century in
England, is the story of William Booth and the Salvation Army.

     L. Booth, William, 1829-1912.   2. Salvation Army.
L. Title.

Voice Lib.   Borge, Victor, 1909-
M1005   Hans Christian Andersen (Television program)
    TV adaptation of film of same title, with
Danny Kaye and Victor Borge.   ABC-TV, Nov. 3,
1966.
     1 reel (7 in.)   7 1/2 in. per sec.
phonotape.

     1. Andersen, Hans Christian, 1805-1875.
I. Kaye, Danny, 1913-   II. Borge,
Victor, 1909-

Voice Lib.
M1659   Borges, Jorge Luis, 1899-
    Borges and his poetry.   Sponsored by
Michigan State University Romance Languages
Department in Music Auditorium.   WKAR,
November 20, 1969.
     45 min.   phonotape (1 r.   7 1/2 i.p.s.)

     I. Title.

Voice Lib.
M1700   Borlaug, Norman Ernst, 1914-
    The green revolution; its genesis, impact,
dangers & hope.   Includes awarding of
honorary D.Sc. degree from Michigan State
University and introduction by President
Wharton.   WKAR, May 12, 1971.
     50 min.   phonotape (1 r.   7 1/2 i.p.s.)

     1. Population.   I. Muelder, Milton E.
II. Wharton, Clifton Reginald, 1926-

Borman, Frank, 1928-
Voice Lib.
M917   Gemini 7 (space flight): Frank McGee's resumé
bd.1   of space flights of astronauts Frank Borman
and James Lovell, Jr., in Gemini 7, commencing
Dec. 4, 1956 to Dec. 18, 1965, and of astronauts Walter Schirra and Thomas Stafford in
Gemini 6, which rendezvoused in space;
including various launching actual reports
and interview with Wally Schirra; comments
by Huntley and Brinkley.   NBC TV, December
18, 1965.
     1 reel (7 in.)   7 1/2 in. per sec.
phonotape.
           (Continued on next card)

Voice Lib.   Borman, Frank, 1928-
M1347-   Apollo 8 (space flight): recovery.   CBS TV
1348,   description of recovery of astronauts and
bd.1   their reception on aircraft carrier "York-
town".   CBS TV, December 27, 1968.
     2 reels (7 in.)   7 1/2 in. per sec.
phonotape.

     1. Project Apollo.   2. Anders, William
Alison, 1933-   3. Lovell, James Arthur, 1928-
4. Borman, Frank, 1928-   I. Anders, William
Alison, 1933-   II. Lovell, James Arthur,
1928-   III. Borman, Frank, 1928-

Voice Lib.   Borman, Frank, 1928-
M1348   Apollo 8 (space flight): reception of Apollo
bd.2   8 astronauts at Joint Session of Congress,
including addresses by the astronauts.
CBS TV, January 1, 1969.
     1 reel (7 in.)   7 1/2 in. per sec.
phonotape.
     1. Project Apollo.   2. Anders, William
Alison, 1933-   3. Lovell, James Arthur, 1928-
4. Borman, Frank, 1928-   I. Anders, William
Alison, 1933-   II. Lovell, James Arthur,
1928-   III. Borman, Frank, 1928-   IV.
McCormack, John William, 1891-

Voice Lib.   Borman, Frank, 1928-
M1351   Apollo 8 (space flight): interview with
bd.1   astronauts William Anders, James Lovell,
and Frank Borman on CBS TV program "Face
the nation".   CBS TV, January 12, 1969.
     1 reel (7 in.)   7 1/2 in. per sec.
phonotape.

     1. Project Apollo.   2. Anders, William
Alison, 1933-   3. Lovell, James Arthur, 1928-
4. Borman, Frank, 1928-   I. Anders, William
Alison, 1933-   II. Lovell, James Arthur,
1928-   III. Borman, Frank, 1928-

Voice Lib.
M1639   Boulding, Kenneth Ewart, 1910-
    Cautious change, or how to prepare for
the next fifty years.   WKAR-AM, February 17,
1974.
     55 min.   phonotape (1 r.   7 1/2 i.p.s.)

     Includes question and answer period.

     1. Ecology.   2. Social sciences.

Bound to be rich, John D. Rockefeller

C1
H79   Whorf, Michael, 1933-
    Bound to be rich, John D. Rockefeller.
    1 tape cassette.   (The visual sounds of
Mike Whorf.   History and heritage, H79)
    Originally presented on his radio program, Kaleidoscope,
WJR, Detroit.
    Duration: 36 min., 30 sec.
    John D. Rockefeller had learned the value of money from his
father and ever since he collected a bit of interest on a loan,
he thought of nothing but money until the day he died.

     L. Rockefeller, John Davison, 1839-1937.   L. Title.

Voice Lib.
X975 Bourne, Francis Alphonsus, Cardinal, 1861-
bd.5   1935.
         Speech on education. Rococo-Can., 1910.
         1 reel (7 in.) 7 1/2 in. per sec.
phonotape.

C1   BOURNE, RICHARD
FA16   Whorf, Michael, 1933-
         Richard Bourne.
         1 tape cassette. (The visual sounds of
Mike Whorf. The forgotten American, FA16)
         Originally presented on his radio program, Kaleidoscope,
WJR, Detroit.
         Duration: 10 min., 25 sec.
         Preacher to the Indians on Cape Cod, Bourne developed a
colony of Christian Indians which blocked an Indian attack
during King Philip's War.

         L Bourne, Richard. L. Title.

Voice Lib.
M1028 Bowes, Edward, 1874-1946.
bd.2   Excerpt from radio's original "Amateur Hour",
with Ted Mack and Teresa Brewer. Michigan
State University, Department of Television and
Radio, 1940's.
         1 reel (7 in.) 7 1/2 in. per sec.
phonotape.

         I. Mack, Ted, 1904-   II. Brewer, Teresa

Voice Lib.   Bowes, Edward, 1874-1946
M655   The Twentieth Century (TV program)
bd.1   "The creative thirties", narrated by
Walter Cronkite. CBS, 1963.
         25 min. phonotape (1 r. 7 1/2 i.p.s.)
         L U.S. - Civilization - 1918-1945. L Bowes, Edward,
1874-1946. IL Geismar, Maxwell David, 1909-
III. MacDonald, Dwight, 1906-   IV. Welles, Orson, 1915-
V. Cronkite, Walter Leland, 1916-   VL Gable, Clark, 1901-
1960. VII. Lewis, Sinclair, 1885-1951. VIII. Houseman,
John, 1902-   IX. Roosevelt, Franklin Delano, Pres. U.S.,
1882-1945.

Voice Lib.   Bowles, Chester Bliss, 1901-
M273- Biography in sound (radio program)
274   Franklin Delano Roosevelt: the friends and
bd.1   former associates of Franklin Roosevelt on
the tenth anniversary of the President's death.
NBC Radio, April, 1955.
         2 reels (7 in.) 7 1/2 in. per sec.
phonotape.
         L Roosevelt, Franklin Delano, Pres. U.S., 1882-1945. L
McIntire, Ross T 1899-   IL Mellett, Lowell, 1884-1960.
III. Tully, Grace   IV. Henderson, Leon, 1895-
V. Roosevelt, Eleanor (Roosevelt) 1884-1962. VL DeGraaf, Albert
VII. Lehman, Herbert Henry, 1878-1963. VIII. Rosenman, Samuel
Irving, 1896-   IX. Arvey, Jacob   X. Moley, Raymond,
1886-   XI. Farley, James Aloysius, 1888-   XII. Roosevelt,
(Continued on next card)

Voice Lib.   Bowman, Robert
M1044 London after dark; on-the-spot recordings of various
points during the London air-raid attacks: the Savoy Hotel
kitchen, Trafalgar Square, anti-aircraft battery near London,
air-raid shelter. With newsmen Edward R. Murrow, Robert
Bowman, Raymond Van Denny, Larry Lesueur, Eric Sevareid,
Vincent Sheean, J. B. Priestley, Michael Standing, and
Winfred Von Thomas. CBS and BBC, August 24, 1940.
         1 reel (7 in.) 7 1/2 in. per sec. phonotape.

         L Murrow, Edward Roscoe, 1908-1965. IL Bowman, Robert
III. Van Denny, Raymond   IV. Lesueur, Laurence Edward,
1909-   V. Sevareid, Arnold Eric, 1912-   VL Sheean,
Vincent, 1899-   VII. Priestley, John Boynton, 1894-
VIII. Standing, Michael   IX. Von Thomas, Winfred

             BOXING
Voice Lib.
M613   Corbett, James John, 1866-1933.
bd.3   Describes his boxing career. Source ?,
1908.
         1 reel (7 in.) 7 1/2 in. per sec.
phonotape.

             BOXING
Voice Lib.
M1064 Dempsey, Jack, 1895-
bd.9   Interview with former heavyweight boxing
champion Jack Dempsey and his associates
regarding their new venture of boxing
promotions. Fox Movietone, 1930.
         1 reel (7 in.) 7 1/2 in. per sec.
phonotape.

             BOXING
Voice Lib.
540   Dempsey, Jack, 1895 -
bd. 17   Sports and boxing. Fox Movietone,
1933.
         1 reel (7 in.) 7 1/2 in. per sec.
phonotape.

         1. Boxing.

Voice Lib. BOXING
M1029 Great moments in sports: boxing. Radio
bd.1   segments of actual sounds: excerpts of
well-known personalities in the boxing
world, centered around the career of
Joe Louis. Speakers: Don Dunphy, narrator;
Jess Willard, Jack Dempsey, James J. Corbett,
Thomas Farr, Max Schmeling, Joe Louis,
Tony Galento, Buddy Baer, Billy Conn,
Grantland Rice. MSU, Dept. of Television
and Radio, 1919-1950.
         1 reel (7 in.) 7 1/2 in. per sec. phonotape.

         L Boxing.

BOY SCOUTS
Voice Lib.
M975 Baden-Powell, Sir Robert Stephenson Smyth
bd.6   Baden-Powell, 1857-1941.
          Address about Wolf Cub Boy Scouts.
          Rococo-Can., 1910.
          1 reel (7 in.) 7 1/2 in. per sec.
          phonotape.

BOY SCOUTS
Voice Lib.
610   Baden-Powell, Sir Robert Stephenson Smyth
bd.2   Baden-Powell, 1857-1941.
          Speech opening Fifth World Scouting
          Jamboree, Holland. NBC, 1936.
          1 reel (7 in.) 7 1/2 in. per sec.
          phonotape.

Voice Lib.
M1257 Baden-Powell, Sir Robert Stephenson Smyth Baden-
bd.4   Powell, 1857-1944.
          Remarks by Lord Baden-Powell addressed to
          Queen Wilhelmina of Holland on the occasion
          of the 5ᵗʰ World Scout Jamboree, held at
          Vogelenzang (near Bloemendaal) Holland.
          Shortwave radio, July 31, 1937.
          1 reel (7 in.) 7 1/2 in. per sec.
          phonotape.

          1. Boy Scouts.

BOY SCOUTS
Voice Lib.
518   Beard, Daniel Carter, 1850-1941.
bd.2   On formation of the Boy Scouts of
          America. CRV, June 21, 1939.
          1 reel (7in.) 7 1/2 in. per sec.
          phonotape.

          1. Boy Scouts.

BOY SCOUTS
C1·
873   Whorf, Michael, 1933-
          The birth of the Boy Scouts.
          1 tape cassette. (The visual sounds of
          Mike Whorf. Social S73)
          Originally presented on his radio program, Kaleidoscope.
          WJR, Detroit.
          Duration 36 min., 35 sec.
          A historic narration of Lord Baden-Powell's life work of
          creating boys into young adults. The history of the Boy Scouts
          from its initiation to the present day world-wide organization is
          presented.

          L. Boy Scouts. 2. Baden-Powell, Sir Robert Stephenson
          Smyth- Baden-Powell, 1857-1944. L. Title.

BOY SCOUTS OF AMERICA
Voice Lib.
608   West, James Edward, 1876-
bd.2   Boy Scouts of America; comments during
          27th Boy Scout Anniversary Week, describes
          Boy Scout Jamboree in Washington, D.C., what
          scouting stands for, future accomplishments,
          presents Boy Scout statue to Fred Waring.
          New York City, WABC (CBS), February 13, 1937.
          1 reel (7 in.) 7 1/2 in. per sec.
          phonotape.

Boyce, Eddy
Voice Lib.
383   I can hear it now (radio program)
          CBS, February 9, 1951.
          1 reel (7 in.) 7 1/2 in. per sec.
          phonotape.
          L. Wilson, Charles Edward, 1886-1972. II. Gabrielson, Guy
          George, 1891-   III. Taft, Robert Alphonso, 1889-1953. IV.
          Martin, Joseph William, 1884-1965. V. McCarthy, Joseph
          Raymond, 1909-1957. VI. Benton, William Burnett, 1900-1973.
          VII. Malone, George Wilson, 1890-1961. VIII. Capehart, Homer
          Earl, 1897-   IX. Eisenhower, Dwight David, Pres. U.S., 1890-
          1969. X. Lee, J   V   XI. Hodge, John Reed, 1893-
          1963. XII. Overton, Watkins   XIII. DiSalle, Michael
          Vincent, 1908-   XIV. Boyce, Eddy   XV. Conklin, Ed
          XVI. Collins, Joseph Lawton, 1896-

Voice Lib.   Boyd, Derwood
M1739 Smith, Dianna
bd.4   Interviews with John Voss and Derwood Boyd,
          county commissioners, who proposed cutting
          their salaries. WKAR, June 14, 1974.
          5 min. phonotape (1 r. 7 1/2 i.p.s.)

          1. County government. 2. County officials
          and employees - Salaries, allowance, etc.
          I. Voss, John. II. Boyd, Derwood.

Voice Lib.   Boyer, Charles, 1899-
M619   Radio in the 1930's (Part II): a series of
bd.1-   excerpts of the 1930's; a sample of radio
14   of the period. NVL, April, 1964.
          1 reel (7 in.) 7 1/2 in. per sec. phonotape.
          L. Allen, Fred, 1894-1956. II. Delmar, Kenny   III. Donald,
          Peter   IV. Pious, Minerva   V. Fennelly, Parker   VI.
          Boyer, Charles, 1899-   VII. Dunne, Irene, 1904-   VIII.
          DeMille, Cecil Blount, 1881-1959. IX. West, Mae, 1893-   X.
          Dafoe, Allan Ray, 1883-1943. XI. Dionne quintuplets. XII. Ortega,
          Santos   XIII. War of the worlds (radio program) XIV. Ives, Burl,
          1909-   XV. Robinson, Earl, 1910-   XVI. Temple, Shirley,
          1928-   XVII. Earhart, Amelia, 1898-1937. XVIII. Lawrence,
          Gertrude, 1901-1952. XIX. Cohan, George Michael, 1878-1942.
          XX. Shaw, George Bernard, 1856-1950. XXI. Hitler, Adolf, 1889-
          1945. XXII. Chamberlain, Neville, 1869-1940. XXIII. Roosevelt,
          Franklin Delano, Pres. U.S., 1882-1945.

Brackett, Charles, 1892-1969
Voice Lib.
M275- Biography in sound (radio program)
276   Alexander Woollcott. N.B.C., date?
bd.1   2 reels (7 in.) 7 1/2 in. per sec.
          phonotape.

          L. Woollcott, Alexander, 1887-1943. L. Woollcott, Alexander,
          1887-1943. II. Banghardt, Kenneth   III. Hecht, Ben, 1893-
          1964. IV. Roosevelt, Eleanor (Roosevelt) 1884-1962. V. Walker,
          Danton   VI. Brackett, Charles, 1892-1969. VII. Grant,
          Jane   VIII. Rude, Robert Barnes   IX. West,
          Rebecca, pseud. X. Henessy, Joseph
          Charles   XII. Welles, Orson, 1915-   XL. Letterer,

C1
R29
BRADFORD, WILLIAM, 1588-1657

Whorf, Michael, 1933-
The best that is in me - William Bradford.
1 tape cassette. (The visual sounds of
Mike Whorf. Religion, R29)

Originally presented on his radio program, Kaleidoscope,
WJR, Detroit.
Duration: 35 min., 45 sec.
In the story of the hardships and the struggles of the Pilgrims'
journey to the New World, William Bradford stands out as a pillar
of strength. Instrumental in the success of the venture, at all
times he gave his best.

L. Bradford, William, 1588-1657. L Title.

Voice Lib.
M1477
Bradley, Benjamin C
Discussion of Supreme Court decision on
publishing Pentagon Papers. William B.
Macomber, deputy under-secretary of state;
Senator Henry Jackson; Max Frankel, head of
New York Times' Washington bureau; Benjamin
Bradley, executive editor of Washington Post.
Questioned by Carl Stern, NBC; Martin Hayden,
Detroit News; James J. Kilpatrick, Washington
Star Syndicate; Kenneth Crawford, Washington
Post; Edwin Newman. NBC-TV, June 30, 1971.
1 reel (7 in.) 7 1/2 in. per sec.
phonotape.

(Continued on next card)

Voice Lib.
M652
bd.16
Bradley, Omar Nelson, 1893-
U.S. does not want war; our problems
and responsibilities pertaining to this
policy. CBS [n.d.]
1 reel (7 in.) 7 1/2 i.p.s. phonotape.

1. U.S. - Foreign relations.

Voice Lib.
197
bd.2
Bradley, Omar Nelson, 1893-
Russian atomic bomb development, a speech
before American Forestry Association.
Detroit, WJR, October 12, 1949.
1 reel (7 in.) 7 1/2 in. per sec.
phonotape.

1. Atomic bomb - Russia.

Voice Lib.
M1368
Bradley, Omar Nelson, 1893-
Some friends of General Eisenhower (TV program)
CBS-TV special recalling anecdotes about
General Eisenhower by some of his friends:
Bob Hope, Kevin McCann, General Omar Bradley,
Robert B. Anderson, General Alfred Gruenther,
with Walter Cronkite acting as emcee. CBS-TV,
March 29, 1969.
1 reel (7 in.) 7 1/2 in. per sec.

L. Eisenhower, Dwight David, Pres. U.S., 1890-1969. L.
Hope, Bob, 1903- II. McCann, Kevin III. Bradley, Omar
Nelson, 1893- IV. Anderson, Robert Bernard, 1910- V.
Gruenther, Alfred Maximilian, 1899- VI. Cronkite, Walter
Leland, 1916-

Voice Lib.
M1286
bd.1
Bradley, Omar Nelson, 1893-
Eisenhower, Dwight David, Pres. U.S., 1890-1969.
Conversation by Harry Reasoner with General
Dwight D. Eisenhower and General Omar N.
Bradley at Eisenhower's office in Gettysburg,
Pennsylvania, about the U.S. military partici-
pation in Vietnam and the conduct of it.
CBS-TV, November 28, 1967.
1 reel (7 in.) 7 1/2 in. per sec.
phonotape.

I. Reasoner, Harry, 1923- II. Bradley,
Omar Nelson, 1893-

Voice Lib.
M344
bd.19
Brandt, Willy, 1913-
Comments made to CBS after his news
conference on Berlin and the wall.
CBS, December 29, 1961.
1 reel (7 in.) 7 1/2 i.p.s. phonotape.

1. Berlin Wall (1961-

Voice Lib.
M312
bd.6
Brandt, Willy, 1913-
Assassination: excerpt of remarks by
Mayor Willy Brandt of Berlin. NBC,
November 23, 1963.
1 reel (7 in.) 7 1/2 in. per sec.
phonotape.

1. Kennedy, John Fitzgerald, Pres U.S.,
1917-1963.

Voice Lib.
131
bd.5
Brannen, Charles Franklin, 1903-
Address at Michigan State University,
with introduction by President John A.
Hannah. WKAR, 1961.
1 reel (7 in.) 7 1/2 in. per sec.
phonotape.

I. Hannah, John Alfred, 1902-

Voice Lib.
M1466
bd.22
Braun, Alfred
Newsreport and ceremony upon the funeral of
Gustav Streseman; eulogy by Alfred Braun.
Peteler, October 6, 1929.
1 reel (7 in.) 7 1/2 in. per sec.
phonotape.

1. Streseman, Gustav, 1878-1929. I. Braun,
Alfred

C1
H9
Brave, bold and bad
Whorf, Michael, 1933-
   Brave, bold and bad.
   1 tape cassette. (The visual sounds of
Mike Whorf. History and heritage, H9)
   Originally presented on his radio program, Kaleidoscope,
WJR, Detroit.
   Duration: 41 min.
   The gunslinger, the desperado, the hero, the villain. Was the
gunman a legend, or was he a paranoid psychopath? They
were men who included William Bonny, Sam Bass, Wyatt Earp
and Bill Hickock - about 250 men in all who were bad, bold
and brave - or were they"
   L. Frontier and pioneer life - The West. 2. Crime and
criminals - The West.   L. Title.

Brewster, Ralph Owen, 1888-1962
Voice Lib.
381-   I can hear it now (radio program)
382   CBS, April 26, 1951.
bd.1   2 reels (7 in.) 7 1/2 in. per sec. phonotape.
   L. Radio Free Europe. 2. Strategic Air Command. L.
Ridgway, Matthew Bunker, 1895-   II. Churchill, Winston Leonard
Spencer, 1874-1965. III. Bevan, Aneurin, 1897-1960. IV. Nixon,
Richard Milhous, Pres. U.S., 1913-   V. Kerr, Robert Samuel, 1896-
1963. VI. Brewster, Ralph Owen, 1888-1962. VII. Wherry, Kenneth
Spicer, 1892-195L VIII. Capehart, Homer Earl, 1897-   IX.
Lehman, Herbert Henry, 1878-1963. X. Taft, Robert Alphonso,
1889-1953. XL. Moody, Arthur Edson Blair, 1902-1954. XII.
Martin, Joseph William, 1884-1968. XIII. McMahon, James O'Brien,
1903-1952. XIV. MacArthur, Douglas, 1880-1964. XVII. Wilson,
Charles Edward, 1886-197?   VIII. Irvine, Clarence T

C1
825
BREAD
Whorf, Michael, 1933-
   The staff of life.
   1 tape cassette. (The visual sounds of
Mike Whorf. Social, S25)
   Originally presented on his radio program, Kaleidoscope,
WJR, Detroit.
   Duration: 41 min.
   This is the story of wheat, of bread, its impact on mankind,
where and how it is processed and utilized.

   L. Wheat. 2. Bread. L. Title.

Brice, Fanny, 1891-1951
Voice Lib.
M617   Radio in the 1920's: a series of excerpts
bd.1-   from important broadcasts of the 1920's,
bd.25   with brief prologue and epilogue; a sample
         of radio of the period. NVL, April, 1964.
         1 reel (7 in.)   7 1/2 in. per sec.
phonotape.
   L. Radio programs. L. Marconi, Guglielmo, marchese, 1874-
1937. IL. Kendall, H   G   III. Coolidge, Calvin, Pres. U.S.,
1872-1933. IV. Wilson, Woodrow, Pres. U.S., 1856-1924. V.
Roosevelt, Franklin Delano, Pres. U.S., 1882-1945. VI. Lodge,
Henry Cabot, 1850-1924. VII. LaGuardia, Fiorello Henry, 1882-1947.
VIII. The Happiness Boys (Radio program) IX. Gallagher and Sheen.
X. Barney Google. XL. Vallee, Rudy, 1901-   XII. The two
                         (Continued on next card)

Voice Lib.
353
bd.18
Bregon, Jack
Outbreak of Korean War and comments by
   various persons. NBC, July, 1950.
   1 reel (7 in.)   7 1/2 in. per sec.
phonotape.

   Original disc off-speed.
   Participants: Henry Cassidy, Merrill Mueller,
Edward Harper, Jack Bregon.

   I. Cassidy, Henry Clarence, 1910-   II.
Mueller, Merrill. III. Harper, Edward. IV.
Bregon, Jack.

C1
M3
BRICE, FANNY, 1891-1951

Whorf, Michael, 1933-
   Fanny.
   1 tape cassette. (The visual sounds of
Mike Whorf. Miscellaneous, M3)
   Originally presented on his radio program, Kaleidoscope,
WJR, Detroit.
   Duration: 30 min.
   Fanny Brice - songstress, comedienne, star of stage and broad-
casting, and girl who brought tears and laughter, who was able to
express on stage those qualities which were found in her own life.

   L. Brice, Fanny, 1891-1   L. Title.

Voice Lib.
M1607
bd.2
Brennan, Thomas E., 1929-
   Off the record. Interviewed by Tim
Skubick, Tom Green, Gary Schuster, and
Paul Weisenfeld. WKAR-TV, January 25, 1974.
   15 min. phonotape (1 r.   7 1/2 in. per
sec.)

   1. Courts - Michigan. I. Skubick, Tim.
II. Green, Tom. III. Schuster, Gary. IV.
Weisenfeld, Paul

C1
H4
BRIDGER, JAMES, 1804-1881
Whorf, Michael, 1933-
   The indispensable, Jim Bridger.
   1 tape cassette. (The visual sounds of
Mike Whorf. History and heritage, H4)
   Originally presented on his radio program, Kaleidoscope,
WJR, Detroit.
   Duration: 37 min., 30 sec.
   The country was unsettled and few men had gone beyond the
Mississippi; yet one man among the few would venture forth, to
trap, hunt, fight, explore, and to discover the marvels of the
frontier.

   L. Bridger, James, 1804-188L L. Title.

Voice Lib.
M1028
bd.2
Brewer, Teresa
Bowes, Edward, 1874-1946.
   Excerpt from radio's original "Amateur Hour",
with Ted Mack and Teresa Brewer. Michigan
State University, Department of Television and
Radio, 1940's.
   1 reel (7 in.)   7 1/2 in. per sec.
phonotape.

   I. Mack, Ted, 1904-   II. Brewer, Teresa

Voice Lib.
351
bd.1
Bridges, Doloris Thauvald
   Recalls her late Senator husband and
announces her desire to succeed him.
CBS, January 10, 1962.
   1 reel (7 in.)   7 1/2 in. per sec.
phonotape.

Voice Lib.
353   Bridges, Henry Styles, 1898-1961.
bd.5   Outbreak of Korean War; now is the time
         to act against Russia. NBC, July, 1950.
         1 reel (7 in.)   7 1/2 in. per sec.
         phonotape.

         Original disc off-speed.

         1. Korean War, 1950-1953

         The brilliant orator - Black Dan
C1
H74   Whorf, Michael, 1933-
         The brilliant orator - Black Dan; Daniel
         Webster.
         1 tape cassette.   (The visual sounds of
         Mike Whorf. History and heritage, H74)
         Originally presented on his radio program, Kaleidoscope,
         WJR, Detroit.
         Duration: 37 min., 45 sec.
         Here is the life and times of America's brilliant orator,
         Daniel Webster, with the emphasis on his deeds and thoughts -
         but primarily on his words.

         L Webster, Daniel, 1782-1852. L Title.

         Bring 'em back alive (radio program)
Voice Lib.
M965   Buck, Frank, 1884-1950.
bd.2   Fifteen-minute radio dramatization of
         RKO Radio pictures series: "Bring 'em
         Back Alive"; episode entitled "Ghost Tiger
         of Sungai". NBC, 1943.
         1 reel (7 in.)   7 1/2 in. per sec.
         phonotape.

         I. Bring 'em back alive (radio program)

Voice Lib.
M1481 Brinkley, David McClure, 1920-
bd.2   David Brinkley interviewed by Elizabeth
         Drew, Washington editor of Atlantic Monthly.
         On believing the government, thoroughness of
         TV news, bias, objectivity of newsmen, personal
         news philosophy, liberal press, visual news.
         1 reel (7 in.)   7 1/2 in. per sec.
         phonotape.

         I. Drew, Elizabeth

Voice Lib.
M935   Brinkley, David McClure, 1920-
bd.1   Interview with David Brinkley discussing
         growth and quality of television broad-
         casting; he compares FCC investigation with
         investigation of "payola"; analyzes types
         of programs that people want; control of
         programs by advertisers and advice on how
         to bring about better broadcasting era;
         stresses the ethic responsibility of broad-
         casters.
         1 reel (7 in.)   7 1/2 in. per sec.
         phonotape.

         Brinkley, David McClure, 1920-
Voice Lib.
M771   Gemini 4 (space flight): excerpts of announce-
bd.2   ments from NBC reporters and Gemini Control,
         regarding preparations for and the actual
         splashdown. Conversation with astronauts
         before pickup by helicopter. Dallas Townsend
         from carrier "Wasp" and David Brinkley and
         Chet Huntley for NBC. NBC TV, June 7, 1965.
         1 reel (7 in.) 7 1/2 in. per sec. phonotape.
         L Project Gemini. 2. McDivitt, James Alton, 1929-   3.
         White, Edward Higgins, 1930-1967. L McDivitt, James Alton,
         1929-   IL White, Edward Higgins, 1930-1967. IIL Townsend,
         Dallas.   IV. Brinkley, David McClure, 1920-   V. Huntley,
         Chet, 1911-1974.

         Brinkley, David McClure, 1920-
Voice Lib.
M772   Gemini 4 (space flight): pickup of astronauts
bd.1   McDivitt and White and the capsule, described
         by Chet Huntley and David Brinkley. NBC TV,
         June 7, 1965.
         1 reel (7 in.)   7 1/2 in. per sec.
         phonotape.

         1. Project Gemini. 2. McDivitt, James Alton,
         1929-   3. White, Edward Higgins, 1930-1967.
         I. McDivitt, James Alton, 1929-   II. White,
         Edward Higgins, 1930-1967. III. Huntley, Chet,
         1911-1974.IV. Brinkley, David McClure, 1920-

Voice Lib.
M796- Brinkley, David McClure, 1920-
799   White Paper, on U.S. foreign policy from
         post World War II period to current hostilities
         in Vietnam, with various commentators, U.S.
         government officials, foreign dignitaries,
         and actual scenes and sound. NBC-TV,
         September 7, 1965.
         4 reels (7 in.) 7 1/2 in. per sec. phonotape.

         Running time approximately 3 hours.

         L U.S. - Foreign policy. L Huntley, Chet, 1911-1974.

         Brinkley, David McClure, 1920-
Voice Lib.
M917   Gemini 7 (space flight): Frank McGee's resumé
bd.1   of space flights of astronauts Frank Borman
         and James Lovell, Jr., in Gemini 7, commencing
         Dec. 4, 1956 to Dec. 18, 1965, and of astro-
         nauts Walter Schirra and Thomas Stafford in
         Gemini 6, which rendezvoused in space;
         including various launching actual reports
         and interview with Wally Schirra; comments
         by Huntley and Brinkley. NBC TV, December
         18, 1965.
         1 reel (7 in.)   7 1/2 in. per sec.
         phonotape.   <del>(Continued on next card)</del>

         Brinkley, David McClure, 1920-
Voice Lib.
M986   Gemini 9 (space flight): a. Take-off of
bd.2   Augmented Target Docking Adaptor (ATDA)
         from Cape Kennedy (June 1); b. re-cap
         by David Brinkley regarding failure of
         shroud to jettison (June 3); c. Gemini 9
         until failure of guidance system computer
         and then scrubbing mission (June 1)
         NBC TV, June 1 and 3, 1966.
         1 reel (7 in.) 7 1/2 in. per sec. phonotape.
         L Project Gemini. 2. Stafford, Thomas P   1931-   3.
         Cernan, Eugene Andrew, 1934-   L Stafford, Thomas P
         1931-   IL Cernan, Eugene Andrew, 1934- IIL Brinkley,
         David McClure, 1920-

Voice Lib. Brinkley, David McClure, 1920-
M968 Gemini 9 (space flight): description of
bd.2 countdown and lift-off of "Agena" by
Gemini Mission Control (voice of Al Chop)
for a period of 11 minutes, 41 seconds,
until Gemini flight was scrubbed. Comments
by NBC's Huntley, Brinkley, and Frank McGee.
NBC TV, May 17, 1966.
1 reel (7 in.) 7 1/2 in. per sec. phonotape.
L. Project Gemini. 2. Stafford, Thomas P 1931- 3.
Cernan, Eugene Andrew, 1934- L Stafford, Thomas P 1931-
H. Cernan, Eugene Andrew, 1934- III. Chop, Al IV.
Huntley, Chet, 1911-1974.V. Brinkley, David McClure, 1920-
VL McGee, Frank, 1921-1974.

Voice Lib. Brinkley, David McClure, 1920-
M1398 From here to the seventies, Part III. NBC-TV
bd.1 two-and-a-half hour documentary pertaining to
events occurring during the 1960's. NBC-TV,
October 7, 1969.
1 reel (7 in.) 7 1/2 in. per sec.
phonotape.
CONTENTS. -L. Style changes: a. clothes; b. sex; c. violence;
d. outlook; e. morals; f. sports and protest. -2. Man's mortality:
a. death of Winston Churchill; b. Bobby Kennedy, speech before
assassination; c. Dr. King, "I've been to the mountain top..." and
"We'll get to the Promised Land"; d. John Kennedy's last speech. -
3. Hunger around the world: a. Green Revolution, problems and
benefits; b. abortions to control population. -4. Communications
(Continued on next card)

Voice Lib. Brinkley, David McClure, 1920-
M1398 From here to the seventies, Part III... 1969.
bd.1 (Card 2)
CONTENTS, cont'd. explosion: a. David Brinkley, TV. -6. Ending:
a. Paul Newman; b. Barbra Streisand.

I. Kennedy, Robert Francis, 1925-1968. II.
King, Martin Luther, 1929-1968. III. Kennedy,
John Fitzgerald, Pres.U.S., 1917-1963. IV.
Brinkley, David McClure, 1920- V. Newman,
Paul, 1925- . VI. Streisand, Barbra, 1942-

Voice Lib. Brinkley, David McClure, 1920-
M1460 Huntley, Chet, 1911-
bd.3 Farewell remarks by Chet Huntley upon
leaving post at NBC after 14 years. Added
comments by David Brinkley. NBC-TV,
June 30, 1970.
1 reel (7 in.) 7 1/2 in. per sec.
phonotape.

I. Brinkley, David McClure, 1920-

Voice Lib. Brinkley, David McClure, 192C-
M1346 Nixon, Richard Milhous, Pres. U.S., 1913-
bd.2 Post-1968 election news described by
Huntley, Brinkley and other NBC staff men.
Statements of victory by Nixon and of defeat
by Humphrey; also by Wallace and LeMay.
Comments from countries overseas. Report of
Congressional elections. NBC-TV, November 6,
1968.
1 reel (7 in.) 7 1/2 in. per sec.
L. Huntley, Chet, 1911- II. Brinkley, David McClure, 1920-
III. Humphrey, Hubert Horatio, 1911- IV. Wallace, George
Corley, 1919- V. LeMay, Curtis Emerson, 1906-

Voice Lib.
M715 British Broadcasting Corporation.
bd.3 Information to British public regarding
the closing of cinema theaters and
instructions on air raid warning signals.
BBC, 1939.
1 reel (7 in.) 7 1/2 in. per sec.
phonotape.

1. Great Britain - Civilian defense

Voice Lib.
M736 British Broadcasting Corporation.
bd.2 Announcing via radio the invasion of
Holland and Belgium by the Nazis. BBC,
May 10, 1940.
1 reel (7 in.) 7 1/2 in. per sec.
phonotape.

Voice Lib.
M1463 British Broadcasting Corporation.
bd.15 BBC beaming songs with German lyrics to
Nazi troops: "Lili Marlene" parody and "Lady
in the dark" parody. Peteler, 1944.
1 reel (7 in.) 7 1/2 i.p.s. phonotape.

1. World War, 1939-1945 - Songs and music.

Voice Lib.
205 British Broadcasting Corporation
D-Day, 1944; being views expressed by
combatants and reporters. BBC, June 6,
1944.
1 reel (7 in.) 7 1/2 in. per sec.
phonotape.

1. World War, 1939-1945 - Campaigns -
Normandy.

Voice Lib.
M316 British Broadcasting Corporation.
bd.1 This was the week that was; comments and
reminiscences of Kennedy by the cast of
weekly BBC show; a rebroadcast of original
live show of November 23, 1963, including
poem "To Jackie" by Dame Sybil Thorndike.
NBC, November 24, 1963.
1 reel (7 in.) 7 1/2 i.p.s. phonotape.

1. Kennedy, John Fitzgerald, Pres. U.S.,
1917-1963 - Assassination. I. Thorndike,
Dame Sybil, 1882-

Voice Lib.
M1053 British Broadcasting Corporation.
Radio program from BBC in London congratulating NBC in U.S. on its 30th anniversary;
featuring stage and screen personalities, also
excerpts of speeches by FDR, Chamberlain, and
Churchill. BBC Radio, 1956.
1 reel (7 in.) 7 1/2 in. per sec.
phonotape.

I. National Broadcasting Company, Inc.

Voice Lib.
M125   British election campaign speeches.
Private recording, 1929.
1 reel (7 in.) 7 1/2 i.p.s.   phonotape.

CONTENTS. -bd. 1. Lloyd George, unemployment. -bd. 2.
Stanley Baldwin, conservative achievements. - bd. 3. William
Joynson-Hicks, why I am a conservative. -bd. 4. Taming
Worthington-Evans, how to vote at election. -bd. 5. Philip
Snowden, finance. -bd. 6. Margaret Bondfield, the women's
opportunity. -bd. 7. Thomas, J. H., the British Empire.

I. Gt. Brit. Parliament - Elections.

                    Brokaw, Tom
Voice Lib.
M1726   Aaron, Hank, 1934-
bd.3   Interviewed on Hank Aaron Day in New York
City, by Curt Gowdy, Joe Garagiola, Tom
Brokaw, and Gene Shalitt. NBC, June 18,
1974.
10 min.   phonotape (1 r.   7 1/2 i.p.s.)

1. Aaron, Hank, 1934-   2. Baseball.
I. Gowdy, Curt. II. Garagiola, Joe.
III. Brokaw, Tom.   Shalitt, Gene.

Voice Lib.
M616   Brokenshire, Norman Ernest, 1898-1965.
bd.1   The minstrel and the story man, a
radio program for children. GRV, 1946.
1 reel (7 in.) 7 1/2 i.p.s.   phonotape.

I. Title.

        Brokenshire, Norman Ernest, 1898-1965
Voice Lib.
M617   Radio in the 1920's: a series of excerpts
bd.1-   from important broadcasts of the 1920's,
bd.25   with brief prologue and epilogue; a sample
of radio of the period. NVL, April, 1964.
1 reel (7 in.) 7 1/2 in. per sec.
phonotape.
I. Radio programs. I. Marconi, Guglielmo, marchese, 1874-
1937. II. Kendall, H   G   III. Coolidge, Calvin, Pres. U.S.,
1872-1933. IV. Wilson, Woodrow, Pres. U.S., 1856-1924. V.
Roosevelt, Franklin Delano, Pres. U.S., 1882-1945. VI. Lodge,
Henry Cabot, 1850-1924. VII. LaGuardia, Fiorello Henry, 1882-1947.
VIII. The Happiness Boys (Radio program) IX. Gallagher and Sheen.
X. Barney Google. XI. Vallee, Rudy, 1901-   XII. The two
(Continued on next card)

Voice Lib.
M1722   Brooke, Edward William, 1919-
Graduation address at Michigan State
University. WKAR-TV, June 9, 1974.
30 min.   phonotape (1 r.   7 1/2 i.p.s.)

Voice Lib.
M791   Brooks, Gwendolyn, 1917-
Reading her poems at Asilomar Negro
Writers Conference. Los Angeles, KPFK,
December 20, 1964.
1 reel (7 in.) 7 1/2 in. per sec.
phonotape.

C1   Brooks Adams
FA22   Whorf, Michael, 1933-
Brooks Adams.
1 tape cassette. (The visual sounds of
Mike Whorf. The forgotten America, FA22)

Originally presented on his radio program, Kaleidoscope,
WJR, Detroit.
Duration: 12 min., 47 sec.
A philosopher of history, he stood alone preaching simplicity,
responsibility, honor, and service.

I. Adams, Brooks, 1848-1927. I. Title.

        Broun, Heywood Campbell, 1888-1939
Voice Lib.
M272   Biography in sound (radio program)
bd.1   Heywood Broun. NBC, date?
1 reel (7 in.) 7 1/2 in. per sec.
phonotape.

I. Broun, Heywood Campbell, 1888-1939. I. Broun,
Heywood Campbell, 1888-1939. II. Swope, Herbert Bayard,
1882-1958. III. Wilson, Mattie   IV. Jackson, Gardner
V. Meany, Thomas   VI. Waldron, Beatrice   VII.
Gordon, Max   VIII. Madison, Connie   IX. Gannett,
Lewis Stiles, 1891-1966. X. Collins, Joseph, 1866-1950. XI.
Brown, Earl Louis, 1900-   XII. Levy, Newman, 1888-
XIII. Growth, John   XIV. Bye, George   XV.
Roosevelt, Franklin Delar   Pres. U.S., 1882-1945. XVI.
Reynolds, Quentin James   -1965.

Voice Lib.
210   Browder, Earl Russell, 1891-
bd.1   Campaign speech for the Presidency, 1940.
CBS, October 10, 1940.
1 reel (7 in.) 7 1/2 in. per sec.
phonotape.

Voice Lib.
M739   Brown, Cecil B   1907-
bd.9   A reading of a report from Brown to
        John Daly, describing Brown's rescue from
        the British ship "Repulse" off the coast of
        Burma. CBS, April 2, 1942.
           1 reel (7 in.)   7 1/2 in. per sec.
        phonotape.

Voice Lib.
M946   Brown, John Mason, 1900-1969.
bd.1   Remarks from his bed in hospital room
        for playback at dinner for Aimee Loveman,
        editor, Saturday Review.   GRV, private
        recording, 1940.
           1 reel (7 in.)   7 1/2 in. per sec.
        phonotape.

                    Brown, Earl Louis, 1900-
Voice Lib.
M272   Biography in sound (radio program)
bd.1   Heywood Broun. NBC, date?
           1 reel (7 in.)   7 1/2 in. per sec.
        phonotape.

           I. Broun, Heywood Campbell, 1888-1939. I. Broun,
        Heywood Campbell, 1888-1939. II. Swope, Herbert Bayard,
        1882-1958. III. Wilson, Mattie   IV. Jackson, Gardner
        V. Meany, Thomas   VI. Waldron, Beatrice   VII.
        Gordon, Max   VIII. Madison, Connie   IX. Gannett,
        Lewis Stiles, 1891-1966. X. Collins, Joseph, 1866-1950. XI.
        Brown, Earl Louis, 1900-   XII. Levy, Newman, 1888-
        XIII. Growth, John   XIV. Bye, George   XV.
        Roosevelt, Franklin Delano, Pres. U.S., 1882-1945. XVI.
        Reynolds, Quentin James, ?-1965.

Voice Lib.
M1701   Brown, Lester Russell, 1934-
           International agricultural development.
        WKAR, October 31, 1968.
           90 min. phonotape (1 r.   7 1/2 i.p.s.)

           1. Agricultural assistance, American.

Voice Lib.
353   Russia and the bomb, discussed by various
bd.19   personalities. NBC, September 25, 1949.
           1 reel (7 in.)   7 1/2 in. per sec.
        phonotape.

           Participants: Harrison Brown, Harold Urey,
        Samuel Allison, Thornton Hugness, Brien McMahon,
        Paul Douglas, John Foster Dulles, Leslie Groves,
        Winston Churchill, Dean Acheson, James Fleming.

           I. Brown, Harrison Scott, 1917-   II.
        Urey, Harold Clayton, 1893-   III. Allison,

                                   (Continued on next card)

Voice Lib.
M1428   Brown, Steve
           Interview with Steve Brown, early New
        Orleans jazz musician, by Frank Gillis,
        Director of Folk Music Archive, Indiana
        University. 1953.
           1 reel (7 in.)   3 3/4 in. per sec.
        phonotape.

           Full track tape.
           I. Gillis, Frank   1. Jazz music

                    Brown, Harrison Scott, 1917-
Voice Lib.
353   Russia and the bomb...   1949.   (Card 2)
bd.19

           Samuel King, 1900-   IV. Hugness, Thornton.
        V. McMahon, James O'Brien, 1903-1952. VI.
        Douglas, Paul Howard, 1892-   VII. Dulles,
        John Foster, 1888-1959. VIII. Groves, Leslie
        R   1896-1970. IX. Churchill, Winston
        Leonard Spencer, 1874-1965. X. Acheson, Dean
        Gooderham, 1893-1971. XI. Fleming, James,
        1915-

           BROWNING, ELIZABETH (BARRETT) 1806-1861
C1
A12   Whorf, Michael, 1933-
           The eternal Romance.
           1 tape cassette. (The visual sounds of
        Mike Whorf. Art, music, and letters, A12)

           Originally presented on his radio program, Kaleidoscope,
        WJR, Detroit.
           Duration: 37 min.
           The tender romance of Elizabeth Barrett and Robert Browning,
        a story of a sickly young woman and her love for the tempestuous
        Browning.

           1. Browning, Elizabeth (Barrett) 1806-1861. 2. Browning,
        Robert, 1812-1889.   I. Title.

           BROWN, JOHN, 1800-1859
C1
H26   Whorf, Michael, 1933-
           The man from Osawattmie - John Brown's story.
           1 tape cassette. (The visual sounds of
        Mike Whorf. History and heritage, H26)
           Originally presented on his radio program, Kaleidoscope,
        WJR, Detroit.
           Duration: 30 min.
           Fanatic or hero, prophet or fool; here is the life and times
        of old John Brown.

           1. Brown, John, 1800-1859. I. Title.

           BROWNING, ROBERT, 1812-1889
C1
A12   Whorf, Michael, 1933-
           The eternal Romance.
           1 tape cassette. (The visual sounds of
        Mike Whorf. Art, music, and letters, A12)

           Originally presented on his radio program, Kaleidoscope,
        WJR, Detroit.
           Duration: 37 min.
           The tender romance of Elizabeth Barrett and Robert Browning,
        a story of a sickly young woman and her love for the tempestuous
        Browning.

           1. Browning, Elizabeth (Barrett) 1806-1861. 2. Browning,
        Robert, 1812-1889.   I. Title.

Voice Lib.
M1470 Brüning, Heinrich, 1885-1970.
bd.2   Explanation of governmental policies in
        the Reichstag. Peteler, October 13, 1931.
        1 reel (7 in.)   7 1/2 in. per sec.
        phonotape.

        1. Germany - Politics and government -
        1918-1933.

Voice Lib.
291   Bryan, William Jennings, 1860-1925.
bd.6   Swollen fortunes. Edison, 1902.
        1 reel (7 in.)   7 1/2 in. per sec.
        phonotape.

Voice Lib.
M1250 Bryan, William Jennings, 1860-1925.
bd.3   Address before Democratic national
        convention, popularly known as his "Cross
        of Gold" speech. Chicago, 1896.
        1 reel (7 in.)   7 1/2 in. per sec.
        phonotape.

        I. Title: Cross of gold.

Voice Lib.
291   Bryan, William Jennings, 1860-1925.
bd.4   Immortality. Edison, 1903.
        1 reel (7 in.)   7 1/2 in. per sec.
        phonotape.

Voice Lib.
291   Bryan, William Jennings, 1860-1925.
bd.3   Cross of Gold speech; address before
        the Democratic Convention in 1896;
        bimetalism.   Gennett, 1896 [1921].
        1 reel (7 in.)   7 1/2 in. per sec.
        phonotape.

Voice Lib.
M756 Bryan, William Jennings, 1860-1925.
bd.2   Immortality; examples of resurrection in
        plant and animal life, giving proof that
        there is a life hereafter. Columbia, 1910.
        1 reel (7 in.)   7 1/2 in. per sec.
        phonotape.

Voice Lib.
M1615 Bryan, William Jennings, 1860-1925.
bd.4   Immortality. Rare Records, Inc., H805
        [19--?]
        2 min., 25 sec.   phonotape (1 r.
        7 1/2 i.p.s.)

Voice Lib.
M756 Bryan, William Jennings, 1860-1925.
bd.3   Mysteries; excerpt from "The Prince of
        Peace" stressing the point that science does
        not explain origin of life. VTM, 1910.
        1 reel (7 in.)   7 1/2 in. per sec.
        phonotape.

Voice Lib.
291   Bryan, William Jennings, 1860-1925.
bd.5   Imperialism. Edison, 1901.
        1 reel (7 in.)   7 1/2 in. per sec.
        phonotape.

Voice Lib.
291   Bryan, William Jennings, 1860-1925.
bd.2   Popular election of senators. Edison,
        1910.
        1 reel (7 in.)   7 1/2 in. per sec.
        phonotape.

Voice Lib.
M756   Bryan, William Jennings, 1860-1925.
bd.5   The tariff question; the burdens of the
        protective tariff on the public.   VTM.
        1910.
            1 reel (7 in.)   7 1/2 in. per sec.
        phonotape.

BRYAN, WILLIAM JENNINGS, 1860-1925

C1
H57   Whorf, Michael, 1933-
            The life and times of William Jennings Bryan.
        1 tape cassette.   (The visual sounds of
        Mike Whorf. History and heritage, H57)

        Originally presented on his radio program, Kaleidoscope,
        WJR, Detroit.
        Duration: 39 min.
        Here is the plea of Bryan for silver, his courageous stand as
        pacifist - his inner conflict, his court battle at the Scopes trial -
        his untimely demise - this is the story of the dauntless persistence
        of William Jennings Bryan.

            L. Bryan, William Jennings, 1860-1925. L. Title.

Voice Lib.
M756   Bryan, William Jennings, 1860-1925.
bd.4   The trust question; explaining the evils
        of monopolies.   VTM, 1910.
            1 reel (7 in.)   7 1/2 in. per sec.
        phonotape.

Voice Lib.
353   Bryan, Wright
bd.12   Outbreak of Korean War; on beginning of
        World War III.   NBC, July, 1950.
            1 reel (7 in.)   7 1/2 in. per sec.
        phonotape.

        Original disc off-speed.

            1. Korean War, 1950-1953

Voice Lib.
653   Bryan, William Jennings, 1860-1925.
bd.6   The labor question, eight-hour day,
        employer's liability act, formation of
        Labor Department, Democratic platform;
        injunctions, law modification.   Edison,
        1912.
            1 reel (7 in.)   7 1/2 in. per sec.
        phonotape.

Voice Lib. Brynner, Yul, 1917-
M669-   The legend of Cecil B. Demille. Yul
670   Brynner, Charlton Heston, Bob Hope, Betty
        Hutton, Edward G. Robinson, Barbara Stanwyck,
        James Stewart, Gloria Swanson, Cornel
        Wilde, Samuel Goldwyn, Billy Graham, Cecil
        B. DeMille.   Recorded 1963.
        2 reels (7 in.) 7 1/2 in. per sec. phonotape.

        L. DeMille, Cecil Blount, 1881-1959. L. Brynner, Yul, 1917-
        II. Heston, Charlton, 1924-   III. Hope, Bob, 1903-   IV.
        Hutton, Betty, 1921-   V. Robinson, Edward G   1893-1973.
        VI. Stanwyck, Barbara, 1907-   VII. Stewart, James Maitland,
        1908-   VIII. Swanson, Gloria, 1899?-   IX. Wilde, Cornel, 1915-
        X. Goldwyn, Samuel, 1884?-   XI. Graham, William Franklin,
        1918-   XII. DeMille, Cecil Blount, 1881-1959.

Voice Lib.
653   Bryan, William Jennings, 1860-1925.
bd.7   The railroad question; I.C.C. enlargement;
        Democratic party policies on railroads.
        Edison, 1912.
            1 reel (7 in.)   7 1/2 in. per sec.
        phonotape.

        Buchanan, Scott Milross, 1895-1968
Voice Lib.
M978   Krauch, Helmut
bd.1   Expressing his opinions about the role of
        the scientist in society, his obligation to
        promote the social welfare. Interview with
        Dr. Krauch at the Center for the Study of
        Democratic Institutions at Santa Barbara by
        Scott Buchanan.   CSDI, 1963.
            1 reel (7 in.)   7 1/2 in. per sec.
        phonotape.

            I. Buchanan, Scott Milross, 1895-1968.

Voice Lib.
M840   Bryan, William Jennings, 1860-1925.
bd.9   Narrating "23rd Psalm".   Gennett, 1920.
            1 reel (7 in.)   7 1/2 in. per sec.
        phonotape.

        Buchanan, Scott Milross, 1895-1968
Voice Lib.
M1079   Meiklejohn, Alexander, 1872-
            Excerpts of reading from his unfinished
        book on education in a free society, the
        American liberal college, etc. Introductory
        remarks by Dr. Scott Buchanan.   CSDI,
        January, 1963.
            1 reel (7 in.)   7 1/2 in. per sec.
        phonotape.

            I. Buchanan, Scott Milross, 1895-1968.

Dictionary Catalog

69

Voice Lib.
M212   Buck, Gene, 1885-1957.
bd.1   American composers and their music at the
          Golden Gate International Exposition.
          ASCAP, September 24, 1940.
          1 reel (7 in.)   7 1/2 i.p.s.   phonotape.

          1. Composers, American.

Voice Lib.
M865   Buck, Frank, 1884-1950.
bd.2   Fifteen-minute radio dramatization of
          RKO Radio pictures series: "Bring 'em
          Back Alive"; episode entitled "Ghost Tiger
          of Sungai". NBC, 1043.
          1 reel (7 in.)   7 1/2 in. per sec.
          phonotape.

          I. Bring 'em back alive (radio program)

Voice Lib.
M300   Buck, Pearl (Sydenstricker), 1892-1973.
bd.1   Gandhi's life and virtue.   Voice
          of America, April 25, 1960.
          1 reel (7 in.)   7 1/2 in. per sec.
          phonotape.

          1. Gandhi, Mohandas Karamchand, 1869-1948.

                    Buckley, William Frank, 1925-
Voice Lib.
M1698   Aspin, Les, 1938-
bd.2   Interviewed on Firing Line by William
          Buckley. WKAR-TV, May 28, 1974.
          15 min.   phonotape (1 r.   7 1/2 i.p.s.)

          1. Industry and state - U.S. 2. U.S. -
          Military policy. I. Buckley, William
          Frank, 1925-

                    Buckley, William Frank, 1925-
Voice Lib.
M1750   Berman, Richard
          Government and the arts; on "Firing Line"
          with William F. Buckley. WKAR, June 28,
          1974.
          45 min.   phonotape (1 r.   7 1/2 i.p.s.)

          1. The Arts - U. S. 2. Art and State. 3.
          State encourgement of science, literature,
          and art - U. S.   I. Buckley, William Frank,
          1925-

Voice Lib.   Buckley, William Frank, 1925-
M1640   Bond, Julian, 1940-
          Politics and Black progress, on "Firing
          Line" with William F. Buckley and John
          Lewis. WKAR-FM, March 17, 1974.
          45 min.   phonotape (1 r.   7 1/2 i.p.s.)

          1. Negroes - Politics and suffrage.
          I. Buckley, William Frank, 1925-
          II. Lewis, John.

                    Buckley, William Frank, 1925-
Voice Lib.
M1731   Clark, Ramsey, 1927-
          Debate on amnesty for draft evaders on
          "Firing Line" with William Buckley. WKAR,
          June 21, 1974.
          45 min.   (1 r.   7 1/2 i.p.s.)

          1. Military service, compulsory - U. S.
          2. Vietnamese conflict, 1961-   I. Buckley,
          William Frank, 19

Voice Lib.   Buckley, William Frank, 1925-
M1665   Hunt, Everette Howard, 1918-
          On "Firing line" about Watergate payments,
          with William Buckley, Ralph Fine, John Owen,
          and Miss Bernstein. WKAR-TV, May 14, 1974.
          50 min.   phonotape (1 r.   7 1/2 i.p.s.)

          1. Watergate Affair, 1972-   I.
          Buckley, William Frank, 1925-   II. Fine,
          Ralph Adam, 1941-   III. Owen, John

                    Buckley, William Frank, 1925-
Voice Lib.
M1561   Muskie, Edmund S   1914-
          Firing line, interviewed by William
          Buckley. WKAR-AM, February 15, 1974.
          25 min.   phonotape (1 r.   7 1/2 i.p.s.)

          1. U.S. - Politics and government - 1969-
          I. Buckley, William Frank, 1925-

                    Buckley, William Frank, 1925-
Voice Lib.
M1546-   Rusk, Dean, 1909-
1547,   Interview on William F. Buckley's Firing
bd.1   Line show. WKAR-FM, February 5, 1974.
          40 min.   phonotape (2 r.   7 1/2 i.p.s.)

          1. Vietnamese Conflict, 1961-   - U.S.
          I. Buckley, William Frank, 1925-

Voice Lib.   Buckley, William Frank, 1925-
M1683   Sayegh, Fayez Abdullah, 1922-
      Interviewed by William Buckley on Firing
    Line. WKAR-TV, May 21, 1974.
      45 min. phonotape (1 r. 7 1/2 i.p.s.)

      1. Arab countries - Relations (general)
with Israel. 2. Israel - Relations (general)
with Arab countries. I. Buckley, William
Frank, 1925-

        The bugler of Balaclava
Voice Lib.
M1008 Ripley, Robert LeRoy, 1893-1949.
bd.2   Rehearsal and discussion regarding text
    of introductory remarks to the recording
    of "The Bugler of Balaclava" with G.R. Vincent,
    followed by 1890 recording of trumpeter
    Kenneth Landfrey. NVL location recording.
    August 7, 1939.
      1 reel (7 in.) 7 1/2 in. per sec.
    phonotape.
      I. Vincent, G   Robert. II. Landfrey, Kenneth.
III. Title: The bugler of Balaclava.

      Buckley, William Frank, 1925-
Voice Lib.
M1740 Williams, Edward Bennett
bd.1   Discusses the Warren Supreme Court on Firing
    Line with William F. Buckley. WKAR, June 14,
    1974.
      20 min. phonotape (1 r. 7 1/2 i.p.s.)

      1. U. S. Supreme Court - Hist. I.
Buckley, William Frank, 1925-

      BULL-FIGHTS
C1
M51   Whorf, Michael, 1933-
      Trumpets in the afternoon --legend and
    sport of bullfight.
      1 tape cassette. (The visual sounds of
    Mike Whorf. Miscellaneous, M51)
      Originally presented on his radio program, Kaleidoscope,
WJR, Detroit.
      Duration: 37 min.
      The unique world of the bullfight arena: the blood, the gore,
the colorful spectacle of brave matadors and their worthy
opponents - the ground-scraping, glaring black bull.
      I. Bull-fights. I. Title.

Voice Lib.
M952 Bülow, Bernhard Heinrich Martin Karl,
bd.9   fürst von, 1849-1929.
      Discussing past German history. H.E. Scholz,
    November 30, 1917.
      1 reel (7 in.) 7 1/2 in. per sec.
    phonotape.

      BUONARROTI, MICHEL ANGELO, 1475-1564
C1
A20   Whorf, Michael, 1933-
      Giant of the age, Michelangelo.
      1 tape cassette. (The visual sounds of
    Mike Whorf. Art, music, and letters, A20)
      Originally published on his radio program, Kaleidoscope,
WJR, Detroit.
      Duration: 28 min., 50 sec.
      His life and the story of his works unfolds in this narrative
dealing with the world of Michelangelo.

      I. Buonarroti, Michel Angelo, 1475-1564. I. Title.

C1   Buffalo Bill
H55   Whorf, Michael, 1933-
      Buffalo Bill.
      1 tape cassette. (The visual sounds of
    Mike Whorf. History and heritage, H55)
      Originally presented on his radio program, Kaleidoscope,
WJR, Detroit.
      Duration: 41 min.
      Scout, soldier, Indian fighter, impressario, entrepreneur;
he was all of these, yet above all, William Frederick Cody was
a legend.

      I. Cody, William Frederick, 1846-1917. I. Title.

Voice Lib.
M715 Burdett, Winston, 1913-
bd.11   Excerpt of broadcast during Israeli-
    Egyptian conflict. CBS, October 31, 1956.
      1 min., 40 sec. phonotape (1 r.
    7 1/2 i.p.s.)

      1. Sinai Campaign, 1956.

Voice Lib.
M341 Bugle call and taps at grave of Roosevelt's
bd.3   Rough Riders; comments by army sergeant.
    Columbia Test Cylinder, June 24, 1898.
      1 reel (7 in.) 7 1/2 i.p.s. phonotape.

      1. Phonorecords - History.

Voice Lib. Burdett, Winston, 1913-
M160 Joannes XXIII, Pope, 1881-1963.
bd.2   Shortwave broadcast of the election of
    Pope John XXIII from St. Peter's Square,
    the Vatican; Winston Burdett announcing.
    CBS, February 7, 1958.
      1 reel (7 in.) 7 1/2 in. per sec.
    phonotape.

      I. Burdett, Winston, 1913-

BUREAUCRACY
Voice Lib.
M1045 Minnow, Newton Norman, 1926-
bd. 2 "Bureaucracy is not muddling through". Address at two-day convocation at the 10th anniversary of the Freedom for the Republic in Los Angeles. Mr. Minnow's address is being narrated for the occasion, the subject being bureaucratic organization and procedures in U.S. government departments; also explains duty of FCC. CDI, 1963.
1 reel (7 in.) 7 1/2 L p. s. phonotape.

L. Bureaucracy.

Voice Lib. Burns, George, 1896-
M1047 Old-time radio excerpts of the 1930's and 1940's... (Card 2)

lecture; Al Jolson singing "Rocka-by-your baby"; and George Burns and Gracie Allen skit. TV&R, 1930's and 1940's.
1 reel (7 in.) 7 1/2 in. per sec.
L. Vallee, Rudy, 1901- II. Rogers, Will, 1879-1935. III. Crosby, Bing, 1901- IV. Cantor, Eddie, 1893-1964. V. Durante, Jimmy, 1893- VI. Clayton, Patti VII. Jackson, Eddie VIII. Hershfield, Harry, 1885- IX. Kyser, Kay, 1906- X. Smith, Kate, 1909- XI. Fields, W. C., 1879-1946. XII. Jolson, Al, 1886-1950. XIII. Burns, George, 1896- XIV. Allen, Gracie, 1906-

---

Voice Lib.
M1461 Burger, Warren Earl, 1907-
State of the judiciary message by Chief Justice Warren E. Burger. CBS, August 10, 1970.
1 reel (7 in.) 7 1/2 in. per sec. phonotape.

Voice Lib.
M313 Burns, James MacGregor, 1918-
bd.4 In an interview, Kennedy's biographer reflects on Kennedy's personality, his dealings with Congress, and his rating by historians. ABC, November 24, 1963.
1 reel (7 in.) 7 1/2 in. per sec. phonotape.

1. Kennedy, John Fitzgerald, Pres. U.S., 1917-1963.

C1
H76 BURKE, EDMUND, 1729?-1797
Whorf, Michael, 1933-
The English patriot, Edmund Burke.
1 tape cassette. (The visual sounds of Mike Whorf. History and heritage, H76)
Originally presented on his radio program, Kaleidoscope, WJR, Detroit.
Duration: 36 min.
This story not only details Edmund Burke's endeavors in America's cause, but also relates his own world.

L. Burke, Edmund, 1729?-1797. L. Title.

BURNS, ROBERT, 1759-1796
Voice Lib.
642 MacDonald, James Ramsay, 1866-1937.
bd.3 "A man amongst men"; eulogy for Robert Burns, poet. BBC, January 25, 1928.
1 reel (7 in.) 7 1/2 in. per sec. phonotape.

1. Burns, Robert, 1759-1796.

Voice Lib.
M1034 Burns, George, 1896-
bd.9 With Gracie Allen in radio comedy skit. TV&R, 1935.
1 reel (7 in.) 7 1/2 in. per sec. phonotape.

I. Allen, Gracie, 1905-

C1
A45 BURNS, ROBERT, 1759-1796
Whorf, Michael, 1933-
The immortal poet. - Robert Burns.
1 tape cassette. (The visual sounds of Mike Whorf. Art, music and letters, A45)
Originally presented on his radio program, Kaleidoscope, WJR, Detroit.
Duration: 37 min., 15 sec.
Romantic, poetic Robert Burns comes to life as his rhythmic verses are set to music. Much of his poetry is read, intimately revealing his various moods throughout his life.

L. Burns, Robert, 1759-1796. L. Title.

Burns, George, 1896-
Voice Lib.
M1047 Old-time radio excerpts of the 1930's and 1940's, including: Rudy Vallee singing "Linger a little longer"; Will Rogers on panaceas for the Depression; Bing Crosby singing "Sweet Georgia Brown"; Eddie Cantor; Jimmy Durante singing "Inka-dinka-do"; musical skit by Clayton, Jackson and Durante; wit by Harry Hershfield; musical selection "Thinking of you" by Kay Kyser; Kate Smith singing theme song, "When the moon comes over the mountain"; W.C. Fields' temperance

(Continued on next card)

C1
A14 BURNS, ROBERT, 1759-1796
Whorf, Michael, 1933-
My love is like a red, red rose.
1 tape cassette. (The visual sounds of Mike Whorf. Art, music, and letters, A14)
Originally presented on his radio program, Kaleidoscope, WJR, Detroit.
Duration: 35 min.
The Scottish highlands, the swirl of tartans, the pipes, the smell of heather, is the setting for the heart-warming story of Robert Burns.

1. Burns, Robert, 1759-1796. L. Title.

Voice Lib.
629   Burns, William John, 1861-1932.
bd.2   On his involvement in the San Francisco
Graft Trials.   Edison Laboratories, 1908.
1 reel (7 in.)   7 1/2 in. per sec.
phonotape.

Voice Lib.
M389   Bush, Vannevar, 1890-
bd.3   Development of nuclear weapons; problems
of outlawing the atomic bomb.   Hearst
Metrotone News, 1963.
1 reel (7 in.)   7 1/2 in. per sec.
phonotape.

1. Atomic weapons

Voice Lib.
611   Burr, Henry, 1885-1941.
bd.2   World War I song "Stay down where you belong."
Victor Talking Machine Co., 1917.
1 reel (7 in.)   7 1/2 in. per sec.
phonotape.

I. Title: Stay down where you belong.

The business of sex
Voice Lib.
M507-   Murrow, Edward Roscoe, 1908-1965.
508.   Narrates "The business of sex", dealing
bd.1   with prostitution and business; various
prostitutes and businessmen talk and
discuss dealings.   CBS, 1957.
2 reels (7 in.)   7 1/2 i.p.s.   phonotape.

1. Prostitution.   I. Title: The business
of sex.

Voice Lib.
M1706   Burton, Richard, 1925-
bd.1   Interview on Merv Griffin Show.
Columbia Broadcasting System, June 5, 1974.
10 min.   phonotape (1 r. 7   7 1/2 i.p.s.)

Burton speaks in English, Irish, Welsh,
and French.

1. Burton, Richard, 1925-   I. Griffin,
Mervyn Edward, 1925-

Voice Lib.
M795   Butler, Nicholas Murray, 1862-1947.
bd.8   "Save America"; a Republican campaign
speech of 1920.   The Nation's Forum, 1920.
1 reel (7 in.)   7 1/2 in. per sec.
phonotape.

1. Republican Party.
I. Title.

Burton, Richard, 1925-
Voice Lib.
126   Lerner, Alan Jay, 1918-
Lerner and Loewe; condensed NBC-TV special
with Julie Andrews, Richard Burton, Robert
Goulet, Alan Lerner and Frederick Loewe.
NBC, February 2, 1962.
1 reel (7 in.)   7 1/2 in. per sec.
phonotape.

I. Andrews, Julie, 1935-   II. Burton,
Richard, 1925-   III. Goulet, Robert
Gerard, 1933-   IV. Loewe, Frederick, 1904-

Voice Lib.
M1800   Butterfield, Alexander Porter, 1926-
WG   Testimony before the Senate Committee
0716.02   investigating the Watergate Affair.
Pacifica, July 16, 1973.
86 min.   phonotape (5 in.   3 3/4 i.p.s.)
(Watergate gavel to gavel, phase 1)

1. Watergate Affair, 1972-

Voice Lib.
M760   Burton, Robert J
bd.14   Excerpt from "The Big Beat" (Program 2);
comments on the content of the audience of
popular music.   Westinghouse Broadcasting
Corporation, 1964.
1 reel (7 in.)   7 1/2 in. per sec.
phonotape.   (The Music Goes Round and Round)

I. Title: The big beat.   II. Series.

By the dawn's early light - Francis Scott Key
C1
H33   Whorf, Michael, 1933-
By the dawn's early light - Francis Scott Key.
1 tape cassette.   (The visual sounds of
Mike Whorf.   History and heritage, H33)

Originally presented on his radio program, Kaleidoscope,
WJR, Detroit.
Duration: 37 min., 30 sec.
It was during the War of 1812 when Francis Scott Key wrote of
the momentous Battle of Fort McHenry.   This is the story of the
life and times of the man who wrote our national anthem.

1. Key, Francis Scott, 1779-1843.   I. Title.

Bye, George

Voice Lib.
M272 Biography in sound (radio program)
bd.1 Heywood Broun. NBC, date?
1 reel (7 in.) 7 1/2 in. per sec.
phonotape.

I. Broun, Heywood Campbell, 1888-1939. I. Broun,
Heywood Campbell, 1888-1939. II. Swope, Herbert Bayard,
1882-1958. III. Wilson, Mattie IV. Jackson, Gardner
V. Meany, Thomas VI. Waldron, Beatrice VII.
Gordon, Max VIII. Madison, Connie IX. Gannett,
Lewis Stiles, 1891-1966. X. Collins, Joseph, 1866-1950. XI.
Brown, Earl Louis, 1900- XII. Levy, Newman, 1888-
XIII. Growth, John XIV. Bye, George XV.
Roosevelt, Franklin Delan Pres. U.S., 1882-1945. XVI.
Reynolds, Quentin Jame ( )2-1965.

Voice Lib.
571 Byrd, Richard Evelyn, 1888-1957.
bd.3 Speech to Explorers' Club in New York
City describing work in Antarctica.
GRV, January 11, 1941.
1 reel (7 in.) 7 1/2 in. per sec.
phonotape.

Voice Lib.
M732 Byrd, Richard Evelyn, 1888-1957.
bd.2 "Keep America's record straight". Address
advocating cooperation with anti-Nazi
forces and support of U.S. government.
WABC Radio, October 8, 1941.
1 reel (7 in.) 7 1/2 in. per sec.
phonotape.

Voice Lib.
640 Byrd, Richard Evelyn, 1888-1957.
bd.4 Telephone conversation with G. R. Vincent
about his appearance on the Fred Allen
Show. GRV, October 10, 1941.
1 reel (7 in.) 7 1/2 in. per sec.
phonotape.

Voice Lib.
M671 Byrd, Richard Evelyn, 1888-1957.
bd.1 "Biography" TV program on exploits in
exploration by R. E. Byrd. Wolper Productions,
1962.
1 reel (7 in.) 7 1/2 in. per sec.
phonotape.

1. Byrd, Richard Evelyn, 1888-1957.

BYRD, RICHARD EVELYN, 1888-1957

Voice Lib.
640 Texaco Star Theater.
bd.6 Admiral Byrd skit. WABC Line, October 22,
1941.
1 reel (7 in.) 7 1/2 in. per sec.
phonotape.

BYRD ANTARCTIC EXPEDITION, 2D, 1933-1935

Voice Lib.
M630 Ober, Norman
bd.2 Interviews Roy Fitzsimons and Dr. Wade
upon their return from the Second Antarctic
Expedition, sponsored by Admiral Richard E.
Byrd. GRV, 1941.
1 reel (7 in.) 7 1/2 i.p.s. phonotape.

1. Byrd Antarctic Expedition, 2d,
1933-1935. I. Wade, Al. II. Fitzsimons,
Roy.

Voice Lib.
M210 Byrnes, James Francis, 1879-1972.
bd.2 An answer to Charles A. Lindbergh.
CBS, May 22, 1940.
1 reel (7 in.) 7 1/2 i.p.s. phonotape.

1. Lindbergh, Charles Augustus, 1902-

Voice Lib.
M856 Byrnes, James Francis, 1879-1972.
Speaking from Stuttgart, Germany, about
America's position in the reconstruction
of Germany. BBC shortwave, September 6,
1946.
36 min., 30 sec. phonotape (1 r.
7 1/2 i.p.s.)

1. Reconstruction (1939-1951)

CABLES, SUBMARINE

Voice Lib.
644 Edison, Thomas Alva, 1847-1931.
bd.4 Fiftieth anniversary of laying of Atlantic
cable; reviews history of electrical communication at opening of Electrical Exposition
at Madison Square Garden, New York City.
GRV (Edison Labs), 1908.
1 reel (7 in.) 7 1/2 in. per sec.
phonotape.

CAESAR, C. JULIUS

C1
H65
Whorf, Michael, 1933–
    Apostles of destruction; Caesar, Alexander,
Ghenghis Khan, Hitler.
    1 tape cassette.. (The visual sounds of Mike Whorf.
History and heritage, H65)

    Originally presented on his radio program, Kaleidoscope,
WJR, Detroit.
    Duration: 39 min.
    Here are graphically related the tales of the despots of the ages -
for though many would strive for goodness and the best in man - a
few were blindly corrupt and evil, and in their time attempted to
bring the world to ruin.
    1. Caesar, C. Julius. 2. Alexander the Great, 356-323 B.C.
3. Jenghis Khan, 1162-1227. 4. Hitler, Adolf, 1889-1945.
L. Title.

Voice Lib.
M762
bd.8
    Caesar, Irving, 1895–
    Excerpt from "Music from Broadway" (Program
5); comments on how he wrote the song "Swanee",
including Al Jolson singing it. Westinghouse
Broadcasting Corporation, 1964.
    1 reel (7 in.) 7 1/2 in. per sec.
phonotape. (The Music Goes Round and Round)

    I. Title: Music from Broadway. II. Series.
    1. Music, Popular (Songs, etc.) - U.S.

Voice Lib.
M761
bd.13
    Caesar, Irving, 1895–
    Excerpt from "Tunesmiths past and present"
(Program 4); comments on writing songs, how
difficult it can be at times but other times
how easy it is. Westinghouse Broadcasting
Corporation, 1964.
    2 min., 58 sec. phonotape (1 r. 7 1/2
i.p.s.) (The music goes round and round)

    1. Music, Popular (Songs, etc.) - Writing
and publishing. I. Title: Tunesmiths past
and present. II. Series.

Voice Lib.
590-
591
bd.1
    Cahn, Sammy, 1913–
    "Today" show salute to Sammy Cahn and
Jimmy Van Heusen; tells how "Three Coins in
the Fountain" came to be written, on winning
an Oscar on "High Hopes", talks about working
with Jimmy Van Heusen, talks about favorite
charity, story behind "Tender Trap", on "It's
Magic", sale of songs in Hollywood, sings and
describes "The Second Time Around", recalls
selling song to Mario Lanza, sings parody on
"Call Me Irresponsible". NBC, March 20, 1964.
    2 reels (7 in.) 7 1/2 in. per sec. phonotape.
L. Van Heusen, James

Voice Lib.
M976-
977
    Calder, Ritchie, 1906–
    Huxley, Aldous Leonard, 1894-1963.
    Leading a discussion group at C.S.D.I. on
ecological effects on technology, the
tragic price we are paying for our conquest
of nature. Other speakers: Ritchie Calder,
Walter J. Ong, S.J., and Robert M. Hutchins,
etc. March, 1962.
    2 reels (7 in.) 7 1/2 in. per sec. phonotape.

    L. Man - Influence on nature. L. Calder, Ritchie, 1906-
II. Ong, Walter Jackson, 1912- III. Hutchins, Robert
Maynard, 1899-

CALIFORNIA - GOLD DISCOVERIES

C1
H14
Whorf, Michael, 1933–
    Tales of the frontier and the forty-niners.
    1 tape cassette. (The visual sounds of
Mike Whorf. History and heritage, H14)
    Originally presented on his radio program, Kaleidoscope,
WJR, Detroit.
    Duration: 39 min.
    The year was 1849, and from every corner of the globe came
all types of men searching for quick wealth. "Gold," was the
cry from California and with their hopes and dreams came the
seekers. For a few months it meant adventure and excitement for
those who confronted the frontier and were called the forty-niners.

    1. California - Gold discoveries. 2. Frontier and pioneer life.
L. Title.

CALIFORNIA - SOCIAL CONDITIONS

Voice Lib.
M879
bd.2-
881
bd.1
    American mood series (Radio program)
    The real American revolution. California,
the real American revolution. Opinions on
liberalism and also opinions by John Birch
Society members and conservatives. Discussion
by magazine editor; San Diego resident talking
about John Birch Society and a discussion
about Barry Goldwater. Discussion of life and
culture in Southern California; cause for the
influx of people; lack of family roots and
analysis of social contacts; broad discussion
of L.A. social problems. Discussions of
    (Continued on next card)

CALIFORNIA - SOCIAL CONDITIONS

Voice Lib.
M879
bd.2-
881
bd.1
    American mood series (Radio program) The
    real American revolution... 1963.
    (Card 2)

uprising of college students and a general
discussion of Southern California compared to
Canada. CBC Radio, 1963.
    2 reels (7 in.) 7 1/2 in. per sec.
phonotape.

    1. California - Soc. condit. I. Hamilton,
John David II. Project '64.

Voice Lib.
M1440
    Calley, William Laws, 1943–
    NBC special program immediately after
conviction of Lieutenant William Calley
for My Lai massacre; with Frank McGee.
NBC-TV, March 29, 1971.
    1 reel (7 in.) 7 1/2 in. per sec.
phonotape.

    1. Calley, William Laws, 1943-
    I. McGee, Frank, 1921-

CALVIN, JEAN, 1509-1564

C1
R25
Whorf, Michael, 1933–
    The accusative - John Calvin.
    1 tape cassette. (The visual sounds of
Mike Whorf. Religion, R25)

    Originally presented on his radio program, Kaleidoscope,
WJR, Detroit.
    Duration: 36 min.
    Born of an affluent family in France, John Calvin turned from the
study of law to the scriptures as his religious convictions deepened.
His work and his life illustrate the burning fires of reformation which
raged through Europe.

    1. Calvin, Jean, 1509-1564. L. Title.

Voice Lib.
M1586   CAMPAIGN FUNDS
         Baker, Howard H., 1925-
             The lessons of Watergate.   WKAR,
         February 28, 1974.
             30 min.   phonotape (1 r.   7 1/2 in. per
         sec.)

             1. Watergate Affair, 1972. 2. Campaign
         funds.

○

Voice Lib.
M1585   CAMPAIGN FUNDS
bd.1   Hays, Wayne L
             Money - politics.   WKAR-AM, February 27,
         1974.
             15 min.   phonotape (1 r.   7 1/2 in. per sec.)

             1. Elections. 2. Campaign funds.
         3. Saxbe, William B., 1916-

○

Voice Lib.   CAMPAIGN FUNDS
M1584   Percy, Charles Harting, 1919-
             Money - politics.   WKAR-AM, February 27,
         1974.
             30 min.   phonotape (1 r.   7 1/2 i.p.s.)

             1. Campaign funds.   2. U.S. - Politics
         and government.

○

Voice Lib.
M765   Campana, Frank
bd.2   Excerpt from "The Anatomy of a Hit"
         (Program 9); comments on the role of the
         promotion man, also the album business.
         Westinghouse Broadcasting Corporation, 1964.
             1 reel (7 in.)   7 1/2 in. per sec.
         phonotape.   (The Music Goes Round and Round)
             1. Phonorecords.
             I. Title: The Anatomy of a Hit. II. Series.

○

Voice Lib.
353   Campbell, Gardner
bd.11   Outbreak of Korean War; supports Truman's
         action as only course of action.   NBC,
         July, 1950.
             1 reel (7 in.)   7 1/2 in. per sec.
         phonotape.

             Original disc off-speed.

             1. Korean War, 1950-1953

○

Voice Lib.
M1483   Campbell, Mrs. Howard, 1869-
bd.2   Interview with Mrs. Campbell (102 years
         old) concerning her experience with the
         birth of the phonograph when she lived near
         Edison's labs in Menlo Park, N.J.   David L.
         Olson, July 21, 1971.
             1 reel (7 in.)   7 1/2 i.p.s.   phonotape.

             1. Phonorecords - History.

○

Voice Lib.
1054   Can you top this? Weekly radio program of
bd.1   contest telling humorous stories; featuring
         Senator Ford, Harry Herschfield, Joe Laurie,
         Jr., Ward Wilson, and Peter Donald.   NBC
         Radio, February 8, 1950.
             1 reel (7 in.)   7 1/2 in. per sec.
         phonotape.

○

C1   CANADA
S64   Whorf, Michael, 1933-
             As big as all outdoors; the story of Canada.
             1 tape cassette.   (The visual sounds of
         Mike Whorf. Social, S64)
             Originally presented on his radio program, Kaleidoscope,
         WJR, Detroit.
             Duration: 37 min., 30 sec.
             As big as all outdoors is the story of America's great neighbor
         to the north - Canada. A country of riches - wealthy in people,
         land, beauty, and raw material, yet a country that has not
         reached its destiny.

             1. Canada. 1. Title. ○

Voice Lib.
M1090   Cantor, Eddie, 1903-1964.
bd.4   Re-recording of 78 rpm phonodisc of
         comedian Eddie Cantor singing "If You Knew
         Susie" by Buddy De Sylva.   Columbia, 1933.
             1 reel (7 in.)   7 1/2 in. per sec.
         phonotape.

( )

Voice Lib.
M710   Cantor, Eddie, 1893-1964.
bd.1   "Eddie Cantor Show"; radio variety show.
         Melchior collection, May 21, 1941.
             1 reel (7 in.)   7 1/2 in. per sec.
         phonotape.

○

Voice Lib.
541   Cantor, Eddie, 1893-1964. ____
bd.2   Documentary program for U.S. Treasury
         Department. Introduction by Deems Taylor.
         WABC-NY, January 25, 1952.
           1 reel (7 in.)   7 1/2 in. per sec.
         phonotape.

           I. Taylor, Deems, 1885-1966. II. U.S.
         Treasury Dept.

Cantor, Eddie, 1893-1964
Voice Lib.
M1047 Old-time radio excerpts of the 1930's and
         1940's, including: Rudy Vallee singing
         "Linger a little longer"; Will Rogers on
         panaceas for the Depression; Bing Crosby
         singing "Sweet Georgia Brown"; Eddie Cantor;
         Jimmy Durante singing "Inka-dinka-do";
         musical skit by Clayton, Jackson and Durante;
         wit by Harry Hershfield; musical selection
         "Thinking of you" by Kay Kyser; Kate Smith
         singing theme song, "When the moon comes over
         the mountain"; W.C. Fields' temperance
                   (Continued on next card)

Cantor, Eddie, 1893-1964
Voice Lib.
M1047 Old-time radio excerpts of the 1930's and
         1940's...   (Card 2)
         lecture; Al Jolson singing "Rocka-by-your
         baby"; and George Burns and Gracie Allen
         skit. TVER, 1930's and 1940's.
           1 reel (7 in.) 7 1/2 in. per sec.
           I. Vallee, Rudy, 1901-   II. Rogers, Will, 1879-1935. III.
         Crosby, Bing, 1901-   IV. Cantor, Eddie, 1893-1964. V. Durante,
         Jimmy, 1893-   VI. Clayton, Patti   VII. Jackson,
         Eddie   VIII. Hershfield, Harry, 1885-   IX. Kyser, Kay,
         1906-   X. Smith, Kate, 1909-   XI. Fields, W.C., 1879-
         1946. XII. Jolson, Al, 1886-1950. XIII. Burns, George, 1896-
         XIV. Allen, Gracie, 1906-

Cantor, Eddie, 1893-1964
Voice Lib.
M621   Radio in the 1940's (Part II): a series of
bd.1-   excerpts from important broadcasts of the
12   1940's; a sample of radio of the period.
         NVL, April, 1964.
           1 reel (7 in.) 7 1/2 in. per sec. phonotape.
           I. Daly, John Charles, 1914-   II. Hall, Josef Washington,
         1894-   III. Shirer, William Lawrence, 1904-   IV. Roosevelt,
         Eleanor (Roosevelt) 1884-1962. V. Roosevelt, Franklin Delano,
         Pres. U.S., 1882-1945. VI. Churchill, Winston Leonard Spencer,
         1874-1965. VII. Wainwright, Jonathan Mayhew, 1883-1953. VIII.
         Cantor, Eddie, 1893-1964. IX. Sinatra, Francis Albert, 1917-
         X. Hope, Bob, 1903-   XI. Crosby, Bing, 1901-   XII. Shore,
         Dinah, 1917(?)-   XIII. Bergen, Edgar, 1903-   XIV. Armstrong,
         Louis, 1900-1971. XV. Eldridge, Roy, 1911-

Canudo, Eugene R
Voice Lib.
M658- Dialogues in depth: the LaGuardia years
659   (TV program from the New York World's Fair).
bd.1   Anecdotes and reminiscences about the late
         New York mayor, Fiorello LaGuardia.
         July 22, 1964.
           2 reels (7 in.)   7 1/2 i.p.s.   phonotape.
           I. LaGuardia, Fiorello Henry, 1882-1947. I. Canudo,
         Eugene R. II. Berle, Adolph Augustus, 1895-1971.
         III. Van Arsdale, Harry, 1905-   IV. Delany, Hubert T.
         V. Morris, Newbold, 1902-1966.

Capehart, Homer Earl, 1897-
Voice Lib.
383   I can hear it now (radio program)
         CBS, February 9, 1951.
           1 reel (7 in.)   7 1/2 in. per sec.
         phonotape.
           I. Wilson, Charles Edward, 1886-1972. II. Gabrielson, Guy
         George, 1891-   III. Taft, Robert Alphonso, 1889-1953. IV.
         Martin, Joseph William, 1884-1965. V. McCarthy, Joseph
         Raymond, 1909-1957. VI. Benton, William Burnett, 1900-1973.
         VII. Malone, George Wilson, 1890-1961. VIII. Capehart, Homer
         Earl, 1897-   IX. Eisenhower, Dwight David, Pres. U.S., 1890-
         1969. X. Lee, J   V   XI. Hodge, John Reed, 1893-
         1963. XII. Overton, Watkins   XIII. DiSalle, Michael
         Vincent, 1908-   XIV. Boyce, Eddy   XV. Conklin, Ed
         XVI. Collins, Joseph Lawton, 1896-

Capehart, Homer Earl, 1897-
Voice Lib.
381-   I can hear it now (radio program)
382   CBS, April 26, 1951.
bd.1   2 reels (7 in.) 7 1/2 in. per sec. phonotape.
           I. Radio Free Europe. 2. Strategic Air Command. I.
         Ridgway, Matthew Bunker, 1895-   II. Churchill, Winston Leonard
         Spencer, 1874-1965. III. Bevan, Aneurin, 1897-1960. IV. Nixon,
         Richard Milhous, Pres. U.S., 1913-   V. Kerr, Robert Samuel, 1896-
         1963. VI. Brewster, Ralph Owen, 1888-1962. VII. Wherry, Kenneth
         Spicer, 1892-1951. VIII. Capehart, Homer Earl, 1897-   IX.
         Lehman, Herbert Henry, 1878-1963. X. Taft, Robert Alphonso,
         1889-1953. XI. Moody, Arthur Edson Blair, 1902-1954. XII.
         Martin, Joseph William, 1884-1968. XIII. McMahon, James O'Brien,
         1903-1952. XIV. MacArthur, Douglas, 1880-1964. XVII. Wilson,
         Charles Edward, 1886-1972. VIII. Irvine, Clarence T

Voice Lib.
1293   Capote, Truman, 1924-
         TV dramatization of story by Capote,
         "Christmas - Thirty Years Ago", with
         descriptions of incidents by the author.
         ABC-TV, December 19, 1967.
           1 reel (7 in.)   7 1/2 in. per sec.
         phonotape.

           I. Title: Christmas - thirty years ago.

Voice Lib.
M1298 Capote, Truman, 1924-
bd.2   Excerpt of interview with Barbara Walters
         of "Today" show, on contemporary music,
         hippies, drugs and being visible. NBC-TV,
         January 3, 1968.
           1 reel (7 in.)   7 1/2 in. per sec.
         phonotape.

           I. Walters, Barbara, 1931-

Voice Lib.
M1402 Capote, Truman, 1924-
bd.1   Discussion with Barbara Walters on the
         Today Show about his book and movie
         "Trilogy". NBC, November 11, 1969.
           1 reel (7 in.)   7 1/2 in. per sec.
         phonotape.

           I. Walters, Barbara, 1931-

Voice Lib.
M325   Cappo, Jo Lynne, 1942-
       Informal remarks pertaining to this MSU
    graduate student's two-month assignment in
    South Vietnam; delivered before Kiwanis
    Club, Mason, Michigan.   NVL location record-
    ing, October 5, 1965.
       1 reel (7 in.)   7 1/2 in. per sec.
    phonotape.

       1. Vietnamese Conflict, 1961-
    Personal narratives, American.

Voice Lib.
302   Carmichael, Hoagy, 1899-
bd.1   Voice of America reviews Carmichael's
       career with the composer; Carmichael
       talks about his favorite songs, motion
       pictures, and contemporary music.
       Voice of America, January 21, 1950.
          1 reel (7 in.)   7 1/2 in. per sec.
       phonotape.

Voice Lib.
M1482 Capra, Frank, 1897-
bd.2   Excerpt of interview with movie producer
       Frank Capra on "Today" show.   NBC,
       August 8, 1971.
          1 reel (7 in.)   7 1/2 in. per sec.
       phonotape.

Voice Lib.
625   Carmichael, Hoagy, 1899-
bd.1   "Salute to Hoagy Carmichael"; condensation
       of special TV program on Today show.
       Carmichael reminiscing, singing "Hong Kong
       Blues" and "Old Buttermilk Sky".   NBC,
       April 24, 1964.
          1 reel (7 in.)   7 1/2 in. per sec.
       phonotape.

          I. Title: Hong Kong blues.   II. Title: Old
       buttermilk sky.

C1   Captain James B. Eads.
FA19
       Whorf, Michael, 1933-
          Captain James B. Eads.
          1 tape cassette.   (The visual sounds of
       Mike Whorf. The forgotten American, FA19)

       Originally presented on his radio program, Kaleidoscope,
       WJR, Detroit.
       Duration: 11 min., 5 sec.
       Eads challenged and tamed the Mississippi river. He
       pioneered in salvaging in the river, designed, and built boats
       used to clear the river during the Civil War, and built the
       first bridge across the river at St. Louis.

       L Eads, James Buchanan, 1820-1887.   L Title.

Voice Lib.
M1204, Carmichael, Stokely, 1941-
bd.2-   Lecture on "black power" and methods of
1205   solving racial problems, held at MSU
       Auditorium.   A/V, February 9, 1967.
          2 reels (7 in.)   7 1/2 in. per sec.
       phonotape.

          1. Race discrimination - U.S.

Voice Lib.
M1673 Captain Midnight (radio program)
bd.3   Captain Midnight.   Golden Age Radio
       Records, 1947.
          10 min.   phonotape (1 r.   7 1/2 i.p.s.)

Voice Lib.
649   Carnegie, Andrew, 1835-1919.
bd.10   The gospel of wealth; Carnegie's thoughts
       on the duties of a man of wealth.   Edison,
       1908.
          1 reel (7 in.)   7 1/2 in. per sec.
       phonotape.

          CARICATURES AND CARTOONS
Voice Lib.
M338   Mauldin, William Henry, 1921-
bd.3   On cartoonists; answers questions on how to
       create effective cartoons, creation of
       "Willy and Joe", New York Star staff,
       control of advertising department,
       editorial policy.   Voice of America,
       May 6, 1967.
          1 reel (7 in.)   7 1/2 i.p.s.   phonotape.

          1. Caricatures and cartoons.

Voice Lib.
M1615 Carnegie, Andrew, 1835-1919.
bd.1   The gospel of wealth.   Rare Records, Inc.,
       #315, 1914.
          2 min., 50 sec.   phonotape (1 r.   7 1/2
       i.p.s.)

          I. Title.

The carpenters from Nazareth

C1
R34   Whorf, Michael, 1933-
       The carpenters from Nazareth; Jesus and
       Joseph.
       1 tape cassette.   (The visual sounds of
       Mike Whorf. Religion, R34)
       Originally presented on his radio program, Kaleidoscope,
       WJR, Detroit.
       Duration: 37 min.
       Jesus emerges from the shadows to walk in a world peopled
       by simple hard-working men in a town named Nazareth.

       1. Jesus Christ. 2. Joseph, Saint. I. Title.

Voice Lib.
352   Carradine, John, 1906-
bd.6   On why actors and actresses attempt to
       succeed on the American stage. NBC, 1949.
          1 reel (7 in.)   7 1/2 in. per sec.
       phonotape.

          1. Acting.

C1
H66   CARSON, CHRISTOPHER, 1809-1868
       Whorf, Michael, 1933-
       Hero of the old west, Kit Carson.
       1 tape cassette.   (The visual sounds of
       Mike Whorf. History and heritage, H66)

       Originally presented on his radio program, Kaleidoscope,
       WJR, Detroit.
       Duration: 37 min., 30 sec.
       Here, set against the background of the American southwest,
       are the exploits of Kit Carson, a two-fisted hard-living frontiers-
       man, who was as much at home in the peaceful hills and mountains
       of the west as he was skulking and scouting for the U. S. Cavalry.

       1. Carson, Christopher, 1809-1868. I. Title.

Voice Lib.
603   Caruso, Enrico, 1873-1921.
bd.2   "Over There"; sings George M. Cohan's
       World War I song (first verse in English,
       second in French).   Victor Talking Machine
       Co., 1917.
          1 reel (7 in.)   7 1/2 in. per sec.
       phonotape.

          I. Title.

Voice Lib.
M1090 Caruso, Enrico, 1873-1921.
bd.2   Re-recording of 78 rpm phonodisc of tenor
       Caruso singing "No, Pagliaccio Non Son"
       from opera Pagliacci, Act II.   Victor,
       1922.
          1 reel (7 in.)   7 1/2 in. per sec.
       phonotape.

          I. Leoncavallo, Ruggiero, 1858-1919./I
       Pagliacci. No, Pagliaccio non son.

Voice Lib.
M1090 Caruso, Enrico, 1873-1921.
bd.3   Re-recording of 78 rpm phonodisc of tenor
       Caruso singing "Vesti La Giubba" from opera
       Pagliacci, Act I.   Victor, 1922.
          1 reel (7 in.)   7 1/2 in. per sec.
       phonotape.

          I. Leoncavallo, Ruggiero, 1858-1919./I
       Pagliacci. Vesti la giubba.

Voice Lib.
652   Casals, Pablo, 1876-
bd.17   Acceptance to participate in concert on
       United Nations Day.   CBS, October 23,
       1958.
          1 reel (7 in.)   7 1/2 in. per sec.
       phonotape.

C1
SC25   The case of the vanishing monsters
       Whorf, Michael, 1933-
       The case of the vanishing monsters.
       1 tape cassette.   (The visual sounds of
       Mike Whorf. Science, SC25)
       Originally presented on his radio program, Kaleidoscope,
       WJR, Detroit.
       Duration: 30 min.
       Here are the great beasts that roamed the earth long before
       the coming of man. The huge dinosaurs prevailed for centuries and
       then suddenly, they disappeared. Here are some of the answers, the
       questions, the conjectures, in a half-hour of gripping scientific fact.

          1. Dinosauria. I. Title.

Casey at the bat

Voice Lib.
526   Hopper, De Wolf, 1858-1935.
bd.4   Reads "Casey at the Bat".   Victor
       Talking Machine Co., 1912.
          1 reel (7 in.)   7 1/2 in. per sec.
       phonotape.

          I. Title: Casey at the bat.

Casey at the Bat

Voice Lib.
654   Hopper, De Wolf, 1858-1935.
bd.9   "Casey at the Bat". Electrical recording
       of De Wolf Hopper narrating famous poem.
       Moran, November, 1926.
          1 reel (7 in.)   7 1/2 in. per sec.
       phonotape.

          I. Title.

Cassidy, Henry Clarence, 1910-
Voice Lib.
353　Outbreak of Korean War and comments by
bd.18　　various persons. NBC, July, 1950.
　　　1 reel (7 in.)　7 1/2 in. per sec.
　　phonotape.

　　　Original disc off-speed.
　　　Participants: Henry Cassidy, Merrill Mueller,
　　Edward Harper, Jack Bregon.

　　　I. Cassidy, Henry Clarence, 1910-　II.
　　Mueller, Merrill. III. Harper, Edward. IV.
　　Bregon, Jack.

Castro, Fidel, 1927-
Voice Lib.
209　Schorr, Daniel Louis, 1916-
bd.1　　Press conference with Fidel Castro and
　　　Anastas Mikoyan.　Source (?), February 13,
　　1960.
　　　1 reel (7 in.)　7 1/2 in. per sec.
　　phonotape.

　　　I. Castro, Fidel, 1927-　　II.
　　Mikoian, Anastas Ivanovich, 1895-

Voice Lib.
652　Cassini, Oleg Loiewski, 1913-
bd.18　　Discussing Jackie Kennedy's wardrobe
　　　with New York fashion editors.　CBS,
　　January 12, 1960.
　　　1 reel (7 in.)　7 1/2 in. per sec.
　　phonotape.

　　　1. Kennedy, Jacqueline (Bouvier) 1929-

CASTRO, FIDEL, 1927-
Voice Lib.
344　Mourison, DeLessepps
bd.7　　On Castro's Communism.　CBS, December 4,
　　1961.
　　　1 reel (7 in.)　7 1/2 in. per sec.
　　phonotape.

　　　1. Castro, Fidel, 1927-

Voice Lib.
M717　Castro, Fidel, 1927-
bd.7　　Explaining reason for friendship of
　　　Cuba with Russia.
　　　1 reel (7 in.)　7 1/2 in. per sec.
　　phonotape.

Voice Lib.
M1800　Caulfield, John, 1929?
WG　　　Testimony before the Senate Committee
0522.03 investigating the Watergate Affair.
　　　Pacifica, May 22, 1973.
　　　89 min.　phonotape (1 r.　3 3/4 i.p.s.)
　　　(Watergate gavel to gavel, phase 1)

　　　1. Watergate Affair, 1972-

Voice Lib.
M652　Castro, Fidel, 1927-
bd.4　　Castro and Cuban rebels speaking from
　　　Cuban hills on U.S. newsman's recorder.
　　CBS, May 19, 1957.
　　　1 reel (7 in.)　7 1/2 i.p.s.　phonotape.

　　　1. Cuba - History - 1933-1959.

Voice Lib.
M1800　Caulfield, John, 1929?-
WG　　　Testimony before the Senate Committee
0523.01 investigating the Watergate Affair.
　　　Pacifica, May 23, 1973.
　　　80 min.　phonotape (1 r.　3 3/4 i.p.s.)
　　　(Watergate gavel to gavel, phase 1)

　　　1. Watergate Affair, 1972-

Voice Lib.
M742　Castro, Fidel, 1927-
vd.10　　Interview with Roger Mudd of CBS, stating
　　　that he is not a Communist.　CBS, 1959.
　　　1 reel (7 in.)　7 1/2 in. per sec.
　　phonotape.

　　　I. Mudd, Roger

Voice Lib.
270　Celestin, Oscar
　　　Oscar "Papa" Celestin and his original
　　　Tuxedo Band; New Orleans Jazz for White
　　　House Correspondents Association and
　　　President Eisenhower. From private
　　　collection of Congressman Hebert, May 8,
　　1953.
　　　1 reel (7 in.)　7 1/2 in. per sec.
　　phonotape.
　　　1. Jazz music

Voice Lib.
M243
bd.8

Celler, Emanuel, 1888–
Martin, Joseph William, 1884-1968.
  Comments on the Senate Jury Trial
Amendment in Civil Rights Bill, by Joseph
Martin and Emanuel Celler. CBS, August 2,
1957.
  1 reel (7 in.)   7 1/2 in. per sec.
phonotape.

  I. Celler, Emanuel, 1888–

C1
S6

The celluloid queen
Whorf, Michael, 1933–
  The celluloid queen.
  1 tape cassette. (The visual sounds of
Mike Whorf. Social, S6)

  Originally presented on his radio program, Kaleidoscope,
WJR, Detroit.
  Duration: 40 min., 30 sec.
  The story of the rise and fall of these glamorous stars who
were legends of their times, Theda Bara, Clara Bow, Gloria
Swanson, Colleen Moore, Lana Turner, Marilyn Monroe, is
outlined here.

  l. Moving-pictures – U.S.   l. Title.

Voice Lib.
M935
bd.2

CENSORSHIP – U.S.
Stanton, Frank, 1908–
  Excerpt wherein Dr. Stanton discusses the
broadcasting investigation and censorship.
Private recording, 1957.
  1 reel (7 in.)   7 1/2 in. per sec.
phonotape.

Voice Lib.
M1063
bd.1

CENTER FOR THE STUDY OF DEMOCRATIC
INSTITUTIONS
Hutchins, Robert Maynard, 1890–
  Explanation of aims of Center for Study
of Democratic Institutions in Santa Barbara,
California. CSDI, 1963.
  1 reel (7 in.)   7 1/2 i.p.s.   phonotape.

  1. Center for the Study of Democratic
Institutions.

Voice Lib.
M1064
bd.6

Cermak, Anton Joseph, 1873-1933.
  Welcoming address by Mayor Cermak of Chicago
to visiting Mayor James J. Walker of New York
City; Mayor Walker's reply. Fox Movietone,
1931.
  1 reel (7 in.)   7 1/2 in. per sec.
phonotape.

  I. Walker, James John Joseph, 1881-1946.

Voice Lib.
540
bd.6

Cermak, Anton Joseph, 1873-1933
Walker, James John Joseph, 1881-1946.
  Welcomed to Chicago by Mayor Anton Cermak.
Fox Movietone, 1931.
  1 reel (7 in.)   7 1/2 in. per sec.
phonotape.

  I. Cermak, Anton Joseph, 1873-1933.

Voice Lib.
M968
bd.2

Cernan, Eugene Andrew, 1934–
Gemini 9 (space flight): description of
countdown and lift-off of "Agena" by
Gemini Mission Control (voice of Al Chop)
for a period of 11 minutes, 41 seconds,
until Gemini flight was scrubbed. Comments
by NBC's Huntley, Brinkley, and Frank McGee.
NBC TV, May 17, 1966.
  1 reel (7 in.)   7 1/2 in. per sec.   phonotape.
  L. Project Gemini. 2. Stafford, Thomas P   1931–   3.
Cernan, Eugene Andrew, 1934–   l. Stafford, Thomas P   1931–
II. Cernan, Eugene Andrew, 1934–   III. Chop, Al   IV.
Huntley, Chet, 1911-19?4. V. Brinkley, David McClure, 1920–
VI. McGee, Frank, 1921-1974.

Voice Lib.
M986
bd.2

Cernan, Eugene Andrew, 1934–
Gemini 9 (space flight): a. Take-off of
Augmented Target Docking Adaptor (ATDA)
from Cape Kennedy (June 1); b. re-cap
by David Brinkley regarding failure of
shroud to jettison (June 3); c. Gemini 9
until failure of guidance system computer
and then scrubbing mission (June 1)
NBC TV, June 1 and 3, 1966.
  1 reel (7 in.)   7 1/2 in. per sec.   phonotape.
  L. Project Gemini. 2. Stafford, Thomas P   1931–   3.
Cernan, Eugene Andrew, 1934–   l. Stafford, Thomas P
1931–   II. Cernan, Eugene Andrew, 1934–   III. Brinkley,
David McClure, 1920–

Voice Lib.
M1377
bd.1

Cernan, Eugene Andrew, 1934–
Apollo 10 (space flight): lift-off. Commentary
by NBC TV news; countdown, lift-off. Astronauts Tom Stafford, John Young, Eugene Cernan.
NBC TV, May 18, 1969.
  1 reel (7 in.)   7 1/2 in. per sec.
phonotape.
  1. Project Apollo. 2. Space flight to the
moon. 3. Stafford, Thomas P   1931–   4.
Young, John Watts, 1930–   5. Cernan, Eugene
Andrew, 1934–   I. Stafford, Thomas P   1931–
II. Young, John Watts, 1930–   III. Cernan,
Eugene Andrew, 1934–

Voice Lib.
M1377
bd.2

Cernan, Eugene Andrew, 1934–
Apollo 10 (space flight): television pictures.
Commentary from astronauts, NBC TV, on
initial separation and docking of Lunar
Landing Module, first live color television
pictures from space, and pictures of the
earth from 6,500 nautical miles out. NBC
TV, May, 1969.
  1 reel (7 in.)   7 1/2 in. per sec.   phonotape.
  L. Project Apollo. 2. Space flight to the moon. 3. Stafford,
Thomas P   1931–   4. Young, John Watts, 1930–   5.
Cernan, Eugene Andrew, 1934–   l. Stafford, Thomas P
1931–   II. Young, John Watts, 1930–   III. Cernan, Eugene
Andrew, 1934–

Cernan, Eugene Andrew, 1934–

Voice Lib.
M1377 Apollo 10 (space flight): splashdown and
bd.3   recovery of Apollo 10; astronauts' first
       words after returning to earth; from the
       recovery ship U.S.S. "Princeton". CBS TV,
       May 26, 1969.
         1 reel (7 in.)   7 1/2 in. per sec.
       phonotape.
         L Project Apollo. 2. Space flight to the moon. 3. Stafford,
       Thomas P   1931–   4. Young, John Watts, 1930–   5.
       Cernan, Eugene Andrew, 1934–   L Stafford, Thomas P
       1931–   IL Young, John Watts, 1930–   III. Cernan, Eugene
       Andrew, 1934–

Cernan, Eugene Andrew, 1934–

Voice Lib.
M1480 Apollo 15 (space flight): walk in deep space
bd.3   by Al Worden to retrieve film packages.
       Commentary of Gene Cernan, who walked in
       space during Gemini 9 flight.   NBC TV,
       August, 1971.
         1 reel (7 in.)   7 1/2 in. per sec.
       phonotape.
         L Project Apollo. 2. Space flight to the moon. 3. Scott,
       David Randolph, 1932–   4. Irwin, James B   1932–   5.
       Worden, Alfred M   1930–   L Scott, David Randolph, 1932–
       IL Irwin, James B   1932–   III. Worden, Alfred M   1930–
       IV. Cernan, Eugene Andrew, 1934–

CHAFFEE, ROGER B., 1936–1967

Voice Lib.
M1030 Huntley, Chet, 1911–1974.
bd.1   Description by Chet Huntley of funeral
       services at burial of astronauts Virgil
       Grissom and Roger Chaffee at Arlington
       Cemetery and of Edward White at West Point,
       New York.   NBC-TV, January 31, 1967.
         1 reel (7 in.)   7 1/2 in. per sec.   phonotape.
         L Grissom, Virgil Ivan, 1926–1967. 2. White, Edward
       Higgins, 1930–1967. 3. Chaffee, Roger B., 1936–1967.

CHAĬKOVSKIĬ, PETR IL'ICH, 1840–1893

C1
PWM21 Whorf, Michael, 1933–
       Tchaikovsky.
         1 tape cassette.   (The visual sounds of
       Mike Whorf. Panorama; a world of music, PWM–21)
         Originally presented on his radio program, Kaleidoscope.
       WJR, Detroit.
         Duration: 28 min., 30 sec.
         The life and times of Tchaikovsky, including excerpts of
       his music.
         L Chaĭkovskiĭ, Petr Il'ich, 1840–1893. L Title.

         The challenge to democracy in the next
Voice Lib.   decade
M1066 Berle, Adolph Augustus, 1895–1971.
         Address in New York at 10th anniversary
       of founding of "Fund for the Republic",
       entitled "The challenge to democracy in
       the next decade"; dealing with corporate
       power and the American economy.   CSDI,
       1962.
         1 reel (7 in.)   7 1/2 in. per sec.
       phonotape.
         I. Title: The challenge to democracy in the
       next decade.

CHAMBER OF COMMERCE OF THE UNITED STATES
OF AMERICA
Voice Lib.
M1642 Rust, Edward Barry, 1918–
         National Press Club luncheon address.
       WKAR-AM, March 14, 1974.
         50 min.   phonotape (1 r.   7 1/2 i.p.s.)
         1. Chamber of Commerce of the United
       States of America.

Voice Lib.
M1227 Chamberlain, Clarence
bd.8   Experiences during his first trans-
       Atlantic flight from New York to Germany,
       from West to East, and his reception in
       Berlin.   Peteler, June 6, 1927.
         1 reel (7 in.)   7 1/2 i.p.s.   phonotape.
         1. Air travel.

Voice Lib.
M1065 Chamberlain, Neville, 1869–1940.
bd.5   Excerpt of address to visiting Indian
       delegation about Britain's position
       regarding self-government for India.
       Fox Movietone, 1931.
         1 reel (7 in.)   7 1/2 in. per sec.
       phonotape.

Voice Lib.
540   Chamberlain, Neville, 1869–1940.
bd.24   Freedom for India from British rule.
       Fox Movietone, 1933.
         1 reel (7 in.)   7 1/2 in. per sec.
       phonotape.

Voice Lib.
M736   Chamberlain, Neville, 1869–1940.
bd.4   Announcing the result of his talks with
       Adolf Hitler.   CBS, September 27, 1938.
         1 reel (7 in.)   7 1/2 in. per sec.
       phonotape.

Voice Lib.
652   Chamberlain, Neville, 1869-1940.
bd.11   At England airport on return from Germany
         and his talk with Hitler, making his
         "Peace in our times" remark. CBS,
         September 27, 1938.
         1 reel (7 in.)   7 1/2 in. per sec.
         phonotape.

Voice Lib.
181   Chamberlain, Neville, 1869-1940.
bd.3   Declaration of war announcement. CBS,
        September 3, 1939.
        1 reel (7 in.)   7 1/2 in. per sec.
        phonotape.

Voice Lib.
M850   Chamberlain, Neville, 1869-1940.
bd.1   Last address as Prime Minister; verifying
        Nazi invasion of Low Countries; announcing
        resignation and formation of new British
        government under Winston Churchill. BBC,
        May 10, 1940.
        1 reel (7 in.)   7 1/2 in. per sec.
        phonotape.

Voice Lib.
M857   Chamberlain, Neville, 1869-1940.
bd.3   Address from London as a member of Prime
        Minister Winston Churchill's war cabinet
        assessing Britain's position before the
        impending Battle of Britain. NBC shortwave,
        June 30, 1940.
        1 reel (7 in.)   7 1/2 in. per sec.
        phonotape.

Voice Lib. Chamberlain, Neville, 1869-1940
M619   Radio in the 1930's (Part II): a series of
bd.1-   excerpts of the 1930's; a sample of radio
14   of the period. NVL, April, 1964.
         1 reel (7 in.) 7 1/2 in. per sec. phonotape.
         I. Allen, Fred, 1894-1956. II. Delmar, Kenny   III. Donald,
         Peter   IV. Pious, Minerva   V. Fennelly, Parker   VI.
         Boyer, Charles, 1899-   VII. Dunne, Irene, 1904-   VIII.
         DeMille, Cecil Blount, 1881-1959. IX. West, Mae, 1893-   X.
         Dafoe, Allan Ray, 1883-1943. XI. Dionne quintuplets. XII. Ortega,
         Santos   XIII. War of the worlds (radio program) XIV. Ives, Burl,
         1909-   XV. Robinson, Earl, 1910-   XVI. Temple, Shirley,
         1928-   XVII. Earhart, Amelia, 1898-1937. XVIII. Lawrence,
         Gertrude, 1901-1952. XIX. Cohan, George Michael, 1878-1942.
         XX. Shaw, George Bernard, 1856-1950. XXI. Hitler, Adolf, 1889-
         1945. XXII. Chamberlain, Neville, 1869-1940. XXIII. Roosevelt,
         Franklin Delano, Pres. U.S., 1882-1945.

Voice Lib. Chamberlain, Neville, 1869-1949
572-   I can hear it now (radio program)
573   1933-1946. CBS, 1948.
bd.1   2 reels (7 in.)   7 1/2 in. per sec.
        phonotape.
        I. Murrow, Edward Roscoe, 1908-1965. II. LaGuardia, Fiorello
        Henry, 1882-1947. III. Chamberlain, Neville, 1869-1949. IV.
        Roosevelt, Franklin Delano, Pres. U.S., 1882-1945. V. Churchill,
        Winston Leonard Spencer, 1874-1965. VI. Gaulle, Charles de,
        Pres. France, 1890-1970. VII. Eisenhower, Dwight David, Pres. U.S.,
        1890-1969. VIII. Willkie, Wendell Lewis, 1892-1944. IX. Martin,
        Joseph William, 1884-1968. X. Elizabeth II, Queen of Great Britain,
        1926-   XI. Margaret Rose, Princess of Gt. Brit., 1930-   XII.
        Johnson, Hugh Samuel, 1882-1942. XIII. Smith, Alfred Emanuel,
        1873-1944. XIV. Lindbergh, Charles Augustus, 1902-   XV. Davis,
        (Continued on next card)

Voice Lib.   CHAMBERLAIN, NEVILLE, 1869-1940
M1463   Alleged BBC broadcast in German about
bd.1   Prime Minister Chamberlain's peace
         mission to Germany. Peteler, September 27,
         1938.
         1 reel (7 in.)   7 1/2 i.p.s.   phonotape.

         1. Chamberlain, Neville, 1869-1940.

Voice Lib.   Chambers, David W
573   I can hear it now (radio program)
bd.2-   1945-1949. CBS, 1950?
574   2 reels (7 in.)   7 1/2 in. per sec.
bd.1   phonotape.
        I. Murrow, Edward Roscoe, 1908-1965. II. Nehru, Jawaharlal,
        1889-1964. III. Philip, duke of Edinburgh, 1921-   IV. Elizabeth II,
        Queen of Great Britain, 1926-   V. Ferguson, Homer, 1889-   VI.
        Hughes, Howard Robard, 1905-   VII. Marshall, George Catlett,
        1880-   VIII. Ruth, George Herman, 1895-1948. IX. Lilienthal,
        David Eli, 1899-   X. Trout, Robert, 1908-   XI. Gage, Arthur.
        XII. Jackson, Robert Houghwout, 1892-1954. XIII. Gromyko, Ana-
        tolii Andreevich, 1908-   XIV. Baruch, Bernard Mannes, 1870-
        1965. XV. Churchill, Winston Leonard Spencer, 1874-1965. XVI.
        Winchell, Walter, 1897-19   XVII. Davis, Elmer Holmes, 1890-
        (Continued on next card)

C1   Champion of the working man
S22   Whorf, Michael, 1922-
       Champion of the working man.
       1 tape cassette. (The visual sounds of
       Mike Whorf. Social, S22)
       Originally presented on his radio program, Kaleidoscope,
       WJR, Detroit.
       Duration: 27 min.
       Amidst the tumult of labor's early struggle to unionize,
       Walter Reuther stood as a pillar of strength in the movement.

       I. Reuther, Walter Philip, 1907-1970. I. Title.

Voice Lib.   Chancellor, John William, 1927-
M1269   Israeli-Arab war; "Victory or Else". NBC-TV
bd.2-   special documentary program, narrated by
1271   John Chancellor and other NBC field
         correspondents in the Middle East, describ-
         ing in detail the entire conflict between
         Israel and its Arab enemies; with inter-
         views of General Eud, General Rabin and
         General Sharan. NBC-TV, July 23, 1967.
         3 reels (7 in.)   7 1/2 in. per sec.
         phonotape.
         (Continued on next card)

Chancellor, John William, 1927-
Voice Lib.
M1454   Nixon, Richard Milhous, Pres. U.S., 1913-
bd.1   Discussion of U.S. foreign policy with
         network newscasters Eric Sevareid (CBS),
         John Chancellor (NBC), and Howard K. Smith
         (ABC).
             1 reel (7 in.)   7 1/2 in. per sec.
         phonotape.

             I. Sevareid, Arnold Eric, 1912-   II.
         Chancellor, John William, 1927-   III.
         Smith, Howard Kingsbury, 1914-

C1   CHAPLAINS, MILITARY
R8
       Whorf, Michael, 1933-
          Left hand of God.
          1 tape cassette.   (The visual sounds of
       Mike Whorf. Religion, R8)
          Originally presented on his radio program, Kaleidoscope,
       WJR, Detroit.
          Duration: 46 min., 30 sec.
          In every conflict in which this country has ever been involved,
       the chaplain has stood beside the fighting man. They are the
       soldiers of God.

          I. Chaplains, Military. I. Title.

Chancellor, John William, 1927-
Voice Lib.
M1479   Nixon, Richard Milhous, Pres. U.S., 1913-
bd.1   President Nixon announces trip to China;
         comment by John Chancellor, Richard Valeriani.
         NBC-TV, July 15, 1971.
             1 reel (7 in.)   7 1/2 in. per sec.
         phonotape.

             I. Chancellor, John William, 1927-
         II. Valeriani, Richard

Voice Lib.
154   Chaplin, Charles, 1889-
bd.5-8   Chaplin sings. Movie soundtracks,
         1936-52.
             1 reel (7 in.)   7 1/2 in. per sec.
         phonotape.

             CONTENTS.-Bd.5. It's love.-bd.6. Life of a
         sardine.-bd.7. Flea satire.-bd.8. Nonsense song.

Chandler, Albert Benjamin, 1898-
Voice Lib.
385   I can hear it now (radio program)
         CBS, February 2, 1951.
             1 reel (7 in.)   7 1/2 in. per sec.
         phonotape.

             I. Austin, Warren Robinson, 1877-1962. II.
         Pandit, Vijaya Lakshmi (Nehru) 1900-   III.
         Roosevelt, Eleanor (Roosevelt) 1884-1962. IV.
         Morse, Wayne Lyman, 1900-   V. Chandler,
         Albert Benjamin, 1898-   VI. Taylor, Telford,
         1908-   VII. White, Jack.

Voice Lib.
M1497   Chaplin, Charles, 1889-
bd.2   Honorary award presentation to Chaplin for
         special achievement by Academy of Motion
         Picture Arts and Sciences. Tribute by
         president of Society and remarks by Chaplin.
         NBC-TV, April 11, 1972.
             1 reel (7 in.)   7 1/2 in. per sec.
         phonotape.

Voice Lib.
M1267   Channing, Carol, 1923-
bd.1   Interview with actress Carol Channing at
         Expo '67, Montreal, Canada, with James Norton
         on TV program "Conversation".   NET, August 15,
         1967.
             1 reel (7 in.)   7 1/2 in. per sec.
         phonotape.

             I. Norton, James.

CHAPLIN, CHARLES, 1889-
Voice Lib.
M787   Chaplin, Charles, 1925-
            Discussion of autobiography of his father,
         Charles Chaplin, with Francis Roberts.
         Los Angeles, KPFK, December 19, 1964.
             1 reel (7 in.)   7 1/2 in. per sec.
         phonotape.

             1. Chaplin, Charles, 1889-   I. Roberts,
         Francis

Chapin, Richard Earl, 1925-
Voice Lib.
M1289   Nye, Russell Blaine, 1913-
            Address on education at Friends of the
         Library dinner held at Kellogg Center,
         including entire proceedings with short
         talk by Professor Crawford and Dr. Richard
         E. Chapin.   December 6, 1967.
             1 reel (7 in.)   7 1/2 in. per sec.
         phonotape.

             I. Chapin, Richard Earl, 1925-

CHAPLIN, CHARLES, 1889-
Voice Lib.
M1498   Safer, Morley
bd.2   Charles Chaplin returns to the U.S.A.
         NBC-TV, April 2, 1972.
             1 reel (7 in.)   7 1/2 i.p.s. phonotape.

             Includes excerpts from "A king in New
         York" and reflections by Sydney and Geraldine
         Chaplin.

             1. Chaplin, Charles, 1889-   I. Chaplin,
         Sydney Earl. II. Chaplin, Geraldine

C1
M45-
M46
CHAPLIN, CHARLES, 1889-
Whorf, Michael, 1933-
The comedian - Charlie Chaplin.
2 tape cassettes. (The visual sounds of
Mike Whorf. Miscellaneous, M45-M46)
Originally presented on his radio program, Kaleidoscope,
WJR, Detroit.
Duration: 37 min.; 37 min.
London to New York to Hollywood - these programs relive the
era in which the little tramp had his beginnings. America, and
then the world, took the humor and pathos of the funny little man
with his hat and cane into their hearts.

1. Chaplin, Charles, 1889-   L. Title.

C1
FA11
Charlemagne Tower
Whorf, Michael, 1933-
Charlemagne Tower.
1 tape cassette. (The visual sounds of
Mike Whorf. The forgotten American, FA11)
Originally presented on his radio program, Kaleidoscope,
WJR, Detroit.
Duration: 11 min., 17 sec.
Tower risked his name and his fortune to provide iron ore
from the Minnesota wilderness, which made the United States
a steel producing giant.

L. Tower, Charlemagne, 1809-1889. L. Title.

Voice Lib.
M787
Chaplin, Charles, 1925-
Discussion of autobiography of his father,
Charles Chaplin, with Francis Roberts.
Los Angeles, KPFK, December 19, 1964.
1 reel (7 in.) 7 1/2 in. per sec.
phonotape.

1. Chaplin, Charles, 1889-   I. Roberts,
Francis

Voice Lib.
M1380
bd.2
Charles, Prince of Wales, 1948-
Investiture ceremonies. BBC, July 1,
1969.
1 reel (7 in.) 7 1/2 in. per sec.
phonotape.

Voice Lib.
M1498
bd.2
Chaplin, Geraldine
Safer, Morley
Charles Chaplin returns to the U.S.A.
NBC-TV, April 2, 1972.
1 reel (7 in.) 7 1/2 i.p.s. phonotape.

Includes excerpts from "A king in New
York" and reflections by Sydney and Geraldine
Chaplin.

1. Chaplin, Charles, 1889-   I. Chaplin,
Sydney Earl. II. Chaplin, Geraldine

C1
FA17
Charles Evans Hughes
Whorf, Michael, 1933-
Charles Evans Hughes.
1 tape cassette. (The visual sounds of
Mike Whorf. The forgotten American, FA17)
Originally presented on his radio program, Kaleidoscope,
WJR, Detroit.
Duration: 10 min., 10 sec.
Although missing the presidency by a small margin, Charles
Evans Hughes was one of the most important public servants of his
time. In 25 years of public life, he served as governor of New
York, Associate Justice of the Supreme Court, Secretary of
State and Chief Justice of the Supreme Court.

L. Hughes, Charles Evans, 1862-1948. L. Title.

Voice Lib.
M1498
bd.2
Chaplin, Sydney Earl
Safer, Morley
Charles Chaplin returns to the U.S.A.
NBC-TV, April 2, 1972.
1 reel (7 in.) 7 1/2 i.p.s. phonotape.

Includes excerpts from "A king in New
York" and reflections by Sydney and Geraldine
Chaplin.

1. Chaplin, Charles, 1889-   I. Chaplin,
Sydney Earl. II. Chaplin, Geraldine

C1
A35
CHAUCER, GEOFFREY, D. 1400
Whorf, Michael, 1933-
England's first poet. - Geoffrey Chaucer.
1 tape cassette. (The visual sounds of
Mike Whorf. Art, music and letters, A35)
Originally presented on his radio program, Kaleidoscope,
WJR, Detroit.
Duration: 40 min.
His works preceded those that were synonymous with the English
contribution to the literary world. Chaucer was poet and author,
and his commentary on life, philosophy, mores, and social aware-
ness was brought to its zenith with a collection of works entitled
Canterbury Tales.

L. Chaucer, Geoffrey,   d. 1400. L. Title.

Voice Lib.
M975
bd.10
The charge of the Light Brigade
Fleming, Canon
Reciting Tennyson's poem: "The Charge
of the Light Brigade". Rococo-Can., 1910.
1 reel (7 in.) 7 1/2 in. per sec.
phonotape.

I. Title: The charge of the Light
Brigade.

Voice Lib.
158
bd.2
Chennault, Claire Lee, 1890-1958.
Interview by Congressman Hébert; China's
political problems. Private recording.
July 14, 1949.
1 reel (7 in.) 7 1/2 in. per sec.
phonotape.

I. Hébert, Felix Edward, 1901-

Voice Lib.
M1735   Chetrick, Myron H
Hardesty, Charles Howard, 1922-
The role of industry in combatting environ-
mental problems; speech delivered at Michigan
State University. Introduction by Myron H.
Chetrick. WKAR, June 20, 1974.
45 min. phonotape (1 r. 7 1/2 i.p.s.)

1. Enviromental policy. 2. Enviromental
eingineering. 3. Factory and trade waste.
I. Chetrick, Myron

Voice Lib.
155
bd.5 Chevalier, Maurice, 1889-1972.
Medley of French music hall songs.
French radio, 1900-1940 (?)
1 reel (7 in.) 7 1/2 in. per sec.
phonotape.

Voice Lib.
M982
bd.3 Chevalier, Maurice, 1889-1972.
Singing "My Love Parade" from Paramount
Pictures' "The Love Parade". Victor,
1927.
1 reel (7 in.) 7 1/2 in. per sec.
phonotape.

I. Title: My love parade.

Voice Lib.
M982
bd.2 Chevalier, Maurice, 1899-1972.
Singing "Nobody's Using It Now" from
Paramount Pictures' "The Love Parade".
Victor, 1927.
1 reel (7 in.) 7 1/2 in. per sec.
phonotape.

I. Title: Nobody's using it now.

Voice Lib.
193-
194 Chevalier, Maurice, 1889-1972.
World of Maurice Chevalier. NBC
Television, 1963.
2 reels (7 in.) 7 1/2 in. per sec.
phonotape.

Voice Lib.
M1265
bd.1 Chevalier, Maurice, 1889-1972.
Biographical sketch in the form of an
interview with stage personality Maurice
Chevalier, covering his entire lifespan.
NET, July 17, 1967.
1 reel (7 in.) 7 1/2 in. per sec.
phonotape.

1. Chevalier, Maurice, 1889-1972.

Voice Lib.
M322 Chevalier, Maurice, 1889-1972
Biography in sound (radio program)
W.C. Fields, the magnificent rogue.
NBC, 1955.
1 reel (7 in.) 7 1/2 in. per sec. phonotape.
I. Fields, W. C., 1879-1946. I. Fields, W. C., 1879-1946.
II. Allen, Fred, 1894-1956. III. LaBaron, William IV.
Taylor, Robert Lewis, 1912- V. McCarey, Thomas Leo, 1898-
1969. VI. Harkins, James - VII. Chevalier, Maurice,
1889-1972. VIII. Kuromoto, Mrs. George IX. Flynn,
Errol Leslie, 1909-1959. X. Wynn, Ed, 1886-1966. XI. Dowling,
Ray Dooley XII. Sennett, Mack XIII. Overacher,
Ronald Leroy XIV. Bergen, Edgar, 1903- XV. Taurog,
Norman, 1899- XVI. Runhell, Ann XVII. Cowen,
Lester

Voice Lib.
M1490
bd.3 Chiang, Mei-ling (Sung), 1897-
Discussing world political situation at
the conclusion of World War II. GRV
location, 1942.
1 reel (7 in.) 7 1/2 in. per sec.
phonotape..

C1
841 CHILDREN
Whorf, Michael, 1933-
The wonderful world of children.
1 tape cassette. (The visual sounds
of Mike Whorf. Social, S41)
Originally presented on his radio program, Kaleidoscope,
WJR, Detroit.
Duration: 40 min., 10 sec.
Kids, kids, kids – a tribute to the small - tenderly and
warmly performed with the accent on how delightful, naive, and
affectionate children can be.

I. Children. I. Title.

Voice Lib.
M1693 CHILDREN - CARE AND HYGIENE
Spock, Benjamin McLane, 1903-
bd.2 On the younger generation and his own
pro-peace activities, anti-obscenity
activities, etc., on Merv Griffin Show.
25 min. phonotape (1 r. 7 1/2 i.p.s.)

1. Women's Liberation Movement.
2. Children - Care & hygiene. 3. Johnson,
Lyndon Baines, Pres. U.S., 1908-
I. Griffin, Mervyn Edward, 1925-

CHILE - POLITICS AND GOVERNMENT

Voice Lib.
M1744   Allende Gossens, Salvador, 1908-1973.
bd.4   Interview with John Wallach. WKAR,
        August, 1973.
          2 min., 40 sec.   phonotape (1 r.   7 1/2
        i.p.s.)

          Wallach in turn was interviewed by Rich Adams.

          1. Chile - Pol & govt. 2. Socialism in
        Chile. 3. Allende Gossens, Salvador, 1908-
        1973. I. Wallach, John. II. Adams, Rich.

C1   CHOPIN, FRYDERYK FRANCISZEK, 1810-1849
PWM2   Whorf, Michael, 1933-
          Chopin.
          1 tape cassette. (The visual sounds of
        Mike Whorf. Panorama; a world of music, PWM-2)
          Originally presented on his radio program, Kaleidoscope,
        WJR, Detroit.
          Duration: 26 min.
          The life and times of Chopin, the poet of the piano,
        including excerpts of his music.

          L. Chopin, Fryderyk Franciszek, 1810-1849. L. Title.

Voice Lib.
352   Ching, Cyrus Stuart, 1876-1968.
bd.2   Federal mediator Ching on the necessity
        of avoiding a coal strike. NBC, 1949.
          1 reel (7 in.)   7 1/2 in. per sec.
        phonotape.

C1   CHOPIN, FRYDERYK FRANCISZEK, 1810-1849
A9   Whorf, Michael, 1933-
          Poet of the piano.
          1 tape cassette. (The visual sounds of
        Mike Whorf. Art, music, and letters, A9)

          Originally published on his radio program, Kaleidoscope,
        WJR, Detroit.
          Duration: 27 min., 30 sec.
          With aspects of his career known only to the devotee, this
        narrative is a portrait of one of the masters, Chopin.

          L. Chopin, Fryderyk Franciszek, 1810-1849. L. Title.

Voice Lib.
M1721   Chisholm, Shirley, 1924-
bd.1   Tells why she ran for President.
        WKAR, June 7, 1974.
          3 min.   phonotape (1 r.   7 1/2 i.p.s.)

          1. Chisholm, Shirley, 1924-
        2. Presidents - U.S. - Elections - 1972.

           Chopin
C1
PWM2   Whorf, Michael, 1933-
          Chopin.
          1 tape cassette. (The visual sounds of
        Mike Whorf. Panorama; a world of music, PWM-2)
          Originally presented on his radio program, Kaleidoscope,
        WJR, Detroit.
          Duration: 26 min.
          The life and times of Chopin, the poet of the piano,
        including excerpts of his music.

          L. Chopin, Fryderyk Franciszek, 1810-1849. L. Title.

Voice Lib.
M1703   Chomsky, Noam
          Address at Michigan State University.
        WKAR, May 9, 1972.
          50 min.   phonotape (1 r.   7 1/2 i.p.s.)

          1. Vietnamese Conflict, 1961-   - U.S.

Voice Lib. Chou-En-Lai, 1898-
M1496   Nixon, Richard Milhous, Pres. U.S., 1913-
bd.2   President's China trip; banquet in Peking
        hosted by President Nixon, including toasts
        by President Nixon and Premier Chou-En-Lai
        and Chinese translations. CBS, February 25,
        1972.
          1 reel (7 in.)   7 1/2 in. per sec.
        phonotape.

          I. Chou-En-Lai, 1898-

           Chop, Al
Voice Lib.
M968   Gemini 9 (space flight): description of
bd.2   countdown and lift-off of "Agena" by
        Gemini Mission Control (voice of Al Chop)
        for a period of 11 minutes, 41 seconds,
        until Gemini flight was scrubbed. Comments
        by NBC's Huntley, Brinkley, and Frank McGee.
        NBC TV, May 17, 1966.
          1 reel (7 in.)   7 1/2 in. per sec.   phonotape.
          L. Project Gemini. 2. Stafford, Thomas P.   1930-   3.
        Cernan, Eugene Andrew, 1934-   L. Stafford, Thomas P   1930-
        H. Cernan, Eugene Andrew, 1934-   III. Chop, Al   IV.
        Huntley, Chet, 1911-19 A.V. Brinkley, David McClure, 1920-
        VL McGee, Frank, 1921-1974.

C1   CHRISTIANITY
R1   Whorf, Michael, 1933-
          The lesson never learned.
          1 tape cassette. (The visual sounds of
        Mike Whorf. Religion, R1)

          Originally presented on his radio program, Kaleidoscope,
        WJR, Detroit.
          Duration: 46 min., 15 sec.
          This is the story of Jesus from His birth, through His ministry and
        teaching, to His death. It is based on the Bible, the stories which
        unfold in the Gospels, and is ecumenical in approach.

          L. Jesus Christ. 2. Christianity. L. Title.

Christmas Carol
Voice Lib.
134   Dickens, Charles, 1812-1870.
          Christmas Carol, dramatized by an all-star
        cast led by Lionel Barrymore and Rudy Vallee.
        NBC, 1941.
          1 reel (7 in.)   7 1/2 in. per sec.
        phonotape.

          I. Barrymore, Lionel, 1878-1954. II.
        Vallee, Rudy, 1901-   III. Title.

Voice Lib.
M715   Churchill, Winston Leonard Spencer, 1874-
bd.4   1965.
          Excerpt of address to the nation. Initial
        speech as Prime Minister.   1940.
          1 reel (7 in.)   7 1/2 in. per sec.
        phonotape.

Christmas day at the workhouse
Voice Lib.
M793   Hilliard, Robert
bd.4   American actor in "Christmas Day at the
        Workhouse".   Victor, 1913.
          1 reel (7 in.)   7 1/2 in. per sec.
        phonotape.

          I. Title: Christmas day at the workhouse.

Voice Lib.
532   Churchill, Winston Leonard Spencer, 1874-
bd.1   1965.
          "In a Solemn Hour", first speech as Prime
        Minister; review of Britain's current war
        position.   BBC, May 19, 1940.
          1 reel (7 in.)   7 1/2 in. per sec.
        phonotape.

          I. Title.

Christmas - thirty years ago
Voice Lib.
1293   Capote, Truman, 1924-
          TV dramatization of story by Capote,
        "Christmas - Thirty Years Ago", with
        descriptions of incidents by the author.
        ABC-TV, December 19, 1967.
          1 reel (7 in.)   7 1/2 in. per sec.
        phonotape.

          I. Title: Christmas - thirty years ago.

Voice Lib.
M714   Churchill, Sir Winston Leonard Spencer,
bd.9   1874-1965.
          Speaking about France's surrender in
        World War II.   June 16-22, 1940.
          7 min., 1 sec.   phonotape (1 r.
        7 1/2 i.p.s.)

          1. World War, 1939-1945 - France.

Church, Samuel Harden, 1858-1943
Voice Lib.
M862   Conrad, Frank
bd.2   Memorial program on his death with eulogies
        on his accomplishments by S.H. Church
        (Pres. Carnegie Institute of Technology),
        L.W. Lamb (Director of Westinghouse Research
        Laboratories) and David Sarnoff (Pres. of
        R.C.A.)   KDKA, December 13, 1944.
          1 reel (7 in.)   7 1/2 in. per sec.
        phonotape.
          I. Church, Samuel Harden, 1858-1943. II. Lamb, L.
        W.   III. Sarnoff, David, 1891-1971.

Voice Lib.
530   Churchill, Winston Leonard Spencer, 1874-1965.
          "This was their finest hour;" on the
        evacuation of troops from France.   BBC,
        June 18, 1940.
          1 reel (7 in.)   7 1/2 in. per sec.
        phonotape.

          1. Dunkirk, France, Battle of, 1940.

Voice Lib.
M975   Churchill, Winston Leonard Spencer, 1874-
bd.3   1965.
          Speech on the budget.   Rococo-Can.,
        1909.
          1 reel (7 in.)   7 1/2 in. per sec.
        phonotape.

Voice Lib.
531   Churchill, Winston Leonard Spencer, 1874-
bd.1   1965.
          "The War of the Unknown Warriors"; on
        sinking of French Navy, liberty of France,
        Britain stands against Germany alone,
        Hitler's Master Plan, British defense.
        BBC, July 14, 1940.
          1 reel (7 in.)   7 1/2 in. per sec.
        phonotape.

Voice Lib.
531   Churchill, Winston Leonard Spencer, 1874-
bd.2   1965.
        "Every Man to His Post"; German air raids
in daylight, reviews British war history and
compares World War II, Home Guard, indiscrim
inate air raids. BBC, September 11, 1940.
        1 reel (7 in.)   7 1/2 in. per sec.
phonotape.

Voice Lib.
M861   Churchill, Winston Leonard Spencer, 1874-
bd.2   1965.
        Report on progress of Allied forces in
Africa.   NBC shortwave, November 29, 1942.
        1 reel (7 in.)   7 1/2 in. per sec.
phonotape.

Voice Lib.
522   Churchill, Winston Leonard Spencer, 1874-1965.
bd.2   Message regarding Britain's state of
war with Japan.   CBS, December 8, 1941.
        1 reel (7 in.)   7 1/2 in. per sec.
phonotape.

Voice Lib.
M607   Churchill, Sir Winston Leonard Spencer,
bd.2   1874-1965.
        Test transmission; difficulties in making
trans-Atlantic transmission from Washington,
D.C., to London on Home Guard work.
U.S. Armed Forces Radio, 1943.
        1 reel (7 in.)   7 1/2 i.p.s.   phonotape.

Voice Lib.
M1303   Churchill, Winston Leonard Spencer, 1874-
bd.1   1965.
        Address before a joint session of Congress,
Washington, D.C.   Peteler, December 26,
1941.
        1 reel (7 in.)   7 1/2 in. per sec.
phonotape.

Voice Lib.
M854   Churchill, Winston Leonard Spencer, 1874-
bd.3   1965.
        VE-Day announcement in detail. Uncond-
itional surrender terms and procedures and
review of the various phases of World War II.
May 8, 1945.
        1 reel (7 in.)   7 1/2 in. per sec.
phonotape.

Voice Lib.
588-   Churchill, Winston Leonard Spencer, 1874-
589   1965.
bd.1   Speech to Canadian Parliament in Ottawa,
Ontario, on Allied efforts to avoid war,
importance of waging total war now that the
enemy has asked for it, "some chicken, some
neck", Canadian war effort, attacks actions
of French generals in refusing to believe
strength of Britain, armament supply.   CBS,
December 30, 1941.
        2 reels (7 in.)   7 1/2 in. per sec.
phonotape.

Voice Lib.
M860   Churchill, Winston Leonard Spencer, 1874-1965.
        Addresses at testimonial dinner held in
Waldorf Astoria hotel, New York, to Winston
Churchill.   NBC, March 15, 1946.
        1 reel (7 in.)   7 1/2 in. per sec.
phonotape.

Voice Lib.
M829   Churchill, Sir Winston Leonard Spencer,
bd.1   1874-1965.
        Shortwave broadcast to the world reviewing
past and current war situation, Russian
military progress, Japan's conquests in the
East; cautioning against discouragement on
the loss of Singapore and Malayan Peninsula.
KIKA, February 14, 1942.
        22 min., 30 sec.   phonotape (1 r.
7 1/2 i.p.s.)

        1. World War, 1939-1945.

Voice Lib.
M1222   Churchill, Winston Leonard Spencer, 1874-
bd.2   1965.
        Excerpt of speech at University of Zurich,
Switzerland, pertaining to his suggestion
for United States of Europe as a way of
peace and prosperity of Europe's future.
Peteler, September 19, 1946.
        1 reel (7 in.)   7 1/2 in. per sec.
phonotape.

Voice Lib.
533   Churchill, Winston Leonard Spencer, 1874-1965.
bd.4   Excerpt from Fulton, Missouri address.
       March of Time, 1948.
          1 reel (7 in.)   7 1/2 in. per sec.
       phonotape.

              Churchill, Sir Winston Leonard Spencer,
Voice Lib.   1874-1965
353   Russia and the bomb, discussed by various
bd.19   personalities.   NBC, September 25, 1949.
          1 reel (7 in.)   7 1/2 in. per sec.
       phonotape.

          Participants: Harrison Brown, Harold Urey,
       Samuel Allison, Thornton Hugness, Brien McMahon,
       Paul Douglas, John Foster Dulles, Leslie Groves,
       Winston Churchill, Dean Acheson, James Fleming.

          I. Brown, Harrison Scott, 1917-   II.
       Urey, Harold Clayton, 1893-   III. Allison,
                         (Continued on next card)

              Churchill, Sir Winston Leonard Spencer,
Voice Lib.   1874-1965
353   Russia and the bomb... 1949.   (Card 2)
bd.19

          Samuel King, 1900-   IV. Hugness, Thornton.
       V. McMahon, James O'Brien, 1903-1952. VI.
       Douglas, Paul Howard, 1892-   VII. Dulles,
       John Foster, 1888-1959. VIII. Groves, Leslie
       R   1896-1970. IX. Churchill, Winston
       Leonard Spencer, 1874-1965. X. Acheson, Dean
       Gooderham, 1893-1971. XI. Fleming, James,
       1915-

Voice Lib.
M1226 Churchill, Winston Leonard Spencer, 1874-
       1965.
          Address before joint session of U.S.
       Congress by Prime Minister Churchill discussing
       Britain's post-war problems and the unity
       of Europe. CBS, January 17, 1952.
          1 reel (7 in.)   7 1/2 in. per sec.
       phonotape.

Voice Lib.
532   Churchill, Winston Leonard Spencer, 1874-1965.
bd.2   Broadcast to the nation on the death of
       King George VI; eulogy of King George VI.
       BBC, February 7, 1952.
          1 reel (7 in.)   7 1/2 in. per sec.
       phonotape.

          1. George VI, king of Great Britain, 1895-
       1952.

Voice Lib.
570-   Churchill, Winston Leonard Spencer, 1874-1965.
571   Winston Spencer Churchill: The Public Years. As a liberal;
       Britain in 20th century; role of government; on conclusion of World
       War I; on Al Smith's 1928 campaign; Bolshevism; Nazis' potential
       invasion power; British vulnerability to being dragged into war;
       fears of dictators; calls for arming of Free World; "the gathering
       storm" excerpt; Russia's future role in World War II; error of
       neutrality; praises Finnish courage; on becoming Prime Minister;
       "blood, tears, toil and sweat"; speaking to France; Thousand Year
       speech; Britain stands alone and prepares for battle; German night
       attacks on London; Britain in Hitler's plan for world dominance;
       "so much owed to so many"; letter from FDR; calls for war
       materials from U.S.; motives of U.S. and Lend-Lease; Mussolini
       joining Hitler; outcome of World War II; "the old lion" stands;
       support for Russia; desire to win; will declare war on Japan if U.S.
                         (Continued on next card)

Voice Lib.
570-   Churchill, Winston Leonard Spencer, 1874-1965.
571   Winston Spencer Churchill: The Public Years.
       1955. (Card 2)

          does; invasion of Pearl Harbor and British declaration of war on
       Japan; before U.S. Congress on Japan's actions; before Canadian
       Parliament on France's failure to judge British strength; trip to
       Kremlin; victory in North Africa; on liberation of Africa; more
       help for Russia; cost of lives in invasion of the continent; Russian
       and U.S. successes; coming of D-Day; comments on Yalta meeting;
       death of FDR; linking of forces on Elbe; German surrender; domestic
       British politics; art of writing; "an iron curtain has descended";
       need for U.S. of Europe; the Cold War; reminiscing; campaigning
       again for Prime Minister; death of King George VI; new attempts
       at reconciliation with Russia; unified defence for Western Europe;
                         (Continued on next card)

Voice Lib.
570-   Churchill, Winston Leonard Spencer, 1874-1965.
571   Winston Spencer Churchill: The Public Years.
       1955. (Card 3)

          80th birthday; and "Lion's Heart of Britain" on retirement.
       Columbia Records Institute, 1955.
          2 reels (7 in.) 7 1/2 in. per sec. phonotape.

          1. Churchill, Winston Leonard Spencer,
       1874-1965.

Voice Lib.
M742   Churchill, Winston Leonard Spencer, 1874-
bd.4   1965.
          Excerpt of speech during British election
       campaign made at Woodford. BBC, September 28,
       1959.
          1 reel (7 in.)   7 1/2 in. per sec.
       phonotape.

              Churchill, Winston Leonard Spencer,
Voice Lib.   1874-1965
M621   Radio in the 1940's (Part II): a series of
bd.1-   excerpts from important broadcasts of the
12   1940's; a sample of radio of the period.
       NVL, April, 1964.
          1 reel (7 in.) 7 1/2 in. per sec. phonotape.
       I. Daly, John Charles, 1914-   II. Hall, Josef Washington,
       1894-   III. Shirer, William Lawrence, 1904-   IV. Roosevelt,
       Eleanor (Roosevelt) 1884-1962. V. Roosevelt, Franklin Delano,
       Pres. U.S., 1882-1945. VI. Churchill, Winston Leonard Spencer,
       1874-1965. VII. Wainwright, Jonathan Mayhew, 1883-1953. VIII.
       Cantor, Eddie, 1893-1964. IX. Sinatra, Francis Albert, 1917-
       X. Hope, Bob, 1903-   XI. Crosby, Bing, 1901-   XII. Shore,
       Dinah, 1917(?)-   XIII. Bergen, Edgar, 1903-   XIV. Armstrong,
       Louis, 1900-1971. XV. Eldridge, Roy, 1911-

Churchill, Winston Leonard Spencer, 1874–
1965
Voice Lib.
M273-   Biography in sound (radio program)
274   Franklin Delano Roosevelt: the friends and
bd.1   former associates of Franklin Roosevelt on
the tenth anniversary of the President's death.
NBC Radio, April, 1955.
    2 reels (7 in.)   7 1/2 in. per sec.
phonotape.
   L. Roosevelt, Franklin Delano, Pres. U.S., 1882-1945. L.
McIntire, Ross T   1899-   II. Mellett, Lowell, 1884-1960.
III. Tully, Grace   IV. Henderson, Leon, 1895-
V. Roosevelt, Eleanor (Roosevelt) 1884-1962. VI. DeGraaf, Albert
VII. Lehman, Herbert Henry, 1878-1963. VIII. Rosenman, Samuel
Irving, 1896-   IX. Arvey, Jacob   X. Moley, Raymond,
1886-   XI. Farley, James Aloysius, 1888-   XII. Roosevelt,
                      (Continued on next card)

Churchill, Winston Leonard Spencer, 1874–
1965
Voice Lib.
572-   I can hear it now (radio program)
573   1933-1946.   CBS, 1948.
bd.1   2 reels (7 in.)   7 1/2 in. per sec.
phonotape.
   L. Murrow, Edward Roscoe, 1908-1965. II. LaGuardia, Fiorello
Henry, 1882-1947. III. Chamberlain, Neville, 1869-1949. IV.
Roosevelt, Franklin Delano, Pres. U.S., 1882-1945. V. Churchill,
Winston Leonard Spencer, 1874-1965. VI. Gaulle, Charles de,
Pres. France, 1890-1970. VII. Eisenhower, Dwight David, Pres. U.S.,
1890-1969. VIII. Willkie, Wendell Lewis, 1892-1944. IX. Martin,
Joseph William, 1884-1968. X. Elizabeth II, Queen of Great Britain,
1926-   XI. Margaret Rose, Princess of Gt. Brit., 1930-   XII.
Johnson, Hugh Samuel, 1882-1942. XIII. Smith, Alfred Emanuel,
1873-1944. XIV. Lindbergh, Charles Augustus, 1902-   XV. Davis,
                       (Continued on next card)

Churchill, Winston Leonard Spencer, 1874–
1965
Voice Lib.
573   I can hear it now (radio program)
bd.2-   1945-1949.   CBS, 1950?
574   2 reels (7 in.)   7 1/2 in. per sec.
bd.1   phonotape.
   L. Murrow, Edward Roscoe, 1908-1965. II. Nehru, Jawaharlal,
1889-1964. III. Philip, duke of Edinburgh, 1921-   IV. Elizabeth II,
Queen of Great Britain, 1926-   V. Ferguson, Homer, 1889-   VI.
Hughes, Howard Robard, 1905-   VII. Marshall, George Catlett,
1880-   VIII. Ruth, George Herman, 1895-1948. IX. Lilienthal,
David Eli, 1899-   X. Trout, Robert, 1909-   XI. Gage, Arthur,
XII. Jackson, Robert Houghwout, 1892-1954. XIII. Gromyko, Ana-
tolii Andreevich, 1908-   XIV. Baruch, Bernard Mannes, 1870-
1965. XV. Churchill, Winston Leonard Spencer, 1874-1965. XVI.
Winchell, Walter, 1897-   XVII. Davis, Elmer Holmes, 1890-
                       (Continued on next card)

Churchill, Winston Leonard Spencer, 1874–1965
Voice Lib.
381-   I can hear it now (radio program)
382   CBS, April 26, 1951.
bd.1   2 reels (7 in.)   7 1/2 in. per sec.   phonotape.
   L. Radio Free Europe. 2. Strategic Air Command. L.
Ridgway, Matthew Bunker, 1895-   II. Churchill, Winston Leonard
Spencer, 1874-1965. III. Bevan, Aneurin, 1897-1960. IV. Nixon,
Richard Milhous, Pres. U.S., 1913-   V. Kerr, Robert Samuel, 1896-
1963. VI. Brewster, Ralph Owen, 1888-1962. VII. Wherry, Kenneth
Spicer, 1892-1951. VIII. Capehart, Homer Earl, 1897-   IX.
Lehman, Herbert Henry, 1878-1963. X. Taft, Robert Alphonso,
1889-1953. XI. Moody, Arthur Edson Blair, 1902-1954. XII.
Martin, Joseph William, 1884-1968. XIII. McMahon, James O'Brien,
1903-1952. XIV. MacArthur, Douglas, 1880-1964. XVII. Wilson,
Charles Edward, 1886-1972. VIII. Irvine, Clarence T

Churchill, Winston Leonard Spencer, 1874-1965
Voice Lib.
M1033   Voice of America.
    Twentieth anniversary program of Voice of
America broadcasts narrated by Henry Fonda,
and including the voices of Carl Sandburg,
Danny Kaye, Jawaharlal Nehru, Franklin D.
Roosevelt, Charles Malik, Arnold Toynbee,
William Faulkner, Harry S. Truman, Dwight D.
Eisenhower, Helen Hayes, Dag Hammarskjöld,
Winston Churchill, and John F. Kennedy.
Voice of America, 1963.
    1 reel (7 in.)   7 1/2 in. per sec.
phonotape.   (Continued on next card)

Churchill, Winston Leonard Spencer, 1874-1965
Voice Lib.
M1033   Voice of America. Twentieth anniversary
       program... 1963.   (Card 2)
   L. Fonda, Henry Jaynes, 1905-   II. Sandburg, Carl,
1878-1967. III. Kaye, Danny, 1913-   IV. Nehru, Jawaharlal,
1889-1964. V. Roosevelt, Franklin Delano, Pres. U.S., 1882-
1945. VI. Malik, Charles Habib, 1906-   VII. Toynbee,
Arnold Joseph, 1889-   VIII. Faulkner, William, 1897-1962.
IX. Truman, Harry S, Pres. U.S., 1884-1972. X. Eisenhower,
Dwight David, Pres. U.S., 1890-1969. XI. Hayes, Helen,
1900-   XII. Hammarskjöld, Dag, 1905-1961. XIII. Churchill,
Winston Leonard Spencer, 1874-1965. XIV. Kennedy, John
Fitzgerald, Pres. U.S., 1917-1963.

CHURCHILL, WINSTON LEONARD SPENCER,
1874-1965
Voice Lib.
M1031   Discussion about Winston Churchill's ability
in military affairs, between Alistair Cooke
and General Dwight Eisenhower, heard at his
home in Gettysburg, Pennsylvania; including
recording of General George C. Marshall's
opinion about the strategic value of U.S.
troops conquering Berlin.   "Studio 67"
production, ABC-TV, January 26, 1967.
1 reel (7 in.)   7 1/2 in. per sec.   phonotape.
   L. Churchill, Winston Leonard Spencer, 1874-1965. L.
Cooke, Alistair, 1908-   II. Eisenhower, Dwight David, Pres.
U.S., 1890-1969.

CHURCHILL, SIR WINSTON LEONARD SPENCER,
1874-1965
Voice Lib.
M722-   Eisenhower, Dwight David, Pres. U.S., 1890-
723   1969.
bd.1   Winston S. Churchill discussed by Walter
Cronkite and Dwight D. Eisenhower, including
Eisenhower's association with Churchill
during and after the war.   CBS, January 25,
1965.
    2 reels (7 in.)   7 1/2 in. per sec.
phonotape.

    I. Churchill, Winston Leonard Spencer, 1874-
1965.   II. Cronkite, Walter Leland, 1916-

CHURCHILL, WINSTON LEONARD SPENCER, 1874-1965
Voice Lib.
M723   Ismay, Hastings Lionel Ismay, baron, 1887-1965.
bd.1   Interview with Edward R. Murrow, dealing
with Ismay's reminiscences about Winston S.
Churchill.   CBS, 1960.
    1 reel (7 in.)   7 1/2 in. per sec.
phonotape.

    1. Churchill, Winston Leonard Spencer, 1874-
1965.   I. Murrow, Edward Roscoe, 1908-1965.

CHURCHILL, WINSTON LEONARD SPENCER,
1874-1965
Voice Lib.
254-   Marshall, Herbert, 1887-
255   Winston Churchill, his finest hour. An
autobiography of Sir Winston Churchill on
the occasion of his 80th birthday.   CBC,
1954.
    2 reels (7 in.)   7 1/2 in. per sec.
phonotape.

    1. Churchill, Winston Leonard Spencer,
1874-1965.

CHURCHILL, SIR WINSTON LEONARD SPENCER,
1874-1965
C1
H44   Whorf, Michael, 1933-
         The prime minister - Winston Churchill.
         1 tape cassette. (The visual sounds of
       Mike Whorf. History and heritage, H44)
           Originally presented on his radio program, Kaleidoscope,
         WJR, Detroit.
           Duration: 61 min., 30 sec.
           The story of Churchill, his background, education, his
         successes and failures make him one of the most admired men in
         history.

           L. Churchill, Sir Winston Leonard Spencer, 1874-1965.
         L. Title.

               Ciano, Galeazzo, conte, 1903-1944
Voice Lib.
M1071   German radio (Nazi controlled)
bd.3   Nazi radio announcement giving text of
        pact made between Germany, Italy, and Japan.
        Read in German by Joachim von Ribbentrop, in
        Italian by Count Ciano, and in Japanese by
        Ambassador Kurusu, stating their spheres of
        interest. Peteler, September 27, 1940.
        1 reel (7 in.)   7 1/2 in. per sec.
        phonotape.
          I. Ribbentrop, Joachim von, 1893-1946. II.
        Ciano, Galeazzo, conte, 1903-1944. III.
        Kuruso, Saburo, 1886-1954.

        CICERO, MARCUS TULLIUS
C1
S68   Whorf, Michael, 1933-
         Statesmen and sages; Demosthenes, Aristotle,
       Socrates, Cicero.
       1 tape cassette. (The visual sounds of Mike Whorf. Social, S68)

           Originally presented on his radio program, Kaleidoscope,
         WJR, Detroit.
           Duration: 36 min.
           As ancient Greece and Rome served as the cradle of our modern
         democracy, so do their citizens serve as shining examples of wisdom
         and statecraft for us today.

           L. Demosthenes. 2. Aristoteles. 3. Socrates. 4. Cicero,
         Marcus Tullius. L. Title.

        CIRCUS - U. S.
C1
M7   Whorf, Michael, 1933-
         The big top.
       1 tape cassette. (The visual sounds of Mike Whorf.
       Miscellaneous, M7)

           Originally presented on his radio program, Kaleidoscope,
         WJR, Detroit.
           Duration: 40 min., 45 sec.
           Here is a fascinating look at the three-ringed world wherein
         lies the greatest show on earth, the animals, the clowns, the
         aerialist, the animal trainer, the marvelous magic of Barnum,
         Bailey and Ringling North.

           L. Circus - U. S. 2. Barnum, Bailey and Ringling North.
         L. Title.

              CITIES AND TOWNS
Voice Lib.
M1718   Alinsky, Saul David, 1909-
        Address at Michigan State University's
       University College Colloquium on the Plight
       of the Cities. WKAR, January 27, 1969.
        50 min. phonotape (1 r. 7 1/2 i.p.s.)

           1. Cities and towns. I. Colloquium on
         the Plight of the Cities, Michigan State
         University, 1969.

              CITIES AND TOWNS
Voice Lib.
M1668- Galbraith, John Kenneth, 1908-
1669   The modern city; speech at Michigan
        State University. WKAR, May 1, 1974.
         1 hr., 15 min. phonotape (2 r. 7 1/2
        i.p.s.)

           1. Cities and towns.

              CITIES AND TOWNS
Voice Lib.
M1682   Harris, Sydney J
          What is wrong with the city; address
        at Michigan State University, with Dr.
        Frederic Reeve. WKAR, January 27, 1969.
         47 min. phonotape (1 r. 7 1/2 i.p.s.)

           1. Cities and towns. I. Reeve, Frederic
         Eugene, 1916-

        CITIES AND TOWNS - PLANNING
Voice Lib.
M1585   Ardrey, Robert
bd.2   Property, status, and self-respect.
        WKAR-TV, February 23, 1974.
         15 min. phonotape (1 r. 7 1/2 in. per sec.)

           1. Territoriality (Zoology) 2. Communism.
         3. Cities & towns - Planning. I. Halverson,
         Craig.

              CITIES AND TOWNS - PLANNING
Voice Lib.
M1011   Doxiadēs, Kōnstantinos Apostolou, 1913-
          Lecture at 158 Natural Resources on MSU
        campus on city planning for the future.
        (1 hour). Auspices of Department of Urban
        Planning. Chapin, October 21, 1966.
         1 reel (7 in.)   7 1/2 in. per sec.
        phonotape.

           1. Cities and towns - Planning.

              CITIES AND TOWNS - U.S.
Voice Lib.
M1725   Rubenstein, Richard L
          The American city; address at Michigan
        State University. WKAR, January, 23, 1969.
         50 min. phonotape (1 r. 7 1/2 i.p.s.)

           1. Cities and towns - U. S.

CIVIL RIGHTS

Voice Lib.
M258   Harper, Robert
bd.9B   Report to CBS News, New York; description
          of military control in Montgomery, Alabama
          under state troops. New York, CBS, May 22,
          1961.
              1 reel (7 in.)   7 1/2 i.p.s.   phonotape.

              1. Civil rights. 2. Montgomery, Ala.

CIVIL RIGHTS

Voice Lib.
M1688   Hook, Sidney, 1902-
              Human rights - what is the philosophical
          basis for them? WKAR, February 28, 1969.
              53 min.   phonotape (1 r.   7 1/2 i.p.s.)

              1. Civil rights.

CIVIL RIGHTS

Voice Lib.
M243   Martin, Joseph William, 1884-1968.
bd.8   Comments on the Senate Jury Trial
          Amendment in Civil Rights Bill, by Joseph
          Martin and Emanuel Celler. CBS, August 2,
          1957.
              1 reel (7 in.)   7 1/2 in. per sec.
          phonotape.

              I. Celler, Emanuel, 1888-

CIVIL RIGHTS

Voice Lib.
267-   Vivian, C   T
268   On segregation and freedom; Provost Lecture
          no. 5, Michigan State University.   National
          Voice Library, spring, 1963.
              2 reels (7 in.)   7 1/2 in. per sec.
          phonotape.

CIVIL RIGHTS

Voice Lib.
M1222   Washington Reports; CBS television news. Reports by CBS
bd.1   news correspondents about President Kennedy's Civil
          Rights message to Congress and interviews with Attorney
          General Robert F. Kennedy pertaining to his views on
          his own work in the Justice Department and his own future.
          CBS-TV News, Bergman, March 3, 1963.
              1 reel (7 in.)   7 1/2 i.p.s.   phonotape.

              1. Civil rights. 2. U.S. Dept. of Justice. 3. Kennedy,
          Robert Francis, 1925-1968.   I. Kennedy, Robert Francis,
          1925-1968.

CIVIL RIGHTS - U.S.

Voice Lib.
M1088   Hannah, John Alfred, 1902-
bd.2   Reading excerpt from 1961 Civil Rights
          Commission report.   Location recording,
          February 8, 1963.
              1 reel (7 in.)   7 1/2 in. per sec.
          phonotape.

Voice Lib.
M743   Civil rights march on Montgomery, Alabama.
              Announcer's description of scene as
          marchers arrive in Montgomery; entertain-
          ment by Harry Belafonte and others; A.F.L.
          speaker; Dr. Ralph Abernathy presiding.
          CBS, March 25, 1965.
              38 min.   phonotape (1 r.   7 1/2 i.p.s.)

              1. Negroes - Civil rights.   I. Belafonte,
          Harold, 1927-   II. Abernathy, Ralph
          David, 1926-

Voice Lib.   CIVILIZATION
M1221   Pearl Harbor to Vietnam; BBC documentary
bd.1   TV program of actual voices and events
          during the 25-year period from 1941 to
          1966. BBC, December, 1966.
              1 reel (7 in.)   7 1/2 i.p.s.   phonotape.

              1. Civilization.

                    Clark, Bob
Voice Lib.
M1321   Kennedy, Robert Francis, 1925-1968.
              Debate consisting of questions and answers.
          Senator Robert Kennedy and Senator Eugene
          McCarthy interviewed by ABC news correspondents
          Bill Lawrence and Bob Clark on program
          "Issues and Answers". ABC-TV, June 1, 1968.
              1 reel (7 in.)   7 1/2 in. per sec.
          phonotape.

              I. McCarthy, Eugene Joseph, 1916-   II.
          Lawrence, Bill. III. Clark, Bob

Voice Lib.
M795   Clark, Champ, 1850-1921.
bd.10   Speaking on Democratic achievements.
          The Nation's Forum, April 20, 1920.
              1 reel (7 in.)   7 1/2 in. per sec.
          phonotape.

Voice Lib.
M1731   Clark, Ramsey, 1927-
         Debate on amnesty for draft evaders on
"Firing Line" with William Buckley.   WKAR,
June 21, 1974.
         45 min.   (1 r.   7 1/2 i.p.s.)

         1. Military service, compulsory - U. S.
2. Vietnamese conflict, 1961-   I. Buckley,
William Frank, 19⁷⁷

Voice Lib.
M1694   Clarke, Arthur Charles, 1917-
         Technological forecasting - the world of
2001; address at Michigan State University.
WKAR, 1973.
         53 min.   phonotape (1 r.   7 1/2 i.p.s.)

         Clay, Cassius Marcellus, 1942-
         see
Muhammad Ali, 1942-

         Clayton, Patti
Voice Lib.
M1047   Old-time radio excerpts of the 1930's and
1940's, including: Rudy Vallee singing
"Linger a little longer"; Will Rogers on
panaceas for the Depression; Bing Crosby
singing "Sweet Georgia Brown"; Eddie Cantor;
Jimmy Durante singing "Inka-dinka-do";
musical skit by Clayton, Jackson and Durante;
wit by Harry Hershfield; musical selection
"Thinking of you" by Kay Kyser; Kate Smith
singing theme song, "When the moon comes over
the mountain"; W.C. Fields' temperance
         (Continued on next card)

Voice Lib.   Clayton, Patti
M1047   Old-time radio excerpts of the 1930's and
         1940's...   (Card 2)

         lecture; Al Jolson singing "Rocka-by-your
baby"; and George Burns and Gracie Allen
skit.   TV&R, 1930's and 1940's.
         1 reel (7 in.)   7 1/2 in. per sec.
         I. Vallee, Rudy, 1901-   II. Rogers, Will, 1879-1935.   III.
Crosby, Bing, 1901-   IV. Cantor, Eddie, 1893-1964.   V. Durante,
Jimmy, 1893-   VI. Clayton, Patti   VII. Jackson,
Eddie   VIII. Hershfield, Harry, 1885-   IX. Kyser, Kay,
1906-   X. Smith, Kate, 1909-   XI. Fields, W.C., 1879-
1946.   XII. Jolson, Al, 1886-1950.   XIII. Burns, George, 1896-
XIV. Allen, Gracie, 1906-

CLEMENS, SAMUEL LANGHORNE, 1835-1910
Voice Lib.
M1067-   Holbrook, Hal, 1925-
1068   Portraying Mark Twain with various humorous
bd.1   anecdotes and tales by the famous author;
special TV performance for NBC.   NBC,
March 6, 1967.
         2 reels (7 in.)   7 1/2 in. per sec.
         phonotape.

CLEMENS, SAMUEL LANGHORNE, 1835-1910
C1
A15   Whorf, Michael, 1933-
       Life and times of Mark Twain.
       1 tape cassette.   (The visual sounds of
Mike Whorf.   Art, music, and letters, A15)

         Originally presented on his radio program, Kaleidoscope,
WJR, Detroit.
         Duration: 44 min., 5 sec.
         Here with the narrator serving in the dual role of story
teller and Mark Twain, is this account of the life and times of
the gifted author.

         L. Clemens, Samuel Langhorne, 1835-1910.   L. Title.

CLEMENS, SAMUEL LANGHORNE, 1835-1910.
Voice Lib.   THE ADVENTURES OF HUCKLEBERRY FINN
M1091   Holbrook, Hal, 1925-
bd.1   Mark Twain impersonation of excerpt
from book "Huckleberry Finn".   (LP phono
album) Bergman, 1953.
         1 reel (7 in.)   7 1/2 in. per sec.
         phonotape.

         1. Clemens, Samuel Langhorne, 1835-1910./
The adventures of Huckleberry Finn.

CLEOPATRA, QUEEN OF EGYPT, D. B.C. 30
C1
S24   Whorf, Michael, 1933-
       Cleopatra.
       1 tape cassette.   (The visual sounds of
Mike Whorf.   Social, S24)
         Originally presented on his radio program, Kaleidoscope,
WJR, Detroit.
         Duration: 35 min.
         Here is the story of the young girl who would one day become
queen of Egypt with her lovers Julius Caesar and Marc Antony.

         L. Cleopatra, queen of Egypt, d. B.C. 30.   L. Title.

Voice Lib.   Clifton, Chester B
M915-   As we knew him; words of reminiscence of
916   friends and relatives about the life of
J.F. Kennedy. Narration by Charles Kuralt;
participants: Charles Bartlett, Lemayne
Billings, Robert Kennedy, Rose Kennedy,
James Reed, Adlai Stevenson, Gen. Chester B.
Clifton, etc.   Columbia Records Inc., 1965.
         2 reels (7 in.)   7 1/2 in. per sec.
         phonotape.

         1. Kennedy, John Fitzgerald, Pres. U.S.,
1917-1963.   I. Kuralt, Charles, 1934-

         (Continued on next card)

Voice Lib.
M828   Cobb, Irvin Shrewsbury, 1876-1944.
bd.1   Scathing campaign speech against Franklin
        Roosevelt and the third term.   Blue Network,
        November 1, 1940.
            1 reel (7 in.)   7 1/2 in. per sec.
        phonotape.

            Incomplete.

            1. Roosevelt, Franklin Delano, Pres. U.S.,
        1882-1945.

Voice Lib.
M620   Radio in the 1940's (Part I): a series of
bd.1-   excerpts from important broadcasts of the 1940's; a
bd.16   sample of radio of the period. NVL, April, 1964.
            1 reel (7 in.) 7 1/2 in. per sec. phonotape.
        I. Radio programs. I. Thomas, Lowell Jackson, 1892-   II.
        Gunther, John, 1901-1970. III. Kaltenborn, Hans von, 1878-1965.
        IV. Delmar, Kenny. V. Those were the good old days (Radio
        program) VI. Elman, Dave. VII. Hall, Frederick Lee, 1916-1970.
        VIII. Hobby lobby (Radio program) IX. Roosevelt, Franklin Delano,
        Pres. U.S., 1882-1945. X. Willkie, Wendell Lewis, 1892-1944.
        XI. Hoover, Herbert Clark, Pres. U.S., 1874-1964. XII. Johnson,
        Hugh Samuel, 1882-1942. XIII. Cobb, Irvin Shrewsbury, 1876-1944.
        XIV. Roosevelt, Theodore, 1858-1919. XV. Nye, Gerald Prentice,
        1892-1971. XVI. Lindbergh, Charles Augustus, 1902-   XVII.
        Toscanini, Arturo, 1867-1957.

Voice Lib.
M1064   Cobb, Tyrus Raymond, 1886-1961.
bd.8   Interview with Ty Cobb in Georgia after
        his retirement from baseball.   Fox Movietone,
        1929.
            1 reel (7 in.)   7 1/2 in. per sec.
        phonotape.

            1. Baseball

Voice Lib.
540   Cobb, Tyrus Raymond, 1886-1961.
bd.16   Baseball. Fox Movietone, 1933.
            1 reel (7 in.)   7 1/2 in. per sec.
        phonotape.

            1. Baseball.

Cody, John Patrick, cardinal, 1907-
Voice Lib.
M1391   Apollo 11 (space flight): reception of
bd.2   Apollo 11 astronauts in Chicago. Descrip-
        tion of motorcade on way to Civic Center
        Plaza and ceremonies there. Cardinal Cody's
        invocation. JFK flashback predicting moon
        landing before decade is out. Mayor Daley
        and Alderman Klene resolution making August
        13 "Astronauts' Day". Senator Percy and
        Governor Ogilvie of Illinois. Presentation
        of honorary citizenship to astronauts.
        [Source?] August 13, 1969.
                        (Continued on next card)

Cody, John Patrick, cardinal, 1907-
Voice Lib.
M1391   Apollo 11 (space flight): reception of Apollo
bd.2   11 astronauts ... 1969.   (Card 2)
            1 reel (7 in.)   7 1/2 in. per sec.
        phonotape.
            I. Project Apollo. 2. Space flight to the moon. 3. Aldrin,
        Edwin E   1930-   4. Collins, Michael, 1930-   5. Armstrong,
        Neil, 1930-   I. Aldrin, Edwin E   1930-   II. Collins,
        Michael, 1930-   III. Armstrong, Neil, 1930-   IV. Cody,
        John Patrick, cardinal, 1907-   V. Kennedy, John Fitzgerald,
        Pres. U.S., 1917-1963. VI. Daley, Richard J   1902-   VII.
        Percy, Charles Harting, 1919-   VIII. Ogilvie, Richard Buell,
        1923-

C1   CODY, WILLIAM FREDERICK, 1846-1917
H55   Whorf, Michael, 1933-
            Buffalo Bill
            1 tape cassette.   (The visual sounds of
        Mike Whorf. History and heritage, H55)

            Originally presented on his radio program, Kaleidoscope,
        WJR, Detroit.
            Duration: 41 min.
            Scout, soldier, Indian fighter, impresario, entrepreneur;
        he was all of these, yet above all, William Frederick Cody was
        a legend.

            I. Cody, William Frederick, 1846-1917. I. Title.

Voice Lib.
394   Cohan, George Michael, 1878-1942.
bd.6   Origin of famous curtain speech; his
        outlook on life.   Private recording,
        April 24, 1939.
            1 reel (7 in.)   7 1/2 in. per sec.
        phonotape.

Voice Lib. Cohan, George Michael, 1878-1942
M619   Radio in the 1930's (Part II): a series of
bd.1-   excerpts of the 1930's; a sample of radio
14   of the period. NVL, April, 1964.
            1 reel (7 in.) 7 1/2 in. per sec. phonotape.
        I. Allen, Fred, 1894-1956. II. Delmar, Kenny   III. Donald,
        Peter   IV. Pious, Minerva   V. Fennelly, Parker   VI.
        Boyer, Charles, 1899-   VII. Dunne, Irene, 1904-   VIII.
        DeMille, Cecil Blount, 1881-1959. IX. West, Mae, 1893-   X.
        Dafoe, Allan Ray, 1883-1943. XI. Dionne quintuplets. XII. Ortega,
        Santos   XIII. War of the worlds (radio program) XIV. Ives, Burl,
        1909-   XV. Robinson, Earl, 1910-   XVI. Temple, Shirley,
        1928-   XVII. Earhart, Amelia, 1898-1937. XVIII. Lawrence,
        Gertrude, 1901-1952. XIX. Cohan, George Michael, 1878-1942.
        XX. Shaw, George Bernard, 1856-1950. XXI. Hitler, Adolf, 1889-
        1945. XXII. Chamberlain, Neville, 1869-1940. XXIII. Roosevelt,
        Franklin Delano, Pres. U.S., 1882-1945.

C1   COHAN, GEORGE MICHAEL, 1878-1942
M23   Whorf, Michael, 1933-
            Cohan is a grand old name.
            1 tape cassette.   (The visual sounds of
        Mike Whorf. Miscellaneous, M23)

            Originally presented on his radio program, Kaleidoscope,
        WJR, Detroit.
            Duration: 37 min., 30 sec.
            The story of George M. Cohan, actor, director, producer, set
        designer, writer, musician and composer, sometimes all at the
        same time.

            I. Cohan, George Michael, 1878-1942. I. Title.

Cohen, Benjamin Victor, 1894-
Voice Lib.
M273- Biography in sound (radio program)
274 Franklin Delano Roosevelt: the friends and
bd.1 former associates of Franklin Roosevelt on
the tenth anniversary of the President's death.
NBC Radio, April, 1955.
2 reels (7 in.) 7 1/2 in. per sec.
phonotape.
I. Roosevelt, Franklin Delano, Pres. U.S., 1882-1945. I.
McIntire, Ross T 1899- II. Mellett, Lowell, 1884-1960.
III. Tully, Grace IV. Henderson, Leon, 1895-
V. Roosevelt, Eleanor (Roosevelt) 1884-1962. VI. DeGraaf, Albert
VII. Lehman, Herbert Henry, 1878-1963. VIII. Rosenman, Samuel
Irving, 1896- IX. Arvey, Jacob X. Moley, Raymond,
1886- XI. Farley, Ja Aloysius, 1888- XII. Roosevelt,
(Continued on next card)

Voice Lib.
M795 Colby, Bainbridge, 1869-1950.
bd.7 Speaking about loyalty. The Nation's
Forum, 1910.
1 reel (7 in.) 7 1/2 in. per sec.
phonotape.

Voice Lib.
M1707 Cohn, Roy M 1927-
bd.3 On the Mike Douglas show recalling the
McCarthy era with no regrets. Includes
Liberace. ABC, May 30, 1974.
7 min. phonotape (1 r. 7 1/2 i.p.s.)

1. McCarthy-Army controversy. I. Douglas,
Mike, 1925?- II. Liberace, 1919-

COLD (DISEASE)
Voice Lib.
M1671 Pauling, Linus Carl, 1901-
Vitamin C and the common cold; controversy
and harassment. WKAR, April 20, 1972.
50 min. phonotape (1 r. 7 1/2 i.p.s.)

1. Cold (Disease) 2. Ascorbic acid.

Cohn, Roy M 1927-
Voice Lib.
M1281 U.S. Congress. Senate. Committee on Government Operations.
Permanent Subcommittee on Investigations.
Proceedings of the 11th session of Senate Army-McCarthy
hearings, May 6, 1954. Sen. McCarthy on witness stand, pertaining
to missing letter from J. Edgar Hoover regarding possible spies at
Ft. Monmouth, N.J. Other speakers: Roy Cohn, Committee Counsel
Jenkins, Robert A. Collier. Summary by CBS' Griffin Bancroft.
CBS Radio, May 6, 1954.
1 reel (7 in.) 7 1/2 in. per sec. phonotape.
I. McCarthy-Army controversy, 1954. I. McCarthy,
Joseph Raymond, 1909-1957. II. Cohn, Roy M 1927-
III. Jenkins, Ray Howard, 1897- IV. Collier, Robert A
V. Bancroft, Griffin

COLLECTIVE BARGAINING
Voice Lib.
352 Lewis, John Llewellyn, 1880-1969.
bd.1 Answering questions of the press on
collective bargaining and its uses, wage
and price freezes. CBS, January 8, 1951.
1 reel (7 in.) 7 1/2 in. per sec.
phonotape.

1. Collective bargaining.

Cohn, Roy M 1927-
Voice Lib.
M1284 U.S. Congress. Senate. Committee on Government Operations.
Permanent Subcommittee on Investigations.
Proceedings of the 13th session of Senate Army-McCarthy
hearings, May 10, 1954. Senator Dirksen suggests they be held
privately; Secretary Stevens makes statement and Senator McCarthy
and his counsel, Roy Cohn, cross-examine Stevens; discussion of
alleged communists at Ft. Monmouth and pressure of favored
treatment for Private Schine. CBS Radio, May 10, 1954.
1 reel (7 in.) 7 1/2 in. per sec. phonotape.
I. McCarthy-Army controversy, 1954. I. Dirksen, Everett
McKinley, 1896-1969. II. Stevens, Robert Ten Broeck, 1899-
III. McCarthy, Joseph Raymond, 1909-1957. IV. Cohn, Roy M
1927-

Voice Lib.
M394 Collier, John, 1884-1968.
bd.4 Talks about Indian affairs during FDR's
administration; tells of the recording made
by Woodrow Wilson to greet Indians on their
reservations. G.R.Vincent, June 14, 1939.
1 reel (7 in.) 7 1/2 i.p.s. phonotape.

1. Indians of North America - Government
Relations.

Cohn, Roy M 1927-
Voice Lib.
M1320 U.S. Congress. Senate. Committee on Government Operations.
Permanent Sub committee on Investigations.
Proceedings of the 17th session of Senate Army-McCarthy
hearings, May 14, 1954. Sen. Mundt questioning Mr. Adams
about high-level meeting dealing with United Nations. Exchanges
between Senator Mundt and Army Counsel Welch. Senator
McCarthy examining Sen. Dirksen. Discussion of purgery charges
against Carr. Cohn and Adams speak about private dinner party.
CBS TV, May 14, 1954.
1 reel (7 in.) 7 1/2 in. per sec. phonotape.
I. McCarthy-Army controversy, 1954. I. Mundt, Karl Earl,
1900- II. Welch, Joseph Nye, 1890-1960. III. McCarthy,
Joseph Raymond, 1909-1957. IV. Dirksen, Everett McKinley, 1896-
1969. V. Cohn, Roy M 1927- VI. Adams, John G

Collier, Robert A
Voice Lib.
M1281 U.S. Congress. Senate. Committee on Government Operations.
Permanent Subcommittee on Investigations.
Proceedings of the 11th session of Senate Army-McCarthy
hearings, May 6, 1954. Sen. McCarthy on witness stand, pertaining
to missing letter from J. Edgar Hoover regarding possible spies at
Ft. Monmouth, N.J. Other speakers: Roy Cohn, Committee Counsel
Jenkins, Robert A. Collier. Summary by CBS' Griffin Bancroft.
CBS Radio, May 6, 1954.
1 reel (7 in.) 7 1/2 in. per sec. phonotape.
I. McCarthy-Army controversy, 1954. I. McCarthy,
Joseph Raymond, 1909-1957. II. Cohn, Roy M 1927-
III. Jenkins, Ray Howard, 1897- IV. Collier, Robert A
V. Bancroft, Griffin

Voice Lib.
M739   Collingwood, Charles Cummings, 1917-
bd.8   Recording he made on the beach during
      D-Day in France, describing activities of the
      invasion, including short interview with a
      sailor. CBS, June 6, 1944.
      1 reel (7 in.)   7 1/2 in. per sec.
      phonotape.

      1. World War, 1939-1945 - Campaigns -
Normandy.

Voice Lib.
M913-   Collingwood, Charles Cummings, 1917-
914   "Where we stand in Vietnam"; CBS Reports pro-
bd.1   gram. Various CBS news correspondents discussing
      current situation of the war in Vietnam,
      including Peter Kalisher, Eric Sevareid, Marvin
      Kalb, Roger Mudd, Harry Reisner, and British
      correspondent James Cameron. CBS-TV,
      December 14, 1964.
      2 reels (7 in.)   7 1/2 in. per sec.
      phonotape.
      1. Vietnamese Conflict, 1961-   - U.S.
I. Title.

      Collingwood, Charles Cummings, 1917-
Voice Lib.
119-   A tour of the White House (Television program)
120   Tour of the White House with Mrs. John F.
      Kennedy. Narrated by Charles Collingwood.
      CBS-TV special, February, 1962.
      2 reels (7 in.)   7 1/2 in. per sec.
      phonotape.

      I. Collingwood, Charles Cummings, 1917-
II. Kennedy, Jacqueline (Bouvier), 1929-

      Collingwood, Charles Cummings, 1917-
Voice Lib.
M317   Johnson, Lyndon Baines, Pres. U.S., 1908-1973.
bd.2   Nancy Dickerson of NBC at Inaugural Ball
      talking to Vice-President and Mrs. Johnson;
      Charles Collingwood and Johnson on Sam Rayburn;
      Johnson in Berlin, audience with Pope John.
      NBC, CBS, November 24, 1963.
      1 reel (7 in.) 7 1/2 in. per sec. phonotape.
      I. Rayburn, Samuel Taliaferro, 1882-1961. I. Dickerson,
      Nancy Hanschman, 1929 (?)-   II. Johnson, Claudia Alta
      (Taylor) 1912-   III. Collingwood, Charles Cummings, 1917-
      IV. Joannes XXIII, Pope, 1881-1963.

Voice Lib.   Collingwood, Charles Cummings, 1917-
M1223   Town meeting of the world (Television program)
bd.1   Discussion and questions by students of
      various countries from Britain about the image
      of America in the eyes of youth. Answers by
      Senator Robert F. Kennedy of New York and
      Governor Ronald Reagan of California, with
      Charles Collingwood as moderator. Principle
      items covered: Vietnam, civil rights. CBS-TV,
      May 15, 1967.
      1 reel (7 in.) 7 1/2 in. per sec. phonotape.
      I. Kennedy, Robert Francis, 1925-1968. II. Reagan, Ronald
      Wilson, 1911-   III. Collingwood, Charles Cummings, 1917-

---

      Collins, Joseph, 1866-1950
Voice Lib.
M272   Biography in sound (radio program)
bd.1   Heywood Broun. NBC, date?
      1 reel (7 in.)   7 1/2 in. per sec.
      phonotape.

      I. Broun, Heywood Campbell, 1888-1939.   I. Broun,
      Heywood Campbell, 1888-1939. II. Swope, Herbert Bayard,
      1882-1958. III. Wilson, Mattie   IV. Jackson, Gardner
      V. Meany, Thomas   VI. Waldron, Beatrice   VII.
      Gordon, Max   VIII. Madison, Connie   IX. Gannett,
      Lewis Stiles, 1891-1966. X. Collins, Joseph, 1866-1950. XI.
      Brown, Earl Louis, 1900-   XII. Levy, Newman, 1888-
      XIII. Growth, John   XIV. Bye, George   XV.
      Roosevelt, Franklin Delano, Pres. U.S., 1882-1945. XVI.
      Reynolds, Quentin James, ( )-1965.

      Collins, Joseph Lawton, 1896-
Voice Lib.
383   I can hear it now (radio program)
      CBS, February 9, 1951.
      1 reel (7 in.)   7 1/2 in. per sec.
      phonotape.
      I. Wilson, Charles Edward, 1886-1972. II. Gabrielson, Guy
      George, 1891-   III. Taft, Robert Alphonso, 1889-1953. IV.
      Martin, Joseph William, 1884-1965. V. McCarthy, Joseph
      Raymond, 1909-1957. VI. Benton, William Burnett, 1900-1973.
      VII. Malone, George Wilson, 1890-1961. VIII. Capehart, Homer
      Earl, 1897-   IX. Eisenhower, Dwight David, Pres. U.S., 1890-
      1969. X. Lee, J   V   XI. Hodge, John Reed, 1893-
      1963. XII. Overton, Watkins   XIII. DiSalle, Michael
      Vincent, 1908-   XIV. Boyce, Eddy   XV. Conklin, Ed
      XVI. Collins, Joseph Lawton, 1896-

      Collins, Michael, 1930-
Voice Lib.
M1384   Apollo 11 (space flight): launch day, July 16,
bd.1   1969. Description of astronauts going up
      the elevator; conversation between Walter
      Cronkite and Walter Schirra at approximately
      2 hours before launch. CBS TV, July 16, 1969.
      1 reel (7 in.)   7 1/2 in. per sec.
      phonotape.
      I. Project Apollo. 2. Space flight to the moon. 3. Aldrin,
      Edwin E   1930-   4. Collins, Michael, 1930-   5. Armstrong,
      Neil, 1930-   I. Aldrin, Edwin E   1930-   II. Collins,
      Michael, 1930-   III. Armstrong, Neil, 1930-   IV. Cronkite,
      Walter Leland, 1916-   V. Schirra, Walter Marty, 1923-

      Collins, Michael, 1930-
Voice Lib.
M1384   Apollo 11 (space flight): biographical sketches
bd.2   of the three astronauts, Edwin Aldrin,
      Michael Collins, and Neil Armstrong, by Chet
      Huntley, at approximately 78 minutes before
      launch time. NBC TV, July 16, 1969.
      1 reel (7 in.)   7 1/2 in. per sec.
      phonotape.
      I. Project Apollo. 2. Space flight to the moon. 3. Aldrin,
      Edwin E   1930-   4. Collins, Michael, 1930-   5. Armstrong,
      Neil, 1930-   I. Aldrin, Edwin E   1930-   II. Collins,
      Michael, 1930-   III. Armstrong, Neil, 1930-   IV. Huntley,
      Chet, 1911-1974.

      Collins, Michael, 1930-
Voice Lib.
M1384   Apollo 11 (space flight): Frank McGee giving
bd.3   an itinerary of space ships, dates, times,
      etc. NBC TV, July 16, 1969.
      1 reel (7 in.)   7 1/2 in. per sec.
      phonotape.

      1. Project Apollo. 2. Space flight to the
      moon. 3. Aldrin, Edwin E   1930-   4.
      Collins, Michael, 1930-   5. Armstrong, Neil,
      1930-   I. Aldrin, Edwin E   1930-   II.
      Collins, Michael, 1930-   III. Armstrong, Neil,
      1930-   IV. McGee, Frank, 1921-1974.

Collins, Michael, 1930-

Voice Lib.
M1384   Apollo 11 (space flight): launch day progress
bd.6   of countdown by Apollo 11 control at 4
         minutes 15 seconds to actual take-off.
         Houston takes over and describes progress
         up to 1,000 miles downrange and successful
         orbit.   NBC TV, July 16, 1969.
           1 reel (7 in.)   7 1/2 in. per sec.
           phonotape.
           1. Project Apollo. 2. Space flight to the moon. 3. Aldrin,
         Edwin E   1930-   4. Collins, Michael, 1930- 5. Armstrong,
         Neil, 1930-   I. Aldrin, Edwin E   1930-   II. Collins,
         Michael, 1930-   III. Armstrong, Neil, 1930-

Collins, Michael, 1930-

Voice Lib.
M1386   Apollo 11 (space flight): excerpts of old
bd.3   Mercury Theatre "War of the Worlds" of
         1938; an interview with Orson Welles by
         Mike Wallace.   CBS TV, July 20, 1969.
           1 reel (7 in.)   7 1/2 in. per sec.
           phonotape.
           1. Project Apollo. 2. Space flight to the moon. 3. Aldrin,
         Edwin E   1930-   4. Collins, Michael, 1930-
         5. Armstrong, Neil, 1930-   I. Aldrin, Edwin E   1930-
         II. Collins, Michael, 1930-   III. Armstrong, Neil, 1930-
         IV. Welles, Orson, 1915-   V. Wallace, Mike, 1918-

Collins, Michael, 1930-

Voice Lib.
M1385   Apollo 11 (space flight): Frank McGee speaking
bd.1   about communications between "Eagle" and
         ground. Conversation between Houston and
         astronauts. Message of "Go for PDI"; "The
         Eagle has landed" (102 hours, 45 minutes,
         40 seconds)   Description of rocks and
         boulders on moon.   NBC TV, July 20, 1969.
           1 reel (7 in.)   7 1/2 in. per sec.   phonotape.
           1. Project Apollo. 2. Space flight to the moon. 3. Aldrin,
         Edwin E   1930-   4. Collins, Michael, 1930-   5.
         II. Collins, Michael, 1930-   III. Armstrong, Neil, 1930-
         IV. McGee, Frank, 1921-1974.

Collins, Michael, 1930-

Voice Lib.
M1587   Apollo 11 (space flight): description of
bd.1   ascent from moon by Frank McGee. Count-
         down, ignition, and lift-off. Meeting the
         command module "Columbia"; docking; trans-
         fer of gear from "Eagle" to "Columbia".
         Recap by ABC's Jules Bergman and Frank
         Reynolds.   NBC and ABC TV, July 21, 1969.
           1 reel (7 in.)   7 1/2 in. per sec.   phonotape.
           1. Project Apollo. 2. Space flight to the moon. 3. Aldrin,
         Edwin E   1930-   4. Collins, Michael, 1930-   5.
         Armstrong, Neil, 1930-   I. Aldrin, Edwin E   1930-   II.
         Collins, Michael, 1930-   III. Armstrong, Neil, 1930-   IV.
         McGee, Frank, 1921-1974. V. Bergman, Jules   VI. Reynolds,
         Frank

Collins, Michael, 1930-

Voice Lib.
M1385   Apollo 11 (space flight): Neil Armstrong
bd.2   requesting everyone everywhere to pause and
         give thanks. Preparing to open hatch and
         walk on the moon. Armstrong backing out
         from hatch, describing lunar surface. "One
         small step for man, one giant step for man-
         kind" (109 hours, 24 minutes, 20 seconds.)
         Bringing down cameras.   CBS TV, July 20, 1969.
           1 reel (7 in.)   7 1/2 in. per sec.   phonotape.
           1. Project Apollo. 2. Space flight to the moon. 3. Aldrin,
         Edwin E   1930-   4. Collins, Michael, 1930- 5. Armstrong,
         Neil, 1930-   I. Aldrin, Edwin E   1930-   II. Collins, Michael,
         1930-   III. Armstrong, Neil, 1930-

Collins, Michael, 1930-

Voice Lib.
M1587   Apollo 11 (space flight): recovery. Walter Cronkite and Wally
bd.2   Schirra announce proceedings from aircraft carrier "Hornet";
         trying to track spacecraft coming down; chutes opening at
         10,500 feet; voice contact with spacecraft; visual of chutes;
         splashdown 9 miles from "Hornet", upside-down. Collar
         attached to spacecraft. NBC and ABC TV, July 24, 1969.
           1 reel (7 in.)   7 1/2 in. per sec.   phonotape.

           1. Project Apollo. 2. Space flight to the moon. 3. Aldrin,
         Edwin E   1930-   4. Collins, Michael, 1930- 5.
         Armstrong, Neil, 1930-   I. Aldrin, Edwin E   1930-
         II. Collins, Michael, 1930-   III. Armstrong, Neil, 1930-
         IV. Cronkite, Walter Leland, 1916-   V. Schirra, Walter Marty,
         1923-

Collins, Michael, 1930-

Voice Lib.
M1386   Apollo 11 (space flight): conversation with
bd.1   broadcasters Walter Cronkite and Wally
         Schirra. Including Armstrong's activities
         on moon alone; pictures, rock descriptions,
         then Aldrin coming down ladder; rock boxes
         put to use. TV cameras put at 30' panoramic
         position. Reading inscription of plaque
         with U.S. flag and setting it up. Telephone
         call from Washington to astronauts and their
         acknowledgement.   CBS TV, July 20, 1969.
           1 reel (7 in.)   7 1/2 in. per sec.
           phonotape.
                              (Continued on next card)

Collins, Michael, 1930-

Voice Lib.
M1388   Apollo 11 (space flight): Walter Cronkite and Wally Schirra
bd.1   describing recovery. Maneuvers by frogmen and helicopters
         at splashdown spot; "air boss" describes close-up scene;
         decontamination process; helicopter landing on "Hornet" with
         astronauts; reception. Description of proceedings on "Hornet"
         by CBS newscasters. CBS TV, July 24, 1969.
           1 reel (7 in.)   7 1/2 in. per sec.   phonotape.

           1. Project Apollo. 2. Space flight to the moon. 3. Aldrin,
         Edwin E   1930-   4. Collins, Michael, 1930-   5. Armstrong,
         Neil, 1930-   I. Aldrin, Edwin E   1930-   II. Collins,
         Michael, 1930-   III. Armstrong, Neil, 1930-   IV. Cronkite,
         Walter Leland, 1916-   V. Schirra, Walter Marty, 1923-

---

Collins, Michael, 1930-

Voice Lib.
M1386   Apollo 11 (space flight): blessing by Pope
bd.2   Paul VI from the Vatican to Apollo 11
         astronauts.   CBS TV, July 20, 1969.
           1 reel (7 in.)   7 1/2 in. per sec.
           phonotape.

           1. Project Apollo. 2. Space flight to the
         moon. 3. Aldrin, Edwin E   1930-   4.
         Collins, Michael, 1930-   5. Armstrong, Neil,
         1930-   I. Aldrin, Edwin E   1930-   II.
         Collins, Michael, 1930-   III. Armstrong, Neil,
         1930-   IV. Paulus VI, Pope, 1897-

Collins, Michael, 1930-

Voice Lib.
M1388   Apollo 11 (space flight): personal greeting
bd.2   by President Nixon to the astronauts on
         the "Hornet" and their replies. Chaplain's
         prayer. Nixon taking off.   CBS and NBC TV,
         July 24, 1969.
           1 reel (7 in.)   7 1/2 in. per sec.
           phonotape.
           1. Project Apollo. 2. Space flight to the moon. 3. Aldrin,
         Edwin E   1930-   4. Collins, Michael, 1930-   5.
         Armstrong, Neil, 1930-   I. Aldrin, Edwin E   1930-
         II. Collins, Michael, 1930-   III. Armstrong, Neil, 1930-
         IV. Nixon, Richard Milhous, Pres. U.S., 1913-

Collins, Michael, 1930-
Voice Lib.
M1389 Apollo 11 (space flight): excerpt of press
bd.1   conference with Apollo 11 astronauts in
          Houston. CBS TV, August 12, 1969.
          1 reel (7 in.)   7 1/2 in. per sec.
          phonotape.

          1. Project Apollo. 2. Space flight to the
          moon. 3. Aldrin, Edwin E   1930-   4.
          Collins, Michael, 1930-   5. Armstrong, Neil,
          1930-   I. Aldrin, Edwin E   1930-   II.
          Collins, Michael, 1930-   III. Armstrong,
          Neil, 1930-

Collins, Michael, 1930-
Voice Lib.
M1391 Apollo 11 (space flight): reception of Apollo
bd.2   11 astronauts ... 1969. (Card 2)

          1 reel (7 in.)   7 1/2 in. per sec.
          phonotape.

          l. Project Apollo. 2. Space flight to the moon. 3. Aldrin,
          Edwin E   1930-   4. Collins, Michael, 1930-   5. Armstrong,
          Neil, 1930-   L. Aldrin, Edwin E   1930-   II. Collins,
          Michael, 1930-   III. Armstrong, Neil, 1930-   IV. Cody,
          John Patrick, cardinal, 1907-   V. Kennedy, John Fitzgerald,
          Pres. U.S., 1917-1963. VL Daley, Richard J   1902- VII.
          Percy, Charles Harting, 1919- VIII. Ogilvie, Richard Buell,
          1923-

Collins, Michael, 1930-
Voice Lib.
M1389 Apollo 11 (space flight): welcome to Apollo 11 astronauts on their
bd.2   arrival at Kennedy Airport at New York; ferried by Marine
          helicopter to Wall Street; boat whistles harbor greeting.
          Flashbacks to former important New York parades (Frank McGee)
          Walter Cronkite, CBS, describing beginning of motorcade
          and parade to city hall. CBS [and NBC] TV, August 13, 1969.
          1 reel (7 in.)   7 1/2 in. per sec. phonotape.

          l. Project Apollo. 2. Space flight to the moon. 3. Aldrin,
          Edwin E   1930-   4. Collins, Michael, 1930-   5.
          Armstrong, Neil, 1930-   L. Aldrin, Edwin E   1930-
          II. Collins, Michael, 1930-   III. Armstrong, Neil, 1930-
          IV. McGee, Frank, 1921-1974. V. Cronkite, Walter Leland, 1916-

---

Colloquium on the Plight of the Cities,
Michigan State University, 1969
Voice Lib.
M1718 Alinsky, Saul David, 1909-
          Address at Michigan State University's
          University College Colloquium on the Plight
          of the Cities. WKAR, January 27, 1969.
          50 min. phonotape (1 r.   7 1/2 i.p.s.)

          1. Cities and towns. I. Colloquium on
          the Plight of the Cities, Michigan State
          University, 1969.

Collins, Michael, 1930-
Voice Lib.
M1390 Apollo 11 (space flight): reception for
          Apollo 11 astronauts in New York. Descrip-
          tion of approach and ceremony at city hall.
          Cardinal Cooke's invocation. Introduction
          by Mayor Lindsay. Presentation of Medal of
          Honor. Reply by all astronauts. Benediction.
          NBC TV, August 13, 1969.
          1 reel (7 in.)   7 1/2 in. per sec. phonotape.
          l. Project Apollo. 2. Space flight to the moon. 3. Aldrin,
          Edwin E   1930-   4. Collins, Michael, 1930-   5.
          Armstrong, Neil, 1930-   L. Aldrin, Edwin E   1930-   II.
          Collins, Michael, 1930-   III. Armstrong, Neil, 1930-   IV.
          Cooke, Terence James, cardinal, 1921-   V. Lindsay, John Vliet,
          1921-

C1   COLOMBO, CRISTOFORO
H22   Whorf, Michael, 1933-
          Birth of a nation; Columbus, the adventurer.
          1 tape cassette. (The visual sounds of
          Mike Whorf. History and heritage, H22)
          Originally presented on his radio program, Kaleidoscope,
          WJR, Detroit.
          Duration: 38 min., 10 sec.
          A generous mixture of poetry and seldom-presented historical
          fact is blended to tell this greatest of all nautical tales. Aboard
          three ships, they sailed into the unknown. "Sail on, sail on and
          on," commanded the admiral and sail they did, into high adventure,
          the like of which the world had never known.

          L. Colombo, Cristoforo   L. Title.

Collins, Michael, 1930-
Voice Lib.
M1391 Apollo 11 (space flight): reception of Apollo 11 astronauts at
bd.1   United Nations Plaza. Statement by U.N. Secretary-
          General U Thant. Reply by Neil Armstrong. Presentation
          of tokens of appreciation to all three astronauts and their
          wives and Dr. Thomas Paine. Presentation of duplicate of
          plaque left on moon to U Thant. NBC TV, August 13, 1969.
          1 reel (7 in.)   7 1/2 in. per sec. phonotape.

          l. Project Apollo. 2. Space flight to the moon. 3. Aldrin,
          Edwin E   1930-   4. Collins, Michael, 1930-   5.
          Armstrong, Neil, 1930-   L. Aldrin, Edwin E   1930-
          II. Collins, Michael, 1930-   III. Armstrong, Neil, 1930-
          IV. Thant, U, 1909-   V. Paine, Thomas Otten, 1921-

---

C1   Colonel William Hill
FA9   Whorf, Michael, 1933-
          Colonel William Hill.
          1 tape cassette. (The visual sounds of
          Mike Whorf. The forgotten American, FA9)

          Originally presented on his radio program, Kaleidoscope,
          WJR, Detroit.
          Duration: 10 min., 5 sec.
          An American civilian in time of war, he was a member of
          the Revolutionary Army of General Sumter. He built the first
          iron forge south of Virginia.

          L. Hill, Captain William. L. Title.

Collins, Michael, 1930-
Voice Lib.
M1391 Apollo 11 (space flight): reception of
bd.2   Apollo 11 astronauts in Chicago. Descrip-
          tion of motorcade on way to Civic Center
          Plaza and ceremonies there. Cardinal Cody's
          invocation. JFK flashback predicting moon
          landing before decade is out. Mayor Daley
          and Alderman Klene resolution making August
          13 "Astronauts' Day". Senator Percy and
          Governor Ogilvie of Illinois. Presentation
          of honorary citizenship to astronauts.
          [Source?] August 13, 1969.

          (Continued on next card)

Voice Lib. Colouris, George
M1677 Dracula (radio program)
          Mercury Theatre production of Dracula
          with Orson Welles, George Colouris, and
          Martin Gabel. Ferris State College, 1937.
          55 min. phonotape (1 r.   7 1/2 i.p.s.)

          I. Welles, Orson, 1915-   II. Colouris,
          George. III. Gabel, Martin, 1912-

Voice Lib.
M566-   Columbia Broadcasting System, Inc.
567   The big news of 1959.   CBS, 1960.
           2 reels (7 in.)   7 1/2 i.p.s.   phonotape.

           1. History - Yearbooks - 1959.

Voice Lib.
M308   Columbia Broadcasting System, inc.
bd.1   Assassination: various news commentators
         describing the event, describing the last
         minutes of the President's life, impact of
         the news on New York City, on Lyndon B.
         Johnson, announcement of arrest of first
         suspect, comments from all over world.
         CBS, November 22, 1963.
           1 reel (7 in.)   7 1/2 in. per sec.
         phonotape.
           1. Kennedy, John Fitzgerald, Pres. U.S.,
         1917-1963 - Assassination.

Voice Lib.
M308   Columbia Broadcasting System, inc.
bd.2   Assassination: announcement of Kennedy's
         death by CBS commentator Walter Cronkite; on
         film of assassination, search for suspect,
         future events and Johnson's oath; announcement
         of shooting of Dallas policeman and arrest
         of Oswald; comments by Eisenhower and Truman.
         CBS, November 22, 1963.
           1 reel (7 in.)   7 1/2 in. per sec.
         phonotape.
         1. Kennedy, John Fitzgerald, Pres. U.S. 1917-1963 - Assassination.
         I. Cronkite, Walter Leland, 1916-   II. Eisenhower, Dwight
         David, Pres. U.S., 1890-1969. III. Truman, Harry S, Pres. U.S.,
         1884-1972.

Voice Lib.
M308   Columbia Broadcasting System, inc.
bd.3   Assassination: description of U.S. Senate
         on announcement of the news of the assassina-
         tion to the Republicans and Democrats in the
         Senate Chamber.   CBS, November 22, 1963.
           1 reel (7 in.)   7 1/2 in. per sec.
         phonotape.
           1. Kennedy, John Fitzgerald, Pres. U.S.,
         1917-1963 - Assassination.

Voice Lib.
M309   Columbia Broadcasting System, inc.
bd.1   Assassination: various news commentators
         on Kennedy trip up to time of shooting;
         description of film taken at Parkland Hospital;
         Kennedy family's departure from Capitol;
         swearing-in of Johnson as 36th President.
         CBS, November 22, 1963.
           1 reel (7 in.)   7 1/2 in. per sec.
         phonotape.
           1. Kennedy, John Fitzgerald, Pres. U.S.,
         1917-1963 - Assassination.

Voice Lib.
M309   Columbia Broadcasting System, inc.
bd.2   Comments on Kennedy assassination from
         people on the street in Chicago.   CBS,
         November 22, 1963.
           1 reel (7 in.)   7 1/2 in. per sec.
         phonotape.
           1. Kennedy, John Fitzgerald, Pres. U.S.,
         1917-1963 - Assassination.

Voice Lib.
M309   Columbia Broadcasting System, inc.
bd.3   Assassination: statements by Senator
         Dirksen and Senator Mansfield, remarks about
         statements and actions of others in Washington.
         CBS, November 22, 1963.
           1 reel (7 in.)   7 1/2 in. per sec.
         phonotape.
           1. Kennedy, John Fitzgerald, Pres. U.S.,
         1917-1963 - Assassination.   I. Dirksen,
         Everett McKinley, 1896-1969.   II. Mansfield,
         Michael Joseph, 1903-

Voice Lib.
M309   Columbia Broadcasting System, inc.
bd.4   Reaction to the assassination: description
         of statement and actions by Gov. Rockefeller
         of New York.   CBS, November 22, 1963.
           1 reel (7 in.)   7 1/2 in. per sec.
         phonotape.
           1. Kennedy, John Fitzgerald, Pres. U.S.,
         1917-1963 - Assassination.

Voice Lib.
M309   Columbia Broadcasting System, inc.
bd.5   On shooting of Oswald and description
         of identity of assassin.   CBS, November
         24, 1963.
           1 reel (7 in.)   7 1/2 in. per sec.
         phonotape.
           1. Oswald, Lee Harvey, 1939-1963.

Voice Lib.
M309   Columbia Broadcasting System, inc.
bd.6   Recount of events, slow-motion replay
         of assassination of Oswald.   CBS,
         November 24, 1963.
           1 reel (7 in.)   7 1/2 in. per sec.
         phonotape.
           1. Oswald, Lee Harvey, 1939-1963.

Voice Lib.
M317   Columbia Broadcasting System, inc.
bd.3   Assassination: activities of the Interfaith
        Assembly in St. Louis.   CBS, November 24, 1963.
            1 reel (7 in.)   7 1/2 in. per sec.
        phonotape.

            1. Kennedy, John Fitzgerald, Pres. U.S.,
        1917-1963 - Assassination.

Voice Lib.
M317   Columbia Broadcasting System, inc.
bd.4   Assassination: description of arrival of
        President DeGaulle and others at Dulles
        Airport.   CBS, November 24, 1963.
            1 reel (7 in.)   7 1/2 in. per sec.
        phonotape.

            1. Kennedy, John Fitzgerald, Pres. U.S.,
        1917-1963 - Assassination.

Voice Lib.
M317   Columbia Broadcasting System, inc.
bd.5   Assassination: description of procession
        of funeral cortege from Capitol to the
        Cathedral in Washington; beginning of
        Requiem Mass.   CBS, November 25, 1963.
            1 reel (7 in.)   7 1/2 in. per sec.
        phonotape.

            1. Kennedy, John Fitzgerald, Pres. U.S.,
        1917-1963 - Assassination.

Voice Lib.
320   Columbia Broadcasting System, inc.
bd.2   Funeral ceremonies for John F. Kennedy at
        grave site: bagpipers of U.S. Air Force,
        planes flying over grave, manual of Irish
        Guard, prayers at graveside by Cardinal
        Cushing, 21 gun salute, taps, Navy Hymn,
        description of everlasting flame, departure
        of distinguished mourners.   CBS, November
        25, 1963.
            1 reel (7 in.)   7 1/2 in. per sec.
        phonotape.
            1. Kennedy, John Fitzgerald, Pres. U.S., 1917-1963 - Assassination.

Voice Lib.
M320   Columbia Broadcasting System, inc.
bd.3   Assassination: description of motion
        picture taken by amateur photographer which
        included complete sequence of the assassination.
        CBS, November 28, 1963.
            1 reel (7 in.)   7 1/2 in. per sec.
        phonotape.

            1. Kennedy, John Fitzgerald, Pres. U.S.,
        1917-1963.- Assassination.

Voice Lib.
M615   Columbia Broadcasting System.
bd.2   Death of MacArthur; return of body from
        New York City to Washington, D.C., and
        delivery of eulogy in Capitol Rotunda.
        CBS, April 5, 1964.
            1 reel (7 in.)   7 1/2 in. per sec.
        phonotape.

            1. MacArthur, Douglas, 1880-1964.

Voice Lib.
M717   Columbia Broadcasting System, Inc.
bd.7   Interview with weather official in New
        York about Hurricane Donna.   September 10,
        1960.
            1 reel (7 in.)   7 1/2 in. per sec.
        phonotape.

            1. Hurricanes.

Voice Lib.
M723   Columbia Broadcasting System, Inc.
bd.2   Memorial broadcast at the death of
        Albert Einstein, with Walter Cronkite.
        CBS, April 18, 1955.
            15 min., 30 sec.   phonotape (1 r.
        7 1/2 i.p.s.)

            1. Einstein, Albert, 1878-1955.
        I. Cronkite, Walter Leland, 1916-

Voice Lib.
M243   Columbia Broadcasting System.
bd.1   Recollection of a tornado, recorded on
        location in Fargo, North Dakota.   CBS
        Radio, June 21, 1957.
            1 reel (7 in.)   7 1/2 i.p.s.   phonotape.

            1. Fargo, N.D. - Tornado.

Voice Lib.
M1696   Columbia Broadcasting System, inc.
bd.6   Special memorial to Duke Ellington, with
        John Hart, Sonny Greer, Russell Procope,
        Billy Taylor, Stanley Dance, and Ella
        Fitzgerald.   CBS-TV, May 24, 1974.
            15 min.   phonotape (1 r.   7 1/2 i.p.s.)

            1. Ellington, Duke, 1899-1974.   I. Hart,
        John. II. Greer, Sonny. III. Procope,
        Russell, 1908-   IV. Taylor, Billy.
        V. Dance, Stanley. VI. Fitzgerald, Ella,
        1918-

Voice Lib.
M1051 Columbia Broadcasting System, Inc. Radio
bd.2 Workshop.
Radio production of program "The Fall of the
City", written by Archibald MacLeish. CBS
Radio, 1934.
1 reel (7 in.) 7 1/2 in. per sec.
phonotape.

I. MacLeish, Archibald, 1892- /The
fall of the city.

Voice Lib.
M603 Columbia Quartet.
bd.4 War song medley from World War I. Columbia Gramaphone
Co., 1917.
1 reel (7 in.) 7 1/2 l.p.s. phonotape.

CONTENTS. –It's a long way to Berlin. –Keep the home fires
burning. –Where do we go from here? –Pack up your troubles in
your old kit bag. –For your country and my country. –Goodbye
Broadway, hello France. –I don't know where I'm going, but I'm
on my way. –Over there.

I. European War, 1914–1918 – Songs and music.

Voice Lib. Come down, ma evenin' star
M948 Russell, Lillian, 1861–1922.
bd.3 Re-recording from Edison cylinder record
of Miss Russell singing "Come Down, Ma Evenin'
Star". Jack Caidin, March 12, 1912.
1 reel (7 in.) 7 1/2 in. per sec.
phonotape.

I. Title: Come down, ma evenin' star.

C1 The comedian – Charlie Chaplin
M45- Whorf, Michael, 1933-
M46 The comedian – Charlie Chaplin.
2 tape cassettes. (The visual sounds of
Mike Whorf. Miscellaneous, M45–M46)
Originally presented on his radio program, Kaleidoscope,
WJR, Detroit.
Duration: 37 min.; 37 min.
London to New York to Hollywood – these programs relive the
era in which the little tramp had his beginnings. America, and
then the world, took the humor and pathos of the funny little man
with his hat and cane into their hearts.

L. Chaplin, Charles, 1889- L. Title.

Voice Lib.
377 Commager, Henry Steele, 1902-
bd.1 Political philosophy. WOED, 1958.
1 reel (7 in.) 7 1/2 in. per sec.
phonotape.

Voice Lib.
M1691 Commager, Henry Steele, 1902-
bd.1 On public service and private
creativity, with Bill Moyers.
WKAR-TV, May 23, 1974.
25 min. phonotape (1 r. 7 1/2 i.p.s.)

1. Impeachments. 2. U.S. – Politics and
government. I. Moyers, Bill D., 1934-

C1 COMMANDMENTS, TEN
R31 Whorf, Michael, 1933-
The Ten Commandments.
1 tape cassette. (The visual sounds of
Mike Whorf. Religion, R31)
Originally presented on his radio program, Kaleidoscope,
WJR, Detroit.
Duration: 37 min.
The graven tables which presented spiritual guidance for
millions have been passed down to us by oral tradition and the
works of the scriptures. The monumental importance of this moral
code has stood the test of time through the ages, and served as a
universal guide to mankind.

L. Commandments, Ten. L. Title.

C1 The commodore – Oliver Hazard Perry
H99 Whorf, Michael, 1933-
The commodore – Oliver Hazard Perry.
1 tape cassette. (The visual sounds of
Mike Whorf. History and heritage, H99)
Originally presented on his radio program, Kaleidoscope,
WJR, Detroit.
Duration: 36 min.
One of the great naval heroes of the U.S., Perry eagerly
bursts into battle. The young officer guarded the seas against the
French after the Revolutionary War. His whole biography sets the
stage for his rich, full, naval career.

L. Perry, Oliver Hazard, 1785–1819. L. Title.

Voice Lib. COMMUNICATION
M902 Ralph, David Clinton, 1922-
Lecture to speech class 101 on credibility
in speech. Direct recording, November 29,
1965.
1 reel (9 in.) 7 1/2 i.p.s. phonotape.

1. Communication.

Voice Lib. COMMUNISM
M1585 Ardrey, Robert
bd.2 Property, status, and self-respect.
WKAR-TV, February 23, 1974.
15 min. phonotape (1 r. 7 1/2 in. per sec.)

1. Territoriality (Zoology) 2. Communism.
3. Cities & towns – Planning. I. Halverson,
Craig.

Voice Lib.
M212
bd.1
COMPOSERS, AMERICAN
Buck, Gene, 1885-1957.
American composers and their music at the Golden Gate International Exposition. ASCAP, September 24, 1940.
1 reel (7 in.)   7 1/2 i.p.s.   phonotape.

1. Composers, American.

Voice Lib.
383
Conklin, Ed
I can hear it now (radio program) CBS, February 9, 1951.
1 reel (7 in.)   7 1/2 in. per sec. phonotape.

L. Wilson, Charles Edward, 1886-1972. II. Gabrielson, Guy George, 1891- III. Taft, Robert Alphonso, 1889-1953. IV. Martin, Joseph William, 1884-1965. V. McCarthy, Joseph Raymond, 1909-1957. VI. Benton, William Burnett, 1900-1973. VII. Malone, George Wilson, 1890-1961. VIII. Capehart, Homer Earl, 1897- IX. Eisenhower, Dwight David, Pres. U.S., 1890-1969. X. Lee, J   V   XI. Hodge, John Reed, 1893-1963. XII. Overton, Watkins   XIII. DiSalle, Michael Vincent, 1908-   XIV. Boyce, Eddy   XV. Conklin, Ed XVI. Collins, Joseph Lawton, 1896-

---

Voice Lib.
M1310
bd.2
Compton, Arthur Holly, 1892-1962
Fermi, Enrico, 1901-1954.
Speaking at the tenth anniversary celebration of the first nuclear chain reaction, held at the University of Chicago. Atomic Energy Commission, December 2, 1952.
1 reel (7 in.)   7 1/2 i.p.s.   phonotape.

1. Nuclear reactions.   I. Compton, Arthur Holly, 1892-1962.

Voice Lib.
M1484,
bd.2-
1485
Connally, John Bowden, 1917-.
News conference, details of Phase two of economic policy.   October 8, 1971.
2 reels (7 in.)   7 1/2 in. per sec. phonotape.

1. U.S. - Economic policy, 1971-

Voice Lib.
M953
bd.3
COMPUTER SOUND PROCESSING
Bell Telephone Laboratories, inc.
Synthesized speech created by digital computer recites soliloquy from "Hamlet", sings "Bicycle built for two". Explanation of computer's operation.   American Telephone and Telegraph Co., 1963.
1 reel (7 in.)   7 1/2 i.p.s.   phonotape.

1. Computer sound processing.   I. Shakespeare, William, 1564-1616./Hamlet.   II. Title: Bicycle built for two.

Voice Lib.
M806
bd.1
Connally, Thomas Terry, 1877-1963.
Excerpt from his speech at disarmament committee criticizing U.S.S.R.   U.N. Archives [no date]
1 reel (7 in.)   7 1/2 in. per sec. phonotape.

On United Nations Special Tape No. 2.

C1
H102
The Confederate hero - Robert E. Lee
Whorf, Michael, 1933-
The Confederate hero - Robert E. Lee.
1 tape cassette.   (The visual sounds of Mike Whorf. History and heritage, H102)
Originally presented on his radio program, Kaleidoscope, WJR, Detroit.
Duration: 37 min.
A narration of new insights into the devoted Confederate general. An exploration into the life and motives of Robert E. Lee. A Confederate general, a religious man, and a hero to his southern countrymen.

L. Lee, Robert Edward, 1807-1870.   L. Title.

Voice Lib.
353
bd.4
Connally, Thomas Terry, 1877-1963.
Outbreak of Korean conflict; preservation of South Korean integrity.   NBC, July, 1950.
1 reel (7 in.)   7 1/2 in. per sec. phonotape.

Original disc off-speed.

1. Korean War, 1950-1953

CONGO QUESTION
Voice Lib.
344
bd.16
Ball, George Wildman, 1909-
Speech in Los Angeles on objectives of U.N. in the Congo.   CBS, December 19, 1961.
1 reel (7in.)   7 1/2 in. per sec. phonotape.

1. Congo question.   2. United Nations.

Voice Lib.
M806
Connally, Thomas Terry, 1877-1963
United Nations Special Tape No. 2.
U.N. Archives [various dates]
1 reel (7 in.)   7 1/2 in. per sec. phonotape.

CONTENTS. -bd. 1. Excerpt from speech by Sen. Tom Connally at disarmament committee criticizing U.S.S.R. -bd. 2. U.N. translators in row, getting into fist fight and interrupting Pakistani delegate. -bd. 3. Nepal U.N. delegate at 771st Plenary Session of General Assembly interrupted by screaming agitator. -bd. 4. Harold MacMillan, honorary president of U.N. Association, welcoming Dag Hammarskjöld to England; interrupted by isolationist heckler conservative, but continuing speech undisturbed. -bd. 5. U.N. delegate from Saudi Arabia arguing with Chairman of Committee about
(Continued on next card)

Voice Lib.
M806   Connally, Thomas Terry, 1877-1963
United Nations Special Tape No. 2. ₍various dates₎ (Card 2)

CONTENTS, cont'd. "point of order". -bd. 6. U. N. delegate speaking about "hamburgers with a college education" and the effect of advertising slogans on the masses. -bd. 7. Turkish U. N. delegate at U. N. replying to Greek delegate on "point of order". -bd. 8. U. N. delegate speaking about white slavery and high cost of women. -bd. 9. U. N. delegate telling an anecdote about an incident in underdeveloped country: "A U. N. Bull". -bd. 10. U. N. delegate balling up anecdote about cats. -bd. 11. U. N. delegate speaking about lizards hindering business in Nigeria. -bd. 12. U. N. delegate advocating more scientific progress on old age rather than the progress on moon exploration. -bd. 13. U. N. delegate telling anecdote about co-operation. -bd. 14. South African delegate

(Continued on next card)

Voice Lib.
M806   Connally, Thomas Terry, 1877-1963
United Nations Special Tape No. 2. ₍various dates₎ (Card 3)

CONTENTS, cont'd. telling anecdote at U. N. -bd. 15. Chairman opening the 714th session of the Second Committee of the 15th session of the U. N. General Assembly. -bd. 16. U. N. delegate indicating the number of seats available for various countries at the U. N. -bd. 17. U. N. delegate instructing delegates how to indicate their vote. -bd. 18. U. N. delegate from Liberia debating on how to address a woman chairman.

I. Connally, Thomas Terry, 1877-1963. II. MacMillan, Harold, 1894-

---

C1
H48   The conquistadors
Whorf, Michael, 1933-
The conquistadors.
1 tape cassette. (The visual sounds of Mike Whorf. History and heritage, H48)

Originally presented on his radio program, Kaleidoscope, WJR, Detroit.
Duration: 44 min., 15 sec.
Sent from Spain to settle and civilize the new world, they plundered, killed, stole, and vanquished the Indian nations of the Southwest, Central America, and Mexico.

I. America - Discovery and exploration - Spanish. I. Title.

Voice Lib.
M788   Conrad, Charles, 1930-
Gemini 5 (space flight): summary of space flight of Gemini Titan V from August 21 to August 29, 1965, including interview with Chris Kraft, flight director. 1965.
1 reel (7 in.) 7 1/2 in. per sec.
phonotape.

1. Project Gemini. 2. Cooper, Leroy Gordon, 1927- 3. Conrad, Charles, 1930- I. Cooper, Leroy Gordon, 1927- II. Conrad, Charles, 1930- III. Kraft, Christopher Columbus, 1924-

---

Voice Lib.
M800   Conrad, Charles, 1930-
Gemini 5 (space flight): press conference with astronauts Cooper and Conrad at NASA Space Center, Houston, Texas, regarding their eight-day space flight with Gemini V. NBC TV, September 9, 1965.
1 reel (7 in.) 7 1/2 in. per sec.
phonotape.

1. Project Gemini. 2. Cooper, Leroy Gordon, 1927- 3. Conrad, Charles, 1930- I. Cooper, Leroy Gordon, 1927- II. Conrad, Charles, 1930-

---

Voice Lib.
M1403   Conrad, Charles, 1930-
bd.1 Apollo 12 (space flight): lift-off of Apollo 12; the electrical "glitch" and instructions and corrections; Dr. Paine and President Nixon speaking from VIP section. CBS TV, November 19, 1969.
1 reel (7 in.) 7 1/2 in. per sec.
phonotape.
L. Project Apollo. 2. Space flight to the moon. 3. Conrad, Charles, 1930- 4. Bean, Alan L 1932- 5. Gordon, Richard F 1929- L Conrad, Charles, 1930- II. Bean, Alan L 1932- III. Gordon, Richard F 1929- IV. Paine, Thomas Otten, 1921- V. Nixon, Richard Milhous, Pres. U. S., 1913-

---

Voice Lib.
M1403   Conrad, Charles, 1930-
bd.2 Apollo 12 (space flight): landing on the moon; conversations of Frank McGee and mission control; dialogue of Pete Conrad preparing to step out on moon; coached on going down ladder; Conrad singing from the moon; trouble with TV camera. NBC TV, November 19, 1969.
1 reel (7 in.) 7 1/2 in. per sec. phonotape.
L. Project Apollo. 2. Space flight to the moon. 3. Conrad, Charles, 1930- 4. Bean, Alan L 1932- 5. Gordon, Richard F 1929- L Conrad, Charles, 1930- II. Bean, Alan L 1932- III. Gordon, Richard F 1929- IV. McGee, Frank, 1921-1974.

Voice Lib.
M1404   Conrad, Charles, 1930-
bd.1 Apollo 12 (space flight): description of last minutes on the moon of Apollo 12 crew; countdown, lift-off from the moon. CBS TV, November 20, 1969.
1 reel (7 in.) 7 1/2 in. per sec.
phonotape.
1. Project Apollo. 2. Space flight to the moon. 3. Conrad, Charles, 1930- 4. Bean, Alan L 1932- 5. Gordon, Richard F 1929- I. Conrad, Charles, 1930- II. Bean, Alan L 1932- III. Gordon, Richard F 1929-

---

Voice Lib.
M1404   Conrad, Charles, 1930-
bd.2 Apollo 12 (space flight): description of splashdown of Apollo 12 and proceeding to aircraft carrier "Hornet". CBS TV, November 24, 1969.
1 reel (7 in.) 7 1/2 in. per sec.
phonotape.
1. Project Apollo. 2. Space flight to the moon. 3. Conrad, Charles, 1930- 4. Bean, Alan L 1932- 5. Gordon, Richard F 1929- I. Conrad, Charles, 1930- II. Bean, Alan L 1932- III. Gordon, Richard F 1929-

---

Conrad, Pete
see
Conrad, Charles, 1930-

Voice Lib.
M1466   Conrad von Hötzendorf, Franz, graf, 1852-
bd.7   1925.
            Order of the day to his troops.   Peteler,
        1916.
            1 reel (7 in.)   7 1/2 in. per sec.
        phonotape.

Voice Lib.
654   Cook, Frederick Albert, 1865-1940.
bd.2   "How I Reached the North Pole".
        Description of Dr. Cook's preparations
        and journey on Artic expedition, 1909.
        Source(?), [n.d.]
            1 reel (7 in.)   7 1/2 in. per sec.
        phonotape.

            1. Arctic regions.   2. Peary, Robert Edwin,
        1856-1920.

Voice Lib.   CONSTITUTIONAL LAW
M1698   Ervin, Samuel James, 1896-
            The lesson of Watergate; address at the
        National Press Club.   WKAR, May 29, 1974.
            45 min.   phonotape (1 r.   7 1/2 i.p.s.)

            1. Constitutional law.   2. Baker, Robert
        Gene, 1928-   3. Sirica, John Joseph, 1904-

Cl   COOK, JAMES, 1728-1779
H84   Whorf, Michael, 1933-
            The last of the great explorers - James Cook.
            1 tape cassette.   (The visual sounds of
        Mike Whorf.   History and heritage.   H84)
            Originally presented on his radio program, Kaleidoscope,
        WJR, Detroit.
            Duration: 37 min., 30 sec.
            James Cook was an extraordinary seaman and an intelligent
        and far-seeing individual who realized that the way to make
        England stronger was to claim for her the lands that lay beyond.

            L Cook, James, 1728-1779.   L Title.

Voice Lib.
M757   Conwell, Russell Herman, 1843-1925.
bd.1   "Acres of Diamonds"; a lecture by Dr. Conwell.
        Rodeheaver Record Co., 1916.
            1 reel (7 in.)   7 1/2 in. per sec.
        phonotape.

            I. Title.

Voice Lib.   Cooke, Alistair, 1908-
M1031   Discussion about Winston Churchill's ability
        in military affairs, between Alistair Cooke
        and General Dwight Eisenhower, heard at his
        home in Gettysburg, Pennsylvania; including
        recording of General George C. Marshall's
        opinion about the strategic value of U.S.
        troops conquering Berlin.   "Studio 67"
        production, ABC-TV, January 26, 1967.
            1 reel (7 in.)   7 1/2 in. per sec.   phonotape.
            L Churchill, Winston Leonard Spencer, 1874-1965.   L
        Cooke, Alistair, 1908-   II. Eisenhower, Dwight David, Pres.
        U.S., 1890-1969.

Voice Lib.
M1611   Conyers, John, 1929-
bd.3   Discusses impeachment and opinion poll
        bias.   WKAR-TV [1974?]
            8 min.   phonotape (1 r.   7 1/2 i.p.s.)

            1. Nixon, Richard Milhous, Pres. U.S., 1913-
        2. U.S. - Politics and government, 1969-

        Cooke, Terence James, cardinal, 1921-
Voice Lib.
M1390   Apollo 11 (space flight): reception for
        Apollo 11 astronauts in New York.   Descrip-
        tion of approach and ceremony at city hall.
        Cardinal Cooke's invocation.   Introduction
        by Mayor Lindsay.   Presentation of Medal of
        Honor.   Reply by all astronauts.   Benediction.
        NBC TV, August 13, 1969.
            1 reel (7 in.)   7 1/2 in. per sec.   phonotape.
            L Project Apollo.   2. Space flight to the moon.   3. Aldrin,
        Edwin E   1930-   4. Collins, Michael, 1930-   5.
        Armstrong, Neil, 1930-   L Aldrin, Edwin E   1930-   II.
        Collins, Michael, 1930-   III. Armstrong, Neil, 1930-   IV.
        Cooke, Terence James, cardinal, 1921-   V. Lindsay, John Vliet,
        1921-

Voice Lib.
M982   Coogan, Jackie
bd.8   In a dialogue with his father.   Made in
        England.   N.V., 1926.
            1 reel (7 in.)   7 1/2 in. per sec.
        phonotape.

Voice Lib.
M1490   Cooley, Mortimer Elwyn, 1855-
bd.1   Candidate for U.S. Senator from Michigan
        (1924) campaign speech.   Arco records,
        1924.
            1 reel (7 in.)   7 1/2 i.p.s.   phonotape.

            1. Michigan - Politics and government.

Voice Lib.
290   Coolidge, Calvin, Pres. U.S., 1872-1933.
bd.4   Law and order; Coolidge's ideas on
       state government in Massachusetts.
       Nation's Forum, 1919.
          1 reel (7 in.)   7 1/2 in. per sec.
       phonotape.

Voice Lib.
M721   Coolidge, Calvin, Pres. U.S., 1872-1933.
bd.3   Address on Republican Party Principles.
       1924.
          1 reel (7 in.)   7 1/2 in. per sec.
       phonotape.

              Coolidge, Calvin, Pres. U.S., 1872-1933
Voice Lib.
M617   Radio in the 1920's: a series of excerpts
bd.1-   from important broadcasts of the 1920's,
bd.25   with brief prologue and epilogue; a sample
       of radio of the period. NVL, April, 1964.
          1 reel (7 in.)   7 1/2 in. per sec.
       phonotape.
          L. Radio programs. L. Marconi, Guglielmo, marchese, 1874-
       1937. IL Kendall, H   G   III. Coolidge, Calvin, Pres. U.S.,
       1872-1933. IV. Wilson, Woodrow, Pres. U.S., 1856-1924. V.
       Roosevelt, Franklin Delano, Pres. U.S., 1882-1945. VI. Lodge,
       Henry Cabot, 1850-1924. VII. LaGuardia, Fiorello Henry, 1882-1947.
       VIII. The Happiness Boys (Radio program) IX. Gallagher and Sheen.
       X. Barney Google. XI. Vallee, Rudy, 1901-   XII. The two
                                  (Continued on next card)

Voice Lib.
M1696   Coolidge, Calvin, Pres. U.S., 1872-1933.
bd.4   President Coolidge welcoming Charles
       Lindbergh.   WJRT-TV, May 27, 1974.
          5 min.   phonotape (1 r.   7 1/2 i.p.s.)

       Taped from the Mike Douglas Show.

          1. Lindbergh, Charles Augustus, 1902-

              COOLIDGE, CALVIN, PRES. U.S., 1872-1933
Voice Lib.
M721   Fuess, Claude Moore, 1885-
bd.2   Eulogy on Calvin Coolidge, the man from
       Vermont. 1938.
          1 reel (7 in.)   7 1/2 in. per sec.
       phonotape.

          1. Coolidge, Calvin, Pres. U.S., 1872-1933.

Cooper, Gordon, 1927-
see
Cooper, Leroy Gordon, 1927-

Voice Lib. Cooper, Jackie, 1922-
M1037   Biography in sound (radio program)
bd.1   "The Actor", narrated by Morgan Beatty.
       Cast includes Tallulah Bankhead, Hy Gardner,
       Rocky Graziano, Arthur Miller, Uta Hagen,
       Jackie Cooper, Sir Laurence Olivier, Gad
       Gayther, Barbara Ashley, Hortense Powdermaker,
       Peter Ustinov, Alfred Hitchcock, Leonard Lyons,
       John Guston, Helen Hayes, Dick Mayne, Ralph
       Bellamy, Lionel Barrymore, Sir Ralph Richardson,
       José Ferrer, and Walter Kerr. NBC Radio, 1950's
          1 reel (7 in.)   7 1/2 in. per sec.
       phonotape.
                         (Continued on next card)

C1   COOPER, JAMES FENIMORE, 1789-1851
A32
       Whorf, Michael, 1933-
          The legend called Leatherstocking - James
       Fenimore Cooper.
          1 tape cassette. (The visual sounds of Mike Whorf.
       Art, music and letters, A32)

          Originally presented on his radio program, Kaleidoscope,
       WJR, Detroit.
          Duration: 27 min., 40 sec.
          In a time of adventure, discovery, and exploration comes the
       man to tell the story of frontier days, of savages both red and white,
       of wilderness and beauty.

          L. Cooper, James Fenimore, 1789-1851. L. Title.

Voice Lib. Cooper, Leroy Gordon, 1927-
M788   Gemini 5 (space flight): summary of space
       flight of Gemini Titan V from August 21 to
       August 29, 1965, including interview with
       Chris Kraft, flight director. 1965.
          1 reel (7 in.)   7 1/2 in. per sec.
       phonotape.
          1. Project Gemini. 2. Cooper, Leroy Gordon,
       1927-   3. Conrad, Charles, 1930-   I.
       Cooper, Leroy Gordon, 1927-   II. Conrad,
       Charles, 1930-   III. Kraft, Christopher
       Columbus, 1924-

       Cooper, Leroy Gordon, 1927-
Voice Lib.
M800   Gemini 5 (space flight): press conference
       with astronauts Cooper and Conrad at NASA
       Space Center, Houston, Texas, regarding
       their eight-day space flight with Gemini V.
       NBC TV, September 9, 1965.
          1 reel (7 in.)   7 1/2 in. per sec.
       phonotape.
          1. Project Gemini. 2. Cooper, Leroy Gordon,
       1927-   3. Conrad, Charles, 1930-   I.
       Cooper, Leroy Gordon, 1927-   II. Conrad,
       Charles, 1930-

C1
FA20   COOPER, PETER, 1791-1883
        Whorf, Michael, 1933-
          Peter Cooper.
          1 tape cassette.   (The visual sounds of
        Mike Whorf. The forgotten American, FA20)
          Originally presented on his radio program, Kaleidoscope,
        WJR, Detroit.
          Duration: 10 min., 40 sec.
          Cooper made and piloted the first steam engine on the
        Baltimore and Ohio railroad. He participated in the laying
        of the Atlantic Cable. Founder of the Cooper Union; he was
        also Greenback candidate for President of the United States.

          L. Cooper, Peter, 1791-1883.   L. Title.

C1
SC27   COPERNICUS, NICOLAUS, 1473-1543
        Whorf, Michael, 1933-
          And then came the light - Copernicus, Galileo.
          1 tape cassette.   (The visual sounds of
        Mike Whorf. Science, SC27)
          Originally presented on his radio program, Kaleidoscope,
        WJR, Detroit.
          Duration: 39 min., 15 sec.
          For the true stargazer here is an accurate account of the great
        astronomers. Included are brief accounts of the lives of Copernicus,
        Galileo, and others who have contributed to the science of
        astronomy.

          L. Copernicus, Nicolaus, 1473-1543.   2. Galilei, Galileo,
        1564-1642.   L. Title.

Voice Lib.
M1726   Coppola, Francis Ford, 1939-
Bd.2   Interviewed on Today Show by Barbara
         Walters and Gene Shalitt.   NBC, June 18,
         1974.
           12 min.   phonotape (1 r.   7 1/2 i.p.s.)

           1. Moving-pictures.   I. Shalitt, Gene.
         II. Walters, Barbara, 1931-

Voice Lib.
M795   Coquelin, Constant, 1841-1909.
bd.5   Excerpt from Rostand play "Cyrano de
         Bergerac: Ballade du duel".   Paris
         Exposition, 1899-1900.
           1 reel (7 in.)   7 1/2 in. per sec.
         phonotape.

           I. Rostand, Edmond, 1868-1918./Cyrano de
         Bergerac.

Voice Lib.
M795   Coquelin, Constant, 1841-1909.
bd.4   Excerpt from Rostand play "Cyrano de
         Bergerac: Ballade du duel."   Paris, 1902.
           1 reel (7 in.)   7 1/2 in. per sec.
         phonotape.

           I. Rostand, Edmond, 1868-1918./Cyrano de
         Bergerac.

Voice Lib.
M613   Corbett, James John, 1866-1933.
bd.3   Describes his boxing career.   Source ?,
         1908.
           1 reel (7 in.)   7 1/2 in. per sec.
         phonotape.

           1. Boxing

             CORNELL UNIVERSITY
Voice Lib.
M847   Dewey, Thomas Edmund, 1902-1971.
bd.2   Address at Cornell University for
         opening of School of Industrial Relations.
         NBC, November 12, 1945.
           14 min.   phonotape (1 r.   7 1/2 i.p.s.)

           1. Cornell University.

             Correll, Charles J   1890-1972
Voice Lib.
M1034   Gosden, Freeman Fisher, 1899-
bd.2   Amos, Andy, and the Kingfish in the
         "Eye Doctor" skit.   TV&R, 1929-1950.
           1 reel (7 in.)   7 1/2 in. per sec.
         phonotape.

           I. Correll, Charles J   1890-1972.

         Correll, Charles J   1890-1972
Voice Lib.
M1034   Gosden, Freeman Fisher, 1899-
bd.4   Andy and Amos (Shorty and Gabby) in a
         "Political Discussion".   TV&R, 1929-1950.
           1 reel (7 in.)   7 1/2 in. per sec.
         phonotape.

           I. Correll, Charles J   1890-1972.

         Correll, Charles J   , 1890-1972
Voice Lib.
M1034   Gosden, Freeman Fisher, 1899-
bd.3   Andy and the Kingfish in the "Funeral
         and Insurance Business" skit.   TV&R,
         1929-1950.
           1 reel (7 in.)   7 1/2 in. per sec.
         phonotape.

           I. Correll, Charles J   1890-1972.

Voice Lib. Correll, Charles J   ,1890-1972
M1034 Gosden, Freeman Fisher, 1899-
bd.1   Andy and the Kingfish in the "New Car"
          skit.   TV&R, 1929-1950.
          1 reel (7 in.)   7 1/2 in. per sec.
          phonotape.

          I. Correll, Charles J   ,1890-1972.

○

C1   The Corsican conqueror
H35   Whorf, Michael, 1933-
          The Corsican conqueror.
          1 tape cassette.   (The visual sounds of
       Mike Whorf. History and heritage, H35)
          Originally presented on his radio program, Kaleidoscope,
       WJR, Detroit.
          Duration: 38 min., 30 sec.
          He was born a Corsican, but would one day serve and command
       the French armies and wage combat against the great armies of
       Europe. He was a brilliant military strategist, often a cruel
       emperor, but always a man of noble spirit.

          L. Napoléon I, Emperor of the French, 1769-1821. L. Title.

○

Voice Lib.
623   Corwin, Norman Lewis, 1910-
          "Twenty-six by Corwin"; presents Earl
       Robinson and Millard Lampell's "Lonesome
       Train", with Earl Robinson, Burl Ives,
       Raymond Massey. CBS, 1940.
          1 reel (7 in.)   7 1/2 in. per sec.
       phonotape.

          I. Robinson, Earl, 1910-   II. Ives,
       Burl, 1909-   III. Massey, Raymond, 1896-

○

Voice Lib.
249   Corwin, Norman Lewis, 1910 -
bd. 2   "Seems Radio is Here to Stay," an excerpt
       from radio play. G. R. Vincent, June 4,
       1940.
          1 reel (7 in.)   7 1/2 in. per sec.
       phonotape.

          I. Title.

○

          Corwin, Norman Lewis, 1910-
Voice Lib.
M1046 World news tonight; radio news commentary.
bd.2   CBS Radio news broadcast from Honolulu,
       London, New York and Washington; including
       William Ewing, Norman Corwin, Albert Leitch
       and Harry Marble. CBS, September 12, 1942.
          1 reel (7 in.)   7 1/2 in. per sec.
       phonotape.

          I. Ewing, William   II. Corwin, Norman
       Lewis, 1910-   III. Leitch, Albert
       IV. Marble, Harry

○

Voice Lib.
M1050-   Corwin, Norman Lewis, 1910-
1051,   CBS Radio Workshop program "On a note of
bd.1   triumph", written and directed by Norman
       Corwin to celebrate Allied war victory in
       Europe. CBS, May 13, 1945.
          2 reels (7 in.)   7 1/2 i.p.s.   phonotape.

          1. World War, 1939-1945. I. Title: On
       a note of triumph.

○

          Corwin, Norman Lewis, 1910-
Voice Lib.
M617   Radio in the 1920's: a series of excerpts
bd.1-   from important broadcasts of the 1920's,
bd.25   with brief prologue and epilogue; a sample
       of radio of the period. NVL, April, 1964.
          1 reel (7 in.)   7 1/2 in. per sec.
       phonotape.
          L. Radio programs. L. Marconi, Guglielmo, marchese, 1874-
       1937. IL Kendall, H   G   III. Coolidge, Calvin, Pres. U. S.,
       1872-1933. IV. Wilson, Woodrow, Pres. U. S., 1856-1924. V.
       Roosevelt, Franklin Delano, Pres. U. S., 1882-1945. VL Lodge,
       Henry Cabot, 1850-1924. VII. LaGuardia, Fiorello Henry, 1882-1947.
       VIII. The Happiness Boys (Radio program) IX. Gallagher and Sheen.
       X. Barney Google. XI. Vallee, Rudy, 1901-   XII. The two
                                     ^Continued on next card)

○

          Corwin, Norman Lewis, 1910-
Voice Lib.
625   Robinson, Earl, 1910-
bd.2   [Battle hymn] Phonotape.
          Battle hymn: musical production by Norman
       Corwin of President Roosevelt's talk to the
       nation on January 6, 1942. Composition by
       Earl Robinson; all-star cast headed by Paul
       Robeson. CBS, January, 1942.

○

          Costello, Frank
Voice Lib.
M1489 U.S. Congress. Senate. Special Committee
bd.2   to Investigate Organized Crime in
          Interstate Commerce.
          Excerpt of examination of racketeer Frank
       Costello by Kefauver Committee Counsel
       Rudolf Halley. New York, WMGM Radio, March
       20, 1951.
          1 reel (7 in.)   7 1/2 in. per sec.
       phonotape.

          I. Costello, Frank   II. Halley,
       Rudolf, 1913-1956.

○

C1   Cotten Mather
FA18   Whorf, Michael, 1933-
          Cotten Mather.
          1 tape cassette.   (The visual sounds of
       Mike Whorf. The forgotten American, FA18)
          Originally presented on his radio program, Kaleidoscope,
       WJR, Detroit.
          Duration: 12 min., 20 sec.
          The most distinguished American of his generation, he made
       contributions in many fields, unrivaled by anyone of his time.
       No other American writer ever exceeded him in volume.

          L. Mather, Cotten, 1663-1728. L. Title.

○

Voice Lib.
M946   Coué, Émile, 1857-1926.
bd.2   Analysis of Coué doctrine. 1024.
      1 reel (7 in.) 7 1/2 in. per sec.
phonotape.

Voice Lib.
196   Coughlin, Charles Edward, 1891-
bd.3   Reading from the Scriptures. Detroit,
WJR, September 27, 1946.
      1 reel (7 in.) 7 1/2 in. per sec.
phonotape.

      Coué, Emil, 1857-1926
Voice Lib.
M617   Radio in the 1920's: a series of excerpts
bd.1-   from important broadcasts of the 1920's,
bd.25   with brief prologue and epilogue; a sample
    of radio of the period. NVL, April, 1964.
      1 reel (7 in.) 7 1/2 in. per sec.
phonotape.
  I. Radio programs. I. Marconi, Guglielmo, marchese, 1874-
1937. II. Kendall, H   G   III. Coolidge, Calvin, Pres. U.S.,
1872-1933. IV. Wilson, Woodrow, Pres. U.S., 1856-1924. V.
Roosevelt, Franklin Delano, Pres. U.S., 1882-1945. VI. Lodge,
Henry Cabot, 1850-1924. VII. LaGuardia, Fiorello Henry, 1882-1947.
VIII. The Happiness Boys (Radio program) IX. Gallagher and Sheen.
X. Barney Google. XI. Vallee, Rudy, 1901-   XII. The two
(Continued on next card)

Voice Lib.
652   Coughlin, Charles Edward, 1891-
bd.24   Excerpt of interview when he was 71
years old. Church of the Little Flower,
Royal Oak, Michigan, 1962.
      1 reel (7 in.) 7 1/2 in. per sec.
phonotape.

Voice Lib.
196   Coughlin, Charles Edward, 1891-
bd.2   Social justice, broadcasts in a series-
Part 1. Detroit, WJR, November 10, 1935 -
November 24, 1935.
      1 reel (7 in.) 7 1/2 in. per sec.
phonotape.

      Coughlin, Charles Edward, 1891-
Voice Lib.
M618   Radio in the 1930's (Part I): a series of
bd.1-   excerpts from important broadcasts of the
14   1930's; a sample of radio of the period.
NVL, April, 1964.
1 reel (7 in.) 7 1/2 in. per sec. phonotape.
  I. Shaw, George Bernard, 1856-1950. II. Crosby, Bing, 1901-
III. Barkley, Alban William, 1877-1956. IV. Roosevelt, Franklin
Delano, Pres. U.S., 1882-1945. V. Hoover, Herbert Clark, Pres.
U.S., 1874-1964. VI. Long, Huey Pierce, 1893-1935. VII. Townsend, Francis Everett, 1867-1960. VIII. Coughlin, Charles Edward,
1891-   IX. Rogers, Will, 1879-1935. X. Pius XII, Pope, 1876-
1958. XI. Edward VIII, king of Great Britain, 1894-1972. XII.
Barrymore, John, 1882-1942. XIII. Woollcott, Alexander, 1887-
1943. XIV. Allen, Fred, 1894-1956. XV. Benchley, Robert Charles,
1889-1945.

Voice Lib.
394   Coughlin, Charles Edward, 1891 -
bd.5   New Year's speech, 1937. Source:
Coughlin's Special Radio Network, January 1,
1937.
      1 reel (7 in.) 7 1/2 in. per sec.
phonotape.

      COUNTY GOVERNMENT
Voice Lib.
M1739   Smith, Dianna
bd.4   Interviews with John Voss and Derwood Boyd,
county commissioners, who proposed cutting
their salaries. WKAR, June 14, 1974.
      5 min. phonotape (1 r. 7 1/2 i.p.s.)

    1. County government. 2. County officials
and employees - Salaries, allowance, etc.
I. Voss, John. II. Boyd, Derwood.

Voice Lib.
377   Coughlin, Charles Edward, 1891-
bd.2   American entry into war; reviews
Spanish Civil War, attacks smear
campaign against himself and Christianity.
Private recording (air check), July 30,
1939.
      1 reel (7 in.) 7 1/2 in. per sec.
phonotape.

      COUNTY OFFICIALS AND EMPLOYEES - SALARIES,
        ALLOWANCE, ETC.
Voice Lib.
M1739   Smith, Dianna
bd.4   Interviews with John Voss and Derwood Boyd,
county commissioners, who proposed cutting
their salaries. WKAR, June 14, 1974.
      5 min. phonotape (1 r. 7 1/2 i.p.s.)

    1. County government. 2. County officials
and employees - Salaries, allowance, etc.
I. Voss, John. II. Boyd, Derwood.

COURTS - MICHIGAN

Voice Lib.
M1607   Brennan, Thomas E., 1929-
bd.2   Off the record. Interviewed by Tim
        Skubick, Tom Green, Gary Schuster, and
        Paul Weisenfeld. WKAR-TV, January 25, 1974.
            15 min.   phonotape (1 r.   7 1/2 in. per
        sec.)

            1. Courts - Michigan.   I. Skubick, Tim.
        II. Green, Tom.   III. Schuster, Gary.   IV.
        Weisenfeld, Paul

COURTS - MICHIGAN

Voice Lib.
M1606   Kavanagh, Thomas R., 1909-
bd.2   Michigan Public Broadcasting presents: an
        evening with Thomas H. Kavanagh. With Tim
        Skubick. Michigan Public Radio, December 10,
        1973.
            30 min.   phonotape (1 r.   7 1/2 in. per
        sec.)

            1. Courts - Michigan.   I. Skubick, Tim

Voice Lib.
129   Coward, Noel Pierce, 1899-
bd.6   Don't let's be beastly to the Germans;
        Coward sings this, his own composition.
        His Majesty's Voice, 1940.
            1 reel (7 in.)   7 1/2 in. per sec.
        phonotape.

            I. Title.

Voice Lib.
155   Coward, Noel Pierce, 1899-1973.
bd.1-4   Original songs.   Private recordings
        from BBC, 1941.
            1 reel (7 in.)   7 1/2 in. per sec.
        phonotape.

            CONTENTS.-bd.1. Imagine the Duchess' feel-
        ings.-bd.2. Something to do with spring.-bd.3.
        The stately homes of England.-bd.4. Lorelie.

The cowboy

C1
H47   Whorf, Michael, 1933-
            The cowboy.
            1 tape cassette.   (The visual sounds of
        Mike Whorf. History and heritage, H47)

            Originally presented on his radio program, Kaleidoscope,
        WJR, Detroit.
            Duration: 40 min., 30 sec.
            This program depicts the cowhand as he was, not as the novel,
        the movie and television has made him but rather as a tough breed
        of man.

            L. Cowboys. L. Title.

COWBOYS

Voice Lib.
376   Hart, William S   1872-1946.
bd.2   On a cowboy's life.   Private
        collection, 1926.
            1 reel (7 in.)   7 1/2 in. per sec.
        phonotape.

            1. Cowboys.

COWBOYS

C1
H47   Whorf, Michael, 1933-
            The cowboy.
            1 tape cassette.   (The visual sounds of
        Mike Whorf. History and heritage, H47)

            Originally presented on his radio program, Kaleidoscope,
        WJR, Detroit.
            Duration: 40 min., 30 sec.
            This program depicts the cowhand as he was, not as the novel,
        the movie and television has made him but rather as a tough breed
        of man.

            L. Cowboys. L. Title.

Cowen, Lester
Voice Lib.
M322   Biography in sound (radio program)
            W.C. Fields, the magnificent rogue.
        NBC, 1955.
            1 reel (7 in.)   7 1/2 in. per sec.   phonotape.
            L. Fields, W.C., 1879-1946.   L. Fields, W.C., 1879-1946.
        II. Allen, Fred, 1894-1956.   III. LaBaron, William   IV.
        Taylor, Robert Lewis, 1912-   V. McCarey, Thomas Leo, 1898-
        1969.   VI. Harkins, James   - VII. Chevalier, Maurice,
        1889-1972.   VIII. Kuromoto, Mrs. George   IX. Flynn,
        Errol Leslie, 1909-1959.   X. Wynn, Ed, 1886-1966.   XI. Dowling,
        Ray Dooley   XII. Sennett, Mack   XIII. Overacher,
        Ronald Leroy   XIV. Bergen, Edgar, 1903-   XV. Taurog,
        Norman, 1899-   XVI. Runnell, Ann   XVII. Cowen,
        Lester

Cowen, Zelman
Voice Lib.
M971-   Tugwell, Rexford Guy, 1891-
972,   "Memoirs of the New Deal"; informal talk
bd.1   with Dean Zelman Cowen (University of
        Melbourne) at Center for the Study of
        Democratic Institutions in Santa Barbara,
        California.   CSDI, 1962.
            2 reels (7 in.)   7 1/2 i.p.s.   phonotape.

            1. U.S. - Social policy.   I. Cowen, Zelman.

Voice Lib.
523   Cox, James Middleton, 1870-1957.
bd.3   1920 campaign speech: the importance of
        America going forward after World War I,
        cites shortcomings of Republican Congress.
        Nation's Forum, 1920.
            1 reel (7 in.)   7 1/2 in. per sec.
        phonotape.

Voice Lib.
654   Cox, James Middleton, 1870-1957.
bd.8   Prevention of war: campaign speech
          stressing preventive measures against war.
          Nation's Forum, 1920.
          1 reel (7 in.)   7 1/2 in. per sec.
          phonotape.

          1. War

Voice Lib.   Crane, Maurice Aaron, 1926-
M1578   Gentile, Eric Anton, 1943-
          The legislative and other social aims of
          NAPH's Civil Presence Group; interview, by
          Maurice Crane.   MSU Voice Library,
          February 13, 1974.
          60 min.   phonotape (1 r.   3 3/4 in. per
          sec.)

          1. Physically handicapped. 2. Physically
          handicapped - Law and legislation.
          I. Crane, Maurice Aaron, 1926-

Voice Lib.   Cox, Patricia (Nixon) 1947-
M1407   Eisenhower, David, 1949-
          Conversation on "Merv Griffin Show" between
          Merv, Merriman Smith, David Eisenhower, Tricia
          Nixon. Various anecdotes about Merriman Smith's
          career as a White House correspondent during
          four administrations.   CBS-TV, November 23, 1969.
          1 reel (7 in.)   7 1/2 in. per sec.
          phonotape.

          I. Griffin, Mervyn Edward, 1925-   II.
          Smith, Merriman   III. Cox, Patricia
          (Nixon) 1947-

Voice Lib.
M1568   Cranston, Alan, 1914-
bd.2   Proposing to the Ervin Committee the
          establishment of a Counsel-General, to be a
          non-Cabinet attorney for the Congress of the
          U.S.   WKAR-AM, March 26, 1974.
          20 min.   phonotape (1 r.   7 1/2 i.p..s)

          1. U.S. - Politics and government - 1969-

         Craig, Elisabeth May
Voice Lib.
656   Kennedy, John Fitzgerald, Pres. U.S., 1917-1963.
bd.3   Press conference excerpt: Mrs. Craig
          questioning President on equal rights for
          women.   CRI, 1962.
          1 reel (7 in.)   7 1/2 in. per sec.
          phonotape.

          1. Woman - Rights of women.   I. Craig,
          Elisabeth May

         CRAWFORD, JOAN, 1908-
Voice Lib.
M1743   Raft, George
bd.2   Reminisces on the Mike Douglas Show.
          WILX-TV, June 27, 1974.
          10 min.   phonotape (1 r.   7 1/2 i.p.s.)

          I. Raft, George. 2. O'Brien, Pat, 1899-   3. Muni,
          Paul, 1895-1967. 4. Crawford, Joan, 1908-   5. West, Mae,
          1893-   6. Richman, Harry. 7. Entertainers - U. S.   I.
          Douglas, Mike, 1925-

Voice Lib.
352   Craig, George North, 1909-
bd.3   On self-help as supported on an exper-
          imental basis in Burnett, Texas.   NBC,
          1949.
          1 reel (7 in.)   7 1/2 in. per sec.
          phonotape.

         Crawford, Kenneth
Voice Lib.
M1369   "The men who covered Ike". CBS-TV Face the Nation program,
bd.2   discussing the late General Dwight David Eisenhower, by the
          newspaper and TV correspondents. UPI, Merriman Smith;
          Newsweek, Kenneth Crawford; Chicago Daily News, Peter
          Lisager; AP, Jack Bell; CBS, George Herman, acting as emcee.
          CBS-TV, March 30, 1969.
          1 reel (7 in.)   7 1/2 l.p.s.   phonotape.

          I. Eisenhower, Dwight David, Pres. U.S., 1890-1969.
          I. Smith, Merriman. II. Crawford, Kenneth. III. Lisager,
          Peter. IV. Bell, Jack. V. Herman, George.

         Craig, May
           see
         Craig, Elisabeth May

Voice Lib.   Crawford, Kenneth
M1477   Discussion of Supreme Court decision on
          publishing Pentagon Papers. William B.
          Macomber, deputy under-secretary of state;
          Senator Henry Jackson; Max Frankel, head of
          New York Times' Washington bureau; Benjamin
          Bradley, executive editor of Washington Post.
          Questioned by Carl Stern, NBC; Martin Hayden,
          Detroit News; James J. Kilpatrick, Washington
          Star Syndicate; Kenneth Crawford, Washington
          Post; Edwin Newman.   NBC-TV, June 30, 1971.
          1 reel (7 in.)   7 1/2 in. per sec.
          phonotape.
          (Continued on next card)

C1
A23

The creator of immortal characters

Whorf, Michael, 1933–
    The creator of immortal characters.
    1 tape cassette.   (The visual sounds of
Mike Whorf. Art, music, and letters, A23)
    Originally presented on his radio program, Kaleidoscope,
WJR, Detroit.
    Duration: 42 min., 30 sec.
    What he was and what he was to the world is forthrightly
told in the story of Dickens, the writer and the man.

    L Dickens, Charles, 1812-1870. L Title.

CRIME AND CRIMINALS – U.S.

Voice Lib.
M540
bd.10

Crowley, "One-Gun"
    Crime; sale of guns to criminals; use
of guns; includes additional comments on
crime of the period, narcotics.   Fox
Movietone, 1932.
    1 reel (7 in.)   7 1/2 i.p.s.   phonotape.

    1. Crime and criminals – U.S.

Voice Lib.
M1577

Creek and Natchi dances.   Victor E.
Riste, December 4, 1931.
    30 min.   phonotape (1 r.   7 1/2 in. per
sec.)

    1. Creek Indians. 2. Natchi Indians.

CRIME AND CRIMINALS – U.S.

Voice Lib.
M990-
995

Organized Crime; a 3 1/2 hour documentary
NBC White Paper TV program. Many actual
voices and sounds.   NBC
    6 reels (7 in.)   7 1/2 in.   per sec.
phonotape.

CREEK INDIANS

Voice Lib.
M1577

Creek and Natchi dances.   Victor E.
Riste, December 4, 1931.
    30 min.   phonotape (1 r.   7 1/2 in. per
sec.)

    1. Creek Indians. 2. Natchi Indians.

CRIMEA CONFERENCE, YALTA, 1945.

Voice Lib.
M851-
852

Roosevelt, Franklin Delano, Pres. U.S., 1882-1945.
    Report to joint session of Congress about Yalta conference of
the Big Three.   Explaining purpose of conference, describing
devastation of Russia, plans for a peace organization in San Francisco to start April 25, 1945, touching on the free elections for
conquered countries; objectives for Poland; France's role in the
future; delays caused by "primadonnas" meeting with King Farouk,
King Ibn Saud and Emperor Haile Selassie; the current Japanese
situation; hopes for United Nations organization.   NBC, March 1,
1945.
    59 min., 30 sec.   phonotape (2 r. 7 1/2 L p. s.)

    L World War, 1939-1945 – Peace. 2. Crimea Conference,
Yalta, 1945.

CRIME AND CRIMINALS

Voice Lib.
M1608

Santarelli, Donald E
    New steps to be taken to reduce crime;
address before the Economic Club of Detroit.
WKAR-FM, March 25, 1974.
    90 min.   phonotape (1 r.   7 1/2 i.p.s.)

    1. Law enforcement. 2. Crime and criminals.

CRIMINAL PROCEDURE – U.S.

Voice Lib.
M1230-
1231,
bd.1

Fair trial, free press; discussion of the Reardon Report of the
American Bar Association about restrictions of the press in
publicizing criminal cases before they are tried.   Participants,
via TV satelite: two British guests and a panel of Americans
of diversified views.   ABC-TV, May 18, 1967.
    2 reel (7 in.)   7 1/2 i. p. s.   phonotape.

    L Liberty of the press – U.S. 2. Criminal procedure – U. S.

C1
H9

CRIME AND CRIMINALS – THE WEST

Whorf, Michael, 1933–
    Brave, bold and bad.
    1 tape cassette.   (The visual sounds of
Mike Whorf. History and heritage, H9)
    Originally presented on his radio program, Kaleidoscope,
WJR, Detroit.
    Duration: 41 min.
    The gunslinger, the desperado, the hero, the villain.   Was the
gunman a legend, or was he a paranoid psychopath? They
were men who included William Bonny, Sam Bass, Wyatt Earp
and Bill Hickock – about 250 men in all who were bad, bold
and brave – or were they?
    L Frontier and pioneer life – The West. 2. Crime and
criminals – The West.   L Title.

Voice Lib.
353
bd.21

Cripps, Sir Richard Stafford, 1889-1952.
    Devaluation of the dollar; change and
lack of changing prices.   NBC, September
25, 1949.
    1 reel (7 in.)   7 1/2 in. per sec.
phonotape.

CROCKETT, DAVID, 1786-1836

C1
H88

Whorf, Michael, 1933-
The frontiersman - Davy Crockett.
1 tape cassette. (The visual sounds of
Mike Whorf. History and heritage, H88)
Originally presented on his radio program, Kaleidoscope,
WJR, Detroit.
Duration: 35 min., 30 sec.
In the rough and ready existence of the American frontier, it
took an exceptional man to live off the land, let alone to rise
above his fellows as did Davy Crockett.

L. Crockett, David, 1786-1836. L. Title.

Voice Lib.
M1699
bd.1

Cromie, Robert Allen, 1909-

Kaplan, Justin
Discusses his book Lincoln Steffens - a
biography on Book Beat with Robert Cromie.
WKAR-TV, May 29, 1974.
20 min. phonotape (1 r. 7 1/2 i.p.s.)

1. Steffens, Joseph Lincoln, 1866-1936.
2. Kaplan, Justin/Lincoln Steffens - a
biography. I. Cromie, Robert Allen, 1909-

Voice Lib.
M1721
bd.4

Cromie, Robert Allen, 1909-

Stout, Rex, 1886-
Interviewed on Book Beat by Robert Cromie.
WKAR-TV, June 12, 1974.
20 min. phonotape (1 r. 7 1/2 i.p.s.)

1. Authors - Correspondence, reminiscences,
etc. I. Cromie, Robert.

CROMWELL, OLIVER, 1599-1658

C1
H87

Whorf, Michael, 1933-
The Puritan protector - Oliver Cromwell.
1 tape cassette. (The visual sounds of
Mike Whorf. History and heritage, H87)
Originally presented on his radio program, Kaleidoscope,
WJR, Detroit.
Duration: 36 min.
Bred to peaceful occupations, Cromwell rebuilt the army of the
Parliament to serve as the powerful military arm of the Puritan
Reformation. He was the leader capable of transforming the royalist
face of England, and establishing the power of the Parliament and
the Independent Party.

L. Cromwell, Oliver, 1599-1658. L. Title.

Voice Lib.
M715
bd.1

Cronkite, Walter Leland, 1916-
Walter Cronkite and Robert Trout
interpolating address by Adolf Hitler,
wherein announcement is made of calling up
of Reichstag; also commentary on prelude
to and beginning of World War II. 1939.
1 reel (7 in.) 7 1/2 in. per sec.
phonotape.

I. Hitler, Adolf, 1889-1945. II. Trout,
Robert, 1908-

Voice Lib.
M740
bd.3

Cronkite, Walter Leland, 1916-
Excerpt from "20ᵗʰ Century" TV program on
race conditions in South Africa. Description
of Sharpville riots and about the awarding
of Nobel Peace Prize to Chief Luthuli.
CBS, 1961.
5 min., 16 sec. phonotape (1 r.
7 1/2 i.p.s.)

1. South Africa - Race question.

Voice Lib.
M1435

Cronkite, Walter Leland, 1916-
Life in other worlds; exploratory discussion about life on other
planets. Arnold J. Toynbee, Dr. G. B. Kiastiakowsky
(professor at Harvard), Dr. Donald M. Michaels, Dr. Otto
Struve, Dr. Harlow Shapley, Walter Cronkite, Chet Huntley,
William L. Laurence. New York, NBC, March 3, 1961.
1 reel (7 in.) 7 1/2 i.p.s. phonotape.

L. Life on other planets. L. Toynbee, Arnold Joseph, 1889-
II. Kiastiakowsky, George Bogdan. III. Michaels, Donald M.
IV. Struve, Otto, 1897-1963. V. Shapley, Harlow, 1885-1972.
VI. Cronkite, Walter Leland, 1916- VII. Huntley, Chet,
1911-1974. VIII. Laurence, William Leonard, 1888-

Voice Lib.
M847
bd.1

Cronkite, Walter Leland, 1914-
Description of launching of Agena spacecraft at 10:04 a.m. Monday, October 25, 1965,
at Cape Kennedy, Florida, until its func-
tional failure. Announcements by Jack King
at Cape Kennedy and Paul Haney at Houston
space center; scrubbing of Gemini VI
launching. CBS-TV, October 25, 1965.
18 min. phonotape (1 r. 7 1/2 i.p.s.)

1. Space flight. I. Project Gemini.

Voice Lib.
M1328
bd.2

Cronkite, Walter Leland, 1916-
Apollo 7 (space flight): description of
launching of Apollo 7 spacecraft, morning
of October 11, 1968, and comments by various
broadcasters, including Walter Cronkite.
Description includes countdown and take-off;
remarks by astronauts. CBS TV, October 11,
1968.
1 reel (7 in.) 7 1/2 in. per sec. phonotape.
L. Project Apollo. 2. Eisele, Donn F 1930- 3. Cunningham, R Walter, 1932- 4. Schirra, Walter Marty, 1923-
L. Eisele, Donn F 1930- II. Cunningham, R Walter,
1932- III. Schirra, Walter Marty, 1923- IV. Cronkite,
Walter Leland, 1916-

Voice Lib.
M1364

Cronkite, Walter Leland, 1916-
Apollo 9 (space flight): splashdown, part 1.
CBS correspondents with anchorman Walter
Cronkite describe recovery of Apollo 9
from the time astronauts are over Australia
to the opening of the hatch. CBS TV,
March 13, 1969.
1 reel (7 in.) 7 1/2 in. per sec.
phonotape.
L. Project Apollo. 2. McDivitt, James Alton, 1929- 3.
Scott, David Randolph, 1932- 4. Schweickart, Russell L
1936- L. McDivitt, James Alton, 1929- II. Scott, David
Randolph, 1932- III. Schweickart, Russell L 1936-
IV. Cronkite, Walter Leland, 1916-

Cronkite, Walter Leland, 1916-
Voice Lib.
M1368   Some friends of General Eisenhower (TV program)
      CBS-TV special recalling anecdotes about
      General Eisenhower by some of his friends:
      Bob Hope, Kevin McCann, General Omar Bradley,
      Robert B. Anderson, General Alfred Gruenther,
      with Walter Cronkite acting as emcee. CBS-TV,
      March 29, 1969.
        1 reel (7 in.) 7 1/2 in. per sec.

        L. Eisenhower, Dwight David, Pres. U.S., 1890-1969. L.
Hope, Bob, 1903-   II. McCann, Kevin   III. Bradley, Omar
Nelson, 1893-   IV. Anderson, Robert Bernerd, 1910-   V.
Gruenther, Alfred Maximilian, 1899-   VI. Cronkite, Walter
Leland, 1916-

Cronkite, Walter Leland, 1916-
Voice Lib.
M1388   Apollo 11 (space flight): Walter Cronkite and Wally Schirra
bd.1   describing recovery. Maneuvers by frogmen and helicopters
      at splashdown spot; "air boss" describes close-up scene;
      decontamination process; helicopter landing on "Hornet" with
      astronauts; reception. Description of proceedings on "Hornet"
      by CBS newscasters. CBS TV, July 24, 1969.
      1 reel (7 in.) 7 1/2 in. per sec. phonotape.

      L. Project Apollo. 2. Space flight to the moon. 3. Aldrin,
Edwin E   1930-   4. Collins, Michael, 1930-   5. Armstrong,
Neil, 1930-   L. Aldrin, Edwin E   1930-   II. Collins,
Michael, 1930-   III. Armstrong, Neil, 1930-   IV. Cronkite,
Walter Leland, 1916-   V. Schirra, Walter Marty, 1923-

Cronkite, Walter Leland, 1916-
Voice Lib.
M1384   Apollo 11 (space flight): launch day, July 16,
bd.1   1969. Description of astronauts going up
      the elevator; conversation between Walter
      Cronkite and Wally Schirra at approximately
      2 hours before launch. CBS TV, July 16, 1969.
      1 reel (7 in.) 7 1/2 in. per sec.
      phonotape.
      L. Project Apollo. 2. Space flight to the moon. 3. Aldrin,
Edwin E   1930-   4. Collins, Michael, 1930-   5. Armstrong,
Neil, 1930-   L. Aldrin, Edwin E   1930-   II. Collins,
Michael, 1930-   III. Armstrong, Neil, 1930-   IV. Cronkite,
Walter Leland, 1916-   V. Schirra, Walter Marty, 1923-

Cronkite, Walter Leland, 1916-
Voice Lib.
M1389   Apollo 11 (space flight): welcome to Apollo 11 astronauts on their
bd.2   arrival at Kennedy Airport at New York; ferried by Marine
      helicopter to Wall Street; boat whistles harbor greeting.
      Flashbacks to former important New York parades (Frank McGee)
      Walter Cronkite, CBS, describing beginning of motorcade
      and parade to city hall. CBS [and NBC] TV, August 13, 1969.
      1 reel (7 in.) 7 1/2 in. per sec. phonotape.

      L. Project Apollo. 2. Space flight to the moon. 3. Aldrin,
Edwin E   1930-   4. Collins, Michael, 1930-   5.
Armstrong, Neil, 1930-   L. Aldrin, Edwin E   1930-
II. Collins, Michael, 1930-   III. Armstrong, Neil, 1930-
IV. McGee, Frank, 1921-1974. V. Cronkite, Walter Leland, 1916-

---

Cronkite, Walter Leland, 1916-
Voice Lib.
M1386   Apollo 11 (space flight): conversation with
bd.1   broadcasters Walter Cronkite and Wally
      Schirra. Including Armstrong's activities
      on moon alone; pictures, rock descriptions,
      then Aldrin coming down ladder; rock boxes
      put to use. TV cameras put at 30' panoramic
      position. Reading inscription of plaque
      with U.S. flag and setting it up. Telephone
      call from Washington to astronauts and their
      acknowledgement. CBS TV, July 20, 1969.
      1 reel (7 in.) 7 1/2 in. per sec.
      phonotape.
         (Continued on next card)

Voice Lib.
M1580   Cronkite, Walter Leland, 1916-
        Accepting Fourth Estate Award of the
    National Press Club. WKAR-AM, February 27,
    1974.
        30 min.   phonotape (1 r. 7 1/2 i.p.s.)

Cronkite, Walter Leland, 1916-
Voice Lib.
M1386   Apollo 11 (space flight): excerpts of
bd.4   interview between Walter Cronkite and
      Lyndon B. Johnson two weeks before the
      moon flight regarding development of American
      space effort. CBS TV, July 20, 1969.
      1 reel (7 in.) 7 1/2 in. per sec.
      phonotape.

      1. Project Apollo. 2. Space flight to the
    moon. I. Cronkite, Walter Leland, 1916-
    II. Johnson, Lyndon Baines, Pres. U.S., 1908-
    1973.

Voice Lib.
M723   Cronkite, Walter Leland, 1916-
bd.2   Columbia Broadcasting System, Inc.
      Memorial broadcast at the death of
    Albert Einstein, with Walter Cronkite.
    CBS, April 18, 1955.
      15 min., 30 sec. phonotape (1 r.
    7 1/2 i.p.s.)

      1. Einstein, Albert, 1878-1955.
    I. Cronkite, Walter Leland, 1916-

Cronkite, Walter Leland, 1916-
Voice Lib.
M1387   Apollo 11 (space flight): recovery. Walter Cronkite and Wally
bd.2   Schirra announce proceedings from aircraft carrier "Hornet";
      trying to track spacecraft coming down; chutes opening at
      10,500 feet; voice contact with spacecraft; visual of chutes;
      splashdown 9 miles from "Hornet", upside-down. Collar
      attached to spacecraft. NBC and ABC TV, July 24, 1969.
      1 reel (7 in.) 7 1/2 in. per sec. phonotape.

      L. Project Apollo. 2. Space flight to the moon. 3. Aldrin,
Edwin E   1930-   4. Collins, Michael, 1930-   5.
Armstrong, Neil, 1930-   L. Aldrin, Edwin E   1930-
II. Collins, Michael, 1930-   III. Armstrong, Neil, 1930-
IV. Cronkite, Walter Leland, 1916-   V. Schirra, Walter Marty,
1923-

Voice Lib.   Cronkite, Walter Leland, 1916-
M308   Columbia Broadcasting System, inc.
bd.2   Assassination: announcement of Kennedy's
      death by CBS commentator Walter Cronkite; on
      film of assassination, search for suspect,
      future events and Johnson's oath; announcement
      of shooting of Dallas policeman and arrest
      of Oswald; comments by Eisenhower and Truman.
      CBS, November 22, 1963.
      1 reel (7 in.) 7 1/2 in. per sec.
    phonotape.
    L. Kennedy, John Fitzgerald, Pres. U.S., 1917-1963 - Assassination.
L. Cronkite, Walter Leland, 1916-   II. Eisenhower, Dwight
David, Pres. U.S., 1890-1969. III. Truman, Harry S, Pres. U.S.,
1884-1972.

Cronkite, Walter Leland, 1916-
Voice Lib.
244-   Eisenhower, Dwight David, Pres. U.S., 1890-1969.
247   Remarks on the Presidency, with Walter
         Cronkite. CBS-TV, September 12-November 26,
         1961.
           4 reels (7 in.)   7 1/2 in. per sec.
         phonotape.

           I. Cronkite, Walter Leland, 1916-

Cronkite, Walter Leland, 1916-
Voice Lib.
M1370 Eisenhower, Dwight David, Pres. U.S., 1890-
bd.2   1969.
           A portion of an interview in London between
         Walter Cronkite, CBS, and Gen. Eisenhower,
         pertaining to the Normandy invasion on its
         20th anniversary. CBS, June 6, 1964.
           1 reel (7 in.)   7 1/2 in. per sec.
         phonotape.

           I. Cronkite, Walter Leland, 1916-

Cronkite, Walter Leland, 1916-
Voice Lib.
650-   Eisenhower, Dwight David, Pres. U.S., 1890-1969.
651   D-Day plus 20 years (CBS Reports); discussion
         of strategy and procedures and preparation for
         invasion of Nazi-occupied France on June 6, 1944
         by former Commander of Allied Expeditionary
         Forces with Walter Cronkite. CBS, June 6, 1964.
           2 reels (7 in.)   7 1/2 in. per sec.
         phonotape.

           I. Cronkite, Walter Leland, 1916-

Cronkite, Walter Leland, 1916-
Voice Lib.
M722- Eisenhower, Dwight David, Pres. U.S., 1890-
723   1969.
bd.1   Winston S. Churchill discussed by Walter
         Cronkite and Dwight D. Eisenhower, including
         Eisenhower's association with Churchill
         during and after the war. CBS, January 25,
         1965.
           2 reels (7 in.)   7 1/2 in. per sec.
         phonotape.

           I. Churchill, Winston Leonard Spencer, 1874-
         1965. II. Cronkite, Walter Leland, 1916-

Cronkite, Walter Leland, 1916-
Voice Lib.
M317   Johnson, Lyndon Baines, Pres. U.S., 1908-1973.
bd.1   Interview of Lyndon B. Johnson on his early
         background. CBS, November 24, 1963.
           1 reel (7 in.)   7 1/2 in. per sec.
         phonotape.

           I. Cronkite, Walter Leland, 1916-

Cronkite, Walter Leland, 1916-
Voice Lib.
M1425 Johnson, Lyndon Baines, Pres. U.S., 1908-
bd.2   1973.
           Interview with ex-President Lyndon
         Johnson regarding Kennedy assassination events
         with CBS commentator Walter Cronkite.
         CBS-TV, March, 1970.
           1 reel (7 in.)   7 1/2 in. per sec.
         phonotape.

           I. Cronkite, Walter Leland, 1916-

Cronkite, Walter Leland, 1916-
Voice Lib.
M1745 al Sadat, Anwar.
bd.4   Sadat: an exclusive interview; an extensive
         interview with Walter Cronkite on the changes
         in U. S. policy regarding Egypt. CBS, June 21,
         1974.
           30 min.   phonotape (1 r.   7 1/2 i.p.s.)

           1. U. S. - For. rel. - Egypt. 2. Egypt -
         For. rel. - U. S. 3. Egypt - Pol. & govt. -
         1952-   I. Cronkite, Walter Leland,
         1916-

Cronkite, Walter Leland, 1916-
Voice Lib.
M655   The Twentieth Century (TV program)
bd.1   "The creative thirties", narrated by
         Walter Cronkite. CBS, 1963.
           25 min.   phonotape (1 r.   7 1/2 i.p.s.)
           1. U.S. - Civilization - 1918-1945. I. Bowes, Edward,
         1874-1946. II. Geismar, Maxwell David, 1909-
         III. MacDonald, Dwight, 1906-   IV. Welles, Orson, 1915-
         V. Cronkite, Walter Leland, 1916-   VI. Gable, Clark, 1901-
         1960. VII. Lewis, Sinclair, 1885-1951. VIII. Houseman,
         John, 1902-   IX. Roosevelt, Franklin Delano, Pres. U.S.,
         1882-1945.

Cronkite, Walter Leland, 1916-
Voice Lib.
M289   Twentieth Century (Television program)
bd.2   Production on career of Alfred E. Smith.
         Various excerpts of addresses by Gov. Smith;
         recollections by Robert Moses on life of
         Gov. Smith; narration by Walter Cronkite;
         placing of Smith's name in nomination for
         President by F.D.R. CBS, 1962.
           1 reel (7 in.)   7 1/2 in. per sec.
         phonotape.
           I. Smith, Alfred Emanuel, 1873-1944. I. Smith, Alfred
         Emanuel, 1873-1944. II. Moses, Robert, 1888-   III. Cronkite,
         Walter Leland, 1916-   IV. Roosevelt, Franklin Delano, Pres. U.S.,
         1882-1945.

Crosby, Bing, 1901-
Voice Lib.
M1047 Old-time radio excerpts of the 1930's and
         1940's, including: Rudy Vallee singing
         "Linger a little longer"; Will Rogers on
         panaceas for the Depression; Bing Crosby
         singing "Sweet Georgia Brown"; Eddie Cantor;
         Jimmy Durante singing "Inka-dinka-do";
         musical skit by Clayton, Jackson and Durante;
         wit by Harry Hershfield; musical selection
         "Thinking of you" by Kay Kyser; Kate Smith
         singing theme song, "When the moon comes over
         the mountain"; W.C. Fields' temperance

(Continued on next card)

Voice Lib.
M1047 Crosby, Bing, 1901-
Old-time radio excerpts of the 1930's and
1940's... (Card 2)

lecture; Al Jolson singing "Rocka-by-your
baby"; and George Burns and Gracie Allen
skit. TV&R 1930's and 1940's.
1 reel (7 in.) 7 1/2 in. per sec.
L. Vallee, Rudy, 1901- II. Rogers, Will, 1879-1935. III.
Crosby, Bing, 1901- IV. Cantor, Eddie, 1893-1964. V. Durante,
Jimmy, 1893- VI. Clayton, Patti VII. Jackson,
Eddie VIII. Hershfield, Harry, 1885- IX. Kyser, Kay,
1906- X. Smith, Kate, 1909- XI. Fields, W. C., 1879-
1946. XII. Jolson, Al, 1886-1950. XIII. Burns, George, 1896-
XIV. Allen, Fracie, 1906-

Voice Lib.
616 Crosby, Bing, 1901-
bd.2 "Let's put out the lights". Brunswick,
1931.
1 reel (7 in.) 7 1/2 in. per sec.
phonotape.

Voice Lib.
591 Crosby, Bing, 1901-
bd.2 Sings sing-along version of Sammy Chan-
Jimmy Van Heusen song "Swinging on a Star",
prepared for use in military hospitals.
Comments on song. V-Disc, 1943.
1 reel (7 in.) 7 1/2 in. per sec.
phonotape.

I. Title: Swinging on a star.

Voice Lib.
M872 Crosby, Bing, 1901-
bd.3 To patients in Army hospitals sings,
"Let Me Call You Sweetheart" and "The Bells
Are Ringing". V Disc. 1943.
1 reel (7 in.) 7 1/2 in. per sec.
phonotape.

Voice Lib.
M709 Crosby, Bing, 1901-
bd.1 "Command Performance"; excerpts of
radio show for Armed Forces Radio Services.
Speaker: Bing Crosby. Melchior collection,
1944.
9 min., 40 sec. phonotape (1 r.
7 1/2 i.p.s.)

Voice Lib.
M618 Crosby, Bing, 1901-
bd.1- Radio in the 1930's (Part I): a series of
14 excerpts from important broadcasts of the
1930's; a sample of radio of the period.
NVL, April, 1964.
1 reel (7 in.) 7 1/2 in. per sec. phonotape.
L. Shaw, George Bernard, 1856-1950. II. Crosby, Bing, 1901-
III. Barkley, Alban William, 1877-1956. IV. Roosevelt, Franklin
Delano, Pres. U.S., 1882-1945. V. Hoover, Herbert Clark, Pres.
U.S., 1874-1964. VI. Long, Huey Pierce, 1893-1935. VII. Townsend, Francis Everett, 1867-1960. VIII. Coughlin, Charles Edward,
1891- IX. Rogers, Will, 1879-1935. X. Pius XII, Pope, 1876-
1958. XI. Edward VIII, king of Great Britain, 1894-1972. XII.
Barrymore, John, 1882-1942. XIII. Woollcott, Alexander, 1887-
1943. XIV. Allen, Fred, 1894-1956. XV. Benchley, Robert Charles,
1889-1945.

Voice Lib.
M621 Crosby, Bing, 1901-
bd.1- Radio in the 1940's (Part II): a series of
12 excerpts from important broadcasts of the
1940's; a sample of radio of the period.
NVL, April, 1964.
1 reel (7 in.) 7 1/2 in. per sec. phonotape.
L. Daly, John Charles, 1914- II. Hall, Josef Washington,
1894- III. Shirer, William Lawrence, 1904- IV. Roosevelt,
Eleanor (Roosevelt) 1884-1962. V. Roosevelt, Franklin Delano,
Pres. U.S., 1882-1945. VI. Churchill, Winston Leonard Spencer,
1874-1965. VII. Wainwright, Jonathan Mayhew, 1883-1953. VIII.
Cantor, Eddie, 1893-1964. IX. Sinatra, Francis Albert, 1917-
X. Hope, Bob, 1903- XI. Crosby, Bing, 1901- XII. Shore,
Dinah, 1917?)- XIII. Bergen, Edgar, 1903- XIV. Armstrong,
Louis, 1900-1971. XV. Eldridge, Roy, 1911-

Voice Lib.
M1264 Crosby, Bing, 1901-
Biographical sketch about the career of
Bing Crosby on "Conversation" program with
John Daly. NET, August 8, 1967.
1 reel (7 in.) 7 1/2 in. per sec.
phonotape.

1. Crosby, Bing, 1901-
I. Daly, John Charles, 1914-

CROSBY, BING, 1901-
Voice Lib.
M763 Whiteman, Paul, 1890-1967.
bd.5 Excerpt from "The Scope of Jazz" (Program
6); comments on Bing Crosby at the beginning
of his career, including song by Crosby,
"Pennies from Heaven." Westinghouse
Broadcasting Corporation, 1964.
1 reel (7 in.) 7 1/2 in. per sec.
phonotape. (The Music Goes Round and Round)

1. Crosby, Bing, 1901- I. Title: The
scope of jazz. II. Series.

Cross of gold
Voice Lib.
M1250 Bryan, William Jennings, 1860-1925.
bd.3 Address before Democratic national
convention, popularly known as his "Cross
of Gold" speech. Chicago, 1896.
1 reel (7 in.) 7 1/2 in. per sec.
phonotape.

I. Title: Cross of gold.

C1
FA15
CROWDER, ENOCH HERBERT, 1859-1932
Whorf, Michael, 1933-
Enoch H. Crowder.
1 tape cassette. (The visual sounds of
Mike Whorf. The forgotten American, FA15)
Originally presented on his radio program, Kaleidoscope,
WJR, Detroit.
Duration: 10 min.
Crowder was a U. S. army officer who administered the
Selective service act during World War I and later served as
Ambassador to Cuba.

I. Crowder, Enoch Herbert, 1859-1932. I. Title.

Voice Lib.
M654
bd.6
Cummings, Homer Stillé, 1870-
Address as temporary chairman of
Democratic Convention of 1920, eulogizing
President Wilson and condemning his
opponents. Nation's Forum, 1920.
1 reel (7 in.) 7 1/2 in. per sec.
phonotape.

1. Wilson, Woodrow, Pres. U.S., 1856-1924.

Voice Lib.
M540
bd.10
Crowley, "One-Gun"
Crime; sale of guns to criminals; use
of guns; includes additional comments on
crime of the period, narcotics. Fox
Movietone, 1932.
1 reel (7 in.) 7 1/2 i.p.s. phonotape.

1. Crime and criminals - U.S.

Voice Lib.
M654
bd.7
Cummings, Homer Stillé, 1870-
Summons to duty. In favor of American
participation of the League of Nations.
Nation's Forum, June 28, 1920.
1 reel (7 in.) 7 1/2 in. per sec.
phonotape.

1. League of Nations.

C1
H49
The crusaders
Whorf, Michael, 1933-
The crusaders.
1 tape cassette. (The visual sounds of
Mike Whorf. History and heritage, H49)
Originally presented on his radio program, Kaleidoscope,
WJR, Detroit.
Duration: 39 min., 15 sec.
The religious wars were led by men who engaged in savage
encounters with the infidels as they attempted to recapture the
cities where Christ once lived. Out of this period came many great
men - none greater than Richard the Lion-Hearted.
I. Richard I, King of England, 1157-1199. 2. Crusades. I. Title.

Cunningham, Paul
Voice Lib.
M273-
274
bd.1
Biography in sound (radio program)
Franklin Delano Roosevelt: the friends and
former associates of Franklin Roosevelt on
the tenth anniversary of the President's death.
NBC Radio, April, 1955.
2 reels (7 in.) 7 1/2 in. per sec.
phonotape.
I. Roosevelt, Franklin Delano, Pres. U.S., 1882-1945. I.
McIntire, Ross T 1899- II. Mellett, Lowell, 1884-1960.
III. Tully, Grace IV. Henderson, Leon, 1895-
V. Roosevelt, Eleanor (Roosevelt) 1884-1962. VI. DeGraaf, Albert
VII. Lehman, Herbert Henry, 1878-1963. VIII. Rosenman, Samuel
Irving, 1896- IX. Arvey, Jacob X. Moley, Raymond,
1886- XI. Farley, James Aloysius, 1888- XII. Roosevelt,
(Continued on next card)

C1
H49
CRUSADES
Whorf, Michael, 1933-
The crusaders.
1 tape cassette. (The visual sounds of
Mike Whorf. History and heritage, H49)
Originally presented on his radio program, Kaleidoscope,
WJR, Detroit.
Duration: 39 min., 15 sec.
The religious wars were led by men who engaged in savage
encounters with the infidels as they attempted to recapture the
cities where Christ once lived. Out of this period came many great
men - none greater than Richard the Lion-Hearted.
I. Richard I, King of England, 1157-1199. 2. Crusades. I. Title.

Voice Lib.
M1328
bd.2
Cunningham, R   Walter, 1932-
Apollo 7 (space flight): description of
launching of Apollo 7 spacecraft, morning
of October 11, 1968, and comments by various
broadcasters, including Walter Cronkite.
Description includes countdown and take-off;
remarks by astronauts. CBS TV, October 11,
1968.
1 reel (7 in.) 7 1/2 in. per sec. phonotape.
I. Project Apollo. 2. Eisele, Donn F 1930- 3. Cunningham, R   Walter, 1932- 4. Schirra, Walter Marty, 1923-
I. Eisele, Donn F 1930- II. Cunningham, R   Walter,
1932- III. Schirra, Walter Marty, 1923- IV. Cronkite,
Walter Leland, 1916-

Voice Lib.
M652
bd.4
CUBA - HISTORY - 1933-1959
Castro, Fidel, 1927-
Castro and Cuban rebels speaking from
Cuban hills on U.S. newsman's recorder.
CBS, May 19, 1957.
1 reel (7 in.) 7 1/2 i.p.s. phonotape.

1. Cuba - History - 1933-1959.

Voice Lib.
M988-
989
Cusack, Cyril, 1910-
Lawrence, Thomas Edward, 1888-1935.
Life of Lawrence of Arabia; one hour
documentary, with Cyril Cusack as T.E.
Lawrence, and actual voices of friends and
contemporaries, including his brother
A.W. Lawrence. BBC, August 21, 1966.
2 reels (7 in.) 7 1/2 in. per sec.
phonotape.

I. Cusack, Cyril, 1910-

Voice Lib.
318   Cushing, Richard James, Cardinal., 1895-
       Requiem Mass for John F. Kennedy at St.
       Matthew's Cathedral in Washington, celebrated
       by Cardinal Cushing. With English
       translation and explanation. CBS,
       November 25, 1963.
       1 reel (7 in.)   7 1/2 in. per sec.
       phonotape.

           1. Kennedy, John Fitzgerald, Pres. U.S.,
       1917-1963. I. Cushing, Richard James,
       Cardinal, 1895-

CZECHOSLOVAK REPUBLIC - FOREIGN RELATIONS -
Voice Lib.   GERMANY
M717   Kaltenborn, Hans von, 1878-1965.
bd.11   Analysis of Hitler speech on Czechoslovakia.
         September 26, 1938.
         1 min., 58 sec.   phonotape (1 r.
         7 1/2 i.p.s.)

             1. Germany - Foreign relations -
         Czechoslovak Republic. 2. Czechoslovak
         Republic - Foreign relations - Germany.

Voice Lib. Cushing, Richard James, Cardinal, 1895-
M319   Funeral of John F. Kennedy: church ceremonies at Washington
        Cathedral; quote of speech segments of JFK and delivery of
        memorial sermon by Most Rev. Philip M. Hannan; prayers
        at bier by Cardinal Richard Cushing; departure of coffin
        from Cathedral to Arlington Cemetery; description of journey
        and arrival. CBS, November 25, 1963.
        1 reel (7 in.)   7 1/2 i.p.s.   phonotape.

        1. Kennedy, John Fitzgerald, Pres. U.S., 1917-1963 -
        Assassination. I. Hannan, Philip Matthew, 1913-   II.
        Cushing, Richard James, Cardinal, 1895-

CZECHOSLOVAK REPUBLIC - HISTORY
Voice Lib.
218   Kaltenborn, Hans von, 1878-1965.
bd.1-2   News reports from Goedesburg on current
          Czechoslovakian situation. CBS, September
          23, 1938.
          1 reel (7 in.)   7 1/2 in. per sec.
          phonotape.

              1. Czechoslovak Republic - History.

Voice Lib.
M1800   Cushman, Robert Everton, 1914-
WG   Testimony before the Senate Committee
0802.03   investigating the Watergate Affair.
           Pacifica, August 2, 1973.
           96 min.   phonotape (2 r.   3 3/4 i.p.s.)
           (Watergate gavel to gavel, phase 1)

               1. Watergate Affair, 1972-

Voice Lib.
M738   Dafoe, Allan Roy, 1883-1943.
bd.2   Telephone conversation with Dr. Dafoe
        pertaining to the condition and care of
        the newly borne Dionne quintuplets in
        Callenier, Ontario. CBC, 1934.
        1 reel (7 in.)   7 1/2 in. per sec.
        phonotape.

            1. Dionne quintuplets.

       CUSTER, GEORGE ARMSTRONG, 1839-1876
C1
H38   Whorf, Michael, 1933-
          General George Armstrong Custer.
          1 tape cassette.   (The visual sounds of
       Mike Whorf. History and heritage, H38)
          Originally presented on his radio program, Kaleidoscope,
       WJR, Detroit.
          Duration: 49 min., 15 sec.
          Yellow Hair, General of the Long Knives, George Armstrong
       Custer, was he the terror of the plains, the egotist, the bombastic,
       or was he a general who followed his orders with flare and dash?

           I. Custer, George Armstrong, 1839-1876. I. Title.

Voice Lib.
M1086   Dafoe, Allan Roy, 1883-1943.
bd.2   Dr. Dafoe in radio broadcast from Callander,
        Ontario, introducing all five Dionne quintup-
        lets, who speak and sing various songs. CBC,
        1938.
        1 reel (7 in.)   7 1/2 in. per sec.
        phonotape.

            I. Dionne quintuplets.

       Customs of marriage
C1
S61   Whorf, Michael, 1933-
          Customs of marriage.
          1 tape cassette.   (The visual sounds of
       Mike Whorf. Social, S61)
          Originally presented on his radio program, Kaleidoscope,
       WJR, Detroit.
          Duration: 37 min., 40 sec.
          The great institution is described with music, prose, and
       poetry which delves into the lore, myth, and legend behind
       marriage customs.

           I. Marriage. I. Title.

Voice Lib. Dafoe, Allan Ray, 1883-1943
M619   Radio in the 1930's (Part II): a series of
bd.1-   excerpts of the 1930's; a sample of radio
14   of the period. NVL, April, 1964.
         1 reel (7 in.) 7 1/2 in. per sec. phonotape.
         I. Allen, Fred, 1894-1956. II. Delmar, Kenny   III. Donald,
         Peter   IV. Pious, Minerva   V. Fennelly, Parker   VI.
         Boyer, Charles, 1899-   VII. Dunne, Irene, 1904-   VIII.
         DeMille, Cecil Blount, 1881-1959. IX. West, Mae, 1893-   X.
         Dafoe, Allan Ray, 1883-1943. XI. Dionne quintuplets. XII. Ortega,
         Santos   XIII. War of the worlds (radio program) XIV. Ives, Burl,
         1909-   XV. Robinson, Earl, 1910-   XVI. Temple, Shirley,
         1928-   XVII. Earhart, Amelia, 1898-1937. XVIII. Lawrence,
         Gertrude, 1901-1952. XIX. Cohan, George Michael, 1878-1942.
         XX. Shaw, George Bernard, 1856-1950. XXI. Hitler, Adolf, 1889-
         1945. XXII. Chamberlain, Neville, 1869-1940. XXIII. Roosevelt,
         Franklin Delano, Pres. U.S., 1882-1945.

Voice Lib.
M529
bd.2
Daladier, Edouard, 1884-1970.
Announcement of war with Germany.
Shortwave, Paris Mondial, September 3, 1939.
1 reel (7 in.)   7 1/2 in. per sec.
phonotape.

In French.

1. World War, 1939-1945

Voice Lib.
M1391
bd.2
Daley, Richard J   1902-
Apollo 11 (space flight): reception of
Apollo 11 astronauts in Chicago. Descrip-
tion of motorcade on way to Civic Center
Plaza and ceremonies there. Cardinal Cody's
invocation. JFK flashback predicting moon
landing before decade is out. Mayor Daley
and Alderman Klene resolution making August
13 "Astronauts' Day". Senator Percy and
Governor Ogilvie of Illinois. Presentation
of honorary citizenship to astronauts.
[Source?] August 13, 1969.
(Continued on next card)

Voice Lib.
M1391
bd.2
Daley, Richard J   1902-
Apollo 11 (space flight): reception of Apollo
11 astronauts ... 1969. (Card 2)

1 reel (7 in.)   7 1/2 in. per sec.
phonotape.
1. Project Apollo. 2. Space flight to the moon. 3. Aldrin,
Edwin E   1930-   4. Collins, Michael, 1930-   5. Armstrong,
Neil, 1930-   L Aldrin, Edwin E   1930-   II. Collins,
Michael, 1930-   III. Armstrong, Neil, 1930-   IV. Cody,
John Patrick, cardinal, 1907-   V. Kennedy, John Fitzgerald,
Pres. U.S., 1917-1963. VI. Daley, Richard J   1902- VII.
Percy, Charles Harting, 1919-   VIII. Ogilvie, Richard Buell,
1923-

Voice Lib.
M1323-
M1328,
bd.1
Daley, Richard J   1902-
Democratic Party. National Convention,
Chicago, 1968.
Hubert Humphrey, Democratic presidential nom. ...,
announcing his selection of Sen. Muskie as his running mate;
convention floor reports; interview with Mrs. Humphrey. Mayor
Daley of Chicago defending police action. Interviews with Sen-
ator McGovern and Jesse Unruh of California. Remote address by
Sen. Edward Kennedy introducing a memorial motion picture on
the late Sen. Robert F. Kennedy. Various reports on riots and
general confusion, reluctance of delegates to come to order.
Nominations for Vice-President; seconding speeches for Sen.
Muskie and nominating speech by Wisconsin delegation of Julian
Bond of Georgia. Interview with Julian Bond, who declined
nomination of the vice-presidency. Story told by chairman of
the New Hampshire [delegation] regarding his arrest. Interview
(Continued on next card)

Voice Lib.
M1323-
M1328,
bd.1
Daley, Richard J   1902-
Democratic Party. National Convention,
Chicago, 1968... (Card 2)
with Paul O'Dwyer of the New York delegation regarding the
nomination of Richard Daley for Vice-President. General
confusion. Nomination of Sen. Edmund Muskie as Vice-President
and resulting confusion with the Oregon delegation. Followed by
Sen. Muskie's acceptance speech. NBC-TV, August 29, 1968.
6 reels (7 in.)   7 1/2 in. per sec. phonotape.
L Humphrey, Hubert Horatio, 1911- II. Humphrey, Muriel Fay
(Buck) 1912-   III. Daley, Richard J   1902-   IV. McGovern,
George Stanley, 1922-   V. Unruh, Jesse Marvin, 1922-   VI.
Kennedy, Edward Moore, 1932-   VII. Bond, Julian, 1940-   VIII.
O'Dwyer, Paul, 1907-   IX. Muskie, Edmund S   1914-

Voice Lib.
M1045
bd.1
Daly, John Charles, 1914-
The world today; radio broadcast with
discussions of George Bernard Shaw by
Alexander Woollcott; John Daly regarding
offensive on Moscow; Edward R. Murrow
from London; Albert Warner concerning
coal miners' strike. CBS Radio, October
30, 1941.
1 reel (7 in.)   7 1/2 in. per sec.
phonotape.
I. Shaw, George Bernard, 1856-1950. I. Woollcott, Alexander,
1887-1943. II. Daly, John Charles, 1914-   III. Murrow, Edward
Roscoe, 1908-1965. IV. Warner, Albert, 1884-1967.

Voice Lib.
M209
bd.4
Daly, John Charles, 1914-
New York Philharmonic interrupted to
announce attack on Pearl Harbor. CBS,
December 7, 1941.
1 reel (7 in.)   7 1/2 i.p.s.   phonotape.

1. Pearl Harbor, Attack on, 1941.

Voice Lib.
M587
bd.2
Daly, John Charles, 1914-
Hosts program "The World Today" on war
status, reports on Russian fighting,
rumored resignation of Pétain, possibility
of German invasion of Spain, surprise
offensive in Mediterranean. CBS,
December 23, 1941.
1 reel (7 in.)   7 1/2 i.p.s.   phonotape.

1. World War, 1939-1945.

Voice Lib.
M774-
775,
bd.1
Daly, John Charles, 1914-
Farewell to Studio Nine; historical broadcasts
made by CBS correspondents at time of action
and reflections by them in retrospect. 1964.
2 reels (7 in.)   7 1/2 in. per sec.
phonotape.

I. Trout, Robert, 1908-   II. Pierpoint,
Robert   III. Murrow, Edward Roscoe,
1908-1965. IV. Kaltenborn, Hans von, 1878-
1965. V. Sevareid, Arnold Eric, 1912-
VI. Daly, John Charles, 1914-

Voice Lib.
M621
bd.1-
12
Daly, John Charles, 1914-
Radio in the 1940's (Part II): a series of
excerpts from important broadcasts of the
1940's; a sample of radio of the period.
NVL, April, 1964.
1 reel (7 in.)   7 1/2 in. per sec. phonotape.
I. Daly, John Charles, 1914-   II. Hall, Josef Washington,
1894-   III. Shirer, William Lawrence, 1904-   IV. Roosevelt,
Eleanor (Roosevelt) 1884-1962. V. Roosevelt, Franklin Delano,
Pres. U.S., 1882-1945. VI. Churchill, Winston Leonard Spencer,
1874-1965. VII. Wainwright, Jonathan Mayhew, 1883-1953. VIII.
Cantor, Eddie, 1893-1964. IX. Sinatra, Francis Albert, 1917-
X. Hope, Bob, 1903-   XI. Crosby, Bing, 1901-   XII. Shore,
Dinah, 1917(?)-   XIII. Bergen, Edgar, 1903-   XIV. Armstrong,
Louis, 1900-1971. XV. Eldridge, Roy, 1911-

Voice Lib.
M1264   Crosby, Bing, 1901-
    Daly, John Charles, 1914-
      Biographical sketch about the career of
  Bing Crosby on "Conversation" program with
  John Daly. NET, August 8, 1967.
    1 reel (7 in.) 7 1/2 in. per sec.
  phonotape.

    I. Daly, John Charles, 1914-

     Dance, Stanley
Voice Lib.
M1696   Columbia Broadcasting System, inc.
bd.6   Special memorial to Duke Ellington, with
  John Hart, Sonny Greer, Russell Procope,
  Billy Taylor, Stanley Dance, and Ella
  Fitzgerald. CBS-TV, May 24, 1974.
    15 min. phonotape (1 r. 7 1/2 i.p.s.)

    1. Ellington, Duke, 1899-1974. I. Hart,
John. II. Greer, Sonny. III. Procope,
Russell, 1908-   IV. Taylor, Billy.
V. Dance, Stanley. VI. Fitzgerald, Ella,
1918-

     Daly, John Charles, 1914-
Voice Lib.
572-   I can hear it now (radio program)
573   1933-1946. CBS, 1948.
bd.1   2 reels (7 in.) 7 1/2 in. per sec.
  phonotape.
    I. Murrow, Edward Roscoe, 1908-1965. II. LaGuardia, Fiorello
Henry, 1882-1947. III. Chamberlain, Neville, 1869-1949. IV.
Roosevelt, Franklin Delano, Pres. U.S., 1882-1945. V. Churchill,
Winston Leonard Spencer, 1874-1965. VI. Gaulle, Charles de,
Pres. France, 1890-1970. VII. Eisenhower, Dwight David, Pres. U.S.,
1890-1969. VIII. Willkie, Wendell Lewis, 1892-1944. IX. Martin,
Joseph William, 1884-1968. X. Elizabeth II, Queen of Great Britain,
1926-   XI. Margaret Rose, Princess of Gt. Brit., 1930-   XII.
Johnson, Hugh Samuel, 1882   2. XIII. Smith, Alfred Emanuel,
1873-1944. XIV. Lindbergh   arles Augustus, 1902-   XV. Davis,

(Continued on next card)

     DANCE MUSIC, AMERICAN
C1
PWM16   Whorf, Michael, 1933-
    The American dance craze.
    1 tape cassette. (The visual sounds of
Mike Whorf. Panorama; a world of music,
PWM-16)

    Originally presented on his radio program, Kaleidoscope,
WJR, Detroit.
    Duration: 25 min.
    A discussion of dancing in the United States, with examples
of dance music.

    1. Dancing. 2. Dance music, American. I. Title.

Voice Lib.
114-   Roosevelt, Franklin Delano, Pres. U.S., 1882-
116   1945.
    The F.D.R. Years. Narrated by John C. Daly.
  Hearst Metrotone News (sound track) 1962.
    3 reels (7 in.) 7 1/2 in. per sec.
  phonotape.

    I. Daly, John Charles, 1914-

     DANCING
C1
PWM16   Whorf, Michael, 1933-
    The American dance craze.
    1 tape cassette. (The visual sounds of
Mike Whorf. Panorama; a world of music,
PWM-16)

    Originally presented on his radio program, Kaleidoscope,
WJR, Detroit.
    Duration: 25 min.
    A discussion of dancing in the United States, with examples
of dance music.

    1. Dancing. 2. Dance music, American. I. Title.

Voice Lib.
M654   Damrosch, Walter Johannes, 1862-1950.
bd.4   Address to Associated Glee Clubs of
  America. First on-the-spot electrical
  recording. Moran, March 31, 1925.
    1 reel (7 in.) 7 1/2 i.p.s.
  phonotape.

    1. Phonorecords - History.

     DANCING - U.S.
C1
M53   Whorf, Michael, 1933-
    The American dance craze.
    1 tape cassette. (The visual sounds of
Mike Whorf. Miscellaneous, M53)

    Originally presented on his radio program, Kaleidoscope,
WJR, Detroit.
    Duration:
    For those that are musically inclined here is a program
concerning the famous dances of the American people.
Along with the music are capsule anecdotes about the life and
times of those who are swept up in the American dance craze.

    1. Dancing - U.S.   I. Title.

    DANA, RICHARD HENRY, 1815-1882
C1
A36   Whorf, Michael, 1933-
    An imposing symposium.
    1 tape cassette. (The visual sounds of Mike Whorf.
Art, music and letters, A36)
    Originally presented on his radio program, Kaleidoscope,
WJR, Detroit.
    Duration: 38 min., 30 sec.
    Longfellow, Agassiz, Emerson, Dana, these were the kings of
the world of literature in the nineteenth century. Every Saturday
night they met at a private club to discuss the current events of
their day.
    1. Longfellow, Henry Wadsworth, 1807-1882. 2. Agassiz,
Louis, 1807-1873. 3. Emerson, Ralph Waldo, 1803-1882.
4. Dana, Richard Henry, 1815-1882. I. Title.

Voice Lib.
629   Daniels, Josephus, 1862-1948.
bd.3   On Thomas A. Edison's contributions to
  the U.S.; reviews Edison's accomplishments
  and looks to future honors for Edison.
  Edison Laboratories, 1915.
    1 reel (7 in.) 7 1/2 in. per sec.
  phonotape.

    1. Edison, Thomas Alva, 1847-1931.

C1
A26
DANTE ALIGHIERI, 1265-1321

Whorf, Michael, 1933-
A man for all ages - Dante.
1 tape cassette. (The visual sounds of
Mike Whorf. Art, music and letters, A26)
Originally presented on his radio program, Kaleidoscope,
WJR, Detroit.
Duration: 38 min.
To many critics the world over Dante's "Divine comedy" is the
finest piece of writing mankind has ever accomplished. Here is a
look at the writing and at the man.

L. Dante Alighieri, 1265-1321. L. Title.

C1
SC20
Daughter of mercy - Clara Barton

Whorf, Michael, 1933-
Daughter of mercy - Clara Barton.
1 tape cassette. (The visual sounds of
Mike Whorf. Science, SC20)
Originally presented on his radio program, Kaleidoscope,
WJR, Detroit.
Duration: 48 min., 55 sec.
This narrative concerns the crusading Clara Barton, the "angel
of the battlefield," and the founder of the Red Cross in America.

L. Barton, Clara Harlowe, 1821-1912. L. Title.

Voice Lib.
M1375
bd.7
Darré, Richard Walther, 1895-1953.
Address to German farmers and peasants.
Peteler, November 17, 1935.
1 reel (7 in.) 7 1/2 in. per sec.
phonotape.

Voice Lib.
M759
bd.7
Davenport, Edgar L
"Lasca"; dramatic recitation about Texas
and the West. VTM, 1909.
1 reel (7 in.) 7 1/2 in. per sec.
phonotape.

I. Title.

C1
SC28
DARWIN, CHARLES ROBERT, 1809-1882

Whorf, Michael, 1933-
Theorist of evolution - Charles Darwin.
1 tape cassette. (The visual sounds of
Mike Whorf. Science, SC28)
Originally presented on his radio program, Kaleidoscope,
WJR, Detroit.
Duration: 36 min., 30 sec.
Throughout his life controversy raged around him, yet this quiet,
self-contained, self-assured man did not engage his detractors, but
forged ahead with his life's work. His life's work was engaging
Nature on Nature's terms, and the result was the storm of disagreement
which surrounds his name.

L. Darwin, Charles Robert, 1809-1882. L. Title.

Voice Lib.
M1084
David Brinkley Journal (television program)

Hoffa, James Riddle, 1913-
"David Brinkley Journal"; TV program on
Jimmy Hoffa and his activities in the
Teamsters' Union, including actual scenes
and statements by his friends and opponents.
Bergman, 1962.
1 reel (7 in.) 7 1/2 in. per sec.
phonotape.

1. Hoffa, James Riddle, 1913- I.
David Brinkley Journal (television program)

Voice Lib.
M17C7
bd.5
Daugherty, Hugh
In an interview Duffy Daugherty talks
about his career, his present job at
Michigan State University and his job as
sports commentator for ABC. Rick Martin,
May 1974.
15 min. phonotape (1 r. 7 1/2 i.p.s.)

1. Daugherty, Hugh. 2. Michigan State
University.

C1
R27
David, King of Israel

Whorf, Michael, 1933-
David, King of Israel.
1 tape cassette. (The visual sounds of
Mike Whorf. Religion, R27)
Originally presented on his radio program, Kaleidoscope,
WJR, Detroit.
Duration: 37 min., 50 sec.
The warrior, the poet, the leader of his people, David was a
bulwark of strength to the Jews.

L. David, king of Israel. L. Title.

Daugherty, Hugh

Voice Lib.
M1742
bd.1
Hannah, John Alfred, 1902-
Address at his retirement dinner at
Michigan State University. Introduction
by Duffy Daugherty. WKAR, March 17, 1968.
29 min. phonotape (1 r. 7 1/2 i.p.s.)

1. U.S. Agency for International
Development. I. Daugherty, Hugh.

Voice Lib.
M1041
bd.2
Davis, Elmer Holmes, 1890-1958
Behind the scenes in the CBS newsroom; CBS
radio news with Elmer Davis, Edward R.
Murrow and Paul White, describing the
operations of radio news broadcasting.
CBS Radio, June 1, 1941.
1 reel (7 in.) 7 1/2 i.p.s. phonotape.

1. Radio journalism. I. Davis, Elmer
Holmes, 1890-1958. II. Murrow, Edward
Roscoe, 1908-1965. III. White, Paul Welrose,
1902-1955.

Voice Lib.
M1028 Davis, Elmer Holmes, 1890-1958.
bd.9   Excerpt from news broadcast about Russian
          demands for withdrawal of British troops
          from Greece. 1947.
             1 reel (7 in.) 7 1/2 in. per sec.
          phonotape.

Davis, Richard Harding, 1864-1916
Voice Lib.
M793 Hilliard, Robert
bd.2   "The littlest girl"; acted and dramatized
          by Hilliard from Richard Harding Davis'
          story "Her first appearance". Victor, 1912.
             8 min., 52 sec. phonotape (1 r. 7 1/2
          i.p.s.)

             I. Title. II. Davis, Richard Harding,
          1864-1916.

Davis, Elmer Holmes, 1890-1958
Voice Lib.
572- I can hear it now (radio program)
573   1933-1946. CBS, 1948.
bd.1   2 reels (7 in.) 7 1/2 in. per sec.
          phonotape.
             L Murrow, Edward Roscoe, 1908-1965. IL LaGuardia, Fiorello
          Henry, 1882-1947. III. Chamberlain, Neville, 1869-1949. IV.
          Roosevelt, Franklin Delano, Pres. U. S., 1882-1945. V. Churchill,
          Winston Leonard Spencer, 1874-1965. VI. Gaulle, Charles de,
          Pres. France, 1890-1970. VII. Eisenhower, Dwight David, Pres. U.S.,
          1890-1969. VIII. Willkie, Wendell Lewis, 1892-1944. IX. Martin,
          Joseph William, 1884-1968. X. Elizabeth II, Queen of Great Britain,
          1926-   XL Margaret Rose, Princess of Gt. Brit., 1930-   XII.
          Johnson, Hugh Samuel, 1882-1942. XIII. Smith, Alfred Emanuel,
          1873-1944. XIV. Lindberg, Charles Augustus, 1902-   XV. Davis,
                     (Continued on next card)

Voice Lib.
262   Davis, Robert H
bd.5   "I am the printing press." O. R. Vincent,
          1937.
             1 reel (7 in.) 7 1/2 in. per sec.
          phonotape.

Davis, Elmer Holmes, 1890-1958
Voice Lib.
573   I can hear it now (radio program)
bd.2-   1945-1949. CBS, 1950?
574   2 reels (7 in.) 7 1/2 in. per sec.
bd.1   phonotape.
             L Murrow, Edward Roscoe, 1908-1965. IL Nehru, Jawaharlal,
          1889-1964. III. Philip, duke of Edinburgh, 1921-   IV. Elizabeth II,
          Queen of Great Britain, 1926-   V. Ferguson, Homer, 1889-   VI
          Hughes, Howard Robard, 1905-   VII. Marshall, George Catlett,
          1880-   VIII. Ruth, George Herman, 1895-1948. IX. Lilienthal,
          David Eli, 1899-   X. Trout, Robert, 1908-   XL Gage, Arthur.
          XII. Jackson, Robert Houghwout, 1892-1954. XIII. Gromyko, Ana-
          tolii Andreevich, 1908-   XIV. Baruch, Bernard Mannes, 1870-
          1965. XV. Churchill, Winston Leonard Spencer, 1874-1965. XVL
          Winchell, Walter, 1897-19 XVII. Davis, Elmer Holmes, 1890-
                     (Continued on next card)

Voice Lib.
M1479 Davis, Sammy, 1925-
bd.2   Sammy Davis Jr. interview, Black Journal,
          on being black, his career, etc. NET-TV,
          August 8, 1971.
             1 reel (7 in.) 7 1/2 in. per sec.
          phonotape.

Voice Lib.
353   Davis, Gary
bd.20   Citizen of the world; discusses his
          reasons for becoming a citizen of
          the world. NBC, September 25, 1949.
             1 reel (7 in.) 7 1/2 in. per sec.
          phonotape.

Voice Lib.
M1056 Dawes, Charles Gates, 1865-1951.
bd.4   Speaking at National Conference of Jews
          and Christians concerning third annual
          Brotherhood Day. Audio Scriptions,
          February 23, 1936.
             1 reel (7 in.) 7 1/2 in. per sec.
          phonotape .

Voice Lib.
M718   Davis, George R
bd.1   Prayer at Presidential Inaugural ceremonies.
          January 20, 1965.
             1 reel (7 in.) 7 1/2 in. per sec.
          phonotape.

The day I drank a glass of water
Voice Lib.
343   Fields, W   C   1879-1946.
bd.3   A humorous dialogue: "The Day I Drank
          a Glass of Water". United Artists,
          1927.
             1 reel (7 in.) 7 1/2 in. per sec.
          phonotape.

             I. Title: The day I drank a glass of water.

The day I drank a glass of water

Voice Lib.
M1359   Fields, W.C., 1879-1946.
bd.1-   "The Temperance Lecture"; "The day I drank
bd 2   a glass of water".   Blue Thumb Records [1968?]
         1 reel (7 in.)   7 1/2 in. per sec.
         phonotape.

         I. Title.   II. Title: The day I drank a
         glass of water.

C1   Days of valor
H41   Whorf, Michael, 1933-
         Days of valor.
         1 tape cassette.   (The visual sounds of
         Mike Whorf. History and heritage, H41)
         Originally presented on his radio program, Kaleidoscope,
         WJR, Detroit.
         Duration: 49 min.
         In each of America's wars there have been given moments,
         certain occasions when men rise above the normal call of duty
         to perform at the peak of their endurance whether in victory or
         defeat.

         1. U.S. - History.   2. War.   L. Title.

Voice Lib.
M1399   A day in October; NBC-TV documentary about
1400   "Moratorium Day" throughout the United
         States in protest to our continued partici-
         pation in the war in Vietnam. Description
         of origin and growth of the moratorium and
         comments by various personalities. Statement
         by President Nixon, "Not affected." NBC-TV,
         October 15, 1969.
         2 reels (7 in.)   7 1/2 in. per sec.
         phonotape.
         1. Vietnamese Conflict, 1961-   - U.S.

Voice Lib.
M344   Dean, Arthur Hobson, 1898-
bd.3   Discusses the resumption of nuclear
         test ban talks in news conference. CBS,
         November 24, 1961.
         1 reel (7 in.)   7 1/2 in. per sec.
         phonotape.

         1. Atomic power - International control.

Voice Lib.
M1497   Dayan, Moshe, 1915-
bd.1   Interview with General Dayan on the present
         Middle East situation and his plans for
         Israel as well as his thoughts on agreement
         with Arabs. CBS-TV, February, 1972.
         1 reel (7 in.)   7 1/2 in. per sec.
         phonotape.

Voice Lib.
M1800   Dean, John Wesley, 1938-
WG   Statement made before the Senate Committee
0625   investigating the Watergate Affair.
         Pacifica, June 25, 1973.
         400 min.   phonotape (5 r.   3 3/4 i.p.s.)
         (Watergate gavel to gavel, phase 1)

         1. Watergate Affair, 1972-

C1   Days of thanks - about Thanksgiving
S42   Whorf, Michael, 1933-
         Days of thanks - about Thanksgiving.
         1 tape cassette.   (The visual sounds of
         Mike Whorf. Social, S42)
         Originally presented on his radio program, Kaleidoscope,
         WJR, Detroit.
         Duration: 48 min., 55 sec.
         Bradford, Brewster, Alden, Mullins, Standish - these were the
         leading figures aboard the Mayflower, who would later colonize
         Plymouth and play out their roles in Europe's age of exploration and
         discovery. Persecuted as Puritans, they came seeking freedom and
         found the beginning of a nation.

         1. Thanksgiving Day.   L. Title.

Voice Lib.
M1800   Dean, John Wesley, 1938-
WG   Testimony before the Senate Committee
0626   investigating the Watergate Affair.
         Pacifica, June 26, 1973.
         343 min.   phonotape (5 r.   3 3/4 i.p.s.)
         (Watergate gavel to gavel, phase 1)

         1. Watergate Affair, 1972-

C1   The days of the iron horse
SC13   Whorf, Michael, 1933-
         The days of the iron horse.
         1 tape cassette.   (The visual sounds of
         Mike Whorf. Science, SC13)
         Originally presented on his radio program, Kaleidoscope,
         WJR, Detroit.
         Duration: 30 min., 50 sec.
         It was a boon to mankind; an invention which would cut
         continents in half. The great iron horse, the trains that would
         fly over nations, serving the millions of people of the world.
         Today its roar of engines and shrill whistles are but dim echoes
         filtering down from the past.

         1. Railroads.   L. Title.

Voice Lib.
M1800   Dean, John Wesley, 1938-
WG   Testimony before the Senate Committee
0627   investigating the Watergate Affair.
         Pacifica, June 27, 1973.
         375 min.   phonotape (5 r.   3 3/4 i.p.s.)
         (Watergate gavel to gavel, phase 1)

         1. Watergate Affair, 1972-

Voice Lib.
M1800   Dean, John Wesley, 1938–
WG   Testimony before the Senate Committee
0628   investigating the Watergate Affair.
         Pacifica, June 28, 1973.
            353 min.   phonotape (5 r.   3 3/4 i.p.s.)
         (Watergate gavel to gavel, phase 1)

            1. Watergate Affair, 1972–

DECATUR, STEPHEN, 1779–1820
C1
H60   Whorf, Michael, 1933–
         Never strike the colors – Stephen Decatur.
         1 tape cassette.   (The visual sounds of
      Mike Whorf. History and heritage, H60)
         Originally presented on his radio program, Kaleidoscope,
      WJR, Detroit.
         Duration: 43 min.
         Handsome, brave, and honorable, Stephen Decatur was one of
      America's most daring naval officers.

         L. Decatur, Stephen, 1779–1820.   L. Title.

Voice Lib.
M1800   Dean, John Wesley, 1938–
WG   Testimony before the Senate Committee
0629   investigating the Watergate Affair.
         Pacifica, June 29, 1973.
            349 min.   phonotape (5 r.   3 3/4 i.p.s.)
         (Watergate gavel to gavel, phase 1)

            1. Watergate Affair, 1972–

Voice Lib.
M961   Decker, Wilhelm
bd.8   Policy on German labor forces.   German
         Radio, Peteler, February 2, 1937.
            1 reel (7 in.)   7 1/2 in. per sec.
         phonotape.

            1. Labor and laboring classes – Germany

Voice Lib.
M1615   Debs, Eugene Victor, 1855–1926.
bd.5   Winning a world.   Rare Records, Inc.,
         H608 [19--?]
            2 min., 15 sec.   phonotape (1 r.
         7 1/2 i.p.s.)

Voice Lib.
M1379   Dedication ceremonies for Great Northern
bd.1   Railway Cascade Tunnel, over NBC Radio
         Network, originating from Philadelphia,
         Washington, D.C., San Francisco, New York
         City, and State of Washington.   NBC Radio,
         January 1929.
            1 reel (7 in.)   7 1/2 in. per sec.
         phonotape.

            1. Great Northern Railway Cascade Tunnel

Voice Lib.
395   Debs, Eugene Victor, 1855–1926.
bd. 1   The Socialist movement.   Edison cylinder
         recording, 1904.
            1 reel (7 in.)   7 1/2 in. per sec.
         phonotape.

            1. Socialism.

Voice Lib.
666   DeForest, Lee, 1873–1961.
bd.2   Broadcast by Dr. DeForest reviewing
         his career. This broadcast carried on
         WLWO, Washington, D.C., and 32 short wave
         stations around the world.   Mrs. DeForest,
         November 30, 1958.
            1 reel (7 in.)   7 1/2 in. per sec.
         phonotape.
            1. DeForest, Lee, 1873–1961

Voice Lib.
M1250   Debs, Eugene Victor, 1855–1926.
bd.6   "Winning a World": socialistic campaign
         speech during presidential election of
         1904, describing benefits of Socialist
         movement.   Col. Ph. Cyl., 1904.
            1 reel (7 in.)   7 1/2 in. per sec.
         phonotape.

Voice Lib.
666   DeForest, Lee, 1873–1961.
bd.1   Memorial program for Dr. DeForest.
         Biographical sketch with excerpts in
         the voice of DeForest, broadcast after his
         death.   Detroit, WWJ, July 3, 1961.
            1 reel (7 in.)   7 1/2 in. per sec.
         phonotape.

            1. DeForest, Lee, 1873–1961

De Gaulle, Charles
see
Gaulle, Charles de, Pres. France, 1890-1970.

VOICE LIBRARY

Voice Lib.   DeMille, Cecil Blount, 1881-1959
M669- The legend of Cecil B. DeMille. Yul
670   Brynner, Charlton Heston, Bob Hope, Betty
Hutton, Edward G. Robinson, Barbara Stanwyck,
James Stewart, Gloria Swanson, Cornel
Wilde, Samuel Goldwyn, Billy Graham, Cecil
B. DeMille. Recorded 1963.
2 reels (7 in.) 7 1/2 in. per sec. phonotape.

I. DeMille, Cecil Blount, 1881-1959. I. Brynner, Yul, 1917-
II. Heston, Charlton, 1924- III. Hope, Bob, 1903- IV.
Hutton, Betty, 1921- V. Robinson, Edward G 1893-1973.
VI. Stanwyck, Barbara, 1907- VII. Stewart, James Maitland,
1908- VIII. Swanson, Gloria, 1899?- IX. Wilde, Cornel, 1915-
X. Goldwyn, Samuel, 1884?- XI. Graham, William Franklin,
1918- XII. DeMille, Cecil Blount, 1881-1959.

Voice Lib.   DeGraaf, Albert
M273- Biography in sound (radio program)
274   Franklin Delano Roosevelt: the friends and
bd.1   former associates of Franklin Roosevelt on
the tenth anniversary of the President's death.
NBC Radio, April, 1955.
2 reels (7 in.) 7 1/2 in. per sec.
phonotape.

I. Roosevelt, Franklin Delano, Pres. U.S., 1882-1945. I.
McIntire, Ross T 1899- II. Mellett, Lowe" 1884-1960.
III. Tully, Grace IV. Henderson, Leon, 1895-
V. Roosevelt, Eleanor (Roosevelt) 1884-1962. VI. DeGraaf, Albert
VII. Lehman, Herbert Henry, 1878-1963. VIII. Rosenman, Samuel
Irving, 1896- IX. Arvey, Jacob X. Moley, Raymond,
1886- XI. Farley, James Aloysius, 1888- XII. Roosevelt,
(continued on next card)

Voice Lib.   DeMille, Cecil Blount, 1881-1959
M619   Radio in the 1930's (Part II): a series of
bd.1- excerpts of the 1930's; a sample of radio
14   of the period. NVL, April, 1964.
1 reel (7 in.) 7 1/2 in. per sec. phonotape.
I. Allen, Fred, 1894-1956. II. Delmar, Kenny III. Donald,
Peter IV. Pious, Minerva V. Fennelly, Parker VI.
Boyer, Charles, 1899- VII. Dunne, Irene, 1904- VIII.
DeMille, Cecil Blount, 1881-1959. IX. West, Mae, 1893- X.
Dafoe, Allan Ray, 1883-1943. XI. Dionne quintuplets. XII. Ortega,
Santos XIII. War of the worlds (radio program) XIV. Ives, Burl,
1909- XV. Robinson, Earl, 1910- XVI. Temple, Shirley,
1928- XVII. Earhart, Amelia, 1898-1937. XVIII. Lawrence,
Gertrude, 1901-1952. XIX. Cohan, George Michael, 1878-1942.
XX. Shaw, George Bernard, 1856-1950. XXI. Hitler, Adolf, 1889-
1945. XXII. Chamberlain, Neville, 1869-1940. XXIII. Roosevelt,
Franklin Delano, Pres. U.S., 1882-1945.

Voice Lib.   Delany, Hubert T
M658- Dialogues in depth: the LaGuardia years
659   (TV program from the New York World's Fair).
bd.1   Anecdotes and reminiscences about the late
New York mayor, Fiorello LaGuardia.
July 22, 1964.
2 reels (7 in.) 7 1/2 i.p.s. phonotape.

I. LaGuardia, Fiorello Henry, 1882-1947. I. Canudo,
Eugene R. II. Berle, Adolph Augustus, 1895-1971.
III. Van Arsdale, Harry, 1905- IV. Delany, Hubert T.
V. Morris, Newbold, 1902-1966.

Voice Lib.
M735   Democracy in Action; composite of excerpts
of proceedings of past presidential
campaigns assembled under the title of
"Democracy in Action". CBS, 1964.
1 reel (7 in.) 7 1/2 in. per sec.
phonotape.

1. Presidents - U.S. - Election

Voice Lib.   Delmar, Kenny
M619   Radio in the 1930's (Part II): a series of
bd.1- excerpts of the 1930's; a sample of radio
14   of the period. NVL, April, 1964.
1 reel (7 in.) 7 1/2 in. per sec. phonotape.
I. Allen, Fred, 1894-1956. II. Delmar, Kenny III. Donald,
Peter IV. Pious, Minerva V. Fennelly, Parker VI.
Boyer, Charles, 1899- VII. Dunne, Irene, 1904- VIII.
DeMille, Cecil Blount, 1881-1959. IX. West, Mae, 1893- X.
Dafoe, Allan Ray, 1883-1943. XI. Dionne quintuplets. XII. Ortega,
Santos XIII. War of the worlds (radio program) XIV. Ives, Burl,
1909- XV. Robinson, Earl, 1910- XVI. Temple, Shirley,
1928- XVII. Earhart, Amelia, 1898-1937. XVIII. Lawrence,
Gertrude, 1901-1952. XIX. Cohan, George Michael, 1878-1942.
XX. Shaw, George Bernard, 1856-1950. XXI. Hitler, Adolf, 1889-
1945. XXII. Chamberlain, Neville, 1869-1940. XXIII. Roosevelt,
Franklin Delano, Pres. U.S., 1882-1945.

Democracy, planning and participation
Voice Lib.
M1080 Mendes-France, Pierre, 1907-
Address by Pierre Mendès-France at New
York on "Democracy, planning and participa-
tion", describing the relevance of the
French plan to American social and economic
practices. CSDI, 1963.
1 reel (7 in.) 7 1/2 in. per sec.
phonotape.

I. Title: Democracy, planning and
participation.

Voice Lib.   Delmar, Kenny
M620   Radio in the 1940's (Part I): a series of
bd.1- excerpts from important broadcasts of the 1940's; a
bd.16 sample of radio of the period. NVL, April, 1964.
1 reel (7 in.) 7 1/2 in. per sec. phonotape.
I. Radio programs. I. Thomas, Lowell Jackson, 1892- II.
Gunther, John, 1901-1970. III. Kaltenborn, Hans von, 1878-1965.
IV. Delmar, Kenny. V. Those were the good old days (Radio
program) VI. Elman, Dave. VII. Hall, Frederick Lee, 1916-1970.
VIII. Hobby lobby (Radio program) IX. Roosevelt, Franklin Delano,
Pres. U.S., 1882-1945. X. Willkie, Wendell Lewis, 1892-1944.
XI. Hoover, Herbert Clark, Pres. U.S., 1874-1964. XII. Johnson,
Hugh Samuel, 1882-1942. XIII. Cobb, Irvin Shrewsbury, 1876-1944.
XIV. Roosevelt, Theodore, 1858-1919. XV. Nye, Gerald Prentice,
1892-1971. XVI. Lindbergh, Charles Augustus, 1902- XVII.
Toscanini, Arturo, 1867-19

DEMOCRATIC PARTY
Voice Lib.
M724   Trout, Robert, 1908-
bd.2   On Democratic loyalty oath, including
Senator Blair Moody of Michigan, Gov. Battle
of Virginia, Speaker Sam Rayburn, Col. Jack
Arvey of Chicago, Gov. Willis of Alabama and
Jim Farley. 1952.
8 min., 12 sec. phonotape (1 r.
7 1/2 i.p.s.)

1. Democratic Party. 2. Presidents - U.S.
- Election - 1952.

DEMOCRATIC PARTY. MICHIGAN
Voice Lib.
M1605   Winograd, Morley
bd.2   Off the record. With Tim Skubick, Tom
        Greene, Gary Schuster, and Hugh Morgan.
        WKAR-TV, February 15, 1974.
          17 min.   phonotape (1 r.   7 1/2 in. per sec.)

          1. Democratic Party. Michigan. 2. Elections -
        Michigan. 3. Youngblood, Charles N., 1932-
        I. Skubick, Tim. II. Greene, Tom. III. Schuster,
        Gary. IV. Morgan, Hugh.

Voice Lib.
540   Dempsey, Jack, 1895 -
bd. 17   Sports and boxing. Fox Movietone,
        1933.
          1 reel (7 in.)   7 1/2 in. per sec.
        phonotape.

          1. Boxing.

Voice Lib.
M1323- Democratic Party. National Convention,
M1328,   Chicago, 1968.
bd.1   Hubert Humphrey, Democratic presidential nom   ,
        announcing his selection of Sen. Muskie as his running, mate;
        convention floor reports; interview with Mrs. Humphrey. Mayor
        Daley of Chicago defending police action. Interviews with Sen-
        ator McGovern and Jesse Unruh of California. Remote address by
        Sen. Edward Kennedy introducing a memorial motion picture on
        the late Sen. Robert F. Kennedy. Various reports on riots and
        general confusion, reluctance of delegates to come to order.
        Nominations for Vice-President; seconding speeches for Sen.
        Muskie and nominating speech by Wisconsin delegation of Julian
        Bond of Georgia. Interview with Julian Bond, who declined
        nomination of the vice-presidency. Story told by chairman of
        the New Hampshire [delegation] regarding his arrest. Interview
                        (Continued on next card)

Voice Lib.
M1353- Denis-Roosevelt expedition to the Congo.
1354   Music re-recorded from original motion
        picture sound track and containing primitive
        music of the negroes of the great Equatorial
        forest and the eastern provinces of the Congo;
        the music of the wandering pigmies of the
        Ituri and Kivu and of the Watusi, the "lost
        tribe", the giants of Ruanda. Mainstream
        Records, App. 1934.
          2 reels (7 in.)   7 1/2 in. per sec.
        phonotape.
          1. Music,   African.

Voice Lib.
M1323- Democratic Party. National Convention,
M1328,   Chicago, 1968...   (Card 2)
bd.1   with Paul O'Dwyer of the New York delegation regarding the
        nomination of Richard Daley for Vice-President. General
        confusion. Nomination of Sen. Edmund Muskie as Vice-President
        and resulting confusion with the Oregon delegation. Followed by
        Sen. Muskie's acceptance speech. NBC-TV, August 29, 1968.
          6 reels (7 in.)   7 1/2 in. per sec.   phonotape.
          L Humphrey, Hubert Horatio, 1911- II. Humphrey, Muriel Fay
        (Buck) 1912-   III. Daley, Richard J   1902-   IV. McGovern,
        George Stanley, 1922-   V. Unruh, Jesse Marvin, 1922-   VL
        Kennedy, Edward Moore, 1932-   VII. Bond, Julian, 1940-   VIII.
        O'Dwyer, Paul, 1907-   IX. Muskie, Edmund S   1914-

            Denison, Jim
Voice Lib.
M1499   Veldhuis, Zachary, 1870-
bd.1   Oldest living Michigan Agricultural College
        alumnus, aged 102, interviewed by Jim Denison
        at National Voice Library. Topic: campus life
        in the past. MSU Voice Library, May 14, 1972.
          1 reel (7 in.)   7 1/2 i.p.s.   phonotape.

          1. Michigan State University.   I. Denison,
        Jim

        DEMOSTHENES
C1
S68   Whorf, Michael, 1933-
          Statesmen and sages; Demosthenes, Aristotle,
        Socrates, Cicero.
          1 tape cassette. (The visual sounds of Mike Whorf. Social, S68)

          Originally presented on his radio program, Kaleidoscope,
        WJR, Detroit.
          Duration: 36 min.
          As ancient Greece and Rome served as the cradle of our modern
        democracy, so do their citizens serve as shining examples of wisdom
        and statecraft for us today.

          L Demosthenes. 2. Aristoteles. 3. Socrates. 4. Cicero,
        Marcus Tullius. L Title.

        The dependables
C1
M52   Whorf, Michael, 1933-
          The dependables; firemen and firefighting.
          1 tape cassette.   (The visual sounds of
        Mike Whorf. Miscellaneous, M52)
          Originally presented on his radio program, Kaleidoscope,
        WJR, Detroit.
          Duration: 37 min.
          The exciting, dangerous world of some of our country's most
        important citizens, the firemen, is told in this visual narrative.
        Beginning with their simple origin as volunteers as the neighbor's
        fire, to the story of the modern day fire brigades - it's all here.

          L Firemen. L Title.

Voice Lib.
M1064   Dempsey, Jack, 1895-
bd.9   Interview with former heavyweight boxing
        champion Jack Dempsey and his associates
        regarding their new venture of boxing
        promotions. Fox Movietone, 1930.
          1 reel (7 in.)   7 1/2 in. per sec.
        phonotape.

          1. Boxing

Voice Lib.
M872   Description of and actual sounds from
bd.2   battle action during D-Day invasion of
        French Coast. NBC shortwave, June 7,
        1944.
          1 reel (7 in.)   7 1/2 in. per sec.
        phonotape.

          1. World War, 1939-1945 - Campaigns -
        Normandy.

Voice Lib.
M652   De Seversky, Alexander Procofieff, 1894–
bd.15   Significance of shooting a rocket around
             the moon. CBS, August 16, 1958.
             1 reel (7 in.)   7 1/2 i.p.s.   phonotape.

             1. Rocket research.

C1   The detective
M24   Whorf, Michael, 1933–
             The detective.
             1 tape cassette.   (The visual sounds of
         Mike Whorf. Miscellaneous, M24)
             Originally presented on his radio program, Kaleidoscope.
         WJR, Detroit.
             Duration: 46 min.
             The adventures of Alan Pinkerton – his rise from obscurity to
         fame as head of the world's foremost detective agency.

             L. Pinkerton, Allan, 1819–1884. L. Title.

Voice Lib.   DETROIT
M1598   Romney, George W   1907–
bd.2   Off the record. With Tim Skubick, Gary
         Schuster, Tom Greene, and Bill Meek.
         WKAR-TV, November 9, 1973.
         .' 20 min.   phonotape (1 r.   7 1/2 in. per
         sec.)

             1. Michigan – Politics and government.
             2. Detroit. I. Skubick, Tim. II. Schuster,
         Gary. III. Greene, Tom. IV. Meek, Bill

Voice Lib.   DETROIT
M1597   Young, Coleman A., 1918–
             Address at the Urban Forum luncheon,
         Michigan State University.   MSU Information
         Services, March 7, 1974.
             40 min.   phonotape (1 r.   7 1/2 in. per
         sec.)

             1. Detroit. 2. Michigan State University.
         College of Urban Development.

              DETROIT. WJR (RADIO STATION)
                 see
              WJR (RADIO STATION) DETROIT

Voice Lib. Deutschland erwache!
M980   German radio (Nazi controlled)
bd.7   Nazi patriotic song "Deutschland erwache!"
             (2 stanzas)   Peteler, 1933.
             1 reel (7 in.)   7 1/2 in. per sec.
         phonotape.

             1. Title: Deutschland erwache!

             Deutschlandlied
Voice Lib.
M1300   Musical ceremonies and bugle calls of
bd.5   German Wehrmacht; also military marches
             and orchestral rendering of "Deutschland-
             lied". Peteler, n.d.
             1 reel (7 in.)   7 1/2 i.p.s.   phonotape.

             1. War-songs, German. I. Title:
         Deutschlandlied.

            Deutschlandlied
Voice Lib.
M1019   Nazi national hymn "Deutschlandlied"
bd.6   (two stanzas). Fred Peteler.
             1 reel (7 in.)   7 1/2 i.p.s.   phonotape.

             1. National music, German. I. Title:
         Deutschlandlied.

Voice Lib.
M1282   DeValera, Eamon, 1882–
bd.2   Speaking from the rostrum of the League of
             Nations in Geneva, urging USSR to accept
             invitation to join the League and declare
             guarantees to the world of liberty and religious
             freedom. League of Nations, September 18, 1934.
             1 reel (7 in.)   7 1/2 in. per sec.
         phonotape.

             1. League of Nations.

Voice Lib.
M265   DeValera, Eamon, 1882–
bd.3   Address to America: Irish political
             problem. Private recording of G. Robert
             Vincent, March 17, 1947.
             1 reel (7 in.)   7 1/2 i.p.s.   phonotape.

             1. Ireland – Politics and government.

C1
H115
DEWEY, GEORGE, 1837-1917

Whorf, Michael, 1933-
A fleeting moment of fame - George Dewey.
1 tape cassette. (The visual sounds of
Mike Whorf. History and heritage, H115)
Originally presented on his radio program, Kaleidoscope,
WJR, Detroit.
Duration: 30 min., 45 sec.
We will learn in this program of the life and times of Admiral
George Dewey, one of naval history's greatest leaders and of the
battles with which his name has become synonymous.

I. Dewey, George, 1837-1917. I. Title.

Voice Lib.
183
bd.1
Dewey, Thomas Edmund, 1902-1971.
Address on return to hometown of
Owosso, Michigan. WJR, September 9,
1944.
1 reel (7 in.) 7 1/2 in. per sec.
phonotape.

Voice Lib.
M847
bd.2
Dewey, Thomas Edmund, 1902-1971.
Address at Cornell University for
opening of School of Industrial Relations.
NBC, November 12, 1945.
14 min. phonotape (1 r. 7 1/2 i.p.s.)

1. Cornell University.

Voice Lib.
M739
bd.5
Dewey, Thomas Edmund, 1902-1971.
Statement in favor of complete mobilization
of productive forces and our propaganda
system for the Korean situation. CBS, 1950.
1 reel (7 in.) 7 1/2 in. per sec.
phonotape.

Dewey, Thomas Edmund, 1902-1971
Voice Lib.
572-
573
bd.1
I can hear it now (radio program)
1933-1946. CBS, 1948.
2 reels (7 in.) 7 1/2 in. per sec.
phonotape.
I. Murrow, Edward Roscoe, 1908-1965. II. LaGuardia, Fiorello
Henry, 1882-1947. III. Chamberlain, Neville, 1869-1949. IV.
Roosevelt, Franklin Delano, Pres. U. S., 1882-1945. V. Churchill,
Winston Leonard Spencer, 1874-1965. VI. Gaulle, Charles de,
Pres. France, 1890-1970. VII. Eisenhower, Dwight David, Pres. U. S.,
1890-1969. VIII. Willkie, Wendell Lewis, 1892-1944. IX. Martin,
Joseph William, 1884-1968. X. Elizabeth II, Queen of Great Britain,
1926- XI. Margaret Rose, Princess of Gt. Brit., 1930- XII.
Johnson, Hugh Samuel, 188?-?2. XIII. Smith, Alfred Emanuel,
1873-1944. XIV. Lindbergh, Charles Augustus, 1902- XV. Davis,
(Continued on next card)

Dewey, Thomas Edmund, 1902-1971
Voice Lib.
573
bd.2-
574
bd.1
I can hear it now (radio program)
1945-1949. CBS, 1950?
2 reels (7 in.) 7 1/2 in. per sec.
phonotape.
I. Murrow, Edward Roscoe, 1908-1965. II. Nehru, Jawaharlal,
1889-1964. III. Philip, duke of Edinburgh, 1921- IV. Elizabeth II,
Queen of Great Britain, 1926- V. Ferguson, Homer, 1889- VI.
Hughes, Howard Robard, 1905- VII. Marshall, George Catlett,
1880- VIII. Ruth, George Herman, 1895-1948. IX. Lilienthal,
David Eli, 1899- X. Trout, Robert, 1908- XI. Gage, Arthur.
XII. Jackson, Robert Houghwout, 1892-1954. XIII. Gromyko, Anatolii Andreevich, 1908- XIV. Baruch, Bernard Mannes, 1870-
1965. XV. Churchill, Winston Leonard Spencer, 1874-1965. XVI.
Winchell, Walter, 1897-1 XVII. Davis, Elmer Holmes, 1890-
(Continued on next card)

Voice Lib.
M658-
659
bd.1
Dialogues in depth: the LaGuardia years
(TV program from the New York World's Fair).
Anecdotes and reminiscences about the late
New York mayor, Fiorello LaGuardia.
July 22, 1964.
2 reels (7 in.) 7 1/2 i.p.s. phonotape.
I. LaGuardia, Fiorello Henry, 1882-1947. I. Canudo,
Eugene R. II. Berle, Adolph Augustus, 1895-1971.
III. Van Arsdale, Harry, 1905- IV. Delany, Hubert T.
V. Morris, Newbold, 1902-1966.

Voice Lib.
249
bd.3
Diaz, Porfirio, Pres. Mexico, 1830-1915.
Message to Thomas Edison from Mexico.
Edison Labs, 1910.
1 reel (7 in.) 7 1/2 in. per sec.
phonotape.

Dick Tracy (radio program)
Voice Lib.
M1675
bd.2
Theme songs from the Green hornet, the Lone
Ranger, Dick Tracy, and Hop Harrigan.
Golden Age Radio Records, 1940's.
10 min. phonotape (1 r. 7 1/2 i.p.s.)

I. Green hornet (radio program) II. Lone
Ranger (radio program) III. Dick Tracy (radio
program) IV. Hop Harrigan (radio program)

Voice Lib.
134
Dickens, Charles, 1812-1870.
Christmas Carol, dramatized by an all-star
cast led by Lionel Barrymore and Rudy Vallee.
NBC, 1941.
1 reel (7 in.) 7 1/2 in. per sec.
phonotape.

I. Barrymore, Lionel, 1878-1954. II.
Vallee, Rudy, 1901- III. Title.

C1
A23
DICKENS, CHARLES, 1812-1870
Whorf, Michael, 1933-
The creator of immortal characters.
1 tape cassette.   (The visual sounds of
Mike Whorf. Art, music, and letters, A23)
Originally presented on his radio program, Kaleidoscope.
WJR, Detroit.
Duration: 42 min., 30 sec.
What he was and what he was to the world is forthrightly
told in the story of Dickens, the writer and the man.

L. Dickens, Charles, 1812-1870. I. Title.

Diles, Ken
Voice Lib.
M622
bd.1-
bd.15
Radio in the 1940's (Part III): a series of
excerpts from important broadcasts of the 1940's; a sample
of radio of the period. NVL, April, 1964.
1 reel (7 in.) 7 1/2 in. per sec. phonotape.
L. Radio programs. L. Miller, Alton Glenn, 1909(?)-1944. II.
Diles, Ken. III. Wilson, Donald Harlow, 1900- IV.
Livingstone, Mary V. Benny, Jack, 1894- VI. Harris,
Phil VII. Merman, Ethel, 1909- VIII. Smith, "Wonderful"
IX. Bennett, Richard Dyer X. Louis, Joe, 1914- XI.
Eisenhower, Dwight David, Pres. U. S., 1890-1969. XII. MacArthur,
Douglas, 1880-1964. XIII. Romulo, Carlos Pena, 1899- XIV.
Welles, Orson, 1915- XV. Jackson, Robert Houghwout, 1892-1954.
XVI. LaGuardia, Fiorello Henry, 1882-1945. XVII. Nehru, Jawa-
harlal, 1889-1964. XVIII. Gandhi, Mohandas Karamchand, 1869-1948.

Dickerson, Nancy Hanschman, 1929(?)-
Voice Lib.
M317
bd.2
Johnson, Lyndon Baines, Pres. U.S., 1908-1973.
Nancy Dickerson of NBC at Inaugural Ball
talking to Vice-President and Mrs. Johnson;
Charles Collingwood and Johnson on Sam Rayburn;
Johnson in Berlin, audience with Pope John.
NBC, CBS, November 24, 1963.
1 reel (7 in.) 7 1/2 in. per sec. phonotape.
L. Rayburn, Samuel Taliaferro, 1882-1961. L. Dickerson,
Nancy Hanschman, 1929 (?)- II. Johnson, Claudia Alta
(Taylor) 1912- III. Collingwood, Charles Cummings, 1917-
IV. Joannes XXIII, Pope, 1881-1963.

C1
877
DILLINGER, JOHN, 1903-1934
Whorf, Michael, 1933-
America's tarnished Robinhood - John Dillinger.
1 tape cassette.   (The visual sounds of
Mike Whorf. Social, 877)
Originally presented on his radio program, Kaleidoscope,
WJR, Detroit.
Duration: 37 min.
1934, with the country climbing out of depression, John
Dillinger arrived upon the scene. The clever criminal's
escapades are fully described as we learn about the tarnished
Robin Hood.

L. Dillinger, John, 1903-1934. I. Title.

Voice Lib. Dickerson, Nancy Hanschman, 1929(?)-
M985-
986
bd.1
Nugent, Luci Baines (Johnson), 1947-
Resumé of ceremonies at wedding of Luci
Baines Johnson, daughter of incumbent President
Lyndon B. Johnson, in Washington, D.C.
Described by Nancy Dickerson, with actual
sounds. NBC-TV, August 6, 1966.
2 reels (7 in.). 7 1/2 in. per sec.
phonotape.

I. Dickerson, Nancy Hanschman, 1929(?)-

Voice Lib.
M742
bd.7
Dillon, Clarence Douglas, 1909-
Statement on Peiping activities. Khrushchev's
agreement to negotiate at Camp David with
President Eisenhower. CBS, 1959.
1 reel (7 in.) 7 1/2 in. per sec.
phonotape.

1. Khrushchev, Nikita Sergeevich, 1894-1971.
2. Eisenhower, Dwight David, Pres U.S., 1890-
1969.

Diem, Pres. Vietnam, 1901-1963.
see
Ngo-Dinh-Diem, Pres. Vietnam, 1901-1963.

Voice Lib.
209
bd.2
Di Maggio, Joseph Paul, 1914-
Joe Di Maggio's farewell to baseball.
Source (?), December 11, 1951.
1 reel (7 in.) 7 1/2 in. per sec.
phonotape.

1. Baseball.

DIET
Voice Lib.
M1734
Pauling, Linus Carl, 1901-
Orthomolecular medicine; address given at
Michigan State University. WKAR, April 19,
1972.
50 min. phonotape (1 r. 7 1/2 i.p.s.)

1. Ascorbic acid. 2. Diet. 3. Human
genetics.

Voice Lib.
M1728
Dinitz, Simcha, 1929-
Speech delivered to National Press Club
on Arab-Israeli relations, with Ken Scheibel.
WKAR, June 13, 1974.
40 min. phonotape (1 r. 7 1/2 i.p.s.)

1. Israel - For. rel. - Arab countries.
2. Arab countries - For. rel. - Israel.
I. Scheibel, Ken.

C1
SC25   DINOSAURIA
      Whorf, Michael, 1933-
        The case of the vanishing monsters.
        1 tape cassette.   (The visual sounds of
      Mike Whorf. Science, SC25)
        Originally presented on his radio program, Kaleidoscope,
      WJR, Detroit.
        Duration: 30 min.
        Here are the great beasts that roamed the earth long before
     the coming of man. The huge dinosaurs prevailed for centuries and
     then suddenly, they disappeared. Here are some of the answers, the
     questions, the conjectures in a half-hour of gripping scientific fact.

       I. Dinosauria. I. Title.

          Dionne quintuplets
Voice Lib.
M1086   Dafoe, Allan Roy, 1883-1943.
bd.2   Dr. Dafoe in radio broadcast from Callander,
    Ontario, introducing all five Dionne quintup-
    lets, who speak and sing various songs.   CBC,
    1938.
      1 reel (7 in.)   7 1/2 in. per sec.
    phonotape.

      I. Dionne quintuplets.

        Dionne quintuplets
voice Lib.
M619   Radio in the 1930's (Part II): a series of
bd.1-   excerpts of the 1930's; a sample of radio
14   of the period. NVL, April, 1964.
      1 reel (7 in.) 7 1/2 in. per sec. phonotape.
    L. Allen, Fred, 1894-1956. II. Delmar, Kenny   III. Donald,
Peter   IV. Pious, Minerva   V. Fennelly, Parker   VI.
Boyer, Charles, 1899-   VII. Dunne, Irene, 1904-   VIII.
DeMille, Cecil Blount, 1881-1959. IX. West, Mae, 1893-   X.
Dafoe, Allan Ray, 1883-1943. XI. Dionne quintuplets. XII. Ortega,
Santos   XIII. War of the worlds (radio program) XIV. Ives, Burl,
1909-   XV. Robinson, Earl, 1910-   XVI. Temple, Shirley,
1928-   XVII. Earhart, Amelia, 1898-1937. XVIII. Lawrence,
Gertrude, 1901-1952. XIX. Cohan, George Michael, 1878-1942.
XX. Shaw, George Bernard, 1856-1950. XXI. Hitler, Adolf, 1889-
1945. XXII. Chamberlain, Neville 1869-1940. XXIII. Roosevelt,
Franklin Delano, Pres. U.S., 1882-1945.

       DIONNE QUINTUPLETS
Voice Lib.
M738   Dafoe, Allan Roy, 1883-1943.
bd.2   Telephone conversation with Dr. Dafoe
    pertaining to the condition and care of
    the newly borne Dionne quintuplets in
    Callender, Ontario.   CBC, 1934.
      1 reel (7 in.)   7 1/2 in. per sec.
    phonotape.

      I. Dionne quintuplets.

Voice Lib.
655   Dirksen, Everett McKinley, 1896-1969.
bd.2   Address at Republican National Convention
    in San Francisco: tribute to ex-President
    Herbert Hoover. NBC, July 13, 1963.
      1 reel (7 in.)   7 1/2 in, per sec.
    phonotape.

      1. Hoover, Herbert Clark, Pres. U.S., 1874-
1964.

Voice Lib.
660   Dirksen, Everett McKinley, 1896-1969.
bd.1   Address at the Republican National
    Convention in San Francisco: nominating
    Senator Barry Goldwater for President.
    NBC, July 15, 1964.
      1 reel (7 in.)   7 1/2 in. per sec.
    phonotape.

      1. Goldwater, Barry Morris, 1909-

Voice Lib.
M1269 Dirksen, Everett McKinley, 1896-1969.
bd.1   Excerpt of conversation with Senator
    Dirksen and his wife at their home in
    Washington, D.C., with F. Lee Bailey from
    TV program "Good Company." Discussion of
    public speaking, forty years of marriage,
    recording ventures, advice to youth, plans
    for another term as senator. NBC-TV,
    September 14, 1967.
      1 reel (7 in.) 7 1/2 in. per sec. phonotape.
    L. Dirksen, Louella Carver, 1899-   II. Bailey, Francis
Lee, 1933-   III. Good Company (Television program)

      1. Dirksen, Everett McKinley, 1896-1969

Voice Lib.
M1383 Dirksen, Everett McKinley, 1896-1969.
bd.1   Special program of obituary of Senator
    Dirksen with various excerpts of interviews.
    NBC, September 7, 1969.
      1 reel (7 in.)   7 1/2 in. per sec.
    phonotape.

       Dirksen, Everett McKinley, 1896-1969
Voice Lib.
M309   Columbia Broadcasting System, inc.
bd.3   Assassination: statements by Senator
    Dirksen and Senator Mansfield, remarks about
    statements and actions of others in Washington.
    CBS, November 22, 1963.
      1 reel (7 in.)   7 1/2 in. per sec.
    phonotape.

      1. Kennedy, John Fitzgerald, Pres. U.S.,
1917-1963 - Assassination. I. Dirksen,
Everett McKinley, 1896-1969. II. Mansfield,
Michael Joseph, 1903-

       Dirksen, Everett McKinley, 1896-1969
Voice Lib.
M725   Republican Party. National Convention.
bd.1   25th, Chicago, 1952.
    Film of excerpts of the Republican National
    Convention in 1952. Clash between Taft and
    Eisenhower forces. Includes speeches by Gen.
    MacArthur, Gen. Eisenhower, Ex-Pres. Hoover,
    Sen. Dirksen, etc. CBS, 1952.
      1 reel (7 in.)   7 1/2 in. per sec.
    phonotape.
    L. MacArthur, Douglas, 1880-1964. II. Eisenhower, Dwight
David, Pres. U.S., 1890-1969. III. Hoover, Herbert Clark, Pres.
U.S., 1874-1964. IV. Dirksen, Everett McKinley, 1896-1969.

Voice Lib.
M1022
bd.2-
1923

Dirksen, Everett McKinley, 1896-1969

U.S. Congress. Senate. Committee on Government Operations.
Permanent Subcommittee on Investigations.
Proceedings of the 9th session of Senate Army-McCarthy hearings, May 4, 1954. Discussion concerning the possibility of shortening the hearings; statements by Senators Dirksen, Mundt, McClellan, Potter, etc.; Aaron Coleman and the stripping of Army files; discussion of FBI confidential letter and how it was obtained by McCarthy; suggestion of night and Saturday sessions. WJR, May 4, 1954.
2 reels (7 in.) 7 1/2 in. per sec. phonotape.

I. McCarthy-Army controversy, 1954. I. Dirksen, Everett McKinley, 1896-1969. II. Mundt, Karl Earl, 1900- III. McClellan, John Little, 1896- IV. Potter, Charles Edward, 1916-

---

Voice Lib.
M1284

Dirksen, Everett McKinley, 1896-1969

U.S. Congress. Senate. Committee on Government Operations.
Permanent Subcommittee on Investigations.
Proceedings of the 13th session of Senate Army-McCarthy hearings, May 10, 1954. Senator Dirksen suggests they be held privately; Secretary Stevens makes statement and Senator McCarthy and his counsel, Roy Cohn, cross-examine Stevens; discussion of alleged communists at Ft. Monmouth and pressure of favored treatment for Private Schine. CBS Radio, May 10, 1954.
1 reel (7 in.) 7 1/2 in. per sec. phonotape.

I. McCarthy-Army controversy, 1954. I. Dirksen, Everett McKinley, 1896-1969. II. Stevens, Robert Ten Broeck, 1899- III. McCarthy, Joseph Raymond, 1909-1957. IV. Cohn, Roy M 1927-

---

Voice Lib.
M1320

Dirksen, Everett McKinley, 1896-1969

U.S. Congress. Senate. Committee on Government Operations.
Permanent Subcommittee on Investigations.
Proceedings of the 17th session of Senate Army-McCarthy hearings, May 14, 1954. Sen. Mundt questioning Mr. Adams about high-level meeting dealing with United Nations. Exchanges between Senator Mundt and Army Counsel Welch. Senator McCarthy examining Sen. Dirksen. Discussion of purgery charges against Carr. Cohn and Adams speak about private dinner party. CBS TV, May 14, 1954.
1 reel (7 in.) 7 1/2 in. per sec. phonotape.

I. McCarthy-Army controversy, 1954. I. Mundt, Karl Earl, 1900- II. Welch, Joseph Nye, 1890-1960. III. McCarthy, Joseph Raymond, 1909-1957. IV. Dirksen, Everett McKinley, 1896-1969. V. Cohn, Roy M 1927- VI. Adams, John G

Voice Lib.
M1269
bd.1

Dirksen, Louella Carver, 1899-

Dirksen, Everett McKinley, 1896-1969.
Excerpt of conversation with Senator Dirksen and his wife at their home in Washington, D.C., with F. Lee Bailey from TV program "Good Company." Discussion of public speaking, forty years of marriage, recording ventures, advice to youth, plans for another term as senator. NBC-TV, September 14, 1967.
1 reel (7 in.) 7 1/2 in. per sec. phonotape.
I. Dirksen, Louella Carver, 1899- II. Bailey, Francis Lee, 1933- III. Good Company (Television program)

Voice Lib.
383

DiSalle, Michael Vincent, 1908-

I can hear it now (radio program)
CBS, February 9, 1951.
1 reel (7 in.) 7 1/2 in. per sec.
phonotape.

I. Wilson, Charles Edward, 1886-1972. II. Gabrielson, Guy George, 1891- III. Taft, Robert Alphonso, 1889-1953. IV. Martin, Joseph William, 1884-1965. V. McCarthy, Joseph Raymond, 1909-1957. VI. Benton, William Burnett, 1900-1973. VII. Malone, George Wilson, 1890-1961. VIII. Capehart, Homer Earl, 1897- IX. Eisenhower, Dwight David, Pres. U.S., 1890-1969. X. Lee, J V XI. Hodge, John Reed, 1893-1963. XII. Overton, Watkins XIII. DiSalle, Michael Vincent, 1908- XIV. Boyce, Eddy XV. Conklin, Ed XVI. Collins, Joseph Lawton, 1896-

---

DISARMAMENT

Voice Lib.
540
bd.20

Addams, Jane, 1860-1935.
Signatures obtained from public on disarmament. Fox Movietone, 1932.
1 reel (7 in.) 7 1/2 in. per sec.
phonotape.

1. Disarmament.

DISARMAMENT

Voice Lib.
M1065
bd.2

Addams, Jane, 1860-1935.
Excerpt of remarks at World Conference on Disarmament, regarding women's fight for universal disarmament. Fox Movietone, 1933.
1 reel (7 in.) 7 1/2 in. per sec.
phonotape.

DISARMAMENT

Voice Lib.
M540
bd.23

Gibson, Hugh, 1883-1954.
First world conference on disarmament: abolition of submarines, bombs, etc. Fox Movietone, 1933.
1 reel (7 in.) 7 1/2 i.p.s. phonotape.

1. Disarmament.

DISARMAMENT

Voice Lib.
M1065
bd.3

Gibson, Hugh, 1883-1954.
Disarmament speech being booed and hissed; interlude music; British delegate opening Disarmament Conference; Hugh Gibson stating U.S. position - abolishing submarine warfare, lethal gas, and bombing by air. Fox Movietone, 1933.
1 reel (7 in.) 7 1/2 in. per sec.
phonotape.

DISARMAMENT

Voice Lib.
565
bd.2

Gromyko, Andrei Andreevich, 1909-
U.N. Disarmament Conference on world food needs. TRV, 1947.
1 reel (7 in.) 7 1/2 in. per sec.
phonotape.

1. Disarmament.

DISARMAMENT

Voice Lib.
209   Gromyko, Andrei Andreevich, 1908-
bd.6   Gromyko's remarks on arrival in
         Geneva for disarmament conference.
         Source (?). May 9, 1959.
            1 reel (7 in.) 7 1/2 in. per sec.
         phonotape.

            1. Disarmament.

Voice Lib.
M1477 Discussion of Supreme Court decision on
       publishing Pentagon Papers. William B.
       Macomber, deputy under-secretary of state;
       Senator Henry Jackson; Max Frankel, head of
       New York Times' Washington bureau; Benjamin
       Bradley, executive editor of Washington Post.
       Questioned by Carl Stern, NBC; Martin Hayden,
       Detroit News; James J. Kilpatrick, Washington
       Star Syndicate; Kenneth Crawford, Washington
       Post; Edwin Newman. NBC-TV, June 30, 1971.
          1 reel (7 in.) 7 1/2 in. per sec.
       phonotape.
                                (Continued on next card)

DISARMAMENT

Voice Lib.
M1065 Kellogg-Briand pact on disarmament; British
bd.1   spokesman in favor of limitation of
         armaments; mood music and effects. Fox
         Movietone, 1930.
            1 reel (7 in.) 7 1/2 in. per sec.
         phonotape.

Voice Lib.
M1477 Discussion of Supreme Court decision on
       publishing Pentagon Papers... June 30, 1971.
       (Card 2)

          1. Pentagon papers. I. Macomber, William
       Butts, 1921-   II. Jackson, Henry Martin,
       1912-   III. Frankel, Max   IV. Bradley,
       Benjamin C   V. Stern, Carl   VI.
       Hayden, Martin S   VII. Kilpatrick,
       James Jackson, 1920-   VIII. Crawford,
       Kenneth   IX. Newman, Edwin Harold, 1919-

DISARMAMENT

Voice Lib.
M1744   Luns, Joseph Marie Antoine Hubert, 1911-
bd.2   At the signing of the Brussels Pact, on
        the "Today Show". WILX-TV, June 25, 1974.
           2 min.   phonotape (1 r.   7 1/2 i.p.s.)

           1. Peace. 2. Disarmament.

DISRAELI, BENJAMIN, 1st EARL OF BEACONSFIELD
SEE
BEACONSFIELD, BENJAMIN DISRAELI, 1st EARL OF,
1804-1881.

VOICE LIBRARY

DISC JOCKEYS

Voice Lib.
M764   Goldmark, Goldie
bd.11   Excerpt from "The world of wax" (Program 8); comments on
       the production of another phenomenon which has had a profound
       effect on the recording industry, the disc jockey. Also comments
       on the dissatisfaction of a large segment of the record industry with
       the radio-record relationship. Westinghouse Broadcasting
       Corporation, 1964.
          7 min., 58 sec. phonotape (1 r.   7 1/2 i.p.s.) (The music
       goes round and round)

          1. Disc jockeys. 1. Title: The world of wax. II. Series.

Voice Lib.
M1100 Dixieland (original jazz band)
bd.4   Playing "Tiger Rag" in Dixieland tempo.
       LaRocca, cornet; Shields, clarinet; Edwards,
       trombone; Regas, piano; Shabaro, drums.
       Forrest, 1918.
          1 reel (7 in.) 7 1/2 in. per sec.
       phonotape.

          1. Jazz music
          I. Title: Tiger rag.

Voice Lib.
M1031 Discussion about Winston Churchill's ability
       in military affairs, between Alistair Cooke
       and General Dwight Eisenhower, heard at his
       home in Gettysburg, Pennsylvania; including
       recording of General George C. Marshall's
       opinion about the strategic value of U.S.
       troops conquering Berlin. "Studio 67"
       production, ABC-TV, January 26, 1967.
          1 reel (7 in.) 7 1/2 in. per sec. phonotape.
          1. Churchill, Winston Leonard Spencer, 1874-1965. I.
       Cooke, Alistair, 1908-   II. Eisenhower, Dwight David, Pres.
       U.S., 1890-1969.

Voice Lib.
M757   Dixon, Calvin P
bd.4   "Dry Bones in the Valley"; a sermon by
       the Rev. Dixon. Columbia U.S., 1925.
          1 reel (7 in.) 7 1/2 in. per sec.
       phonotape.

CL
SC6
DIXON, JEANE

Whorf, Michael, 1933-
A study in prophecy.
1 tape cassette. (The visual sounds of
Mike Whorf. Science, SC6)

Originally presented on his radio program, Kaleidoscope,
WJR, Detroit.
Duration: 55 min.
Jeane Dixon expounds of her faith, tells why she has been
able to see glimpses of another world, and tells of her predictions,
some of which have come true and others which have not.

I. Dixon, Jeane.   I. Title.

Dr. Watson meets Sherlock Holmes

Voice Lib.
111   Doyle, Sir Arthur Conan, 1859-1930.
bd.2   Dr. Watson meets Sherlock Holmes, as
read by John Gielgud and Ralph Richardson.
British Broadcasting Corp., His Master's
Voice, 1947.
1 reel (7 in.)   7 1/2 in. per sec.
phonotape.

I. Gielgud, John, 1904-   II. Richardson,
Ralph David, 1902-   III. Title.

Voice Lib.
M1453   Documentary TV program produced by the
University of Michigan on the Lone Ranger
radio programs, including former participants
of that program.   University of Michigan
TV, 1970.
1 reel (7 in.)   7 1/2 in. per sec.
phonotape.

1. Lone Ranger (Radio program)   I. Lone
Ranger (Radio program)

Voice Lib.
M1361   Dönitz, Karl, 1891-
bd.12   Proclamation to the German Wehrmacht and
to the entire German nation about Hitler's
last will and testament.   Peteler, May 1,
1945.
1 reel (7 in.)   7 1/2 in. per sec.
phonotape.

1. Hitler, Adolf, 1889-1945.

Voice Lib.
M1471   Doenitz, Karl, 1891-
bd.2   Describing the last days of the Third
Reich and his acceptance of the job as
Hitler's successor.   Tells about his plans
for surrender and other matters.   (May 1-8,
1945).   Peteler, 1965.
1 reel (7 in.)   7 1/2 in. per sec.
phonotape.

Doin' the New Low Down

Voice Lib.
262   Robinson, Bill, 1878-1940.
bd.3   "Doin' the New Low Down." Brunswick,
1923.
1 reel (7 in.)   7 1/2 in. per sec.
phonotape.

I. Title.

Voice Lib.
M258   Dominican Government Radio.
bd.7   Assassination of Trujillo and announcement
of his death.   New York, CBS, May 31, 1961.
1 reel (7 in.)   7 1/2 in. per sec.
phonotape.

1. Trujillo Molina, Rafael Leónidas,
Pres. Dominican Republic, 1891-1961.

Voice Lib. Donald, Peter
M619   Radio in the 1930's (Part II): a series of
bd.1-   excerpts of the 1930's; a sample of radio
14   of the period.   NVL, April, 1964.
1 reel (7 in.)   7 1/2 in. per sec.   phonotape.
I. Allen, Fred, 1.894-1956. II. Delmar, Kenny   III. Donald,
Peter   IV. Pious, Minerva   V. Fennelly, Parker   VI.
Boyer, Charles, 1899-   VII. Dunne, Irene, 1904-   VIII.
DeMille, Cecil Blount, 1881-1959. IX. West, Mae, 1893-   X.
Dafoe, Allan Ray, 1883-1943. XI. Dionne quintuplets. XII. Ortega,
Santos   XIII. War of the worlds (radio program) XIV. Ives, Burl,
1909-   XV. Robinson, Earl, 1910-   XVI. Temple, Shirley,
1928-   XVII. Earhart, Amelia, 1898-1937. XVIII. Lawrence,
Gertrude, 1901-1952. XIX. Cohan, George Michael, 1878-1942.
XX. Shaw, George Bernard, 1856-1950. XXI. Hitler, Adolf, 1889-
1945. XXII. Chamberlain, Neville, 1869-1940. XXIII. Roosevelt,
Franklin Delano, Pres. U. S., 1882-1945.

Don't let's be beastly to the Germans

Voice Lib.
129   Coward, Noel Pierce, 1899-
bd.6   Don't let's be beastly to the Germans;
Coward sings this, his own composition.
His Majesty's Voice, 1940.
1 reel (7 in.)   7 1/2 in. per sec.
phonotape.

I. Title.

Voice Lib.
M375   Dooley, Thomas Anthony, 1927-1961.
bd.1   Image of America in Southeast Asia;
communism in Southeast Asia and Laos in schools;
America and its roles in Southeast Asia; Laotian education;
proposes corps of young Americans for Laos; missionaries in
Laos; discusses S. S. "Hope" and its shortcomings; explains
methods of curing native illness; dislike of U. S. people by
people of Laos.   KETC (NET) [n. d.]
1 reel (7 in.)   7 1/2 i. p. s.   phonotape.

I. Laos.

Voice Lib.
M739   Doolittle, James Harold, 1896-
bd.11   Talking on the thirteenth anniversary of
attack of carrier "Hornet" on Japan, April 18,
1942. CBS, April 18, 1955.
1 reel (7 in.) 7 1/2 in. per sec.
phonotape.

Douglas, Mike, 1925?
Voice Lib.
M1745   Knowles, John
bd.2   Explains how to find a capable physician
on the Mike Douglas Show. WILX-TV, June
27, 1974.
6 min. phonotape (1 r. 7 1/2 i.p.s.)

1. Physicians - U. S.   I. Douglas, Mike,
1925?

Voice Lib.
M1467- Dos Passos, John, 1896-1970.
1469   U.S.A.; a 2 1/2 hour dramatization by
Hollywood TV Theatre, based on the three
Dos Passos books dealing with the first
three decades of the 20th century. Host:
Edward G. Robinson. WMSB-TV, May 30, 1971.
3 reels (7 in.) 7 1/2 in. per sec.
phonotape.

I. Robinson, Edward G   1893-1973.
II. Title.

Douglas, Mike, 1925?
Voice Lib.
M1696   Koplin, Mert
bd.2   Appearance of Koplin and Charles Grinker,
of Cinedex, movie archives, on Mike
Douglas Show. WJRT-TV, May 27, 1974.
7 min. phonotape (1 r. 7 1/2 i.p.s.)

1. Moving-pictures - History. I. Grinker,
Charles. II. Douglas, Mike, 1925?

Voice Lib.
344   Douglas, Laura Virginia
bd.18   Author of the letter "Is There a
Santa Claus?" interviewed on her
conception of Christmas. CBS,
December 24, 1961.
1 reel (7 in.) 7 1/2 in. per sec.
phonotape.

I. Title: Is there a Santa Claus?

Douglas, Mike, 1925?-
Voice Lib.
M1691   Miller, Merle, 1918-
Bd.2   On Mike Douglas Show discussing his book
on Truman. Includes Viveca Lindfors and
David Steinberg. WILS-TV, May 23, 1974.
5 min. phonotape (1 r. 7 1/2 i.p.s.)

1. Truman, Harry S, Pres. U.S., 1884-1972.
2. Miller, Merle, 1918-   /Plain speaking.
I. Douglas, Mike, 1925?-   II. Lindfors,
Viveca, 1920-   III. Steinberg, David.

Douglas, Lewis Williams, 1894-
Voice Lib.
266   Elizabeth II, Queen of Great Britain, 1926-
bd.1   Speech at Pilgrims' Dinner; speech and
introduction of the president of the Pilgrims
and closing speech by Lewis Douglas. CBS,
October 21, 1957.
1 reel (7 in.) 7 1/2 in. per sec.
phonotape.

I. Douglas, Lewis Williams, 1894-

Douglas, Mike, 1925?-
Voice Lib.
M1745   O'Connor, Ulick.
bd.1   Interview on Mike Douglas Show. WILS-TV,
June 27, 1974.
10 min. phonotape (1 r. 7 1/2 i.p.s.)

1. Pierce, Patrick/The Mother. 2. O'Connor,
Ulick. I. Douglas, Mike, 1925?-

Voice Lib.   Douglas, Mike, 1925?-
M1707   Cohn, Roy M   1927-
bd.3   On the Mike Douglas show recalling the
McCarthy era with no regrets. Includes
Liberace. ABC, May 30, 1974.
7 min. phonotape (1 r. 7 1/2 i.p.s.)

1. McCarthy-Army controversy. I. Douglas,
Mike, 1925?-   II. Liberace, 1919-

Douglas, Mike, 1925?-
Voice Lib.
M1743   Raft, George
bd.2   Reminisces on the Mike Douglas Show.
WILX-TV, June 27, 1974.
10 min. phonotape (1 r. 7 1/2 i.p.s.)

1. Raft, George. 2. O'Brien, Pat, 1899-   3. Munn,
Paul, 1895-1967. 4. Crawford, Joan, 1908-   5. West, Mae,
1893-   6. Richman, Harry. 7. Entertainers - U. S. I.
Douglas, Mike, 1925?-

Voice Lib.   Douglas, Mike, 1925?
M1706
bd.3   Reuben, David R
   Impotence in marriage; funny discussion
   on parent/child discussions of sex. On
   Mike Douglas Show with Totie Fields and the
   Fifth Dimension. WJRT-TV, June 5, 1974.
     15 min. phonotape (1 r. 7 1/2 i.p.s.)

     1. Sex. I. Douglas, Mike, 1925?
II. Fifth Dimension. III. Fields, Totie.

Voice Lib.   Douglas, William Orville, 1898-
M997   Introduction of Viscount Hailsham, who
   is the main speaker at the Tenth Anniversary
   celebration of "Fund for the Republic".
   CSDI.
     1 reel (7 in.) 7 1/2 in. per sec.
   phonotape.

Voice Lib.   Douglas, Mike, 1925?
M1696
bd.3   Rogers, Charles
   Reminiscing with Mike Douglas on the
   Mike Douglas Show. WJRT-TV, May 27, 1974.
     8 min. phonotape (1 r. 7 1/2 i.p.s.)

     1. Moving-pictures - History. 2. Rogers,
Charles. I. Douglas, Mike, 1925?

C1   DOUGLASS, FREDERICK, 1817-1895
833   Whorf, Michael, 1933-
   Heroes come in many colors; part 3 - The life
   of Frederick Douglas.
     1 tape cassette. (The visual sounds of Mike Whorf. Social, S33)

     Originally presented on his radio program, Kaleidoscope,
WJR, Detroit.
     Duration: 36 min., 45 sec.
     From the heartaches and agonies of slavery came Frederick
Douglass, a giant of a man in mind and spirit, who would express
himself in a manner that no black man had done before.

     1 Douglass, Frederick, 1817-1895. L. Title.

Voice Lib.   Douglas, Mike, 1925?-
M1696
bd.1   Vallee, Rudy, 1901-
   Reminiscing on the Mike Douglas Show.
   ABC-TV, May 27, 1974.
     10 min. phonotape (1 r. 7 1/2 i.p.s.)

     1. Vallee, Rudy, 1901-
I. Douglas, Mike, 1925?

Voice Lib.   Dowling, Ray Dooley
M322   Biography in sound (radio program)
   W.C. Fields, the magnificent rogue.
   NBC, 1955.
     1 reel (7 in.) 7 1/2 in. per sec. phonotape.
     L. Fields, W.C., 1879-1946. L. Fields, W.C., 1879-1946.
II. Allen, Fred, 1894-1956. III. LaBaron, William IV.
Taylor, Robert Lewis, 1912- V. McCarey, Thomas Leo, 1898-
1969. VI. Harkins, James - VII. Chevalier, Maurice,
1889-1972. VIII. Kuromoto, Mrs. George IX. Flynn,
Errol Leslie, 1909-1959. X. Wynn, Ed, 1886-1966. XI. Dowling,
Ray Dooley XII. Sennett, Mack XIII. Overacher,
Ronald Leroy XIV. Bergen, Edgar, 1903- XV. Taurog,
Norman, 1899- XVI. Rumnell, Ann XVII. Cowen,
Lester

Voice Lib.   Douglas, Paul Howard, 1892-
353
bd.19   Russia and the bomb, discussed by various
   personalities. NBC, September 25, 1949.
     1 reel (7 in.) 7 1/2 in. per sec.
   phonotape.

     Participants: Harrison Brown, Harold Urey,
Samuel Allison, Thornton Hugness, Brien McMahon,
Paul Douglas, John Foster Dulles, Leslie Groves,
Winston Churchill, Dean Acheson, James Fleming.

     I. Brown, Harrison Scott, 1917-   II.
Urey, Harold Clayton, 1893-   III. Allison,
     (Continued on next card)

C1   Down to the sea in ships
H63   Whorf, Michael, 1933-
   Down to the sea in ships.
     1 tape cassette. (The visual sounds of
Mike Whorf. History and heritage, H63)
     Originally presented on his radio program, Kaleidoscope,
WJR, Detroit.
     Duration: 38 min., 50 sec.
     What is the lure of the sea that calls men to their destiny?
In this narrative the great tragedies of the ocean are recounted.

     L. Shipwrecks. L. Title.

Voice Lib.   Douglas, Paul Howard, 1892-
353
bd.19   Russia and the bomb... 1949. (Card 2)

     Samuel King, 1900-   IV. Hugness, Thornton.
V. McMahon, James O'Brien, 1903-1952. VI.
Douglas, Paul Howard, 1892- VII. Dulles,
John Foster, 1888-1959. VIII. Groves, Leslie
R   1896-1970. IX. Churchill, Winston
Leonard Spencer, 1874-1965. X. Acheson, Dean
Gooderham, 1893-1971. XI. Fleming, James,
1915-

Voice Lib.   Downey, William
572-   I can hear it now (radio program)
573   1933-1946. CBS, 1948.
bd.1   2 reels (7 in.) 7 1/2 in. per sec.
   phonotape.
     L. Murrow, Edward Roscoe, 1908-1965. II. LaGuardia, Fiorello
Henry, 1882-1947. III. Chamberlain, Neville, 1869-1949. IV.
Roosevelt, Franklin Delano, Pres. U.S., 1882-1945. V. Churchill,
Winston Leonard Spencer, 1874-1965. VI. Gaulle, Charles de,
Pres. France, 1890-1970. VII. Eisenhower, Dwight David, Pres. U.S.,
1890-1969. VIII. Willkie, Wendell Lewis, 1892-1944. IX. Martin,
Joseph William, 1884-1968. X. Elizabeth II, Queen of Great Britain,
1926- XI. Margaret Rose, Princess of Gt. Brit., 1930- XII.
Johnson, Hugh Samuel, 188? 42. XIII. Smith, Alfred Emanuel,
1873-1944. XIV. Lindbergl arles Augustus, 1902- XV. Davis,
     (Continued on next card)

Voice Lib.
580- Downs, Hugh Malcolm, 1921-
581   "Today" show tribute to Fred Allen. Hosts
       show, talks with various personalities, reads
       series of jokes written by Fred Allen, reads
       quote from James Thurber. Excerpt from NBC-TV
       production "The Jazz Age" which Allen narrates,
       recorded shortly before his death on March 17,
       1956. NBC, March 18, 1964.
          2 reels (7 in.)   7 1/2 in. per sec.
       phonotape.
          1. Allen, Fred, 1894-1956.

Voice Lib.   Downs, Hugh Malcolm, 1921-
M1248 Baseball fifty years ago; interviews with four
       famous old time baseball players, on NBC
       "Today" show, by host Hugh Downs, supported by
       sportcaster Joe Garagiola and Dr. Lawrence
       Ritter, author of new book. NBC-TV, June 9,
       1967.
          1 reel (7 in.)   7 1/2 in. per sec.   phonotape.
       L. Baseball. L. Downs, Hugh Malcolm, 1921-   IL. Garagiola,
       Joe. III. Ritter, Lawrence S. /The glory of their times. IV. Roush,
       Edd, 1893-   V. Marquart, Rube, 1890-   VL. O'Doul, Lefty,
       1897-   VII. Meyers, John, 1880-

Voice Lib.
M1279 Downs, Hugh Malcolm, 1921-
       Today show interview pertaining to new
       book, "At Ease - Stories I Tell My Friends";
       recollections, going through Eisenhower's
       entire career. NBC-TV, July 11, 1967.
          1 reel (7 in.)   7 1/2 in. per sec.
       phonotape.
          I. Eisenhower, Dwight David, Pres. U.S.,
       1890-1969.

Voice Lib.   Downs, Hugh Malcolm, 1921-
M1059 Kerenskii, Aleksandr Fedorovich, 1881-
bd.1   Discussion with Hugh Downs and former
       Russian Prime Minister Kerenskii about the
       1917 Russian Revolution on "Today" TV show.
       NBC-TV, February 28, 1967.
          1 reel (7 in.)   7 1/2 in. per sec.
       phonotape.
          I. Downs, Hugh Malcolm, 1921-

Voice Lib.   Downs, Hugh Malcolm, 1921-
M1446 Rockwell, Norman, 1894-
bd.2   Excerpt of conversation between illustrator
       Norman Rockwell and Hugh Downs on the
       "Today" show, pertaining to Rockwell's new
       book of drawings. NBC-TV, 1970.
          1 reel (7 in.)   7 1/2 in. per sec.
       phonotape.
          I. Downs, Hugh Malcolm, 1921-

Voice Lib.   Downs, Hugh Malcolm, 1921-
M1286 Simon, George Thomas
bd.2   Excerpt of "Today" show of conversation
       between emcee Hugh Downs and George T. Simon,
       about name bands and his new book "The Big
       Bands". NBC-TV, December 11, 1967.
          1 reel (7 in.)   7 1/2 in. per sec.
       phonotape.
          I. Downs, Hugh Malcolm, 1921-

Voice Lib.
M1011 Doxiadës, Konstantinos Apostolou, 1913-
       Lecture at 158 Natural Resources on MSU
       campus on city planning for the future.
       (1 hour). Auspices of Department of Urban
       Planning. Chapin, October 21, 1966.
          1 reel (7 in.)   7 1/2 in. per sec.
       phonotape.
          1. Cities and towns - Planning.

Voice Lib.
M1030 Doxiadës, Konstantinos Apostolov, 1913-
bd.2   Questions and answers following lecture at
       ... Natural Resources at MSU campus.
       Chapin, October 21, 1966.
          1 reel (7 in.)   7 1/2 in. per sec.
       phonotape.

Voice Lib.
110   Doyle, Sir Arthur Conan, 1859-1930.
bd.1   Arthur Conan Doyle speaks on creation
       of Sherlock Holmes. British Broadcasting
       Corp., His Master's Voice, 1928.
          1 reel (7 in.)   8 1/2 in. per sec.
       phonotape.

Voice Lib.
537   Doyle, Sir Arthur Conan, 1859-1930.
bd.2   Development of Sherlock Holmes; spiritualism;
       impact of Holmes' stories around the world;
       influence of Thomas Huxley on his spiritual
       belief; ability to answer questions on life
       after death; spiritualism and its compatible
       relationship with other religions; proof of
       spiritualism. BBC, 1928.
          1 reel (7 in.)   7 1/2 in. per sec.
       phonotape.
          1. Spiritualism.

Voice Lib.
111   Doyle, Sir Arthur Conan, 1859-1930.
bd.2   Dr. Watson meets Sherlock Holmes, as
             read by John Gielgud and Ralph Richardson.
             British Broadcasting Corp., His Master's
             Voice, 1947.
                 1 reel (7 in.)   7 1/2 in. per sec.
             phonotape.
                 I. Gielgud, John, 1904-   II. Richardson,
             Ralph David, 1902-   III. Title.

Voice Lib.
110   Doyle, Sir Arthur Conan, 1859-1930.
bd.2   The Final Problem, an episode read by
             John Gielgud, Ralph Richardson, and Orson
             Welles. His Master's Voice, 1947.
                 1 reel (7 in.)   7 1/2 in. per sec.
             phonotape.
                 I. Gielgud, John, 1904-   II. Richardson,
             Ralph David, 1902-   III. Welles, Orson,
             1915-   IV. Title.

Voice Lib.
M1677   Dracula (radio program)
                 Mercury Theatre production of Dracula
             with Orson Welles, George Colouris, and
             Martin Gabel. Ferris State College, 1937.
                 55 min.   phonotape (1 r.   7 1/2 i.p.s.)

                 I. Welles, Orson, 1915-   II. Colouris,
             George. III. Gabel, Martin, 1912-

                 Drainie, John
Voice Lib.
626-   The investigator; satire on the investigations
627   of Senator Joseph McCarthy, written by
             Reuben Ship, with John Drainie playing the
             role of the investigator. CBC, May 30, 1954.
                 2 reels (7 in.)   7 1/2 in. per sec.
             phonotape.

                 I. Ship, Reuben   II. Drainie, John

                 A dream of freedom
C1
31   Whorf, Michael, 1933-
                 A dream of freedom.
                 1 tape cassette. (The visual sounds of
             Mike Whorf. Social, S1)
                 Originally presented on his radio program, Kaleidoscope,
             WJR, Detroit.
                 Duration: 40 min., 45 sec.
                 Utilizing many of his famous speeches and delving into his
             biography, the narrator gives continuity to this story of the life
             and times of Martin Luther King.
                 L. King, Martin Luther, 1929-1968. L. Title.

                 The dream songs
Voice Lib.
M1678   Berryman, John, 1914-1972.
                 Reading from "The dream songs" at
             Michigan State University. WKAR, June 17,
             1969.
                 45 min.   phonotape (1 r.   7 1/2 i.p.s.)

                 I. Title: The dream songs.

Voice Lib.
M863   Dressler, Marie, 1873-1934.
bd.4   In comedy skit: "Rastus, take me back".
             IRCC-cylinder, 1907.
                 1 reel (7 in.)   7 1/2 in. per sec.
             phonotape.

                 I. Title: Rastus, take me back.

                 Drew, Elizabeth
Voice Lib.
M1481   Brinkley, David McClure, 1920-
bd.2   David Brinkley interviewed by Elizabeth
             Drew, Washington editor of Atlantic Monthly.
             On believing the government, thoroughness of
             TV news, bias, objectivity of newsmen, personal
             news philosophy, liberal press, visual news.
                 1 reel (7 in.)   7 1/2 in. per sec.
             phonotape.

                 I. Drew, Elizabeth

Voice Lib.
608   Drinkwater, John, 1882-1937.
bd.1   Reads his poetry. BBC, 1936.
                 1 reel (7 in.)   7 1/2 in. per sec.
             phonotape.

                 CONTENTS.-Mystery, The Vagabond, The Apples,
             Birthright, Cotswold Love, Anthony Crunwald,
             Mrs. Willow, Mamble, A Prayer, Immortality,
             Reciprocity, Gold, Blackbird.

                 DRUG ABUSE
Voice Lib.
M1692   Milliken, William G   1922-
bd.2   Welcoming participants in the Governor's
             Conference on Drug Dependence and Abuse,
             Kellogg Center, East Lansing. WKAR,
             December 8, 1969.
                 10 min.   phonotape (1 r.   7 1/2 i.p.s.)

                 1. Drug abuse.

Voice Lib. DRUG ABUSE
M1692 Swainson, John Burley, 1927-
bd.1 Opening a Governor's Conference on Drug
Dependence and Abuse, and outlining the
scope of the problem. WKAR, December 8,
1969.
10 min. phonotape (1 r. 7 1/2 i.p.s.)

1. Drug abuse.

Duke, Paul
Voice Lib.
M1657 Kennedy, Edward Moore, 1932-
Discusses visit with Brezhnev, Watergate,
Chappaquiddick, and 1976 politics.
Interviewed by Paul Duke. WKAR-TV,
May 7, 1974.
30 min. phonotape (1 r. 7 1/2 i.p.s.)

1. U.S. - Politics and government - 1969-
2. Watergate Affair, 1972- I. Duke,
Paul.

Duke, Paul
Voice Lib.
M1720 O'Neill, Thomas P., 1912-
bd.1 Interview on Washington Straight Talk,
by Paul Duke. WKAR-TV, June 11, 1974.
30 min. phonotape (1 r. 7 1/2 i.p.s.)

1. U.S. - Politics & government.
2. Nixon, Richard Milhous, Pres. U.S., 1913-
I. Duke, Paul.

Duke, Paul
Voice Lib.
M1685 Rodino, Peter Wallace, 1909-
bd.2 Telling PBS that transcript damages Nixon.
Question under investigation is how much?
Interview with Paul Duke on Washington
straight talk. PBS, May 21, 1974.
30 min. phonotape (1 r. 7 1/2 i.p.s.)

1. U.S. - Politics and government - 1969-
2. Nixon, Richard Milhous, Pres. U.S., 1913-
I. Duke, Paul.

Duke, Vernon, 1903-1969
Voice Lib.
M869 The great American song (radio program)
bd.2- Documentary program of CBC on the contribution
870 of American music: discussion of the work of
George Gershwin; American musical comedy;
biographical sketches and interviews with
composers Arthur Schwartz and Vernon Duke, who
discuss the technique of composing. CBC, 1964.
2 reels (7 in.) 7 1/2 in. per sec.
phonotape.

1. Gershwin, George, 1898-1937. I. Schwartz,
Arthur, 1900- II. Duke, Vernon, 1903-1969.

Dulles, John Foster, 1888-1959
Voice Lib.
353 Russia and the bomb, discussed by various
bd.19 personalities. NBC, September 25, 1949.
1 reel (7 in.) 7 1/2 in. per sec.
phonotape.

Participants: Harrison Brown, Harold Urey,
Samuel Allison, Thornton Hugness, Brien McMahon,
Paul Douglas, John Foster Dulles, Leslie Groves,
Winston Churchill, Dean Acheson, James Fleming.

I. Brown, Harrison Scott, 1917- II.
Urey, Harold Clayton, 1893- III. Allison,
(Continued on next card)

Dulles, John Foster, 1888-1959
Voice Lib.
353 Russia and the bomb... 1949. (Card 2)
bd.19
Samuel King, 1900- IV. Hugness, Thornton.
V. McMahon, James O'Brien, 1903-1952. VI.
Douglas, Paul Howard, 1892- VII. Dulles,
John Foster, 1888-1959. VIII. Groves, Leslie
R 1896-1970. IX. Churchill, Winston
Leonard Spencer, 1874-1965. X. Acheson, Dean
Gooderham, 1893-1971. XI. Fleming, James,
1915-

Voice Lib.
M1055 Dulles, John Foster, 1888-1959.
bd.1 Speech at banquet of American Association
for the United Nations at Waldorf Astoria
Hotel in New York; regarding U.S. foreign
policy, outlook at year end of 1950, and
reviewing world political situation,
especially regarding Communism. Mutual,
December 29, 1950.
1 reel (7 in.) 7 1/2 in. per sec.
phonotape.

Voice Lib.
170- Dulles, John Foster, 1888-1959.
171 Speech at AFL Convention, 1953.
AFL-CIO (P.R.O.), 1953.
2 reels (7 in.) 7 1/2 in. per sec.
phonotape.

Voice Lib.
M185 Dulles, John Foster, 1888-1959.
The situation of NATO report upon return
from Paris; first broadcast ever held of a
Cabinet meeting. WJR, October 25, 1954.
1 reel (7 in.) 7 1/2 in. per sec.
phonotape.

1. North Atlantic Treaty Organization.

Voice Lib.
M243   Dulles, John Foster, 1888-1959.
bd.11   On air and ground inspection.   CBS,
August 6, 1957.
1 reel (7 in.)   7 1/2 in. per sec.
phonotape.

1. Atomic power - International control.

Voice Lib.
M345   Dulles, John Foster, 1888-1959.
bd.13   Statement on suspension of nuclear
tests; excerpt from press conference.
CBS, April 1, 1958.
1 reel (7 in.)   7 1/2 in. per sec.
phonotape.

1. Atomic power - International Control.

Voice Lib.   Duncan, Augustin
M225
Packard, Frederick
Styles in Shakespearean acting, 1890-1950.
Creative Associates, 1963?
1 reel (7 in.)   7 1/2 i.p.s.   phonotape.

I. Sothern, Edward Askew, 1826-1881. II. Marlowe,
Julia, 1865-1950. III. Booth, Edwin, 1833-1893. IV. Gielgud,
John, 1904-   V. Robeson, Paul Bustill, 1898-   VI. Terry,
Dame Ellen, 1848-1928. VII. Allen, Viola. VIII. Welles,
Orson, 1915-   IX. Skinner, Otis, 1858-1942. X. Barrymore,
John, 1882-1942. XI. Olivier, Sir Laurence Kerr, 1907-
XII. Forbes-Robertson, Sir Johnston, 1853-   XIII. Evans,
Maurice. XIV. Thorndike, Dame Sybil, 1882-   XV. Robson,
Flora. XVI. LeGallienne, Eva, 1899-   XVII. Anderson,
Judith. XVIII. Duncan, Augustin. XIX. Hampden, Walter.
XX. Speaight, Robert, 190   XXI. Jones, Daniel.

C1
A3
DUNCAN, ISADORA, 1878-1927.

Whorf, Michael, 1933-
The unforgetable Isadora.
1 tape cassette.   (The visual sounds of
Mike Whorf. Art, music, and letters, A3)

Originally presented on his radio program, Kaleidoscope,
WJR, Detroit.
Duration: 29 min.
Isadora Duncan, a carefree, spirited nymph of considerable
ability, was driven by inner urges and pressures that often
possess the gifted.

I. Duncan, Isadora, 1878-1927.   I. Title.

DUNKIRK, FRANCE, BATTLE OF, 1940

Voice Lib.
530   Churchill, Winston Leonard Spencer, 1874-1965.
"This was their finest hour;" on the
evacuation of troops from France.   BBC,
June 18, 1940.
1 reel (7 in.)   7 1/2 in. per sec.
phonotape.

1. Dunkirk, France, Battle of, 1940.

Voice Lib.   Dunne, Irene, 1904-
M619   Radio in the 1930's (Part II): a series of
bd.1-   excerpts of the 1930's; a sample of radio
14   of the period. NVL, April, 1964.
1 reel (7 in.) 7 1/2 in. per sec. phonotape.
I. Allen, Fred, 1894-1956. II. Delmar, Kenny III. Donald,
Peter IV. Pious, Minerva V. Fennelly, Parker   VI.
Boyer, Charles, 1899-   VII. Dunne, Irene, 1904-   VIII.
DeMille, Cecil Blount, 1881-1959. IX. West, Mae, 1893-   X.
Dafoe, Allan Ray, 1883-1943. XI. Dionne quintuplets. XII. Ortega,
Santos XIII. War of the worlds (radio program) XIV. Ives, Burl,
1909-   XV. Robinson, Earl, 1910-   XVI. Temple, Shirley,
1928-   XVII. Earhart, Amelia, 1898-1937. XVIII. Lawrence,
Gertrude, 1901-1952. XIX. Cohan, George Michael, 1878-1942.
XX. Shaw, George Bernard, 1856-1950. XXI. Hitler, Adolf, 1889-
1945. XXII. Chamberlain, Neville, 1869-1940. XXIII. Roosevelt,
Franklin Delano, Pres. U.S., 1882-1945.

Durante, Jimmy, 1893-
Voice Lib.
M1047   Old-time radio excerpts of the 1930's and
1940's, including: Rudy Vallee singing
"Linger a little longer"; Will Rogers on
panaceas for the Depression; Bing Crosby
singing "Sweet Georgia Brown"; Eddie Cantor;
Jimmy Durante singing "Inka-dinka-do";
musical skit by Clayton, Jackson and Durante;
wit by Harry Hershfield; musical selection
"Thinking of you" by Kay Kyser; Kate Smith
singing theme song, "When the moon comes over
the mountain"; W.C. Fields' temperance

(Continued on next card)

Durante, Jimmy, 1893-
Voice Lib.
M1047   Old-time radio excerpts of the 1930's and
1940's...   (Card 2)

lecture; Al Jolson singing "Rocka-by-your
baby"; and George Burns and Gracie Allen
skit.   TV&R, 1930's and 1940's.
1 reel (7 in.) 7 1/2 in. per sec.
I. Vallee, Rudy, 1901-   II. Rogers, Will, 1879-1935. III.
Crosby, Bing, 1901-   IV. Cantor, Eddie, 1893-1964. V. Durante,
Jimmy, 1893-   VI. Clayton, Patti   VII. Jackson,
Eddie   VIII. Hershfield, Harry, 1885-   IX. Kyser, Kay,
1906-   X. Smith, Kate, 1909-   XI. Fields, W.C., 1879-
1946. XII. Jolson, Al, 1886-1950. XIII. Burns, George, 1896-
XIV. Allen, Gracie, 1906-

Durante, Jimmy, 1893-
Voice Lib.
M302   Voice of America (Radio program)
bd.2   Jimmy Durante: Voice of America reviews
Durante's career with the comedian; Durante's
life and times in show business, future trends
in American entertainment.   Voice of America,
November 8, 1961.
1 reel (7 in.)   7 1/2 in. per sec.
phonotape.

1. Durante, Jimmy, 1893-   I. Durante,
Jimmy, 1893-

Voice Lib.
M1383   Duvalier, Francois, Pres. Haiti, 1907-1971.
bd.2   "Papa Doc"; sequence on life in Haiti
from NBC-TV program "First Tuesday in
August".   August 5, 1969.
1 reel (7 in.)   7 1/2 in. per sec.
phonotape.

EADS, JAMES BUCHANAN, 1820-1887

C1
FA19   Whorf, Michael, 1933-
        Captain James B. Eads.
        1 tape cassette.   (The visual sounds of
Mike Whorf. The forgotten American, FA19)

         Originally presented on his radio program, Kaleidoscope,
WJR, Detroit.
         Duration: 11 min., 5 sec.
         Eads challenged and tamed the Mississippi river. He
pioneered in salvaging in the river, designed, and built boats
used to clear the river during the Civil War, and built the
first bridge across the river at St. Louis.

        L Eads, James Buchanan, 1820-1887.   L Title.

        Eagan, Col.

Voice Lib.
M932   Information, please (radio program)
        Panel of experts questioned by Clifton
Fadiman; panel includes Christopher Morley,
John Kieran, Franklin P. Adams, Col. Eagan.
Lloyd Grosse, 1943.
        1 reel (7 in.)   7 1/2 in. per sec.
phonotape.

        I. Fadiman, Clifton, 1904-   II. Morley,
Christopher Darlington, 1890-   III. Kieran,
John, 1892-   IV. Adams, Franklin Pierce,
1881-1960. V. Eagan, Col.

Voice Lib.
541   Earhart, Amelia, 1898-1937.
bd.5   Women's place in aviation; reviewing her
career in aviation and air transportation.
GRV, February 11, 1936.
        1 reel (7 in.)   7 1/2 in. per sec.
phonotape.

Voice Lib.
652   Earhart, Amelia, 1898-1937.
bd.12   Spoken before her take-off on her ill-fated
globe-girdling trip. CBS, 1937.
        1 reel (7 in.)   7 1/2 in. per sec.
phonotape.

Voice Lib.   Earhart, Amelia, 1898-1937
M619   Radio in the 1930's (Part II): a series of
bd.1-   excerpts of the 1930's; a sample of radio
14   of the period. NVL, April, 1964.
        1 reel (7 in.)   7 1/2 in. per sec. phonotape.
        L Allen, Fred, 1894-1956. II. Delmar, Kenny   III. Donald,
Peter   IV. Pious, Minerva   V. Fennelly, Parker   VI.
Boyer, Charles, 1899-   VII. Dunne, Irene, 1904-   VIII.
DeMille, Cecil Blount, 1881-1959. IX. West, Mae, 1893-   X.
Dafoe, Allan Ray, 1883-1943. XI. Dionne quintuplets. XII. Ortega,
Santos   XIII. War of the worlds (radio program) XIV. Ives, Burl,
1909-   XV. Robinson, Earl, 1910-   XVI. Temple, Shirley,
1928-   XVII. Earhart, Amelia, 1898-1937. XVIII. Lawrence,
Gertrude, 1901-1952. XIX. Cohan, George Michael, 1878-1942.
XX. Shaw, George Bernard, 1856-1950. XXI. Hitler, Adolf, 1889-
1945. XXII. Chamberlain, Neville, 1869-1940. XXIII. Roosevelt,
Franklin Delano, Pres. U. S., 1882-1945.

EARHART, AMELIA, 1898-1937

C1
H113   Whorf, Michael, 1933-
        The last flight; Amelia Earhart.
        1 tape cassette.   (The visual sounds of
Mike Whorf. History and heritage, H113)
        Originally presented on his radio program, Kaleidoscope,
WJR, Detroit.
        Duration: 35 min., 45 sec.
        The search for the world's most famous aviatrix has been
kept alive through the years since her disappearance - kept
alive by rumors, half-truths and wild speculations.

        L Earhart, Amelia, 1898-1937.   L Title.

Voice Lib.
M1656 East German radio.
bd.2   Go home, army, army, go home.   Recorded
on home-made metal disk, 1949.
        5 min.   phonotape (1 r.   7 1/2 i.p.s.)

        "Tramp, tramp, tramp" sung in German.

        I. Title.

C1   EATON, WILLIAM, 1764-1811
FA1   Whorf, Michael, 1933-
        William Eaton.
        1 tape cassette.   (The visual sounds of
Mike Whorf. The forgotten American, FA1)

         Originally presented on his radio program, Kaleidoscope,
WJR, Detroit.
         Duration: 11 min., 55 sec.
         Eaton, one-time consul at Tunis, led an expedition
against the Barbary States, landing the U. S. Marines on the
shores of Tripoli.

        L Eaton, William, 1764-1811.   L Title.

Voice Lib.
M1254 Eban, Abba Solomon, 1915-
bd.1   Address by Israel Foreign Minister Eban
at emergency session of U. N. General Assembly meeting in
New York, reviewing Middle East political and military
situations; rebutting the previous speech made by USSR
Premier Kosygin and blaming Russia for Israel-Arab tensions.
NBC-TV, June 19, 1967.
        1 reel (7 in.)   7 1/2 in. per sec. Phonotape.

        Speech incomplete.

        L Israel-Arab War, 1967-   - Diplomatic history.

Voice Lib.
M1466 Ebert, Friedrich, Pres. Germany, 1871-1925.
bd.18   Speaking to the National Assembly upon
assuming presidency of the German Republic.
Peteler, August 21, 1919.
        1 reel (7 in.)   7 1/2 in. per sec.
phonotape.

Voice Lib.
M1464   Ebart, Karl
bd.4   Monologue from "Faust" by Goethe, on the
         occasion of Goethe's birthday.   Peteler,
         1932.
            1 reel (7 in.)   7 1/2 in. per sec.
         phonotape.

            I. Goethe, Johann Wolfgang von, 1749-
         1832. /Faust.

CL   ECOLOGY
837   Whorf, Michael, 1933-
            The ugly land; ecology, part 1.
            1 tape cassette.   (The visual sounds of
         Mike Whorf.   Social, S37)
            Originally presented on his radio program, Kaleidoscope,
         WJR, Detroit.
            Duration: 50 min.
            This program deals with what was here on earth before and
         after man came, and how he unknowingly began the process of
         slow destruction which has caused his great dilemma of the present.

            L. Ecology.   .L. Title.

Voice Lib.
M1464   Eckener, Hugo, 1868-1954.
bd.5   Giving his ideas on dirigibles, their
         future, and the airship "Graf Zeppelin".
         Peteler, 1932.
            1 reel (7 in.)   7 1/2 in. per sec.
         phonotape.

            1. Air-ships.

Voice Lib. ECONOMIC ASSISTANCE, AMERICAN
M873   Truman, Harry S., Pres. U.S., 1884-1972.
bd.1   Address to joint session of Congress on
         European economic needs (Marshall Plan),
         Communist pressure on Czechoslovakia, Finland,
         Italy and Greece requiring economic help in
         order to help free nations recover; also
         requesting support for universal military
         training and temporary selective service.
         KDKA, March 17, 1948.
            1 reel (7 in.)   7 1/2 in. per sec. phonotape.

            L. Economic assistance, American.

Voice Lib.   ECOLOGY
M1639   Boulding, Kenneth Ewart, 1910-
            Cautious change, or how to prepare for
         the next fifty years.   WKAR-AM, February 17,
         1974.
            55 min.   phonotape (1 r.   7 1/2 i.p.s.)

            Includes question and answer period.

            1. Ecology.   2. Social sciences.

                Eddie Cantor Show (radio program)
Voice Lib.
M1025   Fields, W.C., 1879-1946.
bd.4   Excerpt from skit in "Eddie Cantor Show",
         with Martha Raye, Dick Powell, etc.   CBS
         Radio, 1930's.
            1 reel (7 in.)   7 1/2 in. per sec.
         phonotape.

            I. Raye, Martha, 1916-   II. Powell,
         Dick, 1904-1963. III. Eddie Cantor Show
         (radio program)

Voice Lib.   ECOLOGY
M1689   Nelson, Gaylord, 1916-
            Man, the endangered species; address at
         Michigan State University.   Introduction by
         President Wharton.   WKAR, January 19, 1970.
            41 min.   phonotape (1 r.   7 1/2 i.p.s.)

            1. Water - Pollution. 2. Ecology.
         I. Wharton, Clifton Reginald, 1926-

Voice Lib.
353   Eden, Anthony, 1897-
bd.6   Outbreak of Korean War; on Pres. Truman's
         courageous stand.   NBC, July, 1950.
            1 reel (7 in.)   7 1/2 in. per sec.
         phonotape.

            Original disc off-speed.

            1. Korean War, 1950-1953

Voice Lib.   ECOLOGY
M1697   Udall, Stewart L
bd.1   The environmental crisis, the crisis of
         survival; address at Michigan State Univer-
         sity.   WKAR, April 24, 1970.
            37 min.   phonotape (1 r.   7 1/2 i.p.s.)

            1. Ecology. 2. Man - Influence on nature.

         Edinburgh, Philip, 3d duke of, 1921-
             see
         Philip, duke of Edinburgh, 1921-

Voice Lib.
539   Edison, Thomas Alva, 1847-1931.
bd.6   "Liver Story", a humorous story related
by Edison. Introduced by Walter H. Miller.
National Vocarium, 1906.
1 reel (7 in.)   7 1/2 in. per sec.
phonotape.

I. Miller, Walter H   II. Title.

C1
SC26   Whorf, Michael, 1933-
The practical genius - Thomas Edison.
1 tape cassette.   (The visual sounds of
Mike Whorf. Science, SC26)
Originally presented on his radio program, Kaleidoscope,
WJR, Detroit.
Duration: 42 min.
Regarded as a failure in early life, Edison's personal strength and
dogged perseverance bore him above the hardships of life, and
established him as one of the world's greatest and most inventive
minds.

L. Edison, Thomas Alva, 1847-1931. L Title.

Voice Lib.
644   Edison, Thomas Alva, 1847-1931.
bd.4   Fiftieth anniversary of laying of Atlantic
cable; reviews history of electrical communication at opening of Electrical Exposition
at Madison Square Garden, New York City.
GRV (Edison Labs), 1908.
1 reel (7 in.)   7 1/2 in. per sec.
phonotape.

1. Cables, Submarine

EDUCATION
C1
S26   Whorf, Michael, 1933-
Oh, to be a kid again.
1 tape cassette.   (The visual sounds of
Mike Whorf. Social, S26)
Originally presented on his radio program, Kaleidoscope,
WJR, Detroit.
Duration: 28 min. , 30 sec.
An ode to the school, the child and the teacher in this
narrative which deals with a nostalgic look at some of our
experiences.

L Education. L Title.

Voice Lib.
642   Edison, Thomas Alva, 1847-1931.
bd.2   Let us not forget; reviews World War I
and calls for Americans not to forget.
Edison Laboratories, 1918.
1 reel (7 in.)   7 1/2 in. per sec.
phonotape.

1. European War, 1914-1918.

Voice Lib. EDUCATION, HIGHER
M1503 Higher education: who needs it? Hughes Rudd
in a one-hour documentary on employment
problems of college graduates.   CBS-TV,
May 26, 1972.
1 reel (7 in.)   7 1/2 in. per sec.
phonotape.

1. Education, Higher. 2. Labor supply.
I. Rudd, Hughes.

Voice Lib.
539   Edison, Thomas Alva, 1847-1931.
bd.7   First recording ever made: "Mary had a
little lamb". Thomas Edison Laboratories,
1927.
1 reel (7 in.)   7 1/2 in. per sec.
phonotape.

EDUCATION - PHILOSOPHY
Voice Lib.
M1079 Meiklejohn, Alexander, 1872-
Excerpts of reading from his unfinished
book on education in a free society, the
American liberal college, etc. Introductory
remarks by Dr. Scott Buchanan. CSDI,
January, 1963.
1 reel (7 in.)   7 1/2 in. per sec.
phonotape.

I. Buchanan, Scott Milross, 1895-1968.

EDISON, THOMAS ALVA, 1847-1931
Voice Lib.
629   Daniels, Josephus, 1862-1948.
bd.3   On Thomas A. Edison's contributions to
the U.S.; reviews Edison's accomplishments
and looks to future honors for Edison.
Edison Laboratories, 1915.
1 reel (7 in.)   7 1/2 in. per sec.
phonotape.

1. Edison, Thomas Alva, 1847-1931.

C1   Edvard Grieg
PWM22 Whorf, Michael, 1933-
Edvard Grieg.
1 tape cassette.   (The visual sounds of
Mike Whorf. Panorama; a world of music, PWM-22)
Originally presented on his radio program, Kaleidoscope,
WJR, Detroit.
Duration: 25 min.
The life and times of Edvard Grieg, including excerpts
of his music.

L. Grieg, Edvard Hagerup, 1843-1907. L Title.

Voice Lib.
500   Edward VIII, King of Gt. Brit., 1894-1972.
bd.2   On British sportsmanship. HMV, 1919.
        1 reel (7 in.)   7 1/2 in. per sec.
        phonotape.

                    Edward VIII, King of Gt. Brit., 1894-1972
Voice Lib.
572-   I can hear it now (radio program)
573   1933-1946. CBS, 1948.
bd.1   2 reels (7 in.)   7 1/2 in. per sec.
        phonotape.

    I. Murrow, Edward Roscoe, 1908-1965. II. LaGuardia, Fiorello
Henry, 1882-1947. III. Chamberlain, Neville, 1869-1949. IV.
Roosevelt, Franklin Delano, Pres. U. S., 1882-1945. V. Churchill,
Winston Leonard Spencer, 1874-1965. VI. Gaulle, Charles de,
Pres. France, 1890-1970. VII. Eisenhower, Dwight David, Pres. U. S.,
1890-1969. VIII. Willkie, Wendell Lewis, 1892-1944. IX. Martin,
Joseph William, 1884-1968. X. Elizabeth II, Queen of Great Britain,
1926-   XI. Margaret Rose, Princess of Gt. Brit., 1930-   XII.
Johnson, Hugh Samuel, 188? '42. XIII. Smith, Alfred Emanuel,
1873-1944. XIV. Lindbergh   arles Augustus, 1902-   XV. Davis,

(Continued on next card)

Voice Lib.
M928   Edward VIII, King of Great Britain, 1894-
bd.2   1972.
        Abdication and farewell message. BBC,
        December 11, 1926.
        1 reel (7 in.)   7 1/2 in. per sec.
        phonotape.

                    Edwards, Bob
Voice Lib.
M1654-   National Public Radio.
1655   Transcript of conversation between Nixon,
          Dean and Haldeman, read by Linda Wertheimer,
          Bob Edwards, and Mike Waters. NPR, May 1,
          1974.
          1 hr., 40 min.   phonotape (2 r.   7 1/2
          i.p.s.)

          1. Watergate Affair, 1972-
          I. Wertheimer, Linda. II. Edwards, Bob.
          III. Waters, Mike.

Voice Lib.
500   Edward VIII, King of Gt. Brit., 1894-1972.
bd.3   British Legion Festival of Empire and
       Remembrance; delivers "Prayer for the
       Fallen". Wartime choruses of "Tipperary",
       "Who's Your Lady Friend", "Pomp and Circum-
       stance", "Reveille", "Abide with Me", "God
       Save the King". BBC, November 11, 1933.
       1 reel (7 in.)   7 1/2 in. per sec.
       phonotape.

                    Edwards, Douglas
Voice Lib.
M1027   The world today: direct news reports from
bd.3   Belgian front; statement from SHAEF (Supreme
         Headquarters Allied Expeditionary Force);
         news of war in the Pacific discussed by CBS
         correspondents Robert Trout, Douglas Edwards,
         Richard C. Hottelet, and Ned Kalmer. CBS
         News, December 23, 1944.
         1 reel (7 in.)   7 1/2 in. per sec.   phonotape.

    I. Trout, Robert, 1908-   II. Edwards, Douglas
    III. Hottelet, Richard Curt   IV. Kalmer, Ned

Voice Lib.
M1490   Edward VIII, king of Great Britain, 1894-1972.
bd.4   Excerpt of statement before England's entry
         into World War II. BBC, 1939.
         1 reel (7 in.)   7 1/2 in. per sec.
         phonotape.

C1   EDWARDS, JONATHAN, 1703-1758
FA21   Whorf, Michael, 1933-
        Jonathan Edwards.
        1 tape cassette.   (The visual sounds of
        Mike Whorf. The forgotten American, FA21)

        Originally presented on his radio program, Kaleidoscope,
        WJR, Detroit.
        Duration: 12 min., 33 sec.
        Puritan clergyman and theologian, he exerted a permanent
        influence on our American heritage.

        I. Edwards, Jonathan, 1703-1758. I. Title.

            Edward VIII, king of Great Britain, 1894-1972
Voice Lib.
M618   Radio in the 1930's (Part I): a series of
bd.1-   excerpts from important broadcasts of the
14   1930's; a sample of radio of the period.
        NVL, April, 1964.
        1 reel (7 in.)   7 1/2 in. per sec.   phonotape.
        I. Shaw, George Bernard, 1856-1950. II. Crosby, Bing, 1901-
    III. Barkley, Alban William, 1877-1956. IV. Roosevelt, Franklin
    Delano, Pres. U. S., 1882-1945. V. Hoover, Herbert Clark, Pres.
    U. S., 1874-1964. VI. Long, Huey Pierce, 1893-1935. VII. Town-
    send, Francis Everett, 1867-1960. VIII. Coughlin, Charles Edward,
    1891-   IX. Rogers, Will, 1879-1935. X. Pius XII, Pope, 1876-
    1958. XI. Edward VIII, king of Great Britain, 1894-1972. XII.
    Barrymore, John, 1882-1942. XIII. Woollcott, Alexander, 1887-
    1943. XIV. Allen, Fred, 1894-1956, XV. Benchley, Robert Charles,
    1889-1945.

            EGYPT - FOREIGN RELATIONS - U.S.
Voice Lib.
M1745   al Sadat, Anwar.
bd.4   Sadat: an exclusive interview; an extensive
         interview with Walter Cronkite on the changes
         in U. S. policy regarding Egypt. CBS, June 21,
         1974.
         30 min.   phonotape (1 r.   7 1/2 i.p.s.)

         1. U. S. - For. rel. - Egypt. 2. Egypt -
         For. rel. - U. S. 3. Egypt - Pol. & govt. -
         1952-   I. Cronkite, Walter Leland,
         1916-

EGYPT - POLITICS AND GOVERNMENT - 1952-

Voice Lib.
M1745   al Sadat, Anwar.
bd.4   Sadat: an exclusive interview; an extensive
         interview with Walter Cronkite on the changes
         in U. S. policy regarding Egypt. CBS, June 21,
         1974.
             30 min.   phonotape (1 r.   7 1/2 i.p.s.)

             1. U. S. - For. rel. - Egypt. 2. Egypt -
         For. rel. - U. S.   Egypt - Pol. & govt. -
         1952-   I.   Cronkite, Walter Leland,
         1916-

Voice Lib.
M1800   Ehrlichman, John Daniel, 1925-
WG   Testimony before the Senate Committee
0724   investigating the Watergate Affair.
         Pacifica, July 24, 1973.
             292 min.   phonotape (4 r.   3 3/4 i.p.s.)
         (Watergate gavel to gavel, phase 1)

             1. Watergate Affair, 1972-

Voice Lib.
M1800   Ehrlichman, John Daniel, 1925-
WG   Testimony before the Senate Committee
0725   investigating the Watergate Affair.
         Pacifica, July 24, 1973.
             291 min.   phonotape (4 r.   3 3/4 i.p.s.)
         (Watergate gavel to gavel, phase 1)

             1. Watergate Affair, 1972-

Voice Lib.
M1800   Ehrlichman, John Daniel, 1925-
WG   Testimony before the Senate Committee
0726   investigating the Watergate Affair.
         Pacifica, July 26, 1973.
             317 min.   phonotape (4 r.   3 3/4 i.p.s.)
         (Watergate gavel to gavel, phase 1)

             1. Watergate Affair, 1972-

Voice Lib.
M1800   Ehrlichman, John Daniel, 1926-
WG   Testimony before the Senate Committee
0727   investigating the Watergate Affair.
         Pacifica, July 27, 1973.
             296 min.   phonotape (4 r.   3 3/4 i.p.s.)
         (Watergate gavel to gavel, phase 1)

             1. Watergate Affair, 1972-

Voice Lib.
M1800   Ehrlichman, John Daniel, 1925-
WG   Testimony before the Senate Committee
0730.01- investigating the Watergate Affair.
.02   Pacifica, July 30, 1973.
             258 min.   phonotape (4 r.   3 3/4 i.p.s.)
         (Watergate gavel to gavel, phase 1)

             1. Watergate Affair, 1972-

Voice Lib.
M258   Eichmann, Adolph, 1906-1962.
bd.15   Shortwave broadcast from Israel: his
         defense in court in his trial as an
         "enemy of humanity". New York, CBS,
         June 2, 1961.
             1 reel (7 in.)   7 1/2 in. per sec.
         phonotape.

Voice Lib.
M344   Eichmann, Adolph, 1906-1962.
bd.10   Eichmann trial; statements by Gideon
         Hausner, Robert Servatius and Eichmann
         concerning the verdict of the court and
         the death sentence. CBS, December 13,
         1961.
             1 reel (7 in.)   7 1/2 i.p.s.   phonotape.

             1. Eichmann, Adolph, 1906-196..
         1. Hausner, Gideon, 1915-   I. Servatius,
         Robert.

Voice Lib.
M953   Einstein, Albert, 1879-1955.
bd.1   Expounding his principles and philosophy
         of life. Peteler, 1932.
             1 reel (7 in.)   7 1/2 in. per sec.
         phonotape.

Voice Lib.
M1464   Einstein, Albert, 1879-1955.
bd.6   Speaking about his beliefs, in German.
         Peteler, 1932.
             1 reel (7 in.)   7 1/2 in. per sec.
         phonotape.

Voice Lib.
M389   Einstein, Albert, 1879-1955.
bd.5   Development of nuclear weapons; describes
        armament race between U.S. and Russia.
        Hearst Metrotone News, 1963.
          1 reel (7 in.)   7 1/2 in. per sec.
        phonotape.

          1. Atomic weapons

                Einstein, Albert, 1879-1955
Voice Lib.
M858-   Project '63 (Radio program)
859   Einstein and after: a one-hour documentary
        program written by John David Hamilton and
        produced by Harry Boyle as item 6 of a series.
        Project '63 program contains voice of Dr.
        Einstein and many of his distinguished friends
        and colleagues in an appraisal of his life and
        work; a biography in sound made possible through
        the assistance of Princeton, Harvard, Yale,
        Syracuse and Columbia Universities.   CBC, 1963.
          2 reels (7 in.) 7 1/2 in. per sec. phonotape.
          L. Einstein, Albert, 1879-1955. L. Einstein, Albert, 1879-1955.

                EINSTEIN, ALBERT, 1878-1955
Voice Lib.
M723   Columbia Broadcasting System, Inc.
bd.2   Memorial broadcast at the death of
        Albert Einstein, with Walter Cronkite.
        CBS, April 18, 1955.
          15 min., 30 sec.   phonotape (1 r.
        7 1/2 i.p.s.)

          1. Einstein, Albert, 1878-1955.
        I. Cronkite, Walter Leland, 1916-

                EINSTEIN, ALBERT, 1879-1955
C1
SC8   Whorf, Michael, 1933-
          The great Dr. Einstein.
          1 tape cassette.   (The visual sounds of
        Mike Whorf. Science, SC8)

          Originally presented on his radio program, Kaleidoscope,
        WJR, Detroit.
          Duration: 29 min., 30 sec.
          His life in Europe, his coming to America and the theory
        that changed the world is told in this biography of Albert Einstein.

          L. Einstein, Albert, 1879-1955. L. Title.

Voice Lib.
M1407   Eisenhower, David, 1949-
          Conversation on "Merv Griffin Show" between
        Merv, Merriman Smith, David Eisenhower, Tricia
        Nixon. Various anecdotes about Merriman Smith's
        career as a White House correspondent during
        four administrations.   CBS-TV, November 23, 1969.
          1 reel (7 in.)   7 1/2 in. per sec.
        phonotape.

          I. Griffin, Mervyn Edward, 1925-   II.
        Smith, Merriman   III. Cox, Patricia
        (Nixon) 1947-

Voice Lib.   Eisele, Donn F   1930-
M1328   Apollo 7 (space flight): description of
bd.2   launching of Apollo 7 spacecraft, morning
        of October 11, 1968, and comments by various
        broadcasters, including Walter Cronkite.
        Description includes countdown and take-off;
        remarks by astronauts.   CBS TV, October 11,
        1968.
          1 reel (7 in.) 7 1/2 in. per sec. phonotape.
          L. Project Apollo. 2. Eisele, Donn F   1930-   3. Cunning-
        ham, R   Walter, 1932-   4. Schirra, Walter Marty, 1923-
        L. Eisele, Donn F   1930- II. Cunningham, R   Walter,
        1932-   III. Schirra, Walter Marty, 1923-   IV. Cronkite,
        Walter Leland, 1916-

Voice Lib.
350   Eisenhower, Dwight David, Pres. U.S., 1890-1969.
bd.5   Message to people of Western Europe
        on D-Day Invasion (incomplete).   CBS,
        June 6, 1944.
          1 reel (7 in.)   7 1/2 in. per sec.
        phonotape.

          1. World War, 1939-1945 - Campaigns -
        Normandy.

Voice Lib.
350   Eisenhower, Dwight David, Pres. U.S., 1890-1969.
bd.6   Salute to the troops under his command
        on conclusion of the war in Europe.   CBS,
        June, 1945.
          1 reel (7 in.)   7 1/2 in. per sec.
        phonotape.

Voice Lib.
M928   Eisenhower, Dwight David, Pres. U.S., 1890-
bd.3   1969.
          Appreciation of the endowment of a chair at
        Columbia University by Samuel Bronfman and
        congratulations upon Mr. Bronfman's 60th
        birthday.   GRV, March 3, 1951.
          1 reel (7 in.)   7 1/2 in. per sec.
        phonotape.

Voice Lib.
M730   Eisenhower, Dwight David, Pres. U.S., 1890-
bd.10   1969.
          Acceptance speech at the 1952 Republican
        National Convention in Chicago.   CBS,
        July 11, 1952.
          1 reel (7 in.)   7 1/2 in. per sec.
        phonotape.

Voice Lib.
184   Eisenhower, Dwight David, Pres U.S., 1890-1969.
bd.1   Acceptance speech, Republican convention.
       WJR, July 11, 1952.
           1 reel (7 in.)   7 1/2 in. per sec.
       phonotape.

Voice Lib.
198-   Eisenhower, Dwight David, Pres. U.S., 1890-1969.
199   State of the Union address.   Detroit,
       WJR, February 2, 1953.
           2 reels (7 in.)   7 1/2 in. per sec.
       phonotape.

Voice Lib.
209   Eisenhower, Dwight David, Pres. U.S., 1890-1969.
bd.5   Accepting nomination for Presidency
       at 1952 convention, being an excerpt from
       acceptance speech at Republican Convention
       in Chicago.   CBS, 1952.
           1 reel (7 in.)   7 1/2 in. per sec.
       phonotape.

Voice Lib.
127   Eisenhower, Dwight David, Pres. U.S., 1890-1969.
bd.9   A proclamation; an eulogy of Theodore
       Roosevelt.   Recorded on location, June 14,
       1953.
           1 reel (7 in.)   7 1/2 in. per sec.
       phonotape.

           1. Roosevelt, Theodore, Pres. U.S., 1858-
       1919.

Voice Lib.
M926   Eisenhower, Dwight David, Pres. U. S., 1890-
bd.2   1969.
           Pre-election address to public at end of
       1952 campaign.   CBS, November, 1952.
           1 reel (7 in.)   7 1/2 in. per sec.
       phonotape.

Voice Lib.
M715   Eisenhower, Dwight David, Pres. U.S., 1890-
bd.9   1969.
           Statement upon his return from summit
       conference at Geneva.   1955.
           1 reel (7 in.)   7 1/2 in. per sec.
       phonotape.

Voice Lib.
187   Eisenhower, Dwight David, Pres. U.S., 1890-1965.
       Inaugural address. WJR, January 20, 1953.
           1 reel (7 in.)   7 1/2 in. per sec.
       phonotape.

Voice Lib.
M930   Eisenhower, Dwight David, Pres. U.S., 1890-
bd.2   1969.
           News conference held at San Francisco at
       the re-nomination of Richard M. Nixon.
       CBS, September 13, 1956.
           1 reel (7 in.)   7 1/2 in. per sec.
       phonotape.

           1. Nixon, Richard Milhous, Pres. U.S., 1913-

Voice Lib.
186   Eisenhower, Dwight David, Pres. U.S., 1890-
           1969.
           Inauguration ceremonies of President
       Eisenhower and Vice-President Nixon.   WJR,
       January 20, 1953.
           1 reel (7 in.)   7 1/2 in. per sec.
       phonotape.

           I. Nixon, Richard Milhous, Pres. U.S., 1913-

Voice Lib.
M931   Eisenhower, Dwight David, Pres. U.S., 1890-
bd.1   1969.
           Address to the nation reviewing the progress
       of Republican administration during the
       1956 presidential campaign, emanating from
       Washington, D.C.   CBS, September 19, 1956.
           1 reel (7 in.)   7 1/2 in. per sec.
       phonotape.

Voice Lib.
M926   Eisenhower, Dwight David, Pres. U.S., 1890-
bd.3   1969.
           Final pre-election speech to American
       voters, at conclusion of Republican pres-
       idential campaign of 1956. WJR, 1956.
           1 reel (7 in.)   7 1/2 in. per sec.
       phonotape.

Voice Lib.
M345   Eisenhower, Dwight David, Pres. U.S., 1890-1969.
bd.2   Excerpt from news conference: Secretary
       Benson and the farm problem. CBS,
       February 26, 1958.
           1 reel (7 in.)   7 1/2 i.p.s.   phonotape.

           1. Benson, Ezra Taft, 1899-

Voice Lib.
243   Eisenhower, Dwight David, Pres. U.S., 1890-1969.
bd.2   The "clean bomb;" press conference.
       CBS Radio, June 26, 1957.
           1 reel (7 in.)   7 1/2 in. per sec.
       phonotape.

Voice Lib.
345   Eisenhower, Dwight David, Pres. U.S., 1890-1969.
bd.7   Excerpts of speech against new government
       work projects to aid recession. CBS,
       March 18, 1958.
           1 reel (7 in.)   7 1/2 in. per sec.
       phonotape.

Voice Lib.
243   Eisenhower, Dwight David, Pres. U.S., 1890-1969.
bd.6   Remarks on amending Sec. 407, the
       Civil Rights Bill. CBS, July 31, 1957.
           1 reel (7 in.)   7 1/2 in. per sec.
       phonotape.

           1. Negroes - Civil rights

Voice Lib.
M345   Eisenhower, Dwight David, Pres. U.S., 1890-
          1969.
           Discussion, with scientists, of Explorer
       III imperfect orbit and space exploration.
       CBS, March 26, 1958.
           1 reel (7 in.)   7 1/2 i.p.s.   phonotape.

           1. Space flight.

Voice Lib.
256   Eisenhower, Dwight David, Pres. U.S., 1890-1969.
bd.8   Speech while revisiting SHAPE Headquarters.
       CBS News, December 17, 1957.
           1 reel (7 in.)   7 1/2 in. per sec.
       phonotape.

Voice Lib.
345   Eisenhower, Dwight David, Pres. U.S., 1890-1969.
bd.9   Excerpt of statement on recession.
       CBS, March 26, 1958.
           1 reel (7 in.)   7 1/2 in. per sec.
       phonotape.

Voice Lib.
345   Eisenhower, Dwight David, Pres. U.S., 1890-1969.
bd.1   Excerpt from news conference: confidence
       in the country during the recession. CBS,
       February 24, 1958.
           1 reel (7 in.)   7 1/2 in. per sec.
       phonotape.

Voice Lib.
M715   Eisenhower, Dwight David, Pres. U.S., 1890-
bd.13   1969.
           Excerpt of statement on intervention by
       U.S. troops during internal strife in
       Lebanon. July 15, 1958.
           1 reel (7 in.)   7 1/2 in. per sec.
       phonotape.

           1. Lebanon - History - Intervention, 1958.

Voice Lib.
207 Eisenhower, Dwight David, Pres. U.S., 1890-1965.
bd.2   Farewell address to the nation, reviewing
his eight years as president. Detroit,
WJR, January 17, 1961.
    1 reel (7 in.) 7 1/2 in. per sec.
phonotape.

Voice Lib.
244- Eisenhower, Dwight David, Pres. U.S., 1890-1969.
247   Remarks on the Presidency, with Walter
Cronkite. CBS-TV, September 12-November 26,
1961.
    4 reels (7 in.) 7 1/2 in. per sec.
phonotape.

    I. Cronkite, Walter Leland, 1916-

Voice Lib.
351 Eisenhower, Dwight David, Pres. U.S., 1890-1969.
bd.4   Excerpts of speech in Los Angeles on
economy of U.S., business monopoly, legal
review of world laws. CBS, February 1,
1962.
    1 reel (7 in.) 7 1/2 in. per sec.
phonotape.

    1. U.S. - Econ. condit.

Eisenhower, Dwight David, Pres. U.S.,
Voice Lib. 1890-1969
M622 Radio in the 1940's (Part III): a series of
bd.1-   excerpts from important broadcasts of the 1940's; a sample
bd.15   of radio of the period. NVL, April, 1964.
    1 reel (7 in.) 7 1/2 in. per sec. phonotape.
    I. Radio programs. I. Miller, Alton Glenn, 1909(?)-1944. II.
Diles, Ken   III. Wilson, Donald Harlow, 1900-   IV.
Livingstone, Mary   V. Benny, Jack, 1894-   VI. Harris,
Phil   VII. Merman, Ethel, 1909-   VIII. Smith, "Wonderful"
IX. Bennett, Richard Dyer   X. Louis, Joe, 1914-   XI.
Eisenhower, Dwight David, Pres. U.S., 1890-1969. XII. MacArthur,
Douglas, 1880-1964. XIII. Romulo, Carlos Pena, 1899-   XIV.
Welles, Orson, 1915-   XV. Jackson, Robert Houghwout, 1892-1954.
XVI. LaGuardia, Fiorello Henry, 1882-1945. XVII. Nehru, Jawa-
harlal, 1889-1964. XVIII. Gandhi, Mohandas Karamchand, 1869-1948.

Voice Lib.
M1371 Eisenhower, Dwight David, Pres. U.S., 1890-
bd.1   1969.
    Recollections twenty years after VE-Day.
CBS-TV, 1964.
    1 reel (7 in.) 7 1/2 in. per sec.
phonotape.

Voice Lib.
650- Eisenhower, Dwight David, Pres. U.S., 1890-1969.
651   D-Day plus 20 years (CBS Reports); discussion
of strategy and procedures and preparation for
invasion of Nazi-occupied France on June 6, 1944
by former Commander of Allied Expeditionary
Forces with Walter Cronkite. CBS, June 6, 1964.
    2 reels (7 in.) 7 1/2 in. per sec.
phonotape.

    1. World War, 1939-1945 - Campaigns -
Normandy. I. Cronkite, Walter Leland, 1916-

Voice Lib.
M1370 Eisenhower, Dwight David, Pres. U.S., 1890-
bd.2   1969.
    A portion of an interview in London between
Walter Cronkite, CBS, and Gen. Eisenhower,
pertaining to the Normandy invasion on its
20th anniversary. CBS, June 6, 1964.
    1 reel (7 in.) 7 1/2 in. per sec.
phonotape.

    I. Cronkite, Walter Leland, 1916-

Voice Lib.
M722- Eisenhower, Dwight David, Pres. U.S., 1890-
723   1969.
bd.1   Winston S. Churchill discussed by Walter
Cronkite and Dwight D. Eisenhower, including
Eisenhower's association with Churchill
during and after the war. CBS, January 25,
1965.
    2 reels (7 in.) 7 1/2 in. per sec.
phonotape.

    1. Churchill, Winston Leonard Spencer, 1874-
1965. I. Cronkite, Walter Leland, 1916-

Eisenhower, Dwight David, Pres. U.S.,
1890-1969
Voice Lib.
M1031 Discussion about Winston Churchill's ability
in military affairs, between Alistair Cooke
and General Dwight Eisenhower, heard at his
home in Gettysburg, Pennsylvania; including
recording of General George C. Marshall's
opinion about the strategic value of U.S.
troops conquering Berlin. "Studio 67"
production, ABC-TV, January 26, 1967.
    1 reel (7 in.) 7 1/2 in. per sec. phonotape.
    I. Churchill, Winston Leonard Spencer, 1874-1965. I.
Cooke, Alistair, 1908-   II. Eisenhower, Dwight David, Pres.
U.S., 1890-1969.

Voice Lib.
M1277 Eisenhower, Dwight David, Pres. U.S., 1890-
1969.
    Miss Patricia Marks interviews Eisenhower
on occasion of art exhibition at Gallery of
Modern Art of paintings by Ike. The general,
at age 77, reviews and comments on incidents
in his life. NET, June, 1967.
    1 reel (7 in.) 7 1/2 in. per sec.
phonotape.

    I. Marks, Patricia 1. Eisenhower, Dwight
David, Pres. U.S., 1890-1969

Voice Lib.
M1286 Eisenhower, Dwight David, Pres. U.S., 1890-1969.
bd.1   Conversation by Harry Reasoner with General
        Dwight D. Eisenhower and General Omar N.
        Bradley at Eisenhower's office in Gettysburg,
        Pennsylvania, about the U.S. military partici-
        pation in Vietnam and the conduct of it.
        CBS-TV, November 28, 1967.
            1 reel (7 in.)   7 1/2 in. per sec.
        phonotape.
            I. Reasoner, Harry, 1923-   II. Bradley,
        Omar Nelson, 1893-   1. Vietnamese
        Conflict, 1961-

Voice Lib.
M1370 Eisenhower, Dwight David, Pres. U.S., 1890-
bd.1   1969.
        Short quotations and statements by Gen.
        Eisenhower.   ABC, March, 1969.
            1 reel (7 in.)   7 1/2 in. per sec.
        phonotape.

                Eisenhower, Dwight David, Pres. U.S.,
Voice Lib.   1890-1969
M308 Columbia Broadcasting System, inc.
bd.2   Assassination: announcement of Kennedy's
        death by CBS commentator Walter Cronkite; on
        film of assassination, search for suspect,
        future events and Johnson's oath; announcement
        of shooting of Dallas policeman and arrest
        of Oswald; comments by Eisenhower and Truman.
        CBS, November 22, 1963.
            1 reel (7 in.)   7 1/2 in. per sec.
        phonotape.
            L. Kennedy, John Fitzgerald, Pres. U.S., 1917-1963 - Assassination.
        L. Cronkite, Walter Leland, 1916-   II. Eisenhower, Dwight
        David, Pres. U.S., 1890-1969.   III. Truman, Harry S. Pres. U.S.,
        1884-1972.

        Eisenhower, Dwight David, Pres. U.S., 1890-
Voice Lib. 1969
M1279 Downs, Hugh Malcolm, 1921-
        Today show interview pertaining to new
        book, "At Ease - Stories I Tell My Friends";
        recollections, going through Eisenhower's
        entire career.   NBC-TV, July 11, 1967.
            1 reel (7 in.)   7 1/2 in. per sec.
        phonotape.

            I. Eisenhower, Dwight David, Pres. U.S.,
        1890-1969.

            Eisenhower, Dwight David, Pres. U.S.,
Voice Lib.   1890-1969
572- I can hear it now (radio program)
573   1933-1946.   CBS, 1948.
bd.1   2 reels (7 in.)   7 1/2 in. per sec.
        phonotape.
            L. Murrow, Edward Roscoe, 1908-1965. II. LaGuardia, Fiorello
        Henry, 1882-1947. III. Chamberlain, Neville, 1869-1949. IV.
        Roosevelt, Franklin Delano, Pres. U.S., 1882-1945. V. Churchill,
        Winston Leonard Spencer, 1874-1965. VI. Gaulle, Charles de,
        Pres. France, 1890-1970. VII. Eisenhower, Dwight David, Pres. U.S.,
        1890-1969. VIII. Willkie, Wendell Lewis, 1892-1944. IX. Martin,
        Joseph William, 1884-1968. X. Elizabeth II, Queen of Great Britain,
        1926-   XI. Margaret Rose, Princess of Gt. Brit., 1930-   XII.
        Johnson, Hugh Samuel, 1882-1942. XIII. Smith, Alfred Emanuel,
        1873-1944. XIV. Lindbergh, Charles Augustus, 1902-   XV. Davis,
            (Continued on next card)

        Eisenhower, Dwight David, Pres. U.S., 1890-
            1969
Voice Lib.
573   I can hear it now (radio program)
bd.2-   1945-1949.   CBS, 1950?
574   2 reels (7 in.)   7 1/2 in. per sec.
bd.1   phonotape.
            L. Murrow, Edward Roscoe, 1908-1965. II. Nehru, Jawaharlal,
        1889-1964. III. Philip, duke of Edinburgh, 1921- IV. Elizabeth II,
        Queen of Great Britain, 1926-   V. Ferguson, Homer, 1889-   VI.
        Hughes, Howard Robard, 1905- VII. Marshall, George Catlett,
        1880- VIII. Ruth, George Herman, 1895-1948. IX. Lilienthal,
        David Eli, 1899- X. Trout, Robert, 1908-   XI. Gage, Arthur.
        XII. Jackson, Robert Houghwout, 1892-1954. XIII. Gromyko, Ana-
        tolii Andreevich, 1908-   XIV. Baruch, Bernard Mannes, 1870-
        1965. XV. Churchill, Win- - Leonard Spencer, 1874-1965. XVI.
        Winchell, Walter, 1897-19   XVII. Davis, Elmer Holmes, 1890-
            (Continued on next card)

Voice Lib.   Eisenhower, Dwight David, Pres. U.S., 1890-1969
383   I can hear it now (radio program)
        CBS, February 9, 1951.
            1 reel (7 in.)   7 1/2 in. per sec.
        phonotape.
            L. Wilson, Charles Edward, 1886-1972. II. Gabrielson, Guy
        George, 1891-   III. Taft, Robert Alphonso, 1889-1953. IV.
        Martin, Joseph William, 1884-1965. V. McCarthy, Joseph
        Raymond, 1909-1957. VI. Benton, William Burnett, 1900-1973.
        VII. Malone, George Wilson, 1890-1961. VIII. Capehart, Homer
        Earl, 1897-   IX. Eisenhower, Dwight David, Pres. U.S., 1890-
        1969. X. Lee, J   V   XI. Hodge, John Reed, 1893-
        1963. XII. Overton, Watkins   XIII. DiSalle, Michael
        Vincent, 1908-   XIV. Boyce, Eddy   XV. Conklin, Ed
        XVI. Collins, Joseph Lawton, 1896-

        Eisenhower, Dwight David, Pres. U. S.,
Voice Lib.   1890-1969
M1490 Republican Party. National Convention, 25th,
bd.5   Chicago, 1952.
        Description of proceedings at Republican
        National Convention in Chicago, 1952
        (described by commentators George Hicks and
        H.V. Kaltenborn). Includes statements by
        Robert A. Taft and Dwight D. Eisenhower.
        Convention unanimously nominates Eisenhower.
        CBS Radio, 1952.
            1 reel (7 in.)   7 1/2 in. per sec.
        phonotape.

Voice Lib. Eisenhower, Dwight David, Pres. U.S., 1890-
            1969
M725 Republican Party. National Convention.
bd.1   25th, Chicago, 1952.
        Film of excerpts of the Republican National
        Convention in 1952. Clash between Taft and
        Eisenhower forces. Includes speeches by Gen.
        MacArthur, Gen. Eisenhower, Ex-Pres. Hoover,
        Sen. Dirksen, etc.   CBS, 1952.
            1 reel (7 in.)   7 1/2 in. per sec.
        phonotape.
            L. MacArthur, Douglas, 1880-1964. II. Eisenhower, Dwight
        David, Pres. U.S., 1890-1969. III. Hoover, Herbert Clark, Pres.
        U.S., 1874-1964. IV. Dirksen, Everett McKinley, 1896-1969.

        Eisenhower, Dwight David, Pres. U.S.,
            1890-1969
Voice Lib.
238   Trout, Robert, 1908-
bd.1   Description of arrival of Nikita Khrushchev
        in U.S., with welcoming address by President
        Eisenhower and response by Khrushchev.
            1 reel (7 in.)   7 1/2 in. per sec.
        phonotape.

            1. Khrushchev, Nikita Sergeevich, 1894-1971.
        I. Eisenhower, Dwight David, Pres. U.S., 1890-
        1969.

Eisenhower, Dwight David, Pres. U.S.,
Voice Lib. 1890-1969
M1033 Voice of America.
Twentieth anniversary program of Voice of
America broadcasts narrated by Henry Fonda,
and including the voices of Carl Sandburg,
Danny Kaye, Jawaharlal Nehru, Franklin D.
Roosevelt, Charles Malik, Arnold Toynbee,
William Faulkner, Harry S.Truman, Dwight D.
Eisenhower, Helen Hayes, Dag Hammarskjöld,
Winston Churchill, and John F. Kennedy.
Voice of America, 1963.
1 reel (7 in.) 7 1/2 in. per sec.
phonotape.
(Continued on next card)

Eisenhower, Dwight David, Pres. U.S., 1890-
Voice Lib. 1969
M1033 Voice of America. Twentieth anniversary
program... 1963. (Card 2)

L Fonda, Henry Jaynes, 1905-   II. Sandburg, Carl,
1878-1967. III. Kaye, Danny, 1913-   IV. Nehru, Jawaharlal,
1889-1964. V. Roosevelt, Franklin Delano, Pres. U.S., 1882-
1945. VI. Malik, Charles Habib, 1906-   VII. Toynbee,
Arnold Joseph, 1889-   VIII. Faulkner, William, 1897-1962.
IX. Truman, Harry S, Pres. U.S., 1884-1972. X. Eisenhower,
Dwight David, Pres. U.S., 1890-1969. XI. Hayes, Helen,
1900-   XII. Hammarskjöld, Dag, 1905-1961. XIII. Churchill,
Winston Leonard Spencer, 1874-1965. XIV. Kennedy, John
Fitzgerald, Pres. U.S., 1917-1963.

EISENHOWER, DWIGHT DAVID, PRES. U.S.,
1890-1969
Voice Lib.
M350 Adenauer, Konrad, 1876-1967.
bd.1 Tribute to Eisenhower on assuming the
Presidency. CBS, January, 1953.
1 reel (7 in.) 7 1/2 i.p.s. phonotape.

1. Eisenhower, Dwight David, Pres. U.S.,
1890-1969.

EISENHOWER, DWIGHT DAVID, PRES. U.S.,
1890-1969
Voice Lib.
M742 Dillon, Clarence Douglas, 1909-
bd.7 Statement on Peiping activities, Khrushchev's
agreement to negotiate at Camp David with
President Eisenhower. CBS, 1959.
1 reel (7 in.) 7 1/2 in. per sec.
phonotape.

1. Khruschev, Nikita Sergeevich, 1894-1971.
2. Eisenhower, Dwight David, Pres U.S., 1890-
1969.

Voice Lib. EISENHOWER, DWIGHT DAVID, PRES. U.S., 1890-1969
M1371 Funeral ceremonies of General of the Army Dwight David
bd. 2 Eisenhower, beginning with the casket being carried from
the National Cathedral to the U.S. Capitol in Washington,
D.C.; President Nixon's eulogy at the Capitol rotunda;
followed by reconveying the casket to the National Cathedral
where prayers and services are heard. CBS-TV, March 30, 1969.
1 reel (7 in.) 7 1/2 in. per sec. phonotape.

L. Eisenhower, Dwight David, Pres. U.S., 1890-1969.
L. Nixon, Richard Milhous, Pres. U.S., 1913-

EISENHOWER, DWIGHT DAVID, PRES. U.S.,
1890-1969
Voice Lib.
M256 Hagerty, James C   1909-
bd.7 Eisenhower's medical examination. CBS
News, December 10, 1957.
1 reel (7 in.) 7 1/2 in. per sec.
phonotape.

EISENHOWER, DWIGHT DAVID, PRES. U.S.,
1890-1969
Voice Lib.
M350 Ismay, Hastings Lionel Ismay, baron, 1887-
bd.4 Tribute to Eisenhower on assuming the
Presidency. CBS, January, 1953.
1 reel (7 in.) 7 1/2 i.p.s. phonotape.

1. Eisenhower, Dwight David, Pres. U.S.,
1890-1969.

EISENHOWER, DWIGHT DAVID, PRES. U.S.,
1890-1969
Voice Lib.
M1369 "The men who covered Ike". CBS-TV Face the Nation program,
bd. 2 discussing the late General Dwight David Eisenhower, by the
newspaper and TV correspondents. UPI, Merriman Smith;
Newsweek, Kenneth Crawford; Chicago Daily News, Peter
Lisager; AP, Jack Bell; CBS, George Herman, acting as emcee.
CBS-TV, March 30, 1969.
1 reel (7 in.) 7 1/2 i.p.s. phonotape.

L. Eisenhower, Dwight David, Pres. U.S., 1890-1969.
L. Smith, Merriman. II. Crawford, Kenneth. III. Lisager,
Peter. IV. Bell, Jack. V. Herman, George.

EISENHOWER, DWIGHT DAVID, PRES. U.S.,
1890-1969
Voice Lib.
M350 Meyer, René
bd.2 Tribute to Eisenhower on assuming the
Presidency. CBS, January, 1953.
1 reel (7 in.) 7 1/2 i.p.s. phonotape.

1. Eisenhower, Dwight David, Pres. U.S.,
1890-1969.

EISENHOWER, DWIGHT DAVID, PRES. U.S.,
1890-1969
Voice Lib.
256 Nixon, Richard Milhous, Pres. U.S., 1913-
bd.7 Medical report on Ike's health. CBS News,
November 26 and 27, 1957.
1 reel (7 in.) 7 1/2 in. per sec.
phonotape.

1. Eisenhower, Dwight David, Pres. U.S.,
1890-1969.

EISENHOWER, DWIGHT DAVID, PRES. U.S.,
1890-1969
Voice Lib.
M350   Pleven, René, 1901-
bd.3   Tribute to Eisenhower on assuming the
        Presidency. CBS, January, 1953.
        1 reel (7 in.)   7 1/2 i.p.s.   phonotape.

        1. Eisenhower, Dwight David, Pres. U.S.,
        1890-1969.

EISENHOWER, DWIGHT DAVID, PRES. U.S.,
1890-1969
Voice Lib.
M1368   Some friends of General Eisenhower (TV program)
        CBS-TV special recalling anecdotes about
        General Eisenhower by some of his friends:
        Bob Hope, Kevin McCann, General Omar Bradley,
        Robert B. Anderson, General Alfred Gruenther,
        with Walter Cronkite acting as emcee.   CBS-TV,
        March 29, 1969.
        1 reel (7 in.)   7 1/2 in. per sec.

        I. Eisenhower, Dwight David, Pres. U.S., 1890-1969. I.
        Hope, Bob, 1903-   II. McCann, Kevin   III. Bradley, Omar
        Nelson, 1893-   IV. Anderson, Robert Bernard, 1910-   V.
        Gruenther, Alfred Maximilian, 1899-   VI. Cronkite, Walter
        Leland, 1916-

EISENHOWER, DWIGHT DAVID, PRES. U.S.,
1890-1969
C1
H2   Whorf, Michael, 1933-
        The general.
        1 tape cassette.   (The visual sounds of
        Mike Whorf. History and heritage, H2)

        Originally presented on his radio program, Kaleidoscope,
        WJR, Detroit.
        Duration: 30 min., 30 sec.
        The life and times of Dwight Eisenhower, from his boyhood to
        his nomination as president.

        I. Eisenhower, Dwight David, Pres. U.S., 1890-1969.
        I. Title.

Voice Lib.
M1681   Eisenhower, Julie Nixon, 1948-
bd.1   Defense of father. CBS, May 11, 1974.
        1 min.   phonotape (1 r.   7 1/2 i.p.s.)

        1. Nixon, Richard Milhous, Pres. U.S.,
        1913-

Voice Lib.   Eldridge, Florence, 1901-
M310   American Broadcasting Company.
        Tribute to President John Fitzgerald Kennedy
        from the arts. Fredric March emcees; Jerome
        Hines sings "Worship of God and Nature" by
        Beethoven; Florence Eldridge recites "When
        lilacs last in the door-yard bloom'd" by Walt
        Whitman; Marian Anderson in two songs. Includes
        Charlton Heston, Sidney Blackmer, Isaac Stern,
        Nathan Milstein, Christopher Plummer, Albert
        Finney. ABC, November 24, 1963.
        35 min.   phonotape (7 in.   7 1/2 i.p.s.)

        (Continued on next card)

Eldridge, Roy, 1911-
Voice Lib.
M621   Radio in the 1940's (Part II): a series of
bd.1-   excerpts from important broadcasts of the
12   1940's; a sample of radio of the period.
        NVL, April, 1964.
        1 reel (7 in.)   7 1/2 in. per sec.   phonotape.
        I. Daly, John Charles, 1914-   II. Hall, Josef Washington,
        1894-   III. Shirer, William Lawrence, 1904-   IV. Roosevelt,
        Eleanor (Roosevelt) 1884-1962. V. Roosevelt, Franklin Delano,
        Pres. U.S., 1882-1945. VI. Churchill, Winston Leonard Spencer,
        1874-1965. VII. Wainwright, Jonathan Mayhew, 1883-1953. VIII.
        Cantor, Eddie, 1893-1964. IX. Sinatra, Francis Albert, 1917-
        X. Hope, Bob, 1903-   XI. Crosby, Bing, 1901-   XII. Shore,
        Dinah, 1917(?)-   XIII. Bergen, Edgar, 1903-   XIV. Armstrong,
        Louis, 1900-1971. XV. Eldridge, Roy, 1911-

ELECTIONS
Voice Lib.
M1585   Hays, Wayne L
bd.1   Money - politics. WKAR-AM, February 27,
        1974.
        15 min.   phonotape (1 r.   7 1/2 in. per sec.)

        1. Elections. 2. Campaign funds.
        3. Saxbe, William B., 1916-

ELECTIONS - MICHIGAN
Voice Lib.
M1605   Winograd, Morley
bd.2   Off the record. With Tim Skubick, Tom
        Greene, Gary Schuster, and Hugh Morgan.
        WKAR-TV, February 15, 1974.
        17 min.   phonotape (1 r.   7 1/2 in. per sec.)

        1. Democratic Party. Michigan. 2. Elections -
        Michigan. 3. Youngblood, Charles N., 1932-
        I. Skubick, Tim. II. Greene, Tom. III. Schuster,
        Gary. IV. Morgan, Hugh.

Voice Lib.   Eliot, George Fielding, 1894-1971
M1025   Radio news reports concerning U.S. and Allied
bd.3   landings on North Africa, November 7, 1942;
        followed by military analysis by Major George
        Fielding Eliot. CBS Radio, November 7, 1942.
        1 reel (7 in.)   7 1/2 in. per sec.
        phonotape.

        1. World War, 1939-1945.   I. Eliot, George
        Fielding, 1894-1971.

Voice Lib.
M1224   Eliot, Thomas Stearns, 1888-1965.
bd.2-   Various poems read by Eliot, including
1225   "The Love Song of J. Alfred Prufrock".
bd.1   Bergman.
        2 reels (7 in.)   7 1/2 in. per sec.
        phonotape.

        I. Title: The love song of J. Alfred
        Prufrock.

Voice Lib.
M849   Elizabeth II, Queen of Great Britain, 1926-
bd.2   Elizabeth speaking from London to the
          women of France during time of peril.
          EDST, June 14, 1940.
          1 reel (7 in.)   7 1/2 in. per sec.
          phonotape.

          In French.

Voice Lib.
266   Elizabeth II, Queen of Great Britain, 1926-
bd.1   Speech at Pilgrims' Dinner; speech and
          introduction of the president of the Pilgrims
          and closing speech by Lewis Douglas.   CBS,
          October 21, 1957.
          1 reel (7 in.)   7 1/2 in. per sec.
          phonotape.

          I. Douglas, Lewis Williams, 1894-

Voice Lib.
M740   Elizabeth II, Queen of Great Britain, 1926-
bd.7   Excerpt from "The Children's Hour"; a
          radio broadcast from London to children,
          sympathizing with them being sent from their
          country away from their parents during the
          Blitz.   BBC, 1940.
          1 reel (7 in.)   7 1/2 in. per sec.
          phonotape.

            Elizabeth II, Queen of Great Britain,
              1926-
Voice Lib.
572-   I can hear it now (radio program)
573   1933-1946.   CBS, 1948.
bd.1   2 reels (7 in.)   7 1/2 in. per sec.
          phonotape.
          I. Murrow, Edward Roscoe, 1908-1965. II. LaGuardia, Fiorello
          Henry, 1882-1947. III. Chamberlain, Neville, 1869-1949. IV.
          Roosevelt, Franklin Delano, Pres. U. S., 1882-1945. V. Churchill,
          Winston Leonard Spencer, 1874-1965. VI. Gaulle, Charles de,
          Pres. France, 1890-1970. VII. Eisenhower, Dwight David, Pres. U. S.,
          1890-1969. VIII. Willkie, Wendell Lewis, 1892-1944. IX. Martin,
          Joseph William, 1884-1968. X. Elizabeth II, Queen of Great Britain,
          1926-   XI. Margaret Rose, Princess of Gt. Brit., 1930-   XII.
          Johnson, Hugh Samuel, 188?-?42. XIII. Smith, Alfred Emanuel,
          1873-1944. XIV. Lindbergh, Charles Augustus, 1902-   XV. Davis,
                            (Continued on next card)

Voice Lib.
M717   Elizabeth II, Queen of Great Britain, 1926-
bd.9   Excerpts from wedding ceremony.
          November 20, 1947.
          1 min., 14 sec.   phonotape (1 r.
          7 1/2 i.p.s.)

          I. Philip, duke of Edinburgh, 1921-

            Elizabeth II, Queen of Great Britain, 1926-
Voice Lib.
573   I can hear it now (radio program)
bd.2-   1945-1949.   CBS, 1950?
574   2 reels (7 in.)   7 1/2 in. per sec.
bd.1   phonotape.
          I. Murrow, Edward Roscoe, 1908-1965. II. Nehru, Jawaharlal,
          1889-1964. III. Philip, duke of Edinburgh, 1921-   IV. Elizabeth II,
          Queen of Great Britain, 1926-   V. Ferguson, Homer, 1889-   VI.
          Hughes, Howard Robard, 1905-   VII. Marshall, George Catlett,
          1880-   VIII. Ruth, George Herman, 1895-1948. IX. Lilienthal,
          David Eli, 1899-   X. Trout, Robert, 1908-   XI. Gage, Arthur.
          XII. Jackson, Robert Houghwout, 1892-1954. XIII. Gromyko, Ana-
          tolii Andreevich, 1908-   XIV. Baruch, Bernard Mannes, 1870-
          1965. XV. Churchill, Winston Leonard Spencer, 1874-1965. XVI.
          Winchell, Walter, 1897-19   XVII. Davis, Elmer Holmes, 1890-
                            (Continued on next card)

Voice Lib.
M834   Elizabeth II, Queen of Great Britain, 1926-
          Highlights of wedding ceremonies to Prince
          Philip at Westminster Abbey, London, England.
          CBS, November 20, 1947.
          1 reel (7 in.)   7 1/2 in. per sec.
          phonotape.

          I. Philip, duke of Edinburgh, 1921-

Voice Lib.
M1699 Ellington, Duke, 1899-1974.
bd.3   Reminiscences.   [n.d.]
          48 sec.   phonotape (1 r.   7 1/2 i.p.s.)

          1. Ellington, Duke, 1899-1974.

Voice Lib.
M715   Elizabeth II, Queen of Great Britain, 1926-
bd.8   Excerpt of coronation ceremonies, West-
          minster Abbey, London.   June 2, 1953.
          1 reel (7 in.)   7 1/2 in. per sec.
          phonotape.

Voice Lib.   ELLINGTON, DUKE, 1899-1974
M1706 Andrews, Julie, 1935-
bd.2   Discusses her career and her two books
          and her family on the Today Show with
          Barbara Walters.   NBC, June 5, 1974.
          10 min.   phonotape (1 r.   7 1/2 i.p.s.)

          1. Andrews, Julie, 1935-   I. Walters,
          Barbara, 1931-

ELLINGTON, DUKE, 1899-1974

Voice Lib.
M1696 Columbia Broadcasting System, inc.
bd.6   Special memorial to Duke Ellington, with
         John Hart, Sonny Greer, Russell Procope,
         Billy Taylor, Stanley Dance, and Ella
         Fitzgerald. CBS-TV, May 24, 1974.
           15 min. phonotape (1 r.   7 1/2 i.p.s.)

         1. Ellington, Duke, 1899-1974.   I. Hart,
         John. II. Greer, Sonny. III. Procope,
         Russell, 1908-   IV. Taylor, Billy.
         V. Dance, Stanley. VI. Fitzgerald, Ella,
         1918-

Ellis, Handy

Voice Lib.
573   I can hear it now (radio program)
bd.2- 1945-1949. CBS, 1950?
574   2 reels (7 in.)   7 1/2 in. per sec.
bd.1   phonotape.
         I. Murrow, Edward Roscoe, 1908-1965. II. Nehru, Jawaharlal,
         1889-1964. III. Philip, duke of Edinburgh, 1921-   IV. Elizabeth II,
         Queen of Great Britain, 1926-   V. Ferguson, Homer, 1889-   VI.
         Hughes, Howard Robard, 1905-   VII. Marshall, George Catlett,
         1880-   VIII. Ruth, George Herman, 1895-1948. IX. Lilienthal,
         David Eli, 1899-   X. Trout, Robert, 1908-   XI. Gage, Arthur.
         XII. Jackson, Robert Houghwout, 1892-1954. XIII. Gromyko, Ana-
         tolii Andreevich, 1908-   XIV. Baruch, Bernard Mannes, 1870-
         1965. XV. Churchill, Winston Leonard Spencer, 1874-1965. XVI.
         Winchell, Walter, 1897-   XVII. Davis, Elmer Holmes, 1890-
                                    (Continued on next card)

Voice Lib.
M1612- Ellsberg, Daniel, 1931-
1614   Address at Michigan State University.
         MSU Voice Library, February 28, 1974.
           90 min. (3 r.   7 1/2 i.p.s.)

         1.Vietnamese Conflict, 1961-   - U.S.

Elman, Dave

Voice Lib.
M620   Radio in the 1940's (Part I): a series of
bd.1- excerpts from important broadcasts of the 1940's; a
bd.16 sample of radio of the period. NVL, April, 1964.
         1 reel (7 in.) 7 1/2 in. per sec. phonotape.
         I. Radio programs. I. Thomas, Lowell Jackson, 1892-   II.
         Gunther, John, 1901-1970. III. Kaltenborn, Hans von, 1878-1965.
         IV. Delmar, Kenny. V. Those were the good old days (Radio
         program) VI. Elman, Dave. VII. Hall, Frederick Lee, 1916-1970.
         VIII. Hobby lobby (Radio program) IX. Roosevelt, Franklin Delano,
         Pres. U.S., 1882-1945. X. Willkie, Wendell Lewis, 1892-1944.
         XI. Hoover, Herbert Clark, Pres. U.S., 1874-1964. XII. Johnson,
         Hugh Samuel, 1882-1942. XIII. Cobb, Irvin Shrewsbury, 1876-1944.
         XIV. Roosevelt, Theodore, 1858-1919. XV. Nye, Gerald Prentice,
         1892-1971. XVI. Lindbergh, Charles Augustus, 1902-   XVII.
         Toscanini, Arturo, 1867-1957.

Elsie, George

Voice Lib.
M273- Biography in sound (radio program)
274   Franklin Delano Roosevelt: the friends and
bd.1   former associates of Franklin Roosevelt on
         the tenth anniversary of the President's death.
         NBC Radio, April, 1955.
           2 reels (7 in.)   7 1/2 in. per sec.
         phonotape.
         I. Roosevelt, Franklin Delano, Pres. U.S., 1882-1945. I.
         McIntire, Ross T 1899-   II. Mellett, Lowell, 1884-1960.
         III. Tully, Grace   IV. Henderson, Leon, 1895-
         V. Roosevelt, Eleanor (Roosevelt) 1884-1962. VI. DeGraaf, Albert
         VII. Lehman, Herbert Henry, 1878-1963. VIII. Rosenman, Samuel
         Irving, 1896-   IX. Arvey, Jacob   X. Moley, Raymond,
         1886-   XI. Farley, James Aloysius, 1888-   XII. Roosevelt,
                                    (Continued on next card)

EMERSON, RALPH WALDO, 1803-1882

C1
A36   Whorf, Michael, 1933-
         An imposing symposium.
         1 tape cassette. (The visual sounds of Mike Whorf.
         Art, music and letters, A36)
         Originally presented on his radio program, Kaleidoscope,
         WJR, Detroit.
         Duration: 38 min., 30 sec.
         Longfellow, Agassiz, Emerson, Dana, these were the kings of
         the world of literature in the nineteenth century. Every Saturday
         night they met at a private club to discuss the current events of
         their day.
         I. Longfellow, Henry Wadsworth, 1807-1882. 2. Agassiz,
         Louis, 1807-1873. 3. Emerson, Ralph Waldo, 1803-1882.
         4. Dana, Richard Henry, 1815-1882. I. Title.

EMERSON, RALPH WALDO, 1803-1882

C1
A29   Whorf, Michael, 1933-
         The sage of Concord - Ralph Waldo Emerson.
         1 tape cassette. (The visual sounds of
         Mike Whorf. Art, music and letters, A29)
         Originally presented on his radio program, Kaleidoscope,
         WJR, Detroit.
         Duration: 38 min., 45 sec.
         Ralph Waldo Emerson was a witness of his times, able to
         exert influence on the manners and mores of the public. His
         poetry is laced with wisdom and depth, and its meanings are
         as vital today and when first read.
         I. Emerson, Ralph Waldo, 1803-1882. I. Title.

ENERGY SHORTAGE

Voice Lib.
M1733 Sawhill, John Crittenden, 1936-
         Speech at the National Press Club luncheon,
         concerning the international energy picture,
         with Clyde Lamont. WKAR, June 20, 1974.
           50 min. phonotape (1 r.   7 1/2 i.p.s.)

         1. Power resources - U.S. 2. Energy
         shortage. 3. Local transit - U.S.
         I. Lamont, Clyde

ENGINEERING - STUDY AND TEACHING

Voice Lib.
218   Kettering, Charles Franklin, 1876-1958.
bd.3   Address on engineering education at
         Eggleston Award Dinner. WJR, April 14,
         1954.
           1 reel (7 in.)   7 1/2 in. per sec.
         phonotape.

         1. Engineering - Study and teaching.

England's first poet - Geoffrey Chaucer

C1
A35   Whorf, Michael, 1933-
         England's first poet - Geoffrey Chaucer.
         1 tape cassette. (The visual sounds of
         Mike Whorf. Art, music and letters, A35)
         Originally presented on his radio program, Kaleidoscope,
         WJR, Detroit.
         Duration: 40 min.
         His works preceded those that were synonymous with the English
         contribution to the literary world. Chaucer was poet and author,
         and his commentary on life, philosophy, mores, and social aware-
         ness was brought to its zenith with a collection of works entitled
         Canterbury Tales.
         I. Chaucer, Geoffrey, d. 1400. I. Title.

C1
H76

The English patriot, Edmund Burke

Whorf, Michael, 1933-
The English patriot, Edmund Burke.
1 tape cassette. (The visual sounds of
Mike Whorf. History and heritage, H76)
Originally presented on his radio program, Kaleidoscope,
WJR, Detroit.
Duration: 36 min.
This story not only details Edmund Burke's endeavors in
America's cause, but also relates his own world.

L. Burke, Edmund, 1729?-1797. L. Title.

ENVIRONMENTAL POLICY
Voice Lib.
M1735
Hardesty, Charles Howard, 1922-
The role of industry in combatting environ-
mental problems; speech delivered at Michigan
State University. Introduction by Myron H.
Chetrick. WKAR, June 20, 1974.
45 min. phonotape (1 r. 7 1/2 i.p.s.)

1. Enviromental policy. 2. Environmental
eingineering. 3. Factory and trade waste.
I. Chetrick, Myron

C1
S51

The enigma of genius - Voltaire

Whorf, Michael, 1933-
The enigma of genius - Voltaire.
1 tape cassette. (The visual sounds of
Mike Whorf. Social, S51)
Originally presented on his radio program, Kaleidoscope,
WJR, Detroit.
Duration: 37 min.
Voltaire was considered a genius, possessing one of the
finest minds of his day and consorting with his peers and contem-
poraries. His life was complex to the point of being enigmatic,
and we'll give you the right to disagree with our findings.
L. Voltaire, François Marie Arouet de, 1694-1778,
L. Title.

Voice Lib.
M766
bd.6
Ericksen, Espen
Excerpt from "Popular Music of Europe"
(Program 11); comments on music of Norway,
including song "Liebeskummer lohnt sich
nicht" by Siw Malmkvist. Westinghouse
Broadcasting Corporation, 1964.
3 min., 36 sec. phonotape (1 r. 7 1/2
i.p.s.) (The music goes round and round)

1. Music, Popular (Songs, etc.) - Norway.
I. Title: Popular music of Europe. 11. Series.

C1
FA15

Enoch H. Crowder

Whorf, Michael, 1933-
Enoch H. Crowder.
1 tape cassette. (The visual sounds of
Mike Whorf. The forgotten American, FA15)
Originally presented on his radio program, Kaleidoscope,
WJR, Detroit.
Duration: 10 min.
Crowder was a U. S. army officer who administered the
Selective Service act during World War I and later served as
Ambassador to Cuba.

L. Crowder, Enoch Herbert, 1859-1932. L. Title.

Ericson, Leif
see
Leifr Eiriksson, hinn Heppni, d. ca. 1021.

VOICE LIBRA

ENTERTAINERS - U.S.
Voice Lib.
M1743
bd.2
Raft, George
Reminisces on the Mike Douglas Show.
WILX-TV, June 27, 1974.
10 min. phonotape (1 r. 7 1/2 i.p.s.)

L. Raft, George. 2. O'Brien, Pat, 1899- 3. Muni,
Paul, 1895-1967. 4. Crawford, Joan, 1908- 5. West, Mae,
1893- 6. Richman, Harry. 7. Entertainers - U. S. L.
Douglas, Mike, 1925?-

Voice Lib.
M1602
Ervin, Samuel James, 1896-
Summation of the proposed legislation to
reform the office of the Attorney-General,
as a result of the Watergate investigations.
WKAR-AM, April 1, 1974.
30 min. phonotape (1 r. 7 1/2 i.p.s.)

1. U.S. Attorney-General.

ENVIRONMENTAL ENGINEERING
Voice Lib.
M1735
Hardesty, Charles Howard, 1922-
The role of industry in combatting environ-
mental problems; speech delivered at Michigan
State University. Introduction by Myron H.
Chetrick. WKAR, June 20, 1974.
45 min. phonotape (1 r. 7 1/2 i.p.s.)

1. Enviromental policy. 2. Enviromental
eingineering. 3. Factory and trade waste.
I. Chetrick, Myron

Voice Lib.
M1698
Ervin, Samuel James, 1896-
The lesson of Watergate; address at the
National Press Club. WKAR, May 29, 1974.
45 min. phonotape (1 r. 7 1/2 i.p.s.)

1. Constitutional law. 2. Baker, Robert
Gene, 1928- 3. Sirica, John Joseph, 1904-

Ervin, Samuel James, 1896-

Voice Lib.
M1800 U.S. Congress. Senate. Select Committee on Presidential
Campaign Activities.
Watergate gavel to gavel, phase 1: May 17 - August 7, 1973.
Pacifica, May 17 - August 7, 1973.
172 reels (5 in.) 3 3/4 l.p.s. phonotape.

"These tapes include commentaries by Pacifica's Washington
correspondents and interviews with members of the Senate Committee
taped during recesses of the hearings."

I. Presidents - U.S. - Elections - 1972. 2. Watergate Affair,
1972- I. Ervin, Samuel James, 1896- II. Talmadge,
Herman Eugene, 1913- III. Inouye, Daniel Ken, 1924-
IV. Baker, Howard H., 1925- V. Gurney, Edward John, 1914-
VI. Weicker, Lowell P., 19 VII. Title.

Ervin Committee.
see
U.S. Congress. Senate. Select Committee
on Presidential Campaign Activities.

C1
S66 The eternal people - Jews
Whorf, Michael, 1933-
The eternal people - Jews.
1 tape cassette. (The visual sounds of
Mike Whorf. Social, S66)
Originally presented on his radio program, Kaleidoscope,
WJR, Detroit.
Duration: 37 min., 30 sec.
They gave the Western World a philosophy, a culture, and a
religion, yet in many instances they were rejected and despised.
They were the Jews - professing and embracing the Judaic faith -
yet, it was more than a faith. They have been searching for the
promised land, and modern day Israel is but part of it.

I. Jews. I. Title.

The eternal romance

C1
A12 Whorf, Michael, 1933-
The eternal Romance.
1 tape cassette. (The visual sounds of
Mike Whorf. Art, music, and letters, A12)

Originally presented on his radio program, Kaleidoscope,
WJR, Detroit.
Duration: 37 min.
The tender romance of Elizabeth Barrett and Robert Browning,
a story of a sickly young woman and her love for the tempestuous
Browning.

I. Browning, Elizabeth (Barrett) 1806-1861. 2. Browning,
Robert, 1812-1889. I. Title.

EUROPE - HISTORY - 476-1492

Voice Lib.
M1582 Sullivan, Richard Eugene, 1921-
Pre-national Europe; excerpts. WKAR-FM,
February 27, 1974.
25 min. phonotape (1 r. 7 1/2 i.p.s.)

1. Europe - History - 476-1492.

EUROPE - POLITICS - 20TH CENTURY

Voice Lib.
M506 Benes, Edvard, Pres. Czechoslovak Republic, 1884-1948.
Postwar plans for small countries. Responsibilities and
plans for small European countries, treaty of Versailles,
aggression in East, review of Hitler aggressions and dealing with
him, need for true democracy in Europe, advantages of small
nations, modern technological developments and their
influence on politics of Europe, political profile of post-World War
II Europe, politics of post-war Czechoslovakia, need for plans to
form efficient international organization, describes roles of major
post-war countries (Britain, France, USSR), maintenance of U.N.
allies, preparation for future defense of freedom. Speech
delivered in Chicago. CBS, May 22, 1943.
1 reel (7 in.) 7 1/2 l.p.s. phonotape.

I. Europe - Politics - 20th century.

EUROPEAN WAR, 1914-1918

Voice Lib.
M1206
bd.4 Arrival of British troops in France;
British descriptive war scenes of troops
cheering, singing, talking. Br. Col.,
1916.
1 reel (7 in.) 7 1/2 i.p.s. phonotape.

1. European War, 1914-1918.

EUROPEAN WAR, 1914-1918

Voice Lib.
642
bd.2 Edison, Thomas Alva, 1847-1931.
Let us not forget; reviews World War I
and calls for Americans not to forget.
Edison Laboratories, 1918.
1 reel (7 in.) 7 1/2 in. per sec.
phonotape.

EUROPEAN WAR, 1914-1918

Voice Lib.
M1466
bd.1 Wilhelm II, German emperor, 1859-1941.
Call-up of the German people upon entering
World War I. Peteler, August 8, 1914.
1 reel (7 in.) 7 1/2 i.p.s. phonotape.

1. European war, 1914-1918.

EUROPEAN WAR, 1914-1918 - AUSTRIA

Voice Lib.
M1466
bd.8 Karl I, emperor of Austria, 1887-1922.
Talking about the Imperial Austrian fund
to aid military widows and orphans.
Peteler, February 16, 1916.
1 reel (7 in.) 7 1/2 in. per sec.
phonotape.

1. European War, 1914-1918 - Hospitals,
charities, etc. 2. European War, 1914-1918 -
Austria.

EUROPEAN WAR, 1914-1918 - GERMANY

Voice Lib.
M1466 Scheidemann, Philip, 1865-1939.
bd.15 Report on the situation of calling up
soldiers and laborers. Peteler,
November 8, 1918.
1 reel (7 in.) 7 1/2 i.p.s. phonotape.

1. European War, 1914-1918 - Germany.

EUROPEAN WAR, 1914-1918 - HOSPITALS,
CHARITIES, ETC.

Voice Lib.
M1466 Karl I, emperor of Austria, 1887-1922.
bd.8 Talking about the Imperial Austrian fund
to aid military widows and orphans.
Peteler, February 16, 1916.
1 reel (7 in.) 7 1/2 in. per sec.
phonotape.

1. European War, 1914-1918 - Hospitals,
charities, etc. 2. European War, 1914-1918 -
Austria.

EUROPEAN WAR, 1914-1918 - NAVAL OPERATIONS,
GERMAN

Voice Lib.
M952 Tirpitz, Alfred Peter Friedrich von, 1849-1930.
bd.14 Speaking about German U-boat warfare.
F. Peteler, 1915.
1 reel (7 in.) 7 1/2 in. per sec.
phonotape.

1. European War, 1914-1918 - Naval
operations - Submarine. 2. European War,
1914-1918 - Naval operations, German.

EUROPEAN WAR, 1914-1918 - NAVAL OPERATIONS -
SUBMARINE

Voice Lib.
M952 Tirpitz, Alfred Peter Friedrich von, 1849-1930.
bd.14 Speaking about German U-boat warfare.
F. Peteler, 1915.
1 reel (7 in.) 7 1/2 in. per sec.
phonotape.

1. European War, 1914-1918 - Naval
operations - Submarine. 2. European War,
1914-1918 - Naval operations, German.

EUROPEAN WAR, 1914-1918 - PERSONAL NARRATIVES,
GERMAN

Voice Lib.
611 Salay, Julius
bd.5,6 Dramatic description of World War I scenes.
"Life in the trench after the capture of
Warsaw", "Frontier at the German border".
Victor Talking Machine Co., 1916.
1 reel (7 in.) 7 1/2 in. per sec.
phonotape.

In German.

EUROPEAN WAR, 1914-1918 - SONGS AND MUSIC

Voice Lib.
M611 American Quartet.
bd.7 World War I song "You're a grand old flag".
Victor Talking Machine Co., 1918.
1 reel (7 in.) 7 1/2 i.p.s. phonotape.

1. European War, 1914-1918 - Songs and
music. I. Title: You're a grand old flag.

EUROPEAN WAR, 1914-1918 - SONGS AND MUSIC

Voice Lib.
M603 Columbia Quartet.
bd.4 War song medley from World War I. Columbia Gramaphone
Co., 1917.
1 reel (7 in.) 7 1/2 i.p.s. phonotape.

CONTENTS. -It's a long way to Berlin. -Keep the home fires
burning. -Where do we go from here? -Pack up your troubles in
your old kit bag. -For your country and my country. -Goodbye
Broadway, hello France. -I don't know where I'm going, but I'm
on my way. -Over there.

1. European War, 1914-1918 - Songs and music.

EUROPEAN WAR, 1914-1918 - SONGS AND
MUSIC

Voice Lib.
M611 Peerless Quartet.
bd.4 World War I song "Liberty bell (it's time
to ring again)". Victor Talking Machine
Co., 1917.
1 reel (7 in.) 7 1/2 i.p.s. phonotape.

1. European War, 1914-1918 - Songs and
music. I. Title: Liberty bell (it's time
to ring again.)

EUROPEAN WAR, 1914-1918 - SONGS AND
MUSIC

Voice Lib.
M603 Rice, Gitz
bd.8 "Life in a trench in Belgium"; dramatic
skit and songs outlining life on war front
in World War I. Columbia Gramophone Co.,
1917.
1 reel (7 in.) 7 1/2 i.p.s. phonotape.

1. European War, 1914-1918 - Songs and
music.

EUROPEAN WAR, 1914-1918 - SONGS AND MUSIC

Voice Lib.
M611 Shannon Four.
bd.1 World War I song "There's a service flag
flying at our house". Victor Talking
Machine Co., 1917.
1 reel (7 in.) 7 1/2 i.p.s. phonotape.

1. European War, 1914-1918 - Songs and
music. I.Title: There's a service flag
flying at our house.

EUROPEAN WAR, 1914-1918 - U. S.

C1
870   Whorf, Michael, 1933-
            The frenzied home front.
            1 tape cassette.   (The visual sounds of
       Mike Whorf. Social, 870)
            Originally presented on his radio program, Kaleidoscope,
       WJR, Detroit.
            Duration: 36 min., 50 sec.
            The period of the First World War marked a dramatic transition
       in American life. As we consider the "good old days" to be around
       the turn of the century and the end of the Victorian era, so the war
       served as a bridge to the roaring twenties to follow.

            1. European War, 1914-1918 - U. S. 2. U. S. - Social conditions.
       I. Title.

Voice Lib.   Everybody loves me
M975   Terriss, Ellaline, 1871-
bd.9   Singing British popular music hall selection
        "Everybody Loves Me". Rococo-Can., 1909.
             1 reel (7 in.)   7 1/2 in. per sec.
        phonotape.

             I. Title: Everybody loves me.

Voice Lib.   Evans, Maurice
M225   Packard, Frederick
            Styles in Shakespearean acting, 1890-1950.
        Creative Associates, 1963?
             1 reel (7 in.)   7 1/2 L.p.s.   phonotape.

             I. Sothern, Edward Askew, 1826-1881. II. Marlowe,
        Julia, 1865-1950. III. Booth, Edwin, 1833-1893. IV. Gielgud,
        John, 1904-   V. Robeson, Paul Bustill, 1898-   VI. Terry,
        Dame Ellen, 1848-1928. VII. Allen, Viola. VIII. Welles,
        Orson, 1915-   IX. Skinner, Otis, 1858-1942. X. Barrymore,
        John, 1882-1942. XI. Olivier, Sir Laurence Kerr, 1907-
        XII. Forbes-Robertson, Sir Johnston, 1853-   XIII. Evans,
        Maurice. XIV. Thorndike, Dame Sybil, 1882-   XV. Robson,
        Flora. XVI. LeGallienne, Eva, 1899-   XVII. Anderson,
        Judith. XVIII. Duncan, Augustin. XIX. Hampden, Walter.
        XX. Speaight, Robert, 1904-   XXI. Jones, Daniel.

        EVOLUTION
C1
816   Whorf, Michael, 1933-
            The beginning of man.
            1 tape cassette.   (The visual sounds of
       Mike Whorf. Social, 816)
            Originally presented on his radio program, Kaleidoscope,
       WJR, Detroit.
            Duration: 40 min., 35 sec.
            This program takes an open-minded look in a narrative
       which concerns itself with the possibility of evolution and
       how man began.

            1. Evolution. 2. Man - Origin. I. Title.

Voice Lib.
M982   Evans, Robley Dunglison, 1846-1912.
bd.6   Farewell address to the U.S. Navy.   N.Y.,
        1910.
             1 reel (7 in.)   7 1/2 in. per sec.
        phonotape.

Voice Lib.
M1225   Evtushenko, Evgenii Aleksandrovich, 1933-
bd.2   Three poems read by Russian poet Evgenii
        Evtushenko, from a recital for NET entitled
        "Evtushenko in Person". Poems include:
        "Impressions of the Western Cinema", "Town
        Fair", and "Hail in Kharkov".   NET, May 14,
        1967.
             1 reel (7 in.)   7 1/2 in. per sec.
        phonotape.

Voice Lib.
M555   Evatt, Herbert Vere, 1894-1965.
bd.4   Press conference on Australia's position
        on current Conference procedures and charter
        problems of the United Nations Organization.
        GRV, 1945.
             1 reel (7 in.)   7 1/2 i.p.s.   phonotape.

             1. United Nations.

Voice Lib.   Ewing, William
M1046   World news tonight; radio news commentary.
bd.2   CBS Radio news broadcast from Honolulu,
        London, New York and Washington; including
        William Ewing, Norman Corwin, Albert Leitch
        and Harry Marble. CBS, September 12, 1942.
             1 reel (7 in.)   7 1/2 in. per sec.
        phonotape.

             I. Ewing, William   II. Corwin, Norman
        Lewis, 1910-   III. Leitch, Albert
        IV. Marble, Harry

Voice Lib.
M1699   Evers, Charles, 1923-
bd.2   Address at Michigan State University.
        WKAR, October 13, 1971.
             15 min.   phonotape (1 r.   7 1/2 i.p.s.)

             1. Negroes - Civil rights.

Voice Lib.
M1466   Excerpt of ceremonies on opening of new
bd.25   Reichstag Building in Berlin; narrator:
        Alfred Braun.   Pateler, August 1, 1930.
             1 reel (7 in.)   7 1/2 in. per sec.
        phonotape.

             1. Germany - Politics and government -
        1918-1933.

Voice Lib.
M846   Excerpts of political speeches and statements
bd.2   by presidential candidates Lyndon Johnson
        and Barry Goldwater, from TV dramatization
        of Theodore H. White's book "The Making of
        the President, 1964".
        1 reel (7 in.) 7 1/2 in. per sec.
        phonotape.
        I. Johnson, Lyndon Baines, Pres. U.S., 1908-1973. II.
        Goldwater, Barry Morris, 1909-   III. White, Theodore
        Harold, 1915-   /The making of the president, 1964.

F.B.I.
    see
U.S. Federal bureau of investigation.

VOICE LIBRARY

Voice Lib.
M1658   FSM's sounds and songs of the
        demonstration. Berkeley, Calif., FSM
        Records Dept., September 21, 1964.
        50 min. phonotape (1 r. 7 1/2 i.p.s.)

        1. Free Speech Movement. 2. Students -
        Political movements. I. Free Speech
        Movement.

        The face of an angel
Voice Lib.
M844   LaMour, Dorothy
        Radio dramatization entitled: "The Face
        of an Angel", with comments by the new star,
        Marvyn Vey, and Miss Dorothy LaMour.
        November 9, 1947.
        1 reel (7 in.) 7 1/2 in. per sec.
        phonotape.

        I. Vey, Marvyn. II. Title: The face of an
        angel.

        FACTORY AND TRADE WASTE
Voice Lib.
M1735   Hardesty, Charles Howard, 1922-
        The role of industry in combatting environ-
        mental problems; speech delivered at Michigan
        State University. Introduction by Myron H.
        Chetrick. WKAR, June 20, 1974.
        45 min. phonotape (1 r. 7 1/2 i.p.s.)

        1. Environmental policy. 2. Environmental
        engineering. 3. Factory and trade waste.
        I. Chetrick, Myron

Fadiman, Clifton, 1904-
Voice Lib.
M932   Information, please (radio program)
        Panel of experts questioned by Clifton
        Fadiman; panel includes Christopher Morley,
        John Kieran, Franklin P. Adams, Col. Eagan.
        Lloyd Grosse, 1943.
        1 reel (7 in.) 7 1/2 in. per sec.
        phonotape.

        I. Fadiman, Clifton, 1904-   II. Morley,
        Christopher Darlington, 1890-   III. Kieran,
        John, 1892-   IV. Adams, Franklin Pierce,
        1881-1960. V. Eagan, Col.

Voice Lib.
M1230- Fair trial, free press; discussion of the Reardon Report of the
1231,   American Bar Association about restrictions of the press in
bd.1   publicizing criminal cases before they are tried. Participants,
        via TV satelite: two British guests and a panel of Americans
        of diversified views. ABC-TV, May 18, 1967.
        2 reel (7 in.) 7 1/2 i.p.s. phonotape.

        1. Liberty of the press - U.S. 2. Criminal procedure - U.S.

Voice Lib.
662   Faith, Percy
bd.1   Folk songs by Percy Faith and his orchestra.
        CRI, 1964.
        1 reel (7 in.) 7 1/2 in. per sec.
        phonotape.

        CONTENTS.-This Land; Green Back Dollar;
        This Train; Green Fields; John B. Sails;
        Hammer Song; Michael Row the Boat; Blowing
        in the Wind; Darling Corey; 500 Miles;
        Lemon Tree.

C1   FAMILY
S62   Whorf, Michael, 1933-
        The greatest privilege of mankind - the family.
        1 tape cassette. (The visual sounds of
        Mike Whorf. Social, S62)
        Originally presented on his radio program, Kaleidoscope,
        WJR, Detroit.
        Duration: 39 min., 30 sec.
        For a thousand centuries man has received an abundance of
        blessings - but none so rewarding as the family. The family of
        "names" is also encountered with a study of the origin of the
        head of the family.
        1. Family. I. Title.

        FAMILY - ADDRESSES, ESSAYS, LECTURES
Voice Lib.
M1739   Ford, Gerald R., 1915-
bd.3   Acceptance speech for the "Father of the Year"
        award. CBS, June 14, 1974.
        3 min. phonotape (1 r. 7 1/2 i.p.s.)

        1. Family - addresses, essays, lectures.

Fanny

C1
M3   Whorf, Michael, 1933-
         Fanny.
         1 tape cassette.   (The visual sounds of
      Mike Whorf. Miscellaneous, M3)

         Originally presented on his radio program, Kaleidoscope,
      WJR, Detroit.
         Duration: 30 min.
         Fanny Brice - songstress, comedienne, star of stage and broad-
      casting, and girl who brought tears and laughter, who was able to
      express on stage those qualities which were found in her own life.

         I. Brice, Fanny, 1891-   I. Title.

Fehrbelliner Reitermarsch
Voice Lib.
M1073   Nazi martial music; instrumental selection
bd.21   entitled: "Fehrbelliner Reitermarsch".
          Peteler, 1941.
          1 reel (7 in.)   7 1/2 in. per sec.
       phonotape.

          I. Title: Fehrbelliner Reitermarsch.

Voice Lib.
M774-   Farewell to Studio Nine; historical broadcasts
775,   made by CBS correspondents at time of action
bd.1   and reflections by them in retrospect.   1964.
          2 reels (7 in.)   7 1/2 in. per sec.
       phonotape.

          I. Trout, Robert, 1908-   II. Pierpoint,
       Robert   III. Murrow, Edward Roscoe,
       1908-1965. IV. Kaltenborn, Hans von, 1878-
       1965. V. Sevareid, Arnold Eric, 191.'-
       VI. Daly, John Charles, 1914-

FARGO, ND. - TORNADO
Voice Lib.
M243   Columbia Broadcasting System.
bd.1   Recollection of a tornado, recorded on
          location in Fargo, North Dakota.   CBS
       Radio, June 21, 1957.
          1 reel (7 in.)   7 1/2 i.p.s.   phonotape.

          1. Fargo, N.D. - Tornado.

Voice Lib.
M724   Farley, James Aloysius, 1888-
bd.5   Speaking about conventions.
          1 reel (7 in.)   7 1/2 in. per sec.
       phonotape.

Voice Lib.
M276   Farley, James Aloysius, 1888-
bd. 4   Future of the Republican Party; what
       he feels the Republicans need to do if they
       expect to reach the level of the
       Democratic Party.   From private collection
       of G. Robert Vincent, 1938.
          1 reel (7 in.)   7 1/2 in. per sec.
       phonotape.

Voice Lib.
M751   Farley, James Aloysius, 1888-
bd.2   Address at testimonial dinner to Mayor
       Wagner at Lotos Club in New York.   Relates
       experiences with past New York mayors.
       NYC, December 26, 1954.
          1 reel (7 in.)   7 1/2 in. per sec.
       phonotape.

Farley, James Aloysius, 1888-
Voice Lib.
M724   Barkley, Alben William, 1877-1956.
bd.3   Alben Barkley and James Farley at
       Democratic convention of 1940, speaking for
       nomination of Franklin D. Roosevelt for
       third term.   1940.
          1 min., 40 sec.   phonotape (1 r.   7 1/2
       i.p.s.)

          I. Roosevelt, Franklin Delano, Pres. U.S., 1882-1945.
       2. Presidents - U.S. - Election - 1940. I. Farley, James
       Aloysius, 1888-

Farley, James Aloysius, 1888-
Voice Lib.
M273-   Biography in sound (radio program)
274   Franklin Delano Roosevelt: the friends and
bd.1   former associates of Franklin Roosevelt on
       the tenth anniversary of the President's death.
       NBC Radio, April, 1955.
          2 reels (7 in.)   7 1/2 in. per sec.
       phonotape.
          I. Roosevelt, Franklin Delano, Pres. U.S., 1882-1945. I.
       McIntire, Ross T   1899-   II. Mellett, Lowell, 1884-1960.
       III. Tully, Grace   IV. Henderson, Leon, 1895-
       V. Roosevelt, Eleanor (Roosevelt) 1884-1962. VI. DeGraaf, Albert
       VII. Lehman, Herbert Henry, 1878-1963. VIII. Rosenman, Samuel
       Irving, 1896-   IX. Arvey, Jacob   X. Moley, Raymond,
       1886-   XI. Farley, James Aloysius, 1888-   XII. Roosevelt,
       (Continued on next card)

FARRAGUT, DAVID GLASGOW, 1801-1870
C1
H64   Whorf, Michael, 1933-
          Conquer or be conquered, David Farragut.
          1 tape cassette.   (The visual sounds of
       Mike Whorf. History and heritage, H64)

          Originally presented on his radio program, Kaleidoscope,
       WJR, Detroit.
          Duration: 40 min.
          David Farragut was dauntless, brave, courageous - having all
       the attributes of the typical warrior. Yet, with all the notoriety
       that comes with heroism, he was a lonely, much misunderstood
       man.

          I. Farragut, David Glasgow, 1801-1870.

C1
M13 Father of the blues
Whorf, Michael, 1933–
Father of the blues.
1 tape cassette. (The visual sounds of Mike Whorf. Miscellaneous, M13)
Originally presented on his radio program, Kaleidoscope, WJR, Detroit.
Duration: 54 min.
The creator of "St. Louis blues" and a dozen other great blues songs was W. C. Handy. This is the story of a troubled spirit who finally found his life in music. As they said when he died, "The mold is now broken."
I. Handy, William Christopher, 1873–1958. I. Title.

Voice Lib.
M742 Faubus, Orval Eugene, 1910–
bd.2   Concerning school desegregation crisis in Little Rock. CBS, 1957.
1 reel (7 in.) 7 1/2 in. per sec. phonotape.

1. Segregation in education.

Voice Lib.
253 Faubus, Orville Eugene, 1910–
bd.1   Discussion of the problem of integration in the schools of Little Rock. CBS, September 26, 1957.
1 reel (7 in.) 7 1/2 in. per sec. phonotape.

1. Segregation in education.

Voice Lib.
M1300 Faulhaber, Michael von, Cardinal, 1869–1952.
bd.4   Sermon on "All Souls Day" at the cathedral in Munich on the theme of "Cross and Swastika", stressing that the cross is more important to Christian life than the swastika, exhorting congregation to pray for peace and end of war, and that the cross will save the soul. Peteler, November 3, 1941.
1 reel (7 in.) 7 1/2 in. per sec. phonotape.

Voice Lib.
M1303 Faulhaber, Michael von, Cardinal, 1869–1952.
bd.2   New Year's Eve sermon at the cathedral in Munich, Germany entitled "Habt Acht". Peteler, December 31, 1941.
1 reel (7 in.) 7 1/2 in. per sec. phonotape.

I. Title: Habt acht.

Faulkner, William, 1897–1962
Voice Lib.
M1033 Voice of America.
Twentieth anniversary program of Voice of America broadcasts narrated by Henry Fonda, and including the voices of Carl Sandburg, Danny Kaye, Jawaharlal Nehru, Franklin D. Roosevelt, Charles Malik, Arnold Toynbee, William Faulkner, Harry S. Truman, Dwight D. Eisenhower, Helen Hayes, Dag Hammarskjöld, Winston Churchill, and John F. Kennedy. Voice of America, 1963.
1 reel (7 in.) 7 1/2 in. per sec. phonotape.
(Continued on next card)

Faulkner, William, 1897–1962
Voice Lib.
M1033 Voice of America. Twentieth anniversary program... 1963. (Card 2)

I. Fonda, Henry Jaynes, 1905– II. Sandburg, Carl, 1878–1967. III. Kaye, Danny, 1913– IV. Nehru, Jawaharlal, 1889–1964. V. Roosevelt, Franklin Delano, Pres. U.S., 1882–1945. VI. Malik, Charles Habib, 1906– VII. Toynbee, Arnold Joseph, 1889– VIII. Faulkner, William, 1897–1962. IX. Truman, Harry S, Pres. U.S., 1884–1972. X. Eisenhower, Dwight David, Pres. U.S., 1890–1969. XI. Hayes, Helen, 1900– XII. Hammarskjöld, Dag, 1905–1961. XIII. Churchill, Winston Leonard Spencer, 1874–1965. XIV. Kennedy, John Fitzgerald, Pres. U.S., 1917–1963.

Faunce, George, 1894–
Voice Lib.
256 U.S. Congress. Senate. Select committee
bd.5   to investigate racketeering in labor unions.
Senator John Kennedy and Counsel Robert Kennedy questioning Faunce, Vice-President of Continental Baking Company. CBS News, October 23, 1957.
1 reel (7 in.) 7 1/2 in. per sec. phonotape.
I. Faunce, George, 1894– II. Kennedy, John Fitzgerald, Pres. U.S., 1917–1963. III. Kennedy, Robert Francis, 1925–1968.

Voice Lib.
M1256 Fawzi, Mahmoud, 1900–
Address by Deputy Premier of UAR Fawzi attacking Israeli atrocities, aggression, U.S.A. and U.K. help to Israel and ridiculing Pres. Johnson. Complimenting U Thant, praising U.S.S.R., accusing U.S. 6th Fleet. NBC-TV, June 21, 1967.
1 reel (7 in.) 7 1/2 in. per sec. phonotape.
1. Israel-Arab War, 1967–

Federal bureau of investigation.
see
U.S. Federal bureau of investigation.

VOICE LIBRARY

C1
M8

Fennell, Frederick

Whorf, Michael, 1933–
   I love to hear a military band.
   1 tape cassette. (The visual sounds of
Mike Whorf. Miscellaneous, M8)

   Originally presented on his radio program, Kaleidoscope,
WJR, Detroit.
   Duration: 50 min., 30 sec.
   With guest, Frederick Fennell, the tempos are 4/4 and the
music is vibrant and varied, as through narrative and melody, the
story of the march is related.

   I. Marches. I. Fennell, Frederick. II. Title.

Voice Lib. Fennelly, Parker
M619   Radio in the 1930's (Part II): a series of
bd.1-   excerpts of the 1930's; a sample of radio
14   of the period. NVL, April, 1964.
          1 reel (7 in.) 7 1/2 in. per sec. phonotape.
   I. Allen, Fred, 1894–1956. II. Delmar, Kenny   III. Donald,
Peter   IV. Pious, Minerva   V. Fennelly, Parker   VI.
Boyer, Charles, 1899–   VII. Dunne, Irene, 1904–   VIII.
DeMille, Cecil Blount, 1881–1959. IX. West, Mae, 1893–   X.
Dafoe, Allan Ray, 1883–1943. XI. Dionne quintuplets. XII. Ortega,
Santos   XIII. War of the worlds (radio program) XIV. Ives, Burl,
1909–   XV. Robinson, Earl, 1910–   XVI. Temple, Shirley,
1928–   XVII. Earhart, Amelia, 1898–1937. XVIII. Lawrence,
Gertrude, 1901–1952. XIX. Cohan, George Michael, 1878–1942.
XX. Shaw, George Bernard, 1856–1950. XXI. Hitler, Adolf, 1889–
1945. XXII. Chamberlain, Neville, 1869–1940. XXIII. Roosevelt,
Franklin Delano, Pres. U.S., 1882–1945.

Voice Lib.
281   Ferguson, Homer, 1889–
bd.1   "Meet the Press"; Homer Ferguson; answers
reporters' questions concerning irregularities
in the Truman Administration and Communists
in government. Mutual Broadcasting System,
October 1, 1948.
   1 reel (7 in.) 7 1/2 in. per sec.
phonotape.

Ferguson, Homer, 1889–
Voice Lib.
M1491 Hughes, Howard Robard, 1905–
bd.1   Excerpt of testimony before U.S. Senate
War Investigating Committee. Senator
Homer Ferguson of Michigan questions Howard
Hughes. CBS-Radio, 1947.
   1 reel (7 in.) 7 1/2 in. per sec.
phonotape.

   I. Ferguson, Homer, 1889–

Ferguson, Homer, 1889–
Voice Lib.
573   I can hear it now (radio program)
bd.2-   1945–1949. CBS, 1950?
574   2 reels (7 in.) 7 1/2 in. per sec.
bd.1   phonotape.
   I. Murrow, Edward Roscoe, 1908–1965. II. Nehru, Jawaharlal,
1889–1964. III. Philip, duke of Edinburgh, 1921–   IV. Elizabeth II,
Queen of Great Britain, 1926–   V. Ferguson, Homer, 1889–   VI.
Hughes, Howard Robard, 1905–   VII. Marshall, George Catlett,
1880–   VIII. Ruth, George Herman, 1895–1948. IX. Lilienthal,
David Eli, 1899–   X. Trout, Robert, 1908–   XI. Gage, Arthur.
XII. Jackson, Robert Houghwout, 1892–1954. XIII. Gromyko, Ana-
tolii Andreevich, 1908–   XIV. Baruch, Bernard Mannes, 1870–
1965. XV. Churchill, Winston Leonard Spencer, 1874–1965. XVI.
Winchell, Walter, 1897–   XVII. Davis, Elmer Holmes, 1890–
(Continued on next card)

Voice Lib.
M1664   Ferguson, Robert
bd.2   Is seeing always believing? Popular
culture and technology. Recorded live at
National Popular Culture Meetings in Milwaukee,
May 4, 1974.
   20 min. phonotape (1 r.   7 1/2 i.p.s.)

   1. Popular culture.

Voice Lib.
M1068 Ferlinghetti, Lawrence
bd.2   Reading his own poetry at State Theater,
East Lansing, Michigan; sponsored by
"Zeitgeist", with introductory remarks by
Gary Groat. Groat, October 3, 1966.
   1 reel (7 in.) 7 1/2 in. per sec.
phonotape.

   I. Groat, Gary

Voice Lib.
M1342– Ferlinghetti, Lawrence
1343   Reading his own poetry in a public reading
at Cal. Tech. Location recording.
February 2, 1968.
   2 reels (7 in.) 7 1/2 in. per sec.
phonotape.

Voice Lib.
M1310 Fermi, Enrico, 1901–1954.
bd.2   Speaking at the tenth anniversary
celebration of the first nuclear chain
reaction, held at the University of Chicago.
Atomic Energy Commission, December 2, 1952.
   1 reel (7 in.) 7 1/2 i.p.s. phonotape.

   1. Nuclear reactions. I. Compton,
Arthur Holly, 1892–1962.

Ferrer, José, 1912–
Voice Lib.
M1037 Biography in sound (radio program)
bd.1   "The Actor", narrated by Morgan Beatty.
Cast includes Tallulah Bankhead, Hy Gardner,
Rocky Graziano, Arthur Miller, Uta Hagen,
Jackie Cooper, Sir Laurence Olivier, Gad
Gaysher, Barbara Ashley, Hortense Powdermaker,
Peter Ustinov, Alfred Hitchcock, Leonard Lyons,
John Guston, Helen Hayes, Dick Mayne, Ralph
Bellamy, Lionel Barrymore, Sir Ralph Richardson,
José Ferrer, and Walter Kerr. NBC Radio, 1950's.
   1 reel (7 in.) 7 1/2 in. per sec.
phonotape.
(Continued on next card)

Voice Lib.
M1075   Ferry, W. H.
bd.2   Ashmore, Harry Scott, 1916-
         Discussion among three well-known book
publishers about authors of the past, the job
of book editors, the publishing business, book
reviewers, etc. Held in the Library at the
Center for the Study of Democratic Institutions
at Santa Barbara, California. CSDI, 1960.
         1 reel (7 in.) 7 1/2 in. per sec.
phonotape.

         1. Publishers and publishing. I. Knopf, Alfred A., 1892-
II. Ferry, W. H.   ---

Voice Lib.
         FICTION - 20TH CENTURY - HISTORY AND
           CRITICISM
M1732   Aldridge, John W
         Address at Michigan State University.
Introduction by Russel B. Nye. WKAR,
October 28, 1968.
         50 min. phonotape (1 r. 7 1/2 i.p.s.)

         1. Literature, Modern - 20th century - Hist.
& crit. 2. Fiction - 20th century - Hist. &
crit. I. Nye, Russel Blaine, 1913-

Voice Lib.
233   Fiedler, Arthur, 1894-
bd.3   Interview with Arthur Fiedler by Walter
Poole. CBS, March 2, 1957.
         1 reel (7 in.) 7 1/2 in. per sec.
phonotape.

         I. Poole, Walter

         Fields, Lew, 1897-1941
Voice Lib.
649,   Weber, Joe, 1867-
bd.11-   Weber and Fields; two scenes from
12   vaudeville skit by the comedians. VTM,
1906.
         1 reel (7 in.) 7 1/2 in. per sec.
phonotape.
         CONTENTS.-bd.11. Hypnotic scene.-bd.12.
Mike and Meyer's drinking scene.

         I. Fields, Lew, 1897-1941.

         Fields, Totie
Voice Lib.
M1706   Reuben, David R
bd.3   Impotence in marriage; funny discussion
on parent/child discussions of sex. On
Mike Douglas Show with Totie Fields and the
Fifth Dimension. WJRT-TV, June 5, 1974.
         15 min. phonotape (1 r. 7 1/2 i.p.s.)

         1. Sex. I. Douglas, Mike, 1925?
II. Fifth Dimension. III. Fields, Totie.

         Fifth Dimension
Voice Lib.
M1706   Reuben, David R
bd.3   Impotence in marriage; funny discussion
on parent/child discussions of sex. On
Mike Douglas Show with Totie Fields and the
Fifth Dimension. WJRT-TV, June 5, 1974.
         15 min. phonotape (1 r. 7 1/2 i.p.s.)

         1. Sex. I. Douglas, Mike, 1925?
II. Fifth Dimension. III. Fields, Totie.

Voice Lib.
343   Fields, W   C   1879-1946.
bd.3   A humorous dialogue: "The Day I Drank
a Glass of Water". United Artists,
1927.
         1 reel (7 in.) 7 1/2 in. per sec.
phonotape.

         I. Title: The day I drank a glass of water.

Voice Lib.
343   Fields, W   C   1879-1946.
bd.2   Temperance lecture (a dialogue).
United Artists, 1927.
         1 reel (7 in.) 7 1/2 in. per sec.
phonotape.

Voice Lib.
M1025   Fields, W.C., 1879-1946.
bd.4   Excerpt from skit in "Eddie Cantor Show",
with Martha Raye, Dick Powell, etc. CBS
Radio, 1930's.
         1 reel (7 in.) 7 1/2 in. per sec.
phonotape.

         I. Raye, Martha, 1916-   II. Powell,
Dick, 1904-1963. III. Eddie Cantor Show
(radio program)

         Fields, W.C., 1879-1946
Voice Lib.
M1047   Old-time radio excerpts of the 1930's and
1940's, including: Rudy Vallee singing
"Linger a little longer"; Will Rogers on
panaceas for the Depression; Bing Crosby
singing "Sweet Georgia Brown"; Eddie Cantor;
Jimmy Durante singing "Inka-dinka-do";
musical skit by Clayton, Jackson and Durante;
wit by Harry Hershfield; musical selection
"Thinking of you" by Kay Kyser; Kate Smith
singing theme song, "When the moon comes over
the mountain"; W.C. Fields' temperance

(Continued on next card)

Voice Lib. Fields, W.C., 1879-1946
M1047 Old-time radio excerpts of the 1930's and
       1940's... (Card 2)

       lecture; Al Jolson singing "Rocka-by-your
       baby"; and George Burns and Gracie Allen
       skit. TV&R, 1930's and 1940's.
       1 reel (7 in.) 7 1/2 in. per sec.
       L. Vallee, Rudy, 1901-   II. Rogers, Will, 1879-1935. III.
       Crosby, Bing, 1901-   IV. Cantor, Eddie, 1893-1964. V. Durante,
       Jimmy, 1893-   VI. Clayton, Patti   VII. Jackson,
       Eddie   VIII. Hershfield, Harry, 1885-   IX. Kyser, Kay,
       1906-   X. Smith, Kate, 1909-   XI. Fields, W.C., 1879-
       1946. XII. Jolson, Al, 1886-1950. XIII. Burns, George, 1896-
       XIV. Allen, Gracie, 1906-

Voice Lib.
M1098 Fields, W.C., 1879-1946.
bd.1   Documentary program on the career of W.C.
       Fields. April 23, 1939.
          1 reel (7 in.) 7 1/2 in. per sec.
       phonotape.

          1. Fields, W.C., 1879-1946.

Voice Lib.
M1359 Fields, W.C., 1879-1946.
bd.3-   Excerpts of W.C. Fields.   Decca Records
4   (DL 79164), 1968.
          1 reel (7 in.) 7 1/2 in. per sec.
       phonotape.

          CONTENTS. -bd. 3. 1. The philosophy of W.C. Fields. 2. The
       "sound" of W.C. Fields. 3. The rascality of W.C. Fields. 4. The
       chicanery of W.C. Fields. -bd. 4. 1. The braggart and teller of
       tall tales. 2. The spirit of W.C. Fields. 3. W.C. Fields, a man
       against children, motherhood, fatherhood and brotherhood. 4.
       W.C. Fields, creator of weird names.

Voice Lib.
M1359 Fields, W.C., 1879-1946.
bd.1-   "The Temperance Lecture"; "The day I drank
bd 2   a glass of water". Blue Thumb Records (1968?)
          1 reel (7 in.) 7 1/2 in. per sec.
       phonotape.

          I. Title. II. Title: The day I drank a
       glass of water.

          Fields, W.C., 1879-1946
Voice Lib.
M322   Biography in sound (radio program)
          W.C. Fields, the magnificent rogue.
       NBC, 1955.
          1 reel (7 in.) 7 1/2 in. per sec. phonotape.
          L. Fields, W.C., 1879-1946. L. Fields, W.C., 1879-1946.
       II. Allen, Fred, 1894-1956. III. LaBaron, William   IV.
       Taylor, Robert Lewis, 1912-   V. McCarey, Thomas Leo, 1898-
       1969. VI. Harkins, James   - VII. Chevalier, Maurice,
       1889-1972. VIII. Kuromoto, Mrs. George   IX. Flynn,
       Errol Leslie, 1909-1959. X. Wynn, Ed, 1886-1966. XI. Dowling,
       Ray Dooley   XII. Sennett, Mack   XIII. Overacher,
       Ronald Leroy   XIV. Bergen, Edgar, 1903-   XV. Taurog,
       Norman, 1899-   XVI. Runnell, Ann   XVII. Cowen,
       Lester

          Fight for liberty and equality - French
             Revolution
C1
H80   Whorf, Michael, 1933-
          Fight for liberty and equality - French
       Revolution.
          1 tape cassette.   (The visual sounds of
       Mike Whorf. History and heritage, H80)
          Originally presented on his radio program, Kaleidoscope,
       WJR, Detroit.
          Duration: 38 min.
          The story of the French Revolution is one of the greatest sagas of
       the western world. "Liberty, equality and fraternity" was the hue
       and cry of the Frenchmen and the strains of the "Marseillaise" were
       heard everywhere.
          I. France - History - Revolution. I. Title.

Voice Lib.
M1202 Film stars on parade; short excerpts from
bd.2   famous motion pictures in U.S. and England,
       1932 to 1940. Audio Archives, 1942.
          1 reel (7 in.) 7 1/2 in. per sec.
       phonotape.

          1. Moving-pictures.

          The final problem
Voice Lib.
110   Doyle, Sir Arthur Conan, 1859-1930.
bd.2   The Final Problem, an episode read by
       John Gielgud, Ralph Richardson, and Orson
       Welles. His Master's Voice, 1947.
          1 reel (7 in.) 7 1/2 in. per sec.
       phonotape.

          I. Gielgud, John, 1904-   II. Richardson,
       Ralph David, 1902-   III. Welles, Orson,
       1915-   IV. Title.

          Fine, Ralph Adam, 1941-
Voice Lib.
M1665 Hunt, Everette Howard, 1918-
          On "Firing line" about Watergate payments,
       with William Buckley, Ralph Fine, John Owen,
       and Miss Bernstein. WKAR-TV, May 14, 1974.
          50 min. phonotape (1 r. 7 1/2 i.p.s.)

          1. Watergate Affair, 1972-   I.
       Buckley, William Frank, 1925-   II. Fine,
       Ralph Adam, 1941-   III. Owen, John

Voice Lib. Finney, Albert, 1936-
M310   American Broadcasting Company.
          Tribute to President John Fitzgerald Kennedy
       from the arts. Fredric March emcees; Jerome
       Hines sings "Worship of God and Nature" by
       Beethoven; Florence Eldridge recites "When
       lilacs last in the door-yard bloom'd" by Walt
       Whitman; Marian Anderson in two songs. Includes
       Charlton Heston, Sidney Blackmer, Isaac Stern,
       Nathan Milstein, Christopher Plummer, Albert
       Finney. ABC, November 24, 1963.
          35 min. phonotape (7 in. 7 1/2 i.p.s.)

(Continued on next card)

Voice Lib.
M714   Fire on super-aircraft-carrier "Constellation"
bd.2   in the Brooklyn Navy Yard.   On-the-spot
          broadcast, December 19, 1960.
          3 min., 43 sec.   phonotape (1 r.
          7 1/2 i.p.s.)

          1. Ships - Fires and fire protection.

First in the heart of his countrymen
C1
H23   Whorf, Michael, 1933-
         First in the heart of his countrymen.
         1 tape cassette.   (The visual sounds of
      Mike Whorf.   History and heritage, H23)
            Originally presented on his radio program, Kaleidoscope,
      WJR, Detroit.
            A dauntless and fearless commander-in-chief, who led his
      ragged army to victory in war and guided his young nation to
      victory in peace.

         L Washington, George, Pres. U.S., 1732-1799.
      L Title.

Voice Lib.
M936- The fire this time; radio broadcast. A
937   special documentary with actual sounds
bd.1   and comments on the significance of the
          August, 1965 five-day riots in Watts,
          California.   KPFK, August, 1965.
          2 reels (7 in.)   7 1/2 in. per sec.
          phonotape.

          1. Los Angeles - Riots, 1965.

Voice Lib.
M1547 Fisher, John, of General Electric.
bd.2   Energy uses past, present, and future.
          WKAR-FM, January 24, 1974.
          60 min.   phonotape (1 r.   3 3/4 i.p.s.)

          "... from a series of seminar programs
       called Prospectives of Energy, sponsored by
       the Center for Environmental Quality ..."

          1. Force and energy.   2. Power resources.

C1   FIREMEN
M52   Whorf, Michael, 1933-
         The dependables; firemen and firefighting.
         1 tape cassette.   (The visual sounds of
      Mike Whorf. Miscellaneous, M52)
            Originally presented on his radio program, Kaleidoscope,
      WJR, Detroit.
            Duration: 37 min.
            The exciting, dangerous world of some of our country's most
      important citizens, the firemen, is told in this visual narrative.
      Beginning with their simple origin as volunteers as the neighbor's
      fire, to the story of the modern day fire brigades - it's all here.

         L Firemen.   L Title.

C1   The fisher of men
R2   Whorf, Michael, 1933-
         The fisher of men.
         1 tape cassette.   (The visual sounds of
      Mike Whorf.   Religion, R2)

            Originally presented on his radio program, Kaleidoscope,
      WJR, Detroit.
            Duration: 29 min., 30 sec.
            The story of Peter, a man of rough-hewn manner, who became
      the leader of the disciples once the Christ had been crucified.

         L Peter, Saint, Apostle.   L Title.

Voice Lib.
M1362 First broadcast of Soviet military establish-
bd.1   ment from Berlin.   Peteler, May 2, 1945.
          1 reel (7 in.)   7 1/2 in. per sec.
          phonotape.

Fitzgerald, Ella, 1918-
Voice Lib.
M1696 Columbia Broadcasting System, inc.
bd.6   Special memorial to Duke Ellington, with
       John Hart, Sonny Greer, Russell Procope,
       Billy Taylor, Stanley Dance, and Ella
       Fitzgerald.   CBS-TV, May 24, 1974.
          15 min.   phonotape (1 r.   7 1/2 i.p.s.)

          1. Ellington, Duke, 1899-1974.   I. Hart,
       John.   II. Greer, Sonny.   III. Procope,
       Russell, 1908-   IV. Taylor, Billy.
       V. Dance, Stanley.   VI. Fitzgerald, Ella,
       1918-

Voice Lib.
M1090 The first family: satiric dramatization of the
bd.1   Kennedy family.   Scenes: a. the experiment; b.
          after-dinner conversations; c. the Malayan
          ambassador; d. relatively speaking; e. astro-
          nauts; f. motorcade; g. the party; h. the
          tour; i. "But vote !"; j. economy lunch; k.
          the decision; l. the White House visitor; m.
          press conference; n. the dress; o. Saturday
          night; p. Auld Lang Syne; q. bedtime story.
          LP phonodisc, Cadence Records, Inc., October
          22, 1962.
          1 reel (7 in.)   7 1/2 in. per sec.   phonotape.
          L Kennedy, John Fitzgerald, Pres. U.S., 1918-1963.

Voice Lib.
M1610 Fitzgerald, John W., 1924-
bd.1   Interview by Gary Schuster concerning
          his appointment to the State Supreme Court.
          WKAR-TV, November 16, 1973.
          3 min.   phonotape (1 r.   7 1/2 i.p.s.)

          1. Michigan.   Supreme Court.   I. Schuster,
       Gary.

164   *The G. Robert Vincent Voice Library*

Voice Lib.
M1599-
1600
Fitzgerald, Robert, 1910-
A quiet requiem for Ezra Pound, with poets Robert Lowell, Robert Fitzgerald, James Laughlin, and Robert McGregor. Modern Language Center, Harvard University, December 4, 1972.
70 min.   phonotape (2 r.   7 1/2 i.p.s.)

I. Pound, Ezra Loomis, 1885-1972. I. Lowell, Robert, 1917- II. Fitzgerald, Robert, 1910- III. Laughlin, James, 1914- IV. McGregor, Robert,

C1
FA2
FITZPATRICK, THOMAS, 1799-1854
Whorf, Michael, 1933-
Thomas Fitzpatrick.
1 tape cassette.   (The visual sounds of Mike Whorf. The forgotten American, FA2)
Originally presented on his radio program, Kaleidoscope, WJR, Detroit.
Duration: 9 min., 50 sec.
One of the most colorful of the American mountain men, he was noted for his dealings with the Indians.

I. Fitzpatrick, Thomas, 1799-1854. I. Title.

Voice Lib.
M630
bd.2
Fitzsimons, Roy
Ober, Norman
Interviews Roy Fitzsimons and Dr. Wade upon their return from the Second Antarctic Expedition, sponsored by Admiral Richard E. Byrd. GRV, 1941.
1 reel (7 in.)   7 1/2 i.p.s.   phonotape.

1. Byrd Antarctic Expedition, 2d, 1933-1935. I. Wade, Al. II. Fitzsimons, Roy.

C1
H27
The flag is passing by
Whorf, Michael, 1933-
The flag is passing by.
1 tape cassette.   (The visual sounds of Mike Whorf. History and heritage, H27)
Originally presented on his radio program, Kaleidoscope, WJR, Detroit.
Duration: 38 min.
A stirring, patriotic splash of red, white, and blue as the Visual Sounds takes a look at the story of Old Glory.

I. Flags - U.S. I. Title.

C1
PWM19
FLAGS
Whorf, Michael, 1933-
It's a grand old flag.
1 tape cassette.   (The visual sounds of Mike Whorf. Panorama; a world of music, PWM-19)
Originally presented on his radio program, Kaleidoscope, WJR, Detroit.
Duration: 25 min.
The story of the American flag, with selected patriotic music.

I. Flags. I. Patriotic music, American. I. Title.

C1
H27
FLAGS - U.S.
Whorf, Michael, 1933-
The flag is passing by.
1 tape cassette.   (The visual sounds of Mike Whorf. History and heritage, H27)
Originally presented on his radio program, Kaleidoscope, WJR, Detroit.
Duration: 38 min.
A stirring, patriotic splash of red, white, and blue as the Visual Sounds takes a look at the story of Old Glory.

I. Flags - U.S. I. Title.

Voice Lib.
M1012
bd.1
Flannery, Harry W   , 1900-
Sinclair, Upton Beall, 1878-1968.
Interview by Harry W. Flannery with Upton Sinclair for the AFL-CIO radio program "The Upton Sinclair Story". Includes "Sinclair's Early Life". AFL-CIO, April 9, 1960.
1 reel (7 in.)   7 1/2 in. per sec.   phonotape.

I. Flannery, Harry W   1900-

Voice Lib.
M1012
bd.2
Flannery, Harry W   , 1900-
Sinclair, Upton Beall, 1878-1968.
Interview by Harry W. Flannery with Upton Sinclair for the AFL-CIO radio program "The Upton Sinclair Story". Includes "The Jungle". AFL-CIO, April 9, 1960.
1 reel (7 in.)   7 1/2 in. per sec.   phonotape.

I. Flannery, Harry W   1900-

Voice Lib.
M1012
bd.3
Flannery, Harry W   1900-
Sinclair, Upton Beall, 1878-1968.
Interview by Harry W. Flannery with Upton Sinclair for the AFL-CIO radio program "The Upton Sinclair Story". Includes "King Cole" and "The Brass Check". AFL-CIO, April 9, 1960.
1 reel (7 in.)   7 1/2 in. per sec.   phonotape.

I. Flannery, Harry W   1900-

Voice Lib.
M1013
bd.1
Flannery, Harry W   1900-
Sinclair, Upton Beall, 1878-1968.
Interview by Harry W. Flannery with Upton Sinclair for the AFL-CIO radio program "The Upton Sinclair Story". Includes "Oil" and "The Flivver King". AFL-CIO, April 9, 1960.
1 reel (7 in.)   7 1/2 in. per sec.   phonotape.

I. Flannery, Harry W   1900-

Flannery, Harry W   1900–
Voice Lib.
M982   Sinclair, Upton Beall, 1878–1968.
bd.1   Reminiscences by Upton Sinclair during
          interview with Harry W. Flannery, including
          comments on "The Jungle", "The Brass Check",
          "King Coal", "The Flivver King", and others.
          ABC, October 16, 1966.
            1 reel (7 in.)   7 1/2 in. per sec.
          phonotape.

            I. Flannery, Harry W   1900–

Fleming, James, 1915–
Voice Lib.
353   Russia and the bomb...   1949.   (Card 2)
bd.19

            Samuel King, 1900–   IV. Hugness, Thornton.
          V. McMahon, James O'Brien, 1903–1952. VI.
          Douglas, Paul Howard, 1892–   VII. Dulles,
          John Foster, 1888–1959. VIII. Groves, Leslie
          R   1896–1970. IX. Churchill, Winston
          Leonard Spencer, 1874–1965. X. Acheson, Dean
          Gooderham, 1893–1971. XI. Fleming, James,
          1915–

Voice Lib.
M1674   Flash Gordon (radio program)
bd.1   Flash Gordon.   Golden Age Radio Records,
          1935.
            10 min.   phonotape (1 r.   7 1/2 i.p.s.)

Voice Lib. Fleming, James, 1915–
M1278   Hunt, Haroldson Lafayette, 1889–
          H.L. Hunt, "the richest and the rightest".
          A revealing interview with oil millionaire
          Hunt who speaks out on his wealth, his
          philosophy, political patronage, communist
          threat, and other views. By reporter James
          Fleming.   NET, August 27, 1967.
            1 reel (7 in.)   7 1/2 in. per sec.
          phonotape.

            I. Fleming, James, 1915–

           A fleeting moment of fame – George Dewey
C1
M115   Whorf, Michael, 1933–
          A fleeting moment of fame – George Dewey.
          1 tape cassette.   (The visual sounds of
        Mike Whorf. History and heritage, H115)
          Originally presented on his radio program, Kaleidoscope,
        WJR, Detroit.
          Duration: 30 min., 45 sec.
          We will learn in this program of the life and times of Admiral
        George Dewey, one of naval history's greatest leaders; and of the
        battles with which his name has become synonymous.

          L Dewey, George, 1837–1917. L Title.

Voice Lib.
M1590   Fleming, Robben Wright, 1916–
          Who am I; commencement address, Michigan
          State University winter term 1974.
          Introduction by President Clifton Wharton.
          WKAR-AM, March 10, 1974.
            20 min.   phonotape (1 r.   7 1/2 i.p.s.)

            I. Wharton, Clifton Reginald, 1926–

Voice Lib.
M975   Fleming, Canon
bd.10   Reciting Tennyson's poem: "The Charge
          of the Light Brigade". Rococo-Can., 1910.
            1 reel (7 in.)   7 1/2 in. per sec.
          phonotape.

            I. Title: The charge of the Light
          Brigade.

           FLYING SAUCERS
C1
SC30   Whorf, Michael, 1933–
          Great balls of fire; unidentified flying
          saucers.
            1 tape cassette.   (The visual sounds of
        Mike Whorf. Science, SC30)
          Originally presented on his radio program, Kaleidoscope,
        WJR, Detroit.
          Duration: 38 min.
          Of course no one believes in flying saucers. No one believes
        in interplanetary space travel. No one believes in life on distant
        planets. But ... if no one believes in any of this, what's all
        this talk about "great balls of fire"?
          L Flying saucers.   L Title.

Fleming, James, 1915–
Voice Lib.
353   Russia and the bomb, discussed by various
bd.19   personalities.   NBC, September 25, 1949.
            1 reel (7 in.)   7 1/2 in. per sec.
          phonotape.

            Participants: Harrison Brown, Harold Urey,
          Samuel Allison, Thornton Hugness, Brien McMahon,
          Paul Douglas, John Foster Dulles, Leslie Groves,
          Winston Churchill, Dean Acheson, James Fleming.

            I. Brown, Harrison Scott, 1917–   II.
          Urey, Harold Clayton, 1893–   III. Allison,
                         (Continued on next card)

           The Flying Yorkshireman
Voice Lib.
221–   Knight, Eric Mowbray, 1897–1943.
224   "The Flying Yorkshireman", narrated by
          the author.   G.R. Vincent, 1942.
            4 reels (7 in.)   7 1/2 in. per sec.
          phonotape.

            I. Title.

Flynn, Errol Leslie, 1909-1959
Voice Lib.
M322   Biography in sound (radio program)
          W.C. Fields, the magnificent rogue.
          NBC, 1955.
              1 reel (7 in.)   7 1/2 in. per sec.   phonotape.
              L. Fields, W.C., 1879-1946.   L. Fields, W.C., 1879-1946.
          II. Allen, Fred, 1894-1956. III. LaBaron, William   IV.
          Taylor, Robert Lewis, 1912-   V. McCarey, Thomas Leo, 1898-
          1969. VI. Harkins, James   -VII. Chevalier, Maurice,
          1889-1972. VIII. Kuromoto, Mrs. George   IX. Flynn,
          Errol Leslie, 1909-1959. X. Wynn, Ed, 1886-1966. XL Dowling,
          Ray Dooley   XII. Sennett, Mack   XIII. Overacher,
          Ronald Leroy   XIV. Bergen, Edgar, 1903-   XV. Taurog,
          Norman, 1899-   XVI. Runnell, Ann   XVII. Cowen,
          Lester

Voice Lib.
616   Foch, Ferdinand, 1851-1929.
bd.3   Greeting to the American Legion convention
          in Paris; salutes American flag and valor of
          U.S. troops. GRV, 1921.
              1 reel (7 in.)   7 1/2 in. per sec.
          phonotape.

                    Fogg, Sam
Voice Lib.
M1562   Armstrong, Anne
bd.2   Speech to National Press Club, Washington,
          D.C. Introduced by Sam Fogg.   February 14,
          1974.
              25 min.   phonotape (1 r.   7 1/2 i.p.s.)

              1. U.S. - Centennial celebrations, etc.
          I. Fogg, Sam.

          FOLK-LORE, AMERICAN
C1
H39   Whorf, Michael, 1933-
              The tall tales of America - folklore, legends.
              1 tape cassette.   (The visual sounds of
          Mike Whorf. History and heritage, H39)
              Originally presented on his radio program, Kaleidoscope,
          WJR, Detroit.
              Duration: 45 min., 30 sec.
              John Henry, Johnny Appleseed, Paul Bunyan, the great legends
          of American folklore come to life in this amusing account of folk
          tales and folk-songs about America.
              L. Folk-lore, American. 2. Folk-songs, American. L. Title.

          FOLK MUSIC - U.S.
Voice Lib.
M782   Lomax, Alan, 1915-
bd.2-   Dust Bowl songs and conversation with
784   Woody Guthrie. Library of Congress,
bd.1   March 22, 1940.
              3 reels (7 in.)   7 1/2 in. per sec.
          phonotape.

              1. Folk music - U.S.   I. Guthrie,
          Woody, 1912-1967.

          FOLK MUSIC - U.S.
Voice Lib.
M781-   Lomax, Alan, 1915-
782   Folk songs and conversation with Woody
bd.1   Guthrie. Library of Congress, March 21,
          1940.
              2 reels (7 in.)   7 1/2 in. per sec.
          phonotape.

              I. Guthrie, Woody, 1912-1967.

                    The folk singer
C1
S21   Whorf, Michael, 1933-
              The folk singer.   (The visual sounds of
              1 tape cassette.
          Mike Whorf. Social, S21)
              Originally presented on his radio program, Kaleidoscope,
          WJR, Detroit.
              Duration: 41 min.
              Woody Guthrie and his songs depicting the real life
          experiences of his era.
              L. Guthrie, Woody, 1912-1967. L. Title.

          FOLK-SONGS
C1
PWM10   Whorf, Michael, 1933-
              Songbook of the Old World.
              1 tape cassette.   (The visual sounds of
          Mike Whorf. Panorama; a world of music,
          PWM-10)
              Originally presented on his radio program, Kaleidoscope,
          WJR, Detroit.
              Duration: 25 min., 50 sec.
              With many musical examples, here we have the influence
          of other lands on the American folk song.
              L. Folk-songs. L. Title.

          FOLK-SONGS, AMERICAN
C1
H39   Whorf, Michael, 1933-
              The tall tales of America - folklore, legends.
              1 tape cassette.   (The visual sounds of
          Mike Whorf. History and heritage, H39)
              Originally presented on his radio program, Kaleidoscope,
          WJR, Detroit.
              Duration: 45 min., 30 sec.
              John Henry, Johnny Appleseed, Paul Bunyan, the great legends
          of American folklore come to life in this amusing account of folk
          tales and folk-songs about America.
              L. Folk-lore, American. 2. Folk-songs, American. L. Title.

Voice Lib.
M1681   Fonda, Henry Jaynes, 1905-
bd.2   Interviewed on the Today show by Barbara
          Walters. NBC-TV, May 10, 1974.
              5 min.   phonotape (1 r.   7 1/2 i.p.s.)

              1. Fonda, Henry Jaynes, 1905-
          I. Walters, Barbara, 1931-

Fonda, Henry Jaynes, 1905-
Voice Lib.
M1033   Voice of America.
        Twentieth anniversary program of Voice of
America broadcasts narrated by Henry Fonda,
and including the voices of Carl Sandburg,
Danny Kaye, Jawaharlal Nehru, Franklin D.
Roosevelt, Charles Malik, Arnold Toynbee,
William Faulkner, Harry S.Truman, Dwight D.
Eisenhower, Helen Hayes, Dag Hammarskjöld,
Winston Churchill, and John F. Kennedy.
Voice of America, 1963.
        1 reel (7 in.)   7 1/2 in. per sec.
phonotape.
                                    (Continued on next card)

Fonda, Henry Jaynes, 1905-
Voice Lib.
M1033   Voice of America. Twentieth anniversary
        program... 1963.   (Card 2)

        L Fonda, Henry Jaynes, 1905-   IL Sandburg, Carl,
1878-1967. III. Kaye, Danny, 1913-   IV. Nehru, Jawaharlal,
1889-1964. V. Roosevelt, Franklin Delano, Pres. U.S., 1882-
1945. VL Malik, Charles Habib, 1906-   VII. Toynbee,
Arnold Joseph, 1889-   VIII. Faulkner, William, 1897-1962.
IX. Truman, Harry S, Pres. U.S., 1884-1972. X. Eisenhower,
Dwight David, Pres. U.S., 1890-1969. XL Hayes, Helen,
1900-   XII. Hammarskjöld, Dag, 1905-1961. XIII. Churchill,
Winston Leonard Spencer, 1874-1965. XIV. Kennedy, John
Fitzgerald, Pres. U.S., 1917-1963.

        A fool there was
Voice Lib.
M793   Hilliard, Robert
bd.3   American actor in scenes from "A Fool
        There Was", Hilliard's famous success.
        Victor, 1912.
            1 reel (7 in.)   7 1/2 in. per sec.
        phonotape.

            I. Title: A fool there was.

        For God and nation
C1
R26   Whorf, Michael, 1933-
        For God and nation.
        1 tape cassette.   (The visual sound of
Mike Whorf. Religion, R26)
        Originally presented on his radio program, Kaleidoscope,
WJR, Detroit.
        Duration: 35 min., 50 sec.
        Knox's devotion to the cause of reformation and his zeal in
preaching this gospel brought him imprisonment and exile, yet his
beliefs rose above these hardships to transform his native land of
Scotland and influence the world.

        L Knox, John, 1505-1572.   L Title.

Voice Lib.
M1057   Forbes-Robertson, Sir Johnston, 1853-1937.
bd.1   Discussing Shakespearean acting and
        narrating some famous excerpts of his
        plays. HMV, 1931.
            1 reel (7 in.)   7 1/2 i.p.s.   phonotape.

            1. Acting.

Forbes-Robertson, Sir Johnston, 1853-
Voice Lib.
M225   Packard, Frederick
        Styles in Shakespearean acting, 1890-1950.
        Creative Associates, 1963?
        1 reel (7 in.)   7 1/2 i.p.s.   phonotape.

        L Sothern, Edward Askew, 1826-1881. IL Marlowe,
Julia, 1865-1950. III. Booth, Edwin, 1833-1893. IV. Gielgud,
John, 1904-   V. Robeson, Paul Bustill, 1898-   VL Terry,
Dame Ellen, 1848-1928. VII. Allen, Viola. VIII. Welles,
Orson, 1915-   IX. Skinner, Otis, 1858-1942. X. Barrymore,
John, 1882-1942. XL Olivier, Sir Laurence Kerr, 1907-
XII. Forbes-Robertson, Sir Johnston, 1853-   XIII. Evans,
Maurice. XIV. Thorndike, Dame Sybil, 1882-   XV. Robson,
Flora. XVL LeGallienne, Eva, 1899-   XVII. Anderson,
Judith. XVIII. Duncan, Augustin. XIX. Hampden, Walter.
XX. Speaight, Robert, 19??   XXL Jones, Daniel.

Voice Lib.   FORCE AND ENERGY
M1547   Fisher, John, of General Electric.
bd.2   Energy uses past, present, and future.
        WKAR-FM, January 24, 1974.
            60 min.   phonotape (1 r.   3 3/4 i.p.s.)

        "... from a series of seminar programs
called Prospectives of Energy, sponsored by
the Center for Environmental Quality ..."

        1. Force and energy. 2. Power resources.

Voice Lib.   Ford, Clara J. (Bryant)
281   Ford, Henry, 1863-1947.
bd.2   Henry Ford's 75th birthday party; Mrs. Ford
        thanks Detroit for its salute to her husband.
        Detroit, WJR, July 30, 1938.
            1 reel (7 in.)   7 1/2 in. per sec.
        phonotape.

            I. Ford, Clara J. (Bryant)

Voice Lib.
M1560   Ford, Gerald R., 1913-
bd.2   Inauguration of Gerald R. Ford as
        Vice President. CBS-TV, December 6, 1973.
            25 min.   phonotape (1 r.   7 1/2 i.p.s.)

        Commentary by Roger Mudd and William
Miller.

            I. Mudd, Roger. II. Miller, William.

Voice Lib.
M1591   Ford, Gerald R., 1913-
        Privacy; address at the National Governors'
        Conference. WKAR-AM, March 6, 1974.
            20 min.   phonotape (1 r.   7 1/2 i.p.s.)

            1. Privacy, Right of.

Voice Lib.
M1739   Ford, Gerald R., 1913-
bd.3   Acceptance speech for the "Father of the Year"
          award. CBS, June 14, 1974.
          3 min. phonotape (1 r.   7 1/2 i.p.s.)

          1. Family - addresses, essays, lectures.

Voice Lib.
281 .. Ford, Henry, 1863-1947.
bd.2   Henry Ford's 75th birthday party; Mrs. Ford
          thanks Detroit for its salute to her husband.
          Detroit, WJR, July 30, 1938.
          1 reel (7 in.)   7 1/2 in. per sec.
          phonotape.

          I. Ford, Clara J. (Bryant)

          Ford, Gerald R., 1913-
Voice Lib.
M1720   Nixon, Richard Milhous, Pres. U.S., 1913-
bd.5   Departing for the Mideast, with Vice
          President Gerald Ford. NBC-TV, June 10,
          1974.
          5 min. phonotape (1 r.   7 1/2 i.p.s.)

          I. Ford, Gerald R., 1913-

Voice Lib.
183   Ford, Henry, 1863-1947.
bd.2   Memorial tribute to Henry Ford;
          favorite songs of Mr. Ford. WJR,
          April 8, 1947.
          1 reel (7 in.)   7 1/2 in. per sec.
          phonotape.

          FORD, GERALD R., 1913-
Voice Lib.
M1744   Vestal, M   S
bd.1   Discussing his book Jerry Ford, up close,
          on the Today Show with Bill Monroe, Barbara
          Walters, and Jess Marlowe. NBC-TV, June 25,
          1974.
          10 min. phonotape (1 r.   7 1/2 i.p.s.)

          1. Ford, Gerald R., 1913-   2. Vestal,
          M.S./Jerry Ford, up close. I. Monroe, Bill.
          II. Walters, Barb   , 1931-   III. Marlowe,
          Jess.

Voice Lib.
M713   Ford, Patrick K
bd.2   Narrating Westinghouse Time Capsule,
          containing voices and events from 1930 to
          1963. NVL production, December, 1964.
          1 reel (7 in.)   7 1/2 in. per sec.
          phonotape.

          FORD, GERALD R., 1913-
Voice Lib.
M1611   Young, Andrew, 1932-
bd.4   Discusses Vice President Gerald Ford.
          WKAR-TV [1974?]
          4 min. phonotape (1 r.   7 1/2 i.p.s.)

          1. Ford, Gerald R., 1913-

          Forster, Albert
Voice Lib.
M1017   Hitler, Adolf, 1889-1945.
bd.4-   Being introduced by Albert Forster upon
1018   arrival in the city of Danzig, followed by
bd.1   lengthy address by Hitler; stresses unity
          between U.S.S.R. and Germany against
          democracies, inferiority of Polish people,
          and their persecution of Germans. F. Peteler,
          September 19, 1939.
          2 reels (7 in.) 7 1/2 in. per sec.
          phonotape.
          I. Forster, Albert.

Voice Lib.
M1056   Ford, Henry, 1863-1947.
bd.2   Remarks at dedication ceremonies of Ford
          Field Recreation Center at Dearborn, Michigan.
          Audio Scriptions, July 30, 1936.
          1 reel (7 in.)   7 1/2 in. per sec.
          phonotape.

          FOSTER, STEPHEN COLLINS, 1826-1864
C1
M21   Whorf, Michael, 1933-
          The American troubador.
          1 tape cassette. (The visual sounds of
          Mike Whorf. Miscellaneous, M21)

          Originally presented on his radio program, Kaleidoscope,
          WJR, Detroit.
          Duration: 40 min.
          This narrative deals with the life and trials of the gifted, but
          melancholy Stephen Foster.

          I. Foster, Stephen Collins, 1826-1864. I. Title.

C1
PWM7
FOSTER, STEPHEN COLLINS, 1826–1864

Whorf, Michael, 1933–
Stephen Foster.
1 tape cassette. (The visual sounds of
Mike Whorf. Panorama; a world of music, PWM-7)

Originally presented on his radio program, Kaleidoscope,
WJR, Detroit.
Duration: 25 min.
The life and times of Stephen Foster, including excerpts
of his music.

I. Foster, Stephen Collins, 1826-1864. I. Title.

Voice Lib.
M714
bd.6
FRANCE, ARMÉE

Sevareid, Arnold Eric, 1912–
Describes the French soldier during the
early days of World War II.
3 min., 56 sec. phonotape (1 r.
7 1/2 i.p.s.)

1. France. Armée.

C1
R19
Founder of Methodism

Whorf, Michael, 1933–
Founder of Methodism
1 tape cassette. (The visual sounds of
Mike Whorf. Religion, R19)

Originally presented on his radio program, Kaleidoscope,
WJR, Detroit.
Duration: 42 min., 30 sec.
The founders of a new Christian denomination, beset upon by
turmoil and frustration, yet John and Charles Wesley lived to see
a new age in spirituality.

I. Wesley, John, 1703 2. Wesley, Charles, 1707-1788.
I. Title.

C1
H12
FRANCE. ARMÉE. ESCADRILLE LAFAYETTE

Whorf, Michael, 1933–
The Lafayette Escadrille.
1 tape cassette. (The visual sounds of
Mike Whorf. History and heritage, H12)
Originally presented on his radio program, Kaleidoscope,
WJR, Detroit.
Duration: 28 min., 30 sec.
A group of daring young American aviators went to France at
the out-set of World War I to fly and fight for the Allies. Here is
the unlikely adventure of a group of young flyers who were at war
long before their own country entered the conflict.

I. France. Armée. Escadrille Lafayette. I. Title.

C1
SC14-
SC15
Four wheel American dream – the automobile

Whorf, Michael, 1933–
Four wheel American dream – the automobile.
2 tape cassettes. (The visual sounds of
Mike Whorf. Science, SC14-SC15)
Originally presented on his radio program, Kaleidoscope,
WJR, Detroit.
Duration: 54 min., 20 sec.; 50 min., 5 sec.
Two narratives dealing with the automobile industry. The
saga of its invention and a technical approach explaining the
car as a machine.

I. Automobiles. I. Title.

FRANCE – POLITICS AND GOVERNMENT – 1940-1945
Voice Lib.
M714
bd.9
Pétain, Henri Phillippe Bénoni Omer, 1856-1951.
Announcing his assumption as head of state
of France. June 16-22, 1940.
1 reel (7 in.) 7 1/2 in. per sec.
phonotape.

C1
SC7
FOURTH DIMENSION

Whorf, Michael, 1933–
I wouldn't have believed it.
1 tape cassette. (The visual sounds of
Mike Whorf. Science, SC7)
Originally presented on his radio program, Kaleidoscope,
WJR, Detroit.
Duration: 43 min., 45 sec.
Many believe that the fourth dimension is a world of ghosts,
poltergeists, of spirits and ghouls - others do not. Can a person
see things if he or she wants to? Turn down the lights and listen.

I. Fourth dimension. I. Title.

FRANCE – POLITICS AND GOVERNMENT – 1940-1945
Voice Lib.
M848
bd.1
Reynaud, Paul, 1878-1966.
French Prime Minister announcing recall
of Gen. Pétain from Spain to become France's
Deputy Premier in current hour of war
emergency. NBC shortwave, May 18, 1940.
1 reel (7 in.) 7 1/2 in. per sec.
phonotape.

1. Petain, Henri Philippe Bénoni Omer,
1856-1951.

C1
H29
FOURTH OF JULY

Whorf, Michael, 1933–
Freedom day, July 4th.
1 tape cassette. (The visual sounds of
Mike Whorf. History and heritage, H29)

Originally presented on his radio program, Kaleidoscope,
WJR, Detroit.
Duration: 43 min., 50 sec.
The bunting and banners, the bands and the beauty of Indepen-
dence Day. Here, 'midst stirring music and eloquent words is a
tribute to America for Americans.

I. Fourth of July. I. Title.

C1
R6
FRANCIS OF ASSISI, SAINT, 1182-1226

Whorf, Michael, 1933–
The saint from Assisi.
1 tape cassette. (The visual sounds of
Mike Whorf. Religion, R6)

Originally presented on his radio program, Kaleidoscope,
WJR, Detroit.
Duration: 39 min., 30 sec.
This is the tale of Francis of Assisi, who would form the Franciscan
order, would be friend to man and animal, and would teach mankind
the meaning of true humility.

I. Francis of Assisi, Saint, 1182-1226. I. Title.

Voice Lib.
652   Franco Bahamonde, Francisco, 1892-
bd.20   Interview with David Schoenbrun, explaining
         his political philosophy for Spain.   CBS,
         December 6, 1950.
         1 reel (7 in.)   7 1/2 in. per sec.
         phonotape.

         I. Schoenbrun, David Franz, 1915-

C1
H6   FRANKLIN, BENJAMIN, 1706-1790
      Whorf, Michael, 1933-
         The witty sage of Philadelphia.
         1 tape cassette   (The visual sounds of
      Mike Whorf. History and heritage, H6)
         Originally presented on his radio program, Kaleidoscope,
      WJR, Detroit, Michigan.
         Duration: 44 min.
         Franklin found time to invent, innovate, to write,
      philosophize and become his nation's most beloved "grand
      old man."

         L. Franklin, Benjamin, 1706-1790.   L. Title.

Voice Lib.
M1362   Frank, Hans, 1900-1946.
bd.4   Last words before his execution by hanging
        at Nuremberg, Germany.   Peteler, October,
        1946.
           1 reel (7 in.)   7 1/2 in. per sec.
        phonotape.

Voice Lib.
M952   Franz Joseph I, emperor of Austria, 1930-1916.
bd.4   Speaking at Paris World's Fair.   H. E.
        Scholz, 1900.
           1 reel (7 in.)   7 1/2 in. per sec.
        phonotape.

                Frankel, Max
Voice Lib.
M1477   Discussion of Supreme Court decision on
        publishing Pentagon Papers.   William B.
        Macomber, deputy under-secretary of state;
        Senator Henry Jackson; Max Frankel, head of
        New York Times' Washington bureau; Benjamin
        Bradley, executive editor of Washington Post.
        Questioned by Carl Stern, NBC; Martin Hayden,
        Detroit News; James J. Kilpatrick, Washington
        Star Syndicate; Kenneth Crawford, Washington
        Post; Edwin Newman.   NBC-TV, June 30, 1971.
           1 reel (7 in.)   7 1/2 in. per sec.
        phonotape.

(Continued on next card)

Voice Lib.
M1466   Franz Joseph I, emperor of Austria, 1830-1916.
bd.9   Imperial endorsement of fund for Austrian
        military widows and orphans.   Peteler,
        December 14, 1915.
           1 reel (7 in.)   7 1/2 in. per sec.
        phonotape.

                Frankel, Max
Voice Lib.
M1478   The Pentagon Papers; discussion of content,
        meaning.   Bernard Kalb, CBS; Senator J.W.
        Fulbright; Senator John Tower; Arthur
        Schlesinger; Walt Rostow; Max Frankel,
        New York Times; Crosby Noyes, Washington
        Evening Star.   CBS-TV, July 13, 1971.
           1 reel (7 in.)   7 1/2 in. per sec.
        phonotape.
           L. Kalb, Bernard   II. Fulbright, James William, 1905-
        III. Tower, John Goodwin, 1925-   IV. Schlesinger, Arthur
        Meier, 1888-   V. Rostow, Walt Whitman, 1916-   VL
        Frankel, Max   VII. Noyes, Crosby

Voice Lib.   FRAZIER, JOE, 1944-
M1690   Muhammad Ali, 1942-
             Integration, separation, politics, and
          violence.   WKAR, February 27, 1970.
             50 min.   phonotape (1 r.   7 1/2 i.p.s.)

             1. Muhammad Ali, 1942-   2. Frazier,
          Joe, 1944-   3. Black Muslims.

C1
H100   FRANKLIN, BENJAMIN, 1706-1790
        Whorf, Michael, 1933-
           America's grand old man - Benjamin Franklin.
           1 tape cassette.   (The visual sounds of
        Mike Whorf. History and heritage, H100)
           Originally presented on his radio program, Kaleidoscope,
        WJR, Detroit.
           Duration: 36 min.
           The wise man of America has become one of the most quoted,
        most remembered men of the American Revolution. His life revolved
        around his country, his countrymen. His books, his studies, and his
        maxims echo to us throughout history.

           L. Franklin, Benjamin, 1706-1790.   L. Title.

                Frederick, Pauline
Voice Lib.
M1454   United Nations.
bd.2   Ceremonies from 25th anniversary of the
        founding of UN at San Francisco, with
        Pauline Frederick as MC.   ABC, August,
        1971.
           1 reel (7 in.)   7 1/2 in. per sec.
        phonotape.

           I. Frederick, Pauline

Voice Lib.
M1656   Free Speech carols, "Joy to UC"; songs of
bd.1   farce and Christmas in memory of the
            Free Speech Movement's October demonstration
            at the University of California in 1964.
            Berkeley, Calif., Free Speech Movement,
            November 24, 1964.
            20 min.   phonotape (1 r.   7 1/2 i.p.s.)

            1. Free Speech Movement.

                     Free Speech Movement
Voice Lib.
M1658   FSM's sounds and songs of the
            demonstration.   Berkeley, Calif., FSM
            Records Dept., September 21, 1964.
            50 min.   phonotape (1 r.   7 1/2 i.p.s.)

            1. Free Speech Movement. 2. Students -
        Political movements.   I. Free Speech
        Movement.

            FREE SPEECH MOVEMENT
Voice Lib.
M1656   Free Speech carols, "Joy to UC"; songs of
bd.1   farce and Christmas in memory of the
            Free Speech Movement's October demonstration
            at the University of California in 1964.
            Berkeley, Calif., Free Speech Movement,
            November 24, 1964.
            20 min.   phonotape (1 r.   7 1/2 i.p.s.)

            1. Free Speech Movement.

            Freedom day, July 4th
C1
H29   Whorf, Michael, 1933-
            Freedom day, July 4th.
            1 tape cassette.   (The visual sounds of
        Mike Whorf. History and heritage, H29)
            Originally presented on his radio program, Kaleidoscope,
        WJR, Detroit.
            Duration: 43 min., 50 sec.
            The bunting and banners, the bands and the beauty of Indepen-
        dence Day. Here, 'midst stirring music and eloquent words is a
        tribute to America for Americans.

            L Fourth of July.   L 7

Voice Lib.
M1912 Freedom house; special TV program. Filmed
            documentary about men and their methods in
            the fight to combat communist tyranny;
            featuring the Murrow-McCarthy debates from
            "See It Now" TV programs; also excerpts
            from Army-McCarthy Senate hearings, state-
            ments by Gen. Eisenhower and Bishop Sheil.
            CBS, 1954.
            1 reel (7 in.)   7 1/2 i.p.s.   phonotape.
            1. Anti-communist movements. 2. McCarthy-
        Army controversy, 1954.

            FREEHAN, BILL, 1941-
C1
M11   Whorf, Michael, 1933-
            The man in the iron mask.
            1 tape cassette.   (The visual sounds of
        Mike Whorf. Miscellaneous, M11)
            Originally presented on his radio program, Kaleidoscope,
        WJR, Detroit.
            Duration: 42 min., 10 sec.
            An account of the thoughts and ideas of a big league catcher.
        The emphasis is on baseball, but a ball player thinks of other
        things as well.

            L Freehan, Bill, 1941-   2. Baseball. L. Title.

Voice Lib.
M1490   Frensdorf, Edward
bd.2   Candidate for Governor of Michigan (1924);
            campaign speech.   Arco Records, 1924.
            1 reel (7 in.)   7 1/2 i.p.s.   phonotape.

            1. Michigan - Politics and government.

            The frenzied home front
C1
S70   Whorf, Michael, 1933-
            The frenzied home front.
            1 tape cassette.   (The visual sounds of
        Mike Whorf. Social, S70)
            Originally presented on his radio program, Kaleidoscope,
        WJR, Detroit.
            Duration: 36 min., 50 sec.
            The period of the First World War marked a dramatic transition
        in American life. As we consider the "good old days" to be around
        the turn of the century and the end of the Victorian era, so the war
        served as a bridge to the roaring twenties to follow.

            L European War, 1914-1918 - U.S. 2. U.S. - Social conditions.
        L Title.

Voice Lib.
M747   Freud, Sigmund, 1856-1939.
bd.1   Reviewing work in the past, hopes to
            continue study in England after departure
            from Nazi Austria; introduced by Marie
            Coleman Nelson, managing editor of the
            "Psychoanalytical Review".   National
            Psychological, 1938.
            1 reel (7 in.)   7 1/2 in. per sec.
        phonotape.

            I. Nelson, Marie Coleman, 1915-

            FREUD, SIGMUND, 1856-1939
Voice Lib.
M746   Reik, Theodor
bd.1   Reading from his book "Voices from the
            Inaudible" and giving reminiscences of his
            association with Dr. Sigmund Freud.
            Introduced by Marie Coleman Nelson, managing
            editor of the "Psychoanalytical Review."
            Psychoanalytical Review, 1964.
            1 reel (7 in.)   7 1/2 in. per sec.
        phonotape.
            1. Freud, Sigmund, 1856-1939. L Nelson, Marie Coleman,
        1915-   II. Title: Voices from the inaudible.

Voice Lib.
M1376 Frick, Wilhelm, 1877-1946.
bd.7   Remarks at the opening of the public
       exposition in Berlin. Peteler, June 7,
       1936.
          1 reel (7 in.) 7 1/2 in. per sec.
       phonotape.

Voice Lib.
577   Frohman, Daniel, 1851-1940.
bd.2   The theater today and yesterday. CRV,
       October 20, 1937.
          1 reel (7 in.) 7 1/2 in. per sec.
       phonotape.

       1. Theater - Hist.

Voice Lib.
M1667 Friedan, Betty
          Revolution in the consciousness of women;
       speech at Albion College. WKAR, March 3,
       1971.
          47 min.   phonotape (1 r.   7 1/2 i.p.s.)

          1. Women's liberation movement.

Voice Lib.
M1396- From here to the seventies. NBC-TV two-and-a-half hour
1397   documentary pertaining to events occurring during the 1960's.
          NBC-TV, October 7, 1969.
          2 reels (7 in.) 7 1/2 i.p.s.   phonotape.

          CONTENTS. -pt. I. 1. Space sequence, including prediction by
       President Kennedy and excerpts of Apollo 8 mission and first moon
       landing. -2. Sounds of the '60's: a. Joan Baez; b. Berlin Confron-
       tation; c. Bay of Pigs; d. Cuban missile crisis; e. JFK in Berlin;
       f. Dominican invasion; g. LBJ speech on Gulf of Tonkin; h. Vietnam
       i. LBJ declining nomination; j. Peter, Paul and Mary; k. Paul
       Newman on various news items. -3. Civil Rights: a. Dr. Martin
       Luther King, "I have a dream..."; b. schools; c. police; d.
       integration and control; e. riots; f. death of Dr. King; g. Black
       Panthers; h. Black pride. -4. Young generation: a. politics in the

          (Continued on next card)

C1   FRIEDRICH II, DER GROSSE, KING OF PRUSSIA,
H75   1712-1786
       Whorf, Michael, 1933-
          The incomparable emperor, Frederick the Great.
          1 tape cassette. (The visual sounds of
       Mike Whorf. History and heritage, H75)

       Originally presented on his radio program, Kaleidoscope,
       WJR, Detroit.
          Duration: 37 min., 10 sec.
       Frederick the Great was a hero to the Germans - a king, an
       emperor - who ruled as majestically, and at times as oppressively,
       as any of his contemporaries, and this is a story rich in pageantry,
       intrigue and tyranny.

          1. Friedrich II, der Grosse, King of Prussia, 1712-1786.
       1. Title.

Voice Lib.
M1396- From here to the seventies. 1969.   (Card 2)
1397
          CONTENTS (Cont'd) '60's; b. Nixon's "can't kick me around"
       speech and acceptance speech; c. JFK acceptance speech,
       inauguration, and death; d. Bobb. Kennedy "Let us go on to
       Chicago" and funeral service; e. Ted Kennedy, Chappaquiddick;
       f. Humphrey at convention; g. LBJ's "We shall overcome" speech;
       h. Goldwater nomination speech; i. Stokely Carmichael on
       violence; j. Richard Nixon after convention, "We must speak
       quietly". -pt. II. 1. Middle East situation (Paul Newman narration):
       a. Communism; b. hot spots of the world. -2. Problems of the
       good life (Eli Abel narration): a. pollution; b. automation; c. man
       finishing himself off? -3. Generation gap: a. Beatles; b. television;
       c. politics; d. drugs; e. Woodstock. -4. Conflict (problems today,
       predictions). -5. Medical changes: a. birth; b. smoking; c.
       emotions; d. gap between   research and patient.

       FRIML, RUDOLPH, 1881-
Voice Lib.
M761 Harbach, Otto Abels, 1873-1963.
bd.14   Excerpt from "Tunesmiths Past and Present"
       (Program 4); speaking about Rudolph Friml
       and his technique in composing. Westinghouse
       Broadcasting Corporation, 1964.
          1 reel (7 in.) 7 1/2 in. per sec.
       phonotape. (The Music Goes Round and Round)

          1. Friml, Rudolph, 1881-   I. Title:
       Tunesmiths past and present. II. Series.

Voice Lib.
M1398 From here to the seventies, Part III.   NBC-TV
bd.1   two-and-a-half hour documentary pertaining to
       events occurring during the 1960's. NBC-TV,
       October 7, 1969.
          1 reel (7 in.) 7 1/2 in. per sec.
       phonotape.
          CONTENTS. -1. Style changes: a. clothes; b. sex; c. violence;
       d. outlook; e. morals; f. sports and protest. -2. Man's mortality:
       a. death of Winston Churchill; b. Bobby Kennedy, speech before
       assassination; c. Dr. King, "I've been to the mountain top..." and
       "We'll get to the Promised Land"; d. John Kennedy's last speech. -
       3. Hunger around the world: a. Green Revolution, problems and
       benefits; b. abortions to control population. -4. Communications

          (Continued on next card)

       Fritsche, Hans
Voice Lib.
216-   Hitler, Adolph, 1889-1945.
217   Speech before German Parliament,
       announcing annexation of Danzig, with
       introduction by Hermann Göring and comments
       by Hans Fritsche (English translation).
       Detroit, WJR, September 1, 1939.
          2 reels (7 in.) 7 1/2 in. per sec.
       phonotape.

          I. Göring, Hermann, 1893-1946.   II. Fritsche,
       Hans

Voice Lib.
M1398 From here to the seventies, Part III... 1969.
bd.1   (Card 2)
          CONTENTS, cont'd. explosion: a. David Brinkley, TV. -5. Ending:
       a. Paul Newman; b. Barbra Streisand.

          I. Kennedy, Robert Francis, 1925-1968. II.
       King, Martin Luther, 1929-1968. III. Kennedy,
       John Fitzgerald, Pres. U.S., 1917-1963. IV.
       Brinkley, David McClure, 1920-   V. Newman,
       Paul, 1925-   VI. Streisand, Barbra, 1942-

C1
H13

From St. Joe to Sacramento

Whorf, Michael, 1933–
  From St. Joe to Sacramento.
  1 tape cassette. (The visual sounds of
Mike Whorf. History and heritage, H13)
    Originally presented on his radio program, Kaleidoscope,
WJR, Detroit.
    Duration: 29 min.
    It began in Missouri and ended hundreds of miles away in
California. Atop lightning-fast horses, the small wiry riders
braved the elements, the Indians and the loneliness to carry the
mail for the Pony Express.

    L Pony Express. L Title.

C1.
H51

From the halls of Montezuma

Whorf, Michael, 1933–
  From the halls of Montezuma.
  1 tape cassette. (The visual sounds of
Mike Whorf. History and heritage, H51)

    Originally presented on his radio program, Kaleidoscope,
WJR, Detroit.
    Duration: 39 min., 60 sec.
    As America's greatness is often written in the deeds of her
fighting men, so does this moving narrative of the United States
Marine Corps illustrate the countless moments of heroism, the
personal sacrifices and the gallant battles of our country's history.

    L U.S. Marine Corps. L Title.

C1
H14

FRONTIER AND PIONEER LIFE

Whorf, Michael, 1933–
  Tales of the frontier and the forty-niners.
  1 tape cassette. (The visual sounds of
Mike Whorf. History and heritage, H14)
    Originally presented on his radio program, Kaleidoscope,
WJR, Detroit.
    Duration: 39 min.
    The year was 1849, and from every corner of the globe came
all types of men searching for quick wealth. "Gold," was the
cry from California and with their hopes and dreams came the
seekers. For a few months it meant adventure and excitement for
those who confronted the frontier and were called the forty-niners.

    L California – Gold discoveries. 2. Frontier and pioneer life.
L Title.

C1
H9

FRONTIER AND PIONEER LIFE – THE WEST

Whorf, Michael, 1933–
  Brave, bold and bad.
  1 tape cassette. (The visual sounds of
Mike Whorf. History and heritage, H9)
    Originally presented on his radio program, Kaleidoscope,
WJR, Detroit.
    Duration: 41 min.
    The gunslinger, the desperado, the hero, the villain. Was the
gunman a legend, or was he a paranoid psychopath? They
were men who included William Bonny, Sam Bass, Wyatt Earp
and Bill Hickock – about 250 men in all who were bad, bold
and brave – or were they?
    L Frontier and pioneer life – The West. 2. Crime and
criminals – The West.   L Title.

C1
H88

The frontiersman – Davy Crockett

Whorf, Michael, 1933–
  The frontiersman – Davy Crockett.
  1 tape cassette. (The visual sounds of
Mike Whorf. History and heritage, H88)
    Originally presented on his radio program, Kaleidoscope,
WJR, Detroit.
    Duration: 35 min., 30 sec.
    In the rough and ready existence of the American frontier, it
took an exceptional man to live off the land, let alone to rise
above his fellows as did Davy Crockett.

    L Crockett, David, 1786-1836. L Title.

Frost, David Paradine, 1939–
Voice Lib.
M1382 "A look at RFK". Memorial program by David
bd.1   Frost on first anniversary of assassination
         of Senator Robert Kennedy. Includes inter-
         view broadcast originally in David Frost's
         series "The Next President of the U.S."
         ABC-TV, June 5, 1969.
           1 reel (7 in.)   7 1/2 in. per sec.
         phonotape.

           I. Frost, David Paradine, 1939–

Frost, David Paradine, 1939–
Voice Lib.
M1481 Armstrong, Louis, 1900-1971.
bd.1   Tribute after his death by David Frost.
         Replay of last number performed by Louis
         Armstrong on The David Frost Show: "The
         Boy from New Orleans".   Group-W News,
         August 5, 1971.
           1 reel (7 in.)   7 1/2 in. per sec.
         phonotape.

           I. Frost, David Paradine, 1939–

Voice Lib.   Frost, David Paradine, 1939–
M1481   Vanocur, Sander, 1928–
bd.3   Interviewed by David Frost on believing
        the government, being misled, journalistic
        responsibility.   Comments from Sam Levenson.
        July, 1971.
           1 reel (7 in.)   7 1/2 i.p.s.   phonotape.

           1. Journalistic ethics.   I. Frost, David
        Paradine, 1939–   II. Levenson, Samuel,
        1911–

Voice Lib.
M340–   Frost, Robert, 1874-1963.
341   Library of Congress Press Conference.
bd.1   Voice of America, 1958.
           2 reels (7 in.)   7 1/2 i.p.s.
        phonotape.

Voice Lib.
M378   Frost, Robert, 1874-1963.
bd.1   Reads his poetry and talks about it in
        excerpts from programs produced for NET.
        Defines poetry; reads "The pasture", "Stopping
        by the woods"; talks to high school students
        about poetic ideas, writing prose and poetry;
        polishing and creating a work; his start as
        a poet; talks to Jonas Salk on his poetry and
        his life.   WQED (NET), 1959.
           1 reel (7 in.)   7 1/2 i.p.s.   phonotape.

Voice Lib.
M189-
190   Frost, Robert, 1874-1963.
    Reciting and commenting on his own
poetry. Yale University, 1961.
    2 reels (7 in.)   7 1/2 i.p.s.
phonotape.

Voice Lib.
M721
bd.2   Fuess, Claude Moore, 1885-
    Eulogy on Calvin Coolidge, the man from
Vermont. 1938.
    1 reel (7 in.)   7 1/2 in. per sec.
phonotape.

    1. Coolidge, Calvin, Pres. U.S., 1872-1933.

Voice Lib.
M117   Frost, Robert, 1874-1963.
    Robert Frost reads his own works.
Carillon, 1961.
    1 reel (7 in.)   7 1/2 i.p.s.
phonotape.

    Fulbright, James William, 1905-
Voice Lib.
M1478 The Pentagon Papers; discussion of content,
    meaning. Bernard Kalb, CBS; Senator J.W.
    Fulbright; Senator John Tower; Arthur
    Schlesinger; Walt Rostow; Max Frankel,
    New York Times; Crosby Noyes, Washington
    Evening Star. CBS-TV, July 13, 1971.
    1 reel (7 in.)   7 1/2 in. per sec.
phonotape.
    I. Kalb, Bernard   II. Fulbright, James William, 1905-
III. Tower, John Goodwin, 1925-   IV. Schlesinger, Arthur
Meier, 1888-   V. Rostow, Walt Whitman, 1916-   VI.
Frankel, Max   VII. Noyes, Crosby

    Frost, Robert, 1874-1963
C1
A19   Whorf, Michael, 1933-
    The amazing Mr. Frost.
    1 tape cassette. (The visual sounds of
Mike Whorf. Art, music, and letters, A19)
    Originally presented on his radio program, Kaleidoscope,
WJR, Detroit.
    Duration: 43 min., 45 sec.
    Actual recordings of Frost reading his own works make up the
body of this program, yet the narrator brings in important aspects
of his life that made Robert Frost the man he was.

    I. Frost, Robert, 1874-1963. I. Frost, Robert, 1874-1963.
II. Title.

Voice Lib.
M1371
bd. 2   Funeral ceremonies of General of the Army Dwight David
    Eisenhower, beginning with the casket being carried from
    the National Cathedral to the U.S. Capitol in Washington,
    D.C.; President Nixon's eulogy at the Capitol rotunda;
    followed by reconveying the casket to the National Cathedral
    where prayers and services are heard. CBS-TV, March 30, 1969.
    1 reel (7 in.) 7 1/2 in. per sec. phonotape.

    I. Eisenhower, Dwight David, Pres. U.S., 1890-1969.
    I. Nixon, Richard Milhous, Pres. U.S., 1913-

    FROST, ROBERT, 1874-1963
Voice Lib.
M1285 Kennedy, John Fitzgerald, Pres. U.S., 1917-1963.
bd.5   Excerpt from his address at Amherst College
    during a ceremony held in tribute to poet
    Robert Frost. NBC-P.B.L., November 26,
    1967 (1962)
    1 reel (7 in.)   7 1/2 in. per sec.
phonotape.

    1. Frost, Robert, 1874-1963.

Voice Lib.
M319   Funeral of John F. Kennedy: church ceremonies at Washington
    Cathedral; quote of speech segments of JFK and delivery of
    memorial sermon by Most Rev. Philip M. Hannan; prayers
    at bier by Cardinal Richard Cushing; departure of coffin
    from Cathedral to Arlington Cemetery; description of journey
    and arrival. CBS, November 25, 1963.
    1 reel (7 in.) 7 1/2 i.p.s. phonotape.

    I. Kennedy, John Fitzgerald, Pres. U.S., 1917-1963 -
Assassination. I. Hannan, Philip Matthew, 1913-   II.
Cushing, Richard James, Cardinal, 1895-

    FROST, ROBERT, 1874-1963
C1
A19   Whorf, Michael, 1933-
    The amazing Mr. Frost.
    1 tape cassette. (The visual sounds of
Mike Whorf. Art, music, and letters, A19)
    Originally presented on his radio program, Kaleidoscope,
WJR, Detroit.
    Duration: 43 min., 45 sec.
    Actual recordings of Frost reading his own works make up the
body of this program, yet the narrator brings in important aspects
of his life that made Robert Frost the man he was.

    I. Frost, Robert, 1874-1963. I. Frost, Robert, 1874-1963.
II. Title.

    The fur trader - John Jacob Astor
C1
H78   Whorf, Michael, 1933-
    The fur trader - John Jacob Astor.
    1 tape cassette. (The visual sounds of
Mike Whorf. History and heritage, H78)
    Originally presented on his radio program, Kaleidoscope,
WJR, Detroit.
    Duration: 37 min., 50 sec.
    This depicts the life and style of John Jacob Astor, a German
immigrant who literally turned the sidewalks into gold and paved
the streets with silver.

    I. Astor, John Jacob, 1763-1848. I. Title.

Voice Lib. Gabel, Martin, 1912-
M1677   Dracula (radio program)
      Mercury Theatre production of Dracula
    with Orson Welles, George Colouris, and
    Martin Gabel. Ferris State College, 1937.
    55 min. phonotape (1 r. 7 1/2 i.p.s.)

      I. Welles, Orson, 1915-   II. Colouris,
George. III. Gabel, Martin, 1912-

Voice Lib. Gable, Clark, 1901-1960
M655   The Twentieth Century (TV program)
bd.1   "The creative thirties", narrated by
    Walter Cronkite. CBS, 1963.
    25 min. phonotape (1 r. 7 1/2 i.p.s.)

    L. U.S. - Civilization - 1918-1945. L. Bowes, Edward,
1874-1946. II. Geismar, Maxwell David, 1909-
III. MacDonald, Dwight, 1906- IV. Welles, Orson, 1915-
V. Cronkite, Walter Leland, 1916- VI. Gable, Clark, 1901-
1960. VII. Lewis, Sinclair, 1885-1951. VIII. Houseman,
John, 1902-   IX. Roosevelt, Franklin Delano, Pres. U.S.,
1882-1945.

Voice Lib. Gabrielson, Guy George, 1891-
383   I can hear it now (radio program)
    CBS, February 9, 1951.
    1 reel (7 in.) 7 1/2 in. per sec.
phonotape.

    L. Wilson, Charles Edward, 1886-1972. II. Gabrielson, Guy
George, 1891- III. Taft, Robert Alphonso, 1889-1953. IV.
Martin, Joseph William, 1884-1965. V. McCarthy, Joseph
Raymond, 1909-1957. VI. Benton, William Burnett, 1900-1973.
VII. Malone, George Wilson, 1890-1961. VIII. Capehart, Homer
Earl, 1897- IX. Eisenhower, Dwight David, Pres. U.S., 1890-
1969. X. Lee, J   V   XI. Hodge, John Reed, 1893-
1963. XII. Overton, Watkins XIII. DiSalle, Michael
Vincent, 1908-   XIV. Boyce, Eddy   XV. Conklin, Ed
XVI. Collins, Joseph Lawton, 1896-

Voice Lib. Gage, Arthur
573   I can hear it now (radio program)
bd.2-   1945-1949. CBS, 1950?
574   2 reels (7 in.) 7 1/2 in. per sec.
bd.1 phonotape.

    L. Murrow, Edward Roscoe, 1908-1965. II. Nehru, Jawaharlal,
1889-1964. III. Philip, duke of Edinburgh, 1921- IV. Elizabeth II,
Queen of Great Britain, 1926- V. Ferguson, Homer, 1889- VI.
Hughes, Howard Robard, 1905- VII. Marshall, George Catlett,
1880- VIII. Ruth, George Herman, 1895-1948. IX. Lilienthal,
David Eli, 1899- X. Trout, Robert, 1908- XI. Gage, Arthur.
XII. Jackson, Robert Houghwout, 1892-1954. XIII. Gromyko, Ana-
tolii Andreevich, 1908- XIV. Baruch, Bernard Mannes, 1870-
1965. XV. Churchill, Winston Leonard Spencer, 1874-1965. XVI.
Winchell, Walter, 1897-1   )XVII. Davis, Elmer Holmes, 1890-
(Continued on next card)

Voice Lib.
M742   Gaitskell, Hugh Todd Naylor, 1906-1963.
bd.3   Speaking during British election campaign
    in 1959 while he is being heckled by the
    audience. BBC, September 26, 1959.
    1 reel (7 in.) 7 1/2 in. per sec.
phonotape.

Voice Lib. Galbraith, John Kenneth, 1908-
M1668-   The modern city; speech at Michigan
1669   State University. WKAR, May 1, 1974.
    1 hr., 15 min. phonotape (2 r. 7 1/2
i.p.s.)

      1. Cities and towns.

C1   GALILEI, GALILEO, 1564-1642
SC27 Whorf, Michael, 1933-
      And then came the light - Copernicus, Galileo.
    1 tape cassette. (The visual sounds of
Mike Whorf. Science, SC27)
    Originally presented on his radio program, Kaleidoscope,
WJR, Detroit.
    Duration: 39 min., 15 sec.
    For the true stargazer here is an accurate account of the great
astronomers. Included are brief accounts of the lives of Copernicus,
Galileo, and others who have contributed to the science of
astronomy.

    L. Copernicus, Nicolaus, 1473-1543. 2. Galilei, Galileo,
1564-1642. I. Title.

      Gallagher and Sheen
Voice Lib.
M617 Radio in the 1920's: a series of excerpts
bd.1-   from important broadcasts of the 1920's,
bd.25   with brief prologue and epilogue; a sample
    of radio of the period. NVL, April, 1964.
    1 reel (7 in.) 7 1/2 in. per sec.
phonotape.
    L. Radio programs. L. Marconi, Guglielmo, marchese, 1874-
1937. II. Kendall, H   G   III. Coolidge, Calvin, Pres. U.S.,
1872-1933. IV. Wilson, Woodrow, Pres. U.S., 1856-1924. V.
Roosevelt, Franklin Delano, Pres. U.S., 1882-1945. VI. Lodge,
Henry Cabot, 1850-1924. VII. LaGuardia, Fiorello Henry, 1882-1947.
VIII. The Happiness Boys (Radio program) IX. Gallagher and Sheen.
X. Barney Google. XI. Vallee, Rudy, 1901- XII. The two
(Continued on next card)

C1   GAMA, VASCO DA, 1469-1524
H108 Whorf, Michael, 1933-
      The navigator - Vasco de Gama.
    1 tape cassette. (The visual sounds of
Mike Whorf. History and heritage, H108)
    Originally presented on his radio program, Kaleidoscope,
WJR, Detroit.
    Duration: 38 min.
    Hundreds of years ago when the race to expand the world made
rivals of the world's great powers, Portugal sent forth its greatest
soldier and mariner, Vasco de Gama.

    L. Gama, Vasco da, 1469-1524. I. Title.

C1   GAMES
M35 Whorf, Michael, 1933-
      Games people play.
    1 tape cassette. (The visual sounds of
Mike Whorf. Miscellaneous, M35)
    Originally presented on his radio program, Kaleidoscope,
WJR, Detroit.
    Duration: 37 min.
    Not only is this a session on the history of game playing, but also
some instruction as to how and why some games are played. There's
also a brief look into the sociocultural aspect of the games that
people play.

    L. Games. L. Title.

C1
M35
Games people play
Whorf, Michael, 1933-
Games people play.
1 tape cassette. (The visual sounds of
Mike Whorf. Miscellaneous, M35)

Originally presented on his radio program, Kaleidoscope,
WJR, Detroit.
Duration: 37 min.
Not only is this a session on the history of game playing, but also
some instruction as to how and why some games are played. There's
also a brief look into the sociocultural aspect of the games that
people play.

L. Games. L. Title.

GANDHI, MOHANDAS KARAMCHAND, 1869-1948

Voice Lib.
M300   Buck, Pearl (Sydenstricker). 1892-1973.
bd.1   Gandhi's life and virtue.   Voice
of America, April 25, 1960.
1 reel (7 in.) 7 1/2 in. per sec.
phonotape.

Voice Lib.
540   Gandhi, Mohandas Karamchand, 1869-1948.
bd.25   On independence for India. Fox
Movietone, 1933.
1 reel (7 in.)   7 1/2 in. per sec.
phonotape.

1. India.

GANDHI, MOHANDAS KARAMCHAND, 1869-1948

Voice Lib.
M740   Nehru, Jawaharlal, 1889-1964.
bd.5   Excerpt from All-India radio broadcast on
assassination of Gandhi. CBS, January 3,
1948.
1 reel (7 in.) 7 1/2 in. per sec.
phonotape.

Voice Lib.
265   Gandhi, Mohandas Karamchand, 1869-1948.
bd.2   Spiritual message; his conception of
God. BBC, 1934.
1 reel (7 in.) 7 1/2 in. per sec.
phonotape.

GANDHI, MOHANDAS KARAMCHAND, 1869-1948

Voice Lib.
M1402   Shirer, William Lawrence, 1904-
bd.2   Excerpt of conversation with Merv Griffin
about broadcasting during early part of World
War II and about Mahatma Gandhi.   CBS,
November 13, 1969.
1 reel (7 in.) 7 1/2 in. per sec.
phonotape.

1. Gandhi, Mohandas Karamchand, 1869-1948.
I. Griffin, Mervyn Edward, 1925-

Voice Lib.
M1553   Gandhi, Mohandas Karamchand, 1869-1948.
Speech of the 1947 Asian Relations
Conference and excerpts from a 1947
prayer meeting. University of California,
Santa Barbara, 1947.
24 min. phonotape (1 r.   7 1/2 i.p.s.)

GANDHI, MOHANDAS KARAMCHAND, 1869-1948

C1
S2
Whorf, Michael, 1933-
A man named Ghandi.
1 tape cassette. (The visual sounds of
Mike Whorf. Social, S2)

Originally presented on his radio program, Kaleidoscope,
WJR, Detroit.
Duration: 29 min.
Gandhi was counselor, advisor, and spiritual guide to a nation
which upheld the caste system and he alone was able to break
through to open the eyes of the world.

L. Gandhi, Mohandas Karamchand, 1869-1948. L. Title.

Gandhi, Mohandas Karamchand, 1869-1948
Voice Lib.
M622   Radio in the 1940's (Part III): a series of
bd.1-   excerpts from important broadcasts of the 1940's; a sample
bd.15   of radio of the period. NVL, April, 1964.
1 reel (7 in.) 7 1/2 in. per sec. phonotape.

L. Radio programs. L. Miller, Alton Glenn, 1909(?)-1944. II.
Diles, Ken   III. Wilson, Donald Harlow, 1900-   IV.
Livingstone, Mary   V. Benny, Jack, 1894-   VL Harris,
Phil   VII. Merman, Ethel, 1909-   VIII. Smith, "Wonderful"
IX. Bennett, Richard Dyer   X. Louis, Joe, 1914-   XI.
Eisenhower, Dwight David, Pres. U.S., 1890-1969. XII. MacArthur,
Douglas, 1880-1964. XIII. Romulo, Carlos Pena, 1899-   XIV.
Welles, Orson, 1915-   XV. Jackson, Robert Houghwout, 1892-1954.
XVI. LaGuardia, Fiorello Henry, 1882-1945. XVII. Nehru, Jawa-
harlal, 1889-1964. XVIII. Gandhi, Mohandas Karamchand, 1869-1948.

Gannett, Lewis Stiles, 1891-1966
Voice Lib.
M272   Biography in sound (radio program)
bd.1   Heywood Broun. NBC, date?
1 reel (7 in.) 7 1/2 in. per sec.
phonotape.

L. Broun, Heywood Campbell, 1888-1939. L. Broun,
Heywood Campbell, 1888-1939. II. Swope, Herbert Bayard,
1882-1958. III. Wilson, Mattie   IV. Jackson, Gardner
V. Meany, Thomas   VI. Waldron, Beatrice   VII.
Gordon, Max   VIII. Madison, Connie   IX. Gannett,
Lewis Stiles, 1891-1966. X. Collins, Joseph, 1866-1950. XI.
Brown, Earl Louis, 1900-   XII. Levy, Newman, 1888-
XIII. Growth, John   XIV. Bye, George   XV.
Roosevelt, Franklin Delano, Pres. U.S., 1882-1945. XVI.
Reynolds, Quentin James, 1902-1965.

Voice Lib. Garagiola, Joe
M1248 Baseball fifty years ago; interviews with four
famous old time baseball players, on NBC
"Today" show, by host Hugh Downs, supported by
sportcaster Joe Garagiola and Dr. Lawrence
Ritter, author of new book.   NBC-TV, June 9,
1967.
1 reel (7 in.)   7 1/2 in. per sec.   phonotape.

L. Baseball. L. Downs, Hugh Malcolm, 1921-   II. Garagiola,
Joe. III. Ritter, Lawrence S. /The glory of their times. IV. Roush,
Edd, 1893-   V. Marquart, Rube, 1890-   VI. O'Doul, Lefty,
1897-   VII. Meyers, John, 1880-

Voice Lib. Garagiola, Joe
M1726 Aaron, Hank, 1934-
bd.3   Interviewed on Hank Aaron Day in New York
City, by Curt Gowdy, Joe Garagiola, Tom
Brokaw, and Gene Shalitt.   NBC, June 18,
1974.
10 min.   phonotape (1 r.   7 1/2 i.p.s.)

1. Aaron, Hank, 1934-   2. Baseball.
I. Gowdy, Curt. II. Garagiola, Joe.
III. Brokaw, Tom. J. Shalitt, Gene.

Voice Lib. Gardner, Hy, 1904-
M1037 Biography in sound (radio program)
bd.1   "The Actor", narrated by Morgan Beatty.
Cast includes Tallulah Bankhead, Hy Gardner,
Rocky Graziano, Arthur Miller, Uta Hagen,
Jackie Cooper, Sir Laurence Olivier, Gad
Gayther, Barbara Ashley, Hortense Powdermaker,
Peter Ustinov, Alfred Hitchcock, Leonard Lyons,
John Guston, Helen Hayes, Dick Mayne, Ralph
Bellamy, Lionel Barrymore, Sir Ralph Richardson,
José Ferrer, and Walter Kerr.   NBC Radio, 1950's.
1 reel (7 in.)   7 1/2 in. per sec.
phonotape.
(Continued on next card)

Voice Lib.
344   Garin, Vasco Viera
bd.15   Speaking at U.N. just after Adlai
Stevenson: "it is tragic that the brave
but defenseless Goans have been
sacrificed to the idol of power and
force . . ."   CBS, December 19, 1961.
1 reel (7 in.)   7 1/2 in. per sec.
phonotape.

Voice Lib. Garland, Judy, 1922-1969
M764   Harburg, Edgar Y   1896-
bd.3   Excerpts from "Sound Track" (Program 7);
comments on his feelings toward the musical
efforts of the D's. Including example
of movie music: "Over the rainbow", with
Judy Garland; lyrics by Harburg. Westinghouse Broadcasting Corporation, 1964.
3 min., 58 sec.   phonotape (1 r.   7 1/2
i.p.s.) (The music goes round and round)

L. Music, Popular (Songs, etc.) - U.S. L. Garland,
Judy, 1922-196%. L. Title: Sound track. III. Series.

Voice Lib.
M766   Garnier, Jacques
bd.4   Excerpt from "Popular Music of Europe"
(Program 11); comments on French tastes in
music, including song "Cela n'a pas
d'importance" by Les Surfs.   Westinghouse
Broadcasting Corporation, 1964.
2 min., 54 sec.   phonotape (1 r.   7 1/2
i.p.s.) (The music goes round and round)

1. Music, Popular (Songs, etc.) - France.
I. Title: Popular music of Europe. II. Series.

Voice Lib.
M767   Garnier, Jacques
bd.3   Excerpt from "Russia and her swinging satellites" (Program 12);
comments on how effective the ban on rock-and-roll in Russia
actually is, including Soviet pop tune "Lilacs in bloom" and
Russian version of "St. Louis blues" and two numbers recorded
clandestinely in Leningrad: "Let's dance" and "I want to be happy
cha-cha-cha".   Westinghouse Broadcasting Corporation, 1964.
9 min., 42 sec.   phonotape (1 r.   7 1/2 i.p.s.)
(The music goes round and round)

L. Music, Popular (Songs, etc.) - Russia. L. Title: Russia
and her swinging satellites. II. Series.

GAUGUIN, PAUL, 1848-1903
C1
A1   Whorf, Michael, 1933-
The strange life of Paul Gauguin.
1 tape cassette.   (The visual sounds of
Mike Whorf. Art, music and letters, A1)

Originally presented on his radio program, Kaleidoscope,
WJR, Detroit.
Duration: 26 min., 15 sec.
Gauguin forsook the comforts of his world to wander half
way around the globe as a painter.

L. Gauguin, Paul, 1848-1903. L. Title.

Voice Lib.
M714   Gaulle, Charles de, Pres. France, 1890-
bd.9   1970.
Speaking from England against capitulation
to Germany.   June 16-22, 1940.
1 reel (7 in.)   7 1/2 in. per sec.
phonotape.

Voice Lib.
M1225   Gaulle, Charles de, Pres., France, 1890-
bd.5   1970.
Radio appeal made over the BBC about
resistance to the German occupation after
the surrender of France and the founding
of the Free French Forces.   Peteler,
June 23, 1940.
1 reel (7 in.)   7 1/2 in. per sec.
phonotape.

1. Anti-Nazi movement.

Gaulle, Charles de, Pres. France, 1890-1970

Voice Lib.
572- I can hear it now (radio program)
573 1933-1946. CBS, 1948.
bd.1 2 reels (7 in.) 7 1/2 in. per sec.
phonotape.
L. Murrow, Edward Roscoe, 1908-1965. IL LaGuardia, Fiorello Henry, 1882-1947. IIL Chamberlain, Neville, 1869-1949. IV. Roosevelt, Franklin Delano, Pres. U. S., 1882-1945. V. Churchill, Winston Leonard Spencer, 1874-1965. VL Gaulle, Charles de, Pres. France, 1890-1970. VII. Eisenhower, Dwight David, Pres. U.S., 1890-1969. VIII. Willkie, Wendell Lewis, 1892-1944. IX. Martin, Joseph William, 1884-1968. X. Elizabeth II, Queen of Great Britain, 1926- XL Margaret Rose, Princess of Gt. Brit., 1930- XII. Johnson, Hugh Samuel, 188?- '42. XIII. Smith, Alfred Emanuel, 1873-1944. XIV. Lindberg( )arles Augustus, 1902- XV. Davis,
(Continued on next card)

Gaulle, Charles de, Pres. France, 1890-1970

Voice Lib.
624 LaGuardia, Fiorello Henry, 1882-1947.
bd.2 Welcomes DeGaulle on his visit to New
York City at conclusion of World War II,
makes DeGaulle honorary citizen of New
York City. WNYC, August 27, 1945.
1 reel (7 in.) 7 1/2 in. per sec.
phonotape.

GAULLE, CHARLES DE, PRES. FRANCE, 1890-1970

Voice Lib.
M584 LaGuardia, Fiorello Henry, 1882-1947.
bd.2 Welcomes DeGaulle to New York City in his
office in City Hall and later repeated for
the public on the steps of City Hall.
WNYC, July 10, 1944.
1 reel (7 in.) 7 1/2 in. per sec.
phonotape.

Voice Lib.
640 Gay Nineties Revue (radio program)
bd.3 Musical radio program with cast including
Joe Howard and Beatrice Kay. CBS, July, 1940.
1 reel (7 in.) 7 1/2 in. per sec.
phonotape.

I. Howard, Joe   II. Kay, Beatrice

Voice Lib.
539 Gay Nineties Revue (Radio program)
bd.5 The talking machine; skit with Joe Howard,
Al Rinker, and Beatrice Kay concerning
Edison's talking machine. Simulated voices
of P.T. Barnum and Florence Nightingale.
CBS, 1940.
1 reel (7 in.) 7 1/2 in. per sec.
phonotape.

I. Howard, Joe   II. Rinker, Al
III. Kay, Beatrice   IV. Title.

Gayther, Gad

Voice Lib.
M1037 Biography in sound (radio program)
bd.1 "The Actor", narrated by Morgan Beatty.
Cast includes Tallulah Bankhead, Hy Gardner,
Rocky Graziano, Arthur Miller, Uta Hagen,
Jackie Cooper, Sir Laurence Olivier, Gad
Gayther, Barbara Ashley, Hortense Powdermaker,
Peter Ustinov, Alfred Hitchcock, Leonard Lyons,
John Guston, Helen Hayes, Dick Mayne, Ralph
Bellamy, Lionel Barrymore, Sir Ralph Richardson,
José Ferrer, and Walter Kerr. NBC Radio, 1950's.
1 reel (7 in.) 7 1/2 in. per sec.
phonotape.
(Continued on next card)

Gehrig, Lou, 1903-1941

Voice Lib.
M617 Radio in the 1920's: a series of excerpts
bd.1- from important broadcasts of the 1920's,
bd.25 with brief prologue and epilogue; a sample
of radio of the period. NVL, April, 1964.
1 reel (7 in.) 7 1/2 in. per sec.
phonotape.
L. Radio programs. L. Marconi, Guglielmo, marchese, 1874-1937. IL Kendall, H   G   IIL Coolidge, Calvin, Pres. U.S., 1872-1933. IV. Wilson, Woodrow, Pres. U. S., 1856-1924. V. Roosevelt, Franklin Delano, Pres. U. S., 1882-1945. VI. Lodge, Henry Cabot, 1850-1924. VII. LaGuardia, Fiorello Henry, 1882-1947. VIII. The Happiness Boys (Radio program) IX. Gallagher and Sheen. X. Barney Google. XL. Vallee, Rudy, 1901- XII. The two
(Continued on next card)

Gehrig, Lou, 1903-1941

Voice Lib.
572- I can hear it now (radio program)
573 1933-1946. CBS, 1948.
bd.1 2 reels (7 in.) 7 1/2 in. per sec.
phonotape.
L. Murrow, Edward Roscoe, 1908-1965. IL LaGuardia, Fiorello Henry, 1882-1947. IIL Chamberlain, Neville, 1869-1949. IV. Roosevelt, Franklin Delano, Pres. U. S., 1882-1945. V. Churchill, Winston Leonard Spencer, 1874-1965. VL Gaulle, Charles de, Pres. France, 1890-1970. VII. Eisenhower, Dwight David, Pres. U.S., 1890-1969. VIII. Willkie, Wendell Lewis, 1892-1944. IX. Martin, Joseph William, 1884-1968. X. Elizabeth II, Queen of Great Britain, 1926- XL Margaret Rose, Princess of Gt. Brit., 1930- XII. Johnson, Hugh Samuel, 188?- '42. XIII. Smith, Alfred Emanuel, 1873-1944. XIV. Lindberg( )arles Augustus, 1902- XV. Davis,
(Continued on next card)

Gehrig, Lou, 1903-1941

Voice Lib.
M948 Ruth, George Herman, 1894-1948.
bd.7 In a comedy skit with Lou Gehrig. 1938.
1 reel (7 in.) 7 1/2 in. per sec.
phonotape.

I. Gehrig, Lou, 1903-1941.

Geismar, Maxwell David, 1909-

Voice Lib.
M655 The Twentieth Century (TV program)
bd.1 "The creative thirties", narrated by
Walter Cronkite. CBS, 1963.
25 min. phonotape (1 r. 7 1/2 i.p.s.)
L. U.S. - Civilization - 1918-1945. L. Bowes, Edward, 1874-1946. IL Geismar, Maxwell David, 1909- IIL MacDonald, Dwight, 1906- IV. Welles, Orson, 1915-1960. V. Cronkite, Walter Leland, 1916- VL Gable, Clark, 1901-1960. VII. Lewis, Sinclair, 1885-1951. VIII. Houseman, John, 1902- IX. Roosevelt, Franklin Delano, Pres. U.S., 1882-1945.

Voice Lib.
M771   Gemini 4 (space flight): excerpts of descrip-
bd.1   tion of take-off; Gemini 4 and Gemini Control
          announcements.   June 3, 1965.
          1 reel (7 in.)   7 1/2 in. per sec.
       phonotape.

          1. Project Gemini. 2. McDivitt, James Alton,
       1929-   3. White, Edward Higgins, 1930-1967.
       I. McDivitt, James Alton, 1929-   II. White,
       Edward Higgins, 1930-1967.

Voice Lib.
M771   Gemini 4 (space flight): excerpts of announce-
bd.2   ments from NBC reporters and Gemini Control,
          regarding preparations for and the actual
          splashdown. Conversation with astronauts
          before pickup by helicopter. Dallas Townsend
          from carrier "Wasp" and David Brinkley and
          Chet Huntley for NBC.   NBC TV, June 7, 1965.
          1 reel (7 in.)   7 1/2 in. per sec.   phonotape.
          1. Project Gemini. 2. McDivitt, James Alton, 1929-   3.
       White, Edward Higgins, 1930-1967. I. McDivitt, James Alton,
       1929-   II. White, Edward Higgins, 1930-1967. III. Townsend,
       Dallas.   IV. Brinkley, David McClure, 1920-   V. Huntley,
       Chet, 1911-1974.

Voice Lib.
M772   Gemini 4 (space flight): pickup of astronauts
bd.1   McDivitt and White and the capsule, described
          by Chet Huntley and David Brinkley.   NBC TV,
          June 7, 1965.
          1 reel (7 in.)   7 1/2 in. per sec.
       phonotape.

          1. Project Gemini. 2. McDivitt, James Alton,
       1929-   3. White, Edward Higgins, 1930-1967.
       I. McDivitt, James Alton, 1929-   II. White,
       Edward Higgins, 1930-1967. III. Huntley, Chet,
       1911-1974 IV. Brinkley, David McClure, 1920-

Voice Lib.
M788   Gemini 5 (space flight): summary of space
          flight of Gemini Titan V from August 21 to
          August 29, 1965, including interview with
          Chris Kraft, flight director. 1965.
          1 reel (7 in.)   7 1/2 in. per sec.
       phonotape.

          1. Project Gemini. 2. Cooper, Leroy Gordon,
       1927-   3. Conrad, Charles, 1930-   I.
       Cooper, Leroy Gordon, 1927-   II. Conrad,
       Charles, 1930-   III. Kraft, Christopher
       Columbus, 1924-

Voice Lib.
M800   Gemini 5 (space flight): press conference
          with astronauts Cooper and Conrad at NASA
          Space Center, Houston, Texas, regarding
          their eight-day space flight with Gemini V.
          NBC TV, September 9, 1965.
          1 reel (7 in.)   7 1/2 in. per sec.
       phonotape.

          1. Project Gemini. 2. Cooper, Leroy Gordon,
       1927-   3. Conrad, Charles, 1930-   I.
       Cooper, Leroy Gordon, 1927-   II. Conrad,
       Charles, 1930-

Gemini 6 (space flight)
Voice Lib.
M917   Gemini 7 (space flight): Frank McGee's resumé
bd.1   of space flights of astronauts Frank Borman
          and James Lovell, Jr., in Gemini 7, commencing
          Dec. 4, 1956 to Dec. 18, 1965, and of astro-
          nauts Walter Schirra and Thomas Stafford in
          Gemini 6, which rendezvoused in space;
          including various launching actual reports
          and interview with Wally Schirra; comments
          by Huntley and Brinkley.   NBC TV, December
          18, 1965.
          1 reel (7 in.)   7 1/2 in. per sec.
       phonotape.
                              (Continued on next card)

Voice Lib.
M917   Gemini 7 (space flight): Frank McGee's resumé
bd.1   of space flights of astronauts Frank Borman
          and James Lovell, Jr., in Gemini 7, commencing
          Dec. 4, 1956 to Dec. 18, 1965, and of astro-
          nauts Walter Schirra and Thomas Stafford in
          Gemini 6, which rendezvoused in space;
          including various launching actual reports
          and interview with Wally Schirra; comments
          by Huntley and Brinkley.   NBC TV, December
          18, 1965.
          1 reel (7 in.)   7 1/2 in. per sec.
       phonotape.
                              (Continued on next card)

Voice Lib.
M917   Gemini 7 (space flight): Frank McGee's resumé
bd.1   ...   1965.   (Card 2)
          1. Project Gemini. 2. Borman, Frank, 1928-
       3. Lovell, James Arthur, 1928-   4. Schirra,
       Walter Marty, 1923-   5. Stafford, Thomas
       P   1931-   I. Gemini 6 (space flight). II.
       Borman, Frank, 1928-   III. Lovell, James
       Arthur, 1928-   IV. Schirra, Walter Marty,
       1923-   V. Stafford, Thomas P   1931-
       VI. McGee, Frank, 1921-1974. VII. Huntley,
       Chet, 1911-1974. VIII. Brinkley, David
       McClure, 1920-

Voice Lib.
M950- Gemini 8 (space flight): press conference at
951   Houston, Texas, Space Center regarding
          astronauts' space flight on Gemini 8.   NBC
          TV, March 26, 1966.
          2 reels (7 in.)   7 1/2 in. per sec.
       phonotape.

          1. Project Gemini. 2. Armstrong, Neil, 1930-
       3. Scott, David Randolph, 1932-   I. Armstrong,
       Neil, 1930-   II. Scott, David Randolph,
       1932-

Voice Lib.
M968   Gemini 9 (space flight): description of
bd.2   countdown and lift-off of "Agena" by
          Gemini Mission Control (voice of Al Chop)
          for a period of 11 minutes, 41 seconds,
          until Gemini flight was scrubbed. Comments
          by NBC's Huntley, Brinkley, and Frank McGee.
          NBC TV, May 17, 1966.
          1 reel (7 in.)   7 1/2 in. per sec.   phonotape.
          1. Project Gemini. 2. Stafford, Thomas P   1931-   3.
       Cernan, Eugene Andrew, 1934-   I. Stafford, Thomas P   1931-
       II. Cernan, Eugene Andrew, 1934-   III. Chop, Al   IV.
       Huntley, Chet, 1911-1974 V. Brinkley, David McClure, 1920-
       VI. McGee, Frank, 1921-1974.

Voice Lib.
M986 Gemini 9 (space flight): a. Take-off of
bd.2   Augmented Target Docking Adaptor (ATDA)
      from Cape Kennedy (June 1); b. re-cap
      by David Brinkley regarding failure of
      shroud to jettison (June 3); c. Gemini 9
      until failure of guidance system computer
      and then scrubbing mission (June 1)
      NBC TV, June 1 and 3, 1966.
        1 reel (7 in.) 7 1/2 i.p. per sec. phonotape.
      L Project Gemini. 2. Stafford, Thomas P 1931- 3.
      Cernan, Eugene Andrew, 1934- L Stafford, Thomas P
      1931- II. Cernan, Eugene Andrew, 1934- III. Brinkley,
      David McClure, 1920-

      The general
C1
H2   Whorf, Michael, 1933-
        The general.
        1 tape cassette. (The visual sounds of
      Mike Whorf. History and heritage, H2)
        Originally presented on his radio program, Kaleidoscope,
      WJR, Detroit.
        Duration: 30 min., 30 sec.
        The life and times of Dwight Eisenhower, from his boyhood to
      his nomination as president.

        L Eisenhower, Dwight David, Pres. U.S., 1890-1969.
      L Title.

      General George Armstrong Custer
C1
H38   Whorf, Michael, 1933-
        General George Armstrong Custer.
        1 tape cassette. (The visual sounds of
      Mike Whorf. History and heritage, H38)
        Originally presented on his radio program, Kaleidoscope,
      WJR, Detroit.
        Duration: 49 min., 15 sec.
        Yellow Hair, General of the Long Knives, George Armstrong
      Custer; was he the terror of the plains, the egotist, the bombastic,
      or was he a general who followed his orders with flare and dash?

        L Custer, George Armstrong, 1839-1876. L Title.

Voice Lib.
M502- General Motors Corporation.
505,   World's Fair Dinner for selected college
bd.2   students, at GMC Exhibit Building, Flushing
      Meadows, Long Island, N.Y. GRV recording,
      May 6, 1940.
        4 reels (7 in.) 7 1/2 i.p.s. phonotape.

        Contents listed with tapes.

        1. New York, World's Fair, 1939-1940.

      Genius
C1
M43   Whorf, Michael, 1933-
        Genius.
        1 tape cassette. (The visual sounds of
      Mike Whorf. Miscellaneous, M43)
        Originally presented on his radio program, Kaleidoscope,
      WJR, Detroit.
        Duration: 36 min., 15 sec.
        What are the attributes of the giants of the ages that brings
      them their label of genius?

        L Genius. L Title.

Voice Lib.
M1578 Gentile, Eric Anton, 1943-
        The legislative and other social aims of
      NAPH's Civil Presence Group; interview, by
      Maurice Crane. MSU Voice Library,
      February 13, 1974.
        60 min. phonotape (1 r. 3 3/4 in. per
      sec.)

        1. Physically handicapped. 2. Physically
      handicapped - Law and legislation.
      I. Crane, Maurice Aaron, 1926-

Voice Lib.
M1579 Gentile, Eric Anton, 1943-
bd.3   Reading Woody Ayen's State News editorial
      (November 15, 1973) calling for action from
      and/or resignation of MSU Planning Director
      Milton Baron. MSU Voice Library, February
      13, 1974.
        3 min. phonotape (1 r. 7 1/2 i/p.s.)

        1. Physically handicapped. 2. Baron,
      Milton. I. Ayen, Woody.

Voice Lib. Gentile, Eric Anton, 1943-
M1579 Third Civic Presence Group/Legislative
bd.1   luncheon, with Craig Halverson, Lynn
      Jondahl, Gary Owen, Phil Mastin, and
      Eric Gentile. WKAR-TV, February 15, 1973.
        10 min. phonotape (1 r. 7 1/2 i.p.s.)

        1. Physically handicapped - Law and legis-
      lation. I. Halverson, Craig. II. Jondahl,
      H. Lynn, 1936- III. Owen, Gary M., 1944-
      IV. Mastin, Philip O., 1930- V. Gentile,
      Eric Anton, 1943-

      Gentile, Eric Anton, 1943-
Voice Lib.
M1579 Halverson, Craig
bd.2   23 tonight; MSU controversy over curb and
      ramp cuts, with Eric Gentile and Judy K. Taylor.
      WKAR-TV, November 13, 1973.
        15 min. phonotape (1 r. 7 1/2 i.p.s.)

        1. Physically handicapped - Law and legis-
      lation. I. Gentile, Eric Anton, 1943-
      II. Taylor, Judy K

      The gentleman from Virginia
C1
H20   Whorf, Michael, 1933-
        The gentleman from Virginia.
        1 tape cassette. (The visual sounds of
      Mike Whorf. History and heritage, H20)
        Originally presented on his radio program, Kaleidoscope,
      WJR, Detroit.
        Duration: 49 min.
        Gentleman and General was Lee; Lee of the Confederacy; Lee
      of Virginia - a man as noble as his ancestors, as brave as his
      contemporaries. Lee was a patriot, a figure emerging from
      history who would loom as large as anyone on the American scene.

        L Lee, Robert Edward, 1807-1870. L Title.

Voice Lib.
M1228 George V, King of Great Britain, 1865-1936.
bd.1   Reply to introduction by William
Swinburne upon the occasion of the opening
of the Tyne Bridge in Gateshead, England,
and his dedicatory remarks. Peteler,
October 10, 1928.
   1 reel (7 in.)   7 1/2 in. per sec.
phonotape.

GEORGE VI, KING OF GREAT BRITAIN, 1895-1952
Voice Lib.
532   Churchill, Winston Leonard Spencer, 1874-1965.
bd.2   Broadcast to the nation on the death of
King George VI; eulogy of King George VI.
BBC, February 7, 1952.
   1 reel (7 in.)   7 1/2 in. per sec.
phonotape.

    1. George VI, king of Great Britain, 1895-
1952.

Voice Lib.
182   George VI, King of Gt. Brit., 1895-1952.
bd.2   Speech at outbreak of World War II.
CBS, September 3, 1939.
   1 reel (7 in.) 7 1/2 in. per sec.
phonotape.

    George, David Lloyd
      see
Lloyd George, David Lloyd George, 1st earl,
1863-1945.

VOICE LIBRARY

Voice Lib.
523   George VI, King of Gt. Brit., 1895-1952.
bd.2   First anniversary of World War II;
review of early war days. Mutual
Broadcasting System (rebroadcast from
BBC), February 23, 1940.
   1 reel (7 in.)   7 1/2 in. per sec.
phonotape.

Voice Lib.
M1254 George-Brown, George Alfred Brown, baron,
bd.2   1914-
   Portion of address by British Foreign Minister Brown at U.N.
General Assembly emergency session listing U.K. financial aid
to Arab States and recommendations for alleviating current
Arab-Israeli crisis, suggesting new U.N. Middle East military
mission. NBC-TV, June 21, 1967.
   1 reel (7 in.) 7 1/2 in. per sec. phonotape.

    1. Israel-Arab War, 1967-   - Diplomatic history.

Voice Lib.
395   George VI, King of Gt. Brit., 1895-1952.
bd.2   Empire Day speech, 1940. CBS, May 24,
1940.
   1 reel (7 in.)   7 1/2 in. per sec.
phonotape.

C1   George W. Perkins
FA5   Whorf, Michael, 1933-
    George W. Perkins. (The visual sounds of
Mike Whorf. The forgotten American, FA5)
   1 tape cassette.
   Originally presented on his radio program, Kaleidoscope,
WJR, Detroit.
   Duration: 11 min., 30 sec.

   Perkins rose from obscurity to a position of wealth and
power. He used his energies and money to promote the welfare
of his fellow man.

    1. Perkins, George W.   1. Title.

Voice Lib.
526   George VI, King of Gt. Brit., 1895-1952.
bd.2   On Blitzkreig of England. CBS,
September 23, 1940.
   1 reel (7 in.) 7 1/2 in. per sec.
phonotape.

Voice Lib.
M757 Gerard, James Watson, 1867-
bd.2   "Loyalty": discussion of the duty of
German-Americans during war time. Nation's
Forum, 1917.
   1 reel (7 in.)   7 1/2 in. per sec.
phonotape.

Voice Lib.
M795 Gerard, James Watson, 1867-
bd.9 Speaking on "America Safe". The Nation's
  Forum, April 21, 1920.
   1 reel (7 in.) 7 1/2 in. per sec.
  phonotape. .

Voice Lib.
M1018 German radio (Nazi controlled)
bd.8 Nazi radio announcement that, due to British
  and French contemplated aggression, Fuehrer
  Hitler decided to invade Holland, Belgium,
  and Luxemburg. Announcement ending with
  song, "Kamaraden, wir marschieren gegen
  den Westen." Peteler
   1 reel (7 in.) 7 1/2 in. per sec.
  phonotape.

   GERMAN POETRY (COLLECTIONS)
Voice Lib.
M1257 Ysaye, Lisa
bd.3 Various German poems narrated by the author.
  Reeves SS, 1937.
   1 reel (7 in.) 7 1/2 in. per sec.
  phonotape.

   CONTENTS.-Mein Prinz aus Traumland; 2.
  Er schrieb ihr einst; 3. Andante; 4. Ich
  bin eine junge Koenigin; 5. Es war die
  Koenigin von Brabane; 6. Lisette.

Voice Lib.
M1466 German radio (Nazi controlled)
bd.24 Excerpt from celebration at the 3rd zone
  of the Rhineland while being reoccupied by
  Prussian government. Peteler, June 30,
  1950.
   1 reel (7 in.) 7 1/2 in. per sec.
  phonotape.

   I. Nationalsozialistiche Deutsche Arbeiter-
  Partei.

Voice Lib.
M1464 German radio (Nazi controlled)
bd.2 Last broadcast of soldier station "Gustav".
   1 reel (7 in.) 7 1/2 in. per sec.
  phonotape.

Voice Lib.
M1362 German radio (Nazi controlled)
bd.5 Nazi era flashbacks: Nazi liberation of the
  Rhineland and occupation by the Reichwehr
  of the city of Mainz, including speech by
  Ob Kuelb of Mainz. Peteler, July 20, 1930.
   1 reel (7 in.) 7 1/2 in. per sec.
  phonotape.

Voice Lib.
M1019 German radio (Nazi controlled)
bd.7 Nazi era Thanksgiving hymn of the Netherlands
  (instrumental). Fred Peteler.
   1 reel (7 in.) 7 1/2 in. per sec.
  phonotape.

Voice Lib.
M1000 German radio (Nazi controlled)
bd.5 Discussions in Reichstag; enactment of
  laws tending to give unrestricted governmental powers to Chancellor Hitler. Peteler,
  1933.
   1 reel (7 in.) 7 1/2 in. per sec.
  phonotape.

   I. Nationalsozialistiche Deutsche Arbeiter-
  Partei. Reichsparteitag.

Voice Lib.
M981 German radio (Nazi controlled)
bd.5 Nazi march music (instrumental); a. "Alte
  Kameraden"; b. "Preussens gloria"; c.
  Fridericus Rex". Peteler.
   1 reel (7 in.) 7 1/2 in. per sec.
  phonotape.

Voice Lib.
M1000 German radio (Nazi controlled)
bd.2 Nazi German national anthem and three-
  hour adjournment of the Reichstag. Peteler,
  1933.
   1 reel (7 in.) 7 1/2 in. per sec.
  phonotape.

Voice Lib.
M980   German radio (Nazi controlled)
bd.7   Nazi patriotic song "Deutschland erwache!"
(2 stanzas)   Peteler, 1933.
1 reel (7 in.)   7 1/2 in. per sec.
phonotape.

I. Title: Deutschland erwache!

Voice Lib.
M1003   German radio (Nazi controlled)
bd.7   Nazi party campaign speeches; German
authorities in sports, music and the arts
speaking in favor of Hitler in 1934.
Peteler, August 19, 1934.
1 reel (7 in.)   7 1/2 in. per sec.
phonotape.

I. Nationalsozialistische Deutsche Arbeiter-
Partei.

Voice Lib.
M1363   German radio (Nazi controlled)
bd.8   Nazi news report: celebrations in Berlin
after the seizure of power by the Nazis.
Peteler, January 30, 1933.
1 reel (7 in.)   7 1/2 in. per sec.
phonotape.

Voice Lib.
M1376   German radio (Nazi controlled)
bd.9   Unknown speaker at NSDAP Congress in the
city of Weimar.   Peteler, July 5, 1936.
1 reel (7 in.)   7 1/2 in. per sec.
phonotape.

I. Nationalsozialistische Deutsche Arbeiter-
Partei.

Voice Lib.
M1363   German radio (Nazi controlled)
bd.12   Nazi news reports: the burning of outlawed
books in Berlin.   Peteler, May 10, 1933.
1 reel (7 in.)   7 1/2 in. per sec.
phonotape.

Voice Lib.
M1376   German radio (Nazi controlled)
bd.11   Sounds of Nazi Party Day celebration in
Nuremberg.   September 13, 1936.
1 reel (7 in.)   7 1/2 in. per sec.
phonotape.

I. Nationalsozialistische Deutsche Arbeiter-
Partei.

Voice Lib.
M1002   German radio (Nazi controlled)
bd.2   Reichstag session of March 23, 1933, voting
on unrestricted governmental powers for
Chancellor Hitler.   Peteler, March 23, 1933.
1 reel (7 in.)   7 1/2 in. per sec.
phonotape.

I. Nationalsozialistische Deutsche Arbeiter-
Partei.   Reichsparteitag.

Voice Lib.
M1010   German radio (Nazi controlled)
bd.6   Nazi propaganda: marching song about the
unification of Austria and Germany.
Peteler, 1938.
1 reel (7 in.)   7 1/2 in. per sec.
phonotape

Voice Lib.
M1375   German radio (Nazi controlled)
bd.6   Nazi radio announcement: German child
shovelling earth in the Saar section of
Germany and promising that this territory
will be returned to the land of his fathers.
Peteler, July 6, 1934.
1 reel (7 in.)   7 1/2 in. per sec.
phonotape.

Voice Lib.
M1463   German radio (Nazi controlled)
bd.4   Nazi propaganda: alleged broadcast from
England giving news of German POW's.
Peteler, 1940.
1 reel (7 in.)   7 1/2 in. per sec.
phonotape.

Voice Lib.
M1463 German radio (Nazi controlled)
  bd.3   Nazi propaganda; comic sketch by German
           radio actors on enemy broadcasts.   Peteler,
           1940.
               1 reel (7 in.)   7 1/2 in. per sec.
           phonotape.

Voice Lib.
M961   German radio (Nazi controlled)
  bd.1   Nazi news items of Third Reich: special
           news announcements of headquarters of German
           Wehrmacht, stating that German motorized
           troops have crossed Danish frontier on their
           way to the north, followed by march music
           and song on radio.   German Radio, Peteler,
           April 9, 1940.
               1 reel (7 in.)   7 1/2 in. per sec.
           phonotape.

Voice Lib.
M1071 German radio (Nazi controlled)
  bd.2   Nazi air raid alarms in Berlin and in Munich.
           Sirens, anti-aircraft flak, radio warning
           reports.   Peteler, 1940 & 1943.
               1 reel (7 in.)   7 1/2 in. per sec.
           phonotape.

Voice Lib.
M1019 German radio (Nazi controlled)
  bd.1   Nazi radio announcement pertaining to
           German U-boat successes in the Atlantic,
           followed by Nazi martial music.   Fred
           Peteler, May 15, 1940.
               1 reel (7 in.)   7 1/2 in. per sec.
           phonotape.

Voice Lib.
M1016 German radio (Nazi controlled)
  bd.8   Nazi radio report describing jubilation of
           public at the joining of city of Memel to
           greater Germany.   F. Peteler, March 24, 1939.
               1 reel (7 in.)   7 1/2 in. per sec.
           phonotape.

Voice Lib.
M848   German radio (Nazi controlled)
  bd.2   Nazi war news reports on current state of
           military operations; resumé of Nazi conquests
           and booty; situation in Holland, Belgium and
           Flanders.   NBC shortwave, June 4, 1940.
               1 reel (7 in.)   7 1/2 in. per sec.
           phonotape.

Voice Lib.
M1016 German radio (Nazi controlled)
  bd.9   Nazi radio announcement: reading of
           President Roosevelt's letter to Adolf Hitler
           cautioning him against any further annexations
           to Germany by use of force.   F. Peteler,
           April 15, 1939.
               1 reel (7 in.)   7 1/2 in. per sec.
           phonotape.

Voice Lib.
M736   German radio (Nazi controlled)
  bd.11   German radio announcement by German
           headquarters on the fall of Paris and the
           French collapse.   CBS, June 14, 1940.
               1 reel (7 in.)   7 1/2 in. per sec.
           phonotape.

Voice Lib.
M1016 German radio (Nazi controlled)
  bd.14   Nazi radio report: description of victory
           parade in Berlin of the "Legion Condor",
           consisting of returning German troops from
           fighting in Spanish Civil War (including one
           stanza of their marching song).   F. Peteler,
           June 6, 1939.
               1 reel (7 in.)   7 1/2 in. per sec.
           phonotape.

Voice Lib.
M1019 German radio (Nazi controlled)
  bd.2   Nazi radio announcement: German Army
           Supreme Headquarters announcing that Paris
           has been declared an open city; Nazi troops
           advance on the French capital.   Fred
           Peteler, June 14, 1940.
               1 reel (7 in.)   7 1/2 in. per sec.
           phonotape.

Voice Lib.
M1019 German radio (Nazi controlled)
bd.3   Nazi radio announcement; German Army
Supreme Headquarters stating that the new
French President M. Pétain has explained to
the French people that their army has been
forced to lay down its arms and that he is
now discussing with Hitler and Mussolini the
terms for an armistice.   Fred Peteler,
June 17, 1940.
        1 reel (7 in.)   7 1/2 in. per sec.
phonotape.

Voice Lib.
M1071 German radio (Nazi controlled)
bd.3   Nazi radio announcement giving text of
pact made between Germany, Italy, and Japan.
Read in German by Joachim von Ribbentrop, in
Italian by Count Ciano, and in Japanese by
Ambassador Kurusu, stating their spheres of
interest.   Peteler, September 27, 1940.
        1 reel (7 in.)   7 1/2 in. per sec.
phonotape.
        I. Ribbentrop, Joachim von, 1893-1946. II.
Ciano, Galeazzo, conte, 1903-1944. III.
Kuruso, Saburo, 1886-1954.

Voice Lib.
M961   German radio (Nazi controlled)
bd.4   Nazi news bulletins: German newscast of
proceedings at surrender of French army to
German High Command in forest at Compiègne.
German Radio, Peteler, June 21, 1940.
        1 reel (7 in.)   7 1/2 in. per sec.
phonotape.

Voice Lib.
M1073 German radio (Nazi controlled)
bd.17   Nazi martial music: song entitled
"Schwarzbraun ist die Haselnuss".   Peteler,
1941.
        1 reel (7 in.)   7 1/2 in. per sec.
phonotape.

        I. Title: Schwarzbraun ist die Haselnuss.

Voice Lib.
M1019 German radio (Nazi controlled)
bd.4   Nazi special announcement: review by
German commentator on similarity in conditions
at signing of the armistice in 1918; reporting
terms of the present Nazi armistice conditions;
description of proceedings at Compiègne;
telephone conversations with French government
at Bordeaux, ending with Nazi "fill-in" music.
Fred Peteler, June 22, 1940.
        1 reel (7 in.)   7 1/2 in. per sec.
phonotape.

Voice Lib.
M1463 German radio (Nazi controlled)
bd.6   Nazi propaganda: broadcast of "Children's
Hour", with messages to their fathers in
the army, then song of faithfulness by wife,
"Ich bin doch deine Frau".   Peteler, 1941.
        1 reel (7 in.)   7 1/2 in. per sec.
phonotape.

Voice Lib.
M1019 German radio (Nazi controlled)
bd.5   Nazi special radio announcement beginning
with fill-in music and proclaiming end of
hostilities between German and French troops;
ending with praise for German Reichsfuehrer
Hitler.   Fred Peteler, June 25, 1940.
        1 reel (7 in.)   7 1/2 in. per sec.
phonotape.

Voice Lib.
M1463 German radio (Nazi controlled)
bd.5   Nazi propaganda: song parody about German
U-boats and the scare to the British "sea
lord".   Peteler, 1941.
        1 reel (7 in.)   7 1/2 in. per sec.
phonotape.

Voice Lib.
M1019 German radio (Nazi controlled)
bd.11   Nazi radio news commentator: reception of
Adolf Hitler in Berlin after successful conclusion of capitulation of France and signing
of Armistice; expressions of gratitude to the
Fuehrer by various youth groups; ringing of
bells.   Peteler, July 6, 1940.
        1 reel (7 in.)   7 1/2 in. per sec.
phonotape.

        1. Hitler, Adolf, 1889-1945.

Voice Lib.
M1463 German radio (Nazi controlled)
bd.8   Nazi propaganda: song ridiculing Prime
Minister Churchill.   Peteler, 1941.
        1 reel (7 in.)   7 1/2 in. per sec.
phonotape.

Voice Lib.
M1071   German radio (Nazi controlled)
bd.16   Nazi special radio flash: announcement by
German Army High Command stating that fleeing
British fleet lost one Navy cruiser, with
other damage to shipping.   Peteler, 1941.
1 reel (7 in.)   7 1/2 in. per sec.
phonotape.

Voice Lib.
M1071   German radio (Nazi controlled)
bd.13   Nazi special radio flash; announcement by
Germany Army High Command stating that Nazi
tanks have reached Athens and that German
Swastika flag was hissed on the Acropolis.
Peteler, April 27, 1941.
1 reel (7 in.)   7 1/2 in. per sec.
phonotape.

Voice Lib.
M1071   German radio (Nazi controlled)
bd.8   . Nazi special radio flash; announcement that
German army crossed the Wardar River heading
toward Albanian border.   Peteler, April 9,
1941.
1 reel (7 in.)   7 1/2 in. per sec.
phonotape.

Voice Lib.
M1071   German radio (Nazi controlled)
bd.12   Nazi special radio flash: announcement by
German Army High Command that five British
ships sunk in Atlantic by air attacks, thus
slowing British troop movement to Greece.
Peteler, April 24, 1941.
1 reel (7 in.)   7 1/2 in. per sec.
phonotape.

Voice Lib.
M1071   German radio (Nazi controlled)
bd.9   Nazi special radio flash: announcement by
German Army High Command stating that German
and Italian troops are advancing into
Yugoslavia and that tanks have already reached
city of Belgrade.   Peteler, April 13, 1941.
1 reel (7 in.)   7 1/2 in. per sec.
phonotape.

Voice Lib.
M1071   German radio (Nazi controlled)
bd.14   Nazi special radio flash: announcement by
Germany Army High Command, stating that German
paratroops captured Isthmus of Corinth and
occupied the Channel.   Peteler, April 27, 1941.
1 reel (7 in.)   7 1/2 in. per sec.
phonotape.

Voice Lib.
M1071   German radio (Nazi controlled)
bd.10   Nazi special radio flash: announcement by
German Army High Command about the capitulation of the 2nd Yugoslav Army; also Reuter
news dispatch from London about lack of
British aid.   Peteler, April 16, 1941.
1 reel (7 in.)   7 1/2 in. per sec.
phonotape.

Voice Lib.
M1071   German radio (Nazi controlled)
bd.15   Nazi special radio flash: announcement by
German Army High Command stating that Hitler's
elite troops passed the Gulf of Patras in
Greece, entering the Peloponnesus.   Peteler,
April 27, 1941.
1 reel (7 in.)   7 1/2 in. per sec.
phonotape.

Voice Lib.
M1071   German radio (Nazi controlled)
bd.11   Nazi special radio flash; announcement by
German Army High Command stating air raids
on London in retaliation for British air
attacks on Berlin.   Peteler, April 17, 1941.
1 reel (7 in.)   7 1/2 in. per sec.
phonotape.

Voice Lib.
M1071   German radio (Nazi controlled)
bd.18   Nazi radio news item speculating on the
fate of Rudolf Hess, who disappeared while
in flight, disobeying Hitler's order not to
fly.   Peteler, May 12, 1941.
1 reel (7 in.)   7 1/2 in. per sec.
phonotape.

1. Hess, Rudolf, 1894-

Voice Lib.
M1073 German radio (Nazi controlled)
bd.6-A   Nazi actual news reports; on-the-spot
report from Eastern front.   Peteler, June,
1941.
  1 reel (7 in.)   7 1/2 in. per sec.
phonotape.

  CONTENTS.-a. before an attack.-b. description
of action followed by news flash of commencement of attack.-c. on-the-spot enactment of an
execution.

Voice Lib.
M1073 German radio (Nazi controlled)
bd.12   Nazi military announcement stating that
Nazi troops have penetrated Soviet defense
front, and Luftwaffe engaged in air raids
over Moscow.   Peteler, July 24, 1941.
  1 reel (7 in.)   7 1/2 in. per sec.
phonotape.

Voice Lib.
M1073 German radio (Nazi controlled)
bd.9   Nazi special radio flash: announcement from
German Army High Command relating the amount
of war booty captured during first week of
military operation, followed by German anthem.
Peteler, June 3, 1941.
  1 reel (7 in.)   7 1/2 in. per sec.
phonotape.

Voice Lib.
M1073 German radio (Nazi controlled)
bd.14-A Nazi military announcements from German
High Command, describing air fight over
English Channel.   Peteler, July 26-27, 1941.
  1 reel (7 in.)   7 1/2 in. per sec.
phonotape.

Voice Lib.
M1073 German radio (Nazi controlled)
bd.3   Nazi special radio flash; announcement from
Hitler's headquarters of attack on Russia by
German armed forces to defend Reich from
danger in the east. Also giving count of
enemy planes downed.   Peteler, June 22, 1941.
  1 reel (7 in.)   7 1/2 in. per sec.
phonotape.

Voice Lib.
M1073 German radio (Nazi controlled)
bd.14-B Nazi military announcements: further account
of air battle over Channel.   Peteler,
July 26-27, 1941.
  1 reel (7 in.)   7 1/2 in. per sec.
phonotape.

Voice Lib.
M1073 German radio (Nazi controlled)
bd.7   Nazi special radio flash announcing the
capture of city of Lemberg in Russian Poland
and effectiveness of German air support.
Peteler, June 29, 1941.
  1 reel (7 in.)   7 1/2 in. per sec.
phonotape.

Voice Lib.
M1073 German radio (Nazi controlled)
bd.13   Nazi actual report from Russian front
of German aviators during air attack over
Moscow. Peteler, July 27, 1941.
  1 reel (7 in.)   7 1/2 in. per sec.
phonotape.

.Voice Lib.
M1073 German radio (Nazi controlled)
bd.8   Nazi special radio flash: announcement
from Hitler headquarters that Russian troops
at Bialystok are completely surrounded by
German troops. Peteler, June 29, 1941.
  1 reel (7 in.)   7 1/2 in. per sec.
phonotape.

Voice Lib.
M1073 German radio (Nazi controlled)
bd.19   German-Bolivian controversy: denying
conspiracy of German diplomat Wendler with a
Bolivian officer to overthrow Bolivian
government. Peteler, August, 1941.
  1 reel (7 in.)   7 1/2 in. per sec.
phonotape.

  I. Nationalsozialistische Deutsche Arbeiter-
Partei.

Voice Lib.
M1073 German radio (Nazi controlled)
bd.16   Nazi special radio flash from Hitler's
Headquarters, announcing progress of German
troops in Western Ukraine and the encircling
of Odessa. Peteler, August 14, 1941.
    1 reel (7 in.) 7 1/2 in. per sec.
phonotape.

Voice Lib.
M1301 German radio (Nazi controlled)
bd.2   Nazi news bulletin: reports pertaining to
declaration of war by Japan on the U.S.A.;
also of England on Finland, Hungary, and
Rumania. Peteler, December 7, 1941.
    1 reel (7 in.) 7 1/2 in. per sec.
phonotape.

Voice Lib.
M1073 German radio (Nazi controlled)
bd.15   Nazi news report: statement made during
opening of the Great German Art Exhibition
in Munich, followed by the main speaker,
Joseph Goebbels. Peteler, August, 1941.
    1 reel (7 in.) 7 1/2 in. per sec.
phonotape.

    I. Goebbels, Joseph, 1897-1945.

Voice Lib.
M1301 German radio (Nazi controlled)
bd.3   Reporting progress on the Russian front
and the declaration of war by Japan on the
United States. Peteler, December 11, 1941.
    1 reel (7 in.) 7 1/2 in. per sec. phonotape.
    CONTENTS. -a. Göring, Hermann. -b. Hitler, Adolf,
criticizing President Roosevelt and comparing his own actions
with those of FDR.
    I. Göring, Hermann, 1893-1946. II. Hitler, Adolf, 1889-1945.
III. Nationalsozialistische Deutsche Arbeiter-Partei. Reichsparteitag.

Voice Lib.
M1073 German radio (Nazi controlled)
bd.20   Statement by German High Command pertaining
to explanation of Eastern front news blackout,
followed by three current news reports: a.
announcement of penetration of Stalin line by
German troops; b. progress of troops on way to
Leningrad; c. victory in Smolensk; d. announcement of war booty acquired by Army. Peteler,
August 20, 1941.
    1 reel (7 in.) 7 1/2 in. per sec.
phonotape.

Voice Lib.
M1463 German radio (Nazi controlled)
bd.14   Nazi German radio (Belgrade station) with
two stanzas of "Lili Marlene". Peteler, 1942.
    1 reel (7 in.) 7 1/2 in. per sec.
phonotape.

    I. Title: Lili Marlene.

Voice Lib.
M1300 German radio (Nazi controlled)
bd.1   Various special announcements: new German
state laws pertaining to Anti-Comintern Pact
between Germany, Japan and Italy; excerpt of
speech by Nazi Foreign Minister von Ribbentrop.
Peteler, September 12, 1941.
    1 reel (7 in.) 7 1/2 in. per sec.
phonotape.

    I. Nationalsozialistiche Deutsche Arbeiter-
Partei.

Voice Lib.
M1304 German radio (Nazi controlled)
bd.15   Nazi news bulletins: description of the
techniques used by the German Panzer troops
on the Russian front. Peteler, 1942.
    1 reel (7 in.) 7 1/2 in. per sec.
phonotape.

Voice Lib.
M1073 German radio (Nazi controlled)
bd.22   Nazi newsreel motion picture reports
pertaining to campaign on German East Front;
maligning of Jews and Bolsheviks and claiming
German success in every section. Peteler,
October, 1941.
    1 reel (7 in.) 7 1/2 in. per sec.
phonotape.

Voice Lib.
M1304 German radio (Nazi controlled)
bd.13   Nazi news bulletin: four news bulletins
in German language about action during
campaign on Russian front. Peteler, 1942.
    1 reel (7 in.) 7 1/2 in. per sec.
phonotape.

Voice Lib.
M1304 German radio (Nazi controlled)
bd.2   Nazi announcement by German Army Headquarters
        pertaining to North African campaign.   Peteler,
        January 25, 1942.
          1 reel (7 in.)   7 1/2 in. per sec.
        phonotape.

Voice Lib.
M1463 German radio (Nazi controlled)
bd.13   Nazi era special broadcast to German troops
        on Leningrad front, including song "Brave
        Soldier-wife". Peteler, 1943.
          1 reel (7 in.)   7 1/2 in. per sec.
        phonotape.

Voice Lib.
M961   German radio (Nazi controlled)
bd.6   Nazi news items of Third Reich: rules for
        the organization of the Hitler Youth Groups
        and excerpts of speeches and martial music
        pertaining to integration of Hitler Youth
        into war service. German Radio, Peteler,
        January 25, 1942.
          1 reel (7 in.)   7 1/2 in. per sec.
        (phonotape)

Voice Lib.
M1463 German radio (Nazi controlled)
bd.9   Nazi era sketch about soldiers' feelings
        and attitudes during Christmas, 1943.
        Peteler, 1943.
          1 reel (7 in.)   7 1/2 in. per sec.
        phonotape.

Voice Lib.
M1304 German radio (Nazi controlled)
bd.3   Nazi announcement by German Army Headquarters
        pertaining to Allied tonnage sunk by German
        U-boats off the coast of North America.
        Peteler, January 27, 1942.
          1 reel (7 in.)   7 1/2 in. per sec.
        phonotape.

Voice Lib.
M1357 German radio (Nazi controlled)
bd.1   Nazi army headquarters: announcement by
        Army General Headquarters of American and
        British landing and beachhead in Normandy.
        Peteler, June 6, 1944.
          1 reel (7 in.)   7 1/2 in. per sec.
        phonotape.

Voice Lib.
M1304 German radio (Nazi controlled)
bd.4   Nazi announcement by German Army Headquarters;
        further announcement of success of German
        U-boats. Peteler, January 30, 1942.
          1 reel (7 in.)   7 1/2 in. per sec.
        phonotape.

Voice Lib.
M1357 German radio (Nazi controlled)
bd.3   Report of attempted assassination of
        Hitler on July 20, 1944. Peteler, July 20,
        1944.
          1 reel (7 in.)   7 1/2 i.p.s.   phonotape.
          In German.

          1. Hitler, Adolf, 1889-1945.

Voice Lib.
M1463 German radio (Nazi controlled)
bd.12   Nazi era special broadcasts beamed to
        troops in Africa, U.S.S.R., U-boats at sea,
        and on Atlantic coast with Christmas skits,
        songs, greetings. Peteler, December 24,
        1942.
          1 reel (7 in.)   7 1/2 in. per sec.
        phonotape.

Voice Lib.
M1361 German radio (Nazi controlled)
bd.4   Nazi propaganda report; spontaneous report
        of a Hitler Youth Air Force helper. Peteler,
        October, 1944.
          1 reel (7 in.)   7 1/2 in. per sec.
        phonotape.

Voice Lib.
M1361 German radio (Nazi controlled)
bd.1   Nazi propaganda report: weekly news
       announcements; "Volksturm" in Berlin.
       Peteler, January, 1945.
         1 reel (7 in.)   7 1/2 in. per sec.
       phonotape.

Voice Lib.
M1361 German radio (Nazi controlled)
bd.7   Nazi propaganda report on house-to-house
       fighting east of Berlin.   Peteler, March,
       1945.
         1 reel (7 in.)   7 1/2 in. per sec.
       phonotape.

Voice Lib.
M1463 German radio (Nazi controlled)
bd.10   Nazi era radio sketch, with conversations
       between several German soldiers about their
       situation. Peteler, February, 1945.
         1 reel (7 in.)   7 1/2 in. per sec.
       phonotape.

Voice Lib.
M1361 German radio (Nazi controlled)
bd.9   Nazi propaganda report: description of
       street fighting in Berlin.   Peteler,
       April, 1945.
         1 reel (7 in.)   7 1/2 in. per sec.
       phonotape.

Voice Lib.
M1361 German radio (Nazi controlled)
bd.5   Nazi propaganda report; excerpt from weekly
       news reports; Hitler Youth in the Eastern
       War Zone. Peteler, February, 1945.
         1 reel (7 in.)   7 1/2 in. per sec.
       phonotape.

Voice Lib.
M1361 German radio (Nazi controlled)
bd.11   Nazi special announcement: notification
       of the death of Adolf Hitler. Peteler,
       May 1, 1945.
         1 reel (7 in.)   7 1/2 in. per sec.
       phonotape.

         1. Hitler, Adolf, 1889-1945.

Voice Lib.
M1361 German radio (Nazi controlled)
bd.2   Nazi propaganda report: description of
       Hitler Youth, in war-torn city of Breslau.
       Peteler, February 24, 1945.
         1 reel (7 in.)   7 1/2 in. per sec.
       phonotape.

Voice Lib.
M375   German songs of World War II. Private
bd.3-   collection (German radio transcriptions)
6   1942.
         1 reel (7 in.)   7 1/2 in. per sec.
       phonotape.
       In German.
         CONTENTS.-bd.3. "Lili Marlene", Lale Andersen.
       bd.4. "Horst Wessel" song, Stormtroopers SA 33.-
       bd.5."Heil Hitler Dir", Stormtroopers SA 33.-
       bd.6. "Die Jugend marschiert", boys of the
       Berlin Mittelschule.
         1. World War, 1939-1945 - Songs and music.

Voice Lib.
M1361 German radio (Nazi controlled)
bd.6   Nazi propaganda report; on-the-spot reports
       from Stargard (West Prussia). Peteler,
       February 27, 1945.
         1 reel (7 in.)   7 1/2 in. per sec.
       phonotape.

                  GERMANY - CHURCH HISTORY
Voice Lib.
M874   Niemöller, Martin, 1892-
bd.1   Discussing fate of churches and religion
       under the Hitler regime in Germany. KDKA,
       February 11, 1942.
         1 reel (7 in.)   7 1/2 i.p.s.   phonotape.

         1. Germany - Church history.

GERMANY - FOREIGN RELATIONS

Voice Lib.
M1016 Hitler, Adolf, 1889-1945.
bd.10   Excerpt of address at Reichstag pertaining
           to message from President Roosevelt, observing
           that American press should desist its war-
           mongering agitation so that all problems can
           be peacefully resolved. F. Peteler,
           April 28, 1939.
               1 reel (7 in.)   7 1/2 i.p.s.   phonotape.

           1. Germany - Foreign relations.

GERMANY - FOREIGN RELATIONS - YUGOSLAVIA

Voice Lib.
M1071 Ribbentrop, Joachim von, 1893-1946.
bd.7   Excerpt of note to Yugoslavia justifying
           German military intervention because of
           unfriendly policies. Peteler, April 6,
           1941.
               1 reel (7 in.)   7 1/2 i.p.s.   phonotape.

           1. Germany - Foreign relations - Yugoslavia.
           2. Yugoslavia - Foreign relations - Germany.

GERMANY - FOREIGN RELATIONS - CZECHOSLOVAK
           REPUBLIC
Voice Lib.
M717   Kaltenborn, Hans von, 1878-1965.
bd.11   Analysis of Hitler speech on Czechoslovakia.
           September 26, 1938.
               1 min., 58 sec.   phonotape (1 r.
           7 1/2 i.p.s.)

           1. Germany - Foreign relations -
           Czechoslovak Republic. 2. Czechoslovak
           Republic - Foreign relations - Germany.

Voice Lib. GERMANY - HISTORY - 1933-1945
M1470 Warlimont, Walter, 1895-
bd.18   a) Interview with General Warlimont regard-
           ing Hitler's aims in Czechoslovakia and
           his build-up for war in 1938. b) Regarding
           Hitler's military strategy in 1939. Peteler,
           1964.
               1 reel (7 in.)   7 1/2 in. per sec.
           phonotape.

GERMANY - FOREIGN RELATIONS - RUSSIA

Voice Lib.
M1420 Hofer, Walther, 1920-
bd.19   Speaking about the development of
           negotiations between Germany and the Soviet
           Union during the months of April to August,
           1939. Peteler, 1964.
               1 reel (7 in.)   7 1/2 i.p.s.   phonotape.

           1. Germany - Foreign relations - Russia.
           2. Russia - Foreign relations - Germany.

GERMANY - POLITICS AND GOVERNMENT -
Voice Lib.   1888-1918
M1466 Scheidemann, Philip, 1865-1939.
bd.10   Speech to the Imperial German Reichstag.
           Peteler, May 15, 1917.
               1 reel (7 in.)   7 1/2 in. per sec.
           phonotape.

           1. Germany - Politics and government -
           1888-1918.

GERMANY - FOREIGN RELATIONS - RUSSIA

Voice Lib.
M1073 Ribbentrop, Joachim von, 1893-1946.
bd.5   Note to Russian government of Nazi position
           regarding conflict with USSR; Russian demands
           for territory in North and Southeastern
           Europe rejected by Hitler. Peteler,
           June 22, 1941.
               1 reel (7 in.)   7 1/2 i.p.s.   phonotape.

           1. Germany - Foreign relations - Russia.
           2. Russia - Foreign relations - Germany.

Voice Lib. GERMANY - POLITICS AND GOVERNMENT - 1918-1933
M1470 Brüning, Heinrich, 1885-1970.
bd.2   Explanation of governmental policies in
           the Reichstag. Peteler, October 13, 1931.
               1 reel (7 in.)   7 1/2 in. per sec.
           phonotape.

GERMANY - FOREIGN RELATIONS -
Voice Lib.   YUGOSLAVIA
M1071 Goebbels, Joseph, 1897-1945.
           Radio report from Ministry of Propaganda,
           read by Goebbels, stating Hitler's decision
           to end amicable relations with Yugoslavia and
           to occupy it militarily. Peteler, April 6,
           1941.
               1 reel (7 in.)   7 1/2 in. per sec.
           phonotape.
               1. Germany - Foreign relations - Yugoslavia. 2. Yugoslavia -
           Foreign relations - Germany. 3. World War, 1939-1945.

GERMANY - POLITICS AND GOVERNMENT - 1918-1933
Voice Lib.
M1466 Excerpt of ceremonies on opening of new
bd.25   Reichstag Building in Berlin; narrator:
           Alfred Braun. Peteler, August 1, 1930.
               1 reel (7 in.)   7 1/2 in. per sec.
           phonotape.

GERMANY - POLITICS AND GOVERNMENT - 1918-1933

Voice Lib.
M980   Goebbels, Joseph, 1897-1945.
bd.3   Calling up Nazi S.A. troops.   Peteler,
        1932.
            1 reel (7 in.)   7 1/2 in. per sec.
        phonotape.

GERMANY - POLITICS AND GOVERNMENT - 1918-1933

Voice Lib.
M980   Goebbels, Joseph, 1897-1945.
bd.4   Stating his opinions at the occasion of
        the inauguration of von Papen as High
        Commissioner for Prussia at Nazi mass
        meeting in the "Lustgarten" in Berlin.
        Peteler, July 27, 1932.
            1 reel (7 in.)   7 1/2 in. per sec.
        phonotape.

GERMANY - POLITICS AND GOVERNMENT - 1918-1933

Voice Lib.
M1466   Hoersing, Friedrich
bd.19   On the occasion of Founders Day of the
        "Reichsbanners".   Peteler, February 2,
        1924.
            1 reel (7 in.)   7 1/2 in. per sec.
        phonotape.

GERMANY - POLITICS AND GOVERNMENT - 1918-
Voice Lib. 1933
M1466   Noake, Gustav, 1868-1946.
bd.17   About suppressing Communist uprisings in
        Berlin.   Peteler, March 13, 1919.
            1 reel (7 in.)   7 1/2 in. per sec.
        phonotape.

GERMANY - POLITICS AND GOVERNMENT - 1918-1933

Voice Lib.
M1466   Scheidemann, Philip, 1865-1939.
bd.16   Observations on the situation arising from
        the forming of the German Republic and
        suppression of communism in Germany.
        Peteler, 1919.
            1 reel (7 in.)   7 1/2 in. per sec.
        phonotape.

GERMANY - POLITICS AND GOVERNMENT - 1918-1933

Voice Lib.
M1470   Zetkin, Klara, 1857-1933.
bd.9   Opening the first session of the 6th
        election period in the German Reichstag.
        Peteler, August 30, 1932.
            1 reel (7 in.)   7 1/2 in. per sec.
        phonotape.

GERMANY - POLITICS AND GOVERNMENT -
            1933-1945
Voice Lib.
M1471   Boldt, Gerhard, of Lübeck.
bd.1-A   Musical lead-in followed by description
        about the surroundings in the "Fuehrerbunker"
        in Berlin at the beginning of February, 1945.
        1965.
            1 reel (7 in.)   7 1/2 in. per sec.
        phonotape.

            1. Germany - Politics and government -
        1933-1945.

GERMANY - POLITICS AND GOVERNMENT -
            1933-1945
Voice Lib.
M1471   Boldt, Gerhard, of Lübeck
bd.1-B   Description of the last conferences in
        the "Ruehrerbunker" in Berlin, approximately
        April 22, 1945 to April 29, 1945.   1965.
            1 reel (7 in.)   7 i.p.s.   phonotape.

            1. Germany - Politics and government -
        1933-1945.

GERMANY - POLITICS AND GOVERNMENT -
            1933-1945
Voice Lib.
M1300   Goebbels, Joseph, 1875-1945.
bd.2   Address by Nazi propaganda minister
        Goebbels at inauguration of war relief
        work in the winter of 1941. Introducing
        Reichsfuehrer and Adolph Hitler. Peteler,
        October, 1941.
            1 reel (7 in.)   7 1/2 in. per sec.
        phonotape.

            1. Germany - Politics and government -
        1933-1945.

GERMANY - POLITICS AND GOVERNMENT - 1933-1945

Voice Lib.
M953   Göring, Hermann, 1893-1946.
bd.2   Remarks at the take-over of Hitler in the
        Nazi Party.   Peteler, January 30, 1933.
            1 reel (7 in.)   7 1/2 in. per sec.
        phonotape.

GERMANY - POLITICS AND GOVERNMENT -
1933-1945

Voice Lib.
M1373 Hadamovsky, Eugen, 1904-
bd.3   Talking about the so-called "radio affair".
         Peteler, August 12, 1933.
            1 reel (7 in.)   7 1/2 in. per sec.
         phonotape.

            1. Germany - Politics and government -
         1933-1945.

GERMANY - POLITICS AND GOVERNMENT - 1933-1945

Voice Lib.
M952   Hitler, Adolf, 1889-1945.
bd.11   Replying to President von Hindenburg in
        the German Reichstag and discussing his plans
        for the future of Germany.   Peteler, March 21,
        1933.
            1 reel (7 in.)   7 1/2 in. per sec.
        phonotape.

GERMANY - POLITICS AND GOVERNMENT - 1933-1945

Voice Lib.
M1003 Hess, Rudolf, 1894-
bd.1   Address to Nazi S.A. groups warning them
        not to continue their revolutionary tactics
        as they did during the period of the Weimar
        Republic.   Peteler, June 25, 1934.
            1 reel (7 in.)   7 1/2 in. per sec.
        phonotape.

GERMANY - POLITICS AND GOVERNMENT -
1933-1945

Voice Lib.
M999-   Hitler, Adolf, 1889-1945.
1000   Speech at session of German Reichstag
bd.1   stating Nazi policies, including discussions
        of same. Requesting Reichstag for overall
        power in government.   Peteler, March 23, 1933.
            2 reels (7 in.)   7 1/2 in. per sec.
        phonotape.

            1. Germany - Politics and government -
        1933-1945.

GERMANY - POLITICS AND GOVERNMENT - 1933-1945

Voice Lib.
M1003 Hess, Rudolf, 1894-
bd.2   Conciliatory remarks to S.A. group following
        Hitler's smashing of seditious activities
        as practiced by Ernst Roehm.   Peteler,
        July 8, 1934.
            1 reel (7 in.)   7 1/2 in. per sec.
        phonotape.

GERMANY - POLITICS AND GOVERNMENT - 1933-1945

Voice Lib.
M1003 Hitler, Adolf, 1889-1945.
bd.3   Address in German Reichstag defending his
        position in liquidating the disloyal S.A.
        groups and their leader, Ernst Roehm.
        Peteler,   July 13, 1934.
            1 reel (7 in.)   7 1/2 in. per sec.
        phonotape.

GERMANY - POLITICS AND GOVERNMENT - 1933-1945

Voice Lib.
M1376 Himmler, Heinrich, 1900-1945.
bd.2   Speaking to Storm Troop leaders in Frankfurt
        am Main.   Peteler, June 11, 1933.
            1 reel (7 in.)   7 1/2 in. per sec.
        phonotape.

GERMANY - POLITICS AND GOVERNMENT - 1933-1945

Voice Lib.
M1376 Hitler, Adolf, 1889-1945.
bd.6   Speaking at a state function.   Peteler,
        May 1, 1936.
            1 reel (7 in.)   7 1/2 in. per sec.
        phonotape.

GERMANY - POLITICS AND GOVERNMENT - 1933-1945

Voice Lib.
M980   Hitler, Adolf, 1889-1945.
bd.8-   Radio address to the public of Third
981   Reich on the assumption of power by the
bd.1   Nazi regime.   German Radio, Peteler,
        January 30, 1933.
            2 reels (7 in.)   7 1/2 in. per sec.
        phonotape.

            In German.

GERMANY - POLITICS AND GOVERNMENT - 1933-1945.

Voice Lib.
M1376 Hitler, Adolf, 1889-1945.
bd.10   Speaking at the Party Day celebration
        at Nuremberg.   Peteler, September 13,
        1936.
            1 reel (7 in.)   7 1/2 in. per sec.
        phonotape.

Voice Lib.
M1356   GERMANY - POLITICS AND GOVERNMENT -
bd.1   1933-1945
        Ley, Robert, 1890-1945.
        Address at the opening of the Bayreuth
        War Games. Peteler, 1942.
        1 reel (7 in.)   7 1/2 i.p.s.   phonotape.

        1. Germany - Politics and government -
        1933-1945.

Voice Lib.
M1470   GERMANY - POLITICS AND GOVERNMENT - 1933-1945
bd.7   Papen, Franz von, 1879-1969.
        Speaking about the political situation
        in the German province of Prussia and
        announcing his appointment as commissioner
        for the province. Peteler, July 20, 1933.
        1 reel (7 in.)   7 1/2 in. per sec.
        phonotape.

Voice Lib.
M1470   GERMANY - POLITICS AND GOVERNMENT - 1933-1945
bd.11   Schleicher, Kurt von
        Speaking about new government programs.
        Peteler, December 15, 1932.
        1 reel (7 in.)   7 1/2 in. per sec.
        phonotape.

Voice Lib.
540   Gershwin, George, 1898-1937.
bd.3   "Strike Up the Band" rehearsal. Fox
        Movietone, 1927.
        1 reel (7 in.)   7 1/2 in. per sec.
        phonotape.

        I. Title.

Voice Lib.
M1064   Gershwin, George, 1898-1937.
bd.3   Rehearsing for musical show; dialogue and
        singing "I Left My Mademoiselle in New
        Rochelle". Fox Movietone, 1930.
        1 reel (7 in.)   7 1/2 in. per sec.
        phonotape.

        I. Title: I left my mademoiselle in New
        Rochelle.

Voice Lib.
M1065   Gershwin, George, 1898-1937.
bd.7   Playing his composition "I've Got Rhythm"
        at recital. Fox Movietone, 1931.
        1 reel (7 in.)   7 1/2 in. per sec.
        phonotape.

        I. Title: I've got rhythm

Voice Lib. GERSHWIN, GEORGE, 1898-1937
M869   The great American song (radio program)
bd.2-   Documentary program of CBC on the contribution
870   of American music: discussion of the work of
        George Gershwin; American musical comedy;
        biographical sketches and interviews with
        composers Arthur Schwartz and Vernon Duke, who
        discuss the technique of composing. CBC, 1964.
        2 reels (7 in.)   7 1/2 in. per sec.
        phonotape.

        1. Gershwin, George, 1898-1937.   I. Schwartz,
        Arthur, 1900-   II. Duke, Vernon, 1903-1969.

        GERSHWIN, GEORGE, 1898-1937
Voice Lib.
M1026   Journey to Greatness; biographical sketch
bd.1   of the career of George Gershwin. One-
        hour 1963 Ohio State award-winning program
        broadcast by the Voice of America. Voice
        of America, 1963.
        1 reel (7 in.)   7 1/2 in. per sec.
        phonotape.

        1. Gershwin, George, 1898-1937.

        GERSHWIN, GEORGE, 1898-1937
Voice Lib.
M1315   Today (TV program)
bd.2   Celebrating George Gershwin Week in New
        York. Reminiscences of George Gershwin by
        former colleagues and his sister. NBC-TV,
        May 7, 1968.
        1 reel (7 in.)   7 1/2 i.p.s.   phonotape.

        1. Gershwin, George, 1898-1937.

        Gershwin, Ira, 1896-
Voice Lib.
M955   Lawrence, Gertrude, 1901-1952.
bd.11- Singing selections from album of
14   Ira Gershwin-Kurt Weill musical comedy
        "Lady in the dark". RCA, 1938.
        1 reel (7 in.)   7 1/2 in. per sec.
        phonotape.

        CONTENTS.-bd.11. "My ship".-bd.12. "Jenny".-
        bd.13. "This is new".-bd. 14. "One life to live".
        I. Gershwin, Ira, 1896-   II. Weill, Kurt,
        1900-1950.

Getlan, Samuel

Voice Lib.
243   McClellan, John Little, 1896-
bd.9   Senate investigating committee: coin-
machine labor union. Voices of Samuel
Getlan, Karl Mundt, Robert Kennedy and
John McClellan. CBS Radio, August 5, 1957.
1 reel (7 in.)   7 1/2 in. per sec.
phonotape.

I. Getlan, Samuel   II. Mundt, Karl
Earl, 1900-   III. Kennedy, Robert Francis,
1925-1968.

Gettysburg Address

Voice Lib.
112   Lincoln, Abraham, Pres. U.S., 1809-1965.
bd.2   Gettysburg Address, as read by Raymond
Massey. Linguaphone ¸1940¸
1 reel (7 in.)   7 1/2 in. per sec.
phonotape.

I. Massey, Raymond, 1896-   II. Title.

GHOST STORIES

C1
A41   Whorf, Michael, 1933-
Ghost story.
1 tape cassette.   (The visual sounds of
Mike Whorf. Art, music and letters, A41)
Originally presented on his radio program, Kaleidoscope,
WJR, Detroit.
Duration: 37 min., 45 sec.
With stories of the real and the unreal the listener is transported
to a realm in which the dead walk, voices call from the grave,
and ghostly arms reach out for good or ill.

L. Ghost stories. L. Title.

Ghost story

C1
A41   Whorf, Michael, 1933-
Ghost story.
1 tape cassette.   (The visual sounds of
Mike Whorf. Art, music and letters, A41)
Originally presented on his radio program, Kaleidoscope,
WJR, Detroit.
Duration: 37 min., 45 sec.
With stories of the real and the unreal the listener is transported
to a realm in which the dead walk, voices call from the grave,
and ghostly arms reach out for good or ill.

L. Ghost stories. L. Title.

C1
A20   Giant of the age, Michelangelo
Whorf, Michael, 1933-
Giant of the age, Michelangelo.
1 tape cassette.   (The visual sounds of
Mike Whorf. Art, music, and letters, A20)

Originally published on his radio program, Kaleidoscope,
WJR, Detroit.
Duration: 28 min., 50 sec.
His life and the story of his works unfolds in this narrative
dealing with the world of Michelangelo.

L. Buonarroti, Michel Angelo, 1475-1564. L. Title.

C1
S40   GIBSON, CHARLES DANA, 1867-1944
Whorf, Michael, 1933-
The Gibson girl.
1 tape cassette.   (The visual sounds of
Mike Whorf. Social, S40)
Originally presented on his radio program, Kaleidoscope,
WJR, Detroit.
Duration: 29 min., 15 sec.
A charming look at the lovely, illusive American girl. The
drawings of Charles Gibson come to life with the romantic music
of the period, along with an account of the love triangle of the
century.

L. Gibson, Charles Dana, 1867-1944. 2. U.S. - Social
conditions. L. Title.

Voice Lib.
M1065   Gibson, Hugh, 1883-1954.
bd.3   Disarmament speech being booed and hissed;
interlude music; British delegate opening
Disarmament Conference; Hugh Gibson stating
U.S. position - abolishing submarine warfare,
lethal gas, and bombing by air. Fox Movietone,
1933.
1 reel (7 in.)   7 1/2 in. per sec.
phonotape.

1. Disarmament.

Voice Lib.
M540   Gibson, Hugh, 1883-1954.
bd.23   First world conference on disarmament:
abolition of submarines, bombs, etc.
Fox Movietone, 1933.
1 reel (7 in.)   7 1/2 i.p.s.   phonotape.

1. Disarmament.

S

C1
S40   The Gibson girl
Whorf, Michael, 1933-
The Gibson girl.
1 tape cassette.   (The visual sounds of
Mike Whorf. Social, S40)
Originally presented on his radio program, Kaleidoscope,
WJR, Detroit.
Duration: 29 min., 15 sec.
A charming look at the lovely, illusive American girl. The
drawings of Charles Gibson come to life with the romantic music
of the period, along with an account of the love triangle of the
century.

L. Gibson, Charles Dana, 1867-1944. 2. U.S. - Social
conditions. L. Title.

Gielgud, John, 1904-

Voice Lib.
111   Doyle, Sir Arthur Conan, 1859-1930.
bd.2   Dr. Watson meets Sherlock Holmes, as
read by John Gielgud and Ralph Richardson.
British Broadcasting Corp., His Master's
Voice, 1947.
1 reel (7 in.)   7 1/2 in. per sec.
phonotape.
I. Gielgud, John, 1904-   II. Richardson,
Ralph David, 1902-   III. Title.

Gielgud, John, 1904-

Voice Lib.
110   Doyle, Sir Arthur Conan, 1859-1930.
bd.2   The Final Problem, an episode read by
          John Gielgud, Ralph Richardson, and Orson
          Welles. His Master's Voice, 1947.
           1 reel (7 in.)   7 1/2 in. per sec.
          phonotape.

           I. Gielgud, John, 1904-   II. Richardson,
          Ralph David, 1902-   III. Welles, Orson,
          1915-   IV. Title.

Gielgud, John, 1904-

Voice Lib.
M225   Packard, Frederick
           Styles in Shakespearean acting, 1890-1950.
          Creative Associates, 1963?
           1 reel (7 in.) 7 1/2 i.p.s. phonotape.

           I. Sothern, Edward Askew, 1826-1881. II. Marlowe,
          Julia, 1865-1950. III. Booth, Edwin, 1833-1893. IV. Gielgud,
          John, 1904-   V. Robeson, Paul Bustill, 1898-   VI. Terry,
          Dame Ellen, 1848-1928. VII. Allen, Viola. VIII. Welles,
          Orson, 1915-   IX. Skinner, Otis, 1858-1942. X. Barrymore,
          John, 1882-1942. XI. Olivier, Sir Laurence Kerr, 1907-
          XII. Forbes-Robertson, Sir Johnston, 1853-   XIII. Evans,
          Maurice. XIV. Thorndike, Dame Sybil, 1882-   XV. Robson,
          Flora. XVI. LeGallienne, Eva, 1899-   XVII. Anderson,
          Judith. XVIII. Duncan, Augustin. XIX. Hampden, Walter.
          XX. Speaight, Robert, 1904-   XXI. Jones, Daniel.

Voice Lib.
M1046   The gift outright; tribute to John F.
bd.1   Kennedy upon the first anniversary of his
          assassination; broadcast by ABC Radio News.
          Review of President Kennedy's administration
          and comments by various colleagues.   ABC
          Radio, November 22, 1964.
           1 reel (7 in.)   7 1/2 in. per sec.
          phonotape.

           1. Kennedy, John Fitzgerald, Pres. U.S.,
          1917-1963.

Voice Lib.
M1048   Gilbert, L   Wolfe
bd.2   Interview with G. Robert Vincent at his
          office regarding Wolfe Gilbert's song
          "Waiting for the Robert E. Lee"; also,
          rendition of this song. 1952.
           1 reel (7 in.)   7 1/2 in. per sec.
          phonotape.

           I. Vincent, G   Robert   II. Title:
          Waiting for the Robert E. Lee.

Voice Lib.
M761   Gilbert, L   Wolfe
bd.9   Excerpt from "Tunesmiths past and present"
          (Program 4); relates how he began by selling
          six parodies to Al Jolson. Westinghouse
          Broadcasting Corporation, 1964.
           2 min., 23 sec.   phonotape (1 r.
          7 1/2 i.p.s.)   (The music goes round and
          round)

           1. Music, Popular (Songs, etc.) - Writing
          and publishing.   I. Title: Tunesmiths
          past and present.   II. Series.

Voice Lib.
M11   Gillette, William Hooker, 1853-1937.
bd.1   Excerpts from Sherlock Holmes read by
          William Gillette.   Private recording,
          1930.
           1 reel (7 in.)   7 1/2 i.p.s.   phonotape.

Voice Lib.
M1057   Gillette, William Hooker, 1853-1937.
bd.3   Informal characterization of various
          parts of his stage plays on Sherlock
          Holmes, recorded at Harvard University.
          Dr. F.E. Packard taking the part of Dr.
          Watson. Harvard Vocarium, 1934.
           1 reel (7 in.)   7 1/2 in. per sec.
          phonotape.

Gillis, Frank
Voice Lib.
M1428   Brown, Steve
           Interview with Steve Brown, early New
          Orleans jazz musician, by Frank Gillis,
          Director of Folk Music Archive, Indiana
          University. 1953.
           1 reel (7 in.)   3 3/4 in. per sec.
          phonotape.

           Full track tape.
           I. Gillis, Frank

Voice Lib.
M1060-   Ginsberg, Allen, 1926-
1062   Reading his avant garde "stream of
          consciousness" prose-poems at MSU Auditorium
          at invitation of ASMSU; also chanting various
          "mantras". Location recording, February 27,
          1967.
           3 reels (7 in.)   7 1/2 in. per sec.
          phonotape.
           CONTENTS:-"Uptown New York"; "Ken Kesey's First Party
          With Hell's Angels"; "Wings Over the Black Pit", which is a
          part of "From Here on Out"; "Face the Nation"; "Chicago";
          "I Will Haunt These States".

Voice Lib.
M1203-   Ginsberg, Allen, 1926-
1204,   Informal "bull session" at Coral Gables,
bd.1   East Lansing, of MSU students and Allen
          Ginsberg, covering topics of drugs, sex,
          poetry and opinions of MSU. A/V,
          February 28, 1967.
           2 reels (7 in.)   7 1/2 in. per sec.
          phonotape.

Voice Lib. Giovinezza
M1100 Martinelli, Giovanni, 1885-1969.
bd.3   Italian tenor singing "Giovinezza", the
official Fascist song. Complete rendition.
Forrest, 1933.
      1 reel (7 in.)   7 1/2 in. per sec.
phonotape.

      I. Title: Giovinezza.

Voice Lib.
M1695   Gish, Lillian, 1896-
      Interviewed by Edwin Newman on Speaking
freely.   WKAR-TV, 1974.
      37 min.   phonotape (1 r.   7 1/2 i.p.s.)

      1. Moving-pictures - History.
I. Newman, Edwin Harold, 1919-

Voice Lib.
609   Glazer, Tom
bd.7-8   Singing satirical songs.   G. R. Vincent,
1948-49.
      1 reel (7 in.)   7 1/2 in. per sec.
phonotape.

      CONTENTS.-"The Lydia Pinkham Song", "In
New York City".

Voice Lib.
138   Glenn, John Herschel, 1921-
bd.2   An announcer's description of flight
from Cape Canaveral to Washington, with
John Glenn and President Kennedy.
NBC, 1961.
      1 reel (7 in.)   7 1/2 in. per sec.
phonotape.

Voice Lib.
M258   Glenn, John Herschel, 1921-
bd.4   Press conference: future of manned
space flight.   New York, CBS, June 9,
1961.
      1 reel (7 in.)   7 1/2 in. per sec.
phonotape.

Voice Lib.
M103-   Glenn, John Herschel, 1921-
109   The John Glenn story (America's first manned orbital flight).
NBC-TV, February, 1962.
      7 reels (7 in.)   7 1/2 i.p.s.   phonotape.

      CONTENTS. -103, bd. 1. Pre-flight interview. -103, bd. 2.
Preparation at Cape Canaveral. -108, bd. 3. Countdown, delay. -
103, bd. 4. Description of rocket. -103, bd. 5. Excitement at ocean
front. -103, bd. 6. Description of takeoff. -103, bd. 7. Glenn's
first report. -104, bd. 1. Explanation of technical terms. -104, bd. 2,
Glenn's first attempt at food. -104, bd. 3. Glenn observes lights in
Australia. -104, bd. 4. Flash to New Concord, Ohio. -104, bd. 5.
Mercury Control relays reports. -104, bd. 6. Flying by wire, 2d
orbit. -104, bd. 7. Glenn speaks to Canaveral. -105, bd. 1. Spacecraft committed to 3d orbit. -105, bd. 2. Reaction from Moscow. -

                                    (Continued on next card)

Voice Lib.
M103-   Glenn, John Herschel, 1921-   The John Glenn story ...
109   1962.   (Card 2)

      CONTENTS (Cont'd) 105, bd. 3. Description, view and technical
data. -105, bd. 4. Retro rockets fired. -105, bd.5, Capsule's
chutes have opened. -105, bd. 5. Capsule in water, 4 hr. 56 min.
26 sec. -106, bd. 1. Glenn on deck U. S. S. Noa. -106, bd. 2.
Pres. Kennedy speaks. -106, bd. 3, Glenn's parents in New
Concord, Ohio. -106, bd. 4. Glenn's wife in Arlington, Va. -
106, bd. 5. Canaveral reception 2/23/62. -106, bd. 6, Vice-
Pres. Johnson, Glenn decorated. -107, bd. 1. JFK lauds Glenn
and Gilruth. -107, bd. 2. Glenn shows capsule to guests. -107,
bd. 3, The press conference. -108, bd. 1. Press conference continued.

                                    (Continued on next card)

Voice Lib.
M103-   Glenn, John Herschel, 1921-   The John Glenn story ...
109   1962.   (Card 3)

      CONTENTS (Cont'd) 108, bd. 2. Washington ceremonies. -
108, bd. 3. Parade from White House to Capitol. -108, bd. 4.
Glenn speaks to Congress. -109, bd. 1. Glenn speaks to Congress. -
109, bd. 2. Big parade in New York. -109, bd. 3, Ceremonies at
New York City Hall. -109, bd. 4. Boy Scouts ceremonies. -109,
bd. 5. The Waldorf dinner speeches. -109, bd. 6. Mayor Wagner
and Glenn speeches.

      1. Space flight.   2. Glenn, John Herschel, 1921-

Voice Lib.
M1236   Glenn, John Herschel, 1921-
bd.1   Descriptions of proceedings at joint
session of U.S. Congress to honor astronaut
Glenn before his appearance.   Voice of
America, February 26, 1962.
      1 reel (7 in.)   7 1/2 in. per sec.
phonotape.

      1. Glenn, John Herschel, 1921-

Voice Lib.
M1236   Glenn, John Herschel, 1921-
bd.2   Address before joint session of U.S.
Congress about his space flight on "Friendship
7" including humorous anecdotes and
patriotic sentiments.   Voice of America,
February 26, 1962.
      1 reel (7 in.)   7 1/2 in. per sec.
phonotape.

Voice Lib.
351   Glenn, John Herschel, 1921-
bd.6   Before House Space Committee, describing
his space flight before Senate Space Committee,
reviewing public acclaim, describing his
philosophy of life; before U.N. on world
co-operation in space flight. CBS, February
27-28, March 2, 1962.
      1 reel (7 in.)   7 1/2 in. per sec.
phonotape.

      1. Space flight.

C1
SC32   GLENN, JOHN HERSCHEL, 1921-
Whorf, Michael, 1933-
      John Glenn's day of miracles.
      1 tape cassette.   (The visual sounds of
Mike Whorf. Science, SC32)
         Originally presented on his radio program, Kaleidoscope,
WJR, Detroit.
         Duration: 37 min., 15 sec.
         From his days as pilot, to the day he climbed aboard
Friendship Seven, here is the story of the Ohio-born airman who
took the first giant step that led to mankind's gigantic leap.

      1. Glenn, John Herschel, 1921-   1. Title.

Voice Lib.
640   Glick, Carl, 1890-
bd.1   Discusses his book, Shake Hands With the
Dragon. GRV, 1939.
      1 reel (7 in.)   7 1/2 in. per sec.
phonotape.

      1. Glick, Carl, 1890-   /Shake hands with
the dragon. I. Title: Shake hands with the
dragon.

         GLICK, CARL, 1890-
         SHAKE HANDS WITH THE DRAGON
Voice Lib.
640   Glick, Carl, 1890-
bd.1   Discusses his book, Shake Hands With the
Dragon. GRV, 1939.
      1 reel (7 in.)   7 1/2 in. per sec.
phonotape.

      1. Glick, Carl, 1890-   /Shake hands with
the dragon. I. Title: Shake hands with the
dragon.

C1
M37   The glory of the Grecian games
Whorf, Michael, 1933-
      The glory of the Grecian games.
      1 tape cassette.   (The visual sounds of
Mike Whorf. Miscellaneous, M37)
         Originally presented on his radio program, Kaleidoscope,
WJR, Detroit.
         Duration: 36 min.
         From antiquity comes this tale of gods and goddesses, of
athletes who saluted the reigning deities and participated in
peace coexistence. Since a Frenchman revived the games in the
the 1800's, the contests have provided the world with fascinating
spectacle.
      1. Olympic games.   1. Title.

                    Go home, army, army, go home
Voice Lib.
M1656 East German radio.
bd.2   Go home, army, army, go home. Recorded
on home-made metal disk, 1949.
      5 min. phonotape (1 r.   7 1/2 i.p.s.)

      "Tramp, tramp, tramp" sung in German.

      I. Title.

         GOA
Voice Lib.
344   Stevenson, Adlai Ewing, 1900-1965.
bd.13   At the U.N. on the Indian invasion
of Goa. CBS, December 18, 1961.
      1 reel (7 in.)   7 1/2 in. per sec.
phonotape.

         GOA
Voice Lib.
344   Stevenson, Adlai Ewing, 1900-1965.
bd.14   At U.N. following the vote on Goa:
"the failure of the Security Council
tonight to demand a cease-fire is a failure
of the U.N.". CBS, December 19, 1961.
      1 reel (7 in.)   7 1/2 in. per sec.
phonotape.

         God be with you 'til we meet again
Voice Lib.
M987 Sankey, Ira David, 1840-1908.
bd.1   Musical evangelist Ira Sankey singing
excerpt from hymn "God be with you 'til
we meet again". Moody Institute, 1899.
      1 reel (7 in.)   7 1/2 in. per sec.
phonotape.

      I. Title: God be with you 'til we meet
again.

         God bless America
Voice Lib.
M160 Smith, Kate, 1909-
bd.3   Singing Irving Berlin's composition "God
Bless America", with commentary, from
Carnegie Hall, New York. RCA, November 2,
1963.
      1 reel (7 in.)   7 1/2 in. per sec.
phonotape.

      I. Title: God bless America.

C1
SC1   GODDARD, ROBERT HUTCHINGS, 1882-1945

Whorf, Michael, 1933-
The rocket man.
1 tape cassette.   (The visual sounds of
Mike Whorf. Science, SC1)
Originally presented on his radio program, Kaleidoscope,
WJR, Detroit.
Duration: 36 min., 30 sec.
From his early beginnings in New England and New Mexico to
the years of culmination, here is a must for the student of science.
The story of Robert Hutchings Goddard, the rocket man.

L. Goddard, Robert Hutchings, 1882-1945. L. Title.

Voice Lib.
M957 Godfrey, Arthur, 1903-
The magic of broadcasting; variety TV
program about radio and TV broadcasting
with Arthur Godfrey, emcee, and Don Ameche,
Bing Crosby, Lucille Ball, Gale Gordon, John
Scott Trotter, Rod Serling, Sheldon Leonard,
Dianne Sherry, Cary MacLane, and the "Wee
Five".   CBS-TV, May 1, 1966.
1 reel (7 in.) 7 1/2 in. per sec.
phonotape.

I. Godfrey, Arthur, 1903-

Voice Lib.
572- Godfrey, Arthur, 1903-
573   I can hear it now (radio program)
bd.1 1933-1946.   CBS, 1948.
2 reels (7 in.) 7 1/2 in. per sec.
phonotape.
L. Murrow, Edward Roscoe, 1908-1965. II. LaGuardia, Fiorello
Henry, 1882-1947. III. Chamberlain, Neville, 1869-1949. IV.
Roosevelt, Franklin Delano, Pres. U.S., 1882-1945. V. Churchill,
Winston Leonard Spencer, 1874-1965. VI. Gaulle, Charles de,
Pres. France, 1890-1970. VII. Eisenhower, Dwight David, Pres. U.S.,
1890-1969. VIII. Willkie, Wendell Lewis, 1892-1944. IX. Martin,
Joseph William, 1884-1968. X. Elizabeth II, Queen of Great Britain,
1926-   XI. Margaret Rose, Princess of Gt. Brit., 1930-   XII.
Johnson, Hugh Samuel, 188- 42. XIII. Smith, Alfred Emanuel,
1873-1944. XIV. Lindbergh Charles Augustus, 1902-   XV. Davis,
(Continued on next card)

Voice Lib.
M930 Godwin, Charles
bd.3 Conference at the opening of the Abraham
Lincoln Papers at Library of Congress.
Discussion of the contents and value of
these documents by various Lincoln authorities.
Mutual, July 29, 1947.
1 reel (7 in.) 7 1/2 in. per sec.
phonotape.

1. Lincoln, Abraham, Pres. U.S., 1809-1865.

Voice Lib.
M273- Godwin, Earl
274   Biography in sound (radio program)
bd.1 Franklin Delano Roosevelt: the friends and
former associates of Franklin Roosevelt on
the tenth anniversary of the President's death.
NBC Radio, April, 1955.
2 reels (7 in.) 7 1/2 in. per sec.
phonotape.
L. Roosevelt, Franklin Delano, Pres. U.S., 1882-1945. L.
McIntire, Ross T   1899-   II. Mellett, Lowell, 1884-1960.
III. Tully, Grace   IV. Henderson, Leon, 1895-
V. Roosevelt, Eleanor (Roosevelt) 1884-1962. VI. DeGraaf, Albert
VII. Lehman, Herbert Henry, 1878-1963. VIII. Rosenman, Samuel
Irving, 1896-   IX. Arvey, Jacob   X. Moley, Raymond,
1886-   XI. Farley, James Aloysius, 1888-   XII. Roosevelt,
(Continued on next card)

Voice Lib.
M1470 Goebbels, Joseph, 1897-1945.
bd.13 Appeal to the German nation, especially
youth. Peteler, 1932.
1 reel (7 in.) 7 1/2 in. per sec.
phonotape.

Voice Lib.
M980 Goebbels, Joseph, 1897-1945.
bd.3 Calling up Nazi S.A. troops. Peteler,
1932.
1 reel (7 in.) 7 1/2 in. per sec.
phonotape.

1. Germany - Politics and government -
1918-1933

Voice Lib.
M1470 Goebbels, Joseph, 1897-1945.
bd.8 Attacking policies of the existing German
government and speaking as a representative
of the NSDAP (Nazi Party). Peteler, July
15, 1932.
1 reel (7 in.) 7 1/2 in. per sec.
phonotape.

Voice Lib.
M980 Goebbels, Joseph, 1897-1945.
bd.4 Stating his opinions at the occasion of
the inauguration of von Papen as High
Commissioner for Prussia at Nazi mass
meeting in the "Lustgarten" in Berlin.
Peteler, July 27, 1932.
1 reel (7 in.) 7 1/2 in. per sec.
phonotape.

1. Germany - Politics and government -
1918-1933

Voice Lib.
M1373 Goebbels, Joseph, 1897-1945.
bd.4 Talking about the goals of the NSDAP
pertaining to radio broadcast. Peteler,
1933.
1 reel (7 in.) 7 1/2 i.p.s. phonotape.

1. Radio broadcasting. 2. Nationalsozialistische Deutsche Arbeiter-Partei.

Voice Lib.
M1470   Goebbels, Joseph, 1897-1945.
bd.14.   Report on the labor situation in Berlin.
Peteler, January 30, 1933.
    1 reel (7 in.)   7 1/2 i.p.s.   phonotape.

    1. Labor supply - Germany.

Voice Lib.
M1003   Goebbels, Joseph, 1897-1945.
bd.4   Speaking on German radio upon the death
of Reichspresident Paul von Hindenberg, and
giving Nazi-oriented eulogy. Peteler,
August 2, 1934.
    1 reel (7 in.)   7 1/2 in. per sec.
phonotape.

    1. Hindenburg, Paul von, Pres. Germany,
1847-1934.

Voice Lib.
M1363   Goebbels, Joseph, 1897-1945.
bd.9   Memorial ceremonies for SA-Sturmfuehrer
Hans Eberhard Maikowski. Peteler,
February 5, 1933.
    1 reel (7 in.)   7 1/2 in. per sec.
phonotape.

    1. Maikowski, Hans Eberhard

Voice Lib.
M1004   Goebbels, Joseph, 1897-1945.
bd.3-D   Introductory address for the main speaker,
Adolf Hitler, stressing his accomplishments,
at May Day ceremonies. Peteler, May 1,
1935.
    1 reel (7 in.)   7 1/2 in. per sec.
phonotape.

Voice Lib.
M1363   Goebbels, Joseph, 1897-1945.
bd.10   May Day ceremonies in Berlin. Peteler,
May 1, 1933.
    1 reel (7 in.)   7 1/2 in. per sec.
phonotape.

Voice Lib.
M1376   Goebbels, Joseph, 1897-1945.
bd.4   Speaking to the German Culture Commission
on May Day. Peteler, May 1, 1936.
    1 reel (7 in.)   7 1/2 in. per sec.
phonotape.

Voice Lib.
M1375   Goebbels, Joseph, 1897-1945.
bd.1   Tenth anniversary celebration of Munich
"Putsch" of November 11, 1923, held at the
Siemen factory in Berlin. Peteler,
November 8, 1933.
    1 reel (7 in.)   7 1/2 in. per sec.
phonotape.

Voice Lib.
M1016   Goebbels, Joseph, 1897-1945.
bd.6   Announcing in the name of the Fuehrer
the takeover of administering the Czech
provinces of Bohemia and Maehren by Nazis
but permitting autonomous local government
to the Czech people. F. Peteler, March 15,
1939.
    1 reel (7 in.)   7 1/2 in. per sec.
phonotape.

Voice Lib.
M1002   Goebbels, Joseph, 1897-1945.
bd.4   Speech at initial Nazi highway construction
project, near Munich. F. Peteler, March 21,
1934.
    1 reel (7 in.)   7 1/2 in. per sec.
phonotape.

Voice Lib.
M736   Goebbels, Joseph, 1897-1945.
bd.1   Talking about World War II to date and
disavowing Germany's intention of invading
the Low Countries. CBS, January 19, 1940.
    1 reel (7 in.)   7 1/2 in. per sec.
phonotape.

Voice Lib.
M736 Goebbels, Joseph, 1897-1945.
bd.7   Asking German people to demand total
war. CBS, April 9, 1940.
1 reel (7 in.) 7 1/2 in. per sec.
phonotape.

Voice Lib.
M1034 Goebbels, Joseph, 1897-1945.
bd.7   Speaking about the narrow living space
in Germany. Peteler, April, 1942.
1 reel (7 in.) 7 1/2 in. per sec.
phonotape.

Voice Lib.
M736 Goebbels, Joseph, 1897-1945.
bd.9   Talking about the siege of Stalingrad.
CBS, 1941.
1 reel (7 in.) 7 1/2 in. per sec.
phonotape.

Voice Lib.
M1356 Goebbels, Joseph, 1897-1945.
bd.2   Excerpt of address at the Berlin
Sportspalast. Peteler, January 30, 1943.
1 reel (7 in.) 7 1/2 in. per sec.
phonotape.

Voice Lib.
M1071 Goebbels, Joseph, 1897-1945.
Radio report from Ministry of Propaganda,
read by Goebbels, stating Hitler's decision
to end amicable relations with Yugoslavia and
to occupy it militarily. Peteler, April 6,
1941.
1 reel (7 in.) 7 1/2 in. per sec.
phonotape.
    1. Germany - Foreign relations - Yugoslavia. 2. Yugoslavia -
Foreign relations - Germany. 3. World War, 1939-1945.

Voice Lib.
M1356 Goebbels, Joseph, 1897-1945.
bd.3   Address at the Berlin Sportspalast entitled
"Do you want total war?" Peteler, February
18, 1943.
1 reel (7 in.) 7 1/2 in. per sec.
phonotape.

Voice Lib.
M1073 Goebbels, Joseph, 1897-1945.
bd.4   Reading message to the German people from
Hitler, stating that there are now 160
divisions of Soviet troops threatening Europe
and that Nazis are defending the Eastern
front from Arctic Ocean to Black Sea.
Peteler, June 22, 1941.
1 reel (7 in.) 7 1/2 in. per sec.
phonotape.

Voice Lib.
M1361 Goebbels, Joseph, 1897-1945.
bd.8   Talking to the Berlin "Volkssturm".
Peteler, March, 1945.
1 reel (7 in.) 7 1/2 in. per sec.
phonotape.

Voice Lib.
M1300 Goebbels, Joseph, 1875-1945.
bd.2   Address by Nazi propaganda minister
Goebbels at inauguration of war relief
work in the winter of 1941. Introducing
Reichsfuehrer and Adolph Hitler. Peteler,
October, 1941.
1 reel (7 in.) 7 1/2 in. per sec.
phonotape.
    1. Germany - Politics and government -
1933-1945.

Voice Lib.
M1361 Goebbels, Joseph, 1897-1945.
bd.10   Last radio speech, on the occasion of
Hitler's birthday, followed by the German
national anthem (Deutschlandlied), heard
for the last time over Radio Berlin. Peteler,
April 19, 1945.
1 reel (7 in.) 7 1/2 in. per sec.
phonotape.

Voice Lib. Goebbels, Joseph, 1897-1945
M1073 German radio (Nazi controlled)
bd.15   Nazi news report: statement made during
opening of the Great German Art Exhibition
in Munich, followed by the main speaker,
Joseph Goebbels. Peteler, August, 1941.
1 reel (7 in.) 7 1/2 in. per sec.
phonotape.

I. Goebbels, Joseph, 1897-1945.

Voice Lib.
M1001 Göring, Hermann, 1893-1946.
bd.2   Address at German Reichstag session of
March 23, 1933, in defense of Nazi policies
of censorship and condemning false information
published in opposition and foreign newspapers. F. Peteler, March 23, 1933.
1 reel (7 in.) 7 1/2 in. per sec.
phonotape.

Voice Lib.
M1373 Göring, Hermann, 1893-1946.
bd.6   Speech at the celebration of the 10th
anniversary of the Munich Putsch. Peteler,
September 11, 1923.
1 reel (7 in.) 7 1/2 in. per sec.
phonotape.

Voice Lib.
M1375 Göring, Hermann, 1893-1946.
bd.4   Reading new laws pertaining to the government of the Reich. Peteler, January 30,
1934.
1 reel (7 in.) 7 1/2 in. per sec.
phonotape.

Voice Lib.
M1470 Göring, Hermann, 1893-1946.
bd.10   Preventing dissolution of the Reichstag.
Peteler, October 12, 1932.
1 reel (7 in.) 7 1/2 in. per sec.
phonotape.

Voice Lib.
M1003 Göring, Hermann, 1893-1946.
bd.8   Address to German Academy of Jurisprudence
analyzing Nazi conception of justice.
Peteler, November 13, 1934.
1 reel (7 in.) 7 1/2 in. per sec.
phonotape.

1. National socialism.

Voice Lib.
M953 Göring, Hermann, 1893-1946.
bd.2   Remarks at the take-over of Hitler in the
Nazi Party. Peteler, January 30, 1933.
1 reel (7 in.) 7 1/2 in. per sec.
phonotape.

1. Germany - Politics and government -
1933-1945.

Voice Lib.
M1010 Göring, Hermann, 1893-1946.
bd.1   Address upon conclusion of final vote
on Nazi race policies held at a convention
of Nazi Party at Nuremberg. Peteler,
September 15, 1935.
1 reel (7 in.) 7 1/2 in. per sec.
phonotape.

Voice Lib.
M1001 Göring, Hermann, 1893-1946.
bd.2- Address at German Reichstag session of
1002 March 23, 1933 in defense of Nazi policies
bd.1 of censorship and condemning false information
published in opposition and foreign newspapers.
Stressing Nazi fair treatment of Jews, and
German quest for peace. F. Peteler, March 23,
1933.
2 reels (7 in.) 7 1/2 in. per sec.
phonotape.

Voice Lib.
M1376 Göring, Hermann, 1893-1946.
bd.3   Talking to the new German Army on May
Day. Peteler, May 1, 1936.
1 reel (7 in.) 7 1/2 in. per sec.
phonotape.

Voice Lib.
M1016 Göring, Hermann, 1893-1946.
bd.11   Comment in Berlin Reichstag, expressing
words of gratitude and admiration at Hitler's
political genius and continued faith in all
his actions. F. Peteler, April 28, 1939.
1 reel (7 in.) 7 1/2 in. per sec.
phonotape.

Voice Lib. Göring, Hermann, 1893-1946
M1019 Nationalsozialistische Deutsche Arbeiter-Partei.
bd.12   Reichsparteitag.
Reichstag session, July 19, 1940: address
by Adolf Hitler pertaining to armistice with
France; plans for further Nazi aims, such as
the elimination of Jewish financiers domes-
tically and abrogation of all remaining
Versailles treaty demands. Justifying invasion
of Norway as a defense measure. Renewal of
peace proposals with England, followed by Nazi
songs and expressions of gratitude by Hermann
Göring to the vision and strategy of Hitler.
(Continued on next card)

Voice Lib.
M1016 Göring, Hermann, 1893-1946.
bd.13   Congratulating the troops of the Legion
Condor at their accomplishments in Spain in
the Civil War. Peteler, June 6, 1939.
1 reel (7 in.) 7 1/2 i.p.s. phonotape.

1. Spain - History - Civil War, 1936-1939.

Göring, Hermann, 1893-1946
Voice Lib.
M1019 Nationalsozialistische Deutsche Arbeiter-Partei.
bd.12   Reichsparteitag. Reichstag session, July
19, 1940... 1940. (Card 2)

July 19, 1940.
1 reel (7 in.) 7 1/2 in. per sec.
phonotape.

I. Hitler, Adolf, 1889-1945. II. Göring,
Hermann, 1893-1946.

Voice Lib. Göring, Hermann, 1893-1946
M1301 German radio (Nazi controlled)
bd.3   Reporting progress on the Russian front
and the declaration of war by Japan on the
United States. Peteler, December 11, 1941.
1 reel (7 in.) 7 1/2 in. per sec. phonotape.
CONTENTS.--a. Göring, Hermann.--b. Hitler, Adolf,
criticizing President Roosevelt and comparing his own actions
with those of FDR.
L. Göring, Hermann, 1893-1946. II. Hitler, Adolf, 1889-1945.
III. Nationalsozialistische Deutsche Arbeiter-Partei. Reichsparteitag.

Voice Lib. Göring, Hermann, 1893-1946
M1304 Nationalsozialistische Deutsche Arbeiter-Partei.
bd.11   Reichsparteitag.
Reichstag session pertaining to the appointment of Hitler as prime law maker of German
Reich; including addresses by: a. Hitler,
Adolf, about the hardship of German troops at
the Russian front; b. Göring, Hermann, appraisal
of strength of the U.S. entering European
conflict. Peteler, April 26, 1942.
1 reel (7 in.) 7 1/2 in. per sec.
phonotape.
L. Hitler, Adolf, 1889-1945. II. Göring, Hermann, 1893-1946.

Göring, Hermann, 1893-1946
Voice Lib.
216-   Hitler, Adolph, 1889-1945.
217   Speech before German Parliament,
announcing annexation of Danzig, with
introduction by Hermann Göring and comments
by Hans Fritsche (English translation).
Detroit, WJR, September 1, 1939.
2 reels (7 in.) 7 1/2 in. per sec.
phonotape.
I. Göring, Hermann, 1893-1946. II. Fritsche,
Hans

Goethe, Johann Wolfgang von, 1749-1832.
Faust
Voice Lib.
M1464 Ebert, Karl
bd.4   Monologue from "Faust" by Goethe, on the
occasion of Goethe's birthday. Peteler,
1932.
1 reel (7 in.) 7 1/2 in. per sec.
phonotape.

I. Goethe, Johann Wolfgang von, 1749-
1832. /Faust.

Voice Lib. Göring, Hermann, 1893-1946
M1018 Nationalsozialistische Deutsche Arbeiter-Partei.
bd.4   Reichsparteitag.
Reichstag session including remarks by
Hermann Göring, expressing gratitude to
Luftwaffe at Polish victories; and Adolf Hitler
justifying his attack on Poland and his
alliance with Soviets, his aims at European
peace pact and return of German colonies.
Peteler, October 6, 1939.
1 reel (7 in.) 7 1/2 in. per sec.
phonotape.
L. Göring, Hermann, 1893-1946. II. Hitler, Adolf, 1889-1945.

Voice Lib.
M1255 Goldberg, Arthur Joseph, 1908-
bd.2   Address to emergency meeting of U.N.
General Assembly stating current U.S. position
on resolving Arab-Israeli crisis and suggestion
for peace in the Middle East. CBS-TV,
June 20, 1967.
1 reel (7 in.) 7 1/2 in. per sec.
phonotape.

1. Israel-Arab War, 1967-
Diplomatic history.

Voice Lib.
M1058 Golden, Harry Lewis, 1902–
Talking about himself, his books, writing
in general, social problems, early boyhood,
on NET-TV program "The Creative Person".
WMSB, February 26, 1967.
1 reel (7 in.)   7 1/2 in. per sec.
phonotape.

1. Golden, Harry Lewis, 1902–

Voice Lib.
M311 Goldwater, Barry Morris, 1909–
bd.9   Assassination: statement by and interview
of Barry Goldwater.   NBC, November 23, 1963.
1 reel (7 in.)   7 1/2 in. per sec.
phonotape.

1. Kennedy, John Fitzgerald, Pres. U.S.,
1917-1963. - Assassination.

Voice Lib.
M760   Goldmark, Goldie
bd.2   Excerpt from "What All the Screaming's
About" (Program 1); Beatle music is actually
nothing new.   Westinghouse Broadcasting
Corporation, 1964.
23 sec.   phonotape (1 r.   7 1/2 i.p.s.)
(The music goes round and round)

1. Music, Popular (Songs, etc.)   I. Title:
What all the screaming's about. II. Series.

Goldwater, Barry Morris, 1909–
Voice Lib.
M846   Excerpts of political speeches and statements
bd.2   by presidential candidates Lyndon Johnson
and Barry Goldwater, from TV dramatization
of Theodore H. White's book "The Making of
the President, 1964".
1 reel (7 in.)   7 1/2 in. per sec.
phonotape.
I. Johnson, Lyndon Baines, Pres. U. S., 1908-1973. II.
Goldwater, Barry Morris, 1909-   III. White, Theodore
Harold, 1915-   /The making of the president, 1964.

Voice Lib.
M764   Goldmark, Goldie
bd.11   Excerpt from "The world of wax" (Program 8); comments on
the production of another phenomenon which has had a profound
effect on the recording industry, the disc jockey.   Also comments
on the dissatisfaction of a large segment of the record industry with
the radio-record relationship.   Westinghouse Broadcasting
Corporation, 1964.
7 min., 58 sec.   phonotape (1 r.   7 1/2 i.p.s.)   (The music
goes round and round)

1. Disc jockeys.   1. Title: The world of wax.   II. Series.

Voice Lib.
664   Goldwater, Barry Morris, 1908–
bd.1   Acceptance speech at Republican National
Convention in San Francisco; condemning
Democratic administration.   NBC, July 16,
1964.
1 reel (7 in.)   7 1/2 in. per sec.
phonotape.

Speech incomplete.

Voice Lib.
M765   Goldmark, Goldie
bd.4   Excerpt from "The anatomy of a hit"
(Program 9); gives advice on how to get
a new record on a popular music station.
Westinghouse Broadcasting Corporation, 1964.
1 min., 41 sec.   phonotape (1 r.   7 1/2
i.p.s.)   (The music goes round and round)

1. Music, Popular (Songs, etc.)
2. Phonorecords.   I. Title: The anatomy of
a hit. II. Series.

Voice Lib.
M1268 Goldwater, Barry Morris, 1908–
NET program about the 1964 presidential
campaign consisting of informal conversations
by Joseph Stern and Paul Niven with Barry
Goldwater and William E. Miller in
Washington, D.C.   NET, September 25, 1967.
1 reel (7 in.)   7 1/2 in. per sec.
phonotape.

I. Miller, William Edward, 1914–   II.
Stern, Joseph   III. Niven, Paul

Voice Lib.
M763   Goldstein, Chuck
bd.4   Excerpt from "The Scope of Jazz" (Program 6); comments
how each band had their own style and how they adapted
material to fit this style.   Comments on Glenn Miller himself;
also comments on Frank Sinatra, including "Moonlight Serenade"
and an excerpt from "The Hit Parade", with girls screaming
over Frank Sinatra and him singing "Lay That Pistol Down, Babe".
Westinghouse Broadcasting Corporation, 1964.
1 reel (7 in.)   7 1/2 in. per sec.   phonotape.   (The Music
Goes Round and Round)

1. Jazz music.   1. Title: The scope of jazz.   II. Series.

Goldwater, Barry Morris, 1909–
Voice Lib.
M846   The Making of the President, 1964 (TV program)
bd.2   Excerpts of political speeches and state-
ments by presidential candidates Lyndon
Johnson and Barry Goldwater, from TV dramati-
zation of Theodore H. White's book "The
making of the president, 1964".
6 min.   phonotape (1 r.   7 1/2 i.p.s.)
I. Johnson, Lyndon Baines, Pres. U. S., 1908-1973.
II. Goldwater, Barry Morris, 1909-   III. White, Theodore
Harold, 1915-   /The making of the president, 1964.

Voice Lib.
GOLDWATER, BARRY MORRIS, 1909-
660   Dirksen, Everett McKinley, 1896-1969.
bd.1   Address at the Republican National
        Convention in San Francisco: nominating
        Senator Barry Goldwater for President.
        NBC, July 15, 1964.
            1 reel (7 in.)   7 1/2 in. per sec.
        phonotape.

            1. Goldwater, Barry Morris, 1909-

Voice Lib.
654   Gompers, Samuel, 1850-1924.
bd.5   "Labor and the War"; labor's role in
        World War I.   Source(?), 1918.
            1 reel (7 in.)   7 1/2 in. per sec.
        phonotape.

Voice Lib.
GOLDWATER, BARRY MORRIS, 1909-
M656   Kennedy, John Fitzgerald, Pres. U.S., 1917-1963.
bd.2   Press conference excerpt on Senator
        Barry Goldwater.   CRI, 1962.
            1 reel (7 in.)   7 1/2 i.p.s.   phonotape.

            1. Goldwater, Barry Morris, 1909-

C1
PWM12 Whorf, Michael, 1933-
        Gonna sing all over God's Heaven
           Gonna sing all over God's Heaven.
           1 tape cassette.   (The visual sounds of
        Mike Whorf. Panorama; a world of music, PWM-12)

           Originally presented on his radio program, Kaleidoscope,
        WJR, Detroit.
           Duration: 25 min.
           The story of the music in the religious experience of the
        American Negro.

           1. Negro spirituals. 1. Title.

Voice Lib.
GOLDWATER, BARRY MORRIS, 1909-
M1430 Reagan, Ronald Wilson, 1911-
bd.1   "The Speech". Speech in support of Barry
        Goldwater during the 1964 presidential
        campaign. UCLA, October 27, 1964.
            1 reel (7 in.)   7 1/2 in. per sec.
        phonotape.

            1. Goldwater, Barry Morris, 1909-

Voice Lib. Good Company (Television program)
M1269 Dirksen, Everett McKinley, 1896-1969.
bd.1   Excerpt of conversation with Senator
        Dirksen and his wife at their home in
        Washington, D.C., with F. Lee Bailey from
        TV program "Good Company." Discussion of
        public speaking, forty years of marriage,
        recording ventures, advice to youth, plans
        for another term as senator. NBC-TV,
        September 14, 1967.
           1 reel (7 in.) 7 1/2 in. per sec. phonotape.
           1. Dirksen, Louella Carver, 1899-   11. Bailey, Francis
        Lee, 1933-   111. Good Company (Television program)

Voice Lib.
M669- Goldwyn, Samuel, 1884?-
670   The legend of Cecil B. Demille. Yul
        Brynner, Charlton Heston, Bob Hope, Betty
        Hutton, Edward G. Robinson, Barbara Stanwyck,
        James Stewart, Gloria Swanson, Cornel
        Wilde, Samuel Goldwyn, Billy Graham, Cecil
        B. DeMille.   Recorded 1963.
           2 reels (7 in.) 7 1/2 in. per sec. phonotape.
           1. DeMille, Cecil Blount, 1881-1959. 1. Brynner, Yul, 1917-
        11. Heston, Charlton, 1924-   111. Hope, Bob, 1903-   IV.
        Hutton, Betty, 1921-   V. Robinson, Edward G   1893-1973.
        VI. Stanwyck, Barbara, 1907-   VII. Stewart, James Maitland,
        1908-   VIII. Swanson, Gloria, 1899?-   IX. Wilde, Cornel, 1915-
        X. Goldwyn, Samuel, 1884?-   XI. Graham, William Franklin,
        1918-   XII. DeMille, Cecil Blount, 1881-1959.

C1
S7   Whorf, Michael, 1933-
        The good old days
           The good old days.
           1 tape cassette.   (The visual sounds of
        Mike Whorf. Social, S7)

           Originally presented on his radio program, Kaleidoscope,
        WJR, Detroit.
           Duration: 45 min., 30 sec.
           Life as it once was, unhurried, pleasant, "countrified" and
        simple. Here is a nostalgic look at ourselves in the "not so
        long ago."

           1. U.S. - Social life and customs. 1. Title.

Voice Lib.
180   Gompers, Samuel, 1850-1924.
bd.1   Labor and war bond speech during
        World War I. AFI-C10, 1918.
            1 reel (7 in.)   7 1/2 in. per sec.
        phonotape.

Voice Lib.
M763   Goodman, Benny, 1909-
bd.2   Excerpt from "The Scope of Jazz" (Program
        6); relates the early period of his life
        when he was just starting, and the different
        places the band played; including song
        "Let's Dance", theme song of Goodman organiza-
        tion. Westinghouse Broadcasting Corporation,
        1964.
            1 reel (7 in.)   7 1/2 in. per sec.
        phonotape.   (The Music Goes Round and Round)

           I. Title: The scope of jazz. II. Title.
           1. Jazz music

Voice Lib.
M764   Goodman, Benny, 1909-
bd.10   Excerpt from "The World of Wax" (Program
        8); comments on recording with the use of
        electricity. Including music "Blue Skies".
        Westinghouse Broadcasting Corporation, 1964.
        1 reel (7 in.)   7 1/2 in. per sec.
        phonotape.   (The Music Goes Round and Round)

        I. Title: The world of wax. II. Series.
        1. Phonorecords.

Voice Lib.
M775   Goodman, Paul, 1911-1972.
bd.2-   Provost lecture, Kiva, MSU.   October 17,
776   1962.
        2 reels (7 in.)   7 1/2 in. per sec.
        phonotape.

                Goralski, Robert
Voice Lib.
M1202   Westmoreland, William Childs, 1914-
bd.1   Report to joint session of U.S. Congress
        on status of war in Vietnam. Commentary by
        Robert Goralski. NBC-TV, April 28, 1967.
        1 reel (7 in.)   7 1/2 in. per sec.
        phonotape.

        I. Goralski, Robert

                Gordon, Max
Voice Lib.
M272   Biography in sound (radio program)
bd.1   Heywood Broun.   NBC, date?
        1 reel (7 in.)   7 1/2 in. per sec.
        phonotape.

        L Broun, Heywood Campbell, 1888-1939. L Broun,
        Heywood Campbell, 1888-1939. II. Swope, Herbert Bayard,
        1882-1958. III. Wilson, Mattie   IV. Jackson, Gardner
        V. Meany, Thomas   VI. Waldron, Beatrice   VII.
        Gordon, Max   VIII. Madison, Connie   IX. Gannett,
        Lewis Stiles, 1891-1966. X. Collins, Joseph, 1866-1950. XI.
        Brown, Earl Louis, 1900-   XII. Levy, Newman, 1888-
        XIII. Growth, John   XIV. Bye, George   XV.
        Roosevelt, Franklin Delano, Pres. U.S., 1882-1945. XVI.
        Reynolds, Quentin James, 1902-1965.

                Gordon, Richard F   1929-
Voice Lib.
M1404   Apollo 12 (space flight): description of
bd.2   splashdown of Apollo 12 and proceeding
        to aircraft carrier "Hornet".   CBS TV,
        November 24, 1969.
        1 reel (7 in.)   7 1/2 in. per sec.
        phonotape.
        1. Project Apollo. 2. Space flight to the
        moon. 3. Conrad, Charles, 1930-   4. Bean,
        Alan L   1932-   5. Gordon, Richard F
        1929-   I. Conrad, Charles, 1930-   II.
        Bean, Alan L   1932-   III. Gordon, Richard
        F   1929-

                Gordon, Richard F   1929-
Voice Lib.
M1404   Apollo 12 (space flight): description of
bd.1   last minutes on the moon of Apollo 12
        crew; countdown, lift-off from the moon.
        CBS TV, November 20, 1969.
        1 reel (7 in.)   7 1/2 in. per sec.
        phonotape.
        1. Project Apollo. 2. Space flight to the
        moon. 3. Conrad, Charles, 1930-   4. Bean,
        Alan L   1932-   5. Gordon, Richard F
        1929-   I. Conrad, Charles, 1930-   II.
        Bean, Alan L   1932-   III. Gordon, Richard
        F   1929-

                Gordon, Richard F   1929-
Voice Lib.
M1403   Apollo 12 (space flight): landing on the
bd.2   moon; conversations of Frank McGee and
        mission control; dialogue of Pete Conrad
        preparing to step out on moon; coached on
        going down ladder; Conrad singing from the
        moon; trouble with TV camera.   NBC TV,
        November 19, 1969.
        1 reel (7 in.)   7 1/2 in. per sec.   phonotape.
        L Project Apollo. 2. Space flight to the moon. 3. Conrad,
        Charles, 1930-   4. Bean, Alan L   1932-   5. Gordon,
        Richard F   1929-   L Conrad, Charles, 1930-   II. Bean,
        Alan L   1932-   III. Gordon, Richard F   1929-   IV.
        McGee, Frank, 1921-1974.

                Gordon, Richard F   1929
Voice Lib.
M1403   Apollo 12 (space flight): lift-off of Apollo
bd.1   12; the electrical "glitch" and instructions
        and corrections; Dr. Paine and President
        Nixon speaking from VIP section.   CBS TV,
        November 19, 1969.
        1 reel (7 in.)   7 1/2 in. per sec.
        phonotape.
        L Project Apollo. 2. Space flight to the moon. 3. Conrad,
        Charles, 1930-   4. Bean, Alan L   1932-   5. Gordon,
        Richard F   1929-   L Conrad, Charles, 1930-   IL Bean,
        Alan L   1932-   III. Gordon, Richard F   1929-   IV.
        Paine, Thomas Otten, 1921-   V. Nixon, Richard Milhous, Pres.
        U.S., 1913-

Voice Lib.
M761   Gorney, Jay
bd.6   Excerpt from "Whatever happened to Tin Pan
        Alley" (Program 3); comments on methods of
        Max Dreyfus to get great artists to sing his
        songs; also the publisher's degradation from
        a play of creativity to merely a messenger boy.
        Westinghouse Broadcasting Corporation, 1964.
        2 min., 54 sec.   phonotape (1 r.   7 1/2 L p. s.)
        (The music goes round and round)

        L Music, Popular (Songs, etc.) - Writing and publishing.
        L Title: Whatever happened to Tin Pan Alley? IL Series.

Voice Lib.
M1034   Gosden, Freeman Fisher, 1899-
bd.2   Amos, Andy, and the Kingfish in the
        "Eye Doctor" skit.   TV&R, 1929-1950.
        1 reel (7 in.)   7 1/2 in. per sec.
        phonotape.

        I. Correll, Charles J   1890-1972.

Voice Lib.
M1034   Gosden, Freeman Fisher, 1899–
bd.4   Andy and Amos (Shorty and Gabby) in a
        "Political Discussion". TV&R, 1929–1950.
        1 reel (7 in.)   7 1/2 in. per sec.
        phonotape.

        I. Correll, Charles J   1890–1972.

Voice Lib.
M1086   Gouraud, George E
bd.3   "Phonogram message" (1 in. diameter cylinder
        recording) spoken by Colonel Gouraud in London
        and addressed to Mr. Thomas A. Edison in
        New Jersey, about experimental recordings
        made in England and comments on the phono-
        graph by British personalities. Walter
        Miller, 1888.
        1 reel (7 in.)   7 1/2 in. per sec.
        phonotape.
        1. Phonorecords - History.

Voice Lib.
M1034   Gosden, Freeman Fisher, 1899–
bd.3   Andy and the Kingfish in the "Funeral
        and Insurance Business" skit. TV&R,
        1929–1950.
        1 reel (7 in.)   7 1/2 in. per sec.
        phonotape.

        I. Correll, Charles J   1890–1972.

        Gowdy, Curt
Voice Lib.
M1726   Aaron, Hank, 1934–
bd.3   Interviewed on Hank Aaron Day in New York
        City, by Curt Gowdy, Joe Garagiola, Tom
        Brokaw, and Gene Shalitt. NBC, June 18,
        1974.
        10 min.   phonotape (1 r.   7 1/2 i.p.s.)

        1. Aaron, Hank, 1934–   2. Baseball.
        I. Gowdy, Curt. II. Garagiola, Joe.
        III. Brokaw, Tom.   V. Shalitt, Gene.

Voice Lib.
M1034   Gosden, Freeman Fisher, 1899–
bd.1   Andy and the Kingfish in the "New Car"
        skit. TV&R, 1929–1950.
        1 reel (7 in.)   7 1/2 in. per sec.
        phonotape.

        I. Correll, Charles J   ,1890–1972.

Voice Lib.
M1633   Graham, Katherine (Meyer) 1917–
        Speaking on Watergate and the press.
        WKAR-FM, April 15, 1974.
        45 min.   phonotape (1 r.   7 1/2 i.p.s.)

        1. Watergate Affair, 1972–

Voice Lib.   The gospel of wealth
M1615   Carnegie, Andrew, 1835–1919.
bd.1   The gospel of wealth.   Rare Records, Inc.,
        H815, 1914.
        2 min., 50 sec.   phonotape (1 r.   7 1/2
        i.p.s.)

        I. Title.

Voice Lib.   Graham, William Franklin, 1918–
M669–   The legend of Cecil B. Demille. Yul
670   Brynner, Charlton Heston, Bob Hope, Betty
        Hutton, Edward G. Robinson, Barbara Stanwyck,
        James Stewart, Gloria Swanson, Cornel
        Wilde, Samuel Goldwyn, Billy Graham, Cecil
        B. DeMille.   Recorded 1963.
        2 reels (7 in.) 7 1/2 in. per sec. phonotape.
        I. DeMille, Cecil Blount, 1881–1959. I. Brynner, Yul, 1917–
        II. Heston, Charlton, 1924–   III. Hope, Bob, 1903–   IV.
        Hutton, Betty, 1921–   V. Robinson, Edward G   1893–1973.
        VI. Stanwyck, Barbara, 1907–   VII. Stewart, James Maitland,
        1908–   VIII. Swanson, Gloria, 1899?–   IX. Wilde, Cornel, 1915–
        X. Goldwyn, Samuel, 1884?–   XI. Graham, William Franklin,
        1918–   XII. DeMille, Cecil Blount, 1881–1959.

        Goulet, Robert Gerard, 1933–
Voice Lib.
126   Lerner, Alan Jay, 1918–
        Lerner and Loewe; condensed NBC-TV special
        with Julie Andrews, Richard Burton, Robert
        Goulet, Alan Lerner and Frederick Loewe.
        NBC, February 2, 1962.
        1 reel (7 in.)   7 1/2 in. per sec.
        phonotape.

        I. Andrews, Julie, 1935–   II. Burton,
        Richard, 1925–   III. Goulet, Robert
        Gerard, 1933–   IV. Loewe, Frederick, 1904–

Voice Lib.
328   Graham, William Franklin, 1918–
        Evangelistic sermon given in Los Angeles.
        Recorded by G. Robert Vincent, September,
        1963.
        1 reel (7 in.)   7 1/2 in. per sec.
        phonotape.

Graham, William Franklin, 1918-
Voice Lib.
M1329- Republican Party. National Convention, 29m,
1331   Miami, Fla., 1968.
         Proceedings of night session. Attempt to
    nominate Governor Romney for vice-president;
    revolt against Nixon's choice of Governor
    Agnew for running mate. Attempt to nominate
    Mayor Lindsay for vice-president. Roll call
    and nomination of Agnew by acclamation. Richard
    M. Nixon's acceptance speech. Benediction by
    Billy Graham.   NBC-TV, August 8, 1968.
       3 reels (7 in.) 7 1/2 in. per sec. phonotape.
       I. Nixon, Richard Milhous, Pres. U.S., 1913-   II. Graham,
    William Franklin, 1918-

GRANT, ULYSSES SIMPSON, PRES. U.S., 1822-1885
C1
H110   Whorf, Michael, 1933-
         We'll march to Hell and back again - for
    Ulysses Simpson Grant.
         1 tape cassette.   (The visual sounds of
    Mike Whorf. History and heritage, H110)
         Originally presented on his radio program, Kaleidoscope,
    WJR, Detroit.
         Duration: 37 min., 30 sec.
         This program follows Grant from his humble beginnings in Ohio,
    through his education at West Point to the time of his emergence into
    greatness as commander of the Union Army.
         I. Grant, Ulysses Simpson, Pres. U.S., 1822-1885. I. Title.

C1   GRAHAM, WILLIAM FRANKLIN, 1918-
R21
       Whorf, Michael, 1933-
         The phenomenal Billy Graham.
         1 tape cassette.   (The visual sounds of
    Mike Whorf. Religion, R21)
         Originally presented on his radio program, Kaleidoscope,
    WJR, Detroit.
         Duration: 41 min., 30 sec.
         Here are the thoughts and ideas, aspirations and inspirations
    of Billy Graham, a leading personality of our age bent on bringing
    man to God.
         I. Graham, William Franklin, 1918-   I. Title.

Voice Lib.   GRAPHOLOGY
M1611 Hartford, Huntington, 1911-
bd.1   Interview by Edwin Newman on the TV
    program Speaking freely. WKAR-TV,
    March, 1974.
         3 min. phonotape (1 r.   7 1/2 i.p.s.)

         1. Graphology.   I. Newman, Edwin Harold,
    1919-

GRANDMA MOSES
SEE
MOSES, ANNA MARY (ROBERTSON) 1860-1961

VOICE LIBRARY

Voice Lib.
M872   Grauer, Benjamin Franklin, 1908-
bd.1   Describing pre-VJ Day celebration in
    Times Square, N.Y. NBC, August 14, 1945.
         1 reel (7 in.) 7 i.p.s. phonotape.

         1. World War, 1939-1945 - U.S.

Grant, Cary, 1904-
Voice Lib. Stewart, James, 1908-
M1706 bd.4 Discusses his one singing role for MGM; sings "Easy to love".
    Includes part of the sound track of "That's entertainment" with
    Jean Harlow and Cary Grant singing "Did I remember?"
    From the Merv Griffin Show. WJRT-TV, June 6, 1974.
         15 min. phonotape (1 r.   7 1/2 i.p.s.)

         I. Stewart, James, 1908-   2. Harlow, Jean, 1911-1937.
    3. Grant, Cary, 1904-   I. Griffin, Mervyn Edward, 1925-
    II. Grant, Cary, 1904-   III. Harlow, Jean, 1911-1937.

Voice Lib.
M1742 Graves, Gerald
bd.4   Defends Lansing's record of minority hiring
    against attack from Human Relations director
    Richard Letts. WJIM-TV, June 19, 1974.
         2 min. phonotape (1 r.   7 1/2 i.p.s.)

         1. Minorities - Employment - Lansing, Mich.
    I. Letts, Richard

Grant, Jane
Voice Lib.
M275- Biography in sound (radio program)
276   Alexander Woollcott. N.B.C., date?
bd.1   2 reels (7 in.) 7 1/2 in. per sec.
    phonotape.
         I. Woollcott, Alexander, 1887-1943. I. Woollcott, Alexander,
    1887-1943. II. Banghardt, Kenneth   III. Hecht, Ben, 1893-
    1964. IV. Roosevelt, Eleanor (Roosevelt) 1884-1962. V. Walker,
    Danton   VI. Brackett, Charles, 1892-1969. VII. Grant,
    Jane   VIII. Rude, Robert Barnes   IX. West,
    Rebecca, pseud.   X. Henessy, Joseph   XI. Letterer,
    Charles   XII. Welles, Orson, 1915-

Voice Lib.
M1800 Gray, Louis Patrick, 1916-
WG   Testimony before the Senate Committee
0802.02 investigating the Watergate Affair.
    Pacifica, August 3, 1973.
         112 min. phonotape (2 r.   3 3/4 i.p.s.)
    (Watergate gavel to gavel, phase 1)

         1. Watergate Affair, 1972-

Voice Lib.
M1800 Gray, Louis Patrick, 1916-
WG   Testimony before the Senate Committee
0806   investigating the Watergate Affair.
         Pacifica, August 6, 1973.
         325 min. phonotape (4 r. 3 3/4 i.p.s.)
         (Watergate gavel to gavel, phase 1)

         1. Watergate Affair, 1972-

              Graziano, Rocky, 1921-
Voice Lib.
M1037 Biography in sound (radio program)
bd.1   "The Actor", narrated by Morgan Beatty.
         Cast includes Tallulah Bankhead, Hy Gardner,
         Rocky Graziano, Arthur Miller, Uta Hagen,
         Jackie Cooper, Sir Laurence Olivier, Gad
         Gayther, Barbara Ashley, Hortense Powdermaker,
         Peter Ustinov, Alfred Hitchcock, Leonard Lyons,
         John Guston, Helen Hayes, Dick Mayne, Ralph
         Bellamy, Lionel Barrymore, Sir Ralph Richardson,
         José Ferrer, and Walter Kerr. NBC Radio, 1950's.
         1 reel (7 in.) 7 1/2 in. per sec.
         phonotape.
                          (Continued on next card)

C1   The great American buffalo
H42
         Whorf, Michael, 1933-
            The great American buffalo.
            1 tape cassette. (The visual sounds of
         Mike Whorf. History and heritage, H42)
         Originally presented on his radio program, Kaleidoscope,
         WJR, Detroit.
         Duration: 40 min., 45 sec.
         The bison supplied every need for the sustenance of the Indian;
         yet, later he would be wantonly slain for the rugs and coats of the
         American Caucasian. He was a beautiful, gigantic beast, who
         nearly became extinct, but today survives in ever-growing numbers.

         L Bison, American.   L Title.

C1   The great American pastime - baseball
M31
         Whorf, Michael, 1933-
            The great American pastime - baseball.
            1 tape cassette. (The visual sounds of
         Mike Whorf. Miscellaneous, M31)
         Originally presented on his radio program, Kaleidoscope,
         WJR, Detroit.
         Duration: 39 min.
         "Whoever would understand the heart and mind of America had
         better learn the game of baseball ..." As this quotation sums up
         our attitude toward the national pastime, so our program illuminates
         the origin and the history of the great game of baseball.

         L Baseball. L Title.

Voice Lib.
M869   The great American song (radio program)
bd.2-   Documentary program of CBC on the contribution
870   of American music: discussion of the work of
         George Gershwin; American musical comedy;
         biographical sketches and interviews with
         composers Arthur Schwartz and Vernon Duke, who
         discuss the technique of composing. CBC, 1964.
         2 reels (7 in.) 7 1/2 in. per sec.
         phonotape.

            1. Gershwin, George, 1898-1937. I. Schwartz,
         Arthur, 1900-   II. Duke, Vernon, 1903-1969.

              Great balls of fire
C1
SC30   Whorf, Michael, 1933-
            Great balls of fire; unidentified flying
         saucers.
            1 tape cassette. (The visual sounds of
         Mike Whorf. Science, SC30)
         Originally presented on his radio program, Kaleidoscope,
         WJR, Detroit.
         Duration: 38 min.
         Of course no one believes in flying saucers. No one believes
         in interplanetary space travel. No one believes in life on distant
         planets. But ... if no one believes in any of this, what's all
         this talk about "great balls of fire"?
            L Flying saucers.   L Title.

              GREAT BRITAIN - CIVILIAN DEFENSE
Voice Lib.
M715   British Broadcasting Corporation.
bd.3   Information to British public regarding
         the closing of cinema theaters and
         instructions on air raid warning signals.
         BBC, 1939.
         1 reel (7 in.) 7 1/2 in. per sec.
         phonotape.

              GT. BRIT. - ECONOMIC CONDITIONS
Voice Lib.
M1583 Ramsbotham, Sir Peter Edward, 1919-
            National Press Club address. WKAR-AM,
         March 21, 1974.
            50 min. phonotape (1 r. 7 1/2 i.p.s.)

         Includes questions and answer period.

            1. Gt. Brit. - Foreign relations - U.S.
         2. U.S. - Foreign relations - Gt. Brit.
         3. Gt. Brit. - Economic conditions.

              GT. BRIT. - FOREIGN RELATIONS
Voice Lib.
M1470 Steele, Christopher
bd.17   Speaking about the British international
         situation in regard to world problems in
         1939; stressing the problem of Poland.
         Peteler, 1964.
            1 reel (7 in.) 7 1/2 i.p.s. phonotape.

            1. Great Britain - Foreign relations.

              GT. BRIT. - FOREIGN RELATIONS - RUSSIA
Voice Lib.
M1470 Strang, Sir William, 1894-
bd.16   Speaking about the negotiations between
         the British and the Soviets in the year
         1939. Peteler, 1964.
            1 reel (7 in.) 7 1/2 i.p.s. phonotape.

            1. Great Britain - Foreign relations -
         Russia. 2. Russia - Foreign relations -
         Great Britain.

GT. BRIT. - FOREIGN RELATIONS - U.S.
Voice Lib.
M1583   Ramsbotham, Sir Peter Edward, 1919-
National Press Club address. WKAR-AM,
March 21, 1974.
30 min. phonotape (1 r.   7 1/2 i.p.s.)

Includes questions and answer period.

1. Gt. Brit. - Foreign relations - U.S.
2. U.S. - Foreign relations - Gt. Brit.
3. Gt. Brit. - Economic conditions.

C1   GREAT EASTERN (SHIP)
M36   Whorf, Michael, 1933-
The sad, strange saga of the Great Eastern.
1 tape cassette. (The visual sounds of
Mike Whorf. Miscellaneous, M36)
Originally presented on his radio program, Kaleidoscope,
WJR, Detroit.
Duration: 38 min., 15 sec.
Many great ships have sailed the seven seas. Why couldn't
this splendid vessel surmount superstition, obstacle, and nature?
This is the plot of the sad strange saga of the Great Eastern.

1. Great Eastern (Ship) 1. Title.

GT. BRIT. - KINGS AND RULERS
Voice Lib.
M1394- The Royal Family (motion picture)
1395   Motion picture of the life of Britain's
Royal Family at home and in various countries,
including all members of the immediate family
and the palace household. Moderated by
Vincent Price. BBC, Sept. 21, 1969.
2 reels (7 in.)   7 1/2 in. per sec.
phonotape.

I. Price, Vincent, 1911-

Voice Lib.
M1029   Great moments in sports: boxing. Radio
bd.1   segments of actual sounds: excerpts of
well-known personalities in the boxing
world, centered around the career of
Joe Louis. Speakers: Don Dunphy, narrator;
Jess Willard, Jack Dempsey, James J. Corbett,
Thomas Farr, Max Schmeling, Joe Louis,
Tony Galento, Buddy Baer, Billy Conn,
Grantland Rice. MSU, Dept. of Television
and Radio, 1919-1950.
1 reel (7 in.) 7 1/2 in. per sec. phonotape.

1. Boxing.

GT. BRIT. PARLIAMENT - ELECTIONS
Voice Lib.
M125   British election campaign speeches.
Private recording, 1929.
1 reel (7 in.)   7 1/2 i.p.s.   phonotape.

CONTENTS. -bd. 1. Lloyd George, unemployment. -bd. 2.
Stanley Baldwin, conservative achievements. -bd. 3. William
Joynson-Hicks, why I am a conservative. -bd. 4. Taming
Worthington-Evans, how to vote at election. -bd. 5. Philip
Snowden, finance. -bd. 6. Margaret Bondfield, the women's
opportunity. -bd. 7. Thomas, J. H., the British Empire.

1. Gt. Brit. Parliament - Elections.

C1   The great mysteries of science
SC12   Whorf, Michael, 1933-
The great mysteries of science.
1 tape cassette. (The visual sounds of
Mike Whorf. Science, SC12)
Originally presented on his radio program, Kaleidoscope,
WJR, Detroit.
Duration: 31 min.
What is photosynthesis? What caused the ice age? What
causes the common cold? What mysteries do the stars, the sun,
and the sea hold? This program presents a look at some of those
great questions which since the beginning of creation have puzzled
mankind.

1. Natural history. 1. Title.

C1   The great dissenter - Justice Oliver Wendell Holmes
H54   Whorf, Michael, 1933-
The great dissenter - Justice Oliver Wendell
Holmes.
1 tape cassette. (The visual sounds of
Mike Whorf. History and heritage, H54)
Originally presented on his radio program, Kaleidoscope,
WJR, Detroit.
Duration: 41 min.
A heart warming and tender story of Oliver Wendell Holmes,
who was a lawyer, professor and justice of the Supreme Court,
equally adept at each, an inspiration to all who listened to him.

1. Holmes, Oliver   Wendell, 1841-1935. 1. Title.

GREAT NORTHERN RAILWAY CASCADE TUNNEL
Voice Lib.
M1379   Dedication ceremonies for Great Northern
bd.1   Railway Cascade Tunnel, over NBC Radio
Network, originating from Philadelphia,
Washington, D.C., San Francisco, New York
City, and State of Washington. NBC Radio,
January 1929.
1 reel (7 in.)   7 1/2 in. per sec.
phonotape.

C1   The great Dr. Einstein
SC8   Whorf, Michael, 1933-
The great Dr. Einstein.
1 tape cassette. (The visual sounds of
Mike Whorf. Science, SC8)
Originally presented on his radio program, Kaleidoscope,
WJR, Detroit.
Duration: 29 min., 30 sec.
His life in Europe, his coming to America and the theory
that changed the world is told in this biography of Albert Einstein.

1. Einstein, Albert, 1879-1955. 1. Title.

C1   The greatest book ever written
R24   Whorf, Michael, 1933-
The greatest book ever written.
1 tape cassette. (The visual sounds of
Mike Whorf. Religion, R24)
Originally presented on his radio program, Kaleidoscope,
WJR, Detroit.
Duration: 38 min.
Few stories shed such fascinating sidelights on the history
of man as the heritage of the body of literature which we now
know as the Bible.

1. Bible. 1. Title.

C1
862

The greatest privilege of mankind - the family

Whorf, Michael, 1933-
    The greatest privilege of mankind - the family.
    1 tape cassette. (The visual sounds of
Mike Whorf. Social, S62)
        Originally presented on his radio program, Kaleidoscope,
WJR, Detroit.
        Duration: 39 min., 30 sec.
        For a thousand centuries man has received an abundance of
blessings - but none so rewarding as the family. The family of
"names" is also encountered with a study of the origin of the
head of the family.

        1. Family. 1. Title.

C1
M32

The greatest woman in the world

Whorf, Michael, 1933-
    The greatest woman in the world, mother.
    1 tape cassette. (The visual sounds of
Mike Whorf. Miscellaneous, M32)

        Originally presented on his radio program, Kaleidoscope,
WJR, Detroit.
        The selections are those that contain some very basic truths
and sentiments about mothers, yet the presentation is not overly
saccharine in upholding the truth, wisdom, and virtue of the
world's prime example of the unsung heroine.

        1. Mothers. 2. Mother's Day. 1. Title.

Voice Lib.
M1723
bd.2
    Green, Robert Lee
    Address at Martin Luther King Memorial
Service at Michigan State University.
WKAR, April 4, 1969.
    20 min. phonotape (1 r.   7 1/2 i.p.s.)

        1. King, Martin Luther, 1929-1965.

Green, Robert Lee
Voice Lib.
M1551-
1552
    Young, Andrew, 1932-
    A lecture series by the College of Urban
Affairs, Michigan State University, with
Prof. Robert Green and Asst. Prof. Barnes
McConnell. MSU Dept. of Information
Services, January 17, 1974.
    90 min. phonotape (2 r.   7 1/2 i.p.s.)

        1. Local transit. 2. Atlanta.   I. Green,
Robert Lee.   II. McConnell, Barnes.

Green, Tom
Voice Lib.
M1607
bd.2
    Brennan, Thomas E., 1929-
    Off the record. Interviewed by Tim
Skubick, Tom Green, Gary Schuster, and
Paul Weisenfeld. WKAR-TV, January 25, 1974.
    15 min. phonotape (1 r.   7 1/2 in. per
sec.)
        1. Courts - Michigan.   I. Skubick, Tim.
II. Green, Tom. III. Schuster, Gary.   IV.
Weisenfeld, Paul

Green, Tom
Voice Lib.
M1606
bd.1
    Miller, James W
    Off the record. Interviewed by Tim
Skubick, Gary Schuster, Tom Green, and
Bill Meek. WKAR-TV, February 8, 1974.
    10 min. phonotape (1 r.   7 1/2 in. per
sec.)

        1. Singer, Sidney. 2. Michigan. Civil
Service Commission. I. Skubick, Tim.
II. Schuster, Gary. III. Green, Tom.
IV. Meek, Bill.

Green, Tom
Voice Lib.
M1607
bd.1
    Porter, John W   1931-
    Off the record; problems facing Michigan
schools. Interviewed by Tim Skubick, Tom
Green, Bill Meek, and Gary Schuster.
WKAR-TV, February 1, 1974.
    17 min. phonotape (1 r.   7 1/2 in. per
sec.)

        1. Segregation in education. 2. Strikes
and lockouts - Teachers. I. Skubick, Tim.
II. Green, Tom. III. Meek, Bill. IV. Schuster,
Gary.

Green, Tom
Voice Lib.
M1598
bd.2
    Romney, George W   1907-
    Off the record. With Tim Skubick, Gary
Schuster, Tom Greene, and Bill Meek.
WKAR-TV, November 9, 1973.
    20 min. phonotape (1 r.   7 1/2 in. per
sec.)

        1. Michigan - Politics and government.
2. Detroit. I. Skubick, Tim. II. Schuster,
Gary. III. Greene, Tom. IV. Meek, Bill

Green, Tom
Voice Lib.
M1605
bd.2
    Winograd, Morley
    Off the record. With Tim Skubick, Tom
Greene, Gary Schuster, and Hugh Morgan.
WKAR-TV, February 15, 1974.
    17 min. phonotape (1 r.   7 1/2 in. per sec.)

        1. Democratic Party. Michigan. 2. Elections -
Michigan. 3. Youngblood, Charles N., 1932-
I. Skubick, Tim. II. Greene, Tom. III. Schuster,
Gary. IV. Morgan, Hugh.

Voice Lib.
M831
bd.2
    Green, William, 1873-1952.
    Labor Day address at Summit Beach Park,
Akron, Ohio, denouncing Taft-Hartley
Slave Labor Bill. NBC, September 6, 1948.
    1 reel (7 in.)   7 1/2 in. per sec.
phonotape.

        1. U.S. Laws, statutes, etc. Labor
management relations act, 1947.

Voice Lib.
168   Green, William, 1873-1952.
       71st Annual AFL Convention.   AFL-CIO
(P.R.O.), 1952.
       1 reel (7 in.)   7 1/2 in. per sec.
phonotape.

Voice Lib.
M1316- Gregory, Dick, 1932-
1317   Address by Gregory for ASMSU's Great
bd.1   Issues Series in MSU's Auditorium.
       March 8, 1968.
       2 reels (7 in.)   7 1/2 in. per sec.
phonotape.

Green hornet (radio program)
Voice Lib.
M1675   Theme songs from the Green hornet, the Lone
bd.2   Ranger, Dick Tracy, and Hop Harrigan.
       Golden Age Radio Records, 1940's.
       10 min.   phonotape (1 r.   7 1/2 i.p.s.)

       I. Green hornet (radio program) II. Lone
Ranger (radio program) III. Dick Tracy (radio
program) IV. Hop Harrigan (radio program)

Voice Lib.
M1422   Gregory, Dick, 1932-
bd.2   Question and answer conference at MSU.
       December 5, 1969.
       1 reel (7 in.)   7 1/2 in. per sec.
phonotape.

Greensleeves
Voice Lib.
644   Read, Susan
bd.5-6   Sings: "I Know My Love", "Greensleeves".
       V-Discs, 1943.
       1 reel (7 in.)   7 1/2 in. per sec.
phonotape.

       I. Title: I know my love. 2. Title:
Greensleeves.

C1   GREGORY, THOMAS WATT, 1861-1933
FA12   Whorf, Michael, 1933-
       Thomas W. Gregory.
       1 tape cassette.   (The visual sounds of
Mike Whorf. The forgotten American, FA12)
       Originally presented on his radio program, Kaleidoscope,
WJR, Detroit.
       Duration: 11 min., 25 sec.
       Attorney-General during the administrations of Woodrow
Wilson, Gregory was responsible for the internal security of
the United States during World War I.

       L. Gregory, Thomas Watt, 1861-1933.   L. Title.

Greer, Sonny
Voice Lib.
M1696   Columbia Broadcasting System, inc.
bd.6   Special memorial to Duke Ellington, with
       John Hart, Sonny Greer, Russell Procope,
       Billy Taylor, Stanley Dance, and Ella
       Fitzgerald. CBS-TV, May 24, 1974.
       15 min. phonotape (1 r.   7 1/2 i.p.s.)

       1. Ellington, Duke, 1899-1974. I. Hart,
John. II. Greer, Sonny. III. Procope,
Russell, 1908-   IV. Taylor, Billy.
V. Dance, Stanley. VI. Fitzgerald, Ella,
1918-

C1   GRIEG, EDVARD HAGERUP, 1843-1907
PWM22 Whorf, Michael, 1933-
       Edvard Grieg.
       1 tape cassette.   (The visual sounds of
Mike Whorf. Panorama; a world of music, PWM-22)
       Originally presented on his radio program, Kaleidoscope,
WJR, Detroit.
       Duration: 25 min.
       The life and times of Edvard Grieg, including excerpts
of his music.

       L. Grieg, Edvard Hagerup, 1843-1907.   L. Title.

Greer, Thomas Hoag, 1914-
Voice Lib.
M1724   Morse, Wayne Lyman, 1900-
bd.2   Question and answer session with Michigan
       State University students. Includes Dr.
       Thomas H. Greer. WKAR, January 13, 1970.
       20 min. phonotape (1 r.   7 1/2 i.p.s.)

       1. U.S. - Politics and government.
I. Greer, Thomas Hoag, 1914-

Griffin, Mervyn Edward, 1925-
Voice Lib.
M1706   Burton, Richard, 1925-
bd.1   Interview on Merv Griffin Show.
       Columbia Broadcasting System, June 5, 1974.
       10 min. phonotape (1 r. 7 7 1/2 i.p.s.)

       Burton speaks in English, Irish, Welsh,
and French.

       1. Burton, Richard, 1925-   I. Griffin,
Mervyn Edward, 1925-

Griffin, Mervyn Edward, 1925–
Voice Lib.
M1407 Eisenhower, David, 1949–
Conversation on "Merv Griffin Show" between
Merv, Merriman Smith, David Eisenhower, Tricia
Nixon. Various anecdotes about Merriman Smith's
career as a White House correspondent during
four administrations. CBS-TV, November 23, 1969
1 reel (7 in.)   7 1/2 in. per sec.
phonotape.

I. Griffin, Mervyn Edward, 1925–   II.
Smith, Merriman   III. Cox, Patricia
(Nixon) 1947–

Griffin, Mervyn Edward, 1925–
Voice Lib.
M1693 Spock, Benjamin McLane, 1903–
bd.2   On the younger generation and his own
pro-peace activities, anti-obscenity
activities, etc., on Merv Griffin Show.
25 min.   phonotape (1 r.   7 1/2 i.p.s.)

1. Women's Liberation Movement.
2. Children - Care & hygiene. 3. Johnson,
Lyndon Baines, Pres. U.S., 1908–
I. Griffin, Mervyn Edward, 1925–

Griffin, Mervyn Edward, 1925–
Voice Lib.
M1726 Hope, Bob, 1903–
bd.1   Interview on Merv Griffin Show. WJRT-TV,
June 17, 1974.
15 min.   phonotape (1 r.   7 1/2 i.p.s.)

1. Hope, Bob, 1903–   I. Griffin, Mervyn
Edward, 1925–

Griffin, Mervyn Edward, 1925–
Voice Lib.
M1706 Stewart, James, 1908–
bd.4   Discusses his one singing role for MGM; sings "Easy to love".
Includes part of the sound track of "That's entertainment" with
Jean Harlow and Cary Grant singing "Did I remember?"
From the Merv Griffin Show. WJRT-TV, June 6, 1974.
15 min.   phonotape (1 r.   7 1/2 i.p.s.)

1. Stewart, James, 1908–   2. Harlow, Jean, 1911-1937.
3. Grant, Cary, 1904–   I. Griffin, Mervyn Edward, 1925–
II. Grant, Cary, 1904–   III. Harlow, Jean, 1911-1937.

Griffin, Mervyn Edward, 1925–
Voice Lib.
M1401 Kennedy, Rose Fitzgerald, 1890–
bd.1   Informal conversation with Merv Griffin
about her family and her efforts to help
prevent mental retardation in children.
CBS, November 13, 1969.
1 reel (7 in.)   7 1/2 in. per sec.
phonotape.

I. Griffin, Mervyn Edward, 1925–

Griffin, Mervyn Edward, 1925–
Voice Lib.
1294   Susskind, David, 1920–
bd.2   Interview on Merv Griffin Show, discussing
story of Susskind's broadcast with USSR
Chairman Khrushchev. CBS-TV, December 18,
1967.
1 reel (7 in.)   7 1/2 in. per sec.
phonotape.

Griffin, Mervyn Edward, 1925–
Voice Lib.
M1738 Mailer, Norman
bd.2   Interviewed on the Merv Griffin Show.
WJRT-TV, June 19, 1974.
25 min.   phonotape (1 r.   7 1/2 i.p.s.)

I. Griffin, Mervyn Edward, 1925–

GRIMM, JAKOB LUDWIG KARL, 1785-1863
C1
A7   Whorf, Michael, 1933–
They lived happily ever after.
1 tape cassette. (The visual sounds of
Mike Whorf. Art, music, and letters, A7)
Originally presented on his radio program, Kaleidoscope.
WJR, Detroit.
Duration: 41 min., 15 sec.
From their childhood, Jacob and Wilhelm Grimm remembered
the wonderful and magic stories of make-believe, and with their
own special brand of inventiveness they created a heritage for
generations to come.
1. Grimm, Jakob Ludwig Karl, 1785-1863. 2. Grimm, Wilhelm
Karl, 1786-1859.   I. Title.

Griffin, Mervyn Edward, 1925–
Voice Lib.
M1402 Shirer, William Lawrence, 1904–
bd.2   Excerpt of conversation with Merv Griffin
about broadcasting during early part of World
War II and about Mahatma Gandhi. CBS,
November 13, 1969.
1 reel (7 in.)   7 1/2 in. per sec.
phonotape.

1. Gandhi, Mohandas Karamchand, 1869-1948.
I. Griffin, Mervyn Edward, 1925–

GRIMM, WILHELM KARL, 1786-1859
C1
A7   Whorf, Michael, 1933–
They lived happily ever after.
1 tape cassette. (The visual sounds of
Mike Whorf. Art, music, and letters, A7)
Originally presented on his radio program, Kaleidoscope.
WJR, Detroit.
Duration: 41 min., 15 sec.
From their childhood, Jacob and Wilhelm Grimm remembered
the wonderful and magic stories of make-believe, and with their
own special brand of inventiveness they created a heritage for
generations to come.
1. Grimm, Jakob Ludwig Karl, 1785-1863. 2. Grimm, Wilhelm
Karl, 1786-1859.   I. Title.

Voice Lib.
M1696   Grinker, Charles
bd.2   Koplin, Mert
        Appearance of Koplin and Charles Grinker,
        of Cinedex, movie archives, on Mike
        Douglas Show. WJRT-TV, May 27, 1974.
        7 min. phonotape (1 r. 7 1/2 i.p.s.)

        1. Moving-pictures - History. I. Grinker,
        Charles. II. Douglas, Mike, 1925?

Voice Lib.
573   Gromyko, Anatolii Andreevich, 1908-
bd.2-   I can hear it now (radio program)
574   1945-1949. CBS, 1950?
bd.1   2 reels (7 in.) 7 1/2 in. per sec.
        phonotape.
        L. Murrow, Edward Roscoe, 1908-1965. II. Nehru, Jawaharlal,
        1889-1964. III. Philip, duke of Edinburgh, 1921- IV. Elizabeth II,
        Queen of Great Britain, 1926- V. Ferguson, Homer, 1889- VI.
        Hughes, Howard Robard, 1905- VII. Marshall, George Catlett,
        1880- VIII. Ruth, George Herman, 1895-1948. IX. Lilienthal,
        David Eli, 1899- X. Trout, Robert, 1908- XI. Gage, Arthur.
        XII. Jackson, Robert Houghwout, 1892-1954. XIII. Gromyko, Ana-
        tolii Andreevich, 1908- XIV. Baruch, Bernard Mannes, 1870-
        1965. XV. Churchill, Winston Leonard Spencer, 1874-1965. XVI.
        Winchell, Walter, 1897- XVII. Davis, Elmer Holmes, 1890-
        (Continued on next card)

Voice Lib.
M1030   GRISSOM, VIRGIL IVAN, 1926-1967
bd.1   Huntley, Chet, 1911-1974.
        Description by Chet Huntley of funeral
        services at burial of astronauts Virgil
        Grissom and Roger Chaffee at Arlington
        Cemetery and of Edward White at West Point,
        New York. NBC-TV, January 31, 1967.
        1 reel (7 in.) 7 1/2 in. per sec. phonotape.

        L. Grissom, Virgil Ivan, 1926-1967. 2. White, Edward
        Higgins, 1930-1967. 3. Chaffee, Roger B., 1936-1967.

Voice Lib.
353   Gross, Ernest Arnold, 1906-
bd.3   Outbreak of the Korean conflict; U.S.
        resolution to halt Korean conflict. NBC,
        July, 1950.
        1 reel (7 in.) 7 1/2 in. per sec.
        phonotape.

        Original disc off-speed.

        1. Korean War, 1950-1953

Voice Lib.
M1068   Groat, Gary
bd.2   Ferlinghetti, Lawrence
        Reading his own poetry at State Theater,
        East Lansing, Michigan; sponsored by
        "Zeitgeist", with introductory remarks by
        Gary Groat. Groat, October 3, 1966.
        1 reel (7 in.) 7 1/2 in. per sec.
        phonotape.

        I. Groat, Gary

Voice Lib.
353   Groves, Leslie R   1896-1970
bd.19   Russia and the bomb, discussed by various
        personalities. NBC, September 25, 1949.
        1 reel (7 in.) 7 1/2 in. per sec.
        phonotape.

        Participants: Harrison Brown, Harold Urey,
        Samuel Allison, Thornton Hugness, Brien McMahon,
        Paul Douglas, John Foster Dulles, Leslie Groves,
        Winston Churchill, Dean Acheson, James Fleming.

        I. Brown, Harrison Scott, 1917-   II.
        Urey, Harold Clayton, 1893-   III. Allison,

        (Continued on next card)

Voice Lib.
565   Gromyko, Andrei Andreevich, 1908-
bd.2   U.N. Disarmament Conference on
        world food needs. TRV, 1947.
        1 reel (7 in.) 7 1/2 in. per sec.
        phonotape.

        1. Disarmament.

Voice Lib.
353   Groves, Leslie R   1896-1970
bd.19   Russia and the bomb... 1949. (Card 2)

        Samuel King, 1900-   IV. Hugness, Thornton.
        V. McMahon, James O'Brien, 1903-1952. VI.
        Douglas, Paul Howard, 1892-   VII. Dulles,
        John Foster, 1888-1959. VIII. Groves, Leslie
        R   1896-1970. IX. Churchill, Winston
        Leonard Spencer, 1874-1965. X. Acheson, Dean
        Gooderham, 1893-1971. XI. Fleming, James,
        1915-

Voice Lib.
209   Gromyko, Andrei Andreevich, 1908-
bd.6   Gromyko's remarks on arrival in
        Geneva for disarmament conference.
        Source (?), May 9, 1959.
        1 reel (7 in.) 7 1/2 in. per sec.
        phonotape.

        1. Disarmament.

Voice Lib.
M272   Growth, John
bd.1   Biography in sound (radio program)
        Heywood Broun. NBC, date?
        1 reel (7 in.) 7 1/2 in. per sec.
        phonotape.
        L. Broun, Heywood Campbell, 1888-1939. I. Broun,
        Heywood Campbell, 1888-1939. II. Swope, Herbert Bayard,
        1882-1958. III. Wilson, Mattie   IV. Jackson, Gardner
        V. Meany, Thomas   VI. Waldron, Beatrice   VII.
        Gordon, Max   VIII. Madison, Connie   IX. Gannett,
        Lewis Stiles, 1891-1966. X. Collins, Joseph, 1866-1950. XI.
        Brown, Earl Louis, 1900-   XII. Levy, Newman, 1888-
        XIII. Growth, John   XIV. Bye, George   XV.
        Roosevelt, Franklin Delano, Pres. U.S., 1882-1945. XVI.
        Reynolds, Quentin James, 1902-1965.

Voice Lib.
M1589   Gruening, Ernest Henry, 1887-
bd.1   Discussion of his book "Many battles"
            WKAR-AM, March 4, 1974.
            20 min.   phonotape (1 r.   7 1/2 i.p.s.)

            1. Gruening, Ernest Henry, 1887-
            /Many battles.

GRUENING, ERNEST HENRY, 1887-
            MANY BATTLES
Voice Lib.
M1589   Gruening, Ernest Henry, 1887-
bd.1   Discussion of his book "Many battles"
            WKAR-AM, March 4, 1974.
            20 min.   phonotape (1 r.   7 1/2 i.p.s.)

            1. Gruening, Ernest Henry, 1887-
            /Many battles.

Voice Lib.
M1368   Gruenther, Alfred Maximilian, 1899-
            Some friends of General Eisenhower (TV program)
            CBS-TV special recalling anecdotes about
            General Eisenhower by some of his friends:
            Bob Hope, Kevin McCann, General Omar Bradley,
            Robert B. Anderson, General Alfred Gruenther,
            with Walter Cronkite acting as emcee.   CBS-TV,
            March 29, 1969.
            1 reel (7 in.)   7 1/2 in. per sec.
            L. Eisenhower, Dwight David, Pres. U.S., 1890-1969. L.
            Hope, Bob, 1903-   II. McCann, Kevin   III. Bradley, Omar
            Nelson, 1893-   IV. Anderson, Robert Bernard, 1910-   V.
            Gruenther, Alfred Maximilian, 1899-   VI. Cronkite, Walter
            Leland, 1916-

Voice Lib.
M620   Gunther, John, 1901-1970
bd.1-   Radio in the 1940's (Part I): a series of
bd.16   excerpts from important broadcasts of the 1940's; a
            sample of radio of the period.   NVL, April, 1964.
            1 reel (7 in.)   7 1/2 in. per sec.   phonotape.
            L. Radio programs.   L. Thomas, Lowell Jackson, 1892-   II.
            Gunther, John, 1901-1970.   III. Kaltenborn, Hans von, 1878-1965.
            IV. Delmar, Kenny.   V. Those were the good old days (Radio
            program) VI. Elman, Dave.   VII. Hall, Frederick Lee, 1916-1970.
            VIII. Hobby lobby (Radio program) IX. Roosevelt, Franklin Delano,
            Pres. U.S., 1882-1945.   X. Willkie, Wendell Lewis, 1892-1944.
            XL. Hoover, Herbert Clark, Pres. U.S., 1874-1964.   XII. Johnson,
            Hugh Samuel, 1882-1942.   XIII. Cobb, Irvin Shrewsbury, 1876-1944.
            XIV. Roosevelt, Theodore, 1858-1919.   XV. Nye, Gerald Prentice,
            1892-197.   XVI. Lindbergh, Charles Augustus, 1902-   XVII.
            Toscanini, Arturo, 1867-195?

Voice Lib.
1720   Guralski, Robert
bd.2   Train, Russell Errol, 1920-
            Interview on the Today Show with Barbara
            Walters and Robert Guralski.   NBC, June 11,
            1974.
            5 min.   phonotape (1 r.   7 1/2 i.p.s.)

            1. U.S. Environmental Protection Agency.
            I. Walters, Barbara, 1931-   II. Guralski,
            Robert.

Gurney, Edward John, 1914-
Voice Lib.
M1800   U.S. Congress. Senate. Select Committee on Presidential
            Campaign Activities.
            Watergate gavel to gavel, phase I: May 17 - August 7, 1973.
            Pacifica, May 17 - August 7, 1973.
            172 reels (5 in.)   3 3/4 i.p.s.   phonotape.
            "These tapes include commentaries by Pacifica's Washington
            correspondents and interviews with members of the Senate Committee
            taped during recesses of the hearings."
            L. Presidents - U.S. - Elections - 1972.   2. Watergate Affair,
            1972-   L. Ervin, Samuel James, 1896-   II. Talmadge,
            Herman Eugene, 1913-   III. Inouye, Daniel Ken, 1924-
            IV. Baker, Howard H., 1925-   V. Gurney, Edward John, 1914-
            VI. Weicker, Lowell P., 19?   VII. Title.

Voice Lib.
M1037   Guston, John
bd.1   Biography in sound (radio program)
            "The Actor", narrated by Morgan Beatty.
            Cast includes Tallulah Bankhead, Hy Gardner,
            Rocky Graziano, Arthur Miller, Uta Hagen,
            Jackie Cooper, Sir Laurence Olivier, Gad
            Gaythor, Barbara Ashley, Hortense Powdermaker,
            Peter Ustinov, Alfred Hitchcock, Leonard Lyons,
            John Guston, Helen Hayes, Dick Mayne, Ralph
            Bellamy, Lionel Barrymore, Sir Ralph Richardson,
            José Ferrer, and Walter Kerr.   NBC Radio, 1950's.
            1 reel (7 in.)   7 1/2 in. per sec.
            phonotape.
            (Continued on next card)

Voice Lib.
M1721   Guthrie, Mary Ann
bd.2   Catholic nun, running for Democratic
            nomination for Congress from Memphis,
            Tennessee, interviewed by Bruce Hall.
            CBS, June 12, 1974.
            2 min.   phonotape (1 r.   7 1/2 i.p.s.)

            I. Hall, Bruce.

Voice Lib.
M784   Guthrie, Woody, 1912-1967.
bd.2-   Guthrie with Bess Lomax; Dust Bowl Refugees.
785   Library of Congress, March 27, 1940.
            2 reels (7 in.)   7 1/2 in. per sec.
            phonotape.

Voice Lib.
608   Guthrie, Woody, 1912-1962.
bd.4   "Pretty Boy Floyd", "Square Dance"; sings
            and plays his own compositions with Earl
            Robinson on bass.   G.R. Vincent, 1943.
            1 reel (7 in.)   7 1/2 in. per sec.
            phonotape.

Voice Lib.
609   Guthrie, Woody, 1912-1967.
bd.1-6   Singing with guitar accompaniment.   TRV,
        1943.
          1 reel (7 in.)   7 1/2 in. per sec.
        phonotape.

          CONTENTS.-Talking Fish, Railroad Blues,
        Poor Howard, 66 Highway Blues, Jack Hammerjohn,
        If I Lose.

                 Guthrie, Woody, 1912-1967
Voice Lib.
M782   Lomax, Alan, 1915-
bd.2-   Dust Bowl songs and conversation with
784   Woody Guthrie.   Library of Congress,
bd.1   March 22, 1940.
          3 reels (7 in.)   7 1/2 in. per sec.
        phonotape.

          1. Folk music - U.S.   I. Guthrie,
        Woody, 1912-1967.

                 Guthrie, Woody, 1912-1967
Voice Lib.
M781- Lomax, Alan, 1915-
782   Folk songs and conversation with Woody
bd.1   Guthrie.   Library of Congress, March 21,
       1940.
          2 reels (7 in.)   7 1/2 in. per sec.
        phonotape.

          I. Guthrie, Woody, 1912-1967.

                 GUTHRIE, WOODY, 1912-1967
C1
S21   Whorf, Michael, 1933-
         The folk singer.
         1 tape cassette.   (The visual sounds of
       Mike Whorf. Social, S21)

         Originally presented on his radio program, Kaleidoscope,
       WJR, Detroit.
         Duration: 41 min.
         Woody Guthrie and his songs depicting the real life
       experiences of his era.

         L. Guthrie, Woody, 1912-1967. L. Title.

         The gypsies
C1
S67   Whorf, Michael, 1933-
         The gypsies.
         1 tape cassette.   (The visual sounds of
       Mike Whorf. Social, S67)
         Originally presented on his radio program, Kaleidoscope,
       WJR, Detroit.
         Duration: 37 min., 45 sec.
         Like the wayward winds, the gypsies are constantly in motion,
       living for today in a nomadic existence which almost defies
       description.

         L. Gipsies. L. Title.

Voice Lib.
M526   Haakon VII, King of Norway, 1872-1957.
bd.3   Refusal to abdicate Norwegian throne on
       grounds that his people do not desire him
       to, justifies exile government. Speaks from
       his exile headquarters in London; reviews
       early years in Norway.   CBS, 1940.
          1 reel (7 in.)   7 1/2 i.p.s.   phonotape.

          1. World War, 1939-1945 - Norway.
          2. Norway - Politics and government - 1940-
        1945.

                 Haakon VII, King of Norway, 1872-1957
Voice Lib.
572-   I can hear it now (radio program)
573   1933-1946.   CBS, 1948.
bd.1   2 reels (7 in.)   7 1/2 in. per sec.
        phonotape.
         L. Murrow, Edward Roscoe, 1908-1965. II. LaGuardia, Fiorello
       Henry, 1882-1947. III. Chamberlain, Neville, 1869-1949. IV.
       Roosevelt, Franklin Delano, Pres. U.S., 1882-1945. V. Churchill,
       Winston Leonard Spencer, 1874-1965. VI. Gaulle, Charles de,
       Pres. France, 1890-1970. VII. Eisenhower, Dwight David, Pres. U.S.,
       1890-1969. VIII. Willkie, Wendell Lewis, 1892-1944. IX. Martin,
       Joseph William, 1884-1968. X. Elizabeth II, Queen of Great Britain,
       1926-   XI. Margaret Rose, Princess of Gt. Brit., 1930-   XII.
       Johnson, Hugh Samuel, 1882-1942. XIII. Smith, Alfred Emanuel,
       1873-1944. XIV. Lindberg harles Augustus, 1902-   XV. Davis,
                              (Continued on next card)

                 Habt acht
Voice Lib.
M1309 Faulhaber, Michael von, Cardinal, 1869-
bd.2   1952.
         New Year's Eve sermon at the cathedral
       in Munich, Germany entitled "Habt Acht".
       Peteler, December 31, 1941.
          1 reel (7 in.)   7 1/2 in. per sec.
        phonotape.

          I. Title: Habt acht.

Voice Lib.
M1373 Hadamovsky, Eugen, 1904-
bd.3   Talking about the so-called "radio affair".
       Peteler, August 12, 1933.
          1 reel (7 in.)   7 1/2 in. per sec.
        phonotape.

          1. Germany - Politics and government -
        1933-1945.

Voice Lib.
M1429 Hagen, Carlos
         Producer Carlos Hagen of UCLA compares the
       poem "Howl" by Allen Ginsberg with Bob
       Dylan's song "Desolation Row" within the
       social concept of contemporary America.
       Los Angeles, KPFK-FM.
          1 reel (7 in.)   7 1/2 in. per sec.
        phonotape.

          1/2 track; do not play on full track machine.

Voice Lib.
M1262 Hagen, Carlos
bd.2   Interviews by Carlos Hagen and Lawrence
          Lipton with hippies in Golden Gate Park,
          at summer happening; includes chants.
          Hagen, June, 1967.
             1 reel (7 in.)   7 1/2 in. per sec.
          phonotape.

             1. Hippies.
             I. Lipton, Lawrence, 1898-

Voice Lib.
M1261- Hagen, Carlos
1262   Two weeks in Haight-Ashbury district of
bd.1   San Francisco by Lawrence Lipton and Carlos
          Hagen, recording hippie music and philosophy,
          including interview with a priest.   June,
          1967.
             2 reels (7 in.)   7 1/2 in. per sec.
          phonotape.

             1. Hippies.
             I. Lipton, Lawrence, 1898-

          Hagen, Uta Thyra, 1919-
Voice Lib.
M1037 Biography in sound (radio program)
bd.1   "The Actor", narrated by Morgan Beatty.
          Cast includes Tallulah Bankhead, Hy Gardner,
          Rocky Graziano, Arthur Miller, Uta Hagen,
          Jackie Cooper, Sir Laurence Olivier, Gad
          Gayther, Barbara Ashley, Hortense Powdermaker,
          Peter Ustinov, Alfred Hitchcock, Leonard Lyons,
          John Guston, Helen Hayes, Dick Mayne, Ralph
          Bellamy, Lionel Barrymore, Sir Ralph Richardson,
          José Ferrer, and Walter Kerr.   NBC Radio, 1950's
             1 reel (7 in.)   7 1/2 in. per sec.
          phonotape.
                          (Continued on next card)

Voice Lib.
M256   Hagerty, James C   1909-
bd.7   Eisenhower's medical examination.   CBS
          News, December 10, 1957.
             1 reel (7 in.)   7 1/2 in. per sec.
          phonotape.

             1. Eisenhower, Dwight David, Pres. U.S.,
          1890-1969.

Voice Lib.
345   Hagerty, James C   1909-
bd.4   Statement about Presidential disability.
          CBS, March 3, 1958.
             1 reel (7 in.)   7 1/2 in. per sec.
          phonotape.

          Haines, Fred
Voice Lib.
M820, Serett, Maxine
bd.2-   Author Maxine Serett interviewed by Fred
822,   Haines on her ideas about sex and her book:
bd.1   "The Housewife's Handbook of Selective
          Promiscuity".   KPFK, July 20, 1964.
             3 reels (7 in.)   7 1/2 in. per sec.
          phonotape.

             I. Haines, Fred

          Haise, Fred W   1934-
Voice Lib.
M1423 Apollo 13 (space flight): resumé of flight
          of Apollo 13, including lift-off, mal-
          function, and splashdown, and interviews
          on future of space program.   NBC TV,
          April, 1970.
             1 reel (7 in.)   7 1/2 in. per sec.
          phonotape.
             1. Project Apollo. 2. Space flight to the moon. 3. Haise,
          Fred W   1934-   4. Lovell, James Arthur, 1928-   5.
          Swigert, John L   1932-   I. Haise, Fred W   1934-
          II. Lovell, James Arthur, 1928-   III. Swigert, John L   1932-

          Haise, Fred W   1934-
Voice Lib.
M1424 Apollo 13 (space flight): oxygen malfunction
          on Apollo 13 described by NASA, astronauts,
          and Howard K. Smith.   ABC TV, April 14, 1970.
             1 reel (7 in.)   7 1/2 in. per sec.
          phonotape.

             1. Project Apollo. 2. Space flight to the
          moon. 3. Haise, Fred W   1934-   4.
          Lovell, James Arthur, 1928-   5. Swigert,
          John L   1932-   I. Haise, Fred W   1934-
          II. Lovell, James Arthur, 1928-   III. Swigert,
          John L   1932-   IV. Smith, Howard Kingsbury,
          1914-

Voice Lib.
M1800 Haldeman, Harry R., 1926-
WG   Testimony before the Senate Committee
0730.03   investigating the Watergate affair.
          Pacifica, July 30, 1973.
             160 min.   phonotape (2 r.   3 3/4 i.p.s.)
          (Watergate gavel to gavel, phase 1)

             1. Watergate Affair, 1972-

Voice Lib.
M1800 Haldeman, Harry R., 1926-
WG   Testimony before the Senate Committee
0731   investigating the Watergate Affair.
          Pacifica, July 31, 1973.
             418 min.   phonotape (5 r.   3 3/4 i.p.s.)
          (Watergate gavel to gavel, phase 1)

             1. Watergate Affair, 1972-

Voice Lib.
M1800   Haldeman, Harry R., 1926–
WG   Testimony before the Senate Committee
0801   investigating the Watergate Affair.
          Pacifica, August 1, 1973.
            357 min.   phonotape (5 r.   3 3/4 i.p.s.)
          (Watergate gavel to gavel, phase 1)

            1. Watergate Affair, 1972–

Voice Lib.
M711   Haley, Jack
bd.4   "Jack Haley Show"; TV variety show.
          Melchior collection, January 4, 1951.
            1 reel (7 in.)   7 1/2 in. per sec.
          phonotape.

Voice Lib.   Hall, Bruce
M1721   Guthrie, Mary Ann
bd.2   Catholic nun, running for Democratic
          nomination for Congress from Memphis,
          Tennessee, interviewed by Bruce Hall.
          CBS, June 12, 1974.
            2 min.   phonotape (1 r.   7 1/2 i.p.s.)

            I. Hall, Bruce.

Voice Lib.   Hall, Frederick Lee, 1916–1970
M620   Radio in the 1940's (Part I): a series of
bd.1-   excerpts from important broadcasts of the 1940's; a
bd.16   sample of radio of the period. NVL, April, 1964.
          1 reel (7 in.)   7 1/2 in. per sec. phonotape.
            L Radio programs. L Thomas, Lowell Jackson, 1892–   II.
          Gunther, John, 1901-1970. III. Shirer, William Lawrence, 1904– IV.
          Kaltenborn, Hans von, 1878-1965. IV. Delmar, Kenny. V. Those were the good old days (Radio
          program) VL Elman, Dave. VII. Hall, Frederick Lee, 1916-1970.
          VIII. Hobby lobby (Radio program) IX. Roosevelt, Franklin Delano,
          Pres. U.S., 1882-1945. X. Willkie, Wendell Lewis, 1892-1944.
          XI. Hoover, Herbert Clark, Pres. U.S., 1874-1964. XII. Johnson,
          Hugh Samuel, 1882-1942. XIII. Cobb, Irvin Shrewsbury, 1876-1944.
          XIV. Roosevelt, Theodore, 1858-1919. XV. Nye, Gerald Prentice,
          1892-197L. XVI. Lindbergh, Charles Augustus, 1902– XVII.
          Toscanini, Arturo, 1867-1957.

Voice Lib.   Hall, Josef Washington, 1894–
M621   Radio in the 1940's (Part II): a series of
bd.1-   excerpts from important broadcasts of the
12   1940's; a sample of radio of the period.
          NVL, April, 1964.
          1 reel (7 in.)   7 1/2 in. per sec. phonotape.
            L Daly, John Charles, 1914–   II. Hall, Josef Washington,
          1894– III. Shirer, William Lawrence, 1904– IV. Roosevelt,
          Eleanor (Roosevelt) 1884-1962. V. Roosevelt, Franklin Delano,
          Pres. U.S., 1882-1945. VI. Churchill, Winston Leonard Spencer,
          1874-1965. VII. Wainwright, Jonathan Mayhew, 1883-1953. VIII.
          Cantor, Eddie, 1893-1964. IX. Sinatra, Francis Albert, 1917–
          X. Hope, Bob, 1903– XI. Crosby, Bing, 1901– XII. Shore,
          Dinah, 1917(?)– XIII. Bergen, Edgar, 1903– XIV. Armstrong,
          Louis, 1900-197L. XV. Eldridge, Roy, 1911–

                Halley, Rudolf, 1913–1956
Voice Lib.
M1489   U.S. Congress. Senate. Special Committee
bd.2   to Investigate Organized Crime in
          Interstate Commerce.
          Excerpt of examination of racketeer Frank
        Costello by Kefauver Committee Counsel
        Rudolf Halley. New York, WMGM Radio, March
        20, 1951.
            1 reel (7 in.)   7 1/2 in. per sec.
          phonotape.

            I. Costello, Frank   II. Halley,
          Rudolf, 1913–1956.

CL   HALLOWEEN
S30   Whorf, Michael, 1933–
            Seeing things at night – Halloween.
            1 tape cassette.   (The visual sounds of
          Mike Whorf. Social, S30)

            Originally presented on his radio program, Kaleidoscope,
          WJR, Detroit.
            Duration 49 min., 15 sec.
            "Seein' things at night," "The goblins will getcha" and the
          terrifying tale of Sawney Beane and his family are tales appropriate
          for this Halloween special.

            L Halloween. L Title.

                Halverson, Craig
Voice Lib.
M1579   Third Civic Presence Group/Legislative
bd.1   luncheon, with Craig Halverson, Lynn
          Jondahl, Gary Owen, Phil Mastin, and
          Eric Gentile. WKAR-TV, February 15, 1973.
            10 min.   phonotape (1 r.   7 1/2 i.p.s.)

            1. Physically handicapped – Law and legis-
          lation. I. Halverson, Craig. II. Jondahl,
          H. Lynn, 1936–   III. Owen, Gary M., 1944–
          IV. Mastin, Philip O., 1930– V. Gentile,
          Eric Anton, 1943–

Voice Lib.
M1579   Halverson, Craig
bd.2   23 tonight; MSU controversy over curb and
          ramp cuts, with Eric Gentile and Judy K. Taylor.
          WKAR-TV, November 13, 1973.
            15 min.   phonotape (1 r.   7 1/2 i.p.s.)

            1. Physically handicapped – Law and legis-
          lation. I. Gentile, Eric Anton, 1943–
          II. Taylor, Judy K

Voice Lib.   Halverson, Craig
M1585   Ardrey, Robert
bd.2   Property, status, and self-respect.
          WKAR-TV, February 23, 1974.
            15 min.   phonotape (1 r.   7 1/2 in. per sec.)

            1. Territoriality (Zoology) 2. Communism.
          3. Cities & towns – Planning. I. Halverson,
          Craig.

C1
H67

HAMILTON, ALEXANDER, 1757-1804

Whorf, Michael, 1933-
Heart of oak, Alexander Hamilton.
1 tape cassette. (The visual sounds of
Mike Whorf. History and heritage, H67)

Originally presented on his radio program, Kaleidoscope,
WJR, Detroit.
Duration 43 min., 10 sec.
His gifts of intelligence and wisdom had a dramatic impact
on the young nation. Alexander Hamilton was a man of conviction and
ideals, and his perseverance led to his being referred to as the
man with a heart of oak.

L. Hamilton, Alexander, 1757-1804. L. Title.

Voice Lib.
M874
bd.2-
M875

Hamilton, John David

American mood series (Radio program)
Appalachia: first program in a series of
documentaries by John David Hamilton recording
on-the-spot candid sounds and interviews, in
1963. White evangelists' sermons; statements
by teachers and sociologists and natives in
the mountain regions of North Carolina, Tenn-
essee and Kentucky, which include feuding,
square dancing, moon-shining, etc. Native
women recollecting life in the past in Appalachia; origin of feuds; discussion of moon-
shining; native folk songs, including the TVA
(Continued on next card)

Voice Lib.
M874
bd.2-
M875

Hamilton, John David

American mood series (Radio program)
Appalachia... 1963. (Card 2)

song; church service excerpts; the Texas
scene, fundamentalism, philosophy, humor,
songs, etc. CBC, 1963.
2 reels (7 in.) 7 1/2 in. per sec.
phonotape.

1. Appalachian Mountains, Southern - Social
life and customs. I. Hamilton, John David
II. Project '64.

Voice Lib.
M878-
879
bd.1

Hamilton, John David

American mood series (Radio program)
Conversation on a party line: John David
Hamilton talking to people in North Carolina,
Connecticut, New York, Texas, Colorado, New
Mexico, all intellectuals and numerous school
teachers. "Little Boxes" (the conformity song);
description of American life and its meaning;
definition of socialism; discussing Americans'
international ideas; discussion of Texas
University students and attitudes; Berkeley
professor attitudes; discussion on how to make
money; advocating the study of medicine.
CBC, 1963.

Voice Lib.
M878-
879
bd.1

Hamilton, John David

American mood series (Radio program)
Conversation on a party line... 1963.
(Card 2)

2 reels (7 in.) 7 1/2 in. per sec.
phonotape.

1. U.S. - Social life & customs - 20th cent.
I. Hamilton, John David   II. Project
'64.

Voice Lib.
M879
bd.2-
881
bd.1

Hamilton, John David

American mood series (Radio program)
The real American revolution. California,
the real American revolution. Opinions on
liberalism and also opinions by John Birch
Society members and conservatives. Discussion
by magazine editor; San Diego resident talking
about John Birch Society and a discussion
about Barry Goldwater. Discussion of life and
culture in Southern California; cause for the
influx of people; lack of family roots and
analysis of social contacts; broad discussion
of L.A. social problems. Discussions of
(Continued on next card)

Voice Lib.
M879
bd.2-
881
bd.1

Hamilton, John David

American mood series (Radio program) The
real American revolution... 1963.
(Card 2)

uprising of college students and a general
discussion of Southern California compared to
Canada. CBC Radio, 1963.
2 reels (7 in.) 7 1/2 in. per sec.
phonotape.

1. California - Soc. condit. I. Hamilton,
John David   II. Project '64.

Voice Lib.
M881,
bd.2-
882

Hamilton, John David

American mood series (Radio program)
Reverberations from the think tanks. Future of America being
discussed by outstanding thinkers. Final documentary in the
American mood series wherein John David Hamilton visits the
Rand Corp. in Santa Monica, discussing its objectives, type of
work and long-range military strategy. Speakers are: James F.
Digby, Robert D. Specht, Bernard Brody, of the Rand Corporation.
Also interviews with: W. H. Ferry, Walter Millis, and Dr. Robert
Hutchins at the Center for Democratic Institutions in Santa Barbara,
Calif.; the Aspen Institute in Aspen, Colo. Speakers are: business
executives, Robert O. Anderson and William Gomberg discussing
social and economic problems from a business executive's viewpoint;
roles of the individual; distinct optimism. CBC Radio, 1964.
2 reels (7 in.) 7 1/2 i.p.s. phonotape.

I. Hamilton, John David   II. Project '64.

Voice Lib.
M876-
877

Hamilton, John David

American mood series (Radio program)
The Southern moderate: the South as seen
through the eyes of a Canadian, John David
Hamilton. The case of the white moderate;
statements by moderate whites about the racial
situation; sentiments about Negroes by Atlanta,
Georgia newspapermen; appreciation of South-
erners' way of life. New Orleans historian's
appraisal of economic conditions in Louisiana.
Mississippi Chamber of Commerce manager eval-
uating situation in Mississippi. Oldtime
justice described by South Carolina citizen.
(Continued on next card)

Voice Lib.
M876-
877

Hamilton, John David

American mood series (Radio program) The
Southern moderate... 1963. (Card 2)

Mississippi's concealed weapons law; opinions
on violence; discussion of white supremacy
in intellect and education; protests about
taxes to aid colored relief; pro and con
opinions about Negroes' rights from Louisianans
and Georgians. CBC Radio, 1963.
2 reels (7 in.) 7 1/2 in. per sec.
phonotape.

1. Southern states - Civilization. I.
Hamilton, John David   II. Project '64.

Voice Lib. Hamlet's soliloquy
616 Barrymore, John, 1882-1942.
bd.4 "Hamlet's Soliloquy" (excerpt); speaks
informally, narrates excerpt. Famous
Record Company, 1925.
1 reel (7 in.) 7 1/2 in. per sec.
phonotape.

Voice Lib.
M717 Hammarskjöld, Dag, 1905-1961.
bd.7 Replying to Russian demand that he vacate
post as Secretary General of the U.N.
1 reel (7 in.) 7 1/2 in. per sec.
phonotape.

Voice Lib.
M996 Hammarskjöld, Dag, 1905-1961.
Inauguration ceremonies at U.N. upon
assumption of duties as Secretary
General. UN Archives, April 10, 1953.
1 reel (7 in.) 7 1/2 in. per sec.
phonotape.

Voice Lib.
M996 Hammarskjöld, Dag, 1905-1961.
bd.2 Inauguration ceremonies upon acceptance
of second term. UN Archives, September 26,
1957.
1 reel (7 in.) 7 1/2 in. per sec.
phonotape.

Voice Lib.
M996 Hammarskjöld, Dag, 1905-1961.
bd.3 Refutation of Soviet accusation and refusal
to resign. UN Archives, October 3, 1960.
1 reel (7 in.) 7 1/2 in. per sec.
phonotape.

Hammarskjöld, Dag, 1905-1961
Voice Lib.
M1033 Voice of America.
Twentieth anniversary program of Voice of
America broadcasts narrated by Henry Fonda,
and including the voices of Carl Sandburg,
Danny Kaye, Jawaharlal Nehru, Franklin D.
Roosevelt, Charles Malik, Arnold Toynbee,
William Faulkner, Harry S.Truman, Dwight D.
Eisenhower, Helen Hayes, Dag Hammarskjöld,
Winston Churchill, and John F. Kennedy.
Voice of America, 1963.
1 reel (7 in.) 7 1/2 in. per sec.
phonotape.
(Continued on next card)

Hammarskjöld, Dag, 1905-1961
Voice Lib.
M1033 Voice of America. Twentieth anniversary
program... 1963. (Card 2)

L Fonda, Henry Jaynes, 1905- II. Sandburg, Carl,
1878-1967. III. Kaye, Danny, 1913- IV. Nehru, Jawaharlal,
1889-1964. V. Roosevelt, Franklin Delano, Pres. U.S., 1882-
1945. VI. Malik, Charles Habib, 1906- VII. Toynbee,
Arnold Joseph, 1889- VIII. Faulkner, William, 1897-1962.
IX. Truman, Harry S, Pres. U.S., 1884-1972. X. Eisenhower,
Dwight David, Pres. U.S., 1890-1969. XI. Hayes, Helen,
1900- XII. Hammarskjöld, Dag, 1905-1961. XIII. Churchill,
Winston Leonard Spencer, 1874-1965. XIV. Kennedy, John
Fitzgerald, Pres. U.S., 1917-1963.

Voice Lib.
M762 Hammerstein, Oscar, 1895-1960.
bd.6 Excerpt from "Music from Broadway" (Program
5); speaking about Jerome Kern and his style of
writing, including son "They Didn't Believe Me";
also comments on those who followed Jerome Kern
and beginnings of musical comedy, what it was
like in the early days, including song, "Oh,
What a Beautiful Morning". Westinghouse
Broadcasting Corporation, 1964.
1 reel (7 in.) 7 1/2 in. per sec. phonotape. (The Music
Goes Round and Round)
L Kern, Jerome, 1885-1945. I. Title: Music from Broadway.
II. Series.

Voice Lib.
M764 Hammerstein, Oscar, 1895-1960.
bd.2 Excerpt from "Sound Track" (Program 7);
comments on what happened when there was
drop in popularity of Broadway in '30's.
Westinghouse Broadcasting Corporation, 1964.
19 sec. phonotape (1 r. 7 1/2 i.p.s.)
(The music goes round and round)

I. Title: Sound track. II. Series.

Hampden, Walter
Voice Lib.
M225 Packard, Frederick
Styles in Shakespearean acting, 1890-1950.
Creative Associates, 1963?
1 reel (7 in.) 7 1/2 i.p.s. phonotape.

L Sothern, Edward Askew, 1826-1881. II. Marlowe,
Julia, 1865-1950. III. Booth, Edwin, 1833-1893. IV. Gielgud,
John, 1904- V. Robeson, Paul Bustill, 1898- VI. Terry,
Dame Ellen, 1848-1928. VII. Allen, Viola. VIII. Welles,
Orson, 1915- IX. Skinner, Otis, 1858-1942. X. Barrymore,
John, 1882-1942. XI. Olivier, Sir Laurence Kerr, 1907-
XII. Forbes-Robertson, Sir Johnston, 1853- XIII. Evans,
Maurice. XIV. Thorndike, Dame Sybil, 1882- XV. Robson,
Flora. XVI. LeGallienne, Eva, 1899- XVII. Anderson,
Judith. XVIII. Duncan, Augustin. XIX. Hampden, Walter.
XX. Speaight, Robert, 1904- XXI. Jones, Daniel.

Voice Lib.
124   Handy, William Christopher, 1837-1958.
          A visit with William C. Handy.   Private
      recordings [1940-50]
          1 reel (7 in.)   7 1/2 in. per sec.
      phonotape.

HANDY, WILLIAM CHRISTOPHER, 1873-1958
C1
M13   Whorf, Michael, 1933-
          Father of the blues.
          1 tape cassette.   (The visual sounds of
      Mike Whorf.   Miscellaneous, M13)
          Originally presented on his radio program, Kaleidoscope,
      WJR, Detroit.
          Duration: 54 min.
          The creator of "St. Louis blues" and a dozen other great
      blues songs was W. C. Handy. This is the story of a troubled
      spirit who finally found his life in music. As they said when
      he died, "The mold is now broken."

              I. Handy, William Christopher, 1873-1958.   I. Title.

Voice Lib.
M946   Handy, William Christopher, 1873-1958.
bd.8   Singing his own composition "Loveless
       Love" with piano accompaniment.   GRV private
       recording, 1953.
           1 reel (7 in.)   7 1/2 in. per sec.
       phonotape.

           I. Title: Loveless love.

Voice Lib.
M640   Hanna, Mark
bd.5   Telephone conversation with G. Robert
       Vincent, changing date of appearance of
       Admiral Byrd on Fred Allen Show.   GRV,
       October 10, 1941.
           1 reel (7 in.)   7 1/2 i.p.s.   phonotape.

           I. Vincent, G. Robert.

Voice Lib.
M946   Handy, William Christopher, 1873-1958.
bd.9   Singing his own composition "The Big
       Stick Blues".   GRV private recording, 1953.
           1 reel (7 in.)   7 1/2 in. per sec.
       phonotape.

           I. Title: The big stick blues.

Voice Lib.
220   Hannah, John Alfred, 1902-
          Address to Michigan Municipal League on
      the evolution of American higher education.
      Detroit, WJR, October 6, 1950.
          1 reel (7 in.)   7 1/2 in. per sec.
      phonotape.

Voice Lib.
M946   Handy, William Christopher, 1873-1958.
bd.7   Singing folk song "Joe Turner", accompanied
       by his guitar.   GRV private recording,
       1953.
           1 reel (7 in.)   7 1/2 in. per sec.
       phonotape.

           I. Title: Joe Turner

Voice Lib.
M1088   Hannah, John Alfred, 1902-
bd.2   Reading excerpt from 1961 Civil Rights
        Commission report.   Location recording,
        February 8, 1963.
            1 reel (7 in.)   7 1/2 in. per sec.
        phonotape.

            1. Civil rights - U.S.

HANDY, WILLIAM CHRISTOPHER, 1873-1958
Voice Lib.
M652   Armstrong, Louis, 1900-1971.
bd.5   Talks about W.C. Handy.   CBS, March 28,
       1958.
           1 reel (7 in.)   7 1/2 in. per sec.
       phonotape.

           1. Handy, William Christopher, 1873-1958.

Voice Lib.
304   Hannah, John Alfred, 1902-
          Address at MSU Men's Club on the work
      of the Civil Rights Commission.   NVL location
      recording, November 19, 1963.
          1 reel (7 in.)   7 1/2 in. per sec.
      phonotape.

          1. U.S. Commission on Civil Rights.

Voice Lib.
505   Hannah, John Alfred, 1902-
bd.1   Address at M.S.U. Men's Club on the work
         of the Civil Rights Commission.   NVL
         location recording, November 19, 1963.
           1 reel (7 in.)   7 1/2 in. per sec.
         phonotape.

           1. U.S. Commission on Civil Rights.

Voice Lib.
M963-   Hannah, John Alfred, 1902-
968   Subcommittee hearing of Michigan State
bd.1   Legislature pertaining to the controversial
         article in "Ramparts" magazine.   May 16,
         1966.
           6 reels (7 in.)   7 1/2 in. per sec.
         phonotape.

           1. Ramparts.

Voice Lib.
M1238-   Hannah, John Alfred, 1902-
1240   Speakers at recognition dinner held at
         the Lansing Civic Center as a tribute to
         President John A. Hannah, observing his 25th
         year as President of Michigan State University.
         Location recording, November 18, 1966.
           3 reels (7 in.)   7 1/2 in. per sec.
         phonotape.

Voice Lib.
M1251   Hannah, John Alfred, 1902-
           Address at MSU commencement, Spring,
         1967; introductory remarks by Charles
         Stoddard, President of 1967 Senior class.
         WKAR, June 11, 1967.
           1 reel (7 in.)   7 1/2 i.p.s.
         phonotape.

           I. Stoddard, Charles C

Voice Lib.
M1742   Hannah, John Alfred, 1902-
bd.1   Address at his retirement dinner at
         Michigan State University.   Introduction
         by Duffy Daugherty.   WKAR, March 17, 1968.
           29 min.   phonotape (1 r.   7 1/2 i.p.s.)

           1. U.S. Agency for International
         Development.   I. Daugherty, Hugh.

                    Hannah, John Alfred, 1902-
Voice Lib.
131   Anderson, Clinton Presba, 1895-
bd.4   Address at Michigan State University,
         with introduction by President John A.
         Hannah.   WKAR, 1961.
           1 reel (7 in.)   7 1/2 in. per sec.
         phonotape.

           I. Hannah, John Alfred, 1902-

                    Hannah, John Alfred, 1902-
Voice Lib.
132   Benson, Ezra Taft, 1899-
bd.1   Address at Michigan State University,
         with introduction by President John A.
         Hannah.   WKAR, 1961.
           1 reel (7 in.)   7 1/2 in. per sec.
         phonotape.

           I. Hannah, John Alfred, 1902-

                    Hannah, John Alfred, 1902-
Voice Lib.
131   Brannen, Charles Franklin, 1903-
bd.5   Address at Michigan State University,
         with introduction by President John A.
         Hannah.   WKAR, 1961.
           1 reel (7 in.)   7 1/2 in. per sec.
         phonotape.

           I. Hannah, John Alfred, 1902-

                    Hannah, John Alfred, 1902-
Voice Lib.
130-   MacArthur, Douglas, 1880-1964.
131   Commencement address at Michigan State
bd.1   University, with introduction by President
         John A. Hannah.   WKAR, June, 1961.
           2 reels (7 in.)   7 1/2 in. per sec.
         phonotape.

           I. Hannah, John Alfred, 1902-

                    Hannah, John Alfred, 1902-
Voice Lib.
M1311   Ngo-dinh-Diem, Pres. Vietnam, 1901-1963.
bd.1   Special convocation at MSU to present an
         honorary degree to President Diem.   Intro-
         ductory remarks by Dr. John A. Hannah.
         Location recording, May 15, 1957.
           1 reel (7 in.)   7 1/2 in. per sec.
         phonotape.

           I. Hannah, John Alfred, 1902-

Hannah, John Alfred, 1902-
Voice Lib.
131   Wallace, Henry Agard, 1888-1965.
bd.2   Address at Michigan State University,
       with introduction by President John A.
       Hannah. WKAR, 1961.
          1 reel (7 in.)   7 1/2 in. per sec.
       phonotape.

          I. Hannah, John Alfred, 1902-

Hannah, John Alfred, 1902-
Voice Lib.
131   Wickard, Claude Raymond, 1893-1967.
bd.3   Address at Michigan State University,
       with introduction by President John A.
       Hannah. WKAR, 1961.
          1 reel (7 in.)   7 1/2 in. per sec.
       phonotape.

          I. Hannah, John Alfred, 1902-

HANNAH, JOHN ALFRED, 1902-
Voice Lib.
M1417,   Michigan Agricultural Conference.
1418,   Testimonial dinner for John Hannah.
1422,   March 17, 1969.
bd.1   3 reels (7 in.)   7 1/2 i.p.s.   phonotape.

          1. Hannah, John Alfred, 1902-

Hannan, Philip Matthew, 1913-
Voice Lib.
M319   Funeral of John F. Kennedy: church ceremonies at Washington
       Cathedral; quote of speech segments of JFK and delivery of
       memorial sermon by Most Rev. Philip M. Hannan; prayers
       at bier by Cardinal Richard Cushing; departure of coffin
       from Cathedral to Arlington Cemetery; description of journey
       and arrival. CBS, November 25, 1963.
          1 reel (7 in.)   7 1/2 i.p.s.   phonotape.
          1. Kennedy, John Fitzgerald, Pres. U.S., 1917-1963 -
       Assassination. 1. Hannan, Philip Matthew, 1913-   II.
       Cushing, Richard James, Cardinal, 1895-

Voice Lib.
M1306- Hans Christian Anderson (motion picture)
1308   Starring Danny Kaye, with music by Frank
        Loesser. Decommercialized. ABC-TV,
        February 1968 (rerun)
           3 reels (7 in.)   7 1/2 in. per sec.
        phonotape.

Voice Lib.
M1005 Hans Christian Andersen (Television program)
       TV adaptation of film of same title, with
       Danny Kaye and Victor Borge. ABC-TV, Nov. 3,
       1966.
          1 reel (7 in.)   7 1/2 in. per sec.
       phonotape.

          1. Andersen, Hans Christian, 1805-1875.
       I. Kaye, Danny, 1913-   II. Borge,
       Victor, 1909-

The Happiness Boys (Radio program)
Voice Lib.
M617   Radio in the 1920's: a series of excerpts
bd.1-   from important broadcasts of the 1920's,
bd.25   with brief prologue and epilogue; a sample
        of radio of the period. NVL, April, 1964.
          1 reel (7 in.)   7 1/2 in. per sec.
       phonotape.
          1. Radio programs. 1. Marconi, Guglielmo, marchese, 1874-
       1937. II. Kendall, H   G   III. Coolidge, Calvin, Pres. U.S.,
       1872-1933. IV. Wilson, Woodrow, Pres. U.S., 1856-1924. V.
       Roosevelt, Franklin Delano, Pres. U.S., 1882-1945. VI. Lodge,
       Henry Cabot, 1850-1924. VII. LaGuardia, Fiorello Henry, 1882-1947.
       VIII. The Happiness Boys (Radio program) IX. Gallagher and Sheen.
       X. Barney Google. XI. Vallee, Rudy, 1901-   XII. The two
                                           (Continued on next card)

Happiness is the only good
Voice Lib.
M1615   Ingersoll, Robert Green, 1833-1899.
bd.2   Happiness is the only good.   Rare Records,
        Inc., A810 [19--?]
           50 sec.   phonotape (1 r.   7 1/2 i.p.s.)

           I. Title.

Voice Lib.
M761   Harbach, Otto Abels, 1873-1963.
bd.14   Excerpt from "Tunesmiths Past and Present"
       (Program 4); speaking about Rudolph Friml
       and his technique in composing. Westinghouse
       Broadcasting Corporation, 1964.
          1 reel (7 in.)   7 1/2 in. per sec.
       phonotape.   (The Music Goes Round and Round)

          1. Friml, Rudolph, 1881-   I. Title:
       Tunesmiths past and present. II. Series.

Voice Lib.
M762   Harbach, Otto Abels, 1873-1963.
bd.5   Excerpt from "Music from Broadway" (Program
       5); comments on transformation to musical
       comedy as we know it today. Westinghouse
       Broadcasting Corporation, 1964.
          2 min., 43 sec.   phonotape (7 in.
       7 1/2 i.p.s.)   (The music goes round and
       round)

          1. Musical revue, comedy, etc. - New York
       (City) I. Title: Music from Broadway.
       II. Series.

Voice Lib.
M764   Harbach, Otto Abels, 1873-1963.
bd.1   Excerpt from "Sound Track" (Program 7);
        comments on filmdom's first encounter with
        sound tracks; also explains what he feels
        was wrong with the first movie musicals.
        Westinghouse Broadcasting Corporation, 1964.
            1 reel (7 in.)   7 1/2 in. per sec.
        phonotape.   (The Music Goes Round and Round)

            I. Title: Sound track. II. Series.

Voice Lib.
M762   Harburg, Edgar Y   1896-
bd.7   Excerpt from "Music from Broadway" (Program
        5); tells about his relationship with Gershwin
        brothers. Westinghouse Broadcasting Cor-
        poration, 1964.
            1 reel (7 in.)   7 1/2 in. per sec.
        phonotape.   (The Music Goes Round and Round)

            I. Title: Music from Broadway. II. Series.

Voice Lib.
M764   Harburg, Edgar Y.   1896-
bd.3   Excerpts from "Sound Track" (Program 7);
        comments on his feelings toward the musical
        efforts of the 30's.   Including example
        of movie music: "Over the rainbow", with
        Judy Garland; lyrics by Harburg. Westing-
        house Broadcasting Corporation, 1964.
            3 min., 58 sec.   phonotape (1 r.   7 1/2
        i.p.s.) (The music goes round and round)
            L. Music, Popular (Songs, etc.) - U.S. L. Garland,
        Judy, 1922-1969. II. Title: Sound track. III. Series.

Voice Lib.
M1735   Hardesty, Charles Howard, 1922-
            The role of industry in combatting environ-
        mental problems; speech delivered at Michigan
        State University. Introduction by Myron H.
        Chetrick. WKAR, June 20, 1974.
            45 min.   phonotape (1 r.   7 1/2 i.p.s.)

            1. Environmental policy. 2. Environmental
        engineering. 3. Factory and trade waste.
        I. Chetrick, Myron

Voice Lib.
M728   Harding, Warren Gamaliel, Pres. U.S., 1865-
bd.6   1923.
            "An association of nations"; Senator
        Harding's position about limited American
        participation in a League of Nations.
        Nation's Forum, 1920.
            1 reel (7 in.)   7 1/2 in. per sec.
        phonotape.

            1. League of Nations.

Voice Lib.
539   Harding, Warren Gamaliel, Pres. U.S., 1865-1923.
bd.3   Liberty under the law (1920 campaign
        speech). Nation's Forum, 1920.
            1 reel (7 in.)   7 1/2 in. per sec.
        phonotape.

Voice Lib.
M276   Harding, Warren Gamaliel, Pres. U.S., 1865-1923.
bd.3   Speech on the occasion of the return of
        bodies of World War I soldiers. Camden,
        New Jersey, Victor Talking Machine Co.,
        March 23, 1921.
            1 reel (7 in.)   7 1/2 in. per sec.
        phonotape.

            HARDING, WARREN GAMALIEL, PRES. U.S.,
            1865-1923
Voice Lib.
538   Robinson, Mrs. Corrine (Roosevelt), 1861-1933.
bd.2   Republican campaign speech, 1920; gives her
        support to Warren G. Harding for President and
        Calvin Coolidge for Vice-President, attacks
        Woodrow Wilson as a partisan politician.
        Nation's Forum, 1920.
            1 reel (7 in.)   7 1/2 in. per sec.
        phonotape.

            1. Harding, Warren Gamaliel, Pres. U.S.,
        1865-1923.

            Hardwicke, Sir Cedric, 1893-1964
Voice Lib.
M1028   Lux presents Hollywood: montage of excerpts
bd.7   from various Lux radio shows. George Raft,
        Virginia Mayo, Cedric Hardwicke, and
        Ingrid Bergman. Michigan State University,
        Department of Television and Radio, 1940's.
            1 reel (7 in.)   7 1/2 in. per sec.
        phonotape.

            I. Raft, George   II. Mayo, Virginia
        III. Hardwicke, Sir Cedric, 1893-1964. IV.
        Bergman, Ingrid, 1917-

            Hare, Ernie   -1939.
            see
        The Happiness Boys (Radio program)

Voice Lib.
M260
bd.3
Hargrove, Marion Lawton, 1919-
How to become a sergeant in less than twenty years; anecdotes on army life.
G.R. Vincent, 1942.
1 reel (7 in.)   7 1/2 i.p.s.   phonotape.

1. U.S. Army - Military life.

Voice Lib.
M322
Harkins, James
Biography in sound (radio program)
W.C. Fields, the magnificent rogue.
NBC, 1955.
1 reel (7 in.)   7 1/2 in. per sec.   phonotape.
L. Fields, W.C., 1879-1946.   L. Fields, W.C., 1879-1946.
II. Allen, Fred, 1894-1956.   III. LaBaron, William   IV.
Taylor, Robert Lewis, 1912-   V. McCarey, Thomas Leo, 1898-
1969.   VI. Harkins, James   .   VII. Chevalier, Maurice,
1889-1972.   VIII. Kuromoto, Mrs. George   IX. Flynn,
Errol Leslie, 1909-1959.   X. Wynn, Ed, 1886-1966.   XI. Dowling,
Ray Dooley   XII. Sennett, Mack   XIII. Overacher,
Ronald Leroy   XIV. Bergen, Edgar, 1903-   XV. Taurog,
Norman, 1899-   XVI. Runnell, Ann   XVII. Cowen,
Lester

Voice Lib.
M273-
274
bd.1
Harkness, Richard
Biography in sound (radio program)
Franklin Delano Roosevelt: the friends and former associates of Franklin Roosevelt on the tenth anniversary of the President's death.
NBC Radio, April, 1955.
2 reels (7 in.)   7 1/2 in. per sec.
phonotape.
L. Roosevelt, Franklin Delano, Pres. U.S., 1882-1945.   L.
McIntire, Ross T   1899-   II. Mellett, Lowell, 1884-1960.
III. Tully, Grace   IV. Henderson, Leon, 1895-
V. Roosevelt, Eleanor (Roosevelt) 1884-1962.   VI. DeGraaf, Albert
VII. Lehman, Herbert Henry, 1878-1963.   VIII. Rosenman, Samuel
Irving, 1896-   IX. Arvey, Jacob   X. Moley, Raymond,
1886-   XI. Farley, James Aloysius, 1888-   XII. Roosevelt,
(Continued on next card)

Voice Lib.
M1706
bd.4
Harlow, Jean, 1911-1937
Stewart, James, 1908-
Discusses his one singing role for MGM; sings "Easy to love". Includes part of the sound track of "That's entertainment" with Jean Harlow and Cary Grant singing "Did I remember?"
From the Merv Griffin Show.   WJRT-TV, June 6, 1974.
15 min.   phonotape (1 r.   7 1/2 i.p.s.)

L. Stewart, James, 1908-   2. Harlow, Jean, 1911-1937.
3. Grant, Cary, 1904-   L. Griffin, Mervyn Edward, 1925-
II. Grant, Cary, 1904-   III. Harlow, Jean, 1911-1937.

Voice Lib.
M1800
WG
0605.01
Harmony, Sally J
Testimony before the Senate Committee investigating the Watergate Affair.
Pacifica, June 5, 1973.
121 min.   phonotape (1 r.   3 3/4 i.p.s.)
(Watergate gavel to gavel, phase 1)

1. Watergate Affair, 1972-

Voice Lib.
353
bd.18
Harper, Edward
Outbreak of Korean War and comments by various persons.   NBC, July, 1950.
1 reel (7 in.)   7 1/2 in. per sec.
phonotape.

Original disc off-speed.
Participants: Henry Cassidy, Merrill Mueller, Edward Harper, Jack Bregon.

I. Cassidy, Henry Clarence, 1910-   II.
Mueller, Merrill.   III. Harper, Edward.   IV.
Bregon, Jack.

Voice Lib.
M258
bd.9B
Harper, Robert
Report to CBS News, New York; description of military control in Montgomery, Alabama under state troops.   New York, CBS, May 22, 1961.
1 reel (7 in.)   7 1/2 i.p.s.   phonotape.

1. Civil rights.   2. Montgomery, Ala.

Voice Lib.
M258
bd.9A
Harper, Robert
Report to CBS News, New York; description of Gov. Patterson's (Alabama) reaction to the federal protection of Rev. Martin Luther King.   New York, CBS, May 22, 1961.
1 reel (7 in.)   7 1/2 in. per sec.
phonotape.

1. Patterson, John Malcolm, 1921-   2.
King, Martin Luther, 1929-1968.

Voice Lib.
M1707
bd.2
Harrell, Beverley
Announcing her candidacy for the Nevada assembly, Terry Oliver, reporting.
CBS, June 5, 1974.
5 min.   phonotape (1 r.   7 1/2 i.p.s.)

1. Nevada. Legislature - Elections.
I. Oliver, Terry.

Voice Lib.
M1232
Harriman, William Averell, 1891-
A conversation with Averell Harriman at his home in Georgetown, Washington, D.C., and three NBC correspondents covering Mr. Harriman's career in public life from FDR to LBJ.   NBC-TV, May 21, 1967.
1 reel (7 in.)   7 1/2 in. per sec.
phonotape.

Harris, Phil

Voice Lib.
M622   Radio in the 1940's (Part III); a series of
bd.1-   excerpts from important broadcasts of the 1940's; a sample
bd.15   of radio of the period. NVL, April, 1964.
         1 reel (7 in.) 7 1/2 in. per sec. phonotape.
           L Radio programs. L Miller, Alton Glenn, 1909(?)-1944. II.
         Diles, Ken   III. Wilson, Donald Harlow, 1900-   IV.
         Livingstone, Mary   V. Benny, Jack, 1894-   VL Harris,
         Phil   VIL Merman, Ethel, 1909-   VIIL Smith, "Wonderful"
         IX. Bennett, Richard Dyer   X. Louis, Joe, 1914-   XL
         Eisenhower, Dwight David, Pres. U.S., 1890-1969. XIL MacArthur,
         Douglas, 1880-1964. XIII. Romulo, Carlos Pena, 1899-   XIV.
         Welles, Orson, 1915-   XV. Jackson, Robert Houghwout, 1892-1954.
         XVL LaGuardia, Fiorello Henry, 1882-1945. XVIL Nehru, Jawa-
         harlal, 1889-1964. XVIIL Gandhi, Mohandas Karamchand, 1869-1948.

Harry S. Truman - American

C1
H98   Whorf, Michael, 1933-
         Harry S Truman - American.
         1 tape cassette.   (The visual sounds of
       Mike Whorf. History and heritage, H98)
           Originally presented on his radio program, Kaleidoscope,
         WJR, Detroit.
           Duration: 46 min.
           One of the most outspoken and straightforward leaders of all
         our presidents, Harry Truman was praised and cursed, revered and
         reviled.

           L Truman, Harry S, Pres. U.S., 1884-1972. L Title.

Voice Lib.
M731   Harris, Robert
bd.1   Introducing to faculty and student body
         of MSU the Reverend Martin Luther King.
         NVL, February 11, 1965.
           1 reel (7 in.) 7 1/2 i.p.s. phonotape.

           1. King, Martin Luther, 1929-1968.

Harsch, Joseph Close, 1905-
Voice Lib.
M1027   The World Today; CBS News correspondent
bd.2   Joseph C. Harsch discusses the meaning of
         the news of the new German offensive in
         Belgium and Prime Minister Churchill's
         policy in Greece. CBS News, December 20,
         1944.
           1 reel (7 in.) 7 1/2 i.p.s. phonotape.

           1. World War, 1939-1945. I. Harsch,
         Joseph Close, 1905-

Voice Lib.
M1682   Harris, Sydney J
         What is wrong with the city; address
       at Michigan State University, with Dr.
       Frederic Reeve. WKAR, January 27, 1969.
         47 min. phonotape (1 r. 7 1/2 i.p.s.)

           1. Cities and towns. I. Reeve, Frederic
         Eugene, 1916-

Hart, Charles
Voice Lib.
M1206   Popular American patriotic song of World War I
bd.5   entitled "What are you going to do to help
         the boys?" (Gus Kahn-Egbert Van Alstyne)
         Sung by Charles Hart.   Victor, 1917.
         1 reel (7 in.) 7 1/2 in. per sec.
       phonotape.

           I. Hart, Charles   II. Title:
         What are you going to do to help the boys?

Voice Lib.
-M1296 Harrison, George, 1943-
bd.1-A   On effect of Hindu Indian music on
       contemporary musicians and recalling his
       visit to India. P.B.L., December 10,
       1967.
           1 reel (7 in.) 7 1/2 in. per sec.
       phonotape.

Hart, John
Voice Lib.
M1696   Columbia Broadcasting System, inc.
bd.6   Special memorial to Duke Ellington, with
         John Hart, Sonny Greer, Russell Procope,
         Billy Taylor, Stanley Dance, and Ella
         Fitzgerald. CBS-TV, May 24, 1974.
           15 min. phonotape (1 r. 7 1/2 i.p.s.)

           1. Ellington, Duke, 1899-1974. I. Hart,
         John. II. Greer, Sonny. III. Procope,
         Russell, 1908-   IV. Taylor, Billy.
         V. Dance, Stanley. VI. Fitzgerald, Ella,
         1918-

Voice Lib.
394   Harrison, Mary Lord Dimmick, 1858-1948.
bd.8   Looks at world of late '30's, recalls
         life in 1880's and 1890's, compares statesmen
         of two centuries, describes what America
         needs now, younger generation, describes
         value of collection of Voice Library. Inter-
         viewed by G. Robert Vincent.   Vincent studio
         recording, 1938.
           1 reel (7 in.) 7 1/2 in. per sec.
         phonotape.

Voice Lib.
376   Hart, William S   1872-1946.
bd.2   On a cowboy's life.   Private
         collection, 1926.
           1 reel (7 in.) 7 1/2 in. per sec.
       phonotape.

           1. Cowboys.

Voice Lib.
M1611   Hartford, Huntington, 1911-
bd.1   Interview by Edwin Newman on the TV
program Speaking freely. WKAR-TV,
March, 1974.
     3 min.   phonotape (1 r.   7 1/2 i.p.s.)

     1. Graphology.   I. Newman, Edwin Harold,
1919-

HATFIELD-MCCOY FEUD

C1
S27   Whorf, Michael, 1933-
     They was reckless mountain boys - Hatfields
and Martins.
     1 tape cassette.   (The visual sounds of
Mike Whorf. Social, S27)
     Originally presented on his radio program, Kaleidoscope,
WJR, Detroit.
     Duration: 35 min., 30 sec.
     Out from the mountain regions of the Smokies . . . this tale.
It involved two families, the Hatfields and McCoys, and has become
a typical American legend dealing in equal shares of violence and
virtue.
     L. Hatfield-McCoy Feud.   L. Title.

Voice Lib.
M505   Hartung, Edward
bd.3-5   Edward Hartung and Storm Troopers SA33 sing
"Heil Deutschland", medley of German marching
songs, folk songs concerning various neighbor-
hoods in Germany, "Wenn die S.S. und die S.A.
aufmarschiert" ("When the S.S. and the S.A.
march together). Private collection (German
radio transcription), 1942.
     1 reel (7 in.)   7 1/2 in. per sec.
phonotape.

     1. Military music, German.

HAUPTMANN, BRUNO RICHARD, 1899-1936

C1
S75   Whorf, Michael, 1933-
     Kidnap of the century - Lindbergh.
     1 tape cassette.   (The visual sounds of
Mike Whorf. Social, S75)
     Originally presented on his radio program, Kaleidoscope,
WJR, Detroit.
     Duration: 37 min., 30 sec.
     A vivid, exciting account of the notorious Lindbergh kidnapping.
The evening of March 1, 1932, was the scene of the most publicized
abduction of the century. The kidnapping, and the ensuing manhunt
are narrated in this anxious, fearful report.

     L. Lindbergh, Charles Augustus, 1930-1932. 2. Hauptmann,
Bruno Richard, 1899-1936.   L. Title.

Voice Lib.
603   Harvey, Norton
bd.3   "I Didn't Raise My Boy to be a Soldier";
original recording of anti-war song from
World War I era. Victor Talking Machine
Co., 1916.
     1 reel (7 in.)   7 1/2 in. per sec.
phonotape.

     I. Title.

Voice Lib.
M1363   Hauptmann, Gerhart Johann Robert, 1862-1946.
bd.7   Excerpt of radio election speech. Peteler,
1932.
     1 reel (7 in.)   7 1/2 in. per sec.
phonotape.

     Hassett, William D   1880-
Voice Lib.
M273-   Biography in sound (radio program)
274   Franklin Delano Roosevelt: the friends and
bd.1   former associates of Franklin Roosevelt on
the tenth anniversary of the President's death.
NBC Radio, April, 1955.
     2 reels (7 in.)   7 1/2 in. per sec.
phonotape.
     L. Roosevelt, Franklin Delano, Pres. U.S., 1882-1945. L.
McIntire, Ross T   1899-   IL. Mellett, Lowell, 1884-1960.
III. Tully, Grace   IV. Henderson, Leon, 1895-
V. Roosevelt, Eleanor (Roosevelt) 1884-1962. VL. DeGraaf, Albert
VII. Lehman, Herbert Henry, 1878-1963. VIII. Rosenman, Samuel
Irving, 1896-   IX. Arvey, Jacob   X. Moley, Raymond,
1886-   XL. Farley, James Aloysius, 1888-   XII. Roosevelt,
              (Continued on next card)

Voice Lib.   Hausner, Gideon, 1915-
M344   Eichmann, Adolph, 1906-1962.
bd.10   Eichmann trial; statements by Gideon
Hausner, Robert Servatius and Eichmann
concerning the verdict of the court and
the death sentence. CBS, December 13,
1961.
     1 reel (7 in.)   7 1/2 i.p.s.   phonotape.

     1. Eichmann, Adolph, 1906-1962.
I. Hausner, Gideon, 1915-   II. Servatius,
Robert.

Voice Lib.
M772   Hatcher, Harlan Henthorne, 1898-
bd.2   Ceremonies upon presentation of doctorate
degree to astronauts at University of
Michigan, Ann Arbor, Michigan. WUOM,
June 15, 1965.
     1 reel (7 in.)   7 1/2 in. per sec.
phonotape.

Voice Lib.
M1355   Hayakawa, Samuel Ichiyé, 1906-
bd.2   Interview on CBS "Face the Nation" TV
program on Acting President Hayakawa's
opinions on current conditions and future
prospects for San Francisco State College.
CBS, February 2, 1969.
     1 reel (7 in.)   7 1/2 in. per sec.
phonotape.

     1. San Francisco State College.

Hayden, Martin S
Voice Lib.
M1477 Discussion of Supreme Court decision on
publishing Pentagon Papers. William B.
Macomber, deputy under-secretary of state;
Senator Henry Jackson; Max Frankel, head of
New York Times' Washington bureau; Benjamin
Bradley, executive editor of Washington Post.
Questioned by Carl Stern, NBC; Martin Hayden,
Detroit News; James J. Kilpatrick, Washington
Star Syndicate; Kenneth Crawford, Washington
Post; Edwin Newman. NBC-TV, June 30, 1971.
1 reel (7 in.) 7 1/2 in. per sec.
phonotape.

(Continued on next card)

Voice Lib.
M1346 Hayes, Helen, 1900-
bd.1 Reading excerpts from her book to her
grandchildren on the Ed Sullivan Show.
CBS-TV, October 27, 1968.
1 reel (7 in.) 7 1/2 in. per sec.
phonotape.

Voice Lib.
M1458 Hayes, Helen, 1900-
bd.2- Autobiographical narration by Helen Hayes
1459 and her friends about her stage career,
including various parts of her shows. NET, 1971
2 reels (7 in.) 7 1/2 in. per sec.
phonotape.

1. Hayes, Helen, 1900-

Hayes, Helen, 1900-
Voice Lib.
M1037 Biography in sound (radio program)
bd.1 "The Actor", narrated by Morgan Beatty.
Cast includes Tallulah Bankhead, Hy Gardner,
Rocky Graziano, Arthur Miller, Uta Hagen,
Jackie Cooper, Sir Laurence Olivier, Gad
Gaythor, Barbara Ashley, Hortense Powdermaker,
Peter Ustinov, Alfred Hitchcock, Leonard Lyons,
John Guston, Helen Hayes, Dick Mayne, Ralph
Bellamy, Lionel Barrymore, Sir Ralph Richardson,
José Ferrer, and Walter Kerr. NBC Radio, 1950's.
1 reel (7 in.) 7 1/2 in. per sec.
phonotape.

(Continued on next card)

Hayes, Helen, 1900-
Voice Lib.
M1033 Voice of America.
Twentieth anniversary program of Voice of
America broadcasts narrated by Henry Fonda,
and including the voices of Carl Sandburg,
Danny Kaye, Jawaharlal Nehru, Franklin D.
Roosevelt, Charles Malik, Arnold Toynbee,
William Faulkner, Harry S.Truman, Dwight D.
Eisenhower, Helen Hayes, Dag Hammarskjöld,
Winston Churchill, and John F. Kennedy.
Voice of America, 1963.
1 reel (7 in.) 7 1/2 in. per sec.
phonotape.

(Continued on next card)

Hayes, Helen, 1900-
Voice Lib.
M1033 Voice of America. Twentieth anniversary
program... 1963. (Card 2)

I. Fonda, Henry Jaynes, 1905- II. Sandburg, Carl,
1878-1967. III. Kaye, Danny, 1913- IV. Nehru, Jawaharlal,
1889-1964. V. Roosevelt, Franklin Delano, Pres. U.S., 1882-
1945. VI. Malik, Charles Habib, 1906- VII. Toynbee,
Arnold Joseph, 1889- VIII. Faulkner, William, 1897-1962.
IX. Truman, Harry S, Pres. U.S., 1884-1972. X. Eisenhower,
Dwight David, Pres. U.S., 1890-1969. XI. Hayes, Helen,
1900- XII. Hammarskjöld, Dag, 1905-1961. XIII. Churchill,
Winston Leonard Spencer, 1874-1965. XIV. Kennedy, John
Fitzgerald, Pres. U.S., 1917-1963.

Voice Lib.
M1585 Hays, Wayne L
bd.1 Money - politics. WKAR-AM, February 27,
1974.
15 min. phonotape (1 r. 7 1/2 in. per sec.)

1. Elections. 2. Campaign funds.
3. Saxbe, William B., 1916-

C1
H18 He loved her truly
Whorf, Michael, 1933-
He loved her truly.
1 tape cassette. (The visual sounds of Mike Whorf. History
and heritage, H18)

Originally presented on his radio program, Kaleidoscope,
WJR, Detroit.
Duration: 36 min., 30 sec.
Much has been written about the life, times and experiences of
Abraham Lincoln, but perhaps the nicest part of the truth is the
story of Lincoln and his stepmother, Sarah. Here was the motivation
behind Lincoln's quest for greatness.

1. Lincoln, Sarah Bush Johnston, 1788-1869. 2. Lincoln,
Abraham, Pres. U.S., 1809-1865. I. Title.

C1
SC18 HEART - SURGERY
Whorf, Michael, 1933-
The heart of the matter.
1 tape cassette. (The visual sounds of
Mike Whorf. Science, SC18)
Originally presented on his radio program, Kaleidoscope,
WJR, Detroit.
Duration: 45 min.
Here unfolds the amazing story of the heart, its functions, its
disease, its recuperative powers - of transplants and of the men who
devote their hearts, minds and courage in this tremendous endeavor.

1. Heart - Surgery. I. Title.

C1
H67 Heart of oak, Alexander Hamilton
Whorf, Michael, 1933-
Heart of oak, Alexander Hamilton.
1 tape cassette. (The visual sounds of
Mike Whorf. History and heritage, H67)

Originally presented on his radio program, Kaleidoscope,
WJR, Detroit.
Duration: 43 min., 10 sec.
His gifts of intelligence and wisdom had a dramatic impact
on the young nation. Alexander Hamilton was a man of conviction and
ideals, and his perseverance led to his being referred to as the
man with a heart of oak.

1. Hamilton, Alexander, 1757-1804. I. Title.

The heart of the matter

C1
SC18   Whorf, Michael, 1933-
           The heart of the matter.
           1 tape cassette.   (The visual sounds of
        Mike Whorf.   Science, SC18)
           Originally presented on his radio program, Kaleidoscope,
        WJR, Detroit.
           Duration: 45 min.
           Here unfolds the amazing story of the heart, its functions, its
        disease, its recuperative powers - of transplants and of the men who
        devote their hearts, minds and courage in this tremendous endeavor.

           L Heart - Surgery.   L Title.

Voice Lib.
156   Hemingway, Ernest, 1898-1961.
          Reminiscences of Hemingway by
       unidentified contemporaries.   Voice
       of America, January 8, 1963.
          1 reel (7 in.)   7 1/2 in. per sec.
       phonotape.

Voice Lib.
M1091   Heatter, Gabriel, 1890-1972.
bd.2   Commenting on current news items: Churchill
        and domestic problems; ridiculing foreign aid,
        etc.   Bergman, 1953.
           1 reel (7 in.)   7 1/2 in. per sec.
        phonotape.

Voice Lib.
M1447- Hemingway, Ernest, 1898-1961.
1449   Reminiscences of Ernest Hemingway by
        friends and associates, including several
        actual Hemingway voice segments.   NET,
        November 1, 1970.
           3 reels (7 in.)   7 1/2 in. per sec.
        phonotape.

          Hébert, Felix Edward, 1901-

Voice Lib.
158   Chennault, Claire Lee, 1890-1958.
bd.2   Interview by Congressman Hébert; China's
        political problems.   Private recording,
        July 14, 1949.
           1 reel (7 in.)   7 1/2 in. per sec.
        phonotape.

           I. Hébert, Felix Edward, 1901-

                   HEMOGLOBINOPATHY
Voice Lib.
M1676   Pauling, Linus Carl, 1901-
           Abnormal hemoglobin molecules in relation
        to disease; address at Michigan State
        University.   WKAR, April 21, 1972.
           45 min.   phonotape (1 r.   7 1/2 i.p.s.)

           1. Hemoglobinopathy.

          Hecht, Ben, 1893-1964
Voice Lib.
M275-   Biography in sound (radio program)
276   Alexander Woollcott.   N.B.C., date?
bd.1   2 reels (7 in.)   7 1/2 in. per sec.
        phonotape.
           L Woollcott, Alexander, 1887-1943. L Woollcott, Alexander,
        1887-1943. IL Banghardt, Kenneth   IIL Hecht, Ben, 1893-
        1964. IV. Roosevelt, Eleanor (Roosevelt) 1884-1962. V. Walker,
        Danton   VL Brackett, Charles, 1892-1969. VIL Grant,
        Jane   VIIL Rude, Robert Barnes   IX. West,
        Rebecca, pseud.   X. Henessy, Joseph   XL Letterer,
        Charles   XIL Welles, Orson, 1915-

                  Henderson, Leon, 1895-
Voice Lib.
M273-   Biography in sound (radio program)
274   Franklin Delano Roosevelt: the friends and
bd.1   former associates of Franklin Roosevelt on
        the tenth anniversary of the President's death.
        NBC Radio, April, 1955.
           2 reels (7 in.)   7 1/2 in. per sec.
        phonotape.
           L Roosevelt, Franklin Delano, Pres. U.S., 1882-1945. L
        McIntire, Ross T   1891-   IL Mellett, Lowell, 1884-1960.
        IIL Tully, Grace   IV. Henderson, Leon, 1895-
        V. Roosevelt, Eleanor (Roosevelt) 1884-1962. VL DeGraaf, Albert
        VIL Lehman, Herbert Henry, 1878-1963. VIIL Rosenman, Samuel
        Irving, 1896-   IX. Arvey, Jacob   X. Moley, Raymond,
        1886-   XL Farley, James Aloysius, 1888-   XIL Roosevelt,
                                          (Continued on next card)

Voice Lib.
M1800   Helms, Richard, 1913-
WG   Testimony before the Senate Committee
0802.01- investigating the Watergate Affair.
.02   Pacifica, August 2, 1973.
              225 min.   phonotape (4 r.   3 3/4 i.p.s.)
           (Watergate gavel to gavel, phase 1)

           1. Watergate Affair, 1972-

                  Henessy, Joseph
Voice Lib.
M275-   Biography in sound (radio program)
276   Alexander Woollcott.   N.B.C., date?
bd.1   2 reels (7 in.)   7 1/2 in. per sec.
        phonotape.
           L Woollcott, Alexander, 1887-1943. L Woollcott, Alexander,
        1887-1943. IL Banghardt, Kenneth   IIL Hecht, Ben, 1893-
        1964. IV. Roosevelt, Eleanor (Roosevelt) 1884-1962. V. Walker,
        Danton   VL Brackett, Charles, 1892-1969. VIL Grant,
        Jane   VIIL Rude, Robert Barnes   IX. West,
        Rebecca, pseud.   X. Henessy, Joseph   XL Letterer,
        Charles   XIL Welles, Orson, 1915-

C1
H3
HENRY, PATRICK, 1736-1799

Whorf, Michael, 1933-
The patriot, Patrick Henry.
1 tape cassette.   (The visual sounds of
Mike Whorf. History and heritage, H3)
Originally presented on his radio program, Kaleidoscope,
WJR, Detroit.
Duration: 28 min.
From his humble beginnings - to his days as barrister - to
his appointment in Virginia's House of Burgesses, there was about
him the qualities of the patriot.

1. Henry, Patrick, 1736-1799. L. Title.

Herman, George

Voice Lib.
M1560
bd.1
Proxmire, William
Energy speech; rebuttal to President
Nixon's speech. CBS-TV, December 2, 1973.
12 min. phonotape (1 r. 7 1/2 i.p.s.)

Commentary by Dan Rather and George Herman.

1. Power resources - U.S. I. Rather, Dan.
II. Herman, George.

C1
S34
HENSON, MATTHEW ALEXANDER, 1866-1955

Whorf, Michael, 1933-
Heroes come in many colors, part 4 - The life
of Matthew Henson.
1 tape cassette. (The visual sounds of Mike Whorf. Social, S34)

Originally presented on his radio program, Kaleidoscope,
WJR, Detroit.
Duration: 39 min.
The story of the man who accompanied 'Peary the explorer
to the Pole, and whose adventures and exploits are excitingly
and dramatically related in this documentary on the life and
times of Matthew Henson.

1. Henson, Matthew Alexander, 1866-1955. L. Title.

C1
H66
Hero of the old west, Kit Carson

Whorf, Michael, 1933-
Hero of the old west, Kit Carson.
1 tape cassette. (The visual sounds of
Mike Whorf. History and heritage, H66)

Originally presented on his radio program, Kaleidoscope,
WJR, Detroit.
Duration: 37 min., 30 sec.
Here, set against the background of the American southwest,
are the exploits of Kit Carson, a two-fisted hard-living frontiersman, who was as much at home in the peaceful hills and mountains
of the west as he was skulking and scouting for the U. S. Cavalry.

1. Carson, Christopher, 1809-1868. L. Title.

Voice Lib.
M1489
bd.1
Hepburn, Katharine, 1909-
Speaking at an anti "Un-American Activities"
rally in Hollywood, California. GRV location,
May 19, 1947.
1 reel (7 in.) 7 1/2 in. per sec.
phonotape.

C1
S32
Heroes come in many colors.

Whorf, Michael, 1933-
Heroes come in many colors, part 2; the life
of Phyllis Wheatly.
1 tape cassette. (The visual sounds of Mike Whorf. Social, S32)

Originally presented on his radio program, Kaleidoscope,
WJR, Detroit.
Duration: 31 min., 20 sec.
A gentle, frail, quiet girl who grew up in a Caucasion world
and from the love she was given, expressed her inner feelings in the
form of poetry. She was one of the first of her race to bring to the
western world a genuine, artistic talent.

1. Wheatley, Phillis, afterwards Phillis Peters, 1753?-1784.
L. Title.

C1
PWM8
HERBERT, VICTOR, 1859-1924

Whorf, Michael, 1933-
Victor Herbert.
1 tape cassette.   (The visual sounds of
Mike Whorf. Panorama; a world of music, PWM-8)

Originally presented on his radio program, Kaleidoscope,
WJR, Detroit.
Duration: 25 min.
The life and times of Victor Herbert, including excerpts
of his music.

1. Herbert, Victor, 1859-1924. L. Title.

C1
S33
Heroes come in many colors

Whorf, Michael, 1933-
Heroes come in many colors; part 3 - The life
of Frederick Douglas.
1 tape cassette. (The visual sounds of Mike Whorf. Social, S33)

Originally presented on his radio program, Kaleidoscope,
WJR, Detroit.
Duration: 36 min., 45 sec.
From the heartaches and agonies of slavery came Frederick
Douglass, a giant of a man in mind and spirit, who would express
himself in a manner that no black man had done before.

1. Douglass, Frederick, 1817-1895. L. Title.

Herman, George

Voice Lib.
M1369
bd. 2
"The men who covered Ike". CBS-TV Face the Nation program,
discussing the late General Dwight David Eisenhower, by the
newspaper and TV correspondents. UPI, Merriman Smith;
Newsweek, Kenneth Crawford; Chicago Daily News, Peter
Lisager; AP, Jack Bell; CBS, George Herman, acting as emcee.
CBS-TV, March 30, 1969.
1 reel (7 in.) 7 1/2 i.p.s. phonotape.

1. Eisenhower, Dwight David, Pres. U. S., 1890-1969.
1. Smith, Merriman. II. Crawford, Kenneth. III. Lisager,
Peter. IV. Bell, Jack. V. Herman, George.

C1
S34
Heroes come in many colors.

Whorf, Michael, 1933-
Heroes come in many colors, part 4 - The life
of Matthew Henson.
1 tape cassette. (The visual sounds of Mike Whorf. Social, S34)

Originally presented on his radio program, Kaleidoscope,
WJR, Detroit.
Duration: 39 min.
The story of the man who accompanied 'Peary the explorer
to the Pole, and whose adventures and exploits are excitingly
and dramatically related in this documentary on the life and
times of Matthew Henson.

1. Henson, Matthew Alexander, 1866-1955. L. Title.

Heroes come in many colors.

C1
835   Whorf, Michael, 1933–
          Heroes come in many colors, part 5 – The
        life of Dr. Daniel Williams.
          1 tape cassette. (The visual sounds of
        Mike Whorf. Social, 835)
          Originally presented on his radio program, Kaleidoscope,
        WJR, Detroit.
          Duration: 29 min., 30 sec.
          Years before open heart surgery and names like Barnard and
        DeBakey were household words, the name of Daniel Williams was
        prominent in the theatre of medicine.
          L. Williams, Daniel Hale, 1856–1931. L. Title.

          Hershfield, Harry, 1885–
Voice Lib.
M1047 Old-time radio excerpts of the 1930's and
        1940's, including: Rudy Vallee singing
        "Linger a little longer"; Will Rogers on
        panaceas for the Depression; Bing Crosby
        singing "Sweet Georgia Brown"; Eddie Cantor;
        Jimmy Durante singing "Inka-dinka-do";
        musical skit by Clayton, Jackson and Durante;
        wit by Harry Hershfield; musical selection
        "Thinking of you" by Kay Kyser; Kate Smith
        singing theme song, "When the moon comes over
        the mountain"; W.C. Fields' temperance
          (Continued on next card)

        Hershfield, Harry, 1885–
Voice Lib.
M1047 Old-time radio excerpts of the 1930's and
        1940's...   (Card 2)
          lecture; Al Jolson singing "Rocka-by-your
        baby"; and George Burns and Gracie Allen
        skit. TV&R, 1930's and 1940's.
          1 reel (7 in.) 7 1/2 in. per sec.
          I. Vallee, Rudy, 1901–   II. Rogers, Will, 1879–1935. III.
        Crosby, Bing, 1901–   IV. Cantor, Eddie, 1893–1964. V. Durante,
        Jimmy, 1893–   VI. Clayton, Patti   VII. Jackson,
        Eddie   VIII. Hershfield, Harry, 1885–   IX. Kyser, Kay,
        1906–   X. Smith, Kate, 1909–   XI. Fields, W.C., 1879–
        1946. XII. Jolson, Al, 1886–1950. XIII. Burns, George, 1896–
        XIV. Allen, Fracie, 1906–

Voice Lib.
M1003 Hess, Rudolf, 1894–
bd.1   Address to Nazi S.A. groups warning them
        not to continue their revolutionary tactics
        as they did during the period of the Weimar
        Republic. Peteler, June 25, 1934.
          1 reel (7 in.) 7 1/2 in. per sec.
        phonotape.

          1. Germany – Politics and government –
        1933–1945.

Voice Lib.
M1003 Hess, Rudolf, 1894–
bd.2   Conciliatory remarks to S.A. group following
        Hitler's smashing of seditious activities
        as practiced by Ernst Roehm. Peteler,
        July 8, 1934.
          1 reel (7 in.) 7 1/2 in. per sec.
        phonotape.

          1. Germany – Politics and government – 1933–
        1945.

        Hess, Rudolf, 1894–
Voice Lib.
M961   Schirach, Baldur von, 1907–
bd.7   Propaganda speech excerpt to Hitler Youth
        Group; also excerpts by Rudolf Hess and
        Hartmann Lauterbach. German Radio, Peteler,
        April 4, 1934; January 1, 1935.
          1 reel (7 in.) 7 1/2 in. per sec.
        phonotape.

          I. Hess, Rudolf, 1894–   II.
        Lauterbach, Hartmann

        HESS, RUDOLF, 1894–
Voice Lib.
M1071 German radio (Nazi controlled)
bd.18   Nazi radio news item speculating on the
        fate of Rudolf Hess, who disappeared while
        in flight, disobeying Hitler's order not to
        fly. Peteler, May 12, 1941.
          1 reel (7 in.) 7 1/2 in. per sec.
        phonotape.

          1. Hess, Rudolf, 1894–

Voice Lib. Heston, Charlton, 1924–
M669–   The legend of Cecil B. DeMille. Yul
670   Brynner, Charlton Heston, Bob Hope, Betty
        Hutton, Edward G. Robinson, Barbara Stanwyck,
        James Stewart, Gloria Swanson, Cornel
        Wilde, Samuel Goldwyn, Billy Graham, Cecil
        B. DeMille. Recorded 1963.
          2 reels (7 in.) 7 1/2 in. per sec. phonotape.
          I. DeMille, Cecil Blount, 1881–1959. I. Brynner, Yul, 1917–
        II. Heston, Charlton, 1924– III. Hope, Bob, 1903–   IV.
        Hutton, Betty, 1921–   V. Robinson, Edward G   1893–1973.
        VI. Stanwyck, Barbara, 1907–   VII. Stewart, James Maitland,
        1908–   VIII. Swanson, Gloria, 1899– IX. Wilde, Cornel, 1915–
        X. Goldwyn, Samuel, 1884–   XI. Graham, William Franklin,
        1918–   XII. DeMille, Cecil Blount, 1881–1959.

Voice Lib. Heston, Charlton, 1924–
M310   American Broadcasting Company.
          Tribute to President John Fitzgerald Kennedy
        from the arts. Fredric March emcees; Jerome
        Hines sings "Worship of God and Nature" by
        Beethoven; Florence Eldridge recites "When
        lilacs last in the door-yard bloom'd" by Walt
        Whitman; Marian Anderson in two songs. Includes
        Charlton Heston, Sidney Blackmer, Isaac Stern,
        Nathan Milstein, Christopher Plummer, Albert
        Finney. ABC, November 24, 1963.
          55 min. phonotape (7 in. 7 1/2 i.p.s.)
          (Continued on next card)

Voice Lib. Heston, Charlton, 1924–
M1097 Bogart, Humphrey, 1899–1957.
          A biographical documentary program about the
        career of Humphrey Bogart by Flaum-Grimberg
        Productions, including various sequences from
        his motion pictures and comments by his former
        associates, co-ordinated by Charlton Heston.
        ABC-TV, April 23, 1967.
          1 reel (7 in.) 7 1/2 in. per sec.
        phonotape.
          I. Bogart, Humphrey, 1899–1957. I. Heston, Charlton, 1924–

Voice Lib.
172-   Heywood, Alan S
173   Berlin Documentary.   AFL-CIO (P.R.O.),
         July, 1952.
         2 reels (7 in.)   7 1/2 in. per sec.
         phonotape.

                Hicks, George
Voice Lib.
572-   I can hear it now (radio program)
573   1933-1946.   CBS, 1948.
bd.1   2 reels (7 in.)   7 1/2 in. per sec.
         phonotape.
         I. Murrow, Edward Roscoe, 1908-1965. II. LaGuardia, Fiorello
         Henry, 1882-1947. III. Chamberlain, Neville, 1869-1949. IV.
         Roosevelt, Franklin Delano, Pres. U. S., 1882-1945. V. Churchill,
         Winston Leonard Spencer, 1874-1965. VI. Gaulle, Charles de,
         Pres. France, 1890-1970. VII. Eisenhower, Dwight David, Pres. U. S.,
         1890-1969. VIII. Willkie, Wendell Lewis, 1892-1944. IX. Martin,
         Joseph William, 1884-1968. X. Elizabeth II, Queen of Great Britain,
         1926-   XI. Margaret Rose, Princess of Gt. Brit., 1930-   XII.
         Johnson, Hugh Samuel, 188?   42. XIII. Smith, Alfred Emanuel,
         1873-1944. XIV. Lindbergh   arles Augustus, 1902-   XV. Davis,
                            (Continued on next card)

                Hicks, George
Voice Lib.
M1490 Republican Party. National Convention, 25th,
bd.5   Chicago, 1952.
          Description of proceedings at Republican
       National Convention in Chicago, 1952
       (described by commentators George Hicks and
       H.V. Kaltenborn). Includes statements by
       Robert A. Taft and Dwight D. Eisenhower.
       Convention unanimously nominates Eisenhower.
       CBS Radio, 1952.
          1 reel (7 in.)   7 1/2 in. per sec.
       phonotape.

Voice Lib.
M764   Higgins, Joe
bd.7   Excerpt from "The World of Wax" (Program
       8); comments on what the record store was
       like in the early days as compared to today.
       Westinghouse Broadcasting Corporation, 1964.
          1 reel (7 in.)   7 1/2 in. per sec.
       phonotape.   (The Music Goes Round and Round)

          I. Title: The world of wax. II. Series.

Voice Lib.
M1503 Higher education: who needs it? Hughes Rudd
       in a one-hour documentary on employment
       problems of college graduates. CBS-TV,
       May 26, 1972.
          1 reel (7 in.)   7 1/2 in. per sec.
       phonotape.

          1. Education, Higher. 2. Labor supply.
       I. Rudd, Hughes.

Voice Lib.
M707   Hildegarde, 1906-
bd.2   "Hildegarde Show"; radio variety show.
       Melchior collection, April 3, 1946.
          1 reel (7 in.)   7 1/2 in. per sec.
       phonotape.

                Hill, Hugh
Voice Lib.
243   Leopold, Nathan Freudenthal, 1904 or 5-
bd.7   defendant.
          Leopold speaks on his parole denial;
       interviewed by Hugh Hill, WBBM (Chicago).
       CBS Radio, July 31, 1957.
          1 reel (7 in.)   7 1/2 in. per sec.
       phonotape.

          I. Hill, Hugh

                Hill, Hugh
Voice Lib.
243   Stratton, William Grant, 1914-
bd.5   Denial of parole to Nathan Leopold, with
       Hugh Hill of WBBM (Chicago). CBS, July 30,
       1957.
          1 reel (7 in.)   7 1/2 in. per sec.
       phonotape.

          1. Leopold, Nathan Freudenthal, 1904 or 5-
             defendant. I. Hill, Hugh

          HILL, CAPTAIN WILLIAM
C1
FA9   Whorf, Michael, 1933-
          Colonel William Hill.
          1 tape cassette.   (The visual sounds of
       Mike Whorf. The forgotten American, FA9)

          Originally presented on his radio program, Kaleidoscope,
       WJR, Detroit.
          Duration: 10 min., 5 sec.
          An American civilian in time of war, he was a member of
       the Revolutionary Army of General Sumter. He built the first
       iron forge south of Virginia.

          I. Hill, Captain William. L. Title.

Voice Lib.
M793   Hilliard, Robert
bd.3   American actor in scenes from "A Fool
       There Was", Hilliard's famous success.
       Victor, 1912.
          1 reel (7 in.)   7 1/2 in. per sec.
       phonotape.

          I. Title: A fool there was.

Voice Lib.
M793   Hilliard, Robert
bd.2   "The littlest girl"; acted and dramatized
        by Hilliard from Richard Harding Davis'
        story "Her first appearance". Victor, 1912.
        8 min., 52 sec. phonotape (1 r.   7 1/2
        i.p.s.)

            I. Title. II. Davis, Richard Harding,
        1864-1916.

Voice Lib.
M793   Hilliard, Robert
cd.4   American actor in "Christmas Day at the
        Workhouse". Victor, 1913.
        1 reel (7 in.) 7 1/2 in. per sec.
        phonotape.

            I. Title: Christmas day at the workhouse.

Voice Lib.
M1375   Himmler, Heinrich, 1900-1945.
bd.2   Speaking to Storm Troop leaders in Frankfurt
        am Main. Peteler, June 11, 1933.
        1 reel (7 in.) 7 1/2 in. per sec.
        phonotape.

            1. Germany - Politics and government - 1933-
        1945.

Voice Lib.
M1010   Himmler, Heinrich, 1900-1945.
bd.3   Talk to Nazi police officers stressing
        importance of suppressing sex offenders.
        Peteler, January 15, 1937.
        1 reel (7 in.) 7 1/2 in. per sec.
        phonotape.

Voice Lib.
M1356   Himmler, Heinrich, 1900-1945.
bd.4   Speaking to S.S. leaders in Posen, Poland.
        April 10, 1943.
        1 reel (7 in.) 7 1/2 in. per sec.
        phonotape.

Voice Lib.
M1357   Himmler, Heinrich, 1900-1945.
bd.6   Talking to district leaders of Nazi Party
        in Poland. Peteler, August 3, 1944.
        1 reel (7 in.) 7 1/2 in. per sec.
        phonotape.

Voice Lib.
M1358   Himmler, Heinrich, 1900-1945.
bd.3   Speaking to the Nazi leaders in Warthegau.
        Peteler, November, 1944.
        1 reel (7 in.) 7 1/2 in. per sec.
        phonotape.

Voice Lib.
M1358   Himmler, Heinrich, 1900-1945.
bd.2   Reading a passage from the Fuehrer to
        the old comrades of the Munich beer cellar.
        Peteler, November 8, 1944.
        1 reel (7 in.) 7 1/2 in. per sec.
        phonotape.

Voice Lib.
M1466   Hindenburg, Paul von, pres. Germany, 1847-
bd.2   1934.
            Order of the day to the troops of the
        German 8th Army. Peteler, August 31, 1914.
        1 reel (7 in.) 7 1/2 in. per sec.
        phonotape.

Voice Lib.
M952   Hindenburg, Paul von, Pres. Germany, 1847-
bd.13   1934.
            Order of the day to the German 8th Army.
        Peteler, August 31, 1915.
        1 reel (7 in.) 7 1/2 in. per sec.
        phonotape.

Voice Lib.
M1466 Hindenburg, Paul von, pres. Germany, 1847-
bd.11   1934.
     Remarks of appreciation about the honors
paid to him on the occasion of his 70th
birthday. Peteler, October 17, 1917.
     1 reel (7 in.)   7 1/2 in. per sec.
phonotape.

Voice Lib.
M1363 Hindenberg, Paul von, Pres. Germany, 1847-1934.
bd.4   New York oration. Peteler, January 1,
1932.
     1 reel (7 in.)   7 1/2 in. per sec.
phonotape.

Voice Lib.
M1470 Hindenburg, Paul von, Pres. Germany, 1847-
bd.6   1934.
     On the occasion of German presidential
elections; why he will again accept the
post. Peteler, February 16, 1932.
     1 reel (7 in.)   7 1/2 in. per sec.
phonotape.

Voice Lib.
M960 Hindenburg, Paul von, Pres. Germany, 1847-
bd.5   1934.
     Thanking the German people for their
messages of good wishes on his 85th birthday. Peteler, October 3, 1932.
     1 reel (7 in.)   7 1/2 in. per sec.
phonotape.

Voice Lib.
M952 Hindenburg, Paul von, Pres. Germany, 1847-
bd.10   1934.
     Excerpt of remarks in the German Reichstag
on the occasion of "Tag von Potsdam",
wishing Chancellor Hitler god-speed.
Peteler, March 21, 1933.
     1 reel (7 in.)   7 1/2 in. per sec.
phonotape.

HINDENBURG, PAUL VON, PRES. GERMANY,
Voice Lib.   1847-1934
M1003 Goebbels, Joseph, 1897-1945.
bd.4   Speaking on German radio upon the death
of Reichspresident Paul von Hindenberg, and
giving Nazi-oriented eulogy. Peteler,
August 2, 1934.
     1 reel (7 in.)   7 1/2 in. per sec.
phonotape.

     1. Hindenburg, Paul von, Pres. Germany,
1847-1934.

Voice Lib. Hines, Jerome, 1921-
M310 American Broadcasting Company.
     Tribute to President John Fitzgerald Kennedy
from the arts. Fredric March emcees; Jerome
Hines sings "Worship of God and Nature" by
Beethoven; Florence Eldridge recites "When
lilacs last in the door-yard bloom'd" by Walt
Whitman; Marian Anderson in two songs. Includes
Charlton Heston, Sidney Blackmer, Isaac Stern,
Nathan Milstein, Christopher Plummer, Albert
Finney. ABC, November 24, 1963.
     35 min. phonotape (7 in.   7 1/2 i.p.s.)
(Continued on next card)

Voice Lib. HIPPIES
M1262 Hagen, Carlos
bd.2   Interviews by Carlos Hagen and Lawrence
Lipton with hippies in Golden Gate Park,
at summer happening; includes chants.
Hagen, June, 1967.
     1 reel (7 in.)   7 1/2 in. per sec.
phonotape.

     1. Lipton, Lawrence, 1898-

Voice Lib. HIPPIES
M1261- Hagen, Carlos
1262   Two weeks in Haight-Ashbury district of
bd.1   San Francisco by Lawrence Lipton and Carlos
Hagen, recording hippie music and philosophy,
including interview with a priest. June,
1967.
     2 reels (7 in.)   7 1/2 in. per sec.
phonotape.

     1. Lipton, Lawrence, 1898-

HIPPIES
Voice Lib.
M1272 Reasoner, Harry, 1923-
bd.1   Documentary program about the "Hippie
Temptation"; includes interviews with hippies,
doctors, parents, patients, police,
psychiatrists and discussion about use of
LSD. Recorded on location. CBS-TV,
August 22, 1967.
     1 reel (7 in.)   7 1/2 in. per sec.
phonotape.

Hiss, Alger, 1904–
Voice Lib.
573   I can hear it now (radio program)
bd.2–   1945–1949.   CBS, 1950?
574   2 reels (7 in.)   7 1/2 in. per sec.
bd.1   phonotape.
    L. Murrow, Edward Roscoe, 1908–1965. IL Nehru, Jawaharlal,
    1889–1964. III. Philip, duke of Edinburgh, 1921– IV. Elizabeth II,
    Queen of Great Britain, 1926– V. Ferguson, Homer, 1889– VL
    Hughes, Howard Robard, 1905– VII. Marshall, George Catlett,
    1880– VIII. Ruth, George Herman, 1895–1948. IX. Lilienthal,
    David Eli, 1899– X. Trout, Robert, 1908– XL Gage, Arthur.
    XII. Jackson, Robert Houghwout, 1892–1954. XIII. Gromyko, Ana-
    tolii Andreevich, 1908– XIV. Baruch, Bernard Mannes, 1870–
    1965. XV. Churchill, Winston Leonard Spencer, 1874–1965. XVI.
    Winchell, Walter, 1897–19 XVII. Davis, Elmer Holmes, 1890–
    (Continued on next card)

Voice Lib.   Hitchcock, Alfred Joseph, 1899–
M1037   Biography in sound (radio program)
bd.1   "The Actor", narrated by Morgan Beatty.
    Cast includes Tallulah Bankhead, Hy Gardner,
    Rocky Graziano, Arthur Miller, Uta Hagen,
    Jackie Cooper, Sir Laurence Olivier, Gad
    Gayther, Barbara Ashley, Hortense Powdermaker,
    Peter Ustinov, Alfred Hitchcock, Leonard Lyons,
    John Guston, Helen Hayes, Dick Mayne, Ralph
    Bellamy, Lionel Barrymore, Sir Ralph Richardson,
    José Ferrer, and Walter Kerr.   NBC Radio, 1950's.
    1 reel (7 in.)   7 1/2 in. per sec.
    phonotape.
                    (Continued on next card)

HISTORY – YEARBOOKS – 1940
Voice Lib.
M1052   Twelve crowded months; 1940 year-end CBS
    radio correspondents' review of the events
    of the year.   CBS Radio, December 29, 1940.
    1 reel (7 in.)   7 1/2 i.p.s.   phonotape.

    1. History – Yearbooks – 1940.

Voice Lib.
M1090   Hitchcock, Raymond
bd.5   Re-recording of 78 rpm phonodisc of
    comedian Raymond Hitchcock singing "Wal I
    Swan" (Ebenezer Frye).   Columbia, 1919.
    1 reel (7 in.)   7 1/2 in. per sec.
    phonotape.

Voice Lib.   HISTORY – YEARBOOKS – 1959
M566–   Columbia Broadcasting System, Inc.
567   The big news of 1959.   CBS, 1960.
    2 reels (7 in.)   7 1/2 i.p.s.   phonotape.

    1. History – Yearbooks – 1959.

Voice Lib.
M980   Hitler, Adolf, 1889–1945.
bd.2   Appeal for votes to the German public.
    Description of Nazi aims and its causes.
    Peteler, 1932.
    1 reel (7 in.)   7 1/2 in. per sec.
    phonotape.

    1. National socialism

Voice Lib.
667   History speaks; excerpts of voices with
bd.1   narration; copied from NVL l.p. phonograph
    record "Hark ! the Years", side 1.   Carlos
    Hagen, 1964.
    1 reel (7 in.)   7 1/2 in. per sec.
    phonotape.

Voice Lib.
539   Hitler, Adolf, 1889–1945.
bd.1   Reviews German problems following World War
    I; decries unemployment, fate of German
    peasants and lack of money; attacks government
    for turning various factions against each
    other; outlines German problems following World
    War I; complains about injustice of Versailles;
    offers ideas on how to improve conditions and
    raise Germany; promises to make Germany a free
    nation.   Telefunken recording, 1932.
    1 reel (7 in.)   7 1/2 in. per sec.   phonotape.
    In German.

C1
SC5   History's first modern
    Whorf, Michael, 1933–
    History's first modern.
    1 tape cassette.   (The visual sounds of
    Mike Whorf.   Science, SC5)

    Originally presented of his radio program, Kaleidoscope,
    WJR, Detroit.
    Duration: 37 min., 5 sec.
    His world in Italy, his life as a boy and young man, his
    exploits and endeavors as a mature man are given generous
    attention in this account of Leonardo da Vinci.

    L. Leonardo da Vinci, 1452–1519.   L. Title.

Voice Lib.
M980   Hitler, Adolf, 1889–1945.
bd.8–   Radio address to the public of Third
981   Reich on the assumption of power by the
bd.1   Nazi regime.   German Radio, Peteler,
    January 30, 1933.
    2 reels (7 in.)   7 1/2 in. per sec.
    phonotape.

    In German.

    1. Germany – Politics and government –
    1933–1945

Voice Lib.
M1363 Hitler, Adolf, 1889-1945.
bd.11   Installation of NSDAP and other political
       parties. Peteler, 1933.
           1 reel (7 in.)   7 1/2 in. per sec.
       phonotape.

Voice Lib.
M980   Hitler, Adolf, 1889-1945.
bd.6   Excerpt of Hitler's appeal for votes to
       Nazi Party at mass meeting in "Lustgarten".
       Berlin, Peteler, January 30, 1933.
           1 reel (7 in.)   7 1/2 in. per sec.
       phonotape.

Voice Lib.
M981   Hitler, Adolf, 1889-1945.
bd.2   Excerpt of speech at Town Hall in Stuttgart,
       Germany. German Radio, Peteler, February 15,
       1933.
           1 reel (7 in.)   7 1/2 in. per sec.
       phonotape.

Voice Lib.
M981   Hitler, Adolf, 1889-1945.
bd.4   Excerpt of statement at Garrison's Church
       in Potsdam upon assuming post as
       Reichschancellor. Peteler, March 21, 1933.
           1 reel (7 in.)   7 1/2 in. per sec.
       phonotape.

Voice Lib.
M952   Hitler, Adolf, 1889-1945.
bd.11   Replying to President von Hindenburg in
       the German Reichstag and discussing his plans
       for the future of Germany. Peteler, March 21,
       1933.
           1 reel (7 in.)   7 1/2 in. per sec.
       phonotape.

           1. Germany - Politics and government - 1933-
       1945.

Voice Lib.
M999- Hitler, Adolf, 1889-1945.
1000   Speech at session of German Reichstag
bd.1   stating Nazi policies, including discussions
       of same. Requesting Reichstag for overall
       power in government. Peteler, March 23, 1933.
           2 reels (7 in.)   7 1/2 in. per sec.
       phonotape.

           1. Germany - Politics and government -
       1933-1945.

Voice Lib.
M1001 Hitler, Adolf, 1889-1945.
bd.1   Second address at German Reichstag session
       of 1933 replying to Social Democratic
       opponents and attacking their political
       policies. Peteler, March 23, 1933.
           1 reel (7 in.)   7 1/2 in. per sec.
       phonotape.

Voice Lib.
M999   Hitler, Adolf, 1889-1945.
           Speech at session of German Reichstag
       stating Nazi policies, including discussions
       of same. Requesting Reichstag for overall
       power in government. Peteler, March 23,
       1933.
           1 reel (7 in.)   7 1/2 in. per sec.
       phonotape.

           1. National socialism.

Voice Lib.
M1375 Hitler, Adolf, 1889-1945.
bd.2   Tenth anniversary celebration of Munich
       "Putsch" of November 11, held at the Sieman
       factory in Berlin. Peteler, November 8,
       1933.
           1 reel (7 in.)   7 1/2 in. per sec.
       phonotape.

Voice Lib.
M1375 Hitler, Adolf, 1889-1945.
bd.3   Address pertaining to the procedure for the
       Christian churches. Peteler, January 20,
       1934.
           1 reel (7 in.)   7 1/2 in. per sec.
       phonotape.

Voice Lib.
M1375 Hitler,Adolf, 1889 -1945.
bd.5   Excerpt of speech to German students.
Peteler, February 7, 1934.
        1 reel (7 in.)   7 1/2 in. per sec.
phonotape.

Voice Lib.
M1004 Hitler, Adolf, 1°89-1945.
bd.1   Address to huge German Youth group in
Berlin "Lustgarten", stating that German
public is now adopting Nazi philosophy,
and urging youth to uphold and advance
these policies for the future.   Peteler,
May 1, 1935.
        1 reel (7 in.)   7 1/2 in. per sec.
phonotape.

        1. National socialism

Voice Lib.
M1002 Hitler, Adolf, 1889-1945.
bd.5   Address to the workers at initial Nazi
highway construction project near Munich,
Germany, stressing that the project is a
great aid to unemployment. F. Peteler,
March 21, 1934.
        1 reel (7 in.)   7 1/2 in. per sec.
phonotape.

Voice Lib.
M1004 Hitler, Adolf, 1889-1945.
bd.3-3 Address to the German nation on the occasion
of May Day celebration at Tempelhof Field,
Berlin. Peteler, May 1, 1935.
        1 reel (7 in.)   7 1/2 in. per sec.
phonotape.

Voice Lib.
M1002 Hitler, Adolf, 1889-1945.
bd.7   Address to DAF, second workers conference,
stressing the necessity of perseverance in
spite of obstacles, in order to attain
success. F. Peteler, May 16, 1934.
        1 reel (7 in.)   7 1/2 in. per sec.
phonotape.

        1. National socialism

Voice Lib.
M1007 Hitler, Adolf, 1889-1945.
bd.4-D- Address to Reichstag justifying policy of
1009 re-armament and defending democratic principles
in Germany; his peaceful intentions; commending
Woodrow Wilson's ideals, which were not followed
by Allied victors; stating that Allied victors
did not adhere to treaty obligations by dis-
arming, thus Germany is not bound by same rules;
also comparing difference between German
National Socialists and Bolshevism. Peteler,
May 21, 1935.
        3 reels (7 in.)   7 1/2 in. per sec. phonotape.

Voice Lib.
M1003 Hitler, Adolf, 1889-1945.
bd.3   Address in German Reichstag defending his
position in liquidating the disloyal S.A.
groups and their leader, Ernst Roehm.
Peteler,   July 13, 1934.
        1 reel (7 in.)   7 1/2 in. per sec.
phonotape.

        1. Germany - Politics and government -
1933-1945

Voice Lib.
M1376 Hitler, Adolf, 1889-1945.
bd.1   Election speech in Munich. Peteler,
March 14, 1936.
        1 reel (7 in.)   7 1/2 in. per sec.
phonotape.

Voice Lib.
M1003 Hitler, Adolf, 1889-1945.
bd.6   Address to people in city of Hamburg,
appealing for their efforts to advance
Nazi aims. Peteler, August 17, 1934.
        1 reel (7 in.)   7 1/2 in. per sec.
phonotape.

Voice Lib.
M1376 Hitler, Adolf, 1889-1945.
bd.2   Election speech in Cologne. Peteler,
March 28, 1936.
        1 reel (7 in.)   7 1/2 in. per sec.
phonotape.

Voice Lib.
M1376   Hitler, Adolf, 1889-1945.
bd.6   Speaking at a state function.   Peteler,
         May 1, 1936.
            1 reel (7 in.)   7 1/2 in. per sec.
         phonotape.

            1. Germany - Politics and government -
         1933-1945.

Voice Lib.
M1010   Hitler, Adolf, 1889-1945.
bd.7   Speech at Munich regarding referendum on
         a greater Germany.   Peteler, April 3, 1938.
            1 reel (7 in.)   7 1/2 in. per sec.
         phonotape.

Voice Lib.
M1376   Hitler, Adolf, 1889-1945.
bd.5   Speaking to the Hitler Youth on May Day.
         Peteler, May 1, 1936.
            1 reel (7 in.)   7 1/2 in. per sec.
         phonotape.

Voice Lib.
M953   Hitler, Adolf, 1889-1945.
bd.5   Ceremonies in Nuremberg, Germany at the
         Reichsparteitag of the Nazi Party. Commentary
         and interpretation by Ned Kalmer, CBS news
         correspondent, on-the-spot.   Peteler,
         September, 1938.
            1 reel (7 in.)   7 1/2 in. per sec.
         phonotape.

            I. Kalmer, Ned

Voice Lib.
M1376   Hitler, Adolf, 1889-1945.
bd.10   Speaking at the Party Day celebration
         at Nuremberg. Peteler, September 13,
         1936.
            1 reel (7 in.)   7 1/2 in. per sec.
         phonotape.

            1. Germany - Politics and government -
         1933-1945.

Voice Lib.
M736   Hitler, Adolf, 1889-1945.
bd.3   Speaking about his conferences with British
         Prime Minister Chamberlain.   CBS, September 26,
         1938.
            1 reel (7 in.)   7 1/2 in. per sec.
         phonotape.

Voice Lib.
M953   Hitler, Adolf, 1889-1945.
bd.4   Excerpt of his speech in Vienna on the
         occasion of the annexation of Austria
         to Greater Germany. English commentary by
         the BBC.   Peteler, March 12, 1938.
            1 reel (7 in.)   7 1/2 in. per sec.
         phonotape.

Voice Lib.
M736   Hitler, Adolf, 1889-1945.
bd.12   Acknowledges his debt to Prime Minister
         Chamberlain, and assures the world of German
         desire for peace; just wanting to solve
         Sudeten problem.   CBS, September 29, 1938.
            1 reel (7 in.)   7 1/2 in. per sec.
         phonotape.

Voice Lib.
M1010   Hitler, Adolf, 1889-1945.
bd.8   Presentation to German press representatives
         about how to report and interpret the news,
         also stressing propaganda methods to
         enthuse the public. Peteler, March 19 &
         23, 1938.
            1 reel (7 in.)   7 1/2 i.p.s.   phonotape.

            1. Propaganda.

Voice Lib.
M1016   Hitler, Adolf, 1889-1945.
bd.2   Speech to Nazi Press Corps, stressing
         necessity to prepare German public toward
         the use of force in attaining their goals
         declared at the "Fuehrerbau" in Munich.
         F. Peteler, November 10, 1938.
            1 reel (7 in.)   7 1/2 in. per sec.
         phonotape.

Voice Lib.
M1016 Hitler, Adolf, 1889-1945.
bd.3   Speech pertaining to the education of
German youth, pointing out necessity of
changing allegiance from family loyalty to
Nazi cause, by compelling them to join
Hitler Youth groups of all ages. F. Peteler,
December 2, 1938.
     1 reel (7 in.)   7 1/2 in. per sec.
phonotape.

Voice Lib.
M1016 Hitler, Adolf, 1889-1945.
bd.15   Excerpt of speech at opening of the
"Grosse Deutsche Kunstaustellung" art
exhibition in Munich, demanding that the
talent of German artists be used in the
service of Nazi politics. F. Peteler,
July 16, 1939.
     1 reel (7 in.)   7 1/2 in. per sec.
phonotape.

Voice Lib.
M1016 Hitler, Adolf, 1889-1945.
bd.4   Address to Officer's School class, who
were visiting the Chancellery in Berlin,
pertaining to the use of the sword to
attain desired goals. F. Peteler, January
25, 1939.
     1 reel (7 in.)   7 1/2 in. per sec.
phonotape.

Voice Lib.
M736 Hitler, Adolf, 1890-1945.
bd.10   Announcing his intention to solve the
corridor and Polish problem. CBS,
September 1, 1939.
     1 reel (7 in.)   7 1/2 in. per sec.
phonotape.

Voice Lib.
M1016 Hitler, Adolf, 1889-1945.
bd.5   Speech at launching ceremonies of battleship
"Bismarck" in the harbor of Hamburg, Germany.
F. Peteler, February 14, 1939.
     1 reel (7 in.)   7 1/2 in. per sec.
phonotape.

Voice Lib.
216-   Hitler, Adolph, 1889-1945.
217   Speech before German Parliament,
announcing annexation of Danzig, with
introduction by Hermann Göring and comments
by Hans Fritsche (English translation).
Detroit, WJR, September 1, 1939.
     2 reels (7 in.)   7 1/2 in. per sec.
phonotape.
     I. Göring, Hermann, 1893-1946.   II. Fritsche,
Hans

Voice Lib.
M1016   Hitler, Adolf, 1889-1945.
bd.10   Excerpt of address at Reichstag pertaining
to message from President Roosevelt, observing
that American press should desist its war-
mongering agitation so that all problems can
be peacefully resolved. F. Peteler,
April 28, 1939.
     1 reel (7 in.)   7 1/2 i.p.s.   phonotape.

     1. Germany - Foreign relations.

Voice Lib.
M1017 Hitler, Adolf, 1889-1945.
bd.2   Various excerpts of addresses in German
Reichstag after the Nazi invasion of Poland,
mentioning pact with U.S.S.R. and the
collapse of British negotiations, saying he
is the "first soldier of Germany" and will
be victorious or die. Peteler, September 1,
1939.
     1 reel (7 in.)   7 1/2 in. per sec.
phonotape.

Voice Lib.
M1016 Hitler, Adolf, 1889-1945.
bd.12   Excerpt of address to returning German
troops from Spain, commending their valiant
action in the Spanish Civil War. F. Peteler,
June 6, 1939.
     1 reel (7 in.)   7 1/2 in. per sec.
phonotape.

Voice Lib.
M715 Hitler, Adolf, 1889-1945.
bd.2   Address to the Reichstag about German
victory over Poland.   September, 1939.
     1 reel (7 in.)   7 1/2 in. per sec.
phonotape.

Voice Lib.
M1017 Hitler, Adolf, 1889-1945.
bd.4-   Being introduced by Albert Forster upon
1018   arrival in the city of Danzig, followed by
bd.1   lengthy address by Hitler; stresses unity
between U.S.S.R. and Germany against
democracies, inferiority of Polish people,
and their persecution of Germans. F. Peteler,
September 19, 1939.
   2 reels (7 in.) 7 1/2 in. per sec.
phonotape.
   I. Forster, Albert.

Voice Lib.
M1071 Hitler, Adolf, 1889-1945.
bd.1   Excerpt of remarks made at opening of
the first winter welfare program for German
public. Peteler, September 4, 1940.
   1 reel (7 in.) 7 1/2 in. per sec.
phonotape.

Voice Lib.
M1018 Hitler, Adolf, 1889-1945.
bd.5   Speaking to Nazi Party colleagues about
the breach of faith by Britain. Peteler,
November 8, 1939.
   1 reel (7 in.) 7 1/2 in. per sec.
phonotape.

Voice Lib.
M1071 Hitler, Adolf, 1889-1945.
bd.4   Excerpt of speech to members of the SS,
stressing the survival of the fittest.
Peteler, December 24, 1940.
   1 reel (7 in.) 7 1/2 in. per sec.
phonotape.

Voice Lib.
M1019 Hitler, Adolf, 1889-1945.
bd.9   Excerpt from address at May Day celebration
welcoming Mussolini to Berlin. Peteler,
May 1, 1940.
   1 reel (7 in.) 7 1/2 in. per sec.
phonotape.

Voice Lib.
M1071 Hitler, Adolf, 1889-1945.
bd.17   Excerpt of speech in Reichstag pertaining
to Nazi military objectives in the Balkans.
Peteler, May 4, 1941.
   1 reel (7 in.) 7 1/2 in. per sec.
phonotape.

Voice Lib.
527-   Hitler, Adolf, 1889-1945.
529   Final major Reichstag speech: offering
bd.1   Britain final opportunity for peace; denies he
desired war; blames England for causing war
through her economic power; reviews origin of
war; Versailles was untenable; Jews spread
poison; Polish problem; secret documents of
Allied Council proved them warmongers; have
fought overwhelming odds; inadequacy of
British forces; summarizes military aspects of
war to date; notes destruction of main body of
French troops; names leaders; praises troops;
   (Continued on next card)

Voice Lib.
M1300 Hitler, Adolf, 1889-1945.
bd.3   Address at inauguration of war relief
work in the winter of 1941. Peteler,
October, 1941.
   1 reel (7 in.) 7 1/2 in. per sec.
phonotape.

Voice Lib.
527-   Hitler, Adolf, 1889-1945. Final major
529   Reichstag speech... 1940. (Card 2)
bd.1
   praises Hess, Goebbels, Ribbentrop, Göring;
promotes Göring; alliance with Italy; asked
only peace of Britain and France; great empire
will be destroyed; humiliation of World War I
defeat erased. CBS, July 19, 1940.
   3 reels (7 in.) 7 1/2 in. per sec.
phonotape.

Voice Lib.
M1023 Hitler, Adolf, 1889-1945.
bd.23   Excerpt of speech in Berlin Sportpalast
about German victories in Russia. Peteler,
October 3, 1941.
   1 reel (7 in.) 7 1/2 in. per sec.
phonotape.

Voice Lib.
M1304 Hitler, Adolf, 1889-1945.
bd.10   Talking about the Nordic-German woman.
      Peteler, 1942.
        1 reel (7 in.)   7 1/2 in. per sec.
      phonotape.

Voice Lib.
M1358 Hitler, Adolf, 1889-1945.
bd.5   Last radio address. Peteler, January 30,
      1945.
        1 reel (7 in.)   7 1/2 in. per sec.
      phonotape.

Voice Lib.
M961 Hitler, Adolf, 1889-1945.
bd.5   Excerpts of talks to German officers'
      school. German Radio, June 21, 1942.
        1 reel (7 in.)   7 1/2 in. per sec.
      phonotape.

          Hitler, Adolf, 1889-1945
Voice Lib.
M619   Radio in the 1930's (Part II): a series of
bd.1-   excerpts of the 1930's; a sample of radio
14   of the period. NVL, April, 1964.
          1 reel (7 in.) 7 1/2 in. per sec. phonotape.
      L. Allen, Fred, 1894-1956. II. Delmar, Kenny   III. Donald,
      Peter   IV. Pious, Minerva   V. Fennelly, Parker   VI.
      Boyer, Charles, 1899-   VII. Dunne, Irene, 1904-   VIII.
      DeMille, Cecil Blount, 1881-1959. IX. West, Mae, 1893-   X.
      Dafoe, Allan Ray, 1883-1943. XI. Ortega,
      Santos   XIII. War of the worlds (radio program) XIV. Ives, Burl,
      1909-   XV. Robinson, Earl, 1910-   XVI. Temple, Shirley,
      1928-   XVII. Earhart, Amelia, 1898-1937. XVIII. Lawrence,
      Gertrude, 1901-1952. XIX. Cohan, George Michael, 1878-1942.
      XX. Shaw, George Bernard, 1856-1950. XXI. Hitler, Adolf, 1889-
      1945. XXII. Chamberlain, Neville, 1869-1940. XXIII. Roosevelt,
      Franklin Delano, Pres. U.S., 1882-1945.

Voice Lib.
M1463 Hitler, Adolf, 1889-1945.
bd.11   BBC broadcast of montage of Hitler's
      speeches (1943) directed at the German
      soldiers. Peteler, 1943.
        1 reel (7 in.)   7 1/2 in. per sec.
      phonotape.

          Hitler, Adolf, 1889-1945
Voice Lib.
M715   Cronkite, Walter Leland, 1916-
bd.1   Walter Cronkite and Robert Trout
      interpolating address by Adolf Hitler,
      wherein announcement is made of calling up
      of Reichstag; also commentary on prelude
      to and beginning of World War II. 1939.
        1 reel (7 in.)   7 1/2 in. per sec.
      phonotape.

        I. Hitler, Adolf, 1889-1945. II. Trout,
      Robert, 1908-

Voice Lib.
M1357 Hitler, Adolf, 1889-1945.
bd.2   Excerpt of talk to local militia "fuehrers".
      Peteler, June, 1944.
        1 reel (7 in.)   7 1/2 in. per sec.
      phonotape.

Voice Lib. Hitler, Adolf, 1889-1945
M1301 German radio (Nazi controlled)
bd.3   Reporting progress on the Russian front
      and the declaration of war by Japan on the
      United States. Peteler, December 11, 1941.
        1 reel (7 in.) 7 1/2 in. per sec. phonotape.
        CONTENTS. -a. Göring, Hermann. -b. Hitler, Adolf,
      criticizing President Roosevelt and comparing his own actions
      with those of FDR.
        I. Göring, Hermann, 1893-1946. II. Hitler, Adolf, 1889-1945.
      III. Nationalsozialistische Deutsche Arbeiter-Partei. Reichspartei-
      tag.

Voice Lib.
M1358 Hitler, Adolf, 1889-1945.
bd.4   New Year's speech to the German nation.
      Peteler, January 1, 1945.
        1 reel (7 in.)   7 1/2 in. per sec.
      phonotape.

          Hitler, Adolf, 1889-1945
Voice Lib.
572-   I can hear it now (radio program)
573   1933-1946. CBS, 1948.
bd.1   2 reels (7 in.)   7 1/2 in. per sec.
      phonotape.
        I. Murrow, Edward Roscoe, 1908-1965. II. LaGuardia, Fiorello
      Henry, 1882-1947. III. Chamberlain, Neville, 1869-1949. IV.
      Roosevelt, Franklin Delano, Pres. U.S., 1882-1945. V. Churchill,
      Winston Leonard Spencer, 1874-1965. VI. Gaulle, Charles de,
      Pres. France, 1890-1970. VII. Eisenhower, Dwight David, Pres. U.S.,
      1890-1969. VIII. Willkie, Wendell Lewis, 1892-1944. IX. Martin,
      Joseph William, 1884-1968. X. Elizabeth II, Queen of Great Britain,
      1926-   XI. Margaret Rose, Princess of Gt. Brit., 1930-   XII.
      Johnson, Hugh Samuel, 188?   2. XIII. Smith, Alfred Emanuel,
      1873-1944. XIV. Lindbergh, Charles Augustus, 1902-   XV. Davis,

(Continued on next card)

Voice Lib. Hitler, Adolf, 1889-1945
M1019 Nationalsozialistische Deutsche Arbeiter-Partei.
bd.12   Reichsparteitag.
    Reichstag session, July 19, 1940: address
by Adolf Hitler pertaining to armistice with
France; plans for further Nazi aims, such as
the elimination of Jewish financiers domes-
tically and abrogation of all remaining
Versailles treaty demands. Justifying invasion
of Norway as a defense measure. Renewal of
peace proposals with England, followed by Nazi
songs and expressions of gratitude by Hermann
Göring to the vision and strategy of Hitler.
                        (Continued on next card)

        Hitler, Adolf, 1889-1945
Voice Lib.
M1018 Nationalsozialistische Deutsche Arbeiter-Partei.
bd.4   Reichsparteitag.
    Reichstag session including remarks by
Hermann Göring, expressing gratitude to
Luftwaffe at Polish victories; and Adolf Hitler
justifying his attack on Poland and his
alliance with Soviets, his aims at European
peace pact and return of German colonies.
Peteler, October 6, 1939.
    1 reel (7 in.)   7 1/2 in. per sec.
phonotape.
    I. Göring, Hermann, 1893-1946. II. Hitler, Adolf, 1889-1945.

        Hitler, Adolf, 1889-1945
Voice Lib.
M1304 Nationalsozialistische Deutsche Arbeiter-Partei.
bd.11   Reichsparteitag.
    Reichstag session pertaining to the appoint-
ment of Hitler as prime law maker of German
Reich; including addresses by: a. Hitler,
Adolf, about the hardship of German troops at
the Russian front; b. Göring, Hermann, appraisal
of strength of the U.S. entering European
conflict. Peteler, April 26, 1942.
    1 reel (7 in.)   7 1/2 in. per sec.
phonotape.
    I. Hitler, Adolf, 1889-1945. II. Göring, Hermann, 1893-1946.

        Hitler, Adolf, 1889-1945
Voice Lib.
M1019 Nationalsozialistische Deutsche Arbeiter-Partei.
bd.12   Reichsparteitag. Reichstag session, July
        19, 1940... 1940. (Card 2)

July 19, 1940.
    1 reel (7 in.)   7 1/2 in. per sec.
phonotape.

    I. Hitler, Adolf, 1889-1945. II. Göring,
Hermann, 1893-1946.

        Hitler, Adolf, 1889-1945
Voice Lib.
M1465 Olympic games, Berlin, 1936.
bd.1   Hitler opening Olympic Games in 1936
    and   description of proceedings. Various
German announcers make reports on events.
Peteler, 1936.
    1 reel (7 in.)   7 1/2 in. per sec.
phonotape..

    I. Hitler, Adolf, 1889-1945.

        HITLER, ADOLF, 1889-1945
Voice Lib.
M1361 Dönitz, Karl, 1891-
bd.12   Proclamation to the German Wehrmacht and
    to the entire German nation about Hitler's
    last will and testament. Peteler, May 1,
    1945.
    1 reel (7 in.)   7 1/2 in. per sec.
phonotape.

    1. Hitler, Adolf, 1889-1945.

        HITLER, ADOLF, 1889-1945
Voice Lib.
M1019 German radio (Nazi controlled)
bd.11   Nazi radio news commentator: reception of
    Adolf Hitler in Berlin after successful con-
    clusion of capitulation of France and signing
    of Armistice; expressions of gratitude to the
    Fuehrer by various youth groups; ringing of
    bells. Peteler, July 6, 1940.
    1 reel (7 in.)   7 1/2 in. per sec.
phonotape.

    1. Hitler, Adolf, 1889-1945.

        HITLER, ADOLF, 1889-1945
Voice Lib.
M1357 German radio (Nazi controlled)
bd.3   Report of attempted assassination of
    Hitler on July 20, 1944. Peteler, July 20,
    1944.
    1 reel (7 in.)   7 1/2 i.p.s.   phonotape.
    In German.

    1. Hitler, Adolf, 1889-1945.

        HITLER, ADOLF, 1889-1945
Voice Lib.
M1361 German radio (Nazi controlled)
bd.11   Nazi special announcement: notification
    of the death of Adolf Hitler. Peteler,
    May 1, 1945.
    1 reel (7 in.)   7 1/2 in. per sec.
phonotape.

    1. Hitler, Adolf, 1889-1945.

        HITLER, ADOLF, 1889-1945
Voice Lib.
M1357 Remer, Otto Ernst, 1912-
bd.4   Excerpt of broadcast about Hitler's attempted
    assassination. Peteler, July 20, 1944.
    1 reel (7 in.)   7 1/2 in. per sec.
phonotape.

Voice Lib. HITLER, ADOLF, 1889-1945
M1464 Reynolds, Quentin James, 1902-1965.
bd.1   An open letter to Hitler, broadcast over
          BBC in London. Peteler, 1941.
          1 reel (7 in.)   7 1/2 in. per sec.
          phonotape.

          1. Hitler, Adolf, 1889-1945.

C1   Hitler's inferno
H81
        Whorf, Michael, 1933-
          Hitler's inferno.
          1 tape cassette. (The visual sounds of
        Mike Whorf. History and heritage, H81)
          Originally presented on his radio program, Kaleidoscope,
        WJR, Detroit.
          Duration: 39 min., 50 sec.
          Tyrant, dictator, despot, madman - all aptly describe the
        Austrian-born paperhanger who rose from obscurity to become the
        devil in human form. With the sound of storm troopers' boots, and
        the clank of panzer divisions comes this tale of the world's most
        despised man.
          I. Hitler, Adolf, 1889-1945. I. Title.

                HITLER, ADOLF, 1889-1945
Voice Lib.
M1010 Seyss-Inquart, Arthur von, 1892-1946.
bd.5   Speech to Austrian people commending
          Hitler as the great leader of a unified
          greater Germany. Peteler, March 12, 1938.
          1 reel (7 in.)   7 1/2 in. per sec.
          phonotape.

Voice Lib.
M382 Hobart, Garett Augustus, 1844-1899.
bd.2   Talking from Washington, D.C., to New
          York City via telephone for the first
          time, extolling the "electric age" (1898).
          CBS, April 26, 1951.
          1 reel (7 in.)   7 1/2 i.p.s.   phonotape.

          1. Telephone. 2. Phonorecords - History.

C1   HITLER, ADOLF, 1889-1945
H65
        Whorf, Michael, 1933-
          Apostles of destruction; Caesar, Alexander,
        Ghenghis Khan, Hitler.
          1 tape cassette. (The visual sounds of Mike Whorf.
        History and heritage, H65)
          Originally presented on his radio program, Kaleidoscope,
        WJR, Detroit.
          Duration: 39 min.
          Here are graphically related the tales of the despots of the ages -
        for though many would strive for goodness and the best in man - a
        few were blindly corrupt and evil, and in their time attempted to
        bring the world to ruin.
          1. Caesar, C. Julius. 2. Alexander the Great, 356-323 B.C.
        3. Jenghis Khan, 1162-1227. 4. Hitler, Adolf, 1889-1945.
        I. Title.

              Hobby lobby (Radio program)
Voice Lib.
M620 Radio in the 1940's (Part I): a series of
bd.1-   excerpts from important broadcasts of the 1940's; a
bd.16   sample of radio of the period. NVL, April, 1964.
          1 reel (7 in.)   7 1/2 in. per sec.   phonotape.
          I. Radio programs. I. Thomas, Lowell Jackson, 1892-   II.
        Gunther, John, 1901-1970. III. Kaltenborn, Hans von, 1878-1965.
        IV. Delmar, Kenny. V. Those were the good old days (Radio
        program) VI. Elman, Dave. VII. Hall, Frederick Lee, 1916-1970.
        VIII. Hobby lobby (Radio program) IX. Roosevelt, Franklin Delano,
        Pres. U.S., 1882-1945. X. Willkie, Wendell Lewis, 1892-1944.
        XI. Hoover, Herbert Clark, Pres. U.S., 1874-1964. XII. Johnson,
        Hugh Samuel, 1882-1942. XIII. Cobb, Irvin Shrewsbury, 1876-1944.
        XIV. Roosevelt, Theodore, 1858-1919. XV. Nye, Gerald Prentice,
        1892-1971. XVI. Lindbergh, Charles Augustus, 1902-   XVII.
        Toscanini, Arturo, 1867-1957.

C1   HITLER, ADOLF, 1889-1945
H81
        Whorf, Michael, 1933-
          Hitler's inferno.
          1 tape cassette. (The visual sounds of
        Mike Whorf. History and heritage, H81)
          Originally presented on his radio program, Kaleidoscope,
        WJR, Detroit.
          Duration: 39 min., 50 sec.
          Tyrant, dictator, despot, madman - all aptly describe the
        Austrian-born paperhanger who rose from obscurity to become the
        devil in human form. With the sound of storm troopers' boots, and
        the clank of panzer divisions comes this tale of the world's most
        despised man.
          I. Hitler, Adolf, 1889-1945. I. Title.

Voice Lib. Hodge, John Reed, 1893-1963
383   I can hear it now (radio program)
          CBS, February 9, 1951.
          1 reel (7 in.)   7 1/2 in. per sec.
          phonotape.
          I. Wilson, Charles Edward, 1886-1972. II. Gabrielson, Guy
        George, 1891-   III. Taft, Robert Alphonso, 1889-1953. IV.
        Martin, Joseph William, 1884-1965. V. McCarthy, Joseph
        Raymond, 1909-1957. VI. Benton, William Burnett, 1900-1973.
        VII. Malone, George Wilson, 1890-1961. VIII. Capehart, Homer
        Earl, 1897-   IX. Eisenhower, Dwight David, Pres. U.S., 1890-
        1969. X. Lee, J   V   XI. Hodge, John Reed, 1893-
        1963. XII. Overton, Watkins   XIII. DiSalle, Michael
        Vincent, 1908-   XIV. Boyce, Eddy   XV. Conklin, Ed
        XVI. Collins, Joseph Lawton, 1896-

Voice Lib.
M1004 Hitler youth fight song, entitled "Vorwärts".
bd.2   Peteler, 1935.
          1 reel (7 in.)   7 1/2 in. per sec.
          phonotape.

          1. Songs, German.   I. Title: Vorwärts.

Voice Lib.
M1466 Hoersing, Friedrich
bd.19   On the occasion of Founders Day of the
          "Reichsbanners". Peteler, February 2,
          1924.
          1 reel (7 in.)   7 1/2 in. per sec.
          phonotape.

          1. Germany - Politics and government -
          1918-1933.

Voice Lib.
M1420   Hofer, Walther, 1920-
bd.19   Speaking about the development of
            negotiations between Germany and the Soviet
            Union during the months of April to August,
            1939. Peteler, 1964.
               1 reel (7 in.)   7 1/2 i.p.s.   phonotape.

            1. Germany - Foreign relations - Russia.
            2. Russia - Foreign relations - Germany.

Voice Lib.
200-   Hoffa, James Riddle, 1913-
202   Address at Michigan State University.
            Recorded on location, April 2, 1963.
               3 reels (7 in.)   7 1/2 in. per sec.
            phonotape.

               CONTENTS.-200, address.-201, questions and
            answers from the audience.-202, informal
            questions after program.

Voice Lib.
243   Hoffa, James Riddle, 1913-
bd.10   Comments to Blair Clark on accusation
            to lead walk-out from AFL-CIO at Building
            Trades Convention, Atlanta City. CBS
            Radio, August 5, 1957.
               1 reel (7 in.)   7 1/2 in. per sec.
            phonotape.

Voice Lib.
256   Hoffa, James Riddle, 1913-
bd.1   Testimony before Senate Rackets
            Committee, with Senator Ives and
            Counsel Robert Kennedy. CBS News,
            August 22-23, 1957.
               1 reel (7 in.)   7 1/2 in. per sec.
            phonotape.

               I. Ives, Irving McNeil, 1896-1962. II.
            Kennedy, Robert Francis, 1925-1968.

Voice Lib.
259   Hoffman, Clare E   1875-1967.
bd.2   Rep. Hoffman describes happenings when
            firing broke out in the gallery of the
            House of Representatives. CBS, March 1,
            1954.
               1 reel (7 in.)   7 1/2 in. per sec.
            phonotape.

Voice Lib.
M1091   Holbrook, Hal, 1925-
bd.1   Mark Twain impersonation of excerpt
            from book "Huckleberry Finn". (LP phono
            album) Bergman, 1953.
               1 reel (7 in.)   7 1/2 in. per sec.
            phonotape.

            1. Clemens, Samuel Langhorne, 1835-1910./
            The adventures of Huckleberry Finn.

Voice Lib.
M1067-   Holbrook, Hal, 1925-
1068   Portraying Mark Twain with various humorous
bd.1   anecdotes and tales by the famous author;
            special TV performance for NBC. NBC,
            March 6, 1967.
               2 reels (7 in.)   7 1/2 in. per sec.
            phonotape.

               1. Clemens, Samuel Langhorne, 1835-1910.

                        HOLMES, OLIVER WENDELL, 1809-1894
Voice Lib.
M726,   Lunt, Alfred, 1893-
bd.1;   "The Magnificent Yankee", a Hallmark-
727,   sponsored TV dramatization of the life of
bd.1   Justice Oliver Wendell Holmes. NBC, January
            28, 1965.
               2 reels (7 in.)   7 1/2 in. per sec.
            phonotape.

               1. Holmes, Oliver Wendell, 1809-1894.
               I. Fontanne, Lynne   87(?)-   TITLE

                        HOLMES, OLIVER WENDELL, 1809-1894
C1
A40   Whorf, Michael, 1933-
            Autocrat of the breakfast table - O. W. Holmes,
         Sr.
            1 tape cassette. (The visual sounds of
         Mike Whorf. Art, music and letters, A40)
            Originally presented on his radio program, Kaleidoscope.
         WJR, Detroit.
            Duration 36 min., 30 sec.
            Oliver Wendell Holmes, Sr., was a poet and philosopher, and
         here mixed with his works is the story of his life.

            L Holmes, Oliver Wendell, 1809-1894. L Title.

                        HOLMES, OLIVER WENDELL, 1841-1935
C1
H54   Whorf, Michael, 1933-
            The great dissenter - Justice Oliver Wendell
         Holmes.
            1 tape cassette. (The visual sounds of
         Mike Whorf. History and heritage, H54)
            Originally presented on his radio program, Kaleidoscope.
         WJR, Detroit.
            Duration 41 min.
            A heart warming and tender story of Oliver Wendell Holmes,
         who was a lawyer, professor and justice of the Supreme Court,
         equally adept at each, an inspiration to all who listened to him.

            L Holmes, Oliver   Wendell, 1841-1935. L Title.

C1
A27

The Homer of painters - Peter Rubens

Whorf, Michael, 1933-
    The Homer of painters - Peter Rubens.
    1 tape cassette.   (The visual sounds of
Mike Whorf. Art, music and letters, A27)
    Originally presented on his radio program, Kaleidoscope,
WJR, Detroit.
    Duration: 40 min.
    Peter Paul Rubens was diplomat, courtier, and raconteur, but
most of all a brilliant artist. His brilliant technique led to
influencing others of his day and those that were to follow; his
works today are beyond price.

    I. Rubens, Sir Peter Paul, 1577-1640. I. Title.

○

Voice Lib.
M1064
bd.7

Hoover, Herbert Clark, Pres. U.S., 1874-1964.
    Campaign song of 1932 Republican presidential
race: "Let's Get Behind Herbert Hoover";
excerpt from address at Madison Square Garden,
New York, by President Hoover at close of
1932 presidential campaign.   Fox Movietone,
1932.
    1 reel (7 in.)   7 1/2 in. per sec.
phonotape.

    I. Title: Let's get behind Herbert Hoover.

○

HOMOSEXUALITY - U.S.

Voice Lib.
M1719

Wallace, Mike, 1918-
    The press: credible or incredible?
address at Michigan State University.
WKAR, March 5, 1970.
    36 min.   phonotape (1 r.   7 1/2 i.p.s.)

    1. Television broadcasting. 2. Marihuana.
3. Homosexuality - U.S.

○

Voice Lib.
540
bd.15

Hoover, Herbert Clarke, Pres. U.S., 1874-1964.
    1932 campaign speech.   Fox Movietone,
1932.
    1 reel (7 in.)   7 1/2 in. per sec.
phonotape.

○

Hong Kong blues

Voice Lib.
625
bd.1

Carmichael, Hoagy, 1899-
    "Salute to Hoagy Carmichael"; condensation
of special TV program on Today show.
Carmichael reminiscing, singing "Hong Kong
Blues" and "Old Buttermilk Sky".   NBC,
April 24, 1964.
    1 reel (7 in.)   7 1/2 in. per sec.
phonotape.

    I. Title: Hong Kong blues. II. Title: Old
buttermilk sky.

○

Voice Lib.
M728
bd.5

Hoover, Herbert Clark, Pres. U.S., 1874-1964.
    "Shall we send our youth to war?" Advice
against involvement by the U.S. in European
power politics.   RCA Victor, 1938.
    4 min., 8 sec.   phonotape (1 r.
7 1/2 i.p.s.)

    1. U.S. - Foreign relations.

○

Voice Lib.
M1688

Hook, Sidney, 1902-
    Human rights - what is the philosophical
basis for them?   WKAR, February 28, 1969.
    53 min.   phonotape (1 r.   7 1/2 i.p.s.)

    1. Civil rights.

○

Voice Lib.
M736
bd.13

Hoover, Herbert Clark, Pres. U.S., 1874-1964.
    Excerpt from Willkie campaign speech:
settlement of postwar problems.   CBS, 1940.
    1 min., 16 sec.   phonotape (1 r.
7 1/2 i.p.s.)

○

Voice Lib.
141
bd.1-7

Hoover, Herbert Clarke, Pres. U.S., 1874-1964.
    Speeches, addresses, etc.   Various
recordings, 1930-1953.
    1 reel (7 in.)   7 1/2 in. per sec.
phonotape

○

Voice Lib.
259,
bd.3-
260,
bd.1

Hoover, Herbert Clark, Pres. U.S., 1874-1964.
    Food for the occupied democracies in
Europe.   CBS, February 16, 1941.
    2 reels (7 in.)   7 1/2 in. per sec.
phonotape.

○

Voice Lib.
188   Hoover, Herbert Clarke, Pres. U.S., 1874-1964.
        Acceptance speech at Haverford College
    of honorary degree. WJR, June 7, 1941.
        1 reel (7 in.) 7 1/2 in. per sec.
    phonotape.

Voice Lib.
M736   Hoover, Herbert Clark, Pres. U.S., 1874-1964.
bd.15   Excerpt from speech on Korea, stating that
    the Allies should demonstrate actual military
    strength before U.S. should give more troops
    or money. CBS, 1953.
        1 reel (7 in.)   7 1/2 in. per sec.
    phonotape.

        1. Korean War, 1950-1953 - U.S.

Voice Lib.
353   Hoover, Herbert Clark, Pres. U.S., 1874-1964.
bd.8   Outbreak of Korean War; on the importance
    of unity. NBC, July, 1950.
        1 reel (7 in.)   7 1/2 in. per sec.
    phonotape.

    Original disc off-speed.

        1. Korean War, 1950-1953 - U.S.

Voice Lib.
127   Hoover, Herbert Clark, Pres. U.S., 1874-1964.
bd.8   Dedication ceremonies at Sagamore Hill,
    an eulogy of Theodore Roosevelt.
    Recorded on location, June 14, 1953.
        1 reel (7 in.)   7 1/2 in. per sec.
    phonotape.

        1. Roosevelt, Theodore, Pres. U.S., 1858-
    1919.

Voice Lib.
M736   Hoover, Herbert Clark, Pres. U.S., 1874-1964.
bd.14   Excerpt from speech against invasion of
    China's mainland during the Korean conflict,
    and excerpt from speech concerning America's
    defense capabilities. CBS, 1951.
        1 reel (7 in.)   7 1/2 in. per sec.
    phonotape.

        1. Korean War, 1950-1953

Voice Lib.
M736   Hoover, Herbert Clark, Pres. U.S., 1874-1964.
bd.16   Excerpts from speech on his 80th birthday
    celebration. Reviews his life, discusses
    power of Federal and local government and
    separation of their powers; also discusses
    President's power over foreign policy,
    policy of aiding Russia during World War II,
    and communism. CBS, 1954.
        1 reel (7 in.)   7 1/2 in. per sec.
    phonotape.

Voice Lib.
387   Hoover, Herbert Clarke, Pres. U.S., 1874-1964.
bd.2   On the world situation. NBC, 1951.
        1 reel (7 in.)   7 1/2 in. per sec.
    phonotape.

Voice Lib.
652   Hoover, Herbert Clark, Pres. U.S., 1874-1964.
bd.8   Speech on occasion of his 80th birthday at
    West Branch, Iowa.   CBS, August 10, 1954.
        1 reel (7 in.)   7 1/2 in. per sec.
    phonotape.

Voice Lib.
226-   Hoover, Herbert Clarke, Pres. U.S., 1874-1964.
227   Address to Republican convention.
bd.1   CBS, July 8, 1952.
        2 reels (7 in.)   7 1/2 in. per sec.
    phonotape.

Voice Lib.
227   Hoover, Herbert Clark, Pres. U.S., 1874-1964.
bd.2-   Address on country doctors; introduced by
228   Douglas McKay. CBS, August 10, 1955.
bd.1   2 reels (7 in.)   7 1/2 in. per sec.
    phonotape.

        I. McKay, Douglas, 1893-1959.

Voice Lib.
M736   Hoover, Herbert Clark, Pres. U.S., 1874-1964.
bd.17   Excerpt from speech before 1956 Republican
         National Convention.   CBS, 1956.
             1 reel (7 in.)   7 1/2 in. per sec.
         phonotape.

Voice Lib. Hoover, Herbert Clarke, Pres. U.S., 1874-1964
M574   I can hear it now (radio program)
bd.2-   1919-1933.   CBS, 1953.
575   2 reels (7 in.)   7 1/2 in. per sec.
         phonotape.

             I. Murrow, Edward Roscoe, 1908-1965. II.
         Rogers, Will, 1879-1935. III. White, William
         Allen, 1868-1944. IV. Hoover, Herbert Clarke,
         Pres. U.S., 1874-1964. V. Roosevelt, Franklin
         Delano, Pres. U.S., 1882-1945. VI. Rice,
         Grantland, 1880-1954. VII. McNamee, Graham,
         1888-1942.

Voice Lib.
M736   Hoover, Herbert Clark, Pres. U.S., 1874-1964.
bd.18   Excerpt from speech before 1960 Republican
         National Convention.   CBS, 1960.
             1 reel (7 in.)   7 1/2 in. per sec.
         phonotape.

Voice Lib. Hoover, Herbert Clark, Pres. U.S., 1874-1964
M725   Republican Party. National Convention.
bd.1   25th, Chicago, 1952.
             Film of excerpts of the Republican National
         Convention in 1952. Clash between Taft and
         Eisenhower forces. Includes speeches by Gen.
         MacArthur, Gen. Eisenhower, Ex-Pres. Hoover,
         Sen. Dirksen, etc.   CBS, 1952.
             1 reel (7 in.)   7 1/2 in. per sec.
         phonotape.

             I. MacArthur, Douglas, 1880-1964. II. Eisenhower, Dwight
         David, Pres. U.S., 1890-1969. III. Hoover, Herbert Clark, Pres.
         U.S., 1874-1964. IV. Dirksen, Everett McKinley, 1896-1969.

Voice Lib.
M736   Hoover, Herbert Clark, Pres. U.S., 1874-1964.
bd.19   Excerpt from speech on 88th birthday
         celebration. Discusses his life and works;
         recommends the formation of a world-wide
         organization made up of free nations which
         will act when the U.N. cannot, and reminds
         youth that they too have great opportunity.
         CBS, 1962.
             1 reel (7 in.) 7 1/2 in. per sec.
         phonotape.

             HOOVER, HERBERT CLARK, PRES. U.S.,
Voice Lib.   1874-1964
655   Dirksen, Everett McKinley, 1896-1969.
bd.2   Address at Republican National Convention
         in San Francisco: tribute to ex-President
         Herbert Hoover.   NBC, July 13, 1963.
             1 reel (7 in.)   7 1/2 in. per sec.
         phonotape.

             1. Hoover, Herbert Clark, Pres. U.S., 1874-
         1964.

             Hoover, Herbert Clark, Pres. U.S.,
Voice Lib.   1874-1964
M618   Radio in the 1930's (Part I): a series of
bd.1-   excerpts from important broadcasts of the
14   1930's; a sample of radio of the period.
         NVL, April, 1964.
             1 reel (7 in.) 7 1/2 in. per sec. phonotape.
             I. Shaw, George Bernard, 1856-1950. II. Crosby, Bing, 1901-
         III. Barkley, Alban William, 1877-1956. IV. Roosevelt, Franklin
         Delano, Pres. U.S., 1882-1945. V. Hoover, Herbert Clark, Pres.
         U.S., 1874-1964. VI. Long, Huey Pierce, 1893-1935. VII. Town-
         send, Francis Everett, 1867-1960. VIII. Coughlin, Charles Edward,
         1891-   IX. Rogers, Will, 1879-1935. X. Pius XII, Pope, 1876-
         1958. XI. Edward VIII, king of Great Britain, 1894-1972. XII.
         Barrymore, John, 1882-1942. XIII. Woollcott, Alexander, 1887-
         1943. XIV. Allen, Fred, 1894-1956. XV. Benchley, Robert Charles,
         1889-1945.

Voice Lib.
M861   Hoover, John Edgar, 1895-1972.
bd.1   Speech at acceptance of honorary award
         from American Legion, in San Francisco.
         NBC, September 30, 1946.
             1 reel (7 in.) 7 1/2 in. per sec.
         phonotape.

             Hoover, Herbert Clark, Pres. U.S., 1874-
Voice Lib.   1964
M620   Radio in the 1940's (Part I): a series of
bd.1-   excerpts from important broadcasts of the 1940's; a
bd.16   sample of radio of the period. NVL, April, 1964.
             1 reel (7 in.) 7 1/2 in. per sec. phonotape.
             I. Radio programs.   Thomas, Lowell Jackson, 1892-   II.
         Gunther, John, 1901-1970. III. Kaltenborn, Hans von, 1878-1965.
         IV. Delmar, Kenny. V. Those were the good old days (Radio
         program) VI. Elman, Dave. VII. Hall, Frederick Lee, 1916-1970.
         VIII. Hobby lobby (Radio program) IX. Roosevelt, Franklin Delano,
         Pres. U.S., 1882-1945. X. Willkie, Wendell Lewis, 1892-1944.
         XI. Hoover, Herbert Clark, Pres. U.S., 1874-1964. XII. Johnson,
         Hugh Samuel, 1882-1942. XIII. Cobb, Irvin Shrewsbury, 1876-1944.
         XIV. Roosevelt, Theodore, 1858-1919. XV. Nye, Gerald Prentice,
         1892-1971. XVI. Lindbergh, Charles Augustus, 1902-   XVII.
         Toscanini, Arturo, 1867-1957.

Voice Lib. Hop Harrigan (radio program)
M1675   Theme songs from the Green hornet, the Lone
bd.2   Ranger, Dick Tracy, and Hop Harrigan.
         Golden Age Radio Records, 1940's.
             10 min.   phonotape (1 r. 7 1/2 i.p.s.)

             I. Green hornet (radio program) II. Lone
         Ranger (radio program) III. Dick Tracy (radio
         program) IV. Hop Harrigan (radio program)

Voice Lib.
M711   Hope, Bob, 1903-
bd.1   "Elgin Show"; radio variety show. Melchior
        collection, December 25, 1947.
        1 reel (7 in.)   7 1/2 in. per sec.
        phonotape.

Hope, Bob, 1903-
Voice Lib.
M384   I can hear it now (radio program)
bd.1   Biography of a pint of blood.   CBS,
        February, 1951.
        1 reel (7 in.)   7 1/2 in. per sec.
        phonotape.

        1. Blood.   I. McIntire, Ross T., 1899-
        II. Hope, Bob, 1903-   III. Ridgway,
        Matthew Bunker, 1895-   IV. Barkley,
        Alban William, 1877-1956.

Voice Lib. Hope, Bob, 1903-
M669-   The legend of Cecil B. Demille. Yul
670   Brynner, Charlton Heston, Bob Hope, Betty
        Hutton, Edward G. Robinson, Barbara Stanwyck,
        James Stewart, Gloria Swanson, Cornel
        Wilde, Samuel Goldwyn, Billy Graham, Cecil
        B. DeMille. Recorded 1963.
        2 reels (7 in.) 7 1/2 in. per sec. phonotape.
        I. DeMille, Cecil Blount, 1881-1959. I. Brynner, Yul, 1917-
        II. Heston, Charlton, 1924-   III. Hope, Bob, 1903-   IV.
        Hutton, Betty, 1921-   V. Robinson, Edward G   1893-1973.
        VI. Stanwyck, Barbara, 1907-   VII. Stewart, James Maitland,
        1908-   VIII. Swanson, Gloria, 1899?-   IX. Wilde, Cornel, 1915-
        X. Goldwyn, Samuel, 1884?-   XI. Graham, William Franklin,
        1918-   XII. DeMille, Cecil Blount, 1881-1959.

Voice Lib.
396   Hopkins, Harry Lloyd, 1890-1946.
bd.4   The determination of FDR and the
        American people to help Britain through
        lend-lease. BBC, July 21, 1941.
        1 reel (7 in.)   7 1/2 in. per sec.
        phonotape.

        1. Lend-lease operations (1941-1945).

Voice Lib.   Hope, Bob, 1903-
M621   Radio in the 1940's (Part II): a series of
bd.1-   excerpts from important broadcasts of the
12   1940's; a sample of radio of the period.
        NVL, April, 1964.
        1 reel (7 in.) 7 1/2 in. per sec. phonotape.
        I. Daly, John Charles, 1914-   II. Hall, Josef Washington,
        1894-   III. Shirer, William Lawrence, 1904-   IV. Roosevelt,
        Eleanor (Roosevelt) 1884-1962. V. Roosevelt, Franklin Delano,
        Pres. U.S., 1882-1945. VI. Churchill, Winston Leonard Spencer,
        1874-1965. VII. Wainwright, Jonathan Mayhew, 1883-1953. VIII.
        Cantor, Eddie, 1893-1964. IX. Sinatra, Francis Albert, 1917-
        X. Crosby, Bing, 1901-   XI. Shore,
        Dinah, 1917?)-   XIII. Bergen, Edgar, 1903-   XIV. Armstrong,
        Louis, 1900-1971. XV. Eldridge, Roy, 1911-

Voice Lib.
526   Hopper, De Wolf, 1858-1935.
bd.4   Reads "Casey at the Bat".   Victor
        Talking Machine Co., 1912.
        1 reel (7 in.)   7 1/2 in. per sec.
        phonotape.

        I. Title: Casey at the bat.

Voice Lib.   Hope, Bob, 1903-
M1368   Some friends of General Eisenhower (TV program)
        CBS-TV special recalling anecdotes about
        General Eisenhower by some of his friends:
        Bob Hope, Kevin McCann, General Omar Bradley,
        Robert B. Anderson, General Alfred Gruenther,
        with Walter Cronkite acting as emcee. CBS-TV,
        March 29, 1969.
        1 reel (7 in.) 7 1/2 in. per sec.
        I. Eisenhower, Dwight David, Pres. U.S., 1890-1969. I.
        Hope, Bob, 1903-   II. McCann, Kevin   III. Bradley, Omar
        Nelson, 1893-   IV. Anderson, Robert Bernard, 1910-   V.
        Gruenther, Alfred Maximilian, 1899-   VI. Cronkite, Walter
        Leland, 1916-

Voice Lib.
654   Hopper, De Wolf, 1858-1935.
bd.9   "Casey at the Bat". Electrical recording
        of De Wolf Hopper narrating famous poem.
        Moran, November, 1926.
        1 reel (7 in.)   7 1/2 in. per sec.
        phonotape.

        I. Title.

Voice Lib.
M1726   Hope, Bob, 1903-
bd.1   Interview on Merv Griffin Show. WJRT-TV,
        June 17, 1974.
        15 min. phonotape (1 r.   7 1/2 i.p.s.)

        1. Hope, Bob, 1903-   I. Griffin, Mervyn
        Edward, 1925-

Hottelet, Richard Curt
Voice Lib.
M1027   The world today: direct news reports from
bd.3   Belgian front; statement from SHAEF (Supreme
        Headquarters Allied Expeditionary Force);
        news of war in the Pacific discussed by CBS
        correspondents Robert Trout, Douglas Edwards,
        Richard C. Hottelet, and Ned Kalmer. CBS
        News, December 23, 1944.
        1 reel (7 in.) 7 1/2 in. per sec. phonotape.
        I. Trout, Robert, 1908-   II. Edwards, Douglas
        III. Hottelet, Richard Curt   IV. Kalmer, Ned

Voice Lib.
228   Hottelet, Richard Curt
bd.2   Richard C. Hottelet and others on the
        Berlin Airlift and its cessation.   CBS,
        May 12, 1949.
           1 reel (7 in.)   7 1/2 in. per sec.
        phonoreel.

           1. Berlin - Blockade, 1948-1949.

C1
H73   A house united
      Whorf, Michael, 1933-
         A house united; Civil War, part 6.
         1 tape cassette.   (The visual sounds of
      Mike Whorf. History and heritage, H73)
         Originally presented on his radio program, Kaleidoscope,
      WJR, Detroit.
         Duration: 39 min.
            After the Civil War in the South there is the scorched earth,
         the burnt plantation and the carpetbagger, and yet the word
         throughout the land is reconstruction.

            I. Reconstruction.   I. Title.

Voice Lib.
657   Hottelet, Richard Curt
bd.1   The MacArthur Story: narrating continuity
        between speeches by General MacArthur.
        CBS, 1964.
           1 reel (7 in.)   7 1/2 in. per sec.
        phonotape.

           1. MacArthur, Douglas, 1880-1964.
           I. MacArthur, Douglas, 1880-1964.

Voice Lib.   Houseman, John, 1902-
M655   The Twentieth Century (TV program)
bd.1   "The creative thirties", narrated by
         Walter Cronkite. CBS, 1963.
            25 min.   phonotape (1 r. 7 1/2 i.p.s.)

            I. U.S. - Civilization - 1918-1945. I. Bowes, Edward,
         1874-1946. II. Geismar, Maxwell David, 1909-
         III. MacDonald, Dwight, 1906-   IV. Welles, Orson, 1915-
         V. Cronkite, Walter Leland, 1916-   VI. Gable, Clark, 1901-
         1960. VII. Lewis, Sinclair, 1885-1951. VIII. Houseman,
         John, 1902-   IX. Roosevelt, Franklin Delano, Pres. U.S.,
         1882-1945.

Hottelet, Richard Curt
Voice Lib.
235-   Tito, Josip Broz, Pres. Yugoslavia, 1892-
237   Interview by Edward R. Murrow, with comments
bd.1   and analysis by Richard C. Hottelet, Clare
         Boothe Luce, William H. Lawrence, and Hamilton
         F. Armstrong, CBS, June 30, 1957.
            3 reels (7 in.)   7 1/2 in. per sec.
         phonotape.

            I. Hottelet, Richard Curt   II. Luce,
         Clare (Boothe) 1903-   III. Lawrence,
         William H   IV. Armstrong, Hamilton Fish,
         1893-1973.

C1
H37   HOUSTON, SAMUEL, 1793-1863
      Whorf, Michael, 1933-
         Sam Houston.
         1 tape cassette.   (The visual sounds of
      Mike Whorf. History and heritage, H37)
         Originally presented on his radio program, Kaleidoscope,
      WJR, Detroit.
         Duration: 40 min.
            In the days of the young Texas territory many men would ennoble
         themselves for the cause of independence. One man much
         criticized, and yet admired was Sam Houston.

            I. Houston, Samuel, 1793-1863.   I. Title.

C1
M14   HOUDINI, HARRY, 1874-1926
      Whorf, Michael, 1933-
         The incredible Houdini.
         1 tape cassette.   (The visual sounds of
      Mike Whorf. Miscellaneous, M14)
         Originally presented on his radio program, Kaleidoscope,
      WJR, Detroit.
         Duration: 48 min., 10 sec.
            Trickster, magician, seer and scientist - what was it that
         made Harry Houdini the most outstanding slight-of-hand artist,
         the most original prestidigitator of his time? A look behind the
         scenes as one of the world's most incredible performers.

            I. Houdini, Harry, 1874-1926.   I. Title.

Voice Lib.
M1273- How Israel won the war. Interviews with
1274   Arab and Israel military and civilian
         leaders at scene of action at conclusion
         of six-day war in June 1967, including
         resumé of campaign and analysis. CBS-TV,
         July 18, 1967.
            2 reels (7 in.)   7 1/2 in. per sec.
         phonotape.

            Incomplete.
            1. Israel-Arab War, 1967-

Voice Lib.
609   House, Edward Mandell, 1858-1938.
bd.11   A salute to Texas; speaking to fellow Texans
        in New York. Audio Scriptions, April 30,
        1936.
           1 reel (7 in.)   7 1/2 in. per sec.
        phonotape.

C1
M27   How simple a tune
      Whorf, Michael, 1933-
         How simple a tune.
         1 tape cassette.   (The visual sounds of
      Mike Whorf. Miscellaneous, M27)
         Originally presented on his radio program, Kaleidoscope,
      WJR, Detroit.
         Duration: 43 min., 40 sec.
            A heart-warming look at some of the stories that lie behind
         the composition of America's most familiar old tunes.

            I. Music, Popular (Songs, etc.) - U.S.   I. Title.

Howard, Victor
Voice Lib.
M1653   Purdy, Alan
          Reading from his book, Sex and death, and
          receiving the A.J.M. Smith Award ($350)
          given by MSU's Canadian-American Studies
          Division for the outstanding contribution
          to Canadian poetry for the year.   With
          Victor Howard and A.J.M. Smith.   Voice
          Library, May 1, 1974.
          1 hour.   phonotape (1 r.   7 1/2 i.p.s.)

          I. Smith, Arthur James Marshall, 1902-
          II. Howard, Victor

Voice Lib.
M312   Huber, Oscar L
bd.3   Assassination: description of events by
          Reverend Oscar Huber, priest who administered
          last rites to Kennedy.   NBC, November 23,
          1963.
          1 reel (7 in.)   7 1/2 in. per sec.
          phonotape.

          1. Kennedy, John Fitzgerald, Pres. U.S.,
          1917-1963 - Assassination.

C1   HUGHES, CHARLES EVANS, 1862-1948
FA17   Whorf, Michael, 1933-
          Charles Evans Hughes.
          1 tape cassette.   (The visual sounds of
          Mike Whorf.   The forgotten American, FA17)
          Originally presented on his radio program, Kaleidoscope,
          WJR, Detroit.
          Duration: 10 min., 10 sec.
          Although missing the presidency by a small margin, Charles
          Evans Hughes was one of the most important public servants of his
          time.   In 25 years of public life, he served as governor of New
          York, Associate Justice of the Supreme Court, Secretary of
          State and Chief Justice of the Supreme Court.

          I. Hughes, Charles Evans, 1862-1948.   I. Title.

Voice Lib.
M1491   Hughes, Howard Robard, 1905-
bd.1   Excerpt of testimony before U.S. Senate
          War Investigating Committee.   Senator
          Homer Ferguson of Michigan questions Howard
          Hughes.   CBS-Radio, 1947.
          1 reel (7 in.)   7 1/2 in. per sec.
          phonotape.

          I. Ferguson, Homer, 1889-

Hughes, Howard Robard, 1905-
Voice Lib.
573   I can hear it now (radio program)
bd.2-   1945-1949.   CBS, 1950?
574   2 reels (7 in.)   7 1/2 in. per sec.
bd.1   phonotape.
          I. Murrow, Edward Roscoe, 1908-1965.   II. Nehru, Jawaharlal,
          1889-1964.   III. Philip, duke of Edinburgh, 1921-   IV. Elizabeth II,
          Queen of Great Britain, 1926-   V. Ferguson, Homer, 1889-   VI.
          Hughes, Howard Robard, 1905-   VII. Marshall, George Catlett,
          1880-   VIII. Ruth, George Herman, 1895-1948.   IX. Lilienthal,
          David Eli, 1899-   X. Trout, Robert, 1908-   XI. Gage, Arthur.
          XII. Jackson, Robert Houghwout, 1892-1954.   XIII. Gromyko, Ana-
          tolii Andreevich, 1908-   XIV. Baruch, Bernard Mannes, 1870-
          1965.   XV. Churchill, Winston Leonard Spencer, 1874-1965.   XVI.
          Winchell, Walter, 1897-   XVII. Davis, Elmer Holmes, 1890-
          (Continued on next card)

Hughes, Howard Robard, 1905-
Voice Lib.
M1491   Wallace, Mike, 1918-
bd.4   New developments in the mystery case of
          Howard Hughes and Clifford Irving, described
          by Mike Wallace on CBS "60 Minutes".   CBS-TV,
          January 30, 1972.
          1 reel (7 in.)   7 1/2 in. per sec.
          phonotape.

          I. Hughes, Howard Robard, 1905-   II.
          Irving, Clifford Michael, 1930-

Voice Lib.
HUGHES, HOWARD ROBARD, 1905-
M1455   Sixty minutes (Television program)
bd.2   Semi-monthly CBS documentary with a
          biography of Howard Hughes.   CBS TV, 1970.
          1 reel (7 in.)   7 1/2 in. per sec.
          phonotape.

          1. Hughes, Howard Robard, 1905-

HUGHES, HOWARD ROBARD, 1905-
Voice Lib.
M1491   Wallace, Mike, 1918-
bd.2   Segment on alleged Howard Hughes auto-
          biography on CBS "60 Minutes" program,
          describing the controversy, picturing present
          physical appearance of Hughes and bringing
          up loan by Hughes to President Nixon's
          brother of $205,000.   Speakers: Mike Wallace
          and Clifford Irving.   CBS-TV, January 16,
          1972.
          1 reel (7 in.)   7 1/2 in. per sec.
          phonotape.   (Continued on next card)

Voice Lib.   HUGHES, HOWARD ROBARD, 1905-
M1491   Wallace, Mike, 1918-
bd.3   Segment on sequel to the mystery of Howard
          Hughes' alleged autobiography on CBS' "Sixty
          Minutes".   Mystery woman cashes $650,000
          check in Switzerland and description of
          procedures in Swiss banks.   CBS-TV, January 23,
          1972.
          1 reel (7 in.)   7 1/2 in. per sec.
          phonotape.

          1. Hughes, Howard Robard, 1905-

Voice Lib.   Hugness, Thornton
353   Russia and the bomb, discussed by various
bd.19   personalities.   NBC, September 25, 1949.
          1 reel (7 in.)   7 1/2 in. per sec.
          phonotape.

          Participants: Harrison Brown, Harold Urey,
          Samuel Allison, Thornton Hugness, Brien McMahon,
          Paul Douglas, John Foster Dulles, Leslie Groves,
          Winston Churchill, Dean Acheson, James Fleming.

          I. Brown, Harrison Scott, 1917-   II.
          Urey, Harold Clayton, 1893-   III. Allison,

          (Continued on next card)

Hugness, Thornton
Voice Lib.
353   Russia and the bomb... 1949. (Card 2)
bd.19

Samuel King, 1900-   IV. Hugness, Thornton.
V. McMahon, James O'Brien, 1903-1952. VI.
Douglas, Paul Howard, 1892-   VII. Dulles,
John Foster, 1888-1959. VIII. Groves, Leslie
R   1896-1970. IX. Churchill, Winston
Leonard Spencer, 1874-1965. X. Acheson, Dean
Gooderham, 1893-1971. XI. Fleming, James,
1915-

Human nature in politics
Voice Lib.
M729-   Russell, Bertrand Russell, 3d earl, 1872-1970.
730,   "Human nature in politics." A witty
bd.1   address, incorporating some of his ideas,
by Lord Russell. BBC, 1953.
42 min., 45 sec. phonotape (2 r.
7 1/2 i.p.s.)

I. Title.

Hugo, Victor Marie, comte, 1802-1885.
Un peu de musique
Voice Lib.
M795   Bernhardt, Sarah, 1844-1923.
bd.3   Excerpt from Victor Hugo play "Un peu de
Musique". Paris, 1902.
1 reel (7 in.) 7 1/2 in. per sec.
phonotape.

I. Hugo, Victor Marie, comte, 1802-1885./
Un peu de musique.

Voice Lib.
M312   Humphrey, Hubert Horatio, 1911-
bd.5   Ray Shearer of NBC, Washington, speaking
with Senator Hubert Humphrey about his
opinion of the new President, Lyndon B.
Johnson. NBC, November 23, 1963.
1 reel (7 in.) 7 1/2 in. per sec.
phonotape.
1. Johnson, Lyndon Baines, Pres. U.S.,
1908-1973. I. Shearer, Ray

Hugo, Victor Marie, comte, 1802-1885
Voice Lib.
M1464   Beyerlein, Alfred
bd.3   Narrating Victor Hugo's speech on
Voltaire in German translation. Peteler,
1932.
1 reel (7 in.) 7 1/2 i.p.s. phonotape.

1. Voltaire, François Marie Arouet de,
1694-1778. I. Hugo, Victor Marie, comte,
1802-1885.

Voice Lib.
M987   Humphrey, Hubert Horatio, 1911-
bd.2   Commencement address at MSU spring term
1966. WKAR-NVL, June 12, 1966.
1 reel (7 in.) 7 1/2 in. per sec.
phonotape.

C1   HUGO, VICTOR MARIE, COMTE, 1802-1885
A34   Whorf, Michael, 1933-
The romantic poet - Victor Hugo.
1 tape cassette. (The visual sounds of
Mike Whorf. Art, music and letters, A34)
Originally presented on his radio program, Kaleidoscope,
WJR, Detroit.
Duration: 36 min., 45 sec.
He was a gifted author, and a product of the elite French
literary circle, but though his prose and poetry was voluminous
and varied, there was but one novel which insured his
immortality.

I. Hugo, Victor Marie, comte, 1802-1885.

Voice Lib.
M1337-   Humphrey, Hubert Horatio, 1911-
1338   Humphrey's acceptance speech at the
Democratic national convention, Chicago.
NBC-TV, August 28, 1968.
2 reels (7 in.) 7 1/2 in. per sec.
phonotape.

HUMAN GENETICS
Voice Lib.
M1734   Pauling, Linus Carl, 1901-
Orthomolecular medicine; address given at
Michigan State University. WKAR, April 19,
1972.
50 min. phonotape (1 r. 7 1/2 i.p.s.)

1. Ascorbic acid. 2. Diet. 3. Human
genetics.

Voice Lib.
M1336   Humphrey, Hubert Horatio, 1911-
bd.1   TV broadcast by Democratic candidate
Humphrey, clarifying his positions on
Vietnam, crime in the streets, etc.
CBS-TV, September 30, 1968.
1 reel (7 in.) 7 1/2 in. per sec.
phonotape.

Humphrey, Hubert Horatio, 1911-
Voice Lib.
M1323- Democratic Party. National Convention,
M1328,   Chicago, 1968.
bd.1   Hubert Humphrey, Democratic presidential nomi..., announcing his selection of Sen. Muskie as his running mate; convention floor reports; interview with Mrs. Humphrey. Mayor Daley of Chicago defending police action. Interviews with Senator McGovern and Jesse Unruh of California. Remote address by Sen. Edward Kennedy introducing a memorial motion picture on the late Sen. Robert F. Kennedy. Various reports on riots and general confusion, reluctance of delegates to come to order. Nominations for Vice-President; seconding speeches for Sen. Muskie and nominating speech by Wisconsin delegation of Julian Bond of Georgia. Interview with Julian Bond, who declined nomination of the vice-presidency. Story told by chairman of the New Hampshire [delega__] regarding his arrest. Interview (Continued on next card)

Humphrey, Hubert Horatio, 1911-
Voice Lib.
M1323- Democratic Party. National Convention,
M1328,   Chicago, 1968...   (Card 2)
bd.1   with Paul O'Dwyer of the New York delegation regarding the nomination of Richard Daley for Vice-President. General confusion. Nomination of Sen. Edmund Muskie as Vice-President and resulting confusion with the Oregon delegation. Followed by Sen. Muskie's acceptance speech. NBC-TV, August 29, 1968.
   6 reels (7 in.)   7 1/2 in. per sec.   phonotape.
   I. Humphrey, Hubert Horatio, 1911- II. Humphrey, Muriel Fay (Buck) 1912-   III. Daley, Richard J   1902-   IV. McGovern, George Stanley, 1922-   V. Unruh, Jesse Marvin, 1922-   VI. Kennedy, Edward Moore, 1932-   VII. Bond, Julian, 1940-   VIII. O'Dwyer, Paul, 1907-   IX. Muskie, Edmund S   1914-

Humphrey, Hubert Horatio, 1911-
Voice Lib.
M718   McCormack, John William, 1891-
bd.1   Administering oath of office of Vice-President to Hubert H. Humphrey. Presidential inaugural ceremonies. January 20, 1965.
   1 reel (7 in.)   7 1/2 in. per sec. phonotape.

Humphrey, Hubert Horatio, 1911-
Voice Lib.
M1346 Nixon, Richard Milhous, Pres. U.S., 1913-
bd.2   Post-1968 election news described by Huntley, Brinkley and other NBC staff men. Statements of victory by Nixon and of defeat by Humphrey; also by Wallace and LeMay. Comments from countries overseas. Report of Congressional elections.   NBC-TV, November 6, 1968.
   1 reel (7 in.)   7 1/2 in. per sec.
   I. Huntley, Chet, 1911-   II. Brinkley, David McClure, 1920-   III. Humphrey, Hubert Horatio, 1911-   IV. Wallace, George Corley, 1919-   V. LeMay, Curtis Emerson, 1906-

Humphrey, Muriel Fay (Buck) 1912-
Voice Lib.
M1323- Democratic Party. National Convention,
M1328,   Chicago, 1968.
bd.1   Hubert Humphrey, Democratic presidential nom..., announcing his selection of Sen. Muskie as his running mate; convention floor reports; interview with Mrs. Humphrey. Mayor Daley of Chicago defending police action. Interviews with Senator McGovern and Jesse Unruh of California. Remote address by Sen. Edward Kennedy introducing a memorial motion picture on the late Sen. Robert F. Kennedy. Various reports on riots and general confusion, reluctance of delegates to come to order. Nominations for Vice-President; seconding speeches for Sen. Muskie and nominating speech by Wisconsin delegation of Julian Bond of Georgia. Interview with Julian Bond, who declined nomination of the vice-presidency. Story told by chairman of the New Hampshire [delega__] regarding his arrest. Interview (Continued on next card)

Humphrey, Muriel Fay (Buck) 1912-
Voice Lib.
M1323- Democratic Party. National Convention,
M1328,   Chicago, 1968...   (Card 2)
bd.1   with Paul O'Dwyer of the New York delegation regarding the nomination of Richard Daley for Vice-President. General confusion. Nomination of Sen. Edmund Muskie as Vice-President and resulting confusion with the Oregon delegation. Followed by Sen. Muskie's acceptance speech. NBC-TV, August 29, 1968.
   6 reels (7 in.)   7 1/2 in. per sec.   phonotape.
   I. Humphrey, Hubert Horatio, 1911- II. Humphrey, Muriel Fay (Buck) 1912-   III. Daley, Richard J   1902-   IV. McGovern, George Stanley, 1922-   V. Unruh, Jesse Marvin, 1922-   VI. Kennedy, Edward Moore, 1932-   VII. Bond, Julian, 1940-   VIII. O'Dwyer, Paul, 1907-   IX. Muskie, Edmund S   1914-

Voice Lib.
M715   Hungarian Freedom Fighters; excerpt from
bd.10   final broadcast.   October, 1956.
   1 reel (7 in.)   7 1/2 in. per sec.
   phonotape.

   1. Hungary - History - Revolution, 1956.

HUNGARY - HISTORY - REVOLUTION, 1956
Voice Lib.
M715   Hungarian Freedom Fighters; excerpt from
bd.10   final broadcast.   October, 1956.
   1 reel (7 in.)   7 1/2 in. per sec.
   phonotape.

HUNGARY - HISTORY - REVOLUTION, 1956
Voice Lib.
M1471 Last radio appeal by Free Hungary for help
bd.4   against Soviet invasion and occupation by the Democratic Hungarian government. Peteler, 1956.
   1 reel (7 in.)   7 1/2 in. per sec. phonotape.

Voice Lib.
M1665 Hunt, Everette Howard, 1918-
   On "Firing line" about Watergate payments, with William Buckley, Ralph Fine, John Owen, and Miss Bernstein. WKAR-TV, May 14, 1974.
   50 min.   phonotape (1 r.   7 1/2 i.p.s.)

   1. Watergate Affair, 1972-   I. Buckley, William Frank, 1925-   II. Fine, Ralph Adam, 1941-   III. Owen, John

Voice Lib.
M1279   Hunt, Haroldson Lafayette, 1889-
    H.L. Hunt, "the richest and the rightest".
A revealing interview with oil millionaire
Hunt who speaks out on his wealth, his
philosophy, political patronage, communist
threat, and other views. By reporter James
Fleming.   NET, August 27, 1967.
    1 reel (7 in.)   7 1/2 in. per sec.
phonotape.

    I. Fleming, James, 1915-   1. Hunt,
Haroldson   Lafayette, 1889-

           Huntley, Chet, 1911-1974
Voice Lib.
M968   Gemini 9 (space flight): description of
bd.2   countdown and lift-off of "Agena" by
    Gemini Mission Control (voice of Al Chop)
    for a period of 11 minutes, 41 seconds,
    until Gemini flight was scrubbed. Comments
    by NBC's Huntley, Brinkley, and Frank McGee.
    NBC TV, May 17, 1966.
    1 reel (7 in.)   7 1/2 in. per sec.   phonotape.
    1. Project Gemini. 2. Stafford, Thomas P 1931-   3.
Cernan, Eugene Andrew, 1934-   L Stafford, Thomas P   1931-
II. Cernan, Eugene Andrew, 1934-   III. Chop, Al   IV.
Huntley, Chet, 1911-1974 V. Brinkley, David McClure, 1920-
VI. McGee, Frank, 1921-1974.

Voice Lib.
M1435
    Life in other worlds: exploratory discussion about life on other
planets. Arnold J. Toynbee, Dr. G. B. Kiastiakowsky
(professor at Harvard), Dr. Donald M. Michaels, Dr. Otto
Struve, Dr. Harlow Shapley, Walter Cronkite, Chet Huntley,
William L. Laurence. New York, NBC, March 3, 1961.
    1 reel (7 in.)   7 1/2 i.p.s. phonotape.
    1. Life on other planets. I. Toynbee, Arnold Joseph, 1889-
II. Kiastiakowsky, George Bogdan. III. Michaels, Donald M.
IV. Struve, Otto, 1897-1963. V. Shapley, Harlow, 1885-1972.
VI. Cronkite, Walter Leland, 1916-   VII. Huntley, Chet,
1911-1974. VIII. Laurence, William Leonard, 1888-

Voice Lib.
M1030   Huntley, Chet, 1911-1974.
bd.1   Description by Chet Huntley of funeral
    services at burial of astronauts Virgil
    Grisson and Roger Chaffee at Arlington
    Cemetery and of Edward White at West Point,
    New York. NBC-TV, January 31, 1967.
    1 reel (7 in.)   7 1/2 in. per sec.   phonotape.
    1. Grissom, Virgil Ivan, 1926-1967. 2. White, Edward
Higgins, 1930-1967. 3. Chaffee, Roger B., 1936-1967.

        Huntley, Chet, 1911-1974
Voice Lib.
M771   Gemini 4 (space flight): excerpts of announce-
bd.2   ments from NBC reporters and Gemini Control,
    regarding preparations for and the actual
    splashdown. Conversation with astronauts
    before pickup by helicopter. Dallas Townsend
    from carrier "Wasp" and David Brinkley and
    Chet Huntley for NBC.   NBC TV, June 7, 1965.
    1 reel (7 in.)   7 1/2 in. per sec.   phonotape.
    1. Project Gemini. 2. McDivitt, James Alton, 1929-   3.
White, Edward Higgins, 1930-1967. I. McDivitt, James Alton,
1929-   II. White, Edward Higgins, 1930-1967. III. Townsend,
Dallas.   IV. Brinkley, David McClure, 1920-   V. Huntley,
Chet, 1911-1974.

Voice Lib.
M1249   Huntley, Chet, 1911-1974
bd.1   Documentary TV program: "The Talk in
    Vandalia", first capital of state of Illinois,
    prompted by Joseph P. Lyford's book "What's
    Wrong with Vandalia", a small American mid-
    western community. Discussion covers automation
    and unemployment problems, farm problems,
    increasing of intellectual activities. NBC,
    April 30, 1967.
    1 reel (7 in.)   7 1/2 in. per sec.   phonotape.
    1. Vandalia, Ill. 2. Lyford, Joseph P   I. The
talk in Vandalia (Television program)

        Huntley, Chet, 1911-1974
Voice Lib.
M772   Gemini 4 (space flight): pickup of astronauts
bd.1   McDivitt and White and the capsule, described
    by Chet Huntley and David Brinkley.   NBC TV,
    June 7, 1965.
    1 reel (7 in.)   7 1/2 in. per sec.
phonotape.

    1. Project Gemini. 2. McDivitt, James Alton,
1929-   3. White, Edward Higgins, 1930-1967.
I. McDivitt, James Alton, 1929-   II. White,
Edward Higgins, 1930-1967. III. Huntley, Chet,
1911-1974 IV. Brinkley, David McClure, 1920-

        Huntley, Chet, 1911-1974
Voice Lib.
M1384   Apollo 11 (space flight): biographical sketches
bd.2   of the three astronauts, Edwin Aldrin,
    Michael Collins, and Neil Armstrong, by Chet
    Huntley, at approximately 78 minutes before
    launch time. NBC TV, July 16, 1969.
    1 reel (7 in.)   7 1/2 in. per sec.
phonotape.
    1. Project Apollo. 2. Space flight to the moon. 3. Aldrin,
Edwin E   1930-   4. Collins, Michael, 1930-   5. Armstrong,
Neil, 1930-   I. Aldrin, Edwin E   1930-   II. Collins,
Michael, 1930-   III. Armstrong, Neil, 1930-   IV. Huntley,
Chet, 1911-1974.

        Huntley, Chet, 1911-1974
Voice Lib.
M917   Gemini 7 (space flight): Frank McGee's resumé
bd.1   of space flights of astronauts Frank Borman
    and James Lovell, Jr., in Gemini 7, commencing
    Dec. 4, 1956 to Dec. 18, 1965, and of astro-
    nauts Walter Schirra and Thomas Stafford in
    Gemini 6, which rendezvoused in space;
    including various launching actual reports
    and interview with Wally Schirra; comments
    by Huntley and Brinkley.   NBC TV, December
    18, 1965.
    1 reel (7 in.)   7 1/2 in. per sec.
phonotape.
            (Continued on next card)

Voice Lib.
M1460   Huntley, Chet, 1911-1974
bd.3   Farewell remarks by Chet Huntley upon
    leaving post at NBC after 14 years. Added
    comments by David Brinkley.   NBC-TV,
    June 30, 1970.
    1 reel (7 in.)   7 1/2 in. per sec.
phonotape.

    I. Brinkley, David McClure, 1920-

Voice Lib.
M796-   Brinkley, David McClure, 1920–
799   White Paper, on U.S. foreign policy from
           post World War II period to current hostilities
           in Vietnam, with various commentators, U.S.
           government officials, foreign dignitaries,
           and actual scenes and sound.   NBC-TV,
           September 7, 1965.
              4 reels (7 in.)   7 1/2 in. per sec.   phonotape.

              Running time approximately 3 hours.

           I. U.S. – Foreign policy.   I. Huntley, Chet, 1911–1974.

Huntley, Chet, 1911–1974

Voice Lib.
157   Huston, Walter, 1884–1950.
bd.1   "Johnny Appleseed"; a radio play.   CBS,
           1930's.
              1 reel (7 in.)   7 1/2 in. per sec.
           phonotape.

              I. Title.

Voice Lib.
M1346   Nixon, Richard Milhous, Pres. U.S., 1913–
bd.2   Post-1968 election news described by
           Huntley, Brinkley and other NBC staff men.
           Statements of victory by Nixon and of defeat
           by Humphrey; also by Wallace and LeMay.
           Comments from countries overseas. Report of
           Congressional elections.   NBC-TV, November 6,
           1968.
              1 reel (7 in.)   7 1/2 in. per sec.
           I. Huntley, Chet, 1911–   II. Brinkley, David McClure, 1920–
           III. Humphrey, Hubert Horatio, 1911–   IV. Wallace, George
           Corley, 1919–   V. LeMay, Curtis Emerson, 1906–

Huntley, Chet, 1911–1974

Voice Lib.
M982   Huston, Walter, 1884–1950.
bd.4   Reading prose poem by Vachel Lindsay,
           "Abraham Lincoln Walks at Midnight".   Decca
           Specialty, 1930.
              1 reel (7 in.)   7 1/2 in. per sec.
           phonotape.

              I. Lindsay, Nicholas Vachel, 1879–1931./
           Abraham Lincoln walks at midnight.

                  HURRICANES
Voice Lib.
M717   Columbia Broadcasting System, Inc.
bd.7   Interview with weather official in New
           York about Hurricane Donna.   September 19,
           1960.
              1 reel (7 in.)   7 1/2 in. per sec.
           phonotape.

              1. Hurricanes.

Voice Lib.
M982   Huston, Walter, 1884–1950.
bd.5   Reading Walt Whitman's poem "O Captain,
           My Captain".   Decca specialty, 1930.
              1 reel (7 in.)   7 1/2 in. per sec.
           phonotape.

Voice Lib.
M1498   Hussein, King of Jordan, 1935–
bd.3   Interview on "Meet the Press". Regarding
           King Hussein's plans for an autonomous
           Palestine.   NBC, April 2, 1972.
              1 reel (7 in.)   7 1/2 in. per sec.
           phonotape.

Voice Lib.
M972   Hutchins, Robert Maynard, 1899–
bd.2–   "Slightly autobiographical"; interview
973   with Dr. Hutchins, covering early days in
           Brooklyn, N.Y., Oberlin in 1907, Menjou
           Army anecdote, overseas army experiences
           as a teacher, humorous incidents in train-
           ing and spelling, law school at Yale,
           Dean of Yale, and Pres. of University of
           Chicago.   C.S.D.I., 1962.
              2 reels (7 in.)   7 1/2 in. per sec.
           phonotape.

Voice Lib.
M1641   Hussein, King of Jordan, 1935–
           Peace in the Middle East; National Press
           Club Address.   WKAR-AM, March 15, 1974.
              45 min.   phonotape (1 r.   7 1/2 i.p.s.)

           Includes question and answer period.

              1. Arab countries – Foreign relations –
           Israel. 2. Israel – Foreign relations –
           Arab countries.

Voice Lib.
M1063   Hutchins, Robert Maynard, 1890–
bd.1   Explanation of aims of Center for Study
           of Democratic Institutions in Santa Barbara,
           California.   CSDI, 1963.
              1 reel (7 in.)   7 1/2 i.p.s.   phonotape.

              1. Center for the Study of Democratic
           Institutions.

Voice Lib.
M976-   Hutchins, Robert Maynard, 1899–
977   Huxley, Aldous Leonard, 1894-1963.
            Leading a discussion group at C.S.D.I. on
            ecological effects on technology, the
            tragic price we are paying for our conquest
            of nature. Other speakers: Ritchie Calder,
            Walter J. Ong, S.J., and Robert M. Hutchins,
            etc. March, 1962.
                2 reels (7 in.) 7 1/2 in. per sec.   phonotape.

            L. Man – Influence on nature. L. Calder, Ritchie, 1906–
            II. Ong, Walter Jackson, 1912–   III. Hutchins, Robert
            Maynard, 1899–

Voice Lib.
M766   Hutton, Jack
bd.3   Excerpt from "Popular Music of Europe"
            (Program 11); expresses his idea that the
            British sound is not all British; including
            song "I Don't Need You", by the "Panics"
            sextet. Westinghouse Broadcasting Corporation,
            1964.
                1 reel (7 in.) 7 1/2 in. per sec.
            phonotape. (The Music Goes Round and Round)

                I. Title: Popular music of Europe. II. Series.

Voice Lib.
M1078   Hutchins, Robert Maynard, 1899–
bd.2   Huxley, Aldous Leonard, 1894-1963.
            Remarks at symposium at Santa Barbara,
            California on the impact of science and
            technology on democratic institutions,
            especially as regards to population growth,
            arms race, and nationalism. Introductory
            remarks by Dr. Robert M. Hutchins. CSDI,
            1963.
                1 reel (7 in.)   7 1/2 in. per sec.
            phonotape.

                I. Hutchins, Robert Maynard, 1899–

Voice Lib.
M976-   Huxley, Aldous Leonard, 1894-1963.
977   Leading a discussion group at C.S.D.I. on
            ecological effects on technology, the
            tragic price we are paying for our conquest
            of nature. Other speakers: Ritchie Calder,
            Walter J. Ong, S.J., and Robert M. Hutchins,
            etc. March, 1962.
                2 reels (7 in.) 7 1/2 in. per sec.   phonotape.

            L. Man – Influence on nature. L. Calder, Ritchie, 1906–
            II. Ong, Walter Jackson, 1912–   III. Hutchins, Robert
            Maynard, 1899–

Voice Lib.   Hutchins, Robert Maynard, 1899–
M979   Reuther, Walter Philip, 1907-1970.
bd.2   Discussion of moral and social economic
            problems at audience participation session
            in Santa Barbara, California. Introduction
            by Dr. Robert M. Hutchins. CSDI, 1963.
                1 reel (7 in.) 7 1/2 in. per sec.
            phonotape.

                I. Hutchins, Robert Maynard, 1899–

Voice Lib.
M1078   Huxley, Aldous Leonard, 1894-1963.
bd.2   Remarks at symposium at Santa Barbara,
            California on the impact of science and
            technology on democratic institutions,
            especially as regards to population growth,
            arms race, and nationalism. Introductory
            remarks by Dr. Robert M. Hutchins. CSDI,
            1963.
                1 reel (7 in.)   7 1/2 in. per sec.
            phonotape.

                I. Hutchins, Robert Maynard, 1899–

Voice Lib.   Hutchinson, Edward, 1914–
M1656   U.S. Congress. House. Committee on the
bd.3   Judiciary.
            House Judiciary Committee, 1st public
            meeting of impeachment hearings, with
            Chairman Peter Rodino and Edward Hutchinson.
            WKAR, May 9, 1974.
                15 min.   phonotape (1 r.   7 1/2 i.p.s.)

                1. Nixon, Richard Milhous, Pres. U.S., 1913–
            I. Rodino, Peter Wallace, 1909–
            II. Hutchinson, Edward, 1914–

HYMNS
C1
R17   Whorf, Michael, 1933–
            There's nothing like a good old-fashioned
            hymn.
                1 tape cassette. (The visual sounds of
            Mike Whorf. Religion, R17)

            Originally presented on his radio program, Kaleidoscope,
            WJR, Detroit.
            Duration: 54 min., 30 sec.
            A few familiar, well-loved melodies and a close appraisal of
            what makes the song is the content of this program.

            L. Hymns. L. Title.

Voice Lib.   Hutton, Betty, 1921–
M669-   The legend of Cecil B. DeMille. Yul
670   Brynner, Charlton Heston, Bob Hope, Betty
            Hutton, Edward G. Robinson, Barbara Stanwyck,
            James Stewart, Gloria Swanson, Cornel
            Wilde, Samuel Goldwyn, Billy Graham, Cecil
            B. DeMille. Recorded 1963.
                2 reels (7 in.) 7 1/2 in. per sec. phonotape.

            L. DeMille, Cecil Blount, 1881–1959. L. Brynner, Yul, 1917–
            II. Heston, Charlton, 1924–   III. Hope, Bob, 1903–   IV.
            Hutton, Betty, 1921–   V. Robinson, Edward G   1893–1973.
            VI. Stanwyck, Barbara, 1907–   VII. Stewart, James Maitland,
            1908–   VIII. Swanson, Gloria, 1899–   IX. Wilde, Cornel, 1915–
            X. Goldwyn, Samuel, 1884?–   XI. Graham, William Franklin,
            1918–   XII. DeMille, Cecil Blount, 1881–1959.

Voice Lib.
385   I can hear it now (radio program)
            CBS, February 2, 1951.
                1 reel (7 in.) 7 1/2 in. per sec.
            phonotape.

                I. Austin, Warren Robinson, 1877-1962. II.
            Pandit, Vijaya Lakshmi (Nehru) 1900–   III.
            Roosevelt, Eleanor (Roosevelt) 1884-1962. IV.
            Morse, Wayne Lyman, 1900–   V. Chandler,
            Albert Benjamin, 1898–   VI. Taylor, Telford,
            1908–   VII. Whitney, Jack.

Voice Lib.
M384   I can hear it now (radio program)
bd.2   CBS, February 2, 1951.
    1 reel (7 in.) 7 1/2 in. per sec.
phonotape.

    I. Taft, Robert Alphonso, 1889-1953. II.
Rayburn, Samuel Taliaferro, 1882-1961. III.
Barkley, Alban William, 1877-1956. IV. Rabaut,
Louis Charles, 1886-1961. V. Attlee, Clement
Richard Attlee, 1st earl, 1883-1967. VI.
Kelly, Capt., U.S.A.

Voice Lib.
383   I can hear it now (radio program)
    CBS, February 9, 1951.
    1 reel (7 in.) 7 1/2 in. per sec.
phonotape.
    I. Wilson, Charles Edward, 1886-1972. II. Gabrielson, Guy
George, 1891- III. Taft, Robert Alphonso, 1889-1953. IV.
Martin, Joseph William, 1884-1965. V. McCarthy, Joseph
Raymond, 1909-1957. VI. Benton, William Burnett, 1900-1973.
VII. Malone, George Wilson, 1890-1961. VIII. Capehart, Homer
Earl, 1897- IX. Eisenhower, Dwight David, Pres. U.S., 1890-
1969. X. Lee, J   V   XI. Hodge, John Reed, 1893-
1963. XII. Overton, Watkins XIII. DiSalle, Michael
Vincent, 1908- XIV. Boyce, Eddy   XV. Conklin, Ed
XVI. Collins, Joseph Lawton, 1896-

Voice Lib.
381- I can hear it now (radio program)
382   CBS, April 26, 1951.
bd.1   2 reels (7 in.) 7 1/2 in. per sec. phonotape. 1.
Ridgway, Matthew Bunker, 1895- 2. Strategic Air Command. I.
Ridgway, Matthew Bunker, 1895- II. Churchill, Winston Leonard
Spencer, 1874-1965. III. Bevan, Aneurin, 1897-1960. IV. Nixon,
Richard Milhous, Pres. U.S., 1913- V. Kerr, Robert Samuel, 1896-
1963. VI. Brewster, Ralph Owen, 1888-1962. VII. Wherry, Kenneth
Spicer, 1892-1951. VIII. Capehart, Homer Earl, 1897- IX.
Lehman, Herbert Henry, 1878-1963. X. Taft, Robert Alphonso,
1889-1953. XI. Moody, Arthur Edson Blair, 1902-1954. XII.
Martin, Joseph William, 1884-1968. XIII. McMahon, James O'Brien,
1903-1952. XIV. MacArthur, Douglas, 1880-1964. XVII. Wilson,
Charles Edward, 1886-1972. VIII. Irvine, Clarence T

Voice Lib.
M384 I can hear it now (radio program)
bd.1   Biography of a pint of blood. CBS,
   February, 1951.
    1 reel (7 in.) 7 1/2 in. per sec.
phonotape.

    1. Blood. I. McIntire, Ross T., 1899-
II. Hope, Bob, 1903-   III. Ridgway,
Matthew Bunker, 1895-   IV. Barkley,
Alban William, 1877-1956.

Voice Lib.
M574 I can hear it now (radio program)
bd.2- 1919-1933. CBS, 1953.
575   2 reels (7 in.) 7 1/2 in. per sec.
phonotape.
    I. Murrow, Edward Roscoe, 1908-1965. II.
Rogers, Will, 1879-1935. III. White, William
Allen, 1868-1944. IV. Hoover, Herbert Clarke,
Pres. U.S., 1874-1964. V. Roosevelt, Franklin
Delano, Pres. U.S., 1882-1945. VI. Rice,
Grantland, 1880-1954. VII. McNamee, Graham,
1888-1942.

Voice Lib.
572- I can hear it now (radio program)
573   1933-1946. CBS, 1948.
bd.1   2 reels (7 in.) 7 1/2 in. per sec.
    phonotape.
    I. Murrow, Edward Roscoe, 1908-1965. II. LaGuardia, Fiorello
Henry, 1882-1947. III. Chamberlain, Neville, 1869-1949. IV.
Roosevelt, Franklin Delano, Pres. U.S., 1882-1945. V. Churchill,
Winston Leonard Spencer, 1874-1965. VI. Gaulle, Charles de,
Pres. France, 1890-1970. VII. Eisenhower, Dwight David, Pres. U.S.,
1890-1969. VIII. Willkie, Wendell Lewis, 1892-1944. IX. Martin,
Joseph William, 1884-1968. X. Elizabeth II, Queen of Great Britain,
1926- XI. Margaret Rose, Princess of Gt. Brit., 1930- XII.
Johnson, Hugh Samuel, 1882-1942. XIII. Smith, Alfred Emanuel,
1873-1944. XIV. Lindbergh, Charles Augustus, 1902- XV. Davis,
                                (Continued on next card)

Voice Lib.
572- I can hear it now...1933-1946. 1948. (Card 2
573   Elmer Holmes, 1890-1958. XVI. Gehrig, Lou, 1903-1941. XVII.
bd.1 McCarthy, Clem, 1882-1962. XVIII. Morrison, Herbert Stanley,
    1888- XIX. Lewis, John Llewellyn, 1880-1969. XX. Landon,
    Alfred Mossman, 1887- XXI. Edward VIII, King of Gt. Brit.,
    1894-1972. XXII. Long, Huey Pierce, 1893-1935. XXIII. Hitler,
    Adolf, 1889-1945. XXIV. Rogers, Will, 1879-1935. XXV.
    Reynaud, Paul, 1878-1966. XXVI. Shirer, William Lawrence,
    1904- XXVII. Daly, John Charles, 1914- XXVIII. Haakon VII,
    King of Norway, 1872-1957. XXIX. Truman, Harry S, Pres. U.S.,
    1884-1972. XXX. MacArthur, Douglas, 1880-1964. XXXI. Trout,
    Robert, 1908- XXXII. Downey, William XXXIII. Stettinius,
    Edward Reilly, 1900-1949. XXXIV. Godfrey, Arthur Michael, 1903-
    XXXV. Dewey, Thomas Edmund, 1902-1971. XXXVI. Stalin, Iosif,
    1879-1953. XXXVII. Hick   George.

Voice Lib.
573   I can hear it now (radio program)
bd.2- 1945-1949. CBS, 1950?
574   2 reels (7 in.) 7 1/2 in. per sec.
bd.1   phonotape.
    I. Murrow, Edward Roscoe, 1908-1965. II. Nehru, Jawaharlal,
1889-1964. III. Philip, duke of Edinburgh, 1921- IV. Elizabeth II,
Queen of Great Britain, 1926- V. Ferguson, Homer, 1889- VI.
Hughes, Howard Robard, 1905- VII. Marshall, George Catlett,
1880- VIII. Ruth, George Herman, 1895-1948. IX. Lilienthal,
David Eli, 1899- X. Trout, Robert, 1908- XI. Gage, Arthur.
XII. Jackson, Robert Houghwout, 1892-1954. XIII. Gromyko, Anatolii Andreevich, 1908- XIV. Baruch, Bernard Mannes, 1870-
1965. XV. Churchill, Winston Leonard Spencer, 1874-1965. XVI.
Winchell, Walter, 1897-19 XVII. Davis, Elmer Holmes, 1890-
                            (Continued on next card)

Voice Lib.
573   I can hear it now...1945-1949. 1950? (Card 2
bd.2- 1958. XVIII. Kaltenborn, Hans von, 1878-1965. XIX. LaGuardia,
574 Fiorello Henry, 1882-1947. XX. Attlee, Clement Richard Attlee,
bd.1 1st earl, 1883-1967. XXI. Masaryk, Jan Garrigue, 1886-1948. XXII.
    Smith, Howard Kingsbury, 1914- XXIII. Truman, Harry S, Pres.
    U.S., 1884-1972. XXIV. Wallace, Henry Agard, 1888-1965. XXV.
    Dewey, Thomas Edmund, 1902-1971. XXVI. Taylor, Glen Hearst,
    1904- XXVII. Ellis, Handy, XXVIII. Barkley, Alban
    William, 1877-1956. XXIX. Luce, Clare (Boothe) 1903- XXX.
    Eisenhower, Dwight David, Pres. U.S., 1890-1969. XXXI. Chambers,
    David W   XXXII. Hiss, Alger, 1904- XXXIII. Roosevelt,
    Eleanor (Roosevelt) 1884-1962. XXXIV. Tito, Josip Broz, Pres.
    Yugoslavia, 1892- XXXV. Vyshinskii, Andrei Ianuar'evich,
    1883-1954. XXXVI. Pietrillo, James.

          "I Didn't Raise My Boy to be a Soldier"
Voice Lib.
603   Harvey, Morton
bd.3   "I Didn't Raise My Boy to be a Soldier";
    original recording of anti-war song from
    World War I era. Victor Talking Machine
    Co., 1916.
    1 reel (7 in.) 7 1/2 in. per sec.
    phonotape.

    I. Title.

I hear a different drummer

C1
S18
Whorf, Michael, 1933-
I hear a different drummer.
1 tape cassette. (The visual sounds of
Mike Whorf. Social, S18)
Originally presented on his radio program, Kaleidoscope,
WJR, Detroit.
Duration: 54 min.
Henry David Thoreau, American poet and essayist, was
perhaps one of the first outspoken critics of social and economic
problems in 19th century America.

L Thoreau, Henry David, 1817-1862. L Title.

I love to hear a military band

C1
M8
Whorf, Michael, 1933-
I love to hear a military band.
1 tape cassette. (The visual sounds of
Mike Whorf. Miscellaneous, M8)
Originally presented on his radio program, Kaleidoscope,
WJR, Detroit.
Duration: 50 min., 30 sec.
With guest, Frederick Fennell, the tempos are 4/4 and the
music is vibrant and varied, as through narrative and melody, the
story of the march is related.

L Marches. L Fennell, Frederick. II. Title.

I hear America singing

C1
M10
Whorf, Michael, 1933-.
I hear America singing.
1 tape cassette. (The visual sounds of
Mike Whorf. Miscellaneous, M10)
Originally presented on his radio program, Kaleidoscope,
WJR, Detroit.
Duration: 56 min., 30 sec.
The great traditional music of America with authentic, descriptive notes on the background of the writing of these songs. With
each story is a musical example and with each example a familiar
song.

L Music, American. L Title.

I've got my captain working for me

Voice Lib.
611
bd.3
Murray, Billy
Post-World War I song "I've Got My
Captain Working for Me". Victor Talking
Machine Co., 1919.
1 reel (7 in.) 7 1/2 in. per sec.
phonotape.

I. Title: I've got my captain working for
me.

I hear America singing

C1
PWM11
Whorf, Michael, 1933-
I hear America singing.
1 tape cassette. (The visual sounds of
Mike Whorf. Panorama; a world of music, PWM-11)
Originally presented on his radio program, Kaleidoscope,
WJR, Detroit.
Duration: 25 min.
A presentation of songs popular in the U. S. including Barbara
Allen, Yankee Doodle, Auld Lang Syne, Oh Susanna, Pop goes
the weasel, Carry me back to old Virginny, The man on the
flying trapeze, and I've been working on the railroad.

L Music, Popular (Songs, etc.) - U.S. L Title.

I've got rhythm

Voice Lib.
M1065
bd.7
Gershwin, George, 1898-1937.
Playing his composition "I've Got Rhythm"
at recital. Fox Movietone, 1931.
1 reel (7 in.) 7 1/2 in. per sec.
phonotape.

I. Title: I've got rhythm

I know my love

Voice Lib.
644
bd.5-6
Read, Susan
Sings: "I Know My Love", "Greensleeves".
V-Discs, 1943.
1 reel (7 in.) 7 1/2 in. per sec.
phonotape.

I. Title: I know my love. 2. Title:
Greensleeves.

I wouldn't have believed it

C1
SC7
Whorf, Michael, 1933-
I wouldn't have believed it.
1 tape cassette. (The visual sounds of
Mike Whorf. Science, SC7)
Originally presented on his radio program, Kaleidoscope,
WJR, Detroit.
Duration: 43 min., 45 sec.
Many believe that the fourth dimension is a world of ghosts,
poltergeists, of spirits and ghouls - others do not. Can a person
see things if he or she wants to? Turn down the lights and listen.

L Fourth dimension. L Title.

I left my mademoiselle in New Rochelle

Voice Lib.
M1064
bd.3
Gershwin, George, 1898-1937.
Rehearsing for musical show; dialogue and
singing "I Left My Mademoiselle in New
Rochelle". Fox Movietone, 1930.
1 reel (7 in.) 7 1/2 in. per sec.
phonotape.

I. Title: I left my mademoiselle in New
Rochelle.

The immortal poet - Robert Burns

C1
A45
Whorf, Michael, 1933-
The immortal poet - Robert Burns.
1 tape cassette. (The visual sounds of
Mike Whorf. Art, music and letters, A45)
Originally presented on his radio program, Kaleidoscope,
WJR, Detroit.
Duration: 37 min., 15 sec.
Romantic, poetic Robert Burns comes to life as his rhythmic
verses are set to music. Much of his poetry is read, intimately
revealing his various moods throughout his life.

L Burns, Robert, 1759-1796. L Title.

Voice Lib.   IMPEACHMENTS
M1691   Commager, Henry Steele, 1902-
bd.1   On public service and private
creativity, with Bill Moyers.
WKAR-TV, May 23, 1974.
     25 min.   phonotape (1 r.   7 1/2 i.p.s.)

     1. Impeachments. 2. U.S. - Politics and
government. I. Moyers, Bill D., 1934-

C1   In days of old when knights were bold -
H85   knighthood
     Whorf, Michael, 1933-
     In days of old when knights were bold -
knighthood.
     1 tape cassette.   (The visual sounds of
Mike Whorf. History and heritage, H85)
     Originally presented on his radio program, Kaleidoscope.
WJR, Detroit.
     Duration: 36 min., 50 sec.
     The romance and the glories of knighthood are a heritage of
chivalry, but with a misty background in the Arthurian legends.

     L. Knights and knighthood. 2. Arthur, King. L. Title.

Voice Lib.   IMPEACHMENTS
M1692   Jackson, Henry Martin, 1912-
bd.3   Tells the National Press Club his
optimistic estimate of America's economic
future. WKAR, May 23, 1974.
     25 min.   phonotape (1 r.   7 1/2 i.p.s.)

     Includes question & answer session through
Clyde Lamont.

     1. U.S. - Politics and government - 1969-
2. Impeachments. I. Lamont, Clyde.

C1   In the good old summertime
M34   Whorf, Michael, 1933-
     In the good old summertime.
     1 tape cassette.   (The visual sounds of
Mike Whorf. Miscellaneous, M34)

     Originally presented on his radio program, Kaleidoscope.
WJR, Detroit.
     Duration: 37 min., 20 sec.
     It begins and ends with the strains of "In the good old
summertime", and in between is a delightfully warm and
sensitive description of what the season is all about.

     L. Summer. L. Title.

Voice Lib.
644   Impellitteri, Vincent Richard, 1900-
bd.3   Officiates at unveiling of portrait of
Fiorello H. LaGuardia at New York City Hall.
WNYC, December 11, 1950.
     1 reel (7 in.)   7 1/2 in. per sec.
phonotape.

     2. LaGuardia, Fiorello Henry, 1882-1947.

C1   In the shadow of tragedy - Edwin Booth
H53   Whorf, Michael, 1933-
     In the shadow of tragedy - Edwin Booth.
     1 tape cassette.   (The visual sounds of
Mike Whorf. History and heritage, H53)

     Originally presented on his radio program, Kaleidoscope.
WJR, Detroit.
     Duration: 37 min., 45 sec.
     A splendid tragedian, fate would deal with him cruelly.
Despite talent, creative genius and a warm friendly personality,
Edwin Booth would never overcome the blows that destiny dealt him.

     L. Booth, Edwin, 1833-1893. L. Title.

C1   An imposing symposium
A36   Whorf, Michael, 1933-
     An imposing symposium.
     1 tape cassette.   (The visual sounds of Mike Whorf.
Art, music and letters, A36)
     Originally presented on his radio program, Kaleidoscope,
WJR, Detroit.
     Duration: 38 min., 30 sec.
     Longfellow, Agassiz, Emerson, Dana, these were the kings of
the world of literature in the nineteenth century. Every Saturday
night they met at a private club to discuss the current events of
their day.
     L. Longfellow, Henry Wadsworth, 1807-1882. 2. Agassiz,
Louis, 1807-1873. 3. Emerson, Ralph Waldo, 1803-1882-
4. Dana, Richard Henry, 1815-1882. L. Title.

Voice Lib.
M1073   In treue Fest
     Nazi martial music: instrumental band
bd.10   selection entitled, "In treue Fest".
Peteler, 1941.
     1 reel (7 in.)   7 1/2 in. per sec.
phonotape.

     1. Military music, German. I. Title:
In treue Fest.

Voice Lib.   "In a Solemn Hour"
532   Churchill, Winston Leonard Spencer, 1874-
bd.1   1965.
     "In a Solemn Hour", first speech as Prime
Minister; review of Britain's current war
position. BBC, May 19, 1940.
     1 reel (7 in.)   7 1/2 in. per sec.
phonotape.

     I. Title.

C1   The incomparable emperor, Frederick the Great
H75   Whorf, Michael, 1933-
     The incomparable emperor, Frederick the Great.
     1 tape cassette.   (The visual sounds of
Mike Whorf. History and heritage, H75)

     Originally presented on his radio program, Kaleidoscope,
WJR, Detroit.
     Duration: 37 min., 10 sec.
     Frederick the Great was a hero to the Germans - a king, an
emperor - who ruled as majestically, and at times as oppressively,
as any of his contemporaries, and this is a story rich in pageantry,
intrigue and tyranny.

     L. Friedrich II, der Grosse, King of Prussia, 1712-1786.
L. Title.

C1
H58
    The incredible adventurer, Marco Polo

Whorf, Michael, 1933–
    The incredible adventurer, Marco Polo.
    1 tape cassette. (The visual sounds of
Mike Whorf. History and heritage, H58)

    Originally published on his radio program, Kaleidoscope,
WJR, Detroit.
    Duration: 41 min., 30 sec.
    So arduous were the journeys to the ends of the globe, and so
alien was the culture and society of the East, that Marco Polo's
achievements reveal his herculean drive and the audacity of his
vision.

    L. Polo, Marco.   1254-1323? L. Title.

C1
A5
    The incredible Grandma Moses

Whorf, Michael, 1933–
    The incredible Grandma Moses.
    1 tape cassette. (The visual sounds of
Mike Whorf. Art, music, and letters, A5)

    Originally presented on his radio program, Kaleidoscope,
WJR, Detroit.
    Duration: 24 min.
    At the tender young age of 80 she painted quaint pictures
of the America she knew and loved, as a legacy for future
generations.

    L. Moses, Anna Mary (Robertson) 1860-1961. L. Title.

C1
M14
    The incredible Houdini

Whorf, Michael, 1933–
    The incredible Houdini.
    1 tape cassette. (The visual sounds of
Mike Whorf. Miscellaneous, M14)
    Originally presented on his radio program, Kaleidoscope,
WJR, Detroit.
    Duration: 48 min., 10 sec.
    Trickster, magician, seer and scientist – what was it that
made Harry Houdini the most outstanding slight-of-hand artist,
the most original prestidigitator of his time? A look behind the
scenes as one of the world's most incredible performers.

    L. Houdini, Harry, 1874-1926. L. Title.

Voice Lib.
M1265
bd.2
    The incredible victory

Lord, Walter, 1917–
    Interview with author Walter Lord on NBC-TV
"Today" show about his latest book "The incredible victory", pertaining to the Battle of Midway
during World War II. Questioned by Burgess
Meredith. NBC-TV, August 15, 1967.
    1 reel (7 in.) 7 1/2 in. per sec. phonotape.

    L. Midway, Battle of, 1942. L. Meredith, Burgess, 1907–
II. Title: The incredible victory.

INDIA

Voice Lib.
540
bd.25
Gandhi, Mohandas Karamchand, 1869-1948.
    On independence for India. Fox
Movietone, 1933.
    1 reel (7 in.) 7 1/2 in. per sec.
phonotape.

    1. India.

C1
S11
    INDIANS OF NORTH AMERICA

Whorf, Michael, 1933–
    Back to the blankets.
    1 tape cassette. (The visual sounds of
Mike Whorf. Social, S11)
    Originally presented on his radio program, Kaleidoscope,
WJR, Detroit.
    Duration: 52 min., 45 sec.
    The Indian's world for the past 100 years has been on the
reservation, yet he has frequently been induced to compete in the
outside world. What have been and what are the results?

    L. Indians of North America. L. Title.

C1
S9
    INDIANS OF NORTH AMERICA

Whorf, Michael, 1933–
    The stranger.
    1 tape cassette. (The visual sounds of
Mike Whorf. Social, S9)
    Originally presented on his radio program, Kaleidoscope,
WJR, Detroit.
    Duration: 46 min., 30 sec.
    Dealing with the American Indian, it relates the saga of the
warrior from boyhood to manhood, how and why he fought, the
ritual of his ceremony, and the explanation of his way of life.

    L. Indians of North America. L. Title.

C1
S23
    INDIANS OF NORTH AMERICA

Whorf, Michael, 1933–
    Stranger, no more.
    1 tape cassette. (The visual sounds of
Mike Whorf. Social, S23)
    Originally presented on his radio program, Kaleidoscope,
WJR, Detroit.
    Duration: 42 min., 15 sec.
    This is the conclusion to the American Indian series. The
story concerns the redman today. It speaks, as does the Indian,
of his needs, aspirations and hopes.

    L. Indians of North America. L. Title.

C1
S10
    INDIANS OF NORTH AMERICA

Whorf, Michael, 1933–
    Today is a good day to die.
    1 tape cassette. (The visual sounds of
Mike Whorf. Social, S10)
    Originally presented on his radio program, Kaleidoscope,
WJR, Detroit.
    Duration: 45 min., 30 sec.
    This program relates the story of the Indian's ancestry, his
origin, his survival on the continent, the number of nations and
tribes, and their locations, his religion, customs, and the manner
in which he lived in early America.

    L. Indians of North America. L. Title.

Voice Lib.
M394
bd.4
    INDIANS OF NORTH AMERICA – GOVERNMENT
    RELATIONS

Collier, John, 1884-1968.
    Talks about Indian affairs during FDR's
administration; tells of the recording made
by Woodrow Wilson to greet Indians on their
reservations. G.R.Vincent, June 14, 1959.
    1 reel (7 in.) 7 1/2 i.p.s. phonotape.

    1. Indians of North America – Government
Relations.

C1
812

INDIANS OF NORTH AMERICA - GOVERNMENT
RELATIONS

Whorf, Michael, 1933–
The velvet leash.
1 tape cassette. (The visual sounds of
Mike Whorf, Social, S12)
Originally presented on his radio program, Kaleidoscope,
WJR, Detroit.
Duration: 49 min., 15 sec.
This segment deals with the Indian and his involvement with
the Bureau of Indian Affairs. What is the B.I.A. and what
influence does it have on the Indian? What and where were the
forces for good and evil and how has the Indian fared?

1. Indians of North America - Government relations.
2. United States. Bureau of Indian Affairs. L. Title.

C1
H4

The indispensable
Whorf, Michael, 1933–
The indispensable, Jim Bridger.
1 tape cassette. (The visual sounds of
Mike Whorf. History and heritage, H4)
Originally presented on his radio program, Kaleidoscope,
WJR, Detroit.
Duration: 37 min., 30 sec.
The country was unsettled and few men had gone beyond the
Mississippi; yet one man among the few would venture forth, to
trap, hunt, fight, explore, and to discover the marvels of the
frontier.

1. Bridger, James, 1804-1881. L. Title.

INDONESIA - FOREIGN RELATIONS

Voice Lib.
M728   Sukarno, Pres. Indonesia, 1901-1970.
bd.4   Interview with CBS correspondents regarding
the withdrawal of Indonesia from the U.N.
Columbia records, inc., 1965.
1 reel (7 in.)   7 1/2 in. per sec.
phonotape.

INDUSTRY AND STATE - U.S.
Voice Lib.
M1698   Aspin, Les, 1938–
bd.2   Interviewed on Firing Line by William
Buckley. WKAR-TV, May 28, 1974.
15 min.   phonotape (1 r.   7 1/2 i.p.s.)

1. Industry and state - U.S. 2. U.S. -
Military policy. I. Buckley, William
Frank, 1925–

INFLATION (FINANCE)

Voice Lib.
345   Baruch, Bernard Mannes, 1870-1965.
bd. 14   Statement on recession and dangers of
inflation. CBS, April 1, 1958.
1 reel (7in.)   7 1/2 in. per sec.
phonotape.

1. Inflation (finance).

Voice Lib.
M932   Information, please (radio program)
Panel of experts questioned by Clifton
Fadiman; panel includes Christopher Morley,
John Kieran, Franklin P. Adams, Col. Eagan.
Lloyd Grosse, 1943.
1 reel (7 in.)   7 1/2 in. per sec.
phonotape.

I. Fadiman, Clifton, 1904–   II. Morley,
Christopher Darlington, 1890–   III. Kieran,
John, 1892–   IV. Adams, Franklin Pierce,
1881-1960. V. Eag   Col.

Voice Lib.
M757   Ingersoll, Robert Green, 1833-1899.
bd.5   "Hope". Philosophical discussion about
a future life. Berliner, 1898.
1 reel (7 in.)   7 1/2 in. per sec.
phonotape.

Voice Lib.
M1615   Ingersoll, Robert Green, 1833-1899.
bd.2   Happiness is the only good. Rare Records,
Inc., A810 [19--?]
50 sec.   phonotape (1 r.   7 1/2 i.p.s.)

I. Title.

Inouye, Daniel Ken, 1924–

Voice Lib.
M1800   U.S. Congress. Senate. Select Committee on Presidential
Campaign Activities.
Watergate gavel to gavel, phase I: May 17 - August 7, 1973.
Pacifica, May 17 - August 7, 1973.
172 reels (5 in.)   3 3/4 i.p.s.   phonotape.

"These tapes include commentaries by Pacifica's Washington
correspondents and interviews with members of the Senate Committee
taped during recesses of the hearings."

1. Presidents - U.S. - Elections - 1972. 2. Watergate Affair,
1972–   I. Ervin, Samuel James, 1896–   II. Talmadge,
Herman Eugene, 1913–   III. Inouye, Daniel Ken, 1924–
IV. Baker, Howard H., 1925–   V. Gurney, Edward John, 1914–
VI. Weicker, Lowell P., 19   VII. Title.

Voice Lib.
256   Integration; a resident of Little Rock,
bd.2   Arkansas speaks. CBS News, September
22, 1957.
1 reel (7 in.)   7 1/2 in. per sec.
phonotape.

C1
S5

The interracial statesman

Whorf, Michael, 1933-
The interracial statesman.
1 tape cassette. (The visual sounds of
Mike Whorf. Social, S5)

Originally presented on his radio program, Kaleidoscope,
WJR, Detroit.
Duration: 34 min.
Booker T. Washington was one of the first of American Black
men to discover that he must accept the world on its terms. He was
a leader who saw prejudice and bigotry, yet prevailed to become
accepted as an individual, a man deserving of his fellow man's
respect.
L. Washington, Booker Taliaferro, 1859?-1915. I. Title.

Voice Lib.
M265
bd.3

IRELAND - POLITICS AND GOVERNMENT

DeVera, Eamon, 1882-
Address to America: Irish political
problem. Private recording of G. Robert
Vincent, March 17, 1947.
1 reel (7 in.) 7 1/2 i.p.s. phonotape.

1. Ireland - Politics and government.

C1
SC33

INVENTIONS

Whorf, Michael, 1933-
Today, they changed the world; inventions.
1 tape cassette. (The visual sounds of
Mike Whorf. Science, SC33)
Originally presented on his radio program, Kaleidoscope,
WJR, Detroit.
Duration: 37 min., 50 sec.
What causes the creative spark to kindle the flame of a new
idea ... a new process ... a new product? This narrative takes a
look at the march of progress in the individual efforts of the
innovators whose contributions change the course of history.

1. Inventions. I. Title.

C1
R33

The Irish saint, St. Patrick

Whorf, Michael, 1933-
The Irish saint, St. Patrick.
1 tape cassette. (The visual sounds of
Mike Whorf. Religion, R33)
Originally presented on his radio program, Kaleidoscope,
WJR, Detroit.
Duration: 37 min.
From a life shrouded in myth and legend, emerges the
story of the patron saint of Ireland, Saint Patrick.

I. Patrick, Saint, 373?-463? I. Title.

C1
SC10

Inventions in medicine

Whorf, Michael, 1933-
Inventions in medicine.
1 tape cassette. (The visual sounds of
Mike Whorf. Science, SC10)
Originally presented on his radio program, Kaleidoscope,
WJR, Detroit.
Duration: 53 min., 40 sec.
A fast moving account of some of the noblest inventions and
discoveries of medicine and science. Pasteur, Harvey and many
more highlight this adventure of men pitted against disease and
sickness.

I. Medicine - History. I. Title.

C1
H62

The iron duke - Wellington

Whorf, Michael, 1933-
The iron duke - Wellington.
1 tape cassette. (The visual sounds of
Mike Whorf. History and heritage, H62)

Originally presented on his radio program, Kaleidoscope,
WJR, Detroit.
Duration: 38 min., 50 sec.
His military genius, the ability to persevere with his raw and
untrained recruits, and his unquestioned courage in adversity
turned the tide against the Corsican, and earned Wellington his
place as one of England's foremost national heroes.

I. Wellington, Arthur Wellesley, 1st duke of, 1769-1852.
I. Title.

Voice Lib.
626-
627

The investigator; satire on the investigations
of Senator Joseph McCarthy, written by
Reuben Ship, with John Drainie playing the
role of the investigator. CBC, May 30, 1954.
2 reels (7 in.) 7 1/2 in. per sec.
phonotape.

I. Ship, Reuben   II. Drainie, John

Voice Lib.
M906-
908

The irregular verb to love

Skinner, Cornelia Otis, 1901-
In sophisticated comedy play "The Irregular
Verb to Love". NET, December, 1965.
3 reels (7 in.) 7 1/2 in. per sec.
phonotape.

I. Title: The irregular verb to love.

C1
S29

IRELAND

Whorf, Michael, 1933-
A smile and a tear; tribute to the Irish.
1 tape cassette. (The visual sounds of
Mike Whorf. Social, S29)
Originally presented on his radio program, Kaleidoscope,
WJR, Detroit.
Duration: 44 min.
Highlighting this program is a poignant reading of "The
trimmins on the rosary" as the Visual Sounds presents the story
of Ireland; its history, its people, its music, and the tale of
St. Patrick.

I. Ireland. 2. National characteristics, Irish. I. Title.

Voice Lib.
381-
382
bd.1

Irvine, Clarence T
I can hear it now (radio program)
CBS, April 26, 1951.
2 reels (7 in.) 7 1/2 in. per sec. phonotape.
I. Radio Free Europe. 2. Strategic Air Command. I.
Ridgway, Matthew Bunker, 1895- II. Churchill, Winston Leonard
Spencer, 1874-1965. III. Bevan, Aneurin, 1897-1960. IV. Nixon,
Richard Milhous, Pres. U. S., 1913- V. Kerr, Robert Samuel, 1896-
1963. VI. Brewster, Ralph Owen, 1888-1962. VII. Wherry, Kenneth
Spicer, 1892-1951. VIII. Capehart, Homer Earl, 1897- IX.
Lehman, Herbert Henry, 1878-1963. X. Taft, Robert Alphonso,
1889-1953. XI. Moody, Arthur Edson Blair, 1902-1954. XII.
Martin, Joseph William, 1884-1968. XIII. McMahon, James O'Brien,
1903-1952. XIV. MacArthur, Douglas, 1880-1964. XVII. Wilson,
Charles Edward, 1886-1972. XVIII. Irvine, Clarence T

Irving, Clifford Michael, 1930-
Voice Lib.
M1491 Wallace, Mike, 1918-
bd.2   Segment on altered Howard Hughes autobiography on CBS "60 Minutes" program,
describing the controversy, picturing present
physical appearance of Hughes and bringing
up loan by Hughes to President Nixon's
brother of $205,000. Speakers: Mike Wallace
and Clifford Irving. CBS-TV, January 16,
1972.
     1 reel (7 in.)   7 1/2 in. per sec.
phonotape.
             (Continued on next card)

Irving, Clifford Michael, 1930-
Voice Lib.
M1491 Wallace, Mike, 1918-
bd.4   New developments in the mystery case of
Howard Hughes and Clifford Irving, described
by Mike Wallace on CBS "60 Minutes". CBS-TV,
January 30, 1972.
     1 reel (7 in.)   7 1/2 in. per sec.
phonotape.

     I. Hughes, Howard Robard, 1905-   II.
Irving, Clifford Michael, 1930-

Voice Lib.   Irwin, James B   1932-
M1480 Apollo 15 (space flight): lift-off.
bd.1   CBS TV, July 26, 1971.
     1 reel (7 in.)   7 1/2 in. per sec.
phonotape.
     1. Project Apollo. 2. Space flight to the
moon. 3. Scott, David Randolph, 1932-   4.
Irwin, James B   1932- 5. Worden, Alfred
M   1930- I. Scott, David Randolph,
1932- II. Irwin, James B   1932- III.
Worden, Alfred M   1930-

Voice Lib.   Irwin, James B   1932-
M1480 Apollo 15 (space flight): beginning of power
bd.2   descent to moon. NBC TV, July 31, 1971.
     1 reel (7 in.)   7 1/2 in. per sec.
phonotape.
     1. Project Apollo. 2. Space flight to the
moon. 3. Scott, David Randolph, 1932-   4.
Irwin, James B   1932- 5. Worden, Alfred
M   1930- I. Scott, David Randolph,
1932- II. Irwin, James B   1932- III.
Worden, Alfred M   1930-

Voice Lib.   Irwin, James B   1932-
M1480 Apollo 15 (space flight): walk in deep space
bd.3   by Al Worden to retrieve film packages.
Commentary of Gene Cernan, who walked in
space during Gemini 9 flight. NBC TV,
August, 1971.
     1 reel (7 in.)   7 1/2 in. per sec.
phonotape.
     1. Project Apollo. 2. Space flight to the moon. 3. Scott,
David Randolph, 1932-   4. Irwin, James B   1932-   5.
Worden, Alfred M   1930-   I. Scott, David Randolph, 1932-
II. Irwin, James B   1932- III. Worden, Alfred M   1930-
IV. Cernan, Eugene Andrew, 1934-

            Irwin, James B   1932-
Voice Lib.
M1480 Apollo 15 (space flight): splashdown,
bd.4   commentary, speeches. NBC TV, August 7,
1971.
     1 reel (7 in.)   7 1/2 in. per sec.
phonotape.

     1. Project Apollo. 2. Space flight to the
moon. 3. Scott, David Randolph, 1932-   4.
Irwin, James B   1932- 5. Worden, Alfred
M   1930- I. Scott, David Randolph,
1932- II. Irwin, James B   1932- III.
Worden, Alfred M   1930-

          Is there a Santa Claus?
Voice Lib.
344   Douglas, Laura Virginia
bd.18   Author of the letter "Is There a
Santa Claus?" interviewed on her
conception of Christmas. CBS,
December 24, 1961.
     1 reel (7 in.)   7 1/2 in. per sec.
phonotape.

     I. Title: Is there a Santa Claus?

Voice Lib.
M350   Ismay, Hastings Lionel Ismay, baron, 1887-
bd.4   Tribute to Eisenhower on assuming the
Presidency. CBS, January, 1953.
     1 reel (7 in.)   7 1/2 i.p.s.   phonotape.

     1. Eisenhower, Dwight David, Pres. U.S.,
1890-1969.

Voice Lib.
M723   Ismay, Hastings Lionel Ismay, baron, 1887-1965.
bd.1   Interview with Edward R. Murrow, dealing
with Ismay's reminiscences about Winston S.
Churchill. CBS, 1960.
     1 reel (7 in.)   7 1/2 in. per sec.
phonotape.

     1. Churchill, Winston Leonard Spencer, 1874-
1965. I. Murrow, Edward Roscoe, 1908-1965.

      ISRAEL - FOREIGN RELATIONS - ARAB COUNTRIES
Voice Lib.
M1728   Dinitz, Simcha, 1929-
     Speech delivered to National Press Club
on Arab-Israeli relations, with Ken Scheibel.
WKAR, June 13, 1974.
     40 min.   phonotape (1 r.   7 1/2 i.p.s.)

     1. Israel - For. rel. - Arab countries.
2. Arab countries - For. rel. - Israel.
I. Scheibel, Ken.

ISRAEL - FOREIGN RELATIONS - ARAB
COUNTRIES

Voice Lib.
M1641   Hussein, King of Jordan, 1935-
         Peace in the Middle East; National Press
Club Address.   WKAR-AM, March 15, 1974.
    45 min.   phonotape (1 r.   7 1/2 i.p.s.)

    Includes question and answer period.

    1. Arab countries - Foreign relations -
Israel. 2. Israel - Foreign relations -
Arab countries.

ISRAEL - FOREIGN RELATIONS - ARAB COUNTRIES

Voice Lib.
M1241   Reynolds, Frank
         ABC-TV documentary, including reports from
Cairo and Tel Aviv and a review of the
Arab-Israeli conflicts past and present.
ABC-TV, May 25, 1967.
    1 reel (7 in.)   7 1/2 i.p.s.   phonotape.

    1. Israel - Foreign relations - Arab
countries. 2. Arab countries - Foreign
relations - Israel.

ISRAEL - FOREIGN RELATIONS - U.S.

Voice Lib.
M864   Silver, Abba Hillel, 1893-1963.
        Portion of the principal address to the 2000 delegates of the
51st annual convention of the Zionist Organization of America,
held at Syria Mosque in Pittsburgh, Pa. Dr. Silver criticizes
U. S. Government for its vascillating policies on the question
of Palestine partition. Reviews the steps leading to the formation
of Jewish homeland, culminating in a reversal of his policy by
President Truman. KDKA, July 4, 1948
    1 reel (7 in.)   7 1/2 i.p.s.   phonotape.

    1. Zionism. 2. U. S. - Foreign relations - Israel.
3. Israel - Foreign relations - U. S.

ISRAEL - RELATIONS (GENERAL) WITH ARAB
COUNTRIES

Voice Lib.
M1683   Sayegh, Fayez Abdullah, 1922-
         Interviewed by William Buckley on Firing
Line.   WKAR-TV, May 21, 1974.
    45 min.   phonotape (1 r.   7 1/2 i.p.s.)

    1. Arab countries - Relations (general)
with Israel. 2. Israel - Relations (general)
with Arab countries. I. Buckley, William
Frank, 1925-

ISRAEL-ARAB WAR, 1967-

Voice Lib.
M1256   Fawzi, Mahmoud, 1900-
         Address by Deputy Premier of UAR Fawzi
attacking Israeli atrocities, aggression,
U.S.A. and U.K. help to Israel and ridiculing
Pres. Johnson. Complimenting U Thant, praising
U.S.S.R., accusing U.S. 6th Fleet. NBC-TV,
June 21, 1967.
    1 reel (7 in.)   7 1/2 in. per sec.
phonotape.

ISRAEL-ARAB WAR, 1967-

Voice Lib.
M1273-   How Israel won the war. Interviews with
1274   Arab and Israel military and civilian
leaders at scene of action at conclusion
of six-day war in June 1967, including
resumé of campaign and analysis.   CBS-TV,
July 18, 1967.
    2 reels (7 in.)   7 1/2 in. per sec.
phonotape.

    Incomplete.

ISRAEL-ARAB WAR, 1967-

Voice Lib.
M1269   Israeli-Arab war; "Victory or Else". NBC-TV
bd.2-   special documentary program, narrated by
1271   John Chancellor and other NBC field
correspondents in the Middle East, describing in detail the entire conflict between
Israel and its Arab enemies; with interviews of General Hud, General Rabin and
General Sharan. NBC-TV, July 23, 1967.
    3 reels (7 in.)   7 1/2 in. per sec.
phonotape.

(Continued on next card)

ISRAEL-ARAB WAR, 1967-   - DIPLOMATIC
HISTORY

Voice Lib.
M1254   Eban, Abba Solomon, 1915-
bd.1   Address by Israel Foreign Minister Eban
at emergency session of U.N. General Assembly meeting in
New York, reviewing Middle East political and military
situation; rebutting the previous speech made by USSR
Premier Kosygin and blaming Russia for Israel-Arab tensions.
NBC-TV, June 19, 1967.
    1 reel (7 in.)   7 1/2 in. per sec.   Phonotape.

    Speech incomplete.

    1. Israel-Arab War, 1967-   - Diplomatic history.

ISRAEL-ARAB WAR, 1967-   - DIPLOMATIC HISTORY

Voice Lib.
M1254   George-Brown, George Alfred Brown, baron,
bd.2   1914-
        Portion of address by British Foreign Minister Brown at U.N.
General Assembly emergency session listing U.K. financial aid
to Arab States and recommendations for alleviating current
Arab-Israeli crisis, suggesting new U.N. Middle East military
mission. NBC-TV, June 21, 1967.
    1 reel (7 in.)   7 1/2 in. per sec.   phonotape.

    1. Israel-Arab War, 1967-   - Diplomatic history.

ISRAEL-ARAB WAR, 1967-   - DIPLOMATIC
HISTORY

Voice Lib.
M1255   Goldberg, Arthur Joseph, 1908-
bd.2   Address to emergency meeting of U.N.
General Assembly stating current U.S. position
on resolving Arab-Israeli crisis and suggestion
for peace in the Middle East.   CBS-TV,
June 20, 1967.
    1 reel (7 in.)   7 1/2 in. per sec.
phonotape.

ISRAEL-ARAB WAR, 1967-   - DIPLOMATIC
Voice Lib.   HISTORY
M1253 Kosygin, Aleksei Nikolaevich, 1904-
bd.2   Simultaneous interpretation to English of
          Premier Kosygin's address at the emergency
          session of U.N. General Assembly in New
          York pertaining to Middle East crisis.
          Condemns Israel as aggressor.   NBC-TV,
          June 19, 1967.
             1 reel (7 in.)   7 1/2 in. per sec.
          phonotape.

C1
PWM19   Whorf, Michael, 1933-
           It's a grand old flag
           It's a grand old flag.
             1 tape cassette.   (The visual sounds of
           Mike Whorf. Panorama; a world of music,
           PWM-19)
             Originally presented on his radio program, Kaleidoscope,
           WJR, Detroit.
             Duration: 25 min.
             The story of the American flag, with selected patriotic
           music.

             I. Flags. 2. Patriotic music, American. I. Title.

ISRAEL-ARAB WAR, 1967-   - DIPLOMATIC
                              HISTORY
Voice Lib.
M1242-   United Nations. Security Council.
1243   Emergency session of U.N. Security Council
          to discuss the Near East Crisis between
          Israel and Arab States. Main speakers:
          United States delegate; United Arab Republic
          delegate; Danish delegate; and excerpt of
          Israeli delegate.   NBC-TV, May 29, 1967.
             2 reels (7 in.)   7 1/2 i.p.s.   phonotape.

             1. Israel-Arab War, 1967-   - Diplomatic
          history.

Voice Lib.   Ives, Burl, 1909-
M619   Radio in the 1930's (Part II): a series of
bd.1-   excerpts of the 1930's; a sample of radio
14   of the period. NVL, April, 1964.
             1 reel (7 in.)   7 1/2 in. per sec.   phonotape.
          I. Allen, Fred, 1894-1956. II. Delmar, Kenny   III. Donald,
          Peter   IV. Pious, Minerva   V. Fennelly, Parker   VI.
          Boyer, Charles, 1899-   VII. Dunne, Irene, 1904-   VIII.
          DeMille, Cecil Blount, 1881-1959. IX. West, Mae, 1893-   X.
          Dafoe, Allan Ray, 1883-1943. XI. Dionne quintuplets. XII. Ortega,
          Santos   XIII. War of the worlds (radio program) XIV. Ives, Burl,
          1909-   XV. Robinson, Earl, 1910-   XVI. Temple, Shirley,
          1928-   XVII. Earhart, Amelia, 1898-1937. XVIII. Lawrence,
          Gertrude, 1901-1952. XIX. Cohan, George Michael, 1878-1942.
          XX. Shaw, George Bernard, 1856-1950. XXI. Hitler, Adolf, 1889-
          1945. XXII. Chamberlain, Neville, 1869-1940. XXIII. Roosevelt,
          Franklin Delano, Pres. U.S., 1882-1945.

Voice Lib.   ISRAEL-ARAB WAR, 1967-   - DIPLOMATIC HISTORY
M1247 United Nations. Security Council.
          Morning session of U.N. Security Council,
          called by its president, Hans Tabor of Denmark,
          to hear about the outbreak of hostilities
          between Israel and Arab countries. Main speakers:
          U Thant, Secretary General, reading latest
          reports, followed by delegate of Israel and
          delegate of United Arab Republic.   NBC-TV,
          June 5, 1967.
             1 reel (7 in.)   7 1/2 in. per sec.   phonotape.

             I. Israel-Arab War, 1967-   - Diplomatic history.
          I. Thant, U, 1909-

Voice Lib.   Ives, Burl, 1909-
623   Corwin, Norman Lewis, 1910-
          "Twenty-six by Corwin"; presents Earl
          Robinson and Millard Lampell's "Lonesome
          Train", with Earl Robinson, Burl Ives,
          Raymond Massey.   CBS, 1940.
             1 reel (7 in.)   7 1/2 in. per sec.
          phonotape.

             I. Robinson, Earl, 1910-   II. Ives,
          Burl, 1909-   III. Massey, Raymond, 1896-

Voice Lib.
M1269 Israeli-Arab war; "Victory or Else". NBC-TV
bd.2-   special documentary program, narrated by
1271   John Chancellor and other NBC field
          correspondents in the Middle East, describ-
          ing in detail the entire conflict between
          Israel and its Arab enemies; with inter-
          views of General Eud, General Rabin and
          General Sharan.   NBC-TV, July 23, 1967.
             3 reels (7 in.)   7 1/2 in. per sec.
          phonotape.

                           (Continued on next card)

Voice Lib.   Ives, Irving McNeil, 1896-1962
256   Hoffa, James Riddle, 1913-
bd.1   Testimony before Senate Rackets
          Committee, with Senator Ives and
          Counsel Robert Kennedy.   CBS News,
          August 22-23, 1957.
             1 reel (7 in.)   7 1/2 in. per sec.
          phonotape.

             I. Ives, Irving McNeil, 1896-1962. II.
          Kennedy, Robert Francis, 1925-1968.

Voice Lib.
M1269 Israeli-Arab war; "Victory of Else"...
bd.2-   July 23, 1967.   (Card 2)
1271

             1. Israel-Arab war, 1967-   I.
          Chancellor, John William, 1927-

Voice Lib.
339   JFK: son of liberty. Program on the occasion
          of the death of President Kennedy.   London,
          Independent Television, November 25, 1963.
             1 reel (7 in.)   7 1/2 in. per sec.
          phonotape.

             1. Kennedy, John Fitzgerald, Pres. U.S.,
          1917-1963.

Voice Lib.
M1037   Jack Armstrong, the All-American Boy (Radio
bd.2   program)
         Jack Armstrong, the "All-American" boy,
   in one episode entitled "Jack Armstrong and
   the Mutineers"; includes Wheaties commercial.
   NBC Radio, 1944.
         1 reel (7 in.)   7 1/2 in. per sec.
   phonotape.

         1. Radio programs.

Voice Lib.
565   Jack Paar Show tribute to President John F.
bd.1   Kennedy; series of quotes accumulated from
   various press conferences of President,
   recorded between 1961 and 1963.   NBC,
   March 13, 1964.
         1 reel (7 in.)   7 1/2 in. per sec.
   phonotape.

         1. Kennedy, John Fitzgerald, Pres. U.S.,
   1917-1963.

         JACKSON, ANDREW, PRES. U.S., 1767-1845

C1
H30   Whorf, Michael, 1933-
         Old Hickory, Andrew Jackson.
         1 tape cassette.   (The visual sounds of
   Mike Whorf. History and heritage, H30)

         Originally presented on his radio program, Kaleidoscope,
   WJR, Detroit.
         Duration: 30 min., 10 sec.
         The life of Andrew Jackson from his backwoods beginnings,
   through his battles with Indians and British, to his service as
   president.

         1. Jackson, Andrew, Pres. U.S., 1767-1845.   I. Title.

Voice Lib.
M1545   Jackson, Barbara (Ward) 1914-
bd.2   Commencement speech at Michigan State
   University.   WKAR-FM, December 1, 1973.
         22 min.   phonotape (1 r.   7 1/2 i.p.s.)

         Includes introduction by President
   Wharton.

Voice Lib.   Jackson, Eddie
M1047   Old-time radio excerpts of the 1930's and
         1940's, including: Rudy Vallee singing
   "Linger a little longer"; Will Rogers on
   panaceas for the Depression; Bing Crosby
   singing "Sweet Georgia Brown"; Eddie Cantor;
   Jimmy Durante singing "Inka-dinka-do";
   musical skit by Clayton, Jackson and Durante;
   wit by Harry Hershfield; musical selection
   "Thinking of you" by Kay Kyser; Kate Smith
   singing theme song, "When the moon comes over
   the mountain"; W.C. Fields' temperance

         (Continued on next card)

Voice Lib.   Jackson, Eddie
M1047   Old-time radio excerpts of the 1930's and
         1940's...   (Card 2)

         lecture; Al Jolson singing "Rocka-by-your
   baby"; and George Burns and Gracie Allen
   skit.   TV&R, 1930's and 1940's.
         1 reel (7 in.)   7 1/2 in. per sec.
         L. Vallee, Rudy, 1901-   II. Rogers, Will, 1879-1935. III.
   Crosby, Bing, 1901-   IV. Cantor, Eddie, 1893-1964. V. Durante,
   Jimmy, 1893-   VI. Clayton, Patti   VII. Jackson,
   Eddie   VIII. Hershfield, Harry, 1885-   IX. Kyser, Kay,
   1906-   X. Smith, Kate, 1909-   XI. Fields, W.C., 1879-
   1946. XII. Jolson, Al, 1886-1950. XIII. Burns, George, 1896-
   XIV. Allen, Gracie, 1906-

         Jackson, Gardner
Voice Lib.
M272   Biography in sound (radio program)
bd.1   Heywood Broun.   NBC, date?
         1 reel (7 in.)   7 1/2 in. per sec.
   phonotape.

         I. Broun, Heywood Campbell, 1888-1939. I. Broun,
   Heywood Campbell, 1888-1939. II. Swope, Herbert Bayard,
   1882-1958. III. Wilson, Mattie   IV. Jackson, Gardner
   V. Meany, Thomas   VI. Waldron, Beatrice   VII.
   Gordon, Max   VIII. Madison, Connie   IX. Gannett,
   Lewis Stiles, 1891-1966. X. Collins, Joseph, 1866-1950. XI.
   Brown, Earl Louis, 1900-   XII. Levy, Newman, 1888-
   XIII. Growth, John   XIV. Bye, George   XV.
   Roosevelt, Franklin Delano, Pres. U.S., 1882-1945. XVI.
   Reynolds, Quentin James,   )-1965.

         Jackson, Henry Martin, 1912-
Voice Lib.
M1477   Discussion of Supreme Court decision on
   publishing Pentagon Papers. William B.
   Macomber, deputy under-secretary of state;
   Senator Henry Jackson; Max Frankel, head of
   New York Times' Washington bureau; Benjamin
   Bradley, executive editor of Washington Post.
   Questioned by Carl Stern, NBC; Martin Hayden,
   Detroit News; James J. Kilpatrick, Washington
   Star Syndicate; Kenneth Crawford, Washington
   Post; Edwin Newman.   NBC-TV, June 30, 1971.
         1 reel (7 in.)   7 1/2 in. per sec.
   phonotape.   (Continued on next card)

Voice Lib.
M1692   Jackson, Henry Martin, 1912-
bd.3   Tells the National Press Club his
   optimistic estimate of America's economic
   future.   WKAR, May 23, 1974.
         25 min.   phonotape (1 r.   7 1/2 i.p.s.)

         Includes question & answer session through
   Clyde Lamont.

         1. U.S. - Politics and government - 1969-
         2. Impeachments.   I. Lamont, Clyde.

Voice Lib.
M1257   Jackson, Ralph D
bd.2   Acrostic spencerian sonnet written for
   Robert Vincent.   Location recording.
   May 4, 1941.
         1 reel (7 in.)   7 1/2 in. per sec.
   phonotape.

Voice Lib. Jackson, Robert Houghwout, 1892-1954
M622   Radio in the 1940's (Part III): a series of
bd.1-   excerpts from important broadcasts of the 1940's; a sample
bd.15   of radio of the period. NVL, April, 1964.
            1 reel (7 in.) 7 1/2 in. per sec. phonotape.
            I. Radio programs. I. Miller, Alton Glenn, 1909(?)-1944. II.
Diles, Ken   III. Wilson, Donald Harlow, 1900-   IV.
Livingstone, Mary   V. Benny, Jack, 1894-   VI. Harris,
Phil   VII. Merman, Ethel, 1909-   VIII. Smith, "Wonderful"
IX. Bennett, Richard Dyer   X. Louis, Joe, 1914-   XL
Eisenhower, Dwight David, Pres. U.S., 1890-1969. XII. MacArthur,
Douglas, 1880-1964. XIII. Romulo, Carlos Pena, 1899-   XIV.
Welles, Orson, 1915-   XV. Jackson, Robert Houghwout, 1892-1954.
XVI. LaGuardia, Fiorello Henry, 1882-1945. XVII. Nehru, Jawa-
harlal, 1889-1964. XVIII. Gandhi, Mohandas Karamchand, 1869-1948.

Jackson, Robert Houghwout, 1892-1954
Voice Lib.
573   I can hear it now (radio program)
bd.2-   1945-1949. CBS, 1950?
574   2 reels (7 in.) 7 1/2 in. per sec.
bd.1   phonotape.
            I. Murrow, Edward Roscoe, 1908-1965. II. Nehru, Jawaharlal,
1889-1964. III. Philip, duke of Edinburgh, 1921-   IV. Elizabeth II,
Queen of Great Britain, 1926-   V. Ferguson, Homer, 1889-   VI.
Hughes, Howard Robard, 1905-   VII. Marshall, George Catlett,
1880-   VIII. Ruth, George Herman, 1895-1948. IX. Lilienthal,
David Eli, 1899-   X. Trout, Robert, 1908-   XI. Gage, Arthur.
XII. Jackson, Robert Houghwout, 1892-1954. XIII. Gromyko, Anatolii Andreevich, 1908-   XIV. Baruch, Bernard Mannes, 1870-
1965. XV. Churchill, Wi---n Leonard Spencer, 1874-1965. XVI.
Winchell, Walter, 1897-   XVII. Davis, Elmer Holmes, 1890-
            (Continued on next card)

C1   JACKSON, THOMAS JONATHAN, 1824-1863
H107   Whorf, Michael, 1933-
       Stonewall - Thomas Jonathan Jackson.
       1 tape cassette. (The visual sounds of
Mike Whorf. History and heritage, H107)
       Originally presented on his radio program, Kaleidoscope,
WJR, Detroit.
       Duration: 38 min.
       This program tells the exciting story of the life of one of the
Confederacy's most colorful leaders. The humaneness of the man is
stressed as the narrator weaves his tale with equal amounts of
pathos and tender humor.
       I. Jackson, Thomas Jonathan, 1824-1863. I. Title.

Voice Lib.
M611   Janis, Elsie, 1889-
bd.8   Recalls early 20th century theater in song
       parodies; imitates Ethel Barrymore, George M.
       Cohan, Beatrice Lillie and Fanny Brice.
       National Vocarium, 1939.
       1 reel (7 in.) 7 1/2 i.p.s. phonotape.

       1. Theater - U.S.

Voice Lib. JAPAN - CONSTITUTIONAL HISTORY
M740   MacArthur, Douglas, 1880-1964.
bd.8-F   Excerpt of shortwave address to U.N.
       Security Council about Japan's new
       constitution renouncing war. CBS,
       April 17, 1946.
       46 sec. phonotape (1 r. 7 1/2 i.p.s.)

       1. Japan - Constitutional history.

Voice Lib.
352   Javits, Jacob Koppell, 1904-
bd.7   On the National Theater Bill proposed
       in Congress in 1949. NBC, 1949.
       1 reel (7in.) 7 1/2 in per sec.
       phonotape.

JAZZ MUSIC
Voice Lib.
M763   Alexander, Willard
bd.3   Excerpt from "The Scope of Jazz" (Program 6);
       comments on Goodman's success, disappearance
       of swing bands. Westinghouse Broadcasting
       Company, 1964.
       1 reel (7 in.) 7 1/2 in. per sec.
       phonotape. (The Music Goes Round and Round)

       1. Jazz music. I. Title: The scope of jazz.
       II. Series.

JAZZ MUSIC
Voice Lib.
M763   Austin, Bob
bd.6   Excerpt from "The Scope of Jazz" (Program
       6); his reasons for demise of big bands.
       Westinghouse Broadcasting Corporation, 1964.
       1 reel (7 in.) 7 1/2 in. per sec.
       phonotape. (The Music Goes Round and Round)

       I. Title: The scope of jazz. II. Series.

JAZZ MUSIC
Voice Lib.
M1456- Blake, Eubie
1457   Composer and pianist recalls his early
bd.1   career in ragtime music and plays various
       selections. NET, 1970.
       2 reels (7 in.) 7 1/2 in. per sec.
       phonotape.

JAZZ MUSIC
Voice Lib.
M1428   Brown, Steve
       Interview with Steve Brown, early New
       Orleans jazz musician, by Frank Gillis,
       Director of Folk Music Archive, Indiana
       University. 1953.
       1 reel (7 in.) 3 3/4 in. per sec.
       phonotape.

       Full track tape.
       I. Gillis, Frank

JAZZ MUSIC

Voice Lib.
270   Celestin, Oscar
       Oscar "Papa" Celestin and his original
       Tuxedo Band; New Orleans Jazz for White
       House Correspondents Association and
       President Eisenhower. From private
       collection of Congressman Hebert, May 8,
       1953.
            1 reel (7 in.)   7 1/2 in. per sec.
       phonotape.

JAZZ MUSIC

Voice Lib.
M1100   Dixieland (original jazz band)
bd.4   Playing "Tiger Rag" in Dixieland tempo.
         LaRocca, cornet; Shields, clarinet; Edwards,
         trombone; Regas, piano; Shabaro, drums.
         Forrest, 1918.
            1 reel (7 in.)   7 1/2 in. per sec.
         phonotape.

         I. Title: Tiger rag.

JAZZ MUSIC

Voice Lib.
M763   Goldstein, Chuck
bd.4   Excerpt from "The Scope of Jazz" (Program 6); comments
         how each band had their own style and how they adapted
         material to fit this style. Comments on Glenn Miller himself;
         also comments on Frank Sinatra, including "Moonlight Serenade"
         and an excerpt from "The Hit Parade", with girls screaming
         over Frank Sinatra and him singing "Lay That Pistol Down, Babe".
         Westinghouse Broadcasting Corporation, 1964.
            1 reel (7 in.)   7 1/2 in. per sec.   phonotape.   (The Music
         Goes Round and Round)

            1. Jazz music.   I. Title: The scope of jazz.   II. Series.

Voice Lib. JAZZ MUSIC
M763   Goodman, Benny, 1909-
bd.2   Excerpt from "The Scope of Jazz" (Program
         6); relates the early period of his life
         when he was just starting, and the different
         places the band played; including song
         "Let's Dance", theme song of Goodman organiza-
         tion. Westinghouse Broadcasting Corporation,
         1964.
            1 reel (7 in.)   7 1/2 in. per sec.
         phonotape.   (The Music Goes Round and Round)
            I. Title: The scope of jazz.   II. Title.

JAZZ MUSIC

Voice Lib.
M763   Serulli, Dom
bd.1   Excerpt from "The Scope of Jazz" (Program
         6); discusses three biggest factors in the
         establishment of the "swing" era, also his
         reason for decline of big bands. Westing-
         house Broadcasting Corporation, 1964.
            1 reel (7 in.)   7 1/2 in. per sec.
         phonotape.   (The Music Goes Round and Round)
            I. Title: The scope of jazz.   II. Series.

JAZZ MUSIC

Voice Lib.
M763   Whiteman, Paul, 1890-1967.
bd.5   Excerpt from "The Scope of Jazz" (Program
         6); comments on Bing Crosby at the beginning
         of his career, including song by Crosby,
         "Pennies from Heaven." Westinghouse
         Broadcasting Corporation, 1964.
            1 reel (7 in.)   7 1/2 in. per sec.
         phonotape.   (The Music Goes Round and Round)

            1. Crosby, Bing, 1901-   I. Title: The
         scope of jazz.   II. Series.

          JAZZ MUSIC
C1
M47-   Whorf, Michael, 1933-
49   Journey into jazz.
            3 tape cassettes.   (The visual sounds of
         Mike Whorf. Miscellaneous, M47-M49)
            Originally presented on his radio program, Kaleidoscope,
         WJR, Detroit.
            Duration: 36 min., 30 sec.; 37 min.; 37 min.
            A three part series on the unique style of music called
         jazz. The movement of jazz is followed from its origin in
         New Orleans to its rollicking acceptance in the wide open city of
         Chicago. The third part deals with jazz grown-up. That is the
         music form adopted by such greats as Goodman, James and Miller.

            1. Jazz music.   I. Title.

          JAZZ MUSIC
C1
PWM15   Whorf, Michael, 1933-
            A journey into jazz.
            1 tape cassette.   (The visual sounds of
         Mike Whorf. Panorama; a world of music,
         PWM-15)

            Originally presented on his radio program, Kaleidoscope,
         WJR, Detroit.
            Duration: 25 min.
            The capsule story of the development of jazz and
         performances by key contributors to jazz.

            1. Jazz music.   I. Title.

          JEANNE D'ARC, SAINT, 1412-1431
C1
R7   Whorf, Michael, 1933-
            The miracle of Saint Joan.
            1 tape cassette.   (The visual sounds of
         Mike Whorf. Religion, R7)

            Originally presented on his radio program, Kaleidoscope,
         WJR, Detroit.
            Duration: 40 min., 30 sec.
            Her immolation at the stake was the beginning of a legend rather
         than the end of a life, and amidst the splendor and pageantry her
         story is told.

            1. Jeanne d'Arc, Saint, 1412-1431.   I. Title.

          JEFFERSON, THOMAS, PRES. U.S., 1743-1826
C1
H11   Whorf, Michael, 1933-
            Our legacy from Mr. Jefferson.
            1 tape cassette.   (The visual sounds of
         Mike Whorf. History and heritage, H11)
            Originally presented on his radio program, Kaleidoscope,
         WJR, Detroit.
            Duration: 38 min.
            This historical account follows him through his years as a young
         Virginia scholar influenced by Patrick Henry to his days as a patriot
         who left a legacy to each and every American.

            1. Jefferson, Thomas, Pres. U.S., 1743-1826.   I. Title.

C1
H65
JENGHIS KHAN, 1162-1227

Whorf, Michael, 1933-
Apostles of destruction; Caesar, Alexander,
Ghenghis Khan, Hitler.
1 tape cassette.. (The visual sounds of Mike Whorf.
History and heritage, H65)

Originally presented on his radio program, Kaleidoscope,
WJR, Detroit.
Duration: 39 min.
Here are graphically related the tales of the despots of the ages -
for though many would strive for goodness and the best in man - a
few were blindly corrupt and evil, and in their time attempted to
bring the world to ruin.
L Caesar, C. Julius. 2. Alexander the Great, 356-323 B. C.
3. Jenghis Khan, 1162-1227. 4. Hitler, Adolf, 1889-1945.
L Title.

Voice Lib.
M746
bd.2
Jenkins, Ray Howard, 1897-
U.S. Congress. Senate. Committee on Government Operations.
Permanent Subcommittee on Investigations.
Proceedings of the [1st session] of Senate Army-McCarthy
hearings, April 22, 1954. Testimony by various witnesses
regarding pressure put on the Army to obtain a commission for
Private David Schine. Some of the people speaking are:
Griffin Bancroft, CBS announcer, describing the scenes at the
hearings; Joseph N. Welch, counsel for the Army; Ray Jenkins,
counsel for the subcommittee; Army Secretary Robert Stevens;
General Reber and Senator McClellan of Arkansas.   CBS Radio,
April 22, 1954.
1 reel (7 in.) 7 1/2 in. per sec.   phonotape.
L McCarthy-Army controversy, 1954. L Bancroft, Griffin
IL Welch, Joseph Nye, 1890-1960. III. Jenkins, Ray Howard,
1897- IV. Stevens, Robert Ten Broeck, 1899- V.
Reber, Miles VI. McClellan, John Little, 1896-

Voice Lib.
M933
Jenkins, Ray Howard, 1897-
U.S. Congress. Senate. Committee on Government Operations.
Permanent Subcommittee on Investigations.
Proceedings of the 5th session of Senate Army-McCarthy
hearings, April 28, 1954. Cross-examination of Army Secretary
Stevens by Senator McCarthy; Counselor Jenkins questions
Stevens and Private Schine; McCarthy denies charges of special
privileges for Schine. WJR, 10:30 p.m., April 28, 1954.
1 reel (7 in.) 7 1/2 in. per sec. phonotape.
L McCarthy-Army controversy, 1954. L Stevens, Robert
Ten Broeck, 1899- II. McCarthy, Joseph Raymond, 1909-1957.
III. Jenkins, Ray Howard, 1897- IV. Schine, G David,
1927-

Voice Lib.
M934
Jenkins, Ray Howard, 1897-
U.S. Congress. Senate. Committee on Government Operations.
Permanent Subcommittee on Investigations.
Proceedings of the 6th session of Senate Army-McCarthy
sessions, April 29, 1954. Private Schine makes first appearance;
he is cross-examined by Secretary Stevens and Counselor Jenkins;
Schine comments on circumstances of doctoring the "famous
photograph" and delivering it for publication at a Washington
restaurant. Evening session, WJR, April 29, 1954.
1 reel (7 in.) 7 1/2 in. per sec. phonotape.
L McCarthy-Army controversy, 1954. L Schine, G
David, 1927- II. Stevens, Robert Ten Broeck, 1899-
III. Jenkins, Ray Howard, 1897-

Voice Lib.
M1281
Jenkins, Ray Howard, 1897-
U.S. Congress. Senate. Committee on Government Operations.
Permanent Subcommittee on Investigations.
Proceedings of the 11th session of Senate Army-McCarthy
hearings, May 6, 1954. Sen. McCarthy on witness stand, pertaining
to missing letter from J. Edgar Hoover regarding possible spies at
Ft. Monmouth, N.J. Other speakers: Roy Cohn, Committee Counsel
Jenkins, Robert A. Collier.   Summary by CBS' Griffin Bancroft.
CBS Radio, May 6, 1954.
1 reel (7 in.) 7 1/2 in. per sec. phonotape.
L McCarthy-Army controversy, 1954. L McCarthy,
Joseph Raymond, 1909-1957. IL Cohn, Roy M 1927-
III. Jenkins, Ray Howard, 1897- IV. Collier, Robert A
V. Bancroft, Griffin

Voice Lib. Jenkins, Ray Howard, 1897-
M1319
U.S. Congress. Senate. Committee on Government Operations.
Permanent Subcommittee on Investigations.
Proceedings of the 16th session of Senate Army-McCarthy
hearings, May 13, 1954. Ray Jenkins questioning John Adams
about actions of Sec. Stevens. Was Sec. Stevens afraid to ship
Private Schine overseas due to pressure by Roy Cohn and Sen.
McCarthy? Was discussion of Mr. Adams private law practice?
CBS-TV, May 13, 1954.
1 reel (7 in.) 7 1/2 in. per sec. phonotape.
L McCarthy-Army controversy, 1954. L Jenkins, Ray
Howard, 1897- IL Adams, John G

Voice Lib.
138
bd.3-4
Jessel, George Albert, 1808-
The history of show business. Recording (?).
[n.d.]
1 reel (7 in.) 7 1/2 in. per sec.
phonotape.

C1
R34
JESUS CHRIST

Whorf, Michael, 1933-
The carpenters from Nazareth; Jesus and
Joseph.
1 tape cassette.   (The visual sounds of
Mike Whorf. Religion, R34)
Originally presented on his radio program, Kaleidoscope,
WJR, Detroit.
Duration: 37 min.
Jesus emerges from the shadows to walk in a world peopled
by simple hard-working men in a town named Nazareth.
L Jesus Christ. 2. Joseph, Saint. L Title.

C1
R1
JESUS CHRIST

Whorf, Michael, 1933-
The lesson never learned.
1 tape cassette. (The visual sounds of
Mike Whorf. Religion, R1)
Originally presented on his radio program, Kaleidoscope,
WJR, Detroit.
Duration: 46 min. , 15 sec.
This is the story of Jesus from His birth, through His ministry and
teaching to His death. It is based on the Bible, the stories which
unfold in the Gospels, and is ecumenical in approach.
L Jesus Christ. 2. Christianity. L Title.

JEWISH-ARAB RELATIONS
Voice Lib.
M1742
bd.3
Kaul, Triloki Nath
Discussion on capacity for nuclear war
in Egypt and Israel, by Triloki Nath Kaul and
Herbert F. York on the "Today Show". WKAR,
June 21, 1974.
10 min. phonotape (1 r. 7 1/2 i.p.s.)

1. Atomic energy. 2. Jewish-Arab relations.
I. York, Herbert Frank, 1921-

C1
S66
JEWS

Whorf, Michael, 1933-
  The eternal people - Jews.
  1 tape cassette. (The visual sounds of
Mike Whorf. Social, S66)
    Originally presented on his radio program, Kaleidoscope,
WJR, Detroit.
    Duration: 37 min., 30 sec.
    They gave the Western World a philosophy, a culture, and a
religion, yet in many instances they were rejected and despised.
They were the Jews - professing and embracing the Judaic faith -
yet, it was more than a faith. They have been searching for the
promised land, and modern day Israel is but part of it.

    L Jews. L Title.

Voice Lib.
629
bd.1
  The Jimmy Walker Story, from "Twentieth
  Century" TV series. On removing of
  railway tracks from 8th Avenue, welcomes
  Mayor of Berlin to New York, speech before
  Grand Street Boys' Club, says 'hello" to
  New York from Europe, in Cannes, France,
  comments on his tax problems while in
  England, on his return to New York in 1935.
  CBS, April 17, 1964.
    1 reel (7 in.)   7 1/2 in. per sec.
  phonotape.
    1. Walker, James John Joseph, 1881-1946.

Voice Lib.
M160
bd.2
  Joannes XXIII, Pope, 1881-1963.
    Shortwave broadcast of the election of
  Pope John XXIII from St. Peter's Square,
  the Vatican; Winston Burdett announcing.
  CBS, February 7, 1958.
    1 reel (7 in.)   7 1/2 in. per sec.
  phonotape.

    I. Burdett, Winston, 1913-

Voice Lib.
M317
bd.2
  Joannes XXIII, Pope, 1881-1963
  Johnson, Lyndon Baines, Pres. U.S., 1908-1973.
    Nancy Dickerson of NBC at Inaugural Ball
  talking to Vice-President and Mrs. Johnson;
  Charles Collingwood and Johnson on Sam Rayburn;
  Johnson in Berlin, audience with Pope John.
  NBC, CBS, November 24, 1963.
    1 reel (7 in.) 7 1/2 in. per sec. phonotape.
    L Rayburn, Samuel Taliaferro, 1882-1961. L Dickerson,
  Nancy Hanschman, 1929 (?)-   II. Johnson, Claudia Alta
  (Taylor) 1912-   III. Collingwood, Charles Cummings, 1917-
  IV. Joannes XXIII, Pope, 1881-1963.

Voice Lib.
M946
bd.7
  Joe Turner
  Handy, William Christopher, 1873-1958.
    Singing folk song "Joe Turner", accompanied
  by his guitar. CRV private recording,
  1953.
    1 reel (7 in.)   7 1/2 in. per sec.
  phonotape.

C1
FA4
  Joel Barlow

Whorf, Michael, 1933-
  Joel Barlow.
  1 tape cassette.   (The visual sounds of
Mike Whorf. The forgotten American, FA4)
    Originally presented on his radio program, Kaleidoscope,
WJR, Detroit.
    Duration: 13 min., 50 sec.
    Appointed minister to France by President Madison during the
time of the War of 1812, Barlow worked for a trade treaty with
Napoleon.

    L Barlow, Joel, 1754-1812. L Title.

C1
SC32
  John Glenn's day of miracles

Whorf, Michael, 1933-
  John Glenn's day of miracles.
  1 tape cassette. (The visual sounds of
Mike Whorf. Science, SC32)
    Originally presented on his radio program, Kaleidoscope,
WJR, Detroit.
    Duration: 37 min., 15 sec.
    From his days as pilot, to the day he climbed aboard
Friendship Seven, here is the story of the Ohio-born airman who
took the first giant step that led to mankind's gigantic leap.

    L Glenn, John Herschel, 1921-   L Title.

C1
H17
  John Smith's great lady

Whorf, Michael, 1933-
  John Smith's great lady.
  1 tape cassette. (The visual sounds of
Mike Whorf. History and heritage, H17)
    Originally presented on his radio program, Kaleidoscope,
WJR, Detroit.
    Duration: 29 min., 30 sec.
    It is one of America's first romantic histories, fired by an
adventurous spirit of a man and the inner courage of a woman.

    L Pocahontas, d. 1617. 2. Smith, John, 1580-1631.
  L Title.

C1
R4
  JOHN THE BAPTIST

Whorf, Michael, 1933-
  The thunderer.
  1 tape cassette. (The visual sounds of
Mike Whorf. Religion, R4)
    Originally presented on his radio program, Kaleidoscope,
WJR, Detroit.
    Duration: 28 min., 30 sec.
    Here is the narrative that deals with a prophet of God. He was
humble, yet his spirit challenged the brilliance and intelligence of
kings and priests.

    L John the Baptist. L Title.

Voice Lib.
157
bd.1
  "Johnny Appleseed"
  Huston, Walter, 1884-1950.
    "Johnny Appleseed"; a radio play. CBS,
  1930's.
    1 reel (7 in.)   7 1/2 in. per sec.
  phonotape.

    I. Title.

Johnny Bear

Voice Lib.
182   Steinbeck, John, 1902-1968.
bd.1   Reading his short story, "Johnny
        Bear" and briefly commenting.   Columbia
        Records, Inc., 1947.
            1 reel (7 in.)   7 1/2 in. per sec.
        phonotape.

                I. Title: Johnny Bear.

Voice Lib.
M853   John's other wife (radio program).   NBC,
bd.1   June 12, 1940.
            1 reel (7 in.)   7 1/2 in. per sec.
        phonotape.

            1. Radio serials.

Voice Lib.   Johnson, Claudia Alta (Taylor) 1912-
312   Johnson, Lyndon Baines, Pres. U.S., 1908-1973.
bd.1   Excerpts of interview with Vice President
        and Mrs. L. B. Johnson some weeks before the
        assassination, at the Johnsons' ranch.   NBC,
        November 23, 1963.
            1 reel (7 in.)   7 1/2 in. per sec.
        phonotape.

            I. Johnson, Claudia Alta (Taylor) 1912-

            Johnson, Claudia Alta (Taylor) 1912-
Voice Lib.
M317   Johnson, Lyndon Baines, Pres. U.S., 1908-1973.
bd.2   Nancy Dickerson of NBC at Inaugural Ball
        talking to Vice-President and Mrs. Johnson;
        Charles Collingwood and Johnson on Sam Rayburn;
        Johnson in Berlin, audience with Pope John.
        NBC, CBS, November 24, 1963.
            1 reel (7 in.) 7 1/2 in. per sec. phonotape.
            L Rayburn, Samuel Taliaferro, 1882-1961. L Dickerson,
        Nancy Hanschman, 1929 (?)-   II. Johnson, Claudia Alta
        (Taylor) 1912-   III. Collingwood, Charles Cummings, 1917-
        IV. Joannes XXIII, Pope, 1881-1963.

Voice Lib.
376   Johnson, Hugh Samuel, 1882-1942.
bd.3   Liberty of the people: attacks Franklin D.
        Roosevelt for destroying American
        democratic institutions.   Private
        recording, December 11, 1939.
            1 reel (7 in.)   7 1/2 in. per sec.
        phonotape.

            1. Roosevelt, Franklin Delano, Pres. U.S.,
        1882-1945.

                Johnson, Hugh Samuel, 1882-1942
Voice Lib.
572-   I can hear it now (radio program)
573   1933-1946.   CBS, 1948.
bd.1   2 reels (7 in.)   7 1/2 in. per sec.
        phonotape.

            L Murrow, Edward Roscoe, 1908-1965. II. LaGuardia, Fiorello
        Henry, 1882-1947. III. Chamberlain, Neville, 1869-1949. IV.
        Roosevelt, Franklin Delano, Pres. U.S., 1882-1945. V. Churchill,
        Winston Leonard Spencer, 1874-1965. VI. Gaulle, Charles de,
        Pres. France, 1890-1970. VII. Eisenhower, Dwight David, Pres. U.S.,
        1890-1969. VIII. Willkie, Wendell Lewis, 1892-1944.   IX. Martin,
        Joseph William, 1884-1968. X. Elizabeth II, Queen of Great Britain,
        1926-   XI. Margaret Rose, Princess of Gt. Brit. , 1930-   XII.
        Johnson, Hugh Samuel, 188?-'42. XIII. Smith, Alfred Emanuel,
        1873-1944. XIV. Lindbergh, Charles Augustus, 1902- XV. Davis,

                    (Continued on next card)

                Johnson, Hugh Samuel, 1882-1942
Voice Lib.
M620   Radio in the 1940's (Part I): a series of
bd.1-   excerpts from important broadcasts of the 1940's; a
bd.16   sample of radio of the period. NVL, April, 1964.
            1 reel (7 in.) 7 1/2 in. per sec. phonotape.
            L Radio programs. L Thomas, Lowell Jackson, 1892-   II.
        Gunther, John, 1901-1970. III. Kaltenborn, Hans von, 1878-1965.
        IV. Delmar, Kenny. V. Those were the good old days (Radio
        program) VI. Elman, Dave. VII. Hall, Frederick Lee, 1916-1970.
        VIII. Hobby lobby (Radio program) IX. Roosevelt, Franklin Delano,
        Pres. U.S., 1882-1945. X. Willkie, Wendell Lewis, 1892-1944.
        XI. Hoover, Herbert Clark, Pres. U.S., 1874-1964. XII. Johnson,
        Hugh Samuel, 1882-1942. XIII. Cobb, Irvin Shrewsbury, 1876-1944.
        XIV. Roosevelt, Theodore, 1858-1919. XV. Nye, Gerald Prentice,
        1892-1971. XVI. Lindbergh, Charles Augustus, 1902- XVII.
        Toscanini, Arturo, 1867-1957.

Voice Lib.   Johnson, J. Markisha
M1619   Stone, Chuck
bd.2   Perspectives in Black, with Roz Abrahms,
        Cheri Mazingo, and J. Markisha Johnson.
        WKAR, 1974.
            27 min.   phonotape (1 r.   7 1/2 i.p.s.)

            1. Race discrimination - U.S. 2. Watergate
        Affair, 187?-   I. Abrahms, Roz.
        II. Mazingo, Cheri. III. Johnson, J.
        Markisha.

            Johnson, Lady Bird
                see
        Johnson, Claudia Alta (Taylor) 1912-

            Johnson, Luci Baines, 1947-
                see
        Nugent, Luci Baines (Johnson) 1947-

Johnson, Lynda Bird, 1944-
    see
Robb, Lynda Bird (Johnson), 1944-

Voice Lib.
312   Johnson, Lyndon Baines, Pres. U.S., 1908-1973.
bd.1   Excerpts of interview with Vice President
    and Mrs. L. B. Johnson some weeks before the
    assassination, at the Johnsons' ranch. NBC,
    November 23, 1963.
      1 reel (7 in.) 7 1/2 in. per sec.
    phonotape.

      I. Johnson, Claudia Alta (Taylor) 1912-

Voice Lib.
M724 Johnson, Lyndon Baines, Pres. U.S., 1908-
bd.9   1973.
     Acceptance speech for the nomination of
    vice-president. 1960.
      1 min., 56 sec. phonotape (1 r. 7 1/2
    i.p.s.)

Voice Lib.
312   Johnson, Lyndon Baines, Pres. U.S., 1908-1973.
bd.4   Excerpt of remarks by Lyndon B. Johnson at
    Gettysburg, Pennsylvania (July 4, 1963).
    NBC, November 23, 1963.
      1 reel (7 in.) 7 1/2 in. per sec.
    phonotape.

Voice Lib.
M258 Johnson, Lyndon Baines, Pres. U.S., 1908-1973.
bd.10   Press conference on return from Asia;
    report on Southeast Asia journey (excerpts).
    New York, CBS, May 22, 1961.
      1 reel (7 in.) 7 1/2 in. per sec.
    phonotape.

Voice Lib.
M317 Johnson, Lyndon Baines, Pres. U.S., 1908-1973.
bd.1   Interview of Lyndon B. Johnson on his early
    background. CBS, November 24, 1963.
      1 reel (7 in.) 7 1/2 in. per sec.
    phonotape.

      I. Cronkite, Walter Leland, 1916-

Voice Lib.
311   Johnson, Lyndon Baines, Pres. U.S., 1908-1973.
bd.1   Proclamation by President Johnson as Monday,
    November 25, 1963, as a national day of
    mourning for Kennedy; relating of the incident.
    NBC-TV, November 23, 1963.
      1 reel (7 in.) 7 1/2 in. per sec.
    phonotape.

      1. Kennedy, John Fitzgerald, Pres. U.S.,
    1917-1963.

Voice Lib.
M317 Johnson, Lyndon Baines, Pres. U.S., 1908-1973.
bd.2   Nancy Dickerson of NBC at Inaugural Ball
    talking to Vice-President and Mrs. Johnson;
    Charles Collingwood and Johnson on Sam Rayburn;
    Johnson in Berlin, audience with Pope John.
    NBC, CBS, November 24, 1963.
      1 reel (7 in.) 7 1/2 in. per sec. phonotape.
      I. Rayburn, Samuel Taliaferro, 1882-1961. I. Dickerson,
    Nancy Hanschman, 1929 (?)- II. Johnson, Claudia Alta
    (Taylor) 1912- III. Collingwood, Charles Cummings, 1917-
    IV. Joannes XXIII, Pope, 1881-1963.

Voice Lib.
M311 Johnson, Lyndon Baines, Pres. U.S., 1908-1973.
bd.8   Message to the people of the U.S. by
    President Lyndon Johnson; description of
    conditions at White House by NBC. NBC,
    November 23, 1963.
      1 reel (7 in.) 7 1/2 in. per sec.
    phonotape.

      1. Kennedy, John Fitzgerald, Pres. U.S.,
    1917-1963 - Assassination.

Voice Lib.
M1708 Johnson, Lyndon Baines, Pres. U.S., 1908-1973.
     Address to a Joint Session of Congress on
    continuation of current U. S. policies under
    his administration. NBC, November 27, 1963.
      30 min. phonotape (1 r. 7 1/2 i.p.s.)
      Transcript of the address included with
    tape.

      1. U.S. - Politics and government - 1963-
    1969.

Voice Lib.
563-   Johnson, Lyndon Baines, Pres. U.S., 1908-1973.
564   A Conversation with the President: discusses first hours of his
        administration; changes wrought by assassination; pays tribute to
        Jackie Kennedy's courage; stability of Kennedy administration
        following assassination; Presidential succession; selection of
        Vice-President; comments on rift with Robert Kennedy; the press
        and the Presidency; Bobby Baker case; budget; aid to the poor;
        Domestic Peace Corps; discusses name for his administration,
        "The Better Deal"; describes himself as "progressive"; 1964
        campaign; his working day; reasons for giving up smoking;
        analyzes New Hampshire primary; relations with Henry Cabot
        Lodge; Vietnam situation; foresees America's future role in
        world; wisdom in decision-making; Panama situation; comments
        on past actions of DeGaulle; Red China and the U.N.; foreign aid;
        Alliance for Progress; civil rights demonstrations and the Civil
        Rights Bill; responsibilities of the President; personal feelings

Voice Lib.
M758, Johnson, Lyndon Baines, Pres.U.S., 1908-1973.
bd.1-   Address before joint session of Congress
759   requesting new legislation on voting rights
       for Negroes.   CBS line, March 16, 1965.
          2 reels (7 in.)   7 1/2 in. per sec.
       phonotape.

          1. Negroes - Civil rights.

Voice Lib.
563-   Johnson, Lyndon Baines, Pres. U.S., 1908-1973.
564   A Conversation with the President...   1964
       (Card 2)

       about the Presidency and the U.S. CBS, March 15, 1964.
          2 reels (7 in.)   7 1/2 in. per sec. phonotape.

Voice Lib.
M927- Johnson, Lyndon Baines, Pres. U.S., 1908-
928   1973.
bd.1   State of the Union address.   NBC,
       January 12, 1966.
          2 reels.(7 in.)   7 1/2 in. per sec.
       phonotape.

Voice Lib.
577   Johnson, Lyndon Baines, Pres. U.S., 1908-1973.
bd.3   St. Patrick's Day address. NBC,
       March 17, 1964.
          1 reel (7in.)   7 1/2 in. per sec.
       phonotape.

Voice Lib.
M1020- Johnson, Lyndon Baines, Pres. U.S., 1908-
1021   1973.
          State of the Union message delivered before
       joint session of Congress, January 10, 1967,
       with commentaries by Frank McGee, Ray Shearer,
       Chet Huntley, David Brinkley, John K. Galbraith
       and British and French political personalities.
       Main points of address: economic status of
       the country; recommendation of the tax hike;
       United States position in Vietnam, etc.
       NBC-TV, January 10, 1967.
                                    (Continued on next card)

Voice Lib.
645   Johnson, Lyndon Baines, Pres. U.S., 1908-
       1973.
          University of Michigan commencement;
       accepts honorary Doctor of Law degree
       from University of Michigan President
       Harlan Hatcher.   Ann Arbor, WUOM, May 22,
       1964.
          1 reel (7 in.)   7 1/2 in. per sec.
       phonotape.

Voice Lib.
M1020- Johnson, Lyndon Baines, Pres. U.S., 1908-
1021   1973.   State of the Union message...
           January 10, 1967.   (Card 2)

          2 reels (7 in.)   7 1/2 in. per sec.
       phonotape.

Voice Lib.
M718   Johnson, Lyndon Baines, Pres., U.S., 1908-
bd.1   1973.
          Inaugural address.   January 20, 1965.
          1 reel (7 in.)   7 1/2 in. per sec.
       phonotape.

Voice Lib.
M1253 Johnson, Lyndon Baines, Pres. U.S., 1908-1973.
bd.1   Addressing Foreign Policy Conference for
       Education at the State Department Auditorium
       in Washington, prior to the emergency session
       of U.N. General Assembly.   Introductory
       remarks by Secretary Dean Rusk.   NBC-TV,
       June 19, 1967.
          1 reel (7 in.)   7 1/2 in. per sec.
       phonotape.

          I. Rusk, Dean, 1909-

Voice Lib.
M1287   Johnson, Lyndon Baines, Pres. U.S., 1908-
bd.2-   1973.
1288   "A conversation with the President". One
       hour press conference with President Johnson
       by the three TV networks about current
       problems, prior to President's departure
       for Australia. Dan Rather, CBS; Ray Shearer,
       NBC; Frank Reynolds, ABC. NBC-TV,
       December 19, 1967.
          2 reels (7 in.)   7 1/2 in. per sec.
       phonotape.

                                    SEE NEXT CARD

Voice Lib.
M1287   Johnson, Lyndon Baines, Pres. U.S., 1908-
bd.2-   1973. "A conversation with the President"...
1288   1967. (Card 2)

          I. Rather, Dan   II. Shearer, Ray
            III. Reynolds, Frank

Voice Lib.
M1302   Johnson, Lyndon Baines, Pres. U.S., 1908-
       1973.
          State of the Union message, delivered
       before a joint session of Congress. NBC-TV,
       January 17, 1968.   1 reel (7 in.)   7 1/2 in. per sec.
       phonotape.

Voice Lib.
M1309   Johnson, Lyndon Baines, Pres. U.S., 1908-
bd.1   1973.
          Address to the nation by television,
       pertaining to limitation of bombing in
       Vietnam and other current national problems,
       ending with his announcement of withdrawal
       from the 1968 presidential race. NBC-TV,
       March 31, 1968.
          1 reel (7 in.)   7 1/2 in. per sec.
       phonotape.

Voice Lib.
M1317   Johnson, Lyndon Baines, Pres. U.S., 1908-1973.
bd.4   Message of grief by President Johnson
       about Dr. King's death. NBC, April 4, 1968.
          1 reel (7 in.)   7 1/2 in. per sec.
       phonotape.

          1. King, Martin Luther, 1929-1968.

Voice Lib.
M1349- Johnson, Lyndon Baines, Pres. U.S., 1908-
1350   1973.
          State of the Union message delivered to
       joint session of Congress.   January 14,
       1969.
          2 reels (7 in.)   7 1/2 in. per sec.
       phonotape.

        Johnson, Lyndon Baines, Pres. U.S.,
Voice Lib.   1908-1973
M1386   Apollo 11 (space flight): excerpts of
bd.4   interview between Walter Cronkite and
       Lyndon B. Johnson two weeks before the
       moon flight regarding development of American
       space effort.   CBS TV, July 20, 1969.
          1 reel (7 in.)   7 1/2 in. per sec.
       phonotape.
          1. Project Apollo. 2. Space flight to the
       moon. I. Cronkite, Walter Leland, 1916-
       II. Johnson, Lyndon Baines, Pres. U.S., 1908-
       1973.

Voice Lib.
M1425   Johnson, Lyndon Baines, Pres. U.S., 1908-
bd.2   1973.
          Interview with ex-President Lyndon
       Johnson regarding Kennedy assassination events
       with CBS commentator Walter Cronkite.
       CBS-TV, March, 1970.
          1 reel (7 in.)   7 1/2 in. per sec.
       phonotape.

          I. Cronkite, Walter Leland, 1916-

        Johnson, Lyndon Baines, Pres. U.S.,
Voice Lib.   1908-1973
M846   The Making of the President, 1964 (TV program)
bd.2   Excerpts of political speeches and state-
       ments by presidential candidates Lyndon
       Johnson and Barry Goldwater, from TV dramati-
       zation of Theodore H. White's book "The
       making of the president, 1964".
          6 min.   phonotape (1 r.   7 1/2 i.p.s.)

       I. Johnson, Lyndon Baines, Pres. U.S., 1908-1973.
       II. Goldwater, Barry Morris, 1909-   III. White, Theodore
       Harold, 1915-   /The making of the president, 1964.

        JOHNSON, LYNDON BAINES, PRES. U.S.,
Voice Lib.   1908-1973
M312   Humphrey, Hubert Horatio, 1911-
bd.5   Ray Shearer of NBC, Washington, speaking
       with Senator Hubert Humphrey about his
       opinion of the new President, Lyndon B.
       Johnson.   NBC, November 23, 1963.
          1 reel (7 in.)   7 1/2 in. per sec.
       phonotape.

          1. Johnson, Lyndon Baines, Pres. U.S.,
       1908-1973.   I. Shearer, Ray

JOHNSON, LYNDON BAINES, PRES. U.S.,
        1908-1973
Voice Lib.
M312   National Broadcasting Company, inc.
bd.2   Discussion among Texas citizens with
        NBC newsmen about President Lyndon Baines
        Johnson. NBC, November 23, 1963.
        1 reel (7 in.)   7 1/2 in. per sec.
        phonotape.

        1. Johnson, Lyndon Baines, Pres. U.S.,
        1908-1973.

JOHNSON, LYNDON BAINES, PRES. U.S.,
        1908-1973
Voice Lib.
M1310   Newman, Edwin Harold, 1919-
bd.1   Commentary on President Johnson's address
        to the nation and his withdrawal from the
        1968 presidential race. NBC, March 31, 1968.
        1 reel (7 in.)   7 1/2 in. per sec.
        phonotape.

        1. Johnson, Lyndon Baines, Pres. U.S.,
        1908-1973.

JOHNSON, LYNDON BAINES, PRES. U.S.,
        1908-1973
Voice Lib.
M1705   Schlesinger, Arthur Meier, 1917-
        The imperial presidency; address at
        the University of Missouri. WKAR
        (KBIA, Columbia, Mo.), June 3, 1974.
        50 min. phonotape (1 r.   7 1/2 i.p.s.)

        1. Presidents - U.S. 2. Johnson, Lyndon
        Baines, Pres. U.S., 1908-1973. 3. Nixon,
        Richard Milhous, Pres. U.S., 1913-

JOHNSON, LYNDON BAINES, PRES. U.S., 1908-1973
Voice Lib.
M612   Shriver, Robert Sargent, 1915-
        War on poverty; reviews President Lyndon
        Johnson's fight against domestic poverty,
        discusses his role in the fight, briefly
        reviews his own career. NET, March 30, 1964.
        1 reel (7 in.)   7 1/2 i.p.s. phonotape.

        1. U.S. -Economic conditions. 2. Johnson, Lyndon
        Baines, Pres. U.S., 1908-1973. 3. Shriver, Robert Sargent,
        1915-

JOHNSON, LYNDON BAINES, PRES. U.S.,
        1908-1973
Voice Lib.
M1693   Spock, Benjamin McLane, 1903-
bd.2   On the younger generation and his own
        pro-peace activities, anti-obscenity
        activities, etc., on Merv Griffin Show.
        25 min. phonotape (1 r.   7 1/2 i.p.s.)

        1. Women's Liberation Movement.
        2. Children - Care & hygiene. 3. Johnson,
        Lyndon Baines, Pres. U.S., 1908-
        I. Griffin, Mervyn Edward, 1925-

Voice Lib.
M946   Jolson, Al, 1886-1950.
bd.3   Singing World War I novelty song "Sister
        Susie's Sewing Shirts for Soldiers".
        Col. Phonograph, 1916.
        1 reel (7 in.)   7 1/2 in. per sec.
        phonotape.

        I. Title: Sister Susie's sewing shirts for
        soldiers

Voice Lib.
M946   Jolson, Al, 1886-1950.
bd.4   Singing "When the Grown-Up Ladies Act
        Like Babies" (novelty pop song). Col.
        Phono., 1920.
        1 reel (7 in.)   7 1/2 in. per sec.
        phonotape.

        I. Title: When the grown-up ladies act
        like babies.

Voice Lib.   Jolson, Al, 1886-1950
M1047   Old-time radio excerpts of the 1930's and
        1940's, including: Rudy Vallee singing
        "Linger a little longer"; Will Rogers on
        panaceas for the Depression; Bing Crosby
        singing "Sweet Georgia Brown"; Eddie Cantor;
        Jimmy Durante singing "Inka-dinka-do";
        musical skit by Clayton, Jackson and Durante;
        wit by Harry Hershfield; musical selection
        "Thinking of you" by Kay Kyser; Kate Smith
        singing theme song, "When the moon comes over
        the mountain"; W.C. Fields' temperance
        (Continued on next card)

Voice Lib.   Jolson, Al, 1886-1950
M1047   Old-time radio excerpts of the 1930's and
        1940's...   (Card 2)

        lecture; Al Jolson singing "Rocka-by-your
        baby"; and George Burns and Gracie Allen
        skit. TV&R, 1930's and 1940's.
        1 reel (7 in.)   7 1/2 in. per sec.
        I. Vallee, Rudy, 1901-   II. Rogers, Will, 1879-1935. III.
        Crosby, Bing, 1901- IV. Cantor, Eddie, 1893-1964. V. Durante,
        Jimmy, 1893-   VI. Clayton, Patti   VII. Jackson,
        Eddie   VIII. Hershfield, Harry, 1885-   IX. Kyser, Kay,
        1906-   X. Smith, Kate, 1909-   XI. Fields, W.C., 1879-
        1946. XII. Jolson, Al, 1886-1950. XIII. Burns, George, 1896-
        XIV. Allen, Gracie, 1906-

Voice Lib.
M1034   Jolson, Al, 1886-1950.
bd.10   Excerpt of Kraft Music Hall radio program;
        singing "Alabamy Bound". TV & R, 1937.
        1 reel (7 in.)   7 1/2 in. per sec.
        phonotape.

        I. Title: Alabamy bound.

Voice Lib.
M719   Jolson, Al, 1886-1950.
bd.3   Kraft Music Hall with Lauritz Melchior.
        October 9, 1947.
        7 min., 46 sec.   phonotape (1 r.
        7 1/2 i.p.s.)

        I. Melchior, Lauritz Lebrecht Hommel,
        1890-1973

S

Voice Lib.
M225   Jones, Daniel
        Packard, Frederick
            Styles in Shakespearean acting, 1890-1950.
        Creative Associates, 1963?
            1 reel (7 in.)   7 1/2 i.p.s.   phonotape.

            I. Sothern, Edward Askew, 1826-1881. II. Marlowe,
        Julia, 1865-1950. III. Booth, Edwin, 1833-1893. IV. Gielgud,
        John, 1904-   V. Robeson, Paul Bustill, 1898-   VI. Terry,
        Dame Ellen, 1848-1928. VII. Allen, Viola. VIII. Welles,
        Orson, 1915-   IX. Skinner, Otis, 1858-1942. X. Barrymore,
        John, 1882-1942. XI. Olivier, Sir Laurence Kerr, 1907-
        XII. Forbes-Robertson, Sir Johnston, 1853-   XIII. Evans,
        Maurice. XIV. Thorndike, Dame Sybil, 1882-   XV. Robson,
        Flora. XVI. LeGallienne, Eva, 1899-   XVII. Anderson,
        Judith. XVIII. Duncan, Augustin. XIX. Hampden, Walter.
        XX. Speaight, Robert, 190?   XXI. Jones, Daniel.

Voice Lib.
M761   Jolson, Al, 1886-1950
bd.7   Meyer, Joseph
        Excerpt from "Whatever happened to Tin Pan
        Alley?" (Program 3); relates how he got Al Jolson to introduce
        his song "California here I come", including Al Jolson singing
        this song.   Westinghouse Broadcasting Corporation, 1964.
            1 reel (7 in.)   7 1/2 in. per sec.   phonotape. (The music
        goes round and round)

            L. Music, Popular (Songs, etc.) - U.S.   L. Jolson, Al, 1886-
        1950. II. Title: Whatever happened to Tin Pan Alley?
        III. Series.

C1
H36   JONES, JOHN PAUL, 1747-1792
        Whorf, Michael, 1933-
            The admiral - John Paul Jones.
            1 tape cassette.   (The visual sounds of
        Mike Whorf. History and heritage, H36)

            Originally presented on his radio program, Kaleidoscope,
        WJR, Detroit.
            Duration 38 min., 30 sec.
            He was a revolutionary - from his trials and hardships as a
        young Scotsman to his days as the admiral of a brave, young,
        inexperienced navy.

            L. Jones, John Paul, 1747-1792.   L. Title.

C1
FA21   Jonathan Edwards
        Whorf, Michael, 1933-
            Jonathan Edwards.
            1 tape cassette.   (The visual sounds of
        Mike Whorf. The forgotten American, FA21)

            Originally presented on his radio program, Kaleidoscope,
        WJR, Detroit.
            Duration 12 min., 33 sec.
            Puritan clergyman and theologian, he exerted a permanent
        influence on our American heritage.

            L. Edwards, Jonathan, 1703-1758.   L. Title.

Voice Lib.
M792   Jones, LeRoi
            Reading his poems at the Asilomar Negro
        Writers Conference followed by discussion
        by the audience on merits of his work.
        KPFK, December 20, 1964.
            1 reel (7 in.)   7 1/2 in. per sec.
        phonotape.

Voice Lib.
M1579   Jondahl, H. Lynn, 1936-
bd.1   Third Civic Presence Group/Legislative
        luncheon, with Craig Halverson, Lynn
        Jondahl, Gary Owen, Phil Mastin, and
        Eric Gentile.   WKAR-TV, February 15, 1973.
        10 min.   phonotape (1 r.   7 1/2 i.p.s.)

            1. Physically handicapped - Law and legis-
        lation.   I. Halverson, Craig. II. Jondahl,
        H. Lynn, 1936-   III. Owen, Gary M., 1944-
        IV. Mastin, Philip O., 1930-   V. Gentile,
        Eric Anton, 1943-

Voice Lib.
353   Jones, Robert
bd.22   Bob Jones' life; tells of his philosophy.
        Private recording. 1937.
            1 reel (7 in.)   7 1/2 in. per sec.
        phonotape.

Jones, Billy   -1940.
    see
The Happiness Boys (Radio program)

Voice Lib.
540   Jones, Robert Tyre, 1902-
bd.5   Welcoming in New York City by Mayor Jimmy
        Walker; replies.   Fox Movietone, 1930.
            1 reel (7 in.)   7 1/2 in. per sec.
        phonotape.

            I. Walker, James John Joseph, 1881-1946.

Voice Lib.   Jones, Robert Tyre, 1902-
M1064   Walker, James John Joseph, 1881-1946.
bd.5   Excerpt of welcoming remarks by Mayor
Walker of New York at City Hall to golfer
Bobby Jones; reply to Mayor Walker by
Bobby Jones.   Fox Movietone News, 1929.
1 reel (7 in.)   7 1/2 in. per sec.
phonotape.

I. Jones, Robert Tyre, 1902-

C1
PWM14   Whorf, Michael, 1933-
Those ragtime years.
1 tape cassette.   (The visual sounds of
Mike Whorf. Panorama; a world of music, PWM-14

Originally presented on his radio program, Kaleidoscope,
WJR, Detroit.
Duration: 25 min.
Music from the decade between the turn of the century and
World War I, including some by composer Scott Joplin.

1. Ragtime music. 2. Joplin, Scott, 1868-1917. I. Title.

JOPLIN, SCOTT, 1868-1917

Voice Lib.
M871   Jordan, Max
bd.3   Japan's acceptance of Potsdam Declaration.
NBC, August 14, 1945.
1 reel (7 in.)   7 1/2 i.p.s.   phonotape.

1. World War, 1939-1945 - Japan.

C1
R34   Whorf, Michael, 1933-
The carpenters from Nazareth; Jesus and
Joseph.
1 tape cassette.   (The visual sounds of
Mike Whorf. Religion, R34)
Originally presented on his radio program, Kaleidoscope,
WJR, Detroit.
Duration: 37 min.
Jesus emerges from the shadows to walk in a world peopled
by simple hard-working men in a town named Nazareth.

1. Jesus Christ. 2. Joseph, Saint. I. Title.

JOSEPH, SAINT

C1
FA10   Whorf, Michael, 1933-
Joseph Lane.
1 tape cassette.   (The visual sounds of
Mike Whorf. The forgotten American, FA10)
Originally presented on his radio program, Kaleidoscope,
WJR, Detroit.
Duration: 10 min., 24 sec.
Soldier, politician, and pioneer, Lane was one of the
first senators from Oregon. He was the Vice Presidential
candidate on the breakaway Democratic ticket with John C.
Breckinridge in 1860.

1. Lane, Joseph, 1801-1881. I. Title.

Joseph Lane

JOURNALISTIC ETHICS
Voice Lib.
M1481   Vanocur, Sander, 1928-
bd.3   Interviewed by David Frost on believing
the government, being misled, journalistic
responsibility.   Comments from Sam Levenson.
July, 1971.
1 reel (7 in.)   7 1/2 i.p.s.   phonotape.

1. Journalistic ethics.   I. Frost, David
Paradine, 1939-   II. Levenson, Samuel,
1911-

C1
M47-   Whorf, Michael, 1933-
49   Journey into jazz.
3 tape cassettes.   (The visual sounds of
Mike Whorf. Miscellaneous, M47-M49)
Originally presented on his radio program, Kaleidoscope,
WJR, Detroit.
Duration: 36 min., 30 sec.; 37 min.; 37 min.
A three part series on the unique style of music called
jazz. The movement of jazz is followed from its origin in
New Orleans to its rollicking acceptance in the wide open city of
Chicago. The third part deals with jazz grown-up. That is the
music form adopted by such greats as Goodman, James and Miller.

1. Jazz music.   I. Title.

Journey into jazz

C1
PWM15   Whorf, Michael, 1933-
A journey into jazz.
1 tape cassette.   (The visual sounds of
Mike Whorf. Panorama; a world of music,
PWM-15)
Originally presented on his radio program, Kaleidoscope,
WJR, Detroit.
Duration: 25 min.
The capsule story of the development of jazz and
performances by key contributors to jazz.

1. Jazz music.   I. Title.

A journey into jazz

Voice Lib.
M1026   Journey to Greatness; biographical sketch
bd.1   of the career of George Gershwin.   One-
hour 1963 Ohio State award-winning program
broadcast by the Voice of America.   Voice
of America, 1963.
1 reel (7 in.)   7 1/2 in. per sec.
phonotape.

1. Gershwin, George, 1898-1937.

Voice Lib.
M274   Joyce, James, 1882-1941.
bd.2   Reading from "Anna Livia Plurabelle".
Orthonological Institute, Cambridge, 1935.
1 reel (7 in.)   7 1/2 in. per sec.
phonotape.

Voice Lib.
M1463   Joyce, William, 1906-1946.
bd.7   Broadcasting from Germany warning British
           people and farewell to his listeners.
           Peteler, 1940 & April, 1945.
           1 reel (7 in.)   7 1/2 i.p.s.   phonotape.

           1. Propaganda, German.

Voice Lib.
M849   Juliana, Queen of the Netherlands, 1909-
bd.3   Speaking from Canada to the U.S. and
          Canadian people, expressing thanks for aid
          given to war refugees, reviewing war
          devastation, justifying her shelter from war
          zone of her two children, requesting more
          financial aid.   CBC, June 17, 1940.
          1 reel (7 in.)   7 1/2 in. per sec.
          phonotape.

                    Kalb, Bernard
Voice Lib.
M1478 The Pentagon Papers; discussion of content,
          meaning.   Bernard Kalb, CBS; Senator J.W.
          Fulbright; Senator John Tower; Arthur
          Schlesinger; Walt Rostow; Max Frankel,
          New York Times; Crosby Noyes, Washington
          Evening Star.   CBS-TV, July 13, 1971.
          1 reel (7 in.)   7 1/2 in. per sec.
          phonotape.
          I. Kalb, Bernard   II. Fulbright, James William, 1905-
          III. Tower, John Goodwin, 1925-   IV. Schlesinger, Arthur
          Meier, 1888-   V. Rostow, Walt Whitman, 1916-   VI.
          Frankel, Max   VII. Noyes, Crosby

                    Kalb, Marvin L
Voice Lib.
M942   Vietnam perspective (Television program)
          CBS Special Report on Senate Foreign
          Relations Committee hearings and the war
          in Vietnam.   CBS, February 18, 1966.
          1 reel (7 in.)   7 1/2 in. per sec.
          phonotape.

          1. Vietnamese conflict, 1961-   - U.S.
          I. Mudd, Roger   II. Sevareid, Arnold Eric,
          1912-   III. Reasoner, Harry, 1923-   IV.
          Kalb, Marvin L

Voice Lib.
M1040 Kalb, Marvin L
bd.1   Discussion of the significance of Kosygin
          press conference with two political science
          authorities.   CBS, February 9, 1967.
          1 reel (7 in.)   7 1/2 in. per sec.
          phonotape.

          1. Kosygin, Aleksei Nikolaevich, 1904-

                    Kalb, Marvin L
Voice Lib.
M1476 Pentagon Papers.
bd.2   New York times, Washington post, U.S.
          Government arguments before the Supreme
          Court, as represented by CBS News.
          Daniel Schorr (government), Marvin Kalb
          (New York times), Bob Sheafer (Washington
          post), Roger Mudd.   CBS-TV, June 26, 1971.
          1 reel (7 in.)   7 1/2 i.p.s. phonotape.
          I. Security classification (Government documents)
          I. Schorr, Daniel Louis, 1916-   II. Kalb, Marvin L
          III. Sheafer, Bob   IV. Mudd, Roger

                    Kallen, Horace Meyer, 1882-
Voice Lib.
M814   Santayana, George, 1863-1952.
bd.2-   Personal reminiscences about the eminent
815   American philosopher, poet, and novelist by
          Horace H. Kallen and Dr. Corliss Lamont, in
          conversation with Robert Stover of WBAI,
          arranged through the cooperation of the
          American Humanist Association.   KPFK, May 23,
          1964.
          2 reels (7 in.)   7 1/2 in. per sec.   phonotape.
          I. Santayana, George, 1863-1952.   I. Kallen, Horace Meyer,
          1882-   II. Lamont, Corliss, 1902-   III. Stover, Robert

Voice Lib.
M1800 Kalmbach, Herbert Warren, 1921-
WG   Testimony before the Senate Committee
0716.03 investigating the Watergate Affair.
          Pacifica, July 16, 1973.
          105 min.   phonotape (2 r.   3 3/4 i.p.s.)
          (Watergate gavel to gavel, phase 1)

          1. Watergate Affair, 1972-

Voice Lib.
M1800 Kalmbach, Herbert Warren, 1921-
WG   Testimony before the Senate Committee
0717   investigating the Watergate Affair.
          Pacifica, July 17, 1973.
          289 min.   phonotape (4 r.   3 3/4 i.p.s.)
          (Watergate gavel to gavel, phase 1)

          1. Watergate Affair, 1972-

                    Kalmer, Ned
Voice Lib.
M1027 The world today: direct news reports from
bd.3   Belgian front; statement from SHAEF (Supreme
          Headquarters Allied Expeditionary Force);
          news of war in the Pacific discussed by CBS
          correspondents Robert Trout, Douglas Edwards,
          Richard C. Hottelet, and Ned Kalmer.   CBS
          News, December 23, 1944.
          1 reel (7 in.)   7 1/2 in. per sec.   phonotape.
          I. Trout, Robert, 1908-   II. Edwards, Douglas
          III. Hottelet, Richard Curt   IV. Kalmer, Ned

Kalmer, Ned
Voice Lib.
M953   Hitler, Adolf, 1889-1945.
bd.5   Ceremonies in Nuremberg, Germany at the
Reichsparteitag of the Nazi Party. Commentary
and interpretation by Ned Kalmer, CBS news
correspondent, on-the-spot. Peteler,
September, 1938.
    1 reel (7 in.)   7 1/2 in. per sec.
phonotape.

    I. Kalmer, Ned

Voice Lib.
218   Kaltenborn, Hans von, 1878-1965.
bd.1-2   News reports from Goedesburg on current
Czechoslovakian situation.   CBS, September
23, 1938.
    1 reel (7 in.)   7 1/2 in. per sec.
phonotape.

    1. Czechoslovak Republic - History.

Voice Lib.
M717   Kaltenborn, Hans von, 1878-1965.
bd.11   Analysis of Hitler speech on Czechoslovakia.
September 26, 1938.
    1 min., 58 sec.   phonotape (1 r.
7 1/2 i.p.s.)

    1. Germany - Foreign relations -
Czechoslovak Republic.   2. Czechoslovak
Republic - Foreign relations - Germany.

Voice Lib.
522   Kaltenborn, Hans von, 1878-1965.
bd.4   Review of proceedings in Congress on
declaration of war with Germany and
Italy.   CBS, December 11, 1941.
    1 reel (7 in.)   7 1/2 in. per sec.
phonotape.

Voice Lib.
M871   Kaltenborn, Hans von, 1878-1965.
bd.2   Broadcasting news of cessation of
hostilities ending World War II; announcing
acceptance of terms of unconditional surrender
of Japan and the proclamation of a 2-day
holiday for government workers of Great
Britain and U.S.; speculation on zones of
occupation.   NBC, August 14, 1945.
    1 reel (7 in.)   7 1/2 in. per sec.
phonotape.
    1. World War, 1939-1945.

Voice Lib.
K1028   Kaltenborn, Hans von, 1878-1965.
bd.8   Excerpt of news broadcast on foreign
ministers' conference.   1946.
    1 reel (7 in.)   7 1/2 in. per sec.
phonotape.

Voice Lib.
M1048   Kaltenborn, Hans von, 1878-1965.
bd.1   "Recollections at thirty"; one hour
radio program saluting 30 years of network
broadcasting by NBC, featuring dramatic or
humorous actual sounds during that period.
NBC, May 15, 1956.
    1 reel (7 in.)   7 1/2 i.p.s.   phonotape.

    1. National Broadcasting Company, inc.

Kaltenborn, Hans von, 1878-1965.
Voice Lib.
M774-   Farewell to Studio Nine; historical broadcasts
775,   made by CBS correspondents at time of action
bd.1   and reflections by them in retrospect.   1964.
    2 reels (7 in.)   7 1/2 in. per sec.
phonotape.

    I. Trout, Robert, 1908-   II. Pierpoint,
Robert   III. Murrow, Edward Roscoe,
1908-1965.   IV. Kaltenborn, Hans von, 1878-
1965.   V. Sevareid, Arnold Eric, 1912-
VI. Daly, John Charles, 1914-

Kaltenborn, Hans von, 1878-1965
Voice Lib.
M620   Radio in the 1940's (Part I): a series of
bd.1-   excerpts from important broadcasts of the 1940's; a
bd.16   sample of radio of the period.   NVL, April, 1964.
    1 reel (7 in.)   7 1/2 in. per sec.   phonotape.
    I. Radio programs.   I. Thomas, Lowell Jackson, 1892-   II.
Gunther, John, 1901-1970.   III. Kaltenborn, Hans von, 1878-1965.
IV. Delmar, Kenny.   V. Those were the good old days (Radio
program) VI. Elman, Dave.   VII. Hall, Frederick Lee, 1916-1970.
VIII. Hobby lobby (Radio program) IX. Roosevelt, Franklin Delano,
Pres. U.S., 1882-1945.   X. Willkie, Wendell Lewis, 1892-1944.
XI. Hoover, Herbert Clark, Pres. U.S., 1874-1964.   XII. Johnson,
Hugh Samuel, 1882-1942.   XIII. Cobb, Irvin Shrewsbury, 1876-1944.
XIV. Roosevelt, Theodore, 1858-1919.   XV. Nye, Gerald Prentice,
1892-1971.   XVI. Lindbergh, Charles Augustus, 1902-   XVII.
Toscanini, Arturo, 1867-1957.

Voice Lib.
M1029   Kaltenborn, Hans von, 1878-1965.
bd.2   "A Tribute to Hans von Kaltenborn".
Excerpts of various radio news broadcasts by
Mr. Kaltenborn, and comments by his colleagues
upon his death.   Speakers: Morgan Beatty,
narrator; Mary Margaret McBride; H. R. Baukhage;
Harry S Truman.   MSU Dept. of TV and Radio, 1965.
    1 reel (7 in.)   7 1/2 in. per sec.
phonotape.
    I. Kaltenborn, Hans von, 1878-1965.   I. Beatty, Morgan
II. McBride, Mary Margaret, 1899-   III. Baukhage, Hilmar
Robert   IV. Truman, Harry S, Pres. U.S., 1884-1972.

Kaltenborn, Hans von, 1878-1965

Voice Lib.
573 I can hear it now (radio program)
bd.2- 1945-1949. CBS, 1950?
574 2 reels (7 in.) 7 1/2 in. per sec.
bd.1 phonotape.
  L. Murrow, Edward Roscoe, 1908-1965. IL. Nehru, Jawaharlal,
1889-1964. IIL. Philip, duke of Edinburgh, 1921- IV. Elizabeth II,
Queen of Great Britain, 1926- V. Ferguson, Homer, 1889- VL.
Hughes, Howard Robard, 1905- VIL. Marshall, George Catlett,
1880- VIIL. Ruth, George Herman, 1895-1948. IX. Lilienthal,
David Eli, 1899- X. Trout, Robert, 1908- XL. Gage, Arthur.
XIL. Jackson, Robert Houghwout, 1892-1954. XIIL. Gromyko, Ana-
tolii Andreevich, 1908- XIV. Baruch, Bernard Mannes, 1870-
1965. XV. Churchill, Winston Leonard Spencer, 1874-1965. XVL.
Winchell, Walter, 1897- XVIL. Davis, Elmer Holmes, 1890-
   (Continued on next card)

Kaltenborn, Hans von, 1878-1969

Voice Lib.
M1490 Republican Party. National Convention, 25th,
bd.5 Chicago, 1952.
  Description of proceedings at Republican
National Convention in Chicago, 1952
(described by commentators George Hicks and
H.V. Kaltenborn). Includes statements by
Robert A. Taft and Dwight D. Eisenhower.
Convention unanimously nominates Eisenhower.
CBS Radio, 1952.
  1 reel (7 in.) 7 1/2 in. per sec.
phonotape.

Voice Lib.
M1362 Kaltenbrunner, Ernst, 1901-1946.
bd.3 Testimony at the international military
proceedings in Nuremberg, Germany.
Peteler, August 31, 1946.
  1 reel (7 in.) 7 1/2 in. per sec.
phonotape.

  1. Nuremburg Trial of Major German War
Criminals, 1945-1946.

Voice Lib.
M1090 Kane, Joseph Nathan, 1899-
bd.7 Excerpt from radio series "Famous First
Facts" over Mutual Network, of interview
between Tom Slater and G. Robert Vincent,
which included voices of Theodore Roosevelt
and the Bugler of Balaclava. Audio Scriptions,
April 20, 1939.
  1 reel (7 in.) 7 1/2 in. per sec.
phonotape.

Voice Lib.
341 Kantor, MacKinlay, 1904-
bd.2 An interview. Voice of America, 1961.
  1 reel (7 in.) 7 1/2 in. per sec.
phonotape.

Voice Lib.
M1699 Kaplan, Justin
bd.1 Discusses his book Lincoln Steffens - a
biography on Book Beat with Robert Cromie.
WKAR-TV, May 29, 1974.
  20 min. phonotape (1 r. 7 1/2 i.p.s.)

  1. Steffens, Joseph Lincoln, 1866-1936.
2. Kaplan, Justin/Lincoln Steffens - a
biography. I. Cromie, Robert Allen, 1909-

   KAPLAN, JUSTIN
   LINCOLN STEFFENS - A BIOGRAPHY
Voice Lib.
M1699 Kaplan, Justin
bd.1 Discusses his book Lincoln Steffens - a
biography on Book Beat with Robert Cromie.
WKAR-TV, May 29, 1974.
  20 min. phonotape (1 r. 7 1/2 i.p.s.)

  1. Steffens, Joseph Lincoln, 1866-1936.
2. Kaplan, Justin/Lincoln Steffens - a
biography. I. Cromie, Robert Allen, 1909-

Voice Lib.
M764 Kapp, David
bd.6 Excerpt from "The World of Wax" (Program
8); discusses his father when he sold
phonographs door to door. Westinghouse
Broadcasting Corporation, 1964.
  1 reel (7 in.) 7 1/2 in. per sec.
phonotape. (The Music Goes Round and Round)

  I. Title: The world of wax. II. Series.

Voice Lib.
M764 Kapp, Mickey
bd.13 Excerpt from "The World of Wax" (Program 8);
comments on how a small label survives against
the giants. Westinghouse Broadcasting
Corporation, 1964.
  1 reel (7 in.) 7 1/2 in. per sec.
phonotape. (The Music Goes Round and Round)

  I. Title: The world of wax. II. Series.

Voice Lib.
M765 Kapp, Mickey
bd.6 Excerpt from "The Anatomy of a Hit" (Program
9); relates his experience with the record
"Hello, Dolly", including the song as sung
by Louis Armstrong. Westinghouse Broadcasting
Corporation, 1964.
  1 reel (7 in.) 7 1/2 in. per sec.
phonotape. (The Music Goes Round and Round)

  I. Title: The anatomy of a hit. II. Series.

Voice Lib.
M1466   Karl I, emperor of Austria, 1887-1922.
bd.6   Order of the Day to his troops on the
front during World War I.   Peteler, 1916.
1 reel (7 in.)   7 1/2 in. per sec.
phonotape.

Voice Lib.
M1466   Karl I, emperor of Austria, 1887-1922.
bd.8   Talking about the Imperial Austrian fund
to aid military widows and orphans.
Peteler, February 16, 1916.
1 reel (7 in.)   7 1/2 in. per sec.
phonotape.

1. European War, 1914-1918 - Hospitals,
charities, etc. 2. European War, 1914-1918 -
Austria.

Voice Lib.
M233   Karoub, Sheik Hussien, Imam of Moslems.
bd.2   Readings from the Koran.   CBS, July 5, 1945.
1 reel (7 in.)   7 1/2 in. per sec.
phonotape.

Voice Lib.
M1742   Kaul, Triloki Nath
bd.3   Discussion on capacity for nuclear war
in Egypt and Israel, by Triloki Nath Kaul and
Herbert F. York on the "Today Show".   WKAR,
June 21, 1974.
10 min. phonotape (1 r.   7 1/2 i.p.s.)

1. Atomic energy. 2. Jewish-Arab relations.
I. York, Herbert Frank, 1921-

Voice Lib.
M1606   Kavanagh, Thomas H., 1909-
bd.2   Michigan Public Broadcasting presents: an
evening with Thomas H. Kavanagh. With Tim
Skubick. Michigan Public Radio, December 10,
1973.
30 min. phonotape (1 r.   7 1/2 in. per
sec.)

1. Courts - Michigan.   I. Skubick, Tim

Kay, Beatrice
Voice Lib.
640   Gay Nineties Revue (radio program)
bd.3   Musical radio program with cast including
Joe Howard and Beatrice Kay.   CBS, July, 1940.
1 reel (7 in.)   7 1/2 in. per sec.
phonotape.

I. Howard, Joe   II. Kay, Beatrice

Kay, Beatrice
Voice Lib.
539   Gay Nineties Revue (Radio program)
bd.5   The talking machine; skit with Joe Howard,
Al Rinker, and Beatrice Kay concerning
Edison's talking machine. Simulated voices
of P.T. Barnum and Florence Nightingale.
CBS, 1940.
1 reel (7 in.)   7 1/2 in. per sec.
phonotape.

I. Howard, Joe   II. Rinker, Al
III. Kay, Beatrice

Voice Lib.
M708   Kaye, Danny, 1913-
bd.2   "Command Performance"; radio show for
Armed Forces Radio Service. Melchior
collection, 1944.
1 reel (7 in.)   7 1/2 in. per sec.
phonotape.

Voice Lib.
397-   Kaye, Danny, 1913-
398   Good will tour. Matinee performance;
potpourri of songs and gags.   Voice of
America, May 17, 1953.
2 reels (7 in.)   7 1/2 in. per sec.
phonotape.

Kaye, Danny, 1913-
Voice Lib.
M1005   Hans Christian Andersen (Television program)
TV adaptation of film of same title, with
Danny Kaye and Victor Borge. ABC-TV, Nov. 3,
1966.
1 reel (7 in.)   7 1/2 in. per sec.
phonotape.

1. Andersen, Hans Christian, 1805-1875.
I. Kaye, Danny, 1913-   II. Borge,
Victor, 1909-

Kaye, Danny, 1913-
Voice Lib.
M1033 Voice of America.
Twentieth anniversary program of Voice of
America broadcasts narrated by Henry Fonda,
and including the voices of Carl Sandburg,
Danny Kaye, Jawaharlal Nehru, Franklin D.
Roosevelt, Charles Malik, Arnold Toynbee,
William Faulkner, Harry S.Truman, Dwight D.
Eisenhower, Helen Hayes, Dag Hammarskjöld,
Winston Churchill, and John F. Kennedy.
Voice of America, 1963.
1 reel (7 in.)   7 1/2 in. per sec.
phonotape.
(Continued on next card)

Kaye, Danny, 1913-
Voice Lib.
M1033 Voice of America. Twentieth anniversary
program... 1963. (Card 2)

L. Fonda, Henry Jaynes, 1905-   II. Sandburg, Carl,
1878-1967. III. Kaye, Danny, 1913-   IV. Nehru, Jawaharlal,
1889-1964. V. Roosevelt, Franklin Delano, Pres. U.S., 1882-
1945. VI. Malik, Charles Habib, 1906-   VII. Toynbee,
Arnold Joseph, 1889- VIII. Faulkner, William, 1897-1962.
IX. Truman, Harry S, Pres. U.S., 1884-1972. X. Eisenhower,
Dwight David, Pres. U.S., 1890-1969. XI. Hayes, Helen,
1900-   XII. Hammarskjöld, Dag, 1905-1961. XIII. Churchill,
Winston Leonard Spencer, 1874-1965. XIV. Kennedy, John
Fitzgerald, Pres. U.S., 1917-1963.

Voice Lib.
M373 Kazan, Elia, 1909-
Talks with Elliot Norton on drama, etc.
Lowell Institute Co-Operative Broadcasting
Council (NET), October 5, 1961.
1 reel (7 in.)   7 1/2 in. per sec.
phonotape.

I. Norton, Elliot

Voice Lib.
M1059 Kazan, Elia, 1909-
bd.2   Discussion of his work in the past and
his new book, "The Arrangement"; on "Today"
show. NBC-TV, February 20, 1967.
1 reel (7 in.)   7 1/2 in. per sec.
phonotape.

"Keep Your Head Down, Fritzie Boy"
Voice Lib.
603   American Quartet.
bd.5   "Keep Your Head Down, Fritzie Boy",
Lieutenant Gitz Rice's World War I song.
Victor Talking Machine Co., 1918.
1 reel (7 in.)   7 1/2 in. per sec.
phonotape.

I. Title.

Voice Lib.
M724 Kefauver, Estes, 1903-1963.
bd.10   Announcing his candidacy for the
nomination of president on the Democratic
ticket in 1955.
1 min., 4 sec.   phonotape (1 r.
7 1/2 i.p.s.)

1. Presidents - U.S. - Election - 1956.

Voice Lib.
579   Kefauver, Estes, 1903-1963.
bd.1   1956 Democratic National Convention;
accepts Vice-Presidential nomination, gives
his views of the Vice-Presidency. CBS,
August 17, 1956.
1 reel (7 in.)   7 1/2 in. per sec.
phonotape.

Kefauver, Estes, 1903-1963
Voice Lib.
M724 Rayburn, Samuel Taliaferro, 1882-1961.
bd.4   Samuel Rayburn and Estes Kefauver at
Democratic convention. 1952.
45 sec.   phonotape (1 r.   7 1/2 i.p.s.)

1. Presidents - U.S. - Election - 1952.
I. Kefauver, Estes, 1903-1963.

Voice Lib.
M1800 Kehrli, Bruce
WG   Testimony before the Senate Committee
0517.04 investigating the Watergate Affair.
Pacifica, May 17, 1973.
57 min.   phonotape (1 r.   3 3/4 i.p.s.)
(Watergate gavel to gavel, phase 1)

1. Watergate Affair, 1972-

Voice Lib.
M736 Keitel, Wilhelm, 1882-1946.
bd.8   Announcing the armistice required by
France. CBS, June 22, 1940.
25 sec.   phonotape (1 r.   7 1/2 i.p.s.)

1. World War, 1939-1945 - France.

Voice Lib.
M760 Kellem, Manny
bd.4 Excerpt from "What All the Screaming's About" (Program 1); promotion of the Beatles, including remarks by teenaged girls of their feelings toward the new singing group called the Beatles. Westinghouse Broadcasting Corporation, 1964.
1 reel (7 in.) 7 1/2 in. per sec. phonotape. (The Music Goes Round and Round)

I. Title: What all the screaming's about.
II. Series. 1. The Beatles

KELLY, MRS. COLIN

Voice Lib.
M297 McBride, Mary Margaret, 1899-
bd.2 Mrs. Colin Kelly, wife of World War II hero, talks with Miss McBride and Mayor Fiorello H. LaGuardia on living in New York City. NBC, Red Network, 1943.
1 reel (7 in.) 7 1/2 in. per sec. phonotape.

1. Kelly, Mrs. Colin. I. LaGuardia, Fiorello Henry, 1882-1947.

Voice Lib.
540 Kellogg-Briand Pact; futility of war, building
bd.12 of international confidence. Fox Movietone, 1932.
1 reel (7 in.) 7 1/2 in. per sec. phonotape.

Kelly, Frank
Voice Lib.
M969 Tugwell, Rexford Guy, 1891-
Conversation with Frank Kelly at Center for Study of Democratic Institutions in Santa Barbara, Calif., regarding F.D.R., presidential power, campaigning techniques and Tugwell's accomplishments as Governor of Puerto Rico. CSDI, 1964.
1 reel (7 in.) 7 1/2 in. per sec. phonotape.

I. Kelly, Frank

Voice Lib.
M1065 Kellogg-Briand pact on disarmament; British
bd.1 spokesman in favor of limitation of armaments; mood music and effects. Fox Movietone, 1930.
1 reel (7 in.) 7 1/2 in. per sec. phonotape.

1. Disarmament.

Kelly, Frank K., 1914-
Voice Lib.
M970 Pauling, Linus Carl, 1901-
A visit with the Paulings; informal talk with Dr. and Mrs. Pauling about their courtship, their work, the role of women, amusing Kennedy anecdote, questioning by Frank K. Kelly. CSDI, 1964.
1 reel (7 in.) 7 1/2 in. per sec. phonotape.

I. Kelly, Frank K 1914-

Kelly, Capt., U.S.A.F.
Voice Lib.
M384 I can hear it now (radio program)
bd.2 CBS, February 2, 1951.
1 reel (7 in.) 7 1/2 in. per sec. phonotape.

I. Taft, Robert Alphonso, 1889-1953. II. Rayburn, Samuel Taliaferro, 188?-1961. III. Barkley, Alban William, 1877-1956. IV. Mabaut, Louis Charles, 1886-1961. V. Attlee, Clement Richard Attlee, 1st earl, 1883-1967. VI. Kelly, Capt., U.S.A.

Kelly, Patsy
Voice Lib.
640 "A Tree Grows in Brooklyn"; comedy song sung
bd.2 by Barry Wood and Patsy Kelly. NBC, July 15, 1944.
1 reel (7 in.) 7 1/2 in. per sec. phonotape.

I. Wood, Barry II. Kelly, Patsy

Voice Lib.
M1616 Kelly, Clarence M
National Press Club address. WKAR-AM, April 4, 1974.
55 min. phonotape (1 r. 7 1/2 in. per sec.)

1. U.S. Federal Bureau of Investigation.

Kendall, H G
Voice Lib.
M617 Radio in the 1920's: a series of excerpts
bd.1- from important broadcasts of the 1920's,
bd.25 with brief prologue and epilogue; a sample of radio of the period. NVL, April, 1964.
1 reel (7 in.) 7 1/2 in. per sec. phonotape.
1. Radio programs. I. Marconi, Guglielmo, marchese, 1874-1937. II. Kendall, H G III. Coolidge, Calvin, Pres. U.S., 1872-1933. IV. Wilson, Woodrow, Pres. U.S., 1856-1924. V. Roosevelt, Franklin Delano, Pres. U.S., 1882-1945. VI. Lodge, Henry Cabot, 1850-1924. VII. LaGuardia, Fiorello Henry, 1882-1947. VIII. The Happiness Boys (Radio program) IX. Gallagher and Sheen. X. Barney Google. XI. Vallee, Rudy, 1901- XII. The two (Continued on next card)

Voice Lib.
M1336   Kennedy, Caroline, 1957-
bd.2   Launching of aircraft carrier "John F. Kennedy"
        at Newport News, Virginia. Speakers:
        Senator Edward Kennedy, Caroline Kennedy,
        and Robert McNamara. Comments by CBS news-
        caster Steve Rowan. CBS-TV, August, 1968.
        1 reel (7 in.) 7 1/2 in. per sec.
        phonotape.

        I. Kennedy, Edward Moore, 1932-   II.
        Kennedy, Caroline, 1957-   III. McNamara,
        Robert S   1916-

Voice Lib.
M1336   Kennedy, Edward Moore, 1932-
bd.2   Launching of aircraft carrier "John F. Kennedy"
        at Newport News, Virginia. Speakers:
        Senator Edward Kennedy, Caroline Kennedy,
        and Robert McNamara. Comments by CBS news-
        caster Steve Rowan. CBS-TV, August, 1968.
        1 reel (7 in.) 7 1/2 in. per sec.
        phonotape.

        I. Kennedy, Edward Moore, 1932-   II.
        Kennedy, Caroline, 1957-   III. McNamara,
        Robert S   1916-

Voice Lib.
M1378   Kennedy, Edward Moore, 1932-
bd.2   Statement after death of Mary Jo Kopechne
        in an auto accident in which he was involved.
        ABC, July 25, 1969.
        1 reel (7 in.) 7 1/2 in. per sec.
        phonotape.

        1. Kopechne, Mary Jo, 1941-1969.

Voice Lib.
M1657   Kennedy, Edward Moore, 1932-
        Discusses visit with Brezhnev, Watergate,
        Chappaquiddick, and 1976 politics.
        Interviewed by Paul Duke. WKAR-TV,
        May 7, 1974.
        30 min.   phonotape (1 r.   7 1/2 i.p.s.)

        1. U.S. - Politics and government - 1969-
        2. Watergate Affair, 1972-   I. Duke,
        Paul.

Voice Lib.
M1323-   Kennedy, Edward Moore, 1932-
M1328   Democratic Party. National Convention,
bd.1   Chicago, 1968.
        Hubert Humphrey, Democratic presidential nom e,
        announcing his selection of Sen. Muskie as his running mate;
        convention floor reports; interview with Mrs. Humphrey. Mayor
        Daley of Chicago defending police action. Interviews with Sen-
        ator McGovern and Jesse Unruh of California. Remote address by
        Sen. Edward Kennedy introducing a memorial motion picture on
        the late Sen. Robert F. Kennedy. Various reports on riots and
        general confusion, reluctance of delegates to come to order.
        Nominations for Vice-President; seconding speeches for Sen.
        Muskie and nominating speech by Wisconsin delegation of Julian
        Bond of Georgia. Interview with Julian Bond, who declined
        nomination of the vice-presidency. Story told by chairman of
        the New Hampshire [delegation] regarding his arrest. Interview
        (Continued on next card)

Voice Lib.
M1323-   Kennedy, Edward Moore, 1932-
M1328   Democratic Party. National Convention,
bd.1   Chicago, 1968... (Card 2)
        with Paul O'Dwyer of the New York delegation regarding the
        nomination of Richard Daley for Vice-President. General
        confusion. Nomination of Sen. Edmund Muskie as Vice-President
        and resulting confusion with the Oregon delegation. Followed by
        Sen. Muskie's acceptance speech. NBC-TV, August 29, 1968.
        6 reels (7 in.) 7 1/2 in. per sec. phonotape.

        I. Humphrey, Hubert Horatio, 1911- II. Humphrey, Muriel Fay
        (Buck) 1912-   III. Daley, Richard J   1902-   IV. McGovern,
        George Stanley, 1922-   V. Unruh, Jesse Marvin, 1922-   VI.
        Kennedy, Edward Moore, 1932-   VII. Bond, Julian, 1940-   VIII.
        O'Dwyer, Paul, 1907-   IX. Muskie, Edmund S   1914-

Voice Lib.   Kennedy, Edward Moore, 1932-
M315   National Broadcasting Company, inc.
bd.3   Assassination: Henry Cabot Lodge's meeting
        with President Johnson, comments about
        Jacqueline Kennedy, on Jackie's decision
        to walk behind casket; remarks by Senator
        Edward M. Kennedy. NBC, November 24, 1963.
        1 reel (7 in.) 7 1/2 in. per sec.
        phonotape.

        1. Kennedy, Jacqueline (Bouvier) 1929-
        2. Kennedy, John Fitzgerald, Pres. U.S., 1917-
        1963 - Assassination.   I. Kennedy, Edward
        Moore, 1932-

Voice Lib.
344   Kennedy, Jacqueline (Bouvier), 1929-
bd.12   Addressing the formal Bogotá dinner
        in Spanish.   CBS, December 18, 1961.
        1 reel (7 in.) 7 1/2 in. per sec.
        phonotape.

Voice Lib.   Kennedy, Jacqueline (Bouvier), 1929-
119-   A tour of the White House (Television program)
120   Tour of the White House with Mrs. John F.
        Kennedy. Narrated by Charles Collingwood.
        CBS-TV special, February, 1962.
        2 reels (7 in.) 7 1/2 in. per sec.
        phonotape.

        I. Collingwood, Charles Cummings, 1917-
        II. Kennedy, Jacqueline (Bouvier), 1929-

KENNEDY, JACQUELINE (BOUVIER) 1929-
Voice Lib.
652   Cassini, Oleg Loiewski, 1913-
bd.18   Discussing Jackie Kennedy's wardrobe
        with New York fashion editors. CBS,
        January 12, 1960.
        1 reel (7 in.) 7 1/2 in. per sec.
        phonotape.

        1. Kennedy, Jacqueline (Bouvier) 1929-

Voice Lib.
KENNEDY, JACQUELINE (BOUVIER) 1929-
M315   National Broadcasting Company, inc.
bd.3   Assassination: Henry Cabot Lodge's meeting
        with President Johnson, comments about
        Jacqueline Kennedy, on Jackie's decision
        to walk behind casket; remarks by Senator
        Edward M. Kennedy.   NBC, November 24, 1963.
        1 reel (7 in.)   7 1/2 in. per sec.
        phonotape.

           1. Kennedy, Jacqueline (Bouvier) 1929-
        2. Kennedy, John Fitzgerald, Pres. U.S., 1917-
        1963 - Assassination.   I. Kennedy, Edward
        Moore, 1932-

Voice Lib.
M827   Kennedy, John Fitzgerald, Pres. U.S., 1917-
        1963.
          Speaking at the Jefferson-Jackson Day
        dinner in Los Angeles, Calif., where he was
        key-note speaker.   KPFK, November 2, 1959.
        1 reel (7 in.)   7 12/ in. per sec.
        phonotape.

Voice Lib.
652   Kennedy, John Fitzgerald, Pres. U.S., 1917-1963.
bd.13   Announcing his Presidential candidacy.
        CBS, January 2, 1960.
        1 reel (7 in.)   7 1/2 in. per sec.
        phonotape.

Voice Lib.
M724   Kennedy, John Fitzgerald, Pres. U.S., 1917-
bd.7   1963.
          Description of the vote which nominated
        JFK in Los Angeles at Democratic national
        convention and his acceptance speech.
        1 reel (7 in.)   7 1/2 in. per sec.
        phonotape.

Voice Lib.
M724   Kennedy, John Fitzgerald, Pres. U.S., 1917-
bd.8   1963.
          Excerpt of his TV debate with Vice-President
        Richard Nixon in 1960.
        1 reel (7 in.)   7 1/2 in. per sec.
        phonotape.

           I. Nixon, Richard Milhous, Pres. U.S., 1913-

Voice Lib.
M739   Kennedy, John Fitzgerald, Pres. U.S., 1917-1963.
bd.12   Excerpt from the Kennedy-Nixon debates during
        the presidential campaign of 1960, regarding
        the "strong" language charges of Truman against
        the Republican Party, and the Quemoy-Matsu
        Island dispute.   CBS, October 13, 1960.
        1 reel (7 in.)   7 1/2 in. per sec.
        phonotape.

           I. Nixon, Richard Milhous, Pres. U.S., 1913-

Voice Lib.
656   Kennedy, John Fitzgerald, Pres. U.S., 1917-1963.
bd.1   Press conference excerpt: reading
        habits of the President.   CRI, 1961.
        1 reel (7 in.)   7 1/2 in. per sec.
        phonotape.

Voice Lib.
206   Kennedy, John Fitzgerald, Pres. U.S., 1917-1963.
bd.1   Inaugural speech and swearing in
        ceremony by Earl Warren.   Detroit,
        WJR, January 20, 1961.
        1 reel (7 in.)   7 1/2 in. per sec.
        phonotape.

           I. Warren, Earl, 1891-

Voice Lib.
M258   Kennedy, John Fitzgerald, Pres. U.S., 1917-1963.
bd.13   Address to the nation: Russian intervention
        into non-Communist nations and Russian
        political philosophy.   New York, CBS,
        June 6, 1961.
        1 reel (7 in.)   7 1/2 in. per sec.
        phonotape.

Voice Lib.
M258   Kennedy, John Fitzgerald, Pres. U.S., 1917-1963.
bd.12   Address to the nation: the importance of
        America in world politics.   New York,
        CBS, June 6, 1961.
        1 reel (7 in.)   7 1/2 in. per sec.
        phonotape.

Voice Lib.
344   Kennedy, John Fitzgerald, Pres. U.S.,1917-1963.
bd.8   Excerpts of speech to AFL-CIO in Miami,
Florida on the heavy responsibility of
labor; humorous comment on physical
fitness; the economy, the balance of trade.
CBS, December 7, 1961.
          1 reel (7 in.) 7 1/2 in. per sec.
phonotape.

Voice Lib.
344   Kennedy, John Fitzgerald, Pres. U. S., 1917-1963.
bd.11   Addressing formal dinner in Bogotá:
"Leader of Latin America must accept new
responsibilities". CBS, December 18,
1961.
          1 reel (7 in.) 7 1/2 in. per sec.
phonotape.

          I. Title: Leader of Latin America must
accept new responsibilities.

Voice Lib.
656   Kennedy, John Fitzgerald, Pres. U.S., 1917-1963.
bd.8   Address to AFL-CIO convention: humorous
anecdotes.   Columbia records, inc., 1962.
          1 reel (7 in.) 7 1/2 in. per sec.
phonotape.

Voice Lib.
656   Kennedy, John Fitzgerald, Pres. U.S., 1917-1963.
bd.5   Excerpt from address to Newspaper
Publishers Convention: on the under paying
of New York Tribune correspondent, Karl
Marx. CRI, 1962.
          1 reel (7 in.) 7 1/2 in. per sec.
phonotape.

Voice Lib.
M1285   Kennedy, John Fitzgerald, Pres. U.S., 1917-1963.
bd.5   Excerpt from his address at Amherst College
during a ceremony held in tribute to poet
Robert Frost. NBC-P.B.L., November 26,
1967 (1962)
          1 reel (7 in.) 7 1/2 in. per sec.
phonotape.

          1. Frost, Robert, 1874-1963.

Voice Lib.
656   Kennedy, John Fitzgerald, Pres. U.S., 1917-1963
bd.6   Excerpt of a Presidential address to
National Association of Manufacturers'
luncheon, in defense of his administration.
Columbia Records, Inc., 1962.
          1 reel (7 in.) 7 1/2 in. per sec.
phonotape.

Voice Lib.
656   Kennedy, John Fitzgerald, Pres. U.S., 1917-1963.
bd.7   Press conference excerpt: anecdotes about
Senator Smathers. Columbia Records, Inc.,
1962.
          1 reel (7 in.) 7 1/2 in. per sec.
phonotape.

          1. Smathers, George Armistead, 1913-

Voice Lib.
656   Kennedy, John Fitzgerald, Pres. U.S., 1917-1963.
bd.3   Press conference excerpt: Mrs. Craig
questioning President on equal rights for
women. CRI, 1962.
          1 reel (7 in.) 7 1/2 in. per sec.
phonotape.

          1. Woman - Rights of women. I. Craig,
Elisabeth May

Voice Lib.
M656   Kennedy, John Fitzgerald, Pres. U.S., 1917-1963.
bd.2   Press conference excerpt on Senator
Barry Goldwater. CRI, 1962.
          1 reel (7 in.) 7 1/2 i.p.s. phonotape.

          1. Goldwater, Barry Morris, 1909-

Voice Lib.
656   Kennedy, John Fitzgerald, Pres. U.S., 1917-1963.
bd.4   Press conference excerpt: why he likes
being President. CRI, 1962.
          1 reel (7 in.) 7 1/2 in. per sec.
phonotape.

Voice Lib.
346　Kennedy, John Fitzgerald, Pres. U.S., 1917-1963.
　　Press conference on: Russia's resumption
of arms testing; aid to college students;
Viet Nam situation, censorship at Pentagon;
answering criticism by Gov. Rockefeller;
comments on John Birch Society; U.N. Bond
issue; space development progress; steel
strike situation.　CBS, February 7, 1962.
　　1 reel (7 in.)　7 1/2 in. per sec.
phonotape.

Voice Lib.
604　Kennedy, John Fitzgerald, 1917-1963.
　　Press conference: release of Rudolph Abel
and Francis Gary Powers; British nuclear tests
on Easter Island; possibility of Kennedy
entering Geneva Disarmament meeting; automation;
world-wide arms agreement; test ban; purpose
of summit meetings; cost of CIA work; censorship of military speeches and Senator Strom
Thurmond; Viet-Nam; Kashmir dispute; U.S.-
British disarmament agreement; offsetting
changes in Defense Department spending; Red
　　　　　　(Continued on next card)

Voice Lib.
604　Kennedy, John Fitzgerald, 1917-1963.　Press
　　conference ... 1962.　(Card 2)
　　China's place in disarmament; lawmaker exchange
between U.S. and Russia; status of Monroe
Doctrine; exclusion of Cuba from O.A.S.; post-
ponement of Glenn's space flight; summer White
House at Newport, R.I.; postal rate increases;
Laos situation; release of reserves from active
duty; administration foreign policy.　WNYC,
February 14, 1962.
　　1 reel (7 in.)　7 1/2 in. per sec.
phonotape.

Voice Lib.
M159　Kennedy, John Fitzgerald, Pres. U.S., 1917-
bd.1　1963.
　　Statement by President Kennedy at press
conference about the steel price rise.
CBS, April 11, 1962.
　　1 reel (7 in.)　7 1/2 in. per sec.
phonotape.

Voice Lib.
M159　Kennedy, John Fitzgerald, Pres. U.S., 1917-
bd.2　1963.
　　Questions and answers at press conference
between working press and President, concerning the steel price rise and other matters.
CBS, April 11, 1962.
　　1 reel (7 in.)　7 1/2 in. per sec.
phonotape.

Voice Lib.
133　Kennedy, John Fitzgerald, Pres. U.S., 1917-1963.
bd.1　Mississippi crisis, an address to the
　　nation.　NBC, September 30, 1962.
　　1 reel (7 in.)　7 1/2 in. per sec.
phonotape.

Voice Lib.
M133　Kennedy, John Fitzgerald, Pres. U.S., 1917-
bd.2　1963.
　　Cuba blockade, an address to the nation.
NBC, October 22, 1962.
　　1 reel (7 in.)　7 1/2 i.p.s.　phonotape.

　　1. Military bases, Russian - Cuba.
　　2. U.S. - Foreign relations - Russia.
　　3. Russia - Foreign relations - U.S.

Voice Lib.
M161-　Kennedy, John Fitzgerald, Pres. U.S., 1917-1963.
M162　"An Hour with President Kennedy"; informal
　　discussion between JFK and TV newscasters
on the progress of Kennedy administration
during past two years.　CBS, December 17,
1962.
　　2 reels (7 in.)　7 1/2 in. per sec.
phonotape.

　　Continuation on reel 949, band 1.

Voice Lib.
M949　Kennedy, John Fitzgerald, Pres. U.S., 1917-
bd.2　1963.
　　Remarks at ceremonies at lighting of
Christmas tree near the White House.　CBS,
December 24, 1962.
　　1 reel (7 in.)　7 1/2 in. per sec.
phonotape.

Voice Lib.
656　Kennedy, John Fitzgerald, Pres. U.S., 1917-1963.
bd.13　Answer to query at press conference:
America is a peaceful country.　Columbia
records, inc., 1963.
　　1 reel (7 in.)　7 1/2 in. per sec.
phonotape.

Voice Lib.
656   Kennedy, John Fitzgerald, Pres. U.S., 1917-1963.
bd.10   Commencement address at Yale University,
excerpt: remarks about his honorary degree.
Columbia records, inc., 1963.
1 reel (7 in.)   7 1/2 in. per sec.
phonotape.

Voice Lib.
291   Kennedy, John Fitzgerald, Pres. U.S., 1917-1963.
bd.1   Address to U.N. General Assembly: peace
plans and other topics.   CBS, September,
1963.
1 reel (7 in.)   7 1/2 in. per sec.
phonotape.

Voice Lib.
656   Kennedy, John Fitzgerald, Pres. U.S., 1917-1963.
bd.12   Excerpt from press conference: anti-missile
missile, description of consequences of nuclear
attacks.   Columbia records, inc., 1963.
1 reel (7 in.)   7 1/2 in. per sec.
phonotape.

Voice Lib.
M804   Kennedy, John Fitzgerald, Pres. U.S., 1917-
1963.
Address at Plenary Session no. 1209,
United Nations General Assembly in New
York.   U.N. Archives, September 20, 1963.
1 reel (7 in.)   7 1/2 in. per sec.
phonotape.

Voice Lib.
656   Kennedy, John Fitzgerald, Pres. U.S., 1917-1963.
bd.14   Excerpt from press conference: on
remembrance of Pearl Harbor day and the
death of Franklin D. Roosevelt.   Columbia
records, inc., 1963.
1 reel (7 in.)   7 1/2 in. per sec.
phonotape.

Voice Lib.
311   Kennedy, John Fitzgerald, Pres. U.S., 1917-1963.
bd.2   Excerpts of Pres. Kennedy's remarks in
Ireland, with comments by Frank McGee of
NBC.   NBC, November 23, 1963.
1 reel (7 in.)   7 1/2 in. per sec.
phonotape.

I. McGee, Frank

Voice Lib.
656   Kennedy, John Fitzgerald, Pres U.S., 1917-1963.
bd.11   Excerpt from speech on Test Ban Treaty,
describing the horrors of nuclear warfare.
Columbia records, inc., 1963.
1 reel (7 in.)   7 1/2 in. per sec.
phonotape.

Voice Lib.
656   Kennedy, John Fitzgerald, Pres. U.S., 1917-1963.
bd.16   Excerpt of Kennedy's last public address
in Texas: "brinkmanship" and the times we
live in.   Columbia records, inc., [November
22] 1963.
1 reel (7 in.)   7 1/2 in. per sec.
phonotape.

Voice Lib.
656   Kennedy, John Fitzgerald, Pres. U.S., 1917-1963.
bd.9   Excerpt of commencement address at the
United States Military Academy: reflections
on past West Point graduates.   Columbia
records, inc., 1963.
1 reel (7 in.)   7 1/2 in. per sec.
phonotape.

Voice Lib.
656   Kennedy, John Fitzgerald, Pres U.S., 1917-1963.
bd.15   Excerpt of Kennedy's last public address
in Texas: Mrs. Kennedy and fashions.   Columbia
records, inc., November 22, 1963.
1 reel (7 in.)   7 1/2 in. per sec.
phonotape.

Voice Lib.
M511   Kennedy, John Fitzgerald, Pres. U.S., 1917-1963.
bd.2   Excerpts of Pres. Kennedy's remarks in
        Ireland, with comments by Frank McGee of
        NBC. NBC, November 23, 1963.
            1 reel (7 in.)   7 1/2 i.p.s.
        phonotape.

            I. McGee, Frank, 1921-1974.

Voice Lib.
M671   Kennedy, John Fitzgerald, Pres. U.S., 1917-1963.
bd.2   "Years of Lightning, Day of Drums";
        excerpts of comments by JFK on Peace Corps,
        Alliance for Progress, space race, Civil
        Rights. Narrated by Gregory Peck. Voice
        of America, 1964.
            1 reel (7 in.)   7 1/2 in. per sec.
        phonotape.

            I. Peck, Gregory, 1916-   II. Title.

Voice Lib.
565   Kennedy, John Fitzgerald, Pres. U.S., 1917-1963.
bd.1   Jack Paar Show: Tribute to President John
        F. Kennedy. Series of quotes accumulated
        from various press conferences of President,
        recorded between 1961 and 1963. NBC, March
        13, 1964.
            1 reel (7 in.)   7 1/2 in. per sec.
        phonotape.

            I. Paar, Jack Harold, 1918-

Voice Lib.
M712-   Kennedy, John Fitzgerald, Pres. U.S., 1917-
713   1963.
bd.1   Kennedy memorial program; flashbacks in
        sound on career of John F. Kennedy and
        comments from his former colleagues; excerpts
        from his speeches and explanations about
        their preparation and purpose. CBS-TV,
        November 18, 1964.
            2 reels(7 in.)   7 1/2 in. per sec.
        phonotape.

Voice Lib.
M121   Kennedy, John Fitzgerald, Pres. U.S., 1917-1963.
        Nuclear testing, resumption of. NBC,
        March 2, 1965.
            1 reel (7 in.)   7 1/2 i.p.s.   phonotape.

            1. Atomic weapons - Testing.

Voice Lib.
M998   Kennedy, John Fitzgerald, Pres. U.S., 1917-
        1963.
            The John F. Kennedy humor; one-hour tele-
        vision broadcast with Jack Parr as Master
        of Ceremonies. ABC, October 5, 1966.
            1 reel (7 in.)   7 1/2 in. per sec.
        phonotape.

            I. Paar, Jack Harold, 1918-

                Kennedy, John Fitzgerald, Pres. U.S.,
Voice Lib.   1917-1963
M1391   Apollo 11 (space flight): reception of
bd.2   Apollo 11 astronauts in Chicago. Descrip-
        tion of motorcade on way to Civic Center
        Plaza and ceremonies there. Cardinal Cody's
        invocation. JFK flashback predicting moon
        landing before decade is out. Mayor Daley
        and Alderman Klene resolution making August
        13 "Astronauts' Day". Senator Percy and
        Governor Ogilvie of Illinois. Presentation
        of honorary citizenship to astronauts.
        [Source?] August 13, 1969.

                                (Continued on next card)

                Kennedy, John Fitzgerald, Pres. U.S.,
Voice Lib.   1917-1963
M1391   Apollo 11 (space flight): reception of Apollo
bd.2   11 astronauts ... 1969. (Card 2)

            1 reel (7 in.)   7 1/2 in. per sec.
        phonotape.
            1. Project Apollo. 2. Space flight to the moon. 3. Aldrin,
        Edwin E   1930-   4. Collins, Michael, 1930-   5. Armstrong,
        Neil, 1930-   I. Aldrin, Edwin E   1930-   II. Collins,
        Michael, 1930-   III. Armstrong, Neil, 1930-   IV. Cody,
        John Patrick, cardinal, 1907-   V. Kennedy, John Fitzgerald,
        Pres. U.S., 1917-1963. VI. Daley, Richard J   1902- VII.
        Percy, Charles Harting, 1919-   VIII. Ogilvie, Richard Buell,
        1923-

                Kennedy, John Fitzgerald, Pres. U.S.,
Voice Lib.   1917-1963
M1398   From here to the seventies, Part III. NBC-TV
bd.1   two-and-a-half hour documentary pertaining to
        events occurring during the 1960's. NBC-TV,
        October 7, 1969.
            1 reel (7 in.)   7 1/2 in. per sec.
        phonotape.
            CONTENTS. -1. Style changes: a. clothes; b. sex; c. violence;
        d. outlook; e. morals; f. sports and protest. -2. Man's mortality:
        a. death of Winston Churchill; b. Bobby Kennedy, speech before
        assassination; c. Dr. King, "I've been to the mountain top..." and
        "We'll get to the Promised Land"; d. John Kennedy's last speech. -
        3. Hunger around the world: a. Green Revolution, problems and
        benefits; b. abortions to control population. -4. Communications

                                (Continued on next card)

                Kennedy, John Fitzgerald, Pres. U.S.,
Voice Lib.   1917-1963
M1398   From here to the seventies, Part III... 1969.
bd.1   (Card 2)

            CONTENTS, cont'd. explosion: a. David Brinkley, TV. -5. Ending:
        a. Paul Newman; b. Barbra Streisand.

            I. Kennedy, Robert Francis, 1925-1968. II.
        King, Martin Luther, 1929-1968. III. Kennedy,
        John Fitzgerald, Pres.U.S., 1917-1963. IV.
        Brinkley, David McClure, 1920-   V. Newman,
        Paul, 1925-   VI. Streisand, Barbra, 1942-

Kennedy, John Fitzgerald, Pres. U.S., 1917-1963

Voice Lib.
M1033 Voice of America.
    Twentieth anniversary program of Voice of
America broadcasts narrated by Henry Fonda,
and including the voices of Carl Sandburg,
Danny Kaye, Jawaharlal Nehru, Franklin D.
Roosevelt, Charles Malik, Arnold Toynbee,
William Faulkner, Harry S. Truman, Dwight D.
Eisenhower, Helen Hayes, Dag Hammarskjöld,
Winston Churchill, and John F. Kennedy.
Voice of America, 1963.
    1 reel (7 in.)   7 1/2 in. per sec.
phonotape.
                        (Continued on next card)

Kennedy, John Fitzgerald, Pres. U.S., 1917-1963

Voice Lib.
M1033 Voice of America. Twentieth anniversary
        program... 1963. (Card 2)

    I. Fonda, Henry Jaynes, 1905–   II. Sandburg, Carl,
1878-1967. III. Kaye, Danny, 1913–   IV. Nehru, Jawaharlal,
1889-1964. V. Roosevelt, Franklin Delano, Pres. U.S., 1882-
1945. VI. Malik, Charles Habib, 1906–   VII. Toynbee,
Arnold Joseph, 1889–   VIII. Faulkner, William, 1897-1962.
IX. Truman, Harry S., Pres. U.S., 1884-1972. X. Eisenhower,
Dwight David, Pres. U.S., 1890-1969. XI. Hayes, Helen,
1900–   XII. Hammarskjöld, Dag, 1905-1961. XIII. Churchill,
Winston Leonard Spencer, 1874-1965. XIV. Kennedy, John
Fitzgerald, Pres. U.S., 1917-1963.

Kennedy, John Fitzgerald, Pres. U.S., 1917-
Voice Lib.   1963
256   U.S. Congress. Senate. Select committee
bd.5   to investigate racketeering in labor
        unions.
    Senator John Kennedy and Counsel Robert
Kennedy questioning Faunce, Vice-President
of Continental Baking Company. CBS News,
October 23, 1957.
    1 reel (7 in.)   7 1/2 in. per sec.
phonotape.
    I. Faunce, George, 1891–   II. Kennedy, John
Fitzgerald, Pres. U.S., 1917-1963. III. Kennedy, Robert
Francis, 1925-1968.

KENNEDY, JOHN FITZGERALD, PRES. U.S.,
Voice Lib.   1917-1963
315,   American Broadcasting Company.
bd.6-   Tribute to Pres. John Fitzgerald Kennedy
316,   from the arts. Fredric March emcees; Jerome
bd.1   Hines sings "Worship of God and Nature" by
        Beethoven; Florence Eldridge recites "When
        lilacs last in the door-yard bloom'd" by Walt
        Whitman; Marian Anderson in two songs. Includes
        Charlton Heston, Sidney Blackmer, Isaac Stern,
        Nathan Milstein, Christopher Plummer, Albert
        Finney. ABC, November 24, 1963.
    2 reels (7 in.)   7 1/2 in. per sec.
phonotape.
                        (Continued on next card)

KENNEDY, JOHN FITZGERALD, PRES. U.S.,
Voice Lib.   1917-1963
M1083 Analysis and criticism of President Kennedy's
bd.2   administration after a year and a half of
        its incumbency, by Howard K. Smith, Leon
        Keyserling, Roy Wilkins, Theodore Sorensen,
        and various economists, mostly adverse
        opinions; comparison to Wilson and FDR
        administrations. Bergman, July 25, 1962.
    1 reel (7 in.)   7 1/2 in. per sec. phonotape.
    I. Kennedy, John Fitzgerald, Pres. U.S., 1917-1963. I.
Smith, Howard Kingsbury, 1914–   II. Keyserling, Leon Hersch,
1908–   III. Wilkins, Roy, 1901–   IV. Sorensen, Theodore
Chaikin, 1928–

KENNEDY, JOHN FITZGERALD, PRES. U.S.,
Voice Lib.   1917-1963
M915-   As we knew him; words of reminiscence of
916   friends and relatives about the life of
        J.F. Kennedy. Narration by Charles Kuralt;
        participants: Charles Bartlett, Lemayne
        Billings, Robert Kennedy, Rose Kennedy,
        James Reed, Adlai Stevenson, Gen. Chester B.
        Clifton, etc. Columbia Records Inc., 1965.
    2 reels (7 in.)   7 1/2 in. per sec.
phonotape.
    1. Kennedy, John Fitzgerald, Pres. U.S.,
1917-1963. I. Kuralt, Charles, 1934–
                        (Continued on next card)

KENNEDY, JOHN FITZGERALD, PRES. U.S.,
Voice Lib.   1917-1963
317   British Broadcasting Corporation.
bd.1   This was the week that was; comments and
        reminiscences of Kennedy by the cast of
        weekly BBC show; a rebroadcast of original
        live show of November 23, 1963, including
        poem "To Jackie" by Dame Sybil Thorndike.
        NBC, November 24, 1963.
    1 reel (7 in.)   7 1/2 in. per sec.
phonotape.
    1. Kennedy, John Fitzgerald, Pres. U.S.,
1917-1963. I. Thorndike, Dame Sybil, 1882–

KENNEDY, JOHN FITZGERALD, PRES. U.S., 1918-
Voice Lib.   1963
M1090 The first family: satiric dramatization of the
bd.1   Kennedy family. Scenes: a. the experiment; b.
        after-dinner conversations; c. the Malayan
        ambassador; d. relatively speaking; e. astro-
        nauts; f. motorcade; g. the party; h. the
        tour; i. "But vote !"; j. economy lunch; k.
        the decision; l. the White House visitor; m.
        press conference; n. the dress; o. Saturday
        night; p. Auld Lang Syne; q. bedtime story.
        LP phonodisc, Cadence Records, Inc., October
        22, 1962.
    1 reel (7 in.)   7 1/2 in. per sec. phonotape.
    I. Kennedy, John Fitzgerald, Pres. U.S., 1918-1963.

KENNEDY, JOHN FITZGERALD, PRES. U.S.,
Voice Lib.   1917-1963
319   Funeral of John F. Kennedy; church ceremonies
bd.1   at Washington Cathedral, quote of speech
        segments of JFK and delivery of memorial
        sermon by Most Rev. Philip M. Hannan,
        prayers at bier by Cardinal Richard
        Cushing, departure of coffin from cathedral
        to Arlington Cemetery, description of
        journey and arrival. CBS, November 25,
        1963.
    1 reel (7 in.)   7 1/2 in. per sec.
phonotape.
                        (Continued on next card)

Voice Lib. KENNEDY, JOHN FITZGERALD, PRES. U.S., 1917-1963
M1046 The gift outright; tribute to John F.
bd.1   Kennedy upon the first anniversary of his
        assassination; broadcast by ABC Radio News.
        Review of President Kennedy's administration
        and comments by various colleagues. ABC
        Radio, November 22, 1964.
    1 reel (7 in.)   7 1/2 in. per sec.
phonotape.

    1. Kennedy, John Fitzgerald, Pres. U.S.,
1917-1963.

KENNEDY, JOHN FITZGERALD, PRES. U.S.,
1917-1963
Voice Lib.
565   Jack Paar Show tribute to President John F.
bd.1   Kennedy; series of quotes accumulated from
         various press conferences of President,
         recorded between 1961 and 1963. NBC,
         March 13, 1964.
         1 reel (7 in.)   7 1/2 in. per sec.
         phonotape.

         1. Kennedy, John Fitzgerald, Pres. U.S.,
         1917-1963.

KENNEDY, JOHN FITZGERALD, PRES. U.S.,
1917-1963
Voice Lib.
314   Wilkins, Roy, 1901-
bd.9   Statement by Roy Wilkins to NBC newsman
         Frank McGee, at the assassination of
         President Kennedy, his ideas about the
         future of civil rights. NBC, November 24,
         1963.
         1 reel (7 in.)   7 1/2 in. per sec.
         phonotape.

         1. Kennedy, John Fitzgerald, Pres. U.S.,
         1917-1963. I. McGee, Frank

KENNEDY, JOHN FITZGERALD, PRES. U.S.,
1917-1963
Voice Lib.
311   Johnson, Lyndon Baines, Pres. U.S., 1908-1973.
bd.1   Proclamation by President Johnson as Monday,
         November 25, 1963, as a national day of
         mourning for Kennedy; relating of the incident.
         NBC-TV, November 23, 1963.
         1 reel (7 in.)   7 1/2 in. per sec.
         phonotape.

         1. Kennedy, John Fitzgerald, Pres. U.S.,
         1917-1963.

KENNEDY, JOHN FITZGERALD, PRES. U.S.,
1917-1963
Voice Lib.
339   JFK: son of liberty. Program on the occasion
         of the death of President Kennedy. London,
         Independent Television, November 25, 1963.
         1 reel (7 in.)   7 1/2 in. per sec.
         phonotape.

         1. Kennedy, John Fitzgerald, Pres. U.S.,
         1917-1963.

KENNEDY, JOHN FITZGERALD, PRES. U.S.,
1917-1963
Voice Lib.
318   Requiem Mass for John F. Kennedy at St.
         Matthew's Cathedral in Washington, celebrated
         by Cardinal Cushing. With English
         translation and explanation. CBS,
         November 25, 1963.
         1 reel (7 in.)   7 1/2 in. per sec.
         phonotape.

         1. Kennedy, John Fitzgerald, Pres. U.S.,
         1917-1963. I. Cushing, Richard James,
         Cardinal, 1895-

KENNEDY, JOHN FITZGERALD, PRES. U.S.,
1917-1963 - ASSASSINATION
Voice Lib.
M309   Assassination: comments by visitors in
bd.8   Washington. NBC, November 23, 1963.
         1 reel (7 in.)   7 1/2 in. per sec.
         phonotape.

         1. Kennedy, John Fitzgerald, Pres. U.S.,
         1917-1963.

KENNEDY, JOHN FITZGERALD, PRES. U.S.,
1917-1963
Voice Lib.
M909   Stevenson, Adlai Ewing, 1900-1965.
         Remarks about the humor of JFK. RCA,
         1965.
         1 reel (7 in.)   7 1/2 in. per sec.
         phonotape.

         1. Kennedy, John Fitzgerald, Pres. U.S.,
         1917-1963.

KENNEDY, JOHN FITZGERALD, PRES. U.S.,
1917-1963
Voice Lib.
M310   American Broadcasting Company.
         Tribute to President John Fitzgerald Kennedy
         from the arts. Fredric March emcees; Jerome
         Hines sings "Worship of God and Nature" by
         Beethoven; Florence Eldridge recites "When
         lilacs last in the door-yard bloom'd" by Walt
         Whitman; Marian Anderson in two songs. Includes
         Charlton Heston, Sidney Blackmer, Isaac Stern,
         Nathan Milstein, Christopher Plummer, Albert
         Finney. ABC, November 24, 1963.
         35 min. phonotape (7 in.   7 1/2 i.p.s.)

          (Continued on next card)

KENNEDY, JOHN FITZGERALD, PRES. U.S.,
1917-1963
C1
S19   Whorf, Michael, 1933-
         The last full measure.
         1 tape cassette. (The visual sounds of
         Mike Whorf. Social, S19)

         Originally presented on his radio program, Kaleidoscope,
         WJR, Detroit.
         Duration: 47 min., 20 sec.
         John F. Kennedy, his life as a young, wealthy, charming man,
         a Navy Lieutenant, a Senator and finally President is outlined
         in this narrative of a dedicated American.

         L Kennedy, John Fitzgerald, Pres. U.S., 1917-1963.
         L Title.

KENNEDY, JOHN FITZGERALD, PRES. U.S.,
1917-1963 - ASSASSINATION
Voice Lib.
M313   American Broadcasting Company.
bd.1   Assassination: Japanese Ambassador's
         statement; Tokyo reaction; reading of
         telegram from Madame Nhu. ABC, November
         24, 1963.
         1 reel (7 in.)   7 1/2 in. per sec.
         phonotape.

         1. Kennedy, John Fitzgerald, Pres. U.S.,
         1917-1963 - Assassination.

KENNEDY, JOHN FITZGERALD, PRES. U.S.,
1917-1963 - ASSASSINATION
Voice Lib.
M313   American Broadcasting Company.
bd.2   Descriptions of preparations of transfer
        of Oswald from Municipal Jail in Dallas.
        ABC, November 24, 1963.
        1 reel (7 in.)   7 1/2 in. per sec.
        phonotape.

        1. Oswald, Lee Harvey, 1939-1963. 2.
        Kennedy, John Fitzgerald, Pres. U.S., 1917-
        1963 - Assassination.

KENNEDY, JOHN FITZGERALD, PRES. U.S.,
1917-1963 - ASSASSINATION
Voice Lib.
M316   British Broadcasting Corporation.
bd.1   This was the week that was; comments and
        reminiscences of Kennedy by the cast of
        weekly BBC show; a rebroadcast of original
        live show of November 23, 1963, including
        poem "To Jackie" by Dame Sybil Thorndike.
        NBC, November 24, 1963.
        1 reel (7 in.)   7 1/2 i.p.s.   phonotape.

        1. Kennedy, John Fitzgerald, Pres. U.S.,
        1917-1963 - Assassination.   I. Thorndike,
        Dame Sybil, 1882-

KENNEDY, JOHN FITZGERALD, PRES. U.S.,
1917-1963 - ASSASSINATION
Voice Lib.
M313   American Broadcasting Company.
bd.3   Transfer and shooting of Oswald in
        basement of police station; interviews
        with spectators and Policeman Dean in
        Dallas.   ABC, November 24, 1963.
        1 reel (7 in.)   7 1/2 in. per sec.
        phonotape.

        1. Oswald, Lee Harvey, 1939-1963. 2.
        Kennedy, John Fitzgerald, Pres. U.S., 1917-
        1963 - Assassination.

KENNEDY, JOHN FITZGERALD, PRES. U.S.,
1917-1963
Voice Lib.
M313   Burns, James MacGregor, 1918-
bd.4   In an interview, Kennedy's biographer
        reflects on Kennedy's personality, his
        dealings with Congress, and his rating by
        historians.   ABC, November 24, 1963.
        1 reel (7 in.)   7 1/2 in. per sec.
        phonotape.

        1. Kennedy, John Fitzgerald, Pres. U.S.,
        1917-1963.

KENNEDY, JOHN FITZGERALD, PRES. U.S.,
1917-1963 - ASSASSINATION
Voice Lib.
M314   American Broadcasting Company.
bd.2   Comments about Kennedy's assassination;
        on new arrivals in Washington at Dulles
        Airport.   ABC, November 24, 1963.
        1 reel (7 in.)   7 1/2 in. per sec.
        phonotape.

        1. Kennedy, John Fitzgerald, Pres. U.S.,
        1917-1963 - Assassination.

KENNEDY, JOHN FITZGERALD, PRES. U.S.,
1917-1963 - ASSASSINATION
Voice Lib.
M308   Columbia Broadcasting System, inc.
bd.1   Assassination: various news commentators
        describing the event, describing the last
        minutes of the President's life, impact of
        the news on New York City, on Lyndon B.
        Johnson, announcement of arrest of first
        suspect, comments from all over world.
        CBS, November 22, 1963.
        1 reel (7 in.)   7 1/2 in. per sec.
        phonotape.
        1. Kennedy, John Fitzgerald, Pres. U.S.,
        1917-1963 - Assassination.

KENNEDY, JOHN FITZGERALD, PRES. U.S.,
1917-1963 - ASSASSINATION
Voice Lib.
M314   American Broadcasting Company.
bd.4   Assassination: proceedings at the Capitol
        Rotunda in Washington.   ABC, November 24,
        1963.
        1 reel (7 in.)   7 1/2 in. per sec.
        phonotape.

        1. Kennedy, John Fitzgerald, Pres. U.S.,
        1917-1963 - Assassination.

KENNEDY, JOHN FITZGERALD, PRES. U.S.,
1917-1963 - ASSASSINATION
Voice Lib.
M308   Columbia Broadcasting System, inc.
bd.2   Assassination: announcement of Kennedy's
        death by CBS commentator Walter Cronkite; on
        film of assassination, search for suspect,
        future events and Johnson's oath; announcement
        of shooting of Dallas policeman and arrest
        of Oswald; comments by Eisenhower and Truman.
        CBS, November 22, 1963.
        1 reel (7 in.)   7 1/2 in. per sec.
        phonotape.
        1. Kennedy, John Fitzgerald, Pres. U.S., 1917-1963 - Assassination.
        I. Cronkite, Walter Leland, 1916-   II. Eisenhower, Dwight
        David, Pres. U.S., 1890-1969.   III. Truman, Harry S, Pres. U.S.,
        1884-1972.

KENNEDY, JOHN FITZGERALD, PRES. U.S.,
1917-1963
Voice Lib.
M312   Brandt, Willy, 1913-
bd.6   Assassination: excerpt of remarks by
        Mayor Willy Brandt of Berlin.   NBC,
        November 23, 1963.
        1 reel (7 in.)   7 1/2 in. per sec.
        phonotape.

        1. Kennedy, John Fitzgerald, Pres U.S.,
        1917-1963.

KENNEDY, JOHN FITZGERALD, PRES. U.S.,
1917-1963 - ASSASSINATION
Voice Lib.
M308   Columbia Broadcasting System, inc.
bd.3   Assassination: description of U.S. Senate
        on announcement of the news of the assassina-
        tion to the Republicans and Democrats in the
        Senate Chamber.   CBS, November 22, 1963.
        1 reel (7 in.)   7 1/2 in. per sec.
        phonotape.

        1. Kennedy, John Fitzgerald, Pres. U.S.,
        1917-1963 - Assassination.

KENNEDY, JOHN FITZGERALD, PRES. U.S.,
1917-1963 - ASSASSINATION
Voice Lib.
M309   Columbia Broadcasting System, inc.
bd.1   Assassination: various news commentators
on Kennedy trip up to time of shooting;
description of film taken at Parkland Hospital;
Kennedy family's departure from Capitol;
swearing-in of Johnson as 36th President.
CBS, November 22, 1963.
1 reel (7 in.)   7 1/2 in. per sec.
phonotape.

1. Kennedy, John Fitzgerald, Pres. U.S.,
1917-1963 - Assassination.

KENNEDY, JOHN FITZGERALD, PRES. U.S.,
1917-1963 - ASSASSINATION
Voice Lib.
M317   Columbia Broadcasting System, inc.
bd.4   Assassination: description of arrival of
President DeGaulle and others at Dulles
Airport.   CBS, November 24, 1963.
1 reel (7 in.)   7 1/2 in. per sec.
phonotape.

1. Kennedy, John Fitzgerald, Pres. U.S.,
1917-1963 - Assassination.

KENNEDY, JOHN FITZGERALD, PRES. U.S.,
1917-1963 - ASSASSINATION
Voice Lib.
M309   Columbia Broadcasting System, inc.
bd.2   Comments on Kennedy assassination from
people on the street in Chicago.   CBS,
November 22, 1963.
1 reel (7 in.)   7 1/2 in. per sec.
phonotape.

1. Kennedy, John Fitzgerald, Pres. U.S.,
1917-1963 - Assassination.

KENNEDY, JOHN FITZGERALD, PRES. U.S.,
1917-1963 - ASSASSINATION
Voice Lib.
M317   Columbia Broadcasting System, inc.
bd.5   Assassination: description of procession
of funeral cortege from Capitol to the
Cathedral in Washington; beginning of
Requiem Mass.   CBS, November 25, 1963.
1 reel (7 in.)   7 1/2 in. per sec.
phonotape.

1. Kennedy, John Fitzgerald, Pres. U.S.,
1917-1963 - Assassination.

KENNEDY, JOHN FITZGERALD, PRES. U.S.,
1917-1963 - ASSASSINATION
Voice Lib.
M309   Columbia Broadcasting System, inc.
bd.3   Assassination: statements by Senator
Dirksen and Senator Mansfield, remarks about
statements and actions of others in Washington.
CBS, November 22, 1963.
1 reel (7 in.)   7 1/2 in. per sec.
phonotape.

1. Kennedy, John Fitzgerald, Pres. U.S.,
1917-1963 - Assassination.   I. Dirksen,
Everett McKinley, 1896-1969.   II. Mansfield,
Michael Joseph, 1903-

KENNEDY, JOHN FITZGERALD, PRES. U.S.,
1917-1963 - ASSASSINATION
Voice Lib.
320   Columbia Broadcasting System, inc.
bd.2   Funeral ceremonies for John F. Kennedy at
grave site: bagpipers of U.S. Air Force,
planes flying over grave, manual of Irish
Guard, prayers at graveside by Cardinal
Cushing, 21 gun salute, taps, Navy Hymn,
description of everlasting flame, departure
of distinguished mourners.   CBS, November
25, 1963.
1 reel (7 in.)   7 1/2 in. per sec.
phonotape.
1. Kennedy, John Fitzgerald, Pres. U.S., 1917-1963 - Assassination.

KENNEDY, JOHN FITZGERALD, PRES. U.S.,
1917-1963 - ASSASSINATION
Voice Lib.
M309   Columbia Broadcasting System, inc.
bd.4   Reaction to the assassination: description
of statement and actions by Gov. Rockefeller
of New York.   CBS, November 22, 1963.
1 reel (7 in.)   7 1/2 in. per sec.
phonotape.

1. Kennedy, John Fitzgerald, Pres. U.S.,
1917-1963 - Assassination.

KENNEDY, JOHN FITZGERALD, PRES. U.S.,
1917-1963 - ASSASSINATION
Voice Lib.
M320   Columbia Broadcasting System, inc.
bd.3   Assassination: description of motion
picture taken by amateur photographer which
included complete sequence of the assassination.
CBS, November 28, 1963.
1 reel (7 in.)   7 1/2 in. per sec.
phonotape.

1. Kennedy, John Fitzgerald, Pres. U.S.,
1917-1963.- Assassination.

KENNEDY, JOHN FITZGERALD, PRES. U.S.,
1917-1963 - ASSASSINATION
Voice Lib.
M317   Columbia Broadcasting System, inc.
bd.3   Assassination: activities of the Interfaith
Assembly in St. Louis.   CBS, November 24, 1963.
1 reel (7 in.)   7 1/2 in. per sec.
phonotape.

1. Kennedy, John Fitzgerald, Pres. U.S.,
1917-1963 - Assassination.

KENNEDY, JOHN FITZGERALD, PRES. U.S.,
1917-1963 - ASSASSINATION
Voice Lib.
M319   Funeral of John F. Kennedy: church ceremonies at Washington
Cathedral; quote of speech segments of JFK and delivery of
memorial sermon by Most Rev. Philip M. Hannan; prayers
at bier by Cardinal Richard Cushing; departure of coffin
from Cathedral to Arlington Cemetery; description of journey
and arrival.   CBS, November 25, 1963.
1 reel (7 in.)   7 1/2 i.p.s.   phonotape.

1. Kennedy, John Fitzgerald, Pres. U.S., 1917-1963 -
Assassination.   I. Hannan, Philip Matthew, 1913-   II.
Cushing, Richard James, Cardinal, 1895-

KENNEDY, JOHN FITZGERALD, PRES. U.S.,
Voice Lib.   1917-1963 - ASSASSINATION
M311   Goldwater, Barry Morris, 1909-
bd.9   Assassination: statement by and interview
          of Barry Goldwater. NBC, November 23, 1963.
          1 reel (7 in.)   7 1/2 in. per sec.
          phonotape.

          1. Kennedy, John Fitzgerald, Pres. U.S.,
          1917-1963 - Assassination.

KENNEDY, JOHN FITZGERALD, PRES. U.S.,
Voice Lib.   1917-1963 - ASSASSINATION
M311   National Broadcasting Company, inc.
bd.2   Assassination: report on activities in
          Washington the following morning, news
          from Dallas on Oswald. NBC, November
          23, 1963.
          1 reel (7 in.)   7 1/2 in. per sec.
          phonotape.

          1. Kennedy, John Fitzgerald, Pres. U.S.,
          1917-1963 - Assassination. 2. Oswald, Lee
          Harvey, 1939-1963.

KENNEDY, JOHN FITZGERALD, PRES. U.S.,
Voice Lib.   1917-1963 - ASSASSINATION
M312   Huber, Oscar L
bd.3   Assassination: description of events by
          Reverend Oscar Huber, priest who administered
          last rites to Kennedy. NBC, November 23,
          1963.
          1 reel (7 in.)   7 1/2 in. per sec.
          phonotape.

          1. Kennedy, John Fitzgerald, Pres. U.S.,
          1917-1963 - Assassination.

KENNEDY, JOHN FITZGERALD, PRES. U.S.,
Voice Lib.   1917-1963 - ASSASSINATION
M311   National Broadcasting Company, inc.
bd.3   Reading of proclamation written by President
          Johnson of Monday, November 25, 1963, as a
          national day of mourning for Kennedy; announce-
          ment of cancellations in Lansing area. NBC-
          TV, November 23, 1963.
          1 reel (7 in.)   7 1/2 in. per sec.
          phonotape.

          1. Kennedy, John Fitzgerald, Pres. U.S.,
          1917-1963 - Assassination.

KENNEDY, JOHN FITZGERALD, PRES. U.S.,
Voice Lib.   1917-1963 - ASSASSINATION
M311   Johnson, Lyndon Baines, Pres. U.S., 1908-1973.
bd.8   Message to the people of the U.S. by
          President Lyndon Johnson; description of
          conditions at White House by NBC. NBC,
          November 23, 1963.
          1 reel (7 in.)   7 1/2 in. per sec.
          phonotape.

          1. Kennedy, John Fitzgerald, Pres. U.S.,
          1917-1963 - Assassination.

KENNEDY, JOHN FITZGERALD, PRES. U.S.,
Voice Lib.   1917-1963 - ASSASSINATION
M311   National Broadcasting Company, inc.
bd.7   Assassination: comments of servicemen at
          the U.S.O. in Washington. NBC, November
          23, 1963.
          1 reel (7 in.)   7 1/2 in. per sec.
          phonotape.

          1. Kennedy, John Fitzgerald, Pres. U.S.,
          1917-1963 - Assassination.

KENNEDY, JOHN FITZGERALD, PRES. U.S.,
Voice Lib.   1917-1963 - ASSASSINATION
M311   King, Martin Luther, 1929-1968.
bd.4   Martin Luther King interviewed by Ray
          Moore in Atlanta about Kennedy as champion
          of civil rights. NBC, November 23, 1963.
          1 reel (7 in.)   7 1/2 in. per sec.
          phonotape.

          1. Kennedy, John Fitzgerald, Pres. U.S.,
          1917-1963 - Assassination. I. Moore, Ray

KENNEDY, JOHN FITZGERALD, PRES. U.S.,
Voice Lib.   1917-1963 - ASSASSINATION
M315   National Broadcasting Company, inc.
bd.1   Assassination: news from White House, on
          Vietnam, on arrival of President DeGaulle.
          NBC, November 24, 1963.
          1 reel (7 in.)   7 1/2 in. per sec.
          phonotape.

          1. Kennedy, John Fitzgerald, Pres. U.S.,
          1917-1963 - Assassination.

KENNEDY, JOHN FITZGERALD, PRES. U.S.,
Voice Lib.   1917-1963 - ASSASSINATION
M315   Murphy, Franklin David, 1916-
bd.6   Assassination: excerpt of address by
          Chancellor Franklin D. Murphy of UCLA on
          President Kennedy. NBC, November 24,
          1963.
          1 reel (7 in.)   7 1/2 in. per sec.
          phonotape.

          1. Kennedy, John Fitzgerald, Pres. U.S.,
          1917-1963 - Assassination.

KENNEDY, JOHN FITZGERALD, PRES. U.S.,
Voice Lib.   1917-1963 - ASSASSINATION
M315   National Broadcasting Company, inc.
bd.2   Reports from Dulles Airport on arrivals
          of royalty and dignitaries for Kennedy's
          funeral. NBC, November 24, 1963.
          1 reel (7 in.)   7 1/2 in. per sec.
          phonotape.

          1. Kennedy, John Fitzgerald, Pres. U.S.,
          1917-1963 - Assassination.

KENNEDY, JOHN FITZGERALD, PRES. U.S.,
Voice Lib.   1917-1963 - ASSASSINATION
M315   National Broadcasting Company, inc.
bd.3   Assassination: Henry Cabot Lodge's meeting
       with President Johnson, comments about
       Jacqueline Kennedy, on Jackie's decision
       to walk behind casket; remarks by Senator
       Edward M. Kennedy. NBC, November 24, 1963.
         1 reel (7 in.)   7 1/2 in. per sec.
       phonotape.

         1. Kennedy, Jacqueline (Bouvier) 1929-
       2. Kennedy, John Fitzgerald, Pres. U.S., 1917-
       1963 - Assassination.   I. Kennedy, Edward
       Moore, 1932-

KENNEDY, JOHN FITZGERALD, PRES. U.S., 1917-
C1   1963 - ASSASSINATION
869   Whorf, Michael, 1933-
         The long dark hours - J. F. K.
         1 tape cassette. (The visual sounds of
       Mike Whorf. Social, S69)
           Originally presented on his radio program, Kaleidoscope,
       WJR, Detroit.
           Duration: 36 min.
           The reality and the tragedy of the loss of John F. Kennedy
       brings this account of those dark days of November. An account
       of the death of a President, of the shock to a nation, and a
       memorial to the future of mankind.

           L Kennedy, John Fitzgerald, Pres. U.S., 1917-1963 -
       Assassination.   L Title

KENNEDY, JOHN FITZGERALD, PRES. U.S.,
Voice Lib.   1917-1963 - ASSASSINATION
M316   National Broadcasting Company, inc.
bd.2   Description of caisson from Fort Meyer
       arriving in Washington for body of Kennedy;
       departure of body from White House, line of
       procession, drums, playing of "Hail to the
       Chief", "Navy Hymn", etc. NBC, November
       24, 1963.
         1 reel (7 in.)   7 1/2 in. per sec.
       phonotape.

         1. Kennedy, John Fitzgerald, Pres. U.S.,
       1917-1963 - Assassination.

KENNEDY, JOHN FITZGERALD, PRES. U.,
Voice Lib.   1917-1963 - ASSASSINATION
M315   Wilkins, Roy, 1901-
bd.4   Statement by Roy Wilkins to NBC newsman
       Frank McGee, at the assassination of President
       Kennedy, his ideas about the future of civil
       rights. NBC, November 24, 1963.
         1 reel (7 in.)   7 1/2 in. per sec.
       phonotape.

         1. Kennedy, John Fitzgerald, Pres. U.S.,
       1917-1963 - Assassination.   I. McGee, Frank,
       1921-1974.

KENNEDY, JOHN FITZGERALD, PRES. U.S.,
Voice Lib. 1917-1963 - ASSASSINATION
M311   Truman, Harry S, Pres. U.S., 1884-1972.
bd.6   Assassination: statement by Harry Truman
       and description of his mood. NBC, November
       23, 1963.
         1 reel (7 in.)   7 1/2 in. per sec.
       phonotape.

         1. Kennedy, John Fitzgerald, Pres. U.S.,
       1917-1963.

KENNEDY, JOHN FITZGERALD, PRES. U.S.,
Voice Lib.   1917-1963 - ASSASSINATION
M314   Warren, Earl, 1891-
bd.3   Remarks at bier of President Kennedy,
       lying in state at Capitol Rotunda. Also
       remarks by Speaker of the House McCormack;
       beginning of line of dignitaries to pass
       the bier. ABC, November 24, 1963.
         1 reel (7 in.)   7 1/2 in. per sec.
       phonotape.

         1. Kennedy, John Fitzgerald, Pres. U.S.,
       1917-1963 - Assassination.   I. McCormack,
       John William, 1891-

KENNEDY, JOHN FITZGERALD, PRES. U.S.,
Voice Lib.   1917-1963 - ASSASSINATION
M311   Vanocur, Sander, 1928-
bd.5   Assassination: Sander Vanocur of NBC
       compares deaths of FDR and JFK. NBC,
       November 23, 1963.
         1 reel (7 in.)   7 1/2 in. per sec.
       phonotape.

         1. Roosevelt, Franklin Delano, Pres. U.S.,
       1882-1945. 2. Kennedy, John Fitzgerald, Pres.
       U.S., 1917-1963 - Assassination.

Voice Lib.
M258   Kennedy, Robert Francis, 1925-1968.
bd.8   Press conference: announcement of the
       ordering of U.S. forces to Montgomery,
       Alabama. New York, CBS, May 22, 1961.
         1 reel (7 in.)   7 1/2 in. per sec.
       phonotape.

KENNEDY, JOHN FITZGERALD, PRES. U.S.,
Voice Lib.   1917-1963 - ASSASSINATION
M315   Wade, Henry M
bd.5   Report of District Attorney Henry Wade
       of Dallas County; Wade's statement at news
       conference on Oswald case. NBC, November
       24, 1963.
         1 reel (7 in.)   7 1/2 in. per sec.
       phonotape.

         1. Kennedy, John Fitzgerald, Pres. U.S.,
       1917-1963 - Assassination. 2. Oswald, Lee
       Harvey, 1939-1963.

Voice Lib.
351   Kennedy, Robert Francis, 1925-1968.
bd.5   Interview in Berlin on America and the
       future of the world, Berlin conditions,
       the Berlin Wall, world situation. CBS,
       February 25, 1962.
         1 reel (7 in.)   7 1/2 in. per sec.
       phonotape.

Kennedy, Robert Francis, 1925-1968

Voice Lib.
M1222 Washington Reports; CBS television news. Reports by CBS
bd.1 news correspondents about President Kennedy's Civil
Rights message to Congress and interviews with Attorney
General Robert F. Kennedy pertaining to his views on
his own work in the Justice Department and his own future.
CBS-TV News, Bergman, March 3, 1963.
1 reel (7 in.) 7 1/2 i.p.s. phonotape.

1. Civil rights. 2. U.S. Dept. of Justice. 3. Kennedy,
Robert Francis, 1925-1968. I. Kennedy, Robert Francis,
1925-1968.

Kennedy, Robert Francis, 1925-1968

Voice Lib.
M915- As we knew him; words of reminiscence of
916 friends and relatives about the life of
J.F. Kennedy. Narration by Charles Kuralt;
participants: Charles Bartlett, Lemayne
Billings, Robert Kennedy, Rose Kennedy,
James Reed, Adlai Stevenson, Gen. Chester B.
Clifton, etc. Columbia Records Inc., 1965.
2 reels (7 in.) 7 1/2 in. per sec.
phonotape.

1. Kennedy, John Fitzgerald, Pres. U.S.,
1917-1963. I. Kuralt, Charles, 1934-

(Continued on next card)

Kennedy, Robert Francis, 1925-1968

Voice Lib.
M1223 Town meeting of the world (Television program)
bd.1 Discussion and questions by students of
various countries from Britain about the image
of America in the eyes of youth. Answers by
Senator Robert F. Kennedy of New York and
Governor Ronald Reagan of California, with
Charles Collingwood as moderator. Principle
items covered: Vietnam, civil rights. CBS-TV,
May 15, 1967.
1 reel (7 in.) 7 1/2 in. per sec. phonotape.

1. Kennedy, Robert Francis, 1925-1968. II. Reagan, Ronald
Wilson, 1911- III. Collingwood, Charles Cummings, 1917-

Voice Lib.
M1305 Kennedy, Robert Francis, 1925-1968.
Senator Robert F. Kennedy announcing his
candidacy in the race for Democratic presidential nomination in 1968 in press
conference from Senate caucus room,
Washington, D. C. with many questions and
answers. Broadcast switches to Wisconsin for
statement by Senator Eugene McCarthy. CBS-TV,
March 16, 1968.
1 reel (7 in.) 7 1/2 in. per sec.
phonotape.
1. McCarthy, Eugene Joseph, 1916-

Voice Lib.
M1311 Kennedy, Robert Francis, 1923-1968.
bd.2 Press conference at Overseas Press Club
in New York pertaining to President Johnson's
withdrawal from the presidential race of
1968. Followed by questions and answers.
CBS-TV, April 1, 1968.
1 reel (7 in.) 7 1/2 in. per sec.
phonotape.

Voice Lib.
M1321 Kennedy, Robert Francis, 1925-1968.
Debate consisting of questions and answers.
Senator Robert Kennedy and Senator Eugene
McCarthy interviewed by ABC news correspondents
Bill Lawrence and Bob Clark on program
"Issues and Answers". ABC-TV, June 1, 1968.
1 reel (7 in.) 7 1/2 in. per sec.
phonotape.

I. McCarthy, Eugene Joseph, 1916- II.
Lawrence, Bill. III. Clark, Bob

Voice Lib.
M1332- Kennedy, Robert Francis, 1925-1968.
1333 Comments and news regarding condition of
bd.1 Senator Robert F. Kennedy after assassination
attempt in Los Angeles. Statement by Mayor
Yorty and Los Angeles police chief. Statement by Jordanian ambassador regarding
assassin Sirhan; also Mr. and Mrs. Wagner,
former employers. Flashback to scene of
assassination. Views from Washington on
gun legislation. NBC-TV, June 6, 1968.
2 reels (7 in.) 7 1/2 in. per sec.
phonotape.

(Continued on next card)

Voice Lib.
M1332- Kennedy, Robert Francis, 1925-1968. Comments
1333 and news... 1968. (Card 2)
bd.1

1. Sirhan, Sirhan Bishara, 1944-
I. Yorty, Samuel William, 1909-

Kennedy, Robert Francis, 1925-1968

Voice Lib.
M1398 From here to the seventies, Part III. NBC-TV
bd.1 two-and-a-half hour documentary pertaining to
events occurring during the 1960's. NBC-TV,
October 7, 1969.
1 reel (7 in.) 7 1/2 in. per sec.
phonotape.
CONTENTS. -1. Style changes: a. clothes; b. sex; c. violence;
d. outlook; e. morals; f. sports and protest. -2. Man's mortality:
a. death of Winston Churchill; b. Bobby Kennedy, speech before
assassination; c. Dr. King, "I've been to the mountain top..." and
"We'll get to the Promised Land"; d. John Kennedy's last speech. -
3. Hunger around the world: a. Green Revolution, problems and
benefits; b. abortions to control population. -4. Communications

(Continued on next card)

Kennedy, Robert Francis, 1925-1968

Voice Lib.
M1398 From here to the seventies, Part III... 1969.
bd.1 (Card 2)

CONTENTS, cont'd. explosion: a. David Brinkley. TV. -5. Ending:
a. Paul Newman; b. Barbra Streisand.

I. Kennedy, Robert Francis, 1925-1968. II.
King, Martin Luther, 1929-1968. III. Kennedy,
John Fitzgerald, Pres. U.S., 1917-1963. IV.
Brinkley, David McClure, 1920- V. Newman,
Paul, 1925- VI. Streisand, Barbra, 1942-

Kennedy, Robert Francis, 1925-1968
Voice Lib.
256   Hoffa, James Riddle, 1913-
bd.1   Testimony before Senate Rackets
       Committee, with Senator Ives and
       Counsel Robert Kennedy. CBS News,
       August 22-23, 1957.
           1 reel (7 in.)   7 1/2 in. per sec.
       phonotape.

           I. Ives, Irving McNeil, 1896-1962. II.
       Kennedy, Robert Francis, 1925-1968.

KENNEDY, ROBERT FRANCIS, 1925-1968
Voice Lib.
M1335 Reports regarding the California primary victory of Senator
       Kennedy. Recapitulation of occurrences at Ambassador
       Hotel and last speech of Robert F. Kennedy before being
       shot. Description of unidentified suspect. List of others
       wounded. Opinion by Washington neurosurgeon. Statement
       by Senator McCarthy at Beverly Hilton Hotel. NBC-TV,
       June 5, 1968.
           1 reel (7 in.)   7 1/2 i.p.s.   phonotape.

           L. Kennedy, Robert Francis, 1925-1968. L. McCarthy,
       Eugene Joseph, 1916-

Kennedy, Robert Francis, 1925-1968
Voice Lib.
243   McClellan, John Little, 1896-
bd.9   Senate investigating committee: coin-
       machine labor union.   Voices of Samuel
       Getlan, Karl Mundt, Robert Kennedy and
       John McClellan.   CBS Radio, August 3, 1957.
           1 reel (7 in.)   7 1/2 in. per sec.
       phonotape.

           I. Getlan, Samuel   II. Mundt, Karl
       Earl, 1900-   III. Kennedy, Robert Francis,
       1925-1968.

KENNEDY, ROBERT FRANCIS, 1925-1968
Voice Lib.
M1222 Washington Reports; CBS television news. Reports by CBS
bd.1   news correspondents about President Kennedy's Civil
       Rights message to Congress and interviews with Attorney
       General Robert F. Kennedy pertaining to his views on
       his own work in the Justice Department and his own future.
       CBS-TV News, Bergman, March 3, 1963.
           1 reel (7 in.)   7 1/2 i.p.s.   phonotape.

           L. Civil rights. 2. U.S. Dept. of Justice. 3. Kennedy,
       Robert Francis, 1925-1968. L. Kennedy, Robert Francis,
       1925-1968.

Kennedy, Robert Francis, 1925-1968
Voice Lib.
256   U.S. Congress. Senate. Select committee
bd.5   to investigate racketeering in labor
       unions.
       Senator John Kennedy and Counsel Robert
       Kennedy questioning Faunce, Vice-President
       of Continental Baking Company. CBS News,
       October 23, 1957.
           1 reel (7 in.)   7 1/2 in. per sec.
       phonotape.
           L. Faunce, George, 1891-   II. Kennedy, John
       Fitzgerald, Pres. U.S., 1917-1963. III. Kennedy, Robert
       Francis, 1925-1968.

KENNEDY, ROBERT FRANCIS, 1925-1968
C1
S8   Whorf, Michael, 1933-
           Age of anxiety.
           1 tape cassette.   (The visual sour..? of
       Mike Whorf. Social, S8)

           Originally presented on his radio program, Kaleidoscope,
       WJR, Detroit.
           Duration: 48 min., 45 sec.
           A man standing up for an ideal, acting to improve the lot
       of others, striking out against injustice; such was the life of
       Robert F. Kennedy.

           L. Kennedy, Robert Francis, 1925-1968. L. Title.

KENNEDY, ROBERT FRANCIS, 1925-1968
Voice Lib.
M1382 "A look at RFK". Memorial program by David
bd.1   Frost on first anniversary of assassination
       of Senator Robert Kennedy. Includes inter-
       view broadcast originally in David Frost's
       series "The Next President of the U.S."
       ABC-TV, June 5, 1969.
           1 reel (7 in.)   7 1/2 in. per sec.
       phonotape.

           I. Frost, David Paradine, 1939-

Kennedy, Rose Fitzgerald, 1890-
Voice Lib.
M915- As we knew him; words of reminiscence of
916   friends and relatives about the life of
       J.F. Kennedy. Narration by Charles Kuralt;
       participants: Charles Bartlett, Lemayne
       Billings, Robert Kennedy, Rose Kennedy,
       James Reed, Adlai Stevenson, Gen. Chester B.
       Clifton, etc. Columbia Records Inc., 1965.
           2 reels (7 in.)   7 1/2 in. per sec.
       phonotape.

           1. Kennedy, John Fitzgerald, Pres. U.S.,
       1917-1963. I. Kuralt, Charles, 1934-

(Continued on next card)

KENNEDY, ROBERT FRANCIS, 1925-1968
Voice Lib.
M1257 The public and private Robert F. Kennedy;
bd.1   CBS Reports TV documentary program on the
       character, political methods, and ambitions
       of Senator Robert F. Kennedy of New York.
       Narrator: Roger Mudd. CBS-TV, June 20,
       1967.
           1 reel (7 in.)   7 1/2 i.p.s.   phonotape.

           1. Kennedy, Robert Francis, 1925-1968.
       I. Mudd, Roger.

Voice Lib.
M1401 Kennedy, Rose Fitzgerald, 1890-
bd.1   Informal conversation with Merv Griffin
       about her family and her efforts to help
       prevent mental retardation in children.
       CBS, November 13, 1969.
           1 reel (7 in.)   7 1/2 in. per sec.
       phonotape.

           I. Griffin, Merv Edward, 1925-

Kennelly, Martin Henry, 1887-1961

Voice Lib.
204   Truman, Harry S. Pres. U.S., 1884-1972.
bd.1   Campaign speech, with an introduction
       by Mayor Martin H. Kennelly of Chicago.
       Detroit, WJR, October 25, 1948.
          1 reel (7 in.)   7 1/2 in. per sec.
       phonotape.

          I. Kennelly, Martin Henry, 1887-1961.

KENTUCKY DERBY

Voice Lib.
M1040   McCarthy, Clem, 1882-1962.
bd.4   Closing excerpt of Kentucky Derby horse
       race, 1938.   TV & R, 1938.
          1 reel (7 in.)   7 1/2 i.p.s.
       phonotape.

          1. Kentucky Derby.

Voice Lib.
M1059   Kerenskiĭ, Aleksandr Fedorovich, 1881-
bd.1   Discussion with Hugh Downs and former
       Russian Prime Minister Kerenskiĭ about the
       1917 Russian Revolution on "Today" TV show.
       NBC-TV, February 28, 1967.
          1 reel (7 in.)   7 1/2 in. per sec.
       phonotape.

          I. Downs, Hugh Malcolm, 1921-
       1. Russia - History - Revolution, 1917-1921.

KERN, JEROME, 1885-1945
Voice Lib.
M762   Hammerstein, Oscar, 1895-1960.
bd.6   Excerpt from "Music from Broadway" (Program
       5); speaking about Jerome Kern and his style of
       writing, including son "They Didn't Believe Me";
       also comments on those who followed Jerome Kern
       and beginnings of musical comedy, what it was
       like in the early days, including song, "Oh,
       What a Beautiful Morning".   Westinghouse
       Broadcasting Corporation, 1964.
          1 reel (7 in.)   7 1/2 in. per sec.   phonotape.   (The Music
       Goes Round and Round)
          I. Kern, Jerome, 1885-1945.   I. Title: Music from Broadway.
       II. Series.

Voice Lib.
M1237   Kerr, Clark, 1911-
           A conversation with Clark Kerr, former
       president of University of California,
       held at the Harvard Faculty Club with staff
       reporter of NET, dealing with student and
       university problems.   NET, May 28, 1967.
          1 reel (7 in.)   7 1/2 in. per sec.
       phonotape.

Kerr, Robert Samuel, 1896-1963

Voice Lib.
381-   I can hear it now (radio program)
382   CBS, April 26, 1951.
bd.1   2 reels (7 in.)   7 1/2 in. per sec.   phonotape.

          I. Radio Free Europe. 2. Strategic Air Command. I.
       Ridgway, Matthew Bunker, 1895-   II. Churchill, Winston Leonard
       Spencer, 1874-1965.   III. Bevan, Aneurin, 1897-1960.   IV. Nixon,
       Richard Milhous, Pres. U.S., 1913-   V. Kerr, Robert Samuel, 1896-
       1963.   VI. Brewster, Ralph Owen, 1888-1962.   VII. Wherry, Kenneth
       Spicer, 1892-1951.   VIII. Capehart, Homer Earl, 1897-   IX.
       Lehman, Herbert Henry, 1878-1963.   X. Taft, Robert Alphonso,
       1889-1953.   XI. Moody, Arthur Edson Blair, 1902-1954.   XII.
       Martin, Joseph William, 1884-1968.   XIII. McMahon, James O'Brien,
       1903-1952.   XIV. MacArthur, Douglas, 1880-1964.   XVII. Wilson,
       Charles Edward, 1886-197?   XVIII. Irvine, Clarence T

Voice Lib.   Kerr, Walter, 1913-
M1037   Biography in sound (radio program)
bd.1   "The Actor", narrated by Morgan Beatty.
       Cast includes Tallulah Bankhead, Hy Gardner,
       Rocky Graziano, Arthur Miller, Uta Hagen,
       Jackie Cooper, Sir Laurence Olivier, Gad
       Gayther, Barbara Ashley, Hortense Powdermaker,
       Peter Ustinov, Alfred Hitchcock, Leonard Lyons,
       John Guston, Helen Hayes, Dick Mayne, Ralph
       Bellamy, Lionel Barrymore, Sir Ralph Richardson,
       José Ferrer, and Walter Kerr.   NBC Radio, 1950's.
          1 reel (7 in.)   7 1/2 in. per sec.
       phonotape.
(Continued on next card)

Voice Lib.
142   Kettering, Charles Franklin, 1876-1958.
bd.1   Acceptance speech for award from
       American Alumni Council. WJR, July 28,
       1948.
          1 reel (7 in.)   7 1/2 in. per sec.
       phonotape.

Voice Lib.
218   Kettering, Charles Franklin, 1876-1958.
bd.3   Address on engineering education at
       Eggleston Award Dinner.   WJR, April 14,
       1954.
          1 reel (7 in.)   7 1/2 in. per sec.
       phonotape.

          1. Engineering - study and teaching.

Voice Lib.
232-   Kettering, Charles Franklin, 1876-1958.
233   A tribute to Charles F. Kettering,
bd.1   being reminiscences of highlights of his
       career.   CBS, November 30, 1958.
          2 reels (7 in.)   7 1/2 in. per sec.
       phonotape.

C1
H33
KEY, FRANCIS SCOTT, 1779-1843

Whorf, Michael, 1933-
By the dawn's early light - Francis Scott Key.
1 tape cassette.   (The visual sounds of
Mike Whorf. History and heritage, H33)

Originally presented on his radio program, Kaleidoscope,
WJR, Detroit.
Duration: 37 min., 30 sec.
It was during the War of 1812 when Francis Scott Key wrote of
the momentous Battle of Fort McHenry. This is the story of the
life and times of the man who wrote our national anthem.

L. Key, Francis Scott, 1779-1843. L. Title.

C1
M18
KEY, FRANCIS SCOTT, 1779-1929

Whorf, Michael, 1933-
The splendid Americans.
1 tape cassette.   (The visual sounds of
Mike Whorf. Miscellaneous, M18)

Originally presented on his radio program, Kaleidoscope,
WJR, Detroit.
Duration: 54 min., 30 sec.
This is the story of those who wrote the songs of a nation and
a people, songs which gave a different kind of courage to the
people.

L. Bates, Katherine Lee, 1859-1929. 2. Key, Francis Scott,
1779-1929. 3. Patriotic music, American. L. Title.

Voice Lib.   Keyserling, Leon Hersch, 1908-
M1083   Analysis and criticism of President Kennedy's
bd.2   administration after a year and a half of
its incumbency, by Howard K. Smith, Leon
Keyserling, Roy Wilkins, Theodore Sorensen,
and various economists, mostly adverse
opinions; comparison to Wilson and FDR
administrations.   Bergman, July 25, 1962.
1 reel (7 in.) 7 1/2 in. per sec. phonotape.
L. Kennedy, John Fitzgerald, Pres. U.S., 1917-1963. L.
Smith, Howard Kingsbury, 1914-   II. Keyserling, Leon Hersch,
1908-   III. Wilkins, Roy, 1901-   IV. Sorensen, Theodore
Chaikin, 1928-

Voice Lib.
M742   Khrushchev, Nikita Sergeevich, 1894-1971.
bd.8   Excerpt of statement in Russia about his
visit with President Eisenhower at Camp
David.   CBS, 1959.
1 reel (7 in.) 7 1/2 in. per sec.
phonotape.

Voice Lib.
337-   Khrushchev, Nikita Sergeevich, 1894-1971.
338   Face the Nation: talks to American reporters
bd.1   from his office in the Kremlin on farming,
meat production, U.S.-Soviet relations, diplomatic travel restrictions, Voice of America
program jamming, peaceful competition, America's
grandchildren will live under socialism, trading
with U.S., Russian Socialism and its future
success, Chinese and Russian ideology compared,
question of U.S. preparation for war with
Russia, destruction of Russia in war, co-existence, acceptance ( ) .S. proposals for
(Continued on next card)

Voice Lib.
337-   Khrushchev, Nikita Sergeevich, 1894-1971.
338   Face the Nation: talks to American
bd.1   reporters... 1957.   (Card 2)

initial disarmament, size of Soviet army,
secrecy of Soviet nuclear testing, limitations
of military personnel, Russian security,
troop withdrawal inspection, military role in
Eastern Europe, unanimous support of Eastern
Europeans for Communism, fate of Kadiv regime
in Hungary, steps toward easing of tension.
CBS, June 2, 1957.
2 reels (7 in.) 7 1/2 i. per sec. phonotape.

Voice Lib.
347   Khrushchev, Nikita Sergeevich, 1894-1971.
Luncheon for Khrushchev at Hotel
Commodore in New York City. National
anthems of U.S.S.R. and U.S.A..   CBS,
September 17, 1959.
1 reel (7 in.) 7 1/2 in. per sec.
phonotape.

Voice Lib.
348-   Khrushchev, Nikita Sergeevich, 1894-1971.
349   Tells of his feelings about the U.S. and
bd.1   world problems at luncheon in Hotel Commodore
in New York City.   CBS, September 17,
1959.
2 reels (7 in.)   7 1/2 in. per sec.
phonotape.

Voice Lib.
M715   Khrushchev, Nikita Sergeevich, 1894-1971.
bd.14   Excerpt of statement to American workers
during his American visit to San Francisco.
September 21, 1959.
1 reel (7 in.)   7 1/2 in. per sec.
phonotape.

Voice Lib.
M715   Khrushchev, Nikita Sergeevich, 1894-1971.
bd.15   Excerpt of statement to press after collapse
of summit meeting in Paris.   January 20,
1960.
1 reel (7 in.) 7 1/2 in. per sec.
phonotape.

Voice Lib.
M717   Khrushchev, Nikita Sergeevich, 1894-1971.
bd.7   Replying to interrogation by reporters
       from balcony of Russian headquarters in
       New York.   September 19, 1960
            1 reel (7 in.)   7 1/2 in. per sec.
       phonotape.

Voice Lib.
M1266   Khruschev, Nikita Sergeevich, 1894-1971.
        NBC documentary TV program about the life
      and career of Nikita Khrushchev, with
      commentary by Edwin Newman; including Khrushchev's
      opinions on domestic and foreign matters, such as Mao Tse-
      Tung, Eisenhower, Kennedy, Stalin, H. C. Lodge, Nixon,
      the Cuban crisis. NBC-TV, August, 1967.
           1 reel (7 in.)   7 1/2 in. per sec.   Phonotape.

      L. Khrushchev, Nikita Sergeevich, 1894-1971.
      L. Newman, Edwin Harold, 1919-

           KHRUSHCHEV, NIKITA SERGEEVICH, 1894-1971
Voice Lib.
238   Trout, Robert, 1908-
bd.1   Description of arrival of Nikita Khrushchev
        in U.S., with welcoming address by President
        Eisenhower and response by Khrushchev.
             1 reel (7 in.)   7 1/2 in. per sec.
        phonotape.

             1. Khrushchev, Nikita Sergeevich, 1894-1971.
        I. Eisenhower, Dwight David, Pres. U.S., 1890-
        1969.

           KHRUSCHEV, NIKITA SERGEEVICH, 1894-1971
Voice Lib.
M742   Dillon, Clarence Douglas, 1909-
bd.7   Statement on Peiping activities, Khrushchev's
        agreement to negotiate at Camp David with
        President Eisenhower. CBS, 1959.
             1 reel (7 in.)   7 1/2 in. per sec.
        phonotape.

             1. Khruschev, Nikita Sergeevich, 1894-1971.
        2. Eisenhower, Dwight David, Pres U.S., 1890-
        1969.

Voice Lib.
652   Khrushchev, Nina Petrovna
bd.7   Comments in a Paris department store.
        CBS, September 21, 1959.
             1 reel (7 in.)   7 1/2 in. per sec.
        phonotape.

Voice Lib.
M1435   Kiastiakowsky, George Bogdan
        Life in other worlds; exploratory discussion about life on other
        planets. Arnold J. Toynbee, Dr. G. B. Kiastiakowsky
        (professor at Harvard), Dr. Donald M. Michaels, Dr. Otto
        Struve, Dr. Harlow Shapley, Walter Cronkite, Chet Huntley,
        William L. Laurence. New York, NBC, March 3, 1961.
        1 reel (7 in.)   7 1/2 l.p.s.   phonotape.

           L. Life on other planets. L Toynbee, Arnold Joseph, 1889-
        II. Kiastiakowsky, George Bogdan. III. Michaels, Donald M.
        IV. Struve, Otto, 1897-1963. V. Shapley, Harlow, 1885-1972.
        VI. Cronkite, Walter Leland, 1916-   VII. Huntley, Chet,
        1911-1974. VIII. Laurence, William Leonard, 1888-

           Kidnap of the century - Lindbergh
C1
S75   Whorf, Michael, 1933-
        Kidnap of the century - Lindbergh.
        1 tape cassette. (The visual sounds of
        Mike Whorf. Social, S75)
          Originally presented on his radio program, Kaleidoscope,
        WJR, Detroit.
          Duration: 37 min., 30 sec.
          A vivid, exciting account of the notorious Lindbergh kidnapping.
        The evening of March 1, 1932, was the scene of the most publicized
        abduction of the century. The kidnapping, and the ensuing manhunt
        are narrated in this anxious, fearful report.

          L. Lindbergh, Charles Augustus, 1930-1932. 2. Hauptmann,
        Bruno Richard, 1899-1936.   L. Title.

           Kieran, John, 1892-
Voice Lib.
M932   Information, please (radio program)
          Panel of experts questioned by Clifton
        Fadiman; panel includes Christopher Morley,
        John Kieran, Franklin P. Adams, Col. Eagan.
        Lloyd Grosse, 1943.
             1 reel (7 in.)   7 1/2 in. per sec.
        phonotape.

             I. Fadiman, Clifton, 1904-   II. Morley,
        Christopher Darlington, 1890-   III. Kieran,
        John, 1892-   IV. Adams, Franklin Pierce,
        1881-1960. V. Eag—— Col.

Voice Lib.
M1562   Kiker, Douglas
bd.1   Announcement of the resignation of Vice
        President Spiro Agnew; special news report.
        NBC, September 26, 1973.
             3 min.   phonotape (1 r.   7 1/2 i.p.s.)

             1. Agnew, Spiro T., 1918-

           KILMER, JOYCE, 1886-1918
C1
A16   Whorf, Michael, 1933-
        Preserver of love.
        1 tape cassette. (The visual sounds of
        Mike Whorf. Art, music, and letters, A16)
          Originally presented on his radio program, Kaleidoscope,
        WJR, Detroit.
          Duration: 28 min.
          Joyce Kilmer was a writer of verse, a warrior in the trenches
        of France and his untimely death was a tragic loss to the world.

          L. Kilmer, Joyce, 1886-1918.   I. Title.

Kilpatrick, James Jackson, 1920-
Voice Lib.
M1477 Discussion of Supreme Court decision on
publishing Pentagon Papers. William B.
Macomber, deputy under-secretary of state;
Senator Henry Jackson; Max Frankel, head of
New York Times' Washington bureau; Benjamin
Bradley, executive editor of Washington Post.
Questioned by Carl Stern, NBC; Martin Hayden,
Detroit News; James J. Kilpatrick, Washington
Star Syndicate; Kenneth Crawford, Washington
Post; Edwin Newman. NBC-TV, June 30, 1971.
1 reel (7 in.)   7 1/2 in. per sec.
phonotape.

(Continued on next card)

Voice Lib.
M1285 King, Ernest Joseph, 1878-1956.
bd.2   Statement on current military situation
by Admiral King on the occasion of VE-Day,
in the form of a report.   AFRS, May 8,
1945.
1 reel (7 in.)   7 1/2 in. per sec.
phonotape.

1. World War, 1939-1945.

Voice Lib.
M258   King, Martin Luther, 1929-1968.
bd.9D   Report to CBS News; description of the
Freedom Riders' goals and actions in
Montgomery, Alabama.   New York, CBS,
May 22, 1961.
1 reel (7 in.)   7 1/2 in. per sec.
phonotape.

Voice Lib.
M258   King, Martin Luther, 1929-1968.
bd.9E   Report to CBS News; description of the
scene of violence in Montgomery, Alabama.
"Alabama will go to any end to maintain
segregation . . . the federal government
must help."   New York, CBS, May 22, 1961.
1 reel (7 in.)   7 1/2 in. per sec.
phonotape.

Voice Lib.
545   King, Martin Luther, 1929-1968.
bd.1   Address at Lincoln Memorial at march on
Washington ceremonies: "I have a dream..."
WRVR, August 28, 1963.
1 reel (7 in.)   7 1/2 in. per sec.
phonotape.

I. We shall overcome: a lyric affirmation
of freedom.

Voice Lib.
M311   King, Martin Luther, 1929-1968.
bd.4   Martin Luther King interviewed by Ray
Moore in Atlanta about Kennedy as champion
of civil rights.   NBC, November 23, 1963.
1 reel (7 in.)   7 1/2 in. per sec.
phonotape.

1. Kennedy, John Fitzgerald, Pres. U.S.,
1917-1963 - Assassination.   I. Moore, Ray

Voice Lib.
M731. King, Martin Luther, 1929-1968.
bd.1-   "Facing the challenge of a new age".
M732. Address to MSU student body pertaining to
bd.1   civil rights, social justice, voter registra-
tion in Selma, Alabama, and associated topics.
NVL, February 11, 1965.
2 reels (7 in.)   7 1/2 in. per sec.
phonotape.

Voice Lib.
M744   King, Martin Luther, 1929-1968.
Address at Civil Rights rally at Montgomery,
Alabama. Dr. King describes current Negro
crusade for voting right in Alabama; history
of segregated society; "march on ballot
boxes" and "no return to normalcy".
CBS, March 25, 1965.
35 min. phonotape (1 r.   7 1/2 i.p.s.)

1. Negroes - Civil rights.

Voice Lib.
M1318 King, Martin Luther, 1929-1968.
bd.1   Funeral services held at Ebenezer Church
in Atlanta, Georgia. CBS, 1968.
1 reel (7 in.)   7 1/2 in. per sec.
phonotape.

1. King, Martin Luther, 1929-1968.

Voice Lib.
M1317 King, Martin Luther, 1929-1968.
bd.3   Excerpt of peace sermon by Dr. King, for
Massey Lecture Series of Canadian Broadcasting
Corporation made in spring of 1968. NBC,
April 4, 1968.
1 reel (7 in.)   7 1/2 in. per sec.
phonotape.

Voice Lib. King, Martin Luther, 1929-1968
M1398 From here to the seventies, Part III. NBC-TV
bd.1 two-and-a-half hour documentary pertaining to
events occurring during the 1960's. NBC-TV,
October 7, 1969.
1 reel (7 in.) 7 1/2 in. per sec.
phonotape.
CONTENTS. -1. Style changes: a. clothes; b. sex; c. violence;
d. outlook; e. morals; f. sports and protest. -2. Man's mortality:
a. death of Winston Churchill; b. Bobby Kennedy, speech before
assassination; c. Dr. King, "I've been to the mountain top..." and
"We'll get to the Promised Land"; d. John Kennedy's last speech. -
3. Hunger around the world: a. Green Revolution, problems and
benefits; b. abortions to control population. -4. Communications
(Continued on next card)

KING, MARTIN LUTHER, 1929-1968
Voice Lib.
M731 Harris, Robert
bd.1 Introducing to faculty and student body
of MSU the Reverend Martin Luther King.
NVL, February 11, 1965.
1 reel (7 in.) 7 1/2 i.p.s. phonotape.

1. King, Martin Luther, 1929-1968.

King, Martin Luther, 1929-1968
M1398 From here to the seventies, Part III... 1969.
bd.1 (Card 2)
CONTENTS, cont'd. explosion: a. David Brinkley, TV. -5. Ending:
a. Paul Newman; b. Barbra Streisand.

I. Kennedy, Robert Francis, 1925-1968. II.
King, Martin Luther, 1929-1968. III. Kennedy,
John Fitzgerald, Pres.U.S., 1917-1963. IV.
Brinkley, David McClure, 1920- V. Newman,
Paul, 1925- VI. Streisand, Barbra, 1942-

KING, MARTIN LUTHER, 1929-1968
Voice Lib.
M1317 Johnson, Lyndon Baines, Pres. U.S., 1908-1973.
bd.4 Message of grief by President Johnson
about Dr. King's death. NBC, April 4, 1968.
1 reel (7 in.) 7 1/2 in. per sec.
phonotape.

1. King, Martin Luther, 1929-1968.

KING, MARTIN LUTHER, 1929-1968
Voice Lib.
M1723 Adams, Walter, 1922-
bd.1 Speech at Martin Luther King Memorial
Service at Michigan State University.
WKAR, April 4, 1969.
10 min. phonotape (1 r. 7 1/2 i.p.s.)

1. King, Martin Luther, 1929-1968.

KING, MARTIN LUTHER, 1929-1968
Voice Lib.
M1318 Martin Luther King: burial at grave site and
bd.2 description of ceremony. CBS, April 9, 1968.
1 reel (7 in.) 7 1/2 in. per sec.
phonotape.

1. King, Martin Luther, 1929-1968.

KING, MARTIN LUTHER, 1929-1965
Voice Lib.
M1723 Green, Robert Lee
bd.2 Address at Martin Luther King Memorial
Service at Michigan State University.
WKAR, April 4, 1969.
20 min. phonotape (1 r. 7 1/2 i.p.s.)

1. King, Martin Luther, 1929-1965.

KING, MARTIN LUTHER, 1929-1968
C1
S1 Whorf, Michael, 1933-
A dream of freedom.
1 tape cassette. (The visual sounds of
Mike Whorf. Social, S1)
Originally presented on his radio program, Kaleidoscope,
WJR, Detroit.
Duration: 40 min., 45 sec.
Utilizing many of his famous speeches and delving into his
biography, the narrator gives continuity to this story of the life
and times of Martin Luther King.
1. King, Martin Luther, 1929-1968. 1. Title.

KING, MARTIN LUTHER, 1929-1968
Voice Lib.
M258 Harper, Robert
bd.9A Report to CBS News, New York; description
of Gov. Patterson's (Alabama) reaction to
the federal protection of Rev. Martin Luther
King. New York, CBS, May 22, 1961.
1 reel (7 in.) 7 1/2 in. per sec.
phonotape.

1. Patterson, John Malcolm, 1921- 2.
King, Martin Luther, 1929-1968.

The king of the storytellers - Rudyard
Kipling
C1
A30 Whorf, Michael, 1933-
The king of the storytellers - Rudyard Kipling.
1 tape cassette. (The visual sounds of
Mike Whorf. Art, music and letters, A30)
Originally presented on his radio program, Kaleidoscope,
WJR, Detroit.
Duration: 37 min., 45 sec.
Rudyard Kipling was king of the storytellers. From England to
India he wrote of the strange, the fascinating, and became an
international author.
1. Kipling, Rudyard, 1865-1936. 1. Title.

Voice Lib.
537   Kipling, Rudyard, 1865-1936.
bd.1,2   Speaking on the War (incomplete) at the
Royal Society of St. George: Gt. Britain's
loss in World War I, British morality and
war, German war morality. Introduced by
Lord Queensborough.   BBC, 1936.
1 reel (7 in.)   7 1/2 in. per sec.
phonotape.

Knapp, Ruth
Voice Lib.
M1724   Morris, Clyde D   J
bd.1   Next steps to control the military; part
of the MSU Moratorium against the War -
introduces a slogan and a song, sung by
Ruth Knapp, Doug Solomon, and Phyllis Hart.
WKAR, October 15, 1969.
15 min.   phonotape (1 r.   7 1/2 i.p.s.)

1. Vietnamese Conflict, 1961-   - U.S.
I. Knapp, Ruth.   II. Solomon, Douglas S.
III. Hart, Phyllis.

KIPLING, RUDYARD, 1865-1936
C1
A30   Whorf, Michael, 1933-
The king of the storytellers - Rudyard Kipling.
1 tape cassette.   (The visual sounds of
Mike Whorf.   Art, music and letters, A30)
Originally presented on his radio program, Kaleidoscope,
WJR, Detroit.
Duration: 37 min., 45 sec.
Rudyard Kipling was king of the storytellers. From England to
India he wrote of the strange, the fascinating, and became an
international author.

1. Kipling, Rudyard, 1865-1936.   I. Title.

Voice Lib.
221-   Knight, Eric Mowbray, 1897-1943.
224   "The Flying Yorkshireman", narrated by
the author.   G.R. Vincent, 1942.
4 reels (7 in.)   7 1/2 in. per sec.
phonotape.

I. Title.

Voice Lib.
M1720   Kissinger, Henry Alfred, 1923-
bd.3   Emotionally denying ordering wiretapping
of his associates.   NBC-TV, June 12, 1974.
1 min., 15 sec.   phonotape (1 r.
7 1/2 i.p.s.)

1. U.S. - Politics and government - 1969-

KNIGHTS AND KNIGHTHOOD
C1
H85   Whorf, Michael, 1933-
In days of old when knights were bold -
knighthood.
1 tape cassette.   (The visual sounds of
Mike Whorf. History and heritage, H85)
Originally presented on his radio program, Kaleidoscope,
WJR, Detroit.
Duration: 36 min., 50 sec.
The romance and the glories of knighthood are a heritage of
chivalry, but with a misty background in the Arthurian legends.

1. Knights and knighthood. 2. Arthur, King.   I. Title.

Voice Lib.
M1746   Kissinger, Henry Alfred, 1923-
Excerpts of press conference, explaining
that the arms limitations talks with the
Russians will serve the best interests of
both nations; denying secret agreements.
WKAR, June 24, 1974.
50 min.   phonotape (1 r.   7 1/2 i.p.s.)

1. U.S. - Foreign relations - Russia.
2. Russia - Foreign relations - U.S.

Voice Lib.
M1619   Kniseley, William
bd.1   Discussion of the MSU Colloquy on
Sexuality, with J. P. McCarthy.
WJR, January 2, 1969.
22 min.   phonotape (1 r.   7 1/2 i.p.s.)

1. Sex.   I. McCarthy, Joseph Priestley,
1934-

Voice Lib.
M1800   Kleindienst, Richard Gordon, 1923-
WG   Testimony before the Senate Committee
0807.01   investigating the Watergate Affair.
Pacifica, August 7, 1973.
204 min.   phonotape (3 r.   3 3/4 i.p.s.)
(Watergate gavel to gavel, phase 1)

1. Watergate Affair, 1972-

Knopf, Alfred A., 1892-
Voice Lib.
M1075   Ashmore, Harry Scott, 1916-
bd.2   Discussion among three well-known book
publishers about authors of the past, the job
of book editors, the publishing business, book
reviewers, etc. Held in the Library at the
Center for the Study of Democratic Institutions
at Santa Barbara, California.   CSDI, 1960.
1 reel (7 in.)   7 1/2 in. per sec.
phonotape.

1. Publishers and publishing.   I. Knopf, Alfred A., 1892-
II. Ferry, W. H.

Voice Lib.
M1581   Knowles, John
             Rockefeller Foundation.   WVWC, Buchanan,
         W. Va., February 27, 1974.
             30 min. phonotape (1 r.   7 1/2 i.p.s.)

             1. Rockefeller Foundation.

Voice Lib.
M1745   Knowles, John
bd.2   Explains how to find a capable physician
         on the Mike Douglas Show.   WILX-TV, June
         27, 1974.
             6 min.   phonotape (1 r.   7 1/2 i.p.s.)

             1. Physicians - U. S.   I. Douglas, Mike,
         1925?

                 Known but to God - Armistice Day
C1
H52   Whorf, Michael, 1933-
             Known but to God - Armistice Day.
             1 tape cassette.   (The visual sounds of
         Mike Whorf. History and heritage, H52)
             Originally presented on his radio program, Kaleidoscope,
         WJR, Detroit.
             Duration: 38 min., 45 sec.
             A solemn approach to America's fallen - a tribute to the
         unknown soldier - a brief biographical sketch of Sergeant Alvin
         York is the content of this Armistice Day program.
             1. Armistice Day. 2. York, Alvin Cullum, 1887-
         1. Title.

                 KNOX, JOHN, 1505-1572
C1
R26   Whorf, Michael, 1933-
             For God and nation.
             1 tape cassette.   (The visual sounds of
         Mike Whorf. Religion, R26)
             Originally presented on his radio program, Kaleidoscope,
         WJR, Detroit.
             Duration: 35 min., 50 sec.
             Knox's devotion to the cause of reformation and his zeal in
         preaching this gospel brought him imprisonment and exile, yet his
         beliefs rose above these hardships to transform his native land of
         Scotland and influence the world.
             1. Knox, John, 1505-1572. 1. Title.

Voice Lib.
M609   Koch, Frederick Henry, 1877-1944.
bd.9   Carolina playmakers; description of origin
         and history of American folk plays.
         G.R.Vincent, January 3, 1942.
             1 reel (7 in.)   7 1/2 i.p.s.   phonotape.

             1. American drama - History and criticism.

                 KOPECHNE, MARY JO, 1941-1969
Voice Lib.
M1378   Kennedy, Edward Moore, 1932-
bd.2   Statement after death of Mary Jo Kopechne
         in an auto accident in which he was involved.
         ABC, July 25, 1969.
             1 reel (7 in.)   7 1/2 in. per sec.
         phonotape.

             1. Kopechne, Mary Jo, 1941-1969.

Voice Lib.
M1696   Koplin, Mert
bd.2   Appearance of Koplin and Charles Grinker,
         of Cinedex, movie archives, on Mike
         Douglas Show. WJRT-TV, May 27, 1974.
             7 min.   phonotape (1 r.   7 1/2 i.p.s.)

             1. Moving-pictures - History.   I. Grinker,
         Charles. II. Douglas, Mike, 1925?

Voice Lib. KOREAN WAR, 1950-1953
353   Acheson, Dean Gooderham, 1893-1971.
bd.1   Outbreak of the Korean conflict; events
         in State Department on the day the conflict
         began, action of Pres. Truman, U.S. military
         action. NBC, July, 1950.
             1 reel (7 in.)   7 1/2 in. per sec.
         phonotape.

             Original disc off-speed.

                 KOREAN WAR, 1950-1953
Voice Lib.
353   Bridges, Henry Styles, 1898-1961.
bd.5   Outbreak of Korean War; now is the time
         to act against Russia. NBC, July, 1950.
             1 reel (7 in.)   7 1/2 in. per sec.
         phonotape.

             Original disc off-speed.

Voice Lib. KOREAN WAR, 1950-1953
353   Bryan, Wright
bd.12   Outbreak of Korean War; on beginning of
         World War III. NBC, July, 1950.
             1 reel (7 in.)   7 1/2 in. per sec.
         phonotape.

             Original disc off-speed.

Voice Lib.
353   Campbell, Gardner
bd.11   Outbreak of Korean War; supports Truman's
         action as only course of action. NBC,
         July, 1950.
            1 reel (7 in.)   7 1/2 in. per sec.
         phonotape.

            Original disc off-speed.

KOREAN WAR, 1950-1953

Voice Lib.
M353   Lie, Trygve, 1896-1968.
bd.2   Outbreak of the Korean conflict; calling
        of U.N. Security Council to action. NBC,
        July, 1950.
           1 reel (7 in.)   7 1/2 in. per sec.
        phonotape.

           Original disc off-speed.

KOREAN WAR, 1950-1953

Voice Lib.
353   Connally, Thomas Terry, 1877-1963.
bd.4   Outbreak of Korean conflict; preservation
        of South Korean integrity.   NBC, July, 1950.
           1 reel (7 in.)   7 1/2 in. per sec.
        phonotape.

           Original disc off-speed.

KOREAN WAR, 1950-1953

Voice Lib.
353   Magnuson, Warren Grant, 1905-
bd.9   Outbreak of Korean War; meet the enemy
        where they will be, points out this may be
        a bluff. NBC, July, 1950.
           1 reel (7 in.)   7 1/2 in. per sec.
        phonotape.

           Original disc off-speed.

KOREAN WAR, 1950-1953

Voice Lib.
353   Eden, Anthony, 1897-
bd.6   Outbreak of Korean War; on Pres. Truman's
        courageous stand.   NBC, July, 1950.
           1 reel (7 in.)   7 1/2 in. per sec.
        phonotape.

           Original disc off-speed.

KOREAN WAR, 1950-1953

Voice Lib.
353   Marcantonio, Vito, 1902-1954.
bd.17   Outbreak of Korean War; Madison Square
         Garden meeting describing outbreak is not
         in the interest of U.S. NBC, July, 1950.
            1 reel (7 in.)   7 1/2 in. per sec.
         phonotape.

            Original disc off-speed.

KOREAN WAR, 1950-1953

Voice Lib.
353   Gross, Ernest Arnold, 1906-
bd.3   Outbreak of the Korean conflict; U.S.
        resolution to halt Korean conflict.   NBC,
        July, 1950.
           1 reel (7 in.)   7 1/2 in. per sec.
        phonotape.

           Original disc off-speed.

KOREAN WAR, 1950-1953

Voice Lib.
353   Petterson, Elmer
bd.14   Outbreak of Korean War; public opinion
         and editorial opinion supporting Truman.
         NBC, July, 1950.
            1 reel (7 in.)   7 1/2 in. per sec.
         phonotape.

            Original disc off-speed.

KOREAN WAR, 1950-1953

Voice Lib.
M736   Hoover, Herbert Clark, Pres. U.S., 1874-1964.
bd.14   Excerpt from speech against invasion of
         China's mainland during the Korean conflict,
         and excerpt from speech concerning America's
         defense capabilities. CBS, 1951.
            1 reel (7 in.)   7 1/2 in. per sec.
         phonotape.

KOREAN WAR, 1950-1953

Voice Lib.
353   Outbreak of Korean War and comments by
bd.18   various persons. NBC, July, 1950.
            1 reel (7 in.)   7 1/2 in. per sec.
         phonotape.

            Original disc off-speed.
            Participants: Henry Cassidy, Merrill Mueller,
         Edward Harper, Jack Bregon.

            I. Cassidy, Henry Clarence, 1910-   II.
         Mueller, Merrill. III. Harper, Edward. IV.
         Bregon, Jack.

KOREAN WAR, 1950-1953

KOREAN WAR, 1950-1953
Voice Lib.
353   Radio Moscow.
bd.16   Outbreak of Korean War; Russian viewpoint
on starting of Korean conflict.   NBC, July,
1950.
1 reel (7 in.)   7 1/2 in. per sec.
phonotape.

Original disc off-speed.

KOREAN WAR, 1950-1953
Voice Lib.
353   Voice of America (radio program)
bd.15   Outbreak of Korean War; description of
outbreak.   NBC, July, 1950.
1 reel (7 in.)   7 1/2 in. per sec.
phonotape.

In Russian.
Original disc off-speed.

KOREAN WAR, 1950-1953
Voice Lib.
M739   Reuther, Walter Philip, 1907-1970.
bd.4   Speaking on mobilization for Korea,
referring to labor-production capabilities
to meet mobilization demands; price control
importance in mobilization process.   CBS,
1951.
1 reel (7 in.)   7 1/2 in. per sec.
phonotape.

KOREAN WAR, 1950-1953 - U.S.
Voice Lib.
353   Hoover, Herbert Clark, Pres. U.S., 1874-1964.
bd.8   Outbreak of Korean War; on the importance
of unity.   NBC, July, 1950.
1 reel (7 in.)   7 1/2 in. per sec.
phonotape.

Original disc off-speed.

KOREAN WAR, 1950-1953
Voice Lib.
M739   Rickey, Branch (Wesley), 1881-1965.
bd.7   Speaking on mobilization for Korean War
as it affects baseball.   CBS, 1951.
1 reel (7 in.)   7 1/2 in. per sec.
phonotape.

KOREAN WAR, 1950-1953 - U.S.
Voice Lib.
M736   Hoover, Herbert Clark, Pres. U.S., 1874-1964.
bd.15   Excerpt from speech on Korea, stating that
the Allies should demonstrate actual military
strength before U.S. should give more troops
or money.   CBS, 1953.
1 reel (7 in.)   7 1/2 in. per sec.
phonotape.

Voice Lib.   KOREAN WAR, 1950-1953
353   Romulo, Carlos Pena, 1899-
bd.7   Outbreak of Korean War; on acceleration of
military aid to Philippines.   NBC, July, 1950.
1 reel (7 in.)   7 1/2 in. per sec.
phonotape.

Original disc off-speed.

KOREAN WAR, 1950-1953 - U.S.
Voice Lib.
M739   Marshall, George Catlett, 1880-1959.
bd.1   Comments of reassurance of purpose of
U.S. involvement in Korea; in backing up
U.N. forces.   CBS, late 1950.
1 min., 5 sec.   phonotape (1 r.
7 1/2 i.p.s.)

1. Korean War, 1950-1953 - U.S.

KOREAN WAR, 1950-1953
Voice Lib.
353   Villiard, Irving
bd.13   Outbreak of Korean War; Middle West
supports Truman.   NBC, July, 1950.
1 reel (7 in.)   7 1/2 in. per sec.
phonotape.

Original disc off-speed.

KOREAN WAR, 1950-1953 - U.S.
Voice Lib.
249   Ridgway, Matthew Bunker, 1895-
bd.1   Address to joint session of Congress
on conduct of military in Korea.   CBS,
May 22, 1952.
1 reel (7 in.)   7 1/2 in. per sec.
phonotape.

KOREAN WAR, 1950-1953 - U.S.

Voice Lib.
353   Taft, Robert Alphonso, 1889-1953.
bd.10   Outbreak of Korean War; time to give notice
         to Communists to stop, brought on by Pres. [sic]
         administration's bungling. NBC, July, 1950.
             1 reel (7 in.)   7 1/2 in. per sec.
         phonotape.

         Original disc off-speed.

Voice Lib.
M1038- Kosygin, Aleksei Nikolaevich, 1904-
1039   Statements to the press at conference in
         London; followed by questions and answers
         on world political and economic issues.
         CBS, February 9, 1967.
             2 reels (7 in.)   7 1/2 in. per sec.
         phonotape.

Voice Lib.
M1253   Kosygin, Aleksei Nikolaevich, 1904-
bd.2   Simultaneous interpretation to English of
         Premier Kosygin's address at the emergency
         session of U.N. General Assembly in New
         York pertaining to Middle East crisis.
         Condemns Israel as aggressor. NBC-TV,
         June 19, 1967.
             1 reel (7 in.)   7 1/2 in. per sec.
         phonotape.

             1. Israel-Arab War, 1967-   - Diplomatic
         history.

Voice Lib.
M1258- Kosygin, Aleksei Nikolaevich, 1904-
1259   Press conference at U.N. Correspondents
         Association in New York after his week
         at the U.N. and his two meetings with
         President Johnson in Glassboro, N.J.
         Spoken in Russian with English interpretation.
         at United Nations Headquarters on Sunday
         evening at 8 p.m. E.D.T. CBS-TV, June 25,
         1967.
             2 reels (7 in.)   7 1/2 in. per sec.
         phonotape.

KOSYGIN, ALEKSEI NIKOLAEVICH, 1904-

Voice Lib.
M1040   Kalb, Marvin L
bd.1   Discussion of the significance of Kosygin
         press conference with two political science
         authorities. CBS, February 9, 1967.
             1 reel (7 in.)   7 1/2 in. per sec.
         phonotape.

Voice Lib.
M788   Kraft, Christopher Columbus, 1924-
       Gemini 5 (space flight): summary of space
       flight of Gemini Titan V from August 21 to
       August 29, 1965, including interview with
       Chris Kraft, flight director.   1965.
           1 reel (7 in.)   7 1/2 in. per sec.
       phonotape.

           1. Project Gemini. 2. Cooper, Leroy Gordon,
       1927-   3. Conrad, Charles, 1930-   I.
       Cooper, Leroy Gordon, 1927-   II. Conrad,
       Charles, 1930-   III. Kraft, Christopher
       Columbus, 1924-

Voice Lib.
M978   Krauch, Helmut
bd.1   Expressing his opinions about the role of
       the scientist in society, his obligation to
       promote the social welfare. Interview with
       Dr. Krauch at the Center for the Study of
       Democratic Institutions at Santa Barbara by
       Scott Buchanan. CSDI, 1963.
           1 reel (7 in.)   7 1/2 in. per sec.
       phonotape.

           I. Buchanan, Scott Milross, 1895-1968.

Krauch, Helmut

Voice Lib.
M9/8   Pauling, Linus Carl, 1901-
bd.2   Excerpts of discussion between Dr. Helmut
       Krauch and Dr. Pauling at the Center for the
       Study of Democratic Institutions, Pauling
       maintaining that scientists must be free
       to follow their curiosity. CSDI, 1963.
           1 reel (7 in.)   7 1/2 in. per sec.
       phonotape.

           I. Krauch, Helmut

Krauch, Helmut

Voice Lib.
M979   Pauling, Linus Carl, 1901-
bd.1   In discussion with Dr. Krauch at Center
       for the Study of Democratic Institutions,
       recalling creative processes in his
       discoveries. CSDI, 1963.
           1 reel (7 in.)   7 1/2 in. per sec.
       phonotape.

           I. Krauch, Helmut.

Voice Lib.
344   Krishna Menon, Vengalil Krishnan
bd.17   At Idlewild Airport: on the invasion
       of Goa. CBS, December 20, 1961.
           1 reel (7 in.)   7 1/2 in. per sec.
       phonotape.

Voice Lib.
M1351 Krock, Arthur, 1886-
bd.2   Interview with Eric Sevareid pertaining
         to his recent best-selling book, "Presidents
         I Have Known". January 10, 1969.
           1 reel (7 in.) 7 1/2 in. per sec.
         phonotape.

           I. Sevareid, Arnold Eric, 1912-
         Presidents I have known.

Voice Lib.
164   Kroll, Jack, 1885-1971.
bd.2   1949 Labor Day Speech: Labor. AFL-CIO.
       1949.
           1 reel (7 in.) 7 1/2 in. per sec.
         phonotape.

Voice Lib.
M243   Ku Klux Klan (1915-   )
bd.4   Requirements necessary for joining
         the Klan, by the Grand Wizard. CBS,
         July 22, 1957.
           1 reel (7 in.) 7 1/2 i.p.s.   phonotape.

           1. Ku Klux Klan (1915-   )

Voice Lib.
M770   Kuhn, Madison, 1910-
bd.1   Excerpt from proceedings at commencement
         convocation at MSU; interview with Dr. Kuhn,
         university historian, regarding past
         commencements and early customs, also
         explaining preparations for present one.
         WMSB, June 13, 1965.
           15 min., 45 sec.   phonotape (1 r.
         7 1/2 i.p.s.)

           1. Michigan State University - History.

Voice Lib.   KUN, BÉLA, 1886-1937
M1227 Lenin, Vladimir Il'ich, 1820-1924.
bd.7   Report on the conversations with the
         Hungarian communist leader Béla Kun in
         March of 1919. Peteler, 1920.
           1 reel (7 in.) 7 1/2 in. per sec.
         phonotape.

           1. Kun, Béla, 1886-1937.

Voice Lib.   Kuralt, Charles, 1934-
M915- As we knew him; words of reminiscence of
916   friends and relatives about the life of
         J.F. Kennedy. Narration by Charles Kuralt;
         participants: Charles Bartlett, Lemayne
         Billings, Robert Kennedy, Rose Kennedy,
         James Reed, Adlai Stevenson, Gen. Chester B.
         Clifton, etc. Columbia Records Inc., 1965.
           2 reels (7 in.) 7 1/2 in. per sec.
         phonotape.

           1. Kennedy, John Fitzgerald, Pres. U.S.,
         1917-1963. I. Kuralt, Charles, 1934-

           (Continued on next card)

Voice Lib.
M1488 Kuralt, Charles, 1934-
bd.3   "On the Road"; segment pertaining to
         MSU National Voice Library, including
         various actual voices of the past. CBS-TV,
         November 9, 1971.
           1 reel (7 in.) 7 1/2 in. per sec.
         phonotape.

           1. Michigan State University. National
         Voice Library.

Voice Lib.   Kuromoto, Mrs. George
M322   Biography in sound (radio program)
         W.C. Fields, the magnificent rogue.
         NBC, 1955.
           1 reel (7 in.) 7 1/2 in. per sec. phonotape.
           L Fields, W.C., 1879-1946. L Fields, W.C., 1879-1946.
         II. Allen, Fred, 1894-1956. III. LaBaron, William   IV.
         Taylor, Robert Lewis, 1912-   V. McCarey, Thomas Leo, 1898-
         1969. VI. Harkins, James   - VII. Chevalier, Maurice,
         1889-1972. VIII. Kuromoto, Mrs. George   IX. Flynn,
         Errol Leslie, 1909-1959. X. Wynn, Ed, 1886-1966. XI. Dowling,
         Ray Dooley   XII. Sennett, Mack   XIII. Overacher,
         Ronald Leroy   XIV. Bergen, Edgar, 1903-   XV. Taurog,
         Norman, 1899-   XVI. Runnell, Ann   XVII. Cowen,
         Lester

Voice Lib.   Kuruso, Saburo, 1886-1954
M1071 German radio (Nazi controlled)
bd.3   Nazi radio announcement giving text of
         pact made between Germany, Italy, and Japan.
         Read in German by Joachim von Ribbentrop, in
         Italian by Count Ciano, and in Japanese by
         Ambassador Kurusu, stating their spheres of
         interest. Peteler, September 27, 1940.
           1 reel (7 in.) 7 1/2 in. per sec.
         phonotape.
           I. Ribbentrop, Joachim von, 1893-1946. II.
         Ciano, Galeazzo, conte, 1903-1944. III.
         Kuruso, Saburo, 1886-1954.

Voice Lib.
M1047 Kyser, Kay, 1906-
         Old-time radio excerpts of the 1930's and
         1940's, including: Rudy Vallee singing
         "Linger a little longer"; Will Rogers on
         panaceas for the Depression; Bing Crosby
         singing "Sweet Georgia Brown"; Eddie Cantor;
         Jimmy Durante singing "Inka-dinka-do";
         musical skit by Clayton, Jackson and Durante;
         wit by Harry Hershfield; musical selection
         "Thinking of you" by Kay Kyser; Kate Smith
         singing theme song, "When the moon comes over
         the mountain"; W.C. Fields' temperance

           (Continued on next card)

Voice Lib.   Kyser, Kay, 1906-
M1047   Old-time radio excerpts of the 1930's and
      1940's...   (Card 2)

    lecture; Al Jolson singing "Rocka-by-your
    baby"; and George Burns and Gracie Allen
    skit.   TV&R, 1930's and 1940's.
     1 reel (7 in.)   7 1/2 in. per sec.
    L Vallee, Rudy, 1901-   II. Rogers, Will, 1879-1935.   III.
    Crosby, Bing, 1901-   IV. Cantor, Eddie, 1893-1964.   V. Durante,
    Jimmy, 1893-   VI. Clayton, Patti   VII. Jackson,
    Eddie   VIII. Hershfield, Harry, 1885-   IX. Kyser, Kay,
    1906-   X. Smith, Kate, 1909-   XI. Fields, W. C., 1879-
    1946.   XII. Jolson, Al, 1886-1950.   XIII. Burns, George, 1896-
    XIV. Allen, Fracie, 1906-

Voice Lib.
M719   Kyser, Kay, 1906-
bd.2   Excerpt of musical radio program.
     February 5, 1947.
      8 min., 50 sec.   phonotape (1 r.
     7 1/2 i.p.s.)

        LaBaron, William
Voice Lib.
M322   Biography in sound (radio program)
     W.C. Fields, the magnificent rogue.
     NBC, 1955.
      1 reel (7 in.)   7 1/2 in. per sec.   phonotape.
     I. Fields, W. C., 1879-1946.   I. Fields, W. C., 1879-1946.
     II. Allen, Fred, 1894-1956.   III. LaBaron, William   IV.
     Taylor, Robert Lewis, 1912-   V. McCarey, Thomas Leo, 1898-
     1969.   VI. Harkins, James   - VII. Chevalier, Maurice,
     1889-1972.   VIII. Kuromoto, Mrs. George   IX. Flynn,
     Errol Leslie, 1909-1959.   X. Wynn, Ed, 1886-1966.   XI. Dowling,
     Ray Dooley   XII. Sennett, Mack   XIII. Overacher,
     Ronald Leroy   XIV. Bergen, Edgar, 1903-   XV. Taurog,
     Norman, 1899-   XVI. Runnell, Ann   XVII. Cowen,
     Lester

      LABOR AND LABORING CLASSES - GERMANY
Voice Lib.
M961   Decker, Wilhelm
bd.8   Policy on German labor forces.   German
    Radio, Peteler, February 2, 1937.
     1 reel (7 in.)   7 1/2 in. per sec.
    phonotape.

      LABOR AND LABORING CLASSES - U.S.
Voice Lib.
M1430   Patterson, Robert Porter, 1891-1952.
bd.2   In address "Labor for victory".   AFL-
    CIO PRO, April 18, 1942.
     1 reel (7 in.)   7 1/2 i.p.s.   phonotape.

     1. Labor and laboring classes - U.S.

      LABOR AND LABORING CLASSES - U.S.
Voice Lib.
M1572   Ussery, William J
     National Press Club address, plus some
     questions and answers.   WKAR-AM, February 25,
     1974.
      35 min.   phonotape (1 r.   7 1/2 i.p.s.)

     1. U.S. - Social conditions.   2. Labor and
    laboring classes - U.S.

        LABOR SUPPLY
Voice Lib.
M1503   Higher education: who needs it? Hughes Rudd
     in a one-hour documentary on employment
     problems of college graduates.   CBS-TV,
     May 26, 1972.
     1 reel (7 in.)   7 1/2 in. per sec.
    phonotape.

     1. Education, Higher.   2. Labor supply.
    I. Rudd, Hughes.

      LABOR SUPPLY - GERMANY
Voice Lib.
M1470   Goebbels, Joseph, 1897-1945.
bd.14   Report on the labor situation in Berlin.
    Peteler, January 30, 1933.
     1 reel (7 in.)   7 1/2 i.p.s.   phonotape.

     1. Labor supply - Germany.

      The Lafayette Escadrille
C1
H12   Whorf, Michael, 1933-
     The Lafayette Escadrille.
     1 tape cassette.   (The visual sounds of
    Mike Whorf. History and heritage, H12)
      Originally presented on his radio program, Kaleidoscope,
    WJR, Detroit.
     Duration: 28 min., 30 sec.
     A group of daring young American aviators went to France at
    the out-set of World War I to fly and fight for the Allies. Here is
    the unlikely adventure of a group of young flyers who were at war
    long before their own country entered the conflict.

     I. France. Armée. Escadrille Lafayette. I. Title.

Voice Lib.
585   LaGuardia, Fiorello Henry, 1882-1947.
bd.2   Speech before Atlantic States Fishery
    Council.   WNYC, gn. d.;
     1 reel (7 in.)   7 1/2 in. per sec.
    phonotape.

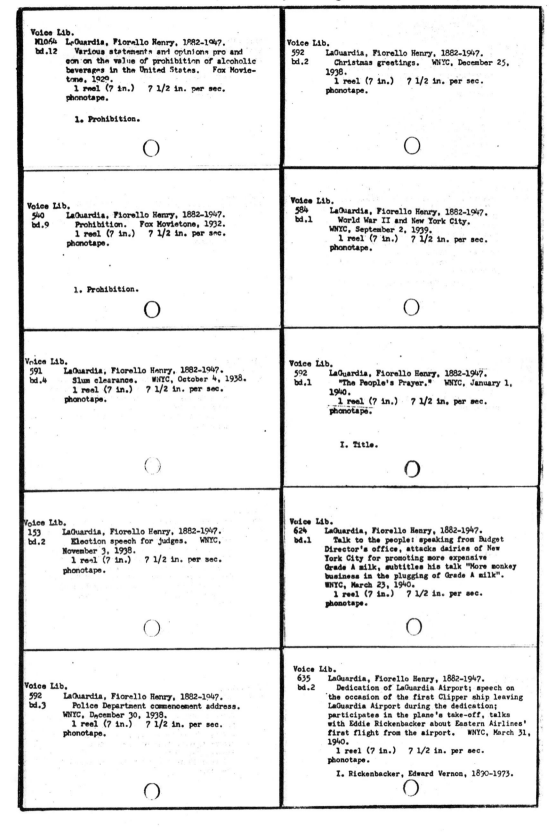

Voice Lib.
M1064 LaGuardia, Fiorello Henry, 1882-1947.
bd.12   Various statements and opinions pro and
        con on the value of prohibition of alcoholic
        beverages in the United States. Fox Movie-
        tone, 1929.
            1 reel (7 in.) 7 1/2 in. per sec.
        phonotape.

            1. Prohibition.

Voice Lib.
592   LaGuardia, Fiorello Henry, 1882-1947.
bd.2   Christmas greetings. WNYC, December 25,
        1938.
            1 reel (7 in.) 7 1/2 in. per sec.
        phonotape.

Voice Lib.
540   LaGuardia, Fiorello Henry, 1882-1947.
bd.9   Prohibition. Fox Movietone, 1932.
            1 reel (7 in.) 7 1/2 in. per sec.
        phonotape.

            1. Prohibition.

Voice Lib.
584   LaGuardia, Fiorello Henry, 1882-1947.
bd.1   World War II and New York City.
        WNYC, September 2, 1939.
            1 reel (7 in.) 7 1/2 in. per sec.
        phonotape.

Voice Lib.
591   LaGuardia, Fiorello Henry, 1882-1947.
bd.4   Slum clearance. WNYC, October 4, 1938.
            1 reel (7 in.) 7 1/2 in. per sec.
        phonotape.

Voice Lib.
592   LaGuardia, Fiorello Henry, 1882-1947.
bd.1   "The People's Prayer." WNYC, January 1,
        1940.
            1 reel (7 in.) 7 1/2 in. per sec.
        phonotape.

            I. Title.

Voice Lib.
153   LaGuardia, Fiorello Henry, 1882-1947.
bd.2   Election speech for judges. WNYC,
        November 3, 1938.
            1 reel (7 in.) 7 1/2 in. per sec.
        phonotape.

Voice Lib.
624   LaGuardia, Fiorello Henry, 1882-1947.
bd.1   Talk to the people: speaking from Budget
        Director's office, attacks dairies of New
        York City for promoting more expensive
        Grade A milk, subtitles his talk "More monkey
        business in the plugging of Grade A milk".
        WNYC, March 23, 1940.
            1 reel (7 in.) 7 1/2 in. per sec.
        phonotape.

Voice Lib.
592   LaGuardia, Fiorello Henry, 1882-1947.
bd.3   Police Department commencement address.
        WNYC, December 30, 1938.
            1 reel (7 in.) 7 1/2 in. per sec.
        phonotape.

Voice Lib.
635   LaGuardia, Fiorello Henry, 1882-1947.
bd.2   Dedication of LaGuardia Airport; speech on
        the occasion of the first Clipper ship leaving
        LaGuardia Airport during the dedication;
        participates in the plane's take-off, talks
        with Eddie Rickenbacker about Eastern Airlines'
        first flight from the airport. WNYC, March 31,
        1940.
            1 reel (7 in.) 7 1/2 in. per sec.
        phonotape.

            I. Rickenbacker, Edward Vernon, 1890-1973.

Voice Lib.
399   LaGuardia, Fiorello Henry, 1882-1947.
bd.3   Induction ceremonies of 500 social
          investigators.   WNYC, April 18, 1940.
            1 reel (7 in.)   7 1/2 in. per sec.
          phonotape.

Voice Lib.
M752   LaGuardia, Fiorello Henry, 1882-1947.
bd.1   Talk to the people; discussion of current
          war news and problems in New York City.
          WNYC, March 15, 1942.
            1 reel (7 in.)   7 1/2 in. per sec.
          phonotape.

Voice Lib.
633   LaGuardia, Fiorello Henry, 1882-1947.
          Willkie vs. Willkie; offers his views on
          the campaign speeches of the Republican
          presidential candidate, Wendell Willkie.
          Sponsored by the National Independent
          Committee for Roosevelt and Wallace.   CBS,
          October 24, 1940.
            1 reel (7 in.)   7 1/2 in. per sec.
          phonotape.

            1. Willkie, Wendell Lewis, 1892-1944.

Voice Lib.
M752   LaGuardia, Fiorello Henry, 1882-1947.
bd.2   Talk to members of National Youth Admin-
          istration Orchestra.   WNYC, April 5, 1942.
            1 reel (7 in.)   7 1/2 in. per sec.
          phonotape.

Voice Lib.
594   LaGuardia, Fiorello Henry, 1882-1947.
bd.2   Brussels proclamation.   WNYC, June 30,
          1941.
            1 reel (7 in.)   7 1/2 in. per sec.
          phonotape.

Voice Lib.
M1034 LaGuardia, Fiorello Henry, 1882-1947.
bd.11   Excerpt of Mayor LaGuardia reading the
          "funnies" regarding Dick Tracy.   Michigan
          State University, Department of Television
          and Radio, 1943.
            1 reel (7 in.)   7 1/2 in. per sec.
          phonotape.

Voice Lib.
585   LaGuardia, Fiorello Henry, 1882-1947.
bd.3   The city and the mayor.   New York, WOR,
          July 21, 1941.
            1 reel (7 in.)   7 1/2 in. per sec.
          phonotape.

Voice Lib.
594   LaGuardia, Fiorello Henry, 1882-1947.
bd.1   New Year's Day program of city of New York;
          delivers New Year's message; reviews
          America's position in world, hardship facing
          U.S. before ultimate victory, God's gift
          to man, greetings to people of New York
          City, sends greetings of people of New York
          to Armed Forces.   WNYC, January 1, 1943.
            1 reel (7 in.)   7 1/2 in. per sec.
          phonotape.

Voice Lib.
585   LaGuardia, Fiorello Henry, 1882-1947.
bd.1   Election returns speech.   WNYC,
          November 5, 1941.
            1 reel (7 in.)   7 1/2 in. per sec.
          phonotape.

Voice Lib.
M294   LaGuardia, Fiorello Henry, 1882-1947.
bd.1   Talk to the people on the invasion of
          Tripoli, War Prod. Board, deferring building,
          bread, smoking ordinance, pedestrian
          safety, dress industry, fire ordinance,
          Grandmother Contest winner.   WNYC,
          January 24, 1943.
            1 reel (7 in.)   7 1/2 in. per sec.
          phonotape.

Voice Lib.
M295   LaGuardia, Fiorello Henry, 1882-1947.
bd.1   Talk to the people on FDR's meeting with
        the Allies, air raid precautions for the
        East Coast, ceiling prices on meat,
        meatless days, implementation of Fire
        Ordinance 25 concerning protection for
        apartments, women in the Navy and Coast
        Guard, Infantile Paralysis Fund. WNYC,
        January 31, 1943.
            1 reel (7 in.) 7 1/2 in. per sec.
        phonotape.

Voice Lib.
  641   LaGuardia, Fiorello Henry, 1882-1947.
            Talk to the people: reasons for meat
        shortage; warning to hotels on meat, kosher
        meat; Bureau of Markets; butter shortage
        appeal to O.P.A.; fish prices; black market
        in eggs; tomato prices and canning; rent
        violations; problems involved in moving;
        displays of Consolidated Edison pressure
        cookers; desire of Northwest Airlines to
        serve New York City; school playground
        openings; reduction ⌢ city fires; salutes

                        (Continued on next card)

Voice Lib.
M394   LaGuardia, Fiorello Henry, 1882-1947.
bd.2   Talk to the people on Lou Valentine's air
        warning system, plant protection, defense
        volunteers, letter from Armenian listener,
        NYC scholarships, TV course for air wardens,
        National Civilian Defense head, alien
        registration (English, Italian, German).
        WNYC, February 8, 1943.
            1 reel (7 in.) 7 1/2 in. per sec.
        phonotape.

Voice Lib.
  641   La Guardia, Fiorello Henry, 1882-1947. Talk
        to the people: reasons for meat shortage...
        1943. (Card 2)
            work of Department of Housing; reads letter
        from jockey Smiky Saunders, offering recipient
        chance to make good bets; points out how
        crooked racing is; names "tin horns" and
        crooked politicians arrested; results of
        gambling on citizenry; techniques of gamblers
        to gain influence with police and courts;
        reviews his action ⌢ against Dutch Schultz;

                        (Continued on next card)

Voice Lib.
M295   LaGuardia, Fiorello Henry, 1882-1947.
bd.2-   Talk to the people on Democrats and
296   Republicans in Albany, Tammany Hall, real
bd.1   estate taxes, wholesale food prices, food
        points at retail and ceiling prices,
        Victory Gardens, air raid siren tests,
        exhibition baseball between Dodgers-Yankees-
        Giants, Boston police corruption, letter
        from New York Teachers' Association, saluting
        a school teacher, Millicent Baum, on her
        death. WNYC, March 28, 1943.
            2 reels (7 in.) 7 1/2 in. per sec. phonotape.

Voice Lib.
  641   LaGuardia, Fiorello Henry, 1882-1947.   Talk
        to the people: reasons for meat shortage...
        1943. (Card 3)
            crooked judges; British anti-aircraft parade;
        New York Herald Tribune Fresh Air Fund;
        announces special radio programs in foreign
        languages, news programs and drama; announces
        resignation of executive secretary. WNYC,
        August 29, 1943.
            1 reel (7 in.) 7 1/2 in. per sec. phonotape.
            First minute of recording missing on master disc.

Voice Lib.
M296   LaGuardia, Fiorello Henry, 1882-1947.
bd.2   Talk to the people on the privileges of
        democracy, food control, details of the
        Office of Price Administration policies,
        child labor law, city swimming pools,
        boarding homeless children. WNYC, July
        4, 1943.
            1 reel (7 in.) 7 1/2 in. per sec.
        phonotape.

Voice Lib.
  637   La Guardia, Fiorello Henry, 1882-1947.
bd.1   "Unity at home - victory abroad"; last in
        a series of programs on the importance of unity
        of American people. Mayor introduces Marian
        Anderson, who sings a selection of songs;
        reviews importance [of] compatible race
        relations. New York City, WOR, September
        11, 1943.
            1 reel (7 in.) 7 1/2 in. per sec.
        phonotape.

Voice Lib.
  635   LaGuardia, Fiorello Henry, 1882-1947.
bd.3   "Unity at home - victory abroad"; comments
        on importance of unity in first of a series
        of programs originating from his home in
        New York City; introduces Eleanor Roosevelt.
        WNYC, August 15, 1943.
            1 reel (7 in.) 7 1/2 in. per sec.
        phonotape.

Voice Lib.
  399,   LaGuardia, Fiorello Henry, 1882-1947.
bd.4;   Talk to the people: on current war news;
500,   O.P.A. prices on fish and other food; waste
bd.1   collection; fuel distribution; admission
        ticket frauds; proposed legislation on 5-cent
        subway fare; state aid to education; sweat
        shop illiteracy plan; juvenile delinquency
        and special court. WNYC, March 5, 1944.
            2 reels (7 in.) 7 1/2 in. per sec.
        phonotape.

Voice Lib.
509   LaGuardia, Fiorello Henry, 1882-1947.
         Talk to the people. WNYC, March 18,
      1944.
         1 reel (7 in.) 7 1/2 in. per sec.
      phonotape.

Voice Lib.
510   LaGuardia, Fiorello Henry, 1882-1947.
         Talk to the people. WNYC, August 27,
      1944.
         1 reel (7 in.) 7 1/2 in. per sec.
      phonotape.

Voice Lib.
511   LaGuardia, Fiorello Henry, 1882-1947.
bd.1   Talk to the people; discussion of current
      food prices, convictions of OPA price
      violators, discussion of clothes prices and
      supply, word of caution to tavern and hotel
      owners about minors, progress of students
      at NYCC, letters to mayor about gambling.
      public service messages, retirement of
      Admiral Marquart, introduction and life of
      Harry T. Burleigh. WNYC, April 2, 1944.
         1 reel (7 in.) 7 1/2 in. per sec.
      phonotape.

Voice Lib.
643   LaGuardia, Fiorello Henry, 1882-1947.
         Talk to the people: talks about Polaski Day
      celebration; starts Polaski Day parade;
      butter shortage, urges use of margarine; 1944
      presidential election and importance of voting;
      voter registration requirements; announces
      presidential panel program on WNYC; new
      manufacturing facilities; creation of co-op
      office building; available post-war finance
      for small business; attacks McCarren Committee
      for wanting to "Freeze" reconstruction;
                        (Continued on next card)

Voice Lib.
399   LaGuardia, Fiorello Henry, 1882-1947.
bd.1   Talk to the people. WNYC, June 4,
      1944.
         1 reel (7 in.) 7 1/2 in. per sec.
      phonotape.

Voice Lib.
643   LaGuardia, Fiorello Henry, 1882-1947.   Talk
         to the people: talks about Polaski Day...
      1944.   (Card 2)
         housing committee; fire problem in New York
      City; warns against use of combustible cleaning
      fluid; Fire Prevention Rally; plays "Sidewalks
      of New York" and talks about Alfred E. Smith,
      who was buried October 7, 1944. WNYC,
      October 8, 1944.
         1 reel (7 in.) 7 1/2 in. per sec.
      phonotape.

Voice Lib.
M584   LaGuardia, Fiorello Henry, 1882-1947.
bd.2   Welcomes DeGaulle to New York City in his
      office in City Hall and later repeated for
      the public on the steps of City Hall.
      WNYC, July 10, 1944.
         1 reel (7 in.) 7 1/2 in. per sec.
      phonotape.

         1. Gaulle, Charles de, Pres. France,
      1890-1970.

Voice Lib.
M753   LaGuardia, Fiorello Henry, 1882-1947.
bd.1   Talk to the people: radio broadcast
      commenting on re-election of FDR; appeal for
      alertness to Volunteer Protective Service;
      concern regarding OPA ceiling price enforcement
      by retailers and wholesalers; cigarette and
      gasoline prices; shortage of children's under-
      wear; answers to letters from listeners;
      protesting the loitering of kids at drugstores
      and bars; attacking child labor; reprimanding
      Railway Express Agency for cheating customers;
                        (Continued on next card)

Voice Lib.
501   LaGuardia, Fiorello Henry, 1882-1947.
         Talk to the people. WNYC, August 6,
      1944.
         1 reel (7 in.) 7 1/2 in. per sec.
      phonotape.

Voice Lib.
M753   LaGuardia, Fiorello Henry, 1882-1947.   Talk
bd.1   to the people: radio broadcast... 1944.
      (Card 2)
         general health problems in the city.
      WNYC, November 12, 1944.
         1 reel (7 in.) 7 1/2 in. per sec.
      phonotape.

Voice Lib.
628   LaGuardia, Fiorello Henry, 1882-1947.
     Talk to the people, from WBBM in Chicago: on cost of telephone line from Chicago where he is broadcasting from on attending the International Civil Aviation Conference; food rationing; children's underwear; ceiling prices; building public housing; gas shortage; traffic violations; returning soldiers; public finance for private housing; exploitation of child labor in bowling alleys; "Tin Horn" gamblers; loan sharks, barbers overcharging
                  (Continued on next card)

Voice Lib.
628   LaGuardia, Fiorello Henry, 1882-1947.   Talk to the people, from WBBM... 1944.   (Card 2)
    servicemen; prohibition of smoking in public places; city water shortage; Henry Street visiting nurses; recommends "Gypsy Baron"; importance of signing off on time; international conferences. WNYC, November 26, 1944.
     1 reel (7 in.)   7 1/2 in. per sec. phonotape.

Voice Lib.
M642   LaGuardia, Fiorello Henry, 1882-1947.
bd.1   Talk to the people: Christmas program featuring Mayor LaGuardia reading from the Scriptures, with Lauritz Melchior and Robert Shaw; offers his own views on America at war; reads prayer of Archbishop Spellman on return from battlefields of World War II; wishes audience a Merry Christmas. WNYC, December 24, 1944.
     1 reel (7 in.)   7 1/2 in. per sec. phonotape.
    I. Melchior, Lauritz Lebrecht Hummel, 1890-1973. II. Shaw, Robert Lawson, 1916-

Voice Lib.
M755   LaGuardia, Fiorello Henry, 1882-1947.
bd.2   Radio talk to N.Y. longshoremen against their strike and work stoppage; pleading with strikers not to break their good record; also talking to their wives; guaranteeing acceptable settlement of their labor dispute. WNYC, 1945.
     1 reel (7 in.)   7 1/2 in. per sec. phonotape.

Voice Lib.
638   LaGuardia, Fiorello Henry, 1882-1947.
     Talk to the people: FDR's annual address to Congress; meat availability; chowder parter at City Fish Market; forced tie-in sales on vegetables; newspaper and magazine recipes; inspection of food facilities by Dept. of Markets; lauds landlords for not trying to raise rent ceilings; fires caused by Christmas trees; attacks operation of Vitamin Corp. of America; Western Union agreement not to transmit betting orders; questions
                 (Continued on next card)

Voice Lib.
638   LaGuardia, Fiorello Henry, 1882-1947.
     Talk to the people: FDR's annual address... 1945. (Card 2)
    integrity of race tracks; attacks betting as denying food to children; reads letter from irate listener attacking his stand on betting; attacks "purveyors of sin"; warns of lethal liquor in New York City; gives recipe for lethal liquor. WNYC, January 7, 1945.
     1 reel (7 in.)   7 1/2 in. per sec. phonotape.

Voice Lib.
644   LaGuardia, Fiorello Henry, 1882-1947.
bd.2   Talk to the people (excerpt): describes previous days Presidential inauguration as making FDR president of all the people; reads from FDR's Inauguration Address, calls it a solace to mothers who have lost sons in war; recounts his trip to Washington; problems confronting FDR, his visit with FDR; wishes all mothers could talk to General G. C. Marshall. WNYC, January 21, 1945.
     1 reel (7 in.)   7 1/2 in. per sec. phonotape.

Voice Lib.
632   LaGuardia, Fiorello Henry, 1882-1947.
     Talk to the people: battlefront conditions in relation to sacrifices at home; defeat of Germany; current freight embargo and its effect on coal and food; meatless Tuesdays and Fridays; attacks New York Times article on food usage; cooperation of hotels and restaurants; meat consumption; fat conservation; price ceiling, tie-in sales; children's clothes; attacks gamblers on bribing of Brooklyn College basketball team; attacks newspapers for gambling coverage, race report
                 (Continued on next card)

Voice Lib.
632   LaGuardia, Fiorello Henry, 1882-1947.
     Talk to the people: battle front conditions... 1945. (Card 2)
    communications; Bingo games and churches. WNYC, February 4, 1945.
     1 reel (7 in.)   7 1/2 in. per sec. phonotape.

Voice Lib.
634-   LaGuardia, Fiorello Henry, 1882-1947.
635,   Talk to the people: meat shortage; Armed
bd.1   Forces food consumption; OPA price violations; warns poultry dealers about overcharging; low cost clothing; New York Times article on meat shortage; manufacture of rayon underwear; coal and kerosene shortage; numbers games and odds and practices of gamblers; admonishes Henry Morgenthau, Jr., to alter number quotations; gambler convictions; thanks New Jersey for fighting gambling; urges listeners to write
                 (Continued on next card)

Voice Lib.
634-   LaGuardia, Fiorello Henry, 1882-1947.   Talk
635   to the people: meat shortage... 1945.
bd.1   (Card 2)

Representative about gambling legislation;
reviews book on life of Mayor Gaynor; asks
James J. Walker if he followed Gaynor's ideas;
Gaynor's handling of police; his philosophy on
police action; compares himself to Gaynor;
traffic problem with interstate busses; transportation problem at Brooklyn Naval Yard,
Brooklyn Civic Center; investigation of college
basketball at Madison Square Garden, proposed
                        (Continued on next card)

Voice Lib.
325   LaGuardia, Fiorello Henry, 1882-1947.
       Talk to the people on conditions in
Germany, meat shortage, egg dealers threat
to strike, appearance before Senate
Committee on Banking and Commerce, Blue
Law. WNYC, March 18, 1945.
       1 reel (7 in.) 7 1/2 in. per sec.
phonotape.

Voice Lib.
634-   LaGuardia, Fiorello Henry, 1882-1947.   Talk
635   to the people: meat shortage... 1945.
bd.1   (Card 3)

changes in seating and gambling; Committee
on Consumer Assistance; usury laws; shelter
for neglected children; WNYC American music
series; creation of music during war period;
Lend-Lease philosophy. WNYC, February 18, 1945.
       2 reels (7 in.) 7 1/2 in. per sec.
phonotape.

Voice Lib.
644   LaGuardia, Fiorello Henry, 1882-1947.
bd.1   Talk to the people (excerpt): urges people
by using dramatic presentation not to try to
obtain drinks after midnight curfew; urges
Briggs Avenue residents not to make test case
out of drinking curfew; describes death of
New York City Patrolman Albert Black; tells of
death on previous day of his old friend, ex-
Senator William Calder. WNYC, March 4, 1945.
       1 reel (7 in.) 7 1/2 in. per sec.
phonotape.

Voice Lib.
151-   LaGuardia, Fiorello Henry, 1882-1947.
152   Talk to the people. WNYC, February 18,
bd.2   1945.
       2 reels (7 in.) 7 1/2 in. per sec.
phonotape.

Voice Lib.
636   LaGuardia, Fiorello Henry, 1882-1947. Talk
       to the people: war conditions... 1945.
       (Card 3)

to gamblers at baseball games. WNYC, March
11, 1945.
       1 reel (7 in.) 7 1/2 in. per sec.
phonotape.

Voice Lib.
631   LaGuardia, Fiorello Henry, 1882-1947.
       Talk to the people: addresses comment to
Churchill on meaning of Atlantic Charter;
conserving heating fuel; meat shortage and
New York Times reporting; warns housewives
on food prices; frozen fish; substitute for
potatoes; poultry dealer cooperation; Red
Cross donations; war prisoner core; New York
quota for Red Cross drive; curfew for entertainment establishments; order to police to
keep speakeasys from developing; honest vs.
crooked judges in regards to illegal sale of
                        (Continued on next card)

Voice Lib.
636   LaGuardia, Fiorello Henry, 1882-1947.
       Talk to the people: war conditions in
Germany and Japan; techniques used to stop
overpricing of poultry; retail fish prices;
restaurant food shortage; egg grading; fuel
crisis; salutes Harold Ickes; donation of
aged people on Welfare Island to City hospitals;
Red Cross donations; basketball scandal at
Brooklyn College; basketball games at Madison
Square Garden; New Jersey phone numbers of
gamblers; history of baseball; importance of
                        (Continued on next card)

Voice Lib.
631   LaGuardia, Fiorello Henry, 1882-1947.   Talk
       to the people: addresses comment... 1945.
       (Card 2)

alcohol; open talk to Governor McNutt on
halting of curfew violations. WNYC, February
25, 1945.
       1 reel (7 in.) 7 1/2 in. per sec.
phonotape.

Voice Lib.
636   LaGuardia, Fiorello Henry, 1882-1947.   Talk
       to the people: war conditions... 1945.
       (Card 2)

good public habits of baseball players;
recalls Lou Gehrig's work on Parole Board;
"Tin Horn" gamblers; Black Sox baseball scandal
of 1919, gambling activities of two New York
Giants; calls for end to rigged sports; public
attitude toward baseball; his own family's
reaction to game between Yankees and Dodgers;
salutes baseball club owners, offers warning
                        (Continued on next card)

Voice Lib.
M297   LaGuardia, Fiorello Henry, 1882-1947.
bd.1   Talk to the people: reasons why the OPA
should use sense in their actions, Police Ath-
letic League memberships, racketeering (Joe
Adonis), basketball betting, student college
scholarships, city finances, referendum on
five cent subway fare increase to ten cents,
future of NYC, invitation from Gen. DeGaulle
to visit Paris, France. WNYC, March 25, 1945.
        1 reel (7 in.)   7 1/2 in. per sec.
phonotape.

Voice Lib.
M292-   LaGuardia, Fiorello Henry, 1882-1947.
293   Talk to the people: city budget and
bd.1   taxes, appropriations for police, fire
hospitals, health services, medical examiner,
health insurance, welfare department, parks
and schools, library, museums, purchase
department, coffee, typewriter repair,
cannery, water, courts, sheriff, elections,
radio, commerce, licenses. WNYC, April 8,
1945.
        2 reels (7 in.)   7 1/2 in. per sec.
phonotape.

Voice Lib.
595   LaGuardia, Fiorello Henry, 1882-1947.
Eulogy to Franklin D. Roosevelt. WNYC,
April 15, 1945.
        1 reel (7 in.)   7 1/2 in. per sec.
phonotape.

        1. Roosevelt, Franklin Delano, Pres. U.S.,
1882-1945.

Voice Lib.
M754-   LaGuardia, Fiorello Henry, 1882-1947.
755,   Talk to the people: broadcast devoted to
bd.1   explanation of Dumbarton Oaks agreement; reviewing principles of Atlantic Charter and
President Wilson's "14 Points"; explaining
origin and functions of forthcoming United
Nations in detail; urging Americans to ratify
U.N. Charter. WNYC, April 22, 1945.
        2 reels (7 in.)   7 1/2 in. per sec.
phonotape.

Voice Lib.
152,   LaGuardia, Fiorello Henry, 1882-1947.
bd.3-   Talk to the people on approaching end of
153,   war; calls Hitler and Mussolini "bums";
bd.1   admonishes New Yorkers to await official
announcement of end of war; approaching
city elections; amazement at longterm success
of his type of city government; recalls his
1929 campaign; thanks Judge Seabury for
investigation of City; refusal to run for
Republican nomination for mayor in 1945;
asks American Labor Party not to nominate him;
reviews decision not to run; continued
                    (Continued on next card)

Voice Lib.
152,   LaGuardia, Fiorello Henry, 1882-1947.   Talk to
bd.3-   the people on approaching end of war...
153,   May 6, 1945.   (Card2)
bd.1
re-election of FDR; his support of FDR;
impossibility of city office heads to control
votes; search for a job, new home; hope for
more kindness from newspapers toward city;
requirements for good New York Mayor; philosophy
of city government; uniqueness of New York City.
WNYC, May 6, 1945.
        2 reels (7 in.)   7 1/2 in. per sec.
phonotape.

Voice Lib.
154   LaGuardia, Fiorello Henry, 1882-1947.
bd.3   Special Message regarding V-E Day.
WNYC, May 7, 1945.
        1 reel (7 in.)   7 1/2 in. per sec.
phonotape.

Voice Lib.
542-   LaGuardia, Fiorello Henry, 1882-1947.
543,   Talk to the people: welcoming troops back
bd.1   from ETO; urges news vendors to return to
work as ordered by War Labor Board; castigates
New York Times for printing erroneous food
price story; food rationing; and the message
from General Eisenhower. WNYC, July 8, 1945.
        2 reels (7 in.)   7 1/2 in. per sec.
phonotape.

Voice Lib.
647   LaGuardia, Fiorello Henry, 1882-1947.
Talk to the people: implications of Bastille
Day; salute to France; Potsdam Conference;
political tyranny; accepts Italy as UN country;
reviews U.S. success in Pacific War; New York
newspaper strike; meat shortage; slaughter-
house control; poultry situation, how poultry
shortage developed; butter shortage; abolition
of ceiling prices; advises against buying green
beans; threatened retail poultry stores in
Queens; anticipation of construction following
war; milk fund scholarships; catching of
                    (Continued on next card)

Voice Lib.
647   LaGuardia, Fiorello Henry, 1882-1947.   Talk
to the people: implications of Bastille
Day...   1945.   (Card 2)

bookmaker; police department must stay alert;
warns juke box owners to keep volume down at
night; OPA trial cases; appointment of City
magistrates; reads comic strip "Little Orphan
Annie" and compares it with his judicial
appointments. WNYC, July 15, 1945.
        1 reel (7 in.)   7 1/2 in. per sec.
phonotape.

Voice Lib.
582   LaGuardia, Fiorello Henry, 1882-1947.
        Talk to the people.   WNYC, August 12,
1945.
        1 reel (7 in.) 7 1/2 in. per sec.
phonotape.

Voice Lib.
591   LaGuardia, Fiorello Henry, 1882-1947.
bd.3   Talk to the people.   WNYC, October 2,
1945.
        1 reel (7 in.)   7 1/2 in. per sec.
phonotape.

Voice Lib.
154   LaGuardia, Fiorello Henry, 1882-1947.
bd.1,2 Presentation of New York City
        Certificate of Merit to Grace Moore.
        WNYC, August 14, 1945.
        1 reel (7 in.)   7 1/2 in. per sec.
phonotape.

        I. Moore, Grace, 1901-1947.

Voice Lib.
648   LaGuardia, Fiorello Henry, 1882-1947.
        Talk to the people: announces Navy Day
        ceremonies with President Truman; numbers
        racket and Judge Lester Patterson; small
        loan "sharks" and quote from Bible on usury;
        traffic control regulations; housing; tribute
        to New York Times; biography of Maj. Gen. Gross;
        discusses 5 cent subway fare; municipal concerts
        and opera at City Center. WNYC, October 21,
1945.
        1 reel (7 in.)   7 1/2 in. per sec.
phonotape.

Voice Lib.
637   LaGuardia, Fiorello Henry, 1882-1947.
bd.2   V-J Day address; speaks from his home on
        the responsibility of U.S. to end of World
        War II, reflects on passing away of FDR,
        reads his official proclamation on conclusion
        of the war. WNYC, August 14, 1945.
        1 reel (7 in.)   7 1/2 in. per sec.
phonotape.

Voice Lib.
152   LaGuardia, Fiorello Henry, 1882-1947.
bd.2   Christmas program for children; excerpts
        from his radio program. WNYC radio,
        December 23, 1945.
        1 reel (7 in.)   7 1/2 in. per sec.
phonotape.

Voice Lib.
624   LaGuardia, Fiorello Henry, 1882-1947.
bd.2   Welcomes DeGaulle on his visit to New
        York City at conclusion of World War II,
        makes DeGaulle honorary citizen of New
        York City. WNYC, August 27, 1945.
        1 reel (7 in.)   7 1/2 in. per sec.
phonotape.

        I. Gaulle, Charles de, Pres. France, 1890-1970.

Voice Lib.
639   LaGuardia, Fiorello Henry, 1882-1947.
        Talk to the people (final broadcast):
        reports on Moscow Conference; urges everyone
        to listen to James Byrnes' report on U.N.;
        WNYC report; library report; future road
        building in New York; letter from boy admitting
        theft of Christmas light from city park;
        textile black market; questions advertising
        of LaSalle School in Chicago; reviews 1945 race
        track receipts in New York; attacks betting,
        false fire alarms, press and radio; suggests
        newspapers are a closed fraternity; reflects
                        (Continued on next card)

Voice Lib.
583   LaGuardia, Fiorello Henry, 1882-1947.
        Talk to the people. WNYC, September 30,
1945.
        1 reel (7 in.) 7 1/2 in. per sec.
phonotape.

Voice Lib.
639   LaGuardia, Fiorello Henry, 1882-1947. Talk
        to the people (final broadcast)... 1945.
        (Card 2)
        on how his terms as mayor have taught him how to
        understand people; sacrifices ahead for
        Americans; offers prayer written by Theodore
        Parker; accepts award from Navy Department
        presented by Admiral Kelly; talks about
        Brooklyn Navy Yard. WNYC, December 30, 1945.
        1 reel (7 in.)   7 1/2 in. per sec.
phonotape.

Voice Lib.
M803   LaGuardia, Fiorello Henry, 1882-1947.
Director-General of UNRRA speaking from
University of Vermont to the country's
wheat farmers aid in feeding little children
of other lands. Entitled: "Little children
must not starve".   UN Archives, April 4,
1946.
1 reel (7 in.)   7 1/2 in. per sec.
phonotape.
I. Title: Little children must not starve.

LaGuardia, Fiorello Henry, 1882-1945
Voice Lib.
M622   Radio in the 1940's (Part III): a series of
bd.1-   excerpts from important broadcasts of the 1940's; a sample
bd.15   of radio of the period. NVL, April, 1964.
1 reel (7 in.) 7 1/2 in. per sec. phonotape.
L. Radio programs. L. Miller, Alton Glenn, 1909(?)-1944. IL.
Diles, Ken   III. Wilson, Donald Harlow, 1900-   IV.
Livingstone, Mary   V. Benny, Jack, 1894-   VL. Harris,
Phil   VII. Merman, Ethel, 1909-   VIII. Smith, "Wonderful"
IX. Bennett, Richard Dyer   X. Louis, Joe, 1914-   XL.
Eisenhower, Dwight David, Pres. U.S., 1890-1969. XIL. MacArthur,
Douglas, 1880-1964. XIII. Romulo, Carlos Pena, 1899-   XIV.
Welles, Orson, 1915-   XV. Jackson, Robert Houghwout, 1892-1954.
XVL. LaGuardia, Fiorello Henry, 1882-1945. XVII. Nehru, Jawa-
harlal, 1889-1964. XVIII. Gandhi, Mohandas Karamchand, 1869-1948.

Voice Lib.
M802   LaGuardia, Fiorello Henry, 1882-1947.
Address for American Red Cross by UNRRA
director LaGuardia from Oklahoma City, Okla.,
about food relief problems.   UN Archives,
June 3, 1946.
1 reel (7 in.)   7 1/2 in. per sec.
phonotape.
Speech incomplete.

Voice Lib.
M737   LaGuardia, Fiorello Henry, 1882-1947.
bd.1   Dramatization and documentary of LaGuardia
era.   WPIX, February 7, 1965.
17 min., 42 sec.   phonotape (1 r.
7 1/2 i.p.s.)
1. LaGuardia, Fiorello Henry, 1882-1947.

Voice Lib.
646   LaGuardia, Marie
bd.2   LaGuardia Memorial Awards Association
(excerpt); presents 1958 Memorial Association
Award to League of Women Voters; recalls
early days in City Hall. WNYC, December 13,
1958.
1 reel (7 in.)   7 1/2 in. per sec.
phonotape.

Voice Lib.
M1439   LaGuardia, Fiorello Henry, 1882-1947.
bd.2   Short description of career of Mayor
LaGuardia, including actual serments.
ABC-TV, May 19, 1971.
1 reel (7 in.)   7 1/2 in. per sec.
phonotape.
1. LaGuardia, Fiorello Henry, 1882-1947

Voice Lib.
512   LaGuardia, Fiorello Henry, 1882-1947.
Luncheon address: various speakers
recall LaGuardia.   WNYC, December 9,
1960.
1 reel (7 in.)   7 1/2 in. per sec.
phonotape.

LaGuardia, Fiorello Henry, 1882-1947
Voice Lib.
572-   I can hear it now (radio program)
573   1933-1946.   CBS, 1948.
bd.1   2 reels (7 in.)   7 1/2 in. per sec.
phonotape.
L. Murrow, Edward Roscoe, 1908-1965. IL. LaGuardia, Fiorello
Henry, 1882-1947. III. Chamberlain, Neville, 1869-1949. IV.
Roosevelt, Franklin Delano, 1882-1945. V. Churchill,
Winston Leonard Spencer, 1874-1965. VL. Gaulle, Charles de,
Pres. France, 1890-1970. VII. Eisenhower, Dwight David, Pres. U.S.,
1890-1969. VIII. Willkie, Wendell Lewis, 1892-1944. IX. Martin,
Joseph William, 1884-1968. X. Elizabeth II, Queen of Great Britain,
1926-   XL. Margaret Rose, Princess of Gt. Brit., 1930-   XIL.
Johnson, Hugh Samuel, 1882-1942. XIII. Smith, Alfred Emanuel,
1873-1944. XIV. Lindbergh, Charles Augustus, 1902-   XV. Davis,
(Continued on next card)

LaGuardia, Fiorello Henry, 1882-1947
Voice Lib.
M617   Radio in the 1920's: a series of excerpts
bd.1-   from important broadcasts of the 1920's,
bd.25   with brief prologue and epilogue; a sample
of radio of the period. NVL, April, 1964.
1 reel (7 in.)   7 1/2 in. per sec.
phonotape.
L. Radio programs. L. Marconi, Guglielmo, marchese, 1874-
1937. IL. Kendall, H   G   III. Coolidge, Calvin, Pres. U.S.,
1872-1933. IV. Wilson, Woodrow, Pres. U.S., 1856-1924. V.
Roosevelt, Franklin Delano, Pres. U.S., 1882-1945. VL. Lodge,
Henry Cabot, 1850-1924. VII. LaGuardia, Fiorello Henry, 1882-1947.
VIII. The Happiness Boys (Radio program) IX. Gallagher and Sheen.
X. Barney Google. XL. Vallee, Rudy, 1901-   XIL. The two
(Continued on next card)

LaGuardia, Fiorello Henry, 1882-1947
Voice Lib.
573   I can hear it now (radio program)
bd.2-   1945-1949.   CBS, 1950?
574   2 reels (7 in.)   7 1/2 in. per sec.
bd.1   phonotape.
L. Murrow, Edward Roscoe, 1908-1965. IL. Nehru, Jawaharlal,
1889-1964. III. Philip, duke of Edinburgh, 1921-   IV. Elizabeth II,
Queen of Great Britain, 1926-   V. Ferguson, Homer, 1889-   VL.
Hughes, Howard Robard, 1905-   VII. Marshall, George Catlett,
1880-   VIII. Ruth, George Herman, 1895-1948. IX. Lilienthal,
David Eli, 1899-   X. Trout, Robert, 1908-   XL. Gage, Arthur.
XIL. Jackson, Robert Houghwout, 1892-1954. XIII. Gromyko, Ana-
tolii Andreevich, 1908-   XIV. Churchill, Winston Leonard Spencer, 1874-1965. XVL.
Winchell, Walter, 1897-19   XVII. Davis, Elmer Holmes, 1890-
(Continued on next card)

LaGuardia, Fiorello Henry, 1882-1947
Voice Lib.
M297   McBride, Mary Margaret, 1899-
bd.2   Mrs. Colin Kelly, wife of World War II
    hero, talks with Miss McBride and Mayor
    Fiorello H. LaGuardia on living in New
    York City. NBC, Red Network, 1943.
       1 reel (7 in.)   7 1/2 in. per sec.
    phonotape.

       1. Kelly, Mrs. Colin. I. LaGuardia,
    Fiorello Henry, 1882-1947.

LAGUARDIA, FIORELLO HENRY, 1882-1947
Voice Lib.
M1439   LaGuardia, Fiorello Henry, 1882-1947.
bd.2   Short description of career of Mayor
    LaGuardia, including actual segments.
    ABC-TV, May 19, 1971.
       1 reel (7 in.)   7 1/2 in. per sec.
    phonotape.

LaGuardia, Fiorello Henry, 1882-1947
Voice Lib.
M293   Whalen, Grover Aloysius, 1886-1962.
    First ticket sale to 1939 World's Fair,
    Flushing Meadows, Long Island, New York.
    Mr. Whalen, president of New York World's
    Fair Committee and New York's official
    welcomer, sells first ticket book to F. H.
    LaGuardia, Mayor of New York. WNYC Radio,
    February 23, 1939.
       1 reel (7 in.) 7 1/2 i.p.s. phonotape.

       l. New York. World's Fair, 1939-1940. l. LaGuardia,
    Fiorello Henry, 1882-1947.

LAGUARDIA, FIORELLO HENRY, 1882-1947
Voice Lib.
399   Siegel, Seymour H
bd.2   Memorial to LaGuardia. WNYC, [n.d.]
       1 reel (7 in.)   7 1/2 in. per sec.
    phonotape.

       1. LaGuardia, Fiorello Henry, 1882-1947.

LAGUARDIA, FIORELLO HENRY, 1882-1947
Voice Lib.
658-   Berle, Adolph Augustus, 1895-1971.
659   Dialogues In Depth: The LaGuardia Years
bd.1   (TV program from the New York World's Fair).
    Anecdotes and reminiscences about the late
    New York Mayor, Fiorello LaGuardia.
    July 28, 1964.
       2 reels (7 in.)   7 1/2 in. per sec.
    phonotape.

       1. LaGuardia, Fiorello Henry, 1882-1947.

LAGUARDIA, FIORELLO HENRY, 1882-1947
Voice Lib.
658-   Van Arsdale, Harry, 1905-
659   Dialogue in depth: The LaGuardia years.
bd.1   (TV program from the New York World's Fair)
    Anecdotes and reminiscences about the
    late New York Mayor Fiorello LaGuardia.
    July 28, 1964.
       2 reels (7 in.)   7 1/2 in. per sec.
    phonotape.

LAGUARDIA, FIORELLO HENRY, 1882-1947
Voice Lib.
M658-   Dialogues in depth: the LaGuardia years
659   (TV program from the New York World's Fair).
bd.1   Anecdotes and reminiscences about the late
    New York mayor, Fiorello LaGuardia.
    July 22, 1964.
       2 reels (7 in.)   7 1/2 i.p.s. phonotape.

       l. LaGuardia, Fiorello Henry, 1882-1947. l. Canudo,
    Eugene R. ll. Berle, Adolph Augustus, 1895-1971.
    lll. Van Arsdale, Harry, 1905- IV. Delany, Hubert T.
    V. Morris, Newbold, 1902-1966.

LaGuire, Al
Voice Lib.
M728   Robinson, Earl, 1910-
bd.1   Interview with Al LaGuire at MSU campus.
    February 2, 1965.
       1 reel (7 in.)   7 1/2 in. per sec.
    phonotape.

       I. LaGuire, Al

LAGUARDIA, FIORELLO HENRY, 1882-1947
Voice Lib.
644   Impellitteri, Vincent Richard, 1900-
bd.3   Officiates at unveiling of portrait of
    Fiorello H. LaGuardia at New York City Hall.
    WNYC, December 11, 1950.
       1 reel (7 in.)   7 1/2 in. per sec.
    phonotape.

       I. LaGuardia, Fiorello Henry, 1882-1947.

Lamb, L   W
Voice Lib.
M862   Conrad, Frank
bd.2   Memorial program on his death with eulogies
    on his accomplishments by S.H. Church
    (Pres. Carnegie Institute of Technology),
    L.W. Lamb (Director of Westinghouse Research
    Laboratories) and David Sarnoff (Pres. of
    R.C.A.) KDKA, December 13, 1944.
       1 reel (7 in.)   7 1/2 in. per sec.
    phonotape.
       l. Church, Samuel Harden, 1858-1943. II. Lamb, L
    W   III. Sarnoff, David, 1891-1971.

Voice Lib.
M1702
    Lamont, Clyde
    Baker, Howard H., 1925-
      On Watergate, with Clyde Lamont, of the
National Press Club. WKAR, May 30, 1974.
      50 min. phonotape (1 r. 7 1/2 i.p.s.)

      1. Watergate Affair, 1972- 2. U.S. -
Politics and government. I. Lamont, Clyde

Voice Lib.
M1692
bd.3
    Lamont, Clyde
    Jackson, Henry Martin, 1912-
      Tells the National Press Club his
optimistic estimate of America's economic
future. WKAR, May 23, 1974.
      25 min. phonotape (1 r. 7 1/2 i.p.s.)

      Includes question & answer session through
Clyde Lamont.
      1. U.S. - Politics and government - 1969-
2. Impeachments. I. Lamont, Clyde.

Voice Lib.
M1733
    Lamont, Clyde
    Sawhill, John Crittenden, 1936-
      Speech at the National Press Club luncheon,
concerning the international energy picture,
with Clyde Lamont. WKAR, June 20, 1974.
      50 min. phonotape (1 r. 7 1/2 i.p.s.)

      1. Power resources - U.S. 2. Energy
shortage. 3. Local transit - U.S.
      I. Lamont, Clyde.

Voice Lib.
M814
bd.2-
815
    Lamont, Corliss, 1902-
    Santayana, George, 1863-1952.
      Personal reminiscences about the eminent
American philosopher, poet, and novelist by
Horace H. Kallen and Dr. Corliss Lamont, in
conversation with Robert Stover of WBAI,
arranged through the cooperation of the
American Humanist Association. KPFK, May 23,
1964.
      2 reels (7 in.) 7 1/2 in. per sec. phonotape.
      I. Santayana, George, 1863-1952. I. Kallen, Horace Meyer,
1882- II. Lamont, Corliss, 1902- III. Stover, Robert

Voice Lib.
M844
    LaMour, Dorothy
      Radio dramatization entitled: "The Face
of an Angel", with comments by the new star,
Marvyn Vey, and Miss Dorothy LaMour.
November 9, 1947.
      1 reel (7 in.) 7 1/2 in. per sec.
phonotape.

      I. Vey, Marvyn. II. Title: The face of an
angel.

Voice Lib.
M1720
bd.4
    LAND
    Udall, Morris K., 1922-
      On the Today Show with Sam Steiger, debating
their opposing bills for land-use funding.
Includes Barbara Walters and Bill Monroe.
NBC-TV, June 10, 1974.
      8 min. phonotape (1 r. 7 1/2 i.p.s.)

      1. Land. 2. Man - Influence on nature.
I. Steiger, Sam, 1929- II. Walters,
Barbara, 1931- III. Monroe, Bill.

C1
A8
    The land of Runyon
    Whorf, Michael, 1933-
      The land of Runyon.
      1 tape cassette. (The visual sounds of
Mike Whorf. Art, music, and letters, A8)
      Originally presented on his radio program, Kaleidoscope,
WJR, Detroit.
      Duration: 28 min., 35 sec.
      Damon Runyon travelled with mugs and molls, gamblers and
their gals, and gave the world humor and human interest.
      I. Runyon, Damon, 1880-1946. I. Title.

Voice Lib.
M948
bd.4
    Landfrey, Kenneth
      The bugler who sounded the Charge of the
Light Brigade resounds same Charge for
Colonel Gouraud at Edison House, London.
G. R. Vincent, re-recording, August 2, 1890.
      1 reel (7 in.) 7 1/2 in. per sec.
phonotape.

Voice Lib.
M1098
bd.2
    Landfrey, Kenneth
    Ripley, Robert LeRoy, 1893-1949.
      Rehearsal and discussion regarding text
of introductory remarks to the recording
of "The Bugler of Balaclava" with G.R. Vincent,
followed by 1890 recording of trumpeter
Kenneth Landfrey. NVL location recording,
August 7, 1939.
      1 reel (7 in.) 7 1/2 in. per sec.
phonotape.
      I. Vincent, G Robert. II. Landfrey, Kenneth.
III. Title: The bugler of Balaclava.

Voice Lib.
M273-
274
bd.1
    Landon, Alfred Mossman, 1887-
    Biography in sound (radio program)
      Franklin Delano Roosevelt: the friends and
former associates of Franklin Roosevelt on
the tenth anniversary of the President's death.
NBC Radio, April, 1955.
      2 reels (7 in.) 7 1/2 in. per sec.
phonotape.
      I. Roosevelt, Franklin Delano, Pres. U.S., 1882-1945. I.
McIntire, Ross T 1899- II. Mellett, Lowell, 1884-1960.
III. Tully, Grace IV. Henderson, Leon, 1895-
V. Roosevelt, Eleanor (Roosevelt) 1884-1962. VI. DeGraaf, Albert
VII. Lehman, Herbert Henry, 1878-1963. VIII. Rosenman, Samuel
Irving, 1896- IX. Arvey, Jacob X. Moley, Raymond,
1886- XI. Farley, James Aloysius, 1888- XII. Roosevelt,
(Continued on next card)

Landon, Alfred Mossman, 1887-

Voice Lib.
572-   I can hear it now (radio program)
573   1933-1946.   CBS, 1948.
bd.1   2 reels (7 in.)   7 1/2 in. per sec.
         phonotape.
         I. Murrow, Edward Roscoe, 1908-1965. II. LaGuardia, Fiorello
         Henry, 1882-1947. III. Chamberlain, Neville, 1869-1949. IV.
         Roosevelt, Franklin Delano, Pres. U. S., 1882-1945. V. Churchill,
         Winston Leonard Spencer, 1874-1965. VI. Gaulle, Charles de,
         Pres. France, 1890-1970. VII. Eisenhower, Dwight David, Pres. U. S.,
         1890-1969. VIII. Willkie, Wendell Lewis, 1892-1944. IX. Martin,
         Joseph William, 1884-1968. X. Elizabeth II, Queen of Great Britain,
         1926-   XI. Margaret Rose, Princess of Gt. Brit., 1930-   XII.
         Johnson, Hugh Samuel, 188?-1942. XIII. Smith, Alfred Emanuel,
         1873-1944. XIV. Lindberg, Charles Augustus, 1902-   XV. Davis,
                    (Continued on next card)

C1
FA10   LANE, JOSEPH, 1801-1881
         Whorf, Michael, 1933-
         Joseph Lane.
         1 tape cassette. (The visual sounds of
         Mike Whorf. The forgotten American, FA10)
         Originally presented on his radio program, Kaleidoscope,
         WJR, Detroit.
         Duration: 10 min., 24 sec.
         Soldier, politician, and pioneer, Lane was one of the
         first senators from Oregon. He was the Vice Presidential
         candidate on the breakaway Democratic ticket with John C.
         Breckinridge in 1860.
         I. Lane, Joseph, 1801-1881. I. Title.

Voice Lib.   LAOS
M375   Dooley, Thomas Anthony, 1927-1961.
bd.1   Image of America in Southeast Asia;
         communism in Southeast Asia and Laos in schools;
         America and its roles in Southeast Asia; Laotian education;
         proposes corps of young Americans for Laos; missionaries in
         Laos; discusses S. S. "Hope" and its shortcomings; explains
         methods of curing native illness; dislike of U. S. people by
         people of Laos. KETC (NET) [n. d.]
         1 reel (7 in.) 7 1/2 i. p. s. phonotape.
         I. Laos.

Voice Lib.
M1800   LaRue, Frederick C., 1928?-
WG   Testimony before the Senate Committee
0718.03 investigating the Watergate Affair.
         Pacifica, July 18, 1973.
         156 min. phonotape (2 r. 3 3/4 i.p.s.)
         (Watergate gavel to gavel, phase 1)
         1. Watergate Affair, 1972-

Voice Lib.
M1800   LaRue, Frederick C., 1928?-
WG   Testimony before the Senate Committee
0719.01 investigating the Watergate Affair.
         Pacifica, July 19, 1973.
         101 min. phonotape (2 r. 3 3/4 i.p.s.)
         (Watergate gavel to gavel, phase 1)
         1. Watergate Affair, 1972-

C1
M109   LASALLE, ROBERT CAVALIER, SIEUR DE, 1643-1687
         Whorf, Michael, 1933-
         The wilderness cavalier - LaSalle.
         1 tape cassette. (The visual sounds of
         Mike Whorf. History and heritage, H109)
         Originally presented on his radio program, Kaleidoscope,
         WJR, Detroit.
         Duration: 36 min., 30 sec.
         This is a program of adventure, of the America of yesterday,
         not today. The adventurous life of LaSalle, explorer, discoverer,
         a pioneer who made an expedition which led to the discovery of
         some of America's richest land.
         I. LaSalle, Robert Cavalier, sieur de, 1643-1687.
         I. Title.

Lasca
Voice Lib.
M759   Davenport, Edgar L
bd.7   "Lasca"; dramatic recitation about Texas
         and the West. VTM, 1909.
         1 reel (7 in.) 7 1/2 in. per sec.
         phonotape.

C1   The last flight
H113   Whorf, Michael, 1933-.
         The last flight; Amelia Earhart.
         1 tape cassette. (The visual sounds of
         Mike Whorf. History and heritage, H113)
         Originally presented on his radio program, Kaleidoscope,
         WJR, Detroit.
         Duration: 35 min., 45 sec.
         The search for the world's most famous aviatrix has been
         kept alive through the years since her disappearance - kept
         alive by rumors, half-truths and wild speculations.
         I. Earhart, Amelia, 1898-1937. I. Title.

C1   The last full measure
S19   Whorf, Michael, 1933-
         The last full measure.
         1 tape cassette. (The visual sounds of
         Mike Whorf. Social, S19)
         Originally presented on his radio program, Kaleidoscope,
         WJR, Detroit.
         Duration: 47 min., 20 sec.
         John F. Kennedy, his life as a young, wealthy, charming man,
         a Navy Lieutenant, a Senator and finally President is outlined
         in this narrative of a dedicated American.
         I. Kennedy, John Fitzgerald, Pres. U. S., 1917-1963.
         I. Title.

C1   The last of the great explorers - James Cook
H84   Whorf, Michael, 1933-
         The last of the great explorers - James Cook.
         1 tape cassette. (The visual sounds of
         Mike Whorf. History and heritage, H84)
         Originally presented on his radio program, Kaleidoscope,
         WJR, Detroit.
         Duration: 37 min., 30 sec.
         James Cook was an extraordinary seaman and an intelligent
         and far-seeing individual who realized that the way to make
         England stronger was to claim for her the lands that lay beyond.
         I. Cook, James, 1728-1779. I. Title.

C1
H1

The last of the heroes

Whorf, Michael, 1933-
The last of the heroes.
1 tape cassette. (The visual sounds of
Mike Whorf. History and heritage, H1)
Originally presented on his radio program, Kaleidoscope,
WJR, Detroit.
Duration: 45 min., 45 sec.
A free verse ode to America's fighting men, tracing our
involvement in wars with other nations; pointing to courage and
bravery as well as the futility of armed conflict. Patriotic music
is used abundantly to create mood and a sense of heritage.

I. U.S. - History, Military. I. Title.

Voice Lib.
129   Lauder, Sir Harry, 1870-1950.
bd.7   Composer singing a medley of his own
choruses. His Majesty's Voice, 1943.
1 reel (7 in.) 7 1/2 in. per sec.
phonotape.

C1
S17

The last of the Queen of Scots

Whorf, Michael, 1933-
The last of the Queen of Scots.
1 tape cassette. (The visual sounds of
Mike Whorf. Social, S17)
Originally presented on his radio program, Kaleidoscope,
WJR, Detroit.
Duration: 42 min.
Against the pageantry of royalty and majesty of kings and queens
of English nobility, comes the story of the last of the queens of
Scotland.

I. Mary Stuart, queen of the Scots, 1542-1587. I. Title.

Voice Lib.   Laughlin, James, 1914-
M1599-   A quiet requiem for Ezra Pound, with poets
1600   Robert Lowell, Robert Fitzgerald, James
Laughlin, and Robert McGregor. Modern
Language Center, Harvard University,
December 4, 1972.
70 min.   phonotape (2 r.   7 1/2 i.p.s.)

I. Pound, Ezra Loomis, 1885-1972. I. Lowell, Robert,
1917-   II. Fitzgerald, Robert, 1910- III. Laughlin,
James, 1914-   IV. McGregor, Robert,

Voice Lib.
M1471   Last radio appeal by Free Hungary for help
bd.4   against Soviet invasion and occupation
by the Democratic Hungarian government.
Peteler, 1956.
1 reel (7 in.)   7 1/2 in. per sec.
phonotape.

1. Hungary - History - Revolution, 1956

LAUGHTER

C1
S4

Whorf, Michael, 1933-
What makes you laugh.
1 tape cassette. (The visual sounds of
Mike Whorf. Social, S4)
Originally presented on his radio program, Kaleidoscope,
WJR, Detroit.
Duration: 34 min.
Philosophers have stated that laughter is the fireworks of the
soul, yet laughter is peculiar, for man is the only creature who
laughs.

I. Laughter. I. Title.

Voice Lib. LATIN AMERICA - FOREIGN RELATIONS - U.S.
M917   Roosevelt, Franklin Delano, Pres. U.S.,
bd.2-   1882-1945.
918   Fireside chat defining position of U.S. on
national defense and alliances with Pan
American republics. May 27, 1941.
2 reels (7 in.)   7 1/2 in. per sec.
phonotape.

1. U.S. - Defenses. 2. U.S. - Foreign
relations - Latin America. 3. Latin America -
Foreign relations - U.S.

Voice Lib.
M1336   Launching of aircraft carrier "John F. Kennedy"
bd.2   at Newport News, Virginia. Speakers:
Senator Edward Kennedy, Caroline Kennedy,
and Robert McNamara. Comments by CBS news-
caster Steve Rowan. CBS-TV, August, 1968.
1 reel (7 in.)   7 1/2 in. per sec.
phonotape.

I. Kennedy, Edward Moore, 1932-   II.
Kennedy, Caroline, 1957-   III. McNamara,
Robert S   1916-

Voice Lib.
M1100   Lauder, Sir Harry, 1870-1950.
bd.2   Complete medley of his most famous songs,
sung by Harry Lauder with orchestral accompaniment and Scottish monologue. HMV, 1943.
1 reel (7 in.)   7 1/2 in. per sec.
phonotape.

Voice Lib.   Laurence, William Leonard, 1888-
M1435
Life in other worlds; exploratory discussion about life on other
planets. Arnold J. Toynbee, Dr. G..B. Kiastiakowsky
(professor at Harvard), Dr. Donald M. Michaels, Dr. Otto
Struve, Dr. Harlow Shapley, Walter Cronkite, Chet Huntley,
William L. Laurence. New York, NBC, March 3, 1961.
1 reel (7 in.)   7 1/2 L.p.s.   phonotape.

I. Life on other planets. I. Toynbee, Arnold Joseph, 1889-
II. Kiastiakowsky, George Bogdan. III. Michaels, Donald M.
IV. Struve, Otto, 1897-1963. V. Shapley, Harlow, 1885-1972.
VI. Cronkite, Walter Leland, 1916-   VII. Huntley, Chet,
1911-1974. VIII. Laurence, William Leonard, 1888-

Lauterbach, Hartmann
Voice Lib.
M961   Schirach, Baldur von, 1907-
bd.7   Propaganda speech excerpt to Hitler Youth
           Group; also excerpts by Rudolf Hess and
           Hartmann Lauterbach. German Radio, Peteler,
           April 4, 1934; January 1, 1935.
              1 reel (7 in.)   7 1/2 in. per sec.
           phonotape.

              I. Hess, Rudolf, 1894-   II.
           Lauterbach, Hartmann

LAW ENFORCEMENT
Voice Lib.
M1608   Santarelli, Donald E
           New steps to be taken to reduce crime;
           address before the Economic Club of Detroit.
           WKAR-FM, March 25, 1974.
              50 min.   phonotape (1 r.   7 1/2 i.p.s.)

              1. Law enforcement. 2. Crime and criminals.

Lawrence, Bill
Voice Lib.
M1321   Kennedy, Robert Francis, 1925-1968.
           Debate consisting of questions and answers.
           Senator Robert Kennedy and Senator Eugene
           McCarthy interviewed by ABC news correspondents
           Bill Lawrence and Bob Clark on program
           "Issues and Answers". ABC-TV, June 1, 1968.
              1 reel (7 in.)   7 1/2 in. per sec.
           phonotape.

              I. McCarthy, Eugene Joseph, 1916-   II.
           Lawrence, Bill. III. Clark, Bob

Voice Lib.
M 386   Lawrence, Sir Geoffrey, 1880-
           Judge's decision on motions by defendants
           Julius Streicher and Martin Bormann, acquisition
           of and use of enemy documents as evidence.
           Private collection, November 22, 1945.
              1 reel (7 in.)   7 1/2 in. per sec.
           phonotape.

              1. Nuremberg Trial of Major German War
           Criminals, 1945-1946.

Voice Lib.
M955   Lawrence, Gertrude, 1901-1952.
bd.11-   Singing selections from album of
14   Ira Gershwin-Kurt Weill musical comedy
           "Lady in the dark". RCA, 1938.
              1 reel (7 in.)   7 1/2 in. per sec.
           phonotape.

              CONTENTS.-bd.11. "My ship".-bd.12. "Jenny".-
           bd.13. "This is new".-bd. 14. "One life to live".
              I. Gershwin, Ira, 1896-   II. Weill, Kurt,
           1900-1950.

Voice Lib.   Lawrence, Gertrude, 1901-1952
M619   Radio in the 1930's (Part II): a series of
bd.1-   excerpts of the 1930's; a sample of radio
14   of the period. NVL, April, 1964.
              1 reel (7 in.) 7 1/2 in. per sec. phonotape.
           I. Allen, Fred, 1894-1956. II. Delmar, Kenny   III. Donald,
           Peter   IV. Pious, Minerva   V. Fennelly, Parker   VL
           Boyer, Charles, 1899-   VII. Dunne, Irene, 1904-   VIII.
           DeMille, Cecil Blount, 1881-1959. IX. West, Mac, 1893-   X.
           Dafoe, Allan Ray, 1883-1943. XL Dionne quintuplets. XIL Ortega,
           Santos   XIII. War of the worlds (radio program)   XIV. Ives, Burl,
           1909-   XV. Robinson, Earl, 1910-   XVL Temple, Shirley,
           1928-   XVII. Earhart, Amelia, 1898-1937. XVIII. Lawrence,
           Gertrude, 1901-1952. XIX. Cohan, George Michael, 1878-1942.
           XX. Shaw, George Bernard, 1856-1950. XXL Hitler, Adolf, 1889-
           1945. XXII. Chamberlain, Neville, 1869-1940. XXIII. Roosevelt,
           Franklin Delano, Pres. U.S., 1882-1945.

Voice Lib.
M988-   Lawrence, Thomas Edward, 1888-1935.
989   Life of Lawrence of Arabia; one hour
           documentary, with Cyril Cusack as T.E.
           Lawrence, and actual voices of friends and
           contemporaries, including his brother
           A.W. Lawrence. BBC, August 21, 1966.
              2 reels (7 in.)   7 1/2 in. per sec.
           phonotape.

              1. Lawrence, Thomas Edward, 1888-1935.
           I. Cusack, Cyril, 1910-

C1   LAWRENCE, THOMAS EDWARD, 1888-1935
H45
        Whorf, Michael, 1933-
           Lawrence of Arabia - T. E. Lawrence.
           1 tape cassette. (The visual sounds of
        Mike Whorf. History and heritage, H45)
           Originally presented on his radio program, Kaleidoscope,
        WJR, Detroit.
           Duration: 42 min., 30 sec.
           He was an enigma, a perplexing figure; yet an intellectual,
        archaeologist, brilliant warrior, and still a man much misunder-
        stood for his depth.

           L. Lawrence, Thomas Edward, 1888-1935. L Title.

Lawrence, William H
Voice Lib.
235-   Tito, Josip Broz, Pres. Yugoslavia, 1892-
237   Interview by Edward R. Murrow, with comments
bd.1   and analysis by Richard C. Hottelet, Clare
        Boothe Luce, William H. Lawrence, and Hamilton
        F. Armstrong, CBS, June 30, 1957.
              3 reels (7 in.)   7 1/2 in. per sec.
           phonotape.

              I. Hottelet, Richard Curt   II. Luce,
           Clare (Boothe) 1903-   III. Lawrence,
           William H   IV. Armstrong, Hamilton Fish,
           1893-1973.

C1   Lawrence of Arabia - T. E. Lawrence
H45
        Whorf, Michael, 1933-
           Lawrence of Arabia - T. E. Lawrence.
           1 tape cassette. (The visual sounds of
        Mike Whorf. History and heritage, H45)
           Originally presented on his radio program, Kaleidoscope,
        WJR, Detroit.
           Duration: 42 min., 30 sec.
           He was an enigma, a perplexing figure; yet an intellectual,
        archaeologist, brilliant warrior, and still a man much misunder-
        stood for his depth.

           L. Lawrence, Thomas Edward, 1888-1935. L Title.

Leaderman, Sy

Voice Lib.
M1379   Osgood, Charles
bd.4   Interviewing Sy Leaderman, blind man, who
         bowls 247 in a league where all others have
         sight.   CBS Morning News, February 21, 1974.
         2 min., 15 sec. phonotape (1 r. 7 1/2
         i.p.s.)

         1. Blind. 2. Physically handicapped.
         I. Leaderman, Sy.

Voice Lib.
M541   League of Nations
bd.3-4   Two Senators speak for and against U.S.
         participation in the League.   Nation's
         Forum, 1919.
         1 reel (7 in.)   7 i.p.s.   phonotape.

         1. League of Nations.

Voice Lib.   LEAGUE OF NATIONS
M654
bd.7   Cummings, Homer Stillé, 1870-
         Summons to duty. In favor of American
         participation of the League of Nations.
         Nation's Forum, June 28, 1920.
         1 reel (7 in.)   7 1/2 in. per sec.
         phonotape.

Voice Lib.   LEAGUE OF NATIONS
M1282   DeValera, Eamon, 1882-
bd.2   Speaking from the rostrum of the League of
         Nations in Geneva, urging USSR to accept
         invitation to join the League and declare
         guarantees to the world of liberty and religious
         freedom.   League of Nations, September 18, 1934.
         1 reel (7 in.)   7 1/2 in. per sec.
         phonotape.

         1. League of Nations.

       LEAGUE OF NATIONS
Voice Lib.
M728   Harding, Warren Gamaliel, Pres. U.S., 1865-
bd.6   1923.
         "An association of nations"; Senator
         Harding's position about limited American
         participation in a League of Nations.
         Nation's Forum, 1920.
         1 reel (7 in.)   7 1/2 in. per sec.
         phonotape.

       LEAGUE OF NATIONS
Voice Lib.
M654   Wise, Stephen Samuel, 1874-1949.
bd.3   "League of Nations"; urging the U.S.
         to participate and uphold the policies of
         Woodrow Wilson.   Nation's Forum, 1920.
         1 reel (7 in.)   7 1/2 in. per sec.
         phonotape.

       LEBANON - HISTORY - INTERVENTION, 1958
Voice Lib.
M715   Eisenhower, Dwight David, Pres. U.S., 1890-
bd.13   1969.
         Excerpt of statement on intervention by
         U.S. troops during internal strife in
         Lebanon.   July 15, 1958.
         1 reel (7 in.)   7 1/2 in. per sec.
         phonotape.

Voice Lib. Lee, J   V
383   I can hear it now (radio program)
         CBS, February 9, 1951.
         1 reel (7 in.)   7 1/2 in. per sec.
         phonotape.

         I. Wilson, Charles Edward, 1886-1972. II. Gabrielson, Guy
         George, 1891-   III. Taft, Robert Alphonso, 1889-1953. IV.
         Martin, Joseph William, 1884-1965. V. McCarthy, Joseph
         Raymond, 1909-1957. VI. Benton, William Burnett, 1900-1973.
         VII. Malone, George Wilson, 1890-1961. VIII. Capehart, Homer
         Earl, 1897-   IX. Eisenhower, Dwight David, Pres. U.S., 1890-
         1969. X. Lee, J   V   XI. Hodge, John Reed, 1893-
         1963. XII. Overton, Watkins   XIII. DiSalle, Michael
         Vincent, 1908-   XIV. Boyce, Eddy   XV. Conklin, Ed
         XVI. Collins, Joseph Lawton, 1896-

       LEE, ROBERT EDWARD, 1807-1870
C1
H102   Whorf, Michael, 1933-
         The Confederate hero - Robert E. Lee.
         1 tape cassette.   (The visual sounds of
       Mike Whorf. History and heritage, H102)
         Originally presented on his radio program, Kaleidoscope,
       WJR, Detroit.
         Duration: 37 min.
         A narration of new insights into the devoted Confederate
       general. An exploration into the life and motives of Robert E.
       Lee. A Confederate general, a religious man, and a hero to
       his southern countrymen.

         I. Lee, Robert Edward, 1807-1870. I. Title.

       LEE, ROBERT EDWARD, 1807-1870
C1
H20   Whorf, Michael, 1933-
         The gentleman from Virginia.
         1 tape cassette.   (The visual sounds of
       Mike Whorf. History and heritage, H20)
         Originally presented on his radio program, Kaleidoscope,
       WJR, Detroit.
         Duration: 49 min.
         Gentleman and General was Lee; Lee of the Confederacy; Lee
       of Virginia - a man as noble as his ancestors, as brave as his
       contemporaries. Lee was a patriot, a figure emerging from
       history who would loom as large as anyone on the American scene.

         I. Lee, Robert Edward, 1807-1870. I. Title.

Voice Lib.
M1800   Leeper, Barrett
WG   Testimony before the Senate Committee
0517.05 investigating the Watergate Affair.
        Pacifica, May 17, 1973.
            67 min.   phonotape (1 r.   3 3/4 i.p.s.)
        (Watergate gavel to gavel, phase 1)

            1. Watergate Affair, 1972-

C1
R8   Left hand of God
        Whorf, Michael, 1933-
            Left hand of God.
            1 tape cassette.   (The visual sounds of
        Mike Whorf. Religion, R8)
            Originally presented on his radio program, Kaleidoscope.
        WJR, Detroit.
            Duration: 46 min., 30 sec.
            In every conflict in which this country has ever been involved,
        the chaplain has stood beside the fighting man. They are the
        soldiers of God.

            L. Chaplains, Military. L. Title.

Voice Lib.   LeGallienne, Eva, 1899-
M225   Packard, Frederick
            Styles in Shakespearean acting, 1890-1950.
        Creative Associates, 1963?
            1 reel (7 in.)   7 1/2 i.p.s.   phonotape.

            L. Sothern, Edward Askew, 1826-1881. II. Markowe,
        Julia, 1865-1950. III. Booth, Edwin, 1833-1893. IV. Gielgud,
        John, 1904-   V. Robeson, Paul Bustill, 1898-   VI. Terry,
        Dame Ellen, 1848-1928. VII. Allen, Viola. VIII. Welles,
        Orson, 1915-   IX. Skinner, Otis, 1858-1942. X. Barrymore,
        John, 1882-1942. XI. Olivier, Sir Laurence Kerr, 1907-
        XII. Forbes-Robertson, Sir Johnston, 1853-   XIII. Evans,
        Maurice. XIV. Thorndike, Dame Sybil, 1882-   XV. Robson,
        Flora. XVI. LeGallienne, Eva, 1899-   XVII. Anderson,
        Judith. XVIII. Duncan, Augustin. XIX. Hampden, Walter.
        XX. Speaight, Robert, 1904-   XXI. Jones, Daniel.

C1   The legend called Leatherstocking - James
A32   Fenimore Cooper
        Whorf, Michael, 1933-
            The legend called Leatherstocking - James
        Fenimore Cooper.
            1 tape cassette. (The visual sounds of Mike Whorf.
        Art, music and letters, A32)
            Originally presented on his radio program, Kaleidoscope.
        WJR, Detroit.
            Duration: 27 min., 40 sec.
            In a time of adventure, discovery, and exploration comes the
        man to tell the story of frontier days, of savages both red and white,
        of wilderness and beauty.

            L. Cooper, James Fenimore, 1789-1851. L. Title.

Voice Lib.
M669-   The legend of Cecil B. DeMille. Yul
670   Brynner, Charlton Heston, Bob Hope, Betty
        Hutton, Edward G. Robinson, Barbara Stanwyck,
        James Stewart, Gloria Swanson, Cornel
        Wilde, Samuel Goldwyn, Billy Graham, Cecil
        B. DeMille. Recorded 1963.
            2 reels (7 in.) 7 1/2 in. per sec. phonotape.
            L. DeMille, Cecil Blount, 1881-1959. L. Brynner, Yul, 1917-
        II. Heston, Charlton, 1924-   III. Hope, Bob, 1903-   IV.
        Hutton, Betty, 1921-   V. Robinson, Edward G.   1893-1973.
        VI. Stanwyck, Barbara, 1907-   VII. Stewart, James Maitland,
        1908-   VIII. Swanson, Gloria, 1899?-   IX. Wilde, Cornel, 1915-
        X. Goldwyn, Samuel, 1884?-   XI. Graham, William Franklin,
        1918-   XII. DeMille, Cecil Blount, 1881-1959.

C1   The legend of Stonehenge
SC11   Whorf, Michael, 1933-
            The legend of Stonehenge.
            1 tape cassette.   (The visual sounds of
        Mike Whorf. Science, SC11)
            Originally presented on his radio program, Kaleidoscope.
        WJR, Detroit.
            Duration: 90 min., 30 sec.
            What were the strange rock formations which had dotted the
        English countryside for centuries? What purpose did these great
        stones serve and where did they come from?

            L. Stonehenge. L. Title.

Voice Lib.   Lehman, Herbert Henry, 1878-1963
M273-   Biography in sound (radio program)
274   Franklin Delano Roosevelt: the friends and
bd.1   former associates of Franklin Roosevelt on
        the tenth anniversary of the President's death.
        NBC Radio, April, 1955.
            2 reels (7 in.)   7 1/2 in. per sec.
        phonotape.
            L. Roosevelt, Franklin Delano, Pres. U.S., 1882-1945. L.
        McIntire, Ross T   1899-   II. Mellett, Lowell, 1884-1960.
        III. Tully, Grace   IV. Henderson, Leon, 1895-
        V. Roosevelt, Eleanor (Roosevelt) 1884-1962. VI. DeGraaf, Albert
        VII. Lehman, Herbert Henry, 1878-1963. VIII. Rosenman, Samuel
        Irving, 1896-   IX. Arvey, Jacob   X. Moley, Raymond,
        1886-   XI. Farley, Ja   Aloysius, 1888-   XII. Roosevelt,
        (continued on next card)

Voice Lib.   Lehman, Herbert Henry, 1878-1963
381-   I can hear it now (radio program)
382   CBS, April 26, 1951.
bd.1   2 reels (7 in.) 7 1/2 in. per sec. phonotape.
            L. Radio Free Europe. 2. Strategic Air Command. L.
        Ridgway, Matthew Bunker, 1895-   II. Churchill, Winston Leonard
        Spencer, 1874-1965. III. Bevan, Aneurin, 1897-1960. IV. Nixon,
        Richard Milhous, Pres. U.S., 1913-   V. Kerr, Robert Samuel, 1896-
        1963. VI. Brewster, Ralph Owen, 1888-1961. VII. Wherry, Kenneth
        Spicer, 1892-1951. VIII. Capehart, Homer Earl, 1897-   IX.
        Lehman, Herbert Henry, 1878-1963. X. Taft, Robert Alphonso,
        1889-1953. XI. Moody, Arthur Edson Blair, 1902-1954. XII.
        Martin, Joseph William, 1884-1968. XIII. McMahon, James O'Brien
        1903-1952. XIV. MacArthur, Douglas, 1880-1964. XVII. Wilson,
        Charles Edward, 1886-1972. XVIII. Irvine, Clarence T

Voice Lib.
240   Lehmann, Lotte, 1902-
        Farewell to the concert world at Town Hall,
        New York City.   Pembroke Records.
        February 16, 1951.
            1 reel (7 in.)   7 1/2 in. per sec.
        phonotape.

Voice Lib.   Lehrer, Jim
M1661   Strauss, Robert Schwartz, 1918-
bd.2   On Nixon tapes and other current political
        issues; interview by Jim Lehrer, on "Straight
        Talk". WKAR-TV, May 14, 1974.
            20 min.   phonotape (1 r.   7 1/2 i.p.s.)

            1. U.S. - Politics and government - 1969-
        I. Lehrer, Jim.

C1
H112   LEIFR EIRIKSSON, HINN HEPPNI, D. CA. 1021
    Whorf, Michael, 1933-
      The viking - Leif Ericson.
      1 tape cassette. (The visual sounds of
    Mike Whorf. History and heritage, H112)
        Originally presented on his radio program, Kaleidoscope,
    WJR, Detroit.
        Duration: 37 min.
        He has been called Leif the Lucky. He was probably the first
    white man to set foot on North America. This program presents
    the story of Leif Ericson, his birth, his infamous father, Eric the
    Red, and his life as an early sea-voyager.

      L. Leifr Eiriksson, hinn Heppni, d. ca. 1021.   L. Title.

Voice Lib.
515   Leighton, Margaret, 1922-
      Dramatic readings from the works of
    Dorothy Parker, from Festival of Performing
    Arts. Talent Associates, May 8, 1962.
      1 reel (7 in.)   7 1/2 in. per sec.
    phonotape.

      CONTENTS.-bd.1. Poem.-bd.4. Telephone call
    (dramatic reading).-bd.5. A lovely leave
    (dramatic reading).

      I. Parker, Dorothy (Rothschild) 1893-1967.

Voice Lib.
516   Leighton, Margaret, 1922-
bd.1   Dramatic readings from the works of
    Dorothy Parker, from Festival of Performing
    Arts. Talent Associates, May 8, 1962.
      1 reel (7 in.)   7 1/2 in. per sec.
    phonotape.

      CONTENTS.-Dusk before fireworks.

      I. Parker, Dorothy (Rothschild) 1893-1967.

      Leitch, Albert
Voice Lib.
M1046 World news tonight; radio news commentary.
bd.2   CBS Radio news broadcast from Honolulu,
    London, New York and Washington; including
    William Ewing, Norman Corwin, Albert Leitch
    and Harry Marble. CBS, September 12, 1942.
      1 reel (7 in.)   7 1/2 in. per sec.
    phonotape.

      I. Ewing, William   II. Corwin, Norman
    Lewis, 1910-   III. Leitch, Albert
    IV. Marble, Harry

Voice Lib.
M1333 LeMay, Curtis Emerson, 1906-
bd.2   Statement by third party vice-presidential
    candidate to press on his thoughts regarding
    the Vietnam situation and the use of nuclear
    weapons. CBS-TV, October 3, 1968.
      1 reel (7 in.)   7 1/2 in. per sec.
    phonotape.

Voice Lib. LeMay, Curtis Emerson, 1906-
M1346 Nixon, Richard Milhous, Pres. U.S., 1913-
bd.2   Post-1968 election news described by
    Huntley, Brinkley and other NBC staff men.
    Statements of victory by Nixon and of defeat
    by Humphrey; also by Wallace and LeMay.
    Comments from countries overseas. Report of
    Congressional elections. NBC-TV, November 6,
    1968.
      1 reel (7 in.)   7 1/2 in. per sec.
      L. Huntley, Chet, 1911-   IL. Brinkley, David McClure, 1920-
    III. Humphrey, Hubert Horatio, 1911-   IV. Wallace, George
    Corley, 1919-   V. LeMay, Curtis Emerson, 1906-

      LEND-LEASE OPERATIONS (1941-1945)
Voice Lib.
396   Hopkins, Harry Lloyd, 1890-1946.
bd.4   The determination of FDR and the
    American people to help Britain through
    lend-lease. BBC, July 21, 1941.
      1 reel (7 in.)   7 1/2 in. per sec.
    phonotape.

      1. Lend-lease operations (1941-1945).

Voice Lib.
M1466 Lenin, Vladimir Ilich, 1870-1924.
bd.12   Calling up of Soviet Army. Peteler, 1917.
      1 reel (7 in.)   7 1/2 in. per sec.
    phonotape.

Voice Lib.
M952 Lenin, Vladimir Ilich, 1870-1924.
bd.16   Message in Russia. Peteler, 1917.
      1 reel (7 in.)   7 1/2 in. per sec.
    phonotape.

Voice Lib.
M1367 Lenin, Vladimir Ilich, 1870-1924.
bd.2   Various speeches by Lenin, recorded between
    1919-1921, on the following subjects:
    a) to the memory of Chairman of the All-
    Russian Central Executive Committee, Comrade
    Yakov Sverdlov; b) speech to the 3rd Communist
    International; c) Comrade Lenin's report on
    radio conversations with the Hungarian
    communist leader, Bela Kun; d) address to the
    Red Army; e) what is Soviet power? f) how
    to deliver the toilers and laborers from

(Continued on next card)

Voice Lib.
M1367   Lenin, Vladimir Ilich, 1870-1924.   Various
bd.2   speeches by Lenin, recorded between
             1919-1921... 1919-1921. (Card 2)

         the oppression of the land-owners and cap-
         italists for all time; g) about the work of
         the transport system; h) about labor discipline.
         Melodiya, All-Union Record Firm (April
         Factory), 1919-1921.
             1 reel (7 in.)   7 1/2 in. per sec.
         phonotape.

Voice Lib.
M1227   Lenin, Vladimir Ilich, 1870-1924.
bd.1   Talk pertaining to "What is Soviet power
             in her relationship to the capitalistic
             West?" Peteler, 1919.
             1 reel (7 in.)   7 1/2 in. per sec.
         phonotape.

Voice Lib.
M1227   Lenin, Vladimir Ilich, 1970-1924.
bd.2   Appeal to the Red Army: the Red army and
             the Socialist workers and peasants as a
             foundation for the new Soviet state.
             Peteler, 1919.
             1 reel (7 in.)   7 1/2 in. per sec.
         phohotape.

Voice Lib.
M1227   Lenin, Vladimir Il'ich, 1820-1924.
bd.7   Report on the conversations with the
             Hungarian communist leader Béla Kun in
             March of 1919. Peteler, 1920.
             1 reel (7 in.)   7 1/2 in. per sec.
         phonotape.

             1. Kun, Béla, 1886-1937.

Voice Lib.
M1227   Lenin, Vladimir Il'ich, 1870-1924.
bd.5   Oration to the memory of Comrade Sverdlov,
             the chairman of the Central Executive
             Committee of the Communist Party of the
             USSR. Peteler, 1919.
             1 reel (7 in.)   7 1/2 in. per sec.
         phonotape.

             1. Sverdlov, Iakov Mikhailovich, 1885-1919.

Voice Lib.
M1227   Lenin, Vladimir Ilich, 1870-1924.
bd.3   Talk to the poor peasants about the
             solution of the peasant problem from the
             Socialist viewpoint. Peteler, 1919.
             1 reel (7 in.)   7 1/2 in. per sec.
         phonotape.

Voice Lib.
M1227   Lenin, Vladimir Ilich, 1870-1924.
bd.6   Talk on the occasion of the Third Communist
             Internationale about the complete leadership
             claims of the various Soviet republics.
             Peteler, 1919.
             1 reel (7 in.)   7 1/2 in. per sec.
         phonotape.

C1   LEONARDO DA VINCI, 1452-1519
SC5
         Whorf, Michael, 1933-
             History's first modern.
             1 tape cassette. (The visual sounds of
         Mike Whorf. Science, SC5)

             Originally presented of his radio program, Kaleidoscope,
         WJR, Detroit.
             Duration: 37 min., 5 sec.
             His world in Italy, his life as a boy and young man, his
         exploits and endeavors as a mature man are given generous
         attention in this account of Leonardo da Vinci.

             1. Leonardo da Vinci, 1452-1519. I. Title.

Voice Lib.
M1227   Lenin, Vladimir Ilich, 1870-1924.
bd.4   Talk pertaining to how the working class
             can be liberated forever from the yoke of
             large landowners. Peteler, 1919.
             1 reel (7 in.)   7 1/2 in. per sec.
         phonotape.

         Leoncavallo, Ruggiero, 1858-1919.
Voice Lib.   I Pagliacci. No, Pagliaccio non son
M1090   Caruso, Enrico, 1873-1921.
bd.2   Re-recording of 78 rpm phonodisc of tenor
         Caruso singing "No, Pagliaccio Non Son"
         from opera Pagliacci, Act II. Victor,
         1922.
             1 reel (7 in.)   7 1/2 in. per sec.
         phonotape.

             I. Leoncavallo, Ruggiero, 1858-1919./I
         Pagliacci. No, Pagliaccio non son.

Leoncavallo, Ruggiero, 1858-1919.
I Pagliacce. Vesti la giubba
Voice Lib.
M1090   Caruso, Enrico, 1873-1921.
bd.3   Re-recording of 78 rpm phonodisc of tenor
        Caruso singing "Vesti La Giubba" from opera
        Pagliacci, Act I.   Victor, 1922.
           1 reel (7 in.)   7 1/2 in. per sec.
        phonotape.

           I. Leoncavallo, Ruggiero, 1858-1919./I
        Pagliacci. Vesti la giubba.

Voice Lib.
118   Lerner, Alan Jay, 1918-
          Lyrics by Lerner.   Heritage, 1961.
          1 reel (7 in.)   7 1/2 in. per sec.
       phonotape.

Voice Lib.
243   Leopold, Nathan Freudenthal, 1904 or 5-
bd.7   defendant.
          Leopold speaks on his parole denial;
       interviewed by Hugh Hill, WBBM (Chicago).
       CBS Radio, July 31, 1957.
          1 reel (7 in.)   7 1/2 in. per sec.
       phonotape.

          I. Hill, Hugh

Voice Lib.
126   Lerner, Alan Jay, 1918-
          Lerner and Loewe; condensed NBC-TV special
       with Julie Andrews, Richard Burton, Robert
       Goulet, Alan Lerner and Frederick Loewe.
       NBC, February 2, 1962.
          1 reel (7 in.)   7 1/2 in. per sec.
       phonotape.

          I. Andrews, Julie, 1935-   II. Burton,
       Richard, 1925-   III. Goulet, Robert
       Gerard, 1933-   IV. Loewe, Frederick, 1904-

Voice Lib.
345   Leopold, Nathan Freudenthal, 1904 or 5-
bd.11   defendant.
          Plea for privacy after being paroled.
       CBS, March 13, 1958.
          1 reel (7 in.)   7 1/2 in. per sec.
       phonotape.

C1
R1   Whorf, Michael, 1933-
          The lesson never learned
          The lesson never learned.
          1 tape cassette.   (The visual sounds of
       Mike Whorf. Religion, R1)

          Originally presented on his radio program, Kaleidoscope,
       WJR, Detroit.
          Duration: 46 min., 15 sec.
          This is the story of Jesus from His birth, through His ministry and
       teaching, to His death.   It is based on the Bible, the stories which
       unfold in the Gospels, and is ecumenical in approach.

          1. Jesus Christ.   2. Christianity.   I. Title.

LEOPOLD, NATHAN FREUDENTHAL, 1904 or 5 -
DEFENDANT
Voice Lib.
243   Stratton, William Grant, 1914-
bd.5   Denial of parole to Nathan Leopold, with
       Hugh Hill of WBBM (Chicago).   CBS, July 30,
       1957.
          1 reel (7 in.)   7 1/2 in. per sec.
       phonotape.

          1. Leopold, Nathan Freudenthal, 1904 or 5-
             defendant.   I. Hill, Hugh

Lesueur, Laurence Edward, 1909-
Voice Lib.
M1044 London after dark; on-the-spot recordings of various
       points during the London air-raid attacks: the Savoy Hotel
       kitchen, Trafalgar Square, anti-aircraft battery near London,
       air-raid shelter.   With newsmen Edward R. Murrow, Robert
       Bowman, Raymond Van Denny, Larry Lesueur, Eric Sevareid,
       Vincent Sheean, J. B. Priestley, Michael Standing, and
       Winfred Von Thomas.   CBS and BBC, August 24, 1940.
       1 reel (7 in.)   7 1/2 in. per sec.   phonotape.

          1. Murrow, Edward Roscoe, 1908-1965.   II. Bowman, Robert
       III. Van Denny, Raymond   IV. Lesueur, Laurence Edward,
       1909-   V. Sevareid, Arnold Eric, 1912-   VI. Sheean,
       Vincent, 1899-   VII. Priestley, John Boynton, 1894-
       VIII. Standing, Michael   IX. Von Thomas, Winfred

Voice Lib.
128   Lerner, Alan Jay
bd.13-15 Singing his own songs.   Private recording.
       [n.d.]
          1 reel (7 in.)   7 1/2 in. per sec.
       phonotape.

          CONTENTS.-Bd.13. Wanderin' star.-bd.14. I
       talk to the trees.-bd.15. Love song.

"Let's All Be Americans Now"
Voice Lib.
603   American Quartet.
bd.6   "Let's All Be Americans Now", Irving
       Berlin's World War I song.   Victor Talking
       Machine Co., 1917.
          1 reel (7 in.)   7 1/2 in. per sec.
       phonotape.

          I. Title.

Voice Lib.   Let's get behind Herbert Hoover
M1064   Hoover, Herbert Clark, Pres. U.S., 1874-1964.
bd.7   Campaign song of 1932 Republican presidential
        race: "Let's Get Behind Herbert Hoover";
        excerpt from address at Madison Square Garden,
        New York, by President Hoover at close of
        1932 presidential campaign. Fox Movietone,
        1932.
            1 reel (7 in.)   7 1/2 in. per sec.
        phonotape.

            I. Title: Let's get behind Herbert Hoover.

Voice Lib.   Letterer, Charles
M275-   Biography in sound (radio program)
276   Alexander Woollcott. N.B.C., date?
bd.1   2 reels (7 in.)   7 1/2 in. per sec.
        phonotape.
            I. Woollcott, Alexander, 1887-1943. I. Woollcott, Alexander,
            1887-1943. II. Banghardt, Kenneth   III. Hecht, Ben, 1893-
            1964. IV. Roosevelt, Eleanor (Roosevelt) 1884-1962. V. Walker,
            Danton   VI. Brackett, Charles, 1892-1969. VII. Grant,
            Jane .   VIII. Rude, Robert Barnes   IX. West,
            Rebecca, pseud. X. Henessy, Joseph   XI. Letterer,
            Charles   XII. Welles, Orson, 1915-

Voice Lib.   Letts, Richard
M1742   Graves, Gerald
bd.4   Defends Lansing's record of minority hiring
        against attack from Human Relations director
        Richard Letts. WJIM-TV, June 19, 1974.
            2 min.   phonotape (1 r.   7 1/2 i.p.s.)

            1. Minorities - Employment - Lansing, Mich.
        I. Letts, Richard

Voice Lib.   LEUKEMIA - PERSONAL NARRATIVES
M1634   Alsop, Stewart, 1914-
bd.4   Interviewed about his terminal leukemia,
        by Barbara Newman. WKAR, April 15, 1974.
            15 min.   phonotape (1 r.   7 1/2 i.p.s.)

            1. Alsop, Stewart, 1914-   2. Leukemia -
        Personal narratives. I. Newman, Barbara.

Voice Lib.   Levenson, Samuel, 1911-
M1481   Vanocur, Sander, 1928-
bd.3   Interviewed by David Frost on believing
        the government, being misled, journalistic
        responsibility. Comments from Sam Levenson.
        July, 1971.
            1 reel (7 in.)   7 1/2 i.p.s.   phonotape.

            1. Journalistic ethics. I. Frost, David
        Paradine, 1939-   II. Levenson, Samuel,
        1911-

Voice Lib.
M760   Levy, Leonard
bd.1   Excerpt from "What All the Screaming's
        About" (Program 1); discusses the effect
        of Beatle music on adolescents. Westing-
        house Broadcasting Corporation, 1964.
            1 reel (7 in.)   7 1/2 in. per sec.
        phonotape.   (The Music Goes Round and Round)

            I. Title: What all the screaming's about.
        II. Series.

Voice Lib.
M760   Levy, Leonard
bd.16   Excerpt from "The Big Beat" (Program 2);
        comments on the many artists who are only
        one-shot record artists and the ones who
        have true talent; including song by Bobby
        Vinton, "Blue Velvet". Westinghouse
        Broadcasting Company, 1964.
            1 reel (7 in.)   7 1/2 in. per sec.
        phonotape.   (The Music Goes Round and Round)

            I. Title: The big beat. II. Series.

Voice Lib.
M765   Levy, Leonard
bd.8   Excerpt from "The Anatomy of a Hit"
        (Program 9); answers the question, "What
        does a company do when one of its artists
        is no longer selling?" Westinghouse
        Broadcasting Corporation, 1964.
            1 reel (7 in.)   7 1/2 in. per sec.
        phonotape.   (The Music Goes Round and Round)

            I. Title: The anatomy of a hit. II. Series.

Voice Lib.   Levy, Newman, 1888-
M272   Biography in sound (radio program)
bd.1   Heywood Broun. NBC, date?
            1 reel (7 in.)   7 1/2 in. per sec.
        phonotape.
            I. Broun, Heywood Campbell, 1888-1939. I. Broun,
            Heywood Campbell, 1888-1939. II. Swope, Herbert Bayard,
            1882-1958. III. Wilson, Mattie   IV. Jackson, Gardner
            V. Meany, Thomas   VI. Waldron, Beatrice   VII.
            Gordon, Max   VIII. Madison, Connie   IX. Gannett,
            Lewis Stiles, 1891-1966. X. Collins, Joseph, 1866-1950. XI.
            Brown, Earl Louis, 1900-   XII. Levy, Newman, 1888-
            XIII. Growth, John   XIV. Bye, George   XV.
            Roosevelt, Franklin Delano Pres. U.S., 1882-1945. XVI.
            Reynolds, Quentin James,   -1965.

Voice Lib.
M1028   Lewis, Fulton, 1903-1966.
bd.1   Radio news broadcast interview with Senator
        Joseph R. McCarthy pertaining to charges
        made against him by Adlai Stevenson, Edward R.
        Murrow, and others. Mutual, January 3,
        1956.
            1 reel (7 in.)   7 1/2 in. per sec.
        phonotape.

            I. McCarthy, Joseph Raymond, 1909-1957.

Voice Lib. Lewis, John
M1640 Bond, Julian, 1940-
Politics and Black progress, on "Firing
Line" with William F. Buckley and John
Lewis. WKAR-FM, March 17, 1974.
45 min. phonotape (1 r. 7 1/2 i.p.s.)

1. Negroes - Politics and suffrage.
I. Buckley, William Frank, 1925-
II. Lewis, John.

Voice Lib.
174- Lewis, John Llewellyn, 1880-1969. Testimonial
177 dinner... 1960. (Card 2)

CONTENTS (cont'd) John L. Lewis.-177, bd.2.
Fred Perkins-177, bd.3. John L. Lewis-177,
bd.4. John Owens.

Voice Lib.
352 Lewis, John Llewellyn, 1880-1969.
bd.1 Answering questions of the press on
collective bargaining and its uses, wage
and price freezes. CBS, January 8, 1951.
1 reel (7 in.) 7 1/2 in. per sec.
phonotape.

1. Collective bargaining.

Voice Lib.
169 Lewis, John Llewellyn, 1880-1969.
bd.2 United Mine Workers District 50
Special Convention. AFL-CIO (P.R.O.),
February 24, 1961.
1 reel (7 in.) 7 1/2 in. per sec.
phonotape.

Voice Lib.
135- Lewis, John Llewellyn, 1880-1969.
136 Testimony before Senate Committee in
regards to mine disasters. United Mine
Workers, January 29, 1952.
2 reels (7 in.) 7 1/2 in. per sec.
phonotape.

Lewis, John Llewellyn, 1880-1969
Voice Lib.
572- I can hear it now (radio program)
573 1933-1946. CBS, 1948.
bd.1 2 reels (7 in.) 7 1/2 in. per sec.
phonotape.
I. Murrow, Edward Roscoe, 1908-1965. II. LaGuardia, Fiorello
Henry, 1882-1947. III. Chamberlain, Neville, 1869-1949. IV.
Roosevelt, Franklin Delano, Pres. U.S., 1882-1945. V. Churchill,
Winston Leonard Spencer, 1874-1965. VI. Gaulle, Charles de,
Pres. France, 1890-1970. VII. Eisenhower, Dwight David, Pres. U.S.,
1890-1969. VIII. Willkie, Wendell Lewis, 1892-1944. IX. Martin,
Joseph William, 1884-1968. X. Elizabeth II, Queen of Great Britain,
1926- XI. Margaret Rose, Princess of Gt. Brit., 1930- XII.
Johnson, Hugh Samuel, 188?-1942. XIII. Smith, Alfred Emanuel,
1873-1944. XIV. Lindberg( )arles Augustus, 1902- XV. Davis,
(Continued on next card)

Voice Lib.
166- Lewis, John Llewellyn, 1880-1969.
167 Speech at Charleston, West Virginia.
AFL-CIO (P.R.O.), October 18, 1952.
2 reels (7 in.) 7 1/2 in. per sec.
phonotape.

Lewis, Sinclair, 1885-1951
Voice Lib.
M655 The Twentieth Century (TV program)
bd.1 "The creative thirties", narrated by
Walter Cronkite. CBS, 1963.
25 min. phonotape (1 r. 7 1/2 i.p.s.)
I. U.S. - Civilization - 1918-1945. II. Bower, Edward,
1874-1946. III. Geismar, Maxwell David, 1909-
III. MacDonald, Dwight, 1906- IV. Welles, Orson, 1915-
V. Cronkite, Walter Leland, 1916- VI. Gable, Clark, 1901-
1960. VII. Lewis, Sinclair, 1885-1951. VIII. Houseman,
John, 1902- IX. Roosevelt, Franklin Delano, Pres. U.S.,
1882-1945.

Voice Lib.
174- Lewis, John Llewellyn, 1880-1969.
177 Testimonial dinner for John L. Lewis.
AFL-CIO, January 14, 1960.
4 reels (7 in.) 7 1/2 in. per sec.
phonotape.

CONTENTS.-174, bd.1. John Owens.-174, bd.2.
Tony Boyle.-174, bd.3. Tom Kennedy.-175, bd.1.
Tom Kennedy.-175, bd.2. John Owens.-175, bd.3.
John L. Lewis.-176. John L.Lewis.-177, bd.1.
(Continued on next card)

Voice Lib.
M1002 Ley, Robert, 1890-1945.
bd.6 Speech at the Second Workers Congress of
the German Workers "Front", which succeeded
the earlier trade unions. Peteler, May 16,
1934.
1 reel (7 in.) 7 1/2 in. per sec.
phonotape.

Voice Lib.
M1004 Ley, Robert, 1890-1945.
bd.3-C   Administering loyalty oath to Hitler to
the members of Labor groups during May Day
activities. Peteler, May 1, 1935.
1 reel (7 in.)   7 1/2 in. per sec.
phonotape.

Voice Lib.
M1304 Ley, Robert, 1890-1945.
bd.9   Speaking to Nazi women about their duty
in raising families as a means of appreciation
to Adolf Hitler. Peteler, 1942.
1 reel (7 in.)   7 1/2 in. per sec.
phonotape.

Voice Lib.
M1018 Ley, Robert, 1890-1945.
bd.2   Speaking to farmers on new Nazi settlement
in Poland, stressing German rights to cultivate
farms due to race superiority which eventually
obliterates Poles and Jews. Peteler,
November, 1939.
1 reel (7 in.)   7 1/2 in. per sec.
phonotape.

1. National socialism

Voice Lib.   Liberace, 1919-
M1707   Cohn, Roy M   1927-
bd.3   On the Mike Douglas show recalling the
McCarthy era with no regrets. Includes
Liberace. ABC, May 30, 1974.
7 min.   phonotape (1 r.   7 1/2 i.p.s.)

1. McCarthy-Army controversy. I. Douglas,
Mike, 1925?-   II. Liberace, 1919-

Voice Lib.
M1356   Ley, Robert, 1890-1945.
bd.1   Address at the opening of the Bayreuth
War Games. Peteler, 1942.
1 reel (7 in.)   7 1/2 i.p.s.   phonotape.

1. Germany - Politics and government -
1933-1945.

Voice Lib.
M543   Liberation of Paris. Radio Diffusion de
la Nation Française, August 25, 1944.
bd.2   1 reel (7 in.)   7 1/2 i.p.s.   phonotape.

1. Paris - History - 1940-1944.

Voice Lib.
M1304 Ley, Robert, 1890-1945.
bd.14   Short and dramatic statement about the
dangers to humanity from the Jewish race.
Peteler, 1942.
1 reel (7 in.)   7 1/2 in. per sec.
phonotape.

The liberator - Simon Bolivar
C1
H86   Whorf, Michael, 1933-
The liberator - Simon Bolivar.
1 tape cassette. (The visual sounds of
Mike Whorf. History and heritage, H86)

Originally presented on his radio program, Kaleidoscope,
WJR, Detroit.
Duration: 34 min., 15 sec.
He was called the Washington of South America and it was a
title richly deserved. Bolivar struck a blow for freedom against the
misrule of Spain, and led his countrymen in the battles that changed
the map of a continent and the future of a people.

1. Bolivar, Simon, 1783-1830. L. Title.

Voice Lib.
M1304 Ley, Robert, 1890-1945.
bd.6   Remarks to German war workers in Troisdorf.
Peteler, February 6, 1942.
1 reel (7 in.)   7 1/2 in. per sec.
phonotape.

Liberty bell (it's time to ring again)
Voice Lib.
M611   Peerless Quartet.
bd.4   World War I song "Liberty bell (it's time
to ring again)". Victor Talking Machine
Co., 1917.
1 reel (7 in.)   7 1/2 i.p.s.   phonotape.

1. European War, 1914-1918 - Songs and
music. I. Title: Liberty bell (it's time
to ring again.)

Voice Lib.
M1230-
1231,
bd.1

LIBERTY OF THE PRESS - U.S.
Fair trial, free press; discussion of the Reardon Report of the
American Bar Association about restrictions of the press in
publicizing criminal cases before they are tried. Participants,
via TV satelite: two British guests and a panel of Americans
of diversified views. ABC-TV, May 18, 1967.
2 reel (7 in.) 7 1/2 i.p.s. phonotape.

1. Liberty of the press - U.S. 2. Criminal procedure - U.S.

C1
H10

Life and times of Daniel Boone
Whorf, Michael, 1933-
   Life and times of Daniel Boone.
   1 tape cassette. (The visual sounds of
Mike Whorf. History and heritage, H10)
   Originally presented on his radio program, Kaleidoscope,
WJR, Detroit.
   Duration: 84 min.
   He was our nation's most illustrious pioneer, a man of action,
a man of determination. Boone was a legend in his own time and a
hero among the many who explored the wilderness of early
America.

1. Boone, Daniel, 1734-1820. I. Title.

Voice Lib.
M981
bd.3

Lichberg, Heinz von
   Nazi news report of a torchlight parade in
Berlin on the assumption of power by Nazi
Party. Reports by Wulf Bley and Heinz
von Lichberg. Peteler, January 30, 1933.
   1 reel (7 in.) 7 1/2 in. per sec.
phonotape.

   I. Bley, Wulf, 1890-   II. Lichberg,
Heinz von

C1
A15

Life and times of Mark Twain
Whorf, Michael, 1933-
   Life and times of Mark Twain.
   1 tape cassette. (The visual sounds of
Mike Whorf. Art, music, and letters, A15)
   Originally presented on his radio program, Kaleidoscope,
WJR, Detroit.
   Duration: 44 min., 5 sec.
   Here with the narrator serving in the dual role of story
teller and Mark Twain, is this account of the life and times of
the gifted author.

1. Clemens, Samuel Langhorne, 1835-1910. I. Title.

Voice Lib.
M353
bd.2

Lie, Trygve, 1896-1968.
   Outbreak of the Korean conflict; calling
of U.N. Security Council to action. NBC,
July, 1950.
   1 reel (7 in.) 7 1/2 in. per sec.
phonotape.

   Original disc off-speed.

   1. Korean War, 1950-1953

C1
H57

The life and times of William Jennings Bryan
Whorf, Michael, 1933-
   The life and times of William Jennings Bryan.
   1 tape cassette. (The visual sounds of
Mike Whorf. History and heritage, H57)
   Originally presented on his radio program, Kaleidoscope,
WJR, Detroit.
   Duration: 39 min.
   Here is the plea of Bryan for silver, his courageous stand as
pacifist - his inner conflict, his court battle at the Scopes trial -
his untimely demise - this is the story of the dauntless persistence
of William Jennings Bryan.

1. Bryan, William Jenn. 1860-1925. I. Title.

Voice Lib.
M762
bd.2

Lieber, Jerry
   Excerpt from "Tunesmiths past and present"
(Program 4); comments on success in relation
to "song writer" vs. "record writing".
Westinghouse Broadcasting Corporation, 1964.
   2 min., 28 sec. phonotape (1 r.
7 1/2 i.p.s.) (The music goes round and
round)

   1. Music, Popular (Songs, etc.) - Publishing
and writing. I. Title: Tunesmiths past and
present.   II. Series.

Voice Lib.
M1028
bd.5

Life Can Be Beautiful; radio program theme
   and introduction to the soap opera.
Michigan State University, Department of
Television and Radio, 1940's.
   1 reel (7 in.) 7 1/2 in. per sec.
phonotape.

Voice Lib.
M762
bd.12

Lieber, Jerry
   Excerpt from "The Big Beat" (Program 2);
changes in the market for rock-and-roll
records; including the song "Surfin' Bird".
Westinghouse Broadcasting Corporation, 1964.
   1 reel (7 in.) 7 1/2 in. per sec.
phonotape. (The Music Goes Round and Round)

   1. Music, Popular (Songs, etc.) - U.S.
I. Title: Surfin' bird. II. Title: The
big beat. III. Series.

Voice Lib.
M1435

Life in other worlds; exploratory discussion about life on other
planets. Arnold J. Toynbee, Dr. G. B. Kiastiakowsky
(professor at Harvard), Dr. Donald M. Michaels, Dr. Otto
Struve, Dr. Harlow Shapley, Walter Cronkite, Chet Huntley,
William L. Laurence. New York, NBC, March 3, 1961.
1 reel (7 in.) 7 1/2 i.p.s. phonotape.

1. Life on other planets. I. Toynbee, Arnold Joseph, 1889-
II. Kiastiakowsky, George Bogdan. III. Michaels, Donald M.
IV. Struve, Otto, 1897-1963. V. Shapley, Harlow, 1885-1972.
VI. Cronkite, Walter Leland, 1916- VII. Huntley, Chet,
1911-1974. VIII. Laurence, William Leonard, 1888-

Voice Lib.
M1435   LIFE ON OTHER PLANETS

Life in other worlds; exploratory discussion about life on other planets. Arnold J. Toynbee, Dr. G. B. Kiastiakowsky (professor at Harvard), Dr. Donald M. Michaels, Dr. Otto Struve, Dr. Harlow Shapley, Walter Cronkite, Chet Huntley, William L. Laurence. New York, NBC, March 3, 1961.
1 reel (7 in.) 7 1/2 i. p. s. phonotape.

I. Life on other planets. L. Toynbee, Arnold Joseph, 1889- II. Kiastiakowsky, George Bogdan. III. Michaels, Donald M. IV. Struve, Otto, 1897-1963. V. Shapley, Harlow, 1885-1972. VI. Cronkite, Walter Leland, 1916- VII. Huntley, Chet, 1911-1974. VIII. Laurence, William Leonard, 1888-

---

Voice Lib.
112   Lincoln, Abraham, Pres. U.S., 1809-1965.
bd.2   Gettysburg Address, as read by Raymond Massey. Linguaphone 1940.
   1 reel (7 in.) 7 1/2 in. per sec. phonotape.

I. Massey, Raymond, 1806-   II. Title.

Voice Lib.
M1504- Light's golden jubilee; ceremony at the
1505   50th anniversary of the invention of the incandescent light bulb. October 21, 1929.
   2 reels (7 in.) 7 1/2 in. per sec. phonotape.

Voice Lib.
112   Lincoln, Abraham, Pres. U.S., 1809-1865.
bd.3   Second inaugural address, as read by Raymond Massey. Linguaphone, 1940.
   1 reel (7 in.) 7 1/2 in. per sec. phonotape.

I. Massey, Raymond, 1896-

     Lili Marlene
Voice Lib.
M1463 German radio (Nazi controlled)
bd.14 Nazi German radio (Belgrade station) with two stanzas of "Lili Marlene". Peteler, 1942.
   1 reel (7 in.) 7 1/2 in. per sec. phonotape.

I. Title: Lili Marlene.

     LINCOLN, ABRAHAM, PRES. U.S., 1809-1865
Voice Lib.
M930 Godwin, Charles
bd.3 Conference at the opening of the Abraham Lincoln Papers at Library of Congress. Discussion of the contents and value of these documents by various Lincoln authorities. Mutual, July 29, 1947.
   1 reel (7 in.) 7 1/2 in. per sec. phonotape.

1. Lincoln, Abraham, Pres. U.S., 1809-1865.

     Lilienthal, David Eli, 1899-
Voice Lib.
573   I can hear it now (radio program)
bd.2- 1945-1949. CBS, 1950?
574   2 reels (7 in.) 7 1/2 in. per sec.
bd.1 phonotape.
   L. Murrow, Edward Roscoe, 1908-1965. II. Nehru, Jawaharlal, 1889-1964. III. Philip, duke of Edinburgh, 1921- IV. Elizabeth II, Queen of Great Britain, 1926- V. Ferguson, Homer, 1889- VI. Hughes, Howard Robard, 1905- VII. Marshall, George Catlett, 1880- VIII. Ruth, George Herman, 1895-1948. IX. Lilienthal, David Eli, 1899- X. Trout, Robert, 1908- XI. Gage, Arthur. XII. Jackson, Robert Houghwout, 1892-1954. XIII. Gromyko, Anatolii Andreevich, 1908- XIV. Baruch, Bernard Mannes, 1870-1965. XV. Churchill, Wins Leonard Spencer, 1874-1965. XVI. Winchell, Walter, 1897-19 XVII. Davis, Elmer Holmes, 1890-

(Continued on next card)

     LINCOLN, ABRAHAM, PRES. U. S., 1809-1865
C1
H18 Whorf, Michael, 1933-
   He loved her truly.
   1 tape cassette. (The visual sounds of Mike Whorf. History and heritage, H18)

Originally presented on his radio program, Kaleidoscope, WJR, Detroit.
Duration: 36 min., 30 sec.
Much has been written about the life, times and experiences of Abraham Lincoln, but perhaps the nicest part of the truth is the story of Lincoln and his stepmother, Sarah. Here was the motivation behind Lincoln's quest for greatness.

1. Lincoln, Sarah Bush Johnston, 1788-1869. 2. Lincoln, Abraham, Pres. U.S., 1809-1865. L Title.

Voice Lib.
M955 Lillie, Beatrice, 1898-
bd.1- Singing selections from album "Beatrice
10   Lillie Sings". JJC Records, 1939.
   1 reel (7 in.) 7 1/2 in. per sec. phonotape.
   CONTENTS. -bd. 1. "Mad about the boy" (school girl version)- bd. 2. "Mad about the boy" (Cockney maid version) -bd. 3. "Three white feathers". -bd. 4. "Weary of it all". -bd. 5. "I went to a marvelous party". -bd. 6. "Get yourself a geisha". -bd. 7. "Paree". - bd. 8. "Mother told me so". -bd. 9. "The gutter song". -bd. 10. "I hate spring".
   I. Title: Beatrice Lillie sings.

     LINCOLN, ABRAHAM, PRES. U.S., 1809-1865
C1
H56 Whorf, Michael, 1933-
   The Lincoln remembered.
   1 tape cassette. (The visual sounds of Mike Whorf. History and heritage, H56)

Originally presented on his radio program, Kaleidoscope, WJR, Detroit.
Duration: 37 min.
Here is a Lincoln that captures the essence of the man, his great humor, his understanding of human nature.

1. Lincoln, Abraham, Pres. U.S., 1809-1865. L Title.

LINCOLN, ABRAHAM, PRES. U.S., 1809-1865

C1
E7
Whorf, Michael, 1933-
The man of steel and velvet.
1 tape cassette. (The visual sounds of
Mike Whorf. History and heritage, H7)
Originally presented on his radio program, Kaleidoscope,
WJR, Detroit.
Duration: 55 min.
A historical account of the young Lincoln, his days as a
struggling young lawyer, his political aspirations, his arduous
years as a president, his tragic death.

L. Lincoln, Abraham, Pres. U.S., 1809-1865. L. Title.

LINCOLN, ABRAHAM, PRES. U.S., 1809-1865

C1
H46
Whorf, Michael, 1933-
The play that Lincoln never saw.
1 tape cassette. (The visual sounds of
Mike Whorf. History and heritage, H46)
Originally presented on his radio program, Kaleidoscope,
WJR, Detroit.
Duration: 36 min.
"Our American cousin" was the play Abraham Lincoln attended on
that fateful night. In the shadows awaited death and the nation went
into shock. But what of the play – its actors and actresses?

L. Taylor, Tom, 1817-1880. /Our American cousin.
2. Lincoln, Abraham, Pres. U.S., 1809-1865. L. Title.

LINCOLN, SARAH BUSH JOHNSTON, 1788-1869

C1
H18
Whorf, Michael, 1933-
He loved her truly.
1 tape cassette. (The visual sounds of Mike Whorf. History
and heritage, H18)
Originally presented on his radio program, Kaleidoscope,
WJR, Detroit.
Duration: 36 min., 30 sec.
Much has been written about the life, times and experiences of
Abraham Lincoln, but perhaps the nicest part of the truth is the
story of Lincoln and his stepmother, Sarah. Here was the motivation
behind Lincoln's quest for greatness.

L. Lincoln, Sarah Bush Johnston, 1788-1869. 2. Lincoln,
Abraham, Pres. U.S., 1809-1865. L. Title.

The Lincoln remembered

C1
H56
Whorf, Michael, 1933-
The Lincoln remembered.
1 tape cassette. (The visual sounds of
Mike Whorf. History and heritage, H56)
Originally presented on his radio program, Kaleidoscope,
WJR, Detroit.
Duration: 37 min.
Here is a Lincoln that captures the essence of the man, his
great humor, his understanding of human nature.

L. Lincoln, Abraham, Pres. U.S., 1809-1865. L. Title.

Voice Lib.
533
bd.1
Lindbergh, Charles Augustus, 1902-
America and foreign wars. NEAF,
September 15, 1939.
1 reel (7 in.) 7 1/2 in. per sec.
phonotape.

Lindbergh, Charles Augustus, 1902-

Voice Lib.
M617
bd.1-
bd.25
Radio in the 1920's: a series of excerpts
from important broadcasts of the 1920's,
with brief prologue and epilogue; a sample
of radio of the period. NVL, April, 1964.
1 reel (7 in.) 7 1/2 in. per sec.
phonotape.
L. Radio programs. L. Marconi, Guglielmo, marchese, 1874-
1937. IL. Kendall, H G III. Coolidge, Calvin, Pres. U.S.,
1872-1933. IV. Wilson, Woodrow, Pres. U.S., 1856-1924. V.
Roosevelt, Franklin Delano, Pres. U.S., 1882-1945. VL. Lodge,
Henry Cabot, 1850-1924. VII. LaGuardia, Fiorello Henry, 1882-1947.
VIII. The Happiness Boys (Radio program) IX. Gallagher and Sheen.
X. Barney Google. XL. Vallee, Rudy, 1901- XIL. The two
(Continued on next card)

Lindbergh, Charles Augustus, 1902-

Voice Lib.
M620
bd.1-
bd.16
Radio in the 1940's (Part I): a series of
excerpts from important broadcasts of the 1940's; a
sample of radio of the period. NVL, April, 1964.
1 reel (7 in.) 7 1/2 in. per sec. phonotape.
L. Radio programs. L. Thomas, Lowell Jackson, 1892- IL.
Gunther, John, 1901-1970. III. Kaltenborn, Hans von, 1878-1965.
IV. Delmar, Kenny. V. Those were the good old days (Radio
program) VL. Elman, Dave. VII. Hall, Frederick Lee, 1916-1970.
VIII. Hobby lobby (Radio program) IX. Roosevelt, Franklin Delano,
Pres. U.S., 1882-1945. X. Willkie, Wendell Lewis, 1892-1944.
XL. Hoover, Herbert Clark, Pres. U.S., 1874-1964. XIL. Johnson,
Hugh Samuel, 1882-1942. XIII. Cobb, Irvin Shrewsbury, 1876-1944.
XIV. Roosevelt, Theodore, 1858-1919. XV. Nye, Gerald Prentice,
1892-1971. XVI. Lindbergh, Charles Augustus, 1902- XVII.
Toscanini, Arturo, 1867-1957.

Lindbergh, Charles Augustus, 1902-

Voice Lib.
572-
573
bd.1
I can hear it now (radio program)
1933-1946. CBS, 1948.
2 reels (7 in.) 7 1/2 in. per sec.
phonotape.
L. Murrow, Edward Roscoe, 1908-1965. IL. LaGuardia, Fiorello
Henry, 1882-1947. III. Chamberlain, Neville, 1869-1949. IV.
Roosevelt, Franklin Delano, Pres. U.S., 1882-1945. V. Churchill,
Winston Leonard Spencer, 1874-1965. VL. Gaulle, Charles de,
Pres. France, 1890-1970. VII. Eisenhower, Dwight David, Pres. U.S.,
1890-1969. VIII. Willkie, Wendell Lewis, 1892-1944. IX. Martin,
Joseph William, 1884-1968. X. Elizabeth II, Queen of Great Britain,
1926- XL. Margaret Rose, Princess of Gt. Brit., 1930- XIL.
Johnson, Hugh Samuel, 1882-1942. XIII. Smith, Alfred Emanuel,
1873-1944. XIV. Lindbergh, Charles Augustus, 1902- XV. Davis,
(Continued on next card)

LINDBERGH, CHARLES AUGUSTUS, 1902-

Voice Lib.
M210
bd.2
Byrnes, James Francis, 1879-1972.
An answer to Charles A. Lindbergh.
CBS, May 22, 1940.
1 reel (7 in.) 7 1/2 i.p.s. phonotape.

1. Lindbergh, Charles Augustus, 1902-

LINDBERGH, CHARLES AUGUSTUS, 1902-

Voice Lib.
M1696
bd.4
Coolidge, Calvin, Pres. U.S., 1872-1933.
President Coolidge welcoming Charles
Lindbergh. WJRT-TV, May 27, 1974.
5 min. phonotape (1 r. 7 1/2 i.p.s.)

Taped from the Mike Douglas Show.

1. Lindbergh, Charles Augustus, 1902-

Cl
875
LINDBERGH, CHARLES AUGUSTUS, 1930-1932

Whorf, Michael, 1933-
Kidnap of the century - Lindbergh.
1 tape cassette. (The visual sounds of
Mike Whorf. Social, 875)
Originally presented on his radio program, Kaleidoscope.
WJR, Detroit.
Duration: 37 min., 30 sec.
A vivid, exciting account of the notorious Lindbergh kidnapping.
The evening of March 1, 1932, was the scene of the most publicized
abduction of the century. The kidnapping, and the ensuing manhunt
are narrated in this anxious, fearful report.
1. Lindbergh, Charles Augustus, 1930-1932. 2. Hauptmann,
Bruno Richard, 1899-1936.   I. Title.

Voice Lib.
M1691
Bd.2
Lindfors, Viveca, 1920-
Miller, Merle, 1918-
On Mike Douglas Show discussing his book
on Truman. Includes Viveca Lindfors and
David Steinberg. WILS-TV, May 23, 1974.
5 min. phonotape (1 r. 7 1/2 i.p.s.)

1. Truman, Harry S, Pres. U.S., 1884-1972.
2. Miller, Merle, 1918-   /Plain speaking.
I. Douglas, Mike, 1925?-   II. Lindfors,
Viveca, 1920-   III. Steinberg, David.

Voice Lib.
M1390
Lindsay, John Vliet, 1921-
Apollo 11 (space flight): reception for
Apollo 11 astronauts in New York. Descrip-
tion of approach and ceremony at city hall.
Cardinal Cooke's invocation. Introduction
by Mayor Lindsay. Presentation of Medal of
Honor. Reply by all astronauts. Benediction.
NBC TV, August 13, 1969.
1 reel (7 in.) 7 1/2 in. per sec. phonotape.
1. Project Apollo. 2. Space flight to the moon. 3. Aldrin,
Edwin E   1930-   4. Collins, Michael, 1930-   5.
Armstrong, Neil, 1930-   I. Aldrin, Edwin E   1930-   II.
Collins, Michael, 1930-   III. Armstrong, Neil, 1930-   IV.
Cooke, Terence James, cardinal, 1921-   V. Lindsay, John Vliet,
1921-

Lindsay, Nicholas Vachel, 1879-1931.
Abraham Lincoln walks at midnight
Voice Lib.
M982
bd.4
Huston, Walter, 1884-1950.
Reading prose poem by Vachel Lindsay,
"Abraham Lincoln Walks at Midnight". Decca
Specialty, 1930.
1 reel (7 in.) 7 1/2 in. per sec.
phonotape.

I. Lindsay, Nicholas Vachel, 1879-1931./
Abraham Lincoln walks at midnight.

Voice Lib.
M1630
bd.2
Linkletter, Arthur Gordon, 1912-
An evening with Art Linkletter.
WKAR, April 16, 1974.
20 min. phonotape (1 r. 7 1/2 i.p.s.)

1. Linkletter, Arthur Gordon, 1912-

Voice Lib.
M342-
343,
bd.1
Lippman, Walter, 1889-
Luncheon for Lippman on his 70th birthday.
Voice of America, October 23, 1959.
2 reels (7 in.) 7 1/2 i.p.s.
phonotape.

1. Lippman, Walter, 1889-

Voice Lib.
614-
615
bd.1
Lippmann, Walter, 1889-
"Walter Lippmann - 1964"; describes his
relationships with high public officials,
threat of nuclear war, influence of balance
of power on world politics, NATO and General
Charles De Gaulle, European conditions,
changing Russian attitude, Communist China,
Southeast Asia, status of South Viet Nam,
De Gaulle and world conditions, appraises
De Gaulle's position in world history,
changing status of cold war, U.S. foreign aid,
(Continued on next card)

Voice Lib.
614-
615
bd.1
Lippmann, Walter, 1889-   "Walter
Lippmann - 1964". 1964. (Card 2)
U.S.-African relations, Cyprus problem,
changing U.S. attitude toward world, Cuban
situation, JFK's presidency, LBJ as president,
potential 1964 Republican presidential candidates and Democratic vice-presidential nomination and 1964 election, civil rights demonstra-
tions. CBS, April 8, 1964.
2 reels (7 in.) 7 1/2 in. per sec.
phonotape.
I. Sevareid, Arnold Eric, 1912-

Voice Lib.
M1285
bd.1
Lippmann, Walter, 1889-
Segment from PLB-TV program conducted by
Edward P. Morgan, containing the questioning
by six college students of Walter Lippmann
on the issues of Vietnam, the Presidency,
and the urban crisis. NBC-TV, November 26,
1967.
1 reel (7 in.) 7 1/2 in. per sec.
phonotape.

Voice Lib.
M1262
bd.2
Lipton, Lawrence, 1898-
Hagen, Carlos
Interviews by Carlos Hagen and Lawrence
Lipton with hippies in Golden Gate Park,
at summer happening; includes chants.
Hagen, June, 1967.
1 reel (7 in.) 7 1/2 in. per sec.
phonotape.

1. Lipton, Lawrence, 1898-

Voice Lib. Lipton, Lawrence, 1898-
M1261- Hagen, Carlos
1262   Two weeks in Haight-Ashbury district of
bd.1   San Francisco by Lawrence Lipton and Carlos
       Hagen, recording hippie music and philosophy,
       including interview with a priest.   June,
       1967.
          2 reels (7 in.)   7 1/2 in. per sec.
       phonotape.

          I. Lipton, Lawrence, 1898-

          ( )

         Lisager, Peter
Voice Lib.
M1369   "The men who covered Ike". CBS-TV Face the Nation program,
bd. 2   discussing the late General Dwight David Eisenhower, by the
        newspaper and TV correspondents. UPI, Merriman Smith;
        Newsweek, Kenneth Crawford; Chicago Daily News, Peter
        Lisager; AP, Jack Bell; CBS, George Herman, acting as emcee.
        CBS-TV, March 30, 1969.
           1 reel (7 in.)   7 1/2 i.p.s.   phonotape.

           I. Eisenhower, Dwight David, Pres. U.S., 1890-1969.
        L. Smith, Merriman. II. Crawford, Kenneth. III. Lisager,
        Peter. IV. Bell, Jack. V. Herman, George.

           O

         "Listen: a Scrapbook in Sound"
Voice Lib.
613   March, Fredric, 1897-
bd.1   "Listen: a Scrapbook In Sound"; condensed
        version of National Voice Library's "Hark I
        The Years", as used in Riverside Radio's
        continuing program series "Listen".   WRVR,
        March, 1964.
           1 reel (7 in.)   7 1/2 in. per sec.
        phonotape.

           I. Title.

           O

         LITERATURE, MODERN - 20TH CENTURY - HISTORY
                  AND CRITICISM
Voice Lib.
M1732   Aldridge, John W
        Address at Michigan State University.
        Introduction by Russel B. Nye.   WKAR,
        October 28, 1968.
           50 min.   phonotape (1 r.   7 1/2 i.p.s.)

           1. Literature, Modern - 20th century - Hist.
        & crit. 2. Fiction - 20th century - Hist. &
        crit. I. Nye, Russel Blaine, 1913-

           O

Voice Lib.
M1089 Little, Malcolm, 1925-1965.
       Speaking at Erickson Kiva on MSU campus to
       students and faculty about race problems and
       the Black Muslim religion and its ideas,
       followed by answers to questions from the
       audience.   Location recording, January 23,
       1963.
          1 reel (7 in.)   7 1/2 in. per sec.
       phonotape.

          O

Voice Lib.
M230   Little, Malcolm, 1925-1965.
bd.2   Excerpts of question and answer session
        with students at Michigan State University.
        January 23, 1963.
           1 reel (7 in.)   7 1/2 i.p.s.   phonotape.

           1. Race discrimination.

           O
                                        OFFICIAL

Voice Lib.
M1087   Little, Malcolm, 1925-1965.
bd.1   Speaking at MSU press conference about
        race problem and aim of Black Muslims;
        Meredith case and Mississippi; followed
        by various takes of interview for MSU film.
        Location recording, June 22, 1963.
           1 reel (7 in.)   7 1/2 i.p.s.   phonotape.

           1. Black Muslims. 2. Race discrimination -
        U.S.

           O

         Little, Malcolm, 1925-1965
Voice Lib.
M866-   Project '64 (Radio program)
867   Harlem, the black ghetto: actual sound and
bd.1   description of life in Harlem and discusses
        Negro residents' problems; Negroes relating
        experiences, impressions, and emotions; opinions
        by various Negroes of more advanced education;
        discussions by white school principals. Covers
        social and economic problems of Negroes,
        juvenile delinquence, drug addiction, broken
        homes, unemployment. Discussion of Harlem
        Negro youths' attempts to achieve manhood;
        religious beliefs and philosophy of the
                              ( )(Continued on next card)

         Little, Malcolm, 1925-1965
Voice Lib.
M866-   Project '64 (Radio program)   Harlem...
867   1964.   (Card 2)
bd.1
        Black Muslims' desire for separate political
        and economic country; includes Malcolm X
        describing his philosophy and ideas in the
        Black Muslim movement. Documentary program
        produced for CBC by Lloyd Chester, written by
        A. Clark and narrated by Percy Rodreguiz [sic]
        CBC, 1964.
           2 reels (7 in.)   7 1/2 in. per sec.   phonotape.
           L. Negroes - Social conditions. L. Little, Malcolm, 1925-1965.

           O

         Little, Malcolm, 1925-1965
Voice Lib.
M867   Project '64 (Radio program)
bd.2-   Negro revolt in Harlem: documentary program describing
M869   the place of the Negro in American society; the Negro search for
bd.1   change, with or without white help; discussion of Negro press;
        Negroes' cultural background and association with black Africa.
        Malcolm X discusses Black Muslim movement, critizing white
        infiltration of NAACP Urban League Corp.; comparison of
        differences between the Muslims and Black Nationalists. Summary
        of Negro revolt and group singing of "We shall overcome".
        CBC, 1964.
           3 reels (7 in.)   7 1/2 in. per sec.   phonotape.

           L. Negroes - Social conditions. L. Little, Malcolm, 1925-1965.

           O

Little children must not starve

Voice Lib.
M803   LaGuardia, Fiorello Henry, 1882-1947.
Director-General of UNRRA speaking from
University of Vermont to the country's
wheat farmers aid in feeding little children
of other lands. Entitled: "Little children
must not starve". UN Archives, April 4,
1946.
1 reel (7 in.)   7 1/2 in. per sec.
phonotape.
I. Title: Little children must not starve.

C1
A6   The little woman
Whorf, Michael, 1933-
The little woman.
1 tape cassette. (The visual sounds of
Mike Whorf. Art, music, and letters, A6)

Originally presented on his radio program, Kaleidoscope,
WJR, Detroit.
Duration: 34 min., 45 sec.
Louisa May Alcott's story is found in her work "Little women,"
but there is another view of her life.

I. Alcott, Louisa May, 1832-1888. I. Title.

"The littlest girl"

Voice Lib.
M793   Hilliard, Robert
bd.2   "The littlest girl"; acted and dramatized
by Hilliard from Richard Harding Davis'
story "Her first appearance." Victor, 1912.
8 min., 52 sec. phonotape (1 r.   7 1/2
i.p.s.)

I. Title. II. Davis, Richard Harding,
1864-1916.

Voice Lib.
396   Litvinoff, Maksim Maksimovich, 1876-1951.
bd.3   League of Nations speech at Geneva.
National Vocarium, September 21, 1938.
1 reel (7 in.)   7 1/2 in. per sec.
phonotape.

"Liver Story"

Voice Lib.
539   Edison, Thomas Alva, 1847-1931.
bd.6   "Liver Story", a humorous story related
by Edison. Introduced by Walter H. Miller.
National Vocarium, 1906.
1 reel (7 in.)   7 1/2 in. per sec.
phonotape.

I. Miller, Walter H   II. Title.

Livingstone, Mary

Voice Lib.
M622   Radio in the 1940's (Part III): a series of
bd.1-   excerpts from important broadcasts of the 1940's; a sample
bd.15   of radio of the period. NVL, April, 1964.
1 reel (7 in.)   7 1/2 in. per sec. phonotape.
I. Radio programs. I. Miller, Alton Glenn, 1909(?)-1944. II.
Diles, Ken   III. Wilson, Donald Harlow, 1900-   IV.
Livingstone, Mary   V. Benny, Jack, 1894-   VI. Harris,
Phil   VII. Merman, Ethel, 1909-   VIII. Smith, "Wonderful"
IX. Bennett, Richard Dyer   X. Louis, Joe, 1914-   XI.
Eisenhower, Dwight David, Pres. U.S., 1890-1969. XII. MacArthur,
Douglas, 1880-1964. XIII. Romulo, Carlos Pena, 1899-   XIV.
Welles, Orson, 1915-   XV. Jackson, Robert Houghwout, 1892-1954.
XVI. LaGuardia, Fiorello Henry, 1882-1945. XVII. Nehru, Jawa-
harlal, 1889-1964. XVIII. Gandhi, Mohandas Karamchand, 1869-1948.

Voice Lib.
M975   Lloyd-George, David Lloyd George, 1st earl,
bd.2   1863-1945.
Speech on the budget. Rococo-Can.,
1909.
1 reel (7 in.)   7 1/2 in. per sec.
phonotape.

LOCAL TRANSIT

Voice Lib.
M1551-   Young, Andrew, 1932-
1552   A lecture series by the College of Urban
Affairs, Michigan State University, with
Prof. Robert Green and Asst. Prof. Barnes
McConnell. MSU Dept. of Information
Services, January 17, 1974.
90 min. phonotape (2 r.   7 1/2 i.p.s.)

1. Local transit. 2. Atlanta. I. Green,
Robert Lee. II. McConnell, Barnes.

LOCAL TRANSIT - U.S.

Voice Lib.
M1733   Sawhill, John Crittenden, 1936-
Speech at the National Press Club luncheon,
concerning the international energy picture,
with Clyde Lamont. WKAR, June 20, 1974.
50 min. phonotape (1 r.   7 1/2 i.p.s.)

1. Power resources - U.S. 2. Energy
shortage. 3. Local transit - U.S.
I. Lamont, Clyde

Lodge, Henry Cabot, 1850-1924

Voice Lib.
M617   Radio in the 1920's: a series of excerpts
bd.1-   from important broadcasts of the 1920's,
bd.25   with brief prologue and epilogue; a sample
of radio of the period. NVL, April, 1964.
1 reel (7 in.)   7 1/2 in. per sec.
phonotape.
I. Radio programs. I. Marconi, Guglielmo, marchese, 1874-
1937. II. Kendall, H   G   III. Coolidge, Calvin, Pres. U.S.,
1872-1933. IV. Wilson, Woodrow, Pres. U.S., 1856-1924. V.
Roosevelt, Franklin Delano, Pres. U.S., 1882-1945. VI. Lodge,
Henry Cabot, 1850-1924. VII. LaGuardia, Fiorello Henry, 1882-1947.
VIII. The Happiness Boys (Radio program) IX. Gallagher and Sheen.
X. Barney Google. XI. Vallee, Rudy, 1901-   XII. The two
(Continued on next card)

Voice Lib.
M737   Lodge, Sir Oliver Joseph, 1851-1940.
bd.2   Time and space; lecture on the measurement of interstellar distances by timing effects of New Star explosions.
8 min., 23 sec. phonotape (1 r. 7 1/2 i.p.s.)

I. Title.

Voice Lib.
M1470 Loebe, Paul, 1875-
bd.1   Radio remarks while president of the "Reichstag". October 16, 1930.
1 reel (7 in.) 7 1/2 in. per sec. phonotape.

Voice Lib.
M1470 Loebe, Paul, 1875-
bd.3   Speaking as acting Reichstag President. May 12, 1932.
1 reel (7 in.) 7 1/2 in. per sec. phonotape.

Loewe, Frederick, 1904-
Voice Lib.
126   Lerner, Alan Jay, 1918-
Lerner and Loewe; condensed NBC-TV special with Julie Andrews, Richard Burton, Robert Goulet, Alan Lerner and Frederick Loewe. NBC, February 2, 1962.
1 reel (7 in.) 7 1/2 in. per sec. phonotape.

I. Andrews, Julie, 1935-   II. Burton, Richard, 1925-   III. Goulet, Robert Gerard, 1933-   IV. Loewe, Frederick, 1904-

---

Voice Lib.
M374 Logan, Joshua Lockwood, 1908-
Talks with Elliot Norton; compares motion picture themes with theater themes, changing mores of American motion pictures, pressure groups and television programs, restraints on free speech, criticism of Hollywood, movie censorship, economics of modern theater. Lowell Institute (NET) September 28, 1961.
1 reel (7 in.) 7 1/2 in. per sec. phonotape.
I. Norton, Elliot

Voice Lib.
M781- Lomax, Alan, 1915-
782   Folk songs and conversation with Woody Guthrie. Library of Congress, March 21, 1940.
bd.1
2 reels (7 in.) 7 1/2 in. per sec. phonotape.

I. Guthrie, Woody, 1912-1967.
1. Folk music - U.S.

Voice Lib.
M782 Lomax, Alan, 1915-
bd.2- Dust Bowl songs and conversation with
784   Woody Guthrie. Library of Congress,
bd.1   March 22, 1940.
3 reels (7 in.) 7 1/2 in. per sec. phonotape.

1. Folk music - U.S.   I. Guthrie, Woody, 1912-1967.

LONDON, JACK, 1876-1916
C1
A21   Whorf, Michael, 1933-
The world of Jack London.
1 tape cassette. (The visual sounds of Mike Whorf. Art, music, and letters, A21)
Originally presented on his radio program, Kaleidoscope, WJR, Detroit.
Duration: 30 min., 30 sec.
Adventures in the north, of roustabouts, rogues, sailors, and longshoremen, this was the world of Jack London, which he brought to the readers of the world in his exciting narratives.
I. London, Jack, 1876-1916   I. Title.

Voice Lib.
M1044 London after dark; on-the-spot recordings of various points during the London air-raid attacks: the Savoy Hotel kitchen, Trafalgar Square, anti-aircraft battery near London, air-raid shelter. With newsmen Edward R. Murrow, Robert Bowman, Raymond Van Denny, Larry Lesueur, Eric Sevareid, Vincent Sheean, J. B. Priestley, Michael Standing, and Winfred Von Thomas. CBS and BBC, August 24, 1940.
1 reel (7 in.) 7 1/2 in. per sec. phonotape.

I. Murrow, Edward Roscoe, 1908-1965. II. Bowman, Robert III. Van Denny, Raymond IV. Lesueur, Laurence Edward, 1909- V. Sevareid, Arnold Eric, 1912- VI. Sheean, Vincent, 1899- VII. Priestley, John Boynton, 1894- VIII. Standing, Michael IX. Von Thomas, Winfred

---

Lone Ranger (radio program)
Voice Lib.
M1675 Theme songs from the Green hornet, the Lone
bd.2   Ranger, Dick Tracy, and Hop Harrigan.
Golden Age Radio Records, 1940's.
10 min. phonotape (1 r. 7 1/2 i.p.s.)

I. Green hornet (radio program) II. Lone Ranger (radio program) III. Dick Tracy (radio program) IV. Hop Harrigan (radio program)

Lone Ranger (Radio program)

Voice Lib.
M1453   Documentary TV program produced by the
        University of Michigan on the Lone Ranger
        radio program, including former participants
        of that program. University of Michigan
        TV, 1970.
        1 reel (7 in.)   7 1/2 in. per sec.
        phonotape.

        1. Lone Ranger (Radio program)   I. Lone
        Ranger (Radio program)

Voice Lib.
M269   Long, Earl Kemp, 1895-1960.
bd.1   Excerpts from various speeches made by
        Governor Long of Louisiana. News Records,
        Inc., 1961.
        1 reel (7 in.)   7 1/2 in. per sec.
        phonotape.

Voice Lib.
522   Long, Huey Pierce, 1893-1935.
bd.1   Excerpt from political speech regarding
        homesteads for every American family.
        CBS, 1934.
        1 reel (7 in.)   7 1/2 in. per sec.
        phonotape.

Long, Huey Pierce, 1893-1935
Voice Lib.
M618   Radio in the 1930's (Part I): a series of
bd.1-   excerpts from important broadcasts of the
14   1930's; a sample of radio of the period.
        NVL, April, 1964.
        1 reel (7 in.)   7 1/2 in. per sec. phonotape.
        L. Shaw, George Bernard, 1856-1950. II. Crosby, Bing, 1901-
        III. Barkley, Alban William, 1877-1956. IV. Roosevelt, Franklin
        Delano, Pres. U.S., 1882-1945. V. Hoover, Herbert Clark, Pres.
        U.S., 1874-1964. VI. Long, Huey Pierce, 1893-1935. VII. Town-
        send, Francis Everett, 1867-1960. VIII. Coughlin, Charles Edward,
        1891-   IX. Rogers, Will, 1879-1935. X. Pius XII, Pope, 1876-
        1958. XI. Edward VIII, king of Great Britain, 1894-1972. XII.
        Barrymore, John, 1882-1942. XIII. Woollcott, Alexander, 1887-
        1943. XIV. Allen, Fred, 1894-1956. XV. Benchley, Robert Charles,
        1889-1945.

Long, Huey Pierce, 1893-1935
Voice Lib.
572-   I can hear it now (radio program)
573   1933-1946. CBS, 1948.
bd.1   2 reels (7 in.)   7 1/2 in. per sec.
        phonotape.
        L. Murrow, Edward Roscoe, 1908-1965. II. LaGuardia, Fiorello
        Henry, 1882-1947. III. Chamberlain, Neville, 1869-1949. IV.
        Roosevelt, Franklin Delano, Pres. U.S., 1882-1945. V. Churchill,
        Winston Leonard Spencer, 1874-1965. VI. Gaulle, Charles de,
        Pres. France, 1890-1970. VII. Eisenhower, Dwight David, Pres. U.S.,
        1890-1969. VIII. Willkie, Wendell Lewis, 1892-1944. IX. Martin,
        Joseph William, 1884-1968. X. Elizabeth II, Queen of Great Britain,
        1926-   XI. Margaret Rose, Princess of Gt. Brit., 1930-   XII.
        Johnson, Hugh Samuel, 1882-1942. XIII. Smith, Alfred Emanuel,
        1873-1944. XIV. Lindberg, [ ]arles Augustus, 1902-   XV. Davis,

        (Continued on next card)

The long dark hours - J. F. K.

C1
S69   Whorf, Michael, 1933-
        The long dark hours - J. F. K.
        1 tape cassette. (The visual sounds of
        Mike Whorf. Social, S69)
        Originally presented on his radio program, Kaleidoscope,
        WJR, Detroit.
        Duration: 36 min.
        The reality and the tragedy of the loss of John F. Kennedy
        brings this account of those dark days of November. An account
        of the death of a President, of the shock to a nation, and a
        memorial to the future of mankind.

        L. Kennedy, John Fitzgerald, Pres. U.S., 1917-1963 -
        Assassination. L. Title

The long drought - prohibition

C1
S76   Whorf, Michael, 1933-
        The long drought - prohibition.
        1 tape cassette. (The visual sour[ ] of
        Mike Whorf. Social, S76)
        Originally presented on his radio program, Kaleidoscope,
        WJR, Detroit.
        Duration: 37 min.
        A nostalgic picture of the Eighteenth Amendment - prohibition.
        A historic picture of alcohol throughout American history from the
        Indian's first intoxication through the repeal of prohibition.

        L. Prohibition. L. Title.

LONGFELLOW, HENRY WADSWORTH, 1807-1882

C1
A36   Whorf, Michael, 1933-
        An imposing symposium.
        1 tape cassette. (The visual sounds of Mike Whorf.
        Art, music and letters, A36)
        Originally presented on his radio program, Kaleidoscope,
        WJR, Detroit.
        Duration: 38 min., 30 sec.
        Longfellow, Agassiz, Emerson, Dana, these were the kings of
        the world of literature in the nineteenth century. Every Saturday
        night they met at a private club to discuss the current events of
        their day.

        L. Longfellow, Henry Wadsworth, 1807-1882. 2. Agassiz,
        Louis, 1807-1873. 3. Emerson, Ralph Waldo, 1803-1882-
        4. Dana, Richard Henry, 1815-1882. L. Title.

LONGFELLOW, HENRY WADSWORTH, 1807-1882

C1
A28   Whorf, Michael, 1933-
        Verses from the heart - Henry W. Longfellow.
        1 tape cassette. (The visual sounds of
        Mike Whorf. Art, music and letters, A28)
        Originally presented on his radio program, Kaleidoscope,
        WJR, Detroit.
        Duration: 37 min., 30 sec.
        He was the dean of poets and held in high esteem by his fellow
        writers; he was nature's poet in the 19th century and a man who
        blended words and beauty in an extraordinarily skillful manner.

        L. Longfellow, Henry Wadsworth, 1807-1882. L. Title.

Voice Lib.
M1382 "A look at RFK". Memorial program by David
bd.1   Frost on first anniversary of assassination
        of Senator Robert Kennedy. Includes inter-
        view broadcast originally in David Frost's
        series "The Next President of the U.S."
        ABC-TV, June 5, 1969.
        1 reel (7 in.)   7 1/2 in. per sec.
        phonotape.

        I. Frost, David Parndine, 1939-
        1. Kennedy, Robert Francis, 1925-1968

Voice Lib.
M1265 Lord, Walter, 1917-
bd.2   Interview with author Walter Lord on NBC-TV
          "Today" show about his latest book "The incredi-
          ble victory", pertaining to the Battle of Midway
          during World War II. Questioned by Burgess
          Meredith. NBC-TV, August 15, 1967.
          1 reel (7 in.) 7 1/2 in. per sec. phonotape.

          L. Midway, Battle of, 1942. L. Meredith, Burgess, 1907-
          IL Title: The incredible victory.

○

Voice Lib. LOS ANGELES - RIOTS, 1965
M936-   The fire this time; radio broadcast. A
937   special documentary with actual sounds
bd.1   and comments on the significance of the
         August, 1965 five-day riots in Watts,
         California. KPFK, August, 1965.
         2 reels (7 in.) 7 1/2 in. per sec.
         phonotape.

         1. Los Angeles - Riots, 1965.

○

LOS ANGELES - RIOTS, 1965
Voice Lib.
M910-   Stout, Bill
911,   Resumé of the Watts riots in Los Angeles
bd.1   County, during the most violent riots in Los
         Angeles history; including actual sounds and
         voices of Police Chief William H. Parker,
         Mayor Yorty, etc. CBS, August, 1965.
         2 reels (7 in.) 7 1/2 i.p.s. phonotape.

         1. Los Angeles - Riots, 1965. I. Parker,
         William H., 1902-   II. Yorty, Samuel
         William, 1909-

○

C1   The lost colony of Roanoke
H40   Whorf, Michael, 1933-
         The lost colony of Roanoke.
         1 tape cassette. (The visual sounds of
         Mike Whorf. History and heritage, H40)

         Originally presented on his radio program, Kaleidoscope,
         WJR, Detroit.
         Duration: 39 min., 30 sec.
         Prior to the coming of the Pilgrims, a group of similar hardy
         souls settled in Virginia. Their colony thrived and grew prosperous
         and then for some unknown reason, it perished.

         L. Raleigh'Roanoke Colonies, 1584-1590. L Title.

○

Louis, Joe, 1914-
Voice Lib.
M622   Radio in the 1940's (Part III): a series of
bd.1-   excerpts from important broadcasts of the 1940's; a sample
bd.15   of radio of the period. NVL, April, 1964.
         1 reel (7 in.) 7 1/2 in. per sec. phonotape.
         L. Radio programs. L. Miller, Alton Glenn, 1909(?)-1944. IL
         Diles, Ken   III. Wilson, Donald Harlow, 1900-   IV.
         Livingstone, Mary   V. Benny, Jack, 1894-   VL Harris,
         Phil   VIL Merman, Ethel, 1909-   VIIL Smith, "Wonderful"
         IX. Bennett, Richard Dyer   X. Louis, Joe, 1914-   XL
         Eisenhower, Dwight David, Pres. U.S., 1890-1969. XIL MacArthur,
         Douglas, 1880-1964. XIIL Romulo, Carlos Pena, 1899-   XIV.
         Welles, Orson, 1915-   XV. Jackson, Robert Houghwout, 1892-1954.
         XVL LaGuardia, Fiorello Henry, 1882-1945. XVIL Nehru, Jawa-
         harlal, 1889-1964. XVIIL Gandhi, Mohandas Karamchand, 1869-1948.

○

LOVE-LETTERS

C1
A39   Whorf, Michael, 1933-
         Love letters.
         1 tape cassette. (The visual sounds of
         Mike Whorf. Art, music and letters, A39)
         Originally presented on his radio program, Kaleidoscope,
         WJR, Detroit.
         Duration: 36 min., 45 sec.
         In this program we take a different tack in looking into the
         infamous and famous characters of history. Though they wrote
         words for the world, there were some words meant for the eyes
         of the few.

         L. Love-letters. L. Title.

○

Love letters

C1
A39   Whorf, Michael, 1933-
         Love letters.
         1 tape cassette. (The visual sounds of
         Mike Whorf. Art, music and letters, A39)
         Originally presented on his radio program, Kaleidoscope,
         WJR, Detroit.
         Duration: 36 min., 45 sec.
         In this program we take a different tack in looking into the
         infamous and famous characters of history. Though they wrote
         words for the world, there were some words meant for the eyes
         of the few.

         L. Love-letters. L. Title.

○

         The love song of J. Alfred Prufrock
Voice Lib.
M1224   Eliot, Thomas Stearns, 1888-1965.
bd.2-   Various poems read by Eliot, including
1225   "The Love Song of J. Alfred Prufrock".
bd.1   Bergman.
         2 reels (7 in.) 7 1/2 in. per sec.
         phonotape.

         I. Title: The love song of J. Alfred
         Prufrock.

○

         Loveless love
Voice Lib.
M946   Handy, William Christopher, 1873-1958.
bd.8   Singing his own composition "Loveless
         Love" with piano accompaniment. GRV private
         recording, 1953.
         1 reel (7 in.) 7 1/2 in. per sec.
         phonotape.

         I. Title: Loveless love.

○

         Lovell, James Arthur, 1928-
Voice Lib.
M917   Gemini 7 (space flight): Frank McGee's resumé
bd.1   of space flights of astronauts Frank Borman
         and James Lovell, Jr., in Gemini 7, commencing
         Dec. 4, 1956 to Dec. 18, 1965, and of astro-
         nauts Walter Schirra and Thomas Stafford in
         Gemini 6, which rendezvoused in space;
         including various launching actual reports
         and interview with Wally Schirra; comments
         by Huntley and Brinkley. NBC TV, December
         18, 1965.
         1 reel (7 in.) 7 1/2 in. per sec.
         phonotape.
         ○ (Continued on next card)

Voice Lib. Lovell, James Arthur, 1928-
M1347- Apollo 8 (space flight): recovery. CBS TV
1348,   description of recovery of astronauts and
bd.1   their reception on aircraft carrier "York-
         town". CBS TV, December 27, 1968.
         2 reels (7 in.)   7 1/2 in. per sec.
         phonotape.
           1. Project Apollo. 2. Anders, William
         Alison, 1933-   3. Lovell, James Arthur, 1928-
         4. Borman, Frank, 1928-   I. Anders, William
         Alison, 1933-   II. Lovell, James Arthur,
         1928-   III. Borman, Frank, 1928-

Voice Lib. Lovell, James Arthur, 1928-
M1348   Apollo 8 (space flight): reception of Apollo
bd.2   8 astronauts at Joint Session of Congress,
        including addresses by the astronauts.
        CBS TV, January 1, 1969.
        1 reel (7 in.)   7 1/2 in. per sec.
        phonotape.
          1. Project Apollo. 2. Anders, William
        Alison, 1933-   3. Lovell, James Arthur, 1928-
        4. Borman, Frank, 1928-   I. Anders, William
        Alison, 1933-   II. Lovell, James Arthur,
        1928-   III. Borman, Frank, 1928-   IV.
        McCormack, John William, 1891-

Voice Lib. Lovell, James Arthur, 1928-
M1351   Apollo 8 (space flight): interview with
bd.1   astronauts William Anders, James Lovell,
        and Frank Borman on CBS TV program "Face
        the nation". CBS TV, January 12, 1969.
        1 reel (7 in.)   7 1/2 in. per sec.
        phonotape.
          1. Project Apollo. 2. Anders, William
        Alison, 1933-   3. Lovell, James Arthur, 1928-
        4. Borman, Frank, 1928-   I. Anders, William
        Alison, 1933-   II. Lovell, James Arthur,
        1928-   III. Borman, Frank, 1928-

Voice Lib. Lovell, James Arthur, 1928-
M1423   Apollo 13 (space flight): resumé of flight
        of Apollo 13, including lift-off, mal-
        function, and splashdown, and interviews
        on future of space program. NBC TV,
        April, 1970.
        1 reel (7 in.)   7 1/2 in. per sec.
        phonotape.
          1. Project Apollo. 2. Space flight to the moon. 3. Haise,
        Fred W   1934-   4. Lovell, James Arthur, 1928-   5.
        Swigert, John L   1932-   I. Haise, Fred W   1934-
        II. Lovell, James Arthur, 1928-   III. Swigert, John L   1932-

Voice Lib. Lovell, James Arthur, 1928-
M1424   Apollo 13 (space flight): oxygen malfunction
        on Apollo 13 described by NASA, astronauts,
        and Howard K. Smith. ABC TV, April 14, 1970.
        1 reel (7 in.)   7 1/2 in. per sec.
        phonotape.
          1. Project Apollo. 2. Space flight to the
        moon. 3. Haise, Fred W   1934-   4.
        Lovell, James Arthur, 1928-   5. Swigert,
        John L   1932-   I. Haise, Fred W   1934-
        II. Lovell, James Arthur, 1928-   III. Swigert,
        John L   1932-   IV. Smith, Howard Kingsbury,
        1914-

                    Lowe, David, 1913 or 14-1965
Voice Lib.
M740   Luthuli, Albert John, 1898-1967.
bd.3   Remarks at interview with David Lowe in
        Oslo, Norway at Oslo University upon awarding
        of Peace Prize: help needed for black natives
        if non-violence in South Africa is to continue,
        and his belief in goodness of man. CBS, 1961.
        1 reel (7 in.)   7 1/2 in. per sec.
        phonotape.

             I. Lowe, David, 1913 or 14-1965.

C1   LOWE, THADDEUS S.C., 1832-1913
FA13   Whorf, Michael, 1933-
           Thaddeus S. C. Lowe.
           1 tape cassette. (The visual sounds of
        Mike Whorf. The forgotten American, FA13)
           Originally presented on his radio program, Kaleidoscope,
        WJR, Detroit.
           Duration: 12 min., 20 sec.
           Aeronaut and inventor, Lowe acted as an aerial spy for the
        Union in the Civil War. He was the father of cold storage and
        invented water gas.

           I. Lowe, Thaddeus, S.C., 1832-1913.   I. Title.

                    Lowell, Robert, 1917-
Voice Lib.
M1599- A quiet requiem for Ezra Pound, with poets
1600   Robert Lowell, Robert Fitzgerald, James
        Laughlin, and Robert McGregor. Modern
        Language Center, Harvard University,
        December 4, 1972.
        70 min.   phonotape (2 r.   7 1/2 i.p.s.)

          I. Pound, Ezra Loomis, 1885-1972.   I. Lowell, Robert,
        1917-   II. Fitzgerald, Robert, 1910-   III. Laughlin,
        James, 1914-   IV. McGregor, Robert,

Voice Lib.
652   Luce, Clare (Boothe), 1903-
bd.19   When she resigned as U.S. Ambassador
        to Brazil. CBS, May 1, 1950.
        1 reel (7 in.)   7 1/2 in. per sec.
        phonotape.

                    Luce, Clare (Boothe) 1903-
Voice Lib.
573   I can hear it now (radio program)
bd.2-   1945-1949. CBS, 1950?
574   2 reels (7 in.)   7 1/2 in. per sec.
bd.1   phonotape.
          I. Murrow, Edward Roscoe, 1908-1965. II. Nehru, Jawaharlal,
        1889-1964. III. Philip, duke of Edinburgh, 1921-   IV. Elizabeth II,
        Queen of Great Britain, 1926-   V. Ferguson, Homer, 1889-   VI.
        Hughes, Howard Robard, 1905-   VII. Marshall, George Catlett,
        1880-   VIII. Ruth, George Herman, 1895-1948. IX. Lilienthal,
        David Eli, 1899-   X. Trout, Robert, 1908-   XI. Gage, Arthur.
        XII. Jackson, Robert Houghwout, 1892-1954. XIII. Gromyko, Ana-
        tolii Andreevich, 1908-   XIV. Baruch, Bernard Mannes, 1870-
        1965. XV. Churchill, Winston Leonard Spencer, 1874-1965. XVI.
        Winchell, Walter, 1897-19   XVII. Davis, Elmer Holmes, 1890-
                                    (Continued on next card)

Luce, Clare (Boothe) 1903–

Voice Lib.
235– Tito, Josip Broz, Pres. Yugoslavia, 1892–
237 Interview by Edward R. Murrow, with comments
bd.1 and analysis by Richard C. Hottelet, Clare
Boothe Luce, William H. Lawrence, and Hamilton
F. Armstrong, CBS, June 30, 1957.
3 reels (7 in.) 7 1/2 in. per sec.
phonotape.

I. Hottelet, Richard Curt II. Luce,
Clare (Boothe) 1903– III. Lawrence,
William H IV. Armstrong, Hamilton Fish,
1893–1973.

C1
R20 **LUTHER, MARTIN, 1483–1546**

Whorf, Michael, 1933–
The reformer – Martin Luther.
1 tape cassette. (The visual sounds of
Mike Whorf. Religion, R20)

Originally presented on his radio program, Kaleidoscope,
WJR, Detroit.
Duration: 43 min., 45 sec.
With the renaissance of culture came also a rebirth of religion;
to spearhead this new age was Martin Luther. Thus Protestantism
was born and here is the man and the movement.

I. Luther, Martin, 1483–1546. I. Title.

Voice Lib. Lucey, Patrick Joseph, 1918–
M1707 Milliken, William G 1922–
bd. Governors Milliken, Lucey and Askew at
the Governors' Conference in Seattle on the
new financing morality. Richard Threlkeld,
reporting. CBS, June 5, 1974.
3 min. phonotape (1 r. 7 1/2 i.p.s.)

1. Watergate Affair, 1972– I. Lucey,
Patrick Joseph, 1918– II. Askew,
Reubin O'D. III. Threlkeld, Richard.

Voice Lib.
M740 Luthuli, Albert John, 1898–1967.
bd.3 Remarks at interview with David Lowe in
Oslo, Norway at Oslo University upon awarding
of Peace Prize: help needed for black natives
if non-violence in South Africa is to continue,
and his belief in goodness of man. CBS, 1961.
1 reel (7 in.) 7 1/2 in. per sec.
phonotape.

I. Lowe, David, 1913 or 14–1965.

LUMUMBA, PATRICE, 1925–1961

Voice Lib.
M811– Nkrumah, Kwame, Pres. of Ghana, 1909–1972.
813 Address at plenary meeting 961 of General
Assembly of the United Nations in New York.
Topics: assassination of Patrice Lumumba;
opinions on the U.N.; analysis of the Congo
situation; African affairs in general;
financial situations in new countries. U.N.
Archives, March 7, 1961.
3 reels (7 in.) 7 1/2 in. per sec.
phonotape.

1. Lumumba, Patrice, 1925–1961.

Voice Lib.
M1028 Lux presents Hollywood: montage of excerpts
bd.7 from various Lux radio shows. George Raft,
Virginia Mayo, Cedric Hardwicke, and
Ingrid Bergman. Michigan State University,
Department of Television and Radio, 1940's.
1 reel (7 in.) 7 1/2 in. per sec.
phonotape.

I. Raft, George II. Mayo, Virginia
III. Hardwicke, Sir Cedric, 1893–1964. IV.
Bergman, Ingrid, 1917–

Voice Lib.
M1744 Luns, Joseph Marie Antoine Hubert, 1911–
bd.2 At the signing of the Brussels Pact, on
the "Today Show". WILX-TV, June 25, 1974.
2 min. phonotape (1 r. 7 1/2 i.p.s.)

1. Peace. 2. Disarmament.

LYFORD, JOSEPH P
Voice Lib.
M1249 Huntley, Chet, 1911–
bd.1 Documentary TV program: "The Talk in
Vandalia", first capital of state of Illinois,
prompted by Joseph P. Lyford's book "What's
Wrong with Vandalia", a small American mid-
western community. Discussion covers automation
and unemployment problems, farm problems,
increasing of intellectual activities. NBC,
April 30, 1967.
1 reel (7 in.) 7 1/2 in. per sec. phonotape.
I. Vandalia, Ill. 2. Lyford, Joseph P I. The
talk in Vandalia (Television program)

Voice Lib.
M726, Lunt, Alfred, 1893–
bd.1; "The Magnificent Yankee", a Hallmark-
727, sponsored TV dramatization of the life of
bd.1 Justice Oliver Wendell Holmes. NBC, January
28, 1965.
2 reels (7 in.) 7 1/2 in. per sec.
phonotape.

1. Holmes, Oliver Wendell, 1809–1894.
I. Fontanne, Lynne 887(?)– TITLE

Lynd, Robert Staughton, 1892–
Middletown
Voice Lib.
M894 Allen, Frederick Lewis, 1890–
bd.4 Reviewing books "Middletown" and
"Middletown in Transition", by Robert S.
Lynd and Helen Merrell Lynd. WQXR,
January 19, 1938.
1 reel (7 in.) 7 1/2 in. per sec.
phonotape.

I. Lynd, Robert Staughton, 1892–
Middletown. II. Lynd, Robert Staughton,
1892– /Middletown in transition.

Voice Lib.
M894   Lynd, Robert Staughton, 1892-
bd.4   Middletown in transition
           Allen, Frederick Lewis, 1890-
               Reviewing books "Middletown" and
           "Middletown in Transition", by Robert S.
           Lynd and Helen Merrell Lynd.   WQXR,
           January 19, 1938.
               1 reel (7 in.)   7 1/2 in. per sec.
           phonotape.

               I. Lynd, Robert Staughton, 1892-   /
           Middletown. II. Lynd, Robert Staughton,
           1892-   /Middletown in transition.

Voice Lib.
M1037   Lyons, Leonard
bd.1   Biography in sound (radio program)
               "The Actor", narrated by Morgan Beatty.
           Cast includes Tallulah Bankhead, Hy Gardner,
           Rocky Graziano, Arthur Miller, Uta Hagen,
           Jackie Cooper, Sir Laurence Olivier, Gad
           Gaylher, Barbara Ashley, Hortense Powdermaker,
           Peter Ustinov, Alfred Hitchcock, Leonard Lyons,
           John Guston, Helen Hayes, Dick Mayne, Ralph
           Bellamy, Lionel Barrymore, Sir Ralph Richardson,
           José Ferrer, and Walter Kerr.   NBC Radio, 1950's.
               1 reel (7 in.)   7 1/2 in. per sec.
           phonotape.

                               (Continued on next card)

Voice Lib.
M795   McAdoo, William Gibbs, 1863-1941.
bd.6   Speaking about plan to revise taxes.
           1910.
               1 reel (7 in.)   7 1/2 in. per sec.
           phonotape.

Voice Lib.
M740   MacArthur, Douglas, 1880-1964.
bd.8-A   Excerpts of remarks made in Australia
           pledging to liberate Philippines, using
           famous quote, "I shall return".   CBS,
           1944.
               1 reel (7 in.)   7 1/2 in. per sec.
           phonotape.

               1. World War, 1939-1945 - Campaigns -
           Philippine Islands.

Voice Lib.
M740   MacArthur, Douglas, 1880-1964.
bd.8-C   Excerpt of shortwave broadcast congratulating
           America on VE-Day, with emphasis on rededica-
           tion to task which lies ahead and the expecta-
           tion of additional reinforcements from West
           to help conclude war against Japan.   CBS,
           1944.
               1 reel (7 in.)   7 1/2 in. per sec.
           phonotape.

Voice Lib.
M740   MacArthur, Douglas, 1880-1964.
bd.8-B   Reviewing steps toward liberation of
           Philippines; "My country has kept the
           faith".   CBS, 1944.
               1 reel (7 in.)   7 1/2 in. per sec.
           phonotape.

Voice Lib.
652   MacArthur, Douglas, 1880-1964.
bd.21   Speech to Australians after his escape
           from Bataan.   CBS, 1944.
               1 reel (7 in.)   7 1/2 in. per sec.
           phonotape.

Voice Lib.
393   MacArthur, Douglas, 1880-1964.
bd.2   World War II speech "I Have Returned", on
           return of U.S. troops to the Philippines;
           tells people to rally for their own good.
           Private recording (U.S. Army), 1944.
               1 reel (7 in.)   7 1/2 in. per sec.
           phonotape.

Voice Lib.
M1285   MacArthur, Douglas, 1880-1964.
bd.3   Speaking to Filipinos at Manila about
           the Philippine liberation during World
           War II.   AFRS, April, 1945.
               1 reel (7 in.)   7 1/2 in. per sec.
           phonotape.

Voice Lib.
M740   MacArthur, Douglas, 1880-1964.
bd.8-E   Excerpt of ceremonies on U.S. Battleship
           Missouri, accepting unconditional surrender
           of Japan.   CBS, September 1, 1945.
               1 reel (7 in.)   7 1/2 in. per sec.
           phonotape.

               1. World War, 1939-1945 - Japan.

Voice Lib.
587   MacArthur, Douglas, 1880-1964.
bd.1   Surrender of Japanese; radio address to
American people upon formal signing of
surrender. Shortwave from Tokyo. Armed
Forces Radio, September 1, 1945.
        1 reel (7 in.)   7 1/2 in. per sec.
phonotape.

Voice Lib.
M740   MacArthur, Douglas, 1880-1964.
bd.8-H Excerpt of address upon arrival in San
Francisco after being relieved of U.N.
command in Japan, including his statement
of no intention to involve himself in
politics. CBS, April, 1951.
        1 reel (7 in.)   7 1/2 in. per sec.
phonotape.

Voice Lib.
586   MacArthur, Douglas, 1880-1964.
        Surrender of Japanese on U.S.S. "Missouri",
Tokyo Bay; outlines purpose of signing,
expresses personal hope for future, explains
his responsibility as Allied Supreme Commander,
leads Allied signing of agreement.   Armed
Forces Radio, September 1, 1945.
        1 reel (7 in.)   7 1/2 in. per sec.
phonotape.

Voice Lib.
380   MacArthur, Douglas, 1880-1964.
bd.1   Voices and events: the Douglas MacArthur
story; describes Rainbow Division in France
in World War I, explains his Soldier's Creed,
tells of return to Manila, statement on
USS "Missouri" (September, 1945), prayer
on occasion of liberation of South Korea
in 1950, complains of restraints on entering Manchuria, talks informally with GI
in Korea. NBC, April 15, 1951.
        1 reel (7 in.)   7 1/2 in. per sec.
phonotape.

Voice Lib.
M717   MacArthur, Douglas, 1880-1964.
bd.12   Shortwave broadcast from Japan about
Japanese surrender. November 15, 1945.
        1 reel (7 in.)   7 1/2 in. per sec.
phonotape.

Voice Lib.
M745   MacArthur, Douglas, 1880-1964.
bd.1   Address before joint session of Congress,
Washington, D.C., after his recall by
President Truman; reviewing his military
career, conduct of the Korean War, and saying
farewell as he closes his army career.
Direct line NVL, April 19, 1951.
        1 reel (7 in.)   7 1/2 in. per sec.
phonotape.

Voice Lib.
M740   MacArthur, Douglas, 1880-1964.
bd.8-G Excerpt of remarks at celebration of
Philippine independence. CBS, July 4,
1946.
        1 reel (7 in.)   7 1/2 in. per sec.
phonotape.

Voice Lib.
M740   MacArthur, Douglas, 1880-1964.
bd.8-I Excerpts of address to combined session
of U.S. Congress, Washington, D.C., after
being relieved from active duty. "Old soldiers
never die; they just fade away". CBS,
April 19, 1951.
        1 reel (7 in.)   7 1/2 in. per sed.
phonotape.

Voice Lib.
M740   MacArthur, Douglas, 1880-1964.
bd.8-F Excerpt of shortwave address to U.N.
Security Council about Japan's new
constitution renouncing war. CBS,
April 17, 1946.
        46 sec.   phonotape (1 r.   7 1/2 i.p.s.)

        1. Japan - Constitutional history.

Voice Lib.
282   MacArthur, Douglas, 1880-1964.
bd.1   Speech delivered before the Michigan
Legislature at the State Capitol in
Lansing on the challenge to America in
a time of faulty leadership. CBS,
May 16, 1952.
        1 reel (7 in.)   7 1/2 in. per sec.
phonotape.

Voice Lib.
239-   MacArthur, Douglas, 1880-1964.
240   Keynote address at the Republican
          Convention, Chicago, Illinois. CBS,
          July 7, 1952.
              2 reels (7 in.)   7 1/2 in. per sec.
          phonotape.

Voice Lib.
M801   MacArthur, Douglas, 1880-1964.
            "Duty-Honor-Country"; farewell address
        delivered at U.S. Military Academy at West
        Point. 1962.
            1 reel (7 in.)   7 1/2 in. per sec.
        phonotape.

Voice Lib.
253   MacArthur, Douglas, 1880-1964.
bd.2   Address at MacArthur Park, Los Angeles,
          dedicating statue of Gen. MacArthur on
          75th birthday.   CBS, January 26, 1955.
              1 reel (7 in.)   7 1/2 in. per sec.
          phonotape.

Voice Lib.
390,   MacArthur, Douglas, 1880-1964.
393   "MacArthur is the Name"; life of General
bd.1   MacArthur.   Hearst Metrotone News, 1962.
              2 reels (7 in.)   7 1/2 in. per sec.
          phonotape.

              1. MacArthur, Douglas, 1880-1964.

Voice Lib.
M740   MacArthur, Douglas, 1880-1964.
bd.8-K   Excerpt from address bidding farewell
        to Philippine people. CBS, 1961.
            1 reel (7 in.)   7 1/2 in. per sec.
        phonotape.

Voice Lib.
M770   MacArthur, Douglas, 1880-1964.
bd.4   Excerpt of remarks at receiving Congressional
        honors in Washington.   CBS, May, 1962.
            1 reel (7 in.)   7 1/2 in. per sec.
        phonotape.

Voice Lib.
130-   MacArthur, Douglas, 1880-1964.
131   Commencement address at Michigan State
bd.1   University, with introduction by President
          John A. Hannah.   WKAR, June, 1961.
              2 reels (7 in.)   7 1/2 in. per sec.
          phonotape.

              I. Hannah, John Alfred, 1902-

Voice Lib.
M740   MacArthur, Douglas, 1880-1964.
bd.8-L   Excerpts of address at the U.S. Military
        Academy, West Point. "Duty, Honor, Country";
        eulogizing the American soldier and bidding
        the cadets farewell.   CBS, May, 1962.
            1 reel (7 in.)   7 1/2 in. per sec.
        phonotape.

Voice Lib.
M740   MacArthur, Douglas, 1880-1964.
bd.8-J   Excerpt from speech to Philippine Congress
        reviewing his past association with Philippines.
        CBS, July, 1961.
            1 reel (7 in.)   7 1/2 in. per sec.
        phonotape.

Voice Lib.
657   MacArthur, Douglas, 1880-1964.
bd.1   The MacArthur story: various addresses
          and statements by General MacArthur,
          including his commencement address at
          West Point in 1962.   CBS, 1964.
              1 reel (7 in.)   7 1/2 in. per sec.
          phonotape.

              1. MacArthur, Douglas, 1880-1964.

MacArthur, Douglas, 1880-1964
Voice Lib.
M622   Radio in the 1940's (Part III): a series of
bd.1-   excerpts from important broadcasts of the 1940's; a sample
bd.15   of radio of the period. NVL, April, 1964.
            1 reel (7 in.) 7 1/2 in. per sec. phonotape.
            I. Radio programs. L. Miller, Alton Glenn, 1909(?)-1944. II.
        Diles, Ken   III. Wilson, Donald Harlow, 1900-   IV.
        Livingstone, Mary   V. Benny, Jack, 1894-   VI. Harris,
        Phil   VII. Merman, Ethel, 1909-   VIII. Smith, "Wonderful"
        IX. Bennett, Richard Dyer   X. Louis, Joe, 1914-   XI.
        Eisenhower, Dwight David, Pres. U.S., 1890-1969. XII. MacArthur,
        Douglas, 1880-1964. XIII. Romulo, Carlos Pena, 1899-   XIV.
        Welles, Orson, 1915-   XV. Jackson, Robert Houghwout, 1892-1954.
        XVI. LaGuardia, Fiorello Henry, 1882-1945. XVII. Nehru, Jawa-
        harlal, 1889-1964. XVIII. Gandhi, Mohandas Karamchand, 1869-1948.

Voice Lib.   MACARTHUR, DOUGLAS, 1880-1964
M615   Columbia Broadcasting System.
bd.2   Death of MacArthur; return of body from
        New York City to Washington, D.C., and
        delivery of eulogy in Capitol Rotunda.
        CBS, April 5, 1964.
            1 reel (7 in.) 7 1/2 in. per sec.
        phonotape.

            1. MacArthur, Douglas, 1880-1964.

Voice Lib. MacArthur, Douglas, 1880-1964
657   Hottelet, Richard Curt
bd.1   The MacArthur Story: narrating continuity
        between speeches by General MacArthur.
        CBS, 1964.
            1 reel (7 in.) 7 1/2 in. per sec.
        phonotape.

            I. MacArthur, Douglas, 1880-1964.

Voice Lib. MACARTHUR, DOUGLAS, 1880-1964
657   Hottelet, Richard Curt
bd.1   The MacArthur Story: narrating continuity
        between speeches by General MacArthur.
        CBS, 1964.
            1 reel (7 in.) 7 1/2 in. per sec.
        phonotape.

            I. MacArthur, Douglas, 1880-1964.

MacArthur, Douglas, 1880-1964
Voice Lib.
381-   I can hear it now (radio program)
382   CBS, April 26, 1951.
bd.1   2 reels (7 in.) 7 1/2 in. per sec. phonotape.
            1. Radio Free Europe. 2. Strategic Air Command. I.
        Ridgway, Matthew Bunker, 1895-   II. Churchill, Winston Leonard
        Spencer, 1874-1965. III. Bevan, Aneurin, 1897-1960. IV. Nixon,
        Richard Milhous, Pres. U.S., 1913-   V. Kerr, Robert Samuel, 1896-
        1963. VI. Brewster, Ralph Owen, 1888-1962. VII. Wherry, Kenneth
        Spicer, 1892-1951. VIII. Capehart, Homer Earl, 1897-   IX.
        Lehman, Herbert Henry, 1878-1963. X. Taft, Robert Alphonso,
        1889-1953. XI. Moody, Arthur Edson Blair, 1902-1954. XII.
        Martin, Joseph William, 1884-1968. XIII. McMahon, James O'Brien,
        1903-1952. XIV. MacArthur, Douglas, 1880-1964. XVII. Wilson,
        Charles Edward, 1886-1972. XVIII. Irvine, Clarence T

MACARTHUR, DOUGLAS, 1880-1964
Voice Lib.
M740   Trout, Robert, 1908-
bd.8-D   News flash announcing termination of
        World War II and promotion of General
        MacArthur to Supreme Commander. CBS,
        1945.
            1 reel (7 in.) 7 1/2 in. per sec.
        phonotape.

            1. World War, 1939-1945. 2. MacArthur,
        Douglas, 1880-1964.

MacArthur, Douglas, 1880-1964
Voice Lib.
572-   I can hear it now (radio program)
573   1933-1946. CBS, 1948.
bd.1   2 reels (7 in.) 7 1/2 in. per sec.
        phonotape.
            I. Murrow, Edward Roscoe, 1908-1965. II. LaGuardia, Fiorello
        Henry, 1882-1947. III. Chamberlain, Neville, 1869-1949. IV.
        Roosevelt, Franklin Delano, Pres. U.S., 1882-1945. V. Churchill,
        Winston Leonard Spencer, 1874-1965. VI. Gaulle, Charles de,
        Pres. France, 1890-1970. VII. Eisenhower, Dwight David, Pres. U.S.,
        1890-1969. VIII. Willkie, Wendell Lewis, 1892-1944. IX. Martin,
        Joseph William, 1884-1968. X. Elizabeth II, Queen of Great Britain,
        1926-   XI. Margaret Rose, Princess of Gt. Brit., 1930-   XII.
        Johnson, Hugh Samuel, 188?   42. XIII. Smith, Alfred Emanuel,
        1873-1944. XIV. Lindbergh   arles Augustus, 1902-   XV. Davis,

        (Continued on next card)

MACARTHUR, DOUGLAS, 1880-1964
Voice Lib.
248   Truman, Harry S, Pres. U.S., 1884-1972.
bd.1   The Korean situation, relieving Gen.
        MacArthur of duty. CBS Radio, April 11, 1951.
            1 reel (7 in.) 7 1/2 in. per sec.
        phonotape.

            1. MacArthur, Douglas, 1880-1964.

Voice Lib. MacArthur, Douglas, 1880-1964
M725   Republican Party. National Convention.
bd.1   25th, Chicago, 1952.
        Film of excerpts of the Republican National
        Convention in 1952. Clash between Taft and
        Eisenhower forces. Includes speeches by Gen.
        MacArthur, Gen. Eisenhower, Ex-Pres. Hoover,
        Sen. Dirksen, etc. CBS, 1952.
            1 reel (7 in.) 7 1/2 in. per sec.
        phonotape.
            I. MacArthur, Douglas, 1880-1964. II. Eisenhower, Dwight
        David, Pres. U.S., 1890-1969. III. Hoover, Herbert Clark, Pres.
        U.S., 1874-1964. IV. Dirksen, Everett McKinley, 1896-1969.

C1   MACARTHUR, DOUGLAS, 1880-1964
H104-   Whorf, Michael, 1933-
H105   Old soldiers never die - General Douglas
        MacArthur.
            2 tape cassettes. (The visual sounds of
        Mike Whorf. History and heritage, H104-H105)
            Originally presented on his radio program, Kaleidoscope,
        WJR, Detroit.
            Duration: 37 min.; 37 min.
            Who was General MacArthur? This questions and others are
        explored, and frequently answered in his own words in this two-part
        series on one of our country's great military leaders.

            I. MacArthur, Douglas, 1880-1964. I. Title.

Voice Lib.
M297 McBride, Mary Margaret, 1899-
bd.2 Mrs. Colin Kelly, wife of World War II
hero, talks with Miss McBride and Mayor
Fiorello H. LaGuardia on living in New
York City. NBC, Red Network, 1943.
1 reel (7 in.) 7 1/2 in. per sec.
phonotape.

1. Kelly, Mrs. Colin. I. LaGuardia,
Fiorello Henry, 1882-1947.

McBride, Mary Margaret, 1899-
Voice Lib.
M1029 Kaltenborn, Hans von, 1878-1965.
bd.2 "A Tribute to Hans von Kaltenborn".
Excerpts of various radio news broadcasts by
Mr. Kaltenborn, and comments by his colleagues
upon his death. Speakers: Morgan Beatty,
narrator; Mary Margaret McBride; H. R. Baukhage;
Harry S Truman. MSU Dept. of TV and Radio, 1965
1 reel (7 in.) 7 1/2 in. per sec.
phonotape.
I. Kaltenborn, Hans von, 1878-1965. I. Beatty, Morgan
II. McBride, Mary Margaret, 1899- III. Baukhage, Hilmar
Robert IV. Truman, Harry S., Pres. U.S., 1884-1972.

McCann, Kevin
Voice Lib.
M1368 Some friends of General Eisenhower (TV program)
CBS-TV special recalling anecdotes about
General Eisenhower by some of his friends:
Bob Hope, Kevin McCann, General Omar Bradley,
Robert B. Anderson, General Alfred Gruenther,
with Walter Cronkite acting as emcee. CBS-TV,
March 29, 1969.
1 reel (7 in.) 7 1/2 in. per sec.

I. Eisenhower, Dwight David, Pres. U.S., 1890-1969. I.
Hope, Bob, 1903- II. McCann, Kevin III. Bradley, Omar
Nelson, 1893- IV. Anderson, Robert Bernerd, 1910- V.
Gruenther, Alfred Maximilian, 1899- VI. Cronkite, Walter
Leland, 1916-

McCarey, Thomas Leo, 1898-1969
Voice Lib.
M322 Biography in sound (radio program)
W.C. Fields, the magnificent rogue.
NBC, 1955.
1 reel (7 in.) 7 1/2 in. per sec. phonotape.
I. Fields, W.C., 1879-1946. I. Fields, W.C., 1879-1946.
II. Allen, Fred, 1894-1956. III. LaBaron, William IV.
Taylor, Robert Lewis, 1912- V. McCarey, Thomas Leo, 1898-
1969. VI. Harkins, James - VII. Chevalier, Maurice,
1889-1972. VIII. Kuromoto, Mrs. George IX. Flynn,
Errol Leslie, 1909-1959. X. Wynn, Ed, 1886-1966. XI. Dowling,
Ray Dooley XII. Sennett, Mack XIII. Overacher,
Ronald Leroy XIV. Bergen, Edgar, 1903- XV. Taurog,
Norman, 1899- XVI. Runnell, Ann XVII. Cowen,
Lester

Voice Lib.
M1040 McCarthy, Clem, 1882-1962.
bd.4 Closing excerpt of Kentucky Derby horse
race, 1938. TV & R, 1938.
1 reel (7 in.) 7 1/2 i.p.s.
phonotape.

1. Kentucky Derby.

McCarthy, Clem, 1882-1962
Voice Lib.
572- I can hear it now (radio program)
573 1933-1946. CBS, 1948.
bd.1 2 reels (7 in.) 7 1/2 in. per sec.
phonotape.
I. Murrow, Edward Roscoe, 1908-1965. II. LaGuardia, Fiorello
Henry, 1882-1947. III. Chamberlain, Neville, 1869-1949. IV.
Roosevelt, Franklin Delano, Pres. U.S., 1882-1945. V. Churchill,
Winston Leonard Spencer, 1874-1965. VI. Gaulle, Charles de,
Pres. France, 1890-1970. VII. Eisenhower, Dwight David, Pres. U.S.,
1890-1969. VIII. Willkie, Wendell Lewis, 1892-1944. IX. Martin,
Joseph William, 1884-1968. X. Elizabeth II, Queen of Great Britain,
1926- XI. Margaret Rose, Princess of Gt. Brit., 1930- XII.
Johnson, Hugh Samuel, 1882-1942. XIII. Smith, Alfred Emanuel,
1873-1944. XIV. Lindbergh, Charles Augustus, 1902- XV. Davis,

(Continued on next card)

Voice Lib.
M1312 McCarthy, Eugene Joseph, 1916-
"MSU Students for McCarthy" session at
campus auditorium to hear speeches and folk
music in furtherance of Sen. McCarthy's
candidacy for Democratic presidential
nomination. Location recording, April 26,
1968.
1 reel (7 in.) 7 1/2 in. per sec.
phonotape.

McCarthy, Eugene Joseph, 1916-
Voice Lib.
M1335 Reports regarding the California primary victory of Senator
Kennedy. Recapitulation of occurrences at Ambassador
Hotel and last speech of Robert F. Kennedy before being
shot. Description of unidentified suspect. List of others
wounded. Opinion by Washington neurosurgeon. Statement
by Senator McCarthy at Beverly Hilton Hotel. NBC-TV,
June 5, 1968.
1 reel (7 in.) 7 1/2 i.p.s. phonotape.

I. Kennedy, Robert Francis, 1925-1968. I. McCarthy,
Eugene Joseph, 1916-

McCarthy, Eugene Joseph, 1916-
Voice Lib.
M1305 Kennedy, Robert Francis, 1925-1968.
Senator Robert F. Kennedy announcing his
candidacy in the race for Democratic presidential nomination in 1968 in press
conference from Senate caucus room,
Washington, D. C. with many questions and
answers. Broadcast switches to Wisconsin for
statement by Senator Eugene McCarthy. CBS-TV,
March 16, 1968.
1 reel (7 in.) 7 1/2 in. per sec.
phonotape.
I. McCarthy, Eugene Joseph, 1916-

McCarthy, Eugene Joseph, 1916-
Voice Lib.
M1321 Kennedy, Robert Francis, 1925-1968.
Debate consisting of questions and answers.
Senator Robert Kennedy and Senator Eugene
McCarthy interviewed by ABC news correspondents
Bill Lawrence and Bob Clark on program
"Issues and Answers". ABC-TV, June 1, 1968.
1 reel (7 in.) 7 1/2 in. per sec.
phonotape.

I. McCarthy, Eugene Joseph, 1916- II.
Lawrence, Bill. III. Clark, Bob

Voice Lib. McCarthy, Joseph Priestley, 1934–
M1619   Kniseley, William
bd.1   Discussion of the MSU Colloquy on
    Sexuality, with J. P. McCarthy.
    WJR, January 2, 1969.
      22 min.   phonotape (1 r.   7 1/2 i.p.s.)

      1. Sex.   I. McCarthy, Joseph Priestley,
1934–

Voice Lib.
652   McCarthy, Joseph Raymond, 1909–1957.
bd.14   Campaign speech in Chicago.   CBS,
    October 27, 1952.
      1 reel (7 in.)   7 1/2 in. per sec.
    phonotape.

Voice Lib.
178   McCarthy, Joseph Raymond, 1909–1957.
bd.1   Attack on Edward R. Murrow.   CBS, I
    Can See It Now, ₍n.d.₎
      1 reel (7 in.)   7 1/2 in. per sec.
    phonotape.

      1. Murrow, Edward Roscoe, 1908–1965.

      McCarthy, Joseph Raymond, 1909–1957
Voice Lib.
383   I can hear it now (radio program)
    CBS, February 9, 1951.
      1 reel (7 in.)   7 1/2 in. per sec.
    phonotape.
      I. Wilson, Charles Edward, 1886–1972. II. Gabrielson, Guy
George, 1891–   III. Taft, Robert Alphonso, 1889–1953. IV.
Martin, Joseph William, 1884–1965. V. McCarthy, Joseph
Raymond, 1909–1957. VI. Benton, William Burnett, 1900–1973.
VII. Malone, George Wilson, 1890–1961. VIII. Capehart, Homer
Earl, 1897–   IX. Eisenhower, Dwight David, Pres. U.S., 1890–
1969. X. Lee, J   V   XI. Hodge, John Reed, 1893–
1963. XII. Overton, Watkins   XIII. DiSalle, Michael
Vincent, 1908–   XIV. Boyce, Eddy   XV. Conklin, Ed
XVI. Collins, Joseph Lawton, 1896–

      McCarthy, Joseph Raymond, 1909–1957
Voice Lib.
M1028   Lewis, Fulton, 1903–1966.
bd.1   Radio news broadcast interview with Senator
    Joseph R. McCarthy pertaining to charges
    made against him by Adlai Stevenson, Edward R.
    Murrow, and others.   Mutual, January 3,
    1956.
      1 reel (7 in.)   7 1/2 in. per sec.
    phonotape.

      I. McCarthy, Joseph Raymond, 1909–1957.

Voice Lib.
219   McCarthy, Joseph Raymond, 1909–1957.
    Address by Sen. McCarthy of Wisconsin
    on "Trumanism."   CBS, November 24, 1953.
      1 reel (7 in.)   7 1/2 in. per sec.
    phonotape.

Voice Lib.
178   McCarthy, Joseph Raymond, 1909–1957.
bd.3–   Army–McCarthy hearings in U.S. Senate.
179   CBS Radio, May 5, 1954.
      2 reels (7 in.)   7 1/2 in. per sec.
    phonotape.

      1. McCarthy–Army controversy, 1954.

      McCarthy, Joseph Raymond, 1909–1957
Voice Lib.
M750   U.S. Congress. Senate. Committee on Government Operations.
bd.1   Permanent Subcommittee on Investigations.
    Proceedings of the 4th session of Senate Army–McCarthy
hearings, continued, April 27, 1954.   Circumstances under
which the altered photograph was taken was questioned; examination of Sec. Stevens in his attempts to sidetrack investigation from
Army to Air Force and Navy; a cross-examination by McCarthy
of Secretary Stevens referring to his attempts to block investigation;
questioning of Stevens by Senator Mundt demanding exact charges
against Carr, Cohn and McCarthy.   CBS Radio, April 27, 1954.
    1 reel (7 in.)   7 1/2 in. per sec.   phonotape.

    I. McCarthy–Army controversy, 1954.   I. Stevens, Robert
Ten Broeck, 1899–   II. McCarthy, Joseph Raymond, 1909–
1957. III. Mundt, Karl Earl, 1900–

Voice Lib.
M715   McCarthy, Joseph Raymond, 1909–1957.
    Army–McCarthy hearings, excerpts of Senate
    subcommittee proceedings discussing publica-
    tion of secret documents.   May 5, 1954.
      1 reel (7 in.)   7 1/2 in. per sec.
    phonotape.

      1. McCarthy–Army Controversy, 1954.

      McCarthy, Joseph Raymond, 1909–1957
Voice Lib.
M933   U.S. Congress. Senate. Committee on Government Operations.
    Permanent Subcommittee on Investigations.
    Proceedings of the 5th session of Senate Army–McCarthy
hearings, April 28, 1954.   Cross-examination of Army Secretary
Stevens by Senator McCarthy; Counselor Jenkins questions
Stevens and Private Schine; McCarthy denies charges of special
privileges for Schine.   WJR, 10:30 p.m., April 28, 1954.
    1 reel (7 in.)   7 1/2 in. per sec.   phonotape.

    I. McCarthy–Army controversy, 1954.   I. Stevens, Robert
Ten Broeck, 1899–   II. McCarthy, Joseph Raymond, 1909–1957.
III. Jenkins, Ray Howard, 1897–   IV. Schine, G   David,
1927–

McCarthy, Joseph Raymond, 1909-1957
Voice Lib.
M1022 U.S. Congress. Senate. Committee on Government Operations.
bd.1   Permanent Subcommittee on Investigations.
    Proceedings of the [8th session] of Senate Army-McCarthy hearings, May 3, 1954. Participants: Secretary of the Army Stevens and Senator McCarthy discussing the case of Major Peress; controversy between Army counsel Adams and McCarthy; McCarthy questioning credibility of Secretary Stevens. WJR, May 3, 1954.
    1 reel (7 in.)   7 1/2 in. per sec.   phonotape.

    I. McCarthy-Army controversy, 1954. I. Stevens, Robert Ten Broeck, 1899-   II. McCarthy, Joseph Raymond, 1909-1957. III. Adams, John G

MCCARTHY, JOSEPH RAYMOND, 1909-1957
Voice Lib.
243   Medina, Harold Raymond, 1888-
bd.12   Judge Medina answers Dr. Frank Stanton on denial of TV access to Senate hearing to censure Sen. McCarthy. CBS, September 2, 1954.
    1 reel (7 in.)   7 1/2 in. per sec. phonotape.

    1. McCarthy, Joseph Raymond, 1909-1957. I. Stanton, Frank, 1908-

---

Voice Lib.
McCarthy, Joseph Raymond, 1909-1957
M1069 U.S. Congress. Senate. Committee on Government Operations.
    Permanent Subcommittee on Investigations.
    Proceedings of the 10th session of Senate Army-McCarthy hearings, May 5, 1954. Senator McCarthy on witness stand; debate concerning letter from FBI files; verbal duel between Counsel Welch and McCarthy; Secretary of Army Stevens on witness stand. CBS Radio, May 5, 1954.
    1 reel (7 in.)   7 1/2 in. per sec. phonotape.

    I. McCarthy-Army controversy, 1954. I. McCarthy, Joseph Raymond, 1909-1957. II. Welch, Joseph Nye, 1890-1960. III. Stevens, Robert Ten Broeck, 1899-

---

Voice Lib.   MCCARTHY-ARMY CONTROVERSY
M1707   Cohn, Roy M   1927-
bd.3   On the Mike Douglas show recalling the McCarthy era with no regrets. Includes Liberace. ABC, May 30, 1974.
    7 min.   phonotape (1 r.   7 1/2 i.p.s.)

    1. McCarthy-Army controversy. I. Douglas, Mike, 1925?-   II. Liberace, 1919-

---

Voice Lib. McCarthy, Joseph Raymond, 1909-1957
M1281 U.S. Congress. Senate. Committee on Government Operations.
    Permanent Subcommittee on Investigations.
    Proceedings of the 11th session of Senate Army-McCarthy hearings, May 6, 1954. Sen. McCarthy on witness stand, pertaining to missing letter from J. Edgar Hoover regarding possible spies at Ft. Monmouth, N.J. Other speakers: Roy Cohn, Committee Counsel Jenkins, Robert A. Collier. Summary by CBS' Griffin Bancroft. CBS Radio, May 6, 1954.
    1 reel (7 in.)   7 1/2 in. per sec. phonotape.

    I. McCarthy-Army controversy, 1954. I. McCarthy, Joseph Raymond, 1909-1957. II. Cohn, Roy M   1927- III. Jenkins, Ray Howard, 1897-   IV. Collier, Robert A V. Bancroft, Griffin

---

MCCARTHY-ARMY CONTROVERSY, 1954
Voice Lib.
M1912 Freedom house; special TV program. Filmed documentary about men and their methods in the fight to combat communist tyranny; featuring the Murrow-McCarthy debates from "See It Now" TV programs; also excerpts from Army-McCarthy Senate hearings, statements by Gen. Eisenhower and Bishop Sheil. CBS, 1954.
    1 reel (7 in.)   7 1/2 i.p.s. phonotape.
    1. Anti-communist movements. 2. McCarthy-Army controversy, 1954.

Voice Lib. McCarthy, Joseph Raymond, 1909-1957
M1284 U.S. Congress. Senate. Committee on Government Operations.
    Permanent Subcommittee on Investigations.
    Proceedings of the 13th session of Senate Army-McCarthy hearings, May 10, 1954. Secretary Stevens makes statement and Senator McCarthy and his counsel, Roy Cohn, cross-examine Stevens; discussion of alleged communists at Ft. Monmouth and pressure of favored treatment for Private Schine. CBS Radio, May 10, 1954.
    1 reel (7 in.)   7 1/2 in. per sec. phonotape.

    I. McCarthy-Army controversy, 1954. I. Dirksen, Everett McKinley, 1896-1969. II. Stevens, Robert Ten Broeck, 1899- III. McCarthy, Joseph Raymond, 1909-1957. IV. Cohn, Roy M 1927-

---

MCCARTHY-ARMY CONTROVERSY, 1954
Voice Lib.
178   McCarthy, Joseph Raymond, 1909-1957.
bd.3-   Army-McCarthy hearings in U.S. Senate.
179   CBS Radio, May 5, 1954.
    2 reels (7 in.)   7 1/2 in. per sec. phonotape.

    1. McCarthy-Army controversy, 1954.

Voice Lib. McCarthy, Joseph Raymond, 1909-1957
M1320 U.S. Congress. Senate. Committee on Government Operations.
    Permanent Subcommittee on Investigations.
    Proceedings of the 17th session of Senate Army-McCarthy hearings, May 14, 1954. Sen. Mundt questioning Mr. Adams about high-level meeting dealing with United Nations. Exchanges between Senator Mundt and Army Counsel Welch. Senator McCarthy examining Sen. Dirksen. Discussion of purgery charges against Carr. Cohn and Adams speak about private dinner party. CBS TV, May 14, 1954.
    1 reel (7 in.)   7 1/2 in. per sec. phonotape.

    I. McCarthy-Army controversy, 1954. I. Mundt, Karl Earl, 1900- II. Welch, Joseph Nye, 1890-1960. III. McCarthy, Joseph Raymond, 1909-1957. IV. Dirksen, Everett McKinley, 1896-1969. V. Cohn, Roy M 1927- VI. Adams, John G

McCARTHY-ARMY CONTROVERSY, 1954
Voice Lib.
X715   McCarthy, Joseph Raymond, 1909-1957.
    Army-McCarthy hearings, excerpts of Senate subcommittee proceedings discussing publication of secret documents. May 5, 1954.
    1 reel (7 in.)   7 1/2 in. per sec. phonotape.

MCCARTHY-ARMY CONTROVERSY, 1954

Voice Lib.
178   Murrow, Edward Roscoe, 1908-1965.
bd.2   Criticism on McCarthy Hearings.   CBS,
       I Can See It Now, _[n.d._]
       1 reel (7 in.)   7 1/2 in. per sec.
       phonotape.

          1. McCarthy-Army controversy, 1954.

MCCARTHY-ARMY CONTROVERSY, 1954

Voice Lib.
M750   U.S. Congress. Senate. Committee on Government Operations.
bd.1   Permanent Subcommittee on Investigations.
       Proceedings of the 4th session of Senate Army-McCarthy
       hearings, continued; April 27, 1954. Circumstances under
       which the altered photograph was taken was questioned; examina-
       tion of Sec. Stevens in his attempts to sidetrack investigation from
       Army to Air Force and Navy; a cross-examination by McCarthy
       of Secretary Stevens referring to his attempts to block investigation;
       questioning of Stevens by Senator Mundt demanding exact charges
       against Carr, Cohn and McCarthy.   CBS Radio, April 27, 1954.
          1 reel (7 in.)   7 1/2 in. per sec.   phonotape.

          L McCarthy-Army controversy, 1954.   L Stevens, Robert
       Ten Broeck, 1899-   II. McCarthy, Joseph Raymond, 1909-
       1957. III. Mundt, Karl Earl, 1900-

MCCARTHY-ARMY CONTROVERSY, 1954

Voice Lib.
M746   U.S. Congress. Senate. Committee on Government Operations.
bd.2   Permanent Subcommittee on Investigations.
       Proceedings of the [1st session] of Senate Army-McCarthy
       hearings, April 22, 1954. Testimony by various witnesses
       regarding pressure put on the Army to obtain a commission for
       Private David Schine. Some of the people speaking are:
       Griffin Bancroft, CBS announcer, describing the scenes at the
       hearings; Joseph N. Welch, counsel for the Army; Ray Jenkins,
       counsel for the subcommittee; Army Secretary Robert Stevens;
       General Reber and Senator McClellan of Arkansas. CBS Radio,
       April 22, 1954.
          1 reel (7 in.)   7 1/2 in. per sec.   phonotape.

          L McCarthy-Army controversy, 1954. L Bancroft, Griffin
       II. Welch, Joseph Nye, 1890-1960. III. Jenkins, Ray Howard,
       1897-   IV. Stevens, Robert Ten Broeck, 1899-   V.
       Reber, Miles   VI. McClellan, John Little, 1896-

MCCARTHY-ARMY CONTROVERSY, 1954

Voice Lib.
M933   U.S. Congress. Senate. Committee on Government Operations.
          Permanent Subcommittee on Investigations.
       Proceedings of the 5th session of Senate Army-McCarthy
       hearings, April 28, 1954. Cross-examination of Army Secretary
       Stevens by Senator McCarthy; Counselor Jenkins questions
       Stevens and Private Schine; McCarthy denies charges of special
       privileges for Schine.   WJR, 10:30 p.m., April 28, 1954.
          1 reel (7 in.)   7 1/2 in. per sec.   phonotape.

          L McCarthy-Army controversy, 1954. L Stevens, Robert
       Ten Broeck, 1899-   II. McCarthy, Joseph Raymond, 1909-1957.
       III. Jenkins, Ray Howard, 1897-   IV. Schine, G   David,
       1927-

MCCARTHY-ARMY CONTROVERSY, 1954

Voice Lib.
M747   U.S. Congress. Senate. Committee on Government Operations.
bd.2   Permanent Subcommittee on Investigations.
       Proceedings of the 2nd session of Senate Army-McCarthy
       hearings, April 23, 1954. Discussion of pressure put upon Army
       Secretary Stevens to obtain direct commission for Private David
       Schine with intimation of dropping the Fort Monmouth
       investigation.   CBS Radio, April 23, 1954.
          1 reel (7 in.)   7 1/2 in. per sec.   phonotape.

          L McCarthy-Army controversy, 1954.

MCCARTHY-ARMY CONTROVERSY, 1954

Voice Lib.
M934   U.S. Congress. Senate. Committee on Government Operations.
          Permanent Subcommittee on Investigations.
       Proceedings of the 6th session of Senate Army-McCarthy
       sessions, April 29, 1954. Private Schine makes first appearance;
       he is cross-examined by Secretary Stevens and Counselor Jenkins;
       Schine comments on circumstances of doctoring the "famous
       photograph" and delivering it for publication at a Washington
       restaurant.   Evening session, WJR, April 29, 1954.
          1 reel (7 in.)   7 1/2 in. per sec.   phonotape.

          L McCarthy-Army controversy, 1954.   L Schine, G
       David, 1927-   II. Stevens, Robert Ten Broeck, 1899-
       III. Jenkins, Ray Howard, 1897-

MCCARTHY-ARMY CONTROVERSY, 1954

Voice Lib.
M748   U.S. Congress. Senate. Committee on Government Operations.
          Permanent Subcommittee on Investigations.
       Proceedings of the 3rd session of Senate Army-McCarthy
       hearings, April 26, 1954. Cross-examination of Secretary of
       the Army Robert Stevens.   CBS Radio, April 26, 1954.
          1 reel (7 in.)   7 1/2 in. per sec.   phonotape.

          L McCarthy-Army controversy, 1954.   L Stevens, Robert
       Ten Broeck, 1899-

MCCARTHY-ARMY CONTROVERSY, 1954

Voice Lib.
M938   U.S. Congress. Senate. Committee on Government Operations.
bd.2   Permanent Subcommittee on Investigations.
       Proceedings of the 7th session of Congressional hearings.
       Continuation of discussion regarding the controversial blow-up
       of photograph of Army Secretary Stevens and Private David
       Schine; discussion about the transfer of General Lawton from
       command at Fort Monmouth, N.J.   CBS, April 30, 1954.
          1 reel (7 in.)   7 1/2 in. per sec.   phonotape.

          L McCarthy-Army controversy, 1954.

MCCARTHY-ARMY CONTROVERSY, 1954

Voice Lib.
M749   U.S. Congress. Senate. Committee on Government Operations.
          Permanent Subcommittee on Investigations.
       Proceedings of the 4th session of Senate Army-McCarthy
       hearings, April 27, 1954. Testimony regarding an altered
       photograph submitted in evidence by McCarthy committee showing
       Secretary Stevens and Private David Schine.   CBS Radio,
       April 27, 1954.
          1 reel (7 in.)   7 1/2 in. per sec.   phonotape.

          L McCarthy-Army controversy, 1954.

MCCARTHY-ARMY CONTROVERSY, 1954

Voice Lib.
M1022 U.S. Congress. Senate. Committee on Government Operations.
bd.1   Permanent Subcommittee on Investigations.
       Proceedings of the [8th session] of Senate Army-McCarthy
       hearings, May 3, 1954. Participants: Secretary of the Army
       Stevens and Senator McCarthy discussing the case of Major
       Peress; controversy between Army counsel Adams and
       McCarthy; McCarthy questioning credibility of Secretary
       Stevens.   WJR, May 3, 1954.
          1 reel (7 in.)   7 1/2 in. per sec.   phonotape.

          L McCarthy-Army controversy, 1954. L Stevens, Robert
       Ten Broeck, 1899-   II. McCarthy, Joseph Raymond, 1909-
       1957. III. Adams, John G

Voice Lib.
M1022   MCCARTHY-ARMY CONTROVERSY, 1954
bd.2-   U.S. Congress. Senate. Committee on Government Operations.
1923   Permanent Subcommittee on Investigations.
          Proceedings of the 9th session of Senate Army-McCarthy
          hearings, May 4, 1954. Discussion concerning the possibility
          of shortening the hearings; statements by Senators Dirksen,
          Mundt, McClellan, Potter, etc.; Aaron Coleman and the
          stripping of Army files; discussion of FBI confidential letter
          and how it was obtained by McCarthy; suggestion of night and
          Saturday sessions. WJR, May 4, 1954.
          2 reels (7 in.)   7 1/2 in. per sec.   phonotape.

          L. McCarthy-Army controversy, 1954.   I. Dirksen, Everett
          McKinley, 1896-1969.   II. Mundt, Karl Earl, 1900-   III. McClellan,
          John Little, 1896-   IV. Potter, Charles Edward, 1916-

Voice Lib.
M1069   MCCARTHY-ARMY CONTROVERSY, 1954
          U.S. Congress. Senate. Committee on Government Operations.
              Permanent Subcommittee on Investigations.
          Proceedings of the 10th session of Senate Army-McCarthy
          hearings, May 5, 1954. Senator McCarthy on witness stand;
          debate concerning letter from FBI files; verbal duel between
          Counsel Welch and McCarthy; Secretary of Army Stevens
          on witness stand. CBS Radio, May 5, 1954.
          1 reel (7 in.)   7 1/2 in. per sec.   phonotape.

          L. McCarthy-Army controversy, 1954.   I. McCarthy,
          Joseph Raymond, 1909-1957.   II. Welch, Joseph Nye, 1890-1960.
          III. Stevens, Robert Ten Broeck, 1899-

Voice Lib.
M1281   MCCARTHY-ARMY CONTROVERSY, 1954
          U.S. Congress. Senate. Committee on Government Operations.
              Permanent Subcommittee on Investigations.
          Proceedings of the 11th session of Senate Army-McCarthy
          hearings, May 6, 1954. Sen. McCarthy on witness stand, pertaining
          to missing letter from J. Edgar Hoover regarding possible spies at
          Ft. Monmouth, N.J. Other speakers: Roy Cohn, Committee Counsel
          Jenkins, Robert A. Collier.   Summary by CBS' Griffin Bancroft.
          CBS Radio, May 6, 1954.
          1 reel (7 in.)   7 1/2 in. per sec.   phonotape.

          L. McCarthy-Army controversy, 1954.   I. McCarthy,
          Joseph Raymond, 1909-1957.   II. Cohn, Roy M   1927-
          III. Jenkins, Ray Howard, 1897-   IV. Collier, Robert A
          V. Bancroft, Griffin

Voice Lib.
M1283   MCCARTHY-ARMY CONTROVERSY, 1954
          U.S. Congress. Senate. Committee on Government Operations.
              Permanent Subcommittee on Investigations.
          Proceedings of the 12th session of Senate Army-McCarthy
          hearings, May 7, 1954. Secretary Stevens alleges he was
          threatened by Sen. McCarthy. Sen. Mundt queries Stevens.
          Much bantering and ribbing. Question of legality of McCarthy
          holding certain documents. Discussion of pressure to give Private
          Schine an Army commission. CBS Radio, May 7, 1954.
          1 reel (7 in.)   7 1/2 in. per sec.   phonotape.

          L. McCarthy-Army controversy, 1954.   I. Stevens, Robert
          Ten Broeck, 1899-   II. Mundt, Karl Earl, 1900-

Voice Lib.
M1284   MCCARTHY-ARMY CONTROVERSY, 1954
          U.S. Congress. Senate. Committee on Government Operations.
              Permanent Subcommittee on Investigations.
          Proceedings of the 13th session of Senate Army-McCarthy
          hearings, May 10, 1954. Senator Dirksen suggests they be held
          privately; Secretary Stevens makes statement and Senator McCarthy
          and his counsel, Roy Cohn, cross-examine Stevens; discussion of
          alleged communists at Ft. Monmouth and pressure of favored
          treatment for Private Schine. CBS Radio, May 10, 1954.
          1 reel (7 in.)   7 1/2 in. per sec.   phonotape.

          L. McCarthy-Army controversy, 1954.   I. Dirksen, Everett
          McKinley, 1896-1969.   II. Stevens, Robert Ten Broeck, 1899-
          III. McCarthy, Joseph Raymond, 1909-1957.   IV. Cohn, Roy M
          1927-

Voice Lib.
M1296   MCCARTHY-ARMY CONTROVERSY, 1954
bd.2   U.S. Congress. Senate. Committee on Government Operations.
              Permanent Subcommittee on Investigations.
          Proceedings of the 15th session of Senate Army-McCarthy
          hearings, Part I, May 12, 1954. Army counsel Adams describes
          resentment of McCarthy counsel Roy Cohn at being restricted
          in certain areas at Ft. Monmouth, N.J. Also, complaints by
          Adams at being abused by Cohn regarding Private David Schine.
          CBS-TV, May 12, 1954.
          1 reel (7 in.)   7 1/2 in. per sec.   phonotape.

          L. McCarthy-Army controversy, 1954.   L. Adams, John G

Voice Lib.
M1299   MCCARTHY-ARMY CONTROVERSY, 1954
bd.2   U.S. Congress. Senate. Committee on Government Operations.
              Permanent Subcommittee on Investigations.
          Proceedings of the 15th session of Senate Army-McCarthy
          hearings, Part II, May 12, 1954. Army Counsel Adams
          describes luncheon with McCarthy, Cohn and himself; further
          abuse and pressure to station Private David Schine; Cohn's
          threat, "We'll wreck the army if Schine is sent overseas".
          CBS-TV, May 12, 1954.
          1 reel (7 in.)   7 1/2 in. per sec.   phonotape.

          L. McCarthy-Army controversy, 1954.   L. Adams, John G

Voice Lib.
M1319   MCCARTHY-ARMY CONTROVERSY, 1954
          U.S. Congress. Senate. Committee on Government Operations.
              Permanent Subcommittee on Investigations.
          Proceedings of the 16th session of Senate Army-McCarthy
          hearings, May 13, 1954. Ray Jenkins questioning John Adams
          about actions of Sec. Stevens. Was Sec. Stevens afraid to ship
          Private Schine overseas due to pressure by Roy Cohn and Sen.
          McCarthy? Was discussion of Mr. Adams private law practice?
          CBS-TV, May 13, 1954.
          1 reel (7 in.)   7 1/2 in. per sec.   phonotape.

          L. McCarthy-Army controversy, 1954.   L. Jenkins, Ray
          Howard, 1897-   II. Adams, John G

Voice Lib.
M1320   MCCARTHY-ARMY CONTROVERSY, 1954
          U.S. Congress. Senate. Committee on Government Operations.
              Permanent Subcommittee on Investigations.
          Proceedings of the 17th session of Senate Army-McCarthy
          hearings, May 14, 1954. Sen. Mundt questioning Mr. Adams
          about high-level meeting dealing with United Nations. Exchanges
          between Senator Mundt and Army Counsel Welch. Senator
          McCarthy examining Sen. Dirksen. Discussion of purgery charges
          against Carr. Cohn and Adams speak about private dinner party.
          CBS TV, May 14, 1954.
          1 reel (7 in.)   7 1/2 in. per sec.   phonotape.

          L. McCarthy-Army controversy, 1954.   I. Mundt, Karl Earl,
          1900-   II. Welch, Joseph Nye, 1890-1960.   III. McCarthy,
          Joseph Raymond, 1909-1957.   IV. Dirksen, Everett McKinley, 1896-
          1969.   V. Cohn, Roy M   1927-   VI. Adams, John G

Voice Lib.
345   McClellan, John Little, 1896-
bd.5   Hearings on Kohler strike in Ohio.
          CBS, March 5, 1958.
              1 reel (7 in.)   7 1/2 in. per sec.
          phonotape.

Voice Lib.
243   McClellan, John Little, 1896-
bd.9   Senate investigating committee: coin-
         machine labor union. Voices of Samuel
         Getlan, Karl Mundt, Robert Kennedy and
         John McClellan. CBS Radio, August 5, 1957.
           1 reel (7 in.) 7 1/2 in. per sec.
         phonotape.
           I. Getlan, Samuel   II. Mundt, Karl
         Earl, 1900-   III. Kennedy, Robert Francis,
         1925-1968.

Voice Lib.
M746   McClellan, John Little, 1896-
bd.2   U.S. Congress. Senate. Committee on Government Operations.
             Permanent Subcommittee on Investigations.
           Proceedings of the [1st session] of Senate Army-McCarthy
         hearings, April 22, 1954. Testimony by various witnesses
         regarding pressure put on the Army to obtain a commission for
         Private David Schine. Some of the people speaking are:
         Griffin Bancroft, CBS announcer, describing the scenes at the
         hearings; Joseph N. Welch, counsel for the Army; Ray Jenkins,
         counsel for the subcommittee; Army Secretary Robert Stevens;
         General Reber and Senator McClellan of Arkansas. CBS Radio,
         April 22, 1954.
           1 reel (7 in.) 7 1/2 in. per sec. phonotape.
           I. McCarthy-Army controversy, 1954. I. Bancroft, Griffin
         II. Welch, Joseph Nye, 1890-1960. III. Jenkins, Ray Howard,
         1897-   IV. Stevens, Robert Ten Broeck, 1899-   V.
         Reber, Miles   VI. McClellan, John Little, 1896-

Voice Lib.
M1022   McClellan, John Little, 1896-
bd.2-   U.S. Congress. Senate. Committee on Government Operations.
1923   Permanent Subcommittee on Investigations.
           Proceedings of the 9th session of Senate Army-McCarthy
         hearings, May 4, 1954. Discussion concerning the possibility
         of shortening the hearings; statements by Senators Dirksen,
         Mundt, McClellan, Potter, etc.; Aaron Coleman and the
         stripping of Army files; discussion of FBI confidential letter
         and how it was obtained by McCarthy; suggestion of night and
         Saturday sessions. WJR, May 4, 1954.
           2 reels (7 in.) 7 1/2 in. per sec. phonotape.
           I. McCarthy-Army controversy, 1954. I. Dirksen, Everett
         McKinley, 1896-1969. II. Mundt, Karl Earl, 1900- III. McClellan,
         John Little, 1896-   IV. Potter, Charles Edward, 1916-

Voice Lib.
M762   McClelland, Douglas
bd.10   Excerpt from "Music from Broadway" (Program
         5); comments on lack of integration of the
         Broadway shows between the script and the
         music. Westinghouse Broadcasting Corporation,
         1964.
           1 reel (7 in.) 7 1/2 in. per sec.
         phonotape. (The Music Goes Round and Round)
           I. Title: Music from Broadway. II. Series.

Voice Lib.
M763   McClelland, Douglas
bd.8   Excerpt from "Sound Track" (Program 7);
         comments how music was used in the production
         of the movie even before the advent of sound;
         on the role of the audience in accepting the
         movies; early stages of sound; the sound
         track album. Westinghouse Broadcasting
         Corporation, 1964.
           1 reel (7 in.) 7 1/2 in. per sec.
         phonotape. (The Music Goes Round and Round)
           I. Title: Sound track. II. Series.

Voice Lib.   McConnell, Barnes
M1551-   Young, Andrew, 1932-
1552   A lecture series by the College of Urban
         Affairs, Michigan State University, with
         Prof. Robert Green and Asst. Prof. Barnes
         McConnell. MSU Dept. of Information
         Services, January 17, 1974.
           90 min. phonotape (2 r. 7 1/2 i.p.s.)

           1. Local transit. 2. Atlanta. I. Green,
         Robert Lee. II. McConnell, Barnes.

Voice Lib.
M1800   McCord, James Walter, 1918?-
WG   Testimony before the Senate Committee
0518.02- investigating the Watergate Affair.
.03   Pacifica, May 18, 1973.
           238 min. phonotape (4 r. 3 3/4 i.p.s.)
         (Watergate gavel to gavel, phase 1)

           1. Watergate Affair, 1972-

Voice Lib.
M1800   McCord, James Walter, 1918?-
WG   Testimony before the Senate Committee
0522.01 investigating the Watergate Affair.
.02   Pacifica, May 22, 1973.
           264 min. phonotape (4 r. 3 3/4 i.p.s.)
         (Watergate gavel to gavel, phase 1)

           1. Watergate Affair, 1972-

Voice Lib.
344   McCormack, John William, 1891-
bd.20   Predicts congressional passage of
         President's foreign aid and national
         defense programs. CBS, January 2,
         1962.
           1 reel (7 in.) 7 1/2 in. per sec.
         phonotape.

Voice Lib.
351   McCormack, John William, 1891-
bd.2   Giving thanks to those who voted for him
         as Speaker of the House, being sworn in as
         Speaker of the House. CBS, January 10, 1962.
           1 reel (7 in.) 7 1/2 in. per sec.
         phonotape.

Voice Lib.
M718   McCormack, John William, 1891-
bd.1   Administering oath of office of Vice-
President to Hubert H. Humphrey. Presidential
inaugural ceremonies.   January 20, 1965.
1 reel (7 in.)   7 1/2 in. per sec.
phonotape.

I1 Humphrey, Hubert Horatio, 1911-

Voice Lib.
M1348 McCormack, John William, 1891-
bd.2   Apollo 8 (space flight): reception of Apollo
8 astronauts at Joint Session of Congress,
including addresses by the astronauts.
CBS TV, January 1, 1969.
1 reel (7 in.)   7 1/2 in. per sec.
phonotape.
1. Project Apollo. 2. Anders, William
Alison, 1933-   3. Lovell, James Arthur, 1928-
4. Borman, Frank, 1928-   I. Anders, William
Alison, 1933-   II. Lovell, James Arthur,
1928-   III. Borman, Frank, 1928-   IV.
McCormack, John William, 1891-

Voice Lib.
M314   McCormack, John William, 1891-
bd.3   Warren, Earl, 1891-
Remarks at bier of President Kennedy,
lying in state at Capitol Rotunda. Also
remarks by Speaker of the House McCormack;
beginning of line of dignitaries to pass
the bier. ABC, November 24, 1963.
1 reel (7 in.)   7 1/2 in. per sec.
phonotape.
1. Kennedy, John Fitzgerald, Pres. U.S.,
1917-1963 - Assassination. I. McCormack,
John William, 1891-

Voice Lib.
M1575- McCracken, Paul Winston, 1915-
1576,   Is American optimism at an end? Economic
bd.1   Club of Detroit address. WKAR-FM, February
25, 1974.
60 min. phonotape (2 r. 7 1/2 in. per.
sec.)

1. U.S. - Economic conditions.

Voice Lib.
298   McCune, Newell Avery
bd.2   Invocation at MSU commencement exercises,
June 9, 1963. National Voice Library
recording, 1963.
1 reel (7 in.)   7 1/2 in. per sec.
phonotape.

McDivitt, James Alton, 1929-
Voice Lib.
M771   Gemini 4 (space flight): excerpts of descrip-
bd.1   tion of take-off; Gemini 4 and Gemini Control
announcements.   June 3, 1965.
1 reel (7 in.)   7 1/2 in. per sec.
phonotape.

1. Project Gemini. 2. McDivitt, James Alton,
1929-   3. White, Edward Higgins, 1930-1967.
I. McDivitt, James Alton, 1929- II. White,
Edward Higgins, 1930-1967.

McDivitt, James Alton, 1929-
Voice Lib.
M771   Gemini 4 (space flight): excerpts of announce-
bd.2   ments from NBC reporters and Gemini Control,
regarding preparations for and the actual
splashdown. Conversation with astronauts
before pickup by helicopter. Dallas Townsend
from carrier "Wasp" and David Brinkley and
Chet Huntley for NBC.   NBC TV, June 7, 1965.
1 reel (7 in.)   7 1/2 in. per sec. phonotape.
1. Project Gemini. 2. McDivitt, James Alton, 3.
White, Edward Higgins, 1930-1967. I. McDivitt, James Alton,
1929-   II. White, Edward Higgins, 1930-1967. III. Townsend,
Dallas.   IV. Brinkley, David McClure, 1920-   V. Huntley,
Chet, 1911-1974.

McDivitt, James Alton, 1929-
Voice Lib.
M772   Gemini 4 (space flight): pickup of astronauts
bd.1   McDivitt and White and the capsule, described
by Chet Huntley and David Brinkley. NBC TV,
June 7, 1965.
1 reel (7 in.)   7 1/2 in. per sec.
phonotape.

1. Project Gemini. 2. McDivitt, James Alton,
1929-   3. White, Edward Higgins, 1930-1967.
I. McDivitt, James Alton, 1929-   II. White,
Edward Higgins, 1930-1967. III. Huntley, Chet,
1911-1974 IV. Brinkley, David McClure, 1920-

McDivitt, James Alton, 1929-
Voice Lib.
M1355 Apollo 9 (space flight): lift-off of Apollo 9
bd.3   space flight at 11 a.m., March 3, 1969.
Description by CBS-TV commentators, Mission
Control, and astronauts. CBS TV, March 3,
1969.
1 reel (7 in.)   7 1/2 in. per sec.
phonotape.
1. Project Apollo. 2. McDivitt, James Alton, 1929-   3.
Scott, David Randolph, 1932-   4. Schweickart, Russell L
1936-   I. McDivitt, James Alton, 1929-   II. Scott, David
Randolph, 1932-   III. Schweickart, Russell L   1936-

McDivitt, James Alton, 1929-
Voice Lib.
M1364 Apollo 9 (space flight): splashdown, part 1.
CBS correspondents with anchorman Walter
Cronkite describe recovery of Apollo 9
from the time astronauts are over Australia
to the opening of the hatch. CBS TV,
March 13, 1969.
1 reel (7 in.)   7 1/2 in. per sec.
phonotape.
1. Project Apollo. 2. McDivitt, James Alton, 1929-   3.
Scott, David Randolph, 1932-   4. Schweickart, Russell L
1936-   I. McDivitt, James Alton, 1929-   II. Scott, David
Randolph, 1932-   III. Schweickart, Russell L   1936-
IV. Cronkite, Walter Leland, 1916-

Voice Lib.   McDivitt, James Alton, 1929-
M1365   Apollo 9 (space flight): splashdown, part 2.
CBS TV description of retrieval of Apollo 9
astronauts, starting with the opening of the
hatch to their examination in sick bay on
the recovery ship. Includes telegram by
President Nixon and brief remarks by the
astronauts. CBS TV, March 13, 1969.
1 reel (7 in.)   7 1/2 in. per sec.
phonotape.
L. Project Apollo. 2. McDivitt, James Alton, 1929-   3.
Scott, David Randolph, 1932-   4. Schweickart, Russell L
1936-   L McDivitt, James Alton, 1929-   IL Scott, David
Randolph, 1932-   IIL Schweickart, Russell L   1936-

Voice Lib.   McDivitt, James Alton, 1929-
M773   Michigan. University.
bd.1   Ceremonies at University of Michigan
presenting White and McDivitt with Doctorate
degrees. Actual presentation to Colonel
McDivitt of the degree of Doctor of Astro-
nautical Science and remarks by McDivitt.
14 min., 50 sec.   phonotape (1 r. 7 1/2
i.p.s.)
1. McDivitt, James Alton, 1929-
I. McDivitt, James Alton, 1929-

Voice Lib.   MacDonald, Dwight, 1906-
M655   The Twentieth Century (TV program)
bd.1   "The creative thirties", narrated by
Walter Cronkite. CBS, 1963.
25 min.   phonotape (1 r.   7 1/2 i.p.s.)
L. U.S. - Civilization - 1918-1945. L. Bowes, Edward,
1874-1946. IL. Geisman, Maxwell David, 1909-
IIL. MacDonald, Dwight, 1906-   IV. Welles, Orson, 1915-
V. Cronkite, Walter Leland, 1916-   VL. Gable, Clark, 1901-
1960. VIL. Lewis, Sinclair, 1885-1951. VIIL. Houseman,
John, 1902-   IX. Roosevelt, Franklin Delano, Pres. U.S.,
1882-1945.

Voice Lib.
M1664   MacDonald, J   Fred
bd.1   Beyond the survey; creating a program
of popular culture courses. Recorded live
at National Popular Culture Meetings in
Milwaukee, May 4, 1974.
20 min.   phonotape (1 r.   7 1/2 i.p.s.)
1. Popular culture.

Voice Lib.
642   MacDonald, James Ramsay, 1866-1937.
bd.3   "A man amongst men"; eulogy for Robert
Burns, poet. BBC, January 25, 1928.
1 reel (7 in.)   7 1/2 in. per sec.
phonotape.
1. Burns, Robert, 1759-1796.

Voice Lib.   McGee, Frank, 1921-1974
M917   Gemini 7 (space flight): Frank McGee's resumé
bd.1   of space flights of astronauts Frank Borman
and James Lovell, Jr., in Gemini 7, commencing
Dec. 4, 1956 to Dec. 18, 1965, and of astronauts Walter Schirra and Thomas Stafford in
Gemini 6, which rendezvoused in space;
including various launching actual reports
and interview with Wally Schirra; comments
by Huntley and Brinkley. NBC TV, December
18, 1965.
1 reel (7 in.)   7 1/2 in. per sec.
phonotape.
(Continued on next card)

Voice Lib.   McGee, Frank, 1921-1974
M968   Gemini 9 (space flight): description of
bd.2   countdown and lift-off of "Agena" by
Gemini Mission Control (voice of Al Chop)
for a period of 11 minutes, 41 seconds,
until Gemini flight was scrubbed. Comments
by NBC's Huntley, Brinkley, and Frank McGee.
NBC TV, May 17, 1966.
1 reel (7 in.)   7 1/2 in. per sec.   phonotape.
L. Project Gemini. 2. Stafford, Thomas P   1931-   3.
Cernan, Eugene Andrew, 1934-   4. Stafford, Thomas P   1931-
II. Cernan, Eugene Andrew, 1934-   III. Chop, Al   IV.
Huntley, Chet, 1911-1974 V. Brinkley, David McClure, 1920-
VL. McGee, Frank, 1921-1974.

McGee, Frank, 1921-
Voice Lib.
M1290-   Same mud, same blood; a one-hour actual
1291   report on the integration of white and
bd.1   colored troops of the 101st Airborne
Division. NBC, December 1, 1967.
2 reels (7 in.)   7 1/2 in. per sec.
phonotape.
1. U.S. Army - Negro troops. I. McGee,
Frank, 1921-

McGee, Frank, 1921-1974
Voice Lib.
M1384   Apollo 11 (space flight): Frank McGee giving
bd.3   an itinerary of space ships, dates, times,
etc. NBC TV, July 16, 1969.
1 reel (7 in.)   7 1/2 in. per sec.
phonotape.
1. Project Apollo. 2. Space flight to the
moon. 3. Aldrin, Edwin E   1930-   4.
Collins, Michael, 1930-   5. Armstrong, Neil,
1930-   I. Aldrin, Edwin E   1930-   II.
Collins, Michael, 1930-   III. Armstrong, Neil,
1930-   IV. McGee, Frank, 1921-1974.

McGee, Frank, 1921-1974
Voice Lib.
M1384   Apollo 11 (space flight): interviews between
bd.4   Frank McGee and Neil Armstrong previous to
the flight of Apollo 11. NBC TV, July 16,
1969.
1 reel (7 in.)   7 1/2 in. per sec.
phonotape.
1. Project Apollo. I. McGee, Frank, 1921-
1974. II. Armstrong, Neil, 1930-

McGee, Frank, 1921-1974

Voice Lib.
M1385 Apollo 11 (space flight): Frank McGee speaking
bd.1   about communications between "Eagle" and
           ground. Conversation between Houston and
           astronauts. Message of "Go for PDI"; "The
           Eagle has landed" (102 hours, 45 minutes,
           40 seconds) Description of rocks and
           boulders on moon. NBC TV, July 20, 1969.
           1 reel (7 in.) 7 1/2 in. per sec. phonotape.
           L. Project Apollo. 2. Space flight to the moon. 3. Aldrin,
           Edwin E   1930-   4. Collins, Michael, 1930-   5.
           Armstrong, Neil, 1930-   L. Aldrin, Edwin E   1930-
           II. Collins, Michael, 1930-   III. Armstrong, Neil, 1930-
           IV. McGee, Frank, 1921-1974.

McGee, Frank, 1921-1974

Voice Lib.
M1387 Apollo 11 (space flight): description of
bd.1   ascent from moon by Frank McGee. Count-
           down, ignition, and lift-off. Meeting the
           command module "Columbia"; docking; trans-
           fer of gear from "Eagle" to "Columbia".
           Recap by ABC's Jules Bergman and Frank
           Reynolds. NBC and ABC TV, July 21, 1969.
           1 reel (7 in.) 7 1/2 in. per sec.   phonotape.
           L. Project Apollo. 2. Space flight to the moon. 3. Aldrin,
           Edwin E   1930-   4. Collins, Michael, 1930-   5.
           Armstrong, Neil, 1930-   L. Aldrin, Edwin E   1930-   II.
           Collins, Michael, 1930-   III. Armstrong, Neil, 1930-   IV.
           McGee, Frank, 1921-1974. V. Bergman, Jules   VI. Reynolds,
           Frank

McGee, Frank, 1921-1974

Voice Lib.
M1389 Apollo 11 (space flight): welcome to Apollo 11 astronauts on their
bd.2   arrival at Kennedy Airport at New York; ferried by Marine
           helicopter to Wall Street; boat whistles brought greeting.
           Flashbacks to former important New York parades (Frank McGee)
           Walter Cronkite, CBS, describing beginning of motorcade
           and parade to city hall. CBS [and NBC] TV, August 13, 1969.
           1 reel (7 in.) 7 1/2 in. per sec. phonotape.
           L. Project Apollo. 2. Space flight to the moon. 3. Aldrin,
           Edwin E   1930-   4. Collins, Michael, 1930-   5.
           Armstrong, Neil, 1930-   L. Aldrin, Edwin E   1930-
           II. Collins, Michael, 1930-   III. Armstrong, Neil, 1930-
           IV. McGee, Frank, 1921-1974. V. Cronkite, Walter Leland, 1916-

McGee, Frank, 1921-1974

Voice Lib.
M1403 Apollo 12 (space flight): landing on the
bd.2   moon; conversations of Frank McGee and
           mission control; dialogue of Pete Conrad
           preparing to step out on moon; coached on
           going down ladder; Conrad singing from the
           moon; trouble with TV camera. NBC TV,
           November 19, 1969.
           1 reel (7 in.) 7 1/2 in. per sec. phonotape.
           L. Project Apollo. 2. Space flight to the moon. 3. Conrad,
           Charles, 1930-   4. Bean, Alan L   1932-   5. Gordon,
           Richard F   1929-   L. Conrad, Charles, 1930-   II. Bean,
           Alan L   1932-   III. Gordon, Richard F   1929-   IV.
           McGee, Frank, 1921-1974.

McGee, Frank, 1921-

Voice Lib.
M1440 Calley, William Laws, 1943-
           NBC special program immediately after
           conviction of Lieutenant William Calley
           for My Lai massacre; with Frank McGee.
           NBC-TV, March 29, 1971.
           1 reel (7 in.) 7 1/2 in. per sec.
           phonotape.

           I. McGee, Frank, 1921-

McGee, Frank, 1921-1974

Voice Lib.
M311   Kennedy, John Fitzgerald, Pres. U.S., 1917-1963.
bd.2   Excerpts of Pres. Kennedy's remarks in
           Ireland, with comments by Frank McGee of
           NBC. NBC, November 23, 1963.
           1 reel (7 in.)   7 1/2 i.p.s.
           phonotape.

           I. McGee, Frank, 1921-1974.

McGee, Frank, 1921-

Voice Lib.
M920   Project '66 (Television program)
bd.2-   NBC year-end TV news analysis. NBC news
923   correspondents analyze 1965 news events and
           make predictions for 1966, headed by Frank
           McGee, with questions by members of Foreign
           Policy Association. NBC, 1965.
           4 reels (7 in.) 7 1/2 in. per sec.
           phonotape.

           I. McGee, Frank, 1921-

McGee, Frank, 1921-1974

Voice Lib.
M315   Wilkins, Roy, 1901-
bd.4   Statement by Roy Wilkins to NBC newsman
           Frank McGee, at the assassination of President
           Kennedy, his ideas about the future of civil
           rights. NBC, November 24, 1963.
           1 reel (7 in.) 7 1/2 in. per sec.
           phonotape.

           1. Kennedy, John Fitzgerald, Pres. U.S.,
           1917-1963 - Assassination. I. McGee, Frank,
           1921-1974.

McGovern, George Stanley, 1922-

Voice Lib.
M1323- Democratic Party. National Convention,
M1328,   Chicago, 1968.
bd.1   Hubert Humphrey, Democratic presidential nom- ...,
           announcing his selection of Sen. Muskie as his running mate;
           convention floor reports; interview with Mrs. Humphrey. Mayor
           Daley of Chicago defending police action. Interviews with Sen-
           ator McGovern and Jesse Unruh of California. Remote address by
           Sen. Edward Kennedy introducing a memorial motion picture on
           the late Sen. Robert F. Kennedy. Various reports on riots and
           general confusion, reluctance of delegates to come to order.
           Nominations for Vice-President; seconding speeches for Sen.
           Muskie and nominating speech by Wisconsin delegation of Julian
           Bond of Georgia. Interview with Julian Bond, who declined
           nomination of the vice-presidency. Story told by chairman of
           the New Hampshire [delegat...] regarding his arrest. Interview
           (Continued on next card)

McGovern, George Stanley, 1922-

Voice Lib.
M1323- Democratic Party. National Convention,
M1328,   Chicago, 1968...   (Card 2)
bd.1   with Paul O'Dwyer of the New York delegation regarding the
           nomination of Richard Daley for Vice-President. General
           confusion. Nomination of Sen. Edmund Muskie as Vice-President
           and resulting confusion with the Oregon delegation. Followed by
           Sen. Muskie's acceptance speech. NBC-TV, August 29, 1968.
           6 reels (7 in.) 7 1/2 in. per sec. phonotape.
           L. Humphrey, Hubert Horatio, 1911- II. Humphrey, Muriel Fay
           (Buck) 1912-   III. Daley, Richard J   1902-   IV. McGovern,
           George Stanley, 1922-   V. Unruh, Jesse Marvin, 1922-   VI.
           Kennedy, Edward Moore, 1932-   VII. Bond, Julian, 1940-   VIII.
           O'Dwyer, Paul, 1907-   IX. Muskie, Edmund S   1914-

McGregor, Robert

Voice Lib.
M1599- A quiet requiem for Ezra Pound, with poets
1600   Robert Lowell, Robert Fitzgerald, James
        Laughlin, and Robert McGregor. Modern
        Language Center, Harvard University,
        December 4, 1972.
        70 min. phonotape (2 r. 7 1/2 i.p.s.)

        L Pound, Ezra Loomis, 1885-1972. L Lowell, Robert,
        1917- IL Fitzgerald, Robert, 1910- IIL Laughlin,
        James, 1914- IV. McGregor, Robert,

Mack, Ted, 1904-

Voice Lib.
M1028 Bowes, Edward, 1874-1946.
bd.2   Excerpt from radio's original "Amateur Hour",
       with Ted Mack and Teresa Brewer. Michigan
       State University, Department of Television and
       Radio, 1940's.
       1 reel (7 in.) 7 1/2 in. per sec.
       phonotape.

       I. Mack, Ted, 1904- II. Brewer, Teresa

McIntire, Ross T   1899-

Voice Lib.
M273- Biography in sound (radio program)
274   Franklin Delano Roosevelt: the friends and
bd.1   former associates of Franklin Roosevelt on
       the tenth anniversary of the President's death.
       NBC Radio, April, 1955.
       2 reels (7 in.) 7 1/2 in. per sec.
       phonotape.
       L Roosevelt, Franklin Delano, Pres. U.S., 1882-1945. L
       McIntire, Ross T   1899- IL Mellett, Lowell, 1884-1960.
       III. Tully, Grace   IV. Henderson, Leon, 1895-
       V. Roosevelt, Eleanor (Roosevelt) 1884-1962. VI. DeGraaf, Albert
       VII. Lehman, Herbert Henry, 1878-1963. VIII. Rosenman, Samuel
       Irving, 1896- IX. Arvey, Jacob   X. Moley, Raymond,
       1886- XI. Farley, James Aloysius, 1888- XII. Roosevelt,
       (Continued on next card)

Voice Lib.
262   Mack and Moran.
bd.2   Two Black Crows: comedy dialogue. WEAF,
       1923.
       1 reel (7 in.) 7 1/2 in. per sec.
       phonotape.

       I. Title.

McIntire, Ross T., 1899-

Voice Lib.
M384   I can hear it now (radio program)
bd.1   Biography of a pint of blood. CBS,
       February, 1951.
       1 reel (7 in.) 7 1/2 in. per sec.
       phonotape.

       1. Blood. I. McIntire, Ross T., 1899-
       II. Hope, Bob, 1903- III. Ridgway,
       Matthew Bunker, 1895- IV. Barkley,
       Alban William, 1877-1956.

Mack and Moran
see also
The two black crows (Radio program)

Voice Lib.
M1745 McIntyre, Thomas James, 1915-
       Debate with Senator John Tower on
       defense spending. WKAR, June 26, 1974.
       15 min. phonotape (1 r. 7 1/2 i.p.s.)

       1. U.S. - Defenses. I. Tower, John
       Goodwin, 1925-

McKay, Douglas, 1893-1959

Voice Lib.
227   Hoover, Herbert Clark, Pres. U.S., 1874-1964.
bd.2- Address on country doctors; introduced by
228   Douglas McKay. CBS, August 10, 1955.
bd.1   2 reels (7 in.) 7 1/2 in. per sec.
       phonotape.

       I. McKay, Douglas, 1893-1959.

Mack, Charles
see
The two black crows (Radio program)

Voice Lib.
341   McKinley, William, Pres. U.S., 1843-1901.
bd.4   Address at Pan-American Exposition.
       Columbia Test Cylinder, 1900.
       1 reel (7 in.) 7 1/2 in. per sec.
       phonotape.

Voice Lib.
M1672 McKissick, Floyd, 1922-
      Black power and white response.
      WKAR, January 27, 1969.
        45 min. phonotape (1 r.   7 1/2 i.p.s.)

      1. Black nationalism.

Voice Lib.
M806 MacMillan, Harold, 1894-
bd.4   Welcoming Dag Hammarskjöld to England;
      interrupted by isolationist heckler conserva-
      tive, but continuing speech undisturbed.
      U.N. Archives [no date]
        1 reel (7 in.) 7 1/2 in. per sec.
      phonotape.

      On United Nations Special Tape No. 2.

          MacLeish, Archibald, 1892-
            The fall of the city
Voice Lib.
M1051 Columbia Broadcasting System, Inc. Radio
bd.2   Workshop.
      Radio production of program "The Fall of the
    City", written by Archibald MacLeish. CBS
    Radio, 1934.
      1 reel (7 in.) 7 1/2 in. per sec.
    phonotape.

      I. MacLeish, Archibald, 1892-   /The
    fall of the city.

Voice Lib.
M742 MacMillan, Harold, 1894-
bd.5   Speaking during British election campaign.
      BBC, 1959.
        1 reel (7 in.) 7 1/2 in. per sec.
      phonotape.

      McMahon, James O'Brien, 1903-1952
Voice Lib.
353 Russia and the bomb, discussed by various
bd.19 personalities. NBC, September 25, 1949.
      1 reel (7 in.) 7 1/2 in. per sec.
    phonotape.

    Participants: Harrison Brown, Harold Urey,
    Samuel Allison, Thornton Hugness, Brien McMahon,
    Paul Douglas, John Foster Dulles, Leslie Groves,
    Winston Churchill, Dean Acheson, James Fleming.

    I. Brown, Harrison Scott, 1917-   II.
    Urey, Harold Clayton, 1893-   III. Allison,
            (Continued on next card)

Voice Lib.
M742 MacMillan, Harold, 1894-
bd.9   Statement of appreciation to British
      public at the result of the 1959 election.
      CBS, 1959.
        1 reel (7 in.) 7 1/2 in. per sec.
      phonotape.

      McMahon, James O'Brien, 1903-1952
Voice Lib.
353 Russia and the bomb... 1949. (Card 2)
bd.19

    Samuel King, 1900-   IV. Hugness, Thornton.
    V. McMahon, James O'Brien, 1903-1952. VI.
    Douglas, Paul Howard, 1892- VII. Dulles,
    John Foster, 1888-1959. VIII. Groves, Leslie
    B   1896-1970. IX. Churchill, Winston
    Leonard Spencer, 1874-1965. X. Acheson, Dean
    Gooderham, 1893-1971. XI. Fleming, James,
    1915-

Voice Lib.
M258 MacMillan, Harold, 1804-
bd.11   BBC address on entering the European
      Free Trade Association. New York, CBS,
      May 29, 1961.
        1 reel (7 in.) 7 1/2 in. per sec.
      phonotape.

      McMahon, James O'Brien, 1903-1952
Voice Lib.
381- I can hear it now (radio program)
382   CBS, April 26, 1951.
bd.1   2 reels (7 in.) 7 1/2 in. per sec. phonotape.
      I. Radio Free Europe. 2. Strategic Air Command. I.
    Ridgway, Matthew Bunker, 1895- II. Churchill, Winston Leonard
    Spencer, 1874-1965. III. Bevan, Aneurin, 1897-1960. IV. Nixon,
    Richard Milhous, Pres. U.S., 1913- V. Kerr, Robert Samuel, 1896-
    1963. VI. Brewster, Ralph Owen, 1888-1962. VII. Wherry, Kenneth
    Spicer, 1892-1951. VIII. Capehart, Homer Earl, 1897- IX.
    Lehman, Herbert Henry, 1878-1963. X. Taft, Robert Alphonso,
    1889-1953. XI. Moody, Arthur Edson Blair, 1902-1954. XII.
    Martin, Joseph William, 1884-1968. XIII. McMahon, James O'Brien,
    1903-1952. XIV. MacArthur, Douglas, 1880-1964. XVII. Wilson,
    Charles Edward, 1886-1972. XVIII. Irvine, Clarence T

Voice Lib.
344 MacMillan, Harold, 1894-
bd.2   Addressing group of business executives
    on East-West relations. CBS, November 8,
    1961.
      1 reel (7 in.) 7 1/2 in. per sec.
    phonotape.

MacMillan, Harold, 1894-

Voice Lib.
M806   United Nations Special Tape No. 2.
       U.N. Archives ₍various dates₎
       1 reel (7 in.)   7 1/2 in. per sec.
       phonotape.

       CONTENTS. -bd. 1. Excerpt from speech by Sen. Tom Connally
       at disarmament committee criticizing U.S.S.R. -bd. 2. U.N.
       translators in row, getting into fist fight and interrupting Pakistani
       delegate. -bd. 3. Nepal U.N. delegate at 771st Plenary Session of
       General Assembly interrupted by screaming agitator. -bd. 4. Harold
       MacMillan, honorary president of U.N. Association, welcoming Dag
       Hammarskjöld to England; interrupted by isolationist heckler conser-
       vative, but continuing speech undisturbed. -bd. 5. U.N. delegate
       from Saudi Arabia arguing with Chairman of Committee about
                                    (Continued on next card)

MacMillan, Harold, 1894-

Voice Lib.
M806   United Nations Special Tape No. 2.   ₍various
       dates₎   (Card 2)
       CONTENTS, cont'd. "point of order". -bd. 6. U.N. delegate
       speaking about "hamburgers with a college education" and the
       effect of advertising slogans on the masses. -bd. 7. Turkish U.N.
       delegate at U.N. replying to Greek delegate on "point of order". -
       bd. 8. U.N. delegate speaking about white slavery and high cost of
       women. -bd. 9. U.N. delegate telling an anecdote about an
       incident in underdeveloped country: "A U.N. Bull". -bd. 10. U.N.
       delegate balling up anecdote about cats. -bd. 11. U.N. delegate
       speaking about lizards hindering business in Nigeria. -bd. 12. U.N.
       delegate advocating more scientific progress on old age rather than
       the progress on moon exploration. -bd. 13. U.N. delegate telling
       anecdote about co-operation. -bd. 14. South African delegate
                                    (Continued on next card)

MacMillan, Harold, 1894-

Voice Lib.
M806   United Nations Special Tape No. 2.   ₍various
       dates₎   (Card 3)
       CONTENTS, cont'd. telling anecdote at U.N. -bd. 15. Chairman
       opening the 714th session of the Second Committee of the 15th
       Session of the U.N. General Assembly. -bd. 16. U.N. delegate
       indicating the number of seats available for various countries at the
       U.N. -bd. 17. Chairman of Committee instructing delegates how to
       indicate their vote. -bd. 18. U.N. delegate from Liberia debating
       on how to address a woman chairman.

       I. Connally, Thomas Terry, 1877-1963.   II.
       MacMillan, Harold, 1894-

Voice Lib.
M954   McNamara, Robert S   1916-
       Testimony at U.S. Senate Foreign
       Relations Committee hearings.   NBC,
       April 20, 1966.
       1 reel (7 in.)   7 1/2 i.p.s.
       phonotape.

       1. U.S. - Foreign relations.   I. U.S.
       Congress.   Senate.   Foreign Relations
       Committee.

McNamara, Robert S   1916-

Voice Lib.
M1336 Launching of aircraft carrier "John F. Kennedy"
bd.2   at Newport News, Virginia.   Speakers:
       Senator Edward Kennedy, Caroline Kennedy,
       and Robert McNamara.   Comments by CBS news-
       caster Steve Rowan.   CBS-TV, August, 1968.
       1 reel (7 in.)   7 1/2 in. per sec.
       phonotape.

       I. Kennedy, Edward Moore, 1932-   II.
       Kennedy, Caroline, 1957-   III. McNamara,
       Robert S   1916-

McNamee, Graham, 1888-1942

Voice Lib.
M617   Radio in the 1920's: a series of excerpts
bd.1-   from important broadcasts of the 1920's,
bd.25   with brief prologue and epilogue; a sample
       of radio of the period.   NVL, April, 1964.
       1 reel (7 in.)   7 1/2 in. per sec.
       phonotape.
           1. Radio programs.   I. Marconi, Guglielmo, marchese, 1874-
       1937. II. Kendall, H   G   III. Coolidge, Calvin, Pres. U.S.,
       1872-1933. IV. Wilson, Woodrow, Pres. U.S., 1856-1924. V.
       Roosevelt, Franklin Delano, Pres. U.S., 1882-1945. VI. Lodge,
       Henry Cabot, 1850-1924. VII. LaGuardia, Fiorello Henry, 1882-1947.
       VIII. The Happiness Boys (Radio program) IX. Gallagher and Sheen.
       X. Barney Google. XI. Vallee, Rudy, 1901-   XII. The two
                                    (Continued on next card)

McNamee, Graham, 1888-1942

Voice Lib.
M574   I can hear it now (radio program)
bd.2-   1919-1933.   CBS, 1953.
575   2 reels (7 in.)   7 1/2 in. per sec.
       phonotape.

       I. Murrow, Edward Roscoe, 1908-1965.   II.
       Rogers, Will, 1879-1935.   III. White, William
       Allen, 1868-1944.   IV. Hoover, Herbert Clarke,
       Pres. U.S., 1874-1964.   V. Roosevelt, Franklin
       Delano, Pres. U.S., 1882-1945.   VI. Rice,
       Grantland, 1880-1954.   VII. McNamee, Graham,
       1888-1942.

Macomber, William Butts, 1921-

Voice Lib.
M1477 Discussion of Supreme Court decision on
       publishing Pentagon Papers.   William B.
       Macomber, deputy under-secretary of state;
       Senator Henry Jackson; Max Frankel, head of
       New York Times' Washington bureau; Benjamin
       Bradley, executive editor of Washington Post.
       Questioned by Carl Stern, NBC; Martin Hayden,
       Detroit News; James J. Kilpatrick, Washington
       Star Syndicate; Kenneth Crawford, Washington
       Post; Edwin Newman.   NBC-TV, June 30, 1971.
       1 reel (7 in.)   7 1/2 in. per sec.
       phonotape.
                                    (Continued on next card)

Voice Lib.
M1064 McPherson, Aimee Semple, 1890-1944.
bd.10   Statement by "Sister" McPherson before
       leaving Los Angeles on a pilgrimage to the
       Holy Land, on prohibition.   Fox Movietone,
       1929.
       1 reel (7 in.)   7 1/2 in. per sec.
       phonotape.

       1. Prohibition.

Voice Lib.
649   McPherson, Aimee Semple, 1890-1944.
bd.6-7   Excerpts from evangelistic sermons.
       Columbia Records Institute, 1931.
       1 reel (7 in.)   7 1/2 in. per sec.
       phonotape.

       CONTENTS.-bd.6. "The Crucifixion".-bd. 7.
       "The Lost Sheep Returns", with David Hutton.

Voice Lib.
M1056   McPherson, Aimee Semple, 1890-1944.
bd.6   Musical sermon, "Calvaries [sic] Rose".
          Salter, 1931.
             1 reel (7 in.)   7 1/2 in. per sec.
          phonotape.

Voice Lib.
M770   Maddox, Joseph A
bd.5   "Motivation"; a prose poem written for
          Education 200 class, narrated by the
          student and author.   NVL recording,
          March 8, 1966.
             1 reel (7 in.)   7 1/2 in. per sec.
          phonotape.

          I. Title.

Voice Lib.
M1056   McPherson, Aimee Semple, 1890-1944.
bd.7   Religious dialogue, "Are You Happy?".
          Salter, 1931.
             1 reel (7 in.)   7 1/2 in. per sec.
          phonotape.

          I. Title: Are you happy?

Voice Lib.
M1567- Maddox, Lester Garfield, 1915-
1568,   Option; television broadcast originating
bd.1   at the University of Buffalo.   WKAR-AM,
          February 19, 1974.
             45 min.   phonotape (2 r.   7 1/2 in. per
          sec.)

          Speech delivered November 1973.

             1. U.S. - Social conditions. 2. U.S. -
          Politics and government.

Voice Lib.
540   McPherson, Aimee Semple, 1890-1944.
bd.18   Prohibition: tells story of prohibition
          on leaving for Europe and the Holy Land.
          Fox Movietone, 1932.
             1 reel (7 in.)   7 1/2 in. per sec.
          phonotape.

          1. Prohibition.

Voice Lib. Madison, Connie
M272   Biography in sound (radio program)
bd.1   Heywood Broun.   NBC, date?
             1 reel (7 in.)   7 1/2 in. per sec.
          phonotape.

             I. Broun, Heywood Campbell, 1888-1939. I. Broun,
          Heywood Campbell, 1888-1939. II. Swope, Herbert Bayard,
          1882-1958. III. Wilson, Mattie   IV. Jackson, Gardner
          V. Meany, Thomas   VI. Waldron, Beatrice   VII.
          Gordon, Max   VIII. Madison, Connie   IX. Gannett,
          Lewis Stiles, 1891-1966. X. Collins, Joseph, 1866-1950. XI.
          Brown, Earl Louis, 1900-   XII. Levy, Newman, 1888-
          XIII. Growth, John   XIV. Bye, George   XV.
          Roosevelt, Franklin Delano, Pres. U.S., 1882-1945. XVI.
          Reynolds, Quentin James,   -1965.

Voice Lib.
554   McPherson, Aimee Semple, 1890-1944.
bd.2   Sermon "Come unto Me"; sings "I ain't
          a gonna grieve" accompanied by choir.
          Columbia Phonograph Company, 1933.
             1 reel (7 in.)   7 1/2 in. per sec.
          phonotape.

C1   MAGIC
S74
        Whorf, Michael, 1933-
          Abracadabra.
             1 tape cassette.   (The visual sounds of
          Mike Whorf. Social, S74)
             Originally presented on his radio program, Kaleidoscope,
          WJR, Detroit.
             Duration: 37 min.
             Magic! Throughout civilization magic has brought men's
          curiosity to a head. Every culture has had its superstitions, its
          sorcerers. Throughout mankind's history magic has been studied,
          has been practiced.
             I. Magic. I. Title.

Voice Lib.   McPherson, Aimee Semple, 1890-1944
M617   Radio in the 1920's: a series of excerpts
bd.1-   from important broadcasts of the 1920's,
bd.25   with brief prologue and epilogue; a sample
          of radio of the period. NVL, April, 1964.
             1 reel (7 in.)   7 1/2 in. per sec.
          phonotape.
             I. Radio programs. I. Marconi, Guglielmo, marchese, 1874-
          1937. II. Kendall, H   G   III. Coolidge, Calvin, Pres. U.S.,
          1872-1933. IV. Wilson, Woodrow, Pres. U.S., 1856-1924. V.
          Roosevelt, Franklin Delano, Pres. U.S., 1882-1945. VI. Lodge,
          Henry Cabot, 1850-1924. VII. LaGuardia, Fiorello Henry, 1882-1947.
          VIII. The Happiness Boys (Radio program) IX. Gallagher and Sheen.
          X. Barney Google. XI. Vallee, Rudy, 1901-   XII. The two
          (Continued on next card)—

Voice Lib.
M957   The magic of broadcasting; variety TV
          program about radio and TV broadcasting
          with Arthur Godfrey, emcee, and Don Ameche,
          Bing Crosby, Lucille Ball, Gale Gordon, John
          Scott Trotter, Rod Serling, Sheldon Leonard,
          Dianne Sherry, Cary MacLane, and the "Wee
          Five".   CBS-TV, May 1, 1966.
             1 reel (7 in.)   7 1/2 in. per sec.
          phonotape.
             1. Television broadcasting.
             I. Godfrey, Arthur, 1903-

C1
A37   The magic of poetry
        Whorf, Michael, 1933-
            The magic of poetry.
            1 tape cassette. (The visual sounds of
        Mike Whorf. Art, music and letters, A37)
            Originally presented on his radio program, Kaleidoscope,
        WJR, Detroit.
            Duration: 37 min., 30 sec.
            Here is a simple and elementary look at the art of reading
        and writing verse. A few quotes from the masters and a few
        dissections help the listener discover the magic of poetry.

            l. Poetry. l. Title.

Voice Lib.
M1322   Mahesh Yogi, Maharishi, 1911 (?)-
bd.2   Interview of Maharishi Yogi of India
        at college seminar held at MSU about
        transcendental meditation. MSU Information
        Service, June 18, 1968.
            1 reel (7 in.) 7 1/2 in. per sec.
        phonotape.

            1. Transcendental meditation

        The Magnificent Yankee
Voice Lib.
M726   Lunt, Alfred, 1893-
bd.1;   "The Magnificent Yankee", a Hallmark-
727,   sponsored TV dramatization of the life of
bd.1   Justice Oliver Wendell Holmes. NBC, January
        28, 1965.
            2 reels (7 in.) 7 1/2 in. per sec.
        phonotape.

            1. Holmes, Oliver Wendell, 1809-1894.
            I. Fontanne, Lynne 887(?)-   TITLE

            MAIKOWSKI, HANS EBERHARD
Voice Lib.
M1363   Goebbels, Joseph, 1897-1945.
bd.0   Memorial ceremonies for SA-Sturmfuehrer
        Hans Eberhard Maikowski. Peteler,
        February 5, 1933.
            1 reel (7 in.) 7 1/2 in. per sec.
        phonotape.

            1. Maikowski, Hans Eberhard

Voice Lib.
353   Magnuson, Warren Grant, 1905-
bd.9   Outbreak of Korean War; meet the enemy
        where they will be, points out this may be
        a bluff. NBC, July, 1950.
            1 reel (7 in.) 7 1/2 in. per sec.
        phonotape.

            Original disc off-speed.

            1. Korean War, 1950-1953

Voice Lib.
M1738   Mailer, Norman
bd.2   Interviewed on the Merv Griffin Show.
        WGRT-TV, June 19, 1974.
            25 min. phonotape (1 r. 7 1/2 i.p.s.)

            I. Griffin, Mervyn Edward, 1925-

Voice Lib.
M1727   Magruder, Jeb Stuart, 1934-
Bd.1   Interviewed by Barbara Walters on the
        Today Show. NBC, June 14, 1974.
            20 min. phonotape (1 r. 7 1/2 i.p.s.)

            1. Watergate Affair, 1972-
            I. Walters, Barbara 1931-

Voice Lib.
M846   The Making of the President, 1964 (TV program)
bd.2   Excerpts of political speeches and state-
        ments by presidential candidates Lyndon
        Johnson and Barry Goldwater, from TV dramati-
        zation of Theodore H. White's book "The
        making of the president, 1964".
            6 min. phonotape (1 r. 7 1/2 i.p.s.)

            I. Johnson, Lyndon Baines, Pres. U.S., 1908-1973.
            II. Goldwater, Barry Morris, 1909-   III. White, Theodore
        Harold, 1915-   /The making of the president, 1964.

Voice Lib.
M1800   Magruder, Jeb Stuart, 1934-
WG   Testimony before the Senate Committee
0614   investigating the Watergate Affair.
            361 min. phonotape (5 r. 3 3/4 i.p.s.)
        (Watergate gavel to gavel, phase 1)

            1. Watergate Affair, 1972-

        Malcolm X
        see
        Little, Malcolm, 1925-1965

VOICE LIBRARY

Malik, Charles Habib, 1906-
Voice Lib.
M1033   Voice of America.
        Twentieth anniversary program of Voice of
        America broadcasts narrated by Henry Fonda,
        and including the voices of Carl Sandburg,
        Danny Kaye, Jawaharlal Nehru, Franklin D.
        Roosevelt, Charles Malik, Arnold Toynbee,
        William Faulkner, Harry S.Truman, Dwight D.
        Eisenhower, Helen Hayes, Dag Hammarskjöld,
        Winston Churchill, and John F. Kennedy.
        Voice of America, 1963.
        1 reel (7 in.)   7 1/2 in. per sec.
        phonotape.
                        (Continued on next card)

Malik, Charles Habib, 1906-
Voice Lib.
M1033   Voice of America. Twentieth anniversary
        program... 1963.   (Card 2)

        I. Fonda, Henry Jaynes, 1905-   II. Sandburg, Carl,
        1878-1967. III. Kaye, Danny, 1913-   IV. Nehru, Jawaharlal,
        1889-1964. V. Roosevelt, Franklin Delano, Pres. U.S., 1882-
        1945. VI. Malik, Charles Habib, 1906-   VII. Toynbee,
        Arnold Joseph, 1889-   VIII. Faulkner, William, 1897-1962.
        IX. Truman, Harry S, Pres. U.S., 1884-1972. X. Eisenhower,
        Dwight David, Pres. U.S., 1890-1969. XI. Hayes, Helen,
        1900-   XII. Hammarskjöld, Dag, 1905-1961. XIII. Churchill,
        Winston Leonard Spencer, 1874-1965. XIV. Kennedy, John
        Fitzgerald, Pres. U.S., 1917-1963.

MALNUTRITION
Voice Lib.
M1611   Mayer, Jean
bd.2   Interview by Edwin Newman on Speaking
        freely. WKAR-TV, March, 1974.
           5 min.   phonotape (1 r.   7 1/2 i.p.s.)

           1. Malnutrition.   I. Newman, Edwin Harold,
        1919-

Voice Lib.   Malone, George Wilson, 1890-1961
383   I can hear it now (radio program)
        CBS, February 9, 1951.
           1 reel (7 in.)   7 1/2 in. per sec.
        phonotape.
           I. Wilson, Charles Edward, 1886-1972. II. Gabrielson, Guy
        George, 1891-   III. Taft, Robert Alphonso, 1889-1953. IV.
        Martin, Joseph William, 1884-1965. V. McCarthy, Joseph
        Raymond, 1909-1957. VI. Benton, William Burnett, 1900-1973.
        VII. Malone, George Wilson, 1890-1961. VIII. Capehart, Homer
        Earl, 1897-   IX. Eisenhower, Dwight David, Pres. U.S., 1890-
        1969. X. Lee, J   V   XI. Hodge, John Reed, 1893-
        1963. XII. Overton, Watkins   XIII. DiSalle, Michael
        Vincent, 1908-   XIV. Boyce, Eddy   XV. Conklin, Ed
        XVI. Collins, Joseph Lawton, 1896-

MAN - INFLUENCE ON NATURE
Voice Lib.
M976-   Huxley, Aldous Leonard, 1894-1963.
977   Leading a discussion group at C.S.D.I. on
        ecological effects on technology, the
        tragic price we are paying for our conquest
        of nature.   Other speakers: Ritchie Calder,
        Walter J. Ong, S.J., and Robert M. Hutchins,
        etc.   March, 1962.
           2 reels (7 in.) 7 1/2 in. per sec.   phonotape.
           I. Man - Influence on nature. I. Calder, Ritchie, 1906-
        II. Ong, Walter Jackson, 1912-   III. Hutchins, Robert
        Maynard, 1899-

MAN - INFLUENCE ON NATURE
Voice Lib.
M1615   Taylor, John Francis Adams
           The social implications of the energy
        crisis.   WKAR-FM, March 28, 1974.
           35 min.   phonotape (1 r.   7 1/2 in. per sec.)
           Part of the "Energy and Life" symposium
        held at Michigan State University.

           1. Man - Influence on nature.   2. Power
        resources - U.S.

MAN - INFLUENCE ON NATURE
Voice Lib.
M1720   Udall, Morris K., 1922-
bd.4   On the Today Show with Sam Steiger, debating
        their opposing bills for land-use funding.
        Includes Barbara Walters and Bill Monroe.
        NBC-TV, June 10, 1974.
           8 min.   phonotape (1 r.   7 1/2 i.p.s.)

           1. Land.   2. Man - Influence on nature.
        I. Steiger, Sam, 1929-   II. Walters,
        Barbara, 1931-   III. Monroe, Bill.

MAN - INFLUENCE ON NATURE
Voice Lib.
M1697   Udall, Stewart L
bd.1   The environmental crisis, the crisis of
        survival; address at Michigan State Univer-
        sity. WKAR, April 24, 1970.
           37 min.   phonotape (1 r.   7 1/2 i.p.s.)

           1. Ecology.   2. Man - Influence on nature.

MAN - ORIGIN
C1
816   Whorf, Michael, 1933-
           The beginning of man.
           1 tape cassette.   (The visual sounds of
        Mike Whorf. Social, S16)
           Originally presented on his radio program, Kaleidoscope,
        WJR, Detroit.
           Duration: 40 min., 35 sec.
           This program takes an open-minded look in a narrative
        which concerns itself with the possibility of evolution and
        how man began.

           1. Evolution.   2. Man - Origin.   I. Title.

        The man called healer
C1
SC2   Whorf, Michael, 1933-
           The man called healer.
           1 tape cassette.   (The visual sounds of
        Mike Whorf. Science, Sc2)
           Originally presented on his radio program, Kaleidoscope,
        WJR, Detroit.
           Duration: 39 min.
           Actual recordings are used to relate the story of medicine -
        its history and progress under difficult conditions.

           1. Physicians.   2. Medicine.   I. Title.

A man for all ages - Dante

C1
A26
Whorf, Michael, 1933–
   A man for all ages - Dante.
   1 tape cassette.   (The visual sounds of
Mike Whorf. Art, music and letters, A26)
   Originally presented on his radio program, Kaleidoscope,
WJR, Detroit.
   Duration: 38 min.
   To many critics the world over Dante's "Divine comedy" is the
finest piece of writing mankind has ever accomplished. Here is a
look at the writing and at the man.

   L Dante Alighieri, 1265-1321.   L Title.

Man from Oklahoma

C1
M4
Whorf, Michael, 1933–
   Man from Oklahoma.
   1 tape cassette.   (The visual sounds of
Mike Whorf. Miscellaneous, M4)

   Originally presented on his radio program, Kaleidoscope,
WJR, Detroit.
   Duration: 40 min.
   The dry, brilliant humor of Will Rogers comes through in this
narrative concerning the cowboy philosopher.

   L Rogers, Will, 1879-1935.   L Title.

Voice Lib.
M388-   The man from Oliver Street; story of Al Smith's life. Sings
399,   "The Bowery", describes himself as an American, reveals
bd. 1   his feelings about the New Deal, at 1928 Democratic
        Convention, youth in New York City, prohibition, democracy,
        politics, acceptance speech for 1928 Democratic nomination,
        attempting to rent space in Empire State Building, action for
        better housing, sings "East side, west side". Hearst
        Metrotone News, 1962.
           2 reels (7 in.)   7 1/2 i. p. s.   phonotape.

           L Smith, Alfred Emanuel, 1873-1944.

The man from Osawattmie - John Brown's story

C1
H26
Whorf, Michael, 1933–
   The man from Osawattmie - John Brown's story.
   1 tape cassette.   (The visual sounds of
Mike Whorf. History and heritage, H26)
   Originally presented on his radio program, Kaleidoscope,
WJR, Detroit.
   Duration: 30 min.
   Fanatic or hero, prophet or fool; here is the life and times
of old John Brown.

   L Brown, John, 1800-1859.   L Title.

The man in the ditch

Voice Lib.
M840   Wallace, Edgar, 1875-1932.
bd.11   Telling his mystery thriller "The Man in
       the Ditch". HMV, 1929.
          1 reel (7 in.)   7 1/2 in. per sec.
       phonotape.

          1. Title: The man in the ditch.

The man in the glass box

C1
SC3–
SC4
Whorf, Michael, 1933–
   The man in the glass box.
   2 tape cassettes.   (The visual sounds of
Mike Whorf. Science, SC3–SC4)
      originally presented on his radio program, Kaleidoscope,
WJR, Detroit.
      Duration: 39 min. , 46 min.
      Two documentary programs on one of today's greatest
medical and social problems ... alcoholism.

   L Alcoholics.   L Title.

The man in the iron mask

C1
M11
Whorf, Michael, 1933–
   The man in the iron mask.
   1 tape cassette.   (The visual sounds of
Mike Whorf. Miscellaneous, M11)

   Originally presented on his radio program, Kaleidoscope,
WJR, Detroit.
   Duration: 42 min., 10 sec.
   An account of the thoughts and ideas of a big league catcher.
The emphasis is on baseball, but a ball player thinks of other
things as well.

   L Freehan, Bill, 1941–   2. Baseball. L Title.

A man named Ghandi

C1
S2
Whorf, Michael, 1933–
   A man named Ghandi.
   1 tape cassette.   (The visual sounds of
Mike Whorf. Social, S2)
   Originally presented on his radio program, Kaleidoscope,
WJR, Detroit.
   Duration: 29 min.
   Gandhi was counselor, advisor, and spiritual guide to a nation
which upheld the caste system and he alone was able to break
through to open the eyes of the world.

   L Gandhi, Mohandas Karamchand, 1869-1948.   L Title.

The man of steel and velvet

C1
H7
Whorf, Michael, 1933–
   The man of steel and velvet.
   1 tape cassette.   (The visual sounds of
Mike Whorf. History and heritage, H7)
   Originally presented on his radio program, Kaleidoscope,
WJR, Detroit.
   Duration: 55 min.
   A historical account of the young Lincoln, his days as a
struggling young lawyer, his political aspirations, his arduous
years as a president, his tragic death.

   L Lincoln, Abraham, Pres. U.S., 1809-1865.   L Title.

The man who wrote Moby Dick - Herman Melville

C1
A25
Whorf, Michael, 1933–
   The man who wrote Moby Dick - Herman Melville.
   1 tape cassette.   (The visual sounds of
Mike Whorf. Art, music and letters, A25)
   Originally presented on his radio program, Kaleidoscope,
WJR, Detroit.
   Duration: 42 min.
   Herman Melville, like his characters, lived a life of adventure
aboard ship. He knew the seas and islands and he drew from his
experiences to write what critics believe is one of the ten best books
ever written.

   L Melville, Herman, 1819-1891.   L Title.

Voice Lib.
M1043 Manchester, William Raymond, 1922-
       "Meet the Press" television program with
       author William Manchester regarding his
       forth-coming book "The Death of A President",
       and discussing the controversy with the
       Kennedy family regarding its contents as
       well as alleged inaccuracies in the present
       serialization in "Look" magazine. Edwin
       Newman, MC. NBC-TV, February 12, 1967.
          1 reel (7 in.) 7 1/2 in. per sec.
       phonotape.
                              SEE NEXT CARD

Voice Lib.
M256   Mann, Woodrow Wilson
  bd.1   Remarks of Mayor Mann preceding first
       day of integration at Little Rock, Arkansas.
       CBS News, September 22, 1957.
          1 reel (7 in.) 7 1/2 i.p.s.   phonotape.

          1. Segregation in education.

Voice Lib.
M1043 Manchester, William Raymond, 1922-   "Meet
       the Press" television program...   1967.
       (Card 2)

          1. Manchester, William Raymond, 1922- /
       The death of a president.   I. Newman, Edwin
       Harold, 1919-

Voice Lib.
M1557- Mansfield, Michael Joseph, 1903-
1558,   Reply to the State of the Union Address
  bd.1   by President Nixon; excerpts. WJIM (CBS),
       February 1, 1974.
          40 min. phonotape (2 r.   7 1/2 in. per
       sec.)

       Includes question and answer period.

          1. U.S. - Politics and government - 1969-

          MANCHESTER, WILLIAM RAYMOND, 1922-
             THE DEATH OF A PRESIDENT
Voice Lib.
M1043 Manchester, William Raymond, 1922-
       "Meet the Press" television program with
       author William Manchester regarding his
       forth-coming book "The Death of A President",
       and discussing the controversy with the
       Kennedy family regarding its contents as
       well as alleged inaccuracies in the present
       serialization in "Look" magazine. Edwin
       Newman, MC. NBC-TV, February 12, 1967.
          1 reel (7 in.) 7 1/2 in. per sec.
       phonotape.

          Mansfield, Michael Joseph, 1903-
Voice Lib.
M309   Columbia Broadcasting System, inc.
  bd.3   Assassination: statements by Senator
       Dirksen and Senator Mansfield, remarks about
       statements and actions of others in Washington.
       CBS, November 22, 1963.
          1 reel (7 in.) 7 1/2 in. per sec.
       phonotape.

          1. Kennedy, John Fitzgerald, Pres. U.S.,
       1917-1963 - Assassination. I. Dirksen,
       Everett McKinley, 1896-1969. II. Mansfield,
       Michael Joseph, 1903-

Voice Lib.
M1675 Mandrake (radio program)
  bd.1   Mandrake.   Golden Age Radio Records,
       1939.
          8 min. phonotape (1 r.   7 1/2 i.p.s.)

          Marble, Harry
Voice Lib.
M1046 World news tonight; radio news commentary.
  bd.2   CBS Radio news broadcast from Honolulu,
       London, New York and Washington; including
       William Ewing, Norman Corwin, Albert Leitch
       and Harry Marble.   CBS, September 12, 1942.
          1 reel (7 in.) 7 1/2 in. per sec.
       phonotape.

          I. Ewing, William   II. Corwin, Norman
       Lewis, 1910-   III. Leitch, Albert
       IV. Marble, Harry

Voice Lib.
M760   Mann, Arthur
  bd.3   Excerpt from "What All The Screaming's
       About" (Program 1); English-based music
       of Beatles; what serious musicians find
       interesting about the music of the Beatles.
       Westinghouse Broadcasting Corporation, 1964.
          1 reel (7 in.) 7 1/2 in. per sec.
       phonotape. (The Music Goes Round and Round)

          1. The Beatles.   I. Title: What all the
       screaming's about. II. Series.

Voice Lib.
353   Marcantonio, Vito, 1902-1954.
  bd.17   Outbreak of Korean War; Madison Square
       Garden meeting describing outbreak is not
       in the interest of U.S. NBC, July, 1950.
          1 reel (7 in.) 7 1/2 in. per sec.
       phonotape.

          Original disc off-speed.

          1. Korean War, 1950-1953

Voice Lib.
M279   March, Frederic, 1897-
bd.1   Hark! the Years; presents the voices of the
           past.   Capitol Records, Inc. (G. R. Vincent),
           1890-1933.
               1 reel (7 in.)   7 1/2 in. per sec.
           phonotape.

Marching as to war
C1
S15   Whorf, Michael, 1933-
           Marching as to war.
               1 tape cassette.   (The visual sounds of
           Mike Whorf.   Social, S15)
               Originally presented on his radio program, Kaleidoscope,
           WJR, Detroit.
               Duration: 42 min.
               Outlined against the background of the 19th century in
           England, is the story of William Booth and the Salvation Army.

               L. Booth, William, 1829-1912. 2. Salvation Army.
           L. Title.

Voice Lib.
613   March, Fredric, 1897-
bd.1   "Listen: a Scrapbook in Sound"; condensed
           version of National Voice Library's "Hark !
           The Years", as used in Riverside Radio's
           continuing program series "Listen".   WRVR,
           March, 1964.
               1 reel (7 in.)   7 1/2 in. per sec.
           phonotape.

               I. Title.

Voice Lib.
M395   Marconi, Guglielmo, Marchese, 1874-1937.
bd.3   Speech to Tribune Women's Club of Chicago
           on modern communications (shortwave broadcast
           from Rome), tells of early communications
           of his first transatlantic broadcast, state
           of radio art in 1930's.   New York, WOR,
           March 1, 1937.
               1 reel (7 in.)   7 1/2 i.p.s.   phonotape.

               1. Radio - History.

March Fredric, 1897-
Voice Lib.
M310   American Broadcasting Company.
           Tribute to President John Fitzgerald Kennedy
           from the arts. Fredric March emcees; Jerome
           Hines sings "Worship of God and Nature" by
           Beethoven; Florence Eldridge recites "When
           lilacs last in the door-yard bloom'd" by Walt
           Whitman; Marian Anderson in two songs. Includes
           Charlton Heston, Sidney Blackmer, Isaac Stern,
           Nathan Milstein, Christopher Plummer, Albert
           Finney.   ABC, November 24, 1963.
               35 min.   phonotape (7 in.   7 1/2 i.p.s.)

                        (Continued on next card)

Marconi, Guglielmo, marchese, 1874-1937
Voice Lib.
M617   Radio in the 1920's: a series of excerpts
bd.1-   from important broadcasts of the 1920's,
bd.25   with brief prologue and epilogue; a sample
           of radio of the period.   NVL, April, 1964.
               1 reel (7 in.)   7 1/2 in. per sec.
           phonotape.
               L. Radio programs. L. Marconi, Guglielmo, marchese, 1874-
           1937. II. Kendall, H   G   III. Coolidge, Calvin, Pres. U.S.,
           1872-1933. IV. Wilson, Woodrow, Pres. U.S., 1856-1924. V.
           Roosevelt, Franklin Delano, Pres. U.S., 1882-1945. VI. Lodge,
           Henry Cabot, 1850-1924. VII. LaGuardia, Fiorello Henry, 1882-1947.
           VIII. The Happiness Boys (Radio program) IX. Gallagher and Sheen.
           X. Barney Google. XI. Vallee, Rudy, 1901-   XII. The two
                        (Continued on next card)

The march to the sea - Sherman
C1
H114   Whorf, Michael, 1933-
           The march to the sea - Sherman.
               1 tape cassette.   (The visual sounds of
           Mike Whorf. History and heritage, H114)
               Originally presented on his radio program, Kaleidoscope,
           WJR, Detroit.
               Duration: 36 min., 15 sec.
               Was he ruthless or merely a genius at the art of warfare?
           Was William Tecumseh Sherman's March to the sea across
           Georgia one of fiery retaliation against the South, or the
           necessary means to an end?

               L. Sherman, William Tecumseh, 1820-1891. I. Title.

Voice Lib.
M1800   Mardian, Robert Charles, 1923-
WG   Testimony before the Senate Committee
0719.02-   investigating the Watergate Affair.
.03   Pacifica, July 19, 1973.
               213 min.   phonotape (3 r.   3 3/4 i.p.s.)
           (Watergate gavel to gavel, phase 1)

               1. Watergate Affair, 1972-

C1
M8   MARCHES
       Whorf, Michael, 1933-
           I love to hear a military band.
               1 tape cassette.   (The visual sounds of
           Mike Whorf. Miscellaneous, M8)
               Originally presented on his radio program, Kaleidoscope,
           WJR, Detroit.
               Duration: 50 min., 30 sec.
               With guest, Frederick Fennell, the tempos are 4/4 and the
           music is vibrant and varied, as through narrative and melody, the
           story of the march is related.

               L. Marches. L. Fennell, Frederick. II. Title.

Voice Lib.
M1800   Mardian, Robert Charles, 1923-
WG   Testimony before the Senate Committee
0720.01-   investigating the Watergate Affair.
.02   Pacifica, July 20, 1973.
               205 min.   phonotape (3 r.   3 3/4 i.p.s.)
           (Watergate gavel to gavel, phase 1)

               1. Watergate Affair, 1972-

Voice Lib.
M740   Margaret Rose, Princess of Great Britain,
bd.7   1930-
            Excerpt from "The Children's Hour", a
       radio broadcast from London to children,
       wishing them a good night after the speech
       by her sister, Princess Elizabeth. BBC,
       1940.
            1 reel (7 in.)   7 1/2 in. per sec.
       phonotape.

                Margaret Rose, Princess of Gt. Brit.,
                   1930-
Voice Lib.
572-   I can hear it now (radio program)
573   1933-1946. CBS, 1948.
bd.1   2 reels (7 in.)   7 1/2 in. per sec.
       phonotape.
         I. Murrow, Edward Roscoe, 1908-1965. II. LaGuardia, Fiorello
       Henry, 1882-1947. III. Chamberlain, Neville, 1869-1949. IV.
       Roosevelt, Franklin Delano, Pres. U.S., 1882-1945. V. Churchill,
       Winston Leonard Spencer, 1874-1965. VI. Gaulle, Charles de,
       Pres. France, 1890-1970. VII. Eisenhower, Dwight David, Pres. U.S.,
       1890-1969. VIII. Willkie, Wendell Lewis, 1892-1944. IX. Martin,
       Joseph William, 1884-1968. X. Elizabeth II, Queen of Great Britain,
       1926-   XI. Margaret Rose, Princess of Gt. Brit., 1930-   XII.
       Johnson, Hugh Samuel, 1882-1942. XIII. Smith, Alfred Emanuel,
       1873-1944. XIV. Lindbergh, Charles Augustus, 1902-   XV. Davis,
                    (Continued on next card)

       MARIHUANA
Voice Lib.
M1719 Wallace, Mike, 1918-
           The press: credible or incredible?
       address at Michigan State University.
       WKAR, March 5, 1970.
           36 min. phonotape (1 r. 7 1/2 i.p.s.)

           1. Television broadcasting. 2. Marihuana.
       3. Homosexuality - U.S.

       MARK TWAIN, PSEUD.
       SEE
       CLEMENS, SAMUEL LANGHORNE, 1835-1910

                    VOICE LIBRARY

C1   Marks, Gerald, 1900-
M20   Whorf, Michael, 1933-
           A tale of a tune, with Gerald Marks.
           1 tape cassette. (The visual sounds of
       Mike Whorf. Miscellaneous, M40)
           Originally presented on his radio program, Kaleidoscope,
       WJR, Detroit.
           Duration: 52 min.
           A delightful nostalgic look at how some of our popular songs
       were written, featuring composer Gerald Marks.
           I. Music, Popular (Songs, etc.) I. Marks, Gerald. II. Title.

C1   Marks, Gerald, 1900-
M29   Whorf, Michael, 1933-
           They don't write 'em like that anymore.
           1 tape cassette. (The visual sounds of
       Mike Whorf. Miscellaneous, M29)
           Originally presented on his radio program, Kaleidoscope,
       WJR, Detroit.
           Duration: 54 min., 30 sec.
           Gerald Marks tells the story of some of America's favorite
       melodies.
           I. Songs, American. 2. Music, Popular (Songs, etc.) - U.S.
       I. Marks, Gerald. II. Title.

C1   Marks, Gerald, 1900-
PMW17 Whorf, Michael, 1933-
           They don't write 'em like that anymore.
           1 tape cassette. (The visual sounds of
       Mike Whorf. Panorama; a world of music, PMW-17)
           Originally presented on his radio program, Kaleidoscope,
       WJR, Detroit.
           Duration: 25 min.
           Composer Gerald Marks relates anecdotes and stories behind
       the composing of several popular American songs.
           I. Music, Popular (Songs, etc.) - U.S. I. Marks, Gerald,
       1900-   II. Title.

Voice Lib.
M761   Marks, Herbert E
bd.1   Excerpt from "Whatever Happened to Tin Pan
       Alley?" (Program 3); comments on rise of
       Tin Pan Alley and the popularity of records.
       Westinghouse Broadcasting Corporation, 1964.
           1 reel (7 in.)   7 1/2 in. per sec.
       phonotape. (The Music Goes Round and Round)
           I. Title: Whatever happened to Tin Pan Alley?
       II. Series.

Voice Lib.
M762   Marks, Herbert E
bd.9   Excerpt from "Music from Broadway"
       (Program 5); comments about Lorenz Hart,
       his partnership with Richard Rodgers;
       including song "Manhattan" from "[The]
       Garrick Gaieties". Westinghouse Broad-
       casting Corporation, 1964.
           1 reel (7 in.)   7 1/2 in. per sec.
       phonotape. (The Music Goes Round and Round)
           I. Title: Music from Broadway. II. Series.

Voice Lib.   Marks, Patricia
M1277 Eisenhower, Dwight David, Pres. U.S., 1890-
                   1969.
           Miss Patricia Marks interviews Eisenhower
       on occasion of art exhibition at Gallery of
       Modern Art of paintings by Ike. The general,
       at age 77, reviews and comments on incidents
       in his life. NET, June, 1967.
           1 reel (7 in.)   7 1/2 in. per sec.
       phonotape.
           I. Marks, Patricia

Marlowe, Jess

Voice Lib.
M1741 Sayegh, Fayez Abdullah, 1922-
bd.1 In an emotional debate with Jess Marlowe
 and Barbara Walters on the Today Show.
 NBC-TV, June 24, 1974.
  15 min. phonotape (1 r. 7 1/2 i.p.s.)

  1. Refuges, Arab. I. Marlowe, Jess.
 II. Walters, Barbara, 1931-

Marlowe, Jess

Voice Lib.
M1744 Vestal, M S
bd.1 Discussing his book Jerry Ford, up close,
 on the Today Show with Bill Monroe, Barbara
 Walters, and Jess Marlowe. NBC-TV, June 25,
 1974.
  10 min. phonotape (1 r. 7 1/2 i.p.s.)

  1. Ford, Gerald R., 1913- 2. Vestal,
 M.S./Jerry Ford, up close. I. Monroe, Bill.
 II. Walters, Barbara, 1931- III. Marlowe,
 Jess.

Voice Lib. Marlowe, Julia, 1865-1950
M225 Packard, Frederick
 Styles in Shakespearean acting, 1890-1950.
 Creative Associates, 1963?
 1 reel (7 in.) 7 1/2 i.p.s. phonotape.

 I. Sothern, Edward Askew, 1826-1881. II. Marlowe,
 Julia, 1865-1950. III. Booth, Edwin, 1833-1893. IV. Gielgud,
 John, 1904- V. Robeson, Paul Bustill, 1898- VI. Terry,
 Dame Ellen, 1848-1928. VII. Allen, Viola. VIII. Welles,
 Orson, 1915- IX. Skinner, Otis, 1858-1942. X. Barrymore,
 John, 1882-1942. XI. Olivier, Sir Laurence Kerr, 1907-
 XII. Forbes-Robertson, Sir Johnston, 1853- XIII. Evans,
 Maurice. XIV. Thorndike, Dame Sybil, 1882- XV. Robson,
 Flora. XVI. LeGallienne, Eva, 1899- XVII. Anderson,
 Judith. XVIII. Duncan, Augustin. XIX. Hampden, Walter.
 XX. Speaight, Robert, 1904- XXI. Jones, Daniel.

Voice Lib. Marquart, Rube, 1890-
M1248 Baseball fifty years ago; interviews with four
 famous old time baseball players, on NBC
 "Today" show, by host Hugh Downs, supported by
 sportcaster Joe Garagiola and Dr. Lawrence
 Ritter, author of new book. NBC-TV, June 9,
 1967.
 1 reel (7 in.) 7 1/2 in. per sec. phonotape.

 I. Baseball. I. Downs, Hugh Malcolm, 1921- II. Garagiola,
 Joe. III. Ritter, Lawrence S. /The glory of their times. IV. Roush,
 Edd, 1893- V. Marquart, Rube, 1890- VI. O'Doul, Lefty,
 1897- VII. Meyers, John, 1880-

C1 MARRIAGE
S61 Whorf, Michael, 1933-
 Customs of marriage.
 1 tape cassette. (The visual sounds of
 Mike Whorf. Social, S61)
 Originally presented on his radio program, Kaleidoscope,
 WJR, Detroit.
 Duration: 37 min., 40 sec.
 The great institution is described with music, prose, and
 poetry which delves into the lore, myth, and legend behind
 marriage customs.

 I. Marriage. I. Title.

Voice Lib.
M871 Marshall, George Catlett, 1880-1959.
bd.1 Accepting Distinguished Service Medal
 from President Truman upon retirement as
 Chief of Staff of U.S. Army. NBC,
 November 26, 1945.
  1 reel (7 in.) 7 1/2 in. per sec.
 phonotape.

Voice Lib.
234 Marshall, George Catlett, 1880-1959.
bd.2 Distinguished Service Medal, awarded
 by Pres. Harry S. Truman. CBS, November 26,
 1945.
  1 reel (7 in.) 7 1/2 in. per sec.
 phonotape.

 I. Truman, Harry S, Pres. U.S., 1884-1972.

Voice Lib.
M899 Marshall, George Catlett, 1880-1959.
 Report on his mission to Moscow, delivered
 from the State Department, Washington, D.C.
 WJR, April 28, 1947.
  1 reel (7 in.) 7 1/2 i.p.s. phonotape.

 1. U.S. - Foreign relations - Russia.
 2. Russia - Foreign relations - U.S.

Voice Lib.
M739 Marshall, George Catlett, 1880-1959.
bd.1 Comments of reassurance of purpose of
 U.S. involvement in Korea; in backing up
 U.N. forces. CBS, late 1950.
  1 min., 5 sec. phonotape (1 r.
 7 1/2 i.p.s.)

  1. Korean War, 1950-1953 - U.S.

Marshall, George Catlett, 1880-

Voice Lib.
573 I can hear it now (radio program)
bd.2- 1945-1949. CBS, 1950?
574 2 reels (7 in.) 7 1/2 in. per sec.
bd.1 phonotape.
 I. Murrow, Edward Roscoe, 1908-1965. II. Nehru, Jawaharlal,
 1889-1964. III. Philip, duke of Edinburgh, 1921- IV. Elizabeth II,
 Queen of Great Britain, 1926- V. Ferguson, Homer, 1889- VI.
 Hughes, Howard Robard, 1905- VII. Marshall, George Catlett,
 1880- VIII. Ruth, George Herman, 1895-1948. IX. Lilienthal,
 David Eli, 1899- X. Trout, Robert, 1908- XI. Gage, Arthur.
 XII. Jackson, Robert Houghwout, 1892-1954. XIII. Gromyko, Ana-
 tolii Andreevich, 1908- XIV. Baruch, Bernard Mannes, 1870-
 1965. XV. Churchill, Winston Leonard Spencer, 1874-1965. XVI.
 Winchell, Walter, 1897-1972 XVII. Davis, Elmer Holmes, 1890-
 (Continued on next card)

Voice Lib.
254-   Marshall, Herbert, 1887-
255   Winston Churchill, his finest hour. An
        autobiography of Sir Winston Churchill on
        the occasion of his 80th birthday. CBC,
        1954.
        2 reels (7 in.)   7 1/2 in. per sec.
        phonotape.

        1. Churchill, Winston Leonard Spencer,
        1874-1965.

Voice Lib.
M1081 Marshall, Thurgood, 1908-
        Speech at convocation during 10th anniver-
        sary of Fund for the Republic, discussing
        the role of federal courts in racial equal-
        ity cases and constitutional rights.
        CSDI, December, 1962.
        1 reel (7 in.)   7 1/2 in. per sec.
        phonotape.

        1. Negroes - Civil rights.

Voice Lib.
M863   Martin, Joseph William, 1884-1968.
bd.1   In Pittsburgh, urging voters to elect
        representative to Congress, commenting on
        loss of American prestige abroad and
        reviewing domestic and social and economic
        conditions in 1946.   KDKA, February 12, 1946.
        1 reel (7 in.)   7 1/2 in. per sec.
        phonotape.

Voice Lib.
M243   Martin, Joseph William, 1884-1968.
bd.8   Comments on the Senate Jury Trial
        Amendment in Civil Rights Bill, by Joseph
        Martin and Emanuel Celler. CBS, August 2,
        1957.
        1 reel (7 in.)   7 1/2 in. per sec.
        phonotape.

        I. Celler, Emanuel, 1888-
        1. Civil rights

        Martin, Joseph William, 1884-1968
Voice Lib.
572-. I can hear it now (radio program)
573   1933-1946. CBS, 1948.
bd.1   2 reels (7 in.)   7 1/2 in. per sec.
        phonotape.
        I. Murrow, Edward Roscoe, 1908-1965. II. LaGuardia, Fiorello
        Henry, 1882-1947. III. Chamberlain, Neville, 1869-1949. IV.
        Roosevelt, Franklin Delano, Pres. U.S., 1882-1945. V. Churchill,
        Winston Leonard Spencer, 1874-1965. VI. Gaulle, Charles de,
        Pres. France, 1890-1970. VII. Eisenhower, Dwight David, Pres. U.S.,
        1890-1969. VIII. Willkie, Wendell Lewis, 1892-1944. IX. Martin,
        Joseph William, 1884-1968. X. Elizabeth II, Queen of Great Britain,
        1926-   XI. Margaret Rose, Princess of Gt. Brit., 1930-   XII.
        Johnson, Hugh Samuel, 1882-'42. XIII. Smith, Alfred Emanuel,
        1873-1944. XIV. Lindbergh arles Augustus, 1902-   XV. Davis,
        -(Continued on next card)

Voice Lib. Martin, Joseph William, 1884-1965
383   I can hear it now (radio program)
        CBS, February 9, 1951.
        1 reel (7 in.)   7 1/2 in. per sec.
        phonotape.
        I. Wilson, Charles Edward, 1886-1972. II. Gabrielson, Guy
        George, 1891-   III. Taft, Robert Alphonso, 1889-1953. IV.
        Martin, Joseph William, 1884-1965. V. McCarthy, Joseph
        Raymond, 1909-1957. VI. Benton, William Burnett, 1900-1973.
        VII. Malone, George Wilson, 1890-1961. VIII. Capehart, Homer
        Earl, 1897-   IX. Eisenhower, Dwight David, Pres. U.S., 1890-
        1969. X. Lee, J   V   XI. Hodge, John Reed, 1893-
        1963. XII. Overton, Watkins   XIII. DiSalle, Michael
        Vincent, 1908-   XIV. Boyce, Eddy   XV. Conklin, Ed
        XVI. Collins, Joseph Lawton, 1896-

        Martin, Joseph William, 1884-1968
Voice Lib.
381-   I can hear it now (radio program)
382   CBS, April 26, 1951.
bd.1   2 reels (7 in.) 7 1/2 in. per sec. phonotape.
        I. Radio Free Europe. 2. Strategic Air Command. I.
        Ridgway, Matthew Bunker, 1895-   II. Churchill, Winston Leonard
        Spencer, 1874-1965. III. Bevan, Aneurin, 1897-1960. IV. Nixon,
        Richard Milhous, Pres. U.S., 1913-   V. Kerr, Robert Samuel, 1896-
        1963. VI. Brewster, Ralph Owen, 1888-1962. VII. Wherry, Kenneth
        Spicer, 1892-1951. VIII. Capehart, Homer Earl, 1897-   IX.
        Lehman, Herbert Henry, 1878-1963. X. Taft, Robert Alphonso,
        1889-1953. XI. Moody, Arthur Edson Blair, 1902-1954. XII.
        Martin, Joseph William, 1884-1968. XIII. McMahon, James O'Brien,
        1903-1952. XIV. MacArthur, Douglas, 1880-1964. XVII. Wilson,
        Charles Edward, 1886-1972. VVIII. Irvine, Clarence T

Voice Lib.
M766   Martin, Neville
bd.2   Excerpt from "Popular Music of Europe"
        (Program 11); discusses extent of American
        influence both today and yesterday in music
        in Europe; including "Ain't Necessarily So"
        by British group "Ian and the Zodiacs."
        Westinghouse Broadcasting Corporation, 1964.
        1 reel (7 in.)   7 1/2 in. per sec.
        phonotape. (The Music Goes Round and Round)
        I. Title: Popular music of Europe. II. Series.

Voice Lib.
M1318 Martin Luther King: burial at grave site and
bd.2   description of ceremony. CBS, April 9, 1968.
        1 reel (7 in.)   7 1/2 in. per sec.
        phonotape.

        1. King, Martin Luther, 1929-1968.

Voice Lib.
M1100 Martinelli, Giovanni, 1885-1969.
bd.3   Italian tenor singing "Giovinezza", the
        official Fascist song. Complete rendition.
        Forrest, 1933.
        1 reel (7 in.)   7 1/2 in. per sec.
        phonotape.

        I. Title: Giovinezza.

Marvin, Johnny
Voice Lib.
M617　Radio in the 1920's: a series of excerpts
bd.1-　　from important broadcasts of the 1920's,
bd.25　　with brief prologue and epilogue; a sample
　　　　of radio of the period.　NVL, April, 1964.
　　　　1 reel (7 in.)　7 1/2 in. per sec.
　　　phonotape.
　　　　L Radio programs.　L Marconi, Guglielmo, marchese, 1874-
　　1937.　IL Kendall, H　G　IIL Coolidge, Calvin, Pres. U. S.,
　　1872-1933.　IV. Wilson, Woodrow, Pres. U. S., 1856-1924.　V.
　　Roosevelt, Franklin Delano, Pres. U. S., 1882-1945.　VL Lodge,
　　Henry Cabot, 1850-1924.　VIL LaGuardia, Fiorello Henry, 1882-1947.
　　VIIL The Happiness Boys (Radio program)　IX. Gallagher and Sheen.
　　X. Barney Google.　XL Vallee, Rudy, 1901-　XIL The two
　　　　　　　　　　　　　　(Continued on next card)

C1　　　MARY CELESTE (BRIG)
M44　Whorf, Michael, 1933-
　　　　The mystery of the Mary Celeste.
　　　　1 tape cassette.　(The visual sounds of
　　Mike Whorf.　Miscellaneous, M44)
　　　　Originally presented on his radio program, Kaleidoscope,
　　WJR, Detroit.
　　　　Duration: 36 min.
　　　　The strange story of a ship and its missing crew.　What
　　happened?　Who was involved?　Over the years since the
　　derelict ship's reappearance, many theories have been
　　expounded.

　　　　L Mary Celeste (Brig)　L Title.

C1　　　MARY STUART, QUEEN OF THE SCOTS, 1542-1587
S17　Whorf, Michael, 1933-
　　　　The last of the Queen of Scots.
　　　　1 tape cassette.　(The visual sounds of
　　Mike Whorf.　Social, S17)
　　　　Originally presented on his radio program, Kaleidoscope,
　　WJR, Detroit.
　　　　Duration: 42 min.
　　　　Against the pageantry of royalty and majesty of kings and queens
　　of English nobility, comes the story of the last of the queens of
　　Scotland.

　　　　L Mary Stuart, queen of the Scots, 1542-1587.　L Title.

Masaryk, Jan Garrigue, 1886-1948
Voice Lib.
573　I can hear it now (radio program)
bd.2-　1945-1949.　CBS, 1950?
574　2 reels (7 in.)　7 1/2 in. per sec.
bd.1　phonotape.
　　　　L Murrow, Edward Roscoe, 1908-1965.　IL Nehru, Jawaharlal,
　　1889-1964.　IIL Philip, duke of Edinburgh, 1921-　IV. Elizabeth II,
　　Queen of Great Britain, 1926-　V. Ferguson, Homer, 1889-　VL
　　Hughes, Howard Robard, 1905-　VII. Marshall, George Catlett,
　　1880-　VIIL Ruth, George Herman, 1895-1948.　IX. Lilienthal,
　　David Eli, 1899-　X. Trout, Robert, 1909-　XL Gage, Arthur.
　　XII. Jackson, Robert Houghwout, 1892-1954.　XIIL Gromyko, Ana-
　　tolii Andreevich, 1908-　XIV. Baruch, Bernard Mannes, 1870-
　　1965.　XV. Churchill, Winston Leonard Spencer, 1874-1965.　XVL
　　Winchell, Walter, 1897-1　XVII. Davis, Elmer Holmes, 1890-
　　　　　　　　　　　　　　(Continued on next card)

Voice Lib.
M1227　Masaryk, Tomáš Garrigue, Pres. Czechoslovak
bd.10　　Republic, 1850-1937.
　　　　Speech of unknown origin.　Peteler,
　　1923.
　　　　1 reel (7 in.)　7 1/2 in. per sec.
　　phonotape.

Voice Lib.
M1227　Masaryk, Tomáš Garrigue, Pres. Czechoslovak
bd.9　　Republic, 1850-1937.
　　　　Speech to Czechoslovakian Parliament.
　　Peteler, May 27, 1928.
　　　　1 reel (7 in.)　7 1/2 in. per sec.
　　phonotape.

Mason, James Neville, 1909-
Voice Lib.
M983-　Sandburg, Carl, 1878-1967.
984　　Parts 1 and 2 of one hour NET-TV program
　　about the songs, prose, poetry, thoughts
　　and sayings of Sandburg.　Narration by
　　James Mason.　NET, June 26, 1966.
　　　　2 reels (7 in.)　7 1/2 in. per sec.
　　phonotape.

　　　　I. Mason, James Neville, 1909-

Voice Lib.　Massey, Raymond, 1896-
623　Corwin, Norman Lewis, 1910-
　　　　"Twenty-six by Corwin"; presents Earl
　　Robinson and Millard Lampell's "Lonesome
　　Train", with Earl Robinson, Burl Ives,
　　Raymond Massey.　CBS, 1940.
　　　　1 reel (7 in.)　7 1/2 in. per sec.
　　phonotape.

　　　　I. Robinson, Earl, 1910-　　II. Ives,
　　Burl, 1909-　　III. Massey, Raymond, 1896-

Massey, Raymond, 1896-
Voice Lib.
112　Lincoln, Abraham, Pres. U.S., 1809-1865.
bd.2　　Gettysburg Address, as read by Raymond
　　Massey.　Linguaphone [1940]
　　　　1 reel (7 in.)　7 1/2 in. per sec.
　　phonotape.

　　　　I. Massey, Raymond, 1896-　　II. Title.

Massey, Raymond, 1896-
Voice Lib.
112　Lincoln, Abraham, Pres. U.S., 1809-1865.
bd.3　　Second inaugural address, as read by
　　Raymond Massey.　Linguaphone, 1940.
　　　　1 reel (7 in.)　7 1/2 in. per sec.
　　phonotape.

　　　　I. Massey, Raymond, 1896-

C1
PWM23- Whorf, Michael, 1933-
24   The masters
        1 tape cassette.   (The visual sounds of
        Mike Whorf. Panorama; a world of music,
        PWM-23-PWM-24)
           Originally presented on his radio program, Kaleidoscope,
        WJR, Detroit.
           Duration: 29 min.; 22 min., 45 sec.
           The great melodies of classical music are set forth here
        under various themes.

           L. Music - History and criticism. L. Title.

Voice Lib.
394   Maxwell, Elsa, 1883-1963.
bd.7   On the outbreak of the war in Europe;
        description of her experiences on her return
        from Europe with Grace Moore and Norma Shearer.
        Vincent recording, September, 1939.
          1 reel (7 in.)   7 1/2 in. per sec.
        phonotape.

Voice Lib.   Mastin, Philip O., 1930-
M1579   Third Civic Presence Group/Legislative
bd.1   luncheon, with Craig Halverson, Lynn
        Jondahl, Gary Owen, Phil Mastin, and
        Eric Gentile.   WKAR-TV, February 15, 1973.
        10 min.   phonotape (1 r.   7 1/2 i.p.s.)

          1. Physically handicapped - Law and legis-
        lation. I. Halverson, Craig. II. Jondahl,
        M. Lynn, 1936-   III. Owen, Gary M., 1944-
        IV. Mastin, Philip O., 1930-   V. Gentile,
        Eric Anton, 1943-

Voice Lib.
M1611   Mayer, Jean
bd.2   Interview by Edwin Newman on Speaking
        freely. WKAR-TV, March, 1974.
          5 min.   phonotape (1 r.   7 1/2 i.p.s.)

          1. Malnutrition.   I. Newman, Edwin Harold,
        1919-

C1
FA18   MATHER, COTTEN, 1663-1728
        Whorf, Michael, 1933-
          Cotten Mather.
          1 tape cassette.   (The visual sounds of
        Mike Whorf. The forgotten American, FA18)
           Originally presented on his radio program, Kaleidoscope,
        WJR, Detroit.
           Duration: 12 min., 20 sec.
           The most distinguished American of his generation, he made
        contributions in many fields, unrivaled by anyone of his time.
        No other American writer ever exceeded him in volume.

           L. Mather, Cotten, 1663-1728. L. Title.

Voice Lib.   Mayes, Bernard
M793   Olde, Lewis
bd.1   Hobo Lewis reads his poetry and tells
        about life on the open road; narration by
        Bernard Mayes of Pacifica Radio in Berkeley.
        KPFK, December 4, 1964.
          21 min., 10 sec.   phonotape (1 r.
        7 1/2 i.p.s.)

          1. Tramps.   I. Mayes, Bernard.

Voice Lib.
M630   Matthews, Kenneth
bd.1   Commentary on Nuremberg War Crimes Trials;
        reviews early days of trial and reflects on
        current courtroom decorum, reviews Justice
        Jackson's view on the case, on defendants'
        knowledge of charges against them. Includes
        trial recording excerpts. BBC, January 30,
        1946.
          1 reel (7 in.)   7 1/2 i.p.s.   phonotape.

          1. Nuremberg Trial of Major German War
        Criminals, 1945-1946.

C1
H97   MAYFLOWER (SHIP)
        Whorf, Michael, 1933-
          The Mayflower story.
          1 tape cassette.   (The visual sounds of
        Mike Whorf. History and heritage, H97)
           Originally presented on his radio program, Kaleidoscope,
        WJR, Detroit.
           Duration: 36 min., 30 sec.
           With the determination born out of persecution and the
        struggle to retain their religious beliefs, the Pilgrims strove to
        establish a new order. This account follows their journey from
        England to the New World, tracing their travels and recounting
        the hardships that accompanied their quest.

           L. Mayflower (Ship)   L. Title.

Voice Lib.
M338   Mauldin, William Henry, 1921-
bd.3   On cartoonists; answers questions on how to
        create effective cartoons, creation of
        "Willy and Joe", New York Star staff,
        control of advertising department,
        editorial policy.   Voice of America,
        May 6, 1967.
          1 reel (7 in.)   7 1/2 i.p.s.   phonotape.

          1. Caricatures and cartoons.

C1
H97   The Mayflower story
        Whorf, Michael, 1933-
          The Mayflower story.
          1 tape cassette.   (The visual sounds of
        Mike Whorf. History and heritage, H97)
           Originally presented on his radio program, Kaleidoscope,
        WJR, Detroit.
           Duration: 36 min., 30 sec.
           With the determination born out of persecution and the
        struggle to retain their religious beliefs, the Pilgrims strove to
        establish a new order. This account follows their journey from
        England to the New World, tracing their travels and recounting
        the hardships that accompanied their quest.

           L. Mayflower (Ship)   L. Title.

Voice Lib.   Mayne, Dick
M1037 Biography in sound (radio program)
bd.1   "The Actor", narrated by Morgan Beatty.
    Cast includes Tallulah Bankhead, Hy Gardner,
    Rocky Graziano, Arthur Miller, Uta Hagen,
    Jackie Cooper, Sir Laurence Olivier, Gad
    Gayther, Barbara Ashley, Hortense Powdermaker,
    Peter Ustinov, Alfred Hitchcock, Leonard Lyons,
    John Guston, Helen Hayes, Dick Mayne, Ralph
    Bellamy, Lionel Barrymore, Sir Ralph Richardson,
    José Ferrer, and Walter Kerr. NBC Radio, 1950's.
      1 reel (7 in.) 7 1/2 in. per sec.
    phonotape.
             (Continued on next card)

Voice Lib.
163 Meany, George, 1894–
bd.1   New York State Federation of Labor
    Convention; labor. AFL-CIO, August 21,
    1944.
      1 reel (7 in.) 7 1/2 in. per sec.
    phonotape.

Voice Lib.   Mayo, Virginia
M1028 Lux presents Hollywood: montage of excerpts
bd.7   from various Lux radio shows. George Raft,
    Virginia Mayo, Cedric Hardwicke, and
    Ingrid Bergman. Michigan State University,
    Department of Television and Radio, 1940's.
      1 reel (7 in.) 7 1/2 in. per sec.
    phonotape.

      I. Raft, George   II. Mayo, Virginia
III. Hardwicke, Sir Cedric, 1893-1964. IV.
Bergman, Ingrid, 1917–

Voice Lib.
256 Meany, George, 1894–
bd.6   Teamsters' suspension from AFL-CIO.
    CBS News, October 24, 1957.
      1 reel (7 in.) 7 1/2 in. per sec.
    phonotape.

Voice Lib.   Mazingo, Cheri
M1619 Stone, Chuck
bd.2   Perspectives in Black, with Roz Abrahms,
    Cheri Mazingo, and J. Markisha Johnson.
    WKAR, 1974.
      27 min. phonotape (1 r. 7 1/2 i.p.s.)

      1. Race discrimination – U.S. 2. Watergate
Affair, 1872–   I. Abrahms, Roz.
II. Mazingo, Cheri. III. Johnson, J.
Markisha.

Meany, Thomas
Voice Lib.
M272 Biography in sound (radio program)
bd.1   Heywood Broun. NBC, date?
      1 reel (7 in.) 7 1/2 in. per sec.
    phonotape.

      L Broun, Heywood Campbell, 1888-1939. L Broun,
Heywood Campbell, 1888-1939. II. Swope, Herbert Bayard,
1882-1958. III. Wilson, Mattie   IV. Jackson, Gardner
V. Meany, Thomas   VI. Waldron, Beatrice   VII.
Gordon, Max   VIII. Madison, Connie   IX. Gannett,
Lewis Stiles, 1891-1966. X. Collins, Joseph, 1866-1950. XI.
Brown, Earl Louis, 1900–   XII. Levy, Newman, 1888–
XIII. Growth, John   XIV. Bye, George   XV.
Roosevelt, Franklin Dela_, Pres. U.S., 1882-1945. XVI.
Reynolds, Quentin James, 2-1965.

Voice Lib.
375 Meadows, Audrey, 1922–
bd.2   Excerpt from "That Was the Week That Was":
    "Nobody's Mad at L.B.J." NBC, January 9,
    1964.
      1 reel (7 in.) 7 1/2 in. per sec.
    phonotape.

      I. That Was the Week That Was (television
program). II. Title: Nobody's mad at L.B.J.

C1
SC2   MEDICINE
    Whorf, Michael, 1933–
      The man called healer.
      1 tape cassette. (The visual sounds of
    Mike Whorf. Science, Sc2)
      Originally presented on his radio program, Kaleidoscope,
    WJR, Detroit.
      Duration: 39 min.
      Actual recordings are used to relate the story of medicine –
    its history and progress under difficult conditions.

      L Physicians. 2. Medicine. L Title.

Voice Lib.
163 Meany, George, 1894–
bd.2   Labor voices of America. AFL-CIO.
    November 5, 1942.
      1 reel (7 in.) 7 1/2 in. per sec.
    phonotape.

C1
SC10   MEDICINE – HISTORY
    Whorf, Michael, 1933–
      Inventions in medicine.
      1 tape cassette. (The visual sounds of
    Mike Whorf. Science, SC10)
      Originally presented on his radio program, Kaleidoscope,
    WJR, Detroit.
      Duration: 53 min., 40 sec.
      A fast moving account of some of the noblest inventions and
    discoveries of medicine and science. Pasteur, Harvey and many
    more highlight this adventure of men pitted against disease and
    sickness.

      L Medicine – History. L Title.

Voice Lib.
M1610
bd.2   Medina, Ernest
     Michigan Public Broadcasting presents an
evening with Ernest Medina. With Tim
Skubick. Michigan Public Radio, December 10,
1973.
     26 min.   phonotape (1 r.   7 1/2 i.p.s.)

     1. My Lai (4),Vietnam - Massacre, 1968.
2. Medina, Ernest.   I. Skubick, Tim.

Voice Lib.
243
bd.12   Medina, Harold Raymond, 1888-
     Judge Medina answers Dr. Frank Stanton
on denial of TV access to Senate hearing
to censure Sen. McCarthy.   CBS,
September 2, 1954.
     1 reel (7 in.)   7 1/2 in. per sec.
phonotape.

     1. McCarthy, Joseph Raymond, 1909-1957.
I. Stanton, Frank, 1908-

       Meek, Bill
Voice Lib.
M1606
bd.1   Miller, James W
     Off the record. Interviewed by Tim
Skubick, Gary Schuster, Tom Green, and
Bill Meek. WKAR-TV, February 8, 1974.
     10 min.   phonotape (1 r.   7 1/2 in. per
sec.)

     1. Singer, Sidney. 2. Michigan. Civil
Service Commission.   I. Skubick, Tim.
II. Schuster, Gary. III. Green, Tom.
IV. Meek, Bill.

       Meek, Bill
Voice Lib.
M1607
bd.1   Porter, John W   1931-
     *Off the record; problems facing Michigan
schools.* Interviewed by Tim Skubick, Tom
Green, Bill Meek, and Gary Schuster.
WKAR-TV, February 1, 1974.
     17 min.   phonotape (1 r.   7 1/2 in. per
sec.)

     1. Segregation in education. 2. Strikes
and lockouts - Teachers.   I. Skubick, Tim.
II. Green, Tom. III. Meek, Bill. IV. Schuster,
Gary.

       Meek, Bill
Voice Lib.
M1598
bd.2   Romney, George W   1907-
     Off the record. With Tim Skubick, Gary
Schuster, Tom Greene, and Bill Meek.
WKAR-TV, November 9, 1973.
     20 min.   phonotape (1 r.   7 1/2 in. per
sec.)

     1. Michigan - Politics and government.
2. Detroit.   I. Skubick, Tim. II. Schuster,
Gary. III. Greene, Tom. IV. Meek, Bill

Voice Lib.
M1079   Meiklejohn, Alexander, 1872-
     Excerpts of reading from his unfinished
book on education in a free society, the
American liberal college, etc. Introductory
remarks by Dr. Scott Buchanan.   CSDI,
January, 1963.
     1 reel (7 in.)   7 1/2 in. per sec.
phonotape.

     1. Education - Philosophy
I. Buchanan, Scott Milross, 1895-1968.

Voice Lib.
577
bd.4   Melba, Dame Nellie, 1861-1931.
     Farewell speech and song, recorded at
Royal Opera House, Covent Garden, London,
England. BBC, June 8, 1926.
     1 reel (7 in.)   7 1/2 in. per sec.
phonotape.

Voice Lib.
M706
bd.2   Melchior, Lauritz Lebrecht Hommel, 1890-
     1973.
     "Duffy's tavern"; radio variety program.
WJZ, January 18, 1944.
     1 reel (7 in.)   7 1/2 in. per sec.
phonotape.

       Melchior, Lauritz Lebrecht Hommel, 1890-1973
Voice Lib.
M719
bd.1   Allen, Fred, 1894-1956.
     "The Big Show", with Tallulah Bankhead
and Lauritz Melchior and all star cast.
December 2, 1951.
     10 min., 56 sec.   phonotape (1 r.
7 1/2 i.p.s.)

     I. Bankhead, Tallulah, 1902-1968. II.
Melchior, Lauritz Lebrecht Hommel, 1890-
1973. III. Title.

       Melchior, Lauritz Lebrecht Hommel, 1890-1973
Voice Lib.
M719
bd.3   Jolson, Al, 1886-1950.
     Kraft Music Hall with Lauritz Melchior.
October 9, 1947.
     7 min., 46 sec.   phonotape (1 r.
7 1/2 i.p.s.)

     I. Melchior, Lauritz Lebrecht Hommel,
1890-1973

Melchior, Lauritz Lebrecht Hummel, 1890–
Voice Lib.   1973
M642   LaGuardia, Fiorello Henry, 1882–1947.
bd.1   Talk to the people: Christmas program
          featuring Mayor LaGuardia reading from the
          Scriptures, with Lauritz Melchior and Robert
          Shaw; offers his own views on America at war;
          reads prayer of Archbishop Spellman on return
          from battlefields of World War II; wishes
          audience a Merry Christmas. WNYC, December 24,
          1944.
             1 reel (7 in.)   7 1/2 in. per sec.
          phonotape.
          L Melchior, Lauritz Lebrecht Hummel, 1890–1973. IL Shaw,
          Robert Lawson, 1916–

Mellett, Lowell, 1884–1960
Voice Lib.
M273– Biography in sound (radio program)
274   Franklin Delano Roosevelt: the friends and
bd.1   former associates of Franklin Roosevelt on
         the tenth anniversary of the President's death.
         NBC Radio, April, 1955.
            2 reels (7 in.)   7 1/2 in. per sec.
         phonotape.
         L Roosevelt, Franklin Delano, Pres. U.S., 1882–1945. L
         McIntire, Ross T   1889–   IL Mellett, Lowell, 1884–1960.
         III. Tully, Grace   IV. Henderson, Leon, 1895–
         V. Roosevelt, Eleanor (Roosevelt) 1884–1962. VI. DeGraaf, Albert
         VII. Lehman, Herbert Henry, 1878–1963. VIII. Rosenman, Samuel
         Irving, 1896–   IX. Arvey, Jacob   X. Moley, Raymond,
         1886–   XI. Farley, James Aloysius, 1888–   XII. Roosevelt,
         (Continued on next card)

Voice Lib.
596   Mellon, Andrew William, 1855–1937.
bd.2   Dedication of Mellon Institute in
          Pittsburgh, Pa. KDKA, May 6, 1937.
             1 reel (7 in.)   7 1/2 in. per sec.
          phonotape.

C1   MELVILLE, HERMAN, 1819–1891
A25   Whorf, Michael, 1933–
          The man who wrote Moby Dick – Herman Melville.
          1 tape cassette.   (The visual sounds of
          Mike Whorf. Art, music and letters, A25)
             Originally presented on his radio program, Kaleidoscope,
          WJR, Detroit.
             Duration: 42 min.
             Herman Melville, like his characters, lived a life of adventure
          aboard ship. He knew the seas and islands and he drew from his
          experiences to write what critics believe is one of the ten best books
          ever written.

          L Melville, Herman, 1819–1891. L Title.

Voice Lib.
M1054 Memories of the movies: radio program
bd.2   pertaining to the early days of movies.
          Joseph Schildkraut, narrator. Westinghouse
          Radio, 1960's.
             1 reel (7 in.)   7 1/2 in. per sec.
          phonotape.

             1. Moving-pictures.
             I. Schildkraut, Joseph, 1896–1964.

"A Memory of Two Mondays"
Voice Lib.
M1462 Miller, Arthur, 1915–
          "A Memory of Two Mondays"; dramatization
          of Arthur Miller play about life in the
          1930's, with introduction by Arthur Miller.
          NET, 1970.
             1 reel (7 in.)   7 1/2 in. per sec.
          phonotape.

             I. Title.

C1   The men before Columbus
H28   Whorf, Michael, 1933–
          The men before Columbus.
          1 tape cassette.   (The visual sounds of
          Mike Whorf. History and heritage, H28)
             Originally presented on his radio program, Kaleidoscope,
          WJR, Detroit.
             Duration: 40 min, 15 sec.
             1000 years before Columbus' exploration of San Salvador came
          the Vikings whose culture and life style made little impression on the
          world, but their knowledge of sailing and their spirit of adventure
          would inspire others to undertake the role of discoverer.

             L Vikings. 2. America – Discovery and exploration – Norse.
          L Title.

Voice Lib.
M1369 "The men who covered Ike". CBS-TV Face the Nation program,
bd.2   discussing the late General Dwight David Eisenhower, by the
          newspaper and TV correspondents. UPI, Merriman Smith;
          Newsweek, Kenneth Crawford; Chicago Daily News, Peter
          Lisager; AP, Jack Bell; CBS, George Herman, acting as emcee.
          CBS-TV, March 30, 1969.
             1 reel (7 in.)   7 1/2 l.p.s.   phonotape.

             L Eisenhower, Dwight David, Pres. U.S., 1890–1969.
          L Smith, Merriman. IL Crawford, Kenneth. III. Lisager,
          Peter. IV. Bell, Jack. V. Herman, George.

Voice Lib.
M929– Mendès-France, Pierre, 1907–
930   Address at Foreign Policy Association in
bd.1   New York dealing primarily with ideas per-
         taining to the unification of Europe and
         thoughts on the North Atlantic Treaty
         Organization. CBS, November 23, 1954.
            2 reels (7 in.)   7 1/2 in. per sec.
         phonotape.

            1. North Atlantic Treaty Organization

Voice Lib.
M1080 Mendès-France, Pierre, 1907–
          Address by Pierre Mendès-France at New
          York on "Democracy, planning and participa-
          tion", describing the relevance of the
          French plan to American social and economic
          practices. CSDI, 1963.
             1 reel (7 in.)   7 1/2 in. per sec.
          phonotape.

             I. Title: Democracy, planning and
          participation.

Voice Lib.
352 Menjou, Adolphe, 1890-1963.
bd.11   On his dress, his early career, the
        size of his wardrobe. NBC, 1947.
        1 reel (7 in.) 7 1/2 in. per sec.
        phonotape.

C1   MENNONITES
R15
        Whorf, Michael, 1933-
        The plain people; the Amish story.
        1 tape cassette. (The visual sounds of
        Mike Whorf. Religion, R15)

        Originally presented on his radio program, Kaleidoscope,
        WJR, Detroit.
        Duration 45 min.
        The life style, traditions, habits, customs and heritage of
        the Amish folk of Pennsylvania.

        L. Mennonites. L. Title.

        Menon, Vengalil Krishnan Krishna
        see
        Krishna Menon, Vengalil Krishnan

VOICE LIBRARY

Voice Lib.
M1296 Menuhin, Yehudi, 1916-
bd.1-B   Discussing Indian music as played by Ravi
        Shankar on the sitar and its effect on
        serious musicians, with Edward P. Morgan.
        PBL, December 10, 1967.
        1 reel (7 in.) 7 1/2 in. per sec.
        phonotape.

        1. Shankar, Ravi, 1920-
        I. Morgan, Edward P   1910-

        Menuhin, Yehudi, 1916-
Voice Lib.
M1296 Shankar, Ravi, 1920-
bd.1-C   Concert on sitar, violin and tabla with
        American violinist Yehudi Menuhin. PBL,
        December 10, 1967.
        1 reel (7 in.) 7 1/2 in. per sec.
        phonotape.

        I. Menuhin, Yehudi, 1916-

        Meredith, Burgess, 1907-
Voice Lib.
M1265 Lord, Walter, 1917-
bd.2   Interview with author Walter Lord on NBC-TV
        "Today" show about his latest book "The incredi-
        ble victory", pertaining to the Battle of Midway
        during World War II. Questioned by Burgess
        Meredith. NBC-TV, August 15, 1967.
        1 reel (7 in.) 7 1/2 in. per sec. phonotape.

        L. Midway, Battle of, 1942. L. Meredith, Burgess, 1907-
        II. Title: The incredible victory.

Voice Lib.
M840 Merman, Ethel, 1909-
bd.10   Introductory greeting to Armed Forces,
        followed by musical selection composed by
        Private Frank Loesser, "Why Do They Call a
        Private a Private?" V-Disc, 1943.
        1 reel (7 in.) 7 1/2 in. per sec.
        phonotape.

        Merman, Ethel, 1909-
Voice Lib.
M622 Radio in the 1940's (Part III): a series of
bd.1-   excerpts from important broadcasts of the 1940's: a sample
bd.15   of radio of the period. NVL, April, 1964.
        1 reel (7 in.) 7 1/2 in. per sec. phonotape.
        L. Radio programs. L. Miller, Alton Glenn, 1909(?)-1944. II.
        Diles, Ken   III. Wilson, Donald Harlow, 1900-   IV.
        Livingstone, Mary   V. Benny, Jack, 1894-   VI. Harris,
        Phil   VII. Merman, Ethel, 1909-   VIII. Smith, "Wonderful"
        IX. Bennett, Richard Dyer   X. Louis, Joe, 1914-   XI.
        Eisenhower, Dwight David, Pres. U.S., 1890-1969. XII. MacArthur,
        Douglas, 1880-1964. XIII. Romulo, Carlos Pena, 1899-   XIV.
        Welles, Orson, 1915-   XV. Jackson, Robert Houghwout, 1892-1954.
        XVI. LaGuardia, Fiorello Henry, 1882-1945. XVII. Nehru, Jawa-
        harlal, 1889-1964. XVIII. Gandhi, Mohandas Karamchand, 1869-1948.

Voice Lib.
M761 Meyer, Joseph
bd.7   Excerpt from "Whatever happened to Tin Pan
        Alley?" (Program 3); relates how he got Al Jolson to introduce
        his song "California here I come", including Al Jolson singing
        this song. Westinghouse Broadcasting Corporation, 1964.
        1 reel (7 in.) 7 1/2 in. per sec. phonotape. (The music
        goes round and round)

        L. Music, Popular (Songs, etc.) - U.S. L. Jolson, Al, 1886-
        1950. II. Title: Whatever happened to Tin Pan Alley?
        III. Series.

Voice Lib.
M350 Meyer, René
bd.2   Tribute to Eisenhower on assuming the
        Presidency. CBS, January, 1953.
        1 reel (7 in.) 7 1/2 i.p.s. phonotape.

        1. Eisenhower, Dwight David, Pres. U.S.,
        1890-1969.

Voice Lib.   Meyers, John, 1880-
M1248   Baseball fifty years ago; interviews with four
         famous old time baseball players, on NBC
         "Today" show, by host Hugh Downs, supported by
         sportcaster Joe Garagiola and Dr. Lawrence
         Ritter, author of new book.   NBC-TV, June 9,
         1967.
         1 reel (7 in.)   7 1/2 in. per sec.   phonotape.

         L Baseball. L Downs, Hugh Malcolm, 1921-   IL Garagiola,
         Joe. III. Ritter, Lawrence S. /The glory of their times. IV. Roush,
         Edd, 1893-   V. Marquart, Rube, 1890-   VL O'Doul, Lefty,
         1897-   VIL Meyers, John, 1880-

Voice Lib.   Michaels, Donald M
M1435
         Life in other worlds; exploratory discussion about life on other
         planets. Arnold J. Toynbee, Dr. G. B. Kiastiakowsky
         (professor at Harvard), Dr. Donald M. Michaels, Dr. Otto
         Struve, Dr. Harlow Shapley, Walter Cronkite, Chet Huntley,
         William L. Laurence. New York, NBC, March 3, 1961.
         1 reel (7 in.)   7 1/2 Lp.s.   phonotape.

         L Life on other planets. L Toynbee, Arnold Joseph, 1889-
         II. Kiastiakowsky, George Bogdan. IIL Michaels, Donald M.
         IV. Struve, Otto, 1897-1963. V. Shapley, Harlow, 1885-1972.
         VL Cronkite, Walter Leland, 1916-   VIL Huntley, Chet,
         1911-1974. VIIL Laurence, William Leonard, 1888-

Voice Lib.
M1027   Michaux, Solomon Lightfoot, 1886-1968.
bd.4   Revival songs recorded on-the-spot at
         Washington, D.C., church of Elder Michaux,
         entitled, "There's Going to be a Meeting
         in the Air".   GRV, 1946.
         1 reel (7 in.)   7 1/2 i.p.s.   phonotape.

         1. Revivals - Hymns.

Voice Lib.
M1027   Michaux, Solomon Lightfoot, 1886-1968.
bd.5   Revival songs recorded on-the-spot at
         Washington, D.C. church of Elder Michaux,
         entitled "Oh, What a Day" and "Everybody
         Will Be Happy Over There".   GRV, 1946.
         1 reel (7 in.)   7 1/2 in. per sec.
         phonotape.

Voice Lib.   MICHIGAN. CIVIL SERVICE COMMISSION
M1606   Miller, James W
bd.1   Off the record.   Interviewed by Tim
         Skubick, Gary Schuster, Tom Green, and
         Bill Meek.   WKAR-TV, February 8, 1974.
         10 min.   phonotape (1 r.   7 1/2 in. per
         sec.)

         1. Singer, Sidney. 2. Michigan. Civil
         Service Commission.   I. Skubick, Tim.
         II. Schuster, Gary. III. Green, Tom.
         IV. Meek, Bill.

Voice Lib.   MICHIGAN - POLITICS AND GOVERNMENT
M1490   Cooley, Mortimer Elwyn, 1855-
bd.1   Candidate for U.S. Senator from Michigan
         (1924) campaign speech.   Arco records,
         1924.
         1 reel (7 in.)   7 1/2 i.p.s.   phonotape.

         1. Michigan - Politics and government.

Voice Lib.   MICHIGAN - POLITICS AND GOVERNMENT
M1490   Frensdorf, Edward
bd.2   Candidate for Governor of Michigan (1924);
         campaign speech.   Arco Records, 1924.
         1 reel (7 in.)   7 1/2 i.p.s.   phonotape.

         1. Michigan - Politics and government.

Voice Lib.   MICHIGAN - POLITICS AND GOVERNMENT
M1601-   Milliken, William G., 1922-
1602,   An evening with the Governor.   With Tim
bd.1   Skubick.   WKAR-TV, December 1973.
         60 min.   phonotape (2 r.   7 1/2 i.p.s.)

         1. Michigan - Politics and government.
         I. Skubick, Tim.

         MICHIGAN - POLITICS AND GOVERNMENT
Voice Lib.
M1550   Milliken, William G., 1922-
bd.2   State of the state address.   WKAR,
         January 1974.
         30 min.   phonotape (1 r.   7 1/2 i.p.s.)

         1. Michigan - Politics and government.

         MICHIGAN - POLITICS AND GOVERNMENT
Voice Lib.
M1598   Romney, George W   1907-
bd.2   Off the record.   With Tim Skubick, Gary
         Schuster, Tom Greene, and Bill Meek.
         WKAR-TV, November 9, 1973.
         20 min.   phonotape (1 r.   7 1/2 in. per
         sec.)

         1. Michigan - Politics and government.
         2. Detroit.   I. Skubick, Tim. II. Schuster,
         Gary. III. Greene, Tom. IV. Meek, Bill

MICHIGAN. STATE POLICE

Voice Lib.
M1598 Plants, John R
bd.1   Safeguards against misuse of state police
         for political purposes. With Tim Skubick.
         WKAR-TV, November 23, 1973.
         10 min. phonotape (1 r.   7 1/2 in. per
         sec.)

         1. Police - Michigan. 2. Michigan. State
Police. I. Skubick, Tim.

MICHIGAN. SUPREME COURT

Voice Lib.
M1610 Fitzgerald, John W., 1924-
bd.1   Interview by Gary Schuster concerning
         his appointment to the State Supreme Court.
         WKAR-TV, November 16, 1973.
         3 min. phonotape (1 r.   7 1/2 i.p.s.)

         1. Michigan. Supreme Court. I. Schuster,
Gary.

Voice Lib.
M773 Michigan. University.
bd.1   Ceremonies at University of Michigan
         presenting White and McDivitt with Doctorate
         degrees. Actual presentation to Colonel
         McDivitt of the degree of Doctor of Astro-
         nautical Science and remarks by McDivitt.
         14 min., 50 sec. phonotape (1 r. 7 1/2
         i.p.s.)
         1. McDivitt, James Alton, 1929-
I. McDivitt, James Alton, 1929-

Voice Lib.
M1417, Michigan Agricultural Conference.
1418,   Testimonial dinner for John Hannah.
1422,   March 17, 1969.
bd.1   3 reels (7 in.)   7 1/2 i.p.s.   phonotape.

         1. Hannah, John Alfred, 1902-

MICHIGAN STATE UNIVERSITY

Voice Lib.
M1707 Daugherty, Hugh
bd.5   In an interview Duffy Daugherty talks
         about his career, his present job at
         Michigan State University and his job as
         sports commentator for ABC. Rick Martin,
         May 1974.
         15 min. phonotape (1 r.   7 1/2 i.p.s.)

         1. Daugherty, Hugh. 2. Michigan State
University.

MICHIGAN STATE UNIVERSITY

Voice Lib.
M1355 Sex colloquium; CBS News program dealing with
bd.1   the six weeks' sex lectures at Michigan
         State University; opinions of students,
         professors, and commentators. Dance at
         Coral Gables. CBS TV (Janak), February 1969.
         1 reel (7 in.)   7 1/2 in. per sec.
         phonotape.

         1. Michigan State University. 2. Sex.

MICHIGAN STATE UNIVERSITY

Voice Lib.
M1499 Veldhuis, Zachary, 1870-
bd.1   Oldest living Michigan Agricultural College
         alumnus, aged 102, interviewed by Jim Denison
         at National Voice Library. Topic: campus life
         in the past. MSU Voice Library, May 14, 1972.
         1 reel (7 in.)   7 1/2 i.p.s.   phonotape.

         1. Michigan State University. I. Denison,
Jim

MICHIGAN STATE UNIVERSITY. COLLEGE OF
                URBAN DEVELOPMENT
Voice Lib.
M1597 Young, Coleman A., 1918-
         Address at the Urban Forum luncheon,
Michigan State University. MSU Information
Services, March 7, 1974.
         40 min. phonotape (1 r.   7 1/2 in. per
sec.)

         1. Detroit. 2. Michigan State University.
College of Urban Development.

         Michigan State University. Colloquium
            on the Plight of the Cities, 1969.
         see
         Colloquium on the Plight of the Cities,
         Michigan State University, 1969.

MICHIGAN STATE UNIVERSITY - HISTORY

Voice Lib.
M770 Kuhn, Madison, 1910-
bd.1   Excerpt from proceedings at commencement
         convocation at MSU; interview with Dr. Kuhn,
         university historian, regarding past
         commencements and early customs, also
         explaining preparations for present one.
         WMSB, June 13, 1965.
         15 min., 45 sec. phonotape (1 r.
         7 1/2 i.p.s.)

         1. Michigan State University - History.

Michigan State University. Midwest Film
Festival, 1st, 1972.
see
Midwest Film Festival. 1st, Michigan State
University, 1972.

Mikoian, Anastas Ivanovich, 1895–
Voice Lib.
209   Schorr, Daniel Louis, 1916–
bd.1   Press conference with Fidel Castro and
Anastas Mikoyan. Source (?), February 13,
1960.
1 reel (7 in.) 7 1/2 in. per sec.
phonotape.

I. Castro, Fidel, 1927–   II.
Mikoian, Anastas Ivanovich, 1895–

MICHIGAN STATE UNIVERSITY. NATIONAL VOICE
LIBRARY
Voice Lib.
M1488 Kuralt, Charles, 1934–
bd.3   "On the Road"; segment pertaining to
MSU National Voice Library, including
various actual voices of the past. CBS-TV,
November 9, 1971.
1 reel (7 in.) 7 1/2 in. per sec.
phonotape.

1. Michigan State University. National
Voice Library.

MILITARY BASES, RUSSIAN – CUBA
Voice Lib.
M133 Kennedy, John Fitzgerald, Pres. U.S., 1917–
bd.2   1963.
Cuba blockade, an address to the nation.
NBC, October 22, 1962.
1 reel (7 in.) 7 1/2 i.p.s. phonotape.

1. Military bases, Russian – Cuba.
2. U.S. – Foreign relations – Russia.
3. Russia – Foreign relations – U.S.

Michigan State University. University
College. Colloquium on the Plight of
the Cities, 1969.
see
Colloquium on the Plight of the Cities,
Michigan State University, 1969.

Voice Lib. MILITARY MUSIC, GERMAN
M505 Hartung, Edward
bd.3-5 Edward Hartung and Storm Troopers SA33 sing
"Heil Deutschland", medley of German marching
songs, folk songs concerning various neighbor-
hoods in Germany, "Wenn die S.S. und die S.A.
aufmarschiert" ("When the S.S. and the S.A.
march together). Private collection (German
radio transcription), 1942.
1 reel (7 in.) 7 1/2 in. per sec.
phonotape.
1. Military music, German.

MIDWAY, BATTLE OF, 1942
Voice Lib.
M1265 Lord, Walter, 1917–
bd.2   Interview with author Walter Lord on NBC-TV
"Today" show about his latest book "The incredible victory", pertaining to the Battle of Midway
during World War II. Questioned by Burgess
Meredith. NBC-TV, August 15, 1967.
1 reel (7 in.) 7 1/2 in. per sec. phonotape.

I. Midway, Battle of, 1942. I. Meredith, Burgess, 1907–
II. Title: The incredible victory.

Voice Lib. MILITARY MUSIC, GERMAN
M1016 Nazi German march music; medley of various
bd.16   military marches. F. Peteler.
1 reel (7 in.) 7 1/2 in. per sec.
phonotape.

Midwest Film Festival. 1st, Michigan
State University, 1972
Voice Lib.
M1670 Serling, Rod, 1924–
Speaking at the First Annual Midwest
Film Festival, at Michigan State University.
WKAR, May 24, 1972.
45 min. phonotape (1 r. 7 1/2 i.p.s.)

1. Television broadcasting. I. Midwest
Film Festival. 1st, Michigan State University, 1972.

MILITARY MUSIC, GERMAN
Voice Lib.
M1301 Nazi march music (instrumental): "Badenweiler
bd.1   Marsch". Peteler, 1941.
1 reel (7 in.) 7 1/2 in. per sec.
phonotape.

I. Title: Badenweiler Marsch.

MILITARY MUSIC, GERMAN
Voice Lib.
M1073   Nazi martial music; instrumental selection
bd.21   entitled: "Fehrbelliner Reitermarsch".
         Peteler, 1941.
         1 reel (7 in.)   7 1/2 in. per sec.
         phonotape.

         I. Title: Fehrbelliner Reitermarsch.

MILITARY MUSIC, GERMAN
Voice Lib.
M1019   Nazi marching song; musical theme from
bd.8   German newsreel film entitled "Wir kommen
         wieder".   Peteler.
         1 reel (7 in.)   7 1/2 in. per sec.
         phonotape.

MILITARY MUSIC, GERMAN
Voice Lib.
M1073   Nazi martial music: instrumental band
bd.10   selection entitled, "In treue Fest".
         Peteler, 1941.
         1 reel (7 in.)   7 1/2 in. per sec.
         phonotape.

         1. Military music, German.   I. Title:
         In treue Fest.

Voice Lib. MILITARY MUSIC, GERMAN
M956   Nazi music; march music of the German Armed
         Forces.   ¿no source, no date¿
         1 reel (7 in.)   7 1/2 in. per sec.
         phonotape.

         CONTENTS.-bd.1. Vorwärts nach Osten.-bd.2.
         Marsch der Deutschen in Polen.-bd.3. Gegen
         Briten und Franzosen.-bd.4. Westerwald.-bd.5.
         Wenn die Sonne scheint, Annemarie.-bd.6. Die
         eiserne Schar (Panzermarsch)-bd.7. Argonnerwald
         um Mitternacht.-bd.8. Ein Heller und ein
         Batzen; bd.9. Der Tod in Flandern.-bd.10. Der
         deutsche U-boot Mann.

MILITARY MUSIC, GERMAN
Voice Lib.
M1073   Nazi martial music; march music entitled
bd.2   "Markische Heide".(three stanzas).
         Peteler, 1941.
         1 reel (7 in.)   7 1/2 in. per sec.
         phonotape.

MILITARY SERVICE, COMPULSORY - U.S.
Voice Lib.
M1731   Clark, Ramsey, 1927-
         Debate on amnesty for draft evaders on
         "Firing Line" with William Buckley.   WKAR,
         June 21, 1974.
         45 min.   (1 r.   7 1/2 i.p.s.)

         1. Military service, compulsory - U. S.
         2. Vietnamese conflict, 1961-   I. Buckley,
         William Frank, 19

MILITARY MUSIC, GERMAN
Voice Lib.
M1071   Nazi martial music; marching song of Nazi
bd.19   paratroopers (3 stanzas).   Peteler, 1941.
         1 reel (7 in.)   7 1/2 i.p.s.   phonotape.

         1. Military music, German.

MILITARY SERVICE, COMPULSORY - U.S.
Voice Lib.
M607   Roosevelt, Franklin Delano, Pres. U.S.,
bd.4   1882-1945.
         Report on President Roosevelt's proposal
         for a peacetime draft.   CBS, June 18, 1940.
         1 reel (7 in.)   7 1/2 i.p.s.   phonotape.

         1. Military service, Compulsory - U.S.

MILITARY MUSIC, GERMAN
Voice Lib.
M1304   Nazi march music; "Marsch der Elisabether".
bd.1   Peteler.
         1 reel (7 in.)   7 1/2 in. per sec.
         phonotape.

         Millay, Edna St. Vincent, 1892-1950.
Voice Lib.   The murder of Lidice
M850   Muni, Paul, 1895-1967.
bd.2   Radio play adaptation of Edna St. Vincent
         Millay's prose-poem "The murder of Lidice",
         relating to the atrocities by Nazis in the
         Czechoslovakian village of Lidice.   All-
         star cast.   NBC, January 6, 1943.
         1 reel (7 in.)   7 1/2 i.p.s.   phonotape.

         I. Millay, Edna St. Vincent, 1892-1950./
         The murder of Lidice. II. Title: The
         murder of Lidice.

Voice Lib.
Millay, Edna St. Vincent, 1892-1950
517- Stickney, Dorothy Hayes, 1903-
518 "A Lovely Night", from Festival of
bd.1 Performing Arts; dramatization of poems and
letters of Edna St. Vincent Millay. Talent
Associates, April 14, 1962.
2 reels (7 in.) 7 1/2 in. per sec.
phonotape.

I. Millay, Edna St. Vincent, 1892-1950.

Voice Lib.
M1426 Miller, Glenn, 1909-1944
Memorial broadcast on Glenn Miller,
including musical selections and anecdotes
by those who knew him. Des Moines, Iowa,
WHO, 1966.
1 reel (7 in.) 7 1/2 in. per sec.
phonotape.

1. Miller, Glenn, 1909-1944.

Voice Lib.
M1462 Miller, Arthur, 1915-
"A Memory of Two Mondays": dramatization
of Arthur Miller play about life in the
1930's, with introduction by Arthur Miller.
NET, 1970.
1 reel (7 in.) 7 1/2 in. per sec.
phonotape.

I. Title.

Voice Lib.
M1606 Miller, James W
bd.1 Off the record. Interviewed by Tim
Skubick, Gary Schuster, Tom Green, and
Bill Meek. WKAR-TV, February 8, 1974.
10 min. phonotape (1 r. 7 1/2 in. per
sec.)

1. Singer, Sidney. 2. Michigan. Civil
Service Commission. I. Skubick, Tim.
II. Schuster, Gary. III. Green, Tom.
IV. Meek, Bill.

Voice Lib.
Miller, Arthur, 1915-
M1037 Biography in sound (radio program)
bd.1 "The Actor", narrated by Morgan Beatty.
Cast includes Tallulah Bankhead, Hy Gardner,
Rocky Graziano, Arthur Miller, Uta Hagen,
Jackie Cooper, Sir Laurence Olivier, Gad
Gayther, Barbara Ashley, Hortense Powdermaker,
Peter Ustinov, Alfred Hitchcock, Leonard Lyons,
John Guston, Helen Hayes, Dick Mayne, Ralph
Bellamy, Lionel Barrymore, Sir Ralph Richardson,
José Ferrer, and Walter Kerr. NBC Radio, 1950's.
1 reel (7 in.) 7 1/2 in. per sec.
phonotape.
(Continued on next card)

Voice Lib.
M1691 Miller, Merle, 1918-
Bd.2 On Mike Douglas Show discussing his book
on Truman. Includes Viveca Lindfors and
David Steinberg. WILS-TV, May 23, 1974.
5 min. phonotape (1 r. 7 1/2 i.p.s.)

1. Truman, Harry S, Pres. U.S., 1884-1972.
2. Miller, Merle, 1918- /Plain speaking.
I. Douglas, Mike, 1925?- II. Lindfors,
Viveca, 1920- III. Steinberg, David.

Voice Lib.
M840 Miller, Glenn, 1909?-1944.
bd.8 Greets American Armed Forces followed
by "St. Louis blues" in march tempo,
recorded especially for V-Discs.
V-Discs, 1944.
9 min., 6 sec. phonotape (1 r.
7 1/2 i.p.s.)

I. Title: St. Louis blues.

MILLER, MERLE, 1918-
PLAIN SPEAKING
Voice Lib.
M1691 Miller, Merle, 1918-
Bd.2 On Mike Douglas Show discussing his book
on Truman. Includes Viveca Lindfors and
David Steinberg. WILS-TV, May 23, 1974.
5 min. phonotape (1 r. 7 1/2 i.p.s.)

1. Truman, Harry S, Pres. U.S., 1884-1972.
2. Miller, Merle, 1918- /Plain speaking.
I. Douglas, Mike, 1925?- II. Lindfors,
Viveca, 1920- III. Steinberg, David.

Voice Lib. Miller, Glenn, 1909?-1944
M622 Radio in the 1940's (Part III): a series of
bd.1- excerpts from important broadcasts of the
bd.15 1940's; a sample of radio of the period.
NVL, April, 1964.
1 reel (7 in.) 7 1/2 i.p.s. phonotape.

Voice Lib.
M760 Miller, Mitch, 1911-
bd.15 Excerpt from "The Big Beat" (Program 2);
criticizing rock-and-roll; feels like people
who like it are lowering themselves.
Westinghouse Broadcasting Corporation, 1964.
1 reel (7 in.) 7 1/2 in. per sec.
phonotape. (The Music Goes Round and Round)

I. Title: The big beat. II. Series.

Miller, Walter H
Voice Lib.
539   Edison, Thomas Alva, 1847-1931.
bd.6   "Liver Story", a humorous story related
             by Edison. Introduced by Walter H. Miller.
             National Vocarium, 1906.
               1 reel (7 in.)   7 1/2 in. per sec.
             phonotape.

               I. Miller, Walter H   II. Title.

Voice Lib.
M1550   Milliken, William G., 1922-
bd.2   State of the state address.   WKAR,
             January 1974.
               30 min.   phonotape (1 r.   7 1/2 i.p.s.)

               1. Michigan - Politics and government.

Miller, William
Voice Lib.
M1560   Ford, Gerald R., 1913-
bd.2   Inauguration of Gerald R. Ford as
             Vice President. CBS-TV, December 6, 1973.
               25 min.   phonotape (1 r.   7 1/2 i.p.s.)

               Commentary by Roger Mudd and William
             Miller.

               I. Mudd, Roger. II. Miller, William.

Voice Lib.
M1707   Milliken, William G   1922-
bd.   Governors Milliken, Lucey and Askew at
             the Governors' Conference in Seattle on the
             new financing morality. Richard Threlkeld,
             reporting.   CBS, June 5, 1974.
               3 min.   phonotape (1 r.   7 1/2 i.p.s.)

               1. Watergate Affair, 1972-   I. Lucey,
             Patrick Joseph, 1918-   II. Askew,
             Reubin O'D. III. Threlkeld, Richard.

Voice Lib. Miller, William Edward, 1914-
M1268   Goldwater, Barry Morris, 1909-
               NET program about the 1964 presidential
             campaign consisting of informal conversations
             by Joseph Stern and Paul Niven with Barry
             Goldwater and William E. Miller in
             Washington, D.C.   NET, September 25, 1967.
               1 reel (7 in.)   7 1/2 in. per sec.
             phonotape.

               I. Miller, William Edward, 1914-   II.
             Stern, Joseph   III. Niven, Paul

Voice Lib. Milstein, Nathan, 1904-
M310   American Broadcasting Company.
               Tribute to President John Fitzgerald Kennedy
             from the arts. Fredric March emcees; Jerome
             Hines sings "Worship of God and Nature" by
             Beethoven; Florence Eldridge recites "When
             lilacs last in the door-yard bloom'd" by Walt
             Whitman; Marian Anderson in two songs. Includes
             Charlton Heston, Sidney Blackmer, Isaac Stern,
             Nathan Milnstein, Christopher Plummer, Albert
             Finney. ABC, November 24, 1963.
               55 min.   phonotape (7 in.   7 1/2 i.p.s.)

                                  (Continued on next card)

Voice Lib.
M1692   Milliken, William G   1922-
bd.2   Welcoming participants in the Governor's
             Conference on Drug Dependence and Abuse,
             Kellogg Center, East Lansing. WKAR,
             December 8, 1969.
               10 min.   phonotape (1 r.   7 1/2 i.p.s.)

               1. Drug abuse.

             MILTON, JOHN, 1608-1674
C1
A31   Whorf, Michael, 1933-
               The Puritan poet - John Milton.
               1 tape cassette. (The visual sounds of
             Mike Whorf. Art, music and letters, A31)
               Originally presented on his radio program, Kaleidoscope,
             WJR, Detroit.
               Duration: 38 min.
               The scene is the old world in the age of Renaissance, and
             Milton discovers a new age of enlightenment as he writes
             Paradise lost - graphically illustrating the new-found path of
             religious conviction and understanding.
               I. Milton, John, 1608-1674. I. Title.

Voice Lib.
M1601-   Milliken, William G., 1922-
1602,   An evening with the Governor. With Tim
bd.1   Skubick. WKAR-TV, December 1973.
               60 min.   phonotape (2 r.   7 1/2 i.p.s.)

               1. Michigan - Politics and government.
               I. Skubick, Tim.

             Minister to millions - Norman Vincent Peale
C1
R32   Whorf, Michael, 1933-
               Minister to millions - Norman Vincent Peale.
               1 tape cassette. (The visual sounds of
             Mike Whorf. Religion, R32)
               Originally presented on his radio program, Kaleidoscope,
             WJR, Detroit.
               Duration: 57 min., 30 sec.
               Norman Vincent Peale, remembered as the author of The
             power of positive thinking, is a man of varied accomplishments,
             some well-known, others which go almost unnoticed.

               I. Peale, Norman Vincent, 1898-   I. Title.

Voice Lib.
M935 Minnow, Newton Norman, 1926-
bd.3   Excerpts of his talks to broadcasters
      about improvements desired and their
      responsibilities. Private recording, 1957.
      1 reel (7 in.) 7 1/2 in. per sec.
      phonotape.

○

C1
R5   Miracle of the twelve
      Whorf, Michael, 1933-
        Miracle of the twelve.
        1 tape cassette. (The visual sounds of
      Mike Whorf. Religion, R5)
        Originally presented on his radio program, Kaleidoscope,
      WJR, Detroit.
        Duration: 35 min., 40 sec.
        Grouped together as a determined force carrying the word of the
      Messiah, were twelve men selected by the Christ to bring to the
      world a philosophy which mankind has never improved on.

        L Apostles. L Title.

○

Voice Lib.
M1045 Minnow, Newton Norman, 1926-
bd.2   "Bureaucracy is not muddling through". Address at two-day
      convocation at the 10th anniversary of the Freedom for the
      Republic in Los Angeles. Mr. Minnow's address is being
      narrated for the occasion, the subject being bureaucratic
      organization and procedures in U.S. government departments;
      also explains duty of FCC. CDI, 1963.
        1 reel (7 in.) 7 1/2 i.p.s. phonotape.

        L Bureaucracy.

○

C1
M39   Mr. Hohner's amazing harmonica
      Whorf, Michael, 1933-
        Mr. Hohner's amazing harmonica.
        1 tape cassette. (The visual sounds of
      Mike Whorf. Miscellaneous, M39)
        Originally presented on his radio program, Kaleidoscope,
      WJR, Detroit.
        Duration: 38 min.
        Never underestimate the power of this six-inch instrument,
      the harmonica. Its history is rich and long, dating from
      ancient China to the twentieth century.

        L Mouth-organ. L Title.

○

        MINORITIES - EMPLOYMENT - LANSING, MICH.
Voice Lib.
M1742 Graves, Gerald
bd.4   Defends Lansing's record of minority hiring
      against attack from Human Relations director
      Richard Letts. WJIM-TV, June 19, 1974.
      2 min. phonotape (1 r. 7 1/2 i.p.s.)

        1. Minorities - Employment - Lansing, Mich.
      I. Letts, Richard

○

             Mitchell, Edgar D   1931-
Voice Lib.
M1438 Apollo 14 (space flight): take-off from Cape
bd.1   Kennedy, including countdown. CBS,
      January 31, 1971.
        1 reel (7 in.) 7 1/2 in. per sec.
      phonotape.

        1. Project Apollo. 2. Space flight to the
      moon. 3. Shepard, Alan Bartlett, 1923- 4.
      Mitchell, Edgar D   1931- 5. Roosa,
      Stuart A   1934- I. Shepard, Alan Bartlett,
      1923- II. Mitchell, Edgar D   1931- III.
      Roosa, Stuart A   1934-

○

       The minstrel and the story man
Voice Lib.
M616   Brokenshire, Norman Ernest, 1898-1965.
bd.1   The minstrel and the story man, a
      radio program for children. GRV, 1946.
        1 reel (7 in.) 7 1/2 i.p.s. phonotape.

        I. Title.

○

             Mitchell, Edgar D   1931-
Voice Lib.
M1458 Apollo 14 (space flight): lunar landed on the
bd.2   moon and moon walk. CBS, February 5, 1971.
        1 reel (7 in.) 7 1/2 in. per sec.
      phonotape.

        1. Project Apollo. 2. Space flight to the
      moon. 3. Shepard, Alan Bartlett, 1923- 4.
      Mitchell, Edgar D   1931- 5. Roosa, Stuart
      A   1934- I. Shepard, Alan Bartlett,
      1923- II. Mitchell, Edgar D   1931- III.
      Roosa, Stuart A   1934-

○

C1
R7   The miracle of Saint Joan
      Whorf, Michael, 1933-
        The miracle of Saint Joan.
        1 tape cassette. (The visual sounds of
      Mike Whorf. Religion, R7)
        Originally presented on his radio program, Kaleidoscope,
      WJR, Detroit.
        Duration: 40 min., 30 sec.
        Her immolation at the stake was the beginning of a legend rather
      than the end of a life, and amidst the splendor and pageantry her
      story is told.

        L Jeanne d'Arc, Saint, 1412-1431. L Title.

○

             Mitchell, Edgar D   1931-
Voice Lib.
M1438 Apollo 14 (space flight): Apollo 14 splash-
bd.3-   down and reception on aircraft carrier.
M1439   CBS, February 9, 1971.
bd.1   2 reels (7 in.) 7 1/2 in. per sec.
      phonotape.

        1. Project Apollo. 2. Space flight to the
      moon. 3. Shepard, Alan Bartlett, 1923- 4.
      Mitchell, Edgar D   1931- 5. Roosa,
      Stuart A   1934- I. Shepard, Alan Bartlett,
      1923- II. Mitchell, Edgar D   1931- III.
      Roosa, Stuart A   1934-

○

Voice Lib.
M1800   Mitchell, John Newton, 1913-
WG   Testimony before the Senate Committee
0710   investigating the Watergate Affair.
           Pacifica, July 10, 1973.
              312 min.   phonotape (4 r.   3 3/4 i.p.s.)
           (Watergate gavel to gavel, phase 1)

              1. Watergate Affair, 1972-

Voice Lib.
M1800   Mitchell, John Newton, 1913-
WG   Testimony before the Senate Committee
0711   investigating the Watergate Affair.
           Pacifica, July 11, 1973.
              325 min.   phonotape (4 r.   3 3/4 i.p.s.)
           (Watergate gavel to gavel, phase 1)

              1. Watergate Affair, 1972-

Voice Lib.
M1800   Mitchell, John Newton, 1913-
WG   Testimony before the Senate Committee
0712.01- investigating the Watergate Affair.
.02   Pacifica, July 12, 1973.
              201 min.   phonotape (3 r.   3 3/4 i.p.s.)
           (Watergate gavel to gavel, phase 1)

              1. Watergate Affair, 1972-

Voice Lib.   MODUGNO, DOMINCO
M766   Stampa, Fred
bd.5   Excerpt from "Popular Music of Europe"
           (Program 11); comments on style of singing
           of Dominco Modugno, including song "Boom
           boom surf" by Peppino Di Capri and the
           Hollerers.   Westinghouse Broadcasting
           Corporation, 1964.
              1 min., 44 sec.   phonotape (1 r.   7 1/2 i.p.s.)
           (The music goes round and round)

              I. Modugno, Dominco.   L. Title: Boom boom surf.
           II. Title: Popular music of Europe.   III. Series.

Voice Lib.
169   Moffett, Elwood
bd.1   District 50 Special Convention.
           AFL-CIO (P.R.O.), February 24, 1961.
              1 reel (7 in.)   7 1/2 in. per sec.
           phonotape.

Voice Lib.   Moley, Raymond, 1886-
M273-   Biography in sound (radio program)
274   Franklin Delano Roosevelt: the friends and
bd.1   former associates of Franklin Roosevelt on
           the tenth anniversary of the President's death.
           NBC Radio, April, 1955.
              2 reels (7 in.)   7 1/2 in. per sec.
           phonotape.
              I. Roosevelt, Franklin Delano, Pres. U.S., 1882-1945.   I.
           McIntire, Ross T   1889-   II. Mellett, Lowell, 1884-1960.
           III. Tully, Grace   IV. Henderson, Leon, 1895-
           V. Roosevelt, Eleanor (Roosevelt) 1884-1962.   VI. DeGraaf, Albert
           VII. Lehman, Herbert Henry, 1878-1963.   VIII. Rosenman, Samuel
           Irving, 1896-   IX. Arvey, Jacob   X. Moley, Raymond,
           1886-   XI. Farley, James Aloysius, 1888-   XII. Roosevelt,
           (continued on next card)

Voice Lib.   Mollenhoff, Clark Raymond, 1921-
M1704   Woodward, Robert
              Woodward and Bernstein, exposers of
           Watergate, at the National Press Club,
           talking to other reporters.   Includes
           Clark Mollenhoff.   WKAR, June 6, 1974.
              50 min.   phonotape (1 r.   7 1/2 i.p.s.)

              1. Watergate Affair, 1972-
           I. Bernstein, Carl.   II. Mollenhoff, Clark
           Raymond, 1921-

C1   The Molly Maguires
S48   Whorf, Michael, 1933-
              The Molly Maguires.
              1 tape cassette.   (The visual sounds of
           Mike Whorf.   Social, S48)
              Originally presented on his radio program, Kaleidoscope,
           WJR, Detroit.
              Duration: 37 min.
              From the green hills of Ireland they came to work in the black
           hills of Pennsylvania.   Because of hardship, ill housing, poor food,
           and intolerable working conditions, they formed themselves into a
           band of marauding vigilantes called the Molly Maguires.

              I. Molly Maguires.   I. Title.

Voice Lib.
M1228   Molotov, Vlacheslav Mikhailovich, 1890-
bd.2   Excerpt of speech on 20th anniversary of
           Russian October Revolution.   Peteler,
           June 11, 1937.
              1 reel (7 in.)   7 1/2 in. per sec.
           phonotape.

MONOPOLIES - U.S.
Voice Lib.
M1729-   Nader, Ralph.
1730   Address at Michigan State University.
           MSU Voice Library, April 11, 1974.
              80 min.   phonotape (2 r.   7 1/2 i.p.s.)

              1. Monopolies - U. S.   2. Pollution.   3.
           Oil industries - U. S.

Monroe, Bill

Voice Lib.
M1720   Udall, Morris K., 1922-
bd.4   On the Today Show with Sam Steiger, debating
          their opposing bills for land-use funding.
          Includes Barbara Walters and Bill Monroe.
          NBC-TV, June 10, 1974.
              8 min.   phonotape (1 r.   7 1/2 i.p.s.)

          1. Land.   2. Man - Influence on nature.
          I. Steiger, Sam, 1929-   II. Walters,
          Barbara, 1931-   III. Monroe, Bill.

Monroe, Bill

Voice Lib.
M1744   Vestal, M   S
bd.1   Discussing his book Jerry Ford, up close,
          on the Today Show with Bill Monroe, Barbara
          Walters, and Jess Marlowe. NBC-TV, June 25,
          1974.
              10 min.   phonotape (1 r.   7 1/2 i.p.s.)

          1. Ford, Gerald R., 1913-   2. Vestal,
          M.S./Jerry Ford, up close. I. Monroe, Bill.
          II. Walters, Barbara, 1931-   III. Marlowe,
          Jess.

Monroe, Bill

Voice Lib.
M1741   Wills, Frank
bd.2   Interview with Bill Monroe. NBC, June
          17, 1974.
              10 min.   phonotape (1 r.   7 1/2 i.p.s.)

          1. Watergate affair, 1972-   I. Monroe,
          Bill.

Voice Lib.
M736   Montgomery of Alamein, Bernard Law Montgomery,
bd.5   1st viscount, 1887-
          Announcing the terms of local German
          surrender in Holland and various islands.
          CBS, May 4, 1945.
          1 reel (7 in.)   7 1/2 in. per sec.
          phonotape.

          1. World War, 1939-1945

MONTGOMERY, ALA.

Voice Lib.
M258   Harper, Robert
bd.9B   Report to CBS News, New York; description
          of military control in Montgomery, Alabama
          under state troops. New York, CBS, May 22,
          1961.
              1 reel (7 in.)   7 1/2 i.p.s.   phonotape.

          1. Civil rights. 2. Montgomery, Ala.

Moody, Arthur Edson Blair, 1902-1954

Voice Lib.
381-   I can hear it now (radio program)
382   CBS, April 26, 1951.
bd.1   2 reels (7 in.)   7 1/2 in. per sec.   phonotape.
          L. Radio Free Europe. 2. Strategic Air Command. L.
          Ridgway, Matthew Bunker, 1895-   IL. Churchill, Winston Leonard
          Spencer, 1874-1965. III. Bevan, Aneurin, 1897-1960. IV. Nixon,
          Richard Milhous, Pres. U.S., 1913-   V. Kerr, Robert Samuel, 1896-
          1963. VL. Brewster, Ralph Owen, 1888-1962. VII. Wherry, Kenneth
          Spicer, 1892-1951. VIII. Capehart, Homer Earl, 1897-   IX.
          Lehman, Herbert Henry, 1878-1963. X. Taft, Robert Alphonso,
          1889-1953. XL. Moody, Arthur Edson Blair, 1902-1954. XII.
          Martin, Joseph William, 1884-1968. XIII. McMahon, James O'Brien,
          1903-1952. XIV. MacArthur, Douglas, 1880-1964. XVII. Wilson,
          Charles Edward, 1886-1972. XVIII. Irvine, Clarence T

Voice Lib.
M978   Moody, Dwight Lyman, 1837-1899.
bd.1   Evangelist Dwight L. Moody in excerpt
          of recitation of Beatitudes. Moody
          Institute, 1899.
              1 reel (7 in.)   7 1/2 in. per sec.
          phonotape.

Voice Lib.
538   Mooney, Thomas J   1882-1942.
bd.1   Address at Tom Mooney Rally at Madison
          Square Garden, New York; appreciation for
          labor's support, feelings as a free man,
          changes in outside world during period
          since 1916, strength of labor today. GRV,
          January, 1939.
              1 reel (7 in.)   7 1/2 in. per sec.
          phonotape.

Voice Lib.
538   Mooney, Thomas J   1882-1942.
bd.1   Tom Mooney Rally at Madison Square
          Garden. GRV, January, 1939.
              1 reel (7 in.)   7 1/2 in. per sec.
          phonotape.

Moore, Grace, 1901-1947

Voice Lib.
154   LaGuardia, Fiorello Henry, 1882-1947.
bd.1,2   Presentation of New York City
          Certificate of Merit to Grace Moore.
          WNYC, August 14, 1945.
              1 reel (7 in.)   7 1/2 in. per sec.
          phonotape.

          I. Moore, Grace, 1901-1947.

Voice Lib.   Moore, Ray
M311   King, Martin Luther, 1929-1968.
bd.4   Martin Luther King interviewed by Ray
          Moore in Atlanta about Kennedy as champion
          of civil rights.   NBC, November 23, 1963.
          1 reel (7 in.)   7 1/2 in. per sec.
          phonotape.

          1. Kennedy, John Fitzgerald, Pres. U.S.,
          1917-1963 - Assassination.   I. Moore, Ray

Voice Lib.
M1800   Moore, Richard Arthur, 1914-
WG   Testimony before the Senate Committee
0712.03   investigating the Watergate Affair.
          Pacifica, July 12, 1973.
          98 min.   phonotape (2 r.   3 3/4 i.p.s.)
          (Watergate gavel to gavel; phase 1)

          1. Watergate Affair, 1972-

Voice Lib.
M1800   Moore, Richard Arthur, 1914-
WG   Testimony before the Senate Committee
0713   investigating the Watergate Affair.
          Pacifica, July 13, 1973.
          360 min.   phonotape (5 r.   3 3/4 i.p.s.)
          (Watergate gavel to gavel, phase 1)

          1. Watergate Affair, 1972-

Voice Lib.
M1800   Moore, Richard Arthur, 1914-
WG   Testimony before the Senate Committee
0716.01   investigating the Watergate Affair.
          Pacifica, July 16, 1973.
          119 min.   phonotape (2 r.   3 3/4 i.p.s.)
          (Watergate gavel to gavel, phase 1)

          1. Watergate Affair, 1972-

                    Moran, George
                      see
          The two black crows (Radio program)

Voice Lib.   Morgan, Al
605-
607   "War and Peace"; narrates story of problems
          of war and peace. G.R. Vincent, 1947.
          3 reels (7 in.)   7 1/2 in. per sec.
          phonotape.

                    Morgan, Edward P   1910-
Voice Lib.
M1296   Menuhin, Yehudi, 1916-
bd.1-B   Discussing Indian music as played by Ravi
          Shankar on the sitar and its effect on
          serious musicians, with Edward P. Morgan.
          PBL, December 10, 1967.
          1 reel (7 in.)   7 1/2 in. per sec.
          phonotape.

          I. Morgan, Edward P   1910-

                    Morgan, Elizabeth
Voice Lib.
M1085   Wilkins, Roy, 1901-
          Radio interview with Roy Wilkins by
          Elizabeth Morgan about methods to attain
          civil rights for Negroes.   Bergman, May 9,
          1962.
          1 reel (7 in.)   7 1/2 in. per sec.
          phonotape.

          1. Negroes - Civil rights.   I. Morgan,
          Elizabeth.

                    Morgan, Helen
Voice Lib.
M617   Radio in the 1920's: a series of excerpts
bd.1-   from important broadcasts of the 1920's,
bd.25   with brief prologue and epilogue; a sample
          of radio of the period. NVL, April, 1964.
          1 reel (7 in.)   7 1/2 in. per sec.
          phonotape.
          1. Radio programs. I. Marconi, Guglielmo, marchese, 1874-
          1937. II. Kendall, H   G   III. Coolidge, Calvin, Pres. U.S.,
          1872-1933. IV. Wilson, Woodrow, Pres. U.S., 1856-1924. V.
          Roosevelt, Franklin Delano, Pres. U.S., 1882-1945. VI. Lodge,
          Henry Cabot, 1850-1924. VII. LaGuardia, Fiorello Henry, 1882-1947.
          VIII. The Happiness Boys (Radio program) IX. Gallagher and Sheen.
          X. Barney Google. XI. Vallee, Rudy, 1901-   XII. The two
                    (Continued on next card)

                    Morgan, Hugh
Voice Lib.
M1605   Winograd, Morley
bd.2   Off the record. With Tim Skubick, Tom
          Greene, Gary Schuster, and Hugh Morgan.
          WKAR-TV, February 15, 1974.
          17 min.   phonotape (1 r.   7 1/2 in. per sec.)

          1. Democratic Party. Michigan. 2. Elections -
          Michigan. 3. Youngblood, Charles N., 1932-
          I. Skubick, Tim. II. Greene, Tom. III. Schuster,
          Gary. IV. Morgan, Hugh.

Morley, Christopher Darlington, 1890-

Voice Lib.
M932   Information, please (radio program)
           Panel of experts questioned by Clifton
        Fadiman; panel includes Christopher Morley,
        John Kieran, Franklin P. Adams, Col. Eagan.
        Lloyd Grosse, 1943.
           1 reel (7 in.)   7 1/2 in. per sec.
        phonotape.
           I. Fadiman, Clifton, 1904-   II. Morley,
        Christopher Darlington, 1890-   III. Kieran,
        John, 1892-   IV. Adams, Franklin Pierce,
        1881-1960. V. Eagan Col.

C1   MORMONS AND MORMONISM
R16
        Whorf, Michael, 1933-
           The way of life - the Mormon story.
           1 tape cassette. (The visual sounds of
        Mike Whorf. Religion, R16)
           Originally presented on his radio program, Kaleidoscope,
        WJR, Detroit.
           Duration: 30 min., 40 sec.
           In the 19th century, Joseph Smith was assassinated in Nauvoo,
        Ill. His successor was Brigham Young, a man who would lead those
        who professed the Mormon faith across hundreds of miles to the
        state of Utah to a religious haven.
           L. Mormons and Mormonism. L. Title.

Voice Lib.
M1724   Morris, Clyde D   J
bd.1   Next steps to control the military; part
        of the MSU Moratorium against the War -
        introduces a slogan and a song, sung by
        Ruth Knapp, Doug Solomon, and Phyllis Hart.
        WKAR, October 15, 1969.
           15 min.   phonotape (1 r.   7 1/2 i.p.s.)
           1. Vietnamese Conflict, 1961-   - U.S.
        I. Knapp, Ruth. II. Solomon, Douglas S.
        III. Hart, Phyllis

Morris, Newbold, 1902-1966
Voice Lib.
M658-   Dialogues in depth: the LaGuardia years
659   (TV program from the New York World's Fair).
bd.1   Anecdotes and reminiscences about the late
        New York mayor, Fiorello LaGuardia.
        July 22, 1964.
           2 reels (7 in.)   7 1/2 i.p.s.   phonotape.
           L. LaGuardia, Fiorello Henry, 1882-1947. L. Canudo,
        Eugene R. IL. Berle, Adolph Augustus, 1895-1971.
        III. Van Arsdale, Harry, 1905-   IV. Delany, Hubert T.
        V. Morris, Newbold, 1902-1966.

Morrison, Herbert Stanley, 1888-
Voice Lib.
572-   I can hear it now (radio program)
573   1933-1946. CBS, 1948.
bd.1   2 reels (7 in.)   7 1/2 in. per sec.
        phonotape.
           L. Murrow, Edward Roscoe, 1908-1965. IL. LaGuardia, Fiorello
        Henry, 1882-1947. III. Chamberlain, Neville, 1869-1949. IV.
        Roosevelt, Franklin Delano, Pres. U.S., 1882-1945. V. Churchill,
        Winston Leonard Spencer, 1874-1965. VI. Gaulle, Charles de,
        Pres. France, 1890-1970. VII. Eisenhower, Dwight David, Pres. U.S.,
        1890-1969. VIII. Willkie, Wendell Lewis, 1892-1944. IX. Martin,
        Joseph William, 1884-1968. X. Elizabeth II, Queen of Great Britain,
        1926-   XI. Margaret Rose, Princess of Gt. Brit., 1930-   XII.
        Johnson, Hugh Samuel, 1882-'42. XIII. Smith, Alfred Emanuel,
        1873-1944. XIV. Lindbergh arles Augustus, 1902-   XV. Davis,
           (Continued on next card)

Voice Lib.
M1724   Morse, Wayne Lyman, 1900-
bd.2   Question and answer session with Michigan
        State University students. Includes Dr.
        Thomas H. Greer. WKAR, January 13, 1970.
           20 min.   phonotape (1 r.   7 1/2 i.p.s.)
           1. U.S. - Politics and government.
        I. Greer, Thomas Hoag, 1914-

Voice Lib.
M1717   Morse, Wayne Lyman, 1900-
           Address at Michigan State University;
        segments. WKAR, January 21, 1970.
           50 min.   phonotape (1 r.   7 1/2 i.p.s.)
           1. Vietnamese Conflict, 1961-   -
        U.S.

Morse, Wayne Lyman, 1900-1974
Voice Lib.
385   I can hear it now (radio program)
           CBS, February 2, 1951.
           1 reel (7 in.)   7 1/2 in. per sec.
        phonotape.
           I. Austin, Warren Robinson, 1877-1962. II.
        Pandit, Vijaya Lakshmi (Nehru) 1900-   III.
        Roosevelt, Eleanor (Roosevelt) 1884-1962. IV.
        Morse, Wayne Lyman, 1900-   V. Chandler,
        Albert Benjamin, 1898-   VI. Taylor, Telford,
        1908-   VII. Wh   Jack.

Voice Lib.   Morton, Bruce
M1628-   Nixon, Richard Milhous, Pres. U.S., 1913-
1629,   Address before the National Radio &
bd.1   Television News Directors Association and
        questions following from the members and
        from the national press. Summary and analysis
        by CBS newsmen Roger Mudd and Bruce Morton.
        CBS, March 19, 1974.
           60 min.   phonotape (2 r.   7 1/2 i.p.s.)
           1. U.S. - Politics and government - 1969-
        2. Power resources - U.S. I. Mudd, Roger.
        II. Morton,   Bruce.

C1   MOSES, ANNA MARY (ROBERTSON) 1860-1961
A5
        Whorf, Michael, 1933-
           The incredible Grandma Moses.
           1 tape cassette. (The visual sounds of
        Mike Whorf. Art, music, and letters, A5)
           Originally presented on his radio program, Kaleidoscope,
        WJR, Detroit.
           Duration: 24 min.
           At the tender young age of 80 she painted quaint pictures
        of the America she knew and loved, as a legacy for future
        generations.
           L. Moses, Anna Mary (Robertson) 1860-1961. L. Title.

Moses, Robert, 1888-
Voice Lib.
M289   Twentieth Century (Television program)
bd.2   Production on career of Alfred E. Smith.
         Various excerpts of addresses by Gov. Smith;
         recollections by Robert Moses on life of
         Gov. Smith; narration by Walter Cronkite;
         placing of Smith's name in nomination for
         President by F.D.R.   CBS, 1962.
             1 reel (7 in.)   7 1/2 in. per sec.
         phonotape.
         I. Smith, Alfred Emanuel, 1873-1944. I. Smith, Alfred
     Emanuel, 1873-1944. II. Moses, Robert, 1888-   III. Cronkite,
     Walter Leland, 1916-   IV. Roosevelt, Franklin Delano, Pres. U.S.,
     1882-1945.

Mountbatten, Philip, 3d duke of Edinburgh,
   1921-
         see
Philip, duke of Edinburgh, 1921-

          Mother Russia - from 1900 to the present
C1
865   Whorf, Michael, 1933-
           Mother Russia - from 1900 to the present.
         1 tape cassette.   (The visual sounds of
         Mike Whorf. Social, 865)
             Originally presented on his radio program, Kaleidoscope,
         WJR, Detroit.
             Duration: 39 min., 25 sec.
             From the age of Czar Nicholas to the present, here is the bigger
         than life story of the great "Mother Russia".

         I. Russia. I. Title.

Voice Lib.
344   Mourison, DeLessepps
bd.7   On Castro's Communism.   CBS, December 4,
         1961.
             1 reel (7 in.)   7 1/2 in. per sec.
         phonotape.

             1. Castro, Fidel, 1927-

          MOTHERS
C1
M32   Whorf, Michael, 1933-
           The greatest woman in the world, mother.
         1 tape cassette.   (The visual sounds of
         Mike Whorf. Miscellaneous, M32)

             Originally presented on his radio program, Kaleidoscope,
         WJR, Detroit.
             The selections are those that contain some very basic truths
         and sentiments about mothers, yet the presentation is not overly
         saccharine in upholding the truth, wisdom, and virtue of the
         world's prime example of the unsung heroine.

         I. Mothers. 2. Mothers' Day. I. Title.

          MOUTH-ORGAN
C1
M39   Whorf, Michael, 1933-
           Mr. Hohner's amazing harmonica.
         1 tape cassette.   (The visual sounds of
         Mike Whorf. Miscellaneous, M39)

             Originally presented on his radio program, Kaleidoscope,
         WJR, Detroit.
             Duration: 38 min.
             Never underestimate the power of this six-inch instrument,
         the harmonica. Its history is rich and long, dating from
         ancient China to the twentieth century.

         I. Mouth-organ. I. Title.

          MOTHERS' DAY
C1
M32   Whorf, Michael, 1933-
           The greatest woman in the world, mother.
         1 tape cassette.   (The visual sounds of
         Mike Whorf. Miscellaneous, M32)

             Originally presented on his radio program, Kaleidoscope,
         WJR, Detroit.
             The selections are those that contain some very basic truths
         and sentiments about mothers, yet the presentation is not overly
         saccharine in upholding the truth, wisdom, and virtue of the
         world's prime example of the unsung heroine.

         I. Mothers. 2. Mothers' Day. I. Title.

          MOVING-PICTURE INDUSTRY
Voice Lib.
M786   Spiegel, Sam
bd.1   Interview on the cinema, discussing his
         personal approach to production, illustrating
         with excerpts from sound tracks of: 1. The
         Bridge over the River Kwai, 2. On the
         waterfront, 3. Suddenly last summer, 4.
         Lawrence of Arabia.   BBC, June 20, 1964.
             29 min.   phonotape (1 r.   7 1/2 i.p.s.)

             1. Moving-picture industry.

          "Motivation"
Voice Lib.
M770   Maddox, Joseph A
bd.5   "Motivation": a prose poem written for
         Education 200 class, narrated by the
         student and author. XVL recording.
         March 8, 1966.
             1 reel (7 in.)   7 1/2 in. per sec.
         phonotape.

             I. Title.

          MOVING-PICTURES
Voice Lib.
M1726   Coppola, Francis Ford, 1939-
Bd.2   Interviewed on Today Show by Barbara
         Walters and Gene Shalitt.   NBC, June 18,
         1974.
             12 min.   phonotape (1 r.   7 1/2 i.p.s.)

             1. Moving-pictures.   I. Shalitt, Gene.
         II. Walters, Barbara, 1931-

Voice Lib. MOVING-PICTURES
M1202 Film stars on parade; short excerpts from
bd.2 famous motion pictures in U.S. and England,
1932 to 1940. Audio Archives, 1942.
1 reel (7 in.) 7 1/2 in. per sec.
phonotape.

1. Moving-pictures.

MOVING-PICTURES - HISTORY
Voice Lib.
M1696 Rogers, Charles
bd.3 Reminiscing with Mike Douglas on the
Mike Douglas Show. WJRT-TV, May 27, 1974.
8 min. phonotape (1 r. 7 1/2 i.p.s.)

1. Moving-pictures - History. 2. Rogers,
Charles. I. Douglas, Mike, 1925?

MOVING-PICTURES
Voice Lib.
M1054 Memories of the movies: radio program
bd.2 pertaining to the early days of movies.
Joseph Schildkraut, narrator. Westinghouse
Radio, 1960's.
1 reel (7 in.) 7 1/2 in. per sec.
phonotape.

1. Moving-pictures.
I. Schildkraut, Joseph, 1896-1964.

MOVING-PICTURES - U.S.
C1
S6 Whorf, Michael, 1933-
The celluloid queen.
1 tape cassette. (The visual sounds of
Mike Whorf. Social, S6)

Originally presented on his radio program, Kaleidoscope,
WJR, Detroit.
Duration: 40 min., 30 sec.
The story of the rise and fall of these glamorous stars who
were legends of their times, Theda Bara, Clara Bow, Gloria
Swanson, Colleen Moore, Lana Turner, Marilyn Monroe, is
outlined here.

1. Moving-pictures - U.S. L. Title.

Voice Lib. MOVING-PICTURES
M1099 Short excerpts from famous pictures of the
bd.2 1930's, featuring the film stars. Released
by Cinematograph Players Benevolent Fund #4
in England. Forrest [no date]
1 reel (7 in.) 7 1/2 in. per sec.
phonotape.

1. Moving-pictures.

MOVING-PICTURES, SILENT
C1
M1 Whorf, Michael, 1933-
The silent screen.
1 tape cassette. (The visual sounds of
Mike Whorf. Miscellaneous, M1)

Originally presented on his radio program, Kaleidoscope,
WJR, Detroit.
Duration: 41 min.
It was a history-making event when Edison came forward with
his moving-picture machine. Mary Pickford, Douglas Fairbanks,
Valentino, Clara Bow - the story of their era would unfold with
stories and stars coming alive on the silent screen.

1. Moving-pictures, Silent. L. Title.

MOVING-PICTURES - HISTORY
Voice Lib.
M1695 Gish, Lillian, 1896-
Interviewed by Edwin Newman on Speaking
freely. WKAR-TV, 1974.
37 min. phonotape (1 r. 7 1/2 i.p.s.)

1. Moving-pictures - History.
I. Newman, Edwin Harold, 1919-

Voice Lib. Moyers, Bill D., 1934-
M1691 Commager, Henry Steele, 1902-
bd.1 On public service and private
creativity, with Bill Moyers.
WKAR-TV, May 23, 1974.
25 min. phonotape (1 r. 7 1/2 i.p.s.)

1. Impeachments. 2. U.S. - Politics and
government. I. Moyers, Bill D., 1934-

MOVING-PICTURES - HISTORY
Voice Lib.
M1696 Koplin, Mert
bd.2 Appearance of Koplin and Charles Grinker,
of Cinedex, movie archives, on Mike
Douglas Show. WJRT-TV, May 27, 1974.
7 min. phonotape (1 r. 7 1/2 i.p.s.)

1. Moving-pictures - History. I. Grinker,
Charles. II. Douglas, Mike, 1925?

MOZART, JOHANN CHRYSOSTOM WOLFGANG AMADEUS,
1756-1791
C1
PWM3 Whorf, Michael, 1933-
Mozart.
1 tape cassette. (The visual sounds of
Mike Whorf. Panorama; a world of music, PWM-3)

Originally presented on his radio program, Kaleidoscope,
WJR, Detroit.
Duration: 25 min.
The life and times of Mozart, including excerpts of his
music.

1. Mozart, Johann Chrysostom Wolfgang Amadeus, 1756-
1791. L. Title.

C1
PWM3   Mozart
      Whorf, Michael, 1933–
        Mozart.
        1 tape cassette.   (The visual sounds of
      Mike Whorf. Panorama; a world of music, PWM-3)

        Originally presented on his radio program, Kaleidoscope,
      WJR, Detroit.
        Duration: 25 min.
        The life and times of Mozart, including excerpts of his
      music.

        L. Mozart, Johann Chrysostom Wolfgang Amadeus, 1756–
      179L. L. Title.

      Mudd, Roger
Voice Lib.
N1559   Nixon, Richard Milhous, Pres. U.S., 1913–
        The Watergate Affair; address to the nation,
    with instant analysis by Roger Mudd and
    Daniel Schorr.   CBS, April 30, 1973.
        30 min.   phonotape (1 r.   7 1/2 i.p.s.)

        1. Watergate affair, 1972. I. Mudd,
    Roger. II. Schorr, Daniel Louis, 1916–

      Mudd, Roger
Voice Lib.
M1257   The public and private Robert F. Kennedy;
bd.1   CBS Reports TV documentary program on the
      character, political methods, and ambitions
      of Senator Robert F. Kennedy of New York.
      Narrator: Roger Mudd. CBS-TV, June 20,
      1967.
      1 reel (7 in1)   7 1/2 i.p.s.   phonotape.

      1. Kennedy, Robert Francis, 1925–1968.
    I. Mudd, Roger.

Voice Lib.   Mudd, Roger
M1628–   Nixon, Richard Milhous, Pres. U.S., 1913–
1629,   Address before the National Radio &
bd.1   Television News Directors Association and
      questions following from the members and
      from the national press. Summary and analysis
      by CBS newsmen Roger Mudd and Bruce Morton.
      CBS, March 19, 1974.
      60 min.   phonotape (2 r.   7 1/2 i.p.s.)

      1. U.S. – Politics and government – 1969–
    2. Power resources – U.S. I. Mudd, Roger.
    II. Morton,   Brude.

      Mudd, Roger
Voice Lib.
M1436   The selling of the Pentagon; CBS documentary
bd.2–   about the excesses of the U.S. Army Infor-
1437   mation Department, with Roger Mudd.
      CBS-TV, March 25, 1971.
      2 reels (7 in.)   7 1/2 in. per sec.
      phonotape.

      I. Mudd, Roger

Voice Lib.   Mudd, Roger
M1476   Pentagon Papers.
bd.2   New York times, Washington post, U.S.
      Government arguments before the Supreme
      Court, as represented by CBS News.
      Daniel Schorr (government), Marvin Kalb
      (New York times), Bob Sheafer (Washington
      post), Roger Mudd.   CBS-TV, June 26, 1971.
      1 reel (7 in.) 7 1/2 i.p.s. phonotape.

      L. Security classification (Government documents)
      L. Schorr, Daniel Louis, 1916–   II. Kalb, Marvin L
      III. Sheafer, Bob   IV. Mudd, Roger

Voice Lib.   Mudd, Roger
M742   Castro, Fidel, 1927–
vd.10   Interview with Roger Mudd of CBS, stating
      that he is not a Communist. CBS, 1959.
      1 reel (7 in.)   7 1/2 in. per sec.
      phonotape.

      I. Mudd, Roger

      Mudd, Roger
Voice Lib.
M942   Vietnam perspective (Television program)
      CBS Special Report on Senate Foreign
      Relations Committee hearings and the war
      in Vietnam. CBS, February 18, 1966.
      1 reel (7 in.)   7 1/2 in. per sec.
      phonotape.

      1. Vietnamese conflict, 1961–   – U.S.
    I. Mudd, Roger   II. Sevareid, Arnold Eric,
    1912–   III. Reasoner, Harry, 1923–   IV.
    Kalb, Marvin L

Voice Lib.   Mudd, Roger
M1560   Ford, Gerald R., 1913–
bd.2   Inauguration of Gerald R. Ford as
      Vice President. CBS-TV, December 6, 1973.
      25 min.   phonotape (1 r.   7 1/2 i.p.s.)

      Commentary by Roger Mudd and William
      Miller.

      I. Mudd, Roger. II. Miller, William.

Voice Lib.   Muelder, Milton E
M1700   Borlaug, Norman Ernst, 1914–
      The green revolution; its genesis, impact,
      dangers & hope. Includes awarding of
      honorary D.Sc. degree from Michigan State
      University and introduction by President
      Wharton. WKAR, May 12, 1971.
      50 min.   phonotape (1 r.   7 1/2 i.p.s.)

      1. Population. I. Muelder, Milton E.
    II. Wharton, Clifton Reginald, 1926–

Mueller, Merrill

Voice Lib.
353   Outbreak of Korean War and comments by
bd.18   various persons. NBC, July, 1950.
          1 reel (7 in.)   7 1/2 in. per sec.
       phonotape.

          Original disc off-speed.
          Participants: Henry Cassidy, Merrill Mueller,
       Edward Harper, Jack Bregon.

          I. Cassidy, Henry Clarence, 1910-   II.
       Mueller, Merrill. III. Harper, Edward. IV.
       Bregon, Jack.

MUHAMMAD, THE PROPHET

Cl
R28   Whorf, Michael, 1933-
         The Arabian prophet - Mahomet.
         1 tape cassette.   (The visual sounds of
      Mike Whorf. Religion, R28)
            Originally presented on his radio program, Kaleidoscope,
         WJR, Detroit.
            Duration: 38 min., 15 sec.
            He was the founder of Islam and became its prophet. Today
         millions of people the world over revere his teachings, and follow
         the precepts which he ordained.

            I. Muhammad, the prophet. I. Title.

Voice Lib.
M1690   Muhammad Ali, 1942-
           Integration, separation, politics, and
        violence. WKAR, February 27, 1970.
           50 min.   phonotape (1 r.   7 1/2 i.p.s.)

           1. Muhammad Ali, 1942-   2. Frazier,
        Joe, 1944-   3. Black Muslims.

Voice Lib. Mullaly, Charles J   1877-
M948   Pius XI, Pope, 1857-1939.
bd.2   First message by a Catholic Pontiff over
          radio to the laity, spoken in Latin with
          English translation by Father Charles Mullaly,
          S.J. Vatican Record Co., 1931.
             1 reel (7 in.)   7 1/2 in. per sec.
          phonotape.

             I. Mullaly, Charles J   1877-

Voice Lib.
M1077- Mumford, Lewis, 1895-
1078   Speeches by Lewis Mumford and Hyman
bd.1   Rickover at convocation in New York for
        10th anniversary of the Fund of the Republic,
        dealing with challenges to democracy in the
        next decade and with authoritarian and
        democratic techniques. CSDI, January,
        1963.
           2 reels (7 in.)   7 1/2 in. per sec.
        phonotape.

           I. Rickover, Hyman George, 1900-

Mundt, Karl Earl, 1900-

Voice Lib.
243   McClellan, John Little, 1896-
bd.9   Senate investigating committee: coin-
      machine labor union. Voices of Samuel
      Getlan, Karl Mundt, Robert Kennedy and
      John McClellan. CBS Radio, August 5, 1957.
         1 reel (7 in.)   7 1/2 in. per sec.
      phonotape.

         I. Getlan, Samuel   II. Mundt, Karl
      Earl, 1900-   III. Kennedy, Robert Francis,
      1925-1968.

Voice Lib. Mundt, Karl Earl, 1900-
M750   U.S. Congress. Senate. Committee on Government Operations.
bd.1   Permanent Subcommittee on Investigations.
          Proceedings of the 4th session of Senate Army-McCarthy
       hearings, continued, April 27, 1954. Circumstances under
       which the altered photograph was taken was questioned; examina-
       tion of Sec. Stevens in his attempts to sidetrack investigation from
       Army to Air Force and Navy; a cross-examination by McCarthy
       of Secretary Stevens referring to his attempts to block investigation;
       questioning of Stevens by Senator Mundt demanding exact charges
       against Carr, Cohn and McCarthy. CBS Radio, April 27, 1954.
          1 reel (7 in.)   7 1/2 in. per sec. phonotape.

          L. McCarthy-Army controversy, 1954. L. Stevens, Robert
       Ten Broeck, 1899-   IL. McCarthy, Joseph Raymond, 1909-
       1957. III. Mundt, Karl Earl, 1900-

Mundt, Karl Earl, 1900-
Voice Lib.
M1022   U.S. Congress. Senate. Committee on Government Operations.
bd.2-   Permanent Subcommittee on Investigations.
1923   Proceedings of the 9th session of Senate Army-McCarthy
        hearings, May 4, 1954. Discussion concerning the possibility
        of shortening the hearings; statements by Senators Dirksen,
        Mundt, McClellan, Potter, etc.; Aaron Coleman and the
        stripping of Army files; discussion of FBI confidential letter
        and how it was obtained by McCarthy; suggestion of night and
        Saturday sessions. WJR, May 4, 1954.
           2 reels (7 in.)   7 1/2 in. per sec. phonotape.

           L. McCarthy-Army controversy, 1954. L. Dirksen, Everett
        McKinley, 1896-1969. IL. Mundt, Karl Earl, 1900- III. McClellan,
        John Little, 1896-   IV. Potter, Charles Edward, 1916-

---

Voice Lib. Mundt, Karl Earl, 1900-
M1283   U.S. Congress. Senate. Committee on Government Operations.
           Permanent Subcommittee on Investigations.
           Proceedings of the 12th session of Senate Army-McCarthy
        hearings, May 7, 1954. Secretary Stevens alleges he was
        threatened by Sen. McCarthy. Sen. Mundt queries Stevens.
        Much bantering and ribbing. Question of legality of McCarthy
        holding certain documents. Discussion of pressure to give Private
        Schine an Army commission. CBS Radio, May 7, 1954.
           1 reel (7 in.)   7 1/2 in. per sec. phonotape.

           L. McCarthy-Army controversy, 1954. L. Stevens, Robert
        Ten Broeck, 1899-   IL. Mundt, Karl Earl, 1900-

Mundt, Karl Earl, 1900-
Voice Lib.
M1320   U.S. Congress. Senate. Committee on Government Operations.
           Permanent Subcommittee on Investigations.
           Proceedings of the 17th session of Senate Army-McCarthy
        hearings, May 14, 1954. Sen. Mundt questioning Mr. Adams
        about high-level meeting dealing with United Nations. Exchanges
        between Senator Mundt and Army Counsel Welch. Senator
        McCarthy examining Sen. Dirksen. Discussion of purgery charges
        against Carr. Cohn and Adams speak about private dinner party.
        CBS TV, May 14, 1954.
           1 reel (7 in.)   7 1/2 in. per sec. phonotape.

           L. McCarthy-Army controversy, 1954. L. Mundt, Karl Earl,
        1900- IL. Welch, Joseph Nye, 1890-1960. III. McCarthy,
        Joseph Raymond, 1909-1957. IV. Dirksen, Everett McKinley, 1896-
        1969. V. Cohn, Roy M   1927-   VL. Adams, John G

Voice Lib.
M850   Muni, Paul, 1895-1967.
bd.2   Radio play adaptation of Edna St. Vincent
        Millay's prose-poem "The murder of Lidice",
        relating to the atrocities by Nazis in the
        Czechoslovakian village of Lidice.   All-
        star cast.   NBC, January 6, 1943.
            1 reel (7 in.)   7 1/2 i.p.s.   phonotape.

        I. Millay, Edna St. Vincent, 1892-1950./
        The murder of Lidice. II. Title: The
        murder of Lidice.

Voice Lib.
M315   Murphy, Franklin David, 1916-
bd.6   Assassination: excerpt of address by
        Chancellor Franklin D. Murphy of UCLA on
        President Kennedy.   NBC, November 24,
        1963.
            1 reel (7 in.)   7 1/2 in. per sec.
        phonotape.

        1. Kennedy, John Fitzgerald, Pres. U.S.,
        1917-1963 - Assassination.

                    MUNI, PAUL, 1895-1967
Voice Lib.
M1743   Raft, George
bd.2   Reminisces on the Mike Douglas Show.
        WILX-TV, June 27, 1974.
            10 min.   phonotape (1 r.   7 1/2 i.p.s.)

        1. Raft, George. 2. O'Brien, Pat, 1899-   3. Muni,
        Paul, 1895-1967. 4. Crawford, Joan, 1908-   5. West, Mae,
        1893-   6. Richman, Harry. 7. Entertainers - U. S.   1.
        Douglas, Mike, 1925-

Voice Lib.
649   Murray, Billy
bd.9   Singing old popular song "Taking a Trip
        up the Hudson".   Re-recorded from Edison
        cylinder record.   Edison, 1906.
            1 reel (7 in.)   7 1/2 in. per sec.
        phonotape.

        I. Title: Taking a trip up the Hudson.

                The murder of Lidice
Voice Lib.
M850   Muni, Paul, 1895-1967.
bd.2   Radio play adaptation of Edna St. Vincent
        Millay's prose-poem "The murder of Lidice",
        relating to the atrocities by Nazis in the
        Czechoslovakian village of Lidice.   All-
        star cast.   NBC, January 6, 1943.
            1 reel (7 in.)   7 1/2 i.p.s.   phonotape.

        I. Millay, Edna St. Vincent, 1892-1950./
        The murder of Lidice. II. Title: The
        murder of Lidice.

Voice Lib.
611   Murray, Billy
bd.3   Post-World War I song "I've Got My
        Captain Working for Me".   Victor Talking
        Machine Co., 1919.
            1 reel (7 in.)   7 1/2 in. per sec.
        phonotape.

        I. Title: I've got my captain working for
        me.

Voice Lib.
M259   Murphy, Frank, 1893-1949.
bd.1   A fair deal for labor.   CBS, September 24,
        1937.
            1 reel (7 in.)   7 1/2 in. per sec.
        phonotape.

Voice Lib.
165   Murray, Philip, 1886-1952.
        Convention in Cleveland, Ohio; section
        prior to vote of expulsion of United
        Electrical Workers from CIO.   AFL-CIO.
        [n.d.].
            1 reel (7 in.)   7 1/2 in. per sec.
        phonotape.

Voice Lib.
101   Murphy, Franklin David, 1916-
        Address to Optimists' Club, Santa Monica,
        Calif.   Recorded on location, March 16,
        1962.
            1 reel (7 in.)   7 1/2 in. per sec.
        phonotape.

Voice Lib.
164   Murray, Philip, 1886-1952.
bd.1   1949 Labor Day Speech.   AFL-CIO,
        1949.
            1 reel (7 in.)   7 1/2 in. per sec.
        phonotape.

Voice Lib.
180   Murray, Philip, 1886-1952.
bd.2   Campaign speech for Adlai Stevenson.
       AFL-CIO, 1952.
          1 reel (7 in.)   7 1/2 in. per sec.
       phonotape.

          1. Stevenson, Adlai Ewing, 1900-1965.

Murrow, Edward Roscoe, 1908-1965
Voice Lib.
M1041   Behind the scenes in the CBS newsroom; CBS
bd.2   radio news with Elmer Davis, Edward R.
       Murrow and Paul White, describing the
       operations of radio news broadcasting.
       CBS Radio, June 1, 1941.
          1 reel (7 in.)   7 1/2 i.p.s.   phonotape.

          1. Radio journalism. I. Davis, Elmer
       Holmes, 1890-1958. II. Murrow, Edward
       Roscoe, 1908-1965. III. White, Paul Welrose,
       1902-1955.

Voice Lib.
178   Murrow, Edward Roscoe, 1908-1965.
bd.2   Criticism on McCarthy Hearings.   CBS,
       I Can See It Now, [n.d.]
          1 reel (7 in.)   7 1/2 in. per sec.
       phonotape.

          1. McCarthy-Army controversy, 1954.

Voice Lib.
522   Murrow, Edward Roscoe, 1909-1965.
bd.5   "London calling" broadcast.   CBS, October,
       1941.
          1 reel (7 in.)   7 1/2 in. per sec.
       phonotape.

Voice Lib.
181   Murrow, Edward Roscoe, 1908-1965.
bd.2   British White Paper; details of calling
       up troops in British Empire.   CBS,
       September 1, 1939.
          1 reel (7 in.)   7 1/2 in. per sec.
       phonotape.

Murrow, Edward Roscoe, 1908-1965
Voice Lib.
M1045   The world today; radio broadcast with
bd.1   discussions of George Bernard Shaw by
       Alexander Woollcott; John Daly regarding
       offensive on Moscow; Edward R. Murrow
       from London; Albert Warner concerning
       coal miners' strike.   CBS Radio, October
       30, 1941.
          1 reel (7 in.)   7 1/2 in. per sec.
       phonotape.
          I. Shaw, George Bernard, 1856-1950. I. Woollcott, Alexander,
       1887-1943. II. Daly, John Charles, 1914-   III. Murrow, Edward
       Roscoe, 1908-1965. IV. Warner, Albert, 1884-1967.

Voice Lib.
526   Murrow, Edward Roscoe, 1908-1965.
bd.1   "London Calling";   on the initiation of
       new anti-aircraft gun installations in
       London, British tactics against German
       cities.   CBS, August, 1940.
          1 reel (7 in.)   7 1/2 in. per sec.
       phonotape.

Voice Lib.
525   Murrow, Edward Roscoe, 1908-1965.
          CBS-sponsored dinner honoring Murrow on
       his return from London; reviews early war
       days in London, his editorial freedom as a
       reporter, British censorship, responsibility
       of reporting from a warring nation, British
       view that U.S. must enter war, general cond-
       itions in Britain, changes in British social
       system that might occur following war.   CBS,
       December 2, 1941.
          1 reel (7 in.)   7 1/2 in. per sec.
       phonotape.

Murrow, Edward Roscoe, 1908-1965
Voice Lib.
M1044   London after dark;   on-the-spot recordings of various
       points during the London air-raid attacks: the Savoy Hotel
       kitchen, Trafalgar Square, anti-aircraft battery near London,
       air-raid shelter. With newsmen Edward R. Murrow, Robert
       Bowman, Raymond Van Denny, Larry Lesueur, Eric Sevareid,
       Vincent Sheean, J. B. Priestley, Michael Standing, and
       Winfred Von Thomas. CBS and BBC, August 24, 1940.
       1 reel (7 in.)   7 1/2 in. per sec.   phonotape.

          I. Murrow, Edward Roscoe, 1908-1965. II. Bowman, Robert
       III. Van Denny, Raymond   IV. Lesueur, Laurence Edward,
       1909-   V. Sevareid, Arnold Eric, 1912-   VI. Sheean,
       Vincent, 1899-   VII. Priestley, John Boynton, 1894-
       VIII. Standing, Michael   IX. Von Thomas, Winfred

Voice Lib.
M717   Murrow, Edward Roscoe, 1908-1965.
bd.4   Excerpt from "Hear it now" news program
       about train wreck of "broker's special" in
       Woodbridge, New Jersey. February 5, 1951.
          1 reel (7 in.)   7 1/2 in. per sec.
       phonotape

Voice Lib.
M1245   Murrow, Edward Roscoe, 1908-1965.
bd.2   News broadcast on current topics, dealing
          primarily with testimony by Attorney General
          Brownell and J. Edgar Hoover, at Un-American
          Activities Committee, condemning Truman
          administration in promoting Harry Dexter
          White, an alleged Communist spy. WJR,
          November 17, 1953.
          1 reel (7 in.) 7 1/2 i.p.s. phonotape.

          1. U.S. - Politics and government - 1945-1953.

Voice Lib.
M1035-   Murrow, Edward Roscoe, 1908-1965.
1036   "An hour with Edward R. Murrow". Memorial
bd.1   broadcast upon the death of Edward R. Murrow
          by his associates at CBS, including excerpts
          of some of his famous broadcasts and inter-
          views. CBS-TV, April 30, 1965.
          2 reels (7 in.) 7 1/2 in. per sec.
          phonotape.

Voice Lib.
M507-   Murrow, Edward Roscoe, 1908-1965.
508,   Narrates "The business of sex", dealing
bd.1   with prostitution and business; various
          prostitutes and businessmen talk and
          discuss dealings. CBS, 1957.
          2 reels (7 in.) 7 1/2 i.p.s. phonotape.

          1. Prostitution. I. Title: The business
          of sex.

         Murrow, Edward Roscoe, 1908-1965
Voice Lib.
372   Armstrong, Louis, 1900-1971.
bd.2   "Satchmo the great;" Paris interview
          with Edward R. Murrow. CBS, 1956.
          1 reel (7 in.) 7 1/2 in. per sec.
          phonotape.

          I. Murrow, Edward Roscoe, 1908-1965.

Voice Lib.
M1024-   Murrow, Edward Roscoe, 1908-1965.
1025,   Television network dramatization "Studio
bd.1   One" entitled "The night America trembled",
          pertaining to the CBS Mercury Theater Show
          "War of the worlds". Westinghouse, 1958.
          2 reels (7 in.) 7 1/2 i.p.s. phonotape.

          1. War of the worlds (radio program.)
          I. Title: The night America trembled.

         Murrow, Edward Roscoe, 1908-1965
Voice Lib.
M574   I can hear it now (radio program)
bd.2-   1919-1933. CBS, 1953.
575   2 reels (7 in.) 7 1/2 in. per sec.
          phonotape.

          I. Murrow, Edward Roscoe, 1908-1965. II.
          Rogers, Will, 1879-1935. III. White, William
          Allen, 1868-1944. IV. Hoover, Herbert Clarke,
          Pres. U.S., 1874-1964. V. Roosevelt, Franklin
          Delano, Pres. U.S., 188.-1945. VI. Rice,
          Grantland, 1880-1954. VII. McNamee, Graham,
          1888-1942.

Voice Lib.
207   Murrow, Edward Roscoe, 1908-1965.
bd.1   Murrow's farewell to CBS before becoming
          Director of U.S.I.A.; a closed circuit
          report to CBS stations by Edward R.
          Murrow and Fred W. Friendly. Detroit.
          WJR, January 31, 1961.
          1 reel (7 in.) 7 1/2 in. per sec.
          phonotape.

         Murrow, Edward Roscoe, 1908-1965
Voice Lib.
572-   I can hear it now (radio program)
573   1933-1946. CBS, 1948.
bd.1   2 reels (7 in.) 7 1/2 in. per sec.
          phonotape.
          I. Murrow, Edward Roscoe, 1908-1965. II. LaGuardia, Fiorello
          Henry, 1882-1947. III. Chamberlain, Neville, 1869-1949. IV.
          Roosevelt, Franklin Delano, Pres. U.S., 1882-1945. V. Churchill,
          Winston Leonard Spencer, 1874-1965. VI. Gaulle, Charles de,
          Pres. France, 1890-1970. VII. Eisenhower, Dwight David, Pres. U.S.,
          1890-1969. VIII. Willkie, Wendell Lewis, 1892-1944. IX. Martin,
          Joseph William, 1884-1968. X. Elizabeth II, Queen of Great Britain,
          1926-   XI. Margaret Rose, Princess of Gt. Brit., 1930-   XII.
          Johnson, Hugh Samuel, 1882-1942. XIII. Smith, Alfred Emanuel,
          1873-1944. XIV. Lindbergh, Charles Augustus, 1902-   XV. Davis,
                                              (Continued on next card)

         Murrow, Edward Roscoe, 1908-1965.
Voice Lib.
M774-   Farewell to Studio Nine; historical broadcasts
775,   made by CBS correspondents at time of action
bd.1   and reflections by them in retrospect. 1964.
          2 reels (7 in.) 7 1/2 in. per sec.
          phonotape.

          I. Trout, Robert, 1908-   II. Pierpoint,
          Robert   III. Murrow, Edward Roscoe,
          1908-1965. IV. Kaltenborn, Hans von, 1878-
          1965. V. Sevareid, Arnold Eric, 191.-
          VI. Daly, John Charles, 1914-

         Murrow, Edward Roscoe, 1908-1965
Voice Lib.
573-   I can hear it now (radio program)
574   1945-1949. CBS, 1950?
bd.2-   2 reels (7 in.) 7 1/2 in. per sec.
bd.1   phonotape.
          I. Murrow, Edward Roscoe, 1908-1965. II. Nehru, Jawaharlal,
          1889-1964. III. Philip, duke of Edinburgh, 1921-   IV. Elizabeth II,
          Queen of Great Britain, 1926-   V. Ferguson, Homer, 1889-   VI.
          Hughes, Howard Robard, 1905-   VII. Marshall, George Catlett,
          1880-   VIII. Ruth, George Herman, 1895-1948. IX. Lilienthal,
          David Eli, 1899-   X. Trout, Robert, 1908-   XI. Gage, Arthur.
          XII. Jackson, Robert Houghwout, 1892-1954. XIII. Gromyko, Ana-
          tolii Andreevich, 1908-   XIV. Baruch, Bernard Mannes, 1870-
          1965. XV. Churchill, Winston Leonard Spencer, 1874-1965. XVI.
          Winchell, Walter, 1897-19   XVII. Davis, Elmer Holmes, 1890-
                                              (Continued on next card)

Murrow, Edward Roscoe, 1908-1965

Voice Lib.
M723   Ismay, Hastings Lionel Ismay, baron, 1887-1965.
bd.1   Interview with Edward R. Murrow, dealing
       with Ismay's reminiscences about Winston S.
       Churchill. CBS, 1960.
          1 reel (7 in.)   7 1/2 in. per sec.
       phonotape.

          1. Churchill, Winston Leonard Spencer, 1874-
       1965. I. Murrow, Edward Roscoe, 1908-1965.

MURROW, EDWARD ROSCOE, 1908-1965

Voice Lib.
178   McCarthy, Joseph Raymond, 1909-1957.
bd.1   Attack on Edward R. Murrow. CBS. I
       Can See It Now, ₍n.d.₎
          1 reel (7 in.)   7 1/2 in. per sec.
       phonotape.

          1. Murrow, Edward Roscoe, 1908-1965.

MUSIC, AFRICAN
Voice Lib.
M1353- Denis-Roosevelt expedition to the Congo.
1354   Music re-recorded from original motion
       picture sound track and containing primitive
       music of the negroes of the great Equatorial
       forest and the eastern provinces of the Congo;
       the music of the wandering pigmies of the
       Ituri and Kivu and of the Watusi, the "lost
       tribe", the giants of Ruanda. Mainstream
       Records, App. 1934.
          2 reels (7 in.)   7 1/2 in. per sec.
       phonotape.

MUSIC, AMERICAN

C1
M10   Whorf, Michael, 1933-
          I hear America singing.
          1 tape cassette. (The visual sound... of
       Mike Whorf. Miscellaneous, M10)
          Originally presented on his radio program, Kaleidoscope,
       WJR, Detroit.
          Duration: 56 min., 30 sec.
          The great traditional music of America with authentic, descrip-
       tive notes on the background of the writing of these songs. With
       each story is a musical example and with each example a familiar
       song.

          L Music, American. L Title.

MUSIC, EUROPEAN

C1
M26   Whorf, Michael, 1933-
          Songbook of the old world; traditional and
       folk songs.
          1 tape cassette. (The visual sounds of
       Mike Whorf. Miscellaneous, M26)
          Originally presented on his radio program, Kaleidoscope,
       WJR, Detroit.
          Duration: 57 min.
          A look at European music and the influence it has had on
       the American song.

          L Music, European. L Title.

MUSIC - HISTORY AND CRITICISM

C1
PWM23- Whorf, Michael, 1933-
24   The masters.
          1 tape cassette. (The visual sounds of
       Mike Whorf. Panorama; a world of music,
       PWM-23-PWM-24)
          Originally presented on his radio program, Kaleidoscope,
       WJR, Detroit.
          Duration: 29 min.; 22 min., 45 sec.
          The great melodies of classical music are set forth here
       under various themes.

          L Music - History and criticism. L Title.

MUSIC, POPULAR (SONGS, ETC.)
Voice Lib.
M760   Goldmark, Goldie
bd.2   Excerpt from "What All the Screaming's
       About" (Program 1); Beatle music is actually
       nothing new. Westinghouse Broadcasting
       Corporation, 1964.
          23 sec. phonotape (1 r.   7 1/2 i.p.s.)
       (The music goes round and round)

          1. Music, Popular (Songs, etc.) I. Title:
       What all the screaming's about. II. Series.

MUSIC, POPULAR (SONGS, ETC.)
Voice Lib.
M765   Goldmark, Goldie
bd.4   Excerpt from "The anatomy of a hit"
       (Program 9); gives advice on how to get
       a new record on a popular music station.
       Westinghouse Broadcasting Corporation, 1964.
          1 min., 41 sec. phonotape (1 r.   7 1/2
       i.p.s.) (The music goes round and round)

          1. Music, Popular (Songs, etc.)
       2. Phonorecords. I. Title: The anatomy of
       a hit. II. Series.

MUSIC, POPULAR (SONGS, ETC.)

C1
M20   Whorf, Michael, 1933-
          A tale of a tune, with Gerald Marks.
          1 tape cassette. (The visual sounds of
       Mike Whorf. Miscellaneous, M40)
          Originally presented on his radio program, Kaleidoscope,
       WJR, Detroit.
          Duration: 52 min.
          A delightful nostalgic look at how some of our popular songs
       were written, featuring composer Gerald Marks.

          L Music, Popular (Songs, etc.) L Marks, Gerald. IL Title.

MUSIC, POPULAR (SONGS, ETC.) - FRANCE
Voice Lib.
M766   Garnier, Jacques
bd.4   Excerpt from "Popular Music of Europe"
       (Program 11); comments on French tastes in
       music, including song "Cela n'a pas
       d'importance" by Les Surfs. Westinghouse
       Broadcasting Corporation, 1964.
          2 min., 54 sec. phonotape (1 r.   7 1/2
       i.p.s.) (The music goes round and round)

          1. Music, Popular (Songs, etc.) - France.
       I. Title: Popular music of Europe. II. Series.

Voice Lib.   MUSIC, POPULAR (SONGS, ETC.) - GT. BRIT.
M1095   Vesta Victoria; old time British song medley.
bd.2   British Col., 1906.
        1 reel (7 in.)   7 1/2 in. per sec.
phonotape.

        CONTENTS.- a. Waiting at the church. b.
He calls me his own Gracie darling. c. It's
all right in the summertime. d. Now I have to
call him "father". e. Poor John. f. Daddy
wouldn't buy me a bow-wow.
        L. Music, Popular (Songs, etc.) - Great Britain.

MUSIC, POPULAR (SONGS, ETC.) - U.S.
Voice Lib.
M760   Aberbach, Jean
bd.7   Excerpt from "What All the Screaming's
About" (Program 1); the real reason for the
success of Elvis Presley and the Beatles.
Westinghouse Broadcasting Corporation, 1964.
        1 min.   phonotape (1 r.   7 1/2 i.p.s.)
(The music goes round and round)

        1. Music, Popular (Songs, etc.) - U.S.
2. Presley, Elvis Aron, 1935-   3. The
Beatles. I. Title: What all the screaming's
about. II. Series.

MUSIC, POPULAR (SONGS, ETC.) - U.S.
Voice Lib.
M762   Caesar, Irving, 1895-
bd.8   Excerpt from "Music from Broadway" (Program
5); comments on how he wrote the song "Swanee",
including Al Jolson singing it. Westinghouse
Broadcasting Corporation, 1964.
        1 reel (7 in.)   7 1/2 in. per sec.
phonotape.   (The Music Goes Round and Round)

        I. Title: Music from Broadway. II. Series.

MUSIC, POPULAR (SONGS, ETC.) - U.S.
Voice Lib.
M764   Harburg, Edgar Y   1896-
bd.3   Excerpts from "Sound Track" (Program 7);
comments on his feelings toward the musical
efforts of the 30's.   Including example
of movie music: "Over the rainbow", with
Judy Garland; lyrics by Harburg. Westinghouse Broadcasting Corporation, 1964.
        3 min., 58 sec.   phonotape (1 r.   7 1/2
i.p.s.) (The music goes round and round)
        L. Music, Popular (Songs, etc.) - U.S. L. Garland,
Judy, 1922-1969. II. Title: Sound track. III. Series.

Voice Lib.   MUSIC, POPULAR (SONGS, ETC.) - NORWAY
M766   Ericksen, Espen
bd.6   Excerpt from "Popular Music of Europe"
(Program 11); comments on music of Norway,
including song "Liebeskummer lohnt sich
nicht" by Siw Malmkvist. Westinghouse
Broadcasting Corporation, 1964.
        3 min., 36 sec.   phonotape (1 r.   7 1/2
i.p.s.) (The music goes round and round)

        1. Music, Popular (Songs, etc.) - Norway.
I. Title: Popular music of Europe. II. Series.

MUSIC, POPULAR (SONGS, ETC.) - U.S.
Voice Lib.
M762   Lieber, Jerry
bd.12   Excerpt from "The Big Beat" (Program 2);
changes in the market for rock-and-roll
records; including the song "Surfin' Bird".
Westinghouse Broadcasting Corporation, 1964.
        1 reel (7 in.)   7 1/2 in. per sec.
phonotape.   (The Music Goes Round and Round)

        I. Title: Surfin' bird. II. Title: The
big beat. III. Series.

MUSIC, POPULAR (SONGS, ETC.) - RUSSIA
Voice Lib.
M767   Garnier, Jacques
bd.3   Excerpt from "Russia and her swinging satellites" (Program 12);
comments on how effective the ban on rock-and-roll in Russia
actually is, including Soviet pop tune "Lilacs in bloom" and
Russian version of "St. Louis blues" and two numbers recorded
clandestinely in Leningrad: "Let's dance" and "I want to be happy
cha-cha-cha". Westinghouse Broadcasting Corporation, 1964.
        9 min., 42 sec.   phonotape (1 r.   7 1/2 i.p.s.)
(The music goes round and round)

        L. Music, Popular (Songs, etc.) - Russia. L. Title: Russia
and her swinging satellites. II. Series.

MUSIC, POPULAR (SONGS, ETC.) - U.S.
Voice Lib.
M761   Meyer, Joseph
bd.7   Excerpt from "Whatever happened to Tin Pan
Alley?" (Program 3); relates how he got Al Jolson to introduce
his song "California here I come", including Al Jolson singing
this song. Westinghouse Broadcasting Corporation, 1964.
        1 reel (7 in.)   7 1/2 in. per sec. phonotape. (The music
goes round and round)

        L. Music, Popular (Songs, etc.) - U.S. L. Jolson, Al, 1886-
1950. II. Title: Whatever happened to Tin Pan Alley?
III. Series.

MUSIC, POPULAR (SONGS, ETC.) - SPAIN
Voice Lib.
M766   Banda, Antonio
bd.7   Excerpt from "Popular Music of Europe"
(Program 11); comments on the popular music
in Spain, including musical number "Chin chin".
Westinghouse Broadcasting Corporation, 1964.
        3 min., 3 sec.   phonotape (1 r.   7 1/2
i.p.s.)   (The music goes round and round)

        1. Music, Popular (Songs, etc.) - Spain.
I. Title: Popular music of Europe.
II. Series.

MUSIC, POPULAR (SONGS, ETC.) - U.S.
Voice Lib.
M760   Sholes, Steven H   1911-1968.
bd.6   Excerpt from "What all the screaming's
about (Program 1); Elvis' progress to fame
and fortune, including one of his first hits,
"That's all right"; a comparison is made
between Elvis and the Beatles. Westinghouse
Broadcasting Corporation, 1964.
        8 min., 6 sec.   phonotape (1 r.   7 1/2 i.p.s.)   (The
music goes round and round)

        L. Presley, Elvis Aron, 1935-   2. Music, Popular (Songs,
etc.) - U.S. L. Title: What all the screaming's about. II.
Series.

MUSIC, POPULAR (SONGS, ETC.) - U.S.

Voice Lib.
M760
bd.8
Stoller, Mike
Excerpt from "What all the screaming's about" (Program 1); anything Elvis had sung at the peak of his career would have been popular. Westinghouse Broadcasting Corporation, 1964.
9 sec. phonotape (1 r. 7 1/2 i.p.s.)
(The music goes round and round)

1. Presley, Elvis Aron, 1935- 2. Music, Popular (Songs, etc.) - U.S. I. Title: What all the screaming's about. II. Series.

C1
PWM11
MUSIC, POPULAR (SONGS, ETC.) - U.S.
Whorf, Michael, 1933-
I hear America singing.
1 tape cassette. (The visual sounds of Mike Whorf. Panorama; a world of music, PWM-11)
Originally presented on his radio program, Kaleidoscope, WJR, Detroit.
Duration: 25 min.
A presentation of songs popular in the U. S., including Barbara Allen, Yankee Doodle, Auld Lang Syne, Oh Susanna, Pop goes the weasel, Carry me back to old Virginny, The man on the flying trapeze, and I've been working on the railroad.

1. Music, Popular (Songs, etc.) - U.S. I. Title.

MUSIC, POPULAR (SONGS, ETC.) - U.S.

Voice Lib.
M761
bd.4
Tobias, Charlie
Excerpt from "Whatever happened to Tin Pan Alley?" (Program 3); tells about his direct method of plugging songs. Westinghouse Broadcasting Corporation, 1964.
53 sec. phonotape (1 r. 7 1/2 i.p.s.)
(The music goes round and round)

1. Music, Popular (Songs, etc.) - U.S.
I. Title: Whatever happened to Tin Pan Alley?
II. Series.

C1
PWM6
MUSIC, POPULAR (SONGS, ETC.) - U.S.
Whorf, Michael, 1933-
The old sweet songs.
1 tape cassette. (The visual sounds of Mike Whorf. Panorama; a world of music, PWM-6)
Originally presented on his radio program, Kaleidoscope, WJR, Detroit.
Duration: 26 min.
The story and instrumental renditions of Greensleeves, My Old Kentucky home, After the ball, and Mighty lak' a rose.

1. Music, Popular (Songs, etc.) - U.S. I. Title.

MUSIC, POPULAR (SONGS, ETC.) - U.S.

Voice Lib.
M761
bd.5
Whitmark, Julius
Excerpt from "Whatever happened to Tin Pan Alley?" (Program 3); comments on importance of vaudeville artist in popularizing songs in the days before radio. Westinghouse Broadcasting Corporation, 1964.
1 min., 35 sec. phonotape (1 r. 7 1/2 i.p.s.) (The music goes round and round)

1. Music, Popular (Songs, etc.) - U.S.
I. Title: Whatever happened to Tin Pan Alley?
II. Series.

C1
PMW18
MUSIC, POPULAR (SONGS, ETC.) - U.S.
Whorf, Michael, 1933-
Songs my father taught me.
1 tape cassette. (The visual sounds of Mike Whorf. Panorama; a world of music, PMW-18)
Originally presented on his radio program, Kaleidoscope, WJR, Detroit.
Duration: 25 min.
Mr. Whorf recounts his father's love for popular American music.

1. Music, Popular (Songs, etc.) - U.S. I. Title.

C1
PWM13
MUSIC, POPULAR (SONGS, ETC.) - U.S.
Whorf, Michael, 1933-
The adolescent years.
1 tape cassette. (The visual sounds of Mike Whorf. Panorama; a world of music, PWM-13)
Originally presented on his radio program, Kaleidoscope, WJR, Detroit.
Duration: 23 min.
A discussion with examples of the music of the gay nineties.

1. Music, Popular (Songs, etc.) - U.S. I. Title.

C1
M29
MUSIC, POPULAR (SONGS, ETC.) - U.S.
Whorf, Michael, 1933-
They don't write 'em like that anymore.
1 tape cassette. (The visual sounds of Mike Whorf. Miscellaneous, M29)
Originally presented on his radio program, Kaleidoscope, WJR, Detroit.
Duration: 54 min., 30 sec.
Gerald Marks tells the story of some of America's favorite melodies.

1. Songs, American. 2. Music, Popular (Songs, etc.) - U.S. I. Marks, Gerald. II. Title.

C1
M27
MUSIC, POPULAR (SONGS, ETC.) - U.S.
Whorf, Michael, 1933-
How simple a tune.
1 tape cassette. (The visual sounds of Mike Whorf. Miscellaneous, M27)
Originally presented on his radio program, Kaleidoscope, WJR, Detroit.
Duration: 43 min., 40 sec.
A heart-warming look at some of the stories that lie behind the composition of America's most familiar old tunes.

1. Music, Popular (Songs, etc.) - U.S. I. Title.

C1
PMW17
MUSIC, POPULAR (SONGS, ETC.) - U.S.
Whorf, Michael, 1933-
They don't write 'em like that anymore.
1 tape cassette. (The visual sounds of Mike Whorf. Panorama; a world of music, PMW-17)
Originally presented on his radio program, Kaleidoscope, WJR, Detroit.
Duration: 25 min.
Composer Gerald Marks relates anecdotes and stories behind the composing of several popular American songs.

1. Music, Popular (Songs, etc.) - U.S. I. Marks, Gerald, 1900- II. Title.

Voice Lib.
M762
bd.4
MUSIC, POPULAR (SONGS, ETC.) - U.S.
Yellen, Jack
Excerpt from "Tunesmiths Past and Present"
(Program 4); relates his view that our
musical future is not as black as many
would believe. Westinghouse Broadcasting
Corporation, 1964.
1 reel (7 in.) 7 1/2 in. per sec.
phonotape. (The Music Goes Round and Round)

I. Title: Tunesmiths past and present. II.
Series.

Music for the heavens

C1
A11
Whorf, Michael, 1933-
Music for the heavens.
1 tape cassette. (The visual sounds of
Mike Whorf. Art, music, and letters, A11)
Originally presented on his radio program, Kaleidoscope,
WJR, Detroit.
Duration: 36 min., 45 sec.
Was Johann Sebastian Bach the most creative and brilliant
musican artist on the European scene? Those aspects and attitudes
can conceivably be confirmed as one delves into his life and times.

L. Bach, Johann Sebastian, 1685-1750. I. Title.

Voice Lib.
M761
bd.13
MUSIC, POPULAR (SONGS, ETC.) - WRITING
AND PUBLISHING
Caesar, Irving, 1895-
Excerpt from "Tunesmiths past and present"
(Program 4); comments on writing songs, how
difficult it can be at times but other times
how easy it is. Westinghouse Broadcasting
Corporation, 1964.
2 min., 58 sec. phonotape (1 r. 7 1/2
i.p.s.) (The music goes round and round)

1. Music, Popular (Songs, etc.) - Writing
and publishing. I. Title: Tunesmiths past
and present.   II. Series.

Music from Broadway

Voice Lib.
M762
bd.8
Caesar, Irving, 1895-
Excerpt from "Music from Broadway" (Program
5); comments on how he wrote the song "Swanee",
including Al Jolson singing it. Westinghouse
Broadcasting Corporation, 1964.
1 reel (7 in.) 7 1/2 in. per sec.
phonotape. (The Music Goes Round and Round)

I. Title: Music from Broadway. II. Series.

Voice Lib.
M761
bd.9
MUSIC, POPULAR (SONGS, ETC.) - WRITING
AND PUBLISHING
Gilbert, L   Wolfe
Excerpt from "Tunesmiths past and present"
(Program 4); relates how he began by selling
six parodies to Al Jolson. Westinghouse
Broadcasting Corporation, 1964.
2 min., 23 sec. phonotape (1 r.
7 1/2 i.p.s.) (The music goes round and
round)

1. Music, Popular (Songs, etc.) - Writing
and publishing. I. Title: Tunesmiths
past and present.   II. Series.

Music from Broadway

Voice Lib.
M762
bd.6
Hammerstein, Oscar, 1895-1960.
Excerpt from "Music from Broadway" (Program
5); speaking about Jerome Kern and his style of
writing, including son "They Didn't Believe Me";
also comments on those who followed Jerome Kern
and beginnings of musical comedy, what it was
like in the early days, including song, "Oh,
What a Beautiful Morning". Westinghouse
Broadcasting Corporation, 1964.
1 reel (7 in.) 7 1/2 in. per sec. phonotape. (The Music
Goes Round and Round)
L. Kern, Jerome, 1885-1945. I. Title: Music from Broadway.
II. Series.

Voice Lib.
M761
bd.6
MUSIC, POPULAR (SONGS, ETC.) - WRITING
AND PUBLISHING
Gorney, Jay
Excerpt from "Whatever happened to Tin Pan
Alley" (Program 3); comments on methods of
Max Dreyfus to get great artists to sing his
songs; also the publisher's degradation from
a play of creativity to merely a messenger boy.
Westinghouse Broadcasting Corporation, 1964.
2 min., 54 sec. phonotape (1 r. 7 1/2 i.p.s.)
(The music goes round and round)

L. Music, Popular (Songs, etc.) - Writing and publishing.
L. Title: Whatever happened to Tin Pan Alley? II. Series.

Music from Broadway

Voice Lib.
M762
bd.5
Harbach, Otto Abels, 1873-1963.
Excerpt from "Music from Broadway" (Program
5); comments on transformation to musical
comedy as we know it today. Westinghouse
Broadcasting Corporation, 1964.
2 min., 43 sec. phonotape (7 in.
7 1/2 i.p.s.) (The music goes round and
round)

1. Musical revue, comedy, etc. - New York
(City) I. Title: Music from Broadway.
II. Series.

Voice Lib.
M765
bd.3
MUSIC, POPULAR (SONGS, ETC.) - WRITING
AND PUBLISHING
Wax, Morty
Excerpt from "The anatomy of a hit"
(Program 9); comments on his role as an
independent record promoter; also answers
question whether or not the songs we are
hearing day after day are being given to us
against our will. Westinghouse Broadcasting
Corporation, 1964.
2 min., 55 sec. phonotape (1 r. 7 1/2 i.p.s.)
(The music goes round and round)

L. Music, Popular (Songs, etc.) - Writing & publishing.
2. Phonorecords.   L. Title: The anatomy of a hit.
II. Series.

Music from Broadway

Voice Lib.
M762
bd.7
Harburg, Edgar Y   1896-
Excerpt from "Music from Broadway" (Program
5); tells about his relationship with Gershwin
brothers. Westinghouse Broadcasting Corporation, 1964.
1 reel (7 in.) 7 1/2 in. per sec.
phonotape. (The Music Goes Round and Round)

I. Title: Music from Broadway. II. Series.

Music from Broadway
Voice Lib.
M762 McClelland, Douglas
bd.10 Excerpt from "Music from Broadway" (Program 5); comments on lack of integration of the Broadway shows between the script and the music. Westinghouse Broadcasting Corporation, 1964.
1 reel (7 in.) 7 1/2 in. per sec. phonotape. (The Music Goes Round and Round)

I. Title: Music from Broadway. II. Series.

The music goes round and round
Voice Lib.
M763 Austin, Bob
bd.6 Excerpt from "The Scope of Jazz" (Program 6); his reasons for demise of big bands. Westinghouse Broadcasting Corporation, 1964.
1 reel (7 in.) 7 1/2 in. per sec. phonotape. (The Music Goes Round and Round)

I. Title: The scope of jazz. II. Series.

Music from Broadway
Voice Lib.
M762 Marks, Herbert E
bd.9 Excerpt from "Music from Broadway" (Program 5); comments about Lorenz Hart, his partnership with Richard Rodgers; including song "Manhattan" from "(The) Garrick Gaieties". Westinghouse Broadcasting Corporation, 1964.
1 reel (7 in.) 7 1/2 in. per sec. phonotape. (The Music Goes Round and Round)

I. Title: Music from Broadway. II. Series.

The music goes round and round
Voice Lib.
M766 Banda, Antonio
bd.7 Excerpt from "Popular Music of Europe" (Program 11); comments on the popular music in Spain, including musical number "Chin chin". Westinghouse Broadcasting Corporation, 1964.
3 min., 3 sec. phonotape (1 r. 7 1/2 i.p.s.) (The music goes round and round)

1. Music, Popular (Songs, etc.) - Spain.
I. Title: Popular music of Europe.
II. Series.

The music goes round and round
Voice Lib.
M760 Aberbach, Jean
bd.7 Excerpt from "What All the Screaming's About" (Program 1); the real reason for the success of Elvis Presley and the Beatles. Westinghouse Broadcasting Corporation, 1964.
1 min. phonotape (1 r. 7 1/2 i.p.s.) (The music goes round and round)

1. Music, Popular (Songs, etc.) - U.S.
2. Presley, Elvis Aron, 1935- 3. The Beatles. I. Title: What all the screaming's about. II. Series.

The music goes round and round
Voice Lib.
M760 Burton, Robert J
bd.14 Excerpt from "The Big Beat" (Program 2); comments on the content of the audience of popular music. Westinghouse Broadcasting Corporation, 1964.
1 reel (7 in.) 7 1/2 in. per sec. phonotape. (The Music Goes Round and Round)

I. Title: The big beat. II. Series.

The music goes round and round
Voice Lib.
M760 Aberbach, Jean
bd.10 Excerpt from "The big beat" (Program 2); comments on decline in band business after World War II; coming to popularity of Negro blues records. Westinghouse Broadcasting Corporation, 1964.
1 min., 10 sec. phonotape (1 r. 7 1/2 i.p.s.) (The music goes round and round)

1. Blues (Songs, etc.) - U.S. I. Title: The big beat. II. Series.

The music goes round and round
Voice Lib.
M761 Caesar, Irving, 1895-
bd.13 Excerpt from "Tunesmiths past and present" (Program 4); comments on writing songs, how difficult it can be at times but other times how easy it is. Westinghouse Broadcasting Corporation, 1964.
2 min., 58 sec. phonotape (1 r. 7 1/2 i.p.s.) (The music goes round and round)

1. Music, Popular (Songs, etc.) - Writing and publishing. I. Title: Tunesmiths past and present. II. Series.

Voice Lib. The music goes round and round
M763 Alexander, Willard
bd.3 Excerpt from "The Scope of Jazz" (Program 6); comments on Goodman's success, disappearance of swing bands. Westinghouse Broadcasting Company, 1964.
1 reel (7 in.) 7 1/2 in. per sec. phonotape. (The Music Goes Round and Round)

1. Jazz music. I. Title: The scope of jazz. II. Series.

The music goes round and round
Voice Lib.
M762 Caesar, Irving, 1895-
bd.8 Excerpt from "Music from Broadway" (Program 5); comments on how he wrote the song "Swanee", including Al Jolson singing it. Westinghouse Broadcasting Corporation, 1964.
1 reel (7 in.) 7 1/2 in. per sec. phonotape. (The Music Goes Round and Round)

I. Title: Music from Broadway. II. Series.

The music goes round and round
Voice Lib.
M765   Campana, Frank
bd.2   Excerpt from "The Anatomy of a Hit"
(Program 9); comments on the role of the
promotion man, also the album business.
Westinghouse Broadcasting Corporation, 1964.
1 reel (7 in.)   7 1/2 in. per sec.
phonotape.   (The Music Goes Round and Round)

I. Title: The Anatomy of a Hit. II. Series.

The music goes round and round
Voice Lib.
M760   Goldmark, Goldie
bd.2   Excerpt from "What All the Screaming's
About" (Program 1); Beatle music is actually
nothing new. Westinghouse Broadcasting
Corporation, 1964.
23 sec. phonotape (1 r.   7 1/2 i.p.s.)
(The music goes round and round)

1. Music, Popular (Songs, etc.) I. Title:
What all the screaming's about. II. Series.

The music goes round and round
Voice Lib.
M766   Ericksen, Espen
bd.6   Excerpt from "Popular Music of Europe"
(Program 11); comments on music of Norway,
including song "Liebeskummer lohnt sich
nicht" by Siw Malnikvist. Westinghouse
Broadcasting Corporation, 1964.
3 min., 36 sec. phonotape (1 r.   7 1/2
i.p.s.) (The music goes round and round)

1. Music, Popular (Songs, etc.) - Norway.
I. Title: Popular music of Europe. II. Series.

The music goes round and round
Voice Lib.
M764   Goldmark, Goldie
bd.11   Excerpt from "The world of wax" (Program 8); comments on
the production of another phenomenon which has had a profound
effect on the recording industry, the disc jockey. Also comments
on the dissatisfaction of a large segment of the record industry with
the radio-record relationship. Westinghouse Broadcasting
Corporation, 1964.
7 min., 58 sec. phonotape (1 r.   7 1/2 i.p.s.) (The music
goes round and round)

1. Disc jockeys. 1. Title: The world of wax. II. Series.

The music goes round and round
Voice Lib.
M766   Garnier, Jacques
bd.4   Excerpt from "Popular Music of Europe"
(Program 11); comments on French tastes in
music, including song "Cela n'a pas
d'importance" by Les Surfs. Westinghouse
Broadcasting Corporation, 1964.
2 min., 54 sec. phonotape (1 r.   7 1/2
i.p.s.) (The music goes round and round)

1. Music, Popular (Songs, etc.) - France.
I. Title: Popular music of Europe. II. Series.

The music goes round and round
Voice Lib.
M765   Goldmark, Goldie
bd.4   Excerpt from "The anatomy of a hit"
(Program 9); gives advice on how to get
a new record on a popular music station.
Westinghouse Broadcasting Corporation, 1964.
1 min., 41 sec. phonotape (1 r.   7 1/2
i.p.s.) (The music goes round and round)

1. Music, Popular (Songs, etc.)
2. Phonorecords. I. Title: The anatomy of
a hit. II. Series.

The music goes round and round
Voice Lib.
M767   Garnier, Jacques
bd.3   Excerpt from "Russia and her swinging satellites" (Program 12);
comments on how effective the ban on rock-and-roll in Russia
actually is, including Soviet pop tune "Lilacs in bloom" and
Russian version of "St. Louis blues" and two numbers recorded
clandestinely in Leningrad: "Let's dance" and "I want to be happy
cha-cha-cha". Westinghouse Broadcasting Corporation, 1964.
9 min., 42 sec. phonotape (1 r.   7 1/2 i.p.s.)
(The music goes round and round)

1. Music, Popular (Songs, etc.) - Russia. 1. Title: Russia
and her swinging satellites. II. Series.

The Music Goes Round and Round
Voice Lib.
M763   Goldstein, Chuck
bd.4   Excerpt from "The Scope of Jazz" (Program 6); comments
how each band had their own style and how they adapted
material to fit this style. Comments on Glenn Miller himself;
also comments on Frank Sinatra, including "Moonlight Serenade"
and an excerpt from "The Hit Parade", with girls screaming
over Frank Sinatra and him singing "Lay That Pistol Down, Babe".
Westinghouse Broadcasting Corporation, 1964.
1 reel (7 in.)   7 1/2 in. per sec. phonotape. (The Music
Goes Round and Round)

1. Jazz music. 1. Title: The scope of jazz. II. Series.

The music goes round and round
Voice Lib.
M761   Gilbert, L   Wolfe
bd.9   Excerpt from "Tunesmiths past and present"
(Program 4); relates how he began by selling
six parodies to Al Jolson. Westinghouse
Broadcasting Corporation, 1964.
2 min., 23 sec. phonotape (1 r.
7 1/2 i.p.s.) (The music goes round and
round)

1. Music, Popular (Songs, etc.) - Writing
and publishing. I. Title: Tunesmiths
past and present. II. Series.

The music goes round and round
Voice Lib.
M763   Goodman, Benny, 1909-
bd.2   Excerpt from "The Scope of Jazz" (Program
6); relates the early period of his life
when he was just starting, and the different
places the band played; including song
"Let's Dance", theme song of Goodman organization. Westinghouse Broadcasting Corporation,
1964.
1 reel (7 in.)   7 1/2 in. per sec.
phonotape. (The Music Goes Round and Round)
I. Title: The scope of jazz. II. Title.

The music goes round and round
Voice Lib.
M764 Goodman, Benny, 1909-
bd.10   Excerpt from "The World of Wax" (Program
8); comments on recording with the use of
electricity. Including music "Blue Skies".
Westinghouse Broadcasting Corporation, 1964.
1 reel (7 in.) 7 1/2 in. per sec.
phonotape. (The Music Goes Round and Round)

I. Title: The world of wax. II. Series.

The music goes round and round
Voice Lib.
M761 Gorney, Jay
bd.6   Excerpt from "Whatever happened to Tin Pan
Alley" (Program 3); comments on methods of
Max Dreyfus to get great artists to sing his
songs; also the publisher's degradation from
a play of creativity to merely a messenger boy.
Westinghouse Broadcasting Corporation, 1964.
3 min., 54 sec. phonotape (1 r. 7 1/2 i.p.s.)
(The music goes round and round)

1. Music, Popular (Songs, etc.) - Writing and publishing.
I. Title: Whatever happened to Tin Pan Alley? II. Series.

The music goes round and round
Voice Lib.
M762 Hammerstein, Oscar, 1895-1960.
bd.6   Excerpt from "Music from Broadway" (Program
5); speaking about Jerome Kern and his style of
writing, including son "They Didn't Believe Me";
also comments on those who followed Jerome Kern
and beginnings of musical comedy, what it was
like in the early days, including song, "Oh,
What a Beautiful Morning". Westinghouse
Broadcasting Corporation, 1964.
1 reel (7 in.) 7 1/2 in. per sec. phonotape. (The Music
Goes Round and Round)
1. Kern, Jerome, 1885-1945. I. Title: Music from Broadway.
II. Series.

Voice Lib. The music goes round and round
M764 Hammerstein, Oscar, 1895-1960.
bd.2   Excerpt from "Sound Track" (Program 7);
comments on what happened when there was
drop in popularity of Broadway in '30's.
Westinghouse Broadcasting Corporation, 1964.
19 sec. phonotape (1 r. 7 1/2 i.p.s.)
(The music goes round and round)

I. Title: Sound track. II. Series.

The music goes round and round
Voice Lib.
M761 Harbach, Otto Abels, 1873-1963.
bd.14   Excerpt from "Tunesmiths Past and Present"
(Program 4); speaking about Rudolph Friml
and his technique in composing. Westinghouse
Broadcasting Corporation, 1964.
1 reel (7 in.) 7 1/2 in. per sec.
phonotape. (The Music Goes Round and Round)

1. Friml, Rudolph, 1881-   I. Title:
Tunesmiths past and present. II. Series.

The music goes round and round
Voice Lib.
M762 Harbach, Otto Abels, 1873-1963.
bd.5   Excerpt from "Music from Broadway" (Program
5); comments on transformation to musical
comedy as we know it today. Westinghouse
Broadcasting Corporation, 1964.
2 min., 43 sec. phonotape (7 in.
7 1/2 i.p.s.) (The music goes round and
round)

1. Musical revue, comedy, etc. - New York
(City) I. Title: Music from Broadway.
II. Series.

The music goes round and round
Voice Lib.
M764 Harbach, Otto Abels, 1873-1963.
bd.1   Excerpt from "Sound Track" (Program 7);
comments on filmdom's first encounter with
sound tracks; also explains what he feels
was wrong with the first movie musicals.
Westinghouse Broadcasting Corporation, 1964.
1 reel (7 in.) 7 1/2 in. per sec.
phonotape. (The Music Goes Round and Round)

I. Title: Sound track. II. Series.

The music goes round and round
Voice Lib.
M762 Harburg, Edgar Y   1896-
bd.7   Excerpt from "Music from Broadway" (Program
5); tells about his relationship with Gershwin
brothers. Westinghouse Broadcasting Corporation, 1964.
1 reel (7 in.) 7 1/2 in. per sec.
phonotape. (The Music Goes Round and Round)

I. Title: Music from Broadway. II. Series.

The music goes round and round
Voice Lib.
M764 Harburg, Edgar Y   1896-
bd.3   Excerpts from "Sound Track" (Program 7);
comments on his feelings toward the musical
efforts of the 30's. Including example
of movie music: "Over the rainbow", with
Judy Garland; lyrics by Harburg. Westinghouse Broadcasting Corporation, 1964.
3 min., 58 sec. phonotape (1 r. 7 1/2
i.p.s.) (The music goes round and round)
1. Music, Popular (Songs, etc.) - U.S. I. Garland,
Judy, 1922-1969. II. Title: Sound track. III. Series.

The music goes round and round
Voice Lib.
M764 Higgins, Joe
bd.7   Excerpt from "The World of Wax" (Program
8); comments on what the record store was
like in the early days as compared to today.
Westinghouse Broadcasting Corporation, 1964.
1 reel (7 in.) 7 1/2 in. per sec.
phonotape. (The Music Goes Round and Round)

I. Title: The world of wax. II. Series.

The music goes round and round
Voice Lib.
M766　Hutton, Jack
bd.3　　Excerpt from "Popular Music of Europe"
(Program 11); expresses his idea that the
British sound is not all British; including
song "I Don't Need You", by the "Panics"
sextet. Westinghouse Broadcasting Corporation,
1964.
　　1 reel (7 in.)　7 1/2 in. per sec.
phonotape.　(The Music Goes Round and Round)

　　I. Title: Popular music of Europe. II. Series.

The music goes round and round
Voice Lib.
M764　Kapp, David
bd.6　　Excerpt from "The World of Wax" (Program
8); discusses his father when he sold
phonographs door to door. Westinghouse
Broadcasting Corporation, 1964.
　　1 reel (7 in.)　7 1/2 in. per sec.
phonotape.　(The Music Goes Round and Round)

　　I. Title: The world of wax. II. Series.

The music goes round and round
Voice Lib.
M764　Kapp, Mickey
bd.13　　Excerpt from "The World of Wax" (Program 8);
comments on how a small label survives against
the giants. Westinghouse Broadcasting
Corporation, 1964.
　　1 reel (7 in.)　7 1/2 in. per sec.
phonotape.　(The Music Goes Round and Round)

　　I. Title: The world of wax. II. Series.

The music goes round and round
Voice Lib.
M765　Kapp, Mickey
bd.6　　Excerpt from "The Anatomy of a Hit" (Program
9); relates his experience with the record
"Hello, Dolly", including the song as sung
by Louis Armstrong. Westinghouse Broadcasting
Corporation, 1964.
　　1 reel (7 in.)　7 1/2 in. per sec.
phonotape.　(The Music Goes Round and Round)

　　I. Title: The anatomy of a hit. II. Series.

The music goes round and round
Voice Lib.
M760　Kellem, Manny
bd.4　　Excerpt from "What All the Screaming's
About" (Program 1); promotion of the Beatles,
including remarks by teenaged girls of their
feelings toward the new singing group called
the Beatles. Westinghouse Broadcasting
Corporation, 1964.
　　1 reel (7 in.)　7 1/2 in. per sec.
phonotape.　(The Music Goes Round and Round)

　　I. Title: What all the screaming's about.
II. Series.

The music goes round and round
Voice Lib.
M766　Levy, Leonard
bd.1　　Excerpt from "What All the Screaming's
About" (Program 1); discusses the effect
of Beatle music on adolescents. Westinghouse Broadcasting Corporation, 1964.
　　1 reel (7 in.)　7 1/2 in. per sec.
phonotape.　(The Music Goes Round and Round)

　　I. Title: What all the screaming's about.
II. Series.

The music goes round and round
Voice Lib.
M760　Levy, Leonard
bd.16　　Excerpt from "The Big Beat" (Program 2);
comments on the many artists who are only
one-shot record artists and the ones who
have true talent; including song by Bobby
Vinton, "Blue Velvet". Westinghouse
Broadcasting Company, 1964.
　　1 reel (7 in.)　7 1/2 in. per sec.
phonotape.　(The Music Goes Round and Round)

　　I. Title: The big beat. II. Series.

The music goes round and round
Voice Lib.
M765　Levy, Leonard
bd.8　　Excerpt from "The Anatomy of a Hit"
(Program 9); answers the question, "What
does a company do when one of its artists
is no longer selling?" Westinghouse
Broadcasting Corporation, 1964.
　　1 reel (7 in.)　7 1/2 in. per sec.
phonotape.　(The Music Goes Round and Round)

　　I. Title: The anatomy of a hit. II. Series.

The music goes round and round
Voice Lib.
M762　Lieber, Jerry
bd.2　　Excerpt from "Tunesmiths past and present"
(Program 4); comments on success in relation
to "song writer" vs. "record writing".
Westinghouse Broadcasting Corporation, 1964.
　　2 min., 28 sec.　phonotape (1 r.
7 1/2 i.p.s.)　(The music goes round and
round)

　　1. Music, Popular (Songs, etc.) - Publishing
and writing.　I. Title: Tunesmiths past and
present.　　II. Series.

The music goes round and round
Voice Lib.
M762　Lieber, Jerry
bd.12　　Excerpt from "The Big Beat" (Program 2);
changes in the market for rock-and-roll
records; including the song "Surfin' Bird".
Westinghouse Broadcasting Corporation, 1964.
　　1 reel (7 in.)　7 1/2 in. per sec.
phonotape.　(The Music Goes Round and Round)

　　I. Title: Surfin' bird. II. Title: The
big beat. III. Series.

The music goes round and round
Voice Lib.
M762 McClelland, Douglas
bd.10   Excerpt from "Music from Broadway" (Program
5); comments on lack of integration of the
Broadway shows between the script and the
music. Westinghouse Broadcasting Corporation,
1964.
    1 reel (7 in.)   7 1/2 in. per sec.
phonotape. (The Music Goes Round and Round)

    I. Title: Music from Broadway. II. Series.

The music goes round and round
Voice Lib.
M766 Martin, Neville
bd.2   Excerpt from "Popular Music of Europe"
(Program 11); discusses extent of American
influence both today and yesterday in music
in Europe; including "Ain't Necessarily So"
by British group "Ian and the Zodiacs."
Westinghouse Broadcasting Corporation, 1964.
    1 reel (7 in.)   7 1/2 in. per sec.
phonotape. (The Music Goes Round and Round)
    I. Title: Popular music of Europe. II. Series.

Voice Lib. The music goes round and round
M763 McClelland, Douglas
bd.8   Excerpt from "Sound Track" (Program 7);
comments how music was used in the production
of the movie even before the advent of sound;
on the role of the audience in accepting the
movies; early stages of sound; the sound
track album. Westinghouse Broadcasting
Corporation, 1964.
    1 reel (7 in.)   7 1/2 in. per sec.
phonotape. (The Music Goes Round and Round)

    I. Title: Sound track. II. Series.

The Music Goes Round and Round
Voice Lib.
M761 Meyer, Joseph
bd.7   Excerpt from "Whatever happened to Tin Pan
Alley?" (Program 3); relates how he got Al Jolson to introduce
his song "California here I come", including Al Jolson singing
this song. Westinghouse Broadcasting Corporation, 1964.
    1 reel (7 in.) 7 1/2 in. per sec. phonotape. (The music
goes round and round)

    I. Music, Popular (Songs, etc.) - U.S. I. Jolson, Al, 1886-
1950. II. Title: Whatever happened to Tin Pan Alley?
III. Series.

The music goes round and round
Voice Lib.
M760 Mann, Arthur
bd.3   Excerpt from "What All The Screaming's
About" (Program 1); English-based music
of Beatles; what serious musicians find
interesting about the music of the Beatles.
Westinghouse Broadcasting Corporation, 1964.
    1 reel (7 in.)   7 1/2 in. per sec.
phonotape. (The Music Goes Round and Round)

    1. The Beatles. I. Title: What all the
screaming's about. II. Series.

The music goes round and round
Voice Lib.
M760 Miller, Mitch, 1911-
bd.15   Excerpt from "The Big Beat" (Program 2);
criticizing rock-and-roll; feels like people
who like it are lowering themselves.
Westinghouse Broadcasting Corporation, 1964.
    1 reel (7 in.)   7 1/2 in. per sec.
phonotape. (The Music Goes Round and Round)

    I. Title: The big beat. II. Series.

The music goes round and round
Voice Lib.
M761 Marks, Herbert E
bd.1   Excerpt from "Whatever Happened to Tin Pan
Alley?" (Program 3); comments on rise of
Tin Pan Alley and the popularity of records.
Westinghouse Broadcasting Corporation, 1964.
    1 reel (7 in.)   7 1/2 in. per sec.
phonotape. (The Music Goes Round and Round)

    I. Title: Whatever happened to Tin Pan Alley?
II. Series.

Voice Lib. The music goes round and round
M761 Olman, Abe
bd.3   Excerpt from "Whatever Happened to Tin Pan
Alley?" (Program 3); composed "Down Among the
Sheltering Palms" and "Oh, Johnny, Oh";
comments on how he went about plugging songs.
Westinghouse Broadcasting Corporation, 1964.
    1 reel (7 in.)   7 1/2 in. per sec.
phonotape. (The Music Goes Round and Round)

    I. Title: Whatever happened to Tin Pan Alley?
II. Series.

The music goes round and round
Voice Lib.
M762 Marks, Herbert E
bd.9   Excerpt from "Music from Broadway"
(Program 5); comments about Lorenz Hart,
his partnership with Richard Rodgers;
including song "Manhattan" from "The
Garrick Gaieties". Westinghouse Broadcasting Corporation, 1964.
    1 reel (7 in.)   7 1/2 in. per sec.
phonotape. (The Music Goes Round and Round)

    I. Title: Music from Broadway. II. Series.

The music goes round and round
Voice Lib.
M761 Olman, Abe
bd.15   Excerpt from "Tunesmiths Past and Present
(Program 4); pessimistic outlook for present-
day song writers. Westinghouse Broadcasting
Corporation, 1964.
    1 reel (7 in.)   7 1/2 in. per sec.
phonotape. (The Music Goes Round and Round)

    I. Title: Tunesmiths past and present.
II. Series.

Voice Lib.   The music goes round and round
M763   Perado, Al
bd.7   Excerpt from "Sound track" (Program 7);
          discusses importance of music in bringing
          out emotions of actors. Westinghouse
          Broadcasting Corporation, 1964.
          . 1 min., 10 sec.   phonotape (1 r.
          7 1/2 i.p.s.)   (The music goes round and
          round)
              I. Title: Sound track. II. Series.

Voice Lib.   The music goes round and round
M767   Rapoport, Azaria
bd.1   Excerpt from "Popular Music of Europe"
          (Program 11); comments on effects of British
          music on Israel, including song "With a Little
          Bit of Luck" from "My Fair Lady", sung in
          Hebrew, Italian and Spanish. Westinghouse
          Broadcasting Corporation, 1964.
          1 reel (7 in.)   7 1/2 in. per sec.
          phonotape.   (The Music Goes Round and Round)
              I. Title: Popular music of Europe. II. Series.

Voice.Lib.   The music goes round and round
M764   Robbins, Oscar, 1912-1965.
bd.5   Excerpt from "Sound Track" (Program 7);
          gives his reasons for the apparent dearth
          of initiative from Hollywood which is so
          famous for originality and innovation.
          Westinghouse Broadcasting Corporation, 1964.
          1 reel (7 in.)   7 1/2 in. per sec.
          phonotape.   (The Music Goes Round and Round)

              I. Title: Sound track. II. Series.

Voice Lib. The music goes round and round
M761   Ruby, Harry
bd.2   Excerpt from "Whatever Happened to Tin Pan
          Alley?" (Program 3); comments on how he
          plugged his songs and others. Westinghouse
          Broadcasting Corporation, 1964.
          1 reel (7 in.)   7 1/2 in. per sec.
          phonotape.   (The Music Goes Round and Round)

              I. Title: Whatever happened to Tin Pan Alley?
          II. Series.

Voice Lib. The music goes round and round
M761   Ruby, Harry
bd.10   Excerpt from "Tunesmiths Past and Present"
          (Program 4); tells about the big composers
          in the days before the golden era of the
          '20's and '30's. Westinghouse Broadcasting
          Corporation, 1964.
          1 reel (7 in.)   7 1/2 in. per sec.
          phonotape.   (The Music Goes Round and Round)

              I. Title: Tunesmiths past and present.
          II. Series.

Voice Lib. The music goes round and round
M760   Schimmel, John L
bd.5   Excerpt from "What All the Screaming's
          About" (Program 1); psychiatrist's approach
          to Beatlemania and its effects on teenage
          girls. Westinghouse Broadcasting Corporation,
          1964.
          1 reel (7 in.)   7 1/2 in. per sec.
          phonotape.   (The Music Goes Round and Round)

              I. Title: What all the screaming's about.
          II. Series.

Voice Lib.   The music goes round and round
M763   Serulli, Dom
bd.1   Excerpt from "The Scope of Jazz" (Program
          6); discusses three biggest factors in the
          establishment of the "swing" era, also his
          reason for decline of big bands. Westing-
          house Broadcasting Corporation, 1964.
          1 reel (7 in.)   7 1/2 in. per sec.
          phonotape.   (The Music Goes Round and Round)
              I. Title: The scope of jazz. II. Series.

Voice Lib.   The music goes round and round
M760   Sholes, Steven H   1911-1968.
bd.6   Excerpt from "What all the screaming's
          about (Program 1); Elvis' progress to fame
          and fortune, including one of his first hits,
          "That's all right"; a comparison is made
          between Elvis and the Beatles. Westinghouse
          Broadcasting Corporation, 1964.
          8 min., 6 sec. phonotape (1 r.   7 1/2 i.p.s.) (The
          music goes round and round)

              1. Presley, Elvis Aron, 1935-   2. Music, Popular (Songs,
          etc.) - U. S.   I. Title: What all the screaming's about. II.
          Series.

Voice Lib. The music goes round and round
M760   Sholes, Steven H   1911-1968.
bd.11   Excerpt from "The Big Beat" (Program 2);
          formation of popular music, including a
          song by Eddie Arnold, "There's a Star-
          Spangled Banner Waving Somewhere". Westing-
          house Broadcasting Corporation, 1964.
          1 reel (7 in.)   7 1/2 in. per sec.
          phonotape.   (The Music Goes Round and Round)

              I. Title: The big beat. II. Series.

Voice Lib.   The music goes round and round
M762   Sholes, Steven H   1911-1968.
bd.3   Excerpt from "Tunesmiths Past and Present"
          (Program 4); comments on today's emphasis
          on youth as song writers and as the audience
          of these songs. Westinghouse Broadcasting
          Corporation, 1964.
          1 reel (7 in.)   7 1/2 in. per sec.
          phonotape.   (The Music Goes Round and Round)

              I. Title: Tunesmiths past and present.
          II. Series.

The music goes round and round
Voice Lib.
M764 Sholes, Steven H   1911-1968.
bd.9   Excerpt from "The World of Wax" (Program
        8); discusses why radio almost killed the
        record business, and the biggest change in
        the record business. Westinghouse Broad-
        casting Corporation, 1964.
          1 reel (7 in.)   7 1/2 in. per sec.
        phonotape. (The Music Goes Round and Round)

          I. Title: The world of wax. II. Series.

The music goes round and round
Voice Lib.
M765 Spector, Phil
bd.7   Excerpt from "The Anatomy of a Hit"
        (Program 9); answers the questions, Was
        the popularity of "Hello, Dolly" a freak?
        Could it happen again and how did it happen
        in the first place? Westinghouse Broad-
        casting Corporation, 1964.
          1 reel (7 in.)   7 1/2 in. per sec.
        phonotape. (The Music Goes Round and Round)

          I. Title: The anatomy of a hit. II. Series.

The music goes round and round
Voice Lib.
M765 Sholes, Steven H   1911-1968.
bd.1   Excerpt from "The Anatomy of a Hit"
        (Program 9); comments on why the A&R man
        is the most important person in the production
        of a hit record; the changing attitude of
        the juke box operator. Westinghouse
        Broadcasting Corporation, 1964.
          1 reel (7 in.)   7 1/2 in. per sec.
        phonotape. (The Music Goes Round and Round)

          I. Title: The anatomy of a hit. II. Series.

The music goes round and round
Voice Lib.
M766 Stampa, Fred
bd.5   Excerpt from "Popular Music of Europe"
        (Program 11); comments on style of singing
        of Dominco Modugno, including song "Boom
        boom surf" by Peppino Di Capri and the
        Hollerers. Westinghouse Broadcasting
        Corporation, 1964.
          1 min., 44 sec. phonotape (1 r.   7 1/2 i.p.s.)
        (The music goes round and round)

          1. Modugno, Dominco. L. Title: Boom boom surf.
        II. Title: Popular music of Europe. III. Series.

The music goes round and round
Voice Lib.
M761 Spaeth, Sigmund, 1885-1965.
bd.8   Excerpt from "Whatever Happened to Tin Pan
        Alley?" (Program 3); comments on the replace-
        ment of pianos with records. Westinghouse
        Broadcasting Corporation, 1964.
          1 reel (7 in.)   7 1/2 in. per sec.
        phonotape. (The Music Goes Round and Round)

          I. Title: Whatever happened to Tin Pan Alley?
        II. Series.

The music goes round and round
Voice Lib.
M765 Steinberg, Dick
bd.5   Excerpt from "The Anatomy of a Hit" (Program
        9); comments on the difficulty of compiling
        sheet list of the top records in the country.
        Westinghouse Broadcasting Corporation, 1964.
          1 reel (7 in.)   7 1/2 in. per sec.
        phonotape. (The Music Goes Round and Round)

          I. Title: The anatomy of a hit. II. Series.

The music goes round and round
Voice Lib.
M762 Spector, Phil
bd.1   Excerpt from "Tunesmiths Past and Present"
        (Program 4); explanation as to why many of
        the old writers apparently can no longer make
        the grade, also comments on his goal in the
        business; including two songs, "Be My Baby"
        and "Spanish Harlem". Westinghouse Broad-
        casting Corporation, 1964.
          1 reel (7 in.)   7 1/2 in. per sec.
        phonotape. (The Music Goes Round and Round)
          I. Title: Tunesmiths past and present. II.
        Series.

The music goes round and round
Voice Lib.
M760 Stoller, Mike
bd.8   Excerpt from "What all the screaming's
        about" (Program 1); anything Elvis had sung
        at the peak of his career would have been
        popular. Westinghouse Broadcasting
        Corporation, 1964.
          9 sec.   phonotape (1 r.   7 1/2 i.p.s.)
        (The music goes round and round)

          1. Presley, Elvis Aron, 1935-   2. Music, Popular (Songs,
        etc.) - U.S. L. Title: What all the screaming's about.
        II. Series.

The music goes round and round
Voice Lib.
M764 Spector, Phil
bd.12   Excerpt from "The World of Wax" (Program
        8); discusses the effect of all the factors
        on the quality of the records being produced,
        after the advent of rock-and-roll. Westing-
        house Broadcasting Corporation, 1964.
          1 reel (7 in.)   7 1/2 in. per sec.
        phonotape. (The Music Goes Round and Round)

          I. Title: The world of wax. II. Series.

The music goes round and round
Voice Lib.
M760 Stoller, Mike
bd.13   Excerpt from "The Big Beat" (Program 2);
        comments on how the musical tastes of people
        change and have changed. Westinghouse
        Broadcasting Corporation, 1964.
          1 reel (7 in.)   7 1/2 in. per sec.
        phonotape. (The Music Goes Round and Round)

          I. Title: The big beat. II. Series.

Voice Lib.   The music goes round and round
M761
bd.4   Tobias, Charlie
          Excerpt from "Whatever happened to Tin Pan
          Alley?" (Program 3); tells about his direct
          method of plugging songs. Westinghouse
          Broadcasting Corporation, 1964.
              53 sec. phonotape (1 r.   7 1/2 i.p.s.)
          (The music goes round and round)

              1. Music, Popular (Songs, etc.) - U.S.
          I. Title: Whatever happened to Tin Pan Alley?
          II. Series.

Voice Lib.   The music goes round and round
M761
bd.5   Whitmark, Julius
          Excerpt from "Whatever happened to Tin Pan
          Alley?" (Program 3); comments on importance
          of vaudeville artist in popularizing songs
          in the days before radio. Westinghouse
          Broadcasting Corporation, 1964.
              1 min., 35 sec. phonotape (1 r.   7 1/2
          i.p.s.) (The music goes round and round)

              1. Music, Popular (Songs, etc.) - U.S.
          I. Title: Whatever happened to Tin Pan Alley?
          II. Series.

Voice Lib.   The music goes round and round
M765
bd.3   Wax, Morty
          Excerpt from "The anatomy of a hit"
          (Program 9); comments on his role as an
          independent record promoter; also answers
          question whether or not the songs we are
          hearing day after day are being given to us
          against our will. Westinghouse Broadcasting
          Corporation, 1964.
              2 min., 55 sec. phonotape (1 r.   7 1/2 i.p.s.)
          (The music goes round and round)

              1. Music, Popular (Songs, etc.) - Writing & publishing.
              2. Phonorecords.   I. Title: The anatomy of a hit.
          II. Series.

Voice Lib.   The music goes round and round
M762
bd.4   Yellen, Jack
          Excerpt from "Tunesmiths Past and Present"
          (Program 4); relates his view that our
          musical future is not as black as many
          would believe. Westinghouse Broadcasting
          Corporation, 1964.
              1 reel (7 in.)   7 1/2 in. per sec.
          phonotape.   (The Music Goes Round and Round)

              I. Title: Tunesmiths past and present. II.
          Series.

Voice Lib.   The music goes round and round
M764
bd.4   Waxman, Frank
          Excerpt from "Sound Track" (Program 7);
          comments on where the new group of composers
          came from besides Broadway. Westinghouse
          Broadcasting Corporation, 1964.
              1 min., 5 sec.   phonotape (1 r.
          7 1/2 i.p.s.) (The music goes round and round)

              1. Music, Popular (Songs, etc.) -
          Writing and publishing. I. Title: Sound
          track. II. Series.

Voice Lib.
M1300
bd.5   Musical ceremonies and bugle calls of
          German Wehrmacht; also military marches
          and orchestral rendering of "Deutschland-
          lied". Peteler, n.d.
              1 reel (7 in.)   7 1/2 i.p.s.   phonotape.

              1. War-songs, German.   I. Title:
          Deutschlandlied.

Voice Lib.   The music goes round and round
M763
bd.5   Whiteman, Paul, 1890-1967.
          Excerpt from "The Scope of Jazz" (Program
          6); comments on Bing Crosby at the beginning
          of his career, including song by Crosby,
          "Pennies from Heaven." Westinghouse
          Broadcasting Corporation, 1964.
              1 reel (7 in.)   7 1/2 in. per sec.
          phonotape.   (The Music Goes Round and Round)

              1. Crosby, Bing, 1901-   I. Title: The
          scope of jazz. II. Series.

Voice Lib.
587
bd.3   Musick, Edwin K
          Air transportation in 1935; acknowledges
          NBC salute to Pan-American Airways for
          China Clipper flights in 1935. NBC,
          January 1, 1936.
              1 reel (7 in.)   7 1/2 in. per sec.
          phonotape.

              1. Aeronautics, Commercial

Voice Lib.   The music goes round and round
M764
bd.8   Whiteman, Paul, 1890-1967.
          Excerpt from "The World of Wax" (Program 8);
          comments on how the recording was accomplished;
          including music "Whispering". Westinghouse
          Broadcasting Corporation, 1964.
              1 reel (7 in.)   7 1/2 in. per sec.
          phonotape.   (The Music Goes Round and Round)

              I. Title: The world of wax. II. Series.

Voice Lib.
M1561   Muskie, Edmund S   1914-
          Firing line, interviewed by William
          Buckley. WKAR-AM, February 15, 1974.
              25 min. phonotape (1 r.   7 1/2 i.p.s.)

              1. U.S. - Politics and government - 1969-
          I. Buckley, William Frank, 1925-

Muskie, Edmund S   1914-
Voice Lib.
M1323- Democratic Party. National Convention,
M1328,   Chicago, 1968.
  bd.1   Hubert Humphrey, Democratic presidential nom...,
          announcing his selection of Sen. Muskie as his running mate;
          convention floor reports; interview with Mrs. Humphrey. Mayor
          Daley of Chicago defending police action. Interviews with Sen-
          ator McGovern and Jesse Unruh of California. Remote address by
          Sen. Edward Kennedy introducing a memorial motion picture on
          the late Sen. Robert F. Kennedy. Various reports on riots and
          general confusion, reluctance of delegates to come to order.
          Nominations for Vice-President; seconding speeches for Sen.
          Muskie and nominating speech by Wisconsin delegation of Julian
          Bond of Georgia. Interview with Julian Bond, who declined
          nomination of the vice-presidency. Story told by chairman of
          the New Hampshire [delegation] regarding his arrest. Interview
                                    (Continued on next card)

Muskie, Edmund S   1914-
Voice Lib.
M1323- Democratic Party. National Convention,
M1328,   Chicago, 1968...   (Card 2)
  bd.1   with Paul O'Dwyer of the New York delegation regarding the
          nomination of Richard Daley for Vice-President. General
          confusion. Nomination of Sen. Edmund Muskie as Vice-President
          and resulting confusion with the Oregon delegation. Followed by
          Sen. Muskie's acceptance speech. NBC-TV, August 29, 1968.
          6 reels (7 in.) 7 1/2 in. per sec. phonotape.
          L. Humphrey, Hubert Horatio, 1911- II. Humphrey, Muriel Fay
          (Buck) 1912-   III. Daley, Richard J   1902-   IV. McGovern,
          George Stanley, 1922-   V. Unruh, Jesse Marvin, 1922-   VI.
          Kennedy, Edward Moore, 1932-   VII. Bond, Julian, 1940-   VIII.
          O'Dwyer, Paul, 1907-   IX. Muskie, Edmund S   1914-

---

Voice Lib.
M961   Mussolini, Benito, 1883-1945.
  bd.9   Excerpt of speech in Italian celebrating
          twentieth anniversary of Fascist march on
          Rome. German Radio; Peteler, October 27,
          1939.
          1 reel (7 in.) 7 1/2 in. per sec.
          phonotape.

Voice Lib.
M1019 Mussolini, Benito, 1883-1945.
  bd.10   Excerpt from address given in German,
          at May Day celebration, expressing his
          friendship with Hitler. Peteler, May 1,
          1940.
          1 reel (7 in.) 7 1/2 in. per sec.
          phonotape.

Voice Lib.
607   Mussolini, Benito, 1883-1945.
  bd.5   Declaration of war on Great Britain and
          France, in special shortwave broadcast
          from Rome, Italy. CBS, June 10, 1940.
          1 reel (7 in.) 7 1/2 in. per sec.
          phonotape.

          In Italian.

Voice Lib.
M961   Mussolini, Benito, 1883-1945.
  bd.3   Excerpt from his speech in Italian declaring
          war against Britain and France. German
          Radio; Peteler, June 10, 1940.
          1 reel (7 in.) 7 1/2 in. per sec.
          phonotape.

Voice Lib.
M714   Mussolini, Benito, 1883-1945.
  bd.8   Speaking in broadcast from Rome, Italy
          announcing Italy's entrance into World War
          II on the side of the Axis. July 10, 1940.
          1 min., 1 sec. phonotape (1 r.
          7 1/2 i.p.s.)

          1. World War, 1939-1945 - Italy.

             MY LAI (4), VIETNAM - MASSACRE, 1968
Voice Lib.
M1610 Medina, Ernest
  bd.2   Michigan Public Broadcasting presents an
          evening with Ernest Medina. With Tim
          Skubick. Michigan Public Radio, December 10,
          1973.
          26 min. phonotape (1 r. 7 1/2 i.p.s.)

          1. My Lai (4), Vietnam - Massacre, 1968.
          2. Medina, Ernest. I. Skubick, Tim.

          My love is like a red, red rose
C1
A14   Whorf, Michael, 1933-
          My love is like a red, red rose.
          1 tape cassette. (The visual sounds of
          Mike Whorf. Art, music, and letters, A14)

          Originally presented on his radio program, Kaleidoscope,
          WJR, Detroit.
          Duration: 35 min.
          The Scottish highlands, the swirl of tartans, the pipes, the
          smell of heather, is the setting for the heart-warming story of
          Robert Burns.

          1. Burns, Robert, 1759-1796. L Title.

          My love parade
Voice Lib.
M982   Chevalier, Maurice, 1889-1972.
  bd.3   Singing "My Love Parade" from Paramount
          Pictures' "The Love Parade". Victor,
          1927.
          1 reel (7 in.) 7 1/2 in. per sec.
          phonotape.

          I. Title: My love parade.

C1
M44
    The mystery of the Mary Celeste

Whorf, Michael, 1933–
    The mystery of the Mary Celeste.
    1 tape cassette. (The visual sounds of
Mike Whorf. Miscellaneous, M44)
    Originally presented on his radio program, Kaleidoscope,
WJR, Detroit.
    Duration: 36 min.
    The strange story of a ship and its missing crew. What
happened? Who was involved? Over the years since the
derelict ship's reappearance, many theories have been
expounded.

    L Mary Celeste (Brig) L Title.

Voice Lib.
M1729–
1730
    Nader, Ralph.
    Address at Michigan State University.
MSU Voice Library, April 11, 1974.
    80 min. phonotape (2 r. 7 1/2 i.p.s.)

    1. Monopolies – U. S. 2. Pollution. 3.
Oil industries – U. S.

C1
A46
    The mystery of William Porter – O. Henry

Whorf, Michael, 1933–
    The mystery of William Porter – O. Henry.
    1 tape cassette. (The visual sounds of
Mike Whorf. Art, music and letters, A46)
    Originally presented on his radio program, Kaleidoscope,
WJR, Detroit.
    Duration: 36 min., 30 sec.
    The man spent many of his years behind bars, movements
inhibited, freedom gone. But his mind was free, free to imagine,
then to put down on paper his short stories.

    L Porter, William Sydney, 1862–1910. L Title.

Voice Lib.
M1726
bd.5
    Namath, Joe Willie, 1943–
    On the Mike Douglas Show.
NBC–TV, June 18, 1974.
    5 min. phonotape (1 r. 7 1/2 i.p.s.)

    1. Namath, Joe Willie, 1943–

C1
R22
    MYTHOLOGY

Whorf, Michael, 1933–
    Of myths and gods.
    1 tape cassette. (The visual sounds of
Mike Whorf. Religion, R22)
    Originally presented on his radio program, Kaleidoscope,
WJR, Detroit.
    Duration: 48 min., 30 sec.
    From antiquity comes the history of gods and legends. Who were
the great Egyptian, Greek and Roman gods – and what part did man
play in their world and they in his?

    L Mythology. L Title.

C1
H35
    NAPOLÉON I, EMPEROR OF THE FRENCH, 1769–1821

Whorf, Michael, 1933–
    The Corsican conqueror.
    1 tape cassette. (The visual sounds of
Mike Whorf. History and heritage, H35)
    Originally presented on his radio program, Kaleidoscope,
WJR, Detroit.
    Duration: 38 min., 30 sec.
    He was born a Corsican, but would one day serve and command
the French armies and wage combat against the great armies of
Europe. He was a brilliant military strategist, often a cruel
emperor, but always a man of noble spirit.

    L Napoléon I, Emperor of the French, 1769–1821 L Title.

    NSDAP
    see
Nationalsozialistische Deutsche Arbeiter-Partei.

VOICE LIBRARY

Voice Lib.
M1064
bd.13
    Narcotics: statements by New York police
officials and FBI agents about the sale
of firearms to criminals; musical bridge;
sociologist speaking about drug addicts;
and member of U.S. Narcotic Bureau commenting
about seizures and destruction of illegal
narcotics. Fox Movietone, 1929.
    1 reel (7 in.) 7 1/2 in. per sec.
phonotape.

    1. Narcotics, Control of.

Voice Lib.
M1206
bd.2
    Nach der Einnahme von Warschau; German
descriptive war scene of life in trenches
and in the field. Victor, 1916.
    1 reel (7 in.) 7 1/2 in. per sec.
phonotape.

Voice Lib. NARCOTICS, CONTROL OF
M1064
bd.13
    Narcotics: statements by New York police
officials and FBI agents about the sale
of firearms to criminals; musical bridge;
sociologist speaking about drug addicts;
and member of U.S. Narcotic Bureau commenting
about seizures and destruction of illegal
narcotics. Fox Movietone, 1929.
    1 reel (7 in.) 7 1/2 in. per sec.
phonotape.

NATCHI INDIANS

Voice Lib.
M1577   Creek and Natchi dances.   Victor E.
         Riste, December 4, 1931.
         30 min.   phonotape (1 r.   7 1/2 in. per
sec.)

         1. Creek Indians.   2. Natchi Indians.

Voice Lib.
M524   National Broadcasting Company, inc.
        Special NBC program on first anniversary
of the war, featuring NBC news commentators.
September 3, 1940.
        1 reel (7 in.)   7 1/2 in. per sec.
phonotape.

        1. World War, 1939-1945

Voice Lib.
M846
        National broadcasting company, inc.
        Closed circuit broadcast to affiliated radio stations by N.B.C.
network officials on the subject of radio program promotion. 1947.
        1 reel (7 in.)   7 1/2 in. per sec.   phonotape.

        CONTENTS. -bd. 1. Announcement of promotional plans for a
written contest of an essay "What America means to me" by "The
Quiz Kids Program" to stations on NBC Red network, including a ten-
second message by Joe Kelly, emcee of "Quiz Kids" program. -Oct.
14, 1947. -bd. 2. Announcing Van Heflin program for Advertising
Council to all network radio stations.   Dec. 10, 1947. -bd. 3. Instructions about build-up of new program line-up on NBC network for 1947,
including comments by Fred Waring and Advertising Manager of
Proctor & Gamble.   Sept. 23, 1947.

Voice Lib.
M311   National Broadcasting Company, inc.
bd.1   Assassination: excerpts from the three
hour "Today" show; comments about Lyndon
B. Johnson, reading of New York Times
editorial.   NBC, November 23, 1963.
        1 reel (7 in.)   7 1/2 in. per sec.
phonotape.

        1. Kennedy, John Fitzgerald, Pres. U.S.,
1917-1963 - Assassination.   I. Agronski, Martin

Voice Lib.
M311   National Broadcasting Company, inc.
bd.2   Assassination: report on activities in
Washington the following morning, news
from Dallas on Oswald.   NBC, November
23, 1963.
        1 reel (7 in.)   7 1/2 in. per sec.
phonotape.

        1. Kennedy, John Fitzgerald, Pres. U.S.,
1917-1963 - Assassination.   2. Oswald, Lee
Harvey, 1939-1963.

Voice Lib.
M311   National Broadcasting Company, inc.
bd.3   Reading of proclamation written by President
Johnson of Monday, November 25, 1963, as a
national day of mourning for Kennedy; announcement of cancellations in Lansing area.   NBC-
TV, November 23, 1963.
        1 reel (7 in.)   7 1/2 in. per sec.
phonotape.

        1. Kennedy, John Fitzgerald, Pres. U.S.,
1917-1963 - Assassination.

Voice Lib.
M311   National Broadcasting Company, inc.
bd.7   Assassination: comments of servicemen at
the U.S.O. in Washington.   NBC, November
23, 1963.
        1 reel (7 in.)   7 1/2 in. per sec.
phonotape.

        1. Kennedy, John Fitzgerald, Pres. U.S.,
1917-1963 - Assassination.

Voice Lib.
M312   National Broadcasting Company, inc.
bd.2   Discussion among Texas citizens with
NBC newsmen about President Lyndon Baines
Johnson.   NBC, November 23, 1963.
        1 reel (7 in.)   7 1/2 in. per sec.
phonotape.

        1. Johnson, Lyndon Baines, Pres. U.S.,
1908-1973.

Voice Lib.
M315   National Broadcasting Company, inc.
bd.1   Assassination: news from White House, on
Vietnam, on arrival of President DeGaulle.
NBC, November 24, 1963.
        1 reel (7 in.)   7 1/2 in. per sec.
phonotape.

        1. Kennedy, John Fitzgerald, Pres. U.S.,
1917-1963 - Assassination.

Voice Lib.
M315   National Broadcasting Company, inc.
bd.2   Reports from Dulles Airport on arrivals
of royalty and dignitaries for Kennedy's
funeral.   NBC, November 24, 1963.
        1 reel (7 in.)   7 1/2 in. per sec.
phonotape.

        1. Kennedy, John Fitzgerald, Pres. U.S.,
1917-1963 - Assassination.

Voice Lib.
M315   National Broadcasting Company, inc.
 bd.3   Assassination: Henry Cabot Lodge's meeting
        with President Johnson, comments about
        Jacqueline Kennedy, on Jackie's decision
        to walk behind casket; remarks by Senator
        Edward M. Kennedy. NBC, November 24, 1963.
          1 reel (7 in.)   7 1/2 in. per sec.
        phonotape.
          1. Kennedy, Jacqueline (Bouvier) 1929-
        2. Kennedy, John Fitzgerald, Pres. U.S., 1917-
        1963 - Assassination. I. Kennedy, Edward
        Moore, 1932-

National Gallery of Art, Washington, D.C.
see
U.S. National Gallery of Art.

VOICE LIBRARY

Voice Lib.
M316   National Broadcasting Company, inc.
 bd.2   Description of caisson from Fort Meyer
        arriving in Washington for body of Kennedy;
        departure of body from White House, line of
        procession, drums, playing of "Hail to the
        Chief", "Navy Hymn", etc. NBC, November
        24, 1963.
          1 reel (7 in.)   7 1/2 in. per sec.
        phonotape.
          1. Kennedy, John Fitzgerald, Pres. U.S.,
        1917-1963 - Assassination.

NATIONAL MUSIC, GERMAN
Voice Lib.
M1019   Nazi national hymn "Deutschlandlied"
 bd.6   (two stanzas). Fred Peteler.
          1 reel (7 in.)   7 1/2 i.p.s.   phonotape.
          1. National music, German. I. Title:
        Deutschlandlied.

        National Broadcasting Company, Inc.
Voice Lib.
M1053 British Broadcasting Corporation.
        Radio program from BBC in London congratu-
        lating NBC in U.S. on its 30th anniversary;
        featuring stage and screen personalities, also
        excerpts of speeches by FDR, Chamberlain, and
        Churchill. BBC Radio, 1956.
          1 reel (7 in.)   7 1/2 in. per sec.
        phonotape.
          I. National Broadcasting Company, Inc.

Voice Lib.
M1654- National Public Radio.
1655   Transcript of conversation between Nixon,
        Dean and Haldeman, read by Linda Wertheimer,
        Bob Edwards, and Mike Waters. NPR, May 1,
        1974.
          1 hr., 40 min.   phonotape (2 r.   7 1/2
        i.p.s.)
          1. Watergate Affair, 1972-
        I. Wertheimer, Linda. II. Edwards, Bob.
        III. Waters, Mike.

NATIONAL BROADCASTING COMPANY, INC.
Voice Lib.
M1048 Kaltenborn, Hans von, 1878-1965.
 bd.1   "Recollections at thirty"; one hour
        radio program saluting 30 years of network
        broadcasting by NBC, featuring dramatic or
        humorous actual sounds during that period.
        NBC, May 15, 1956.
          1 reel (7 in.)   7 1/2 i.p.s.   phonotape.
          1. National Broadcasting Company, inc.

NATIONAL SOCIALISM
Voice Lib.
M1003 Göring, Hermann, 1893-1946.
 bd.8   Address to German Academy of Jurisprudence
        analyzing Nazi conception of justice.
        Peteler, November 13, 1934.
          1 reel (7 in.)   7 1/2 in. per sec.
        phonotape.

NATIONAL CHARACTERISTICS, IRISH
C1
S29   Whorf, Michael, 1933-
        A smile and a tear; tribute to the Irish.
        1 tape cassette. (The visual sounds of
      Mike Whorf. Social, S29)
        Originally presented on his radio program, Kaleidoscope.
      WJR, Detroit.
        Duration 44 min.
        Highlighting this program is a poignant reading of "The
      trimmins on the rosary" as the Visual Sounds presents the story
      of Ireland; its history, its people, its music, and the tale of
      St. Patrick.
          1. Ireland. 2. National characteristics, Irish. I. Title.

NATIONAL SOCIALISM
Voice Lib.
M980 Hitler, Adolf, 1889-1945.
 bd.2   Appeal for votes to the German public.
        Description of Nazi aims and its causes.
        Peteler, 1932.
          1 reel (7 in.)   7 1/2 in. per sec.
        phonotape.

NATIONAL SOCIALISM

Voice Lib.
.M999   Hitler, Adolf, 1889-1945.
Speech at session of German Reichstag stating Nazi policies, including discussions of same. Requesting Reichstag for overall power in government.   Peteler, March 23, 1933.
1 reel (7 in.)   7 1/2 in. per sec. phonotape.

NATIONAL SOCIALISM

Voice Lib.
M1002   Hitler, Adolf, 1889-1945.
bd.7   Address to DAF, second workers conference, stressing the necessity of perseverance in spite of obstacles, in order to attain success. F. Peteler, May 16, 1934.
1 reel (7 in.)   7 1/2 in. per sec. phonotape.

NATIONAL SOCIALISM

Voice Lib.
M1004   Hitler, Adolf, 1889-1945.
bd.1   Address to huge German Youth group in Berlin "Lustgarten", stating that German public is now adopting Nazi philosophy, and urging youth to uphold and advance these policies for the future. Peteler, May 1, 1935.
1 reel (7 in.)   7 1/2 in. per sec. phonotape.

NATIONAL SOCIALISM

Voice Lib.
M1018   Ley, Robert, 1890-1945.
bd.2   Speaking to farmers on new Nazi settlement in Poland, stressing German rights to cultivate farms due to race superiority which eventually obliterates Poles and Jews.   Peteler, November, 1939.
1 reel (7 in.)   7 1/2 in. per sec. phonotape.

NATIONAL SOCIALISM

Voice Lib.
M1470   Nationalsozialistiche Deutsche Arbeiter-Partei.
bd.12   S.A. oath of loyalty. Peteler, 1932.
1 reel (7 in.)   7 1/2 in. per sec. phonotape.

1. National socialism.

NATIONAL SOCIALISM

Voice Lib.
M1201   Rockwell, George Lincoln, 1918-1967.
Address to MSU students in Auditorium at the invitation of ASMSU for the "Controversial Issues" series of lectures. Introduction by Greg Hopkins, followed by Rockwell explaining his position; maligns press; introduces documents; blames Jews for Bolshevism; quotes "G2" report of 1920; exposes alleged graft for stamping "Kosher" on all foods; commends Hitler; ridicules Eleanor Roosevelt, Rusk, Acheson; WWII made world safe for Soviets and Israel; commends Malcolm X on Negro solution and calls Martin Luther King a communist.   Questions and answers follow lecture.   A/V, April 20, 1967.
1 reel (7 in.)   7 1/2 L.p.s. phonotape.

1. National socialism.

NATIONAL SOCIALISM

Voice Lib.
M1010   Streicher, Julius, 1885-1946.
bd.2   Speech in which Streicher compares Hitler's ideas to those of Jesus Christ, as both wished to eliminate Jewish capitalists. Peteler, January 22, 1936.
1 reel (7 in.)   7 1/2 in. per sec. phonotape.

NATIONAL SONGS

C1
M6   Whorf, Michael, 1933-
Symbols of nationhood, national anthems.
1 tape cassette.   (The visual sounds of Mike Whorf. Miscellaneous, M6)

Originally presented on his radio program, Kaleidoscope, WJR, Detroit.
Duration: 41 min.
A program devoted to the national anthems of the world, with many musical illustrations and comments concerning the composition, and conditions under which they were written.

1. National songs. L. Title.

NATIONAL VOCARIUM

Voice Lib.
M994   Watrous, Richard B
bd.2   Talks about the National Vocarium, tells of his feelings of the past coming to life, of his relations with T. R. Roosevelt, P.T. Barnum.   G.R. Vincent, May 12, 1939.
1 reel (7 in.)   7 1/2 i.p.s.   phonotape.

1. National Vocarium.

NATIONAL VOICE LIBRARY.
see
MICHIGAN STATE UNIVERSITY. NATIONAL VOICE LIBRARY.

Voice Lib.
M953   Nationalsozialistische Deutsche Arbeiter-Partei.
bd.3   War songs of the Nazi Party: a. Wir sind das
       Heer von Hakenkreuz; b. Brüder in Zechen und
       Gruben; c. Es pfeift von allen Dächern; d. Zum
       Kampfe wollen wir marschieren; e. Als die
       gold'ne Abendsonne; f. Durch Berlin marschieren
       wir; g. Deutschland, du Land der treue; h. Wenn
       die SS und die SA aufmarschiert. Peteler, 1930's.
          1 reel (7 in.)   7 1/2 in. per sec.
       phonotape.

          1. War-songs, German.

Voice Lib.
M1470 Nationalsozialistiche Deutsche Arbeiter-Partei.
bd.12   S.A. oath of loyalty.   Peteler, 1932.
          1 reel (7 in.)   7 1/2 in. per sec.
       phonotape.

          1. National socialism.

          Nationalsozialistiche Deutsche Arbeiter-
Voice Lib.   Partei
M1466 German radio (Nazi-controlled)
bd.24   Excerpt from celebration at the 3rd zone
       of the Rhineland while being reoccupied by
       Prussian government. Peteler, June 30,
       1930.
          1 reel (7 in.)   7 1/2 in. per sec.
       phonotape.

          I. Nationalsozialistiche Deutsche Arbeiter-
       Partei.

          Nationalsozialistiche Deutsche Arbeiter-
Voice Lib.   Partei
M1003 German radio (Nazi controlled)
bd.7   Nazi party campaign speeches; German
       authorities in sports, music and the arts
       speaking in favor of Hitler in 1934.
       Peteler, August 19, 1934.
          1 reel (7 in.)   7 1/2 in. per sec.
       phonotape.

          I. Nationalsozialistiche Deutsche Arbeiter-
       Partei.

          Nationalsozialistiche Deutsche Arbeiter-
Voice Lib.   Partei
M1376 German radio (Nazi controlled)
bd.9   Unknown speaker at NSDAP Congress in the
       city of Weimar. Peteler, July 5, 1936.
          1 reel (7 in.)   7 1/2 in. per sec.
       phonotape.

          I. Nationalsozialistiche Deutsche Arbeiter-
       Partei.

                  Nationalsozialistische Deutsche Arbeiter-
Voice Lib.   Partei
M1376 German radio (Nazi controlled)
bd.11   Sounds of Nazi Party Day celebration in
       Nuremberg. September 15, 1936.
          1 reel (7 in.)   7 1/2 in. per sec.
       phonotape.

          I. Nationalsozialistische Deutsche Arbeiter-
       Partei.

                  Nationalsozialistische Deutsche Arbeiter-
Voice Lib.   Partei
M1300 German radio (Nazi controlled)
bd.1   Various special announcements: new German
       state laws pertaining to Anti-Comintern Pact
       between Germany, Japan and Italy; excerpt of
       speech by Nazi Foreign Minister von Ribbentrop.
       Peteler, September 12, 1941.
          1 reel (7 in.)   7 1/2 in. per sec.
       phonotape.

          I. Nationalsozialistische Deutsche Arbeiter-
       Partei.

                  Nationalsozialistische Deutsche Arbeiter-
Voice Lib.   Partei
M1073 German radio (Nazi controlled)
bd.19   German-Bolivian controversy: denying
       conspiracy of German diplomat Wendler with a
       Bolivian officer to overthrow Bolivian
       government. Peteler, August, 1941.
          1 reel (7 in.)   7 1/2 in. per sec.
       phonotape.

          I. Nationalsozialistische Deutsche Arbeiter-
       Partei.

            NATIONALSOZIALISTISCHE DEUTSCHE ARBEITER-
            PARTEI
Voice Lib.
M1373 Goebbels, Joseph, 1897-1945.
bd.4   Talking about the goals of the NSDAP
       pertaining to radio broadcast.   Peteler,
       1933.
          1 reel (7 in.)   7 1/2 i.p.s.   phonotape.

          1. Radio broadcasting. 2. National-
       sozialistische Deutsche Arbeiter-Partei.

            NATIONALSOZIALISTISCHE DEUTSCHE ARBEITER-
Voice Lib.   PARTEI
M1345 Strasser, Gregor, 1892-1934.
          First radio broadcast of a member of the
       NSDAP; subject: The state concept of
       national socialism. Peteler, June 1, 1932.
          1 reel (7 in.)   7 1/2 i.p.s.   phonotape.
          Strasser was chief of staff of operations of the NSDAP;
       denounced Party membership in November, 1932, and became a
       bitter enemy of Hitler; assassinated June 1934, during the Rohm
       purge.
          1. Nationalsozialistische Deutsche Arbeiter-Partei.

Voice Lib.
M1363   Nationalsozialistische Deutsche Arbeiter-
bd.3   Partei. Reichsparteitag.
        Excerpts from Reichstag session.
        February 11, 1931.
            1 reel (7 in.)   7 1/2 in. per sec.
        phonotape.

                  Nationalsozialistische Deutsche Arbeiter-
Voice Lib.   Partei. Reichsparteitag
M1000   German radio (Nazi controlled)
bd.5   Discussions in Reichstag; enactment of
        laws tending to give unrestricted govern-
        mental powers to Chancellor Hitler.   Peteler,
        1933.
            1 reel (7 in.)   7 1/2 in. per sec.
        phonotape.

            I. Nationalsozialistiche Deutsche Arbeiter-
        Partei.   Reichsparteitag.

Voice Lib.
M1018   Nationalsozialistiche Deutsche Arbeiter-Partei.
bd.4   Reichsparteitag.
        Reichstag session including remarks by
        Hermann Göring, expressing gratitude to
        Luftwaffe at Polish victories; and Adolf Hitler
        justifying his attack on Poland and his
        alliance with Soviets, his aims at European
        peace pact and return of German colonies.
        Peteler, October 6, 1939.
            1 reel (7 in.)   7 1/2 in. per sec.
        phonotape.
            I. Göring, Hermann, 1893-1946. II. Hitler, Adolf, 1889-1945.

                  Nationalsozialistische Deutsche Arbeiter-
Voice Lib.   Partei. Reichsparteitag
M1002   German radio (Nazi controlled)
bd.2   Reichstag session of March 23, 1933, voting
        on unrestricted governmental powers for
        Chancellor Hitler.   Peteler, March 23, 1933.
            1 reel (7 in.)   7 1/2 in. per sec.
        phonotape.

            I. Nationalsozialistiche Deutsche Arbeiter-
        Partei.   Reichsparteitag.

Voice Lib.
M1019   Nationalsozialistische Deutsche Arbeiter-Partei.
bd.12   Reichsparteitag.
        Reichstag session, July 19, 1940: address
        by Adolf Hitler pertaining to armistice with
        France; plans for further Nazi aims, such as
        the elimination of Jewish financiers domes-
        tically and abrogation of all remaining
        Versailles treaty demands. Justifying invasion
        of Norway as a defense measure. Renewal of
        peace proposals with England, followed by Nazi
        songs and expressions of gratitude by Hermann
        Göring to the vision and strategy of Hitler.
                                    (Continued on next card)

                  Nationalsozialistiche Deutsche Arbeiter-Partei. Reichsparteitag
Voice Lib.
M1301   German radio (Nazi controlled)
bd.3   Reporting progress on the Russian front
        and the declaration of war by Japan on the
        United States.   Peteler, December 11, 1941.
            1 reel (7 in.)   7 1/2 in. per sec.   phonotape.
        CONTENTS. -a. Göring, Hermann. -b. Hitler, Adolf,
        criticizing President Roosevelt and comparing his own actions
        with those of FDR.
            I. Göring, Hermann, 1893-1946. II. Hitler, Adolf, 1889-1945.
        III. Nationalsozialistische Deutsche Arbeiter-Partei. Reichspartei-
        tag.

Voice Lib.
M1019   Nationalsozialistiche Deutsche Arbeiter-Partei.
bd.12   Reichsparteitag. Reichstag session, July
            19, 1940... 1940.   (Card 2)

        July 19, 1940.
            1 reel (7 in.)   7 1/2 in. per sec.
        phonotape.

            I. Hitler, Adolf, 1889-1945. II. Göring,
        Hermann, 1893-1946.

            NATURAL HISTORY
C1
SC12   Whorf, Michael, 1933-
        The great mysteries of science.
            1 tape cassette.   (The visual sounds of
        Mike Whorf.   Science, SC12)
            Originally presented on his radio program, Kaleidoscope,
        WJR, Detroit.
            Duration: 31 min.
            What is photosynthesis? What caused the ice age? What
        causes the common cold? What mysteries do the stars, the sun,
        and the sea hold? This program presents a look at some of those
        great questions which since the beginning of creation have puzzled
        mankind.
            I. Natural history. I. Title.

Voice Lib.
M1304   Nationalsozialistiche Deutsche Arbeiter-Partei.
bd.11   Reichsparteitag.
        Reichstag session pertaining to the appoint-
        ment of Hitler as prime law maker of German
        Reich; including addresses by: a. Hitler,
        Adolf, about the hardship of German troops at
        the Russian front; b. Göring, Hermann, appraisal
        of strength of the U.S. entering European
        conflict.   Peteler, April 26, 1942.
            1 reel (7 in.)   7 1/2 in. per sec.
        phonotape.
            I. Hitler, Adolf, 1889-1945. II. Göring, Hermann, 1893-1946.

            NATURE - INFLUENCE OF MAN ON
C1
S38   Whorf, Michael, 1933-
        America the beautiful; pollution, part 2.
            1 tape cassette.   (The visual sounds of
        Mike Whorf.   Social, S38)
            Originally presented on his radio program, Kaleidoscope,
        WJR, Detroit.
            Duration: 54 min.
            This second narration looks at the types of pollution which have
        engulfed the globe. Here are the acts of water and air poisoning
        which man has slowly but deliberately committed, and the results
        of his carelessness and negligence.
            I. Pollution. 2. Nature - Influence of man on. I. Title.

C1
H108
The navigator - Vasco de Gama
Whorf, Michael, 1933-
The navigator - Vasco de Gama.
1 tape cassette. (The visual sounds of
Mike Whorf. History and heritage, H108)
Originally presented on his radio program, Kaleidoscope,
WJR, Detroit.
Duration: 38 min.
Hundreds of years ago when the race to expand the world made
rivals of the world's great powers, Portugal sent forth its greatest
soldier and mariner, Vasco de Gama.

I. Gama, Vasco da, 1469-1524.   I. Title.

Voice Lib.
M1304   Nazi march music; "Marsch der Elisabether".
bd.1   Peteler.
1 reel (7 in.)   7 1/2 in. per sec.
phonotape.

1. Military music, German

Voice Lib.
M1071   Nazi actual on-the-spot reports of paratroop
bd.20-   invasion on the island of Crete, given by
1073   correspondents; also narration of exper-
bd.1   iences of captured Nazi soldier. Peteler,
May 20-27, 1941.
3 reels (7 in.)   7 1/2 in. per sec.
phonotape.

1. World War, 1939-1945 - Crete.

Voice Lib.
M1301   Nazi march music (instrumental): "Badenweiler
bd.1   Marsch".   Peteler, 1941.
1 reel (7 in.)   7 1/2 in. per sec.
phonotape.

1. Military music, German
I. Title: Badenweiler Marsch.

Voice Lib.
M1016   Nazi German march music; medley of various
bd.16   military marches. F. Peteler.
1 reel (7 in.)   7 1/2 in. per sec.
phonotape.

1. Military music, German

Voice Lib.
M1019   Nazi marching song; musical theme from
bd.8   German newsreel film entitled "Wir kommen
wieder".   Peteler
1 reel (7 in.)   7 1/2 in. per sec.
phonotape.

1. Military music, German

Voice Lib.
M1007   Nazi Hitler Youth fight song, "Es zittern
bd.2   die marschen Knochen".   Various stanzas
of song, "Today we have Germany, tomorrow
the entire world..." Peteler, April 30,
1935.
1 reel (7 in.)   7 1/2 i.p.s.   phonotape.

1. Songs, German.

Voice Lib.
M980   Nazi martial music: "Die Fahne hoch", war
bd.1   song of the NSDAP (Nazi Party); 3 stanzas.
Peteler, 1938.
1 reel (7 in.)   7 1/2 in. per sec.
phonotape.

1. War songs, German

Voice Lib.
M1007   Nazi Hitler Youth marching song entitled
bd.3   "Youth Marching for Germany". Peteler,
April 30, 1935.
1 reel (7 in.)   7 1/2 in. per sec.
phonotape.

1. Songs, German

Voice Lib.
M1073   Nazi martial music; instrumental selection
bd.21   entitled: "Fehrbelliner Reitermarsch".
Peteler, 1941.
1 reel (7 in.)   7 1/2 in. per sec.
phonotape.

1. Military music, German
I. Title: Fehrbelliner Reitermarsch.

Voice Lib.
M1073   Nazi martial music: instrumental band
bd.10   selection entitled, "In treue Fest".
    Peteler, 1941.
    1 reel (7 in.)   7 1/2 in. per sec.
    phonotape.

      1. Military music, German.   I. Title:
In treue Fest.

Voice Lib.
M1019   Nazi national hymn "Deutschlandlied"
bd.6   (two stanzas).   Fred Peteler.
    1 reel (7 in.)   7 1/2 i.p.s.   phonotape.

      1. National music, German.   I. Title:
Deutschlandlied.

Voice Lib.
M1073   Nazi martial music; march music entitled
bd.2   "Markische Heide".(three stanzas).
    Peteler, 1941.
    1 reel (7 in.)   7 1/2 in. per sec.
    phonotape.

      1. Military music, German

Voice Lib.
M981   Nazi news report of a torchlight parade in
bd.3   Berlin on the assumption of power by Nazi
    Party. Reports by Wulf Bley and Heinz
    von Lichberg.   Peteler, January 30, 1933.
    1 reel (7 in.)   7 1/2 in. per sec.
  phonotape.

      I. Bley, Wulf, 1890-   II. Lichberg,
Heinz von

Voice Lib.
M1071   Nazi martial music; marching song of Nazi
bd.19   paratroopers (3 stanzas).   Peteler, 1941.
    1 reel (7 in.)   7 1/2 i.p.s.   phonotape.

      1. Military music, German.

Voice Lib.
M1018   Nazi parody song on "We're gonna hang our
bd.7   washing on the Siegfried line".   Peteler.
    1 reel (7 in.)   7 1/2 i.p.s.   phonotape.

      1. World War, 1939-1945 - Songs and music.

Voice Lib.
M1004   Nazi May Day ceremonies. Male choir singing
bd.3-B   (3 stanzas) of song "Wir glauben an die
    neue Zeit".   Peteler, May 1, 1935.
    1 reel (7 in.)   7 1/2 i.p.s.   phonotape.

      1. Songs, German.   I. Title: Wir glauben
an die neue Zeit.

Voice Lib.
M1018   Nazi propaganda song; three stanzas of song
bd.6   ridiculing Neville Chamberlain.   Peteler
    1 reel (7 in.)   7 1/2 in. per sec.
  phonotape.

      1. Songs, German

Voice Lib.
M956   Nazi music; march music of the German Armed
    Forces.   [no source, no date]
    1 reel (7 in.)   7 1/2 in. per sec.
    phonotape.
     CONTENTS.-bd.1. Vorwärts nach Osten.-bd.2.
Marsch der Deutschen in Polen.-bd.3. Gegen
Briten und Franzosen.-bd.4. Westerwald.-bd.5.
Wenn die Sonne scheint, Annemarie.-bd.6. Die
eiserne Schar (Panzermarsch)-bd.7. Argonnerwald
um Mitternacht.-bd.8. Ein Heller und ein
Batzen; bd.9. Der Tod in Flandern.-bd.10. Der
deutsche U-boot M .
     1. Military music, German

Voice Lib.
M1361   Nazi war songs; stormtroopers singing Nazi
bd.3   war song, "Heil unserem Führer".
    Peteler, 1945.
    1 reel (7 in.)   7 1/2 i.p.s.   phonotape.

      1. War songs, German.

Voice Lib.
M1304 Nazi war songs: three stanzas of "We're
bd.5　　on our way to conquer England" ("Wir
　　　　fahren gegen England").　Peteler, n.d.
　　　　1 reel (7 in.)　7 1/2 i.p.s.　phonotape.

　　　　1. War-songs, German.　2. World War, 1939-
　　　1945 - Songs and music.

C1　　　NEGRO SPIRITUALS
PWM12 Whorf, Michael, 1933-
　　　　Gonna sing all over God's Heaven.
　　　　1 tape cassette.　(The visual sounds of
　　　Mike Whorf. Panorama; a world of music, PWM-12)

　　　Originally presented on his radio program, Kaleidoscope,
　　WJR, Detroit.
　　Duration: 25 min.
　　The story of the music in the religious experience of the
　　American Negro.

　　　L. Negro spirituals.　L. Title.

　　　　NEGROES
Voice Lib.
M1687　Abernathy, Ralph David, 1926-
　　　　Address at Michigan State University.
　　　　WKAR, 1972.
　　　　50 min.　phonotape (1 r.　7 1/2 i.p.s.)

　　　　1. Negroes.　2. U.S. - Social conditions.

　　　　NEGROES
Voice Lib.
M1063 Weaver, Robert Clifton, 1907-
bd.2　　Address at Symposium of Race Relations
　　　in Chicago under the auspices of the Center
　　　for the Study of Democratic Institutions
　　　entitled, "The Negro as an American".
　　　CSDI, 1963.
　　　　1 reel (7 in.)　7 1/2 in. per sec.
　　　phonotape.

NEGROES - CIVIL RIGHTS
Voice Lib.
M743　Civil rights march on Montgomery, Alabama.
　　　Announcer's description of scene as
　　　marchers arrive in Montgomery; entertain-
　　　ment by Harry Belafonte and others; A.F.L.
　　　speaker; Dr. Ralph Abernathy presiding.
　　　CBS, March 25, 1965.
　　　　38 min.　phonotape (1 r.　7 1/2 i.p.s.)

　　　　1. Negroes - Civil rights.　I. Belafonte,
　　　Harold, 1927-　　II. Abernathy, Ralph
　　　David, 1926-

NEGROES - CIVIL RIGHTS
Voice Lib.
243　　Eisenhower, Dwight David, Pres. U.S., 1890-1969.
bd.6　　Remarks on amending Sec. 407, the
　　　Civil Rights Bill.　CBS, July 31, 1957.
　　　　1 reel (7 in.)　7 1/2 in. per sec.
　　　phonotape.

NEGROES - CIVIL RIGHTS
Voice Lib.
M1699　Evers, Charles, 1923-
bd.2　　Address at Michigan State University.
　　　WKAR, October 13, 1971.
　　　　15 min.　phonotape (1 r.　7 1/2 i.p.s.)

　　　　1. Negroes - Civil rights.

Voice Lib.　NEGROES - CIVIL RIGHTS
M758,　Johnson, Lyndon Baines, Pres.U.S., 1908-1973.
bd.1-　　Address before joint session of Congress
759　　requesting new legislation on voting rights
　　　for Negroes.　CBS line, March 16, 1965.
　　　　2 reels (7 in.)　7 1/2 in. per sec.
　　　phonotape.

　　　　1. Negroes - Civil rights.

NEGROES - CIVIL RIGHTS
Voice Lib.
M744　King, Martin Luther, 1929-1968.
　　　Address at Civil Rights rally at Montgomery,
　　　Alabama.　Dr. King describes current Negro
　　　crusade for voting right in Alabama; history
　　　of segregated society; "march on ballot
　　　boxes" and "no return to normalcy".
　　　CBS, March 25, 1965.
　　　　35 min.　phonotape (1 r.　7 1/2 i.p.s.)

　　　　1. Negroes - Civil rights.

NEGROES - CIVIL RIGHTS
Voice Lib.
M1081 Marshall, Thurgood, 1908-
　　　Speech at convocation during 10th anniver-
　　　sary of Fund for the Republic discussing
　　　the role of federal courts in racial equal-
　　　ity cases and constitutional rights.
　　　CSDI, December, 1962.
　　　　1 reel (7 in.)　7 1/2 in. per sec.
　　　phonotape.

NEGROES - CIVIL RIGHTS
Voice Lib.
M1611   Parks, Rosa Lee
bd.5   Montgomery, Alabama, bus test case.
            WKAR-TV ₍1974?₎
            9 min.   phonotape (1 r.   7 1/2 i.p.s.)

            1. Negroes - Civil rights.

NEGROES - CIVIL RIGHTS
Voice Lib.
544   "We shall overcome: a lyric affirmation of
            freedom"; a montage of actual sounds:
            speeches, statements, songs. WRVR,
            August 28, 1963.
            1 reel (7 in.)   7 1/2 in. per sec.
            phonotape.

NEGROES - CIVIL RIGHTS
Voice Lib.
M1085   Wilkins, Roy, 1901-
            Radio interview with Roy Wilkins by
            Elizabeth Morgan about methods to attain
            civil rights for Negroes. Bergman, May 9,
            1962.
            1 reel (7 in.)   7 1/2 in. per sec.
            phonotape.

            1. Negroes - Civil rights.   I. Morgan,
            Elizabeth.

Voice Lib.   NEGROES - CIVIL RIGHTS
M314   Wilkins, Roy, 1901-
bd.9   Statement by Roy Wilkins to NBC newsman
            Frank McGee, at the assassination of
            President Kennedy, his ideas about the
            future of civil rights. NBC, November 24,
            1963.
            1 reel (7 in.)   7 1/2 i.p.s.   phonotape.

            1. Kennedy, John Fitzgerald, Pres. U.S.,
            1917-1963 - Assassination. 2. Negroes -
            Civil rights.   I. McGee, Frank, 1921-1974.

Voice Lib.   NEGROES - POLITICS AND SUFFRAGE
M1640   Bond, Julian, 1940-
            Politics and Black progress, on "Firing
            Line" with William F. Buckley and John
            Lewis. WKAR-FM, March 17, 1974.
            45 min.   phonotape (1 r.   7 1/2 i.p.s.)

            1. Negroes - Politics and suffrage.
            I. Buckley, William Frank, 1925-
            II. Lewis, John.

NEGROES - SOCIAL CONDITIONS
Voice Lib.
M866-   Project '64 (Radio program)
867   Harlem, the black ghetto: actual sound and
bd.1   description of life in Harlem and discusses
            Negro residents' problems; Negroes relating
            experiences, impressions, and emotions; opinions
            by various Negroes of more advanced education;
            discussions by white school principals. Covers
            social and economic problems of Negroes,
            juvenile delinquence, drug addiction, broken
            homes, unemployment. Discussion of Harlem
            Negro youths' attempts to achieve manhood;
            religious beliefs and philosophy of the
                                            (Continued on next card)

NEGROES - SOCIAL CONDITIONS
Voice Lib.
M866-   Project '64 (Radio program)   Harlem...
867   1964.   (Card 2)
bd.1
            Black Muslims' desire for separate political
            and economic country; includes Malcolm X
            describing his philosophy and ideas in the
            Black Muslim movement.   Documentary program
            produced for CBC by Lloyd Chester, written by
            A. Clark and narrated by Percy Rodreguiz ₍sic₎
            CBC, 1964.
            2 reels (7 in.)   7 1/2 in. per sec.   phonotape.
            I. Negroes - Social conditions.   I. Little, Malcolm, 1925-1965.

NEGROES - SOCIAL CONDITIONS
Voice Lib.
M867   Project '64 (Radio program)
bd.2-   Negro revolt in Harlem: documentary program describing
M869   the place of the Negro in American society; the Negro search for
bd.1   change, with or without white help; discussion of Negro press;
            Negroes' cultural background and association with black Africa.
            Malcolm X discusses Black Muslim movement, critizing white
            infiltration of NAACP Urban League Corp.; comparison of
            differences between the Muslims and Black Nationalists. Summary
            of Negro revolt and group singing of "We shall overcome".
            CBC, 1964.
            3 reels (7 in.)   7 1/2 in. per sec.   phonotape.

            I. Negroes - Social conditions.   I. Little, Malcom, 1925-1965.

NEGROES - U.S.
Voice Lib.
M1082-   Baldwin, James, 1924-
1083,   An interview with James Baldwin by Studs
bd.1   Turkel about "The Black man in America".
            Credo Records, 1963.
            2 reels (7 in.)   7 1/2 in. per sec.
            phonotape.

            1. Negroes - U.S.   I. Turkel, Studs.

NEGROES - U.S.
C1
S13   Whorf, Michael, 1933-
            Some lessons in history.
            1 tape cassette.   (The visual sounds of
            Mike Whorf. Social, S13)

            Originally presented on his radio program, Kaleidoscope,
            WJR, Detroit.
            Duration: 41 min., 10 sec.
            Here is a detailed account of the contributions of the Black
            American.

            I. Negroes - U.S.   I. Title.

C1
S14
NEGROES AS COWBOYS
Whorf, Michael, 1933-
The black cowboy.
1 tape cassette. (The visual sounds of Mike Whorf. Social, S14)

Originally presented on his radio program, Kaleidoscope, WJR, Detroit.
Duration: 30 min.
Along with the rustlers, wranglers, badmen and heroes, were Black men who rode the same trails and equalled the exploits of Earp, Bass, Bonney and Hickok.

1. Negroes as cowboys. I. Title.

Voice Lib.
M740
bd.5
Nehru, Jawaharlal, 1889-1964.
Excerpt from All-India radio broadcast on assassination of Gandhi. CBS, January 3, 1948.
1 reel (7 in.) 7 1/2 in. per sec. phonotape.

1. Gandhi, Mohandas Karamchand, 1869-1948.

Voice Lib.
243
bd.3
Nehru, Jawaharlal, 1889-1964.
On foreign alliances and foreign domination: "We will not submit to foreign domination." CBS, June 26, 1957.
1 reel (7 in.) 7 1/2 in. per sec. phonotape.

Voice Lib.
M740
bd.6
Nehru, Jawaharlal, 1889-1964.
Excerpts from speech given in New Delhi commemorating January 6, 1950, the birth of independence for India. CBS, January 26, 1959.
1 reel (7 in.) 7 1/2 in. per sec. phonotape.

Nehru, Jawaharlal, 1889-1964
Voice Lib.
M622
bd.1-
bd.15
Radio in the 1940's (Part III): a series of excerpts from important broadcasts of the 1940's; a sample of radio of the period. NVL, April, 1964.
1 reel (7 in.) 7 1/2 in. per sec. phonotape.
1. Radio programs. I. Miller, Alton Glenn, 1909(?)-1944. II. Diles, Ken III. Wilson, Donald Harlow, 1900- IV. Livingstone, Mary V. Benny, Jack, 1894- VI. Harris, Phil VII. Merman, Ethel, 1909- VIII. Smith, "Wonderful" IX. Bennett, Richard Dyer X. Louis, Joe, 1914- XI. Eisenhower, Dwight David, Pres. U.S., 1890-1969. XII. MacArthur, Douglas, 1880-1964. XIII. Romulo, Carlos Pena, 1899- XIV. Welles, Orson, 1915- XV. Jackson, Robert Houghwout, 1892-1954. XVI. LaGuardia, Fiorello Henry, 1882-1945. XVII. Nehru, Jawaharlal, 1889-1964. XVIII. Gandhi, Mohandas Karamchand, 1869-1948.

Voice Lib.
573
bd.2-
574
bd.1
Nehru, Jawaharlal, 1889-1964
I can hear it now (radio program)
1945-1949. CBS, 1950?
2 reels (7 in.) 7 1/2 in. per sec. phonotape.
I. Murrow, Edward Roscoe, 1908-1965. II. Nehru, Jawaharlal, 1889-1964. III. Philip, duke of Edinburgh, 1921- IV. Elizabeth II, Queen of Great Britain, 1926- V. Ferguson, Homer, 1889- VI. Hughes, Howard Robard, 1905- VII. Marshall, George Catlett, 1880- VIII. Ruth, George Herman, 1895-1948. IX. Lilienthal, David Eli, 1899- X. Trout, Robert, 1908- XI. Gage, Arthur. XII. Jackson, Robert Houghwout, 1892-1954. XIII. Gromyko, Anatolii Andreevich, 1908- XIV. Baruch, Bernard Mannes, 1870-1965. XV. Churchill, Winston Leonard Spencer, 1874-1965. XVI. Winchell, Walter, 1897-1972. XVII. Davis, Elmer Holmes, 1890-
(Continued on next card)

Nehru, Jawaharlal, 1889-1964
Voice Lib.
M1033
Voice of America.
Twentieth anniversary program of Voice of America broadcasts narrated by Henry Fonda, and including the voices of Carl Sandburg, Danny Kaye, Jawaharlal Nehru, Franklin D. Roosevelt, Charles Malik, Arnold Toynbee, William Faulkner, Harry S. Truman, Dwight D. Eisenhower, Helen Hayes, Dag Hammarskjöld, Winston Churchill, and John F. Kennedy.
Voice of America, 1963.
1 reel (7 in.) 7 1/2 in. per sec. phonotape.
(Continued on next card)

Nehru, Jawaharlal, 1889-1964
Voice Lib.
M1033
Voice of America. Twentieth anniversary program... 1963. (Card 2)

I. Fonda, Henry Jaynes, 1905- II. Sandburg, Carl, 1878-1967. III. Kaye, Danny, 1913- IV. Nehru, Jawaharlal, 1889-1964. V. Roosevelt, Franklin Delano, Pres. U.S., 1882-1945. VI. Malik, Charles Habib, 1906- VII. Toynbee, Arnold Joseph, 1889- VIII. Faulkner, William, 1897-1962. IX. Truman, Harry S, Pres. U.S., 1884-1972. X. Eisenhower, Dwight David, Pres. U.S., 1890-1969. XI. Hayes, Helen, 1900- XII. Hammarskjöld, Dag, 1905-1961. XIII. Churchill, Winston Leonard Spencer, 1874-1965. XIV. Kennedy, John Fitzgerald, Pres. U.S., 1917-1963.

Voice Lib.
M1689
Nelson, Gaylord, 1916-
Man, the endangered species; address at Michigan State University. Introduction by President Wharton. WKAR, January 19, 1970.
41 min. phonotape (1 r. 7 1/2 i.p.s.)

1. Water - Pollution. 2. Ecology. I. Wharton, Clifton Reginald, 1926-

---

Nelson, Marie Coleman, 1915-
Voice Lib.
M747
bd.1
Freud, Sigmund, 1856-1939.
Reviewing work in the past, hopes to continue study in England after departure from Nazi Austria; introduced by Marie Coleman Nelson, managing editor of the "Psychoanalytical Review". National Psychological, 1938.
1 reel (7 in.) 7 1/2 in. per sec. phonotape.

I. Nelson, Marie Coleman, 1915-

Voice Lib. Nelson, Marie Coleman, 1915–
M746 Reik, Theodor
bd.1   Reading from his book "Voices from the
Inaudible" and giving reminiscenc s of his
association with Dr. Sigmund Freud.
Introduced by Marie Coleman Nelson, managing
editor of the "Psychoanalytical Review."
Psychoanalytical Review, 1964.
  1 reel (7 in.)   7 1/2 in. per sec.
phonotape.
    1. Freud, Sigmund, 1856–1939. L. Nelson, Marie Coleman,
1915–   II. Title: Voices from the i~~~~~.

Voice Lib. NEVADA. LEGISLATURE – ELECTIONS
M1707 Harrell, Beverley
bd.2   Announcing her candidacy for the Nevada
assembly, Terry Oliver, reporting.
CBS, June 3, 1974.
  5 min.   phonotape (1 r.   7 1/2 i.p.s.)

    1. Nevada. Legislature – Elections.
I. Oliver, Terry.

    Never strike the colors – Stephen Decatur
C1
H60
  Whorf, Michael, 1933–
    Never strike the colors – Stephen Decatur.
  1 tape cassette.   (The visual sounds of
Mike Whorf. History and heritage, H60)
    Originally presented on his radio program, Kaleidoscope,
WJR, Detroit.
    Duration: 43 min.
    Handsome, brave, and honorable, Stephen Decatur was one of
America's most daring naval officers.
    L. Decatur, Stephen, 1779–1820. L. Title.

NEW YORK (CITY) – NEWSPAPER STRIKE, 1963
Voice Lib.
M883– Project '63 (Radio program)
884   City without newspapers: documentary. actual
bd.1 program describing effects of New York City's
newspaper strike; comments by New Yorkers;
union members and company representatives;
reports of various businessmen and touching
upon the cultural stoppage and the business
slump caused by the strike. CBC, 1963.
  2 reels (7 in.)   7 1/2 in. per sec.
phonotape.
    1. New York (City) – Newspaper strike, 1963.

NEW YORK (CITY) – NEWSPAPER STRIKE, 1963
Voice Lib.
M884 Project '63 (Radio program)
bd.2   City without newspapers: continuation.
Comparison of the public's credibility of
newswriters as compared to television commentators; comparison of the intelligence of
readers of tabloids as compared with those
reading New York Times and Tribune; comments by
newspaper publishers on their responsibility
to the public; assumption that the greatest
void left by strike is in the lack of
advertisement and entertainments. CBC, 1963.
  1 reel (7 in.) 7 1/2 in. per sec. phonotape.
  L. New York (City) – Newspaper strike, 1963.

NEW YORK (CITY) – NEWSPAPER STRIKE, 1963
Voice Lib.
M885 Project '63 (Radio program)
  City without newspapers: continuation of program; views
about the values of the printed word as against the spoken word
(radio vs. newspapers); opinions about the elimination and
consolidation of newspapers; opinions by journalistic authorities
about the quality and the necessity of newspapers; discussion
of the values of editorials; pro and con, the idea of "too much
communication"; the Cuban crisis in the news. CBC, 1963.
  1 reel (7 in.) 7 1/2 in. per sec. phonotape.
  L. New York (City) – Newspaper strike, 1963.

Voice Lib. NEW YORK. BASEBALL CLUB (AMERICAN LEAGUE)
609 Ruppert, Jacob
bd.10   Interview about New York Yankee baseball
team; review of past Yankee victories on
radio program "Famous Firsts". WOR,
October 10, 1938.
  1 reel (7 in.)   7 1/2 in. per sec.
phonotape.

    1. New York. Baseball club (American league)

Voice Lib. NEW YORK. WORLD'S FAIR, 1939–1940
M502– General Motors Corporation.
505,   World's Fair Dinner for selected college
bd.2 students, at GMC Exhibit Building, Flushing
Meadows, Long Island, N.Y.   ORV recording,
May 6, 1940.
  4 reels (7 in.)   7 1/2 i.p.s.   phonotape.

  Contents listed with tapes.

    1. New York, World's Fair, 1939–1940.

NEW YORK. WORLD'S FAIR, 1939–1940
Voice Lib.
M293 Whalen, Grover Aloysius, 1886–1962.
  First ticket sale to 1939 World's Fair,
Flushing Meadows, Long Island, New York.
Mr. Whalen, president of New York World's
Fair Committee and New York's official
welcomer, sells first ticket book to F. H.
LaGuardia, Mayor of New York.   WNYC Radio,
February 23, 1939.
  1 reel (7 in.) 7 1/2 i.p.s. phonotape.

  L. New York. World's Fair, 1939–1940. L. LaGuardia,
Fiorello Henry, 1882–1947.

Voice Lib. NEWARK, N.J.
M1274, Newark race riots, midsummer 1967. Discussion
bd.2– of mass meeting in Newark between city
1276 officials, black and white citizens and
sociologists about the causes of Newark race
riots and suggestions for improved
conditions.   NET, August 20, 1967.
  3 reels (7 in.)   7 1/2 i.p.s.   phonotape.

    1. Newark, N.J. 2. Race discrimination –
U.S.

Voice Lib.
M1274,   Newark race riots, midsummer 1967. Discussion
bd.2-   of mass meeting in Newark between city
1276   officials, black and white citizens and
          sociologists about the causes of Newark race
          riots and suggestions for improved
          conditions. NET, August 20, 1967.
          3 reels (7 in.) 7 1/2 i.p.s. phonotape.

          1. Newark, N.J. 2. Race discrimination -
U.S.

Voice Lib. Newman, Barbara
M1634   Alsop, Stewart, 1914-
bd.4   Interviewed about his terminal leukemia,
          by Barbara Newman. WKAR, April 15, 1974.
          15 min. phonotape (1 r.   7 1/2 i.p.s.)

          1. Alsop, Stewart, 1914-   2. Leukemia -
Personal narratives. I. Newman, Barbara.

Voice Lib.
M1510   Newman, Edwin Harold, 1919-
bd.1   Commentary on President Johnson's address
          to the nation and his withdrawal from the
          1968 presidential race. NBC, March 31, 1968.
          1 reel (7 in.) 7 1/2 in. per sec.
          phonotape.

          1. Johnson, Lyndon Baines, Pres. U.S.,
1908-1973.

Voice Lib. Newman, Edwin Harold, 1919-
M1477   Discussion of Supreme Court decision on
          publishing Pentagon Papers. William B.
          Macomber, deputy under-secretary of state;
          Senator Henry Jackson; Max Frankel, head of
          New York Times' Washington bureau; Benjamin
          Bradley, executive editor of Washington Post.
          Questioned by Carl Stern, NBC; Martin Hayden,
          Detroit News; James J. Kilpatrick, Washington
          Star Syndicate; Kenneth Crawford, Washington
          Post; Edwin Newman. NBC-TV, June 30, 1971.
          1 reel (7 in.) 7 1/2 in. per sec.
          phonotape.

                    (Continued on next card)

          Newman, Edwin Harold, 1919-
Voice Lib.
M1695   Gish, Lillian, 1896-
          Interviewed by Edwin Newman on Speaking
          freely. WKAR-TV, 1974.
          37 min. phonotape (1 r.   7 1/2 i.p.s.)

          1. Moving-pictures - History.
I. Newman, Edwin Harold, 1919-

          Newman, Edwin Harold, 1919-
Voice Lib.
M1611   Hartford, Huntington, 1911-
bd.1   Interview by Edwin Newman on the TV
          program Speaking freely. WKAR-TV,
          March, 1974.
          3 min. phonotape (1 r.   7 1/2 i.p.s.)

          1. Graphology.   I. Newman, Edwin Harold,
1919-

          Newman, Edwin Harold, 1919-
Voice Lib.
M1266   Khruschev, Nikita Sergeevich, 1894-1971.
          NBC documentary TV program about the life
          and career of Nikita Khrushchev, with
          commentary by Edwin Newman; including Khrushchev's
          opinions on domestic and foreign matters, such as Mao Tse-
          Tung, Eisenhower, Kennedy, Stalin, H. C. Lodge, Nixon,
          the Cuban crisis. NBC-TV, August, 1967.
          1 reel (7 in.) 7 1/2 in. per sec. Phonotape.

          1. Khrushchev, Nikita Sergeevich, 1894-1971.
          1. Newman, Edwin Harold, 1919-

          Newman, Edwin Harold, 1919-
Voice Lib.
M1043   Manchester, William Raymond, 1922-
          "Meet the Press" television program with
          author William Manchester regarding his
          forth-coming book "The Death of A President",
          and discussing the controversy with the
          Kennedy family regarding its contents as
          well as alleged inaccuracies in the present
          serialization in "Look" magazine. Edwin
          Newman, MC. NBC-TV, February 12, 1967.
          1 reel (7 in.) 7 1/2 in. per sec.
          phonotape.

          Newman, Edwin Harold, 1919-
Voice Lib.
M1611   Mayer, Jean
bd.2   Interview by Edwin Newman on Speaking
          freely. WKAR-TV, March, 1974.
          5 min. phonotape (1 r.   7 1/2 i.p.s.)

          1. Malnutrition.   I. Newman, Edwin Harold,
1919-

          Newman, Edwin Harold, 1919-
Voice Lib.
M1475-   Rusk, Dean, 1909-
1476,   Dean Rusk, former Secretary of State,
bd.1   discusses the Pentagon Papers with Edwin
          Newman and Barbara Walters. NBC, July 2,
          1971.
          2 reels (7 in.) 7 1/2 i.p.s. phonotape.

          1. Pentagon papers. 2. Vietnamese
Conflict, 1961-   - U.S.   I. Newman,
Edwin Harold, 1919-   II. Walters,
Barbara, 1931-

Newman, Paul, 1925-
Voice Lib.
M1398 From here to the seventies, Part III.   NBC-TV
bd.1   two-and-a-half hour documentary pertaining to
        events occurring during the 1960's.   NBC-TV,
        October 7, 1969.
        1 reel (7 in.)   7 1/2 in. per sec.
        phonotape.
            CONTENTS. -1. Style changes: a. clothes; b. sex; c. violence;
        d. outlook; e. morals; f. sports and protest. -2. Man's mortality:
        a. death of Winston Churchill; b. Bobby Kennedy, speech before
        assassination; c. Dr. King, "I've been to the mountain top..." and
        "We'll get to the Promised Land"; d. John Kennedy's last speech. -
        3. Hunger around the world: a. Green Revolution, problems and
        benefits; b. abortions to control population. -4. Communications

(Continued on next card)

Newman, Paul, 1925-
Voice Lib.
M1398 From here to the seventies, Part III...   1969.
bd.1   (Card 2)
            CONTENTS, cont'd. explosion: a. David Brinkley, TV. -5. Ending:
        a. Paul Newman; b. Barbra Streisand.

            I. Kennedy, Robert Francis, 1925-1968.   II.
        King, Martin Luther, 1929-1968.   III. Kennedy,
        John Fitzgerald, Pres.U.S., 1917-1963.   IV.
        Brinkley, David McClure, 1920-   V. Newman,
        Paul, 1925-   VI. Streisand, Barbra, 1942-

Voice Lib.
M1466 Newsreport and ceremony upon the funeral of
bd.22   Gustav Streseman; eulogy by Alfred Braun.
        Peteler, October 6, 1929.
        1 reel (7 in.)   7 1/2 in. per sec.
        phonotape.

            1. Streseman, Gustav, 1878-1929.   I. Braun,
        Alfred

Voice Lib.
M1311 Ngo-dinh-Diem, Pres. Vietnam, 1901-1963.
bd.1   Special convocation at MSU to present an
        honorary degree to President Diem.   Intro-
        ductory remarks by Dr. John A. Hannah.
        Location recording, May 15, 1957.
        1 reel (7 in.)   7 1/2 in. per sec.
        phonotape.

            I. Hannah, John Alfred, 1902-

Niemöller, Fredrich Gustav Emil Martin,
    1892-
    see
Niemöller, Martin, 1892-

Voice Lib.
M874   Niemöller, Martin, 1892-
bd.1   Discussing fate of churches and religion
        under the Hitler regime in Germany.   KDKA,
        February 11, 1947.
        1 reel (7 in.)   7 1/2 i.p.s.   phonotape.

            1. Germany - Church history.

The night America trembled
Voice Lib.
M1024- Murrow, Edward Roscoe, 1908-1965.
1025,   Television network dramatization "Studio
bd.1   One" entitled "The night America trembled",
        pertaining to the CBS Mercury Theater Show
        "War of the worlds".   Westinghouse, 1958.
        2 reels (7 in.)   7 1/2 i.p.s.   phonotape.

            1. War of the worlds (radio program.)
        I. Title: The night America trembled.

Nightingale, Florence, 1820-1910
Voice Lib.
M1000 Nutting, Mary Adelaide, 1858-1948.
bd.6   Appraisal of the legacy of Florence
        Nightingale and the value of schools of
        schools of nursing, followed by introduction
        of voice of Miss Nightingale from recording
        made in 1890.   National Vocarium, 1933.
        1 reel (7 in.)   7 1/2 in. per sec.
        phonotape.

            I. Nightingale, Florence, 1820-1910.

NIGHTINGALE, FLORENCE, 1820-1910
C1
8C19   Whorf, Michael, 1933-
        The woman in white - Florence Nightingale.
        1 tape cassette.   (The visual sounds of
        Mike Whorf.   Science, SC19)

            Originally presented on his radio program, Kaleidoscope,
        WJR, Detroit.
            Duration: 47 min., 30 sec.
            The account of one of history's most famous nurses, Florence
        Nightingale, who persevered to bring her ideals and thoughts to
        the world.

            1. Nightingale, Florence, 1820-1910.   1. Title.

Voice Lib.
596   Nimitz, Chester William, 1885-1966.
bd.1   Banquet for Admiral Nimitz; words of
        appreciation, giving credit to others,
        reading poem.   WNYC, October 9, 1945.
        1 reel (7 in.)   7 1/2 in. per sec.
        phonotape.

Voice Lib.
Niven, Paul
M1268 Goldwater, Barry Morris, 1909-
        NET program about the 1964 presidential
campaign consisting of informal conversations
by Joseph Stern and Paul Niven with Barry
Goldwater and William E. Miller in
Washington, D.C.   NET, September 25, 1967.
        1 reel (7 in.)   7 1/2 in. per sec.
phonotape.

        I. Miller, William Edward, 1914-   II.
Stern, Joseph   III. Niven, Paul

Voice Lib.
256   Nixon, Richard Milhous, Pres. U.S., 1913-
bd.7   Medical report on Ike's health.   CBS News,
November 26 and 27, 1957.
        1 reel (7 in.)   7 1/2 in. per sec.
phonotape.

        1. Eisenhower, Dwight David, Pres. U.S.,
1890-1969.

Niven, Paul
Voice Lib.
M1295 Nixon, Richard Milhous, Pres. U.S., 1913-
        A conversation on the science of politics
with Paul Niven of NET.   NET, December 3,
1967.
        1 reel (7 in.)   7 1/2 in. per sec.
phonotape.

        I. Niven, Paul.

Voice Lib.
257   Nixon, Richard Milhous, Pres. U.S., 1913-
bd.1   Address at the airport on arrival
from South American trip, with description
of reception at airport.   CBS, May 15,
1958.
        1 reel (7 in.)   7 1/2 in. per sec.
phonotape.

Voice Lib.
M1454 Nixon, Richard Milhous, Pres. U.S., 1913-
bd.1   Discussion of U.S. foreign policy with
network newscasters Eric Sevareid (CBS),
John Chancellor (NBC), and Howard K. Smith
(ABC).
        1 reel (7 in.)   7 1/2 in. per sec.
phonotape.
        1. U.S. - Foreign policy
        I. Sevareid, Arnold Eric, 1912-   II.
Chancellor, John William, 1927-   III.
Smith, Howard Kingsbury, 1914-

Voice Lib.
M1295 Nixon, Richard Milhous, Pres. U.S., 1913-
        A conversation on the science of politics
with Paul Niven of NET.   NET, December 3,
1967.
        1 reel (7 in.)   7 1/2 in. per sec.
phonotape.

        I. Niven, Paul.

Voice Lib.
184   Nixon, Richard Milhous, Pres. U.S., 1913-
bd.2   Acceptance speech for vice-president
at Republican convention.   WJR, July 11,
1952.
        1 reel (7 in.)   7 1/2 in. per sec.
phonotape.

Voice Lib.
M1346 Nixon, Richard Milhous, Pres. U.S., 1913-
bd.2   Post-1968 election news described by
Huntley, Brinkley and other NBC staff men.
Statements of victory by Nixon and of defeat
by Humphrey; also by Wallace and LeMay.
Comments from countries overseas. Report of
Congressional elections.   NBC-TV, November 6,
1968.
        1 reel (7 in.)   7 1/2 in. per sec.
        I. Huntley, Chet, 1911-   II. Brinkley, David McClure, 1920-
III. Humphrey, Hubert Horatio, 1911-   IV. Wallace, George
Corley, 1919-   V. LeMay, Curtis Emerson, 1906-

Voice Lib.
283   Nixon, Richard Milhous, Pres. U.S., 1913-
bd.1   Speech presented under the auspices of
the Republican State Central Committee
at Lansing, Michigan on the issues of
the 1954 Congressional and state race.
Detroit, WJR, September 21, 1954.
        1 reel (7 in.)   7 1/2 in. per sec.
phonotape.

Voice Lib.
M1352 Nixon, Richard Milhous, Pres. U.S., 1913-
        Inaugural ceremonies for Richard M.
Nixon and Vice-President Spiro T. Agnew in
Washington, D.C., and commentary by NBC
correspondents.   NBC-TV, January 20, 1969.
        1 reel (7 in.)   7 1/2 in. per sec.
phonotape.

Voice Lib.
M1360 Nixon, Richard Milhous, Pres. U.S., 1913-
bd.1 Press conference and report to the nation
on his European trip; held in the East Room
of the White House, Washington, D.C. ABC-TV,
March 4, 1969.
1 reel (7 in.) 7 1/2 in. per sec.
phonotape.

Voice Lib.
M1406 Nixon, Richard Milhous, Pres. U.S., 1913-
President Nixon's address to nation on
current U.S. position on the war in Vietnam.
November 3, 1969.
1 reel (7 in.) 7 1/2 in. per sec.
phonotape.

1. Vietnamese Conflict, 1961- - U.S.

Voice Lib. Nixon, Richard Milhous, Pres. U.S., 1913-
M1371 Funeral ceremonies of General of the Army Dwight David
bd.2 Eisenhower, beginning with the casket being carried from
the National Cathedral to the U.S. Capitol in Washington,
D.C.; President Nixon's eulogy at the Capitol rotunda;
followed by reconveying the casket to the National Cathedral
where prayers and services are heard. CBS-TV, March 30, 1969.
1 reel (7 in.) 7 1/2 in. per sec. phonotape.

L Eisenhower, Dwight David, Pres. U.S., 1890-1969.
L Nixon, Richard Milhous, Pres. U.S., 1913-

Nixon, Richard Milhous, Pres. U.S.,
Voice Lib. 1913-
M1403 Apollo 12 (space flight): lift-off of Apollo
bd.1 12; the electrical "glitch" and instructions
and corrections; Dr. Paine and President
Nixon speaking from VIP section. CBS TV,
November 19, 1969.
1 reel (7 in.) 7 1/2 in. per sec.
phonotape.
L Project Apollo. 2. Space flight to the moon. 3. Conrad,
Charles, 1930- 4. Bean, Alan L 1932- 5. Gordon,
Richard F 1929- L Conrad, Charles, 1930- IL Bean,
Alan L 1932- III. Gordon, Richard F 1929- IV.
Paine, Thomas Otten, 1921- V. Nixon, Richard Milhous, Pres.
U.S., 1913-

Voice Lib.
M1381 Nixon, Richard Milhous, Pres. U.S., 1913-
bd.1 Commencement address at U.S. Air Force
Academy, Colorado Springs, Colorado.
CBS-TV, June 4, 1969.
1 reel (7 in.) 7 1/2 in. per sec.
phonotape.

Voice Lib.
M1410 Nixon, Richard Milhous, Pres. U.S., 1913-
bd.3 Nixon's report to the nation on further
withdrawal of troops from Vietnam. CBS-TV,
December 15, 1969.
1 reel (7 in.) 7 1/2 in. per sec.
phonotape.

1. Vietnamese Conflict, 1961- - U.S.

Nixon, Richard Milhous, Pres. U.S.,
Voice Lib. 1913-
M1386 Apollo 11 (space flight): conversation with
bd.1 broadcasters Walter Cronkite and Wally
Schirra. Including Armstrong's activities
on moon alone; pictures, rock descriptions,
then Aldrin coming down ladder; rock boxes
put to use. TV cameras put at 30' panoramic
position. Reading inscription of plaque
with U.S. flag and setting it up. Telephone
call from Washington to astronauts and their
acknowledgement. CBS TV, July 20, 1969.
1 reel (7 in.) 7 1/2 in. per sec.
phonotape.
(Continued on next card)

Voice Lib.
M1460 Nixon, Richard Milhous, Pres. U.S., 1913-
bd.1 Message to the nation on new peace initiative
in Vietnam. 1970.
1 reel (7 in.) 7 1/2 in. per.sec.
phonotape.

1. Vietnamese conflict, 1961- - U.S.

Nixon, Richard Milhous, Pres. U.S., 1913-
Voice Lib.
M1388 Apollo 11 (space flight): personal greeting
bd.2 by President Nixon to the astronauts on
the "Hornet" and their replies. Chaplain's
prayer. Nixon taking off. CBS and NBC TV,
July 24, 1969.
1 reel (7 in.) 7 1/2 in. per sec.
phonotape.
L Project Apollo. 2. Space flight to the moon. 3. Aldrin,
Edwin E 1930- 4. Collins, Michael, 1930- 5.
Armstrong, Neil, 1930- L Aldrin, Edwin E 1930-
IL Collins, Michael, 1930- III. Armstrong, Neil, 1930-
IV. Nixon, Richard Milhous, Pres. U.S., 1913-

Voice Lib.
M1409-Nixon, Richard Milhous, Pres. U.S., 1913-
1410 State of Union message. CBS-TV.
bd.1 January 22, 1970.
2 reels (7 in.) 7 1/2 in. per sec.
phonotape.

Voice Lib.
M1416 Nixon, Richard Milhous, Pres. U.S., 1913-
         Nixon's comments and actions on postal
         workers' strike.   CBS-TV, March 23, 1970.
         1 reel (7 in.)   7 1/2 in. per sec.
         phonotape.

Voice Lib.
M1419 Nixon, Richard Milhous, Pres. U.S., 1913-
         TV address to nation regarding troop
         withdrawals from Vietnam.   CBS-TV, April 20,
         1970.
         1 reel (7 in.)   7 1/2 in. per sec.
         phonotape.

         1. Vietnamese Conflict, 1961-   - U.S.

Voice Lib.
M1420 Nixon, Richard Milhous, Pres. U.S., 1913-
         Press conference held at White House
         regarding present status of war in Vietnam
         and regarding Cambodia.   CBS-TV, May 8,
         1970.
         1 reel (7 in.)   7 1/2 in. per sec.
         phonotape.

         1. Vietnamese Conflict, 1961-   - U.S.

Voice Lib.
M1452 Nixon, Richard Milhous, Pres. U.S., 1913-
         State of the Union message.   NBC-TV,
         January 22, 1971.
         1 reel (7 in.)   7 1/2 in. per sec.
         phonotape.

Voice Lib.
M1436 Nixon, Richard Milhous, Pres. U.S., 1913-
bd.1   On Vietnam troop withdrawals.   NBC-TV,
         April 7, 1971.
         1 reel (7 in.)   7 1/2 in. per sec.
         phonotape.

         1. Vietnamese Conflict, 1961-   - U.S.

Voice Lib.
M1479 Nixon, Richard Milhous, Pres. U.S., 1913-
bd.1   President Nixon announces trip to China;
         comment by John Chancellor, Richard Valeriani.
         NBC-TV, July 15, 1971.
         1 reel (7 in.)   7 1/2 in. per sec.
         phonotape.

         I. Chancellor, John William, 1927-
        II. Valeriani, Richard

Voice Lib.
M1482 Nixon, Richard Milhous, Pres. U.S., 1913-
bd.1   Address at joint session of Congress
         asking for implementation of the President's
         new economic policies.   CBS, September 9,
         1971.
         1 reel (7 in.)   7 1/2 in. per sec.
         phonotape.

         1. U.S. - Economic policy, 1971-

Voice Lib.
M1483 Nixon, Richard Milhous, Pres. U.S., 1913-
bd.1   Speech before the Economic Club of
         Detroit at Cobo Hall.   NBC, September 23,
         1971.
         1 reel (7 in.)   7.1/2 in. per sec.
         phonotape.

Voice Lib.
M1484 Nixon, Richard Milhous, Pres. U.S., 1913-
bd.1   National broadcast describing Phase Two
         of the wage-price freeze.   CBS, October 7,
         1971.
         1 reel (7 in.)   7 1/2 in. per sec.
         phonotape.

         1. U.S. - Economic policy - 1971-

Voice Lib.
M1486 Nixon, Richard Milhous, Pres. U.S., 1913-
         One hour documentary describing an entire
         day in the life of Pres. Richard M. Nixon
         in the White House, with NBC's John Batchellor,
         including visit of Canadian Prime Minister
         Pierre Trudeau.   NBC-TV, December 6, 1971.
         1 reel (7 in.)   7 1/2 in. per sec.
         phonotape.

         I. Batchellor, John.

Voice Lib.
M1487- Nixon, Richard Milhous, Pres. U.S., 1913-
1488   One hour question and answer session
bd.1   with Pres. Nixon and CBS's Dan Rather,
       dealing with all current topics.   CBS,
       January 2, 1972.
         2 reels (7 in.)   7 1/2 in. per sec.
       phonotape.

         I. Rather, Dan

Voice Lib.
M1502   Nixon, Richard Milhous, Pres. U.S., 1913-
        Address to joint session of Congress
        immediately after his return from visit to
        USSR and other countries.   CBS-TV, June 1,
        1972.
          1 reel (7 in.)   7 1/2 in. per sec.
        phonotape.

Voice Lib.
M1492   Nixon, Richard Milhous, Pres. U.S., 1913-
        State of Union message to joint session
        of Congress, rehearsing Administration's
        progress and plans for the future.   NBC-TV,
        January 20, 1972.
          1 reel (7 in.)   7 1/2 in. per sec.
        phonotape.

Voice Lib.
M1559   Nixon, Richard Milhous, Pres. U.S., 1913-
        The Watergate Affair; address to the nation,
        with instant analysis by Roger Mudd and
        Daniel Schorr.   CBS, April 30, 1973.
          30 min.   phonotape (1 r.   7 1/2 i.p.s.)

          1. Watergate affair, 1972.   I. Mudd,
        Roger.   II. Schorr, Daniel Louis, 1916-

Voice Lib.
M1493   Nixon, Richard Milhous, Pres. U.S., 1913-
        Trip to China: take-off from Washington;
        arrival in Peking; tour of city of Peking;
        Nixon address at dinner attended by Chou-
        En-Lai.   CBS, February 21, 1972.
          1 reel (7 in.)   7 1/2 in. per sec.
        phonotape.

Voice Lib.
M1549-   Nixon, Richard Milhous, Pres. U.S., 1913-
1550,   News conference recorded over CBS
bd.1   television network.   CBS, October 26, 1973.
           35 min.   phonotape (2 r.   7 1/2 i.p.s.)

           Includes question and answer session, including Nelson
         Benton.

           1. U.S. - Politics and government - 1969-
         2. Watergate Affair, 1972.   3. Power resources - U. S.
         I. Benton, Nelson

Voice Lib.
M1496   Nixon, Richard Milhous, Pres. U.S., 1913-
bd.2   President's China trip; banquet in Peking
        hosted by President Nixon, including toasts
        by President Nixon and Premier Chou-En-Lai
        and Chinese translations.   CBS, February 25,
        1972.
          1 reel (7 in.)   7 1/2 in. per sec.
        phonotape.

          I. Chou En-Lai, 1898-

Voice Lib.
M1556   Nixon, Richard Milhous, Pres. U.S., 1913-
        State of the Union address; excerpts.
        WKAR-FM, January 30, 1974.
          42 min.   phonotape (1 r.   7 1/2 in. per
        sec.)

          1. U.S. - Politics and government - 1969-

Voice Lib.
M1500   Nixon, Richard Milhous, Pres. U.S., 1913-
        Special TV broadcast to the nation regarding
        start of blockade of shipping to North
        Vietnam and mining of Haiphong harbor;
        also extended bombing of North Vietnam.
        Followed by commentary of NBC and CBS
        correspondents.   NBC, May 8, 1972.
          1 reel (7 in.)   7 1/2 in. per sec.
        phonotape.
          1. Vietnamese Conflict, 1961-   - U.S.

Voice Lib.
M1545   Nixon, Richard Milhous, Pres. U.S., 1913-
bd.1   Transportation message.   CBS, February 9,
        1974.
          12 min.   phonotape (1 r.   7 1/2 i.p.s.)

          1. Transportation - U.S.

Voice Lib.
M1558   Nixon, Richard Milhous, Pres. U.S., 1913-
bd.2   Comments on invasion of privacy; radio
         address. Followup to State of the Union
         Address. With commentary by Russ Ward.
         NBC, February 23, 1974.
            22 min.   phonotape (1 r.   7 1/2 in. per
         sec.)

            1. Privacy, Right of.   I. Ward, Russ.

Voice Lib.
M1566   Nixon, Richard Milhous, Pres. U.S., 1913-
bd.2   Address on the energy crisis, followed by
         excerpts from question and answer period with
         the press. WKAR-FM, February 24, 1974.
            20 min.   phonotape. 7 1/2 in. per sec.

            1. Power resources - U. S. 2. U. S. - Economic conditions.
            3. Nixon, Richard Milhous, Pres. U. S., 1913-

Voice Lib.
M1609   Nixon, Richard Milhous, Pres. U.S., 1913-
            Address before the Executive Club of
         Chicago. WKAR-AM, March 15, 1974.
            40 min.   phonotape (1 r.   7 1/2 i.p.s.)

            Includes question & answer session.

            1. U.S. - Politics and government - 1969-

Voice Lib.
M1628-   Nixon, Richard Milhous, Pres. U.S., 1913-
1629,   Address before the National Radio &
bd.1   Television News Directors Association and
         questions following from the members and
         from the national press. Summary and analysis
         by CBS newsmen Roger Mudd and Bruce Morton.
         CBS, March 19, 1974.
            60 min.   phonotape (2 r.   7 1/2 i.p.s.)

            1. U.S. - Politics and government - 1969-
         2. Power resources - U.S.   I. Mudd, Roger.
         II. Morton,   Bruce.

Voice Lib.
M1634   Nixon, Richard Milhous, Pres. U.S., 1913-
bd.2   Speaking at Bad Axe, Michigan, in support
         of James Sparling, Republican candidate for
         Congress.   MSU Dept. of Journalism, April,
         1974.
            10 min.   phonotape (1 r.   7 1/2 i.p.s.)

            1. U.S. - Politics and government - 1969-
         2. Sparling, James

Voice Lib.
M1720   Nixon, Richard Milhous, Pres. U.S., 1913-
bd.5   Departing for the Mideast, with Vice
         President Gerald Ford.   NBC-TV, June 10,
         1974.
            5 min.   phonotape (1 r.   7 1/2 i.p.s.)

            I. Ford, Gerald R., 1913-

            Nixon, Richard Milhous, Pres. U.S., 1913-
Voice Lib.
186   Eisenhower, Dwight David, Pres. U.S., 1890-
         1969.
            Inauguration ceremonies of President
         Eisenhower and Vice-President Nixon. WJR,
         January 20, 1953.
            1 reel (7 in.)   7 1/2 in. per sec.
         phonotape.

            I. Nixon, Richard Milhous, Pres. U.S., 1913-

            Nixon, Richard Milhous, Pres. U.S., 1913-
Voice Lib.
381-   I can hear it now (radio program)
382   CBS, April 26, 1951.
bd.1   2 reels (7 in.) 7 1/2 in. per sec. phonotape.
            1. Radio Free Europe. 2. Strategic Air Command. I.
         Ridgway, Matthew Bunker, 1895-   II. Churchill, Winston Leonard
         Spencer, 1874-1965. III. Bevan, Aneurin, 1897-1960. IV. Nixon,
         Richard Milhous, Pres. U. S., 1913-   V. Kerr, Robert Samuel, 1896-
         1963. VI. Brewster, Ralph Owen, 1888-1962. VII. Wherry, Kenneth
         Spicer, 1892-1951. VIII. Capehart, Homer Earl, 1897-   IX.
         Lehman, Herbert Henry, 1878-1963. X. Taft, Robert Alphonso,
         1889-1953. XI. Moody, Arthur Edson Blair, 1902-1954. XII.
         Martin, Joseph William, 1884-1968. XIII. McMahon, James O'Brien,
         1903-1952. XIV. MacArthur, Douglas, 1880-1964. XVII. Wilson,
         Charles Edward, 1886-1972. XVIII. Irvine, Clarence T

            Nixon, Richard Milhous, Pres. U.S., 1913-
Voice Lib.
M724   Kennedy, John Fitzgerald, Pres. U.S., 1917-
bd.8   1963.
            Excerpt of his TV debate with Vice-President
         Richard Nixon in 1960.
            1 reel (7 in.)   7 1/2 in. per sec.
         phonotape.

            I. Nixon, Richard Milhous, Pres. U.S., 1913-

            Nixon, Richard Milhous, Pres. U.S., 1913-
Voice Lib.
M739   Kennedy, John Fitzgerald, Pres. U.S., 1917-1963.
bd.12   Excerpt from the Kennedy-Nixon debates during
         the presidential campaign of 1960, regarding
         the "strong" language charges of Truman against
         the Republican Party, and the Quemoy-Matsu
         Island dispute.   CBS, October 13, 1960.
            1 reel (7 in.)   7 1/2 in. per sec.
         phonotape.

            I. Nixon, Richard Milhous, Pres. U.S., 1913-

Nixon, Richard Milhous, Pres. U.S., 1913-
Voice Lib.
M1329-   Republican Party. National Convention, 29th,
1331   Miami, Fla., 1968.
           Proceedings of night session. Attempt to
           nominate Governor Romney for vice-president;
           revolt against Nixon's choice of Governor
           Agnew for running mate. Attempt to nominate
           Mayor Lindsay for vice-president. Roll call
           and nomination of Agnew by acclamation. Richard
           M. Nixon's acceptance speech. Benediction by
           Billy Graham. NBC-TV, August 8, 1968.
           3 reels (7 in.) 7 1/2 in. per sec. phonotape.
           L. Nixon, Richard Milhous, Pres. U.S., 1913-   II. Graham,
           William Franklin, 1918-

NIXON, RICHARD MILHOUS, PRES.,
1913-
Voice Lib.
M1685   Rodino, Peter Wallace, 1909-
bd.2   Telling PBS that transcript damages Nixon.
         Question under investigation is how much?
         Interview with Paul Duke on Washington
         straight talk. PBS, May 21, 1974.
            30 min. phonotape (1 r.   7 1/2 i.p.s.)

            1. U.S. - Politics and government - 1969-
         2. Nixon, Richard Milhous, Pres. U.S., 1913-
         I. Duke, Paul.

NIXON, RICHARD MILHOUS, PRES. U.S.,
1913-
Voice Lib.
M1611   Conyers, John, 1929-
bd.3   Discusses impeachment and opinion poll
         bias. WKAR-TV (1974?)
            8 min. phonotape (1 r.   7 1/2 i.p.s.)

            1. Nixon, Richard Milhous, Pres. U.S., 1913-
         2. U.S. - Politics and government, 1969-

NIXON, RICHARD MILHOUS, PRES. U.S., 1913-
Voice Lib.
M1705   Schlesinger, Arthur Meier, 1917-
            The imperial presidency; address at
         the University of Missouri. WKAR
         (KBIA, Columbia, Mo.), June 3, 1974.
            50 min. phonotape (1 r.   7 1/2 i.p.s.)

            1. Presidents - U.S. 2. Johnson, Lyndon
         Baines, Pres. U.S., 1908-1973. 3. Nixon,
         Richard Milhous, Pres. U.S., 1913-

NIXON, RICHARD MILHOUS, PRES. U.S., 1913-
Voice Lib.
M930   Eisenhower, Dwight David, Pres. U.S., 1890-
bd.2   1969.
            News conference held at San Francisco at
         the re-nomination of Richard M. Nixon.
         CBS, September 13, 1956.
            1 reel (7 in.)   7 1/2 in. per sec.
         phonotape.

            1. Nixon, Richard Milhous, Pres. U.S., 1913-

NIXON, RICHARD MILHOUS, PRES. U.S., 1913-
Voice Lib.
M1421   Smith, Howard Kingsbury, 1914-
            Comments by Howard K. Smith and guests
         regarding Nixon's press conference.
         ABC-TV, May 8, 1970.
            1 reel (7 in.)   7 1/2 in. per sec.
         phonotape.

NIXON, RICHARD MILHOUS, PRES. U.S.,
1913-
Voice Lib.
M1681   Eisenhower, Julie Nixon, 1948-
bd.1   Defense of father. CBS, May 11, 1974.
            1 min. phonotape (1 r.   7 1/2 i.p.s.)

            1. Nixon, Richard Milhous, Pres. U.S.,
         1913-

NIXON, RICHARD MILHOUS, PRES. U.S., 1913-
Voice Lib.
M1656   U.S. Congress. House. Committee on the
bd.3   Judiciary.
            House Judiciary Committee, 1st public
         meeting of impeachment hearings, with
         Chairman Peter Rodino and Edward Hutchinson.
         WKAR, May 9, 1974.
            15 min. phonotape (1 r.   7 1/2 i.p.s.)

            1. Nixon, Richard Milhous, Pres. U.S., 1913-
         I. Rodino, Peter Wallace, 1909-
         II. Hutchinson, Edward, 1914-

NIXON, RICHARD MILHOUS, PRES. U.S., 1913-
Voice Lib.
M1720   O'Neill, Thomas P., 1912-
bd.1   Interview on Washington Straight Talk,
         by Paul Duke. WKAR-TV, June 11, 1974.
            30 min. phonotape (1 r.   7 1/2 i.p.s.)

            1. U.S. - Politics & government.
         2. Nixon, Richard Milhous, Pres. U.S., 1913-
         I. Duke, Paul.

Voice Lib.
M811-   Nkrumah, Kwame, Pres. of Ghana, 1909-1972.
813   Address at plenary meeting 961 of General
         Assembly of the United Nations in New York.
         Topics: assassination of Patrice Lumumba;
         opinions on the U.N.; analysis of the Congo
         situation; African affairs in general;
         financial situations in new countries. U.N.
         Archives, March 7, 1961.
            3 reels (7 in.)   7 1/2 in. per sec.
         phonotape.

            1. Lumumba, Patrice, 1925-1961.

No news, or, what killed the dog?
Voice Lib.
611   Wills, Nat M
bd.9   Comedy monologue "No news, or, what killed
the dog?" Victor Talking Machine Co., 1917.
1 reel (7 in.)   7 1/2 in. per sec.
phonotape.

I. Title: No news, or, what killed the
dog?

Nobody's mad at L.B.J.
Voice Lib.
375   Meadows, Audrey, 1922-
bd.2   Excerpt from "That Was the Week That Was":
"Nobody's Mad at L.B.J." NBC, January 9,
1964.
1 reel (7 in.)   7 1/2 in. per sec.
phonotape.

I. That Was the Week That Was (television
program). II. Title: Nobody's mad at L.B.J.

Nobody's using it now
Voice Lib.
M982   Chevalier, Maurice, 1899-1972.
bd.2   Singing "Nobody's Using It Now" from
Paramount Pictures' "The Love Parade".
Victor, 1927.
1 reel (7 in.)   7 1/2 in. per sec.
phonotape.

I. Title: Nobody's using it now.

NORTH ATLANTIC TREATY ORGANIZATION
Voice Lib.
M185   Dulles, John Foster, 1888-1959.
The situation of NATO report upon return
from Paris; first broadcast ever held of a
Cabinet meeting. WJR, October 25, 1954.
1 reel (7 in.)   7 1/2 in. per sec.
phonotape.

1. North Atlantic Treaty Organization.

NORTH ATLANTIC TREATY ORGANIZATION
Voice Lib.
M929- Mendès-France, Pierre, 1907-
930   Address at Foreign Policy Association in
bd.1   New York dealing primarily with ideas pertaining to the unification of Europe and
thoughts on the North Atlantic Treaty
Organization. CBS, November 23, 1954.
2 reels (7 in.)   7 1/2 in. per sec.
phonotape.

Norton, Elliot
Voice Lib.
M373   Kazan, Elia, 1909-
Talks with Elliot Norton on drama, etc.
Lowell Institute Co-Operative Broadcasting
Council (NET), October 5, 1961.
1 reel (7 in.)   7 1/2 in. per sec.
phonotape.

I. Norton, Elliot

Norton, Elliot
Voice Lib.
M374   Logan, Joshua Lockwood, 1908-
Talks with Elliot Norton; compares
motion picture themes with theater memes,
changing mores of American motion pictures,
pressure groups and television programs,
restraints on free speech, criticism of
Hollywood, movie censorship, economics of
modern theater. Lowell Institute (NET)
September 28, 1961.
1 reel (7 in.)   7 1/2 in. per sec.
phonotape.
I. Norton, Elliot

Norton, James
Voice Lib.
M1267 Channing, Carol, 1923-
bd.1   Interview with actress Carol Channing at
Expo '67, Montreal, Canada, with James Norton
on TV program "Conversation". NET, August 15,
1967.
1 reel (7 in.)   7 1/2 in. per sec.
phonotape.

I. Norton, James.

NORWAY - POLITICS AND GOVERNMENT - 1940-
Voice Lib.   1945
M526   Haakon VII, King of Norway, 1872-1957.
bd.3   Refusal to abdicate Norwegian throne on
grounds that his people do not desire him
to, justifies exile government. Speaks from
his exile headquarters in London; reviews
early years in Norway. CBS, 1940.
1 reel (7 in.)   7 1/2 i.p.s.   phonotape.

1. World War, 1939-1945 - Norway.
2. Norway - Politics and government - 1940-
1945.

Voice Lib.
M1466 Noske, Gustav, 1868-1946.
bd.17   About suppressing Communist uprisings in
Berlin. Peteler, March 13, 1919.
1 reel (7 in.)   7 1/2 in. per sec.
phonotape.

1. Germany - Politics and government -
1918-1933.

Notre Dame University. Band

Voice Lib.
649   Notre Dame Victory March, from sound track
bd.14   of Universal motion picture "The Spirit of
           Notre Dame".   Universal Pictures, 1938.
           1 reel (7 in.)   7 1/2 in. per sec.
           phonotape.

I. Notre Dame University. Band.

Voice Lib.
649 ·   Notre Dame Victory March, from sound track
bd.14   of Universal motion picture "The Spirit of
           Notre Dame".   Universal Pictures, 1938.
           1 reel (7 in.)   7 1/2 in. per sec.
           phonotape.

I. Notre Dame University. Band.

Novin, Stuart

Voice Lib.
242   Rayburn, Samuel Taliaferro, 1882-1961.
           A tribute to Sam Rayburn, with Stuart
         Novin and Robert Trout.   CBS Radio,
         November 16, 1961.
           1 reel (7 in.)   7 1/2 in. per sec.
         phonotape.

           I. Novin, Stuart   II. Trout, Robert,
         1908-

Now batting for the New York Yankees

C1
M16   Whorf, Michael, 1933-
           Now batting for the New York Yankees.
           1 tape cassette. (The visual sounds of
         Mike Whorf. Miscellaneous, M16)

           Originally presented on his radio program, Kaleidoscope,
         WJR, Detroit.
             Duration: 40 min., 30 sec.
             This is the story of Babe Ruth, the orphan boy of Baltimore who
         would one day become the great New York Yankee slugger.

           I. Ruth, George Herman, 1894-1948. I. Title.

Noyes, Crosby

Voice Lib.
M1478   The Pentagon Papers; discussion of content,
         meaning.   Bernard Kalb, CBS; Senator J.W.
         Fulbright; Senator John Tower; Arthur
         Schlesinger; Walt Rostow; Max Frankel,
         New York Times; Crosby Noyes, Washington
         Evening Star.   CBS-TV, July 13, 1971.
           1 reel (7 in.)   7 1/2 in. per sec.
         phonotape.
           I. Kalb, Bernard   II. Fulbright, James William, 1905-
         III. Tower, John Goodwin, 1925-   IV. Schlesinger, Arthur
         Meier, 1888-   V. Rostow, Walt Whitman, 1916-   VI.
         Frankel, Max   VII. Noyes, Crosby

NUCLEAR REACTIONS

Voice Lib.
M1310   Fermi, Enrico, 1901-1954.
bd.2   Speaking at the tenth anniversary
         celebration of the first nuclear chain
         reaction, held at the University of Chicago.
         Atomic Energy Commission, December 2, 1952.
           1 reel (7 in.)   7 1/2 i.p.s.   phonotape.

           1. Nuclear reactions.   I. Compton,
         Arthur Holly, 1892-1962.

Voice Lib.
M985-   Nugent, Luci Baines (Johnson), 1947-
986   Resumé of ceremonies at wedding of Luci
bd.1   Baines Johnson, daughter of incumbent President
         Lyndon B. Johnson, in Washington, D.C.
         Described by Nancy Dickerson, with actual
         sounds.   NBC-TV, August 6, 1966.
           2 reels (7 in.)   7 1/2 in. per sec.
         phonotape.
           I. Dickerson, Nancy Hanschman, 1929(?)-

NUREMBURG TRIAL OF MAJOR GERMAN WAR
CRIMINALS, 1945-1946

Voice Lib.
M1362   Kaltenbrunner, Ernst, 1901-1946.
bd.3   Testimony at the international military
         proceedings in Nuremberg, Germany.
         Peteler, August 31, 1946.
           1 reel (7 in.)   7 1/2 in. per sec.
         phonotape.

           1. Nuremburg Trial of Major German War
         Criminals, 1945-1946.

NUREMBERG TRIAL OF MAJOR GERMAN WAR
CRIMINALS, 1945-1946

Voice Lib.
M386   Lawrence, Sir Geoffrey, 1880-
           Judge's decision on motions by defendants
         Julius Streicher and Martin Bormann, acquisition
         of and use of enemy documents as evidence.
         Private collection, November 2, 1945.
           1 reel (7 in.)   7 1/2 in. per sec.
         phonotape.

           1. Nuremberg Trial of Major German War
         Criminals, 1945-1946.

NUREMBERG TRIAL OF MAJOR GERMAN WAR
CRIMINALS, 1945-1946

Voice Lib.
M630   Matthews, Kenneth
bd.1   Commentary on Nuremberg War Crimes Trials;
         reviews early days of trial and reflects on
         current courtroom decorum, reviews Justice
         Jackson's view on the case, on defendants'
         knowledge of charges against them.   Includes
         trial recording excerpts.   BBC, January 30,
         1946.
           1 reel (7 in.)   7 1/2 i.p.s.   phonotape.

           1. Nuremberg Trial of Major German War
         Criminals, 1945- 1946.

NUREMBERG TRIAL OF MAJOR GERMAN WAR
CRIMINALS, 1945-1946
Voice Lib.
M354-   War Crimes Trials - Nuremberg, 1945-1949.
361   Pleas of defendants, opening address.
             Official Government Recording, November 21,
             1945.
                 8 reels (7 in.)   7 1/2 i.p.s.   phonotape.

                 1. Nuremberg Trial of Major German War
             Criminals, 1945-1946.

Voice Lib.
M1090   Nutting, Mary Adelaide, 1858-1948.
bd.6   Appraisal of the legacy of Florence
             Nightingale and the value of schools of
             schools of nursing, followed by introduction
             of voice of Miss Nightingale from recording
             made in 1890. National Vocarium, 1938.
                 1 reel (7 in.)   7.1/2 in. per sec.
             phonotape.

                 I. Nightingale, Florence, 1820-1910.

Nye, Gerald Prentice, 1892-1971
Voice Lib.
M620   Radio in the 1940's (Part I): a series of
bd.1-   excerpts from important broadcasts of the 1940's; a
bd.16   sample of radio of the period. NVL, April, 1964.
                 1 reel (7 in.)   7 1/2 in. per sec.   phonotape.
             I. Radio programs. L. Thomas, Lowell Jackson, 1892-   IL.
             Gunther, John, 1901-1970. III. Kaltenborn, Hans von, 1878-1965.
             IV. Delmar, Kenny. V. Those were the good old days (Radio
             program) VI. Elman, Dave. VII. Hall, Frederick Lee, 1916-1970.
             VIII. Hobby lobby (Radio program) IX. Roosevelt, Franklin Delano,
             Pres. U.S., 1882-1945. X. Willkie, Wendell Lewis, 1892-1944.
             XI. Hoover, Herbert Clark, Pres. U.S., 1874-1964. XII. Johnson,
             Hugh Samuel, 1882-1942. XIII. Cobb, Irvin Shrewsbury, 1876-1944.
             XIV. Roosevelt, Theodore, 1858-1919. XV. Nye, Gerald Prentice,
             1892-1971. XVI. Lindbergh, Charles Augustus, 1902- XVII.
             Toscanini, Arturo, 1867-1957

Voice Lib.
M1289   Nye, Russell Blaine, 1913-
                 Address on education at Friends of the
             Library dinner held at Kellogg Center,
             including entire proceedings with short
             talk by Professor Crawford and Dr. Richard
             E. Chapin. December 6, 1967.
                 1 reel (7 in.)   7 1/2 in. per sec.
             phonotape.

                 I. Chapin, Richard Earl, 1925-

Voice Lib.
M630   Ober, Norman
bd.2   Interviews Roy Fitzsimons and Dr. Wade
             upon their return from the Second Antarctic
             Expedition, sponsored by Admiral Richard E.
             Byrd. GRV, 1941.
                 1 reel (7 in.)   7 1/2 i.p.s.   phonotape.

                 1. Byrd Antarctic Expedition, 2d,
             1933-1935. I. Wade, Al. II. Fitzsimons,
             Roy.

Oboler, Arch, 1907-
Voice Lib.
M1026   West, Mae, 1893-
bd.2   "Adam and Eve"; skit written by Arch
             Oboler, from Charlie McCarthy radio program.
             NBC, December 12, 1937.
                 1 reel (7 in.)   7 1/2 in. per sec.
             phonotape.

                 I. Oboler, Arch, 1907-

Voice Lib.
649   O'Brien, Pat, 1899-
bd.13   Knute Rockne talks to his team;
             sequence from motion picture film "The
             Spirit of Notre Dame". Universal Pictures,
             1938.
                 1 reel (7 in.)   7 1/2 in. per sec.
             phonotape.

                 I. The spirit of Notre Dame (Motion picture)

O'BRIEN, PAT, 1899-
Voice Lib.
M1743   Raft, George
bd.2   Reminisces on the Mike Douglas Show.
             WILX-TV, June 27, 1974.
                 10 min.   phonotape (1 r.   7 1/2 i.p.s.)

                 L. Raft, George. 2. O'Brien, Pat, 1899-   3. Muni,
             Paul, 1895-1967. 4. Crawford, Joan, 1908-   5. West, Mae,
             1893-   6. Richman, Harry. 7. Entertainers - U. S. L.
             Douglas, Mike, 1925-

O'Connor, Basil, 1892-1972
Voice Lib.
231   Salk, Jonas Edward, 1914-
bd.2   Discussion of Salk vaccine, introduced
             by Basil O'Connor. CBS, May 3, 1954.
                 1 reel (7 in.)   7 1/2 in. per sec.
             phonotape.

                 1. Poliomyelitis vaccine. I. O'Connor,
             Basil, 1892-1972.

Voice Lib.
M1745   O'Connor, Ulick
bd.1   Interview on Mike Douglas Show. WILS-TV,
             June 27, 1974.
                 10 min.   phonotape (1 r.   7 1/2 i.p.s.)

                 1. Pierce, Patrick/The Mother. 2. O'Connor,
             Ulick. I. Douglas, Mike, 1925-

Voice Lib.
M1245 Odetta.
bd.3 Singing Freedom Trilogy: 1. "Come All Ye
Young Fellas"; 2. "This Land is Your Land";
3. "A Mighty Hard Road". CRI, 1962.
1 reel (7 in.) 7 1/2 in. per sec.
phonotape.

Voice Lib.
132 O'Dwyer, William, 1890-1964.
bd.2 Refusing renomination, an address
at New York City Hall. Recorded on
location, June 9, 1949.
1 reel (7 in.) 7 1/2 in. per sec.
phonotape.

Voice Lib.
M1800 Odle, Robert C., 1944?-
WG Testimony before the Senate Committee
0517.02- investigating the Watergate Affair.
.03 Pacifica, May 17, 1973.
218 min. phonotape (2 r. 3 3/4 i.p.s.)
(Watergate gavel to gavel, phase 1)

1. Watergate Affair, 1972-

Of men and legends
C1
H8 Whorf, Michael, 1933-
Of men and legends.
1 tape cassette. (The visual sounds of
Mike Whorf. History and heritage, H8)
Originally presented on his radio program, Kaleidoscope,
WJR, Detroit.
Duration: 50 min., 30 sec.
Beloved and revered, despised and dislike, they were figures
in our history that helped to make a great land. Here are brief
character sketches of personalities in our heritage whose contri-
butions and efforts are gratefully acknowledged by an appreciative
nation.

L. U.S. - Biography. L. Title.

Voice Lib. O'Doul, Lefty, 1897-
M1248 Baseball fifty years ago; interviews with four
famous old time baseball players, on NBC
"Today" show, by host Hugh Downs, supported by
sportcaster Joe Garagiola and Dr. Lawrence
Ritter, author of new book. NBC-TV, June 9,
1967.
1 reel (7 in.) 7 1/2 in. per sec. phonotape.

L. Baseball. L. Downs, Hugh Malcolm, 1921- II. Garagiola,
Joe. III. Ritter, Lawrence S./The glory of their times. IV. Roush,
Edd, 1893- V. Marquart, Rube, 1890- VI. O'Doul, Lefty,
1897- VII. Meyers, John, 1880-

Of myths and gods
C1
R22 Whorf, Michael, 1933-
Of myths and gods.
1 tape cassette. (The visual sounds of
Mike Whorf. Religion, R22)
Originally presented on his radio program, Kaleidoscope,
WJR, Detroit.
Duration: 48 min., 30 sec.
From antiquity comes the history of gods and legends. Who were
the great Egyptian, Greek and Roman gods - and what part did man
play in their world and they in his?

L. Mythology. L. Title.

O'Dwyer, Paul, 1907-
Voice Lib.
M1323- Democratic Party. National Convention,
M1328, Chicago, 1968.
bd.1 Hubert Humphrey, Democratic presidential nom. e,
announcing his selection of Sen. Muskie as his running mate;
convention floor reports; interview with Mrs. Humphrey. Mayor
Daley of Chicago defending police action. Interviews with Senator McGovern and Jesse Unruh of California. Remote address by
Sen. Edward Kennedy introducing a memorial motion picture on
the late Sen. Robert F. Kennedy. Various reports on riots and
general confusion, reluctance of delegates to come to order.
Nominations for Vice-President; seconding speeches for Sen.
Muskie and nominating speech by Wisconsin delegation of Julian
Bond of Georgia. Interview with Julian Bond, who declined
nomination of the vice-presidency. Story told by chairman of
the New Hampshire [delegation] regarding his arrest. Interview
(Continued on next card)

Ogilvie, Richard Buell, 1923-
Voice Lib.
M1391 Apollo 11 (space flight): reception of
bd.2 Apollo 11 astronauts in Chicago. Description of motorcade on way to Civic Center
Plaza and ceremonies there. Cardinal Cody's
invocation. JFK flashback predicting moon
landing before decade is out. Mayor Daley
and Alderman Klene resolution making August
13 "Astronauts' Day". Senator Percy and
Governor Ogilvie of Illinois. Presentation
of honorary citizenship to astronauts.
[Source?] August 13, 1969.

(Continued on next card)

O'Dwyer, Paul, 1907-
Voice Lib.
M1323- Democratic Party. National Convention,
M1328, Chicago, 1968... (Card 2)
bd.1 with Paul O'Dwyer of the New York delegation regarding the
nomination of Richard Daley for Vice-President. General
confusion. Nomination of Sen. Edmund Muskie as Vice-President
and resulting confusion with the Oregon delegation. Followed by
Sen. Muskie's acceptance speech. NBC-TV, August 29, 1968.
6 reels (7 in.) 7 1/2 in. per sec. phonotape.

L. Humphrey, Hubert Horatio, 1911- II. Humphrey, Muriel Fay
(Buck) 1912- III. Daley, Richard J 1902- IV. McGovern,
George Stanley, 1922- V. Unruh, Jesse Marvin, 1922- VI.
Kennedy, Edward Moore, 1932- VII. Bond, Julian, 1940- VIII.
O'Dwyer, Paul, 1907- IX. Muskie, Edmund S 1914-

Ogilvie, Richard Buell, 1923-
Voice Lib.
M1391 Apollo 11 (space flight): reception of Apollo
bd.2 11 astronauts ... 1969. (Card 2)

1 reel (7 in.) 7 1/2 in. per sec.
phonotape.

L. Project Apollo. 2. Space flight to the moon. 3. Aldrin,
Edwin E 1930- 4. Collins, Michael, 1930- 5. Armstrong,
Neil, 1930- L. Aldrin, Edwin E 1930- II. Collins,
Michael, 1930- III. Armstrong, Neil, 1930- IV. Cody,
John Patrick, cardinal, 1907- V. Kennedy, John Fitzgerald,
Pres. U.S., 1917-1963. VI. Daley, Richard J 1902- VII.
Percy, Charles Harting, 1919- VIII. Ogilvie, Richard Buell,
1923-

Oh, to be a kid again

C1
826   Whorf, Michael, 1933-
      Oh, to be a kid again.
      1 tape cassette. (The visual sounds of
Mike Whorf. Social, S26)
      Originally presented on his radio program, Kaleidoscope,
WJR, Detroit.
      Duration: 28 min., 30 sec.
      An ode to the school, the child and the teacher in this
narrative which deals with a nostalgic look at some of our
experiences.

      I. Education. L. Title.

OIL INDUSTRIES - U.S.

Voice Lib.
M1729- Nader, Ralph.
1730   Address at Michigan State University.
MSU Voice Library, April 11, 1974.
      80 min. phonotape (2 r. 7 1/2 i.p.s.)

      1. Monopolies - U.S. 2. Pollution. 3.
Oil industries - U. S.

Old buttermilk sky

Voice Lib.
625   Carmichael, Hoagy, 1899-
bd.1   "Salute to Hoagy Carmichael"; condensation
of special TV program on Today show.
Carmichael reminiscing, singing "Hong Kong
Blues" and "Old Buttermilk Sky". NBC,
April 24, 1964.
      1 reel (7 in.) 7 1/2 in. per sec.
phonotape.

      I. Title: Hong Kong blues. II. Title: Old
buttermilk sky.

Old Hickory, Andrew Jackson

C1
H30   Whorf, Michael, 1933-
      Old Hickory, Andrew Jackson.
      1 tape cassette. (The visual sounds of
Mike Whorf. History and heritage, H30)

      Originally presented on his radio program, Kaleidoscope,
WJR, Detroit.
      Duration: 30 min., 10 sec.
      The life of Andrew Jackson from his backwoods beginnings,
through his battles with Indians and British, to his service as
president.

      I. Jackson, Andrew, Pres. U.S., 1767-1845. L. Title.

Old man river

Voice Lib.
555   Robeson, Paul Bustill, 1898-
bd.2   Singing "Old Man River" from Showboat.
Victor, 1927.
      1 reel (7 in.) 7 1/2 in. per sec.
phonotape.

      I. Title: Old man river.

Old man river

Voice Lib.
555   Rollickers (radio quartet)
bd.3   Singing their arrangement of "Old Man
River". Edison, 1926.
      1 reel (7 in.) 7 1/2 in. per sec.
phonotape.

      I. Title: Old man river.

Old soldiers never die - General Douglas
    MacArthur

C1
H104- Whorf, Michael, 1933-
H105   Old soldiers never die - General Douglas
MacArthur.
      2 tape cassettes. (The visual sounds of
Mike Whorf. History and heritage, H104-H105)

      Originally presented on his radio program, Kaleidoscope,
WJR, Detroit.
      Duration: 37 min.; 37 min.
      Who was General MacArthur? This questions and others are
explored, and frequently answered in his own words in this two-part
series on one of our country's great military leaders.

      I. MacArthur, Douglas, 1880-1964. L. Title.

The old sweet songs

C1
PWM6 Whorf, Michael, 1933-
      The old sweet songs.
      1 tape cassette. (The visual sounds of
Mike Whorf. Panorama; a world of music, PWM-6)

      Originally presented on his radio program, Kaleidoscope,
WJR, Detroit.
      Duration: 26 min.
      The story and instrumental renditions of Greensleeves,
My Old Kentucky home, After the ball, and Mighty lak' a
rose.

      I. Music, Popular (Songs, etc.) - U.S. L. Title.

Voice Lib.
M1047 Old-time radio excerpts of the 1930's and
      1940's, including: Rudy Vallee singing
"Linger a little longer"; Will Rogers on
panaceas for the Depression; Bing Crosby
singing "Sweet Georgia Brown"; Eddie Cantor;
Jimmy Durante singing "Inka-dinka-do";
musical skit by Clayton, Jackson and Durante;
wit by Harry Hershfield; musical selection
"Thinking of you" by Kay Kyser; Kate Smith
singing theme song, "When the moon comes over
the mountain"; W.C. Fields' temperance

      (Continued on next card)

Voice Lib.
M1047 Old-time radio excerpts of the 1930's and
      1940's... (Card 2)

      lecture; Al Jolson singing "Rocka-by-your
baby"; and George Burns and Gracie Allen
skit. TV&R, 1930's and 1940's.
      1 reel (7 in.) 7 1/2 in. per sec.
      I. Vallee, Rudy, 1901- II. Rogers, Will, 1879-1935. III.
Crosby, Bing, 1901- IV. Cantor, Eddie, 1893-1964. V. Durante,
Jimmy, 1893- VI. Clayton, Patti VII. Jackson,
Eddie VIII. Hershfield, Harry, 1885- IX. Kyser, Kay,
1906- X. Smith, Kate, 1909- XI. Fields, W.C., 1879-
1946. XII. Jolson, Al, 1886-1950. XIII. Burns, George, 1896-
XIV. Allen, Gracie, 1906-

Voice Lib.
N793   Olde, Lewis
bd.1   Hobo Lewis reads his poetry and tells
        about life on the open road; narration by
        Bernard Mayes of Pacifica Radio in Berkeley.
        KPFK, December 4, 1964.
        21 min., 10 sec.   phonotape (1 r.
        7 1/2 i.p.s.)

        1. Tramps.   I. Mayes, Bernard.

Voice Lib.   Oliver, Terry
M1707   Harrell, Beverley
bd.2   Announcing her candidacy for the Nevada
        assembly, Terry Oliver, reporting.
        CBS, June 5, 1974.
        5 min.   phonotape (1 r.   7 1/2 i.p.s.)

        1. Nevada. Legislature - Elections.
        I. Oliver, Terry.

Voice Lib.
M1280   Olivier, Sir Laurence Kerr, 1907-
        A conversation at Expo 67, Montreal, with
        Sir Laurence Olivier discussing the National
        Theatre of Great Britain, his interpretation
        of Othello and of the techniques of acting.
        NET, July 30, 1967.
        1 reel (7 in.)   7 1/2 in. per sec.
        phonotape.

        1. Acting as a profession.

             Olivier, Sir Laurence Kerr, 1907-
Voice Lib.
M1037   Biography in sound (radio program)
bd.1   "The Actor", narrated by Morgan Beatty.
        Cast includes Tallulah Bankhead, Hy Gardner,
        Rocky Graziano, Arthur Miller, Uta Hagen,
        Jackie Cooper, Sir Laurence Olivier, Gad
        Gayther, Barbara Ashley, Hortense Powdermaker,
        Peter Ustinov, Alfred Hitchcock, Leonard Lyons,
        John Guston, Helen Hayes, Dick Mayne, Ralph
        Bellamy, Lionel Barrymore, Sir Ralph Richardson,
        José Ferrer, and Walter Kerr.   NBC Radio, 1950's
        1 reel (7 in.)   7 1/2 in. per sec.
        phonotape.
                        (Continued on next card)

             Olivier, Sir Laurence Kerr, 1907-
Voice Lib.
M225   Packard, Frederick
        Styles in Shakespearean acting, 1890-1950.
        Creative Associates, 1963?
        1 reel (7 in.) 7 1/2 i.p.s. phonotape.

        I. Sothern, Edward Askew, 1826-1881. II. Marlowe,
        Julia, 1865-1950. III. Booth, Edwin, 1833-1893. IV. Gielgud,
        John, 1904-   V. Robeson, Paul Bustill, 1898-   VI. Terry,
        Dame Ellen, 1848-1928. VII. Allen, Viola. VIII. Welles,
        Orson, 1915-   IX. Skinner, Otis, 1858-1942. X. Barrymore,
        John, 1882-1942. XI. Olivier, Sir Laurence Kerr, 1907-
        XII. Forbes-Robertson, Sir Johnston, 1853-   XIII. Evans,
        Maurice. XIV. Thorndike, Dame Sybil, 1882-   XV. Robson,
        Flora. XVI. LeGallienne, Eva, 1899-   XVII. Anderson,
        Judith. XVIII. Duncan, Augustin. XIX. Hampden, Walter.
        XX. Speaight, Robert, 1904-   XXI. Jones, Daniel.

Voice Lib.
N761   Olman, Abe
bd.3   Excerpt from "Whatever Happened to Tin Pan
        Alley?" (Program 3); composed "Down Among the
        Sheltering Palms" and "Oh, Johnny, Oh";
        comments on how he went about plugging songs.
        Westinghouse Broadcasting Corporation, 1964.
        1 reel (7 in.)   7 1/2 in. per sec.
        phonotape.   (The Music Goes Round and Round)

        I. Title: Whatever happened to Tin Pan Alley?
        II. Series.

Voice Lib.
N761   Olman, Abe
bd.15   Excerpt from "Tunesmiths Past and Present
        (Program 4); pessimistic outlook for present-
        day song writers.   Westinghouse Broadcasting
        Corporation, 1964.
        1 reel (7 in.)   7 1/2 in. per sec.
        phonotape.   (The Music Goes Round and Round)

        I. Title: Tunesmiths past and present.
        II. Series.

Voice Lib.
M1465   Olympic games, Berlin, 1936.
bd.1   Hitler opening Olympic Games in 1936
        and   description of proceedings.   Various
        German announcers make reports on events.
        Peteler, 1936.
        1 reel (7 in.)   7 1/2 in. per sec.
        phonotape.

        I. Hitler, Adolf, 1889-1945.

C1   OLYMPIC GAMES
M37   Whorf, Michael, 1933-
        The glory of the Grecian games.
        1 tape cassette.   (The visual sounds of
        Mike Whorf. Miscellaneous, M37)

        Originally presented on his radio program, Kaleidoscope,
        WJR, Detroit.
        Duration: 36 min.
        From antiquity comes this tale of gods and goddesses, of
        athletes who saluted the reigning deities and participated in
        peace coexistence. Since a Frenchman revived the games in the
        the 1800's, the contests have provided the world with fascinating
        spectacle.
        I. Olympic games.   I. Title.

             On a note of triumph
Voice Lib.
M1050- Corwin, Norman Lewis, 1910-
1051,   CBS Radio Workshop program "On a note of
bd.1   triumph", written and directed by Norman
        Corwin to celebrate Allied war victory in
        Europe.   CBS, May 13, 1945.
        2 reels (7 in.)   7 1/2 i.p.s.   phonotape.

        1. World War, 1939-1945.   I. Title: On
        a note of triumph.

O'NEILL, EUGENE GLADSTONE, 1888-1953.
Voice Lib.
M1092 A tribute to Eugene O'Neill; excerpt from
bd.2   his play "Anna Christie"; presented by
          the Speech Department, University of Cali-
          fornia at Berkeley. Bergman, 1963.
          1 reel (7 in.) 7 1/2 in. per sec.
          phonotape.

          I. O'Neill, Eugene Gladstone, 1888-1953./
          Anna Christie.

O'Neill, Eugene Gladstone, 1888-1953
          Mourning becomes Electra
Voice Lib.
M1092 A tribute to Eugene O'Neill, excerpt from
bd.3   his play "Mourning Becomes Electra";
          presented by the Speech Department, Univer-
          sity of California at Berkeley. Bergman,
          1963.
          1 reel (7 in.) 7 1/2 in. per sec.
          phonotape.

          I. O'Neill, Eugene Gladstone, 1888-1953./
          Mourning becomes Electra.

Voice Lib. O'NEILL, EUGENE GLADSTONE, 1888-1953
M1092 A tribute to Eugene O'Neill; excerpt from
bd.3   his play "Mourning Becomes Electra";
          presented by the Speech Department, Univer-
          sity of California at Berkeley. Bergman,
          1963.
          1 reel (7 in.) 7 1/2 in. per sec.
          phonotape.

          I. O'Neill, Eugene Gladstone, 1888-1953./
          Mourning becomes Electra.

          O'Neill, Eugene Gladstone, 1888-1953
          Strange interlude
Voice Lib.
M1092 A tribute to Eugene O'Neill; excerpt from
bd.4   his play "Strange Interlude"; presented
          by the Speech Department, University of
          California at Berkeley. Bergman, 1963.
          1 reel (7 in.) 7 1/2 in. per sec.
          phonotape.

          I. O'Neill, Eugene Gladstone, 1888-1953./
          Strange interlude.

Voice Lib. O'NEILL, EUGENE GLADSTONE, 1888-1953
M1092 A tribute to Eugene O'Neill; excerpt from
bd.4   his play "Strange Interlude"; presented
          by the Speech Department, University of
          California at Berkeley. Bergman, 1963.
          1 reel (7 in.) 7 1/2 in. per sec.
          phonotape.

          I. O'Neill, Eugene Gladstone, 1888-1953./
          Strange interlude.

Voice Lib.
M1720 O'Neill, Thomas P., 1912-
bd.1   Interview on Washington Straight Talk,
          by Paul Duke. WKAR-TV, June 11, 1974.
          30 min. phonotape (1 r. 7 1/2 i.p.s.)

          1. U.S. - Politics & government.
          2. Nixon, Richard Milhous, Pres. U.S., 1913-
          I. Duke, Paul.

          O'Neill, Eugene Gladstone, 1888-1953
          Anna Christie
Voice Lib.
M1092 A tribute to Eugene O'Neill; excerpt from
bd.2   his play "Anna Christie"; presented by
          the Speech Department, University of Cali-
          fornia at Berkeley. Bergman, 1963.
          1 reel (7 in.) 7 1/2 in. per sec.
          phonotape.

          I. O'Neill, Eugene Gladstone, 1888-1953./
          Anna Christie.

          Ong, Walter Jackson, 1912-
Voice Lib.
M976- Huxley, Aldous Leonard, 1894-1963.
977   Leading a discussion group at C.S.D.I. on
          ecological effects on technology, the
          tragic price we are paying for our conquest
          of nature. Other speakers: Ritchie Calder,
          Walter J. Ong, S.J., and Robert M. Hutchins,
          etc. March, 1962.
          2 reels (7 in.) 7 1/2 in. per sec. phonotape.

          I. Man - influence on nature. I. Calder, Ritchie, 1906-
          II. Ong, Walter Jackson, 1912- III. Hutchins, Robert
          Maynard, 1899-

          O'Neill, Eugene Gladstone, 1888-1953.
          Beyond the horizon
Voice Lib.
M1092 A tribute to Eugene O'Neill; excerpt from
bd.1   his play "Beyond the Horizon"; presented
          by the Speech Department, University of
          California at Berkeley. Bergman, 1963.
          1 reel (7 in.) 7 1/2 in. per sec.
          phonotape.

          I. O'Neill, Eugene Gladstone, 1888-1953./
          Beyond the horizon.

C1   Operetta memories
PWM5   Whorf, Michael, 1933-
          Operetta memories.
          1 tape cassette. (The visual sounds of
          Mike Whorf. Panorama; a world of music, PMW-5
          Originally presented on his radio program, Kaleidoscope.
          WJR, Detroit.
          Duration: 27 min., 45 sec.
          A history of operettas including excerpts from The merry
          widow and The chocolate soldier.

          I. Musical revues, comedies, etc. I. Title.

Voice Lib.
M389   Oppenheimer, Julius Robert, 1904-1967.
bd.2   Development of nuclear weapons; describes
        effect atomic bombs could have on U.S.,
        describes inability to develop a deterrent
        force. Hearst Metrotone News, 1963.
            1 reel (7 in.)   7 1/2 in. per sec.
        phonotape.

            1. Atomic weapons.

---

voice Lib. Ortega, Santos
M619   Radio in the 1930's (Part II): a series of
bd.1-   excerpts of the 1930's; a sample of radio
14   of the period. NVL, April, 1964.
            1 reel (7 in.) 7 1/2 in. per sec. phonotape.
            L Allen, Fred, 1.894-1956. II. Delmar, Kenny   III. Donald,
        Peter   IV. Pious, Minerva   V. Fennelly, Parker   VI.
        Boyer, Charles, 1899-   VII. Dunne, Irene, 1904-   VIII.
        DeMille, Cecil Blount, 1881-1959. IX. West, Mae, 1893-   X.
        Dafoe, Allan Ray, 1883-1943. XI. Dionne quintuplets. XII. Ortega,
        Santos   XIII. War of the worlds (radio program) XIV. Ives, Burl,
        1909-   XV. Robinson, Earl, 1910-   XVI. Temple, Shirley,
        1928-   XVII. Earhart, Amelia, 1898-1937. XVIII. Lawrence,
        Gertrude, 1901-1952. XIX. Cohan, George Michael, 1878-1942.
        XX. Shaw, George Bernard, 1856-1950. XXI. Hitler, Adolf, 1889-
        1945. XXII. Chamberlain, Neville, 1869-1940. XXIII. Roosevelt,
        Franklin Delano, Pres. U.S., 1882-1945.

VOICE LIBRARY
D
16   Oral history.
.07   no.1-
        Colchester, University of Essex, Dept. of
        Sociology, 1972-
            no.   irreg.

        Journal of the Oral History Society, 1974-

            1. Oral history - Period. I. University of
        Essex. Dept. of Sociology. II. Oral History
        Society.

CHECK LIST

Voice Lib.
M1379   Osgood, Charles
bd.4   Interviewing Sy Leaderman, blind man, who
        bowls 247 in a league where all others have
        sight. CBS Morning News, February 21, 1974.
            2 min., 15 sec. phonotape (1 r.   7 1/2
        i.p.s.)

            1. Blind. 2. Physically handicapped.
        I. Leaderman, Sy.

Voice Lib.
M990-   Organized Crime: a 3 1/2 hour documentary
995   NBC White Paper TV program. Many actual
        voices and sounds. NBC
            6 reels (7 in.)   7 1/2 in. per sec.
        phonotape.

            1. Crime and criminals - U.S.

Voice Lib.
M392   Oswald, Lee Harvey, 1939-1963.
bd.2   Interview with Oswald on WDSU-TV in New
        Orleans, Louisiana in 1963, while he was
        active in pro-Castro Cuban activity.
        Segment of "Today" show. NBC-TV, December 27,
        1966.
            1 reel (7 in.)   7 1/2 in. per sec.
        phonotape.

        The original big-little book
C1
A38   Whorf, Michael, 1933-
            The original big-little book.
            1 tape cassette. (The visual sounds of
        Mike Whorf. Art, music and letters, A38)
            Originally presented on his radio program, Kaleidoscope,
        WJR, Detroit.
            Duration: 40 min.
            Here is the story of the Reader's digest, the people who write it,
        why they write it and how this popular magazine is compiled.

            I. The Reader's digest. 2. Wallace, DeWitt, 1889-
        I. Title.

        OSWALD, LEE HARVEY, 1939-1963
Voice Lib.
M313   American Broadcasting Company.
bd.2   Descriptions of preparations of transfer
        of Oswald from Municipal Jail in Dallas.
        ABC, November 24, 1963.
            1 reel (7 in.)   7 1/2 in. per sec.
        phonotape.

            1. Oswald, Lee Harvey, 1939-1963. 2.
        Kennedy, John Fitzgerald, Pres. U.S., 1917-
        1963 - Assassination.

Voice Lib.
M853   Orphans of divorce (radio program).   NBC,
bd.2   June 7, 1940.
            1 reel (7 in.)   7 1/2 in. per sec.
        phonotape.

            1. Radio serials.

        OSWALD, LEE HARVEY, 1939-1963
Voice Lib.
M313   American Broadcasting Company.
bd.3   Transfer and shooting of Oswald in
        basement of police station; interviews
        with spectators and Policeman Dean in
        Dallas. ABC, November 24, 1963.
            1 reel (7 in.)   7 1/2 in. per sec.
        phonotape.

            1. Oswald, Lee Harvey, 1939-1963. 2.
        Kennedy, John Fitzgerald, Pres. U.S., 1917-
        1963 - Assassination.

Voice Lib. OSWALD, LEE HARVEY, 1939-1963
M314   American Broadcasting Company.
  bd.1   Assassination: on death of Oswald.   Dallas,
        WFAA-TV (ABC), November 24, 1963.
          1 reel (7 in.)   7 1/2 i.p.s.   phonotape.

          1. Oswald, Lee Harvey, 1939-1963.

                Our legacy from Mr. Jefferson
C1
H11   Whorf, Michael, 1933-
          Our legacy from Mr. Jefferson.
          1 tape cassette.   (The visual sounds of
        Mike Whorf. History and heritage, H11)
          Originally presented on his radio program, Kaleidoscope,
        WJR, Detroit
          Duration: 38 min.
          This historical account follows him through his years as a young
        Virginia scholar influenced by Patrick Henry to his days as a patriot
        who left a legacy to each and every American.

          I. Jefferson, Thomas, Pres. U.S., 1743-1826. I. Title.

            OSWALD, LEE HARVEY, 1939-1963
Voice Lib.
M309   Columbia Broadcasting System, inc.
  bd.5   On shooting of Oswald and description
        of identity of assassin.   CBS, November
        24, 1963.
          1 reel (7 in.)   7 1/2 in. per sec.
        phonotape.

          1. Oswald, Lee Harvey, 1939-1963.

Voice Lib.
353   Outbreak of Korean War and comments by
  bd.18   various persons.   NBC, July, 1950.
          1 reel (7 in.)   7 1/2 in. per sec.
        phonotape.

          Original disc off-speed.
          Participants: Henry Cassidy, Merrill Mueller,
        Edward Harper, Jack Bregon.

          I. Cassidy, Henry Clarence, 1910-   II.
        Mueller, Merrill. III. Harper, Edward. IV.
        Bregon, Jack.   1. Korean War, 1950-1953.

            OSWALD, LEE HARVEY, 1939-1963
Voice Lib.
M309   Columbia Broadcasting System, inc.
  bd.6   Recount of events, slow-motion replay
        of assassination of Oswald.   CBS,
        November 24, 1963.
          1 reel (7 in.)   7 1/2 in. per sec.
        phonotape.

          1. Oswald, Lee Harvey, 1939-1963.

            OUTER SPACE - EXPLORATION
Voice Lib.
M1233-   U.S. Congress. Senate. Special Committee
1235,   on Astronautics and Space Exploration.
  bd.1   Discussion between various U.S. Senators
        on Space Committee and astronauts and NASA
        officials regarding their opinions and
        experiences.   Voice of America, March 1,
        1962.
          3 reels (7 in.)   7 1/2 i.p.s.   phonotape.

          1. Outer space - Exploration.

            OSWALD, LEE HARVEY, 1939-1963
Voice Lib.
M311   National Broadcasting Company, inc.
  bd.2   Assassination: report on activities in
        Washington the following morning, news
        from Dallas on Oswald.   NBC, November
        23, 1963.
          1 reel (7 in.)   7 1/2 in. per sec.
        phonotape.

          1. Kennedy, John Fitzgerald, Pres. U.S.,
        1917-1963 - Assassination. 2. Oswald, Lee
        Harvey, 1939-1963.

            "Over There"
Voice Lib.
603   Bayes, Nora
  bd.1   "Over There"; sings original recording of
        George M. Cohan's World War I song.   Victor
        Talking Machine Co., 1917.
          1 reel (7 in.)   7 1/2 in. per sec.
        phonotape.

          I. Title.

Voice Lib. OSWALD, LEE HARVEY, 1939-1963
M315   Wade, Henry M.
  bd.5   Report of District Attorney Henry Wade
        of Dallas County; Wade's statement at news
        conference on Oswald case.   NBC, November
        24, 1963.
          1 reel (7 in.)   7 1/2 in. per sec.
        phonotape.

          1. Kennedy, John Fitzgerald, Pres. U.S.,
        1917-1963 - Assassination. 2. Oswald, Lee
        Harvey, 1939-1963.

            "Over There"
Voice Lib.
603   Caruso, Enrico, 1873-1921.
  bd.2   "Over There"; sings George M. Cohan's
        World War I song (first verse in English,
        second in French).   Victor Talking Machine
        Co., 1917.
          1 reel (7 in.)   7 1/2 in. per sec.
        phonotape.

          I. Title.

Overacher, Ronald Leroy
Voice Lib.
M322 Biography in sound (radio program)
W.C. Fields, the magnificent rogue.
NBC, 1955.
1 reel (7 in.) 7 1/2 in. per sec. phonotape.
I. Fields, W.C., 1879-1946. I. Fields, W.C., 1879-1946.
II. Allen, Fred, 1894-1956. III. LaBaron, William IV.
Taylor, Robert Lewis, 191.- V. McCarey, Thomas Leo, 1898-
1969. VI. Harkins, James - VII. Chevalier, Maurice,
1889-1972. VIII. Kuromoto, Mrs. George IX. Flynn,
Errol Leslie, 1909-1959. X. Wynn, Ed, 1886-1966. XI. Dowling,
Ray Dooley XII. Sennett, Mack XIII. Overacher,
Ronald Leroy XIV. Bergen, Edgar, 1903- XV. Taurog,
Norman, 1899- XVI. Russell, Ann XVII. Cowen,
Lester

Voice Lib. Overton, Watkins
383 I can hear it now (radio program)
CBS, February 9, 1951.
1 reel (7 in.) 7 1/2 in. per sec. phonotape.
I. Wilson, Charles Edward, 1886-1972. II. Gabrielson, Guy
George, 1891- III. Taft, Robert Alphonso, 1889-1953. IV.
Martin, Joseph William, 1884-1968. V. McCarthy, Joseph
Raymond, 1909-1957. VI. Benton, William Burnett, 1900-1973.
VII. Malone, George Wilson, 1890-1961. VIII. Capehart, Homer
Earl, 1897- IX. Eisenhower, Dwight David, Pres. U.S., 1890-
1969. X. Lee, J V XI. Hodge, John Reed, 1893-
1963. XII. Overton, Watkins XIII. DiSalle, Michael
Vincent, 1908- XIV. Boyce, Eddy XV. Conklin, Ed
XVI. Collins, Joseph Lawton, 1896-

Voice Lib. Owen, Gary M., 1944-
M1579 Third Civic Presence Group/Legislative
bd.1 luncheon, with Craig Halverson, Lynn
Jondahl, Gary Owen, Phil Mastin, and
Iris Gentile. WKAR-TV, February 15, 1973.
10 min. phonotape (1 r. 7 1/2 i.p.s.)

1. Physically handicapped - Law and legis-
lation. I. Halverson, Craig. II. Jondahl,
E. Lynn, 1936- III. Owen, Gary M., 1944-
IV. Mastin, Philip O., 1930- V. Gentile,
Iris Anton, 1943-

Voice Lib. Owen, John
M1665 Hunt, Everette Howard, 1918-
On "Firing line" about Watergate payments,
with William Buckley, Ralph Fine, John Owen,
and Miss Bernstein. WKAR-TV, May 14, 1974.
50 min. phonotape (1 r. 7 1/2 i.p.s.)

1. Watergate Affair, 1972- I.
Buckley, William Frank, 1925- II. Fine,
Ralph Adam, 1941- III. Owen, John

Voice Lib.
M975 Oxford and Asquith, Herbert Henry Asquith,
bd.1 1st earl of, 1852-1928.
Speech on the budget. Rococo, 1909.
1 reel (7 in.) 7 1/2 in. per sec. phonotape.

Paar, Jack Harold, 1918-
Voice Lib.
565 Kennedy, John Fitzgerald, Pres. U.S., 1917-1963.
bd.1 Jack Paar Show: Tribute to President John
F. Kennedy. Series of quotes accumulated
from various press conferences of President,
recorded between 1961 and 1963. NBC, March
13, 1964.
1 reel (7 in.) 7 1/2 in. per sec.
phonotape.

I. Paar, Jack Harold, 1918-

Paar, Jack Harold, 1918-
Voice Lib.
M998 Kennedy, John Fitzgerald, Pres. U.S., 1917-
1963.
The John F. Kennedy humor; one-hour television broadcast with Jack Parr as Master
of Ceremonies. ABC, October 5, 1966.
1 reel (7 in.) 7 1/2 in. per sec.
phonotape.

I. Paar, Jack Harold, 1918-

Pacelli, Eugenio [secular name]
see
Pius XII, Pope, 1876-1958.

VOICE LIBRARY

Voice Lib.
M228 Packard, Frederick
Styles in Shakespearean acting, 1890-1950.
Creative Associates, 1963?
1 reel (7 in.) 7 1/2 i.p.s. phonotape.

I. Sothern, Edward Askew, 1826-1881. II. Marlowe,
Julia, 1865-1950. III. Booth, Edwin, 1833-1893. IV. Gielgud,
John, 1904- V. Robeson, Paul Bustill, 1898- VI. Terry,
Dame Ellen, 1848-1928. VII. Allen, Viola, VIII. Welles,
Orson, 1915- IX. Skinner, Otis, 1858-1942. X. Barrymore,
John, 1882-1942. XI. Olivier, Sir Laurence Kerr, 1907-
XII. Forbes-Robertson, Sir Johnston, 1853- XIII. Evans,
Maurice, XIV. Thorndike, Dame Sybil, 1882- XV. Robson,
Flora. XVI. LeGallienne, Eva, 1899- XVII. Anderson,
Judith. XVIII. Duncan, Augustin. XIX. Hampden, Walter,
XX. Speaight, Robert, 190? XXI. Jones, Daniel.

Voice Lib.
396 Paderewski, Ignacy Jan, 1860-1941.
bd.2 Speech to U.S. people (shortwave
broadcast from Switzerland). NBC,
April 16, 1940.
1 reel (7 in.) 7 1/2 in. per sec.
phonotape.

Paine, Thomas Otten, 1921-
Voice Lib.
M1391   Apollo 11 (space flight): reception of Apollo 11 astronauts at
bd.1   United Nations Plaza. Statement by U. N. Secretary-
General U Thant. Reply by Neil Armstrong. Presentation
of tokens of appreciation to all three astronauts and their
wives and Dr. Thomas Paine. Presentation of duplicate of
plaque left on moon to U Thant. NBC TV, August 13, 1969.
1 reel (7 in.)   7 1/2 in. per sec.   phonotape.
    1. Project Apollo. 2. Space flight to the moon. 3. Aldrin,
Edwin E   1930-   4. Collins, Michael, 1930-   5.
Armstrong, Neil, 1930-   I. Aldrin, Edwin E   1930-
II. Collins, Michael, 1930-   III. Armstrong, Neil, 1930-
IV. Thant, U, 1909-   V. Paine, Thomas Otten, 1921-

Paine, Thomas Otten, 1921-
Voice Lib.
M1403   Apollo 12 (space flight): lift-off of Apollo
bd.1   12; the electrical "glitch" and instructions
and corrections; Dr. Paine and President
Nixon speaking from VIP section.   CBS TV,
November 19, 1969.
    1 reel (7 in.)   7 1/2 in. per sec.
phonotape.
    1. Project Apollo. 2. Space flight to the moon. 3. Conrad,
Charles, 1930-   4. Bean, Alan L   1932-   5. Gordon,
Richard F   1929-   I. Conrad, Charles, 1930-   II. Bean,
Alan L   1932-   III. Gordon, Richard F   1929-   IV.
Paine, Thomas Otten, 1921-   V. Nixon, Richard Milhous, Pres.
U. S., 1913-

Painter of the plains
C1·
A4   Whorf, Michael, 1933-
Painter of the plains.
1 tape cassette.   (The visual sounds of
Mike Whorf. Art, music, and letters, A4)

Originally presented on his radio program, Kaleidoscope,
WJR, Detroit.
Duration 30 min.
Those who never saw the American West in its greatness can
thank the creativeness of Frederic Remington, who seemed to know
that a way of life, a people, and a time would quickly vanish,
and so he captured it on canvas.
    1. Remington, Frederic   1861-1909. I. Title.

Voice Lib.
529   Palmer, Alexander Mitchell, 1872-
bd.3   The Democratic Party and the conclusion
of World War I; Americans and their courageous
action during World War I, importance of
mixing party philosophies in time of war.
Nation's Forum, 1920.
    1 reel (7 in.)   7 1/2 in. per sec.
phonotape.

Palmer, George
Voice Lib.
M273-   Biography in sound (radio program)
274   Franklin Delano Roosevelt: the friends and
bd.1   former associates of Franklin Roosevelt on
the tenth anniversary of the President's death.
NBC Radio, April, 1955.
    2 reels (7 in.)   7 1/2 in. per sec.
phonotape.
    1. Roosevelt, Franklin Delano, Pres. U. S., 1882-1945. I.
McIntire, Ross T   1899-   II. Mellett, Lowell, 1884-1960.
III. Tully, Grace   IV. Henderson, Leon, 1895-
V. Roosevelt, Eleanor (Roosevelt) 1884-1962. VI. DeGraaf, Albert
VII. Lehman, Herbert Henry, 1878-1963. VIII. Rosenman, Samuel
Irving, 1896-   IX. Arvey, Jacob   X. Moley, Raymond,
1886-   XI. Farley, James Aloysius, 1888-   XII. Roosevelt,
(Continued on next card)

PANAMA
Voice Lib.
M816-   The Panama crisis, outlook and prospects.
817   A panel discussion sponsored by UCLA's
Latin American Studies Center. Recorded
by Carlos Hagen and edited by David Wolfe.
KPFK, May 17, 1964.
    2 reels (7 in.)   7 1/2 in. per sec.
phonotape.

Voice Lib.
M816-   The Panama crisis, outlook and prospects.
817   A panel discussion sponsored by UCLA's
Latin American Studies Center. Recorded
by Carlos Hagen and edited by David Wolfe.
KPFK, May 17, 1964.
    2 reels (7 in.)   7 1/2 in. per sec.
phonotape.

    1. Panama

Pandit, Vijaya Lakshmi (Nehru) 1900-
Voice Lib.
385   I can hear it now (radio program)
CBS, February 2, 1951.
    1 reel (7 in.)   7 1/2 in. per sec.
phonotape.

    I. Austin, Warren Robinson, 1877-1962. II.
Pandit, Vijaya Lakshmi (Nehru) 1900-   III.
Roosevelt, Eleanor (Roosevelt) 1884-1962. IV.
Morse, Wayne Lyman, 1900-   V. Chandler,
Albert Benjamin, 1898-   VI. Taylor, Telford,
1908-   VII. Whit   Jack.

Voice Lib.
M1363   Papen, Franz von, 1879-1969.
bd.6   Excerpt of radio election speech.
Peteler, 1932.
    1 reel (7 in.)   7 1/2 in. per sec.
phonotape.

Voice Lib.
M1470   Papen, Franz von, 1879-1969.
bd.7   Speaking about the political situation
in the German province of Prussia and
announcing his appointment as commissioner
for the province. Peteler, July 20, 1933.
    1 reel (7 in.)   7 1/2 in. per sec.
phonotape.

    1. Germany - Politics and government -
1933-1945

PARIS - HISTORY - 1940-1944
Voice Lib.
M543
bd.2 Liberation of Paris. Radio Diffusion de
la Nation Française, August 25, 1944.
1 reel (7 in.) 7 1/2 i.p.s. phonotape.

1. Paris - History - 1940-1944.

Parker, Dorothy (Rothschild) 1893-1967
Voice Lib.
515 Leighton, Margaret, 1922-
Dramatic readings from the works of
Dorothy Parker, from Festival of Performing
Arts. Talent Associates, May 8, 1962.
1 reel (7 in.) 7 1/2 in. per sec.
phonotape.
CONTENTS.-bd.1. Poem.-bd.2. Telephone call
(dramatic reading).-bd.3. A lovely leave
(dramatic reading).

1. Parker, Dorothy (Rothschild) 1893-1967.

Parker, Dorothy (Rothschild) 1893-1967
Voice Lib.
516
bd.1 Leighton, Margaret, 1922-
Dramatic readings from the works of
Dorothy Parker, from Festival of Performing
Arts. Talent Associates, May 8, 1962.
1 reel (7 in.) 7 1/2 in. per sec.
phonotape.
CONTENTS.-Dusk before fireworks.

1. Parker, Dorothy (Rothschild) 1893-1967.

Parker, William H., 1902-
Voice Lib.
M910- Stout, Bill
911,
bd.1 Resumé of the Watts riots in Los Angeles
County, during the most violent riots in Los
Angeles history; including actual sounds and
voices of Police Chief William H. Parker,
Mayor Yorty, etc. CBS, August, 1965.
2 reels (7 in.) 7 1/2 i.p.s. phonotape.

1. Los Angeles - Riots, 1965. I. Parker,
William H., 1902- II. Yorty, Samuel
William, 1909-

Voice Lib.
M1611
bd.5 Parks, Rosa Lee
Montgomery, Alabama, bus test case.
WKAR-TV [1974?]
9 min. phonotape (1 r. 7 1/2 i.p.s.)

1. Negroes - Civil rights.

PASSIVE RESISTANCE TO GOVERNMENT
Voice Lib.
M1663 Powell, Adam Clayton, 1908-1972.
Speech to Great Issues Class at MSU,
co-sponsored by ASMSU. WKAR, January 17,
1969.
35 min., 30 sec. phonotape (1 r.
7 1/2 i.p.s.)

1. Passive resistance to government.
2. U.S. - Politics and government.

PATRICK, SAINT, 373?-463?
C1
R33 Whorf, Michael, 1933-
The Irish saint, St. Patrick.
1 tape cassette. (The visual sounds of
Mike Whorf. Religion, R33)
Originally presented on his radio program, Kaleidoscope,
WJR, Detroit.
Duration: 37 min.
From a life shrouded in myth and legend, emerges the
story of the patron saint of Ireland, Saint Patrick.

1. Patrick, Saint, 373?-463? I. Title.

The patriot, Patrick Henry
C1
H3 Whorf, Michael, 1933-
The patriot, Patrick Henry.
1 tape cassette. (The visual sounds of
Mike Whorf. History and heritage, H3)
Originally presented on his radio program, Kaleidoscope,
WJR, Detroit.
Duration: 28 min.
From his humble beginnings - to his days as barrister - to
his appointment in Virginia's House of Burgesses, there was about
him the qualities of the patriot.

1. Henry, Patrick, 1736-1799. I. Title.

PATRIOTIC MUSIC, AMERICAN
C1
PWM19 Whorf, Michael, 1933-
It's a grand old flag.
1 tape cassette. (The visual sounds of
Mike Whorf. Panorama; a world of music,
PWM-19)
Originally presented on his radio program, Kaleidoscope,
WJR, Detroit.
Duration: 25 min.
The story of the American flag, with selected patriotic
music.

1. Flags. 2. Patriotic music, American. I. Title.

PATRIOTIC MUSIC, AMERICAN
C1
M18 Whorf, Michael, 1933-
The splendid Americans.
1 tape cassette. (The visual sounds of
Mike Whorf. Miscellaneous, M18)
Originally presented on his radio program, Kaleidoscope,
WJR, Detroit.
Duration: 54 min., 30 sec.
This is the story of those who wrote the songs of a nation and
a people, songs which gave a different kind of courage to the
people.

1. Bates, Katherine Lee, 1859-1929. 2. Key, Francis Scott,
1779-1929. 3. Patriotic music, American. I. Title.

C1
H5
PATRIOTIC POETRY

Whorf, Michael, 1933–
   The voice of the patriot.
   1 tape cassette. (The visual sounds of
Mike Whorf. History and heritage, H5)

   Originally presented on his radio program, Kaleidoscope,
WJR, Detroit.
   Duration: 46 min., 30 sec.
   Here are poems of devotion and love expressed by those who
lived through perilous and difficult times, and these words are
the living testimony of a nation's struggle.

   L Patriotic poetry. L Title.

C1
R3
PAUL, SAINT, APOSTLE

Whorf, Michael, 1933–
   The apostle.
   1 tape cassette. (The visual sounds of
Mike Whorf. Religion, R3)

   Originally presented on his radio program, Kaleidoscope,
WJR, Detroit.
   Duration: 35 min., 30 sec.
   Paul of Tarsus was a man who persecuted and tormented the early
believers of the Christian following. Yet he would one day become
one of them and bring organization and firmness to the early church.

   L Paul, Saint, apostle. L Title.

Voice Lib.
M258
bd.9A
PATTERSON, JOHN MALCOLM, 1921–
Harper, Robert
   Report to CBS News, New York; description
of Gov. Patterson's (Alabama) reaction to
the federal protection of Rev. Martin Luther
King. New York, CBS, May 22, 1961.
   1 reel (7 in.) 7 1/2 in. per sec.
phonotape.

   1. Patterson, John Malcolm, 1921–   2.
King, Martin Luther, 1929-1968.

Voice Lib.
M389
bd.6
Pauling, Linus Carl, 1901–
   Development of nuclear weapons; foresees
future for world if atomic testing continues,
tells of his suit against the nations of the
world. Hearst Metrotone News, 1963.
   1 reel (7 in.) 7 1/2 in. per sec.
phonotape.

   1. Atomic weapons

Voice Lib.
M1430
bd.2
Patterson, Robert Porter, 1891-1952.
   In address "Labor for victory". AFL-
CIO PRO, April 18, 1942.
   1 reel (7 in.) 7 1/2 i.p.s. phonotape.

   1. Labor and laboring classes – U.S.

Voice Lib.
M979
bd.1
Pauling, Linus Carl, 1901–
   In discussion with Dr. Krauch at Center
for the Study of Democratic Institutions,
recalling creative processes in his
discoveries. CSDI, 1963.
   1 reel (7 in.) 7 1/2 in. per sec.
phonotape.

   I. Krauch, Helmut.

C1
H34
PATTON, GEORGE SMITH, 1885-1945

Whorf, Michael, 1933–
   Patton.
   1 tape cassette. (The visual sounds of
Mike Whorf. History and heritage, H34)

   Originally presented on his radio program, Kaleidoscope,
WJR, Detroit.
   Duration: 54 min.
   A cavalry officer in W. W. I, a tank commander in the
second global holocaust, here is the story of the brilliant bold
general who led his armament against Rommel in Africa, and
fought one of the great campaigns shortly before the end of W. W. II.

   L Patton, George Smith 5-1945. L Title.

Voice Lib.
M970
Pauling, Linus Carl, 1901–
   A visit with the Paulings; informal talk
with Dr. and Mrs. Pauling about their courtship, their work, the role of women,
amusing Kennedy anecdote, questioning by
Frank K. Kelly. CSDI, 1964.
   1 reel (7 in.) 7 1/2 in. per sec.
phonotape.

   1. Pauling, Linus Carl, 1901–
   I. Kelly, Frank K   1914–

C1
H34
Patton

Whorf, Michael, 1933–
   Patton.
   1 tape cassette. (The visual sounds of
Mike Whorf. History and heritage, H34)

   Originally presented on his radio program, Kaleidoscope,
WJR, Detroit.
   Duration: 54 min.
   A cavalry officer in W. W. I, a tank commander in the
second global holocaust, here is the story of the brilliant bold
general who led his armament against Rommel in Africa, and
fought one of the great campaigns shortly before the end of W. W. II.

   L Patton, George Smith 85-1945. L Title.

Voice Lib.
M1734
Pauling, Linus Carl, 1901–
   Orthomolecular medicine; address given at
Michigan State University. WKAR, April 19,
1972.
   50 min. phonotape (1 r. 7 1/2 i.p.s.)

   1. Ascorbic acid. 2. Diet. 3. Human
genetics.

Voice Lib.
M1671   Pauling, Linus Carl, 1901-
           Vitamin C and the common cold; controversy
         and harassment. WKAR, April 20, 1972.
           50 min. phonotape (1 r.   7 1/2 i.p.s.)

           1. Cold (Disease) 2. Ascorbic acid.

Voice Lib.
M1676   Pauling, Linus Carl, 1901-
           Abnormal hemoglobin molecules in relation
         to disease; address at Michigan State
         University. WKAR, April 21, 1972.
           45 min.   phonotape (1 r.   7 1/2 i.p.s.)

           1. Hemoglobinopathy.

Voice Lib.
M823-   Paulus VI, Pope, 1897-
824   The Pope's visit to the United States;
         High Mass for peace, held at Yankee Stadium,
         New York. Description and sound of
         ceremonies. NBC, October 4, 1965.
           2 reels (7 in.)   7 1/2 in. per sec.
         phonotape.

Voice Lib.
M841   Paulus VI, Pope, 1897-
           Address of His Holiness Pope Paul VI at
         the UN General Assembly. Official English
         translation. U.N. Archives, October 4, 1965.
           1 reel (7 in.)   7 1/2 in. per sec.
         phonotape.

Voice Lib.
M842   Paulus VI, Pope, 1897-
           Address of His Holiness Pope Paul VI at
         the UN General Assembly, speaking in French.
         UN Archives, October 4, 1965.
           1 reel (7 in.)   7 1/2 in. per sec.
         phonotape.

Voice Lib.
M818   Paulus VI, Pope, 1897-
           The Pope's visit to the United States.
         CBS, October 4, 1965.
           1 reel (7 in.)   7 1/2 in. per sec.
         phonotape.

           CONTENTS.-a. statement by Bill Moyers,
         White House press officer, on meeting between
         the Pope and U.S. President Johnson at
         Waldorf Astoria Hotel in New York.-b. des-
         cription of arrival of Pope Paul VI at
                                    (Continued on next card)

Voice Lib.
M818   Paulus VI, Pope, 1897-   The Pope's
           visit to the United States.   October 4,
         1965. (Card 2)

           CONTENTS, cont'd.-the U.N. in New York.-
         c. description of Pope entering assembly
         chamber.-d. remarks by President of the
         General Assembly of the U.N. Fanfani.-
         e. remarks by Secretary General of the U.N.
         U Thant.-f. address by Pope Paul VI at the
         United Nations.

Voice Lib.   Paulus VI, Pope, 1897-
M1386   Apollo 11 (space flight): blessing by Pope
bd.2   Paul VI from the Vatican to Apollo 11
         astronauts.   CBS TV, July 20, 1969.
           1 reel (7 in.)   7 1/2 in. per sec.
         phonotape.

           1. Project Apollo. 2. Space flight to the
         moon. 3. Aldrin, Edwin E   1930-   4.
         Collins, Michael, 1930-   5. Armstrong, Neil,
         1930-   I. Aldrin, Edwin E   1930-   II.
         Collins, Michael, 1930-   III. Armstrong, Neil,
         1930-   IV. Paulus VI, Pope, 1897-

                      PEACE
Voice Lib.
M1744   Luns, Joseph Marie Antoine Hubert, 1911-
bd.2   At the signing of the Brussels Pact, on
         the "Today Show". WTLX-TV, June 25, 1974.
           2 min. phonotape (1 r.   7 1/2 i.p.s.)

           1. Peace. 2. Disarmament.

                      PEACE
Voice Lib.
M1076   Spaak, Paul Henri Charles, 1899-1972.
           Convocation of representatives of twenty
         nations on the requirements for peace, held
         at General Assembly hall of the United
         Nations; discussion of Pope John XXIII
         encyclical; Germany's re-unification, etc.,
         under auspices of Center for Democratic
         Institutions. CSDI, February, 1965.
           1 reel (7 in.)   7 1/2 in. per sec.
         phonotape.

C1
R32
PEALE, NORMAN VINCENT, 1898-
Whorf, Michael, 1933-
   Minister to millions - Norman Vincent Peale.
   1 tape cassette.   (The visual sounds of
Mike Whorf.   Religion, R32)
     Originally presented on his radio program, Kaleidoscope,
WJR, Detroit.
     Duration: 57 min., 30 sec.
     Norman Vincent Peale, remembered as the author of The
power of positive thinking, is a man of varied accomplishments,
some well-known, others which go almost unnoticed.

     L. Peale, Norman Vincent, 1898-   L. Title.

Voice Lib.
541
bd.1
Peary, Robert Edwin, 1856-1920.
   Address to Peary Arctic Club in New York;
log of voyage of S.S. "Roosevelt" and adventures
in discovery of the North Pole; introductory
remarks by Robert Bartlett.   Edison, 1909.
   1 reel (7 in.)   7 1/2 in. per sec.
phonotape.

     I. Bartlett, Robert Abram, 1875-1946.

Voice Lib.
M209
bd.4
PEARL HARBOR, ATTACK ON, 1941
Daly, John Charles, 1914-
   New York Philharmonic interrupted to
announce attack on Pearl Harbor.   CBS,
December 7, 1941.
   1 reel (7 in.)   7 1/2 i.p.s.   phonotape.

     1. Pearl Harbor, Attack on, 1941.

Voice Lib.
654
bd.2
PEARY, ROBERT EDWIN, 1856-1920
Cook, Frederick Albert, 1865-1940.
   "How I Reached the North Pole".
Description of Dr. Cook's preparations
and journey on Arctic expedition, 1909.
Source(?), [n.d.]
   1 reel (7 in.)   7 1/2 in. per sec.
phonotape.

     1. Arctic regions.   2. Peary, Robert Edwin,
1856-1920.

C1
H25
PEARL HARBOR, ATTACK ON, 1941
Whorf, Michael, 1933-
   There are some days you don't forget - Pearl
Harbor.
   1 tape cassette.   (The visual sounds of
Mike Whorf.   History and heritage, H25)
     Originally presented on his radio program, Kaleidoscope,
WJR, Detroit.
     Duration: 42 min., 50 sec.
     December 7th, 1941 - from out of the skies came the enemy at
8 o'clock Sunday morning - less than an hour later they had gone,
leaving in their wake wreckage and death.

     L. Pearl Harbor, Attack on, 1941. L. Title.

Voice Lib.
M671
bd.2
Peck, Gregory, 1916-
Kennedy, John Fitzgerald, Pres. U.S., 1917-1963.
   "Years of Lightning, Day of Drums";
excerpts of comments by JFK on Peace Corps,
Alliance for Progress, space race, Civil
Rights.   Narrated by Gregory Peck.   Voice
of America, 1964.
   1 reel (7 in.)   7 1/2 in. per sec.
phonotape.

     I. Peck, Gregory, 1916-   II. Title.

Voice Lib.
M1221
bd.1
Pearl Harbor to Vietnam; BBC documentary
TV program of actual voices and events
during the 25-year period from 1941 to
1966.   BBC, December, 1966.
   1 reel (7 in.)   7 1/2 i.p.s.   phonotape.

     1. Civilization.

Voice Lib.
603
bd.7
Peerless Quartet.
   "America, Here's My Boy", World War I song.
Victor Talking Machine Company, 1917.
   1 reel (7 in.)   7 1/2 in. per sec.
phonotape.

     I. Title.

Voice Lib.
654
bd.1
Peary, Robert Edwin, 1856-1920.
   Address before leaving for the North
Pole in 1905.   Incentives of the explorer
to reach new frontiers.   Moran, July 13,
1905.
   1 reel (7 in.)   7 1/2 in. per sec.
phonotape.

Voice Lib.
M611
bd.4
Peerless Quartet.
   World War I song "Liberty bell (it's time
to ring again)".   Victor Talking Machine
Co., 1917.
   1 reel (7 in.)   7 1/2 i.p.s.   phonotape.

     1. European War, 1914-1918 - Songs and
music.   I. Title: Liberty bell (it's time
to ring again.)

Voice Lib.
M1476   Pentagon Papers.
bd.2   New York times, Washington post, U.S.
         Government arguments before the Supreme
         Court, as represented by CBS News.
         Daniel Schorr (government), Marvin Kalb
         (New York times), Bob Sheafer (Washington
         post), Roger Mudd. CBS-TV, June 26, 1971.
            1 reel (7 in.) 7 1/2 i.p.s. phonotape.

            I. Security classification (Government documents)
         L Schorr, Daniel Louis, 1916-   II. Kalb, Marvin L
         III. Sheafer, Bob   IV. Mudd, Roger

          PENTAGON PAPERS
Voice Lib.
M1477 Discussion of Supreme Court decision on
        publishing Pentagon Papers. William B.
        Macomber, deputy under-secretary of state;
        Senator Henry Jackson; Max Frankel, head of
        New York Times' Washington bureau; Benjamin
        Bradley, executive editor of Washington Post.
        Questioned by Carl Stern, NBC; Martin Hayden,
        Detroit News; James J. Kilpatrick, Washington
        Star Syndicate; Kenneth Crawford, Washington
        Post; Edwin Newman.   NBC-TV, June 30, 1971.
           1 reel (7 in.)   7 1/2 in. per sec.
        phonotape.

                        (Continued on next card)

          PENTAGON PAPERS
Voice Lib.
M1475- Rusk, Dean, 1909-
1476,   Dean Rusk, former Secretary of State,
bd.1   discusses the Pentagon Papers with Edwin
        Newman and Barbara Walters.   NBC, July 2,
        1971.
           2 reels (7 in.)   7 1/2 i.p.s.   phonotape.

           1. Pentagon papers. 2. Vietnamese
        Conflict, 1961-   - U.S.   I. Newman,
        Edwin Harold, 1919-   II. Walters,
        Barbara, 1931-

Voice Lib.
M1478 The Pentagon Papers; discussion of content,
        meaning. Bernard Kalb, CBS; Senator J.W.
        Fulbright; Senator John Tower; Arthur
        Schlesinger; Walt Rostow; Max Frankel,
        New York Times; Crosby Noyes, Washington
        Evening Star.   CBS-TV, July 13, 1971.
           1 reel (7 in.)   7 1/2 in. per sec.
        phonotape.
           I. Kalb, Bernard   II. Fulbright, James William, 1905-
        III. Tower, John Goodwin, 1925-   IV. Schlesinger, Arthur
        Meier, 1888-   V. Rostow, Walt Whitman, 1916-   VI.
        Frankel, Max   VII. Noyes, Crosby
        I. Vietnamese Conflict, 1961-   U.S.

Voice Lib.
M763   Perado, Al
bd.7   Excerpt from "Sound track" (Program 7);
         discusses importance of music in bringing
         out emotions of actors.   Westinghouse
         Broadcasting Corporation, 1964.
            1 min., 10 sec. phonotape (1 r.
         7 1/2 i.p.s.)   (The music goes round and
         round)

            I. Title: Sound track. II. Series.

                    Percy, Charles Harting, 1919-
Voice Lib.
M1391 Apollo 11 (space flight): reception of
bd.2   Apollo 11 astronauts in Chicago. Descrip-
         tion of motorcade on way to Civic Center
         Plaza and ceremonies there. Cardinal Cody's
         invocation. JFK flashback predicting moon
         landing before decade is out. Mayor Daley
         and Alderman Klene resolution making August
         13 "Astronauts' Day". Senator Percy and
         Governor Ogilvie of Illinois. Presentation
         of honorary citizenship to astronauts.
         [Source?] August 13, 1969.

              (Continued on next card)

                  Percy, Charles Harting, 1919-
Voice Lib.
M1391 Apollo 11 (space flight): reception of Apollo
bd.2   11 astronauts ... 1969. (Card 2)

            1 reel (7 in.)   7 1/2 in. per sec.
         phonotape.
            1. Project Apollo. 2. Space flight to the moon. 3. Aldrin,
         Edwin E   1930-   4. Collins, Michael, 1930-   5. Armstrong,
         Neil, 1930-   L Aldrin, Edwin E   1930-   II. Collins,
         Michael, 1930-   III. Armstrong, Neil, 1930-   IV. Cody,
         John Patrick, cardinal, 1907-   V. Kennedy, John Fitzgerald,
         Pres. U.S., 1917-1963. VI. Daley, Richard J   1902- VII.
         Percy, Charles Harting, 1919-   VIII. Ogilvie, Richard Buell,
         1923-

Voice Lib.
M1573- Percy, Charles Harting, 1919-
1574,   The government's response to change;
bd.1   Eisenhower Symposium, Johns Hopkins Univer-
        sity. WBJC, Baltimore, October 29, 1973.
           45 min.   phonotape (2 r.   7 1/2 i.p.s.)

           Includes question and answer period.

           1. U.S. - Politics and government.
           2. Watergate Affair, 1972-

Voice Lib.
M1584   Percy, Charles Harting, 1919-
         Money - politics. WKAR-AM, February 27,
         1974.
            30 min.   phonotape (1 r.   7 1/2 i.p.s.)

            1. Campaign funds.   2. U.S. - Politics
         and government.

          The perfect legend - George Washington
Cl
H106   Whorf, Michael, 1933-
            The perfect legend - George Washington.
         1 tape cassette.   (The visual sounds of
         Mike Whorf. History and heritage, H106)
            Originally presented on his radio program, Kaleidoscope,
         WJR, Detroit.
            Duration: 37 min., 30 sec.
            As commander of a new country, General George Washington
         watched his soldiers falter. His faith, trust and heroics led his
         men to a nearly impossible victory.

            I. Washington, George, Pres. U.S., 1732-1799.   I. Title.

Perkins, Frances, 1882-1965
Voice Lib.
M273-   Biography in sound (radio program)
274   Franklin Delano Roosevelt: the friends and
bd.1   former associates of Franklin Roosevelt on
         the tenth anniversary of the President's death.
         NBC Radio, April, 1955.
         2 reels (7 in.)   7 1/2 in. per sec.
         phonotape.
         I. Roosevelt, Franklin Delano, Pres. U.S., 1882-1945. I.
         McIntire, Ross T   1899-   II. Mellett, Lowell, 1884-1960.
         III. Tully, Grace   IV. Henderson, Leon, 1895-
         V. Roosevelt, Eleanor (Roosevelt) 1884-1962. VI. DeGraaf, Albert
         VII. Lehman, Herbert Henry, 1878-1963. VIII. Rosenman, Samuel
         Irving, 1896-   IX. Arvey, Jacob   X. Moley, Raymond,
         1886-   XI. Farley, James Aloysius, 1888-   XII. Roosevelt,
         (Continued on next card)

C1
FA5   PERKINS, GEORGE W
         Whorf, Michael, 1933-
         George W. Perkins.
         1 tape cassette.   (The visual sounds of
         Mike Whorf. The forgotten American, FA5)
         Originally presented on his radio program, Kaleidoscope,
         WJR, Detroit.
         Duration: 11 min., 30 sec.
         Perkins rose from obscurity to a position of wealth and
         power. He used his energies and money to promote the welfare
         of his fellow man.
         I. Perkins, George W.   I. Title.

Perkins, Jack
Voice Lib.
M1378   Sirhan, Sirhan Bishara, 1944-
bd.1   Interview by Jack Perkins.   NBC, June 3,
         1969.
         1 reel (7 in.)   7 1/2 in. per sec.
         phonotape.
         I. Perkins, Jack.

C1
H99   PERRY, OLIVER HAZARD, 1785-1819
         Whorf, Michael, 1933-
         The commodore - Oliver Hazard Perry.
         1 tape cassette.   (The visual sounds of
         Mike Whorf. History and heritage, H99)
         Originally presented on his radio program, Kaleidoscope,
         WJR, Detroit.
         Duration: 36 min.
         One of the great naval heroes of the U.S., Perry eagerly
         bursts into battle. The young officer guarded the seas against the
         French after the Revolutionary War. His whole biography sets the
         stage for his rich, full, naval career.
         I. Perry, Oliver Hazard, 1785-1819.   I. Title.

Voice Lib.
M757   Pershing, John Joseph, 1860-1948.
bd.3   Message from the battlefields of France
         requesting support of American public in
         the war effort. Nation's Forum, 1917.
         1 reel (7 in.)   7 1/2 in. per sec.
         phonotape.

                                              The perspectives of four major constituen-
                                              cies
Voice Lib.
M1565-   Wharton, Clifton Reginald, 1926-
1566,   The perspectives of four major constituen-
bd.1   cies: faculty, student, administrative, and
         legislative perspectives; state of the
         university address.   WKAR, February 14, 1974.
         40 min.   phonotape (2 r.   7 1/2 in. per
         sec.)

         I. Title.

Voice Lib.
M714   Pétain, Henri Phillippe Bénoni Omer, 1856-1951.
bd.9   Announcing his assumption as head of state
         of France.   June 16-22, 1940.
         1 reel (7 in.)   7 1/2 in. per sec.
         phonotape.

         1. France - Politics and government -
         1940-1945.

Voice Lib.
M714   Pétain, Henri Phillippe Bénoni Omer, 1856-
bd.9   1951.
         Explaining the reason for France's
         surrender.   June 16-22, 1940.
         1 reel (7 in.)   7 1/2 in. per sec.
         phonotape.

         PETAIN, HENRI PHILIPPE BÉNONI OMER, 1856-1951
Voice Lib.
M848   Reynaud, Paul, 1878-1966.
bd.1   French Prime Minister announcing recall
         of Gen. Petain from Spain to become France's
         Deputy Premier in current hour of war
         emergency.   NBC shortwave, May 18, 1940.
         1 reel (7 in.)   7 1/2 in. per sec.
         phonotape.

         1. Petain, Henri Philippe Bénoni Omer,
         1856-1951.

Voice Lib.
M1362   Peteler, Fred E
bd.6   Summation and closing of the recorded
         series "The Third Reich". Peteler, 1965.
         1 reel (7 in.)   7 1/2 in. per sec.
         phonotape.
         In German.

C1
R2
    PETER, SAINT, APOSTLE

Whorf, Michael, 1933–
    The fisher of men.
    1 tape cassette. (The visual sounds of
Mike Whorf. Religion, R2)

    Originally presented on his radio program, Kaleidoscope,
WJR, Detroit.
    Duration: 29 min., 30 sec.
    The story of Peter, a man of rough-hewn manner, who became
the leader of the disciples once the Christ had been crucified.

    l. Peter, Saint, Apostle. L. Title.

Voice Lib.
M649
bd.1
    Phelps, William Lyon, 1865–1943.
    Introduction to recordings of Hoosier
poet James Whitcomb Riley. G.R. Vincent,
1940.
    1 reel (7 in.) 7 1/2 i.p.s. phonotape.

    1. Riley, James Whitcomb, 1849–1916.

OFFICIAL

C1
FA20
    Peter Cooper

Whorf, Michael, 1933–
    Peter Cooper.
    1 tape cassette. (The visual sounds of
Mike Whorf. The forgotten American, FA20)

    Originally presented on his radio program, Kaleidoscope,
WJR, Detroit.
    Duration: 10 min., 40 sec.
    Cooper made and piloted the first steam engine on the
Baltimore and Ohio railroad. He participated in the laying
of the Atlantic Cable. Founder of the Cooper Union; he was
also Greenback candidate for President of the United States.

    l. Cooper, Peter, 1791–1883. L. Title.

C1
R21
    The phenomenal Billy Graham

Whorf, Michael, 1933–
    The phenomenal Billy Graham.
    1 tape cassette. (The visual sounds of
Mike Whorf. Religion, R21)

    Originally presented on his radio program, Kaleidoscope,
WJR, Detroit.
    Duration: 41 min., 30 sec.
    Here are the thoughts and ideas, aspirations and inspirations
of Billy Graham, a leading personality of our age bent on bringing
man to God.

    l. Graham, William Franklin, 1918– L. Title.

Voice Lib.
M1800
WG
0807.02
    Peterson, Henry E
    Testimony before the Senate Committee
investigating the Watergate Affair.
Pacifica, August 7, 1973.
    173 min. phonotape (2 r. 3 3/4 i.p.s.)
(Watergate gavel to gavel, phase 1)

    1. Watergate Affair, 1972–

Voice Lib.
M717
bd.9
    Philip, duke of Edinburgh, 1921–
    Elizabeth II, Queen of Great Britain, 1926–
    Excerpts from wedding ceremony.
November 20, 1947.
    1 min., 14 sec. phonotape (1 r.
7 1/2 i.p.s.)

    I. Philip, duke of Edinburgh, 1921–

Voice Lib.
353
bd.14
    Petterson, Elmer
    Outbreak of Korean War; public opinion
and editorial opinion supporting Truman.
NBC, July, 1950.
    1 reel (7 in.) 7 1/2 in. per sec.
phonotape.

    Original disc off-speed.

    1. Korean War, 1950–1953

Voice Lib.
M834
    Philip, duke of Edinburgh, 1921–
    Elizabeth II, Queen of Great Britain, 1926–
    Highlights of wedding ceremonies to Prince
Philip at Westminster Abbey, London, England.
CBS, November 20, 1947.
    1 reel (7 in.) 7 1/2 in. per sec.
phonotape.

    I. Philip, duke of Edinburgh, 1921–

Voice Lib.
526
bd.5-6
    Phelps, William Lyon, 1865–1943.
    Interlude on cats; the joy of teaching.
Linguaphone, 1939.
    1 reel (7 in.) 7 1/2 in. per sec.
phonotape.

Voice Lib.
573
bd.2-
574
bd.1
    Philip, duke of Edinburgh, 1921–
    I can hear it now (radio program)
    1945–1949. CBS, 1950?
    2 reels (7 in.) 7 1/2 in. per sec.
phonotape.

    L. Murrow, Edward Roscoe, 1908–1965. II. Nehru, Jawaharlal,
1889–1964. III. Philip, duke of Edinburgh, 1921– IV. Elizabeth II,
Queen of Great Britain, 1926– V. Ferguson, Homer, 1889– VI.
Hughes, Howard Robard, 1905– VII. Marshall, George Catlett,
1880– VIII. Ruth, George Herman, 1895–1948. IX. Lilienthal,
David Eli, 1899– X. Trout, Robert, 1908– XI. Gage, Arthur.
XII. Jackson, Robert Houghwout, 1892–1954. XIII. Gromyko, Ana-
tolii Andreevich, 1908– XIV. Baruch, Bernard Mannes, 1870–
1965. XV. Churchill, Winston Leonard Spencer, 1874–1965. XVI.
Winchell, Walter, 1897–19   XVII. Davis, Elmer Holmes, 1890–
(Continued on next card)

PHONORECORDS

Voice Lib.
M765   Campana, Frank
bd.2   Excerpt from "The Anatomy of a Hit"
        (Program 9); comments on the role of the
        promotion man, also the album business.
        Westinghouse Broadcasting Corporation, 1964.
           1 reel (7 in.)   7 1/2 in. per sec.
        phonotape.   (The Music Goes Round and Round)

           I. Title: The Anatomy of a Hit. II. Series.

PHONORECORDS

Voice Lib.
M765   Goldmark, Goldie
bd.4   Excerpt from "The anatomy of a hit"
        (Program 9); gives advice on how to get
        a new record on a popular music station.
        Westinghouse Broadcasting Corporation, 1964.
           1 min., 41 sec. phonotape (1 r.   7 1/2
        i.p.s.) (The music goes round and round)
           1. Music, Popular (Songs, etc.)
           2. Phonorecords. I. Title: The anatomy of
        a hit. II. Series.

PHONORECORDS

Voice Lib.
M764   Goodman, Benny, 1909-
bd.10   Excerpt from "The World of Wax" (Program
        8); comments on recording with the use of
        electricity. Including music "Blue Skies".
        Westinghouse Broadcasting Corporation, 1964.
           1 reel (7 in.)   7 1/2 in. per sec.
        phonotape.   (The Music Goes Round and Round)

           I. Title: The world of wax. II. Series.

PHONORECORDS

Voice Lib.
M640   Savory, William
bd.7   Experiments with magnet and human voice
        (Somnivox).   GRV, September 22, 1941.
           1 reel (7 in.)   7 1/2 i.p.s.   phonotape.

           1. Phonorecords.

PHONORECORDS

Voice Lib.
M765   Wax, Morty
bd.3   Excerpt from "The anatomy of a hit"
        (Program 9); comments on his role as an
        independent record promoter; also answers
        question whether or not the songs we are
        hearing day after day are being given to us
        against our will.   Westinghouse Broadcasting
        Corporation, 1964.
           2 min., 55 sec. phonotape (1 r.   7 1/2 i.p.s.)
        (The music goes round and round)
           1. Music, Popular (Songs, etc.) - Writing & publishing.
           2. Phonorecords.   I. Title: The anatomy of a hit.
        II. Series.

PHONORECORDS

Voice Lib.
M764   Whiteman, Paul, 1890-1967.
bd.8   Excerpt from "The World of Wax" (Program 8);
        comments on how the recording was accomplished;
        including music "Whispering". Westinghouse
        Broadcasting Corporation, 1964.
           1 reel (7 in.)   7 1/2 in. per sec.
        phonotape.   (The Music Goes Round and Round)

           I. Title: The world of wax. II. Series.

PHONORECORDS - HISTORY

Voice Lib.
M952   Berliner, Emile, 1851-1929.
bd.1   First phonograph recording made in
        Germany by Dr. Emile Berliner; march
        music. H. C. Scholz, 1892.
           1 reel (7 in.)   7 1/2 i.p.s.   phonotape.

           1. Phonorecords - History.

PHONORECORDS - HISTORY

Voice Lib.
M952   Berliner, Emile, 1851-1929.
bd.2   Message of greetings by Dr. Berliner in
        Philadelphia, Pennsylvania to Mrs. Hahn in
        Hannover, Germany on her 70th birthday.
        H.E. Scholz, November 18, 1890.
           1 reel (7 in.)   7 1/2 in. per sec.
        phonotape.

PHONORECORDS - HISTORY

Voice Lib.
M952   Berliner, Emile, 1851-1929.
bd.3   Dr. Berliner discussing his experiments
        on recording and playing back cylinder
        phonograph records. H.E. Scholz, 1900.
           1 reel (7 in.)   7 1/2 i.p.s.   phonotape.

           1. Phonorecords - History.

PHONORECORDS - HISTORY

Voice Lib.
M943   Big Ben; first sound effect record made
bd.5   by technicians at Edison House, London,
        of Big Ben striking 10:30, 10:45 and 11:00.
        G. R. Vincent re-recording. July 16, 1890.
           1 reel (7 in.)   7 1/2 in. per sec.
        phonotape.

           1. Phonorecords - History.

PHONORECORDS - HISTORY

Voice Lib.
M341   Bugle call and taps at grave of Roosevelt's
bd.3   Rough Riders; comments by army sergeant.
        Columbia Test Cylinder, June 24, 1898.
        1 reel (7 in.)   7 1/2 i.p.s.   phonotape.

        1. Phonorecords - History.

PHONORECORDS - HISTORY

Voice Lib.
249   Stanley, Sir Henry Morton, 1841-1904.
bd.4   Greeting through phonograph.   Edison
        Labs, 1888.
        1 reel (7 in.)   7 1/2 in. per sec.
        phonotape.

PHONORECORDS - HISTORY

Voice Lib.
M1483   Campbell, Mrs. Howard, 1869-
bd.2   Interview with Mrs. Campbell (102 years
        old) concerning her experience with the
        birth of the phonograph when she lived near
        Edison's labs in Menlo Park, N.J.   David L.
        Olson, July 21, 1971.
        1 reel (7 in.)   7 1/2 i.p.s.   phonotape.

        1. Phonorecords - History.

PHONORECORDS - HISTORY

Voice Lib.
M613   Sullivan, Sir Arthur Seymour, 1842-1900.
bd.5   Preservation of sound through records.
        Source (?), 1890-1900?
        1 reel (7 in.)   7 1/2 in. per sec.
        phonotape.

PHONORECORDS - HISTORY

Voice Lib.
M654   Damrosch, Walter Johannes, 1862-1950.
bd.4   Address to Associated Glee Clubs of
        America. First on-the-spot electrical
        recording. Moran, March 31, 1925.
        1 reel (7 in.)   7 1/2 i.p.s.
        phonotape.

        1. Phonorecords - History.

PHONORECORDS - HISTORY

Voice Lib.
M1099   Tinney, Frank, 1878-1940.
bd.3-   Humorous monologue by Frank Tinney and
bd.4   Charles A. Prince with musical accompaniment,
        entitled: "Frank Tinney's First Record" and
        "Frank Tinney's Second Record", depicting
        the making of an acoustic phonograph record.
        Colonel Graph, 1917.
        1 reel (7 in.)   7 1/2 in. per sec.
        phonotape.

        I. Prince, Charles A

PHONORECORDS - HISTORY

Voice Lib.
M1086   Gouraud, George E
bd.3   "Phonogram message" (1 in. diameter cylinder
        recording) spoken by Colonel Gouraud in London
        and addressed to Mr. Thomas A. Edison in
        New Jersey, about experimental recordings
        made in England and comments on the phono-
        graph by British personalities.   Walter
        Miller, 1888.
        1 reel (7 in.)   7 1/2 in. per sec.
        phonotape.

PHOTOGRAPHY

Voice Lib.
M1466   Stresemann, Gustav, 1878-1929.
bd.20   Remarks at the opening of the German
        photographic and motion picture exhibition.
        Peteler, 1925.
        1 reel (7 in.)   7 1/2 i.p.s.   phonotape.

        1. Photography.

PHONORECORDS - HISTORY

Voice Lib.
M382   Hobart, Garett Augustus, 1844-1899.
bd.2   Talking from Washington, D.C., to New
        York City via telephone for the first
        time, extolling the "electric age" (1898)
        CBS, April 26, 1951.
        1 reel (7 in.)   7 1/2 i.p.s.   phonotape.

        1. Telephone.   2. Phonorecords - History.

PHYSICALLY HANDICAPPED

Voice Lib.
M1579   Gentile, Eric Anton, 1943-
bd.3   Reading Woody Ayen's State News editorial
        (November 15, 1973) calling for action from
        and/or resignation of MSU Planning Director
        Milton Baron.   MSU Voice Library, February
        13, 1974.
        3 min.   phonotape (1 r.   7 1/2 i/p.s.)

        1. Physically handicapped.   2. Baron,
        Milton.   I. Ayen, Woody.

PHYSICALLY HANDICAPPED

Voice Lib.
M1578   Gentile, Eric Anton, 1943-
         The legislative and other social aims of
         NAPH's Civil Presence Group; interview, by
         Maurice Crane. MSU Voice Library,
         February 13, 1974.
         60 min.   phonotape (1 r.   3 3/4 in. per
         sec.)

         1. Physically handicapped. 2. Physically
         handicapped - Law and legislation.
         I. Crane, Maurice Aaron, 1926-

PHYSICALLY HANDICAPPED

Voice Lib.
M1579   Osgood, Charles
bd.4   Interviewing Sy Leaderman, blind man, who
         bowls 247 in a league where all others have
         sight. CBS Morning News, February 21, 1974.
         2 min., 15 sec. phonotape (1 r.   7 1/2
         i.p.s.)

         1. Blind. 2. Physically handicapped.
         I. Leaderman, Sy.

PHYSICALLY HANDICAPPED

Voice Lib.
M1592   Stigma I.
         What is it like to be crippled?
         Center for Independent Living, University
         of California at Berkeley, 1973.
         25 min. phonotape (1 r.   7 1/2 i.p.s.)

         1. Physically handicapped.   I. Title.

PHYSICALLY HANDICAPPED

Voice Lib.
M1593   Stigma II.
         The physically disabled and the world.
         Center for Independent Living, University
         of California at Berkeley, 1973.
         25 min. phonotape (1 r.   7 1/2 i.p.s.)

         1. Physically handicapped.

PHYSICALLY HANDICAPPED - LAW AND LEGISLATION

Voice Lib.
M1578   Gentile, Eric Anton, 1943-
         The legislative and other social aims of
         NAPH's Civil Presence Group; interview, by
         Maurice Crane. MSU Voice Library,
         February 13, 1974.
         60 min.   phonotape (1 r.   3 3/4 in. per
         sec.)

         1. Physically handicapped. 2. Physically
         handicapped - Law and legislation.
         I. Crane, Maurice Aaron, 1926-

PHYSICALLY HANDICAPPED - LAW AND LEGISLATION

Voice Lib.
M1579   Halverson, Craig
bd.2   23 tonight; MSU controversy over curb and
         ramp cuts, with Eric Gentile and Judy K. Taylor.
         WKAR-TV, November 13, 1973.
         15 min.   phonotape (1 r.   7 1/2 i.p.s.)

         1. Physically handicapped - Law and legis-
         lation. I. Gentile, Eric Anton, 1943-
         II. Taylor, Judy K

PHYSICALLY HANDICAPPED - LAW AND LEGISLATION

Voice Lib.
M1579   Third Civic Presence Group/Legislative
bd.1   luncheon, with Craig Halverson, Lynn
         Jondahl, Gary Owen, Phil Mastin, and
         Eric Gentile. WKAR-TV, February 15, 1973.
         10 min.   phonotape (1 r.   7 1/2 i.p.s.)

         1. Physically handicapped - Law and legis-
         lation. I. Halverson, Craig. II. Jondahl,
         H. Lynn, 1936-   III. Owen, Gary M., 1944-
         IV. Mastin, Philip O., 1930-   V. Gentile,
         Eric Anton, 1943-

PHYSICIANS

C1
SC2   Whorf, Michael, 1933-
         The man called healer.
         1 tape cassette.   (The visual sounds of
         Mike Whorf. Science, Sc2)

         Originally presented on his radio program, Kaleidoscope,
         WJR, Detroit.
         Duration: 39 min.
         Actual recordings are used to relate the story of medicine -
         its history and progress under difficult conditions.

         1. Physicians. 2. Medicine. I. Title.

PHYSICIANS - U.S.

Voice Lib.
M1745   Knowles, John
bd.2   Explains how to find a capable physician
         on the Mike Douglas show. WILX-TV, June
         27, 1974.
         6 min.   phonotape (1 r.   7 1/2 i.p.s.)

         1. Physicians - U. S.   I. Douglas, Mike,
         1925?

Voice Lib.
352   Pickens, Jane
bd.5   Talks of her role in the play "Regina"
         opening on Broadway. NBC, 1949.
         1 reel (7 in.)   7 1/2 in. per sec.
         phonotape.

PIERCE, PATRICK.
THE MOTHER
Voice Lib.
M1745   O'Connor, Ulick.
bd.1   Interview on Mike Douglas Show.   WILS-TV,
June 27, 1974.
10 min.   phonotape (1 r.   7 1/2 i.p.s.)

1. Pierce, Patrick/The Mother. 2. O'Connor,
Ulick. I. Douglas, Mike, 1925?-

C1   PIRATES
H32   Whorf, Michael, 1933-
The bold buccaneers - Kidd, Teach, Lafitte.
1 tape cassette.   (The visual sounds of
Mike Whorf. History and heritage, H32)
Originally presented on his radio program, Kaleidoscope,
WJR, Detroit.
Duration: 55 min., 20 sec.
William Kidd, Edward Teach, Jean Lafitte were bold captains
who sailed the bounding main in search of rich prizes. Who were
they and why did they sail under the Jolly Roger? Here is the
picturesque account of the bold buccaneers.

L. Pirates. L. Title.

Pierpoint, Robert
Voice Lib.
M774-   Farewell to Studio Nine; historical broadcasts
775,   made by CBS correspondents at time of action
bd.1   and reflections by them in retrospect.   1964.
2 reels (7 in.)   7 1/2 in. per sec.
phonotape.

I. Trout, Robert, 1908-   II. Pierpoint,
Robert   III. Murrow, Edward Roscoe,
1908-1965. IV. Kaltenborn, Hans von, 1878-
1965. V. Sevareid, Arnold Eric, 191?-
VI. Daly, John Charles, 1914-

Voice Lib.
M948   Pius XI, Pope, 1857-1939.
bd.2   First message by a Catholic Pontiff over
radio to the laity, spoken in Latin with
English translation by Father Charles Mullaly,
S.J. Vatican Record Co., 1931.
1 reel (7 in.)   7 1/2 in. per sec.
phonotape.

I. Mullaly, Charles J   1877-

Pietrillo, James
Voice Lib.
573   I can hear it now (radio program)
bd.2-   1945-1949.   CBS, 1950?
574   2 reels (7 in.)   7 1/2 in. per sec.
bd.1   phonotape.
L. Murrow, Edward Roscoe, 1908-1965. II. Nehru, Jawaharlal,
1889-1964. III. Philip, duke of Edinburgh, 1921- IV. Elizabeth II,
Queen of Great Britain, 1926- V. Ferguson, Homer, 1889-   VI.
Hughes, Howard Robard, 1905-   VII. Marshall, George Catlett,
1880-   VIII. Ruth, George Herman, 1895-1948. IX. Lilienthal,
David Eli, 1899- X. Trout, Robert, 1908-   XI. Gage, Arthur.
XII. Jackson, Robert Houghwout, 1892-1954. XIII. Gromyko, Ana-
tolii Andreevich, 1908-   XIV. Baruch, Bernard Mannes, 1870-
1965. XV. Churchill, Wi... g Leonard Spencer, 1874-1965. XVI.
Winchell, Walter, 1897-?   XVII. Davis, Elmer Holmes, 1890-
(Continued on next card).

Voice Lib.
M587   Pius XI, pope, 1857-1939.
bd.4   Christmas message, 1936.   Shortwave
broadcast from Vatican City.   New York,
WEAF, December 24, 1936.
1 reel (7 in.)   7 1/2 i.p.s.   phonotape.

In Latin.

C1   PINKERTON, ALLAN, 1819-1884
M24   Whorf, Michael, 1933-
The detective.
1 tape cassette.   (The visual sounds of
Mike Whorf. Miscellaneous, M24)
Originally presented on his radio program, Kaleidoscope,
WJR, Detroit.
Duration: 46 min.
The adventures of Alan Pinkerton - his rise from obscurity to
fame as head of the world's foremost detective agency.

L. Pinkerton, Allan, 1819-1884. L. Title.

Voice Lib.
M1465   Pius XI, Pope, 1857-1939.
bd.2   Message from Pope Pius XI from Vatican
and apostolic blessing to International
Euraistic Congress in Manila.   Peteler,
1937.
1 reel (7 in.)   7 1/2 in. per sec.
phonotape.

Pious, Minerva
Voice Lib.
M619   Radio in the 1930's (Part II): a series of
bd.1-   excerpts of the 1930's; a sample of radio
14   of the period. NVL, April, 1964.
1 reel (7 in.)   7 1/2 in. per sec.   phonotape.
L. Allen, Fred, 1894-1956. II. Delmar, Kenny   III. Donald,
Peter   IV. Pious, Minerva   V. Fennelly, Parker   VI.
Boyer, Charles, 1899-   VII. Dunne, Irene, 1904-   VIII.
DeMille, Cecil Blount, 1881-1959. IX. West, Mae, 1893-   X.
Dafoe, Allan Ray, 1883-1943. XI. Dionne quintuplets. XII. Ortega,
Santos   XIII. War of the worlds (radio program) XIV. Ives, Burl,
1909-   XV. Robinson, Earl, 1910-   XVI. Temple, Shirley,
1928-   XVII. Earhart, Amelia, 1898-1937. XVIII. Lawrence,
Gertrude, 1901-1952. XIX. Cohan, George Michael, 1878-1942.
XX. Shaw, George Bernard, 1856-1950. XXI. Hitler, Adolf, 1889-
1945. XXII. Chamberlain, Neville, 1869-1940. XXIII. Roosevelt,
Franklin Delano, Pres. U.S., 1882-1945.

Voice Lib.
M1055   Pius XII, Pope, 1876-1958.
bd.3   Coronation at St. Peter's Cathedral and
description of the ceremony.   Vatican
Radio, March 3, 1939.
1 reel (7 in.)   7 1/2 in. per sec.
phonotape.

Voice Lib.
M773 Pius XII, Pope, 1876-1958.
bd.2   Ceremony at St. Peter's Church for children
        of Rome; aided by UNRRA. Vatican Radio
        via shortwave, January 26, 1946.
          1 reel (7 in.)   7 1/2 in. per sec.
        phonotape.

The play that Lincoln never saw

Cl
H46   Whorf, Michael, 1933-
        The play that Lincoln never saw.
        1 tape cassette. (The visual sounds of
      Mike Whorf. History and heritage, H46)
        Originally presented on his radio program, Kaleidoscope,
      WJR, Detroit.
        Duration: 30 min.
        "Our American cousin" was the play Abraham Lincoln attended on
      that fateful night. In the shadows awaited death and the nation went
      into shock. But what of the play - its actors and actresses?

        1. Taylor, Tom, 1817-1880. /Our American cousin.
      2. Lincoln, Abraham, Pres. U.S., 1809-1865. L. Title.

              Pius XII, Pope, 1876-1958
Voice Lib.
M618   Radio in the 1930's (Part I): a series of
bd.1-   excerpts from important broadcasts of the
14   1930's; a sample of radio of the period.
        NVL, April, 1964.
          1 reel (7 in.) 7 1/2 in. per sec. phonotape.
        1. Shaw, George Bernard, 1856-1950. II. Crosby, Bing, 1901-
      III. Barkley, Alban William, 1877-1956. IV. Roosevelt, Franklin
      Delano, Pres. U.S., 1882-1945. V. Hoover, Herbert Clark, Pres.
      U.S., 1874-1964. VI. Long, Huey Pierce, 1893-1935. VII. Town-
      send, Francis Everett, 1867-1960. VIII. Coughlin, Charles Edward,
      1891-   IX. Rogers, Will, 1879-1935. X. Pius XII, Pope, 1876-
      1958. XI. Edward VIII, king of Great Britain, 1894-1972. XII.
      Barrymore, John, 1882-1942. XIII. Woollcott, Alexander, 1887-
      1943. XIV. Allen, Fred, 1894-1956. XV. Benchley, Robert Charles,
      1889-1945.

Voice Lib.
M350   Pleven, René, 1901-
bd.3   Tribute to Eisenhower on assuming the
        Presidency. CBS, January, 1953.
          1 reel (7 in.)   7 1/2 i.p.s. phonotape.

          1. Eisenhower, Dwight David, Pres. U.S.,
        1890-1969.

Cl
R15   The plain people

       Whorf, Michael, 1933-
        The plain people; the Amish story.
        1 tape cassette. (The visual sounds of
      Mike Whorf. Religion, R15)

        Originally presented on his radio program, Kaleidoscope,
      WJR, Detroit.
        Duration: 45 min.
        The life style, traditions, habits, customs and heritage of
      the Amish folk of Pennsylvania.

        1. Mennonites. L. Title.

Voice Lib.
M1380   Plimpton, Calvin H
bd.1   Commencement address at Michigan State
        University on "Musings about the contemporary
        college scene". Introduced by Acting President
        Walter Adams. On-campus recording, June 8,
        1969.
          1 reel (7 in.)   7 1/2 in. per sec.
        phonotape.

          I. Adams, Walter, 1922-

Voice Lib.
M1464   Planck, Max Karl Ernst Ludwig, 1858-1947.
bd.7   Address about the desire of the public
        for freedom. Peteler, 1932.
          1 reel (7 in.)   7 1/2 in. per sec.
        phonotape.

          In German.

Voice Lib. Plummer, Christopher, 1929-
M310   American Broadcasting Company.
        Tribute to President John Fitzgerald Kennedy
        from the arts. Fredric March emcees; Jerome
        Hines sings "Worship of God and Nature" by
        Beethoven; Florence Eldridge recites "When
        lilacs last in the door-yard bloom'd" by Walt
        Whitman; Marian Anderson in two songs. Includes
        Charlton Heston, Sidney Blackmer, Isaac Stern,
        Nathan Milstein, Christopher Plummer, Albert
        Finney. ABC, November 24, 1963.
          35 min. phonotape (7 in. 7 1/2 i.p.s.)

          (Continued on next card)

Voice Lib.
M1598   Plants, John R
bd.1   Safeguards against misuse of state police
        for political purposes. With Tim Skubick.
        WKAR-TV, November 23, 1973.
          10 min. phonotape (1 r. 7 1/2 in. per
        sec.)

          1. Police - Michigan. 2. Michigan. State
        Police. I. Skubick, Tim.

Cl   POCAHONTAS, D. 1617
H17   Whorf, Michael, 1933-
        John Smith's great lady.
        1 tape cassette. (The visual sounds of
      Mike Whorf. History and heritage, H17)
        Originally presented on his radio program, Kaleidoscope,
      WJR, Detroit.
        Duration: 29 min., 30 sec.
        It is one of America's first romantic histories, fired by an
      adventurous spirit of a man and the inner courage of a woman.

        1. Pocahontas, d. 1617. 2. Smith, John, 1580-1631.
      L. Title.

Dictionary Catalog

447

POE, EDGAR ALLAN, 1809-1849

C1
A17

Whorf, Michael, 1933-
Poe, evermore.
1 tape cassette. (The visual sounds of
Mike Whorf. Art, music, and letters, A17)

Originally presented on his radio program, Kaleidoscope,
WJR, Detroit.
Duration: 47 min., 40 sec.
Works of Poe are featured, as well as a close look at the
man who was an enigma to his friends as well as himself.

I. Poe, Edgar Allan, 1809-1849. I. Title.

Poe, evermore

C1
A17

Whorf, Michael, 1933-
Poe, evermore.
1 tape cassette. (The visual sounds of
Mike Whorf. Art, music, and letters, A17)

Originally presented on his radio program, Kaleidoscope,
WJR, Detroit.
Duration: 47 min., 40 sec.
Works of Poe are featured, as well as a close look at the
man who was an enigma to his friends as well as himself.

I. Poe, Edgar Allan, 1809-1849. I. Title.

The poet of democracy - Walt Whitman

C1
A44

Whorf, Michael, 1933-
The poet of democracy - Walt Whitman.
1 tape cassette. (The visual sounds of
Mike Whorf. Art, music and letters, A44)
Originally presented on his radio program, Kaleidoscope,
WJR, Detroit.
Duration: 37 min.
The likeable, candid Whitman has become the poet of
America. During his life he strived for freedom; for the
country, for his poetry.

I. Whitman, Walt, 1819-1892. I. Title.

Poet of the piano

C1
A9

Whorf, Michael, 1933-
Poet of the piano.
1 tape cassette. (The visual sounds of
Mike Whorf. Art, music, and letters, A9)

Originally published on his radio program, Kaleidoscope,
WJR, Detroit.
Duration: 27 min., 30 sec.
With aspects of his career known only to the devotee, this
narrative is a portrait of one of the masters, Chopin.

I. Chopin, Fryderyk Franciszek, 1810-1849. I. Title.

POETRY

C1
A37

Whorf, Michael, 1933-
The magic of poetry.
1 tape cassette. (The visual sounds of
Mike Whorf. Art, music and letters, A37)

Originally presented on his radio program, Kaleidoscope,
WJR, Detroit.
Duration: 37 min., 30 sec.
Here is a simple and elementary look at the art of reading
and writing verse. A few quotes from the masters and a few
dissections help the listener discover the magic of poetry.

I. Poetry. I. Title.

POLICE - MICHIGAN

Voice Lib.
M1598
bd.1

Plants, John R
Safeguards againt misuse of state police
for political purposes. With Tim Skubick.
WKAR-TV, November 23, 1973.
10 min. phonotape (1 r. 7 1/2 in. per
sec.)

1. Police - Michigan. 2. Michigan. State
Police. I. Skubick, Tim.

POLIOMYELITIS VACCINE

Voice Lib.
M717
bd.1

Burdett, Winston M   1913-
Interview with Dr. Jonas E. Salk regarding
polio vaccine, at University of Michigan.
CBS, April 13, 1955.
1 reel (7 in.) 7 1/2 in. per sec.
phonotape.

I. Salk, Jonas Edward, 1914-

POLIOMYELITIS VACCINE

Voice Lib.
231
bd.2

Salk, Jonas Edward, 1914-
Discussion of Salk vaccine, introduced
by Basil O'Connor. CBS, May 3, 1954.
1 reel (7 in.) 7 1/2 in. per sec.
phonotape.

1. Poliomyelitis vaccine. I. O'Connor,
Basil, 1892-1972.

POLLUTION

Voice Lib.
M1729-
1730

Nader, Ralph.
Address at Michigan State University.
MSU Voice Library, April 11, 1974.
80 min. phonotape (2 r. 7 1/2 i.p.s.)

1. Monopolies - U. S. 2. Pollution. 3.
Oil industries - U. S.

POLLUTION

C1
S38

Whorf, Michael, 1933-
America the beautiful; pollution, part 2.
1 tape cassette. (The visual sounds of
Mike Whorf. Social, S38)
Originally presented on his radio program, Kaleidoscope,
WJR, Detroit.
Duration: 54 min.
This second narration looks at the types of pollution which have
engulfed the globe. Here are the acts of water and air poisoning
which man has slowly but deliberately committed, and the results
of his carelessness and negligence.

1. Pollution. 2. Nature - Influence of man on. I. Title.

C1
H58
POLO, MARCO, 1254-1323?

Whorf, Michael, 1933-
    The incredible adventurer, Marco Polo.
1 tape cassette. (The visual sounds of
Mike Whorf. History and heritage, H58)
    Originally published on his radio program, Kaleidoscope.
WJR, Detroit.
    Duration: 41 min., 30 sec.
    So arduous were the journeys to the ends of the globe, and so
alien was the culture and society of the East, that Marco Polo's
achievements reveal his herculean drive and the audacity of his
vision.

L Polo, Marco.   1254-1323? L Title.

POPULAR CULTURE

Voice Lib.
M1664   Ferguson, Robert
bd.2   Is seeing always believing? Popular
         culture and technology. Recorded live at
         National Popular Culture Meetings in Milwaukee.
         May 4, 1974.
            20 min.   phonotape (1 r.   7 1/2 i.p.s.)

         1. Popular culture.

C1
H13
PONY EXPRESS

Whorf, Michael, 1933-
    From St. Joe to Sacramento.
1 tape cassette. (The visual sounds of
Mike Whorf. History and heritage, H13)
    Originally presented on his radio program, Kaleidoscope.
WJR, Detroit.
    Duration: 29 min.
    It began in Missouri and ended hundreds of miles away in
California. Atop lightning-fast horses, the small wiry riders
braved the elements, the Indians and the loneliness to carry the
mail for the Pony Express.

L Pony Express. L Title.

POPULAR CULTURE

Voice Lib.
M1664   MacDonald, J   Fred
bd.1   Beyond the survey; creating a program
         of popular culture courses. Recorded live
         at National Popular Culture Meetings in
         Milwaukee, May 4, 1974.
            20 min.   phonotape (1 r.   7 1/2 i.p.s.)

         1. Popular culture.

Voice Lib.
M1041   Pool, David de Sola, 1885-
bd.1   "Gevuroth". An address to the Spanish
         and Portuguese synagogue in New York upon
         the occasion of his 80th birthday.
         Private recording, 1960.
            1 reel (7 in.)   7 1/2 in. per sec.
         phonotape.

Voice Lib.   Popular music of Europe
M766   Banda, Antonio
bd.7   Excerpt from "Popular Music of Europe"
         (Program 11); comments on the popular music
         in Spain, including musical number "Chin chin".
         Westinghouse Broadcasting Corporation, 1964.
            3 min., 3 sec.   phonotape (1 r.   7 1/2
         i.p.s.)   (The music goes round and round)

         1. Music, Popular (Songs, etc.) - Spain.
         I. Title: Popular music of Europe.
         II. Series.

            Poole, Walter
Voice Lib.
233   Fiedler, Arthur, 1894-
bd.3   Interview with Arthur Fiedler by Walter
         Poole.   CBS, March 2, 1957.
            1 reel (7 in.)   7 1/2 in. per sec.
         phonotape.

         I. Poole, Walter

Voice Lib.   Popular music of Europe
M766   Ericksen, Espen
bd.6   Excerpt from "Popular Music of Europe"
         (Program 11); comments on music of Norway,
         including song "Liebeskummer lohnt sich
         nicht" by Siw Malnikvist.   Westinghouse
         Broadcasting Corporation, 1964.
            3 min., 36 sec.   phonotape (1 r.   7 1/2
         i.p.s.)   (The music goes round and round)

         1. Music, Popular (Songs, etc.) - Norway.
         I. Title: Popular music of Europe. II. Series.

Voice Lib.
M1206   Popular American patriotic song of World War I
bd.5   entitled "What are you going to do to help
         the boys?" (Gus Kahn-Egbert Van Alstyne)
         Sung by Charles Hart.   Victor, 1917.
            1 reel (7 in.)   7 1/2 in. per sec.
         phonotape.

         I. Hart, Charles   II. Title:
         What are you going to do to help the boys?

Voice Lib.   Popular music of Europe
M766   Garnier, Jacques
bd.4   Excerpt from "Popular Music of Europe"
         (Program 11); comments on French tastes in
         music, including song "Cela n'a pas
         d'importance" by Les Surfs.   Westinghouse
         Broadcasting Corporation, 1964.
            2 min., 54 sec.   phonotape (1 r.   7 1/2
         i.p.s.)   (The music goes round and round)

         1. Music, Popular (Songs, etc.) - France.
         I. Title: Popular music of Europe. II. Series.

Popular music of Europe
Voice Lib.
M766   Hutton, Jack
bd.3   Excerpt from "Popular Music of Europe"
(Program 11); expresses his idea that the
British sound is not all British; including
song "I Don't Need You", by the "Panics"
sextet. Westinghouse Broadcasting Corporation,
1964.
1 reel (7 in.) 7 1/2 in. per sec.
phonotape. (The Music Goes Round and Round)

I. Title: Popular music of Europe. II. Series.

Voice Lib.
M1800   Porter, Herbert L., 1938?-
WG   Testimony before the Senate Committee
0607.02 investigating the Watergate Affair.
Pacifica, June, 7, 1973.
168 min. phonotape (2 r. 3 3/4 i.p.s.)
(Watergate gavel to gavel, phase 1)

1. Watergate Affair, 1972-

Popular music of Europe
Voice Lib.
M766   Martin, Neville
bd.2   Excerpt from "Popular Music of Europe"
(Program 11); discusses extent of American
influence both today and yesterday in music
in Europe; including "Ain't Necessarily So"
by British group "Ian and the Zodiacs."
Westinghouse Broadcasting Corporation, 1964.
1 reel (7 in.) 7 1/2 in. per sec.
phonotape. (The Music Goes Round and Round)
I. Title: Popular music of Europe. II. Series.

Voice Lib.
M1800   Porter, Herbert L., 1938?-
WG   Testimony before the Senate Committee
0612.01 investigating the Watergate Affair.
Pacifica, June 12, 1973.
87 min. phonotape (1 r. 3 3/4 i.p.s.)
(Watergate gavel to gavel, phase 1)

1. Watergate Affair, 1972-

Popular music of Europe
Voice Lib.
M767   Rapoport, Azaria
bd.1   Excerpt from "Popular Music of Europe"
(Program 11); comments on effects of British
music on Israel, including song "With a Little
Bit of Luck" from "My Fair Lady", sung in
Hebrew, Italian and Spanish. Westinghouse
Broadcasting Corporation, 1964.
1 reel (7 in.) 7 1/2 in. per sec.
phonotape. (The Music Goes Round and Round)
I. Title: Popular music of Europe. II. Series.

Voice Lib.
M1607   Porter, John W   1931-
bd.1   Off the record; problems facing Michigan
schools. Interviewed by Tim Skubick, Tom
Green, Bill Meek, and Gary Schuster.
WKAR-TV, February 1, 1974.
17 min. phonotape (1 r. 7 1/2 in. per
sec.)

1. Segregation in education. 2. Strikes
and lockouts - Teachers. I. Skubick, Tim.
II. Green, Tom. III. Meek, Bill. IV. Schuster.
Gary.

Voice Lib. Popular music of Europe
M766   Stampa, Fred
bd.5   Excerpt from "Popular Music of Europe"
(Program 11); comments on style of singing
of Dominco Modugno, including song "Boom
boom surf" by Peppino Di Capri and the
Hollerers. Westinghouse Broadcasting
Corporation, 1964.
1 min., 44 sec. phonotape (1 r. 7 1/2 i.p.s.)
(The music goes round and round)

I. Modugno, Dominco. L. Title: Boom boom surf.
II. Title: Popular music of Europe. III. Series.

Voice Lib.
613   Porter, William Sydney, 1862-1910.
bd.4   Reviews his writing techniques.
Source (?), 1900-1910?
1 reel (7 in.) 7 1/2 in. per sec.
phonotape.

POPULATION
Voice Lib.
M1700   Borlaug, Norman Ernst, 1914-
The green revolution; its genesis, impact,
dangers & hope. Includes awarding of
honorary D.Sc. degree from Michigan State
University and introduction by President
Wharton. WKAR, May 12, 1971.
50 min. phonotape (1 r. 7 1/2 i.p.s.)

1. Population. I. Muelder, Milton E.
II. Wharton, Clifton Reginald, 1926-

PORTER, WILLIAM SYDNEY, 1862-1910
C1
A46   Whorf, Michael, 1933-
The mystery of William Porter - O. Henry.
1 tape cassette. (The visual sounds of
Mike Whorf. Art, music and letters, A46)

Originally presented on his radio program, Kaleidoscope,
WJR, Detroit.
Duration: 36 min., 30 sec.
The man spent many of his years behind bars, movements
inhibited, freedom gone. But his mind was free, free to imagine,
then to put down on paper his short stories.

I. Porter, William Sydney, 1862-1910. I. Title.

C1
H61
Portrait of a patriot - Ethan Allen

Whorf, Michael, 1933–
Portrait of a patriot - Ethan Allen.
1 tape cassette. (The visual sounds of
Mike Whorf. History and heritage, H61)
Originally presented on his radio program, Kaleidoscope.
WJR, Detroit.
Duration 40 min.
Ethan Allen's small band of Green Mountain boys captured the
heavily- fortified garrison at Fort Ticonderoga in a daring attack
at dawn, and gave the struggling Continental Congress a much-
needed victory.

L Allen, Ethan, 1738-1789.   L Title.

Voice Lib.
M1022 Potter, Charles Edward, 1916–
bd.2- U.S. Congress. Senate. Committee on Government Operations.
1923 Permanent Subcommittee on Investigations.
Proceedings of the 9th session of Senate Army-McCarthy
hearings, May 4, 1954. Discussion concerning the possibility
of shortening the hearings; statements by Senators Dirksen,
Mundt, McClellan, Potter, etc.; Aaron Coleman and the
stripping of Army files; discussion of FBI confidential letter
and how it was obtained by McCarthy; suggestion of night and
Saturday sessions. WJR, May 4, 1954.
2 reels (7 in.) 7 1/2 in. per sec. phonotape.

L McCarthy-Army controversy, 1954.   L Dirksen, Everett
McKinley, 1896-1969.   II. Mundt, Karl Earl, 1900–   III. McClellan,
John Little, 1896–   IV. Potter, Charles Edward, 1916–

Voice Lib.
M1599- POUND, EZRA LOOMIS, 1885-1972
1600 A quiet requiem for Ezra Pound, with poets
Robert Lowell, Robert Fitzgerald, James
Laughlin, and Robert McGregor. Modern
Language Center, Harvard University,
December 4, 1972.
70 min. phonotape (2 r. 7 1/2 i.p.s.)

L Pound, Ezra Loomis, 1885-1972.   L Lowell, Robert,
1917–   II. Fitzgerald, Robert, 1910–   III. Laughlin,
James, 1914–   IV. McGregor, Robert,

Voice Lib.
M1037 Powdermaker, Hortense, 1903-1970
bd.1 Biography in sound (radio program)
"The Actor", narrated by Morgan Beatty.
Cast includes Tallulah Bankhead, Hy Gardner,
Rocky Graziano, Arthur Miller, Uta Hagen,
Jackie Cooper, Sir Laurence Olivier, Gad
Gayther, Barbara Ashley, Hortense Powdermaker,
Peter Ustinov, Alfred Hitchcock, Leonard Lyons,
John Guston, Helen Hayes, Dick Mayne, Ralph
Bellamy, Lionel Barrymore, Sir Ralph Richardson,
José Ferrer, and Walter Kerr. NBC Radio, 1950's.
1 reel (7 in.) 7 1/2 in. per sec.
phonotape.
(Continued on next card)

Voice Lib.
M1413 Powell, Adam Clayton, 1908-1972.
Address at "Great Issues" series at MSU.
MSU Information Services, Spring 1967.
1 reel (7 in.) 7 1/2 in. per sec.
phonotape.

Voice Lib.
M1663 Powell, Adam Clayton, 1908-1972.
Speech to Great Issues Class at MSU,
co-sponsored by ASMSU. WKAR, January 17,
1969.
35 min., 30 sec. phonotape (1 r.
7 1/2 i.p.s.)

1. Passive resistance to government.
2. U.S. - Politics and government.

Voice Lib.
M1454 Powell, Adam Clayton, 1908-1972.
bd.3 On loss of nomination for representative
to the 92nd Congress. CBS, March, 1970.
1 reel (7 in.) 7 1/2 in. per sec.
phonotape.

1. Powell, Adam Clayton, 1908-1972.

Voice Lib. Powell, Dick, 1904-1963
M1025 Fields, W.C., 1879-1946.
bd.4 Excerpt from skit in "Eddie Cantor Show",
with Martha Raye, Dick Powell, etc. CBS
Radio, 1930's.
1 reel (7 in.) 7 1/2 in. per sec.
phonotape.

I. Raye, Martha, 1916–   II. Powell,
Dick, 1904-1963. III. Eddie Cantor Show
(radio program)

Voice Lib. POWER RESOURCES
M1547 Fisher, John, of General Electric.
bd.2 Energy uses past, present, and future.
WKAR-FM, January 24, 1974.
60 min. phonotape (1 r. 3 3/4 i.p.s.)

"... from a series of seminar programs
called Prospectives of Energy, sponsored by
the Center for Environmental Quality ..."

1. Force and energy. 2. Power resources.

Voice Lib. POWER RESOURCES - U.S.
M1549- Nixon, Richard Milhous, Pres. U.S., 1913–
1550, News conference recorded over CBS
bd.1 television network. CBS, October 26, 1973.
35 min. phonotape (2 r. 7 1/2 i.p.s.)
Includes question and answer session, including Nelson
Benton.

L U.S. - Politics and government - 1969–
2. Watergate Affair, 1972. 3. Power resources - U.S.
L Benton, Nelson

POWER RESOURCES - U.S.

Voice Lib.
M1566   Nixon, Richard Milhous, Pres. U.S., 1913-
bd.2   Address on the energy crisis, followed by
         excerpts from question and answer period with
         the press. WKAR-FM, February 24, 1974.
         20 min. phonotape. 7 1/2 in. per sec.

         1. Power resources - U.S. 2. U.S. - Economic conditions.
         3. Nixon, Richard Milhous, Pres. U.S., 1913-

POWER RESOURCES - U.S.

Voice Lib.
M1554   Simon, William Edward, 1927-
         Address to the National Press Club.
         WKAR, February 4, 1974.
         40 min. phonotape (1 r. 7 1/2 i.p.s.)

         Includes 25 min. question and answer period.

         1. Power resources - U.S.

POWER RESOURCES - U.S.

Voice Lib.
M1628-   Nixon, Richard Milhous, Pres. U.S., 1913-
1629,   Address before the National Radio &
bd.1   Television News Directors Association and
         questions following from the members and
         from the national press. Summary and analysis
         by CBS newsmen Roger Mudd and Bruce Morton.
         CBS, March 19, 1974.
         60 min. phonotape (2 r. 7 1/2 i.p.s.)

         1. U.S. - Politics and government - 1969-
         2. Power resources - U.S. I. Mudd, Roger.
         II. Morton, Bruce.

POWER RESOURCES - U.S.

Voice Lib.
M1615   Taylor, John Francis Adams
         The social implications of the energy
         crisis. WKAR-FM, March 28, 1974.
         35 min. phonotape (1 r. 7 1/2 in. per sec.)

         Part of the "Energy and Life" symposium
         held at Michigan State University.

         1. Man - Influence on nature. 2. Power
         resources - U.S.

POWER RESOURCES - U.S.

Voice Lib.
M1560   Proxmire, William
bd.1   Energy speech; rebuttal to President
         Nixon's speech. CBS-TV, December 2, 1973.
         12 min. phonotape (1 r. 7 1/2 i.p.s.)

         Commentary by Dan Rather and George Herman.

         1. Power resources - U.S. I. Rather, Dan.
         II. Herman, George.

The practical genius - Thomas Edison

C1
SC26   Whorf, Michael, 1933-
         The practical genius - Thomas Edison.
         1 tape cassette. (The visual sounds of
         Mike Whorf. Science, SC26)
         Originally presented on his radio program, Kaleidoscope,
         WJR, Detroit.
         Duration: 42 min.
         Regarded as a failure in early life, Edison's personal strength and
         dogged perseverance bore him above the hardships of life, and
         established him as one of the world's greatest and most inventive
         minds.

         1. Edison, Thomas Alva, 1847-1931. I. Title.

POWER RESOURCES - U.S.

Voice Lib.
M1733   Sawhill, John Crittenden, 1936-
         Speech at the National Press Club luncheon,
         concerning the international energy picture,
         with Clyde Lamont. WKAR, June 20, 1974.
         50 min. phonotape (1 r. 7 1/2 i.p.s.)

         1. Power resources - U.S. 2. Energy
         shortage. 3. Local transit - U.S.
         I. Lamont, Clyde.

The preacher and the bear

Voice Lib.
M982   Bernard, Al
bd.7   Comedy song selection "The Preacher and
         the Bear". Perfect Records, 1912.
         1 reel (7 in.) 7 1/2 in. per sec.
         phonotape.

         I. Title: The preacher and the bear.

POWER RESOURCES - U.S.

Voice Lib.
M1570-   Shapp, Milton J   1912-
1571,   National Press Club address. WKAR-AM,
bd.1   February 21, 1974.
         50 min. phonotape (2 r. 7 1/2 i.p.s.)

         1. Railroads - U.S. 2. Power resources -
         U.S.

Preserver of love

C1
A16   Whorf, Michael, 1933-
         Preserver of love.
         1 tape cassette. (The visual sounds of
         Mike Whorf. Art, music, and letters, A16)
         Originally presented on his radio program, Kaleidoscope,
         WJR, Detroit.
         Duration: 28 min.
         Joyce Kilmer was a writer of verse, a warrior in the trenches
         of France and his untimely death was a tragic loss to the world.

         1. Kilmer, Joyce, 1886-1918. I. Title.

PRESIDENTS - U.S.

Voice Lib.
M1705   Schlesinger, Arthur Meier, 1917-
         The imperial presidency; address at
         the University of Missouri. WKAR
         (KBIA, Columbia, Mo.), June 3, 1974.
         50 min. phonotape (1 r.   7 1/2 i.p.s.)

         1. Presidents - U.S. 2. Johnson, Lyndon
         Baines, Pres. U.S., 1908-1973. 3. Nixon,
         Richard Milhous, Pres. U.S., 1913-

PRESIDENTS - U.S.

C1
H111   Whorf, Michael, 1933-
        Vision of America.
        1 tape cassette. (The visual sounds of
        Mike Whorf. History and heritage, H111)
        Originally presented on his radio program, Kaleidoscope,
        WJR, Detroit.
        Duration: 37 min.
        In this narration we are presented with cameo portraits of
        Presidents of the United States. In their speeches, philosophies
        and maxims, these past leaders bring us a stirring vision of
        America.

        1. Presidents - U.S. 1. Title.

PRESIDENTS - U.S. - ELECTION

Voice Lib.
M735   Democracy in Action; composite of excerpts
        of proceedings of past presidential
        campaigns assembled under the title of
        "Democracy in Action". CBS, 1964.
        1 reel (7 in.)   7 1/2 in. per sec.
        phonotape.

PRESIDENTS - U.S. - ELECTION

C1
H82   Whorf, Michael, 1933-
        America's first citizen, the President.
        1 tape cassette. (The visual sounds of
        Mike Whorf. History and heritage, H82)

        Originally presented on his radio program, Kaleidoscope,
        WJR, Detroit.
        Duration: 37 min., 30 sec.
        Here are the ins and outs, the political aspects and
        attributes of the election of a president.

        1. Presidents - U.S. - Election. 1. Title.

PRESIDENTS - U.S. - ELECTION - 1940

Voice Lib.
M724   Barkley, Alben William, 1877-1956.
bd.3   Alben Barkley and James Farley at
        Democratic convention of 1940, speaking for
        nomination of Franklin D. Roosevelt for
        third term. 1940.
        1 min., 40 sec. phonotape (1 r.   7 1/2
        i.p.s.)

        1. Roosevelt, Franklin Delano, Pres. U.S., 1882-1945.
        2. Presidents - U.S. - Election - 1940. 1. Farley, James
        Aloysius, 1888-

PRESIDENTS - U.S. - ELECTION - 1948

Voice Lib.
M724   Wallace, Henry Agard, 1888-1965.
bd.1   Repudiating the Truman doctrince,
        followed by Wallace campaign song. 1948.
        51 sec. phonotape (1 r.   7 1/2 i.p.s.)

        1. Presidents - U.S. - Election - 1948.

PRESIDENTS - U.S. - ELECTION - 1952

Voice Lib.
M724   Rayburn, Samuel Taliaferro, 1882-1961.
bd.4   Samuel Rayburn and Estes Kefauver at
        Democratic convention. 1952.
        45 sec. phonotape (1 r.   7 1/2 i.p.s.)

        1. Presidents - U.S. - Election - 1952.
        I. Kefauver, Estes, 1903-1963.

PRESIDENTS - U.S. - ELECTION - 1952

Voice Lib.
M724   Trout, Robert, 1908-
bd.2   On Democratic loyalty oath, including
        Senator Blair Moody of Michigan, Gov. Battle
        of Virginia, Speaker Sam Rayburn, Col. Jack
        Arvey of Chicago, Gov. Willis of Alabama and
        Jim Farley. 1952.
        8 min., 12 sec. phonotape (1 r.
        7 1/2 i.p.s.)

        1. Democratic Party. 2. Presidents - U.S.
        - Election - 1952.

PRESIDENTS - U.S. - ELECTION - 1956

Voice Lib.
M724   Kefauver, Estes, 1903-1963.
bd.10   Announcing his candidacy for the
        nomination of president on the Democratic
        ticket in 1955.
        1 min., 4 sec. phonotape (1 r.
        7 1/2 i.p.s.)

        1. Presidents - U.S. - Election - 1956.

PRESIDENTS - U.S. - ELECTIONS - 1972

Voice Lib.
M1721   Chisholm, Shirley, 1924-
bd.1   Tells why she ran for President.
        WKAR, June 7, 1974.
        3 min. phonotape (1 r.   7 1/2 i.p.s.)

        1. Chisholm, Shirley, 1924-
        2. Presidents - U.S. - Elections - 1972.

PRESIDENTS - U.S. - ELECTIONS - 1972

Voice Lib.
M1800 U.S. Congress. Senate. Select Committee on Presidential
Campaign Activities.
Watergate gavel to gavel, phase I: May 17 - August 7, 1973.
Pacifica, May 17 - August 7, 1973.
172 reels (5 in.) 3 3/4 L.p. s. phonotape.

"These tapes include commentaries by Pacifica's Washington
correspondents and interviews with members of the Senate Committee
taped during recesses of the hearings."

1. Presidents - U.S. - Elections - 1972. 2. Watergate Affair,
1972- 1. Ervin, Samuel James, 1896- II. Talmadge,
Herman Eugene, 1913- III. Inouye, Daniel Ken, 1924-
IV. Baker, Howard H., 1925- V. Gurney, Edward John, 1914-
VI. Weicker, Lowell P., 19 VII. Title.

C1
S53

PRESIDENTS - U.S. - WIVES

Whorf, Michael, 1933-
That woman in the White House; wives of
Presidents.
1 tape cassette. (The visual sounds of Mike Whorf. Social, S53)

Originally presented on his radio program, Kaleidoscope,
WJR, Detroit.
Duration: 28 min., 20 sec.
Along with the many presidents that have served our nation,
are the wives and hostesses who have served as well. From Washington to Nixon; here is a capsule comment on the vivacious,
intelligent women in the White House.

1. Presidents - U.S. - Wives. I. Title.

PRESLEY, ELVIS ARON, 1935-

Voice Lib.
M760 Aberbach, Jean
bd.7 Excerpt from "What All the Screaming's
About" (Program 1); the real reason for the
success of Elvis Presley and the Beatles.
Westinghouse Broadcasting Corporation, 1964.
1 min. phonotape (1 r. 7 1/2 i.p.s.)
(The music goes round and round)

1. Music, Popular (Songs, etc.) - U.S.
2. Presley, Elvis Aron, 1935- 3. The
Beatles. I. Title: What all the screaming's
about. II. Series.

PRESLEY, ELVIS ARON, 1935-

Voice Lib.
M760 Sholes, Steven H 1911-1968.
bd.6 Excerpt from "What all the screaming's
about (Program 1); Elvis' progress to fame
and fortune, including one of his first hits,
"That's all right"; a comparison is made
between Elvis and the Beatles. Westinghouse
Broadcasting Corporation, 1964.
8 min., 6 sec. phonotape (1 r. 7 1/2 i.p. s.) (The
music goes round and round)

1. Presley, Elvis Aron, 1935- 2. Music, Popular (Songs,
etc.) - U.S. I. Title: What all the screaming's about. II.
Series.

PRESLEY, ELVIS ARON, 1935-

Voice Lib.
M760 Stoller, Mike
bd.8 Excerpt from "What all the screaming's
about" (Program 1); anything Elvis had sung
at the peak of his career would have been
popular. Westinghouse Broadcasting
Corporation, 1964.
9 sec. phonotape (1 r. 7 1/2 i.p.s.)
(The music goes round and round)

1. Presley, Elvis Aron, 1935- 2. Music, Popular (Songs,
etc.) - U.S. I. Title: What all the screaming's about.
II. Series.

Voice Lib.
M718 Price, Leontyne, 1929-
bd.1 Singing "America, the Beautiful".
Presidential Inaugural ceremonies.
January 20, 1965.
1 reel (7 in.) 7 1/2 in. per sec.
phonotape..

I. Title: America, the beautiful.

Price, Vincent, 1911-

Voice Lib.
M1394- The Royal Family (motion picture)
1395 Motion picture of the life of Britain's
Royal Family at home and in various countries,
including all members of the immediate family
and the palace household. Moderated by
Vincent Price. BBC, Sept. 21, 1969.
2 reels (7 in.) 7 1/2 in. per sec.
phonotape.

I. Price, Vincent, 1911-

Priestley, John Boynton, 1894-

Voice Lib.
M1044 London after dark; on-the-spot recordings of various
points during the London air-raid attacks: the Savoy Hotel
kitchen, Trafalgar Square, anti-aircraft battery near London,
air-raid shelter. With newsmen Edward R. Murrow, Robert
Bowman, Raymond Van Denny, Larry Lesueur, Eric Sevareid,
Vincent Sheean, J. B. Priestley, Michael Standing, and
Winfred Von Thomas. CBS and BBC, August 24, 1940.
1 reel (7 in.) 7 1/2 in. per sec. phonotape.

1. Murrow, Edward Roscoe, 1908-1965. II. Bowman, Robert
III. Van Denny, Raymond IV. Lesueur, Laurence Edward,
1909- V. Sevareid, Arnold Eric, 1912- VI. Sheean,
Vincent, 1899- VII. Priestley, John Boynton, 1894-
VIII. Standing, Michael IX. Von Thomas, Winfred

C1
H44

The prime minister - Winston Churchill

Whorf, Michael, 1933-
The prime minister - Winston Churchill.
1 tape cassette. (The visual sounds of
Mike Whorf. History and heritage, H44)
Originally presented on his radio program, Kaleidoscope,
WJR, Detroit.
Duration: 61 min., 30 sec.
The story of Churchill, his background, education, his
successes and failures make him one of the most admired men in
history.

1. Churchill, Sir Winston Leonard Spencer, 1874-1965.
I. Title.

Prince, Charles A

Voice Lib.
M1099 Tinney, Frank, 1878-1940.
bd.3- Humorous monologue by Frank Tinney and
bd.4 Charles A. Prince with musical accompaniment,
entitled: "Frank Tinney's First Record" and
"Frank Tinney's Second Record", depicting
the making of an acoustic phonograph record.
Colonel Graph, 1917.
1 reel (7 in.) 7 1/2 in. per sec.
phonotape.

I. Prince, Charles A

PRIVACY, RIGHT OF
Voice Lib.
M1591   Ford, Gerald R., 1913-
        Privacy; address at the National Governors'
        Conference. WKAR-AM, March 6, 1974.
        20 min. phonotape (1 r. 7 1/2 i.p.s.)

        1. Privacy, Right of.

PROHIBITION
Voice Lib.
M1064   LaGuardia, Fiorello Henry, 1882-1947.
bd.12   Various statements and opinions pro and
        con on the value of prohibition of alcoholic
        beverages in the United States. Fox Movie-
        tone, 1929.
        1 reel (7 in.) 7 1/2 in. per sec.
        phonotape.

PRIVACY, RIGHT OF
Voice Lib.
M1558   Nixon, Richard Milhous, Pres. U.S., 1913-
bd.2   Comments on invasion of privacy; radio
        address. Followup to State of the Union
        Address. With commentary by Russ Ward.
        NBC, February 23, 1974.
        22 min. phonotape (1 r. 7 1/2 in. per
        sec.)

        1. Privacy, Right of. I. Ward, Russ.

PROHIBITION
Voice Lib.
540   LaGuardia, Fiorello Henry, 1882-1947.
bd.9   Prohibition. Fox Movietone, 1932.
        1 reel (7 in.) 7 1/2 in. per sec.
        phonotape.

        1. Prohibition.

Procope, Russell, 1908-
Voice Lib.
M1696   Columbia Broadcasting System, inc.
bd.6   Special memorial to Duke Ellington, with
        John Hart, Sonny Greer, Russell Procope,
        Billy Taylor, Stanley Dance, and Ella
        Fitzgerald. CBS-TV, May 24, 1974.
        15 min. phonotape (1 r. 7 1/2 i.p.s.)

        1. Ellington, Duke, 1899-1974. I. Hart,
        John. II. Greer, Sonny. III. Procope,
        Russell, 1908- IV. Taylor, Billy.
        V. Dance, Stanley. VI. Fitzgerald, Ella,
        1918-

PROHIBITION
Voice Lib.
M1064   McPherson, Aimee Semple, 1890-1944.
bd.10   Statement by "Sister" McPherson before
        leaving Los Angeles on a pilgrimage to the
        Holy Land, on prohibition. Fox Movietone,
        1929.
        1 reel (7 in.) 7 1/2 in. per sec.
        phonotape.

PROGRESSIVE PARTY (FOUNDED 1912)
Voice Lib.
M127   Roosevelt, Theodore, Pres. U.S., 1858-1919.
bd.6   Why the trusts and bosses oppose the
        Progressive Party. Victor, 1912.
        1 reel (7 in.) 7 1/2 in. per sec.
        phonotape.

PROHIBITION
Voice Lib.
540   McPherson, Aimee Semple, 1890-1944.
bd.18   Prohibition: tells story of prohibition
        on leaving for Europe and the Holy Land.
        Fox Movietone, 1932.
        1 reel (7 in.) 7 1/2 in. per sec.
        phonotape.

PROHIBITION
Voice Lib.
M540   Boole, Ella Alexander, 1858-1952.
bd.7   Prohibition; advantages of prohibition for
        all Americans. Fox Movietone, 1932.
        1 reel (7 in.) 7 1/2 in. per sec.
        phonotape.

PROHIBITION
Voice Lib.
290   Sunday, William Ashley, 1862-1935.
bd.2   Regulation of liquor; statement on ideas
        regarding prohibition. Pathe, 1925.
        1 reel (7 in.) 7 1/2 in. per sec.
        phonotape.

PROHIBITION

Voice Lib.
514 Sunday, William Ashley, 1862-1935.
bd.2   On the control of intoxicating beverages.
      Fox Movietone News, 1928.
      1 reel (7 in.) 7 1/2 in. per sec.
      phonotape.

PROHIBITION

C1
S76
      Whorf, Michael, 1933-
      The long drought - prohibition.
      1 tape cassette. (The visual sounds of
      Mike Whorf. Social, S76)
          Originally presented on his radio program, Kaleidoscope,
      WJR, Detroit.
          Duration: 37 min.
          A nostalgic picture of the Eighteenth Amendment - prohibition.
      A historic picture of alcohol throughout American history from the
      Indian's first intoxication through the repeal of prohibition.

          1. Prohibition. 1. Title.

PROJECT APOLLO

Voice Lib.
M1328 Apollo 7 (space flight): description of
bd.2   launching of Apollo 7 spacecraft, morning
      of October 11, 1968, and comments by various
      broadcasters, including Walter Cronkite.
      Description includes countdown and take-off;
      remarks by astronauts. CBS TV, October 11,
      1968.
      1 reel (7 in.) 7 1/2 in. per sec. phonotape.
          1. Project Apollo. 2. Eisele, Donn F   1930-   3. Cunning-
      ham, R   Walter, 1932-   4. Schirra, Walter Marty, 1923-
      1. Eisele, Donn F   1930-   II. Cunningham, R   Walter,
      1932-   III. Schirra, Walter Marty, 1923-   IV. Cronkite,
      Walter Leland, 1916-

PROJECT APOLLO

Voice Lib.
M1347- Apollo 8 (space flight): recovery. CBS TV
1348,   description of recovery of astronauts and
bd.1   their reception on aircraft carrier "York-
      town". CBS TV, December 27, 1968.
      2 reels (7 in.) 7 1/2 in. per sec.
      phonotape.

          1. Project Apollo. 2. Anders, William
      Alison, 1933-   3. Lovell, James Arthur, 1928-
      4. Borman, Frank, 1928-   I. Anders, William
      Alison, 1933-   II. Lovell, James Arthur,
      1928-   III. Borman, Frank, 1928-

PROJECT APOLLO

Voice Lib.
M1348 Apollo 8 (space flight): reception of Apollo
bd.2   8 astronauts at Joint Session of Congress,
      including addresses by the astronauts.
      CBS TV, January 1, 1969.
      1 reel (7 in.) 7 1/2 in. per sec.
      phonotape.
          1. Project Apollo. 2. Anders, William
      Alison, 1933-   3. Lovell, James Arthur, 1928-
      4. Borman, Frank, 1928-   I. Anders, William
      Alison, 1933-   II. Lovell, James Arthur,
      1928-   III. Borman, Frank, 1928-   IV.
      McCormack, John William, 1891-

PROJECT APOLLO

Voice Lib.
M1351 Apollo 8 (space flight): interview with
bd.1   astronauts William Anders, James Lovell,
      and Frank Borman on CBS TV program "Face
      the nation". CBS TV, January 12, 1969.
      1 reel (7 in.) 7 1/2 in. per sec.
      phonotape.

          1. Project Apollo. 2. Anders, William
      Alison, 1933-   3. Lovell, James Arthur, 1928-
      4. Borman, Frank, 1928-   I. Anders, William
      Alison, 1933-   II. Lovell, James Arthur,
      1928-   III. Borman, Frank, 1928-

PROJECT APOLLO

Voice Lib.
M1355 Apollo 9 (space flight): lift-off of Apollo 9
bd.3   space flight at 11 a.m., March 3, 1969.
      Description by CBS-TV commentators, Mission
      Control, and astronauts. CBS TV, March 3,
      1969.
      1 reel (7 in.) 7 1/2 in. per sec.
      phonotape.
          1. Project Apollo. 2. McDivitt, James Alton, 1929-   3.
      Scott, David Randolph, 1932-   4. Schweickart, Russell L
      1936-   1. McDivitt, James Alton, 1929-   II. Scott, David
      Randolph, 1932-   III. Schweickart, Russell L   1936-

PROJECT APOLLO

Voice Lib.
M1364 Apollo 9 (space flight): splashdown, part 1.
      CBS correspondents with anchorman Walter
      Cronkite describe recovery of Apollo 9
      from the time astronauts are over Australia
      to the opening of the hatch. CBS TV,
      March 13, 1969.
      1 reel (7 in.) 7 1/2 in. per sec.
      phonotape.
          1. Project Apollo. 2. McDivitt, James Alton, 1929-   3.
      Scott, David Randolph, 1932-   4. Schweickart, Russell L
      1936-   1. McDivitt, James Alton, 1929-   II. Scott, David
      Randolph, 1932-   III. Schweickart, Russell L   1936-
      IV. Cronkite, Walter Leland, 1916-

PROJECT APOLLO

Voice Lib.
M1365 Apollo 9 (space flight): splashdown, part 2.
      CBS TV description of retrieval of Apollo 9
      astronauts, starting with the opening of the
      hatch to their examination in sick bay on
      the recovery ship. Includes telegram by
      President Nixon and brief remarks by the
      astronauts. CBS TV, March 13, 1969.
      1 reel (7 in.) 7 1/2 in. per sec.
      phonotape.
          1. Project Apollo. 2. McDivitt, James Alton, 1929-   3.
      Scott, David Randolph, 1932-   4. Schweickart, Russell L
      1936-   1. McDivitt, James Alton, 1929-   II. Scott, David
      Randolph, 1932-   III. Schweickart, Russell L   1936-

PROJECT APOLLO

Voice Lib.
M1377 Apollo 10 (space flight): lift-off. Commentary
bd.1   by NBC TV news; countdown, lift-off. Astro-
      nauts Tom Stafford, John Young, Eugene Cernan.
      NBC TV, May 18, 1969.
      1 reel (7 in.) 7 1/2 in. per sec.
      phonotape.
          1. Project Apollo. 2. Space flight to the
      moon. 3. Stafford, Thomas P   1931-   4.
      Young, John Watts, 1930-   5. Cernan, Eugene
      Andrew, 1934-   I. Stafford, Thomas P   1931-
      II. Young, John Watts, 1930-   III. Cernan,
      Eugene Andrew, 1934-

PROJECT APOLLO

Voice Lib.
M1377 Apollo 10 (space flight): television pictures.
bd.2   Commentary from astronauts, NBC TV, on
        initial separation and docking of Lunar
        Landing Module, first live color television
        pictures from space, and pictures of the
        earth from 6,500 nautical miles out.   NBC
        TV, May, 1969.
          1 reel (7 in.) 7 1/2 in. per sec. phonotape.
          L Project Apollo. 2. Space flight to the moon. 3. Stafford,
        Thomas P   1931-   4. Young, John Watts, 1930-   5.
        Cernan, Eugene Andrew, 1934-   L Stafford, Thomas P
        1931-   IL Young, John Watts, 1930-   IIL Cernan, Eugene
        Andrew, 1934-

PROJECT APOLLO

Voice Lib.
M1377 Apollo 10 (space flight): splashdown and
bd.3   recovery of Apollo 10; astronauts' first
        words after returning to earth; from the
        recovery ship U.S.S. "Princeton".   CBS TV,
        May 26, 1969.
          1 reel (7 in.) 7 1/2 in. per sec.
        phonotape.
          L Project Apollo. 2. Space flight to the moon. 3. Stafford,
        Thomas P   1931-   5.
        Cernan, Eugene Andrew, 1934-   L Stafford, Thomas P
        1931-   IL Young, John Watts, 1930-   III. Cernan, Eugene
        Andrew, 1934-

PROJECT APOLLO

Voice Lib.
M1384 Apollo 11 (space flight): launch day, July 16,
bd.1   1969. Description of astronauts going up
        the elevator; conversation between Walter
        Cronkite and Walter Schirra at approximately
        2 hours before launch. CBS TV, July 16, 1969.
          1 reel (7 in.) 7 1/2 in. per sec.
        phonotape.
          L Project Apollo. 2. Space flight to the moon. 3. Aldrin,
        Edwin E   1930-   4. Collins, Michael, 1930-   5. Armstrong,
        Neil, 1930-   L Aldrin, Edwin E   1930-   IL Collins,
        Michael, 1930-   IIL Armstrong, Neil, 1930-   IV. Cronkite,
        Walter Leland, 1916-   V. Schirra, Walter Marty, 1923-

PROJECT APOLLO

Voice Lib.
M1384 Apollo 11 (space flight): biographical sketches
bd.2   of the three astronauts, Edwin Aldrin,
        Michael Collins, and Neil Armstrong, by Chet
        Huntley, at approximately 78 minutes before
        launch time. NBC TV, July 16, 1969.
          1 reel (7 in.) 7 1/2 in. per sec.
        phonotape.
          L Project Apollo. 2. Space flight to the moon. 3. Aldrin,
        Edwin E   1930-   4. Collins, Michael, 1930-   5. Armstrong,
        Neil, 1930-   L Aldrin, Edwin E   1930-   IL Collins,
        Michael, 1930-   IIL Armstrong, Neil, 1930-   IV. Huntley,
        Chet, 1911-1974.

PROJECT APOLLO

Voice Lib.
M1384 Apollo 11 (space flight): Frank McGee giving
bd.3   an itinerary of space ships, dates, times,
        etc. NBC TV, July 16, 1969.
          1 reel (7 in.) 7 1/2 in. per sec.
        phonotape.

          1. Project Apollo. 2. Space flight to the
        moon. 3. Aldrin, Edwin E   1930-   4.
        Collins, Michael, 1930-   5. Armstrong, Neil,
        1930-   I. Aldrin, Edwin E   1930-   II.
        Collins, Michael, 1930-   III. Armstrong, Neil,
        1930-   IV. McGee, Frank, 1921-1974.

PROJECT APOLLO

Voice Lib.
M1384 Apollo 11 (space flight): interviews between
bd.4   Frank McGee and Neil Armstrong previous to
        the flight of Apollo 11.   NBC TV, July 16,
        1969.
          1 reel (7 in.) 7 1/2 in. per sec.
        phonotape.

          1. Project Apollo. I. McGee, Frank, 1921-
        1974. II. Armstrong, Neil, 1930-

PROJECT APOLLO

Voice Lib.
M1384 Apollo 11 (space flight): launch day progress
bd.6   of countdown by Apollo 11 control at 4
        minutes 15 seconds to actual take-off.
        Houston takes over and describes progress
        up to 1,000 miles downrange and successful
        orbit.   NBC TV, July 16, 1969.
          1 reel (7 in.) 7 1/2 in. per sec.
        phonotape.
          L Project Apollo. 2. Space flight to the moon. 3. Aldrin,
        Edwin E   1930-   4. Collins, Michael, 1930-   5. Armstrong,
        Neil, 1930-   L Aldrin, Edwin E   1930-   IL Collins,
        Michael, 1930-   IIL Armstrong, Neil, 1930-

PROJECT APOLLO

Voice Lib.
M1385 Apollo 11 (space flight): Frank McGee speaking
bd.1   about communications between "Eagle" and
        ground. Conversation between Houston and
        astronauts. Message of "Go for PDI"; "The
        Eagle has landed" (102 hours, 45 minutes,
        40 seconds)   Description of rocks and
        boulders on moon. NBC TV, July 20, 1969.
          1 reel (7 in.) 7 1/2 in. per sec. phonotape.
          L Project Apollo. 2. Space flight to the moon. 3. Aldrin,
        Edwin E   1930-   4. Collins, Michael, 1930-   5.
        Armstrong, Neil, 1930-   L Aldrin, Edwin E   1930-
        IL Collins, Michael, 1930-   IIL Armstrong, Neil, 1930-
        IV. McGee, Frank, 1921-1974.

PROJECT APOLLO

Voice Lib.
M1385 Apollo 11 (space flight): Neil Armstrong
bd.2   requesting everyone everywhere to pause and
        give thanks. Preparing to open hatch and
        walk on the moon. Armstrong backing out
        from hatch, describing lunar surface. "One
        small step for man, one giant step for man-
        kind" (109 hours, 24 minutes, 20 seconds.)
        Bringing down cameras. CBS TV, July 20, 1969.
          1 reel (7 in.) 7 1/2 in. per sec. phonotape.
          L Project Apollo. 2. Space flight to the moon. 3. Aldrin,
        Edwin E   1930-   4. Collins, Michael, 1930-   5. Armstrong,
        Neil, 1930-   L Aldrin, Edwin E   1930-   IL Collins, Michael,
        1930-   IIL Armstrong, Neil, 1930-

PROJECT APOLLO

Voice Lib.
M1386 Apollo 11 (space flight): conversation with
bd.1   broadcasters Walter Cronkite and Wally
        Schirra. Including Armstrong's activities
        on moon alone; pictures, rock descriptions,
        then Aldrin coming down ladder; rock boxes
        put to use. TV cameras put at 30' panoramic
        position. Reading inscription of plaque
        with U.S. flag and setting it up. Telephone
        call from Washington to astronauts and their
        acknowledgement. CBS TV, July 20, 1969.
          1 reel (7 in.) 7 1/2 in. per sec.
        phonotape.
                               (Continued on next card)

PROJECT APOLLO

Voice Lib.
M1386 Apollo 11 (space flight): blessing by Pope
bd.2   Paul VI from the Vatican to Apollo 11
       astronauts.   CBS TV, July 20, 1969.
       1 reel (7 in.)   7 1/2 in. per sec.
       phonotape.

       1. Project Apollo. 2. Space flight to the
       moon. 3. Aldrin, Edwin E   1930-   4.
       Collins, Michael, 1930-   5. Armstrong, Neil,
       1930-   I. Aldrin, Edwin E   1930-   II.
       Collins, Michael, 1930-   III. Armstrong, Neil,
       1930-   IV. Paulus VI, Pope, 1897-

PROJECT APOLLO

Voice Lib.
M1388 Apollo 11 (space flight): Walter Cronkite and Wally Schirra
bd.1   describing recovery. Maneuvers by frogmen and helicopters
       at splashdown spot; "air boss" describes close-up scene;
       decontamination process; helicopter landing on "Hornet" with
       astronauts; reception. Description of proceedings on "Hornet"
       by CBS newscasters. CBS TV, July 24, 1969.
       1 reel (7 in.)   7 1/2 in. per sec.   phonotape.

       1. Project Apollo. 2. Space flight to the moon. 3. Aldrin,
       Edwin E   1930-   4. Collins, Michael, 1930-   5. Armstrong,
       Neil, 1930-   I. Aldrin, Edwin E   1930-   II. Collins,
       Michael, 1930-   III. Armstrong, Neil, 1930-   IV. Cronkite,
       Walter Leland, 1916-   V. Schirra, Walter Marty, 1923-

PROJECT APOLLO

Voice Lib.
M1386 Apollo 11 (space flight): excerpts of old
bd.3   Mercury Theatre "War of the Worlds" of
       1938; an interview with Orson Welles by
       Mike Wallace. CBS TV, July 20, 1969.
       1 reel (7 in.)   7 1/2 in. per sec.
       phonotape.
       1. Project Apollo. 2. Space flight to the moon. 3. Aldrin,
       Edwin E   1930-   4. Collins, Michael, 1930-
       5. Armstrong, Neil, 1930-   I. Aldrin, Edwin E   1930-
       II. Collins, Michael, 1930-   III. Armstrong, Neil, 1930-
       IV. Welles, Orson, 1915-   V. Wallace, Mike, 1918-

PROJECT APOLLO

Voice Lib.
M1388 Apollo 11 (space flight): personal greeting
bd.2   by President Nixon to the astronauts on
       the "Hornet" and their replies. Chaplain's
       prayer. Nixon taking off. CBS and NBC TV,
       July 24, 1969.
       1 reel (7 in.)   7 1/2 in. per sec.
       phonotape.
       1. Project Apollo. 2. Space flight to the moon. 3. Aldrin,
       Edwin E   1930-   4. Collins, Michael, 1930-   5.
       Armstrong, Neil, 1930-   I. Aldrin, Edwin E   1930-
       II. Collins, Michael, 1930-   III. Armstrong, Neil, 1930-
       IV. Nixon, Richard Milhous, Pres. U.S., 1913-

PROJECT APOLLO

Voice Lib.
M1386 Apollo 11 (space flight): excerpts of
bd.4   interview between Walter Cronkite and
       Lyndon B. Johnson two weeks before the
       moon flight regarding development of American
       space effort. CBS TV, July 20, 1969.
       1 reel (7 in.)   7 1/2 in. per sec.
       phonotape.

       1. Project Apollo. 2. Space flight to the
       moon. I. Cronkite, Walter Leland, 1916-
       II. Johnson, Lyndon Baines, Pres. U.S., 1908-
       1973.

PROJECT APOLLO

Voice Lib.
M1389 Apollo 11 (space flight): excerpt of press
bd.1   conference with Apollo 11 astronauts in
       Houston.   CBS TV, August 12, 1969.
       1 reel (7 in.)   7 1/2 in. per sec.
       phonotape.

       1. Project Apollo. 2. Space flight to the
       moon. 3. Aldrin, Edwin E   1930-   4.
       Collins, Michael, 1930-   5. Armstrong, Neil,
       1930-   I. Aldrin, Edwin E   1930-   II.
       Collins, Michael, 1930-   III. Armstrong,
       Neil, 1930-

PROJECT APOLLO

Voice Lib.
M1387 Apollo 11 (space flight): description of
bd.1   ascent from moon by Frank McGee. Count-
       down, ignition, and lift-off. Meeting the
       command module "Columbia"; docking; trans-
       fer of gear from "Eagle" to "Columbia".
       Recap by ABC's Jules Bergman and Frank
       Reynolds.   NBC and ABC TV, July 21, 1969.
       1 reel (7 in.)   7 1/2 in. per sec.   phonotape.
       1. Project Apollo. 2. Space flight to the moon. 3. Aldrin,
       Edwin E   1930-   4. Collins, Michael, 1930-   5.
       Armstrong, Neil, 1930-   I. Aldrin, Edwin E   1930-   II.
       Collins, Michael, 1930-   III. Armstrong, Neil, 1930-   IV.
       McGee, Frank, 1921-1974. V. Bergman, Jules VI. Reynolds,
       Frank

PROJECT APOLLO

Voice Lib.
M1389 Apollo 11 (space flight): welcome to Apollo 11 astronauts on their
bd.2   arrival at Kennedy Airport at New York; ferried by Marine
       helicopter to Wall Street; boat whistles harbor greeting.
       Flashbacks to former important New York parades (Frank McGee)
       Walter Cronkite, CBS, describing beginning of motorcade
       and parade to city hall. CBS [and NBC] TV, August 13, 1969.
       1 reel (7 in.)   7 1/2 in. per sec.   phonotape.

       1. Project Apollo. 2. Space flight to the moon. 3. Aldrin,
       Edwin E   1930-   4. Collins, Michael, 1930-   5.
       Armstrong, Neil, 1930-   I. Aldrin, Edwin E   1930-
       II. Collins, Michael, 1930-   III. Armstrong, Neil, 1930-
       IV. McGee, Frank, 1921-1974. V. Cronkite, Walter Leland, 1916-

PROJECT APOLLO

Voice Lib.
M1387 Apollo 11 (space flight): recovery. Walter Cronkite and Wally
bd.2   Schirra announce proceedings from aircraft carrier "Hornet";
       trying to track spacecraft coming down; chutes opening at
       10,500 feet; voice contact with spacecraft; visual of chutes;
       splashdown 9 miles from "Hornet", upside-down. Collar
       attached to spacecraft. NBC and ABC TV, July 24, 1969.
       1 reel (7 in.)   7 1/2 in. per sec.   phonotape.

       1. Project Apollo. 2. Space flight to the moon. 3. Aldrin,
       Edwin E   1930-   4. Collins, Michael, 1930-   5.
       Armstrong, Neil, 1930-   I. Aldrin, Edwin E   1930-
       II. Collins, Michael, 1930-   III. Armstrong, Neil, 1930-
       IV. Cronkite, Walter Leland, 1916-   V. Schirra, Walter Marty,
       1923-

PROJECT APOLLO

Voice Lib.
M1390 Apollo 11 (space flight): reception for
       Apollo 11 astronauts in New York. Descrip-
       tion of approach and ceremony at city hall.
       Cardinal Cooke's invocation. Introduction
       by Mayor Lindsay. Presentation of Medal of
       Honor. Reply by all astronauts. Benediction.
       NBC TV, August 13, 1969.
       1 reel (7 in.)   7 1/2 in. per sec.   phonotape.
       1. Project Apollo. 2. Space flight to the moon. 3. Aldrin,
       Edwin E   1930-   4. Collins, Michael, 1930-   5.
       Armstrong, Neil, 1930-   I. Aldrin, Edwin E   1930-   II.
       Collins, Michael, 1930-   III. Armstrong, Neil, 1930-   IV.
       Cooke, Terence James, cardinal, 1921-   V. Lindsay, John Vliet,
       1921-

PROJECT APOLLO

Voice Lib.
M1391   Apollo 11 (space flight): reception of Apollo 11 astronauts at
bd.1   United Nations Plaza. Statement by U. N. Secretary-
         General U Thant. Reply by Neil Armstrong. Presentation
         of tokens of appreciation to all three astronauts and their
         wives and Dr. Thomas Paine. Presentation of duplicate of
         plaque left on moon to U Thant. NBC TV, August 13, 1969.
         1 reel (7 in.) 7 1/2 in. per sec. phonotape.

         1. Project Apollo. 2. Space flight to the moon. 3. Aldrin,
         Edwin E   1930–   4. Collins, Michael, 1930–   5.
         Armstrong, Neil, 1930–   I. Aldrin, Edwin E   1930–
         II. Collins, Michael, 1930–   III. Armstrong, Neil, 1930–
         IV. Thant, U, 1909–   V. Paine, Thomas Otten, 1921–

PROJECT APOLLO

Voice Lib.
M1391   Apollo 11 (space flight): reception of
bd.2   Apollo 11 astronauts in Chicago. Descrip-
         tion of motorcade on way to Civic Center
         Plaza and ceremonies there. Cardinal Cody's
         invocation. JFK flashback predicting moon
         landing before decade is out. Mayor Daley
         and Alderman Klene resolution making August
         13 "Astronauts' Day". Senator Percy and
         Governor Ogilvie of Illinois. Presentation
         of honorary citizenship to astronauts.
         [Source?] August 13, 1969.

         (Continued on next card)

PROJECT APOLLO

Voice Lib.
M1391   Apollo 11 (space flight): reception of Apollo
bd.2   11 astronauts ... 1969. (Card 2)

         1 reel (7 in.) 7 1/2 in. per sec.
         phonotape.

         1. Project Apollo. 2. Space flight to the moon. 3. Aldrin,
         Edwin E   1930–   4. Collins, Michael, 1930–   5. Armstrong,
         Neil, 1930–   I. Aldrin, Edwin E   1930–   II. Collins,
         Michael, 1930–   III. Armstrong, Neil, 1930–   IV. Cody,
         John Patrick, cardinal, 1907–   V. Kennedy, John Fitzgerald,
         Pres. U.S., 1917–1963. VI. Daley, Richard J   1902– VII.
         Percy, Charles Harting, 1919–   VIII. Ogilvie, Richard Buell,
         1923–

PROJECT APOLLO

Voice Lib.
M1403   Apollo 12 (space flight): lift-off of Apollo
bd.1   12; the electrical "glitch" and instructions
         and corrections; Dr. Paine and President
         Nixon speaking from VIP section. CBS TV,
         November 19, 1969.
         1 reel (7 in.) 7 1/2 in. per sec.
         phonotape.
         1. Project Apollo. 2. Space flight to the moon. 3. Conrad,
         Charles, 1930–   4. Bean, Alan L   1932– 5. Gordon,
         Richard F   1929–   I. Conrad, Charles, 1930– II. Bean,
         Alan L   1932–   III. Gordon, Richard F   1929– IV.
         Paine, Thomas Otten, 1921–   V. Nixon, Richard Milhous, Pres.
         U.S., 1913–

PROJECT APOLLO

Voice Lib.
M1403   Apollo 12 (space flight): landing on the
bd.2   moon; conversations of Frank McGee and
         mission control; dialogue of Pete Conrad
         preparing to step out on moon; coached on
         going down ladder; Conrad singing from the
         moon; trouble with TV camera. NBC TV,
         November 19, 1969.
         1 reel (7 in.) 7 1/2 in. per sec. phonotape.
         1. Project Apollo. 2. Space flight to the moon. 3. Conrad,
         Charles, 1930–   4. Bean, Alan L   1932– 5. Gordon,
         Richard F   1929–   I. Conrad, Charles, 1930– II. Bean,
         Alan L   1932–   III. Gordon, Richard F   1929– IV.
         McGee, Frank, 1921–1974.

PROJECT APOLLO

Voice Lib.
M1404   Apollo 12 (space flight): description of
bd.1   last minutes on the moon of Apollo 12
         crew; countdown, lift-off from the moon.
         CBS TV, November 20, 1969.
         1 reel (7 in.) 7 1/2 in. per sec.
         phonotape.
         1. Project Apollo. 2. Space flight to the
         moon. 3. Conrad, Charles, 1930–   4. Bean,
         Alan L   1932– 5. Gordon, Richard F
         1929–   I. Conrad, Charles, 1930–   II.
         Bean, Alan L   1932–   III. Gordon, Richard
         F   1929–

PROJECT APOLLO

Voice Lib.
M1404   Apollo 12 (space flight): description of
bd.2   splashdown of Apollo 12 and proceeding
         to aircraft carrier "Hornet". CBS TV,
         November 24, 1969.
         1 reel (7 in.) 7 1/2 in. per sec.
         phonotape.
         1. Project Apollo. 2. Space flight to the
         moon. 3. Conrad, Charles, 1930–   4. Bean,
         Alan L   1932– 5. Gordon, Richard F
         1929–   I. Conrad, Charles, 1930–   II.
         Bean, Alan L   1932–   III. Gordon, Richard
         F   1929–

PROJECT APOLLO

Voice Lib.
M1423   Apollo 13 (space flight): resumé of flight
         of Apollo 13, including lift-off, mal-
         function, and splashdown, and interviews
         on future of space program. NBC TV,
         April, 1970.
         1 reel (7 in.) 7 1/2 in. per sec.
         phonotape.
         1. Project Apollo. 2. Space flight to the moon. 3. Haise,
         Fred W   1934–   4. Lovell, James Arthur, 1928–   5.
         Swigert, John L   1932–   I. Haise, Fred W   1934–
         II. Lovell, James Arthur, 1928–   III. Swigert, John L   1932–

PROJECT APOLLO

Voice Lib.
M1424   Apollo 13 (space flight): oxygen malfunction
         on Apollo 13 described by NASA, astronauts,
         and Howard K. Smith. ABC TV, April 14, 1970.
         1 reel (7 in.) 7 1/2 in. per sec.
         phonotape.
         1. Project Apollo. 2. Space flight to the
         moon. 3. Haise, Fred W   1934–   4.
         Lovell, James Arthur, 1928–   5. Swigert,
         John L   1932–   I. Haise, Fred W   1934–
         II. Lovell, James Arthur, 1928–   III. Swigert,
         John L   1932–   IV. Smith, Howard Kingsbury,
         1914–

PROJECT APOLLO

Voice Lib.
M1438   Apollo 14 (space flight): take-off from Cape
bd.1   Kennedy, including countdown. CBS,
         January 31, 1971.
         1 reel (7 in.) 7 1/2 in. per sec.
         phonotape.

         1. Project Apollo. 2. Space flight to the
         moon. 3. Shepard, Alan Bartlett, 1923–   4.
         Mitchell, Edgar D   1931– 5. Roosa,
         Stuart A   1934–   I. Shepard, Alan Bartlett,
         1923–   II. Mitchell, Edgar D   1931–   III.
         Roosa, Stuart A   1934–

PROJECT APOLLO
Voice Lib.
M1458   Apollo 14 (space flight): lunar landed on the
bd.2   moon and moon walk. CBS, February 5, 1971.
           1 reel (7 in.) 7 1/2 in. per sec.
        phonotape.

           1. Project Apollo. 2. Space flight to the
        moon. 3. Shepard, Alan Bartlett, 1923- 4.
        Mitchell, Edgar D   1931-   5. Roosa, Stuart
        A   1934-   I. Shepard, Alan Bartlett,
        1923-   II. Mitchell, Edgar D   1931- III.
        Roosa, Stuart A   1934-

PROJECT APOLLO
Voice Lib.
M1438   Apollo 14 (space flight): Apollo 14 splash-
bd.3-   down and reception on aircraft carrier.
M1439   CBS, February 9, 1971.
bd.1   2 reels(7 in.) 7 1/2 in. per sec.
        phonotape.

           1. Project Apollo. 2. Space flight to the
        moon. 3. Shepard, Alan Bartlett, 1923- 4.
        Mitchell, Edgar D   1931-   5. Roosa,
        Stuart A   1934-   I. Shepard, Alan Bartlett,
        1923- II. Mitchell, Edgar D   1931- III.
        Roosa, Stuart A   1934-

PROJECT APOLLO
Voice Lib.
M1480   Apollo 15 (space flight): lift-off.
bd.1   CBS TV, July 26, 1971.
           1 reel (7 in.) 7 1/2 in. per sec.
        phonotape.

           1. Project Apollo. 2. Space flight to the
        moon. 3. Scott, David Randolph, 1932-   4.
        Irwin, James B   1932-   5. Worden, Alfred
        M   1930-   I. Scott, David Randolph,
        1932- II. Irwin, James B   1932- III.
        Worden, Alfred M   1930-

PROJECT APOLLO
Voice Lib.
M1480   Apollo 15 (space flight): beginning of power
bd.2   descent to moon. NBC TV, July 31, 1971.
           1 reel (7 in.) 7 1/2 in. per sec.
        phonotape.

           1. Project Apollo. 2. Space flight to the
        moon. 3. Scott, David Randolph, 1932-   4.
        Irwin, James B   1932- 5. Worden, Alfred
        M   1930-   I. Scott, David Randolph,
        1932- II. Irwin, James B   1932- III.
        Worden, Alfred M   1930-

PROJECT APOLLO
Voice Lib.
M1480   Apollo 15 (space flight): walk in deep space
bd.3   by Al Worden to retrieve film packages.
        Commentary of Gene Cernan, who walked in
        space during Gemini 9 flight. NBC TV,
        August, 1971.
           1 reel (7 in.) 7 1/2 in. per sec.
        phonotape.

           L Project Apollo. 2. Space flight to the moon. 3. Scott,
        David Randolph, 1932- 4. Irwin, James B   1932- 5.
        Worden, Alfred M   1930-   L Scott, David Randolph, 1932-
        IL Irwin, James B   1932- IIL Worden, Alfred M   1930-
        IV. Cernan, Eugene Andrew, 1934-

PROJECT APOLLO
Voice Lib.
M1480   Apollo 15 (space flight): splashdown,
bd.4   commentary, speeches. NBC TV, August 7,
        1971.
           1 reel (7 in.) 7 1/2 in. per sec.
        phonotape.

           1. Project Apollo. 2. Space flight to the
        moon. 3. Scott, David Randolph, 1932- 4.
        Irwin, James B   1932-   5. Worden, Alfred
        M   1930-   I. Scott, David Randolph,
        1932- II. Irwin, James B   1932- III.
        Worden, Alfred M   1930-

Project Gemini
Voice Lib.
M847   Cronkite, Walter Leland, 1914-
bd.1   Description of launching of Agena space-
        craft at 10:04 a.m. Monday, October 25, 1965,
        at Cape Kennedy, Florida, until its func-
        tional failure. Announcements by Jack King
        at Cape Kennedy and Paul Haney at Houston
        space center; scrubbing of Gemini VI
        launching. CBS-TV, October 25, 1965.
           18 min.   phonotape (1 r.   7 1/2 i.p.s.)

           1. Space flight. I. Project Gemini.

PROJECT GEMINI
Voice Lib.
M771   Gemini 4 (space flight): excerpts of descrip-
bd.1   tion of take-off; Gemini 4 and Gemini Control
        announcements. June 3, 1965.
           1 reel (7 in.) 7 1/2 in. per sec.
        phonotape.

           1. Project Gemini. 2. McDivitt, James Alton,
        1929- 3. White, Edward Higgins, 1930-1967.
        I. McDivitt, James Alton, 1929- II. White,
        Edward Higgins, 1930-1967.

PROJECT GEMINI
Voice Lib.
M771   Gemini 4 (space flight): excerpts of announce-
bd.2   ments from NBC reporters and Gemini Control,
        regarding preparations for and the actual
        splashdown. Conversation with astronauts
        before pickup by helicopter. Dallas Townsend
        from carrier "Wasp" and David Brinkley and
        Chet Huntley for NBC. NBC TV, June 7, 1965.
        1 reel (7 in.) 7 1/2 in. per sec. phonotape.
           L Project Gemini. 2. McDivitt, James Alton, 1929- 3.
        White, Edward Higgins, 1930-1967. L McDivitt, James Alton,
        1929-   IL White, Edward Higgins, 1930-1967. IIL Townsend,
        Dallas. IV. Brinkley, David McClure, 1920-   V. Huntley,
        Chet, 1911-1974.

PROJECT GEMINI
Voice Lib.
M772   Gemini 4 (space flight): pickup of astronauts
bd.1   McDivitt and White and the capsule, described
        by Chet Huntley and David Brinkley. NBC TV,
        June 7, 1965.
           1 reel (7 in.) 7 1/2 in. per sec.
        phonotape.

           1. Project Gemini. 2. McDivitt, James Alton,
        1929- 3. White, Edward Higgins, 1930-1967.
        I. McDivitt, James Alton, 1929-   II. White,
        Edward Higgins, 1930-1967. III. Huntley, Chet,
        1911-1974 IV. Brinkley, David McClure, 1920-

PROJECT GEMINI

Voice Lib.
M788 Gemini 5 (space flight): summary of space
flight of Gemini Titan V from August 21 to
August 29, 1965, including interview with
Chris Kraft, flight director. 1965.
1 reel (7 in.) 7 1/2 in. per sec.
phonotape.
1. Project Gemini. 2. Cooper, Leroy Gordon,
1927- 3. Conrad, Charles, 1930- I.
Cooper, Leroy Gordon, 1927- II. Conrad,
Charles, 1930- III. Kraft, Christopher
Columbus, 1924-

PROJECT GEMINI

Voice Lib.
M800 Gemini 5 (space flight): press conference
with astronauts Cooper and Conrad at NASA
Space Center, Houston, Texas, regarding
their eight-day space flight with Gemini V.
NBC TV, September 9, 1965.
1 reel (7 in.) 7 1/2 in. per sec.
phonotape.
1. Project Gemini. 2. Cooper, Leroy Gordon,
1927- 3. Conrad, Charles, 1930- I.
Cooper, Leroy Gordon, 1927- II. Conrad,
Charles, 1930-

PROJECT GEMINI

Voice Lib.
M917 Gemini 7 (space flight): Frank McGee's resumé
bd.1 of space flights of astronauts Frank Borman
and James Lovell, Jr., in Gemini 7, commencing
Dec. 4, 1956 to Dec. 18, 1965, and of astronauts Walter Schirra and Thomas Stafford in
Gemini 6, which rendezvoused in space;
including various launching actual reports
and interview with Wally Schirra; comments
by Huntley and Brinkley. NBC TV, December
18, 1965.
1 reel (7 in.) 7 1/2 in. per sec.
phonotape. (Continued on next card)

PROJECT GEMINI

Voice Lib.
M950- Gemini 8 (space flight): press conference at
951 Houston, Texas, Space Center regarding
astronauts' space flight on Gemini 8. NBC
TV, March 26, 1966.
2 reels (7 in.) 7 1/2 in. per sec.
phonotape.
1. Project Gemini. 2. Armstrong, Neil, 1930-
3. Scott, David Randolph, 1932- I. Armstrong,
Neil, 1930- II. Scott, David Randolph,
1932-

PROJECT GEMINI

Voice Lib.
M968 Gemini 9 (space flight): description of
bd.2 countdown and lift-off of "Agena" by
Gemini Mission Control (voice of Al Chop)
for a period of 11 minutes, 41 seconds,
until Gemini flight was scrubbed. Comments
by NBC's Huntley, Brinkley, and Frank McGee.
NBC TV, May 17, 1966.
1 reel (7 in.) 7 1/2 in. per sec. phonotape.
1. Project Gemini. 2. Stafford, Thomas P 1931- 3.
Cernan, Eugene Andrew, 1934- L. Stafford, Thomas P 1931-
II. Cernan, Eugene Andrew, 1934- III. Chop, Al IV.
Huntley, Chet, 1911-1974 V. Brinkley, David McClure, 1920-
VI. McGee, Frank, 1921-1974.

PROJECT GEMINI

Voice Lib.
M986 Gemini 9 (space flight): a. Take-off of
bd.2 Augmented Target Docking Adaptor (ATDA)
from Cape Kennedy (June 1); b. re-cap
by David Brinkley regarding failure of
shroud to jettison (June 3); c. Gemini 9
until failure of guidance system computer
and then scrubbing mission (June 1)
NBC TV, June 1 and 3, 1966.
1 reel (7 in.) 7 1/2 in. per sec. phonotape.
L. Project Gemini. 2. Stafford, Thomas P 1931- 3.
Cernan, Eugene Andrew, 1934- L. Stafford, Thomas P
1931- II. Cernan, Eugene Andrew, 1934- III. Brinkley,
David McClure, 1920-

Voice Lib.
M866- Project '64 (Radio program)
867 Harlem, the black ghetto: actual sound and
bd.1 description of life in Harlem and discusses
Negro residents' problems; Negroes relating
experiences, impressions, and emotions; opinions
by various Negroes of more advanced education;
discussions by white school principals. Covers
social and economic problems of Negroes,
juvenile delinquence, drug addiction, broken
homes, unemployment. Discussion of Harlem
Negro youths' attempts to achieve manhood;
religious beliefs and philosophy of the
(Continued on next card)

Voice Lib.
M866- Project '64 (Radio program) Harlem...
867 1964. (Card 2)
bd.1
Black Muslims' desire for separate political
and economic country; includes Malcolm X
describing his philosophy and ideas in the
Black Muslim movement. Documentary program
produced for CBC by Lloyd Chester, written by
A. Clark and narrated by Percy Rodreguiz [sic]
CBC, 1964.
2 reels (7 in.) 7 1/2 in. per sec. phonotape.
L. Negroes - Social conditions. I. Little, Malcolm, 1925-1965.

Voice Lib.
M867 Project '64 (Radio program)
bd.2- Negro revolt in Harlem: documentary program describing
the place of the Negro in American society; the Negro search for
M869 change, with or without white help; discussion of Negro press;
bd.1 Negroes' cultural background and association with black Africa.
Malcolm X discusses Black Muslim movement, critizing white
infiltration of NAACP Urban League Corp.; comparison of
differences between the Muslims and Black Nationalists. Summary
of Negro revolt and group singing of "We shall overcome".
CBC, 1964.
3 reels (7 in.) 7 1/2 in. per sec. phonotape.

L. Negroes - Social conditions. I. Little, Malcolm, 1925-1965.

Project '64
Voice Lib.
M874 American mood series (Radio program)
bd.2- Appalachia: first program in a series of
M 875 documentaries by John David Hamilton recording
on-the-spot candid sounds and interviews, in
1963. White evangelists' sermons; statements
by teachers and sociologists and natives in
the mountain regions of North Carolina, Tenn-
essee and Kentucky, which include feuding,
square dancing, moon-shining, etc. Native
women recollecting life in the past in Appalachia; origin of feuds; discussion of moon-
shining; native folk songs, including the TVA
(Continued on next card)

Voice Lib.
M874   Project '64
bd.2-   American mood series (Radio program)
M875   Appalachia... 1963. (Card 2)

song; church service excerpts; the Texas
scene, fundamentalism, philosophy, humor,
songs, etc. CBC, 1963.
2 reels (7 in.) 7 1/2 in. per sec.
phonotape.

1. Appalachian Mountains, Southern - Social
life and customs. I. Hamilton, John David
II. Project '64.

Voice Lib.   Project '64
M881,   American mood series (Radio program)
bd.2-   Reverberations from the think tanks. Future of America being
882   discussed by outstanding thinkers. Final documentary in the
American mood series wherein John David Hamilton visits the
Rand Corp. in Santa Monica, discussing its objectives, type of
work and long-range military strategy. Speakers are: James F.
Digby, Robert D. Specht, Bernard Brody, of the Rand Corporation.
Also interviews with: W. H. Ferry, Walter Millis, and Dr. Robert
Hutchins at the Center for Democratic Institutions in Santa Barbara,
Calif.; the Aspen Institute in Aspen, Colo. Speakers are: business
executives, Robert O. Anderson and William Gomberg discussing
social and economic problems from a business executive's viewpoint;
roles of the individual; distinct optimism. CBC Radio, 1964.
2 reels (7 in.) 7 1/2 i.p.s. phonotape.

I. Hamilton, John David   II. Project '64.

Voice Lib.   Project '64
M878-   American mood series (Radio program)
879   Conversation on a party line: John David
bd.1   Hamilton talking to people in North Carolina,
Connecticut, New York, Texas, Colorado, New
Mexico, all intellectuals and numerous school
teachers. "Little Boxes" (the conformity song);
description of American life and its meaning;
definition of socialism; discussing Americans'
international ideas; discussion of Texas
University students and attitudes; Berkeley
professor attitudes; discussion on how to make
money; advocating the study of medicine.
CBC, 1963.

Voice Lib.   Project '64
M876-   American mood series (Radio program)
877   The Southern moderate: the South as seen
through the eyes of a Canadian, John David
Hamilton. The case of the white moderate;
statements by moderate whites about the racial
situation; sentiments about Negroes by Atlanta,
Georgia newspapermen; appreciation of South-
erners' way of life. New Orleans historian's
appraisal of economic conditions in Louisiana.
Mississippi Chamber of Commerce manager eval-
uating situation in Mississippi. Oldtime
justice described by South Carolina citizen.
(Continued on next card)

Voice Lib.   Project '64
M878-   American mood series (Radio program)
879   Conversation on a party line... 1963.
bd.1   (Card 2)

2 reels (7 in.) 7 1/2 in. per sec.
phonotape.

1. U.S. - Social life & customs - 20th cent.
I. Hamilton, John David   II. Project
'64.

Voice Lib.   Project '64
M876-   American mood series (Radio program) The
877   Southern moderate... 1963. (Card 2)

Mississippi's concealed weapons law; opinions
on violence; discussion of white supremacy
in intellect and education; protests about
taxes to aid colored relief; pro and con
opinions about Negroes' rights from Louisianans
and Georgians. CBC Radio, 1963.
2 reels (7 in.) 7 1/2 in. per sec.
phonotape.

1. Southern states - Civilization. I.
Hamilton, John David   II. Project '64.

Voice Lib.   Project '64
M879   American mood series (Radio program)
bd.2-   The real American revolution. California,
881   the real American revolution. Opinions on
bd.1   liberalism and also opinions by John Birch
Society members and conservatives. Discussion
by magazine editor; San Diego resident talking
about John Birch Society and a discussion
about Barry Goldwater. Discussion of life and
culture in Southern California; cause for the
influx of people; lack of family roots and
analysis of social contacts; broad discussion
of L.A. social problems. Discussions of
(Continued on next card)

Voice Lib.
M920   Project '66 (Television program)
bd.2-   NBC year-end TV news analysis. NBC news
923   correspondents analyze 1965 news events and
make predictions for 1966, headed by Frank
McGee, with questions by members of Foreign
Policy Association. NBC, 1965.
4 reels (7 in.) 7 1/2 in. per sec.
phonotape.

I. McGee, Frank, 1921-

Voice Lib.   Project '64
M879   American mood series (Radio program) The
bd.2-   real American revolution... 1963.
881   (Card 2)
bd.1

uprising of college students and a general
discussion of Southern California compared to
Canada. CBC Radio, 1963.
2 reels (7 in.) 7 1/2 in. per sec.
phonotape.

1. California - Soc. condit. I. Hamilton,
John David   II. Project '64.

Voice Lib.
M883-   Project '63 (Radio program)
884   City without newspapers: documentary actual
bd.1   program describing effects of New York City's
newspaper strike; comments by New Yorkers;
union members and company representatives;
reports of various businessmen and touching
upon the cultural stoppage and the business
slump caused by the strike. CBC, 1963.
2 reels (7 in.) 7 1/2 in. per sec.
phonotape.

1. New York (City) - Newspaper strike, 1963.

Voice Lib.
M884   Project '63 (Radio program)
bd.2   City without newspapers: continuation.
          Comparison of the public's credibility of
          newswriters as compared to television commen-
          tators; comparison of the intelligence of
          readers of tabloids as compared with those
          reading New York Times and Tribune; comments by
          newspaper publishers on their responsibility
          to the public; assumption that the greatest
          void left by strike is in the lack of
          advertisement and entertainments. CBC, 1963.
              1 reel (7 in.) 7 1/2 in. per sec. phonotape.
              L New York (City) - Newspaper strike, 1963.

Voice Lib.
M885   Project '63 (Radio program)
              City without newspapers: continuation of program; views
          about the values of the printed word as against the spoken word
          (radio vs. newspapers); opinions about the elimination and
          consolidation of newspapers; opinions by journalistic authorities
          about the quality and the necessity of newspapers; discussion
          of the values of editorials; pro and con, the idea of "too much
          communication"; the Cuban crisis in the news. CBC, 1963.
              1 reel (7 in.) 7 1/2 in. per sec. phonotape.

              L New York (City) - Newspaper strike, 1963.

Voice Lib.
M858-   Project '63 (Radio program)
859   Einstein and after: a one-hour documentary
          program written by John David Hamilton and
          produced by Harry Boyle as item 6 of a series.
          Project '63 program contains voice of Dr.
          Einstein and many of his distinguished friends
          and colleagues in an appraisal of his life and
          work; a biography in sound made possible through
          the assistance of Princeton, Harvard, Yale,
          Syracuse and Columbia Universities. CBC, 1963.
              2 reels (7 in.) 7 1/2 in. per sec. phonotape.
              L Einstein, Albert, 1879-1955. L Einstein, Albert, 1879-1955.

PROPAGANDA
Voice Lib.
M1010   Hitler, Adolf, 1889-1945.
bd.8   Presentation to German press representatives
          about how to report and interpret the news,
          also stressing propaganda methods to
          enthuse the public. Peteler, March 19 &
          23, 1938.
              1 reel (7 in.) 7 1/2 i.p.s. phonotape.

              1. Propaganda.

PROPAGANDA, GERMAN
Voice Lib.
M1463   Joyce, William, 1906-1946.
bd.7   Broadcasting from Germany warning British
          people and farewell to his listeners.
          Peteler, 1940 & April, 1945.
              1 reel (7 in.) 7 1/2 i.p.s. phonotape.

              1. Propaganda, German.

Voice Lib.   PROSTITUTION
M507-   Murrow, Edward Roscoe, 1908-1965.
508,   Narrates "The business of sex", dealing
bd.1   with prostitution and business; various
          prostitutes and businessmen talk and
          discuss dealings. CBS, 1957.
              2 reels (7 in.) 7 1/2 i.p.s. phonotape.

              1. Prostitution. I. Title: The business
          of sex.

Voice Lib.
M1560   Proxmire, William
bd.1   Energy speech; rebuttal to President
          Nixon's speech. CBS-TV, December 2, 1973.
              12 min. phonotape (1 r. 7 1/2 i.p.s.)

              Commentary by Dan Rather and George Herman.

              1. Power resources - U.S. I. Rather, Dan.
          II. Herman, George.

Voice Lib.
M1257   The public and private Robert F. Kennedy;
bd.1   CBS Reports TV documentary program on the
          character, political methods, and ambitions
          of Senator Robert F. Kennedy of New York.
          Narrator: Roger Mudd. CBS-TV, June 20,
          1967.
              1 reel (7 in1) 7 1/2 i.p.s. phonotape.

              1. Kennedy, Robert Francis, 1925-1968.
          I. Mudd, Roger.

PUBLISHERS AND PUBLISHING
Voice Lib.
M1075   Ashmore, Harry Scott, 1916-
bd.2   Discussion among three well-known book
          publishers about authors of the past, the job
          of book editors, the publishing business, book
          reviewers, etc. Held in the Library at the
          Center for the Study of Democratic Institutions
          at Santa Barbara, California. CSDI, 1960.
              1 reel (7 in.) 7 1/2 in. per sec.
          phonotape.

              L Publishers and publishing. L Knopf, Alfred A., 1892-
          II. Ferry, W. H.

Voice Lib.
M1653   Purdy, Alan
              Reading from his book, Sex and death, and
          receiving the A.J.M. Smith Award ($350)
          given by MSU's Canadian-American Studies
          Division for the outstanding contribution
          to Canadian poetry for the year. With
          Victor Howard and A.J.M. Smith. Voice
          Library, May 1, 1974.
              1 hour. phonotape (1 r. 7 1/2 i.p.s.)

              I. Smith, Arthur James Marshall, 1902-
          II. Howard, Victor

C1
A31

The Puritan poet - John Milton

Whorf, Michael, 1933-
The Puritan poet - John Milton.
1 tape cassette.   (The visual sounds of
Mike Whorf. Art, music and letters, A31)
Originally presented on his radio program, Kaleidoscope,
WJR, Detroit.
Duration: 38 min.
The scene is the old world in the age of Renaissance, and
Milton discovers a new age of enlightenment as he writes
Paradise lost - graphically illustrating the new-found path of
religious conviction and understanding.
L. Milton, John, 1608-1674.   L. Title.

C1
H87

The Puritan protector - Oliver Cromwell

Whorf, Michael, 1933-
The Puritan protector - Oliver Cromwell.
1 tape cassette.   (The visual sounds of
Mike Whorf. History and heritage, H87)
Originally presented on his radio program, Kaleidoscope,
WJR, Detroit.
Duration: 36 min.
Bred to peaceful occupations, Cromwell rebuilt the army of the
Parliament to serve as the powerful military arm of the Puritan
Reformation. He was the leader capable of transforming the royalist
face of England, and establishing the power of the Parliament and
the Independent Party.
L. Cromwell, Oliver,   1599-1658.   L. Title.

Voice Lib.
M1220

The pursuit of pleasure

Vanocur, Sander, 1928-
Narrating NBC-TV special documentary program:
"The Pursuit of Pleasure" dealing with such
topics as narcotics, sex, promiscuity, fads,
morals of the current era.   NBC-TV, May 8,
1967.
1 reel (7 in.)   7 1/2 in. per sec.
phonotape.

I. Title: The pursuit of pleasure.

Voice Lib.
M1599-
1600

A quiet requiem for Ezra Pound, with poets
Robert Lowell, Robert Fitzgerald, James
Laughlin, and Robert McGregor.   Modern
Language Center, Harvard University,
December 4, 1972.
70 min.   phonotape (2 r.   7 1/2 i.p.s.)

L. Pound, Ezra Loomis, 1885-1972.   L. Lowell, Robert,
1917-   II. Fitzgerald, Robert, 1910-   III. Laughlin,
James, 1914-   IV. McGregor, Robert,

Voice Lib.
M384
bd.2

Rabaut, Louis Charles, 1886-1961

I can hear it now (radio program)
CBS, February 2, 1951.
1 reel (7 in.)   7 1/2 in. per sec.
phonotape.

I. Taft, Robert Alphonso, 1889-1953. II.
Rayburn, Samuel Taliaferro, 1882-1961. III.
Barkley, Alben William, 1877-1956. IV. Rabaut,
Louis Charles, 1886-1961. V. Attlee, Clement
Richard Attlee, 1st earl, 1883-1967. VI.
Kelly, Capt., U.S.A.

Voice Lib.
M230
bd.2

RACE DISCRIMINATION

Little, Malcolm, 1925-1965.
Excerpts of question and answer session
with students at Michigan State University,
January 23, 1963.
1 reel (7 in.)   7 1/2 i.p.s.   phonotape.

1. Race discrimination.

Voice Lib.
M362-
372,
bd.1

RACE DISCRIMINATION - U.S.

Birmingham: a testament of non-violence.   In six parts.
WRVR, May 1963.
11 reels (7 in.)   7 1/2 i.p.s.   phonotape.

CONTENTS. -pt. 1. "A happy day in Birmingham". -pt. 2.
"The Klan, two bombs, and a riot"; Alabama crowd, bombing
of a home and motel, rioting that followed, interviews with
citizens of Birmingham. -pt. 3. "Mother's Day, 1963". -pt. 4.
"Back to school in Birmingham"; students in non-violence
movement, methods of organization. -pt. 5. "Keep Birmingham
southern"; unidentified 78-year old Birmingham citizen, white,
analyzes integration problem; Birmingham Medical College
faculty member analyzes situation; Birmingham College white
student gives ideas od integration; white Birmingham mothers
chatting about integration problem; Birmingham insurance

(Continued on next card)

Voice Lib.
M362-
372,
bd.1

RACE DISCRIMINATION - U.S.

Birmingham: a testament of non-violence.   1963.
(Card 2)

CONTENTS (Cont'd)   executive's opinion on situation. -
pt. 6. "Blacks and whites together".

L. Birmingham, Ala.   2. Race discrimination - U.S.

Voice Lib.
M1204,
bd.2-
1205

RACE DISCRIMINATION - U.S.

Carmichael, Stokely, 1941-
Lecture on "black power" and methods of
solving racial problems, held at MSU
Auditorium.   A/V, February 9, 1967.
2 reels (7 in.)   7 1/2 in. per sec.
phonotape.

Voice Lib.
M1087
bd.1

RACE DISCRIMINATION - U.S.

Little, Malcolm, 1925-1965.
Speaking at MSU press conference about
race problem and aim of Black Muslims;
Meredith case and Mississippi; followed
by various takes of interview for MSU film.
Location recording, June 22, 1963.
1 reel (7 in.)   7 1/2 i.p.s.   phonotape.

1. Black Muslims.   2. Race discrimination -
U.S.

Voice Lib.
M1274,
bd.2-
1276
RACE DISCRIMINATION - U.S.
Newark race riots, midsummer 1967. Discussion of mass meeting in Newark between city officials, black and white citizens and sociologists about the causes of Newark race riots and suggestions for improved conditions. NET, August 20, 1967.
3 reels (7 in.)   7 1/2 i.p.s.   phonotape.

1. Newark, N.J. 2. Race discrimination - U.S.

Voice Lib.
M1619
bd.2
RACE DISCRIMINATION - U.S.
Stone, Chuck
Perspectives in Black, with Roz Abrahms, Cheri Mazingo, and J. Markisha Johnson. WKAR, 1974.
27 min.   phonotape (1 r.   7 1/2 i.p.s.)

1. Race discrimination - U.S. 2. Watergate Affair, 1872-   I. Abrahms, Roz.
II. Mazingo, Cheri. III. Johnson, J. Markisha.

RACE DISCRIMINATION - U.S.
Voice Lib.
M1088
bd.3
Wilkins, Roy, 1901-
Interview on Barry Gray Show with Roy Wilkins, Executive Secretary of NAACP, pertaining to social and economic problems of Negroes in America and equal rights for all minority groups. WMCA, 1962.
1 reel (7 in.)   7 1/2 in. per sec. phonotape.

Voice Lib.
M539
bd.4
RACE PROBLEMS - ADDRESSES, ESSAYS, LECTURES
Washington, Booker Taliaferro, 1859?-1915.
The American Negro (Atlanta Exposition address); improvement of race relations, conditions in the South. Columbia Gramophone Company, 1906.
1 reel (7 in.)   7 1/2 i.p.s.   phonotape.

1. Race problems - Addresses, essays, lectures.

Voice Lib.
M795
bd.2
Racine, Jean Baptiste, 1639-1699.
Phèdre
Bernhardt, Sarah, 1844-1923.
Excerpt from Racine play "Phèdre". G&T, 1903.
1 reel (7 in.)   7 1/2 in. per sec. phonotape.

I. Racine, Jean Baptiste, 1639-1699./ Phèdre.

RADIO
Voice Lib.
M1472
The way it was and the way it is. Fiftieth anniversary of radio broadcasting in U.S. Voice of America, 1970.
1 reel (7 in.)   7 1/2 in. per sec. phonotape.

CONTENTS.-Lee De Forest describes Hughes-Wilson election; KDKA Harding-Cox election broadcast; Harold Arlend, first radio announcer; Lowell Thomas reports Lindbergh landing; Herb Morrison reports "Hindenberg" crash; H. V. Kaltenborn, Spanish Civil War broadcast; East Coast (Continued on next card)

RADIO
Voice Lib.
M1472
The way it was and the way it is... 1970.
(Card 2)

CONTENTS, cont'd.-power failure bulletins; miscellaneous station calls, program excerpts, jingles.

1. Radio.

Voice Lib.
M395
bd.3
RADIO - HISTORY
Marconi, Guglielmo, Marchese, 1874-1937.
Speech to Tribune Women's Club of Chicago on modern communications (shortwave broadcast from Rome), tells of early communications of his first transatlantic broadcast, state of radio art in 1930's. New York, WOR, March 1, 1937.
1 reel (7 in.)   7 1/2 i.p.s.   phonotape.

1. Radio - History.

Voice Lib.
M1373
bd.4
RADIO BROADCASTING
Goebbels, Joseph, 1897-1945.
Talking about the goals of the NSDAP pertaining to radio broadcast. Peteler, 1933.
1 reel (7 in.)   7 1/2 i.p.s.   phonotape.

1. Radio broadcasting. 2. Nationalsozialistische Deutsche Arbeiter-Partei.

C1
M19
RADIO BROADCASTING
Whorf, Michael, 1933-
The big broadcast.
1 tape cassette. (The visual sounds of Mike Whorf. Miscellaneous, M19)

Originally presented on his radio program, Kaleidoscope. WJR, Detroit.
Duration: 53 min.
The history and the personalities who made the radio a fixture in the household.

L Radio broadcasting. L Title.

RADIO FREE EUROPE

Voice Lib.
381-   I can hear it now (radio program)
382   CBS, April 26, 1951.
bd.1   2 reels (7 in.) 7 1/2 in. per sec. phonotape.
        L Radio Free Europe. 2. Strategic Air Command. L
Ridgway, Matthew Bunker, 1895-   IL Churchill, Winston Leonard
Spencer, 1874-1965.   IIL Bevan, Aneurin, 1897-1960.   IV. Nixon,
Richard Milhous, Pres. U. S., 1913-   V. Kerr, Robert Samuel, 1896-
1963.   VL Brewster, Ralph Owen, 1888-1962.   VII. Wherry, Kenneth
Spicer, 1892-195L VIII. Capehart, Homer Earl, 1897-   IX.
Lehman, Herbert Henry, 1878-1963.   X. Taft, Robert Alphonso,
1889-1953.   XL Moody, Arthur Edson Blair, 1902-1954.   XII.
Martin, Joseph William, 1884-1968.   XIII. McMahon, James O'Brien,
1903-1952.   XIV. MacArthur, Douglas, 1880-1964.   XVII. Wilson,
Charles Edward, 1886-197   XVIII. Irvine, Clarence T

Voice Lib.
M620   Radio in the 1940's (Part I): a series of
bd.1-   excerpts from important broadcasts of the 1940's; a
bd.16   sample of radio of the period. NVL, April, 1964.
         1 reel (7 in.) 7 1/2 in. per sec. phonotape.
         L Radio programs. L Thomas, Lowell Jackson, 1892-   IL
Gunther, John, 1901-1970.   IIL Kaltenborn, Hans von, 1878-1965.
IV. Delmar, Kenny.   V. Those were the good old days (Radio
program) VL Elman, Dave.   VII. Hall, Frederick Lee, 1916-1970.
VIII. Hobby lobby (Radio program) IX. Roosevelt, Franklin Delano,
Pres. U. S., 1882-1945.   X. Willkie, Wendell Lewis, 1892-1944.
XL Hoover, Herbert Clark, Pres. U. S., 1874-1964.   XII. Johnson,
Hugh Samuel, 1882-1942.   XIII. Cobb, Irvin Shrewsbury, 1876-1944.
XIV. Roosevelt, Theodore, 1858-1919.   XV. Nye, Gerald Prentice,
1892-197L XVL Lindbergh, Charles Augustus, 1902-   XVII.
Toscanini, Arturo, 1867-1957

Voice Lib.
M621   Radio in the 1940's (Part II): a series of
bd.1-   excerpts from important broadcasts of the
12   1940's; a sample of radio of the period.
         NVL, April, 1964.
         1 reel (7 in.) 7 1/2 in. per sec. phonotape.
         L Daly, John Charles, 1914-   IL Hall, Josef Washington,
1894-   IIL Shirer, William Lawrence, 1904-   IV. Roosevelt,
Eleanor (Roosevelt) 1884-1962.   V. Roosevelt, Franklin Delano,
Pres. U. S., 1882-1945.   VL Churchill, Winston Leonard Spencer,
1874-1965.   VII. Wainwright, Jonathan Mayhew, 1883-1953.   VIII.
Cantor, Eddie, 1893-1964.   IX. Sinatra, Francis Albert, 1917-
X. Hope, Bob, 1903-   XL Crosby, Bing, 1901-   XII. Shore,
Dinah, 1917(?)-   XIII. Bergen, Edgar, 1903-   XIV. Armstrong,
Louis, 1900-1971.   XV. Eldridge, Roy, 1911-

Voice Lib.
M622   Radio in the 1940's (Part III): a series of
bd.1-   excerpts from important broadcasts of the 1940's; a sample
bd.15   of radio of the period. NVL, April, 1964.
         1 reel (7 in.) 7 1/2 in. per sec. phonotape.
         L Radio programs. L Miller, Alton Glenn, 1909(?)-1944. IL
Diles, Ken   IIL Wilson, Donald Harlow, 1900-   IV.
Livingstone, Mary   V. Benny, Jack, 1894-   VL Harris,
Phil   VIL Merman, Ethel, 1909-   VIII. Smith, "Wonderful"
IX. Bennett, Richard Dyer   X. Louis, Joe, 1914-   XL
Eisenhower, Dwight David, Pres. U. S., 1890-1969.   XII. MacArthur,
Douglas, 1880-1964.   XIII. Romulo, Carlos Pena, 1899-   XIV.
Welles, Orson, 1915-   XV. Jackson, Robert Houghwout, 1892-1954.
XVL LaGuardia, Fiorello Henry, 1882-1945.   XVII. Nehru, Jawa-
harlal, 1889-1964.   XVIII. Gandhi, Mohandas Karamchand, 1869-1948.

Voice Lib.
M618   Radio in the 1930's (Part I): a series of
bd.1-   excerpts from important broadcasts of the
14   1930's; a sample of radio of the period.
         NVL, April, 1964.
         1 reel (7 in.) 7 1/2 in. per sec. phonotape.
         L Shaw, George Bernard, 1856-1950. IL Crosby, Bing, 1901-
IIL Barkley, Alban William, 1877-1956.   IV. Roosevelt, Franklin
Delano, Pres. U. S., 1882-1945.   V. Hoover, Herbert Clark, Pres.
U. S., 1874-1964.   VL Long, Huey Pierce, 1893-1935.   VIL Townsend, Francis Everett, 1867-1960.   VIII. Coughlin, Charles Edward,
1891-   IX. Rogers, Will, 1879-1935.   X. Pius XII, Pope, 1876-
1958.   XL Edward VIII, king of Great Britain, 1894-1972.   XII.
Barrymore, John, 1882-1942.   XIII. Woollcott, Alexander, 1887-
1943.   XIV. Allen, Fred, 1894-1956.   XV. Benchley, Robert Charles,
1889-1945.

Voice Lib.
M619   Radio in the 1930's (Part II): a series of
bd.1-   excerpts of the 1930's; a sample of radio
14   of the period. NVL, April, 1964.
         1 reel (7 in.) 7 1/2 in. per sec. phonotape.
         L Allen, Fred, 1894-1956. IL Delmar, Kenny   IIL Donald,
Peter   IV. Pious, Minerva   V. Fennelly, Parker   VL
Boyer, Charles, 1899-   VIL Dunne, Irene, 1904-   VIII.
DeMille, Cecil Blount, 1881-1959.   IX. West, Mae, 1893-   X.
Dafoe, Allan Ray, 1883-1943.   XL Dionne quintuplets.   XII. Ortega,
Santos   XIII. War of the worlds (radio program) XIV. Ives, Burl,
1909-   XV. Robinson, Earl, 1910-   XVL Temple, Shirley,
1928-   XVII. Earhart, Amelia, 1898-1937.   XVIII. Lawrence,
Gertrude, 1901-1952.   XIX. Cohan, George Michael, 1878-1942.
XX. Shaw, George Bernard, 1856-1950.   XXL Hitler, Adolf, 1889-
1945.   XXII. Chamberlain, Neville, 1869-1940.   XXIII. Roosevelt,
Franklin Delano, Pres. U. S., 1882-1945.

Voice Lib.
M617   Radio in the 1920's: a series of excerpts
bd.1-   from important broadcasts of the 1920's,
bd.25   with brief prologue and epilogue; a sample
         of radio of the period. NVL, April, 1964.
         1 reel (7 in.) 7 1/2 in. per sec.
phonotape.
         L Radio programs. L Marconi, Guglielmo, marchese, 1874-
1937. IL Kendall, H   G   IIL Coolidge, Calvin, Pres. U. S.,
1872-1933. IV. Wilson, Woodrow, Pres. U. S., 1856-1924. V.
Roosevelt, Franklin Delano, Pres. U. S., 1882-1945. VL Lodge,
Henry Cabot, 1850-1924. VII. LaGuardia, Fiorello Henry, 1882-1947.
VIII. The Happiness Boys (Radio program) IX. Gallagher and Sheen.
X. Barney Google. XL Vallee, Rudy, 1901-   XIL The two
(Continued on next card)

Voice Lib.
M617   Radio in the 1920's... 1964. (Card 2)
bd.1-
bd.25   black crows (Radio program). XIII. The Rollickers. XIV. Marvin,
Johnny   XV. Brokenshire, Norman Ernest, 1898-1965. XVL
Smith, "Whispering Jack"   XVII. Brice, Fanny, 1891-1951.
XVIII. Rogers, Will, 1879-1935. XIX. Morgan, Helen
XX. Sunday, William Ashley, 1862-1935. XXL McPherson,
Aimee Semple, 1890-1944. XXIL Ruth, George Herman, 1894-
1948. XXIIL Gehrig, Lou, 1903-194L XXIV. Coué, Emil, 1857-
1926. XXV. McNamee, Graham, 1888-1942. XXVL Lindbergh,
Charles Augustus, 1902-   XXVIL Corwin, Norman Lewis,
1910-

RADIO JOURNALISM

Voice Lib.
M1041   Behind the scenes in the CBS newsroom; CBS
bd.2   radio news with Elmer Davis, Edward R.
        Murrow and Paul White, describing the
        operations of radio news broadcasting.
        CBS Radio, June 1, 1941.
        1 reel (7 in.) 7 1/2 i.p.s. phonotape.

        1. Radio journalism. I. Davis, Elmer
Holmes, 1890-1958. II. Murrow, Edward
Roscoe, 1908-1965. III. White, Paul Welrose,
1902-1955.

Voice Lib.
353   Radio Moscow.
bd.16   Outbreak of Korean War; Russian viewpoint
        on starting of Korean conflict. NBC, July,
        1950.
        1 reel (7 in.) 7 1/2 in. per sec.
phonotape.

        Original disc off-speed.

        1. Korean War, 1950-1953

Voice Lib.
M1025 Radio news reports concerning U.S. and Allied
bd.3   landings on North Africa, November 7, 1942;
        followed by military analysis by Major George
        Fielding Eliot. CBS Radio, November 7, 1942.
        1 reel (7 in.)   7 1/2 in. per sec.
        phonotape.

        1. World War, 1939-1945.   I. Eliot, George
        Fielding, 1894-1971.

Voice Lib.
M1025 Radio news special report regarding first
bd.2   use of atomic bomb on Japan, August 7, 1945;
        description by pilot of actual detonation.
        CBS Radio, August 7, 1945.
        1 reel (7 in.)   7 1/2 in. per sec.
        phonotape.

        1. Atomic bomb

                    RADIO PROGRAMS
Voice Lib.
M1037 Jack Armstrong, the All-American Boy (Radio
bd.2   program)
        Jack Armstrong, the "All-American" boy,
        in one episode entitled "Jack Armstrong and
        the Mutineers"; includes Wheaties commercial.
        NBC Radio, 1944.
        1 reel (7 in.)   7 1/2 in. per sec.
        phonotape.

        1. Radio programs.

                    RADIO PROGRAMS
Voice Lib.
M620   Radio in the 1940's (Part I): a series of
bd.1-   excerpts from important broadcasts of the 1940's; a
bd.16   sample of radio of the period. NVL, April, 1964.
        1 reel (7 in.)   7 1/2 in. per sec. phonotape.
        I. Radio programs. I. Thomas, Lowell Jackson, 1892-   II.
        Gunther, John, 1901-1970. III. Kaltenborn, Hans von, 1878-1965.
        IV. Delmar, Kenny. V. Those were the good old days (Radio
        program) VI. Elman, Dave. VII. Hall, Frederick Lee, 1916-1970.
        VIII. Hobby lobby (Radio program) IX. Roosevelt, Franklin Delano,
        Pres. U.S., 1882-1945. X. Willkie, Wendell Lewis, 1892-1944.
        XI. Hoover, Herbert Clark, Pres. U.S., 1874-1964. XII. Johnson,
        Hugh Samuel, 1882-1942. XIII. Cobb, Irvin Shrewsbury, 1876-1944.
        XIV. Roosevelt, Theodore, 1858-1919. XV. Nye, Gerald Prentice,
        1892-1971. XVI. Lindbergh, Charles Augustus, 1902-   XVII.
        Toscanini, Arturo, 1867-195?

                    RADIO PROGRAMS
Voice Lib.
M622   Radio in the 1940's (Part III): a series of
bd.1-   excerpts from important broadcasts of the 1940's; a sample
bd.15   of radio of the period. NVL, April, 1964.
        1 reel (7 in.)   7 1/2 in. per sec. phonotape.
        I. Radio programs. I. Miller, Alton Glenn, 1909(?)-1944. II.
        Diles, Ken   III. Wilson, Donald Harlow, 1900-   IV.
        Livingstone, Mary   V. Benny, Jack, 1894-   VI. Harris,
        Phil   VII. Merman, Ethel, 1909-   VIII. Smith, "Wonderful"
        IX. Bennett, Richard Dyer   X. Louis, Joe, 1914-   XI.
        Eisenhower, Dwight David, Pres. U.S., 1890-1969. XII. MacArthur,
        Douglas, 1880-1964. XIII. Romulo, Carlos Pena, 1899-   XIV.
        Welles, Orson, 1915-   XV. Jackson, Robert Houghwout, 1892-1954.
        XVI. LaGuardia, Fiorello Henry, 1882-1945. XVII. Nehru, Jawa-
        harlal, 1889-1964. XVIII. Gandhi, Mohandas Karamchand, 1869-1948.

                    RADIO PROGRAMS
Voice Lib.
M617   Radio in the 1920's: a series of excerpts
bd.1-   from important broadcasts of the 1920's,
bd.25   with brief prologue and epilogue; a sample
        of radio of the period. NVL, April, 1964.
        1 reel (7 in.)   7 1/2 in. per sec.
        phonotape.
        I. Radio programs. I. Marconi, Guglielmo, marchese, 1874-
        1937. II. Kendall, H   G   III. Coolidge, Calvin, Pres. U.S.,
        1872-1933. IV. Wilson, Woodrow, Pres. U.S., 1856-1924. V.
        Roosevelt, Franklin Delano, Pres. U.S., 1882-1945. VI. Lodge,
        Henry Cabot, 1850-1924. VII. LaGuardia, Fiorello Henry, 1882-1947.
        VIII. The Happiness Boys (Radio program) IX. Gallagher and Sheen.
        X. Barney Google. XI. Vallee, Rudy, 1901-   XII. The two
        (Continued on next card)

                    RADIO SERIALS
Voice Lib.
M853   John's other wife (radio program). NBC,
bd.1   June 12, 1940.
        1 reel (7 in.)   7 1/2 in. per sec.
        phonotape.

        1. Radio serials.

                    RADIO SERIALS
Voice Lib.
M853   Orphans of divorce (radio program). NBC,
bd.2   June 7, 1940.
        1 reel (7 in.)   7 1/2 in. per sec.
        phonotape.

        1. Radio serials.

                    Raft, George
Voice Lib.
M1028 Lux presents Hollywood: montage of excerpts
bd.7   from various Lux radio shows. George Raft,
        Virginia Mayo, Cedric Hardwicke, and
        Ingrid Bergman. Michigan State University,
        Department of Television and Radio, 1940's.
        1 reel (7 in.)   7 1/2 in. per sec.
        phonotape.

        I. Raft, George   II. Mayo, Virginia
        III. Hardwicke, Sir Cedric, 1893-1964. IV.
        Bergman, Ingrid, 1917-

Voice Lib.
M1743 Raft, George
bd.2   Reminisces on the Mike Douglas Show.
        WILX-TV, June 27, 1974.
        10 min. phonotape (1 r.   7 1/2 i.p.s.)

        I. Raft, George. 2. O'Brien, Pat, 1899-   3. Muni,
        Paul, 1895-1967. 4. Crawford, Joan, 1908-   5. West, Mae,
        1893-   6. Richman, Harry. 7. Entertainers - U. S. I.
        Douglas, Mike, 1925-

C1 PWM14
RAGTIME MUSIC
Whorf, Michael, 1933-
Those ragtime years.
1 tape cassette. (The visual sounds of Mike Whorf. Panorama; a world of music, PWM-14)

Originally presented on his radio program, Kaleidoscope, WJR, Detroit.
Duration: 25 min.
Music from the decade between the turn of the century and World War I, including some by composer Scott Joplin.

1. Ragtime music. 2. Joplin, Scott, 1868-1917. I. Title.

C1 SC13
RAILROADS
Whorf, Michael, 1933-
The days of the iron horse.
1 tape cassette. (The visual sounds of Mike Whorf. Science, SC13)

Originally presented on his radio program, Kaleidoscope, WJR, Detroit.
Duration: 30 min., 50 sec.
It was a boon to mankind, an invention which would cut continents in half. The great iron horse, the trains that would fly over nations, serving the millions of people of the world. Today its roar of engines and shrill whistles are but dim echoes filtering down from the past.

1. Railroads. I. Title.

Voice Lib. M1570-1571, bd.1
RAILROADS - U.S.
Shapp, Milton J 1912-
National Press Club address. WKAR-AM, February 21, 1974.
50 min. phonotape (2 r. 7 1/2 i.p.s.)

1. Railroads - U.S. 2. Power resources - U.S.

C1 H40
RALEIGH'S ROANOKE COLONIES, 1584-1590
Whorf, Michael, 1933-
The lost colony of Roanoke.
1 tape cassette. (The visual sounds of Mike Whorf. History and heritage, H40)

Originally presented on his radio program, Kaleidoscope, WJR, Detroit.
Duration: 39 min., 30 sec.
Prior to the coming of the Pilgrims, a group of similar hardy souls settled in Virginia. Their colony thrived and grew prosperous and then for some unknown reason, it perished.

1. Raleigh's Roanoke Colonies, 1584-1590. I. Title.

Voice Lib. M902
Ralph, David Clinton, 1922-
Lecture to speech class 101 on credibility in speech. Direct recording, November 29, 1965.
1 reel (7 in.) 7 1/2 i.p.s. phonotape.

1. Communication.

Voice Lib. M963-968 bd.1
RAMPARTS
Hannah, John Alfred, 1902-
Subcommittee hearing of Michigan State Legislature pertaining to the controversial article in "Ramparts" magazine. May 16, 1966.
6 reels (7 in.) 7 1/2 in. per sec. phonotape.

1. Ramparts.

Voice Lib. M1583
Ramsbotham, Sir Peter Edward, 1919-
National Press Club address. WKAR-AM, March 21, 1974.
50 min. phonotape (1 r. 7 1/2 i.p.s.)

Includes questions and answer period.

1. Gt. Brit. - Foreign relations - U.S.
2. U.S. - Foreign relations - Gt. Brit.
3. Gt. Brit. - Economic conditions.

Voice Lib. M837 bd.2
The Rape of Nanking (symphonic selection); musical description of Japanese attacks on China in 1942. Columbia Records, Inc., 1943.
1 reel (7 in.) 7 1/2 in. per sec. phonotape.

Voice Lib. M767 bd.1
Rapoport, Azaria
Excerpt from "Popular Music of Europe" (Program 11); comments on effects of British music on Israel, including song "With a Little Bit of Luck" from "My Fair Lady", sung in Hebrew, Italian and Spanish. Westinghouse Broadcasting Corporation, 1964.
1 reel (7 in.) 7 1/2 in. per sec. phonotape. (The Music Goes Round and Round)
I. Title: Popular music of Europe. II. Series.

Voice Lib. M863 bd.4
Rastus, take me back
Dressler, Marie, 1873-1934.
In comedy skit: "Rastus, take me back". IRCC-cylinder, 1907.
1 reel (7 in.) 7 1/2 in. per sec. phonotape.

I. Title: Rastus, take me back.

Rather, Dan
Voice Lib.
M1287   Johnson, Lyndon Baines, Pres. U.S., 1908-
bd.2-   1973.
1288   "A conversation with the President". One
hour press conference with President Johnson
by the three TV networks about current
problems, prior to President's departure
for Australia. Dan Rather, CBS; Ray Shearer,
NBC; Frank Reynolds, ABC.   NBC-TV,
December 19, 1967.
    2 reels (7 in.)   7 1/2 in. per sec.
phonotape.

Voice Lib.
158   Rayburn, Samuel Taliaferro, 1882-1961.
bd.1   Interview by Congressman Hebert.
Private recording, June 26, 1944.
    1 reel (7 in.)   7 1/2 in. per sec.
phonotape.

Rather, Dan
Voice Lib.
M1487-   Nixon, Richard Milhous, Pres. U.S., 1913-
1488   One hour question and answer session
bd.1   with Pres. Nixon and CBS's Dan Rather,
dealing with all current topics.   CBS,
January 2, 1972.
    2 reels (7 in.)   7 1/2 in. per sec.
phonotape.

    I. Rather, Dan

Voice Lib.
M724   Rayburn, Samuel Taliaferro, 1882-1961.
bd.4   Samuel Rayburn and Estes Kefauver at
Democratic convention.   1952.
    45 sec.   phonotape (1 r.   7 1/2 i.p.s.)

    1. Presidents - U.S. - Election - 1952.
I. Kefauver, Estes, 1903-1963.

Rather, Dan
Voice Lib.
M1560   Proxmire, William
bd.1   Energy speech; rebuttal to President
Nixon's speech.   CBS-TV, December 2, 1973.
    12 min.   phonotape (1 r.   7 1/2 i.p.s.)

    Commentary by Dan Rather and George Herman.

    1.Power resources - U.S.   I. Rather, Dan.
II. Herman, George.

Voice Lib.
578   Rayburn, Samuel Taliaferro, 1882-1961.
1956 Democratic National Convention;
introduces former President Harry S Truman
and Vice-Presidential nominee Estes Kefauver
to delegates.   CBS, August 17, 1956.
    1 reel (7 in.)   7 1/2 in. per sec.
phonotape.

Rather, Dan
Voice Lib.
M1286   Robb, Lynda Bird (Johnson), 1944-
bd.3   Excerpt of description of wedding ceremony
at White House by Dan Rather, including
statements of Lynda and her bridegroom,
Captain Charles Robb.   December 9, 1967.
    1 reel (7 in.)   7 1/2 in. per sec.
phonotape.

    I. Rather, Dan   II. Robb, Charles
Spittal, 1939-

Voice Lib.
M724   Rayburn, Samuel Taliaferro, 1882-1961.
Nominating for President, Lyndon B.
Johnson in Los Angeles in 1960.   1960.
    1 reel (7 in.)   7 1/2 in. per sec.
phonotape.

    1. Johnson, Lyndon Baines, Pres. U.S.,
1908-1973.

Ratti, Achille, 1857-1939.
    see
Pius XI, pope, 1857-1939.

Voice Lib.
M258   Rayburn, Samuel Taliaferro, 1882-1961.
bd.14   CBS Radio interview discussing his long
service in the House of Representatives.
New York, CBS, June 12, 1961.
    1 reel (7 in.)   7 1/2 in. per sec.
phonotape.

Voice Lib.
242   Rayburn, Samuel Taliaferro, 1882-1961.
          A tribute to Sam Rayburn, with Stuart
       Novin and Robert Trout. CBS Radio,
       November 16, 1961.
          1 reel (7 in.) 7 1/2 in. per sec.
       phonotape.

          I. Novin, Stuart   II. Trout, Robert,
       1908-

              Rayburn, Samuel Taliaferro, 1882-1961
Voice Lib.
M384   I can hear it now (radio program)
bd.2   CBS, February 2, 1951.
            1 reel (7 in.) 7 1/2 in. per sec.
         phonotape.

            I. Taft, Robert Alphonso, 1889-1953. II.
         Rayburn, Samuel Taliaferro, 1882-1961. III.
         Barkley, Alban William, 1877-1956. IV. Rabaut,
         Louis Charles, 1886-1961. V. Attlee, Clement
         Richard Attlee, 1st earl, 1883-1967. VI.
         Kelly, Capt., U.S.A.

              RAYBURN, SAMUEL TALIAFERRO, 1882-1961
Voice Lib.
M317   Johnson, Lyndon Baines, Pres. U.S., 1908-1973.
bd.2   Nancy Dickerson of NBC at Inaugural Ball
         talking to Vice-President and Mrs. Johnson;
         Charles Collingwood and Johnson on Sam Rayburn;
         Johnson in Berlin, audience with Pope John.
         NBC, CBS, November 24, 1963.
           1 reel (7 in.) 7 1/2 in. per sec. phonotape.
           L. Rayburn, Samuel Taliaferro, 1882-1961. L. Dickerson,
         Nancy Hanschman, 1929 (?)-   II. Johnson, Claudia Alta
         (Taylor) 1912-   III. Collingwood, Charles Cummings, 1917-
         IV. Joannes XXIII, Pope, 1881-1963.

              Raye, Martha, 1916-
Voice Lib.
K1025 Fields, W.C., 1879-1946.
bd.4   Excerpt from skit in "Eddie Cantor Show",
       with Martha Raye, Dick Powell, etc. CBS
       Radio, 1930's.
          1 reel (7 in.) 7 1/2 in. per sec.
       phonotape.

          I. Raye, Martha, 1916-   II. Powell,
       Dick, 1904-1963. III. Eddie Cantor Show
       (radio program)

Voice Lib.
644   Read, Susan
bd.5-6   Sings: "I Know My Love", "Greensleeves".
       V-Discs, 1943.
          1 reel (7 in.) 7 1/2 in. per sec.
       phonotape.

          I. Title: I know my love. 2. Title:
       Greensleeves.

               THE READER'S DIGEST
C1
A38   Whorf, Michael, 1933-
            The original big-little book.
          1 tape cassette.   (The visual sounds of
       Mike Whorf. Art, music and letters, A38)
          Originally presented on his radio program, Kaleidoscope,
       WJR, Detroit.
          Duration: 40 min.
          Here is the story of the Reader's digest, the people who write it,
       why they write it and how this popular magazine is compiled.
          L. The Reader's digest. 2. Wallace, DeWitt, 1889-
       L. Title.

Voice Lib.
M1430 Reagan, Ronald Wilson, 1911-
bd.1   "The Speech". Speech in support of Barry
       Goldwater during the 1964 presidential
       campaign. UCLA, October 27, 1964.
          1 reel (7 in.) 7 1/2 in. per sec.
       phonotape.

          1. Goldwater, Barry Morris, 1909-

Voice Lib.
M1299 Reagan, Ronald Wilson, 1911-
bd.1   A presentation of some of the ideas of
       Governor Ronald Reagan of California, as
       they are expressed by him in four days of
       "examination" at Yale University. Conversation
       and confrontation with students. PBL
       program, December 31, 1967.
          1 reel (7 in.) 7 1/2 in. per sec.
       phonotape.

Voice Lib. Reagan, Ronald Wilson, 1911-
M1223 Town meeting of the world (Television program)
bd.1   Discussion and questions by students of
       various countries from Britain about the image
       of America in the eyes of youth. Answers by
       Senator Robert F. Kennedy of New York and
       Governor Ronald Reagan of California, with
       Charles Collingwood as moderator. Principle
       items covered: Vietnam, civil rights. CBS-TV,
       May 15, 1967.
          1 reel (7 in.) 7 1/2 in. per sec. phonotape.
          L. Kennedy, Robert Francis, 1925-1968. II. Reagan, Ronald
       Wilson, 1911-   III. Collingwood, Charles Cummings, 1917-

---

              Reasoner, Harry, 1923-
Voice Lib.
M942   Vietnam perspective (Television program)
          CBS Special Report on Senate Foreign
       Relations Committee hearings and the war
       in Vietnam. CBS, February 18, 1966.
          1 reel (7 in.) 7 1/2 in. per sec.
       phonotape.

          1. Vietnamese conflict, 1961-   - U.S.
       I. Mudd, Roger   II. Severeid, Arnold Eric,
       1912-   III. Reasoner, Harry, 1923-   IV.
       Kalb, Marvin L

Voice Lib.
M1272   Reasoner, Harry, 1923-
bd.1   Documentary program about the "Hippie
         Temptation"; includes interviews with hippies,
         doctors, parents, patients, police,
         psychiatrists and discussion about use of
         LSD. Recorded on location.   CBS-TV,
         August 22, 1967.
            1 reel (7 in.)   7 1/2 in. per sec.
         phonotape.
            1. Hippies.

Voice Lib.   Reasoner, Harry, 1923-
M1286   Eisenhower, Dwight David, Pres. U.S., 1890-1969.
bd.1   Conversation by Harry Reasoner with General
         Dwight D. Eisenhower and General Omar N.
         Bradley at Eisenhower's office in Gettysburg,
         Pennsylvania, about the U.S. military partici-
         pation in Vietnam and the conduct of it.
         CBS-TV, November 28, 1967.
            1 reel (7 in.)   7 1/2 in. per sec.
         phonotape.
            I. Reasoner, Harry, 1923-   II. Bradley,
         Omar Nelson, 1893-

Voice Lib.   Reber, Miles
M746   U.S. Congress. Senate. Committee on Government Operations.
bd.2   Permanent Subcommittee on Investigations.
            Proceedings of the [1st session] of Senate Army-McCarthy
         hearings, April 22, 1954. Testimony by various witnesses
         regarding pressure put on the Army to obtain a commission for
         Private David Schine. Some of the people speaking are:
         Griffin Bancroft, CBS announcer, describing the scenes at the
         hearings; Joseph N. Welch, counsel for the Army; Ray Jenkins,
         counsel for the subcommittee; Army Secretary Robert Stevens;
         General Reber and Senator McClellan of Arkansas. CBS Radio,
         April 22, 1954.
            1 reel (7 in.) 7 1/2 in. per sec. phonotape.
            L. McCarthy-Army controversy, 1954. L. Bancroft, Griffin
         II. Welch, Joseph Nye, 1890-1960. III. Jenkins, Ray Howard,
         1897-   IV. Stevens, Robert Ten Broeck, 1899-   V.
         Reber, Miles   VI. McClellan, John Little, 1896-

Voice Lib.
M331   Reception for George VI and Elizabeth by
bd.3   Anglo-American performers at Hyde Park.
         Vincent private recording, June 11, 1939.
            3 min.   phonotape (1 r.   7 1/2 i.p.s.)

            Includes George M. Cohan and Gertrude
         Lawrence.

C1   RECONSTRUCTION
H73   Whorf, Michael, 1933-
          A house united; Civil War, part 6.
          1 tape cassette.   (The visual sounds of
        Mike Whorf. History and heritage, H73)
          Originally presented on his radio program, Kaleidoscope,
        WJR, Detroit.
          Duration: 39 min.
          After the Civil War in the South there is the scorched earth,
        the burnt plantation and the carpetbagger, and yet the word
        throughout the land is reconstruction.

          L. Reconstruction. L. Title.

                   RECONSTRUCTION (1939-1951)
Voice Lib.
M856   Byrnes, James Francis, 1879-1972.
            Speaking from Stuttgart, Germany, about
         America's position in the reconstruction
         of Germany. BBC shortwave, September 6,
         1946.
            36 min., 30 sec.   phonotape (1 r.
         7 1/2 i.p.s.)

            1. Reconstruction (1939-1951)

Voice Lib.
M1471   Red Cross. International Committee, Geneva.
bd.3-B   Report by a German journalist about his
         experiences as an allied prisoner-of-war.
         May 5, 1965.
            1 reel (7 in.)   7 1/2 i.p.s.   phonotape.

            1. World War, 1939-1945 - Prisons and
         prisoners.

Voice Lib.
M1471   Red Cross. International Committee, Geneva.
bd.3-A   Round Robin broadcasts by International
         Red Cross to all liberated countries in
         various languages. Greetings at twentieth
         anniversary since Hitler's surrender.
         May 5, 1965.
            1 reel (7 in.)   7 1/2 in. per sec.
         phonotape.

Voice Lib.   Reed, James
M915-   As we knew him; words of reminiscence of
916   friends and relatives about the life of
         J.F. Kennedy. Narration by Charles Kuralt;
         participants: Charles Bartlett, Lemayne
         Billings, Robert Kennedy, Rose Kennedy,
         James Reed, Adlai Stevenson, Gen. Chester B.
         Clifton, etc. Columbia Records Inc., 1965.
            2 reels (7 in.)   7 1/2 in. per sec.
         phonotape.
            1. Kennedy, John Fitzgerald, Pres. U.S.,
         1917-1963. I. Kuralt, Charles, 1934-

(Continued on next card)

                   REED, WALTER, 1851-1902
C1
SC9-   Whorf, Michael, 1933-
          Walter Reed, M.D.
          1 tape cassette.   (The visual sounds of
        Mike Whorf. Science, SC9)

          Originally presented on his radio program, Kaleidoscope,
        WJR, Detroit.
          Duration: 28 min.
          The story of the man who fought and conquered the dreaded
        mosquito and yellow fever.

          L. Reed, Walter, 1851-1902. L. Title.

Voice Lib. Reeve, Frederic Eugene, 1916–
M1682   Harris, Sydney J
        What is wrong with the city; address
        at Michigan State University, with Dr.
        Frederic Reeve. WKAR, January 27, 1969.
        47 min. phonotape (1 r. 7 1/2 i.p.s.)

        1. Cities and towns. I. Reeve, Frederic
        Eugene, 1916–

○

C1   Remember the Alamo
H15 Whorf, Michael, 1933–
     Remember the Alamo. (The visual sounds of
     Mike Whorf. History and heritage, H15)
       Originally presented on his radio program, Kaleidoscope,
     WJR, Detroit.
       Duration: 39 min.
       Travis, Crockett, Bowie – these were the heroes of the Alamo,
     where a handful of Texans took on the forces of Santa Anna's Mexican
     army.

       L. Alamo – Siege. 1836. L. Title.

○

C1   The reformer – Martin Luther
R20 Whorf, Michael, 1933–
     The reformer – Martin Luther.
     1 tape cassette. (The visual sounds of
     Mike Whorf. Religion, R20)

       Originally presented on his radio program, Kaleidoscope,
     WJR, Detroit.
       Duration: 43 min., 45 sec.
       With the renaissance of culture came also a rebirth of religion;
     to spearhead this new age was Martin Luther. Thus Protestantism
     was born and here is the man and the movement.

       L. Luther, Martin, 1483–1546. L. Title.

○

Voice Lib.
M1357 Remer, Otto Ernst, 1912–
bd.4   Excerpt of broadcast about Hitler's attempted
        assassination. Peteler, July 20, 1944.
        1 reel (7 in.) 7 1/2 in. per sec.
        phonotape.

        1. Hitler, Adolf, 1889–1945

○

           REFUGES, ARAB
Voice Lib.
M1741   Sayegh, Fayez Abdullah, 1922–
bd.1   In an emotional debate with Jess Marlowe
        and Barbara Walters on the Today Show.
        NBC-TV, June 24, 1974.
        15 min. phonotape (1 r. 7 1/2 i.p.s.)

        1. Refuges, Arab. I. Marlowe, Jess.
        II. Walters, Barbara, 1931–

○

        REMINGTON, FREDERIC, 1861–1909
C1
A4   Whorf, Michael, 1933–
     Painter of the plains.
     1 tape cassette. (The visual sounds of
     Mike Whorf. Art, music, and letters, A4)

       Originally presented on his radio program, Kaleidoscope,
     WJR, Detroit.
       Duration: 30 min.
       Those who never saw the American West in its greatness can
     thank the creativeness of Frederic Remington, who seemed to know
     that a way of life, a people, and a time would quickly vanish,
     and so he captured it on canvas.

       L. Remington, Frederic, 1861–1909. L. Title.

○

Voice Lib.
M746 Reik, Theodor
bd.1   Reading from his book "Voices from the
        Inaudible" and giving reminiscences of his
        association with Dr. Sigmund Freud.
        Introduced by Marie Coleman Nelson, managing
        editor of the "Psychoanalytical Review."
        Psychoanalytical Review, 1964.
        1 reel (7 in.) 7 1/2 in. per sec.
        phonotape.
          1. Freud, Sigmund, 1856–1939. L. Nelson, Marie Coleman,
        1915– II. Title: Voices from the inaudible.

○

C1   Rendezvous with destiny
S54 Whorf, Michael, 1933–
     Rendezvous with destiny; the 1930's.
     1 tape cassette. (The visual sounds of
     Mike Whorf. Social, S54)
       Originally presented on his radio program, Kaleidoscope,
     WJR, Detroit.
       Duration: 47 min.
       Apple stands on the street corners, dust bowls, the unemployed,
     the dispossessed – this was the depression of the 1930's. It was the
     era of Roosevelt, the NRA, the CCC, and the TVA.

       L. U.S. – Civilization – 1918–1945. 2. U.S. – History –
     1933–1945. L. Title.

○

Voice Lib.
M1800 Reisner, Robert Alan Fernon, 1946–
WG   Testimony before the Senate Committee
0605.02 investigating the Watergate Affair.
        Pacifica, June 5, 1973.
        158 min. phonotape (2 r. 3 3/4 i.p.s.)
        (Watergate gavel to gavel, phase 1)

        1. Watergate Affair, 1972–

○

Voice Lib.
M1335 Reports regarding the California primary victory of Senator
       Kennedy. Recapitulation of occurrences at Ambassador
       Hotel and last speech of Robert F. Kennedy before being
       shot. Description of unidentified suspect. List of others
       wounded. Opinion by Washington neurosurgeon. Statement
       by Senator McCarthy at Beverly Hilton Hotel. NBC-TV,
       June 5, 1968.
       1 reel (7 in.) 7 1/2 i.p.s. phonotape.

       L. Kennedy, Robert Francis, 1925–1968. L. McCarthy,
     Eugene Joseph, 1916–

○

REPUBLICAN PARTY

Voice Lib.
M795   Butler, Nicholas Murray, 1862-1947.
bd.8   "Save America"; a Republican campaign
          speech of 1920.   The Nation's Forum, 1920.
          1 reel (7 in.)   7 1/2 in. per sec.
          phonotape.

          I. Title.

Voice Lib.
M1490 Republican Party. National Convention, 25th,
bd.5   Chicago, 1952.
          Description of proceedings at Republican
          National Convention in Chicago, 1952
          (described by commentators George Hicks and
          H.V. Kaltenborn). Includes statements by
          Robert A. Taft and Dwight D. Eisenhower.
          Convention unanimously nominates Eisenhower.
          CBS Radio, 1952.
          1 reel (7 in.)   7 1/2 in. per sec.
          phonotape.

Voice Lib.
M1490 Republican Party. National Convention, 25th,
bd.5   Chicago, 1952.   Description of proceedings..
          1952.   (Card 2)

          I. Taft, Robert Alphonso, 1889-1953. II.
          Eisenhower, Dwight David, Pres. U.S., 1890-
          1969. III. Hicks, George   IV.
          Kaltenborn, Hans von, 1878-1965.

Voice Lib.
M725   Republican Party. National Convention.
bd.1   25th, Chicago, 1952.
          Film of excerpts of the Republican National
          Convention in 1952. Clash between Taft and
          Eisenhower forces. Includes speeches by Gen.
          MacArthur, Gen. Eisenhower, Ex-Pres. Hoover,
          Sen. Dirksen, etc. CBS, 1952.
          1 reel (7 in.)   7 1/2 in. per sec.
          phonotape.
          I. MacArthur, Douglas, 1880-1964. II. Eisenhower, Dwight
          David, Pres. U.S., 1890-1969. III. Hoover, Herbert Clark, Pres.
          U.S., 1874-1964. IV. Dirksen, Everett McKinley, 1896-1969.

Voice Lib.
M1329- Republican Party. National Convention, 29th,
1331   Miami, Fla., 1968.
          Proceedings of night session. Attempt to
          nominate Governor Romney for vice-president;
          revolt against Nixon's choice of Governor
          Agnew for running mate. Attempt to nominate
          Mayor Lindsay for vice-president. Roll call
          and nomination of Agnew by acclamation. Richard
          M. Nixon's acceptance speech. Benediction by
          Billy Graham.   NBC-TV, August 8, 1968.
          3 reels (7 in.)   7 1/2 in. per sec.   phonotape.
          I. Nixon, Richard Milhous, Pres. U.S., 1913-   II. Graham,
          William Franklin, 1918-

Voice Lib.
318   Requiem Mass for John F. Kennedy at St.
      Matthew's Cathedral in Washington, celebrated
      by Cardinal Cushing. With English
      translation and explanation.   CBS,
      November 25, 1963.
      1 reel (7 in.)   7 1/2 in. per sec.
      phonotape.

      1. Kennedy, John Fitzgerald, Pres. U.S.,
      1917-1963. I. Cushing, Richard James,
      Cardinal, 1895-

Voice Lib.
M1706 Reuben, David R
bd.3   Impotence in marriage; funny discussion
          on parent/child discussions of sex. On
          Mike Douglas Show with Totie Fields and the
          Fifth Dimension.   WJRT-TV, June 5, 1974.
          15 min.   phonotape (1 r.   7 1/2 i.p.s.)

          1. Sex.   I. Douglas, Mike, 1925?
          II. Fifth Dimension. III. Fields, Totie.

Voice Lib.
180   Reuther, Walter Philip, 1907-1970.
bd.3   Speech to the workers of Australia.
          WJR, June 2, 1944.
          1 reel (7 in.)   7 1/2 in. per sec.
          phonotape.

Voice Lib.
230   Reuther, Walter Philip, 1907-1970.
bd.1   The Ford contract. CBS, August 5,
          1949.
          1 reel (7 in.)   7 1/2 in. per sec.
          phonotape.

Voice Lib.
251   Reuther, Walter Philip, 1907-1970.
bd.2   Labor Day address: labor and democracy's
          unfinished business. CBS, September 5,
          1949.
          1 reel (7 in.)   7 1/2 in. per sec.
          phonotape.

Voice Lib.
260   Reuther, Walter Philip, 1907-1970.
bd.2   Religion in a world of tension. CBS,
        March 14, 1950.
            1 reel (7 in.)   7 1/2 in. per sec.
        phonotape.

Voice Lib.
M979   Reuther, Walter Philip, 1907-1970.
bd.2   Discussion of moral and social economic
        problems at audience participation session
        in Santa Barbara, California.   Introduction
        by Dr. Robert M. Hutchins. CSDI, 1963.
            1 reel (7 in.)   7 1/2 in. per sec.
        phonotape.

            I. Hutchins, Robert Maynard, 1899-

Voice Lib.
K739   Reuther, Walter Philip, 1907-1970.
bd.4   Speaking on mobilization for Korea,
        referring to labor-production capabilities
        to meet mobilization demands; price control
        importance in mobilization process.   CBS,
        1951.
            1 reel (7 in.)   7 1/2 in. per sec.
        phonotape.

            1. Korean War, 1950-1953

                                REUTHER, WALTER PHILIP, 1907-1970
C1
S22   Whorf, Michael, 1922-
            Champion of the working man.
            1 tape cassette.   (The visual sounds of
        Mike Whorf. Social, S22)
            Originally presented on his radio program, Kaleidoscope.
        WJR, Detroit.
            Duration: 27 min.
            Amidst the tumult of labor's early struggle to unionize,
        Walter Reuther stood as a pillar of strength in the movement.

            L. Reuther, Walter Philip, 1907-1970.   L. Title.

Voice Lib.
229   Reuther, Walter Philip, 1907-1970.
bd.1   The Dave Beck story.   Source (?),
        March 28, 1957.
            1 reel (7 in.)   7 1/2 in. per sec.
        phonotape.

            I. Beck, Dave, 1894-

                        REVIVALS - HYMNS
Voice Lib.
M1027   Michaux, Solomon Lightfoot, 1886-1968.
bd.4   Revival songs recorded on-the-spot at
        Washington, D.C., church of Elder Michaux,
        entitled, "There's Going to be a Meeting
        in the Air". GRW, 1946.
            1 reel (7 in.)   7 1/2 i.p.s.   phonotape.

            1. Revivals - Hymns.

Voice Lib.
208   Reuther, Walter Philip, 1907-1970.
bd.1   Walter Reuther reports on meeting with
        Khrushchev. Los Angeles, KCBS,
        September 20, 1959.
            1 reel (7 in.)   7 1/2 in. per sec.
        phonotape.

Voice Lib.
M819-   Rexroth, Kenneth, 1905-
820,   The artist and his social and personal
bd.1   morals; a discussion about Picasso, Brecht,
        Dostoevsky and other artists. KPFK,
        July 11, 1964.
            58 min., 30 sec.   phonotape (2 r.
        7 1/2 i.p.s.)

            1. Art and morals. 2. Artists.

Voice Lib.
M258   Reuther, Walter Philip, 1907-1970.
bd.6   Tractors for Cuba. New York, May 22,
        1961.
            1 reel (7 in.)   7 1/2 in. per sec.
        phonotape.

Voice Lib.
M848   Reynaud, Paul, 1878-1966.
bd.1   French Prime Minister announcing recall
        of Gen. Petain from Spain to become France's
        Deputy Premier in current hour of war
        emergency. NBC shortwave, May 18, 1940.
            1 reel (7 in.)   7 1/2 in. per sec.
        phonotape.

            1. Petain, Henri Philippe Bénoni Omer,
        1856-1951. 2. France - Politics and government
        - 1940-1945

Voice Lib.
Reynaud, Paul, 1878-1966
572- I can hear it now (radio program)
573 1933-1946. CBS, 1948.
bd.1 2 reels (7 in.) 7 1/2 in. per sec.
phonotape.

L. Murrow, Edward Roscoe, 1908-1965. II. LaGuardia, Fiorello Henry, 1882-1947. III. Chamberlain, Neville, 1869-1949. IV. Roosevelt, Franklin Delano, Pres. U.S., 1882-1945. V. Churchill, Winston Leonard Spencer, 1874-1965. VI. Gaulle, Charles de, Pres. France, 1890-1970. VII. Eisenhower, Dwight David, Pres. U.S., 1890-1969. VIII. Willkie, Wendell Lewis, 1892-1944. IX. Martin, Joseph William, 1884-1968. X. Elizabeth II, Queen of Great Britain, 1926- XI. Margaret Rose, Princess of Gt. Brit., 1930- XII. Johnson, Hugh Samuel, 1882- 42. XIII. Smith, Alfred Emanuel, 1873-1944. XIV. Lindbergh, Charles Augustus, 1902- XV. Davis,

(Continued on next card)

Voice Lib.
M1241 Reynolds, Frank
ABC-TV documentary, including reports from Cairo and Tel Aviv and a review of the Arab-Israeli conflicts past and present. ABC-TV, May 25, 1967.
1 reel (7 in.) 7 1/2 i.p.s. phonotape.

1. Israel - Foreign relations - Arab countries. 2. Arab countries - Foreign relations - Israel.

Voice Lib.
M1587 Reynolds, Frank
bd.1 Apollo 11 (space flight): description of ascent from moon by Frank McGee. Countdown, ignition, and lift-off. Meeting the command module "Columbia"; docking; transfer of gear from "Eagle" to "Columbia". Recap by ABC's Jules Bergman and Frank Reynolds. NBC and ABC TV, July 21, 1969.
1 reel (7 in.) 7 1/2 in. per sec. phonotape.
1. Project Apollo. 2. Space flight to the moon. 3. Aldrin, Edwin E 1930- 4. Collins, Michael, 1930- 5. Armstrong, Neil, 1930- I. Aldrin, Edwin E 1930- II. Collins, Michael, 1930- III. Armstrong, Neil, 1930- IV. McGee, Frank, 1921-1974. V. Bergman, Jules VI. Reynolds, Frank

Voice Lib.
M1287 Reynolds, Frank
bd.2- Johnson, Lyndon Baines, Pres. U.S., 1908-1973.
1288 "A conversation with the President". One hour press conference with President Johnson by the three TV networks about current problems, prior to President's departure for Australia. Dan Rather, CBS; Ray Shearer, NBC; Frank Reynolds, ABC. NBC-TV, December 19, 1967.
2 reels (7 in.) 7 1/2 in. per sec. phonotape.

Voice Lib.
M1464 Reynolds, Quentin James, 1902-1965.
bd.1 An open letter to Hitler, broadcast over BBC in London. Peteler, 1941.
1 reel (7 in.) 7 1/2 in. per sec. phonotape.

1. Hitler, Adolf, 1889-1945.

Voice Lib.
M1463 Reynolds, Quentin James, 1902-1965.
bd.16 Satirical song broadcast over the BBC.
1. Letter from Hirohito to Hitler. 2. Letter from Hitler to Hirohito. Peteler, 1945.
1 reel (7 in.) 7 1/2 in. per sec. phonotape.

Voice Lib.
M272 Reynolds, Quentin James, 1902-1965
bd.1 Biography in sound (radio program)
Heywood Broun. NBC, date?
1 reel (7 in.) 7 1/2 in. per sec. phonotape.

L. Broun, Heywood Campbell, 1888-1939. I. Broun, Heywood Campbell, 1888-1939. II. Swope, Herbert Bayard, 1882-1958. III. Wilson, Mattie IV. Jackson, Gardner V. Meany, Thomas VI. Waldron, Beatrice VII. Gordon, Max VIII. Madison, Connie IX. Gannett, Lewis Stiles, 1891-1966. X. Collins, Joseph, 1866-1950. XI. Brown, Earl Louis, 1900- XII. Levy, Newman, 1888- XIII. Growth, John XIV. Bye, George XV. Roosevelt, Franklin Delano, Pres. U.S., 1882-1945. XVI. Reynolds, Quentin James, 1902-1965.

Voice Lib.
M1028 Rhythm Boys.
bd.6 Excerpt from radio program sketch about the origin of the Rhythm Boys, with Al Rinker, Harry Barris, and Bing Crosby. Michigan State University, TV & R, 1940's.

Voice Lib.
M1016 Ribbentrop, Joachim von, 1893-1946.
Reading the official Nazi terms of administering the protectorate of Bohemia and Maehren in Czechoslovakia. Peteler, March 16, 1939.
1 reel (7 in.) 7 1/2 i.p.s. phonotape.

1. World War, 1939-1945 - Czechoslovak Republic.

Voice Lib.
M1071 Ribbentrop, Joachim von, 1893-1946.
bd.7 Excerpt of note to Yugoslavia justifying German military intervention because of unfriendly policies. Peteler, April 6, 1941.
1 reel (7 in.) 7 1/2 i.p.s. phonotape.

1. Germany - Foreign relations - Yugoslavia.
2. Yugoslavia - Foreign relations - Germany.

Voice Lib.
M1073 Ribbentrop, Joachim von, 1893–1946.
bd.5 Note to Russian government of Nazi position
regarding conflict with USSR; Russian demands
for territory in North and Southeastern
Europe rejected by Hitler. Peteler,
June 22, 1941.
1 reel (7 in.) 7 1/2 i.p.s. phonotape.

1. Germany - Foreign relations - Russia.
2. Russia - Foreign relations - Germany.

Voice Lib.
Ribbentrop, Joachim von, 1893–1946
M1071 German radio (Nazi controlled)
bd.3 Nazi radio announcement giving text of
pact made between Germany, Italy, and Japan.
Read in German by Joachim von Ribbentrop, in
Italian by Count Ciano, and in Japanese by
Ambassador Kurusu, stating their spheres of
interest. Peteler, September 27, 1940.
1 reel (7 in.) 7 1/2 in. per sec.
phonotape.
I. Ribbentrop, Joachim von, 1893–1946. II.
Ciano, Galeazzo, conte, 1903–1944. III.
Kuruso, Saburo, 1886–1954.

Voice Lib.
M603 Rice, Gitz
bd.8 "Life in a trench in Belgium"; dramatic
skit and songs outlining life on war front
in World War I. Columbia Gramophone Co.,
1917.
1 reel (7 in.) 7 1/2 i.p.s. phonotape.

1. European War, 1914–1918 - Songs and
music.

Voice Lib.
Rice, Grantland, 1880–1954
M574 I can hear it now (radio program)
bd.2– 1919–1933. CBS, 1953.
575 2 reels (7 in.) 7 1/2 in. per sec.
phonotape.
I. Murrow, Edward Roscoe, 1908–1965. II.
Rogers, Will, 1879–1935. III. White, William
Allen, 1868–1944. IV. Hoover, Herbert Clarke,
Pres. U.S., 1874–1964. V. Roosevelt, Franklin
Delano, Pres. U.S., 1882–1945. VI. Rice,
Grantland, 1880–1954. VII. McNamee, Graham,
1888–1942.

C1
H49 RICHARD I, KING OF ENGLAND, 1157–1199
Whorf, Michael, 1933–
The crusaders.
1 tape cassette. (The visual sounds of
Mike Whorf. History and heritage, H49)

Originally presented on his radio program, Kaleidoscope,
WJR, Detroit.
Duration: 39 min., 15 sec.
The religious wars were led by men who engaged in savage
encounters with the Infidels as they attempted to recapture the
cities where Christ once lived. Out of this period came many great
men - none greater than Richard the Lion-Hearted.
1. Richard I, King of England, 1157–1199. 2. Crusades. I. Title.

C1
FA16 Richard Bourne
Whorf, Michael, 1933–
Richard Bourne.
1 tape cassette. (The visual sounds of
Mike Whorf. The forgotten American, FA16)
Originally presented on his radio program, Kaleidoscope,
WJR, Detroit.
Duration: 10 min., 25 sec.
Preacher to the Indians on Cape Cod. Bourne developed a
colony of Christian Indians which blocked an Indian attack
during King Philip's War.

I. Bourne, Richard. I. Title.

Voice Lib.
Richardson, Sir Ralph David, 1902–
M1037 Biography in sound (radio program)
bd.1 "The Actor", narrated by Morgan Beatty.
Cast includes Tallulah Bankhead, Hy Gardner,
Rocky Graziano, Arthur Miller, Uta Hagen,
Jackie Cooper, Sir Laurence Olivier, Gad
Gayther, Barbara Ashley, Hortense Powdermaker,
Peter Ustinov, Alfred Hitchcock, Leonard Lyons,
John Guston, Helen Hayes, Dick Mayne, Ralph
Bellamy, Lionel Barrymore, Sir Ralph Richardson,
José Ferrer, and Walter Kerr. NBC Radio, 1950's.
1 reel (7 in.) 7 1/2 in. per sec.
phonotape.
(Continued on next card)

Voice Lib.
Richardson, Ralph David, 1902–
111 Doyle, Sir Arthur Conan, 1859–1930.
bd.2 Dr. Watson meets Sherlock Holmes, as
read by John Gielgud and Ralph Richardson.
British Broadcasting Corp., His Master's
Voice, 1947.
1 reel (7 in.) 7 1/2 in. per sec.
phonotape.
I. Gielgud, John, 1904– II. Richardson,
Ralph David, 1902– III. Title.

Voice Lib.
Richardson, Ralph David, 1902–
110 Doyle, Sir Arthur Conan, 1859–1930.
bd.2 The Final Problem, an episode read by
John Gielgud, Ralph Richardson, and Orson
Welles. His Master's Voice, 1947.
1 reel (7 in.) 7 1/2 in. per sec.
phonotape.

I. Gielgud, John, 1904– II. Richardson,
Ralph David, 1902– III. Welles, Orson,
1915– IV. Title.

Voice Lib.
RICHMAN, HARRY
M1743 Raft, George
bd.2 Reminisces on the Mike Douglas Show.
WILX-TV, June 27, 1974.
10 min. phonotape (1 r. 7 1/2 i.p.s.)

I. Raft, George. 2. O'Brien, Pat, 1899– 3. Muni,
Paul, 1895–1967. 4. Crawford, Joan, 1908– 5. West, Mae,
1893– 6. Richman, Harry. 7. Entertainers - U. S. I.
Douglas, Mike, 1925–

Voice Lib.
251   Rickenbacker, Edward Vernon, 1890-1973.
bd.1   Report to the people of the U.S. on his
       3 month tour of the Russian war machine in
       action and behind the lines.   CBS,
       August 17, 1943.
          1 reel (7 in.)   7 1/2 in. per sec.
       phonotape.

Voice Lib.
250   Rickenbacker, Edward Vernon, 1890-1973.
       Address to Detroit Economics Club,
       being excerpts from speech foretelling
       the future of aviation.   Detroit, WJR,
       July 30, 1957.
          1 reel (7 in.)   7 1/2 in. per sec.
       phonotape.

                 Rickenbacker, Edward Vernon, 1890-1973
Voice Lib.
635   LaGuardia, Fiorello Henry, 1882-1947.
bd.2   Dedication of LaGuardia Airport; speech on
       the occasion of the first Clipper ship leaving
       LaGuardia Airport during the dedication;
       participates in the plane's take-off, talks
       with Eddie Rickenbacker about Eastern Airlines'
       first flight from the airport.   WNYC, March 31,
       1940.
          1 reel (7 in.)   7 1/2 in. per sec.
       phonotape.

          I. Rickenbacker, Edward Vernon, 1890-1973.

Voice Lib.
M730 Rickey, Branch (Wesley), 1881-1965.
bd.7   Speaking on mobilization for Korean War
       as it affects baseball.   CBS, 1951.
          1 reel (7 in.)   7 1/2 in. per sec.
       phonotape.

          1. Korean War, 1950-1953. 2. Baseball

Voice Lib.
376   Rickey, Branch (Wesley), 1881-1965.
bd.1   "Baseball: the Game"; on origin of, as a
       national past-time; his youth and sports;
       college sports and professionalism; eligibility
       in college sports; professional sports; career
       for college graduates; review of career in
       World War I; development of modern farm system.
       WOED, 1958.
          1 reel (7 in.)   7 1/2 in. per sec.
       phonotape.

          1. Baseball.

                 Rickover, Hyman George, 1900-
Voice Lib.
M1077- Mumford, Lewis, 1895-
1078   Speeches by Lewis Mumford and Hyman
bd.1   Rickover at convocation in New York for
       10th anniversary of the Fund of the Republic,
       dealing with challenges to democracy in the
       next decade and with authoritarian and
       democratic techniques.   CSDI, January,
       1963.
          2 reels (7 in.)   7 1/2 in. per sec.
       phonotape.

          I. Rickover, Hyman George, 1900-

Voice Lib.
249   Ridgway, Matthew Bunker, 1895-
bd.1   Address to joint session of Congress
       on conduct of military in Korea.   CBS,
       May 22, 1952.
          1 reel (7 in.)   7 1/2 in. per sec.
       phonotape.

          1. Korean War, 1950-1953 - U.S.

                 Ridgway, Matthew Bunker, 1895-
Voice Lib.
381-   I can hear it now (radio program)
382   CBS, April 26, 1951.
bd.1   2 reels (7 in.) 7 1/2 in. per sec.   phonotape.
          I. Radio Free Europe. 2. Strategic Air Command. I.
       Ridgway, Matthew Bunker, 1895- II. Churchill, Winston Leonard
       Spencer, 1874-1965. III. Bevan, Aneurin, 1897-1960. IV. Nixon,
       Richard Milhous, Pres. U.S., 1913-   V. Kerr, Robert Samuel, 1896-
       1963. VI. Brewster, Ralph Owen, 1888-1962. VII. Wherry, Kenneth
       Spicer, 1892-1951. VIII. Capehart, Homer Earl, 1897-   IX.
       Lehman, Herbert Henry, 1878-1963. X. Taft, Robert Alphonso,
       1889-1953. XI. Moody, Arthur Edson Blair, 1902-1954. XII.
       Martin, Joseph William, 1884-1968. XIII. McMahon, James O'Brien,
       1903-1952. XIV. MacArthur, Douglas, 1880-1964. XVII. Wilson,
       Charles Edward, 1886-1972. XVIII. Irvine, Clarence T

                 Ridgway, Matthew Bunker, 1895-
Voice Lib.
M384 I can hear it now (radio program)
bd.1   Biography of a pint of blood.   CBS,
       February, 1951.
          1 reel (7 in.)   7 1/2 in. per sec.
       phonotape.

          1. Blood.   I. McIntire, Ross T., 1899-
       II. Hope, Bob, 1903-   III. Ridgway,
       Matthew Bunker, 1895-   IV. Barkley,
       Alban William, 1877-1956.

                 The right of the people to rule
Voice Lib.
M1250 Roosevelt, Theodore, Pres. U.S., 1858-1919.
bd.4   Campaign speech entitled "The right of
       the people to rule," cautioning against
       political extremes of the right and left.
       VTM, 1912.
          1 reel (7 in.)   7 1/2 in. per sec.
       phonotape.

          I. Title: The right of the people to
       rule.

Voice Lib.
649 Riley, James Whitcomb, 1849-1916.
bd.2-5 Reciting his own poems. National
Vocarium, 1908.
1 reel (7 in.) 7 1/2 in. per sec.
phonotape.

CONTENTS.-bd.2. Out to Old Aunt Mary's.-bd.3.
Little Orphan Annie.-bd.4. The Raggedy Man.-
bd.5. The Happy Little Cripple.

Rise and fall of the Third Reich
Voice Lib.
M1313 Shirer, William Lawrence, 1904-
David L. Wolper production of filmed
documentary "Rise and Fall of the Third
Reich"; (Part 3) with actual voices of
Nazi generals, Eric Kempke (Hitler's chauffeur)
Hitler and Goebbels; (period from 1941-
1945). NBC-TV; March, 1968.
1 reel (7 in.) 7 1/2 in. per sec.
phonotape.

I. Title: Rise and fall of the Third
Reich.

RILEY, JAMES WHITCOMB, 1849-1916

Voice Lib.
M649 Phelps, William Lyon, 1865-1943.
bd.1 Introduction to recordings of Hoosier
poet James Whitcomb Riley. G.R. Vincent,
1940.
1 reel (7 in.) 7 1/2 i.p.s. phonotape.

1. Riley, James Whitcomb, 1849-1916.

Ritter, Lawrence S.
The glory of their times
Voice Lib.
M1248 Baseball fifty years ago; interviews with four
famous old time baseball players, on NBC
"Today" show, by host Hugh Downs, supported by
sportscaster Joe Garagiola and Dr. Lawrence
Ritter, author of new book. NBC-TV, June 9,
1967.
1 reel (7 in.) 7 1/2 in. per sec. phonotape.

I. Baseball. I. Downs, Hugh Malcolm, 1921- II. Garagiola,
Joe. III. Ritter, Lawrence S./The glory of their times. IV. Roush,
Edd, 1893- V. Marquart, Rube, 1890- VI. O'Doul, Lefty,
1897- VII. Meyers, John, 1880-

Voice Lib.
649 Ring, Blanche
bd.15- Comedienne singing old novelty songs.
16 Victor Talking Machine Co., 1908-1909.
1 reel (7 in.) 7 1/2 in. per sec.
phonotape.

CONTENTS.-bd.15. Yip ! I Adee I Aye (Cobb-
Flynn).-bd.16. I've got rings on my fingers
(Weston-Scott).

C1
S45- The roaring twenties
S47 Whorf, Michael, 1933-
The roaring twenties. (The visual sounds of
Mike Whorf. Social, S45-S47)
Originally presented on his radio program, Kaleidoscope,
WJR, Detroit.
Duration: 40 min., 30 sec.; 40 min., 30 sec.; 52 min.
The voices of the famous and infamous relating the times as to
what transpired and why. Part 2 has the banner stories of the decade.
The year 1929 brought the depression, but the '20's were doomed to
die.

I. U.S. - Social conditions. I. Title.

Voice Lib.
539 Rinker, Al
bd.5 Gay Nineties Revue (Radio program)
The talking machine; skit with Joe Howard,
Al Rinker, and Beatrice Kay concerning
Edison's talking machine. Simulated voices
of P.T. Barnum and Florence Nightingale.
CBS, 1940.
1 reel (7 in.) 7 1/2 in. per sec.
phonotape.

I. Howard, Joe   II. Rinker, Al
III. Kay, Beatrice

Robb, Charles Spittal, 1939-
Voice Lib.
M1286 Robb, Lynda Bird (Johnson), 1944-
bd.3 Excerpt of description of wedding ceremony
at White House by Dan Rather, including
statements of Lynda and her bridegroom,
Captain Charles Robb. December 9, 1967.
1 reel (7 in.) 7 1/2 in. per sec.
phonotape.

I. Rather, Dan   II. Robb, Charles
Spittal, 1939-

Voice Lib.
M1098 Ripley, Robert LeRoy, 1893-1949.
bd.2 Rehearsal and discussion regarding text
of introductory remarks to the recording
of "The Bugler of Balaclava" with G.R. Vincent,
followed by 1890 recording of trumpeter
Kenneth Landfrey. NVL location recording.
August 7, 1939.
1 reel (7 in.) 7 1/2 in. per sec.
phonotape.
I. Vincent, G   Robert. II. Landfrey, Kenneth.
III. Title: The bugler of Balaclava.

Voice Lib.
M1286 Robb, Lynda Bird (Johnson), 1944-
bd.3 Excerpt of description of wedding ceremony
at White House by Dan Rather, including
statements of Lynda and her bridegroom,
Captain Charles Robb. December 9, 1967.
1 reel (7 in.) 7 1/2 in. per sec.
phonotape.

I. Rather, Dan   II. Robb, Charles
Spittal, 1939-

Voice Lib.
M764   Robbins, Oscar, 1912-1965.
bd.5   Excerpt from "Sound Track" (Program 7);
gives his reasons for the apparent dearth
of initiative from Hollywood which is so
famous for originality and innovation.
Westinghouse Broadcasting Corporation, 1964.
    1 reel (7 in.)   7 1/2 in. per sec.
phonotape.   (The Music Goes Round and Round)

    I. Title: Sound track.   II. Series.

            Roberts, Francis
Voice Lib.
M787   Chaplin, Charles, 1925-
        Discussion of autobiography of his father,
Charles Chaplin, with Francis Roberts.
Los Angeles, KPFK, December 19, 1964.
    1 reel (7 in.)   7 1/2 in. per sec.
phonotape.

        1. Chaplin, Charles, 1889-   I. Roberts,
Francis

Voice Lib.
M840   Robeson, Paul Bustill, 1898-
bd.1-5   Singing various selections during 1920's.
    1 reel (7 in.)   7 1/2 in. per sec.
phonotape.

    CONTENTS.-bd.1. "Ah Still Suits Me" from
Showboat by Jerome Kern (duet with orchestra;
Paul Robeson and Elizabeth Welch) recorded
in Europe.-bd.2. "Ol' Man River" from Showboat by Oscar Hammerstein 2nd with orchestral
accompaniment; recorded in Europe.-bd.3. "Deep
                (Continued on next card)

Voice Lib.
M840   Robeson, Paul Bustill, 1898-   Singing
bd.1-5   various selections during 1920's...
            1920's.   (Card 2)

    CONTENTS. cont'd.-River" by H.J. Burleigh,
piano accompaniment by Lawrence Brown.-
bd.4. "I'm Goin' to Tell God All O' My
Troubles"; spiritual piano accompaniment by
Lawrence Brown.-bd.5. (a) "Git on Board, Lil'
Chillun"; spiritual, (b) "Dere's No Hidin'
Place"; spiritual piano accompaniment by
Lawrence Brown.

Voice Lib.
555   Robeson, Paul Bustill, 1898-
bd.2   Singing "Old Man River" from Showboat.
Victor, 1927.
    1 reel (7 in.)   7 1/2 in. per sec.
phonotape.

        I. Title: Old man river.

Voice Lib.
M838-   Robeson, Paul Bustill, 1898-
839   Mr. Robeson's testimony before the U.S.
Senate's Mundt Bill hearings. He is questioned
by Senator Ferguson and others and he outlines
denial of rights to Negroes; discusses the
definition of a communist; refuses to reveal
his membership; points out absence of prejudice
toward Negroes in Russia; discusses fascism.
Implies that he would refuse to adhere to Mundt
bill if passed by Congress; pleads for human
dignities; defines laws he would support or
oppose; discussion of his allegiance to U.S.
                (Continued on next card)

Voice Lib.
M838-   Robeson, Paul Bustill, 1898-   Mr. Robeson's
839   testimony... 1948. (Card 2)

    Government and participation in a war with
USSR, if one were to occur; mentions New
Deal legislation to aid Negroes not passed,
names other minority groups. Washington,
WOL, May 31, 1948.
    2 reels (7 in.)   7 1/2 in. per sec.
phonotape.

Voice Lib.   Robeson, Paul Bustill, 1898-
M225   Packard, Frederick
        Styles in Shakespearean acting, 1890-1950.
Creative Associates, 1963?
    1 reel (7 in.)   7 1/2 l.p.s.   phonotape.

    I. Sothern, Edward Askew, 1826-188L II. Marlowe,
Julia, 1865-1950. III. Booth, Edwin, 1833-1893. IV. Gielgud,
John, 1904-   V. Robeson, Paul Bustill, 1898-   VI. Terry,
Dame Ellen, 1848-1928. VII. Allen, Viola. VIII. Welles,
Orson, 1915-   IX. Skinner, Otis, 1858-1942. X. Barrymore,
John, 1882-1942. XI. Olivier, Sir Laurence Kerr, 1907-
XII. Forbes-Robertson, Sir Johnston, 1853-   XIII. Evans,
Maurice. XIV. Thorndike, Dame Sybil, 1882-   XV. Robson,
Flora. XVI. LeGallienne, Eva, 1899-   XVII. Anderson,
Judith. XVIII. Duncan, Augustin. XIX. Hampden, Walter.
XX. Speaight, Robert, 1904-   XXI. Jones, Daniel.

        Robeson, Paul Bustill, 1898-
Voice Lib.
289   Robinson, Earl, 1910-
bd.1   [Battle hymn] Phonotape.
        Battle Hymn: Earl Robinson's cantata
about Pres. Franklin D. Roosevelt's message
on the state of the Union in January, 1942.
CBS, January, 1942.
    1 reel (7 in.)   7 1/2 in. per sec.
phonotape.

        I. Robeson, Paul Bustill, 1898-

        Robeson, Paul Bustill, 1898-
Voice Lib.
625   Robinson, Earl, 1910-
bd.2   [Battle hymn] Phonotape.
        Battle hymn: musical production by Norman
Corwin of President Roosevelt's talk to the
nation on January 6, 1942. Composition by
Earl Robinson; all-star cast headed by Paul
Robeson. CBS, January, 1942.
    1 reel (7 in.)   7 1/2 in. per sec.
phonotape.

        I. Corwin, Norman Lewis, 1910-
        II. Robeson, Paul Bustill, 1898-

Voice Lib.
262   Robinson, Bill, 1878-1949.
bd.4   "Ain't Misbehavin'."   Brunswick,
       1923.
          1 reel (7 in.)   7 1/2 in. per sec.
       phonotape.

          I. Title.

Voice Lib.
625   Robinson, Earl, 1910-
bd.2   [Battle hymn]   Phonotape.
          Battle hymn: musical production by Norman
       Corwin of President Roosevelt's talk to the
       nation on January 6, 1942. Composition by
       Earl Robinson; all-star cast headed by Paul
       Robeson. CBS, January, 1942.
          1 reel (7 in.)   7 1/2 in. per sec.
       phonotape.

          I. Corwin, Norman Lewis, 1910-
          II. Robeson, Paul Bustill, 1898-

Voice Lib.
262   Robinson, Bill, 1878-1940.
bd.3   "Doin' the New Low Down."   Brunswick,
       1923.
          1 reel (7 in.)   7 1/2 in. per sec.
       phonotape.

          I. Title.

Voice Lib.
289   Robinson, Earl, 1910-
bd.1   [Battle hymn]   Phonotape.
          Battle Hymn: Earl Robinson's cantata
       about Pres. Franklin D. Roosevelt's message
       on the state of the Union in January, 1942.
       CBS, January, 1942.
          1 reel (7 in.)   7 1/2 in. per sec.
       phonotape.

          I. Robeson, Paul Bustill, 1898-

Voice Lib.
538   Robinson, Mrs. Corrine (Roosevelt), 1861-1933.
bd.2   Republican campaign speech, 1920; gives her
       support to Warren G. Harding for President and
       Calvin Coolidge for Vice-President, attacks
       Woodrow Wilson as a partisan politician.
       Nation's Forum, 1920.
          1 reel (7 in.)   7 1/2 in. per sec.
       phonotape.

          1. Harding, Warren Gamaliel, Pres. U.S.,
       1865-1923.

Voice Lib.
213-   Robinson, Earl, 1910-
215   Recording his own works for G. Robert
       Vincent. Recorded on location, 1944-
       1946.
          3 reels (7 in.)   7 1/2 in. per sec.
       phonotape.

Voice Lib.
113   Robinson, Earl, 1910-
bd.2   [The lonesome train]   Phonotape.
          The lonesome train (Lincoln Cantata).
       Private recording [n.d.]
          1 reel (7 in.)   7 1/2 in. per sec.
       phonotape.

Voice Lib. Robinson, Earl, 1910-
M619   Radio in the 1930's (Part II): a series of
bd.1-   excerpts of the 1930's; a sample of radio
14   of the period. NVL, April, 1964.
          1 reel (7 in.)   7 1/2 in. per sec.   phonotape.
       I. Allen, Fred, 1894-1956. II. Delmar, Kenny   III. Donald,
       Peter   IV. Pious, Minerva   V. Fennelly, Parker   VI.
       Boyer, Charles, 1899-   VII. Dunne, Irene, 1904-   VIII.
       DeMille, Cecil Blount, 1881-1959. IX. West, Mae, 1893-   X.
       Dafoe, Allan Ray, 1883-1943. XI. Dionne quintuplets. XII. Ortega,
       Santos   XIII. War of the worlds (radio program) XIV. Ives, Burl,
       1909-   XV. Robinson, Earl, 1910-   XVI. Temple, Shirley,
       1928-   XVII. Earhart, Amelia, 1898-1937. XVIII. Lawrence,
       Gertrude, 1901-1952. XIX. Cohan, George Michael, 1878-1942.
       XX. Shaw, George Bernard, 1856-1950. XXI. Hitler, Adolf, 1889-
       1945. XXII. Chamberlain, Neville, 1869-1940. XXIII. Roosevelt,
       Franklin Delano, Pres. U.S., 1882-1945.

Voice Lib.
129   Robinson, Earl, 1910-
bd.8   Singing his own composition. Recorded
       on location, 1942.
          1 reel (7 in.)   7 1/2 in. per sec.
       phonotape.

          CONTENTS.-The house I live in (1942)

Voice Lib.
M728   Robinson, Earl, 1910-
bd.1   Interview with Al LaGuire at MSU campus.
       February 2, 1965.
          1 reel (7 in.)   7 1/2 in. per sec.
       phonotape.

          I. LaGuire, Al

Voice Lib.
K728   Robinson, Earl, 1910-
bd.3   Singing his musical composition "Black
        and White". NVL, February 2, 1965.
            1 reel (7 in.)   7 1/2 in. per sec.
        phonotape.

Voice Lib.
M225   Robson, Flora
        Packard, Frederick
        Styles in Shakespearean acting, 1890-1950.
        Creative Associates, 1963?
            1 reel (7 in.)   7 1/2 i.p.s.   phonotape.

            L. Sothern, Edward Askew, 1826-1881. II. Marlowe,
        Julia, 1865-1950. III. Booth, Edwin, 1833-1893. IV. Gielgud,
        John, 1904-   V. Robeson, Paul Bustill, 1898-   VI. Terry,
        Dame Ellen, 1848-1928. VII. Allen, Viola. VIII. Welles,
        Orson, 1915-   IX. Skinner, Otis, 1858-1942. X. Barrymore,
        John, 1882-1942. XI. Olivier, Sir Laurence Kerr, 1907-
        XII. Forbes-Robertson, Sir Johnston, 1853-   XIII. Evans,
        Maurice. XIV. Thorndike, Dame Sybil, 1882-   XV. Robson,
        Flora. XVI. LeGallienne, Eva, 1899-   XVII. Anderson,
        Judith. XVIII. Duncan, Augustin. XIX. Hampden, Walter.
        XX. Speaight, Robert, 1904-   XXI. Jones, Daniel.

Voice Lib.
K728   Robinson, Earl, 1910-
bd.2   Singing his musical composition "Free and
        Equal Blues". NVL, February 2, 1965.
            1 reel (7 in.)   7 1/2 in. per sec.
        phonotape.

Voice Lib.
M1065   Rockefeller, John Davison, 1839-1937.
bd.8   Statement from his residence in Florida
        about his faith and hope in America. Fox
        Movietone, 1930.
            1 reel (7 in.)   7 1/2 in. per sec.
        phonotape.

Voice Lib.
623   Robinson, Earl, 1910-
        Corwin, Norman Lewis, 1910-
        "Twenty-six by Corwin"; presents Earl
        Robinson and Millard Lampell's "Lonesome
        Train", with Earl Robinson, Burl Ives,
        Raymond Massey. CBS, 1940.
            1 reel (7 in.)   7 1/2 in. per sec.
        phonotape.

            I. Robinson, Earl, 1910-   II. Ives,
        Burl, 1909-   III. Massey, Raymond, 1896-

C1
H79   ROCKEFELLER, JOHN DAVISON, 1839-1937
        Whorf, Michael, 1933-
        Bound to be rich, John D. Rockefeller.
            1 tape cassette.   (The visual sounds of
        Mike Whorf. History and heritage, H79)
            Originally presented on his radio program, Kaleidoscope,
        WJR, Detroit.
            Duration: 36 min., 30 sec.
            John D. Rockefeller had learned the value of money from his
        father and ever since he collected a bit of interest on a loan,
        he thought of nothing but money until the day he died.

            I. Rockefeller, John Davison, 1839-1937. I. Title.

Voice Lib.   Robinson, Edward G   1893-1973
M1467-   Dos Passos, John, 1896-1970.
1469   U.S.A.; a 2 1/2 hour dramatization by
        Hollywood TV Theatre, based on the three
        Dos Passos books dealing with the first
        three decades of the 20th century. Host:
        Edward G. Robinson. WMSB-TV, May 30, 1971.
            3 reels (7 in.)   7 1/2 in. per sec.
        phonotape.
            I. Robinson, Edward G   1893-1973.
        II. Title.

Voice Lib.
351   Rockefeller, Nelson Aldrich, 1908-
bd.3   Speaks about the Presidency on "At the
        Source". CBS, January 12, 1962.
            1 reel (7 in.)   7 1/2 in. per sec.
        phonotape.

Voice Lib.   Robinson, Edward G   1893-1973
M669-   The legend of Cecil B. Demille. Yul
670   Brynner, Charlton Heston, Bob Hope, Betty
        Hutton, Edward G. Robinson, Barbara Stanwyck,
        James Stewart, Gloria Swanson, Cornel
        Wilde, Samuel Goldwyn, Billy Graham, Cecil
        B. DeMille. Recorded 1963.
            2 reels (7 in.)   7 1/2 in. per sec. phonotape.
            I. DeMille, Cecil Blount, 1881-1959. I. Brynner, Yul, 1917-
        II. Heston, Charlton, 1924-   III. Hope, Bob, 1903-   IV.
        Hutton, Betty, 1921-   V. Robinson, Edward G   1893-1973.
        VI. Stanwyck, Barbara, 1907-   VII. Stewart, James Maitland,
        1908-   VIII. Swanson, Gloria, 1899'-   IX. Wilde, Cornel, 1915-
        X. Goldwyn, Samuel, 1884?-   XI. Graham, William Franklin,
        1918-   XII. DeMille, Cecil Blount, 1881-1959.

Voice Lib.   ROCKEFELLER FOUNDATION
M1581   Knowles, John
        Rockefeller Foundation. WVWC, Buchanan,
        W. Va., February 27, 1974.
            30 min. phonotape (1 r.   7 1/2 i.p.s.)

            1. Rockefeller Foundation.

C1
SC1
The rocket man

Whorf, Michael, 1933-
The rocket man.
1 tape cassette.   (The visual sounds of
Mike Whorf. Science, SC1)
Originally presented on his radio program, Kaleidoscope,
WJR, Detroit.
Duration: 36 min., 30 sec.
From his early beginnings in New England and New Mexico to
the years of culmination, here is a must for the student of science.
The story of Robert Hutchings Goddard, the rocket man.

L. Goddard, Robert Hutchings, 1882-1945. L. Title.

ROCKET RESEARCH
Voice Lib.
M652   De Seversky, Alexander Procofieff, 1894-
bd.15   Significance of shooting a rocket around
the moon.   CBS, August 16, 1958.
1 reel (7 in.)   7 1/2 i.p.s.   phonotape.

1. Rocket research.

Voice Lib.
540   Rockne, Knute Kenneth, 1888-1931.
bd.4   Notre Dame football: spring football talk
before team of South Bend, Indiana.   Fox
Movietone, 1929.
1 reel (7 in.)   7 1/2 in. per sec.
phonotape.

Voice Lib.
M1201   Rockwell, George Lincoln, 1918-1967.
Address to MSU students in Auditorium at the invitation of
ASMSU for the "Controversial Issues" series of lectures.
Introduction by Greg Hopkins, followed by Rockwell explaining
his position; maligns press; introduces documents; blames Jews for
Bolshevism; quotes "G2" report of 1920; exposes alleged graft for
stamping "Kosher" on all foods; commends Hitler; ridicules
Eleanor Roosevelt, Rusk, Acheson; WWII made world safe for
Soviets and Israel; commends Malcolm X on Negro solution and
calls Martin Luther King a communist.   Questions and answers
follow lecture.   A/V, April 20, 1967.
1 reel (7 in.)   7 1/2 i.p.s.   phonotape.

L. National socialism.

Voice Lib.
M1446   Rockwell, Norman, 1894-
bd.2   Excerpt of conversation between illustrator
Norman Rockwell and Hugh Downs on the
"Today" show, pertaining to Rockwell's new
book of drawings.   NBC-TV, 1970.
1 reel (7 in.)   7 1/2 in. per sec.
phonotape.

I. Downs, Hugh Malcolm, 1921-

Voice Lib.
M1685   Rodino, Peter Wallace, 1909-
bd.2   Telling PBS that transcript damages Nixon.
Question under investigation is how much?
Interview with Paul Duke on Washington
straight talk.   PBS, May 21, 1974.
30 min.   phonotape (1 r.   7 1/2 i.p.s.)

1. U.S. - Politics and government - 1969-
2. Nixon, Richard Milhous, Pres. U.S., 1913-
I. Duke, Paul.

Rodino, Peter Wallace, 1909-
Voice Lib.
M1656   U.S. Congress. House. Committee on the
bd.3   Judiciary.
House Judiciary Committee, 1st public
meeting of impeachment hearings, with
Chairman Peter Rodino and Edward Hutchinson.
WKAR, May 9, 1974.
15 min.   phonotape (1 r.   7 1/2 i.p.s.)

1. Nixon, Richard Milhous, Pres. U.S., 1913-
I. Rodino, Peter Wallace, 1909-
II. Hutchinson, Edward, 1914-

Voice Lib.
M1002   Roehm, Ernst, 1887-1934.
bd.3   Speech in Saxony to the S.A. exhorting
them to uphold Nazi doctrines.   Peteler,
March 25, 1934.
1 reel (7 in.)   7 1/2 in. per sec.
phonotape.

Voice Lib.
M1260   Rodgers, Richard, 1902-
"Richard Rodgers 65"; TV program celebrating
65th birthday anniversary of songwriter and
composer Richard Rodgers.   Interviews and
reminiscences with Rodgers and his co-workers
and friends; various musical selections from
former shows, including film clip of "The
Sound of Music".   NBC-TV, June 28, 1967.
1 reel (7 in.)   7 1/2 in. per sec.
phonotape.

Rogers, Buddy
see
Rogers, Charles

Voice Lib.
M1696 Rogers, Charles
bd.3   Reminiscing with Mike Douglas on the
          Mike Douglas Show. WJRT-TV, May 27, 1974.
          8 min. phonotape (1 r. 7 1/2 i.p.s.)

          1. Moving-pictures - History. 2. Rogers,
          Charles. I. Douglas, Mike, 1925?

Voice Lib.
M1040 Rogers, Will, 1879-1935.
bd.6   Excerpt of radio broadcast; satire about
          plowing under cotton and birth control of
          hogs. TV&R, 1933.
          1 reel (7 in.) 7 1/2 in. per sec.
          phonotape.

Voice Lib.
122-   Rogers, Will, 1879-1935.
123   Will Rogers and son. Columbia, 1952.
          2 reels (7 in.) 7 1/2 in. per sec.
          phonotape.

                Rogers, Will, 1879-1935
Voice Lib.
M1047 Old-time radio excerpts of the 1930's and
          1940's, including: Rudy Vallee singing
          "Linger a little longer"; Will Rogers on
          panaceas for the Depression; Bing Crosby
          singing "Sweet Georgia Brown"; Eddie Cantor;
          Jimmy Durante singing "Inka-dinka-do";
          musical skit by Clayton, Jackson and Durante;
          wit by Harry Hershfield; musical selection
          "Thinking of you" by Kay Kyser; Kate Smith
          singing theme song, "When the moon comes over
          the mountain"; W.C. Fields' temperance.
          (Continued on next card)

                Rogers, Will, 1879-1935
Voice Lib.
M1047 Old-time radio excerpts of the 1930's and
          1940's... (Card 2)

          lecture; Al Jolson singing "Rocka-by-your
          baby"; and George Burns and Gracie Allen
          skit. TV&R, 1930's and 1940's.
          1 reel (7 in.) 7 1/2 in. per sec.
          I. Vallee, Rudy, 1901-   II. Rogers, Will, 1879-1935. III.
          Crosby, Bing, 1901-   IV. Cantor, Eddie, 1893-1964. V. Durante,
          Jimmy, 1893-   VI. Clayton, Patti   VII. Jackson,
          Eddie   VIII. Hershfield, Harry, 1885-   IX. Kyser, Kay,
          1906-   X. Smith, Kate, 1909-   XI. Fields, W.C., 1879-
          1946. XII. Jolson, Al, 1886-1950. XIII. Burns, George, 1896-
          XIV. Allen, Gracie, 1906-

                    Rogers, Will, 1879-1935
Voice Lib.
M618   Radio in the 1930's (Part I): a series of
bd.1-   excerpts from important broadcasts of the
14   1930's; a sample of radio of the period.
          NVL, April, 1964.
          1 reel (7 in.) 7 1/2 in. per sec. phonotape.
          I. Shaw, George Bernard, 1856-1950. II. Crosby, Bing, 1901-
          III. Barkley, Alban William, 1877-1956. IV. Roosevelt, Franklin
          Delano, Pres. U.S., 1882-1945. V. Hoover, Herbert Clark, Pres.
          U.S., 1874-1964. VI. Long, Huey Pierce, 1893-1935. VII. Town-
          send, Francis Everett, 1867-1960. VIII. Coughlin, Charles Edward,
          1891-   IX. Rogers, Will, 1879-1935. X. Pius XII, Pope, 1876-
          1958. XI. Edward VIII, king of Great Britain, 1894-1972. XII.
          Barrymore, John, 1882-1942. XIII. Woollcott, Alexander, 1887-
          1943. XIV. Allen, Fred, 1894-1956. XV. Benchley, Robert Charles,
          1889-1945.

                Rogers, Will, 1879-1935
Voice Lib.
M617   Radio in the 1920's: a series of excerpts
bd.1-   from important broadcasts of the 1920's,
bd.25   with brief prologue and epilogue; a sample
          of radio of the period. NVL, April, 1964.
          1 reel (7 in.) 7 1/2 in. per sec.
          phonotape.
          I. Radio programs. L. Marconi, Guglielmo, marchese, 1874-
          1937. II. Kendall, H   G   III. Coolidge, Calvin, Pres. U.S.,
          1872-1933. IV. Wilson, Woodrow, Pres. U.S., 1856-1924. V.
          Roosevelt, Franklin Delano, Pres. U.S., 1882-1945. VI. Lodge,
          Henry Cabot, 1850-1924. VII. LaGuardia, Fiorello Henry, 1882-1947.
          VIII. The Happiness Boys (Radio program) IX. Gallagher and Sheen.
          X. Barney Google. XI. Vallee, Rudy, 1901-   XII. The two
          (Continued on next card)

                Rogers, Will, 1879-1935
Voice Lib.
M323   Biography in sound (radio program)
          Will Rogers of Oklahoma. "All I know ...",
          singing "In the blue of the night", marriage
          is a poker game, on acting, excerpt from radio
          program (Rogers' Lottery Plan), excerpt
          closing broadcast with his famous alarm
          clock. NBC, 1955.
          1 reel (7 in.) 7 1/2 in. per sec.
          phonotape.

          I. Rogers, Will, 1879-1935. I. Rogers, Will, 1879-1935.

Voice Lib. Rogers, Will, 1879-1935
M574   I can hear it now (radio program)
bd.2-   1919-1933. CBS, 1953.
575   2 reels (7 in.) 7 1/2 in. per sec.
          phonotape.

          I. Murrow, Edward Roscoe, 1908-1965. II.
          Rogers, Will, 1879-1935. III. White, William
          Allen, 1868-1944. IV. Hoover, Herbert Clarke,
          Pres. U.S., 1874-1964. V. Roosevelt, Franklin
          Delano, Pres. U.S., 1882-1945. VI. Rice,
          Grantland, 1880-1954. VII. McNamee, Graham,
          1888-1942.

                Rogers, Will, 1879-1935
Voice Lib.
572-   I can hear it now (radio program)
573   1933-1946. CBS, 1948.
bd.1   2 reels (7 in.) 7 1/2 in. per sec.
          phonotape.

          I. Murrow, Edward Roscoe, 1908-1965. II. LaGuardia, Fiorello
          Henry, 1882-1947. III. Chamberlain, Neville, 1869-1949. IV.
          Roosevelt, Franklin Delano, Pres. U.S., 1882-1945. V. Churchill,
          Winston Leonard Spencer, 1874-1965. VI. Gaulle, Charles de,
          Pres. France, 1890-1970. VII. Eisenhower, Dwight David, Pres. U.S.,
          1890-1969. VIII. Willkie, Wendell Lewis, 1892-1944. IX. Martin,
          Joseph William, 1884-1968. X. Elizabeth II, Queen of Great Britain,
          1926-   XI. Margaret Rose, Princess of Gt. Brit., 1930-   XII.
          Johnson, Hugh Samuel, 188   42. XIII. Smith, Alfred Emanuel,
          1873-1944. XIV. Lindberg   arles Augustus, 1902-   XV. Davis,
          (Continued on next card)

ROGERS, WILL, 1879-1935

C1
M4
   Whorf, Michael, 1933-
     Man from Oklahoma.
     1 tape cassette. (The visual sounds of
Mike Whorf. Miscellaneous, M4)

    Originally presented on his radio program, Kaleidoscope,
WJR, Detroit.
    Duration: 40 min.
    The dry, brilliant humor of Will Rogers comes through in this
narrative concerning the cowboy philosopher.

     L. Rogers, Will, 1879-1935. L. Title.

Voice Lib.
555   The Rollickers (radio quartet)
bd.3   Singing their arrangement of "Old Man
River". Edison, 1926.
     1 reel (7 in.) 7 1/2 in. per sec.
phonotape.

     I. Title: Old man river.

     The Rollickers
Voice Lib.
M617 Radio in the 1920's: a series of excerpts
bd.1-   from important broadcasts of the 1920's,
bd.25 with brief prologue and epilogue; a sample
    of radio of the period. NVL, April, 1964.
     1 reel (7 in.) 7 1/2 in. per sec.
phonotape.
    L. Radio programs. L. Marconi, Guglielmo, marchese, 1874-
1937. IL. Kendall, H G III. Coolidge, Calvin, Pres. U.S.,
1872-1933. IV. Wilson, Woodrow, Pres. U.S., 1856-1924. V.
Roosevelt, Franklin Delano, Pres. U.S., 1882-1945. VI. Lodge,
Henry Cabot, 1850-1924. VII. LaGuardia, Fiorello Henry, 1882-1947.
VIII. The Happiness Boys (Radio program) IX. Gallagher and Sheen.
X. Barney Google. XI. Vallee, Rudy, 1901- XII. The two
          (Continued on next card)

C1   Romance of the Audubons--John and Lucy
A24 Whorf, Michael, 1933-
     Romance of the Audubons--John and Lucy.
     1 tape cassette. (The visual sounds of
Mike Whorf. Art, music, and letters, A24)
    Originally presented on his radio program, Kaleidoscope,
WJR, Detroit.
    Duration: 46 min.
    From the reaches of time is drawn this story of romance, of
the love of John Audubon and his wife, Lucy, who survived the
struggles and hardships of the wilderness so that her gifted husband
would achieve his ambition and dreams.

    L. Audubon, John James, 1788-1851. 2. Audubon, Lucy
(Bakewell) L. Title.

Voice Lib.
511   Rome, Harold Jacob, 1908-
bd.2   Writer of the words to "United Nations
Hymn" as sung by choir. Source (?), 1945.
     1 reel (7 in.) 7 1/2 in. per sec.
phonotape.

Voice Lib.
154   Rome, Harold Jacob, 1908-
bd.9   Money song, an original composition.
Private recording, 1949.
     1 reel (7 in.) 7 1/2 in. per sec.
phonotape.

Voice Lib.
128   Rome, Harold Jacob, 1908-
bd.4-12 On his own works. Private recording,
1937-52.
     1 reel (7 in.) 7 1/2 in. per sec.
phonotape.

    CONTENTS.-Bd.4. Sunday in the park (1937).-
bd.5. It's better with a union man (1937).-
bd.6. Franklin D. Roosevelt Jones (1938).-bd.7.
The money song (1948).-bd.8. Military life
         (Continued on next card)

Voice Lib.
128   Rome, Harold Jacob, 1908-
bd.4-12 On his own works... 1937-52. (Card 2)

    CONTENTS(cont'd) (The Jerk Song) (1946).-
bd.9. Call me Mister (1946).-bd.10. Where
did the night go? (1952).-bd.11. Don José
from Far Rockaway (1952).-bd.12. Wish you
were here (1952).

Voice Lib.
M720 Romney, George W   1907-
bd.1   Inaugural address. Lansing, Michigan,
12 noon, January 1, 1965.
     1 reel (7 in.) 7 1/2 in. per sec.
phonotape.

Voice Lib.
M772 Romney, George W   1907-
bd.2   Ceremonies at presentation of doctorate
degrees to astronauts at University of
Michigan, Ann Arbor. Appreciation of
accomplishments by McDivitt and White,
proclamation of White-McDivitt Day in Michigan
and presentation of clocks. Ann Arbor,
WUOM-Radio, June 15, 1965.
     1 reel (7 in.) 7 1/2 in. per sec.
phonotape.

The G. Robert Vincent Voice Library

Voice Lib.
M1282 Romney, George W   1907-
bd.1   Press conference with Governor Romney
          in which he announces his decision to enter
          the presidential race for Republican
          nomination in 1968.
              1 reel (7 in.)   7 1/2 in. per sec.
          phonotape.

Voice Lib.
352   Rooney, Pat
bd.4   On the reviving of vaudeville in the
          late 40's.   NBC, 1949.
              1 reel (7 in.)   7 1/2 in. per sec.
          phonotape.

          1. Vaudeville.

Voice Lib.
M1598 Romney, George W   1907-
bd.2   Off the record.   With Tim Skubick, Gary
          Schuster, Tom Greene, and Bill Meek.
          WKAR-TV, November 9, 1973.
          .' 20 min.   phonotape (1 r.   7 1/2 in. per
          sec.)

              1. Michigan - Politics and government.
          2. Detroit. I. Skubick, Tim. II. Schuster,
          Gary. III. Greene, Tom. IV. Meek, Bill

Voice Lib.   Roosa, Stuart A   1934-
M1438 Apollo 14 (space flight): take-off from Cape
bd.1   Kennedy, including countdown.   CBS,
          January 31, 1971.
              1 reel (7 in.)   7 1/2 in. per sec.
          phonotape.

              1. Project Apollo. 2. Space flight to the
          moon. 3. Shepard, Alan Bartlett, 1923-   4.
          Mitchell, Edgar D   1931- 5. Roosa,
          Stuart A   1934-   I. Shepard, Alan Bartlett,
          1923-   II. Mitchell, Edgar D   1931-   III.
          Roosa, Stuart A   ^934-

Voice Lib.
353   Romulo, Carlos Pena, 1899-
bd.7   Outbreak of Korean War; on acceleration of
          military aid to Philippines.   NBC, July, 1950.
              1 reel (7 in.)   7 1/2 in. per sec.
          phonotape.

          Original disc off-speed.

          1. Korean War, 1950-1953

             Roosa, Stuart A   1934-
Voice Lib.
M1438 Apollo 14 (space flight): lunar landed on the
bd.2   moon and moon walk.   CBS, February 5, 1971.
              1 reel (7 in.)   7 1/2 in. per sec.
          phonotape.

              1. Project Apollo. 2. Space flight to the
          moon. 3. Shepard, Alan Bartlett, 1923- 4.
          Mitchell, Edgar D   1931- 5. Roosa, Stuart
          A   1934-   I. Shepard, Alan Bartlett,
          1923-   II. Mitchell, Edgar D   1931- III.
          Roosa, Stuart A   1934-

             Romulo, Carlos Pena, 1899-
Voice Lib.
M622   Radio in the 1940's (Part III): a series of
bd.1-   excerpts from important broadcasts of the 1940's; a sample
bd.15   of radio of the period.   NVL, April, 1964.
          1 reel (7 in.)   7 1/2 in. per sec.   phonotape.
          I. Radio programs. L Miller, Alton Glenn, 1909(?)-1944. II.
          Diles, Ken   III. Wilson, Donald Harlow, 1900-   IV.
          Livingstone, Mary   V. Benny, Jack, 1894-   VI. Harris,
          Phil   VII. Merman, Ethel, 1909-   VIII. Smith, "Wonderful"
          IX. Bennett, Richard Dyer   X. Louis, Joe, 1914-   XI.
          Eisenhower, Dwight David, Pres. U. S., 1890-1969. XII. MacArthur,
          Douglas, 1880-1984. XIII. Romulo, Carlos Pena, 1899-   XIV.
          Welles, Orson, 1915-   XV. Jackson, Robert Houghwout, 1892-1954.
          XVI. LaGuardia, Fiorello Henry, 1882-1945. XVII. Nehru, Jawa-
          harlal, 1889-1964. XVIII. Gandhi, Mohandas Karamchand, 1869-1948.

Voice Lib.   Roosa, Stuart A   1934-
M1438 Apollo 14 (space flight): Apollo 14 splash-
bd.3-   down and reception on aircraft carrier.
M1439   CBS, February 9, 1971.
bd.1   2 reels (7 in.)   7 1/2 in. per sec.
          phonotape.

              1. Project Apollo. 2. Space flight to the
          moon. 3. Shepard, Alan Bartlett, 1923- 4.
          Mitchell, Edgar D   1931- 5. Roosa,
          Stuart A   1934-   I. Shepard, Alan Bartlett,
          1923-   II. Mitchell, Edgar D   1931- III.
          Roosa, Stuart A   1934-

             Roncalli, Angelo Giuseppe, Cardinal.
             see
             Joannes XXIII, Pope, 1881-1963.

Voice Lib.
M1096 Roosevelt, Eleanor (Roosevelt) 1884-1962.
bd.1   Weekly panel of guests on live television
          program entitled, "Today with Mrs. Roosevelt",
          discussing the future of atomic energy and
          the hydrogen bomb.   NBC-TV, February 12,
          1950.
              1 reel (7 in.)   7 1/2 i.p.s.   phonotape.

              1. Atomic energy. I. Title: Today with
          Mrs. Roosevelt.

Voice Lib.
306   Roosevelt, Eleanor (Roosevelt), 1884-1962.
      Address to the American Library
Association; discussion of books and
American image in foreign lands.
From WNYC program "Books are Basic",
October 13, 1952.
      1 reel (7 in.)   7 1/2 in. per sec.
phonotape.

Voice Lib.
256   Roosevelt, Eleanor (Roosevelt), 1884-1962.
bd.4   Interview by Dan Schorr following her
tour through the Soviet Union and her
conference with Khrushchev.   CBS News,
October 27, 1957.
      1 reel (7 in.)   7 1/2 in. per sec.
phonotape.

      I. Schorr, Daniel Louis, 1916-

Voice Lib.
203   Roosevelt, Eleanor (Roosevelt), 1884-1962.
      A speech at Jefferson-Jackson Day
Dinner at Masonic Temple. Detroit,
WJR, March 7, 1953.
      1 reel (7 in.)   7 1/2 in. per sec.
phonotape.

Voice Lib.
M724   Roosevelt, Eleanor Roosevelt, 1884-1962.
bd.7   Speaking in favor of nomination of Adlai
Stevenson in 1960 at convention in Los
Angeles, Calif.
      1 reel (7 in.)   7 1/2 in. per sec.
phonotape.

      1. Stevenson, Adlai Ewing, 1900-1965.

Voice Lib.
307   Roosevelt, Eleanor (Roosevelt), 1884-1962.
      Address at AFL-CIO Unity Convention:
labor's part in our political life.
WNYC, December 9, 1955.
      1 reel (7 in.)   7 1/2 in. per sec.
phonotape.

Voice Lib.
M258   Roosevelt, Eleanor (Roosevelt), 1884-1962.
bd.5   Tractors for Cuba. New York, CBS,
May 31, 1961.
      1 reel (7 in.)   7 1/2 in. per sec.
phonotape.

Voice Lib.
M931   Roosevelt, Eleanor Roosevelt, 1884-1962.
bd.2   Introducing Adlai Stevenson from Los
Angeles; he speaks about current condition
of schools. CBS, September 28, 1956.
      1 reel (7 in.)   7 1/2 in. per sec.
phonotape.

      I. Stevenson, Adlai Ewing, 1900-1965.

Voice Lib.
M778
Roosevelt, Eleanor (Roosevelt) 1884-1962.
    Reminiscences: reminiscences of her childhood; how she met
FDR and his earlier life; his interest in conservation; description of
FDR inauguration, of her marriage ceremony, life at Hyde Park, and
FDR's childhood; description of Campo Bello and life there; 1920
Democratic convention; relates fighting fire and then swimming in
Bay of Fundy; examinations for polio and his reactions; FDR's
nomination for governor of New York and his campaign for governor;
also life in Albany. Columbia Records Inc., 1962.
    1 reel (7 in.) 7 1/2 in. per sec. phonotape.

    1. Roosevelt, Eleanor (Roosevelt) 1884-1962. 2. Roosevelt,
Franklin Delano, Pres. U.S., 1882-1945.

Voice Lib.
652   Roosevelt, Eleanor (Roosevelt), 1884-1962.
bd.3   Interview with Daniel Schorr following
her tour through Russia. CBS, September 29,
1957.
      1 reel (7 in.)   7 1/2 in. per sec.
phonotape.

      I. Schorr, Daniel Louis, 1916-

Voice Lib.
M779   Roosevelt, Eleanor (Roosevelt) 1894-1962.
    Reminiscences: description of FDR nomination in 1932 and
the trip to Chicago for acceptance; election night of 1932 and
FDR's feelings; FDR as a father and children's education and
discipline; attempted assassination and ideas thereon; inauguration
day 1932, impressions; life in the White House in all respects;
about Miss Thompson, her secretary; FDR and the radio and
recognition of the American scene on the first 100 days.
Columbia Records Inc., 1962.
    1 reel (7 in.) 7 1/2 in. per sec. phonotape.

    1. Roosevelt, Eleanor (Roosevelt) 1894-1962.

Voice Lib.
M 780   Roosevelt, Eleanor (Roosevelt) 1884-1962.
bd.1   Reminiscences: her political influence; FDR hiding from guards
         and P.S. at Hyde Park; King's and Queen's visit to Hyde Park;
         Churchill at White House; FDR on the third term and 1940 conven-
         tion, Vice-President Wallace nomination; December 7, 1941; Mrs.
         Roosevelt at White House and FDR's reactions about General Eisen-
         hower and his promotion; her travels to military installations in U.S.
         and abroad; campaign of 1944; her last visit with FDR. Columbia
         Records, Inc., 1962.
         1 reel (7 in.)   7 1/2 in. per sec.   phonotape.

         L. Roosevelt, Eleanor (Roosevelt) 1884-1962. 2. Roosevelt,
         Franklin Delano, Pres. U.S., 1882-1945.

         Roosevelt, Eleanor (Roosevelt) 1884-1962
Voice Lib.
M621   Radio in the 1940's (Part II): a series of
bd.1-   excerpts from important broadcasts of the
12   1940's; a sample of radio of the period.
         NVL, April, 1964.
         1 reel (7 in.)   7 1/2 in. per sec.   phonotape.
         L. Daly, John Charles, 1914-   IL. Hall, Josef Washington,
         1894-   III. Shirer, William Lawrence, 1904-   IV. Roosevelt,
         Eleanor (Roosevelt) 1884-1962. V. Roosevelt, Franklin Delano,
         Pres. U.S., 1882-1945. VI. Churchill, Winston Leonard Spencer,
         1874-1965. VII. Wainwright, Jonathan Mayhew, 1883-1953. VIII.
         Cantor, Eddie, 1893-1964. IX. Sinatra, Francis Albert, 1917-
         X. Hope, Bob, 1903-   XI. Crosby, Bing, 1901-   XII. Shore,
         Dinah, 191?7?-   XIII. Bergen, Edgar, 1903-   XIV. Armstrong,
         Louis, 1900-1971. XV. Eldridge, Roy, 1911-

         Roosevelt, Eleanor (Roosevelt) 1884-1962
Voice Lib.
M275-   Biography in sound (radio program)
276   Alexander Woollcott. N.B.C., date?
bd.1   2 reels (7 in.)   7 1/2 in. per sec.
         phonotape.
         L. Woollcott, Alexander, 1887-1943. L. Woollcott, Alexander,
         1887-1943. IL. Banghardt, Kenneth   III. Hecht, Ben, 1893-
         1964. IV. Roosevelt, Eleanor (Roosevelt) 1884-1962. V. Walker,
         Danton   VI. Brackett, Charles, 1892-1969. VII. Grant,
         Jane   VIII. Rude, Robert Barnes   IX. West,
         Rebecca, pseud. X. Henessy, Joseph   XI. Letterer,
         Charles   XII. Welles, Orson, 1915-

         Roosevelt, Eleanor (Roosevelt) 1884-1962
Voice Lib.
M273-   Biography in sound (radio program)
274   Franklin Delano Roosevelt: the friends and
bd.1   former associates of Franklin Roosevelt on
         the tenth anniversary of the President's death.
         NBC Radio, April, 1955.
         2 reels (7 in.)   7 1/2 in. per sec.
         phonotape.
         L. Roosevelt, Franklin Delano, Pres. U.S., 1882-1945. L.
         McIntire, Ross T   1899-   IL. Mellett, Lowell, 1884-1960.
         III. Tully, Grace   IV. Henderson, Leon, 1895-
         V. Roosevelt, Eleanor (Roosevelt) 1884-1962. VI. DeGraaf, Albert
         VII. Lehman, Herbert Henry, 1878-1963. VIII. Rosenman, Samuel
         Irving, 1896-   IX. Arvey, Jacob   X. Moley, Raymond,
         1886-   XI. Farley, Jai   Aloysius, 1888-   XII. Roosevelt,
         (Continued on next card)

         Roosevelt, Eleanor (Roosevelt) 1884-
                     1962
Voice Lib.
385   I can hear it now (radio program)
         CBS, February 2, 1951.
         1 reel (7 in.)   7 1/2 in. per sec.
         phonotape.

         I. Austin, Warren Robinson, 1877-1962. II.
         Pandit, Vijaya Lakshmi (Nehru) 1900-   III.
         Roosevelt, Eleanor (Roosevelt) 1884-1962. IV.
         Morse, Wayne Lyman, 1900-   V. Chandler,
         Albert Benjamin, 1898-   VI. Taylor, Telford,
         1908-   VII. Why   Jack.

                 Roosevelt, Eleanor (Roosevelt) 1884-1962
Voice Lib.
573   I can hear it now (radio program)
bd.2-   1945-1949. CBS, 1950?
574   2 reels (7 in.)   7 1/2 in. per sec.
bd.1   phonotape.
         L. Murrow, Edward Roscoe, 1908-1965. IL. Nehru, Jawaharlal,
         1889-1964. III. Philip, duke of Edinburgh, 1921-   IV. Elizabeth II,
         Queen of Great Britain, 1926-   V. Ferguson, Homer, 1889-   VL.
         Hughes, Howard Robard, 1905-   VII. Marshall, George Catlett,
         1880-   VIII. Ruth, George Herman, 1895-4948. IX. Lilienthal,
         David Eli, 1899-   X. Trout, Robert, 1908-   XL Gage, Arthur.
         XII. Jackson, Robert Houghwout, 1892-1954. XIII. Gromyko, Ana-
         tolii Andreevich, 1908-   XIV. Baruch, Bernard Mannes, 1870-
         1965. XV. Churchill, Win---n Leonard Spencer, 1874-1965. XVL.
         Winchell, Walter, 1897-1   XVII. Davis, Elmer Holmes, 1890-
         (Continued on next card)

              Roosevelt, Eleanor (Roosevelt) 1884-1962
Voice Lib.
M891   Roosevelt, Franklin Delano, Pres. U.S.,
bd.2   1882-1945.
         Address to the National Education Association
         delivered at the N.Y. World's Fair in 1938.
         Introduction of the President by Mrs.
         Eleanor Roosevelt; discussion of the
         necessity of government aid to educational
         institutions in poorer communities without
         curbing freedom of teaching. WJR, June 30,
         1938.
         (Continued on next card)

              Roosevelt, Eleanor (Roosevelt) 1884-1962
Voice Lib.
M891   Roosevelt, Franklin Delano, Pres. U.S.,
bd.2   1882-1945. Address to the National
         Education Association... 1938. (Card 2)

         1 reel (7 in.)   7 1/2 in. per sec.
         phonotape.

         I. Roosevelt, Eleanor (Roosevelt) 1884-1962.

              ROOSEVELT, ELEANOR (ROOSEVELT), 1884-1962
Voice Lib.
M1460   Stevenson, Adlai Ewing, 1900-1965.
bd.2   Adlai Stevenson gives eulogy of Eleanor
         Roosevelt at U.N.   U.N., November 9, 1962.
         1 reel (7 in.)   7 1/2 in. per sec.
         phonotape.

         I. Roosevelt, Eleanor (Roosevelt), 1884-1962.

Voice Lib.
M717   Roosevelt, Franklin Delano, Pres. U.S., 1882-
         1945.
         Drawing the first draft number from the
         "fish bowl."
         1 reel (7 in.)   7 1/2 in. per sec.
         phonotape.

Voice Lib.
M1285   Roosevelt, Franklin Delano, Pres. U.S.,
bd.4   1882-1945.
             Talking about Americanism, the U.S. part
         in World War I, and hope for permanent peace.
         Talk recorded during presidential campaign
         of 1920. Nation's Forum, 1920.
             1 reel (7 in.)   7 1/2 in. per sec.
         phonotape..

Voice Lib.
M716   Roosevelt, Franklin Delano, Pres. U.S.,
             1882-1945.
             Fireside chat about changes needed in the
         U.S. Supreme Court. CBS, March 9, 1937.
             1 reel (7 in.)   7 1/2 in. per sec.
         phonotape.

Voice Lib.
M1034   Roosevelt, Franklin Delano, Pres. U.S.,
bd.6   1882-1945.
             Excerpt of acceptance of nomination by
         Franklin D. Roosevelt at 1932 Democratic
         National Convention. CBS, 1932.
             1 reel (7 in.)   7 1/2 in. per sec.
         phonotape.

Voice Lib.
M891   Roosevelt, Franklin Delano, Pres. U.S.,
bd.2   1882-1945.
             Address to the National Education Association
         delivered at the N.Y. World's Fair in 1938.
         Introduction of the President by Mrs.
         Eleanor Roosevelt; discussion of the
         necessity of government aid to educational
         institutions in poorer communities without
         curbing freedom of teaching. WJR, June 30,
         1938.

(Continued on next card)

Voice Lib.
M714   Roosevelt, Franklin Delano, Pres. U.S.,
bd.3   1882-1945.
             First fireside chat, on banking situation
         in the U.S. (opening and closing statements
         of this broadcast). March 12, 1933.
             2 min., 9 sec.   phonotape (1 r.   7 1/2
         i.p.s.)

             1. U.S. - Economic conditions. 2. Banks
         & banking - U.S.

Voice Lib.
M891   Roosevelt, Franklin Delano, Pres. U.S.,
bd.2   1882-1945. Address to the National
             Education Association...   1938.   (Card 2)

             1 reel (7 in.)   7 1/2 in. per sec.
         phonotape.

             I. Roosevelt, Eleanor (Roosevelt) 1884-1962.

Voice Lib.
514   Roosevelt, Franklin Delano, Pres. U.S.,
bd.3   1882-1945.
             Brotherhood Day Address to National
         Conference of Jews and Christians on the
         importance of brotherhood. New York,
         WJZ, February 23, 1936.
             1 reel (7 in.)   7 1/2 in. per sec.
         phonotape.

Voice Lib.
M894   Roosevelt, Franklin Delano, Pres. U.S.,
bd.2   1882-1945.
             Radio talk to the nation on America's
         position on outbreak of war in Europe.
         CBS, September 3, 1939.
             1 reel (7 in.)   7 1/2 in. per sec.
         phonotape.

Voice Lib.
211   Roosevelt, Franklin Delano, Pres. U.S., 1882-
             1945.
             Fireside Talk: reorganization of the
         judicial branch of government. CBS,
         March 9, 1937.
             1 reel (7 in.)   7 1/2 in. per sec.
         phonotape.

Voice Lib.
M892   Roosevelt, Franklin Delano, Pres. U.S.,
             1882-1945.
             Address to the special session of Congress
         which he called to request repeal of the
         embargo act of trading with belligerents
         in war materials. WJR, September 21, 1939.
             1 reel (7 in.)   7 1/2 i.p.s.   phonotape.

             1. U.S. - Politics and government -
         1933-1945.

Voice Lib.
M865   Roosevelt, Franklin Delano, Pres. U.S.,
bd.1   1882-1945.
            Address to inaugural session of the 8th
Pan American Scientific Congress from Constitutional Hall, Washington, D.C.   NBC, May 10,
1940.
        1 reel (7 in.)   7 1/2 in. per sec.
phonotape.

Voice Lib.
M898   Roosevelt, Franklin Delano, Pres. U.S.,
bd.1   1882-1945.
            Remarks at community Christmas tree lighting
in Washington, D.C.   WJR, December 24, 1940.
        1 reel (7 in.)   7 1/2 in. per sec.
phonotape.

Voice Lib.
M897   Roosevelt, Franklin Delano, Pres. U.S.,
            1882-1945.
            Addressing joint session of Congress on
measures to strengthen United States' national
defense; asking for funds for general
preparedness. WJR, May 16, 1940.
        1 reel (7 in.)   7 1/2 in. per sec.
phonotape.

Voice Lib.
M901   Roosevelt, Franklin Delano, Pres. U.S.,
            1882-1945.
            Fireside chat on national defense program,
giving reasons for American aid to Britain.
CBS, December 29, 1940.
        1 reel (7 in.)   7 1/2 i.p.s.   phonotape.

        1. U.S. - Defenses.

Voice Lib.
M905   Roosevelt, Franklin Delano, Pres. U.S.,
            1882-1945.
            Fireside talk discussing necessity of
speed-up in national defense and reviewing
accomplishments of military and economic
preparedness so far. CBS, May 26, 1940.
        1 reel (7 in.)   7 1/2 i.p.s.   phonotape.

        1. U.S. - Defenses. 2. U.S. - Politics and
government - 1933-1945.

Voice Lib.
M893-   Roosevelt, Franklin Delano, Pres. U.S.,
894   1882-1945.
bd.1   Address on state of the Union to the
combined first session of the 77th Congress
requesting U.S. support of armaments to
those nations resisting aggression (Lend-
Lease), also stressing domestic aims; including
famous quotation on "The Four Freedoms".
CBS, January 6, 1941.
        2 reels (7 in.)   7 1/2 in. per sec.
phonotape.

Voice Lib.
M607   Roosevelt, Franklin Delano, Pres. U.S.,
bd.4   1882-1945.
            Report on President Roosevelt's proposal
for a peacetime draft. CBS, June 18, 1940.
        1 reel (7 in.)   7 1/2 i.p.s.   phonotape.

        1. Military service, Compulsory - U.S.

Voice Lib.
M780   Roosevelt, Franklin Delano, Pres. U.S.,
bd.2   1882-1945.
            Inaugural address, Washington, D.C.   CBS,
January 20, 1941.
        1 reel (7 in.)   7 1/2 in. per sec.
phonotape.

Voice Lib.
M724   Roosevelt, Franklin Delano, Pres. U.S.,
bd.5   1882-1945.
            Excerpt of his 1940 acceptance speech.
        1 reel (7 in.)   7 1/2 in. per sec.
phonotape.

Voice Lib.
M914   Roosevelt, Franklin Delano, Pres. U.S.,
bd.2   1882-1945.
            Remarks at second annual National Farm
Day, stressing the necessity of aiding the
warring democracies with farm products.
CBS, March 8, 1941.
        1 reel (7 in.)   7 1/2 in. per sec.
phonotape.

Voice Lib.
M904   Roosevelt, Franklin Delano, Pres. U.S.,
    1882-1945.
    Address on necessity of our full aid
to Britain. CBS, March 15, 1941.
    1 reel (7 in.) 7 1/2 in. per sec.
phonotape.

Voice Lib.
M900   Roosevelt, Franklin Delano, Pres. U.S.,
bd.1   1882-1945.
    Radio talk to the people explaining his
message to Congress regarding extension of
selective military service, the Reserve,
and National Guard. WJR, July 21, 1941.
    1 reel (7 in.) 7 1/2 in. per sec.
phonotape.

Voice Lib.
M903   Roosevelt, Franklin Delano, Pres. U.S.,
    1882-1945.
    Dedication of National Gallery of Art in
Washington, D.C. CBS, March 17, 1941.
    1 reel (7 in.) 7 1/2 i.p.s. phonotape.

    1. U.S. National Gallery of Art.

Voice Lib.
533   Roosevelt, Franklin Delano, Pres. U.S.,
bd.2   1882-1945.
    Labor Day address; comparison of U.S.
labor's progress to that of Axis powers.
Source ?, September, 1941.
    1 reel (7 in.) 7 1/2 in. per sec.
phonotape.

Voice Lib.
M898   Roosevelt, Franklin Delano, Pres. U.S.,
bd.2   1882-1945.
    Addressing the Jackson Day dinners through-
out the country. Delivered from the
Presidential yacht "Potomac" in Fort
Lauderdale waters. WJR, March 29, 1941.
    1 reel (7 in.) 7 1/2 in. per sec.
phonotape.

Voice Lib.
M831   Roosevelt, Franklin Delano, Pres. U.S.,
bd.1   1882-1945.
    Message delivered in person by President
requesting declaration of war on Japan,
before joint session of Congress. NBC,
December 8, 1941.
    1 reel (7 in.) 7 1/2 in. per sec.
phonotape.

Voice Lib.
M917   Roosevelt, Franklin Delano, Pres. U.S.,
bd.2-   1882-1945.
918   Fireside chat defining position of U.S. on
national defense and alliances with Pan
American republics. May 27, 1941.
    2 reels (7 in.) 7 1/2 in. per sec.
phonotape.

    1. U.S. - Defenses. 2. U.S. - Foreign
relations - Latin America. 3. Latin America -
Foreign relations - U.S.

Voice Lib.
M830   Roosevelt, Franklin Delano, Pres. U.S., 1882-1945.
    Description of proceedings at Joint Session of Congress on
December 8, 1941, prior to President's address asking for
declaration of war; including news flashes by NBC correspondents
Carlton Smith, Morgan Beatty, and Baukhage. NBC, December 8,
1941.
    32 min. phonotape (1 r. 7 1/2 i. p. s.)

    I. World War, 1939-1945 - U.S. I. Smith, Carlton.
II. Beatty, Morgan. III. Baukhage, Hilmar Robert.

Voice Lib.
M900   Roosevelt, Franklin Delano, Pres. U.S.,
bd.2   1882-1945.
    Speaking from the F.D.R. Library at Hyde
Park, New York, on the subject of allegiance
to the flag; over the CBS radio network,
including the pledge by Chief Justice Harlan
Stone. WJR, July 4, 1941.
    1 reel (7 in.) 7 1/2 in. per sec.
phonotape.

    I. Stone, Harlan Fiske, 1872-1946.

Voice Lib.
522   Roosevelt, Franklin Delano, Pres. U.S., 1882-
bd.3   1945.
    Asking Congress to recognize a state of
war between U.S., Germany and Italy. CBS,
December 11, 1941.
    1 reel (7 in.) 7 1/2 in. per sec.
phonotape.

Voice Lib.
M863   Roosevelt, Franklin Delano, Pres. U.S.,
bd.2   1882-1945.
     Address to delegates of Allied Nations
Food Conference from the East Room of White
House.   NBC, June 7, 1943.
     1 reel (7 in.)   7 1/2 in. per sec.
phonotape.

Voice Lib.
533   Roosevelt, Franklin Delano, Pres. U.S.,
bd.3   1882-1945.
     D-Day Prayer; announcement of troops
crossing channel on D-Day and offering
prayer.   WIZ, June 6, 1944.
     1 reel (7 in.)   7 1/2 in. per sec.
phonotape.

Voice Lib.
M851-   Roosevelt, Franklin Delano, Pres. U.S., 1882-1945.
852   Report to joint session of Congress about Yalta conference of
the Big Three. Explaining purpose of conference, describing
devastation of Russia, plans for a peace organization in San Francisco to start April 25, 1945, touching on the free elections for
conquered countries; objectives for Poland; France's role in the
future; delays caused by "primadonnas" meeting with King Farouk,
King Ibn Saud and Emperor Haile Selassie; the current Japanese
situation; hopes for United Nations organization. NBC, March 1,
1945.
     59 min., 30 sec.   phonotape (2 r. 7 1/2 i.p.s.)

     1. World War, 1939-1945 - Peace. 2. Crimea Conference,
Yalta, 1945.

Voice Lib.
593   Roosevelt, Franklin Delano, Pres. U.S., 1882-
     1945.
     Memorial service upon his death.   City Hall
Plaza, New York City, WNYC, April 14, 1945.
     1 reel (7 in.)   7 1/2 in. per sec.
phonotape.

     1. Roosevelt, Franklin Delano, pres. U.S.,
1882-1945.

Voice Lib.
114-   Roosevelt, Franklin Delano, Pres. U.S., 1882-
116   1945.
     The F.D.R. Years.   Narrated by John C. Daly.
Hearst Metrotone News (sound track) 1962.
     3 reels (7 in.)   7 1/2 in. per sec.
phonotape.

     I. Daly, John Charles, 1914-
     1. Roosevelt, Franklin Delano, Pres. U.S.,
1882-1945.

         Roosevelt, Franklin Delano, Pres. U.S.,
Voice Lib.   1882-1945
M620   Radio in the 1940's (Part I): a series of
bd.1-   excerpts from important broadcasts of the 1940's; a
bd.16   sample of radio of the period.   NVL, April, 1964.
     1 reel (7 in.)   7 1/2 in. per sec.   phonotape.
     I. Radio programs.   I. Thomas, Lowell Jackson, 1892-   II.
Gunther, John, 1901-1970.   III. Kaltenborn, Hans von, 1878-1965.
IV. Delmar, Kenny.   V. Those were the good old days (Radio
program)   VI. Elman, Dave.   VII. Hall, Frederick Lee, 1916-1970.
VIII. Hobby lobby (Radio program)   IX. Roosevelt, Franklin Delano,
Pres. U.S., 1882-1945.   X. Willkie, Wendell Lewis, 1892-1944.
XI. Hoover, Herbert Clark, Pres. U.S., 1874-1964.   XII. Johnson,
Hugh Samuel, 1882-1942.   XIII. Cobb, Irvin Shrewsbury, 1876-1944.
XIV. Roosevelt, Theodore, 1858-1919.   XV. Nye, Gerald Prentice,
1892-1971.   XVI. Lindbergh, Charles Augustus, 1902-   XVII.
Toscanini, Arturo, 1867-1957.

         Roosevelt, Franklin Delano, Pres. U.S.,
Voice Lib.   1882-1945
M621   Radio in the 1940's (Part II): a series of
bd.1-   excerpts from important broadcasts of the
12   1940's; a sample of radio of the period.
     NVL, April, 1964.
     1 reel (7 in.)   7 1/2 in. per sec.   phonotape.
     I. Daly, John Charles, 1914-   II. Hall, Josef Washington,
1894-   III. Shirer, William Lawrence, 1904-   IV. Roosevelt,
Eleanor (Roosevelt) 1884-1962.   V. Roosevelt, Franklin Delano,
Pres. U.S., 1882-1945.   VI. Churchill, Winston Leonard Spencer,
1874-1965.   VII. Wainwright, Jonathan Mayhew, 1883-1953.   VIII.
Cantor, Eddie, 1893-1964.   IX. Sinatra, Francis Albert, 1917-
X. Hope, Bob, 1903-   XI. Crosby, Bing, 1901-   XII. Shore,
Dinah, 1917?)-   XIII. Bergen, Edgar, 1903-   XIV. Armstrong,
Louis, 1900-1971.   XV. Eldridge, Roy, 1911-

         Roosevelt, Franklin Delano, Pres. U.S., 1882-
Voice Lib.   1945
M618   Radio in the 1930's (Part I): a series of
bd.1-   excerpts from important broadcasts of the
14   1930's; a sample of radio of the period.
     NVL, April, 1964.
     1 reel (7 in.)   7 1/2 in. per sec.   phonotape.
     I. Shaw, George Bernard, 1856-1950.   II. Crosby, Bing, 1901-
III. Barkley, Alban William, 1877-1956.   IV. Roosevelt, Franklin
Delano, Pres. U.S., 1882-1945.   V. Hoover, Herbert Clark, Pres.
U.S., 1874-1964.   VI. Long, Huey Pierce, 1893-1935.   VII. Townsend, Francis Everett, 1867-1960.   VIII. Coughlin, Charles Edward,
1891-   IX. Rogers, Will, 1879-1935.   X. Pius XII, Pope, 1876-
1958.   XI. Edward VIII, king of Great Britain, 1894-1972.   XII.
Barrymore, John, 1882-1942.   XIII. Woollcott, Alexander, 1887-
1943.   XIV. Allen, Fred, 1894-1956.   XV. Benchley, Robert Charles,
1889-1945.

         Roosevelt, Franklin Delano, Pres. U.S.,
Voice Lib.   1882-1945
M619   Radio in the 1930's (Part II): a series of
bd.1-   excerpts of the 1930's; a sample of radio
14   of the period. NVL, April, 1964.
     1 reel (7 in.)   7 1/2 in. per sec.   phonotape.
     I. Allen, Fred, 1894-1956.   II. Delmar, Kenny   III. Donald,
Peter   IV. Pious, Minerva   V. Fennelly, Parker   VI.
Boyer, Charles, 1899-   VII. Dunne, Irene, 1904-   VIII.
DeMille, Cecil Blount, 1881-1959.   IX. West, Mae, 1893-   X.
Dafoe, Allan Roy, 1883-1943.   XI. Dionne quintuplets.   XII. Ortega,
Santos   XIII. War of the worlds (radio program)   XIV. Ives, Burl,
1909-   XV. Robinson, Earl, 1910-   XVI. Temple, Shirley,
1928-   XVII. Earhart, Amelia, 1898-1937.   XVIII. Lawrence,
Gertrude, 1901-1952.   XIX. Cohan, George Michael, 1878-1942.
XX. Shaw, George Bernard, 1856-1950.   XXI. Hitler, Adolf, 1889-
1945.   XXII. Chamberlain, Neville, 1869-1940.   XXIII. Roosevelt,
Franklin Delano, Pres. U.S., 1882-1945.

         Roosevelt, Franklin Delano, Pres. U.S.,
Voice Lib.   1882-1945
M617   Radio in the 1920's: a series of excerpts
bd.1-   from important broadcasts of the 1920's,
bd.25   with brief prologue and epilogue; a sample
     of radio of the period. NVL, April, 1964.
     1 reel (7 in.)   7 1/2 in. per sec.
phonotape.
     I. Radio programs.   I. Marconi, Guglielmo, marchese, 1874-
1937.   II. Kendall, H   G   III. Coolidge, Calvin, Pres. U.S.,
1872-1933.   IV. Wilson, Woodrow, Pres. U.S., 1856-1924.   V.
Roosevelt, Franklin Delano, Pres. U.S., 1882-1945.   VI. Lodge,
Henry Cabot, 1850-1924.   VII. LaGuardia, Fiorello Henry, 1882-1947.
VIII. The Happiness Boys (Radio program)   IX. Gallagher and Sheen.
X. Barney Google.   XI. Vallee, Rudy, 1901-   XII. The two
(Continued on next card)

Roosevelt, Franklin Delano, Pres. U.S., 1882-
Voice Lib.   1945
M273-   Biography in sound (radio program)
274   Franklin Delano Roosevelt: the friends and
bd.1   former associates of Franklin Roosevelt on
         the tenth anniversary of the President's death.
         NBC Radio, April, 1955.
             2 reels (7 in.)   7 1/2 in. per sec.
         phonotape.
             L. Roosevelt, Franklin Delano, Pres. U.S., 1882-1945. L.
         McIntire, Ross T   1899-   II. Mellett, Lowell, 1884-1960.
         III. Tully, Grace   IV. Henderson, Leon, 1895-
         V. Roosevelt, Eleanor (Roosevelt) 1884-1962. VI. DeGraaf, Albert
         VII. Lehman, Herbert Henry, 1878-1963. VIII. Rosenman, Samuel
         Irving, 1896-   IX. Arvey, Jacob   X. Moley, Raymond,
         1886-   XI. Farley, James Aloysius, 1888-   XII. Roosevelt,
                                (Continued on next card)

Roosevelt, Franklin Delano, Pres. U.S.,
Voice Lib.   1882-1945
M272   Biography in sound (radio program)
bd.1   Heywood Broun.   NBC, date?
             1 reel (7 in.)   7 1/2 in. per sec.
         phonotape.
             L. Broun, Heywood Campbell, 1888-1939. L. Broun,
         Heywood Campbell, 1888-1939. II. Swope, Herbert Bayard,
         1882-1958. III. Wilson, Mattie   IV. Jackson, Gardner
         V. Meany, Thomas   VI. Waldron, Beatrice   VII.
         Gordon, Max   VIII. Madison, Connie   IX. Gannett,
         Lewis Stiles, 1891-1966. X. Collins, Joseph, 1866-1950. XI.
         Brown, Earl Louis, 1900-   XII. Levy, Newman, 1888-
         XIII. Growth, John   XIV. Bye, George   XV.
         Roosevelt, Franklin Delano, Pres. U.S., 1882-1945. XVI.
         Reynolds, Quentin James, 1902-1965.

ROOSEVELT, FRANKLIN DELANO, PRES. U.S.,
Voice Lib.   1882-1945
M273-   Biography in sound (radio program)
274   Franklin Delano Roosevelt: the friends and
bd.1   former associates of Franklin Roosevelt on
         the tenth anniversary of the President's death.
         NBC Radio, April, 1955.
             2 reels (7 in.)   7 1/2 in. per sec.
         phonotape.
             L. Roosevelt, Franklin Delano, Pres. U.S., 1882-1945. L.
         McIntire, Ross T   1899-   II. Mellett, Lowell, 1884-1960.
         III. Tully, Grace   IV. Henderson, Leon, 1895-
         V. Roosevelt, Eleanor (Roosevelt) 1884-1962. VI. DeGraaf, Albert
         VII. Lehman, Herbert Henry, 1878-1963. VIII. Rosenman, Samuel
         Irving, 1896-.   IX. Arvey, Jacob   X. Moley, Raymond,
         1886-   XI. Farley, James Aloysius, 1888-   XII. Roosevelt,
                                (Continued on next card)

Roosevelt, Franklin Delano, Pres. U.S.,
Voice Lib.   1882-1945
M574   I can hear it now (radio program)
bd.2-   1919-1933.   CBS, 1953.
575   2 reels (7 in.)   7 1/2 in. per sec.
         phonotape.
             I. Murrow, Edward Roscoe, 1908-1965. II.
         Rogers, Will, 1879-1935. III. White, William
         Allen, 1868-1944. IV. Hoover, Herbert Clarke,
         Pres. U.S., 1874-1964. V. Roosevelt, Franklin
         Delano, Pres. U.S., 1882-1945. VI. Rice,
         Grantland, 1880-1954. VII. McNamee, Graham,
         1888-1942.

Roosevelt, Franklin Delano, Pres. U.S.,
Voice Lib.   1882-1945
572-   I can hear it now (radio program)
573   1933-1946.   CBS, 1948.
bd.1   2 reels (7 in.)   7 1/2 in. per sec.
         phonotape.
             L. Murrow, Edward Roscoe, 1908-1965. II. LaGuardia, Fiorello
         Henry, 1882-1947. III. Chamberlain, Neville, 1869-1949. IV.
         Roosevelt, Franklin Delano, Pres. U.S., 1882-1945. V. Churchill,
         Winston Leonard Spencer, 1874-1965. VI. Gaulle, Charles de,
         Pres. France, 1890-1970. VII. Eisenhower, Dwight David, Pres. U.S.,
         1890-1969. VIII. Willkie, Wendell Lewis, 1892-1944. IX. Martin,
         Joseph William, 1884-1968. X. Elizabeth II, Queen of Great Britain,
         1926-   XI. Margaret Rose, Princess of Gt. Brit., 1930-   XII.
         Johnson, Hugh Samuel, 1882-1942. XIII. Smith, Alfred Emanuel,
         1873-1944. XIV. Lindbergh, Charles Augustus, 1902-   XV. Davis,
                                -(Continued on next card)

ROOSEVELT, FRANKLIN DELANO, PRES. U.S.,
Voice Lib.   1882-1945
M778
         Roosevelt, Eleanor (Roosevelt) 1884-1962.
             Reminiscences: reminiscences of her childhood; how she met
         FDR and his earlier life; his interest in conservation; description of
         FDR inauguration, of her marriage ceremony, life at Hyde Park, and
         FDR's childhood; description of Campo Bello and life there; 1920
         Democratic convention; relates fighting fire and then swimming in
         Bay of Fundy; examinations for polio and his reactions; FDR's
         nomination for governor of New York and his campaign for governor;
         also life in Albany.   Columbia Records Inc., 1962.
             1 reel (7 in.)   7 1/2 in. per sec.   phonotape.

             L. Roosevelt, Eleanor (Roosevelt) 1884-1962. 2. Roosevelt,
         Franklin Delano, Pres. U.S., 1882-1945.

ROOSEVELT, FRANKLIN DELANO, PRES. U.S.,
Voice Lib.   1882-1945
M714   Trout, Robert, 1908-
bd.5   Recollecting events in preparing the
         first "Fireside Chat" with Franklin D.
         Roosevelt on the banking situation, in
         March, 1933.   CBS, 1963.
             1 reel (7 in.)   7 1/2 in. per sec.
         phonotape.

Roosevelt, Franklin Delano, Pres. U.S.,
Voice Lib.   1882-1945
M655   The Twentieth Century (TV program)
bd.1   "The creative thirties", narrated by
         Walter Cronkite.   CBS, 1963.
             25 min.   phonotape (1 r.   7 1/2 i.p.s.)

             L. U.S. - Civilization - 1918-1945. L. Bowes, Edward,
         1874-1946. II. Geismar, Maxwell David, 1909-
         III. MacDonald, Dwight, 1906-   IV. Welles, Orson, 1915-
         V. Cronkite, Walter Leland, 1916-   VI. Gable, Clark, 19..-
         1960. VII. Lewis, Sinclair, 1895-1951. VIII. Houseman,
         John, 1902-   IX. Roosevelt, Franklin Delano, Pres. U.S.,
         1882-1945.

Roosevelt, Franklin Delano, Pres. U.S.,
Voice Lib.   1882-1945
M289   Twentieth Century (Television program)
bd.2   Production on career of Alfred E. Smith.
         Various excerpts of addresses by Gov. Smith;
         recollections by Robert Moses on life of
         Gov. Smith; narration by Walter Cronkite;
         placing of Smith's name in nomination for
         President by F.D.R.   CBS, 1962.
             1 reel (7 in.)   7 1/2 in. per sec.
         phonotape.
             L. Smith, Alfred Emanuel, 1873-1944. L. Smith, Alfred
         Emanuel, 1873-1944. II. Moses, Robert, 1888-   III. Cronkite,
         Walter Leland, 1916-   IV. Roosevelt, Franklin Delano, Pres. U.S.,
         1882-1945.

Roosevelt, Franklin Delano, Pres. U.S., 1882-1945
Voice Lib.
M1033   Voice of America.
             Twentieth anniversary program of Voice of
         America broadcasts narrated by Henry Fonda,
         and including the voices of Carl Sandburg,
         Danny Kaye, Jawaharlal Nehru, Franklin D.
         Roosevelt, Charles Malik, Arnold Toynbee,
         William Faulkner, Harry S. Truman, Dwight D.
         Eisenhower, Helen Hayes, Dag Hammarskjöld,
         Winston Churchill, and John F. Kennedy.
         Voice of America, 1963.
             1 reel (7 in.)   7 1/2 in. per sec.
         phonotape.
                                (Continued on next card)

Roosevelt, Franklin Delano, Pres. U.S., 1882-1945
Voice Lib.
M1033 Voice of America. Twentieth anniversary
program... 1963. (Card 2)

I. Fonda, Henry Jaynes, 1905-   II. Sandburg, Carl,
1878-1967. III. Kaye, Danny, 1913-   IV. Nehru, Jawaharlal,
1889-1964. V. Roosevelt, Franklin Delano, Pres. U.S., 1882-
1945. VI. Malik, Charles Habib, 1906-   VII. Toynbee,
Arnold Joseph, 1889-   VIII. Faulkner, William, 1897-1962.
IX. Truman, Harry S, Pres. U.S., 1884-1972. X. Eisenhower,
Dwight David, Pres. U.S., 1890-1969. XI. Hayes, Helen,
1900-   XII. Hammarskjöld, Dag, 1905-1961. XIII. Churchill,
Winston Leonard Spencer, 1874-1965. XIV. Kennedy, John
Fitzgerald, Pres. U.S., 1917-1963.

ROOSEVELT, FRANKLIN DELANO, PRES. U.S.,
1882-1945
Voice Lib.
376   Johnson, Hugh Samuel, 1882-1942.
bd.3   Liberty of the people: attacks Franklin D.
Roosevelt for destroying American
democratic institutions. Private
recording, December 11, 1939.
1 reel (7 in.)   7 1/2 in. per sec.
phonotape.

1. Roosevelt, Franklin Delano, Pres. U.S.,
1882-1945.

ROOSEVELT, FRANKLIN DELANO, PRES. U.S.,
Voice Lib. 1882-1945
M1034 Barkley, Alben William, 1877-1956.
bd.5   Excerpt of nominating speech for Franklin D.
Roosevelt at 1932 Democratic National
Convention. CBS, 1932.
1 reel (7 in.)   7 1/2 in. per sec.
phonotape.

ROOSEVELT, FRANKLIN DELANO, PRES. U.S.,
1882-1945.
Voice Lib.
595   LaGuardia, Fiorello Henry, 1882-1947.
Eulogy to Franklin D. Roosevelt. WNYC,
April 15, 1945.
1 reel (7 in.)   7 1/2 in. per sec.
phonotape.

1. Roosevelt, Franklin Delano, Pres. U.S.,
1882-1945.

ROOSEVELT, FRANKLIN DELANO, PRES. U.S.,
1882-1945
Voice Lib.
M724   Barkley, Alben William, 1877-1956.
bd.3   Alben Barkley and James Farley at
Democratic convention of 1940, speaking for
nomination of Franklin D. Roosevelt for
third term. 1940.
1 min., 40 sec.   phonotape (1 r.   7 1/2
i.p.s.)

1. Roosevelt, Franklin Delano, Pres. U.S., 1882-1945.
2. Presidents - U.S. - Election - 1940. I. Farley, James
Aloysius, 1888-

ROOSEVELT, FRANKLIN DELANO, PRES. U.S.,
1882-1945
Voice Lib.
M780   Roosevelt, Eleanor (Roosevelt) 1884-1962.
bd.1   Reminiscences: her political influence; FDR hiding from guards
and P.S. at Hyde Park; King's and Queen's visit to Hyde Park;
Churchill at White House; FDR on the third term and 1940 convention, Vice-President Wallace nomination; December 7, 1941; Mrs.
Roosevelt at White House and FDR's reactions about General Eisenhower and his promotion; her travels to military installations in U.S.
and abroad; campaign of 1944; her last visit with FDR. Columbia
Records, Inc., 1962.
1 reel (7 in.)   7 1/2 in. per sec.   phonotape.

1. Roosevelt, Eleanor (Roosevelt) 1884-1962. 2. Roosevelt,
Franklin Delano, Pres. U.S., 1882-1945.

ROOSEVELT, FRANKLIN DELANO, PRES. U.S.,
Voice Lib. 1882-1945
M724   Barkley, Alben William, 1877-1956.
bd.5   Introducing President Roosevelt to
the convention in 1940. 1940.
1 reel (7 in.)   7 1/2 in. per sec.
phonotape.

ROOSEVELT, FRANKLIN DELANO, PRES. U.S.,
Voice Lib. 1882-1945
M714   Trout, Robert, 1908-
bd.5   Recollecting events in preparing the
first "Fireside chat" with Franklin D.
Roosevelt on the banking situation, in
March, 1933. CBS, 1963.
2 min., 30 sec.   phonotape (1 r.
7 1/2 i.p.s.)

1. Roosevelt, Franklin Delano, Pres. U.S.,
1882-1945.

ROOSEVELT, FRANKLIN DELANO, PRES. U.S.,
1882-1945
Voice Lib.
M828   Cobb, Irvin Shrewsbury, 1876-1944.
bd.1   Scathing campaign speech against Franklin
Roosevelt and the third term. Blue Network,
November 1, 1940.
1 reel (7 in.)   7 1/2 in. per sec.
phonotape.

Incomplete.

1. Roosevelt, Franklin Delano, Pres. U.S.,
1882-1945.

ROOSEVELT, FRANKLIN DELANO, PRES. U.S.,
1882-1945
Voice Lib.
M311   Vanocur, Sander, 1928-
bd.5   Assassination: Sander Vanocur of NBC
compares deaths of FDR and JFK. NBC,
November 23, 1963.
1 reel (7 in.)   7 1/2 in. per sec.
phonotape.

1. Roosevelt, Franklin Delano, Pres. U.S.,
1882-1945. 2. Kennedy, John Fitzgerald, Pres.
U.S., 1917-1963 - Assassination.

Voice Lib.
M1250   Roosevelt, Theodore, Pres. U.S., 1858-1919.
bd.4   Campaign speech entitled "The right of
the people to rule," cautioning against
political extremes of the right and left.
VTM, 1912.
1 reel (7 in.)   7 1/2 in. per sec.
phonotape.

I. Title: The right of the people to
rule.

Voice Lib.
M127   Roosevelt, Theodore, Pres. U.S., 1858-1919.
bd.5   Social and industrial justice. Edison,
1912.
1 reel (7 in.)   7 1/2 in. per sec.
phonotape.

Voice Lib.
M127   Roosevelt, Theodore, Pres. U.S., 1858-1919.
bd.1   A covenant with the people, accepting
the "Bull Moose" nomination. Edison, 1912.
1 reel (7 in.)   7 1/2 in. per sec.
phonotape.

Voice Lib.
653   Roosevelt, Theodore, Pres. U.S., 1858-1919.
bd.4   Why the bosses oppose the Progressive
Party; Theodore Roosevelt's opinions on
Messrs. Penrose and Archbold, and the
Standard Oil Corporation. Defines his
policy of the Abyssinian Treatment of
Corporations; also his stand on labor.
Source (?), 1912.
1 reel (7 in.)   7 1/2 in. per sec.
phonotape.

Voice Lib.
M127   Roosevelt, Theodore, Pres. U.S., 1858-
bd.4   1919.
The farmer and the business man. Victor,
1912.
1 reel (7 in.)   7 1/2 in. per sec.
phonotape.

Voice Lib.
M770   Roosevelt, Theodore, Pres. U.S., 1858-1910.
bd.2   Why the bosses oppose the Progressive
party; comparing Republican and Democratic
parties to Progressive party; administering
the "Abyssinian Treatment" to the Standard
Oil Company; defending his policies. VTM,
1912.
1 reel (7 in.)   7 1/2 in. per sec.
phonotape.

Voice Lib.
M759   Roosevelt, Theodore, Pres. U.S., 1858-
bd.6   1919.
The farmer and the businessman; campaign
speech by Roosevelt. VTM, 1912.
1 reel (7 in.)   7 1/2 in. per sec.
phonotape.

Voice Lib.
M127   Roosevelt, Theodore, Pres. U.S., 1858-1919.
bd.6   Why the trusts and bosses oppose the
Progressive Party. Victor, 1912.
1 reel (7 in.)   7 1/2 in. per sec.
phonotape.

1. Progressive Party (Founded 1912)

Voice Lib.
M127   Roosevelt, Theodore, Pres. U.S., 1858-1919.
bd.7   The liberty of the people. Victor, 1912.
1 reel (7 in.)   7 1/2 in. per sec.
phonotape.

Voice Lib.
M127   Roosevelt, Theodore, Pres. U.S., 1858-1919.
bd.2   Greeting to the American boy. Private
recording, 1913.
1 reel (7 in.)   7 1/2 in. per sec.
phonotape.

Voice Lib.
M757   Roosevelt, Theodore, Pres. U.S., 1858-
bd.6   1919.
            A Message to the American Boys; University
        Society's 10 inch disc of old Theodore
        Roosevelt cylinder record, with musical
        accompaniment and introductory remarks by
        G. Robert Vincent. University Society.
        1913 (1937).
            1 reel (7 in.)   7 1/2 in. per sec.
        phonotape.

Voice Lib.
M396   Roosevelt, Theodore, 1887-1944.
bd.1   American Legion speech at Providence,
        Rhode Island; need to maintain liberty,
        minorities in government, reasons for not
        entering World War II, duty of America is
        to itself. Private recording, May 4,
        1939.
            1 reel (7 in.)   7 1/2 i.p.s.   phonotape.

            ROOSEVELT, THEODORE, PRES. U.S.,
                1858-1919.
Voice Lib.
127   Eisenhower, Dwight David, Pres. U.S., 1890-1969.
bd.9   A proclamation; an eulogy of Theodore
        Roosevelt. Recorded on location, June 14,
        1953.
            1 reel (7 in.)   7 1/2 in. per sec.
        phonotape.

            1. Roosevelt, Theodore, Pres. U.S., 1858-
        1919.

            Roosevelt, Theodore, Pres. U.S., 1858-1919.
Voice Lib.
M620   Radio in the 1940's (Part I): a series of
bd.1-   excerpts from important broadcasts of the 1940's; a
bd.16   sample of radio of the period. NVL, April, 1964.
            1 reel (7 in.) 7 1/2 in. per sec. phonotape.
                L Radio programs. L Thomas, Lowell Jackson, 1892-   IL
        Gunther, John, 1901-1970. III. Kaltenborn, Hans von, 1878-1965.
        IV. Delmar, Kenny. V. Those were the good old days (Radio
        program) VL Elman, Dave. VIL Hall, Frederick Lee, 1916-1970.
        VIII. Hobby lobby (Radio program) IX. Roosevelt, Franklin Delano,
        Pres. U.S., 1882-1945. X. Willkie, Wendell Lewis, 1892-1944.
        XL Hoover, Herbert Clark, Pres. U.S., 1874-1964. XII. Johnson,
        Hugh Samuel, 1882-1942. XIII. Cobb, Irvin Shrewsbury, 1876-1944.
        XIV. Roosevelt, Theodore, 1858-1919. XV. Nye, Gerald Prentice,
        1892-1971. XVL Lindbergh, Charles Augustus, 1902-   XVII.
        Toscanini, Arturo, 1867-195?

            ROOSEVELT, THEODORE, PRES. U.S.,
                1858-1919
Voice Lib.
127   Hoover, Herbert Clark, Pres. U.S., 1874-1964.
bd.8   Dedication ceremonies at Sagamore Hill,
        an eulogy of Theodore Roosevelt.
        Recorded on location, June 14, 1953.
            1 reel (7 in.)   7 1/2 in. per sec.
        phonotape.

            1. Roosevelt, Theodore, Pres. U.S., 1858-
        1919.

Voice Lib.
382   Roper, Daniel Calhoun, 1867-1943.
bd.3   Speaking about current times in 1938.
        CBS, 1938.
            1 reel (7 in.)   7 1/2 in. per sec.
        phonotape.

            ROOSEVELT, THEODORE, PRES., U.S., 1858-1919
C1
H77   Whorf, Michael, 1933-
            The apostle of the strenuous life, Theodore
        Roosevelt.
            1 tape cassette.   (The visual sounds of
        Mike Whorf. History and heritage, H77)
            Originally presented on his radio program, Kaleidoscope.
        WJR, Detroit.
            Duration: 38 min., 45 sec.
            America's favorite hero is the underdog, the frail, ninety-
        seven pound weakling who rises to accept no threat from any
        adversary. One such man was Theodore Roosevelt, a weak and
        frail youth who builds his body and character, and one day reaches
        the highest office in the land.
            L Roosevelt, Theodore, Pres., U.S., 1858-1919. L Title.

Voice Lib.
M1434   Rosenberg, Barnett
            MSU professor of biophysics, Dr. Barnett
        Rosenberg, in lecture pertaining to new
        anti-tumor agent. MSU Information Services,
        April 24, 1969.
            1 reel (7 in.)   7 1/2 i.p.s.   phonotape.

            1. Antineoplastic agents.

            ROOSEVELT, THEODORE, PRES. U.S., 1858-
Voice Lib. 1919.
653   Wood, Leonard, 1860-1927.
bd.5   Tribute to Theodore Roosevelt. Analysis
        of Teddy Roosevelt's character. Nation's
        Forum, 1920.
            1 reel (7 in.)   7 1/2 in. per sec.
        phonotape.

            1. Roosevelt, Theodore, Pres. U.S., 1858-
        1919.

            Rosenman, Samuel Irving, 1896-
Voice Lib.
M273-   Biography in sound (radio program)
274   Franklin Delano Roosevelt: the friends and
bd.1   former associates of Franklin Roosevelt on
        the tenth anniversary of the President's death.
        NBC Radio, April, 1955.
            2 reels (7 in.)   7 1/2 in. per sec.
        phonotape.
            L Roosevelt, Franklin Delano, Pres. U.S., 1882-1945. L
        McIntire, Ross T   1899-   IL Mellett, Lowell, 1884-1960.
        III. Tully, Grace   IV. Henderson, Leon, 1895-
        V. Roosevelt, Eleanor (Roosevelt) 1884-1962. VI. DeGraaf, Albert
        VII. Lehman, Herbert Henry, 1878-1963. VIII. Rosenman, Samuel
        Irving, 1896-   IX. Arvey, Jacob   X. Moley, Raymond,
        1886-   XL Farley, James Aloysius, 1888-   XII. Roosevelt,
            (Continued on next card)

Rostand, Edmond, 1868-1918.
Cyrano de Bergerac
Voice Lib.
M795 Coquelin, Constant, 1841-1909.
bd.4   Excerpt from Rostand play "Cyrano de
Bergerac: Ballade du duel." Paris, 1902.
1 reel (7 in.) 7 1/2 in. per sec.
phonotape.

I. Rostand, Edmond, 1868-1918./Cyrano de
Bergerac.

Voice Lib.
M1394- The Royal Family (motion picture)
1395   Motion picture of the life of Britain's
Royal Family at home and in various countries,
including all members of the immediate family
and the palace household. Moderated by
Vincent Price. BBC, Sept. 21, 1969.
2 reels (7 in.) 7 1/2 in. per sec.
phonotape.
1. Gt. Brit. - Kings and rulers.
I. Price, Vincent, 1911-

Rostand, Edmond, 1868-1918.
Cyrano de Bergerac
Voice Lib.
M795 Coquelin, Constant, 1841-1909.
bd.5   Excerpt from Rostand play "Cyrano de
Bergerac: Ballade du duel". Paris
Exposition, 1899-1900.
1 reel (7 in.) 7 1/2 in. per sec.
phonotape.

I. Rostand, Edmond, 1868-1918./Cyrano de
Bergerac.

C1   RUBENS, SIR PETER PAUL, 1577-1640
A27   Whorf, Michael, 1933-
The Homer of painters - Peter Rubens.
1 tape cassette. (The visual sounds of
Mike Whorf. Art, music and letters, A27)
Originally presented on his radio program, Kaleidoscope,
WJR, Detroit.
Duration: 40 min.
Peter Paul Rubens was diplomat, courtier, and raconteur, but
most of all a brilliant artist. His brilliant technique led to
influencing others of his day and those that were to follow; his
works today are beyond price.

1. Rubens, Sir Peter Paul, 1577-1640. 1. Title.

Rostand, Edmond, 1868-1918.
La Samaritaine
Voice Lib.
M795 Bernhardt, Sarah, 1844-1923.
bd.1   Excerpt from Rostand play "La Samaritaine".
G&T, 1903.
1 reel (7 in.) 7 1/2 in. per sec.
phonotape.

I. Rostand, Edmond, 1868-1918./La Samaritaine.

Voice Lib.
M1725   Rubenstein, Richard L
The American city; address at Michigan
State University. WKAR, January, 23, 1969.
50 min. phonotape (1 r. 7 1/2 i.p.s.)

1. Cities and towns - U. S.

Rostow, Walt Whitman, 1916-
Voice Lib.
M1478 The Pentagon Papers; discussion of content,
meaning. Bernard Kalb, CBS; Senator J.W.
Fulbright; Senator John Tower; Arthur
Schlesinger; Walt Rostow; Max Frankel,
New York Times; Crosby Noyes, Washington
Evening Star. CBS-TV, July 13, 1971.
1 reel (7 in.) 7 1/2 in. per sec.
phonotape.
1. Kalb, Bernard   II. Fulbright, James William, 1905-
III. Tower, John Goodwin, 1925-   IV. Schlesinger, Arthur
Meier, 1888-   V. Rostow, Walt Whitman, 1916-   VI.
Frankel, Max   VII. Noyes, Crosby

Voice Lib.
M1432- Rubinstein, Artur, 1889-
1433,   Biographical comments and piano performances
bd.1   by Rubinstein and his wife. CBS-TV, 1970.
2 reels (7 in.) 7 1/2 i.p.s. phonotape.

1. Rubinstein, Artur, 1889-

Roush, Edd, 1893-
Voice Lib.
M1248 Baseball fifty years ago; interviews with four
famous old time baseball players, on NBC
"Today" show, by host Hugh Downs, supported by
sportcaster Joe Garagiola and Dr. Lawrence
Ritter, author of new book. NBC-TV, June 9,
1967.
1 reel (7 in.) 7 1/2 in. per sec. phonotape.
1. Baseball. 1. Downs, Hugh Malcolm, 1921-   II. Garagiola,
Joe. III. Ritter, Lawrence S./The glory of their times. IV. Roush,
Edd, 1893-   V. Marquart, Rube, 1890-   VI. O'Doul, Lefty,
1897-   VII. Meyers, John, 1880-

Voice Lib.
M761 Ruby, Harry
bd.2   Excerpt from "Whatever Happened to Tin Pan
Alley?" (Program 3); comments on how he
plugged his songs and others. Westinghouse
Broadcasting Corporation, 1964.
1 reel (7 in.) 7 1/2 in. per sec.
phonotape. (The Music Goes Round and Round)

I. Title: Whatever happened to Tin Pan Alley?
II. Series.

Voice Lib.
M761   Ruby, Harry
bd.10   Excerpt from "Tunesmiths Past and Present"
        (Program 4); tells about the big composers
        in the days before the golden era of the
        '20's and '30's. Westinghouse Broadcasting
        Corporation, 1964.
          1 reel (7 in.)   7 1/2 in. per sec.
        phonotape. (The Music Goes Round and Round)

          I. Title: Tunesmiths past and present.
        II. Series.

RUNYON, DAMON, 1880-1946

C1
A8   Whorf, Michael, 1933-
        The land of Runyon.
          1 tape cassette. (The visual sounds of
        Mike Whorf. Art, music, and letters, A8)

        Originally presented on his radio program, Kaleidoscope,
        WJR, Detroit.
        Duration: 28 min., 35 sec.
        Damon Runyon travelled with mugs and molls, gamblers and
        their gals, and gave the world humor and human interest.

          I. Runyon, Damon, 1880-1946. I. Title.

Voice Lib.
562   Ruby, Jack, 1912-1967.
          Jack Ruby trial jury delivers verdict
        before Judge Joseph B. Brown (video tape
        replay of original verdict). CBS, March 14,
        1964.
          1 reel (7 in.)   7 1/2 in. per sec.
        phonotape.

Voice Lib.
609   Ruppert, Jacob
bd.10   Interview about New York Yankee baseball
        team; review of past Yankee victories on
        radio program "Famous Firsts". WOR,
        October 10, 1938.
          1 reel (7 in.)   7 1/2 in. per sec.
        phonotape.

          1. New York. Baseball club (American league)

Voice Lib.
M1503   Rudd, Hughes
          Higher education: who needs it? Hughes Rudd
        in a one-hour documentary on employment
        problems of college graduates. CBS-TV,
        May 26, 1972.
          1 reel (7 in.)   7 1/2 in. per sec.
        phonotape.

          1. Education, Higher. 2. Labor supply.
        I. Rudd, Hughes.

Voice Lib.
M1040   Rusk, Dean, 1909-
bd.2   Excerpt of press conference at State
        Department, Washington, D.C., with Secretary
        Rusk clarifying the U.S. position regarding
        peace in Vietnam. CBS, February 9, 1967.
          1 reel (7 in.)   7 1/2 in. per sec.
        phonotape.

Voice Lib.
M275-   Rude, Robert Barnes
276   Biography in sound (radio program)
bd.1   Alexander Woollcott. N.B.C., date?
          2 reels (7 in.)   7 1/2 in. per sec.
        phonotape.

          I. Woollcott, Alexander, 1887-1943. I. Woollcott, Alexander,
        1887-1943. II. Banghardt, Kenneth   III. Hecht, Ben, 1893-
        1964. IV. Roosevelt, Eleanor (Roosevelt) 1884-1962. V. Walker,
        Danton   VI. Brackett, Charles, 1892-1969. VII. Grant,
        Jane   VIII. Rude, Robert Barnes   IX. West,
        Rebecca, pseud. X. Henessy, Joseph   XI. Letterer,
        Charles   XII. Welles, Orson, 1915-

Voice Lib.
M1372-   Rusk, Dean, 1909-
1373   Interview with Dean Rusk pertaining to
bd.1   events which occurred during his term in
        office, including Vietnam controversy.
        Presented on NBC "Today" show. NBC-TV,
        March 24-28, 1969.
          2 reels (7 in.)   7 1/2 in. per sec.
        phonotape.

Voice Lib.
M322   Runnell, Ann
          Biography in sound (radio program)
          W.C. Fields, the magnificent rogue.
        NBC, 1955.
          1 reel (7 in.)   7 1/2 in. per sec. phonotape.
          I. Fields, W.C., 1879-1946. I. Fields, W.C., 1879-1946.
        II. Allen, Fred, 1894-1956. III. LaBaron, William   IV.
        Taylor, Robert Lewis, 1912-   V. McCarey, Thomas Leo, 1898-
        1969. VI. Harkins, James   - VII. Chevalier, Maurice,
        1889-1972. VIII. Kuromoto, Mrs. George   IX. Flynn,
        Errol Leslie, 1909-1959. X. Wynn, Ed, 1886-1966. XI. Dowling,
        Ray Dooley   XII. Sennett, Mack   XIII. Overacher,
        Ronald Leroy   XIV. Bergen, Edgar, 1903-   XV. Taurog,
        Norman, 1899-   XVI. Runnell, Ann   XVII. Cowen,
        Lester

Voice Lib.
M1475-   Rusk, Dean, 1909-
1476,   Dean Rusk, former Secretary of State,
bd.1   discusses the Pentagon Papers with Edwin
        Newman and Barbara Walters. NBC, July 2,
        1971.
          2 reels (7 in.)   7 1/2 in.p.s.   phonotape.

          1. Pentagon papers. 2. Vietnamese
        Conflict, 1961-   - U.S. I. Newman,
        Edwin Harold, 1919-   II. Walters,
        Barbara, 1931-

Voice Lib.
M1546-   Rusk, Dean, 1909-
1547,   Interview on William F. Buckley's Firing
bd.1   Line show.   WKAR-FM, February 5, 1974.
         40 min.   phonotape (2 r.   7 1/2 i.p.s.)

         1. Vietnamese Conflict, 1961-   - U.S.
         I. Buckley, William Frank, 1925-

Voice Lib.
M948   Russell, Lillian, 1861-1922.
bd.3   Re-recording from Edison cylinder record
        of Miss Russell singing "Come Down, Ma Evenin'
        Star".   Jack Caidin, March 12, 1912.
        1 reel (7 in.)   7 1/2 in. per sec.
        phonotape.

          I. Title: Come down, ma evenin' star.

              Rusk, Dean, 1909-
Voice Lib.
M1253   Johnson, Lyndon Baines, Pres. U.S., 1908-1973.
bd.1   Addressing Foreign Policy Conference for
        Education at the State Department Auditorium
        in Washington, prior to the emergency session
        of U.N. General Assembly.   Introductory
        remarks by Secretary Dean Rusk.   NBC-TV,
        June 19, 1967.
        1 reel (7 in.)   7 1/2 in. per sec.
        phonotape.

          I. Rusk, Dean, 1909-

        RUSSIA
C1
S65   Whorf, Michael, 1933-
        Mother Russia - from 1900 to the present.
        1 tape cassette.   (The visual sounds of
        Mike Whorf. Social, S65)
          Originally presented on his radio program, Kaleidoscope,
        WJR, Detroit.
          Duration: 39 min., 25 sec.
          From the age of Czar Nicholas to the present, here is the bigger
        than life story of the great "Mother Russia".

          L Russia.   L Title.

Voice Lib.
M729-   Russell, Bertrand Russell, 3d earl, 1872-1970.
730,   "Human nature in politics." A witty
bd.1   address, incorporating some of his ideas,
        by Lord Russell.   BBC, 1953.
        42 min., 45 sec.   phonotape (2 r.
        7 1/2 i.p.s.)

          I. Title.

S

        RUSSIA - FOREIGN RELATIONS - GERMANY
Voice Lib.
M1420   Hofer, Walther, 1920-
bd.19   Speaking about the development of
        negotiations between Germany and the Soviet
        Union during the months of April to August,
        1939.   Peteler, 1964.
        1 reel (7 in.)   7 1/2 i.p.s.   phonotape.

          1. Germany - Foreign relations - Russia.
          2. Russia - Foreign relations - Germany.

Voice Lib.
M730   Russell, Bertrand Russell,   3rd earl,
bd.2   1872-1970.
          Forum address. Conference pertaining to
        the statement about the significance of
        nuclear warfare issued by various scientists.
        BBC, 1955.
        1 reel (7 in.)   7 1/2 in. per sec.
        phonotape.

          1. Atomic weapons

        RUSSIA - FOREIGN RELATIONS - GERMANY
Voice Lib.
M1073   Ribbentrop, Joachim von, 1893-1946.
bd.5   Note to Russian government of Nazi position
        regarding conflict with USSR; Russian demands
        for territory in North and Southeastern
        Europe rejected by Hitler.   Peteler,
        June 22, 1941.
        1 reel (7 in.)   7 1/2 i.p.s.   phonotape.

          1. Germany - Foreign relations - Russia.
          2. Russia - Foreign relations - Germany.

Voice Lib.
M911   Russell, Bertrand Russell, 3rd earl, 1872-
bd.2   1970.
912   Interview with Russell at age 91 and with
        various friends and associates who have
        known him throughout his lifetime.   BBC,
        1965.
        2 reels (7 in.)   7 1/2 in. per sec.
        phonotape.

          1. Russell, Bertrand Russell, 3rd earl,
        1872-1970.

        RUSSIA - FOREIGN RELATIONS - GT. BRIT.
Voice Lib.
M1470   Strang, Sir William, 1894-
bd.16   Speaking about the negotiations between
        the British and the Soviets in the year
        1939.   Peteler, 1964.
        1 reel (7 in.)   7 1/2 i.p.s.   phonotape.

          1. Great Britain - Foreign relations -
        Russia. 2. Russia - Foreign relations -
        Great Britain.

RUSSIA - FOREIGN RELATIONS - U.S.

Voice Lib.
M133   Kennedy, John Fitzgerald, Pres. U.S., 1917-
bd.2   1963.
           Cuba blockade, an address to the nation.
        NBC, October 22, 1962.
           1 reel (7 in.)   7 1/2 i.p.s.   phonotape.

           1. Military bases, Russian - Cuba.
           2. U.S. - Foreign relations - Russia.
           3. Russia - Foreign relations - U.S.

           O

RUSSIA - FOREIGN RELATIONS - U.S.

Voice Lib.
M1746   Kissinger, Henry Alfred, 1923-
           Excerpts of press conference, explaining
        that the arms limitations talks with the
        Russians will serve the best interests of
        both nations; denying secret agreements.
        WKAR, June 24, 1974.
           50 min.   phonotape (1 r.   7 1/2 i.p.s.)

           1. U.S. - Foreign relations - Russia.
           2. Russia - Foreign relations - U.S.

           O

RUSSIA - FOREIGN RELATIONS - U.S.

Voice Lib.
M899   Marshall, George Catlett, 1880-1959.
           Report on his mission to Moscow, delivered
        from the State Department, Washington, D.C.
        WJR, April 28, 1947.
           1 reel (7 in.)   7 1/2 i.p.s.   phonotape.

           1. U.S. - Foreign relations - Russia.
           2. Russia - Foreign relations - U.S.

           O

RUSSIA - HISTORY - REVOLUTION, 1917-1921

Voice Lib.
M1059   Kérenskiĭ, Aleksandr Fedorovich, 1881-
bd.1   Discussion with Hugh Downs and former
        Russian Prime Minister Kerenskiĭ about the
        1917 Russian Revolution on "Today" TV show.
        NBC-TV, February 28, 1967.
           1 reel (7 in.)   7 1/2 in. per sec.
        phonotape.

           I. Downs, Hugh Malcolm, 1921-

           O

Russia and her swinging satellites

Voice Lib.
M767   Garnier, Jacques
bd.3   Excerpt from "Russia and her swinging satellites" (Program 12);
        comments on how effective the ban on rock-and-roll in Russia
        actually is, including Soviet pop tune "Lilacs in bloom" and
        Russian version of "St. Louis blues" and two numbers recorded
        clandestinely in Leningrad: "Let's dance" and "I want to be happy
        cha-cha-cha".   Westinghouse Broadcasting Corporation, 1964.
           9 min., 42 sec.   phonotape (1 r.   7 1/2 i.p.s.)
        (The music goes round and round)

           I. Music, Popular (Songs, etc.) - Russia.   I. Title: Russia
        and her swinging satellites.   II. Series.

           O

Voice Lib.
353   Russia and the bomb, discussed by various
bd.19   personalities.   NBC, September 25, 1949.
           1 reel (7 in.)   7 1/2 in. per sec.
        phonotape.

           Participants: Harrison Brown, Harold Urey,
        Samuel Allison, Thornton Hugness, Brien McMahon,
        Paul Douglas, John Foster Dulles, Leslie Groves,
        Winston Churchill, Dean Acheson, James Fleming.
           I. Atomic bomb.
           I. Brown, Harrison Scott, 1917-   II.
        Urey, Harold Clayton, 1893-   III. Allison,

           O   (Continued on next card)

Voice Lib.
353   Russia and the bomb...   1949.   (Card 2)
bd.19

           Samuel King, 1900-   IV. Hugness, Thornton.
        V. McMahon, James O'Brien, 1903-1952.   VI.
        Douglas, Paul Howard, 1892-   VII. Dulles,
        John Foster, 1888-1959.   VIII. Groves, Leslie
        R   1896-1970.   IX. Churchill, Winston
        Leonard Spencer, 1874-1965.   X. Acheson, Dean
        Gooderham, 1893-1971.   XI. Fleming, James,
        1915-

           O

Voice Lib.
M1073   Russian marching song; song of the Russian
bd.11   army guardsmen (vocal).   Peteler, 1941.
           1 reel (7 in.)   7 1/2 in. per sec.
        phonotape.

           1. War songs, Russian

           O

Voice Lib.
M1073   Russian marching song; song of the USSR
bd.18   artillery (vocal   and instrumental).
           Peteler, 1941.
           1 reel (7 in.)   7 1/2 in. per sec.
        phonotape.

           1. War-songs, Russian.

           O

Voice Lib.
M1304   Rust, Bernhard, 1883-
bd.8   Remarks to students preparing to enter
        German armed forces.   Peteler, 1942.
           1 reel (7 in.)   7 1/2 in. per sec.
        phonotape.

           O

Voice Lib.
M1642 Rust, Edward Barry, 1918-
       National Press Club luncheon address.
      WKAR-AM, March 14, 1974.
        50 min. phonotape (1 r. 7 1/2 i.p.s.)

      1. Chamber of Commerce of the United
  States of America.

Ruth, George Herman, 1895-1948
Voice Lib.
573   I can hear it now (radio program)
bd.2-   1945-1949. CBS, 1950?
574   2 reels (7 in.) 7 1/2 in. per sec.
bd.1 phonotape.
    L. Murrow, Edward Roscoe, 1908-1965. II. Nehru, Jawaharlal,
1889-1964. III. Philip, duke of Edinburgh, 1921- IV. Elizabeth II,
Queen of Great Britain, 1926- V. Ferguson, Homer, 1889- VI.
Hughes, Howard Robard, 1905- VII. Marshall, George Catlett,
1880- VIII. Ruth, George Herman, 1895-1948. IX. Lilienthal,
David Eli, 1899- X. Trout, Robert, 1908- XI. Gage, Arthur.
XII. Jackson, Robert Houghwout, 1892-1954. XIII. Gromyko, Ana-
toiii Andreevich, 1908- XIV. Baruch, Bernard Mannes, 1870-
1965. XV. Churchill, Wir---g Leonard Spencer, 1874-1965. XVI.
Winchell, Walter, 1897- XVII. Davis, Elmer Holmes, 1890-
(Continued on next card)

Voice Lib.
M757 Ruth, George Herman, 1894-1948.
bd.7   Babe Ruth's home run story; monologue.
    Humorous recitation. Actuelle (Pathes
    Frères), 1923.
      1 reel (7 in.) 7 1/2 in. per sec.
    phonotape.

      1. Baseball

      RUTH, GEORGE HERMAN, 1894-1948
C1
M16   Whorf, Michael, 1933-
      Now batting for the New York Yankees.
      1 tape cassette. (The visual sounds of
    Mike Whorf. Miscellaneous, M16)

      Originally presented on his radio program, Kaleidoscope,
WJR, Detroit.
      Duration: 40 min., 30 sec.
      This is the story of Babe Ruth, the orphan boy of Baltimore who
would one day become the great New York Yankee slugger.

      L. Ruth, George Herman, 1894-1948. L. Title.

Voice Lib.
M948 Ruth, George Herman, 1894-1948.
bd.7   In a comedy skit with Lou Gehrig. 1938.
      1 reel (7 in.) 7 1/2 in. per sec.
    phonotape.

      1. Baseball.
      I. Gehrig, Lou, 1903-1941.

C1   The sad, strange saga of the Great Eastern
M36   Whorf, Michael, 1933-
      The sad, strange saga of the Great Eastern.
      1 tape cassette. (The visual sounds of
    Mike Whorf. Miscellaneous, M36)

      Originally presented on his radio program, Kaleidoscope,
WJR, Detroit.
      Duration: 38 min., 15 sec.
      Many great ships have sailed the seven seas. Why couldn't
this splendid vessel surmount superstition, obstacle, and nature?
This is the plot of the sad strange saga of the Great Eastern.

      L. Great Eastern (Ship) L. Title.

Voice Lib.
M948 Ruth, George Herman, 1894-1948.
bd.6   Pep talk to American boys about baseball.
    1948.
      1 reel (7 in.) 7 1/2 in. per sec.
    phonotape.

      1. Baseball.

Voice Lib.
M1745 al Sadat, Anwar.
bd.4   Sadat: an exclusive interview; an extensive
    interview with Walter Cronkite on the changes
    in U. S. policy regarding Egypt. CBS, June 21,
    1974.
      30 min. phonotape (1 r. 7 1/2 i.p.s.)

      1. U. S. - For. rel. - Egypt. 2. Egypt -
  For. rel. - U. S. 3. Egypt - Pol. & govt. -
  1952-   I. Cronkite, Walter Leland,
  1916-

Ruth, George Herman, 1894-1948
Voice Lib.
M617 Radio in the 1920's: a series of excerpts
bd.1-   from important broadcasts of the 1920's,
bd.25   with brief prologue and epilogue; a sample
    of radio of the period. NVL, April, 1964.
      1 reel (7 in.) 7 1/2 in. per sec.
    phonotape.
      L. Radio programs. L. Marconi, Guglielmo, marchese, 1874-
1937. II. Kendall, H G III. Coolidge, Calvin, Pres. U.S.,
1872-1933. IV. Wilson, Woodrow, Pres. U. S., 1856-1924. V.
Roosevelt, Franklin Delano, Pres. U. S., 1882-1945. VI. Lodge,
Henry Cabot, 1850-1924. VII. LaGuardia, Fiorello Henry, 1882-1947.
VIII. The Happiness Boys (Radio program) IX. Gallagher and Sheen.
X. Barney Google. XI. Vallee, Rudy, 1901- XII. The two
(Continued on next card)

Voice Lib.
M1498 Safer, Morley
bd.2   Charles Chaplin returns to the U.S.A.
    NBC-TV, April 2, 1972.
      1 reel (7 in.) 7 1/2 i.p.s. phonotape.

      Includes excerpts from "A king in New
  York" and reflections by Sydney and Geraldine
  Chaplin.

      1. Chaplin, Charles, 1889-   I. Chaplin,
  Sydney Earl. II. Chaplin, Geraldine

The sage of Concord - Ralph Waldo Emerson

C1
A29   Whorf, Michael, 1933-
       The sage of Concord - Ralph Waldo Emerson.
       1 tape cassette.   (The visual sounds of
       Mike Whorf. Art, music and letters, A29)
       Originally presented on his radio program, Kaleidoscope,
       WJR, Detroit.
       Duration: 38 min., 45 sec.
       Ralph Waldo Emerson was a witness of his times, able to
       exert influence on the manners and mores of the public. His
       poetry is laced with wisdom and depth, and its meanings are
       as vital today and when first read.

       L Emerson, Ralph Waldo, 1803-1882.   L Title.

The saint from Assisi

C1
R6   Whorf, Michael, 1933-
       The saint from Assisi.
       1 tape cassette.   (The visual sounds of
       Mike Whorf. Religion, R6)

       Originally presented on his radio program, Kaleidoscope,
       WJR, Detroit.
       Duration: 39 min., 30 sec.
       This is the tale of Francis of Assisi, who would form the Franciscan
       order, would be friend to man and animal, and would teach mankind
       the meaning of true humility.

       L Francis of Assisi, Saint, 1182-1226.   L Title.

St. Louis blues

Voice Lib.
M840   Miller, Glenn, 1909?-1944.
bd.8   Greets American Armed Forces followed
        by "St. Louis blues" in march tempo,
        recorded especially for V-Discs.
        V-Discs, 1944.
           9 min., 6 sec.   phonotape (1 r.
        7 1/2 i.p.s.)

           I. Title: St. Louis blues.

Voice Lib.
611   Salay, Julius
bd.5,6   Dramatic description of World War I scenes.
        "Life in the trench after the capture of
        Warsaw", "Frontier at the German border".
        Victor Talking Machine Co., 1916.
           1 reel (7 in.)   7 1/2 in. per sec.
        phonotape.

           In German.

           1. European War, 1914-1918 - Personal
        narratives, German.

Voice Lib.
231   Salk, Jonas Edward, 1914-
bd.2   Discussion of Salk vaccine, introduced
        by Basil O'Connor. CBS, May 3, 1954.
           1 reel (7 in.)   7 1/2 in. per sec.
        phonotape.

           1. Poliomyelitis vaccine.   I. O'Connor,
        Basil, 1892-1972.

Voice Lib.
266   Salk, Jonas Edward, 1914-
bd.2   Dr. Jonas Salk and others discuss the
        vaccine, its significance, effectiveness,
        etc. CBS, April 12, 1955.
           1 reel (7 in.)   7 1/2 in. per sec.
        phonotape.

Salk, Jonas Edward, 1914-

Voice Lib.
M717   Burdett, Winston M   1913-
bd.1   Interview with Dr. Jonas E. Salk regarding
        polio vaccine, at University of Michigan.
        CBS, April 13, 1955.
           1 reel (7 in.)   7 1/2 in. per sec.
        phonotape.

           I. Salk, Jonas Edward, 1914-

SALVATION ARMY

Voice Lib.
M756   Booth, William, 1829-1912.
bd.6   "Don't forget"; an address by the late
        General Booth, founder of the Salvation
        Army. VTM, 1910.
           1 reel (7 in.)   7 1/2 in. per sec.
        phonotape.

SALVATION ARMY

Voice Lib.
M756   Booth, William, 1829-1912.
bd.9   "Please, sir, save me !" An address by
        the late General William Booth, founder of
        the Salvation Army.   VTM, 1910.
           1 reel (7 in.)   7 1/2 in. per sec.
        phonotape.

SALVATION ARMY

Voice Lib.
M756   Booth, William, 1829-1912.
bd.7   "Rope wanted"; an address by the late
        General Booth, founder of the Salvation
        Army. VTM, 1910.
           1 reel (7 in.)   7 1/2 in. per sec.
        phonotape.

'SALVATION ARMY

Voice Lib.
M756   Booth, William, 1829-1912.
bd.8   "Through Jordan"; an address in verse
        by the late General Booth, founder of the
        Salvation Army.   VTM, 1910.
            1 reel (7 in.)   7 1/2 in. per sec.
        phonotape.

            1. Salvation Army.   I. Title.

SALVATION ARMY

C1
S15   Whorf, Michael, 1933-
           Marching as to war.
           1 tape cassette.   (The visual sounds of
       Mike Whorf.   Social, S15)
           Originally presented on his radio program, Kaleidoscope,
       WJR, Detroit.
           Duration: 42 min.
           Outlined against the background of the 19th century in
       England, is the story of William Booth and the Salvation Army.

           1. Booth, William, 1829-1912. 2. Salvation Army.
       I. Title.

Sam Houston

C1
H37   Whorf, Michael, 1933-
           Sam Houston.
           1 tape cassette.   (The visual sounds of
       Mike Whorf.   History and heritage, H37)
           Originally presented on his radio program, Kaleidoscope,
       WJR, Detroit.
           Duration: 40 min.
           In the days of the young Texas territory many men would ennoble
       themselves for the cause of independence. One man much
       criticized, and yet admired was Sam Houston.

           1. Houston, Samuel, 17 -1863. I. Title.

Voice Lib.
M1290- Same mud, same blood; a one-hour actual
1291   report on the integration of white and
bd.1   colored troops of the 101st Airborne
        Division.   NBC, December 1, 1967.
            2 reels (7 in.)   7 1/2 in. per sec.
        phonotape.

            1. U.S. Army - Negro troops.   I. McGee,
        Frank, 1921-

San Francisco State College

Voice Lib.
M1355   Hayakawa, Samuel Ichiyé, 1906-
bd.2   Interview on CBS "Face the Nation" TV
        program on Acting President Hayakawa's
        opinions on current conditions and future
        prospects for San Francisco State College.
        CBS, February 2, 1969.
            1 reel (7 in.)   7 1/2 in. per sec.
        phonotape.

            1. San Francisco State College.

Voice Lib.
M769   Sandburg, Carl, 1878-1967.
bd.1   Readings from his prose, "The People, Yes".
            1 reel (7 in.)   7 1/2 in. per sec.
        phonotape.

            CONTENTS.-Colorado Graveyard; Father and Son;
        Infantryman; Man and Sphinx; Salzman; Every Man;
        An Even Whack; Struggle; The Arch; The Two
        Maggots - A Story; proverbs from The People,
        Yes"; opening sequence from "The People, Yes"
        (The Tower of Babel and other readings); Many
        Occupations; Grand Canyon of Humanity; Gags.

Voice Lib.
113   Sandburg, Carl, 1878-1967.
bd.1   The people, yes. The Lincoln sequence as
        read by Carl Sandburg.   Private recording,
        (n.d.)
            1 reel (7 in.)   7 1/2 in. per sec.
        phonotape.

Voice Lib.
M739   Sandburg, Carl, 1878-1967.
bd.3   Reading his poetry "On freedom". Excerpt
        from "The people, yes"; Ed Murrow introduces
        second part.
            3 min., 34 sec.   phonotape (1 r.
        7 1/2 i.p.s.)

Voice Lib.
112   Sandburg, Carl, 1878-1967.
bd.4   Lincoln now, as read by Carl Sandburg.
        Private recording, 1940.
            1 reel (7 in.)   7 1/2 in. per sec.
        phonotape.

Voice Lib.
M768   Sandburg, Carl, 1878-1967.
bd.1-5   Readings.   Muzak, 1942.
            1 reel (7 in.)   7 1/2 in. per sec.
        phonotape.

            CONTENTS.-bd.1. The Man With the Broken
        Fingers, a reading.-bd.2. I.W.W. Lumber
        Workers song.-bd.3. Gallows Song.-bd.4. Free
        America, 1775, a patriotic song of 1775.-
        bd.5. Foggy Dew, old English folk song.

Voice Lib.
M768   Sandburg, Carl, 1868-1967.
bd.6   Series of readings from "Smoke and Steel"
        and "Good Morning, America", and free verse.
        Muzak, 1942.
            1 reel (7 in.)   7 1/2 in. per sec.
        phonotape.

            CONTENTS.-Cahoots; Ossawatomie; Night Stuff;
        snatch of Sliphorn Jazz; Maybe; Phizzog;
        fragment from The Windy City; Upstream;
        Primer Lesson; Is God; Too; Lonely; Sea
                                (Continued on next card)

Voice Lib.
M769   Sandburg, Carl, 1878-1967.
bd.2   Waillie, a song.   Muzak, 1942.
            1 reel (7 in.)   7 1/2 in. per sec.
        phonotape.

Voice Lib.
M768   Sandburg, Carl, 1868-1967. Series of
bd.6   readings from "Smoke and Steel"...
        1942.   (Card 2)

        CONTENTS. cont'd.-Chest; end lines from
        Good Morning, America; Bells and Heavens;
        Precious Moments; Baby Song of the Four
        Winds; They All Want to Play Hamlet.

Voice Lib.
M1223   Sandburg, Carl, 1878-1967.
bd.2-   Reading assorted verse and prose, including
1224   sections of "The People, Yes".   Bergman.
bd.1   1949.
            2 reels (7 in.)   7 1/2 in. per sec.
        phonotape.

Voice Lib.
327   Sandburg, Carl, 1878-1967.
bd.2   Reading his work in prose, "Snider's
        Vinegar, Inc.".   From private collection,
        1942.
            1 reel (7 in.)   7 1/2 in. per sec.
        phonotape.

            I. Title: Snider's Vinegar, Inc.

Voice Lib.
327   Sandburg, Carl, 1878-1967.
bd.1   Meet the Press interview. On Chicago,
        Lincoln, personalities, etc..   Voice of
        America, 1957.
            1 reel (7 in.)   7 1/2 in. per sec.
        phonotape.

Voice Lib.
349   Sandburg, Carl, 1868-1967.
bd.2   Prologue from the book "The People - Yes".
        Private collection (Muzak pressing), 1942.
            1 reel (7 in.)   7 1/2 in. per sec.
        phonotape.

Voice Lib.
663   Sandburg, Carl, 1878-1967.
bd.1   Columbia Radio Workshop Program: talks,
        songs and poems by Sandburg celebrating
        his 79th birthday.   CBS, January 4, 1957.
            1 reel (7 in.)   7 1/2 in. per sec.
        phonotape.

Voice Lib.
349   Sandburg, Carl, 1868-1967.
bd.3   "Skyline America" from the book "The
        People - Yes".   Private collection (Muzak
        pressing), 1942.
            1 reel (7 in.)   7 1/2 in. per sec.
        phonotape.

Voice Lib.
652   Sandburg, Carl, 1878-1967.
bd.22   Address to Congress on 150th anniversary
        of Lincoln's birthday.   CBS, February 12,
        1959.
            1 reel (7 in.)   7 1/2 in. per sec.
        phonotape.

Voice Lib.
M963- Sandburg, Carl, 1878-1967.
984   Parts 1 and 2 of one hour NET-TV program
about the songs, prose, poetry, thoughts
and sayings of Sandburg. Narration by
James Mason. NET, June 26, 1966.
2 reels (7 in.) 7 1/2 in. per sec.
phonotape.

1. Sandburg, Carl, 1878-1967
I. Mason, James Neville, 1909-

Voice Lib.
M814 Santayana, George, 1863-1952.
bd.2- Personal reminiscences about the eminent
815   American philosopher, poet, and novelist by
Horace H. Kallen and Dr. Corliss Lamont, in
conversation with Robert Stover of WBAI,
arranged through the cooperation of the
American Humanist Association. KPFK, May 23,
1964.
2 reels (7 in.) 7 1/2 in. per sec. phonotape.
L. Santayana, George, 1863-1952. L. Kallen, Horace Meyer,
1882- II. Lamont, Corliss, 1902- III. Stover, Robert

Sandburg, Carl, 1878-1967
M1033 Voice of America.
Twentieth anniversary program of Voice of
America broadcasts narrated by Henry Fonda,
and including the voices of Carl Sandburg,
Danny Kaye, Jawaharlal Nehru, Franklin D.
Roosevelt, Charles Malik, Arnold Toynbee,
William Faulkner, Harry S.Truman, Dwight D.
Eisenhower, Helen Hayes, Dag Hammarskjöld,
Winston Churchill, and John F. Kennedy.
Voice of America, 1963.
1 reel (7 in.) 7 1/2 in. per sec.
phonotape.
(Continued on next card)

Voice Lib.
M1488 Sarnoff, David, 1891-1971.
bd.2   Memorial documentary on his death. NBC,
December 12, 1971.
1 reel (7 in.) 7 1/2 in. per sec.
phonotape.

Sandburg, Carl, 1878-1967
M1033 Voice of America. Twentieth anniversary
program... 1963. (Card 2)

L. Fonda, Henry Jaynes, 1905- II. Sandburg, Carl,
1878-1967. III. Kaye, Danny, 1913- IV. Nehru, Jawaharlal,
1889-1964. V. Roosevelt, Franklin Delano, Pres. U.S., 1882-
1945. VI. Malik, Charles Habib, 1906- VII. Toynbee,
Arnold Joseph, 1889- VIII. Faulkner, William, 1897-1962.
IX. Truman, Harry S, Pres. U.S., 1884-1972. X. Eisenhower,
Dwight David, Pres. U.S., 1890-1969. XI. Hayes, Helen,
1900- XII. Hammarskjöld, Dag, 1905-1961. XIII. Churchill,
Winston Leonard Spencer, 1874-1965. XIV. Kennedy, John
Fitzgerald, Pres. U.S., 1917-1963.

Voice Lib.
M640 Savory, William
bd.7   Experiments with magnet and human voice
(Somnivox). GRV, September 22, 1941.
1 reel (7 in.) 7 1/2 i.p.s. phonotape.

1. Phonorecords.

Voice Lib.
M987 Sankey, Ira David, 1840-1908.
bd.1   Musical evangelist Ira Sankey singing
excerpt from hymn "God be with you 'til
we meet again". Moody Institute, 1899.
1 reel (7 in.) 7 1/2 in. per sec.
phonotape.

I. Title: God be with you 'til we meet
again.

Voice Lib.
M1733 Sawhill, John Crittenden, 1936-
Speech at the National Press Club luncheon,
concerning the international energy picture,
with Clyde Lamont. WKAR, June 20, 1974.
50 min. phonotape (1 r. 7 1/2 i.p.s.)

1. Power resources - U.S. 2. Energy
shortage. 3. Local transit - U.S.
I. Lamont, Clyde.

Voice Lib.
M1608 Santarelli, Donald E
New steps to be taken to reduce crime;
address before the Economic Club of Detroit.
WKAR-FM, March 25, 1974.
50 min. phonotape (1 r. 7 1/2 i.p.s.)

1. Law enforcement. 2. Crime and criminals.

SAXBE, WILLIAM B., 1916-
Voice Lib.
M1585 Hays, Wayne L
bd.1   Money - politics. WKAR-AM, February 27,
1974.
15 min. phonotape (1 r. 7 1/2 in. per sec.)

1. Elections. 2. Campaign funds.
3. Saxbe, William B., 1916-

Voice Lib.
M683   Sayegh, Fayez Abdullah, 1922-
        Interviewed by William Buckley on Firing
Line. WKAR-TV, May 21, 1974.
        45 min.   phonotape (1 r.   7 1/2 i.p.s.)

        1. Arab countries - Relations (general)
with Israel. 2. Israel - Relagions (general)
with Arab countries.   I. Buckley, William
Frank, 1925-

Voice.Lib.
M952   Scheidemann, Philipp, 1865-1939.
bd.18   Stressing the necessity for peace during
World War I in the German Reichstag.
F. Peteler, May 15, 1917.
        1 reel (7 in.)   7 1/2 in. per sec.
phonotape.

Voice Lib.
M1741   Sayegh, Fayez Abdullah, 1922-
bd.1   In an emotional debate with Jess Marlowe
and Barbara Walters on the Today Show.
NBC-TV, June 24, 1974.
        15 min.   phonotape (1 r.   7 1/2 i.p.s.)

        1. Refuges, Arab.   I. Marlowe, Jess.
II. Walters, Barbara, 1931-

Voice Lib.
M952   Scheidemann, Philipp, 1865-1939.
bd.8   Political speech. H.E. Scholz, May 15,
1918.
        1 reel (7 in.)   7 1/2 in. per sec.
phonotape.

Voice Lib.
M718   Schachtel, Hyman Judah, 1907-
bd.1   Prayer by Rabbi of Beth Israel Congregation
of Houston, Texas, at Presidential
Inaugural ceremonies. January 20, 1965.
        1 reel (7 in.)   7 1/2 in. per sec.
phonotape.

Voice Lib.
M1466   Scheidemann, Philip, 1865-1939.
bd.15   Report on the situation of calling up
soldiers and laborers. Peteler,
November 8, 1918.
        1 reel (7 in.)   7 1/2 i.p.s.   phonotape.

        1. European War, 1914-1918 - Germany.

                    Scheibel, Ken
Voice Lib.
M1728   Dinitz, Simcha, 1929-
        Speech delivered to National Press Club
on Arab-Israeli relations, with Ken Scheibel.
WKAR, June 13, 1974.
        40 min.   phonotape (1 r.   7 1/2 i.p.s.)

        1. Israel - For. rel. - Arab countries.
2. Arab countries - For. rel. - Israel.
I. Scheibel, Ken.

Voice Lib.
M1466   Scheidemann, Philip, 1865-1939.
bd.16   Observations on the situation arising from
the forming of the German Republic and
suppression of communism in Germany.
Peteler, 1919.
        1 reel (7 in.)   7 1/2 in. per sec.
phonotape.

        1. Germany - Politics and government -
1918-1933.

Voice Lib.
M1466   Scheidemann, Philip, 1865-1939.
bd.10   Speech to the Imperial German Reichstag.
Peteler, May 15, 1917.
        1 reel (7 in.)   7 1/2 in. per sec.
phonotape.

        1. Germany - Politics and government -
1888-1918.

Voice Lib. Schildkraut, Joseph, 1896-1964
M1054   Memories of the movies: radio program
bd.2   pertaining to the early days of movies.
        Joseph Schildkraut, narrator. Westinghouse
Radio, 1960's.
        1 reel (7 in.)   7 1/2 in. per sec.
phonotape.

        1. Moving-pictures.
I. Schildkraut, Joseph, 1896-1964.

Voice Lib.
M760   Schimmel, John L
bd.5   Excerpt from "What All the Screaming's
        About" (Program 1); psychiatrist's approach
        to Beatlemania and its effects on teenage
        girls.   Westinghouse Broadcasting Corporation,
        1964.
        1 reel (7 in.)   7 1/2 in. per sec.
        phonotape.   (The Music Goes Round and Round)

        I. Title: What all the screaming's about.
        II. Series.   1. The Beatles.

Voice Lib.
M933   Schine, G   David, 1927-
        U. S. Congress. Senate. Committee on Government Operations.
        Permanent Subcommittee on Investigations.
            Proceedings of the 5th session of Senate Army-McCarthy
        hearings, April 28, 1954.   Cross-examination of Army Secretary
        Stevens by Senator McCarthy; Counselor Jenkins questions
        Stevens and Private Schine; McCarthy denies charges of special
        privileges for Schine.   WJR, 10:30 p. m., April 28, 1954.
            1 reel (7 in.)   7 1/2 in. per sec.   phonotape.

            I. McCarthy-Army controversy, 1954.   I. Stevens, Robert
        Ten Broeck, 1899-   II. McCarthy, Joseph Raymond, 1909-1957.
        III. Jenkins, Ray Howard, 1897-   IV. Schine, G   David,
        1927-

Voice Lib.
M934   Schine, G   David, 1927-
        U. S. Congress. Senate. Committee on Government Operations.
        Permanent Subcommittee on Investigations.
            Proceedings of the 6th session of Senate Army-McCarthy
        sessions, April 29, 1954.   Private Schine makes first appearance;
        he is cross-examined by Secretary Stevens and Counselor Jenkins;
        Schine comments on circumstances of doctoring the "famous
        photograph" and delivering it for publication at a Washington
        restaurant.   Evening session, WJR, April 29, 1954.
            1 reel (7 in.)   7 1/2 in. per sec.   phonotape.

            I. McCarthy-Army controversy, 1954.   I. Schine, G
        David, 1927-   II. Stevens, Robert Ten Broeck, 1899-
        III. Jenkins, Ray Howard, 1897-

Voice Lib.
M961   Schirach, Baldur von, 1907-
bd.7   Propaganda speech excerpt to Hitler Youth
        Group; also excerpts by Rudolf Hess and
        Hartmann Lauterbach.   German Radio, Peteler,
        April 4, 1934; January 1, 1935.
            1 reel (7 in.)   7 1/2 in. per sec.
        phonotape.

            I. Hess, Rudolf, 1894-   II.
        Lauterbach, Hartmann

Voice Lib.
M1376   Schirach, Baldur von, 1907-
bd.8   Speaking to Hitler Youth celebration.
        Peteler, June 21, 1936.
            1 reel (7 in.)   7 1/2 in. per sec.
        phonotape.

Voice Lib.
M917   Schirra, Walter Marty, 1923-
bd.1   Gemini 7 (space flight): Frank McGee's resumé
        of space flights of astronauts Frank Borman
        and James Lovell, Jr., in Gemini 7, commencing
        Dec. 4, 1956 to Dec. 18, 1965, and of astro-
        nauts Walter Schirra and Thomas Stafford in
        Gemini 6, which rendezvoused in space;
        including various launching actual reports
        and interview with Wally Schirra; comments
        by Huntley and Brinkley.   NBC TV, December
        18, 1965.
            1 reel (7 in.)   7 1/2 in. per sec.
        phonotape.   (Continued on next card)

Voice Lib.
M1384   Schirra, Walter Marty, 1923-
bd.1   Apollo 11 (space flight): launch day, July 16,
        1969.   Description of astronauts going up
        the elevator; conversation between Walter
        Cronkite and Walter Schirra at approximately
        2 hours before launch.   CBS TV, July 16, 1969.
            1 reel (7 in.)   7 1/2 in. per sec.
        phonotape.
            I. Project Apollo.   2. Space flight to the moon.   3. Aldrin,
        Edwin E   1930-   4. Collins, Michael, 1930-   5. Armstrong,
        Neil, 1930-   I. Aldrin, Edwin E   1930-   II. Collins,
        Michael, 1930-   III. Armstrong, Neil, 1930-   IV, Cronkite,
        Walter Leland, 1916-   V. Schirra, Walter Marty, 1923-

---

Voice Lib.
M1386   Schirra, Walter Marty, 1923-
bd.1   Apollo 11 (space flight): conversation with
        broadcasters Walter Cronkite and Wally
        Schirra.   Including Armstrong's activities
        on moon alone; pictures, rock descriptions,
        then Aldrin coming down ladder; rock boxes
        put to use.   TV cameras put at 30' panoramic
        position.   Reading inscription of plaque
        with U.S. flag and setting it up.   Telephone
        call from Washington to astronauts and their
        acknowledgement.   CBS TV, July 20, 1969.
            1 reel (7 in.)   7 1/2 in. per sec.
        phonotape.   (Continued on next card)

Voice Lib.
M1387   Schirra, Walter Marty, 1923-
bd.2   Apollo 11 (space flight): recovery.   Walter Cronkite and Wally
        Schirra announce proceedings from aircraft carrier "Hornet";
        trying to track spacecraft coming down;   chutes opening at
        10,500 feet; voice contact with spacecraft; visual of chutes;
        splashdown 9 miles from "Hornet", upside-down.   Collar
        attached to spacecraft.   NBC and ABC TV, July 24, 1969.
            1 reel (7 in.)   7 1/2 in. per sec.   phonotape.
            I. Project Apollo.   2. Space flight to the moon.   3. Aldrin,
        Edwin E   1930-   4. Collins, Michael, 1930-   5.
        Armstrong, Neil, 1930-   I. Aldrin, Edwin E   1930-
        II. Collins, Michael, 1930-   III. Armstrong, Neil, 1930-
        IV. Cronkite, Walter Leland, 1916-   V. Schirra, Walter Marty,
        1923-

Voice Lib.
M1388   Schirra, Walter Marty, 1923-
bd.1   Apollo 11 (space flight): Walter Cronkite and Wally Schirra
        describing recovery.   Maneuvers by frogmen and helicopters
        at splashdown spot; "air boss" describes close-up scene;
        decontamination process; helicopter landing on "Hornet" with
        astronauts; reception.   Description of proceedings on "Hornet"
        by CBS newscasters.   CBS TV, July 24, 1969.
            1 reel (7 in.)   7 1/2 in. per sec.   phonotape.
            I. Project Apollo.   2. Space flight to the moon.   3. Aldrin,
        Edwin E   1930-   4. Collins, Michael, 1930-   5. Armstrong,
        Neil, 1930-   I. Aldrin, Edwin E   1930-   II. Collins,
        Michael, 1930-   III. Armstrong, Neil, 1930-   IV. Cronkite,
        Walter Leland, 1916-   V. Schirra, Walter Marty, 1923-

Voice Lib.   Schirra, Walter Marty, 1923-
M1328 Apollo 7 (space flight): description of
bd.2   launching of Apollo 7 spacecraft, morning
     of October 11, 1968, and comments by various
     broadcasters, including Walter Cronkite.
     Description includes countdown and take-off;
     remarks by astronauts. CBS TV, October 11,
     1968.
       1 reel (7 in.) 7 1/2 in. per sec. phonotape.
       I. Project Apollo. 2. Eisele, Donn F 1930- 3. Cunning-
ham, R   Walter, 1932- 4. Schirra, Walter Marty, 1923-
I. Eisele, Donn F 1930- II. Cunningham, R   Walter,
1932- III. Schirra, Walter Marty, 1923- IV. Cronkite,
Walter Leland, 1916-

Voice Lib.
M1470 Schleicher, Kurt von
bd.11   Speaking about new government programs.
     Peteler, December 15, 1932.
       1 reel (7 in.) 7 1/2 in. per sec.
     phonotape.

       1. Germany - Politics and government -
     1918-1933.

Voice Lib.   Schlesinger, Arthur Meier, 1888-
M1478 The Pentagon Papers; discussion of content,
     meaning. Bernard Kalb, CBS; Senator J.W.
     Fulbright; Senator John Tower; Arthur
     Schlesinger; Walt Rostow; Max Frankel,
     New York Times; Crosby Noyes, Washington
     Evening Star. CBS-TV, July 13, 1971.
       1 reel (7 in.) 7 1/2 in. per sec.
     phonotape.
       I. Kalb, Bernard II. Fulbright, James William, 1905-
   III. Tower, John Goodwin, 1925- IV. Schlesinger, Arthur
   Meier, 1888-   V. Rostow, Walt Whitman, 1916-   VI.
   Frankel, Max   VII. Noyes, Crosby

Voice Lib.
M1705 Schlesinger, Arthur Meier, 1917-
     The imperial presidency; address at
     the University of Missouri. WKAR
     (KBIA, Columbia, Mo.), June 3, 1974.
       50 min. phonotape (1 r. 7 1/2 i.p.s.)

       1. Presidents - U.S. 2. Johnson, Lyndon
    Baines, Pres. U.S., 1908-1973. 3. Nixon,
    Richard Milhous, Pres. U.S., 1913-

Voice Lib.
M1470 Schmidt, Paul Karl
bd.15   a. Recalling the occupation of the
     Rhineland by Hitler, March 7, 1936. b.
     Recalling the Hitler-Chamberlain visits,
     August, 1938. c. Recalling Hitler's consterna-
     tion at Allied ultimatum of September 3, 1939;
     description of mood in the Chancellory.
     Peteler, 1964.
       1 reel (7 in.) 7 1/2 in. per sec.
     phonotape.

Voice Lib.   Schoenbrun, David Franz, 1915-
652   Franco Bahamonde, Francisco, 1892-
bd.20   Interview with David Schoenbrun, explaining
     his political philosophy for Spain. CBS,
     December 6, 1950.
       1 reel (7 in.) 7 1/2 in. per sec.
     phonotape.

       I. Schoenbrun, David Franz, 1915-

Voice Lib.
209   Schorr, Daniel Louis, 1916-
bd.1   Press conference with Fidel Castro and
     Anastas Mikoyan. Source (?), February 13,
     1960.
       1 reel (7 in.) 7 1/2 in. per sec.
     phonotape.

       I. Castro, Fidel, 1927-   II.
    Mikoian, Anastas Ivanovich, 1895-

Voice Lib.   Schorr, Daniel Louis, 1916-
M714 Adenauer, Konrad, 1876-1967.
bd.4   Interview with West German Chancellor
     pertaining to origin of Nazi regime,
     Rhineland occupation, Hitler, etc., by
     Daniel Schorr. CBS.
       5 min., 42 sec. phonotape (1 r.
     7 1/2 i.p.s.)

       I. Schorr, Daniel Louis, 1916-

Voice Lib.   Schorr, Daniel Louis, 1916-
M1559 Nixon, Richard Milhous, Pres. U.S., 1913-
     The Watergate Affair; address to the nation,
     with instant analysis by Roger Mudd and
     Daniel Schorr. CBS, April 30, 1973.
       30 min. phonotape (1 r. 7 1/2 i.p.s.)

       1. Watergate affair, 1972. I. Mudd,
    Roger. II. Schorr, Daniel Louis, 1916-

Voice Lib.   Schorr, Daniel Louis, 1916-
M1476 Pentagon Papers.
bd.2   New York times, Washington post, U.S.
     Government arguments before the Supreme
     Court, as represented by CBS News.
     Daniel Schorr (government), Marvin Kalb
     (New York times), Bob Sheafer (Washington
     post), Roger Mudd. CBS-TV, June 26, 1971.
       1 reel (7 in.) 7 1/2 i.p.s. phonotape.
       1. Security classification (Government documents)
   I. Schorr, Daniel Louis, 1916- II. Kalb, Marvin L
   III. Sheafer, Bob   IV. Mudd, Roger

Schorr, Daniel Louis, 1916-

Voice Lib.
652   Roosevelt, Eleanor (Roosevelt), 1884-1962.
bd.3   Interview with Daniel Schorr following
       her tour through Russia.   CBS, September 29,
       1957.
            1 reel (7 in.)   7 1/2 in. per sec.
       phonotape.

            I. Schorr, Daniel Louis, 1916-

SCHUMANN, ROBERT ALEXANDER, 1810-1856

C1
PWM4   Whorf, Michael, 1933-
            Schumann.
            1 tape cassette.   (The visual sounds of
       Mike Whorf. Panorama; a world of music,
       PWM-4)

            Originally presented on his radio program, Kaleidoscope,
       WJR, Detroit.
            Duration: 25 min., 50 sec.
            The life and times of Robert Schumann, including excerpts
       of his music.

            1. Schumann, Robert Alexander, 1810-1856.   L Title .

Schorr, Daniel Louis, 1916-

Voice Lib.
256   Roosevelt, Eleanor (Roosevelt), 1884-1962.
bd.4   Interview by Dan Schorr following her
       tour through the Soviet Union and her
       conference with Khrushchev.   CBS News,
       October 27, 1957.
            1 reel (7 in.)   7 1/2 in. per sec.
       phonotape.

            I. Schorr, Daniel Louis, 1916-

Voice Lib.
392   Schumann-Heink, Ernestine, 1861-
bd.3   Rehearsal of skit for radio program
       "House of Glass" celebrating her 75th
       birthday anniversary.   Private recording,
       1937.
            1 reel (7 in.)   7 1/2 in. per sec.
       phonotape.

Voice Lib.
394   Schulte, Paul
bd.3   "The Flying Priest" (later sentenced as
       a German spy and sent to a concentration
       camp) tells of his career as the Flying
       Priest.   G.R. Vincent, June 14, 1930.
            1 reel (7 in.)   7 1/2 in. per sec.
       phonotape.

C1
PWM4   Schumann
       Whorf, Michael, 1933-
            Schumann.
            1 tape cassette.   (The visual sounds of
       Mike Whorf. Panorama; a world of music,
       PWM-4)

            Originally presented on his radio program, Kaleidoscope,
       WJR, Detroit.
            Duration: 25 min., 50 sec.
            The life and times of Robert Schumann, including excerpts
       of his music.

            1. Schumann, Robert Alexander, 1810-1856.   L Title .

Voice Lib.
M1470 Schumacher, Kurt, 1895-1952.
bd.4   Attacking the Nazi Party at German Reichstag
       session.   Peteler, February 23, 1932.
            1 reel (7 in.)   7 1/2 in. per sec.
       phonotape.

Voice Lib.
M1010 Schuschnigg, Kurt, 1897-
bd.4   Announcement of Hitler's ultimatum to
       Austria, his resignation as Chancellor, and
       recommending non-resistance to Nazi troops
       by Austrian armed forces.   Peteler,
       March 11, 1938.
            1 reel (7 in.)   7 1/2 i.p.s.   phonotape.

            1. World War, 1939-1945 - Austria.

Voice Lib.
       Schumaker, Neil
379   Sitwell, Edith, 1897-1964.
bd.1   Talks to Oliver Waldrop and Neil Schumaker
       on becoming a poet, creation of poetry,
       technique for reading poetry.   WOED (NET),
       1959.
            1 reel (7 in.)   7 1/2 in. per sec.
       phonotape.

            I. Waldrop, Oliver   II. Schumaker,
       Neil

Voice Lib.   Schuster, Gary
M1607 Brennan, Thomas E., 1929-
bd.2   Off the record.   Interviewed by Tim
       Skubick, Tom Green, Gary Schuster, and
       Paul Weisenfeld.   WKAR-TV, January 25, 1974.
            15 min.   phonotape (1 r.   7 1/2 in. per
       sec.)

            1. Courts - Michigan.   I. Skubick, Tim.
       II. Green, Tom. III. Schuster, Gary. IV.
       Weisenfeld, Paul

Voice Lib.
M1610   Schuster, Gary
bd.1   Fitzgerald, John W., 1924–
    Interview by Gary Schuster concerning
    his appointment to the State Supreme Court.
    WKAR-TV, November 16, 1973.
    3 min.   phonotape (1 r.   7 1/2 i.p.s.)

    1. Michigan.   Supreme Court.   I. Schuster,
Gary.

Voice Lib.
M1606   Schuster, Gary
bd.1   Miller, James W
    Off the record.   Interviewed by Tim
    Skubick, Gary Schuster, Tom Green, and
    Bill Meek.   WKAR-TV, February 8, 1974.
    10 min.   phonotape (1 r.   7 1/2 in. per
sec.)

    1. Singer, Sidney. 2. Michigan. Civil
Service Commission.   I. Skubick, Tim.
II. Schuster, Gary. III. Green, Tom.
IV. Meek, Bill.

Voice Lib.
M1607   Schuster, Gary
bd.1   Porter, John W   1931–
    Off the record; problems facing Michigan
    schools. Interviewed by Tim Skubick, Tom
    Green, Bill Meek, and Gary Schuster.
    WKAR-TV, February 1, 1974.
    17 min.   phonotape (1 r.   7 1/2 in. per
sec.)

    1. Segregation in education. 2. Strikes
and lockouts - Teachers.   I. Skubick, Tim.
II. Green, Tom.   III. Meek, Bill. IV. Schuster,
Gary.

Voice Lib.
M1598   Schuster, Gary
bd.2   Romney, George W   1907–
    Off the record.   With Tim Skubick, Gary
    Schuster, Tom Greene, and Bill Meek.
    WKAR-TV, November 9, 1973.
    20 min.   phonotape (1 r.   7 1/2 in. per
sec.)

    1. Michigan - Politics and government.
2. Detroit.   I. Skubick, Tim. II. Schuster,
Gary. III. Greene, Tom. IV. Meek, Bill

Voice Lib.
M1605   Schuster, Gary
bd.2   Winograd, Morley
    Off the record. With Tim Skubick, Tom
    Greene, Gary Schuster, and Hugh Morgan.
    WKAR-TV, February 15, 1974.
    17 min.   phonotape (1 r.   7 1/2 in. per sec.)

    1. Democratic Party. Michigan. 2. Elections -
Michigan. 3. Youngblood, Charles N., 1932–
I. Skubick, Tim. II. Greene, Tom. III. Schuster,
Gary. IV. Morgan, Hugh.

Voice Lib.
M869   Schwartz, Arthur, 1900–
bd.2-   The great American song (radio program)
870   Documentary program of CBC on the contribution
    of American music: discussion of the work of
    George Gershwin; American musical comedy;
    biographical sketches and interviews with
    composers Arthur Schwartz and Vernon Duke, who
    discuss the technique of composing.   CBC, 1964.
    2 reels (7 in.)   7 1/2 in. per sec.
    phonotape.

    1. Gershwin, George, 1898-1937.   I. Schwartz,
Arthur, 1900–   II. Duke, Vernon, 1903-1969.

Voice Lib.
M1073   Schwarzbraun ist die Haselnuss
bd.17   German radio (Nazi controlled)
    Nazi martial music: song entitled
    "Schwarzbraun ist die Haselnuss".   Peteler,
    1941.
    1 reel (7 in.)   7 1/2 in. per sec.
    phonotape.

    I. Title: Schwarzbraun ist die Haselnuss.

Voice Lib.
M1355   Schweickart, Russell L   1936–
bd.3   Apollo 9 (space flight): lift-off of Apollo 9
    space flight at 11 a.m., March 3, 1969.
    Description of CBS-TV commentators, Mission
    Control, and astronauts.   CBS TV, March 3,
    1969.
    1 reel (7 in.)   7 1/2 in. per sec.
    phonotape.
    1. Project Apollo. 2. McDivitt, James Alton, 1929- 3.
Scott, David Randolph, 1932- 4. Schweickart, Russell L
1936-   I. McDivitt, James Alton, 1929- II. Scott, David
Randolph, 1932-   III. Schweickart, Russell L   1936-

Voice Lib.
M1364   Schweickart, Russell L   1936–
    Apollo 9 (space flight): splashdown, part 1.
    CBS correspondents with anchorman Walter
    Cronkite describe recovery of Apollo 9
    from the time astronauts are over Australia
    to the opening of the hatch.   CBS TV,
    March 13, 1969.
    1 reel (7 in.)   7 1/2 in. per sec.
    phonotape.
    1. Project Apollo. 2. McDivitt, James Alton, 1929- 3.
Scott, David Randolph, 1932- 4. Schweickart, Russell L
1936-   I. McDivitt, James Alton, 1929-   II. Scott, David
Randolph, 1932-   III. Schweickart, Russell L   1936-
IV. Cronkite, Walter Leland, 1916-

Voice Lib.   Schweickart, Russell L   1936–
M1365   Apollo 9 (space flight): splashdown, part 2.
    CBS TV description of retrieval of Apollo 9
    astronauts, starting with the opening of the
    hatch to their examination in sick bay on
    the recovery ship. Includes telegram by
    President Nixon and brief remarks by the
    astronauts.   CBS TV, March 13, 1969.
    1 reel (7 in.)   7 1/2 in. per sec.
    phonotape.
    1. Project Apollo. 2. McDivitt, James Alton, 1929- 3.
Scott, David Randolph, 1932- 4. Schweickart, Russell L
1936-   I. McDivitt, James Alton, 1929-   II. Scott, David
Randolph, 1932-   III. Schweickart, Russell L   1936-

Voice Lib.
M717   Schweitzer, Albert, 1875-1965.
bd.2   Discussing his life's work and his
       philosophy on his 85th birthday.   CBS,
       1960.
          1 reel (7 in.)   7 1/2 in. per sec.
       phonotape.

SCIENCE - SOCIAL ASPECTS
Voice Lib.
M1501 Wigner, Eugene Paul, 1902-
          Lecture on social responsibility of the
       scientist, and other topics, visiting the
       campus of MSU at Wells Hall.   Location
       recording, May 23, 1972.
          1 reel (7 in.)   7 1/2 in. per sec.
       phonotape.

Voice Lib.
M789- Schweitzer, Albert, 1875-1965.
790   A mix of Bach organ works played by
       Dr. Schweitzer and the folk music of the
       place where he practices, French Equatorial
       Africa.   KPFK, January 1, 1965.
          2 reels (7 in.)   7 1/2 in. per sec.
       phonotape.

SCIENCE FICTION
Voice Lib.
M1587- Asimov, Isaac, 1920-
1588   Utopian change; excerpts.   WKAR-AM,
       March 3, 1974.
          60 min.   phonotape (2 r.   7 1/2 in. per
       sec.)

          1. Science fiction. 2. Atomic weapons.

          Schweitzer, Albert, 1875-1965
Voice Lib.
324   Biography in sound (radio program)
          Albert Schweitzer: at Aspen, Colorado;
       Goethe Conference (in French, translation
       by Emery Ross); excerpt from Schweitzer
       film; Schweitzer at piano, speaks in German
       on Bach.   NBC, 1954.
          1 reel (7 in.)   7 1/2 in. per sec.
       phonotape.

          1. Schweitzer, Albert, 1875-1965.   I.
       Schweitzer, Albert, 1875-1965.

Voice Lib.
513   Scofield, Paul, 1922-
          A duet of poetry and drama from Festival
       of Performing Arts, Part I; with Joy Parker,
       reads "Ozymandias" by P.B. Shelley, "Kubla
       Khan" by S.T. Coleridge, 7th century Chinese
       courtship songs, lyrics from the first
       and second centuries, duet from Don Juan,
       Canto I by Lord Byron. Dress rehearsal.
       Talent Associates, March 23, 1962.
          1 reel (7 in.)   7 1/2 in. per sec.
       phonotape.

Voice Lib.
M1466 Schwerin-Loewitz, Hans
bd.13   Excerpt of speech in the Imperial German
       Parliament.   Peteler, March 3, 1918.
          1 reel (7 in.)   7 1/2 in. per sec.
       phonotape.

Voice Lib.
514   Scofield, Paul, 1922-
bd.1   A duet of poetry and drama from Festival
       of Performing Arts, Part II; with Joy
       Parker reads "Porphyria's Lover" by Robert
       Browning, "Bats" by D.H. Lawrence, dialogue
       from "The Family Reunion" by T.S. Eliot,
       "A Line of Beauty" by A.W. O'Shaughnessy,
       two short poems by Walter de la Mare.
       Talent Associates, March 23, 1962.
          1 reel (7 in.)   7 1/2 in. per sec.
       phonotape.

          SCIENCE - ADDRESSES, ESSAYS, LECTURES
Voice Lib.
M1686 Wald, George
          Address at Michigan State University.
       WKAR, March 4, 1970.
          50 min.   phonotape (1 r.   7 1/2 i.p.s.)

          1. Science - Addresses, essays, lectures.
       2. Abortion.

          The scope of jazz
Voice Lib.
M763   Alexander, Willard
bd.3   Excerpt from "The Scope of Jazz" (Program 6);
       comments on Goodman's success, disappearance
       of swing bands.   Westinghouse Broadcasting
       Company, 1964.
          1 reel (7 in.)   7 1/2 in. per sec.
       phonotape.   (The Music Goes Round and Round)

          1. Jazz music. I. Title: The scope of jazz.
       II. Series.

Voice Lib.
M763   The scope of jazz
bd.6   Austin, Bob
        Excerpt from "The Scope of Jazz" (Program
        6); his reasons for demise of big bands.
        Westinghouse Broadcasting Corporation, 1964.
        1 reel (7 in.)   7 1/2 in. per sec.
        phonotape.   (The Music Goes Round and Round)

            I. Title: The scope of jazz. II. Series.

Voice Lib.
M763   The scope of jazz
bd.4   Goldstein, Chuck
            Excerpt from "The Scope of Jazz" (Program 6); comments
        how each band had their own style and how they adapted
        material to fit this style. Comments on Glenn Miller himself;
        also comments on Frank Sinatra, including "Moonlight Serenade"
        and an excerpt from "The Hit Parade", with girls screaming
        over Frank Sinatra and him singing "Lay That Pistol Down, Babe".
        Westinghouse Broadcasting Corporation, 1964.
            1 reel (7 in.)   7 1/2 in. per sec.   phonotape.   (The Music
        Goes Round and Round)

            1. Jazz music.   1. Title: The scope of jazz. II. Series.

Voice Lib.
M763   The scope of jazz
bd.2   Goodman, Benny, 1909-
        Excerpt from "The Scope of Jazz" (Program
        6); relates the early period of his life
        when he was just starting, and the different
        places the band played; including song
        "Let's Dance", theme song of Goodman organiza-
        tion. Westinghouse Broadcasting Corporation,
        1964.
            1 reel (7 in.)   7 1/2 in. per sec.
        phonotape.   (The Music Goes Round and Round)
            I. Title: The scope of jazz. II. Title.

Voice Lib.
M763   The scope of jazz
bd.1   Serulli, Dom
            Excerpt from "The Scope of Jazz" (Program
        6); discusses three biggest factors in the
        establishment of the "swing" era, also his
        reason for decline of big bands. Westing-
        house Broadcasting Corporation, 1964.
            1 reel (7 in.)   7 1/2 in. per sec.
        phonotape.   (The Music Goes Round and Round)

            I. Title: The scope of jazz. II. Series.

Voice Lib.
M763   The scope of jazz
bd.5   Whiteman, Paul, 1890-1967.
            Excerpt from "The Scope of Jazz" (Program
        6); comments on Bing Crosby at the beginning
        of his career, including song by Crosby,
        "Pennies from Heaven." Westinghouse
        Broadcasting Corporation, 1964.
            1 reel (7 in.)   7 1/2 in. per sec.
        phonotape.   (The Music Goes Round and Round)

            1. Crosby, Bing, 1901-   I. Title: The
        scope of jazz. II. Series.

C1
M42   SCOTLAND

        Whorf, Michael, 1933-
            The bonny land of Scotland.
            1 tape cassette.   (The visual sounds of
        Mike Whorf. Miscellaneous, M42)

            Originally presented on his radio program, Kaleidoscope,
        WJR, Detroit.
            Duration: 36 min., 10 sec.
            An ancient land with a proud people, Scotland is a heritage
        for its descendants, and a state of mind for all.

            1. Scotland.   1. Title.

Voice Lib.
M950-   Scott, David Randolph, 1932-
951   Gemini 8 (space flight): press conference at
        Houston, Texas, Space Center regarding
        astronauts' space flight on Gemini 8.   NBC
        TV, March 26, 1966.
            2 reels (7 in.)   7 1/2 in. per sec.
        phonotape.

            1. Project Gemini. 2. Armstrong, Neil, 1930-
        3. Scott, David Randolph, 1932-   I. Armstrong,
        Neil, 1930-   II. Scott, David Randolph,
        1932-

Voice Lib.
M1355   Scott, David Randolph, 1932-
bd.3   Apollo 9 (space flight): lift-off of Apollo 9
        space flight at 11 a.m., March 3, 1969.
        Description by CBS-TV commentators, Mission
        Control, and astronauts.   CBS TV, March 3,
        1969.
            1 reel (7 in.)   7 1/2 in. per sec.
        phonotape.
            1. Project Apollo. 2. McDivitt, James Alton, 1929- 3.
        Scott, David Randolph, 1932- 4. Schweickart, Russell L.
        1936-   1. McDivitt, James Alton, 1929-   II. Scott, David
        Randolph, 1932-   III. Schweickart, Russell L.   1936-

---

Voice Lib.
M1364   Scott, David Randolph, 1932-
        Apollo 9 (space flight): splashdown, part 1.
        CBS correspondents with anchorman Walter
        Cronkite describe recovery of Apollo 9
        from the time astronauts are over Australia
        to the opening of the hatch.   CBS TV,
        March 13, 1969.
            1 reel (7 in.)   7 1/2 in. per sec.
        phonotape.
            1. Project Apollo. 2. McDivitt, James Alton, 1929-   3.
        Scott, David Randolph, 1932- 4. Schweickart, Russell L.
        1936-   1. McDivitt, James Alton, 1929-   II. Scott, David
        Randolph, 1932-   III. Schweickart, Russell L.   1936-
        IV. Cronkite, Walter Leland, 1916-

Voice Lib.
M1365   Scott, David Randolph, 1932-
        Apollo 9 (space flight): splashdown, part 2.
        CBS TV description of retrieval of Apollo 9
        astronauts, starting with the opening of the
        hatch to their examination in sick bay on
        the recovery ship. Includes telegram by
        President Nixon and brief remarks by the
        astronauts.   CBS TV, March 13, 1969.
            1 reel (7 in.)   7 1/2 in. per sec.
        phonotape.
            1. Project Apollo. 2. McDivitt, James Alton, 1929-   3.
        Scott, David Randolph, 1932- 4. Schweickart, Russell L.
        1936-   1. McDivitt, James Alton, 1929-   II. Scott, David
        Randolph, 1932-   III. Schweickart, Russell L.   1936-

Voice Lib.
Scott, David Randolph, 1932-
M1480 Apollo 15 (space flight): lift-off.
bd.1   CBS TV, July 26, 1971.
        1 reel (7 in.) 7 1/2 in. per sec.
phonotape.

        1. Project Apollo. 2. Space flight to the
moon. 3. Scott, David Randolph, 1932-   4.
Irwin, James B   1932-   5. Worden, Alfred
M   1930-   I. Scott, David Randolph,
1932-   II. Irwin, James B   1932-   III.
Worden, Alfred M   1930-

Voice Lib.
Scott, David Randolph, 1932-
M1480 Apollo 15 (space flight): beginning of power
bd.2   descent to moon. NBC TV, July 31, 1971.
        1 reel (7 in.) 7 1/2 in. per sec.
phonotape.

        1. Project Apollo. 2. Space flight to the
moon. 3. Scott, David Randolph, 1932-   4.
Irwin, James B   1932-   5. Worden, Alfred
M   1930-   I. Scott, David Randolph,
1932-   II. Irwin, James B   1932-   III.
Worden, Alfred M   1930-

Voice Lib.
Scott, David Randolph, 1932-
M1480 Apollo 15 (space flight): walk in deep space
bd.3   by Al Worden to retrieve film packages.
        Commentary of Gene Cernan, who walked in
space during Gemini 9 flight. NBC TV,
August, 1971.
        1 reel (7 in.) 7 1/2 in. per sec.
phonotape.
        1. Project Apollo. 2. Space flight to the moon. 3. Scott,
David Randolph, 1932- 4. Irwin, James B   1932-   5.
Worden, Alfred M   1930-   I. Scott, David Randolph, 1932-
II. Irwin, James B   1932-   III. Worden, Alfred M   1930-
IV. Cernan, Eugene Andrew, 1934-

Voice Lib.
Scott, David Randolph, 1932-
M1480 Apollo 15 (space flight): splashdown,
bd.4   commentary, speeches. NBC TV, August 7,
1971.
        1 reel (7 in.) 7 1/2 in. per sec.
phonotape.

        1. Project Apollo. 2. Space flight to the
moon. 3. Scott, David Randolph, 1932-   4.
Irwin, James B   1932-   5. Worden, Alfred
M   1930-   I. Scott, David Randolph,
1932-   II. Irwin, James B   1932-   III.
Worden, Alfred M   1930-

Voice Lib.
Scourby, Alexander, 1913-
M919- Stevenson, Adlai Ewing, 1900-1965.
920   The voice of the uncommon man; narrated by
bd.1   Alexander Scourby. RCA, 1965.
        2 reels (7 in.) 7 1/2 in. per sec.
phonotape.

        1. Stevenson, Adlai Ewing, 1900-1965. I.
Scourby, Alexander, 1913-

SECURITY CLASSIFICATION (GOVERNMENT
DOCUMENTS)
Voice Lib.
M1476 Pentagon Papers.
bd.2   New York times, Washington post, U.S.
Government arguments before the Supreme
Court, as represented by CBS News.
Daniel Schorr (government), Marvin Kalb
(New York times), Bob Sheafer (Washington
post), Roger Mudd.   CBS-TV, June 26, 1971.
        1 reel (7 in.) 7 1/2 L.p.s. phonotape.

        1. Security classification (Government documents)
L. Schorr, Daniel Louis, 1916-   II. Kalb, Marvin L
III. Sheafer, Bob   IV. Mudd, Roger.

Voice Lib.
M974 Seeger, Peter, May 3, 1919-
bd.2-   Selections from Carnegie Hall Concert.
bd.4   New York City.
        1 reel (7 in.) 7 1/2 in. per sec.
phonotape.

        CONTENTS.-bd.2. "We Shall Overcome".-
bd.3. "What Did You Learn in School Today?".-
bd.4. "Little Boxes".

C1
S30   Seeing things at night - Halloween
        Whorf, Michael, 1933-
        Seeing things at night - Halloween.
        1 tape cassette. (The visual sounds of
Mike Whorf. Social, S30)

        Originally presented on his radio program, Kaleidoscope,
WJR, Detroit.
        Duration: 49 min., 15 sec.
        "Seein' things at night," "The goblins will getcha" and the
terrifying tale of Sawney Beane and his family are tales appropriate
for this Halloween special.

        1. Halloween. I. Title.

"Seems Radio is Here to Stay"
Voice Lib.
249   Corwin, Norman Lewis, 1910 -
bd. 2   "Seems Radio is Here to Stay," an excerpt
from radio play. G. R. Vincent, June 4,
1940.
        1 reel (7 in.) 7 1/2 in. per sec.
phonotape.

        I. Title.

SEGREGATION IN EDUCATION
Voice Lib.
M742 Faubus, Orval Eugene, 1910-
bd.2   Concerning school desegregation crisis
in Little Rock. CBS, 1957.
        1 reel (7 in.) 7 1/2 in. per sec.
phonotape.

        1. Segregation in education.

Voice Lib.
253   SEGREGATION IN EDUCATION
bd.1   Faubus, Orville Eugene, 1910-
        Discussion of the problem of integration
        in the schools of Little Rock.   CBS,
        September 26, 1957.
            1 reel (7 in.)   7 1/2 in. per sec.
        phonotape.

            1. Segregation in education.

Voice Lib. SEGREGATION IN EDUCATION
M256   Mann, Woodrow Wilson
bd.1   Remarks of Mayor Mann preceding first
        day of integration at Little Rock, Arkansas.
        CBS News, September 22, 1957.
            1 reel (7 in.)   7 1/2 i.p.s.   phonotape.

            1. Segregation in education.

Voice Lib. SEGREGATION IN EDUCATION
M1607   Porter, John W   1931-
bd.1   Off the record; problems facing Michigan
        schools. Interviewed by Tim Skubick, Tom
        Green, Bill Meek, and Gary Schuster.
        WKAR-TV, February 1, 1974.
            17 min.   phonotape (1 r.   7 1/2 in. per
        sec.)

            1. Segregation in education. 2. Strikes
        and lockouts - Teachers. I. Skubick, Tim.
        II. Green, Tom. III. Meek, Bill. IV. Schuster,
        Gary.

Voice Lib.
M1436   The selling of the Pentagon; CBS documentary
bd.2-   about the excesses of the U.S. Army Infor-
1437   mation Department, with Roger Mudd.
        CBS-TV, March 25, 1971.
            2 reels (7 in.)   7 1/2 in. per sec.
        phonotape.

            I. Mudd, Roger

Voice Lib.
M1366- Selznick, David Oliver, 1902-1965.
1367   "The Selznick Years"; about the life and
bd.1   work of David O. Selznick and reminiscences
        by his friends and associates. Various
        excerpts from Selznick motion pictures.
        NBC-TV, March, 1969.
            2 reels (7 in.)   7 1/2 in. per sec.
        phonotape.

            1. Selznick, David Oliver, 1902-1965

Senate Rackets Committee.
    see
U.S. Congress. Senate. Select Committee to
    investigate racketeering in labor unions.

Voice Lib. Sennett, Mack
M322   Biography in sound (radio program)
        W.C. Fields, the magnificent rogue.
        NBC, 1955.
            1 reel (7 in.)   7 1/2 in. per sec.   phonotape.
            I. Fields, W.C., 1879-1946. I. Fields, W.C., 1879-1946.
        II. Allen, Fred, 1894-1956. III. LaBaron, William   IV.
        Taylor, Robert Lewis, 1912-   V. McCarey, Thomas Leo, 1898-
        1969. VI. Harkins, James   - VII. Chevalier, Maurice,
        1889-1972. VIII. Kuromoto, Mrs. George   IX. Flynn,
        Errol Leslie, 1909-1959. X. Wynn, Ed, 1886-1966. XI. Dowling,
        Ray Dooley   XII. Sennett, Mack   XIII. Overacher,
        Ronald Leroy   XIV. Bergen, Edgar, 1903-   XV. Taurog,
        Norman, 1899-   XVI. Runhell, Ana   . XVII. Cowen,
        Lester

Voice Lib.
M820,   Serett, Maxine
bd.2-   Author Maxine Serett interviewed by Fred
822   Haines on her ideas about sex and her book:
bd.1   "The Housewife's Handbook of Selective
        Promiscuity". KPFK, July 20, 1964.
            3 reels (7 in.)   7 1/2 in. per sec.
        phonotape.

            I. Haines, Fred

Voice Lib.
M1670   Serling, Rod, 1924-
        Speaking at the First Annual Midwest
        Film Festival, at Michigan State University.
        WKAR, May 24, 1972.
            45 min.   phonotape (1 r.   7 1/2 i.p.s.)

            1. Television broadcasting.   I. Midwest
        Film Festival. 1st, Michigan State Univer-
        sity, 1972.

Voice Lib.
M763   Serulli, Dom
bd.1   Excerpt from "The Scope of Jazz" (Program
        6); discusses three biggest factors in the
        establishment of the "swing" era, also his
        reason for decline of big bands. Westing-
        house Broadcasting Corporation, 1964.
            1 reel (7 in.)   7 1/2 in. per sec.
        phonotape.   (The Music Goes Round and Round)
            I. Title: The scope of jazz. II. Series.
        1. Jazz music.

Voice Lib.
M344
bd.10
Servatius, Robert
Eichmann, Adolph, 1906-1962.
Eichmann trial; statements by Gideon
Hausner, Robert Servatius and Eichmann
concerning the verdict of the court and
the death sentence. CBS, December 13,
1961.
1 reel (7 in.) 7 1/2 i.p.s. phonotape.

1. Eichmann, Adolph, 1906-1962.
I. Hausner, Gideon, 1915-   II. Servatius,
Robert.

C1
A42
SERVICE, ROBERT WILLIAM, 1874-1958
Whorf, Michael, 1933-
The spell of the Yukon; Robert Service.
1 tape cassette. (The visual sounds of
Mike Whorf. Art, music, and letters, A42)
Originally presented on his radio program, Kaleidoscope,
WJR, Detroit.
Duration: 44 min., 55 sec.
From the frontier towns of Whitehorse and Dawson, Service
sang the glories of the North Country. A prospector himself, he
was able to capture the rolling spirit of the brawling, boisterous
life of the Yukon in the days of the Gold Rush.

1. Service, Robert William, 1874-1958. I. Title.

Voice Lib.
M714
bd.6
Sevareid, Arnold Eric, 1912-
Describes the French soldier during the
early days of World War II.
3 min., 56 sec. phonotape (1 r.
7 1/2 i.p.s.)

1. France. Armée.

Voice Lib.
M1044
London after dark; on-the-spot recordings of various
points during the London air-raid attacks: the Savoy Hotel
kitchen, Trafalgar Square, anti-aircraft battery near London,
air-raid shelter. With newsmen Edward R. Murrow, Robert
Bowman, Raymond Van Denny, Larry Lesueur, Eric Sevareid,
Vincent Sheean, J. B. Priestley, Michael Standing, and
Winfred Von Thomas. CBS and BBC, August 24, 1940.
1 reel (7 in.) 7 1/2 in. per sec. phonotape.

I. Murrow, Edward Roscoe, 1908-1965. II. Bowman, Robert
III. Van Denny, Raymond IV. Lesueur, Laurence Edward,
1909- V. Sevareid, Arnold Eric, 1912- VI. Sheean,
Vincent, 1899- VII. Priestley, John Boynton, 1894-
VIII. Standing, Michael IX. Von Thomas, Winfred

Voice Lib.
M774-
775,
bd.1
Sevareid, Arnold Eric, 1912-
Farewell to Studio Nine; historical broadcasts
made by CBS correspondents at time of action
and reflections by them in retrospect. 1964.
2 reels (7 in.) 7 1/2 in. per sec.
phonotape.

I. Trout, Robert, 1908-   II. Pierpoint,
Robert   III. Murrow, Edward Roscoe,
1908-1965. IV. Kaltenborn, Hans von, 1878-
1965. V. Sevareid, Arnold Eric, 1912-
VI. Daly, John Charles, 1914-

Voice Lib.
M1351
bd.2
Sevareid, Arnold Eric, 1912-
Presidents I have known
Krock, Arthur, 1886-
Interview with Eric Sevareid pertaining
to his recent best-selling book, "Presidents
I Have Known". January 10, 1969.
1 reel (7 in.) 7 1/2 in. per sec.
phonotape.

I. Sevareid, Arnold Eric, 1912-
Presidents I have known.

Voice Lib.
614-
615
bd.1
Sevareid, Arnold Eric, 1912-
Lippmann, Walter, 1889-
"Walter Lippmann - 1964"; describes his
relationships with high public officials,
threat of nuclear war, influence of balance
of power on world politics, NATO and General
Charles De Gaulle, European conditions,
changing Russian attitude, Communist China,
Southeast Asia, status of South Viet Nam,
De Gaulle and world conditions, appraises
De Gaulle's position in world history,
changing status of cold war, U.S. foreign aid,
(Continued on next card)

Voice Lib.
614-
615
bd.1
Sevareid, Arnold Eric, 1912-
Lippmann, Walter, 1889-   "Walter
Lippmann - 1964". 1964. (Card 2)
U.S.-African relations, Cyprus problem,
changing U.S. attitude toward world, Cuban
situation, JFK's presidency, LBJ as president,
potential 1964 Republican presidential candidates and Democratic vice-presidential nomination and 1964 election, civil rights demonstra-
tions. CBS, April 8, 1964.
2 reels (7 in.) 7 1/2 in. per sec.
phonotape.
I. Sevareid, Arnold Eric, 1912-

Voice Lib.
M1454
bd.1
Sevareid, Arnold Eric, 1912-
Nixon, Richard Milhous, Pres. U.S., 1913-
Discussion of U.S. foreign policy with
network newscasters Eric Sevareid (CBS),
John Chancellor (NBC), and Howard K. Smith
(ABC).
1 reel (7 in.) 7 1/2 in. per sec.
phonotape.

I. Sevareid, Arnold Eric, 1912-   II.
Chancellor, John William, 1927-   III.
Smith, Howard Kingsbury, 1914-

Voice Lib.
M942
Sevareid, Arnold Eric, 1912-
Vietnam perspective (Television program)
CBS Special Report on Senate Foreign
Relations Committee hearings and the war
in Vietnam. CBS, February 18, 1966.
1 reel (7 in.) 7 1/2 in. per sec.
phonotape.

1. Vietnamese conflict, 1961-   - U.S.
I. Mudd, Roger   II. Sevareid, Arnold Eric,
1912-   III. Reasoner, Harry, 1923-   IV.
Kalb, Marvin L

Voice Lib.
M1363 Severing, Carl, 1875-1952.
bd.5   Excerpt of radio election speech.   Peteler,
1932.
1 reel (7 in.)   7 1/2 in. per sec.
phonotape.

Seversky, Alexander Procofieff de
see
De Seversky, Alexander Frocofieff, 1894-

VOICE LIBRARY

C1
H116   SEWARD, WILLIAM HENRY, 1801-1872
Whorf, Michael, 1933-
Seward's big deal - purchase of Alaska.
1 tape cassette.   (The visual sounds of
Mike Whorf. History and heritage, H116)
Originally presented on his radio program, Kaleidoscope,
WJR, Detroit.
Duration: 36 min., 10 sec.
They called it Seward's ice box or Seward's folly - this big deal
made by William Seward. This program tells the story of Seward,
the man, the man responsible for the purchase of Alaska.

L. Seward, William Henry, 1801-1872. 2. Alaska - History :
To 1867. L. Title.

C1
H116   Seward's big deal - purchase of Alaska
Whorf, Michael, 1933-
Seward's big deal - purchase of Alaska.
1 tape cassette.   (The visual sounds of
Mike Whorf. History and heritage, H116)
Originally presented on his radio program, Kaleidoscope,
WJR, Detroit.
Duration: 36 min., 10 sec.
They called it Seward's ice box or Seward's folly - this big deal
made by William Seward. This program tells the story of Seward,
the man, the man responsible for the purchase of Alaska.

L. Seward, William Henry, 1801-1872. 2. Alaska - History :
To 1867. L. Title.

SEX
Voice Lib.
M1619   Kniseley, William
bd.1   Discussion of the MSU Colloquy on
Sexuality, with J. P. McCarthy.
WJR, January 2, 1969.
22 min. phonotape (1 r. 7 1/2 i.p.s.)

1. Sex. I. McCarthy, Joseph Priestley,
1934-

SEX
Voice Lib.
M1706   Reuben, David R
bd.3   Impotence in marriage; funny discussion
on parent/child discussions of sex. On
Mike Douglas Show with Totie Fields and the
Fifth Dimension. WJRT-TV, June 5, 1974.
15 min. phonotape (1 r.   7 1/2 i.p.s.)

1. Sex. I. Douglas, Mike, 1925?
II. Fifth Dimension. III. Fields, Totie.

SEX
Voice Lib.
M1355   Sex colloquium; CBS News program dealing with
bd.1   the six weeks' sex lectures at Michigan
State University; opinions of students,
professors, and commentators. Dance at
Coral Gables. CBS TV (Janak), February 1969.
1 reel (7 in.)   7 1/2 in. per sec.
phonotape.

1. Michigan State University. 2. Sex.

Voice Lib.
M1355   Sex colloquium; CBS News program dealing with
bd.1   the six weeks' sex lectures at Michigan
State University; opinions of students,
professors, and commentators. Dance at
Coral Gables. CBS TV (Janak), February 1969.
1 reel (7 in.)   7 1/2 in. per sec.
phonotape.

1. Michigan State University. 2. Sex.

Voice Lib.
M1010   Seyss-Inquart, Arthur von, 1892-1946.
bd.5   Speech to Austrian people commending
Hitler as the great leader of a unified
greater Germany. Peteler, March 12, 1938.
1 reel (7 in.)   7 1/2 in. per sec.
phonotape.

1. Hitler, Adolf, 1889-1945

Voice Lib.
M975   Shackleton, Sir Ernest Henry, 1874-1922.
bd.8   Description of a dash for the South Pole.
Rococo-Can., 1909.
1 reel (7 in.)   7 1/2 i.p.s.   phonotape.

1. South Pole.

Voice Lib.
M1673   The Shadow (radio program)
bd.1   The white god.   Golden Age Radio
         Records, 1937.
             25 min.   phonotape (1 r.   7 1/2 i.p.s.)

Shakespeare, William, 1564-1616.
    Twelfth night
Voice Lib.
M299   Barrymore, John, 1882-1942.
bd.2   Excerpts from Shakespeare's Twelfth Night.
        Voice of America - NBC (rebroadcast 1950),
        1937.
            1 reel (7 in.)   7 1/2 in. per sec.
        phonotape.

            I. Shakespeare, William, 1564-1616./
        Twelfth night.

Shakespeare, William, 1564-1616.
    Hamlet
Voice Lib.
M1494   Barrymore, John, 1882-1942.
        Excerpts of "Hamlet", acted by John Barrymore,
        with his own narration as bridges.
        Shakespeare Society, 1947.
            1 reel (7 in.)   7 1/2 in. per sec.
        phonotape.

            I. Shakespeare, William, 1564-1616./Hamlet.

C1
A22   SHAKESPEARE, WILLIAM, 1564-1616
       Whorf, Michael, 1933-
           All the world's a stage, Shakespeare.
           1 tape cassette.   (The visual sounds of
       Mike Whorf.   Art, music, and letters, A22)

           Originally presented on his radio program, Kaleidoscope,
       WJR, Detroit.
           Duration: 44 min., 10 sec.
           William Shakespeare is considered the father of literature, for
       this prolific author composed plays, stories, sonnets and poems that
       are as popular today as when he first wrote them.

           I. Shakespeare, William, 1564-1616.   I. Title.

Shakespeare, William, 1564-1616.
    Hamlet
Voice Lib.
M553   Bell Telephone Laboratories, inc.
bd.3   Synthesized speech created by digital
        computer recites soliloquy from "Hamlet",
        sings "Bicycle built for two".   Explanation
        of computer's operation.   American Telephone
        and Telegraph Co., 1963.
            1 reel (7 in.)   7 1/2 i.p.s.   phonotape.

            1. Computer sound processing.   I. Shake-
        speare, William, 1564-1616./Hamlet.   II.
        Title: Bicycle built for two.

Shalitt, Gene
Voice Lib.
M1726   Aaron, Hank, 1934-
bd.3   Interviewed on Hank Aaron Day in New York
        City, by Curt Gowdy, Joe Garagiola, Tom
        Brokaw, and Gene Shalitt.   NBC, June 18,
        1974.
            10 min.   phonotape (1 r.   7 1/2 i.p.s.)

            1. Aaron, Hank, 1934-   2. Baseball.
        I. Gowdy, Curt.   II. Garagiola, Joe.
        III. Brokaw, Tom.   IV. Shalitt, Gene.

Shakespeare, William, 1564-1616.
    The merchant of Venice
Voice Lib.
567   Skinner, Ctis. 1858-1942.
bd.2   Portrays all characters in scenes
        from Shakespeare's "The Merchant of
        Venice."   Ted Packard of Harvard
        University Vocarium. 1931.
            1 reel (7 in.)   7 1/2 in. per sec.
        phonotape.

            I. Shakespeare, William, 1564-1616./
        The merchant of Venice.

Shalitt, Gene
Voice Lib.
M1726   Coppola, Francis Ford, 1939-
Bd.2   Interviewed on Today Show by Barbara
        Walters and Gene Shalitt.   NBC, June 18,
        1974.
            12 min.   phonotape (1 r.   7 1/2 i.p.s.)

            1. Moving-pictures.   I. Shalitt, Gene.
        II. Walters, Barbara, 1931-

Shakespeare, William, 1564-1616.
    Richard III
Voice Lib.
M301   Barrymore, John, 1882-1942.
bd.1   Excerpts from Shakespeare's Richard III.
        Voice of America - NBC, 1937 (rebroadcast
        1950).
            1 reel (7 in.)   7 1/2 in. per sec.
        phonotape.

            I. Shakespeare, William, 1564-1616./
        Richard III.

Voice Lib.
M1296   Shankar, Ravi, 1920-
bd.1-C Concert on sitar, violin and tabla with
        American violinist Yehudi Menuhin.   PRL,
        December 10, 1967.
            1 reel (7 in.)   7 1/2 in. per sec.
        phonotape.

            I. Menuhin, Yehudi, 1916-

SHANKAR, RAVI, 1920-
Voice Lib.
M1296   Menuhin, Yehudi, 1916-
bd.1-B   Discussing Indian music as played by Ravi
        Shankar on the sitar and its effect on
        serious musicians, with Edward P. Morgan.
        PBL, December 10, 1967.
            1 reel (7 in.)   7 1/2 in. per sec.
        phonotape.

            I. Morgan, Edward P   1910-

Voice Lib.
M611   Shannon Four.
bd.1   World War I song "There's a service flag
        flying at our house".   Victor Talking
        Machine Co., 1917.
            1 reel (7 in.)   7 1/2 i.p.s.   phonotape.

            1. European War, 1914-1918 - Songs and
        music. I.Title: There's a service flag
        flying at our house.

Voice Lib.
M1435
        Shapley, Harlow, 1885-1972
        Life in other worlds; exploratory discussion about life on other
        planets. Arnold J. Toynbee, Dr. G. B. Klastiakowsky
        (professor at Harvard), Dr. Donald M. Michaels, Dr. Otto
        Struve, Dr. Harlow Shapley, Walter Cronkite, Chet Huntley,
        William L. Laurence. New York, NBC, March 3, 1961.
        1 reel (7 in.)   7 1/2 i.p.s   phonotape.

            I. Life on other planets. I. Toynbee, Arnold Joseph, 1889-
        II. Klastiakowsky, George Bogdan. III. Michaels, Donald M.
        IV. Struve, Otto, 1897-1963. V. Shapley, Harlow, 1885-1972.
        VI. Cronkite, Walter Leland, 1916-   VII. Huntley, Chet,
        1911-1974. VIII. Laurence, William Leonard, 1888-

Voice Lib.
M1570- Shapp, Milton J   1912-
1571,   National Press Club address.   WKAR-AM,
bd.1   February 21, 1974.
            50 min.   phonotape (2 r.   7 1/2 i.p.s.)

            1. Railroads - U.S. 2. Power resources -
        U.S.

Voice Lib.
102   Shaw, George Bernard, 1856-1950.
bd.2   It seems to me (the folly of war).
        BBC, [n.d.]
            1 reel (7 in.)   7 1/2 in. per sec.
        phonotape.

Voice Lib.
102   Shaw, George Bernard, 1856-1950.
bd.1   Spoken English and broken English.
        Linguaphone, 1927.
            1 reel (7 in.)   7 1/2 in. per sec.
        phonotape.

Voice Lib.
537   Shaw, George Bernard, 1856-1950.
bd.3   Acceptance of honorary title of Freeman in
        a British borough; justifies use of recording
        for his speech (speech made via recording),
        alternatives to parliamentary government, views
        on British parliamentary procedure, experience
        in British politics, suggests British Parlia-
        ment to return to the committee system as
        practiced in municipalities, advises young
        people on entering politics. BBC, 1935.
            1 reel (7 in.)   7 1/2 in. per sec.
        phonotape.

            Shaw, George Bernard, 1856-1950
Voice Lib.
M618   Radio in the 1930's (Part I): a series of
bd.1-   excerpts from important broadcasts of the
14   1930's; a sample of radio of the period.
        NVL, April, 1964.
            1 reel (7 in.) 7 1/2 in. per sec. phonotape.
            I. Shaw, George Bernard, 1856-1950. II. Crosby, Bing, 1901-
        III. Barkley, Alban William, 1877-1956. IV. Roosevelt, Franklin
        Delano, Pres. U.S., 1882-1945. V. Hoover, Herbert Clark, Pres.
        U.S., 1874-1964. VI. Long, Huey Pierce, 1893-1935. VII. Town-
        send, Francis Everett, 1867-1960. VIII. Coughlin, Charles Edward,
        1891-   IX. Rogers, Will, 1879-1935. X. Pius XII, Pope, 1876-
        1958. XI. Edward VIII, king of Great Britain, 1894-1972. XII.
        Barrymore, John, 1882-1942. XIII. Woollcott, Alexander, 1887-
        1943. XIV. Allen, Fred, 1894-1956. XV. Benchley, Robert Charles,
        1889-1945.

            Shaw, George Bernard, 1856-1950
Voice Lib.
M619   Radio in the 1930's (Part II): a series of
bd.1-   excerpts of the 1930's; a sample of radio
14   of the period. NVL, April, 1964.
            1 reel (7 in.) 7 1/2 in. per sec. phonotape.
            I. Allen, Fred, 1894-1956. II. Delmar, Kenny   III. Donald,
        Peter   IV. Pious, Minerva   V. Fennelly, Parker   VI.
        Boyer, Charles, 1899-   VII. Dunne, Irene, 1904-   VIII.
        DeMille, Cecil Blount, 1881-1959. IX. West, Mae, 1893-   X.
        Dafoe, Allan Ray, 1883-1943. XI. Dionne quintuplets. XII. Ortega,
        Santos   XIII. War of the worlds (radio program) XIV. Ives, Burl,
        1909-   XV. Robinson, Earl, 1910-   XVI. Temple, Shirley,
        1928-   XVII. Earhart, Amelia, 1898-1937. XVIII. Lawrence,
        Gertrude, 1901-1952. XIX. Cohan, George Michael, 1878-1942.
        XX. Shaw, George Bernard, 1856-1950. XXI. Hitler, Adolf, 1889-
        1945. XXII. Chamberlain, Neville, 1869-1940. XXIII. Roosevelt,
        Franklin Delano, Pres. U.S., 1882-1945.

Voice Lib.
M1013   Shaw, George Bernard, 1856-1950.
bd.3   "Biography": Wolper Productions film on
        the life of George Bernard Shaw with
        various [segments] of George Bernard Shaw['s]
        voice. Wolper Productions, 1965.
            1 reel (7 in.)   7 1/2 in. per sec.
        phonotape.

            1. Shaw, George Bernard, 1856-1950.

SHAW, GEORGE BERNARD, 1859-1950
Voice Lib.
M1045 The world today; radio broadcast with
bd.1 discussions of George Bernard Shaw by
Alexander Woollcott; John Daly regarding
offensive on Moscow; Edward R. Murrow
from London; Albert Warner concerning
coal miners' strike. CBS Radio, October
30, 1941.
1 reel (7 in.) 7 1/2 in. per sec.
phonotape.
L. Shaw, George Bernard, 1856-1950. L. Woollcott, Alexander,
1887-1943. IL. Daly, John Charles, 1914- III. Murrow, Edward
Roscoe, 1908-1965. IV. Warner, Albert, 1884-1967.

Shaw, Robert Lawson, 1916-
Voice Lib.
M642 LaGuardia, Fiorello Henry, 1882-1947.
bd.1 Talk to the people: Christmas program
featuring Mayor LaGuardia reading from the
Scriptures, with Lauritz Melchior and Robert
Shaw; offers his own views on America at war;
reads prayer of Archbishop Spellman on return
from battlefields of World War II; wishes
audience a Merry Christmas. WNYC, December 24,
1944.
1 reel (7 in.) 7 1/2 in. per sec.
phonotape.
L. Melchior, Lauritz Lebrecht Hummel, 1890-1973. IL. Shaw,
Robert Lawson, 1916-

Sheafer, Bob
Voice Lib.
M1476 Pentagon Papers.
bd.2 New York times, Washington post, U.S.
Government arguments before the Supreme
Court, as represented by CBS News.
Daniel Schorr (government), Marvin Kalb
(New York times), Bob Sheafer (Washington
post), Roger Mudd. CBS-TV, June 26, 1971.
1 reel (7 in.) 7 1/2 i.p.s. phonotape.

L. Security classification (Government documents)
L. Schorr, Daniel Louis, 1916- IL. Kalb, Marvin L
III. Sheafer, Bob IV. Mudd, Roger

Shearer, Ray
Voice Lib.
M312 Humphrey, Hubert Horatio, 1911-
bd.5 Ray Shearer of NBC, Washington, speaking
with Senator Hubert Humphrey about his
opinion of the new President, Lyndon B.
Johnson. NBC, November 23, 1963.
1 reel (7 in.) 7 1/2 in. per sec.
phonotape.
1. Johnson, Lyndon Baines, Pres. U.S.,
1908-1973. I. Shearer, Ray

Shearer, Ray
Voice Lib.
M1287 Johnson, Lyndon Baines, Pres. U.S., 1908-
bd.2- 1973.
1288 "A conversation with the President". One
hour press conference with President Johnson
by the three TV networks about current
problems, prior to President's departure
for Australia. Dan Rather, CBS; Ray Shearer,
NBC; Frank Reynolds, ABC. NBC-TV,
December 19, 1967.
2 reels (7 in.) 7 1/2 in. per sec.
phonotape.

Sheean, Vincent, 1899-
Voice Lib.
M1044 London after dark; on-the-spot recordings of various
points during the London air-raid attacks: the Savoy Hotel
kitchen, Trafalgar Square, anti-aircraft battery near London,
air-raid shelter. With newsmen Edward R. Murrow, Robert
Bowman, Raymond Van Denny, Larry Lesueur, Eric Sevareid,
Vincent Sheean, J. B. Priestley, Michael Standing, and
Winfred Von Thomas. CBS and BBC, August 24, 1940.
1 reel (7 in.) 7 1/2 in. per sec. phonotape.
L. Murrow, Edward Roscoe, 1908-1965. IL. Bowman, Robert
III. Van Denny, Raymond IV. Lesueur, Laurence Edward,
1909- V. Sevareid, Arnold Eric, 1912- VI. Sheean,
Vincent, 1899- VII. Priestley, John Boynton, 1894-
VIII. Standing, Michael IX. Von Thomas, Winfred

Voice Lib.
516 Sheen, Fulton John, Bp., 1895-
bd.2 The needs of man; man's search for
happiness. GRV, 1935.
1 reel (7 in.) 7 1/2 in. per sec.
phonotape.

Shepard, Alan Bartlett, 1923-
Voice Lib.
M1438 Apollo 14 (space flight): lunar landed on the
bd.2 moon and moon walk. CBS, February 5, 1971.
1 reel (7 in.) 7 1/2 in. per sec.
phonotape.

1. Project Apollo. 2. Space flight to the
moon. 3. Shepard, Alan Bartlett, 1923- 4.
Mitchell, Edgar D 1931- 5. Roosa, Stuart
A 1934- I. Shepard, Alan Bartlett,
1923- II. Mitchell, Edgar D 1931- III.
Roosa, Stuart A 1934-

Shepard, Alan Bartlett, 1923-
Voice Lib.
M1438 Apollo 14 (space flight): Apollo 14 splash-
bd.3- down and reception on aircraft carrier.
M1439 CBS, February 9, 1971.
bd.1 2 reels (7 in.) 7 1/2 in. per sec.
phonotape.

1. Project Apollo. 2. Space flight to the
moon. 3. Shepard, Alan Bartlett, 1923- 4.
Mitchell, Edgar D 1931- 5. Roosa,
Stuart A 1934- I. Shepard, Alan Bartlett,
1923- II. Mitchell, Edgar D 1931- III.
Roosa, Stuart A 1934-

Shepard, Alan Bartlett, 1923-
Voice Lib.
M1438 Apollo 14 (space flight): take-off from Cape
bd.1 Kennedy, including countdown. CBS,
January 31, 1971.
1 reel (7 in.) 7 1/2 in. per sec.
phonotape.

1. Project Apollo. 2. Space flight to the
moon. 3. Shepard, Alan Bartlett, 1923- 4.
Mitchell, Edgar D 1931- 5. Roosa,
Stuart A 1934- I. Shepard, Alan Bartlett,
1923- II. Mitchell, Edgar D 1931- III.
Roosa, Stuart A 1934-

C1
H114

SHERMAN, WILLIAM TECUMSEH, 1820-1891

Whorf, Michael, 1933-
The march to the sea - Sherman.
1 tape cassette.   (The visual sounds of
Mike Whorf. History and heritage, H114)
Originally presented on his radio program, Kaleidoscope,
WJR, Detroit.
Duration: 36 min., 15 sec.
Was he ruthless or merely a genius at the art of warfare?
Was William Tecumseh Sherman's March to the sea across
Georgia one of fiery retaliation against the South, or the
necessary means to an end?

L. Sherman, William Tecumseh, 1820-1891.   I. Title.

Voice Lib.
M607
bd.3

Shirer, William Lawrence, 1904-
Fall of France; reports on fall of France
in special shortwave report from Berlin,
reviews states falling to Germany to date.
CBS, June 17, 1940.
1 reel (7 in.)   7 1/2 i.p.s.   phonotape.

1. World War, 1939-1945 - France.

Voice Lib.
M273-
274
bd.1

Sherwood, Robert Emmet, 1896-1955

Biography in sound (radio program)
Franklin Delano Roosevelt: the friends and
former associates of Franklin Roosevelt on
the tenth anniversary of the President's death.
NBC Radio, April, 1955.
2 reels (7 in.)   7 1/2 in. per sec.
phonotape.

L. Roosevelt, Franklin Delano, Pres. U.S., 1882-1945. L.
McIntire, Ross T   1899-   II. Mellett, Lowell, 1884-1960.
III. Tully, Grace   IV. Henderson, Leon, 1895-
V. Roosevelt, Eleanor (Roosevelt) 1884-1962. VI. DeGraaf, Albert
VII. Lehman, Herbert Henry, 1878-1963. VIII. Rosenman, Samuel
Irving, 1896-   IX. Arvey, Jacob   X. Moley, Raymond,
1886-   XI. Farley, Ja... Aloysius, 1888-   XII. Roosevelt,
(Continued on next card)

Voice Lib.
M621
bd.1-
12

Shirer, William Lawrence, 1904-

Radio in the 1940's (Part II): a series of
excerpts from important broadcasts of the
1940's; a sample of radio of the period.
NVL, April, 1964.
1 reel (7 in.)   7 1/2 in. per sec.   phonotape.
L. Daly, John Charles, 1914-   II. Hall, Josef Washington,
1894-   III. Shirer, William Lawrence, 1904-   IV. Roosevelt,
Eleanor (Roosevelt) 1884-1962. V. Roosevelt, Franklin Delano,
Pres. U.S., 1882-1945. VI. Churchill, Winston Leonard Spencer,
1874-1965. VII. Wainwright, Jonathan Mayhew, 1883-1953. VIII.
Cantor, Eddie, 1893-1964. IX. Sinatra, Francis Albert, 1917-
X. Hope, Bob, 1903-   XI. Crosby, Bing, 1901-   XII. Shore,
Dinah, 1917(?)-   XIII. Bergen, Edgar, 1903-   XIV. Armstrong,
Louis, 1900-1971. XV. Eldridge, Roy, 1911-

Voice Lib.
626-
627

Ship, Reuben

The investigator; satire on the investigations
of Senator Joseph McCarthy, written by
Reuben Ship, with John Drainie playing the
role of the investigator.   CBC, May 30, 1954.
2 reels (7 in.)   7 1/2 in. per sec.
phonotape.

I. Ship, Reuben   II. Drainie, John

Voice Lib.
M1313

Shirer, William Lawrence, 1904-
David L. Wolper production of filmed
documentary "Rise and Fall of the Third
Reich"; (Part 3) with actual voices of
Nazi generals, Eric Kempke (Hitler's chauffeur)
Hitler and Goebbels; (period from 1941-
1945).   NBC-TV; March, 1968.
1 reel (7 in.)   7 1/2 in. per sec.
phonotape.

I. Title: Rise and fall of the Third
Reich.

Voice Lib.
M714
bd.2

SHIPS - FIRES AND FIRE PROTECTION

Fire on super-aircraft-carrier "Constellation"
in the Brooklyn Navy Yard.   On-the-spot
broadcast, December 19, 1960.
3 min., 43 sec.   phonotape (1 r.
7 1/2 i.p.s.)

1. Ships - Fires and fire protection.

Voice Lib.
M1402
bd.2

Shirer, William Lawrence, 1904-
Excerpt of conversation with Merv Griffin
about broadcasting during early part of World
War II and about Mahatma Gandhi.   CBS,
November 13, 1969.
1 reel (7 in.)   7 1/2 in. per sec.
phonotape.

1. Gandhi, Mohandas Karamchand, 1869-1948.
I. Griffin, Mervyn Edward, 1925-

C1
H63

SHIPWRECKS

Whorf, Michael, 1933-
Down to the sea in ships.
1 tape cassette.   (The visual sounds of
Mike Whorf. History and heritage, H63)
Originally presented on his radio program, Kaleidoscope,
WJR, Detroit.
Duration: 38 min., 50 sec.
What is the lure of the sea that calls men to their destiny?
In this narrative the great tragedies of the ocean are recounted.

L. Shipwrecks. L. Title.

Voice Lib.
572-
573
bd.1

Shirer, William Lawrence, 1904-
I can hear it now (radio program)
1933-1946.   CBS, 1948.
2 reels (7 in.)   7 1/2 in. per sec.
phonotape.

L. Murrow, Edward Roscoe, 1908-1965. II. LaGuardia, Fiorello
Henry, 1882-1947. III. Chamberlain, Neville, 1869-1949. IV.
Roosevelt, Franklin Delano, Pres. U.S., 1882-1945. V. Churchill,
Winston Leonard Spencer, 1874-1965. VI. Gaulle, Charles de,
Pres. France, 1890-1970. VII. Eisenhower, Dwight David, Pres. U.S.,
1890-1969. VIII. Willkie, Wendell Lewis, 1892-1944. IX. Martin,
Joseph William, 1884-1968. X. Elizabeth II, Queen of Great Britain,
1926-   XI. Margaret Rose, Princess of Gt. Brit., 1930-   XII.
Johnson, Hugh Samuel, 1882-... XIII. Smith, Alfred Emanuel,
1873-1944. XIV. Lindbergh... arles Augustus, 1902-   XV. Davis,
(Continued on next card)

Voice Lib.
M1800   Shoffler, Carl
WG   Testimony before the Senate Committee
0518.01   investigating the Watergate Affair.
         Pacifica, May 18, 1973.
             34 min.   phonotape (1 r.   3 3/4 i.p.s.)
         (Watergate gavel to gavel, phase 1)

         1. Watergate Affair, 197.-

Voice Lib.
M765   Sholes, Steven H   1911-1968.
bd.1   Excerpt from "The Anatomy of a Hit"
         (Program 9); comments on why the A&R man
         is the most important person in the production
         of a hit record; the changing attitude of
         the juke box operator. Westinghouse
         Broadcasting Corporation, 1964.
             1 reel (7 in.)   7 1/2 in. per sec.
         phonotape.   (The Music Goes Round and Round)

             I. Title: The anatomy of a hit. II. Series.

Voice Lib.
M760   Sholes, Steven H   1911-1968.
bd.6   Excerpt from "What all the screaming's
         about (Program 1); Elvis' progress to fame
         and fortune, including one of his first hits,
         "That's all right"; a comparison is made
         between Elvis and the Beatles. Westinghouse
         Broadcasting Corporation, 1964.
             8 min., 6 sec.   phonotape (1 r.   7 1/2 i.p.s.) (The
         music goes round and round)

         1. Presley, Elvis Aron, 1935-   2. Music, Popular (Songs,
         etc.) - U.S.   3. Title: What all the screaming's about. II.
         Series.

Voice Lib.   Shore, Dinah, 1917(?)-
M621   Radio in the 1940's (Part II): a series of
bd.1-   excerpts from important broadcasts of the
12   1940's; a sample of radio of the period.
         NVL, April, 1964.
             1 reel (7 in.)   7 1/2 in. per sec.   phonotape.
             1. Daly, John Charles, 1914-   II. Hall, Josef Washington,
         1894-   III. Shirer, William Lawrence, 1904-   IV. Roosevelt,
         Eleanor (Roosevelt) 1884-1962. V. Roosevelt, Franklin Delano,
         Pres. U.S., 1882-1945. VI. Churchill, Winston Leonard Spencer,
         1874-1965. VII. Wainwright, Jonathan Mayhew, 1883-1953. VIII.
         Cantor, Eddie, 1893-1964. IX. Sinatra, Francis Albert, 1917-
         X. Hope, Bob, 1903-   XI. Crosby, Bing, 1901-   XII. Shore,
         Dinah, 1917(?)-   XIII. Bergen, Edgar, 1903-   XIV. Armstrong,
         Louis, 1900-1971. XV. Eldridge, Roy, 1911-

Voice Lib.
M760   Sholes, Steven H   1911-1968.
bd.11   Excerpt from "The Big Beat" (Program 2);
         formation of popular music, including a
         song by Eddie Arnold, "There's a Star-
         Spangled Banner Waving Somewhere". Westing-
         house Broadcasting Corporation, 1964.
             1 reel (7 in.)   7 1/2 in. per sec.
         phonotape.   (The Music Goes Round and Round)

             I. Title: The big beat. II. Series.

Voice Lib.
M1099   Short excerpts from famous pictures of the
bd.2   1930's, featuring the film stars. Released
         by Cinematograph Players Benevolent Fund #4
         in England. Forrest ₍no date₎
             1 reel (7 in.)   7 1/2 in. per sec.
         phonotape.

             1. Moving-pictures.

Voice Lib.
M762   Sholes, Steven H   1911-1968.
bd.3   Excerpt from "Tunesmiths Past and Present"
         (Program 4); comments on today's emphasis
         on youth as song writers and as the audience
         of these songs. Westinghouse Broadcasting
         Corporation, 1964.
             1 reel (7 in.)   7 1/2 in. per sec.
         phonotape.   (The Music Goes Round and Round)

             I. Title: Tunesmiths past and present.
         II. Series.

Voice Lib.
M612   Shriver, Robert Sargent, 1915-
             War on poverty; reviews President Lyndon
         Johnson's fight against domestic poverty,
         discusses his role in the fight, briefly
         reviews his own career. NET, March 30, 1964.
             1 reel (7 in.)   7 1/2 i.p.s.   phonotape.

             1. U.S. -Economic conditions. 2. Johnson, Lyndon
         Baines, Pres. U.S., 1908-1973. 3. Shriver, Robert Sargent,
         1915-

Voice Lib.
M764   Sholes, Steven H   1911-1968.
bd.9   Excerpt from "The World of Wax" (Program
         8); discusses why radio almost killed the
         record business, and the biggest change in
         the record business. Westinghouse Broad-
         casting Corporation, 1964.
             1 reel (7 in.)   7 1/2 in. per sec.
         phonotape.   (The Music Goes Round and Round)

             I. Title: The world of wax. II. Series.

Voice Lib.
399   Siegel, Seymour H
bd.2   Memorial to LaGuardia. WNYC, ₍n.d.₎
             1 reel (7 in.)   7 1/2 in. per sec.
         phonotape.

             1. LaGuardia, Fiorello Henry, 1882-1947.

The silent screen

CI
M1   Whorf, Michael, 1933-
      The silent screen.
      1 tape cassette. (The visual sounds of
      Mike Whorf. Miscellaneous, M1)

         Originally presented on his radio program, Kaleidoscope,
      WJR, Detroit.
         Duration: 41 min.
         It was a history-making event when Edison came forward with
      his moving-picture machine. Mary Pickford, Douglas Fairbanks,
      Valentino, Clara Bow - the story of their era would unfold with
      stories and stars coming alive on the silent screen.

         I. Moving-pictures.   Silent. I. Title.

Voice Lib.
M864   Silver, Abba Hillel, 1893-1963.
         Portion of the principal address to the 2000 delegates of the
      81st annual convention of the Zionist Organization of America,
      held at Syria Mosque in Pittsburgh, Pa. Dr. Silver criticizes
      U.S. Government for its vascillating policies on the question
      of Palestine partition. Reviews the steps leading to the formation
      of Jewish homeland, culminating in a reversal of his policy by
      President Truman. KDKA, July 4, 1948
         1 reel (7 in.) 7 1/2 i.p.s. phonotape.

         I. Zionism. 2. U.S. - Foreign relations - Israel.
      3. Israel - Foreign relations - U.S.

Voice Lib.
M1286 Simon, George Thomas
  bd.2   Excerpt of "Today" show of conversation
      between emcee Hugh Downs and George T. Simon,
      about name bands and his new book "The Big
      Bands". NBC-TV, December 11, 1967.
         1 reel (7 in.) 7 1/2 in. per sec.
      phonotape.

         I. Downs, Hugh Malcolm, 1921-

Voice Lib.
M1554 Simon, William Edward, 1927-
      Address to the National Press Club.
      WKAR, February 4, 1974.
      40 min. phonotape (1 r. 7 1/2 i.p.s.)

      Includes 25 min. question and answer period.

         1. Power resources - U.S.

SINAI CAMPAIGN, 1956

Voice Lib.
M715   Burdett, Winston, 1913-
  bd.11   Excerpt of broadcast during Israeli-
      Egyptian conflict. CBS, October 31, 1956.
      1 min., 40 sec. phonotape (1 r.
      7 1/2 i.p.s.)

         1. Sinai Campaign, 1956.

Voice Lib.
393   Sinatra, Francis Albert, 1917-
  bd.5   Parody on song "Sunday, Monday and
      Always". From radio program V-Disc's
      "For the Record". Produced by G.R.
      Vincent. CBS Reference Recording,
      October 23, 1944.
         1 reel (7 in.) 7 1/2 in. per sec.
      phonotape.

Voice Lib.
652   Sinatra, Francis Albert, 1917-
  bd.2   At luncheon for Khrushchev for the
      movie "CanCan". CBS, September 19, 1959.
         1 reel (7 in.) 7 1/2 in. per sec.
      phonotape.

Sinatra, Francis Albert, 1917-

Voice Lib.
M621   Radio in the 1940's (Part II): a series of
  bd.1-   excerpts from important broadcasts of the
  12   1940's; a sample of radio of the period.
      NVL, April, 1964.
         1 reel (7 in.) 7 1/2 in. per sec. phonotape.
      I. Daly, John Charles, 1914-   II. Hall, Josef Washington,
      1894-   III. Shirer, William Lawrence, 1904-   IV. Roosevelt,
      Eleanor (Roosevelt) 1884-1962. V. Roosevelt, Franklin Delano,
      Pres. U.S., 1882-1945. VI. Churchill, Winston Leonard Spencer,
      1874-1965. VII. Wainwright, Jonathan Mayhew, 1883-1953. VIII.
      Cantor, Eddie, 1893-1964. IX. Sinatra, Francis Albert, 1917-
      X. Hope, Bob, 1903-   XI. Crosby, Bing, 1901-   XII. Shore,
      Dinah, 1917(?)-   XIII. Bergen, Edgar, 1903-   XIV. Armstrong,
      Louis, 1900-1971. XV. Eldridge, Roy, 1911-

Voice Lib.
338   Sinclair, Upton Beall, 1878-1968.
  bd.2   On free democratic socialism; disclaims
      misuse of his name by Russian critics.
      Voice of America, June 22, 1949.
         1 reel (7 in.) 7 1/2 in. per sec.
      phonotape.

Voice Lib.
M1012 Sinclair, Upton Beall, 1878-1968.
  bd.1   Interview by Harry W. Flannery with Upton
      Sinclair for the AFL-CIO radio program
      "The Upton Sinclair Story". Includes
      "Sinclair's Early Life". AFL-CIO, April 9,
      1960.
         1 reel (7 in.) 7 1/2 in. per sec.
      phonotape.

         I. Flannery, Harry W   1900-

Voice Lib.
M1012 Sinclair, Upton Beall, 1878-1968.
bd.2 Interview by Harry W. Flannery with Upton
Sinclair for the AFL-CIO radio program
"The Upton Sinclair Story". Includes "The
Jungle". AFL-CIO, April 9, 1960.
1 reel (7 in.) 7 1/2 in. per sec.
phonotape.

I. Flannery, Harry W   1900-

SINGER, SIDNEY
Voice Lib.
M1606 Miller, James W
bd.1   Off the record.   Interviewed by Tim
Skubick, Gary Schuster, Tom Green, and
Bill Meek. WKAR-TV, February 8, 1974.
10 min. phonotape (1 r. 7 1/2 in. per
sec.)

1. Singer, Sidney. 2. Michigan. Civil
Service Commission. I. Skubick, Tim.
II. Schuster, Gary. III. Green, Tom.
IV. Meek, Bill.

Voice Lib.
M1012 Sinclair, Upton Beall, 1878-1968.
bd.3   Interview by Harry W. Flannery with Upton
Sinclair for the AFL-CIO radio program
"The Upton Sinclair Story". Includes "King
Cole" and "The Brass Check". AFL-CIO,
April 9, 1960.
1 reel (7 in.) 7 1/2 in. per sec.
phonotape.

I. Flannery, Harry W   1900-

The sinking of the Bismarck
C1
M15 Whorf, Michael, 1933-
The sinking of the Bismarck.
1 tape cassette. (The visual sounds of
Mike Whorf. Miscellaneous, M15)

Originally presented on his radio program, Kaleidoscope,
WJR, Detroit.
Duration: 25 min.
During the early years of World War II, the German ship
Bismarck, was the terror of the high seas. Challenged by the
ships of the English fleet, it was a day of retribution and one
that changed the course of battle in the north Atlantic.

L. Bismarck (Battleship) 2. World War, 1939-1945 - Naval
operations, British.   L Title.

Voice Lib.
M1013 Sinclair, Upton Beall, 1878-1968.
bd.1   Interview by Harry W. Flannery with Upton
Sinclair for the AFL-CIO radio program
"The Upton Sinclair Story". Includes "Oil"
and "The Flivver King". AFL-CIO, April 9,
1960.
1 reel (7 in.) 7 1/2 in. per sec.
phonotape.

I. Flannery, Harry W   1900-

Voice Lib.
M1378 Sirhan, Sirhan Bishara, 1944-
bd.1   Interview by Jack Perkins. NBC, June 3,
1969.
1 reel (7 in.) 7 1/2 in. per sec.
phonotape.

I. Perkins, Jack.

Voice Lib.
M960 Sinclair, Upton Beall, 1878-1968.
bd.2   O, my America! Anecdotes and reminiscences.
C.S.D.I., 1963.
1 reel (7 in.) 7 1/2 in. per sec.
phonotape.

Voice Lib. SIRHAN, SIRHAN BISHARA, 1944-
M1332- Kennedy, Robert Francis, 1925-1968.
1333   Comments and news regarding condition of
bd.1   Senator Robert F. Kennedy after assassination
attempt in Los Angeles. Statement by Mayor
Yorty and Los Angeles police chief. Statement by Jordanian ambassador regarding
assassins Sirhan; also Mr. and Mrs. Wagner,
former employers. Flashback to scene of
assassination. Views from Washington on
gun legislation. NBC-TV, June 6, 1968.
2 reels (7 in.) 7 1/2 in. per sec.
phonotape.
(Continued on next card)

Voice Lib.
M982 Sinclair, Upton Beall, 1878-1968.
bd.1   Reminiscences by Upton Sinclair during
interview with Harry W. Flannery, including
comments on "The Jungle", "The Brass Check",
"King Coal", "The Flivver King", and others.
ABC, October 16, 1966.
1 reel (7 in.) 7 1/2 in. per sec.
phonotape.

I. Flannery, Harry W   1900-

SIRICA, JOHN JOSEPH, 1904-
Voice Lib.
M1698   Ervin, Samuel James, 1896-
The lesson of Watergate; address at the
National Press Club. WKAR, May 29, 1974.
45 min. phonotape (1 r. 7 1/2 i.p.s.)

1. Constitutional law. 2. Baker, Robert
Gene, 1928-   3. Sirica, John Joseph, 1904-

Sister Susie's sewing shirts for soldiers
Voice Lib.
M946   Jolson, Al, 1886-1950.
bd.3   Singing World War I novelty song "Sister
        Susie's Sewing Shirts for Soldiers".
        Col. Phonograph, 1916.
           1 reel (7 in.)   7 1/2 in. per sec.
        phonotape.

Voice Lib.
M1455   Sixty minutes (Television program)
bd.2   Semi-monthly CBS documentary with a
        biography of Howard Hughes.   CBS TV, 1970.
           1 reel (7 in.)   7 1/2 in. per sec.
        phonotape.

           1. Hughes, Howard Robard, 1905-

Voice Lib.
379   Sitwell, Edith, 1887-1964.
bd.2-4   From "Facade" with music by William
        Walton: "Mariner Man", "Trio for Two
        Cats and Trombone", "Through Gilded
        Trellises".   Columbia Records, 1953.
           1 reel (7 in.)   7 1/2 in. per sec.
        phonotape.

Voice Lib.
M1455   Sixty minutes (Television program)
bd.1   Semi-monthly CBS documentary with a
        biography of Vice-President Spiro Agnew.
        CBS TV, 1970.
           1 reel (7 in.)   7 1/2 in. per sec.
        phonotape.

           1. Agnew, Spiro T   · 1918-

Voice Lib.
379   Sitwell, Edith, 1887-1964.
bd.1   Talks to Oliver Waldrop and Neil Schumaker
        on becoming a poet, creation of poetry,
        technique for reading poetry.   WOED (NET),
        1959.
           1 reel (7 in.)   7 1/2 in. per sec.
        phonotape.

           I. Waldrop, Oliver   II. Schumaker,
        Neil   1. Sitwell, Edith, 1887-1964.

Voice Lib.
M906-   Skinner, Cornelia Otis, 1901-
908   In sophisticated comedy play "The
        Irregular Verb to Love".   NET,
        December, 1965.
           3 reels (7 in.)   7 1/2 i.p.s.
        phonotape.

           I. Title: The irregular verb to love.

Sitwell, Sir Osbert, bart., 1892-1969
Voice Lib.
M836   Beecham, Sir Thomas, bart., 1879-1961.
bd.2   Interviewing with Sir Osbert Sitwell on
        the occasion of Sir Thomas' 70th birthday.
        RCA, 1949.
           1 reel (7 in.)   7 1/2 in. per sec.
        phonotape.

           I. Sitwell, Sir Osbert, bart., 1892-1969.

Voice Lib.
567   Skinner, Otis, 1858-1942.
bd.2   Portrays all characters in scenes
        from Shakespeare's "The Merchant of
        Venice."   Ted Packard of Harvard
        University Vocarium, 1931.
           1 reel (7 in.)   7 1/2 in. per sec.
        phonotape.

           I. Shakespeare, William, 1564-1616./
        The merchant of Venice.

Voice Lib.
M1405   Sixty minutes (Television program)
           Agnew TV controversy: CBS TV program
        devoted entirely to defending the
        television newscasters' points of view
        regarding the criticism of the media by
        Vice-President Spiro T. Agnew.   CBS-TV,
        November 25, 1969.
           1 reel (7 in.)   7 1/2 in. per sec.
        phonotape.

           1. Agnew, Spiro T   1918-

Voice Lib.   Skinner, Otis, 1858-1942
M225   Packard, Frederick
           Styles in Shakespearean acting, 1890-1950.
        Creative Associates, 1963?
           1 reel (7 in.)   7 1/2 i.p.s. phonotape.

           I. Sothern, Edward Askew, 1826-1881. II. Marlowe,
        Julia, 1865-1950. III. Booth, Edwin, 1833-1893. IV. Gielgud,
        John, 1904-   V. Robeson, Paul Bustill, 1898-   VI. Terry,
        Dame Ellen, 1848-1928. VII. Allen, Viola. VIII. Welles,
        Orson, 1915-   IX. Skinner, Otis, 1858-1942. X. Barrymore,
        John, 1882-1942. XI. Olivier, Sir Laurence Kerr, 1907-
        XII. Forbes-Robertson, Sir Johnston, 1853-   XIII. Evans,
        Maurice. XIV. Thorndike, Dame Sybil, 1882-   XV. Robson,
        Flora. XVI. LeGallienne, Eva, 1899-   XVII. Anderson,
        Judith. XVIII. Duncan, Augustin. XIX. Hampden, Walter.
        XX. Speaight, Robert, 1904-   XXI. Jones, Daniel.

Voice Lib.
M1607
bd.2
Skubick, Tim
Brennan, Thomas E., 1929-
Off the record. Interviewed by Tim
Skubick, Tom Green, Gary Schuster, and
Paul Weisenfeld. WKAR-TV, January 25, 1974.
15 min. phonotape (1 r. 7 1/2 in. per
sec.)

1. Courts - Michigan. I. Skubick, Tim.
II. Green, Tom. III. Schuster, Gary. IV.
Weisenfeld, Paul

Voice Lib.
M1598
bd.1
Skubick, Tim
Plants, John R
Safeguards againt misuse of state police
for political purposes. With Tim Skubick.
WKAR-TV, November 23, 1973.
10 min. phonotape (1 r. 7 1/2 in. per
sec.)

1. Police - Michigan. 2. Michigan. State
Police. I. Skubick, Tim.

Voice Lib.
M1606
bd.2
Skubick, Tim
Kavanagh, Thomas H., 1909-
Michigan Public Broadcasting presents: an
evening with Thomas H. Kavanagh. With Tim
Skubick. Michigan Public Radio, December 10,
1973.
30 min. phonotape (1 r. 7 1/2 in. per
sec.)

1. Courts - Michigan. I. Skubick, Tim

Voice Lib.
M1607
bd.1
Skubick, Tim
Porter, John W 1931-
Off the record; problems facing Michigan
schools. Interviewed by Tim Skubick, Tom
Green, Bill Meek, and Gary Schuster.
WKAR-TV, February 1, 1974.
17 min. phonotape (1 r. 7 1/2 in. per
sec.)

1. Segregation in education. 2. Strikes
and lockouts - Teachers. I. Skubick, Tim.
II. Green, Tom. III. Meek, Bill. IV. Schuster,
Gary.

Voice Lib.
M1610
bd.2
Skubick, Tim
Medina, Ernest
Michigan Public Broadcasting presents an
evening with Ernest Medina. With Tim
Skubick. Michigan Public Radio, December 10,
1973.
26 min. phonotape (1 r. 7 1/2 i.p.s.)

1. My Lai (4), Vietnam - Massacre, 1968.
2. Medina, Ernest. I. Skubick, Tim.

Voice Lib.
M1598
bd.2
Skubick, Tim
Romney, George W 1907-
Off the record. With Tim Skubick, Gary
Schuster, Tom Greene, and Bill Meek.
WKAR-TV, November 9, 1973.
20 min. phonotape (1 r. 7 1/2 in. per
sec.)

1. Michigan - Politics and government.
2. Detroit. I. Skubick, Tim. II. Schuster,
Gary. III. Greene, Tom. IV. Meek, Bill

Voice Lib.
M1606
bd.1
Skubick, Tim
Miller, James W
Off the record. Interviewed by Tim
Skubick, Gary Schuster, Tom Green, and
Bill Meek. WKAR-TV, February 8, 1974.
10 min. phonotape (1 r. 7 1/2 in. per
sec.)

1. Singer, Sidney. 2. Michigan. Civil
Service Commission. I. Skubick, Tim.
II. Schuster, Gary. III. Green, Tom.
IV. Meek, Bill.

Voice Lib.
M1605
bd.2
Skubick, Tim
Winograd, Morley
Off the record. With Tim Skubick, Tom
Greene, Gary Schuster, and Hugh Morgan.
WKAR-TV, February 15, 1974.
17 min. phonotape (1 r. 7 1/2 in. per sec.)

1. Democratic Party. Michigan. 2. Elections -
Michigan. 3. Youngblood, Charles N., 1932-
I. Skubick, Tim. II. Greene, Tom. III. Schuster,
Gary. IV. Morgan, Hugh.

Voice Lib.
M1601-
1602,
bd.1
Skubick, Tim
Milliken, William G., 1922-
An evening with the Governor. With Tim
Skubick. WKAR-TV, December 1973.
60 min. phonotape (2 r. 7 1/2 i.p.s.)

1. Michigan - Politics and government.
I. Skubick, Tim.

C1
S63
SLAVERY
Whorf, Michael, 1933-
Slaves.
1 tape cassette. (The visual sounds of
Mike Whorf. Social, S63)
Originally presented on his radio program, Kaleidoscope,
WJR, Detroit.
Duration: 39 min., 30 sec.
This presentation deals with one of man's most despicable
acts - that of making slaves of men. From time immemorial, to
the late 19th and early 20th century, man has placed his fellow
man in chains - and this is the story of slavery.

1. Slavery. I. Title.

Cl
863   Slaves
        Whorf, Michael, 1933-
        Slaves.
        1 tape cassette.   (The visual sounds of
        Mike Whorf. Social, S63)
        Originally presented on his radio program, Kaleidoscope,
        WJR, Detroit.
        Duration: 39 min., 30 sec.
        This presentation deals with one of man's most despicable
        acts – that of making slaves of men. From time immemorial, to
        the late 19th and early 20th century, man has placed his fellow
        man in chains – and this is the story of slavery.

        L Slavery. L Title.

Voice Lib.
M1800   Sloan, Hugh W., 1941?-
WG   Testimony before the Senate Committee
0606   investigating the Watergate Affair.
        Pacifica, June 6, 1973.
        261 min.   phonotape (4 r.   3 3/4 i.p.s.)
        (Watergate gavel to gavel, phase 1)

        1. Watergate Affair, 1972-

Voice Lib.
M1800   Sloan, Hugh W., 1941?-
WG   Testimony before the Senate Committee
0607.01 investigating the Watergate Affair.
        Pacifica, June 7, 1973.
        130 min.   phonotape (2 r.   3 3/4 i.p.s.)
        (Watergate gavel to gavel, phase 1)

        1. Watergate Affair, 1972-

            SMATHERS, GEORGE ARMISTEAD, 1913-
Voice Lib.
656   Kennedy, John Fitzgerald, Pres. U.S., 1917-1963.
bd.7   Press conference excerpt: anecdotes about
        Senator Smathers.   Columbia Records, Inc.,
        1962.
        1 reel (7 in.)   7 1/2 in. per sec.
        phonotape.

        1. Smathers, George Armistead, 1913-

Cl
529   A smile and a tear
        Whorf, Michael, 1933-
        A smile and a tear; tribute to the Irish.
        1 tape cassette.   (The visual sounds of
        Mike Whorf. Social, S29)
        Originally presented on his radio program, Kaleidoscope,
        WJR, Detroit.
        Duration: 44 min.
        Highlighting this program is a poignant reading of "The
        trimmins on the rosary" as the Visual Sounds presents the story
        of Ireland; its history, its people, its music, and the tale of
        St. Patrick.

        L Ireland. 2. National characteristics, Irish. L Title.

Voice Lib.
M1064   Smith, Alfred Emanuel, 1873-1944.
bd.1   Al Smith talking to children in the
        vicinity of Beekman Street hospital, New
        York, and distributing Christmas gifts.
        Fox Movietone, 1929.
        1 reel (7 in.)   7 1/2 in. per sec.
        phonotape.

Voice Lib.
540   Smith, Alfred Emanuel, 1873-1944.
bd.1   Christmas party at Beekman Street
        Hospital for children; gives presents to
        children.   Fox Movietone News, 1929.
        1 reel (7 in.)   7 1/2 in. per sec.
        phonotape.

Voice Lib.
M1064   Smith, Alfred Emanuel, 1873-1944.
bd.2   Excerpts of remarks of appreciation to
        Notre Dame University faculty and alumni
        for appearing at testimonial reception.
        Fox Movietone, 1929.
        1 reel (7 in.)   7 1/2 in. per sec.
        phonotape.

Voice Lib.
540   Smith, Alfred Emanuel, 1873-1944.
bd.2   Accepts honors from Notre Dame
        University at alumni meeting.   Fox
        Movietone, 1930.
        1 reel (7 in.)   7 1/2 in. per sec.
        phonotape.

Voice Lib.
197   Smith, Alfred Emanuel, 1873-1944.
bd.1   Neutrality, a speech before American
        Peace Union.   Detroit, WJR, October 1,
        1939.
        1 reel (7 in.)   7 1/2 in. per sec.
        phonotape.

Smith, Alfred Emanuel, 1873-1944

Voice Lib.
572-   I can hear it now (radio program)
573   1933-1946. CBS, 1948.
bd.1   2 reels (7 in.) 7 1/2 in. per sec.
        phonotape.
        L. Murrow, Edward Roscoe, 1908-1965. IL. LaGuardia, Fiorello
        Henry, 1882-1947. III. Chamberlain, Neville, 1869-1949. IV.
        Roosevelt, Franklin Delano, Pres. U. S., 1882-1945. V. Churchill,
        Winston Leonard Spencer, 1874-1965. VI. Gaulle, Charles de,
        Pres. France, 1890-1970. VII. Eisenhower, Dwight David, Pres. U. S.,
        1890-1969. VIII. Willkie, Wendell Lewis, 1892-1944. IX. Martin,
        Joseph William, 1884-1968. X. Elizabeth II, Queen of Great Britain,
        1926-   XI. Margaret Rose, Princess of Gt. Brit., 1930-   XII.
        Johnson, Hugh Samuel, 188?-1942. XIII. Smith, Alfred Emanuel,
        1873-1944. XIV. Lindbergh, Charles Augustus, 1902-   XV. Davis,

(Continued on next card)

Smith, Alfred Emanuel, 1873-1944

Voice Lib.
M289   Twentieth Century (Television program)
bd.2   Production on career of Alfred E. Smith.
        Various excerpts of addresses by Gov. Smith;
        recollections by Robert Moses on life of
        Gov. Smith; narration by Walter Cronkite;
        placing of Smith's name in nomination for
        President by F.D.R. CBS, 1962.
        1 reel (7 in.) 7 1/2 in. per sec.
        phonotape.
        L. Smith, Alfred Emanuel, 1873-1944. L. Smith, Alfred
        Emanuel, 1873-1944. IL. Moses, Robert, 1888-   III. Cronkite,
        Walter Leland, 1916-   IV. Roosevelt, Franklin Delano, Pres. U. S.,
        1882-1945.

SMITH, ALFRED EMANUEL, 1873-1944

Voice Lib.
M388-   The man from Oliver Street; story of Al Smith's life. Sings
399,   "The Bowery", describes himself as an American, reveals
bd.1   his feelings about the New Deal, at 1928 Democratic
        Convention, youth in New York City, prohibition, democracy,
        politics, acceptance speech for 1928 Democratic nomination,
        attempting to rent space in Empire State Building, action for
        better housing, sings "East side, west side". Hearst
        Metrotone News, 1962.
        2 reels (7 in.) 7 1/2 L. p. s. phonotape.

        L. Smith, Alfred Emanuel, 1873-1944.

Voice Lib.
M1595- Smith, Arthur James Marshall, 1902-
1996,   Arthur J. M. Smith reading his own poetry.
bd.1   MSU Voice Library, March 11, 1974.
        45 min. phonotape (2 r. 7 1/2 in. per sec.)

Voice Lib.
M1653   Smith, Arthur James Marshall, 1902-
        Purdy, Alan
        Reading from his book, Sex and death, and
        receiving the A.J.M. Smith Award ($350)
        given by MSU's Canadian-American Studies
        Division for the outstanding contribution
        to Canadian poetry for the year. With
        Victor Howard and A.J.M. Smith. Voice
        Library, May 1, 1974.
        1 hour. phonotape (1 r. 7 1/2 i.p.s.)

        I. Smith, Arthur James Marshall, 1902-
        II. Howard, Victor

Smith, Carlton

Voice Lib.
M830   Roosevelt, Franklin Delano, Pres. U. S., 1882-1945.
        Description of proceedings at Joint Session of Congress on
        December 8, 1941, prior to President's address asking for
        declaration of war; including news flashes by NBC correspondents
        Carlton Smith, Morgan Beatty, and Baukhage. NBC, December 8,
        1941.
        32 min. phonotape (1 r. 7 1/2 L.p.s.)

        L. World War, 1939-1945 - U.S. L. Smith, Carlton.
        IL. Beatty, Morgan. III. Baukhage, Hilmar Robert.

Smith, Cecil Michener, 1906-

Voice Lib.
M1291   Bergman, Ingrid, 1917-
bd.2   Conversation conducted by Cecil Smith,
        drama critic of Los Angeles Times, about
        her entire career and present activities.
        NET, December 3, 1967.
        1 reel (7 in.) 7 1/2 in. per sec.
        phonotape.

        I. Smith, Cecil Michener, 1906-

Voice Lib.
M1739   Smith, Dianna
bd.4   Interviews with John Voss and Derwood Boyd,
        county commissioners, who proposed cutting
        their salaries. WKAR, June 14, 1974.
        5 min. phonotape (1 r. 7 1/2 i.p.s.)

        1. County government. 2. County officials
        and employees - Salaries, allowance, etc.
        I. Voss, John. II. Boyd, Derwood.

Smith, Howard Kingsbury, 1914-

Voice Lib.
M1083   Analysis and criticism of President Kennedy's
bd.2   administration after a year and a half of
        its incumbency, by Howard K. Smith, Leon
        Keyserling, Roy Wilkins, Theodore Sorensen,
        and various economists, mostly adverse
        opinions; comparison to Wilson and FDR
        administrations. Bergman, July 25, 1962.
        1 reel (7 in.) 7 1/2 in. per sec. phonotape.
        L. Kennedy, John Fitzgerald, Pres. U. S., 1917-1963. L.
        Smith, Howard Kingsbury, 1914-   IL. Keyserling, Leon Hersch,
        1908-   III. Wilkins, Roy, 1901-   IV. Sorensen, Theodore
        Chaikin, 1928-

Voice Lib.
M1680   Smith, Howard Kingsbury, 1914-
        Speaking at MSU Mass Communications
        Colloquium. WKAR, April 7, 1967.
        50 min. phonotape (1 r. 7 1/2 i.p.s.)

        1. Vietnamese Conflict, 1961-   - U.S.
        2. U.S. - Politics and government - 1963-
        1969.

Voice Lib.
M1424 Smith, Howard Kingsbury, 1914-
Apollo 13 (space flight): oxygen malfunction
on Apollo 13 described by NASA, astronauts,
and Howard K. Smith. ABC TV, April 14, 1970.
1 reel (7 in.) 7 1/2 in. per sec.
phonotape.

1. Project Apollo. 2. Space flight to the
moon. 3. Haise, Fred W 1934- 4.
Lovell, James Arthur, 1928- 5. Swigert,
John L 1932- I. Haise, Fred W 1934-
II. Lovell, James Arthur, 1928- III. Swigert,
John L 1932- IV. Smith, Howard Kingsbury,
1914-

Voice Lib.
M1421 Smith, Howard Kingsbury, 1914-
Comments by Howard K. Smith and guests
regarding Nixon's press conference.
ABC-TV, May 8, 1970.
1 reel (7 in.) 7 1/2 in. per sec.
phonotape.

1. Nixon, Richard Milhous, Pres. U.S.,
1913-

Smith, Howard Kingsbury, 1914-
Voice Lib.
573 I can hear it now (radio program)
bd.2- 1945-1949. CBS, 1950?
574 2 reels (7 in.) 7 1/2 in. per sec.
bd.1 phonotape.
L. Murrow, Edward Roscoe, 1908-1965. IL. Nehru, Jawaharlal,
1889-1964. III. Philip, duke of Edinburgh, 1921- IV. Elizabeth II,
Queen of Great Britain, 1926- V. Ferguson, Homer, 1889- VL
Hughes, Howard Robard, 1905- VII. Marshall, George Catlett,
1880- VIII. Ruth, George Herman, 1895-1948. IX. Lilienthal,
David Eli, 1899- X. Trout, Robert, 1908- XL Gage, Arthur.
XII. Jackson, Robert Houghwout, 1892-1954. XIII. Gromyko, Ana-
toili Andreevich, 1908- XIV. Baruch, Bernard Mannes, 1870-
1965. XV. Churchill, Wi... Leonard Spencer, 1874-1965. XVL
Winchell, Walter, 1897-1... XVII. Davis, Elmer Holmes, 1890-
(Continued on next card)

Smith, Howard Kingsbury, 1914-
Voice Lib.
M1454 Nixon, Richard Milhous, Pres. U.S., 1913-
bd.1 Discussion of U.S. foreign policy with
network newscasters Eric Sevareid (CBS),
John Chancellor (NBC), and Howard K. Smith
(ABC).
1 reel (7 in.) 7 1/2 in. per sec.
phonotape.

I. Sevareid, Arnold Eric, 1912- II.
Chancellor, John William, 1927- III.
Smith, Howard Kingsbury, 1914-

C1 SMITH, JOHN, 1580-1631
H7 Whorf, Michael, 1933-
John Smith's great lady.
1 tape cassette. (The visual sounds of
Mike Whorf. History and heritage, H7)
Originally presented on his radio program, Kaleidoscope,
WJR, Detroit.
Duration: 29 min., 30 sec.
It is one of America's first romantic histories, fired by an
adventurous spirit of a man and the inner courage of a woman.

L. Pocahontas, d. 1617. 2. Smith, John, 1580-1631.
L. Title.

Voice Lib.
M1047 Smith, Kate, 1909-
Old-time radio excerpts of the 1930's and
1940's, including: Rudy Vallee singing
"Linger a little longer"; Will Rogers on
panaceas for the Depression; Bing Crosby
singing "Sweet Georgia Brown"; Eddie Cantor;
Jimmy Durante singing "Inka-dinka-do";
musical skit by Clayton, Jackson and Durante;
wit by Harry Hershfield; musical selection
"Thinking of you" by Kay Kyser; Kate Smith
singing theme song, "When the moon comes over
the mountain"; W.C. Fields' temperance

(Continued on next card)

Voice Lib. Smith, Kate, 1909-
M1047 Old-time radio excerpts of the 1930's and
1940's... (Card 2)
lecture; Al Jolson singing "Rocka-by-your
baby"; and George Burns and Gracie Allen
skit. TV&R, 1930's and 1940's.
1 reel (7 in.) 7 1/2 in. per sec.
L. Vallee, Rudy, 1901- IL. Rogers, Will, 1879-1935. III.
Crosby, Bing, 1901- IV. Cantor, Eddie, 1893-1964. V. Durante,
Jimmy, 1893- VL. Clayton, Patti VII. Jackson,
Eddie VIII. Hershfield, Harry, 1885- IX. Kyser, Kay,
1906- X. Smith, Kate, 1909- XL. Fields, W.C., 1879-
1946. XII. Jolson, Al, 1886-1950. XIII. Burns, George, 1896-
XIV. Allen, Gracie, 1906-

Voice Lib.
M711 Smith, Kate, 1909-
bd.3 "The Kate Smith Show"; TV variety show.
Melchior collection, December 28, 1950.
1 reel (7 in.) 7 1/2 in. per sec.
phonotape.

Voice Lib.
M160 Smith, Kate, 1909-
bd.3 Singing Irving Berlin's composition "God
Bless America", with commentary, from
Carnegie Hall, New York. RCA, November 2,
1963.
1 reel (7 in.) 7 1/2 in. per sec.
phonotape.

I. Title: God bless America.

Voice Lib.
M160 Smith, Kate, 1909-
bd.4 Singing her theme song "When the Moon
Comes Over the Mountain", and remarks by
Kate Smith at Carnegie Hall, New York.
RCA, November 2, 1963.
1 reel (7 in.) 7 1/2 in. per sec.
phonotape.

I. Title: When the moon comes over the
mountain.

Smith, Merriman

Voice Lib.
M1407 Eisenhower, David, 1949-
Conversation on "Merv Griffin Show" between Merv, Merriman Smith, David Eisenhower, Tricia Nixon. Various anecdotes about Merriman Smith's career as a White House correspondent during four administrations. CBS-TV, November 23, 1969.
1 reel (7 in.) 7 1/2 in. per sec. phonotape.

I. Griffin, Mervyn Edward, 1925- II. Smith, Merriman III. Cox, Patricia (Nixon) 1947-

---

Smith, Merriman

Voice Lib.
M1369 "The men who covered Ike". CBS-TV Face the Nation program,
bd. 2 discussing the late General Dwight David Eisenhower, by the newspaper and TV correspondents. UPI, Merriman Smith; Newsweek, Kenneth Crawford; Chicago Daily News, Peter Lisager; AP, Jack Bell; CBS, George Herman, acting as emcee. CBS-TV, March 30, 1969.
1 reel (7 in.) 7 1/2 l.p.s. phonotape.

I. Eisenhower, Dwight David, Pres. U.S., 1890-1969. I. Smith, Merriman. II. Crawford, Kenneth. III. Lisager, Peter. IV. Bell, Jack. V. Herman, George.

Smith, "Whispering Jack"

Voice Lib.
M617 Radio in the 1920's: a series of excerpts
bd.1- from important broadcasts of the 1920's,
bd.25 with brief prologue and epilogue; a sample of radio of the period. NVL, April, 1964.
1 reel (7 in.) 7 1/2 in. per sec. phonotape.
I. Radio programs. I. Marconi, Guglielmo, marchese, 1874-1937. II. Kendall, H G III. Coolidge, Calvin, Pres. U.S., 1872-1933. IV. Wilson, Woodrow, Pres. U.S., 1856-1924. V. Roosevelt, Franklin Delano, Pres. U.S., 1882-1945. VI. Lodge, Henry Cabot, 1850-1924. VII. LaGuardia, Fiorello Henry, 1882-1947. VIII. The Happiness Boys (Radio program) IX. Gallagher and Sheen. X. Barney Google. XI. Vallee, Rudy, 1901- XII. The two
(Continued on next card)

Smith, "Wonderful"

Voice Lib.
M622 Radio in the 1940's (Part III): a series of
bd.1- excerpts from important broadcasts of the 1940's; a sample
bd.15 of radio of the period. NVL, April, 1964.
1 reel (7 in.) 7 1/2 in. per sec. phonotape.
I. Radio programs. I. Miller, Alton Glenn, 1909(?)-1944. II. Diles, Ken III. Wilson, Donald Harlow, 1900- IV. Livingstone, Mary V. Benny, Jack, 1894- VI. Harris, Phil VII. Merman, Ethel, 1909- VIII. Smith, "Wonderful" IX. Bennett, Richard Dyer X. Louis, Joe, 1914- XI. Eisenhower, Dwight David, Pres. U.S., 1890-1969. XII. MacArthur, Douglas, 1880-1964. XIII. Romulo, Carlos Pena, 1899- XIV. Welles, Orson, 1915- XV. Jackson, Robert Houghwout, 1892-1954. XVI. LaGuardia, Fiorello Henry, 1882-1945. XVII. Nehru, Jawaharlal, 1889-1964. XVIII. Gandhi, Mohandas Karamchand, 1869-1948.

Snake

Voice Lib.
181 Steinbeck, John, 1902-1968.
bd.1 Reading his short story, "Snake," and reviewing public reaction. CRI, 1947.
1 reel (7 in.) 7 1/2 in. per sec. phonotape.

I. Title: Snake.

Snider's Vinegar, Inc.

Voice Lib.
327 Sandburg, Carl, 1878-1967.
bd.2 Reading his work in prose, "Snider's Vinegar, Inc.". From private collection, 1942.
1 reel (7 in.) 7 1/2 in. per sec. phonotape.

I. Title: Snider's Vinegar, Inc.

Voice Lib.
M794 Snyder, Gary
Professor of English at Berkeley, a Zen Buddhist monk, reading his own poetry. Carlos Hagen, 1964.
1 reel (7 in.) 7 1/2 in. per sec. phonotape.

So this is the little lady who started a war

C1
A18 Whorf, Michael, 1933-
So this is the little lady who started a war.
1 tape cassette. (The visual sounds of Mike Whorf. Art, music, and letters, A18)
Originally presented on his radio program, Kaleidoscope, WJR, Detroit.
Duration: 45 min.
Harriet Beecher Stowe's "Uncle Tom's cabin" certainly had its effect on the nation, causing such a division of emotion and belief that the country fought a war.

I. Stowe, Harriet Elizabeth (Beecher) 1811-1896. I. Title.

Voice Lib. SOCIAL SCIENCES
M1639 Boulding, Kenneth Ewart, 1910-
Cautious change, or how to prepare for the next fifty years. WKAR-AM, February 17, 1974.
55 min. phonotape (1 r. 7 1/2 i.p.s.)

Includes question and answer period.

1. Ecology. 2. Social sciences.

SOCIALISM

Voice Lib.
395 Debs, Eugene Victor, 1855-1926.
bd. 1 The Socialist movement. Edison cylinder recording, 1904.
1 reel (7 in.) 7 1/2 in. per sec. phonotape.

1. Socialism.

SOCIALISM IN CHILE

Voice Lib.
M1744 Allende Gossens, Salvador, 1908-1973.
bd.4 Interview with John Wallach. WKAR,
August, 1973.
2 min., 40 sec. phonotape (1 r. 7 1/2
i.p.s.)

Wallach in turn was interviewed by Rich Adams.

1. Chile - Pol & govt. 2. Socialism in
Chile. 3. Allende Gossens, Salvador, 1908-
1973. I. Wallach, John. II. Adams, Rich.

SOCRATES

C1
S68 Whorf, Michael, 1933-
Statesmen and sages; Demosthenes, Aristotle,
Socrates, Cicero.
1 tape cassette. (The visual sounds of Mike Whorf. Social, S68)

Originally presented on his radio program, Kaleidoscope,
WJR, Detroit.
Duration: 36 min.
As ancient Greece and Rome served as the cradle of our modern
democracy, so do their citizens serve as shining examples of wisdom
and statecraft for us today.

1. Demosthenes. 2. Aristoteles. 3. Socrates. 4. Cicero,
Marcus Tullius. I. Title.

Solomon, Douglas S.

Voice Lib.
M1724 Morris, Clyde D   J
bd.1 Next steps to control the military; part
of the MSU Moratorium against the War -
introduces a slogan and a song, sung by
Ruth Knapp, Doug Solomon, and Phyllis Hart.
WKAR, October 15, 1969.
15 min. phonotape (1 r. 7 1/2 i.p.s.)

1. Vietnamese Conflict, 1961-   - U.S.
I. Knapp, Ruth. II. Solomon, Douglas S.

III. Hart, Phyllis.

Voice Lib.
M1368 Some friends of General Eisenhower (TV program)
CBS-TV special recalling anecdotes about
General Eisenhower by some of his friends:
Bob Hope, Kevin McCann, General Omar Bradley,
Robert B. Anderson, General Alfred Gruenther,
with Walter Cronkite acting as emcee. CBS-TV,
March 29, 1969.
1 reel (7 in.) 7 1/2 in. per sec.

1. Eisenhower, Dwight David, Pres. U.S., 1890-1969. I.
Hope, Bob, 1903-   II. McCann, Kevin   III. Bradley, Omar
Nelson, 1893-   IV. Anderson, Robert Bernerd, 1910-   V.
Gruenther, Alfred Maximilian, 1899-   VI. Cronkite, Walter
Leland, 1916-

Some lessons in history

C1
S13 Whorf, Michael, 1933-
Some lessons in history.
1 tape cassette. (The visual sounds of
Mike Whorf. Social, S13)

Originally presented on his radio program, Kaleidoscope,
WJR, Detroit.
Duration: 41 min., 10 sec.
Here is a detailed account of the contributions of the Black
American.

1. Negroes - U.S. I. Title.

Some of these days

Voice Lib.
M1100 Tucker, Sophie, 1884-1966.
bd.5 Singing her well-known number, "Some of
These Days". Forrest, 1928.
1 reel (7 in.) 7 1/2 in. per sec.
phonotape.

I. Title: Some of these days.

Songbook of the old world

C1
M26 Whorf, Michael, 1933-
Songbook of the old world; traditional and
folk songs.
1 tape cassette. (The visual sounds of
Mike Whorf. Miscellaneous, M26)

Originally presented on his radio program, Kaleidoscope,
WJR, Detroit.
Duration: 57 min.
A look at European music and the influence it has had on
the American song.

1. Music, European. I. Title.

Songbook of the Old World

C1
PWM10 Whorf, Michael, 1933-
Songbook of the Old World.
1 tape cassette. (The visual sounds of
Mike Whorf. Panorama; a world of music,
PWM-10)

Originally presented on his radio program, Kaleidoscope,
WJR, Detroit.
Duration: 25 min., 50 sec.
With many musical examples, here we have the influence
of other lands on the American folk song.

1. Folk-songs. I. Title.

SONGS, AMERICAN

C1
M29 Whorf, Michael, 1933-
They don't write 'em like that anymore.
1 tape cassette. (The visual sounds of
Mike Whorf. Miscellaneous, M29)

Originally presented on his radio program, Kaleidoscope,
WJR, Detroit.
Duration: 54 min., 30 sec.
Gerald Marks tells the story of some of America's favorite
melodies.

1. Songs, American. 2. Music, Popular (Songs, etc.) - U.S.
I. Marks, Gerald. II. Title.

SONGS, GERMAN

Voice Lib.
M1004 Hitler youth fight song, entitled "Vorwärts".
bd.2 Peteler, 1935.
1 reel (7 in.) 7 1/2 in. per sec.
phonotape.

1. Songs, German. I. Title: Vorwärts.

SONGS, GERMAN
Voice Lib.
M1007   Nazi Hitler Youth fight song, "Es zittern
bd.2   die marschen Knochen".   Various stanzas
          of song, "Today we have Germany, tomorrow
          the entire world..." Peteler, April 30,
          1935.
          1 reel (7 in.)   7 1/2 i.p.s.   phonotape.

          1. Songs, German.

SONGS, GERMAN
Voice Lib.
M1007   Nazi Hitler Youth marching song entitled
bd.3   "Youth Marching for Germany".   Peteler,
          April 30, 1935.
          1 reel (7 in.)   7 1/2 in. per sec.
          phonotape.

SONGS, GERMAN
Voice Lib.
M1004   Nazi May Day ceremonies. Male choir singing
bd.3-B   (3 stanzas) of song "Wir glauben an die
          neue Zeit". Peteler, May 1, 1935.
          1 reel (7 in.)   7 1/2 i.p.s.   phonotape.

          1. Songs, German.   I. Title: Wir glauben
          an die neue Zeit.

SONGS, GERMAN
Voice Lib.
M1018   Nazi propaganda song; three stanzas of song
bd.6   ridiculing Neville Chamberlain.   Peteler
          1 reel (7 in.)   7 1/2 in. per sec.
          phonotape.

C1   Songs my father taught me
PMW18   Whorf, Michael, 1933-
          Songs my father taught me.
          1 tape cassette. (The visual sounds of
          Mike Whorf. Panorama; a world of music, PMW-18)
          Originally presented on his radio program, Kaleidoscope,
          WJR, Detroit.
          Duration: 25 min.
          Mr. Whorf recounts his father's love for popular American
          music.

          1. Music, Popular (Songs, etc.) - U.S.   1. Title.

Voice Lib.   Sorensen, Theodore Chaikin, 1928-
M1083   Analysis and criticism of President Kennedy's
bd.2   administration after a year and a half of
          its incumbency, by Howard K. Smith, Leon
          Keyserling, Roy Wilkins, Theodore Sorensen,
          and various economists, mostly adverse
          opinions; comparison to Wilson and FDR
          administrations.   Bergman, July 25, 1962.
          1 reel (7 in.) 7 1/2 per sec. phonotape.
          1. Kennedy, John Fitzgerald, Pres. U.S., 1917-1963. I.
          Smith, Howard Kingsbury, 1914-   II. Keyserling, Leon Hersch,
          1908-   III. Wilkins, Roy, 1901-   IV. Sorensen, Theodore
          Chaikin, 1928-

Voice Lib.   Sothern, Edward Askew, 1826-1881
M225   Packard, Frederick
          Styles in Shakespearean acting, 1890-1950.
          Creative Associates, 1963?
          1 reel (7 in.) 7 1/2 i.p.s. phonotape.

          1. Sothern, Edward Askew, 1826-1881. II. Marlowe,
          Julia, 1865-1950. III. Booth, Edwin, 1833-1893. IV. Gielgud,
          John, 1904-   V. Robeson, Paul Bustill, 1898-   VI. Terry,
          Dame Ellen, 1848-1928. VII. Allen, Viola. VIII. Welles,
          Orson, 1915-   IX. Skinner, Otis, 1858-1942. X. Barrymore,
          John, 1882-1942. XI. Forbes-Robertson, Sir Johnston, 1853- XIII. Evans,
          XII. Forbes-Robertson, Sir Johnston, 1853-   XIII. Evans,
          Maurice. XIV. Thorndike, Dame Sybil, 1882-   XV. Robson,
          Flora. XVI. LeGallienne, Eva, 1899-   XVII. Anderson,
          Judith. XVIII. Duncan, Augustin. XIX. Hampden, Walter.
          XX. Speaight, Robert, 1904-   XXI. Jones, Daniel.

Voice Lib.   Sound track
M764   Hammerstein, Oscar, 1895-1960.
bd.2   Excerpt from "Sound Track" (Program 7);
          comments on what happened when there was
          drop in popularity of Broadway in '30's.
          Westinghouse Broadcasting Corporation, 1964.
          19 sec.   phonotape (1 r.   7 1/2 i.p.s.)
          (The music goes round and round)

          I. Title: Sound track. II. Series.

Sound track
Voice Lib.
M764   Harbach, Otto Abels, 1873-1963.
bd.1   Excerpt from "Sound Track" (Program 7);
          comments on filmdom's first encounter with
          sound tracks; also explains what he feels
          was wrong with the first movie musicals.
          Westinghouse Broadcasting Corporation, 1964.
          1 reel (7 in.)   7 1/2 in. per sec.
          phonotape. (The Music Goes Round and Round)

          I. Title: Sound track. II. Series.

Voice Lib. Sound track
M764   Harburg, Edgar Y   1896-
bd.3   Excerpts from "Sound Track" (Program 7);
          comments on his feelings toward the musical
          efforts of the 30's. Including example
          of movie music: "Over the rainbow", with
          Judy Garland; lyrics by Harburg. Westing-
          house Broadcasting Corporation, 1964.
          3 min., 58 sec.   phonotape (1 r.   7 1/2
          i.p.s.) (The music goes round and round)
          1. Music, Popular (Songs, etc.) - U.S. 1. Garland,
          Judy, 1922-1969. II. Title: Sound track. III. Series.

Voice Lib.   Sound track
M763   McClelland, Douglas
bd.8   Excerpt from "Sound Track" (Program 7);
       comments how music was used in the production
       of the movie even before the advent of sound;
       on the role of the audience in accepting the
       movies; early stages of sound; the sound
       track album. Westinghouse Broadcasting
       Corporation, 1964.
          1 reel (7 in.)   7 1/2 in. per sec.
       phonotape. (The Music Goes Round and Round)

          I. Title: Sound track. II. Series.

Voice Lib.   Sound track
M763   Perado, Al
bd.7   Excerpt from "Sound track" (Program 7);
       discusses importance of music in bringing
       out emotions of actors. Westinghouse
       Broadcasting Corporation, 1964.
          1 min., 10 sec.   phonotape (1 r.
       7 1/2 i.p.s.) (The music goes round and
       round)

          I. Title: Sound track. II. Series.

Voice Lib.   Sound track
M764   Bobbins, Oscar, 1912-1965.
bd.5   Excerpt from "Sound Track" (Program 7);
       gives his reasons for the apparent dearth
       of initiative from Hollywood which is so
       famous for originality and innovation.
       Westinghouse Broadcasting Corporation, 1964.
          1 reel (7 in.)   7 1/2 in. per sec.
       phonotape. (The Music Goes Round and Round)

          I. Title: Sound track. II. Series.

Voice Lib.   Sound track
M764   Waxman, Frank
bd.4   Excerpt from "Sound Track" (Program 7);
       comments on where the new group of composers
       came from besides Broadway. Westinghouse
       Broadcasting Corporation, 1964.
          1 min., 5 sec.   phonotape (1 r.
       7 1/2 i.p.s.) (The music goes round and round)

          I. Music, Popular (Songs, etc.) -
       Writing and publishing. I. Title: Sound
       track. II. Series.

Voice Lib.
M1096 Sousa, John Philip, 1854-1932.
bd.2   Sousa's band playing his own march,
       "Stars and Stripes Forever". Victor,
       1920.
          1 reel (7 in.)   7 1/2 in. per sec.
       phonotape.

          I. Title: Stars and stripes forever.

Voice Lib.
M1095 Sousa, John Philip, 1854-1932.
bd.3   Sousa's band playing "Under the Double
       Eagle March". Victor, 1920.
          1 reel (7 in.)   7 1/2 in. per sec.
       phonotape.

          I. Title: Under the double eagle march.

C1   SOUSA, JOHN PHILIP, 1854-1932
M22   Whorf, Michael, 1933-
          A blare of bugles and a ruffle of drums.
          1 tape cassette. (The visual sounds of
       Mike Whorf. Miscellaneous, M22)

       Originally presented on his radio program, Kaleidoscope,
       WJR, Detroit.
       Duration: 39 min., 30 sec.
       He was called the "march king" and indeed he was, for
       John Philip Sousa gave the world hundreds of stirring melodies.

          I. Sousa, John Philip, 1854-1932. I. Title.

C1   SOUSA, JOHN PHILIP, 1854-1932
PWM20 Whorf, Michael, 1933-
          Blare of bugles, ruffle of drums.
          1 tape cassette. (The visual sounds of
       Mike Whorf. Panorama; a world of music,
       PWM-20)

       Originally presented on his radio program, Kaleidoscope,
       WJR, Detroit.
       Duration: 28 min.
       The life and times of John Philip Sousa, with excerpts of
       his music.

          I. Sousa, John Philip, 1854-1932. I. Title.

              SOUTH AFRICA - RACE QUESTION
Voice Lib.
M740   Cronkite, Walter Leland, 1916-
bd.3   Excerpt from "20th Century" TV program on
       race conditions in South Africa. Description
       of Sharpville riots and about the awarding
       of Nobel Peace Prize to Chief Luthuli.
       CBS, 1961.
          5 min., 16 sec.   phonotape (1 r.
       7 1/2 i.p.s.)

          1. South Africa - Race question.

              SOUTH POLE
Voice Lib.
M975   Shackleton, Sir Ernest Henry, 1874-1922.
bd.8   Description of a dash for the South Pole.
       Rococo-Can., 1909.
          1 reel (7 in.)   7 1/2 i.p.s.   phonotape.

          1. South Pole.

Voice Lib.
M876- SOUTHERN STATES - CIVILIZATION
877 American mood series (Radio program)
The Southern moderate: the South as seen
through the eyes of a Canadian, John David
Hamilton. The case of the white moderate;
statements by moderate whites about the racial
situation; sentiments about Negroes by Atlanta,
Georgia newspapermen; appreciation of South-
erners' way of life. New Orleans historian's
appraisal of economic conditions in Louisiana.
Mississippi Chamber of Commerce manager eval-
uating situation in Mississippi. Oldtime
justice described by South Carolina citizen.
(Continued on next card)

Voice Lib.
M876- SOUTHERN STATES - CIVILIZATION
877 American mood series (Radio program) The
Southern moderate... 1963. (Card 2)

Mississippi's concealed weapons law; opinions
on violence; discussion of white supremacy
in intellect and education; protests about
taxes to aid colored relief; pro and con
opinions about Negroes' rights from Louisianans
and Georgians. CBC Radio, 1963.
2 reels (7 in.) 7 1/2 in. per sec.
phonotape.
1. Southern states - Civilization. I.
Hamilton, John David II. Project '64.

Voice Lib.
M1076 Spaak, Paul Henri Charles, 1899-1972.
Convocation of representatives of twenty
nations on the requirements for peace, held
at General Assembly hall of the United
Nations; discussion of Pope John XXIII
encyclical; Germany's re-unification, etc.,
under auspices of Center for Democratic
Institutions. CSDI, February, 1965.
1 reel (7 in.) 7 1/2 in. per sec.
phonotape.

1. Peace.

Voice Lib.
M847 SPACE FLIGHT
bd.1 Cronkite, Walter Leland, 1914-
Description of launching of Agena spacecraft at 10:04 a.m. Monday, October 25, 1965,
at Cape Kennedy, Florida, until its func-
tional failure. Announcements by Jack King
at Cape Kennedy and Paul Haney at Houston
space center; scrubbing of Gemini VI
launching. CBS-TV, October 25, 1965.
18 min. phonotape (1 r. 7 1/2 i.p.s.)

1. Space flight. I. Project Gemini.

Voice Lib.
M345 SPACE FLIGHT
Eisenhower, Dwight David, Pres. U.S., 1890-
1969.
Discussion, with scientists, of Explorer
III imperfect orbit and space exploration.
CBS, March 26, 1958.
1 reel (7 in.) 7 1/2 i.p.s. phonotape.

1. Space flight.

Voice Lib.
M103- SPACE FLIGHT
109 Glenn, John Herschel, 1921-
The John Glenn story (America's first manned orbital flight).
NBC-TV, February, 1962.
7 reels (7 in.) 7 1/2 i.p.s. phonotape.

CONTENTS. -103, bd. 1. Pre-flight interview. -103, bd. 2.
Preparation at Cape Canaveral. -103, bd. 3. Countdown, delay. -
103, bd. 4. Description of rocket. -103, bd. 5. Excitement at ocean
front. -103, bd. 6. Description of takeoff. -103, bd. 7. Glenn's
first report. -104, bd. 1. Explanation of technical terms. -104, bd. 2.
Glenn's first attempt at food. -104, bd. 3. Glenn observes lights in
Australia. -104, bd. 4. Flash to New Concord, Ohio. -104, bd. 5.
Mercury Control relays reports. -104, bd. 6. Flying by wire, 2d
orbit. -104, bd. 7. Glenn speaks to Canaveral. -105, bd. 1. Spacecraft committed to 3d orbit. -105, bd. 2. Reaction from Moscow. -
(Continued on next card)

Voice Lib.
M103- SPACE FLIGHT
109 Glenn, John Herschel, 1921- The John Glenn story ...
1962. (Card 2)

CONTENTS (Cont'd) 105, bd. 3. Description, view and technical
data. -105, bd. 4. Retro rockets fired. -105, bd.5. Capsule's
chutes have opened. -105, bd. 6. Capsule in water, 4 hr. 56 min.
26 sec. -106, bd. 1. Glenn on deck U.S.S. Noa. -106, bd. 2.
Pres. Kennedy speaks. -106, bd. 3. Glenn's parents in New
Concord, Ohio. -106, bd. 4. Glenn's wife in Arlington, Va. -
106, bd. 5. Canaveral reception 2/23/62. -106, bd. 6. Vice-
Pres. Johnson, Glenn decorated. -107, bd. 1. JFK lauds Glenn
and Gilruth. -107, bd. 2. Glenn shows capsule to guests. -107,
bd. 3. The press conference. -108, bd. 1. Press conference continued.

(Continued on next card)

Voice Lib.
M103- SPACE FLIGHT
109 Glenn, John Herschel, 1921- The John Glenn story ...
1962. (Card 3)

CONTENTS (Cont'd) 108, bd. 2. Washington ceremonies. -
108, bd. 3. Parade from White House to Capitol. -108, bd. 4.
Glenn speaks to Congress. -109, bd. 1. Glenn speaks to Congress. -
109, bd. 2. Big parade in New York. -109, bd. 3. Ceremonies at
New York City Hall. -109, bd. 4. Boy Scouts ceremonies. -109,
bd. 5. The Waldorf dinner speeches. -109, bd. 6. Mayor Wagner
and Glenn speeches.

1. Space flight. 2. Glenn, John Herschel, 1921-

Voice Lib.
351 SPACE FLIGHT
bd.6 Glenn, John Herschel, 1921-
Before House Space Committee, describing
his space flight before Senate Space Committee,
reviewing public acclaim, describing his
philosophy of life; before U.N. on world
co-operation in space flight. CBS, February
27-28, March 2, 1962.
1 reel (7 in.) 7 1/2 in. per sec.
phonotape.

1. Space flight.

Voice Lib.
M1577 SPACE FLIGHT TO THE MOON
bd.1 Apollo 10 (space flight): lift-off. Commentary
by NBC TV news; countdown, lift-off. Astronauts Tom Stafford, John Young, Eugene Cernan.
NBC TV, May 18, 1969.
1 reel (7 in.) 7 1/2 in. per sec.
phonotape.
1. Project Apollo. 2. Space flight to the
moon. 3. Stafford, Thomas F 1931- 4.
Young, John Watts, 1930- 5. Cernan, Eugene
Andrew, 1934- I. Stafford, Thomas F 1931-
II. Young, John Watts, 1930- III. Cernan,
Eugene Andrew, 1934-

SPACE FLIGHT TO THE MOON

Voice Lib.
M1377 Apollo 10 (space flight): television pictures.
bd.2   Commentary from astronauts, NBC TV, on
         initial separation and docking of Lunar
         Landing Module, first live color television
         pictures from space, and pictures of the
         earth from 6,500 nautical miles out.   NBC
         TV, May, 1969.
         1 reel (7 in.) 7 1/2 in. per sec. phonotape.
         1. Project Apollo. 2. Space flight to the moon. 3. Stafford,
         Thomas P 1931- 4. Young, John Watts, 1930- 5.
         Cernan, Eugene Andrew, 1934- I. Stafford, Thomas P
         1931- II. Young, John Watts, 1930- III. Cernan, Eugene
         Andrew, 1934-

SPACE FLIGHT TO THE MOON

Voice Lib.
M1377 Apollo 10 (space flight): splashdown and
bd.3   recovery of Apollo 10; astronauts' first
         words after returning to earth; from the
         recovery ship U.S.S. "Princeton".   CBS TV,
         May 26, 1969.
         1 reel (7 in.)   7 1/2 in. per sec.
         phonotape.
         1. Project Apollo. 2. Space flight to the moon. 3. Stafford,
         Thomas P 1931- 4. Young, John Watts, 1930- 5.
         Cernan, Eugene Andrew, 1934- I. Stafford, Thomas P
         1931- II. Young, John Watts, 1930- III. Cernan, Eugene
         Andrew, 1934-

SPACE FLIGHT TO THE MOON

Voice Lib.
M1384 Apollo 11 (space flight): launch day, July 16,
bd.1   1969. Description of astronauts going up
         the elevator; conversation between Walter
         Cronkite and Walter Schirra at approximately
         2 hours before launch. CBS TV, July 16, 1969.
         1 reel (7 in.)   7 1/2 in. per sec.
         phonotape.
         1. Project Apollo. 2. Space flight to the moon. 3. Aldrin,
         Edwin E   1930- 4. Collins, Michael, 1930- 5. Armstrong,
         Neil, 1930- I. Aldrin, Edwin E   1930- II. Collins,
         Michael, 1930- III. Armstrong, Neil, 1930- IV. Cronkite,
         Walter Leland, 1916- V. Schirra, Walter Marty, 1923-

SPACE FLIGHT TO THE MOON

Voice Lib.
M1384 Apollo 11 (space flight): biographical sketches
bd.2   of the three astronauts, Edwin Aldrin,
         Michael Collins, and Neil Armstrong, by Chet
         Huntley, at approximately 78 minutes before
         launch time. NBC TV, July 16, 1969.
         1 reel (7 in.)   7 1/2 in. per sec.
         phonotape.
         1. Project Apollo. 2. Space flight to the moon. 3. Aldrin,
         Edwin E   1930- 4. Collins, Michael, 1930- 5. Armstrong,
         Neil, 1930- I. Aldrin, Edwin E   1930- II. Collins,
         Michael, 1930- III. Armstrong, Neil, 1930- IV. Huntley,
         Chet, 1911-1974.

SPACE FLIGHT TO THE MOON

Voice Lib.
M1384 Apollo 11 (space flight): Frank McGee giving
bd.3   an itinerary of space ships, dates, times,
         etc. NBC TV, July 16, 1969.
         1 reel (7 in.)   7 1/2 in. per sec.
         phonotape.
         1. Project Apollo. 2. Space flight to the
         moon. 3. Aldrin, Edwin E   1930-   4.
         Collins, Michael, 1930-   5. Armstrong, Neil,
         1930-   I. Aldrin, Edwin E   1930-   II.
         Collins, Michael, 1930-   III. Armstrong, Neil,
         1930-   IV. McGee, Frank, 1921-1974.

SPACE FLIGHT TO THE MOON

Voice Lib.
M1384 Apollo 11 (space flight): launch day progress
bd.6   of countdown by Apollo 11 control at 4
         minutes 15 seconds to actual take-off.
         Houston takes over and describes progress
         up to 1,000 miles downrange and successful
         orbit.   NBC TV, July 16, 1969.
         1 reel (7 in.)   7 1/2 in. per sec.
         phonotape.
         1. Project Apollo. 2. Space flight to the moon. 3. Aldrin,
         Edwin E   1930- 4. Collins, Michael, 1930- 5. Armstrong,
         Neil, 1930- I. Aldrin, Edwin E   1930- II. Collins,
         Michael, 1930- III. Armstrong, Neil, 1930-

SPACE FLIGHT TO THE MOON

Voice Lib.
M1385 Apollo 11 (space flight): Frank McGee speaking
bd.1   about communications between "Eagle" and
         ground. Conversation between Houston and
         astronauts. Message of "Go for PDI"; "The
         Eagle has landed" (102 hours, 45 minutes,
         40 seconds) Description of rocks and
         boulders on moon.   NBC TV, July 20, 1969.
         1 reel (7 in.) 7 1/2 in. per sec. phonotape.
         1. Project Apollo. 2. Space flight to the moon. 3. Aldrin,
         Edwin E   1930- 4. Collins, Michael, 1930- 5.
         Armstrong, Neil, 1930- I. Aldrin, Edwin E   1930-
         II. Collins, Michael, 1930- III. Armstrong, Neil, 1930-
         IV. McGee, Frank, 1921-1974.

SPACE FLIGHT TO THE MOON

Voice Lib.
M1385 Apollo 11 (space flight): Neil Armstrong
bd.2   requesting everyone everywhere to pause and
         give thanks. Preparing to open hatch and
         walk on the moon. Armstrong backing out
         from hatch, describing lunar surface. "One
         small step for man, one giant step for man-
         kind" (109 hours, 24 minutes, 20 seconds.)
         Bringing down cameras. CBS TV, July 20, 1969.
         1 reel (7 in.) 7 1/2 in. per sec. phonotape.
         1. Project Apollo. 2. Space flight to the moon. 3. Aldrin,
         Edwin E   1930- 4. Collins, Michael, 1930- 5. Armstrong,
         Neil, 1930- I. Aldrin, Edwin E   1930- II. Collins, Michael,
         1930- III. Armstrong, Neil, 1930-

SPACE FLIGHT TO THE MOON

Voice Lib.
M1386 Apollo 11 (space flight): conversation with
bd.1   broadcasters Walter Cronkite and Wally
         Schirra. Including Armstrong's activities
         on moon alone; pictures, rock descriptions,
         then Aldrin coming down ladder; rock boxes
         put to use. TV cameras put at 30' panoramic
         position. Reading inscription of plaque
         with U.S. flag and setting it up. Telephone
         call from Washington to astronauts and their
         acknowledgement. CBS TV, July 20, 1969.
         1 reel (7 in.)   7 1/2 in. per sec.
         phonotape.
                        (Continued on next card)

SPACE FLIGHT TO THE MOON

Voice Lib.
M1386 Apollo 11 (space flight): blessing by Pope
bd.2   Paul VI from the Vatican to Apollo 11
         astronauts. CBS TV, July 20, 1969.
         1 reel (7 in.)   7 1/2 in. per sec.
         phonotape.
         1. Project Apollo. 2. Space flight to the
         moon. 3. Aldrin, Edwin E   1930-   4.
         Collins, Michael, 1930-   5. Armstrong, Neil,
         1930-   I. Aldrin, Edwin E   1930-   II.
         Collins, Michael, 1930-   III. Armstrong, Neil,
         1930-   IV. Paulus VI, Pope, 1897-

SPACE FLIGHT TO THE MOON
Voice Lib.
M1386 Apollo 11 (space flight): excerpts of old
bd.3 Mercury Theatre "War of the Worlds" of
1938; an interview with Orson Welles by
Mike Wallace. CBS TV, July 20, 1969.
1 reel (7 in.) 7 1/2 in. per sec.
phonotape.
1. Project Apollo. 2. Space flight to the moon. 3. Aldrin,
Edwin E 1930- 4. Collins, Michael, 1930-
5. Armstrong, Neil, 1930- I. Aldrin, Edwin E 1930-
II. Collins, Michael, 1930- III. Armstrong, Neil, 1930-
IV. Welles, Orson, 1915- V. Wallace, Mike, 1918-

SPACE FLIGHT TO THE MOON
Voice Lib.
M1388 Apollo 11 (space flight): personal greeting
bd.2 by President Nixon to the astronauts on
the "Hornet" and their replies. Chaplain's
prayer. Nixon taking off. CBS and NBC TV,
July 24, 1969.
1 reel (7 in.) 7 1/2 in. per sec.
phonotape.
1. Project Apollo. 2. Space flight to the moon. 3. Aldrin,
Edwin E 1930- 4. Collins, Michael, 1930-
Armstrong, Neil, 1930- I. Aldrin, Edwin E 1930-
II. Collins, Michael, 1930- III. Armstrong, Neil, 1930-
IV. Nixon, Richard Milhous, Pres. U.S., 1913-

SPACE FLIGHT TO THE MOON
Voice Lib.
M1386 Apollo 11 (space flight): excerpts of
bd.4 interview between Walter Cronkite and
Lyndon B. Johnson two weeks before the
moon flight regarding development of American
space effort. CBS TV, July 20, 1969.
1 reel (7 in.) 7 1/2 in. per sec.
phonotape.
1. Project Apollo. 2. Space flight to the
moon. I. Cronkite, Walter Leland, 1916-
II. Johnson, Lyndon Baines, Pres. U.S., 1908-
1973.

SPACE FLIGHT TO THE MOON
Voice Lib.
M1389 Apollo 11 (space flight): excerpt of press
bd.1 conference with Apollo 11 astronauts in
Houston. CBS TV, August 12, 1969.
1 reel (7 in.) 7 1/2 in. per sec.
phonotape.
1. Project Apollo. 2. Space flight to the
moon. 3. Aldrin, Edwin E 1930- 4.
Collins, Michael, 1930- 5. Armstrong, Neil,
1930- I. Aldrin, Edwin E 1930- II.
Collins, Michael, 1930- III. Armstrong,
Neil, 1930-

SPACE FLIGHT TO THE MOON
Voice Lib.
M1387 Apollo 11 (space flight): description of
bd.1 ascent from moon by Frank McGee. Count-
down, ignition, and lift-off. Meeting the
command module "Columbia"; docking; trans-
fer of gear from "Eagle" to "Columbia".
Recap by ABC's Jules Bergman and Frank
Reynolds. NBC and ABC TV, July 21, 1969.
1 reel (7 in.) 7 1/2 in. per sec. phonotape.
1. Project Apollo. 2. Space flight to the moon. 3. Aldrin,
Edwin E 1930- 4. Collins, Michael, 1930- 5.
Armstrong, Neil, 1930- I. Aldrin, Edwin E 1930- II.
Collins, Michael, 1930- III. Armstrong, Neil, 1930- IV.
McGee, Frank. 1921-1974. V. Bergman, Jules VI. Reynolds,
Frank

SPACE FLIGHT TO THE MOON
Voice Lib.
M1389 Apollo 11 (space flight): welcome to Apollo 11 astronauts on their
bd.2 arrival at Kennedy Airport at New York; ferried by Marine
helicopter to Wall Street; boat whistles harbor greeting.
Flashbacks to former important New York parades (Frank McGee)
Walter Cronkite, CBS, describing beginning of motorcade
and parade to city hall. CBS [and NBC] TV, August 13, 1969.
1 reel (7 in.) 7 1/2 in. per sec. phonotape.
1. Project Apollo. 2. Space flight to the moon. 3. Aldrin,
Edwin E 1930- 4. Collins, Michael, 1930- 5.
Armstrong, Neil, 1930- I. Aldrin, Edwin E 1930-
II. Collins, Michael, 1930- III. Armstrong, Neil, 1930-
IV. McGee, Frank. 1921-1974. V. Cronkite, Walter Leland, 1916-

SPACE FLIGHT TO THE MOON
Voice Lib.
M1387 Apollo 11 (space flight): recovery. Walter Cronkite and Wally
bd.2 Schirra announce proceedings from aircraft carrier "Hornet";
trying to track spacecraft coming down; chutes opening at
10,500 feet; voice contact with spacecraft; visual of chutes;
splashdown 9 miles from "Hornet", upside-down. Collar
attached to spacecraft. NBC and ABC TV, July 24, 1969.
1 reel (7 in.) 7 1/2 in. per sec. phonotape.
1. Project Apollo. 2. Space flight to the moon. 3. Aldrin,
Edwin E 1930- 4. Collins, Michael, 1930- 5.
Armstrong, Neil, 1930- I. Aldrin, Edwin E 1930-
II. Collins, Michael, 1930- III. Armstrong, Neil, 1930-
IV. Cronkite, Walter Leland, 1916- V. Schirra, Walter Marty,
1923-

SPACE FLIGHT TO THE MOON
Voice Lib.
M1390 Apollo 11 (space flight): reception for
Apollo 11 astronauts in New York. Descrip-
tion of approach and ceremony at city hall.
Cardinal Cooke's invocation. Introduction
by Mayor Lindsay. Presentation of Medal of
Honor. Reply by all astronauts. Benediction.
NBC TV, August 13, 1969.
1 reel (7 in.) 7 1/2 in. per sec. phonotape.
1. Project Apollo. 2. Space flight to the moon. 3. Aldrin,
Edwin E 1930- 4. Collins, Michael, 1930- 5.
Armstrong, Neil, 1930- I. Aldrin, Edwin E 1930- II.
Collins, Michael, 1930- III. Armstrong, Neil, 1930- IV.
Cooke, Terence James, cardinal, 1921- V. Lindsay, John Vliet,
1921-

SPACE FLIGHT TO THE MOON
Voice Lib.
M1388 Apollo 11 (space flight): Walter Cronkite and Wally Schirra
bd.1 describing recovery. Maneuvers by frogmen and helicopters
at splashdown spot; "air boss" describes close-up scene;
decontamination process; helicopter landing on "Hornet" with
astronauts; reception. Description of proceedings on "Hornet"
by CBS newscasters. CBS TV, July 24, 1969.
1 reel (7 in.) 7 1/2 in. per sec. phonotape.
1. Project Apollo. 2. Space flight to the moon. 3. Aldrin,
Edwin E 1930- 4. Collins, Michael, 1930- 5. Armstrong,
Neil, 1930- I. Aldrin, Edwin E 1930- II. Collins,
Michael, 1930- III. Armstrong, Neil, 1930- IV. Cronkite,
Walter Leland, 1916- V. Schirra, Walter Marty, 1923-

SPACE FLIGHT TO THE MOON
Voice Lib.
M1391 Apollo 11 (space flight): reception of Apollo 11 astronauts at
bd.1 United Nations Plaza. Statement by U.N. Secretary-
General U Thant. Reply by Neil Armstrong. Presentation
of tokens of appreciation to all three astronauts and their
wives and Dr. Thomas Paine. Presentation of duplicate of
plaque left on moon to U Thant. NBC TV, August 13, 1969.
1 reel (7 in.) 7 1/2 in. per sec. phonotape.
1. Project Apollo. 2. Space flight to the moon. 3. Aldrin,
Edwin E 1930- 4. Collins, Michael, 1930- 5.
Armstrong, Neil, 1930- I. Aldrin, Edwin E 1930-
II. Collins, Michael, 1930- III. Armstrong, Neil, 1930-
IV. Thant, U, 1909- V. Paine, Thomas Otten, 1921-

SPACE FLIGHT TO THE MOON

Voice Lib.
M1391 Apollo 11 (space flight): reception of
bd.2   Apollo 11 astronauts in Chicago. Descrip-
          tion of motorcade on way to Civic Center
          Plaza and ceremonies there. Cardinal Cody's
          invocation. JFK flashback predicting moon
          landing before decade is out. Mayor Daley
          and Alderman Klene resolution making August
          13 "Astronauts' Day". Senator Percy and
          Governor Ogilvie of Illinois. Presentation
          of honorary citizenship to astronauts.
          ₍Source?₎ August 13, 1969.

                              (Continued on next card)

SPACE FLIGHT TO THE MOON

Voice Lib.
M1391 Apollo 11 (space flight): reception of Apollo
bd.2   11 astronauts ... 1969. (Card 2)

          1 reel (7 in.)   7 1/2 in. per sec.
          phonotape.
          L. Project Apollo. 2. Space flight to the moon. 3. Aldrin,
          Edwin E   1930-   4. Collins, Michael, 1930-   5. Armstrong,
          Neil, 1930-   L. Aldrin, Edwin E   1930-   II. Collins,
          Michael, 1930-   III. Armstrong, Neil, 1930-   IV. Cody,
          John Patrick, cardinal, 1907-   V. Kennedy, John Fitzgerald,
          Pres. U.S., 1917-1963. VI. Daley, Richard J   1902- VII.
          Percy, Charles Harting, 1919-   VIII. Ogilvie, Richard Buell,
          1923-

SPACE FLIGHT TO THE MOON

Voice Lib.
M1403 Apollo 12 (space flight): lift-off of Apollo
bd.1   12; the electrical "glitch" and instructions
          and corrections; Dr. Paine and President
          Nixon speaking from VIP section. CBS TV,
          November 19, 1969.
          1 reel (7 in.)   7 1/2 in. per sec.
          phonotape.
          L. Project Apollo. 2. Space flight to the moon. 3. Conrad,
          Charles, 1930-   4. Bean, Alan L   1932-   5. Gordon,
          Richard F   1929-   L. Conrad, Charles, 1930-   II. Bean,
          Alan L   1932-   III. Gordon, Richard F   1929-   IV.
          Paine, Thomas Otten, 1921-   V. Nixon, Richard Milhous, Pres.
          U.S., 1913-

SPACE FLIGHT TO THE MOON

Voice Lib.
M1403 Apollo 12 (space flight): landing on the
bd.2   moon; conversations of Frank McGee and
          mission control; dialogue of Pete Conrad
          preparing to step out on moon; coached on
          going down ladder; Conrad singing from the
          moon; trouble with TV camera. NBC TV,
          November 19, 1969.
          1 reel (7 in.) 7 1/2 in. per sec. phonotape.
          L. Project Apollo. 2. Space flight to the moon. 3. Conrad,
          Charles, 1930-   4. Bean, Alan L   1932-   5. Gordon,
          Richard F   1929-   L. Conrad, Charles, 1930-   II. Bean,
          Alan L   1932-   III. Gordon, Richard F   1929-   IV.
          McGee, Frank, 1921-1974.

SPACE FLIGHT TO THE MOON

Voice Lib.
M1404 Apollo 12 (space flight): description of
bd.1   last minutes on the moon of Apollo 12
          crew; countdown, lift-off from the moon.
          CBS TV, November 20, 1969.
          1 reel (7 in.)   7 1/2 in. per sec.
          phonotape.
          1. Project Apollo. 2. Space flight to the
          moon. 3. Conrad, Charles, 1930-   4. Bean,
          Alan L   1932-   5. Gordon, Richard F
          1929-   I. Conrad, Charles, 1930-   II.
          Bean, Alan L   1932-   III. Gordon, Richard
          F   1929-

SPACE FLIGHT TO THE MOON

Voice Lib.
M1404 Apollo 12 (space flight): description of
bd.2   splashdown of Apollo 12 and proceeding
          to aircraft carrier "Hornet". CBS TV,
          November 24, 1969.
          1 reel (7 in.)   7 1/2 in. per sec.
          phonotape.
          1. Project Apollo. 2. Space flight to the
          moon. 3. Conrad, Charles, 1930-   4. Bean,
          Alan L   1932-   5. Gordon, Richard F
          1929-   I. Conrad, Charles, 1930-   II.
          Bean, Alan L   1932-   III. Gordon, Richard
          F   1929-

SPACE FLIGHT TO THE MOON

Voice Lib.
M1423 Apollo 13 (space flight): resumé of flight
          of Apollo 13, including lift-off, mal-
          function, and splashdown, and interviews
          on future of space program. NBC TV,
          April, 1970.
          1 reel (7 in.)   7 1/2 in. per sec.
          phonotape.
          1. Project Apollo. 2. Space flight to the moon. 3. Haise,
          Fred W   1934-   4. Lovell, James Arthur, 1928-   5.
          Swigert, John L   1932-   L. Haise, Fred W   1934-
          II. Lovell, James Arthur, 1928-   III. Swigert, John L   1932-

---

SPACE FLIGHT TO THE MOON

Voice Lib.
M1424 Apollo 13 (space flight): oxygen malfunction
          on Apollo 13 described by NASA, astronauts,
          and Howard K. Smith. ABC TV, April 14, 1970.
          1 reel (7 in.)   7 1/2 in. per sec.
          phonotape.
          1. Project Apollo. 2. Space flight to the
          moon. 3. Haise, Fred W   1934-   4.
          Lovell, James Arthur, 1928-   5. Swigert,
          John L   1932-   I. Haise, Fred W   1934-
          II. Lovell, James Arthur, 1928-   III. Swigert,
          John L   1932-   IV. Smith, Howard Kingsbury,
          1914-

SPACE FLIGHT TO THE MOON

Voice Lib.
M1438 Apollo 14 (space flight): take-off from Cape
bd.1   Kennedy, including countdown. CBS,
          January 31, 1971.
          1 reel (7 in.)   7 1/2 in. per sec.
          phonotape.

          1. Project Apollo. 2. Space flight to the
          moon. 3. Shepard, Alan Bartlett, 1923-   4.
          Mitchell, Edgar D   1931-   5. Roosa,
          Stuart A   1934-   I. Shepard, Alan Bartlett,
          1923-   II. Mitchell, Edgar D   1931-   III.
          Roosa, Stuart A   1934-

SPACE FLIGHT TO THE MOON

Voice Lib.
M1438 Apollo 14 (space flight): lunar landed on the
bd.2   moon and moon walk. CBS, February 5, 1971.
          1 reel (7 in.)   7 1/2 in. per sec.
          phonotape.

          1. Project Apollo. 2. Space flight to the
          moon. 3. Shepard, Alan Bartlett, 1923-   4.
          Mitchell, Edgar D   1931-   5. Roosa, Stuart
          A   1934-   I. Shepard, Alan Bartlett,
          1923-   II. Mitchell, Edgar D   1931- III.
          Roosa, Stuart A   1934-

Voice Lib.　SPACE FLIGHT TO THE MOON
M1438　Apollo 14 (space flight): Apollo 14 splash-
bd.3-　　down and reception on aircraft carrier.
M1439　　CBS, February 9, 1971.
bd.1　　　2 reels(7 in.)　7 1/2 in. per sec.
phonotape.

　　　1. Project Apollo.　2. Space flight to the
moon.　3. Shepard, Alan Bartlett, 1923-　4.
Mitchell, Edgar D　1931-　　5. Roosa,
Stuart A　1934-　I. Shepard, Alan Bartlett,
1923-　II. Mitchell, Edgar D　1931-　III.
Roosa, Stuart A　　1934-

Voice Lib.　SPACE FLIGHT TO THE MOON
M1480　Apollo 15 (space flight): lift-off.
bd.1　　CBS TV, July 26, 1971.
　　　1 reel (7 in.)　7 1/2 in. per sec.
phonotape.

　　　1. Project Apollo.　2. Space flight to the
moon.　3. Scott, David Randolph, 1932-　4.
Irwin, James B　1932-　5. Worden, Alfred
M　　1930-　I. Scott, David Randolph,
1932-　II. Irwin, James B　1932-　III.
Worden, Alfred M　　1930-

Voice Lib.　SPACE FLIGHT TO THE MOON
M1480　Apollo 15 (space flight): beginning of power
bd.2　　descent to moon.　NBC TV, July 31, 1971.
　　　1 reel (7 in.)　7 1/2 in. per sec.
phonotape.

　　　1. Project Apollo.　2. Space flight to the
moon.　3. Scott, David Randolph, 1932-　4.
Irwin, James B　1932-　5. Worden, Alfred
M　　1930-　I. Scott, David Randolph,
1932-　II. Irwin, James B　1932-　III.
Worden, Alfred M　　1930-

Voice Lib.　SPACE FLIGHT TO THE MOON
M1480　Apollo 15 (space flight): walk in deep space
bd.3　　by Al Worden to retrieve film packages.
　　　Commentary of Gene Cernan, who walked in
　　　space during Gemini 9 flight.　NBC TV,
　　　August, 1971.
　　　1 reel (7 in.)　7 1/2 in. per sec.
phonotape.
　L. Project Apollo.　2. Space flight to the moon.　3. Scott,
David Randolph, 1932-　4. Irwin, James B　1932-　5.
Worden, Alfred M　1930-　L. Scott, David Randolph, 1932-
II. Irwin, James B　1932-　III. Worden, Alfred M　1930-
IV. Cernan, Eugene Andrew, 1934-

Voice Lib.　SPACE FLIGHT TO THE MOON
M1480　Apollo 15 (space flight): splashdown,
bd.4　　commentary, speeches.　NBC TV, August 7,
　　　1971.
　　　1 reel (7 in.)　7 1/2 in. per sec.
phonotape.

　　　1. Project Apollo.　2. Space flight to the
moon.　3. Scott, David Randolph, 1932-　4.
Irwin, James B　1932-　5. Worden, Alfred
M　　1930-　I. Scott, David Randolph,
1932-　II. Irwin, James B　1932-　III.
Worden, Alfred M　　1930-

Voice Lib.
M761　Spaeth, Sigmund, 1885-1965.
bd.8　　Excerpt from "Whatever Happened to Tin Pan
　　　Alley?" (Program 3); comments on the replace-
　　　ment of pianos with records.　Westinghouse
　　　Broadcasting Corporation, 1964.
　　　1 reel (7 in.)　7 1/2 in. per sec.
phonotape.　(The Music Goes Round and Round)

　　　I. Title: Whatever happened to Tin Pan Alley?
II. Series.

　　　　　　SPAIN - HISTORY - CIVIL WAR, 1936-1939
Voice Lib.
M1016　Göring, Hermann, 1893-1946.
bd.13　　Congratulating the troops of the Legion
　　　Condor at their accomplishments in Spain in
　　　the Civil War.　Peteler, June 6, 1939.
　　　1 reel (7 in.)　7 1/2 i.p.s.　phonotape.

　　　1. Spain - History - Civil War, 1936-1939.

Voice Lib.
M833　The spark at Sarajevo, an actual and dramatized
bd.2　　radio program produced by Triangle Program
　　　Sales, 320 Park Avenue, New York, for WFIL,
　　　Philadelphia.　Excerpts taken from "Hark,
　　　the Years", vol. I.　Philadelphia, WFIL,
　　　September 2, 1965.
　　　1 reel (7 in.)　7 1/2 in. per sec.
phonotape.

　　　　　　SPARLING, JAMES
Voice Lib.
M1634　Nixon, Richard Milhous, Pres. U.S., 1913-
bd.2　　Speaking at Bad Axe, Michigan, in support
　　　of James Sparling, Republican candidate for
　　　Congress.　MSU Dept. of Journalism, April,
　　　1974.
　　　10 min.　phonotape (1 r.　7 1/2 i.p.s.)

　　　1. U.S. - Politics and government - 1969-
2. Sparling, James

Voice Lib.　　Speaight, Robert, 1904-
M225　Packard, Frederick
　　　Styles in Shakespearean acting, 1890-1950.
　　　Creative Associates, 1963?
　　　1 reel (7 in.)　7 1/2 i.p.s.　phonotape.
　L. Sothern, Edward Askew, 1826-1881.　II. Marlowe,
Julia, 1865-1950.　III. Booth, Edwin, 1833-1893.　IV. Gielgud,
John, 1904-　V. Robeson, Paul Bustill, 1898-　VI. Terry,
Dame Ellen, 1848-1928.　VII. Allen, Viola.　VIII. Welles,
Orson, 1915-　IX. Skinner, Otis, 1858-1942.　X. Barrymore,
John, 1882-1942.　XI. Olivier, Sir Laurence Kerr, 1907-
XII. Forbes-Robertson, Sir Johnston, 1853-　XIII. Evans,
Maurice.　XIV. Thorndike, Dame Sybil, 1882-　XV. Robson,
Flora.　XVI. LeGallienne, Eva, 1899-　XVII. Anderson,
Judith.　XVIII. Duncan, Augustin.　XIX. Hampden, Walter.
XX. Speaight, Robert, 1904-　XXI. Jones, Daniel.

Voice Lib.
M762   Spector, Phil
bd.1   Excerpt from "Tunesmiths Past and Present"
        (Program 4); explanation as to why many of
        the old writers apparently can no longer make
        the grade, also comments on his goal in the
        business; including two songs, "Be My Baby"
        and "Spanish Harlem". Westinghouse Broad-
        casting Corporation, 1964.
            1 reel (7 in.)   7 1/2 in. per sec.
        phonotape.   (The Music Goes Round and Round)
            I. Title: Tunesmiths past and present. II.
        Series.

Voice Lib.
M764   Spector, Phil
bd.12   Excerpt from "The World of Wax" (Program
        8); discusses the effect of all the factors
        on the quality of the records being produced,
        after the advent of rock-and-roll. Westing-
        house Broadcasting Corporation, 1964.
            1 reel (7 in.)   7 1/2 in. per sec.
        phonotape.   (The Music Goes Round and Round)

            I. Title: The world of wax. II. Series.

Voice Lib.
M765   Spector, Phil
bd.7   Excerpt from "The Anatomy of a Hit"
        (Program 9); answers the questions, Was
        the popularity of "Hello, Dolly" a freak?
        Could it happen again and how did it happen
        in the first place? Westinghouse Broad-
        casting Corporation, 1964.
            1 reel (7 in.)   7 1/2 in. per sec.
        phonotape.   (The Music Goes Round and Round)

            I. Title: The anatomy of a hit. II. Series.

C1   The spell of the Yukon
A42   Whorf, Michael, 1933-
            The spell of the Yukon; Robert Service.
            1 tape cassette.   (The visual sounds of
        Mike Whorf. Art, music, and letters, A42)
            Originally presented on his radio program, Kaleidoscope.
        WJR, Detroit.
            Duration: 44 min., 55 sec.
            From the frontier towns of Whitehorse and Dawson, Service
        sang the glories of the North Country. A prospector himself, he
        was able to capture the rolling spirit of the brawling, boisterous
        life of the Yukon in the days of the Gold Rush.

            1. Service, Robert William, 1874-1958. I. Title.

Voice Lib.
M303   Spellman, Francis Joseph, Cardinal, 1889-1967.
bd.1   Being saluted at George Washington
        Carver Memorial Luncheon.   Voice of America,
        March 9, 1956.
            1 reel (7 in.)   7 1/2 in. per sec.
        phonotape.

            1. Spellman, Francis Joseph, Cardinal,
        1889-1967.

Voice Lib.
M786   Spiegel, Sam
bd.1   Interview on the cinema, discussing his
        personal approach to production, illustrating
        with excerpts from sound tracks of: 1. The
        Bridge over the River Kwai, 2. On the
        waterfront, 3. Suddenly last summer, 4.
        Lawrence of Arabia. BBC, June 20, 1964.
            29 min.   phonotape (1 r.   7 1/2 i.p.s.)

            1. Moving-picture industry.

Voice Lib.   The spirit of Notre Dame (Motion picture)
649   O'Brien, Pat, 1899-
bd.13   Knute Rockne talks to his team;
        sequence from motion picture film "The
        Spirit of Notre Dame".   Universal Pictures,
        1938.
            1 reel (7 in.)   7 1/2 in. per sec.
        phonotape.

            I. The spirit of Notre Dame(Motion picture)

                SPIRITUALISM
Voice Lib.
537   Doyle, Sir Arthur Conan, 1859-1930.
bd.2   Development of Sherlock Holmes; spiritualism;
        impact of Holmes' stories around the world;
        influence of Thomas Huxley on his spiritual
        belief; ability to answer questions on life
        after death; spiritualism and its compatible
        relationship with other religions; proof of
        spiritualism. BBC, 1928.
            1 reel (7 in.)   7 1/2 in. per sec.
        phonotape.

            The splendid Americans
C1
M18   Whorf, Michael, 1933-
            The splendid Americans.
            1 tape cassette.   (The visual sounds of
        Mike Whorf. Miscellaneous, M18)

            Originally presented on his radio program, Kaleidoscope,
        WJR, Detroit.
            Duration: 54 min., 30 sec.
            This is the story of those who wrote the songs of a nation and
        a people, songs which gave a different kind of courage to the
        people.

            1. Bates, Katherine Lee, 1859-1929. 2. Key, Francis Scott,
        1779-1929. 3. Patriotic music, American. I. Title.

Voice Lib.
M1693   Spock, Benjamin McLane, 1903-
bd.2   On the younger generation and his own
        pro-peace activities, anti-obscenity
        activities, etc., on Merv Griffin Show.
            25 min.   phonotape (1 r.   7 1/2 i.p.s.)

            1. Women's Liberation Movement.
        2. Children - Care & hygiene. 3. Johnson,
        Lyndon Baines, Pres. U.S., 1908-1973.
        I. Griffin, Mervyn Edward, 1925-

SPORTS

Voice Lib.
M1064   Sports highlights of the 1920's and 1930's.
bd.4   Various segments about the activities of
    famous sports personalities during the
    era. Fox Movietone, 1930.
    1 reel (7 in.)   7 1/2 in. per sec.
phonotape.

Voice Lib.
M1064   Sports highlights of the 1920's and 1930's.
bd.4   Various segments about the activities of
    famous sports personalities during the
    era. Fox Movietone, 1930.
    1 reel (7 in.)   7 1/2 in. per sec.
phonotape.

      1. Sports.

Spring
C1
M30   Whorf, Michael, 1933-
    Spring.
    1 tape cassette.   (The visual sounds of
Mike Whorf. Miscellaneous, M30)

Originally presented on his radio program, Kaleidoscope,
WJR, Detroit.
Duration: 36 min., 15 sec.
For the nature lover - for the poetry enthusiast - for those
who love the season of promise, here is a delightful and
refreshing episode devoted to spring.

    1. Spring. 1. Title.

Voice Lib.
M715   Sputnik: first earth satellite to orbit
bd.12   the globe announced over Moscow radio by
    U.S.S.R., followed by sound signals from
    satellite. October 4, 1957.
    1 reel (7 in.)   7 1/2 in. per sec.
phonotape.

      1. Artificial satellites.

Squanto
C1
H43   Whorf, Michael, 1933-
    Squanto.
    1 tape cassette.   (The visual sounds of
Mike Whorf. History and heritage, H43)

Originally presented on his radio program, Kaleidoscope,
WJR, Detroit.
Duration: 45 min., 40 sec.
He was guide, interpreter, agricultural agent and comrade,
yet his life was as strange and as bizarre as the tale of the white
man he would greet on the shores of Cape Cod.

    1. Squanto. 1. Title.

The staff of life
C1
S25   Whorf, Michael, 1933-
    The staff of life.
    1 tape cassette.   (The visual sounds of
Mike Whorf. Social, S25)

Originally presented on his radio program, Kaleidoscope,
WJR, Detroit.
Duration: 41 min.
This is the story of wheat, of bread, its impact on mankind,
where and how it is processed and utilized.

    1. Wheat. 2. Bread. 1. Title.

          Stafford, Thomas P   1931-
Voice Lib.
M917   Gemini 7 (space flight): Frank McGee's resumé
bd.1   of space flights of astronauts Frank Borman
    and James Lovell, Jr., in Gemini 7, commencing
    Dec. 4, 1956 to Dec. 18, 1965, and of astro-
    nauts Walter Schirra and Thomas Stafford in
    Gemini 6, which rendezvoused in space;
    including various launching actual reports
    and interview with Wally Schirra; comments
    by Huntley and Brinkley.   NBC TV, December
    18, 1965.
    1 reel (7 in.)   7 1/2 in. per sec.
phonotape.
                    (Continued on next card)

          Stafford, Thomas P   1931-
Voice Lib.
M968   Gemini 9 (space flight): description of
bd.2   countdown and lift-off of "Agena" by
    Gemini Mission Control (voice of Al Chop)
    for a period of 11 minutes, 41 seconds,
    until Gemini flight was scrubbed. Comments
    by NBC's Huntley, Brinkley, and Frank McGee.
    NBC TV, May 17, 1966.
    1 reel (7 in.)   7 1/2 in. per sec.
1. Project Gemini. 2. Stafford, Thomas P   1931-   3.
Cernan, Eugene Andrew, 1934-   I. Stafford, Thomas P   1931-
II. Cernan, Eugene Andrew, 1934-   III. Chop, Al   IV.
Huntley, Chet, 1911-19   V. Brinkley, David McClure, 1920-
VI. McGee, Frank, 1921-1974.

          Stafford, Thomas P   1931-
Voice Lib.
M986   Gemini 9 (space flight): a. Take-off of
bd.2   Augmented Target Docking Adaptor (ATDA)
    from Cape Kennedy (June 1); b. re-cap
    by David Brinkley regarding failure of
    shroud to jettison (June 3); c. Gemini 9
    until failure of guidance system computer
    and then scrubbing mission (June 1)
    NBC TV, June 1 and 3, 1966.
    1 reel (7 in.)   7 1/2 in. per sec.   phonotape.
    1. Project Gemini. 2. Stafford, Thomas P   1931-   3.
Cernan, Eugene Andrew, 1934-   I. Stafford, Thomas P
1931-   II. Cernan, Eugene Andrew, 1934-   III. Brinkley,
David McClure, 1920-

          Stafford, Thomas P   1931-
Voice Lib.
M1377   Apollo 10 (space flight): lift-off. Commentary
bd.1   by NBC TV news; countdown, lift-off. Astro-
    nauts Tom Stafford, John Young, Eugene Cernan.
    NBC TV, May 18, 1969.
    1 reel (7 in.)   7 1/2 in. per sec.
phonotape.
    1. Project Apollo. 2. Space flight to the
moon. 3. Stafford, Thomas P   1931-   4.
Young, John Watts, 1930-   5. Cernan, Eugene
Andrew, 1934-   I. Stafford, Thomas P   1931-
II. Young, John Watts, 1930-   III. Cernan,
Eugene Andrew, 1934-

Voice Lib.
M1377 Stafford, Thomas P   1931-
bd.2   Apollo 10 (space flight): television pictures.
       Commentary from astronauts, NBC TV, on
       initial separation and docking of Lunar
       Landing Module, first live color television
       pictures from space, and pictures of the
       earth from 6,500 nautical miles out.   NBC
       TV, May, 1969.
         1 reel (7 in.)   7 1/2 in. per sec. phonotape.
         L. Project Apollo. 2. Space flight to the moon. 3. Stafford,
       Thomas P   1931-   4. Young, John Watts, 1930-   5.
       Cernan, Eugene Andrew, 1934-   L. Stafford, Thomas P
       1931-   IL. Young, John Watts, 1930-   III. Cernan, Eugene
       Andrew, 1934-

Voice Lib.
M1377 Stafford, Thomas P   1931-
bd.3   Apollo 10 (space flight): splashdown and
       recovery of Apollo 10; astronauts' first
       words after returning to earth; from the
       recovery ship U.S.S. "Princeton".   CBS TV,
       May 26, 1969.
         1 reel (7 in.)   7 1/2 in. per sec.
       phonotape.
         L. Project Apollo. 2. Space flight to the moon. 3. Stafford,
       Thomas P   1931-   4. Young, John Watts, 1930-   5.
       Cernan, Eugene Andrew, 1934-   L. Stafford, Thomas P
       1931-   IL. Young, John Watts, 1930-   III. Cernan, Eugene
       Andrew, 1934-

Voice Lib.
M1228 Stalin, Iosif, 1879-1953.
bd.3   Speech previous to election to the Supreme
       Soviet in Moscow.   Peteler, December 11,
       1937.
         1 reel (7 in.)   7 1/2 in. per sec.
       phonotape.

Voice Lib.
290   Stalin, Iosif, 1879-1953.
bd.3   Talking to the Russian people; excerpt
       of address on 25th anniversary of
       Soviet Revolution.   Gotham Recording,
       1942.
         1 reel (7 in.)   7 1/2 in. per sec.
       phonotape.

Voice Lib.
M1229; Stalin, Iosif, 1879-1953.
1221   Speech to the electorate of the
bd.2   Otalinskij district of Moscow.   Peteler,
       February 9, 1946.
         2 reels (7 in.)   7 1/2 in. per sec.
       phonotape.

Voice Lib.
M715 Stalin, Iosif, 1879-1953.
bd.6   Stalin's death; Radio Moscow excerpt
      announcing the death of Stalin.   March 5,
      1953.
        1 reel (7 in.)   7 1/2 in. per sec.
      phonotape.

Voice Lib.
572-   Stalin, Iosif, 1879-1953
573   I can hear it now (radio program)
bd.1   1933-1946.   CBS, 1948.
         2 reels (7 in.)   7 1/2 in. per sec.
       phonotape.
         L. Murrow, Edward Roscoe, 1908-1965. II. LaGuardia, Fiorello
       Henry, 1882-1947. III. Chamberlain, Neville, 1869-1949. IV.
       Roosevelt, Franklin Delano, Pres. U.S., 1882-1945. V. Churchill,
       Winston Leonard Spencer, 1874-1965. VI. Gaulle, Charles de,
       Pres. France, 1890-1970. VII. Eisenhower, Dwight David, Pres. U.S.,
       1890-1969. VIII. Willkie, Wendell Lewis, 1892-1944. IX. Martin,
       Joseph William, 1884-1968. X. Elizabeth II, Queen of Great Britain,
       1926-   XI. Margaret Rose, Princess of Gt. Brit., 1930-   XII.
       Johnson, Hugh Samuel, 188?-?42. XIII. Smith, Alfred Emanuel,
       1873-1944. XIV. Lindbergh, Charles Augustus, 1902-   XV. Davis,
         (Continued on next card)

Stalin, Svetlana
  see
Allilueva, Svetlana, 1925-

VOICE LIBRARY

C1   STALINGRAD, BATTLE OF, 1942-1943
S?   Whorf, Michael, 19??-
      We who are about to die.
        1 tape cassette.   (The visual sounds of
      Mike Whorf. Social, S?)
        Originally presented on his radio program, Kaleidoscope,
      WJR, Detroit.
        Duration: 39 min., 30 sec.
        Caught at Stalingrad, 300,000 German soldiers question their
      fathers, wives, mothers, sweethearts, friends and relations as
      they prepare to die, and in their final moments see the utter
      futility of conflict.
        L. Stalingrad, Battle of, 1942-1943. I. Title.

Voice Lib.
M766 Stampa, Fred
bd.5   Excerpt from "Popular Music of Europe"
      (Program 11); comments on style of singing
      of Dominco Modugno, including song "Boom
      boom surf" by Peppino Di Capri and the
      Hollerers.   Westinghouse Broadcasting
      Corporation, 1964.
        1 min., 44 sec. phonotape (1 r.   7 1/2 i.p.s.)
      (The music goes round and round)
        L. Modugno, Dominco. L. Title: Boom boom surf.
      II. Title: Popular music of Europe. III. Series.

Standing, Michael
Voice Lib.
M1044   London after dark; on-the-spot recordings of various
         points during the London air-raid attacks: the Savoy Hotel
         kitchen, Trafalgar Square, anti-aircraft battery near London,
         air-raid shelter. With newsmen Edward R. Murrow, Robert
         Bowman, Raymond Van Denny, Larry Lesueur, Eric Sevareid,
         Vincent Sheean, J. B. Priestley, Michael Standing, and
         Winfred Von Thomas.   CBS and BBC, August 24, 1940.
         1 reel (7 in.)   7 1/2 in. per sec.   phonotape.

         I. Murrow, Edward Roscoe, 1908-1965. II. Bowman, Robert
         III. Van Denny, Raymond   IV. Lesueur, Laurence Edward,
         1909-   V. Sevareid, Arnold Eric, 1912-   VI. Sheean,
         Vincent, 1899-   VII. Priestley, John Boynton, 1894-
         VIII. Standing, Michael   IX. Von Thomas, Winfred

Voice Lib.
249   Stanley, Sir Henry Morton, 1841-1904.
bd.4   Greeting through phonograph.   Edison
         Labs, 1888.
             1 reel (7 in.)   7 1/2 in. per sec.
         phonotape.

             1. Phonorecords - History

Voice Lib.
M1800   Stans, Maurice Hubert, 1908-
WG   Testimony before the Senate Committee
0612.02 investigating the Watergate Affair.
         Includes statement by Robert W. Barker,
         counsel. Pacifica, June 12, 1973.
             46 min.   phonotape (1 r.   3 3/4 i.p.s.)
         (Watergate gavel to gavel, phase 1)

             1. Watergate Affair, 1972-
         I. Barker, Robert

Voice Lib.
M1800   Stans, Maurice Hubert, 1908-
WG   Testimony before the Senate Committee
0612.03 investigating the Watergate Affair.
         Pacifica, June 12, 1973.
             161 min.   phonotape (2 r.   3 3/4 i.p.s.)
         (Watergate gavel to gavel, phase 1)

             1. Watergate Affair, 1972-

Voice Lib.
M1800   Stans, Maurice Hubert, 1908-
WG   Testimony before the Senate Committee
0613   investigating the Watergate Affair.
         Pacifica, June 13, 1973.
             299 min.   phonotape (4 r.   3 3/4 i.p.s.)
         (Watergate gavel to gavel, phase 1)

             1. Watergate Affair, 1972-

Voice Lib.
M935   Stanton, Frank, 1908-
bd.2   Excerpt wherein Dr. Stanton discusses the
         broadcasting investigation and censorship.
         Private recording, 1957.
             1 reel (7 in.)   7 1/2 in. per sec.
         phonotape.

             1. Censorship - U.S.

Stanton, Frank, 1908-
Voice Lib.
243   Medina, Harold Raymond, 1888-
bd.12   Judge Medina answers Dr. Frank Stanton
         on denial of TV access to Senate hearing
         to censure Sen. McCarthy.   CBS,
         September 2, 1954.
             1 reel (7 in.)   7 1/2 in. per sec.
         phonotape.

             1. McCarthy, Joseph Raymond, 1909-1957.
         I. Stanton, Frank, 1908-

Stanwyck, Barbara, 1907-
Voice Lib.
M669-   The legend of Cecil B. Demille. Yul
670   Brynner, Charlton Heston, Bob Hope, Betty
         Hutton, Edward G. Robinson, Barbara Stanwyck,
         James Stewart, Gloria Swanson, Cornel
         Wilde, Samuel Goldwyn, Billy Graham, Cecil
         B. DeMille.   Recorded 1963.
         2 reels (7 in.)   7 1/2 in. per sec.   phonotape.

         I. DeMille, Cecil Blount, 1881-1959.   I. Brynner, Yul, 1917-
         II. Heston, Charlton, 1924-   III. Hope, Bob, 1903-   IV.
         Hutton, Betty, 1921-   V. Robinson, Edward G   1893-1973.
         VI. Stanwyck, Barbara, 1907-   VII. Stewart, James Maitland,
         1908-   VIII. Swanson, Gloria, 1899?-   IX. Wilde, Cornel, 1915-
         X. Goldwyn, Samuel, 1884?-   XI. Graham, William Franklin,
         1918-   XII. DeMille, Cecil Blount, 1881-1959.

Stars and stripes forever
Voice Lib.
M1096   Sousa, John Philip, 1854-1932.
bd.2   Sousa's band playing his own march,
         "Stars and Stripes Forever".   Victor,
         1920.
             1 reel (7 in.)   7 1/2 in. per sec.
         phonotape.

             I. Title: Stars and stripes forever.

STATE ENCOURAGEMENT OF SCIENCE, LITERATURE,
AND ART - U.S.
Voice Lib.
M1750   Berman, Richard
             Government and the arts; on "Firing Line"
         with William F. Buckley.   WKAR, June 28,
         1974.
             45 min.   phonotape (1 r.   7 1/2 i.p.s.)

             1. The Arts - U. S.   2. Art and State.   3.
         State encouragement of science, literature,
         and art - U. S.   I. Buckley, William Frank,
         1925-

C1
868
Whorf, Michael, 1933-
Statesmen and sages
Statesmen and sages; Demosthenes, Aristotle, Socrates, Cicero.
1 tape cassette. (The visual sounds of Mike Whorf. Social, S68)
Originally presented on his radio program, Kaleidoscope, WJR, Detroit.
Duration: 36 min.
As ancient Greece and Rome served as the cradle of our modern democracy, so do their citizens serve as shining examples of wisdom and statecraft for us today.
1. Demosthenes. 2. Aristoteles. 3. Socrates. 4. Cicero, Marcus Tullius. I. Title.

Voice Lib.
M1450-
1451
Stein, Gertrude, 1874-1946.
Reminiscences of Gertrude Stein by her friends and associates with many actual segments of her voice. NET, December 20, 1970.
2 reels (7 in.) 7 1/2 in. per sec. phonotape.
1. Stein, Gertrude, 1874-1946.

Voice Lib.
611
bd.2
Burr, Henry, 1885-1941.
Stay down where you belong
World War I song "Stay down where you belong." Victor Talking Machine Co., 1917.
1 reel (7 in.) 7 1/2 in. per sec. phonotape.
I. Title: Stay down where you belong.

Voice Lib.
610
bd.3
Steinbeck, John, 1902-1968.
Reads "The Chrysanthemums"; reads his own short story. Columbia Records, Inc., 1947.
1 reel (7 in.) 7 1/2 in. per sec. phonotape.

Voice Lib.
M1470
bd.17
Steele, Christopher
Speaking about the British international situation in regard to world problems in 1939; stressing the problem of Poland. Peteler, 1964.
1 reel (7 in.) 7 1/2 i.p.s. phonotape.
1. Great Britain - Foreign relations.

Voice Lib.
182
bd.1
Steinbeck, John, 1902-1968.
Reading his short story, "Johnny Bear" and briefly commenting. Columbia Records, Inc., 1947.
1 reel (7 in.) 7 1/2 in. per sec. phonotape.
I. Title: Johnny Bear.

Voice Lib.
M1699
bd.1
STEFFENS, JOSEPH LINCOLN, 1866-1936
Kaplan, Justin
Discusses his book Lincoln Steffens - a biography on Book Beat with Robert Cromie. WKAR-TV, May 29, 1974.
20 min. phonotape (1 r. 7 1/2 i.p.s.)
1. Steffens, Joseph Lincoln, 1866-1936. 2. Kaplan, Justin/Lincoln Steffens - a biography. I. Cromie, Robert Allen, 1909-

Voice Lib.
181
bd.1
Steinbeck, John, 1902-1968.
Reading his short story, "Snake," and reviewing public reaction. CRI, 1947.
1 reel (7 in.) 7 1/2 in. per sec. phonotape.
I. Title: Snake.

Voice Lib.
M1720
bd.4
Steiger, Sam, 1929-
Udall, Morris K., 1922-
On the Today Show with Sam Steiger, debating their opposing bills for land-use funding. Includes Barbara Walters and Bill Monroe. NBC-TV, June 10, 1974.
8 min. phonotape (1 r. 7 1/2 i.p.s.)
1. Land. 2. Man - Influence on nature. I. Steiger, Sam, 1929- II. Walters, Barbara, 1931- III. Monroe, Bill.

Voice Lib.
M1691
Bd.2
Steinberg, David
Miller, Merle, 1918-
On Mike Douglas Show discussing his book on Truman. Includes Viveca Lindfors and David Steinberg. WILS-TV, May 23, 1974.
5 min. phonotape (1 r. 7 1/2 i.p.s.)
1. Truman, Harry S, Pres. U.S., 1884-1972. 2. Miller, Merle, 1918- /Plain speaking. I. Douglas, Mike, 1925?- II. Lindfors, Viveca, 1920- III. Steinberg, David.

Voice Lib.
M765 Steinberg, Dick
bd.5   Excerpt from "The Anatomy of a Hit" (Program
       9); comments on the difficulty of compiling
       sheet list of the top records in the country.
       Westinghouse Broadcasting Corporation, 1964.
          1 reel (7 in.)   7 1/2 in. per sec.
       phonotape.   (The Music Goes Round and Round)

          I. Title: The anatomy of a hit. II. Series.

Voice Lib.
M717 Stengel, Casey
bd.7   Interview after dismissal as manager of
       New York Yankee baseball team.   1960.
          1 reel (7 in.)   7 1/2 in. per sec.
       phonotape.

Voice Lib.
M263- Stengel, Casey
265   U.S. Congress. Senate. Special Committee to
bd.1   investigate organized crime in interstate
          commerce.
          Committee anti-trust hearing on baseball;
       interrogation and testimony of Casey Stengel.
       CBS, July 9, 1958.
          3 reels (7 in.)   7 1/2 in. per sec.
       phonotape.

          1. Baseball.   I. Stengel, Casey

C1   Stephen Foster
PWM7 Whorf, Michael, 1933-
          Stephen Foster.
          1 tape cassette.   (The visual sounds of
       Mike Whorf. Panorama; a world of music, PWM-7)

          Originally presented on his radio program, Kaleidoscope,
       WJR, Detroit.
          Duration: 25 min.
          The life and times of Stephen Foster, including excerpts
       of his music.

          I. Foster, Stephen Collins, 1826-1864.   I. Title.

Voice Lib. Stern, Carl
M1477 Discussion of Supreme Court decision on
       publishing Pentagon Papers. William B.
       Macomber, deputy under-secretary of state;
       Senator Henry Jackson; Max Frankel, head of
       New York Times' Washington bureau; Benjamin
       Bradley, executive editor of Washington Post.
       Questioned by Carl Stern, NBC; Martin Hayden,
       Detroit News; James J. Kilpatrick, Washington
       Star Syndicate; Kenneth Crawford, Washington
       Post; Edwin Newman.   NBC-TV, June 30, 1971.
          1 reel (7 in.)   7 1/2 in. per sec.
       phonotape.   (Continued on next card)

Voice Lib. Stern, Isaac, 1920-
M310 American Broadcasting Company.
          Tribute to President John Fitzgerald Kennedy
       from the arts. Fredric March emcees; Jerome
       Hines sings "Worship of God and Nature" by
       Beethoven; Florence Eldridge recites "When
       lilacs last in the door-yard bloom'd" by Walt
       Whitman; Marian Anderson in two songs. Includes
       Charlton Heston, Sidney Blackmer, Isaac Stern,
       Nathan Milstein, Christopher Plummer, Albert
       Finney.   ABC, November 24, 1963.
          35 min.   phonotape (7 in.   7 1/2 i.p.s.)

                              (Continued on next card)

Voice Lib. Stern, Joseph
M1268 Goldwater, Barry Morris, 1909-
          NET program about the 1964 presidential
       campaign consisting of informal conversations
       by Joseph Stern and Paul Niven with Barry
       Goldwater and William E. Miller in
       Washington, D.C.   NET, September 25, 1967.
          1 reel (7 in.)   7 1/2 in. per sec.
       phonotape.

          I. Miller, William Edward, 1914-   II.
       Stern, Joseph   III. Niven, Paul

Stettinius, Edward Reilly, 1900-1949
Voice Lib.
572- I can hear it now (radio program)
573   1933-1946. CBS, 1948.
bd.1   2 reels (7 in.)   7 1/2 in. per sec.
       phonotape.

          I. Murrow, Edward Roscoe, 1908-1965. II. LaGuardia, Fiorello
       Henry, 1882-1947. III. Chamberlain, Neville, 1869-1949. IV.
       Roosevelt, Franklin Delano, Pres. U.S., 1882-1945. V. Churchill,
       Winston Leonard Spencer, 1874-1965. VI. Gaulle, Charles de,
       Pres. France, 1890-1970. VII. Eisenhower, Dwight David, Pres. U.S.,
       1890-1969. VIII. Willkie, Wendell Lewis, 1892-1944. IX. Martin,
       Joseph William, 1884-1968. X. Elizabeth II, Queen of Great Britain,
       1926-   XI. Margaret Rose, Princess of Gt. Brit., 1930-   XII.
       Johnson, Hugh Samuel, 18 942. XIII. Smith, Alfred Emanuel,
       1873-1944. XIV. Lindberg harles Augustus, 1902-   XV. Davis,
                                   (Continued on next card)

Voice Lib. Stevens, Robert Ten Broeck, 1899-
M746 U.S. Congress. Senate. Committee on Government Operations.
          Permanent Subcommittee on Investigations.
bd.2   Proceedings of the [1st session] of Senate Army-McCarthy
       hearings, April 22, 1954. Testimony by various witnesses
       regarding pressure put on the Army to obtain a commission for
       Private David Schine. Some of the people speaking are:
       Griffin Bancroft, CBS announcer, describing the scenes at the
       hearings; Joseph N. Welch, counsel for the Army; Ray Jenkins,
       counsel for the subcommittee; Army Secretary Robert Stevens;
       General Reber and Senator McClellan of Arkansas.   CBS Radio,
       April 22, 1954.
          1 reel (7 in.)   7 1/2 in. per sec.   phonotape.

          I. McCarthy-Army controversy, 1954. I. Bancroft, Griffin
       II. Welch, Joseph Nye, 1890-1960. III. Jenkins, Ray Howard,
       1897-   IV. Stevens, Robert Ten Broeck, 1899-   V.
       Reber, Miles   VI. McClellan, John Little, 1896-

Voice Lib. Stevens, Robert Ten Broeck, 1899-
M748 U.S. Congress. Senate. Committee on Government Operations.
          Permanent Subcommittee on Investigations.
          Proceedings of the 3rd session of Senate Army-McCarthy
       hearings, April 26, 1954. Cross-examination of Secretary of
       the Army Robert Stevens.   CBS Radio, April 26, 1954.
          1 reel (7 in.)   7 1/2 in. per sec.   phonotape.

          I. McCarthy-Army controversy, 1954. I. Stevens, Robert
       Ten Broeck, 1899-

Voice Lib.
M750
bd.1
Stevens, Robert Ten Broeck, 1899-
U.S. Congress. Senate. Committee on Government Operations.
Permanent Subcommittee on Investigations.
Proceedings of the 4th session of Senate Army-McCarthy hearings, continued, April 27, 1954. Circumstances under which the altered photograph was taken was questioned; examination of Sec. Stevens in his attempts to sidetrack investigation from Army to Air Force and Navy; a cross-examination by McCarthy of Secretary Stevens referring to his attempts to block investigation; questioning of Stevens by Senator Mundt demanding exact charges against Carr, Cohn and McCarthy. CBS Radio, April 27, 1954.
1 reel (7 in.) 7 1/2 in. per sec. phonotape.

I. McCarthy-Army controversy, 1954. I. Stevens, Robert Ten Broeck, 1899- II. McCarthy, Joseph Raymond, 1909-1957. III. Mundt, Karl Earl, 1900-

---

Voice Lib.
M933
Stevens, Robert Ten Broeck, 1899-
U.S. Congress. Senate. Committee on Government Operations.
Permanent Subcommittee on Investigations.
Proceedings of the 5th session of Senate Army-McCarthy hearings, April 28, 1954. Cross-examination of Army Secretary Stevens by Senator McCarthy; Counselor Jenkins questions Stevens and Private Schine; McCarthy denies charges of special privileges for Schine. WJR, 10:30 p.m., April 28, 1954.
1 reel (7 in.) 7 1/2 in. per sec. phonotape.

I. McCarthy-Army controversy, 1954. I. Stevens, Robert Ten Broeck, 1899- II. McCarthy, Joseph Raymond, 1909-1957. III. Jenkins, Ray Howard, 1897- IV. Schine, G. David, 1927-

---

Voice Lib.
M934
Stevens, Robert Ten Broeck, 1899-
U.S. Congress. Senate. Committee on Government Operations.
Permanent Subcommittee on Investigation.
Proceedings of the 6th session of Senate Army-McCarthy sessions, April 29, 1954. Private Schine makes first appearance; he is cross-examined by Secretary Stevens and Counselor Jenkins; Schine comments on circumstances of doctoring the "famous photograph" and delivering it for publication at a Washington restaurant. Evening session, WJR, April 29, 1954.
1 reel (7 in.) 7 1/2 in. per sec. phonotape.

I. McCarthy-Army controversy, 1954. I. Schine, G. David, 1927- II. Stevens, Robert Ten Broeck, 1899- III. Jenkins, Ray Howard, 1897-

---

Voice Lib.
M1022
bd.1
Stevens, Robert Ten Broeck, 1899-
U.S. Congress. Senate. Committee on Government Operations.
Permanent Subcommittee on Investigations.
Proceedings of the [8 th session] of Senate Army-McCarthy hearings, May 3, 1954. Participants: Secretary of the Army Stevens and Senator McCarthy discussing the case of Major Peress; controversy between Army counsel Adams and McCarthy; McCarthy questioning creditability of Secretary Stevens. WJR, May 3, 1954.
1 reel (7 in.) 7 1/2 in. per sec. phonotape.

I. McCarthy-Army controversy, 1954. I. Stevens, Robert Ten Broeck, 1899- II. McCarthy, Joseph Raymond, 1909-1957. III. Adams, John G.

Voice Lib.
M1069
Stevens, Robert Ten Broeck, 1899-
U.S. Congress. Senate. Committee on Government Operations.
Permanent Subcommittee on Investigations.
Proceedings of the 10th session of Senate Army-McCarthy hearings, May 5, 1954. Senator McCarthy on witness stand; debate concerning letter from FBI files; verbal duel between Counsel Welch and McCarthy; Secretary of Army Stevens on witness stand. CBS Radio, May 5, 1954.
1 reel (7 in.) 7 1/2 in. per sec. phonotape.

I. McCarthy-Army controversy, 1954. I. McCarthy, Joseph Raymond, 1909-1957. II. Welch, Joseph Nye, 1890-1960. III. Stevens, Robert Ten Broeck, 1899-

---

Voice Lib.
M1283
Stevens, Robert Ten Broeck, 1899-
U.S. Congress. Senate. Committee on Government Operations.
Permanent Subcommittee on Investigations.
Proceedings of the 12th session of Senate Army-McCarthy hearings, May 7, 1954. Secretary Stevens alleges he was threatened by Sen. McCarthy. Sen. Mundt queries Stevens. Much bantering and ribbing. Question of legality of McCarthy holding certain documents. Discussion of pressure to give Private Schine an Army commission. CBS Radio, May 7, 1954.
1 reel (7 in.) 7 1/2 in. per sec. phonotape.

I. McCarthy-Army controversy, 1954. I. Stevens, Robert, 1899- II. Mundt, Karl Earl, 1900-

---

Voice Lib.
M1284
Stevens, Robert Ten Broeck, 1899-
U.S. Congress. Senate. Committee on Government Operations.
Permanent Subcommittee on Investigations.
Proceedings of the 13th session of Senate Army-McCarthy hearings, May 10, 1954. Senator Dirksen suggests they be held privately; Secretary Stevens makes statement and Senator McCarthy and his counsel, Roy Cohn, cross-examine Stevens; discussion of alleged communists at Ft. Monmouth and pressure of favored treatment for Private Schine. CBS Radio, May 10, 1954.
1 reel (7 in.) 7 1/2 in. per sec. phonotape.

I. McCarthy-Army controversy, 1954. I. Dirksen, Everett McKinley, 1896-1969. II. Stevens, Robert Ten Broeck, 1899- III. McCarthy, Joseph Raymond, 1909-1957. IV. Cohn, Roy M. 1927-

---

Voice Lib.
M805
Stevenson, Adlai Ewing, 1900-1965
United Nations Special Tape no. 1.
U.N. Archives, various dates.
33 min., 40 sec. phonotape (1 r. 7 1/2 i.p.s.)

CONTENTS. - bd. 1 African member of Judicial Committee on international law (5 min., 32 sec.). -bd. 2. U.N. Indian delegate describing Mahatma Gandhi as a "half-naked fakir" (54 sec.). -bd. 3. Woman president of a committee adjourning meeting because of lack of speakers, amidst laughter (1 min., 38 sec.). -bd. 4. U.N. sound crew testing equiment: "take your pot up there" (1 min., 22 sec.). -bd. 5. "Song of United Nations" rehearsal (3 min., 4 sec.). -bd. 6. Address by Minister of External Affairs of Cuba at U.N., delivered in

(Continued on next card)

Voice Lib.
M805
Stevenson, Adlai Ewing, 1900-1965
United Nations Special Tape no. 1. Various dates (Card 2)

CONTENTS (cont'd.) Spanish, starting a riot from the galleries; warning given, then meeting adjourned (5 min., 41 sec.). -bd. 7 Khrushchev quote; arguments among U.N. Secretariat (1 min., 50 sec.). -bd. 8. Adlai Stevenson speaking about the Congo situation; outbreak of rioting of African visitors until session is suspended; galleries ordered cleared (10 min., 26 sec.). -bd. 9. U.N. delegate, Social and Economic Council, pleading "don't send underdeveloped persons to underdeveloped areas" (1 min., 8 sec.). -bd. 10. Adlai Stevenson speaking at the U.N. and making an error of speech, covered up by humorous remark (40 sec.). -bd. 11. U.K. delegate enthusiastically endorsing U.S.S.R. proposal to adjourn (1 min., 25 sec.)

I. United Nations. I. Stevenson, Adlai Ewing, 1900-1965.

Voice Lib.
M805
bd.10
Stevenson, Adlai Ewing, 1900-1965.
Speaking at the U.N. and making an error of speech, covered up by humorous remark.
U.N. Archives [no date]
1 reel (7 in.) 7 1/2 in. per sec. phonotape.

On United Nations Special Tape No. 1.

Voice Lib.
M805   Stevenson, Adlai Ewing, 1900-1965.
bd.8   Speaking about the Congo situation;
        outbreak of rioting of African visitors
        until session is suspended; galleries
        ordered cleared.   U.N. Archives [n.d.]
        10 min., 26 sec.   phonotape (1 r.
        7 1/2 i.p.s.)

        On United Nations Special Tape no. 1.

        1. Zaire - Politics and government.

Voice Lib.
252   Stevenson, Adlai Ewing, 1900-1965.
        Acceptance speech at Democratic
        National Convention, 1956. Detroit,
        WJR, September 6, 1956.
        1 reel (7 in.)   7 1/2 in. per sec.
        phonotape.

Voice Lib.
M724   Stevenson, Adlai Ewing, 1900-1965.
bd.5   Excerpt of acceptance speech in 1952.
        1 reel (7 in.)   7 1/2 in. per sec.
        phonotape.

Voice Lib.
M924   Stevenson, Adlai Ewing, 1900-1965.
bd.2   Opening address at start of Democratic
        presidential campaign of 1956 at Harrisburg,
        Pennsylvania.   WJR, September 13, 1956.
        1 reel (7 in.)   7 1/2 in. per sec.
        phonotape.

Voice Lib.
M924   Stevenson, Adlai Ewing, 1900-1965.
bd.1   Excerpts of witty remarks on various
        occasions.   CRI, February 14, 1953.
        1 reel (7 in.)   7 1/2 in. per sec.
        phonotape.

        CONTENTS.-a) commenting on distinction of
        talking at $250 a plate dinner.-b) politics
        should stop at water's edge but that should
        not prevent pulling Mr. Dulles back onto dry
        ground.-c) remarks about Senator Cooper (Ky.)
        (Continued on next card)

Voice Lib.
237   Stevenson, Adlai Ewing, 1900-1965.
bd.2   Conceding loss of Presidential election.
        CBS, November 7, 1956.
        1 reel (7 in.)   7 1/2 in. per sec.
        phonotape.

Voice Lib.
M924   Stevenson, Adlai Ewing, 1900-1965.   Excerpts
bd.1   of witty remarks on various occasions.
        February 14, 1953.   (Card 2)

        CONTENTS, cont'd.-d) acknowledging gratification
        to be asked to speak about ethics.-
        e) reminiscing about 30 year alumni reunion
        classes.- f) remarks at American Legion
        banquet.-g) about a speech of his old boss,
        Col. Frank Knox.-h) remarks about General
        Motors at Jefferson Day dinner.

Voice Lib.
M898   Stevenson, Adlai Ewing, 1900-1964.
bd.3   Speaking from Pittsburgh, Pa., during
        national political campaign of 1956.
        WJR, October 3, 1956.
        1 reel (7 in.)   7 1/2 in. per sec.
        phonotape.

Voice Lib.
M721   Stevenson, Adlai Ewing, 1900-1965.
bd.1   Address discussing U.S. position on Formosa
        crisis.   April 11, 1955.
        1 reel (7 in.)   7 1/2 in. per sec.
        phonotape.

Voice Lib.
M925-   Stevenson, Adlai Ewing, 1900-1965.
926   Final network program of the Democratic
bd.1   presidential campaign of 1956.   WJR,
        November 5, 1956.
        2 reels (7 in.)   7 1/2 in. per sec.
        phonotape.

Voice Lib.
351   Stevenson, Adlai Ewing, 1900-1965.
bd.7   Review of his South American trip; on
          changing social structure of Latin America,
          Bay of Pigs incident, view of Latin America
          on U.S., appeal of Communism for Latin
          Americans, propaganda from Cuba to Latin
          America. CBS, 1961.
            1 reel (7 in.)   7 1/2 in. per sec.
          phonotape.

Voice Lib.
M1460   Stevenson, Adlai Ewing, 1900-1965.
bd.2   Adlai Stevenson gives eulogy of Eleanor
          Roosevelt at U.N.   U.N., November 9, 1962.
            1 reel (7 in.)   7 1/2 in. per sec.
          phonotape.

            1. Roosevelt, Eleanor (Roosevelt), 1884-1962.

Voice Lib.
M344   Stevenson, Adlai Ewing, 1900-1965.
bd.5   Speech at the U.N. on admittance of Red
          China to the United Nations. CBS,
          December 1, 1961.
            1 reel (7 in.)   7 1/2 i.p.s.   phonotape.

            1. United Nations - Membership.

Voice Lib.
M974   Stevenson, Adlai Ewing, 1900-1965.
bd.1   Address at convocation celebrating the
          10th anniversary of the Fund for the
          Republic, entitled: "The prospects for
          democracy around the world".   CSDI,
          January 22, 1963.
            1 reel (7 in.)   7 1/2 in. per sec.
          phonotape.

Voice Lib.
344   Stevenson, Adlai Ewing, 1900-1965.
bd.13   At the U.N. on the Indian invasion
          of Goa. CBS, December 18, 1961.
            1 reel (7 in.)   7 1/2 in. per sec.
          phonotape.

            1. Goa.

Voice Lib. Stevenson, Adlai Ewing, 1900-1965
M915-   As we knew him; words of reminiscence of
916   friends and relatives about the life of
          J.F. Kennedy. Narration by Charles Kuralt;
          participants: Charles Bartlett, Lemayne
          Billings, Robert Kennedy, Rose Kennedy,
          James Reed, Adlai Stevenson, Gen. Chester B.
          Clifton, etc. Columbia Records Inc., 1965.
            2 reels (7 in.)   7 1/2 in. per sec.
          phonotape.

            1. Kennedy, John Fitzgerald, Pres. U.S.,
          1917-1963. I. Kuralt, Charles, 1934-

(Continued on next card)

Voice Lib.
344   Stevenson, Adlai Ewing, 1900-1965.
bd.14   At U.N. following the vote on Goa:
          "the failure of the Security Council
          tonight to demand a cease-fire is a failure
          of the U.N.". CBS, December 19, 1961.
            1 reel (7 in.)   7 1/2 in. per sec.
          phonotape.

            1. Goa.

Voice Lib.
M909   Stevenson, Adlai Ewing, 1900-1965.
            Remarks about the humor of JFK.   RCA,
          1965.
            1 reel (7 in.)   7 1/2 in. per sec.
          phonotape.

            1. Kennedy, John Fitzgerald, Pres. U.S.,
          1917-1963.

Voice Lib.
M715   Stevenson, Adlai Ewing, 1900-1965.
bd.16   Excerpt of statement at U.N. Security
          Council meeting on U.S. position on Cuban
          missile build up October 23, 1962 and his
          reply to USSR Ambassador Zorin at U.N.
          Security Council meeting of October 25,
          1962.   October 23-25, 1962.
            2 min., 24 sec.   phonotape (1 r.
          7 1/2 i.p.s.)

            1. United Nations.

Voice Lib.
M919-   Stevenson, Adlai Ewing, 1900-1965.
920   The voice of the uncommon man; narrated by
bd.1   Alexander Scourby. RCA, 1965.
            2 reels (7 in.)   7 1/2 in. per sec.
          phonotape.

            1. Stevenson, Adlai Ewing, 1900-1965. I.
          Scourby, Alexander, 1913-

Stevenson, Adlai Ewing, 1900-1965

Voice Lib.
M931   Roosevelt, Eleanor Roosevelt, 1884-1962.
bd.2   Introducing Adlai Stevenson from Los
        Angeles; he speaks about current condition
        of schools.   CBS, September 28, 1956.
            1 reel (7 in.)   7 1/2 in. per sec.
        phonotape.

                I. Stevenson, Adlai Ewing, 1900-1965.

STEVENSON, ADLAI EWING, 1900-1965

Voice Lib.
180   Murray, Philip, 1886-1952.
bd.2   Campaign speech for Adlai Stevenson.
        AFL-CIO, 1952.
            1 reel (7 in.)   7 1/2 in. per sec.
        phonotape.

                1. Stevenson, Adlai Ewing, 1900-1965.

STEVENSON, ADLAI EWING, 1900-1965

Voice Lib.
M724   Roosevelt, Eleanor Roosevelt, 1884-1962.
bd.7   Speaking in favor of nomination of Adlai
        Stevenson in 1960 at convention in Los
        Angeles, Calif.
            1 reel (7 in.)   7 1/2 in. per sec.
        phonotape.

                . Stevenson, Adlai Ewing, 1900-1965.

Voice Lib.
M1706   Stewart, James, 1908-
bd. 4   Discusses his one singing role for MGM; sings "Easy to love".
        Includes part of the sound track of "That's entertainment" with
        Jean Harlow and Cary Grant singing "Did I remember?"
        From the Merv Griffin Show. WJRT-TV, June 6, 1974.
            15 min. phonotape (1 r.   7 1/2 i.p.s.)

                1. Stewart, James, 1908-   2. Harlow, Jean, 1911-1937.
            3. Grant, Cary, 1904-   I. Griffin, Mervyn Edward, 1925-
            II. Grant, Cary, 1904-   III. Harlow, Jean, 1911-1937.

Voice Lib.
517-   Stickney, Dorothy Hayes, 1903-
518   "A Lovely Night", from Festival of
bd.1   Performing Arts; dramatization of poems and
        letters of Edna St. Vincent Millay.   Talent
        Associates, April 14, 1962.
            2 reels (7 in.)   7 1/2 in. per sec.
        phonotape.

                I. Millay, Edna St. Vincent, 1892-1950.

Voice Lib.
M1592   Stigma I.
            What is it like to be crippled?
        Center for Independent Living, University
        of California at Berkeley, 1973.
            25 min.   phonotape (1 r.   7 1/2 i.p.s.)

                1. Physically handicapped.   I. Title.

Voice Lib.
M1593   Stigma II.
            The physically disabled and the world.
        Center for Independent Living, University
        of California at Berkeley, 1973.
            25 min.   phonotape (1 r.   7 1/2 i.p.s.)

                1. Physically handicapped.

Voice Lib.
M982   Stilwell, Joseph Warren, 1883-1946.
bd.10   Excerpt of short-wave radio message
        about conditions and the welfare of American
        troops in the Pacific during World War II.
        N.Y., 1944.
            1 reel (7 in.)   7 1/2 in. per sec.
        phonotape.

                1. World War, 1939-1945 - Pacific Ocean.

Voice Lib.
M715   Stock market slump of 1962; newscast and
bd.5   "on-the-spot" interview with customers
        in brokerage firm.   May 29, 1962.
            2 min., 52 sec.   phonotape (1 r.
        7 1/2 i.p.s.)

                1. U.S. - Economic conditions.

Stoddard, Charles C

Voice Lib.
M1251   Hannah, John Alfred, 1902-
            Address at MSU commencement, Spring,
        1967; introductory remarks by Charles
        Stoddard, President of 1967 Senior class.
        WKAR, June 11, 1967.
            1 reel (7 in.)   7 1/2 in. per sec.
        phonotape.

                I. Stoddard, Charles C

Voice Lib.
M1470   Stoehr, Franz
bd.5   Speaking in the German Reichstag, among
much shouting and commotion and singing.
Peteler, February 11, 1932.
    1 reel (7 in.)   7 1/2 in. per sec.
phonotape.

STONEHENGE

C1
SC11   Whorf, Michael, 1933-
    The legend of Stonehenge.
    1 tape cassette.   (The visual sounds of
Mike Whorf. Science, SC11)
     Originally presented on his radio program, Kaleidoscope,
WJR, Detroit.
     Duration: 30 min., 30 sec.
     What were the strange rock formations which had dotted the
English countryside for centuries? What purpose did these great
stones serve and where did they come from?

     L Stonehenge. L Title.

Voice Lib.
M760   Stoller, Mike
bd.8   Excerpt from "What all the screaming's
about" (Program 1); anything Elvis had sung
at the peak of his career would have been
popular. Westinghouse Broadcasting
Corporation, 1964.
    9 sec.   phonotape (1 r.   7 1/2 i.p.s.)
(The music goes round and round)

    L Presley, Elvis Aron, 1935-   2. Music, Popular (Songs,
etc.) - U.S.   L Title: What all the screaming's about.
II. Series.

C1
H107   Stonewall - Thomas Jonathan Jackson
    Whorf, Michael, 1933-
    Stonewall - Thomas Jonathan Jackson.
    1 tape cassette.   (The visual sounds of
Mike Whorf. History and heritage, H107)
     Originally presented on his radio program, Kaleidoscope,
WJR, Detroit.
     Duration: 38 min.
     This program tells the exciting story of the life of one of the
Confederacy's most colorful leaders. The humanness of the man is
stressed as the narrator weaves his tale with equal amounts of
pathos and tender humor.

     L Jackson, Thomas Jonathan, 1824-1863. L Title.

Voice Lib.
M760   Stoller, Mike
bd.13   Excerpt from "The Big Beat" (Program 2);
comments on how the musical tastes of people
change and have changed. Westinghouse
Broadcasting Corporation, 1964.
    1 reel (7 in.)   7 1/2 in. per sec.
phonotape.   (The Music Goes Round and Round)

    I. Title: The big beat. II. Series.

Voice Lib.
M910-   Stout, Bill
911,   Resumé of the Watts riots in Los Angeles
bd.1   County, during the most violent riots in Los
Angeles history; including actual sounds and
voices of Police Chief William H. Parker,
Mayor Yorty, etc. CBS, August, 1965.
    2 reels (7 in.)   7 1/2 i.p.s.   phonotape.

    1. Los Angeles - Riots, 1965.   I. Parker,
William H., 1902-   II. Yorty, Samuel
William, 1909-

Voice Lib.
M1619   Stone, Chuck
bd.2   Perspectives in Black, with Roz Abrahms,
Cheri Mazingo, and J. Markisha Johnson.
WKAR, 1974.
    27 min.   phonotape (1 r.   7 1/2 i.p.s.)

    1. Race discrimination - U.S. 2. Watergate
Affair, 1972-   I. Abrahms, Roz.
II. Mazingo, Cheri. III. Johnson, J.
Markisha.

Voice Lib.
M1721   Stout, Rex, 1886-
bd.4   Interviewed on Book Beat by Robert Cromie.
WKAR-TV, June 12, 1974.
    20 min.   phonotape (1 r.   7 1/2 i.p.s.)

    1. Authors - Correspondence, reminiscences,
etc. I. Cromie, Robert.

    Stone, Harlan Fiske, 1872-1946
Voice Lib.
M900   Roosevelt, Franklin Delano, Pres. U.S.,
bd.2   1882-1945.
    Speaking from the F.D.R. Library at Hyde
Park, New York, on the subject of allegiance
to the flag; over the CBS radio network,
including the pledge by Chief Justice Harlan
Stone. WJR, July 4, 1941.
    1 reel (7 in.)   7 1/2 in. per sec.
phonotape.

    I. Stone, Harlan Fiske, 1872-1946.

    Stover, Robert
Voice Lib.
M814   Santayana, George, 1863-1952.
bd.2-   Personal reminiscences about the eminent
815   American philosopher, poet, and novelist by
Horace H. Kallen and Dr. Corliss Lamont, in
conversation with Robert Stover of WBAI,
arranged through the cooperation of the
American Humanist Association. KPFK, May 23,
1964.
    2 reels (7 in.)   7 1/2 in. per sec.   phonotape.
    L Santayana, George, 1863-1952. L Kallen, Horace Meyer,
1882-   II. Lamont, Corliss, 1902-   III. Stover, Robert

C1
A18
STOWE, HARRIET ELIZABETH (BEECHER) 1811-1896

Whorf, Michael, 1933-
So this is the little lady who started
a war.
1 tape cassette. (The visual sounds of
Mike Whorf. Art, music, and letters, A18)
Originally presented on his radio program, Kaleidoscope,
WJR, Detroit.
Duration: 45 min.
Harriet Beecher Stowe's "Uncle Tom's cabin" certainly had
its effect on the nation, causing such a division of emotion and
belief that the country fought a war.

L. Stowe, Harriet Elizabeth (Beecher) 1811-1896. L. Title.

Voice Lib.
M1800
WG
0720.03
Strachan, Gordon Creighton, 1943-
Testimony before the Senate Committee
investigating the Watergate Affair.
27 min. phonotape (1 r.   3 3/4 i.p.s.)
(Watergate gavel to gavel, phase 1)

1. Watergate Affair, 1972-

Voice Lib.
M1800
WG
0723
Strachan, Gordon Creighton, 1943-
Testimony before the Senate Committee
investigating the Watergate Affair.
Pacifica, July 23, 1973.
274 min. phonotape (4 r.   3 3/4 i.p.s.)
(Watergate gavel to gavel, phase 1)

1. Watergate Affair, 1972-

Voice Lib.
M1470
bd.16
Strang, Sir William, 1894-
Speaking about the negotiations between
the British and the Soviets in the year
1939. Peteler, 1964.
1 reel (7 in.) 7 1/2 i.p.s. phonotape.

1. Great Britain - Foreign relations -
Russia. 2. Russia - Foreign relations -
Great Britain.

C1
A1
The strange life of Paul Gauguin

Whorf, Michael, 1933-
The strange life of Paul Gauguin.
1 tape cassette. (The visual sounds of
Mike Whorf. Art, music, and letters, A1)
Originally presented on his radio program, Kaleidoscope,
WJR, Detroit.
Duration: 28 min., 15 sec.
Gauguin forsook the comforts of his world to wander half
way around the globe as a painter.

L. Gauguin, Paul, 1848-1903. L. Title.

C1
S9
The stranger

Whorf, Michael, 1933-
The stranger.
1 tape cassette. (The visual sounds of
Mike Whorf. Social, S9)
Originally presented on his radio program, Kaleidoscope,
WJR, Detroit.
Duration: 46 min., 30 sec.
Dealing with the American Indian, it relates the saga of the
warrior from boyhood to manhood, how and why he fought, the
ritual of his ceremony, and the explanation of his way of life.

L. Indians of North America. L. Title.

C1
S23
Stranger, no more

Whorf, Michael, 1933-
Stranger, no more.
1 tape cassette. (The visual sounds of
Mike Whorf. Social, S23)
Originally presented on his radio program, Kaleidoscope,
WJR, Detroit.
Duration: 42 min., 15 sec.
This is the conclusion to the American Indian series. The
story concerns the redman today. It speaks, as does the indian,
of his needs, aspirations and hopes.

L. Indians of North America. L. Title.

C1
M50
Stranger then fiction

Whorf, Michael, 1933-
Stranger then fiction.
1 tape cassette. (The visual sounds of
Mike Whorf. Miscellaneous, M50)
Originally presented on his radio program, Kaleidoscope,
WJR, Detroit.
Duration: 36 min., 30 sec.
Are these short stories fact or fiction, which elements are
true, which untrue?

L. Title.

Voice Lib.
M1345
Strasser, Gregor, 1892-1934.
First radio broadcast of a member of the
NSDAP; subject: The state concept of
national socialism. Peteler, June 1, 1932.
1 reel (7 in.) 7 1/2 i.p.s. phonotape.

Strasser was chief of staff of operations of the NSDAP;
denounced Party membership in November, 1932, and became a
bitter enemy of Hitler; assassinated June 1934, during the Rohm
purge.

L. Nationalsozialistische Deutsche Arbeiter-Partei.

STRATEGIC AIR COMMAND
Voice Lib.
381-
382
bd.1
I can hear it now (radio program)
CBS, April 26, 1951.
2 reels (7 in.) 7 1/2 in. per sec. phonotape.
L. Radio Free Europe. 2. Strategic Air Command. L.
Ridgway, Matthew Bunker, 1895- II. Churchill, Winston Leonard
Spencer, 1874-1965. III. Bevan, Aneurin, 1897-1960. IV. Nixon,
Richard Milhous, Pres. U.S., 1913- V. Kerr, Robert Samuel, 1896-
1963. VI. Brewster, Ralph Owen, 1888-1962. VII. Wherry, Kenneth
Spicer, 1892-1951. VIII. Capehart, Homer Earl, 1897- IX.
Lehman, Herbert Henry, 1878-1963. X. Taft, Robert Alphonso,
1889-1953. XI. Moody, Arthur Edson Blair, 1902-1954. XII.
Martin, Joseph William, 1884-1968. XIII. McMahon, James O'Brien,
1903-1952. XIV. MacArthur, Douglas, 1880-1964. XVII. Wilson,
Charles Edward, 1886-1972. VIII. Irvine, Clarence T

Voice Lib.
243   Stratton, William Grant, 1914–
bd.5   Denial of parole to Nathan Leopold, with
           Hugh Hill of WBBM (Chicago).   CBS, July 30,
           1957.
             1 reel (7 in.)   7 1/2 in. per sec.
           phonotape.

             1. Leopold, Nathan Freudenthal, 1904 or 5–
                defendant.   I. Hill, Hugh

C1   STRAUSS, JOHANN, 1825–1899
PWM9   Whorf, Michael, 1933–
          Strauss.
            1 tape cassette.   (The visual sounds of
          Mike Whorf. Panorama; a world of music,
          PWM-9)
            Originally presented on his radio program, Kaleidoscope,
          WJR, Detroit.
            Duration: 25 min.
            The life and times of Johann Strauss, the younger, the
          waltz king, including excerpts of his music.
            1. Strauss, Johann, 1825–1899.   1. Title.

Voice Lib.
M1661   Strauss, Robert Schwartz, 1918–
bd.2   On Nixon tapes and other current political
           issues; interview by Jim Lehrer, on "Straight
           Talk".   WKAR-TV, May 14, 1974.
             20 min.   phonotape (1 r.   7 1/2 i.p.s.)

             1. U.S. – Politics and government – 1969–
           I. Lehrer, Jim.

C1   Strauss
PWM9   Whorf, Michael, 1933–
          Strauss.
            1 tape cassette.   (The visual sounds of
          Mike Whorf. Panorama; a world of music,
          PWM-9)
            Originally presented on his radio program, Kaleidoscope,
          WJR, Detroit.
            Duration: 25 min.
            The life and times of Johann Strauss, the younger, the
          waltz king, including excerpts of his music.
            1. Strauss, Johann, 1825–1899.   1. Title.

Voice Lib.
M1010   Streicher, Julius, 1885–1946.
bd.2   Speech in which Streicher compares Hitler's
           ideas to those of Jesus Christ, as both
           wished to eliminate Jewish capitalists.
           Peteler, January 22, 1936.
             1 reel (7 in.)   7 1/2 in. per sec.
           phonotape.

             1. National socialism

                    Streisand, Barbra, 1942–
Voice Lib.
M1398   From here to the seventies, Part III.   NBC-TV
bd.1   two-and-a-half hour documentary pertaining to
           events occurring during the 1960's.   NBC-TV,
           October 7, 1969.
             1 reel (7 in.)   7 1/2 in. per sec.
           phonotape.
             CONTENTS. –1. Style changes: a. clothes; b. sex; c. violence;
           d. outlook; e. morals; f. sports and protest. –2. Man's mortality:
           a. death of Winston Churchill; b. Bobby Kennedy, speech before
           assassination; c. Dr. King, "I've been to the mountain top..." and
           "We'll get to the Promised Land"; d. John Kennedy's last speech. –
           3. Hunger around the world: a. Green Revolution, problems and
           benefits; b. abortions to control population. –4. Communications
                                    (Continued on next card)

                    Streisand, Barbra, 1942–
Voice Lib.
M1398   From here to the seventies, Part III...   1969.
bd.1   (Card 2)
             CONTENTS, cont'd. explosion: a. David Brinkley, TV. –5. Ending:
           a. Paul Newman; b. Barbra Streisand.

             I. Kennedy, Robert Francis, 1925–1968.   II.
           King, Martin Luther, 1929–1968.   III. Kennedy,
           John Fitzgerald, Pres.U.S., 1917–1963.   IV.
           Brinkley, David McClure, 1920–   V. Newman,
           Paul, 1925–   VI. Streisand, Barbra, 1942–

Voice Lib.
M1466   Stresemann, Gustav, 1878–1929.
bd.20   Remarks at the opening of the German
           photographic and motion picture exhibition.
           Peteler, 1925.
             1 reel (7 in.)   7 1/2 i.p.s.   phonotape.

             1. Photography.

Voice Lib.
M1466   Stresemann, Gustav, 1878–1929.
bd.22   Speech on the occasion of German Reichstag
           elections.   Peteler, May 1928.
             1 reel (7 in.)   7 1/2 in. per sec.
           phonotape.

                    STRESEMAN, GUSTAV, 1878–1929
Voice Lib.
M1466   Newsreport and ceremony upon the funeral of
bd.22   Gustav Stresemann; eulogy by Alfred Braun.
           Peteler, October 6, 1929.
             1 reel (7 in.)   7 1/2 in. per sec.
           phonotape.

             1. Streseman, Gustav, 1878–1929.   I. Braun,
           Alfred

Voice Lib.
129   Strickland, Lily Teresa, 1887-1958.
bd.1-5   Talking about, singing, playing own
         composition.   Private recording on location,
         1942.
            1 reel (7 in.)   7 1/2 in. per sec.
         phonotape.

            CONTENTS.-Bd.1. Lindy Lou.-bd.2. Moanin'
         wind.-bd.3. Smiling on.-bd.4. Why can't I?.-
         bd.5. Down South.

C1
8C6   Whorf, Michael, 1933-
            A study in prophecy.
            1 tape cassette.   (The visual sounds of
         Mike Whorf.   Science, SC6)

            Originally presented on his radio program, Kaleidoscope,
         WJR, Detroit.
            Duration: 55 min.
            Jeane Dixon expounds of her faith, tells why she has been
         able to see glimpses of another world, and tells of her predictions,
         some of which have come true and others which have not.

            L Dixon, Jeane.   L Title.

               "Strike Up the Band" rehearsal
Voice Lib.
540   Gershwin, George, 1898-1937.
bd.3   "Strike Up the Band" rehearsal.   Fox
         Movietone, 1927.
            1 reel (7 in.)   7 1/2 in. per sec.
         phonotape.

            I. Title.

Voice Lib.
M807-   Sukarno, Pres. Indonesia, 1901-1970.
810   Address at United Nations General Assembly,
         New York.   U.N. Archives, September 30, 1960.
            4 reels (7 in.)   7 1/2 in. per sec.
         phonotape.

            STRIKES AND LOCKOUTS - TEACHERS
Voice Lib.
M1607   Porter, John W   1931-
bd.1   Off the record; problems facing Michigan
         schools.   Interviewed by Tim Skubick, Tom
         Green, Bill Meek, and Gary Schuster.
         WKAR-TV, February 1, 1974.
            17 min.   phonotape (1 r.   7 1/2 in. per
         sec.)

            1. Segregation in education. 2. Strikes
         and lockouts - Teachers.   I. Skubick, Tim.
         II. Green, Tom.   III. Meek, Bill. IV. Schuster.
         Gary.

Voice Lib.
M728   Sukarno, Pres. Indonesia, 1901-1970.
bd.4   Interview with CBS correspondents regarding
         the withdrawal of Indonesia from the U.N.
         Columbia records, inc., 1965.
            1 reel (7 in.)   7 1/2 in. per sec.
         phonotape.

            1. Indonesia - Foreign relations.

Voice Lib.
M1435   Struve, Otto, 1897-1963
            Life in other worlds; exploratory discussion about life on other
         planets. Arnold J. Toynbee, Dr. G. B. Kiastiakowsky
         (professor at Harvard), Dr. Donald M. Michaels, Dr. Otto
         Struve, Dr. Harlow Shapley, Walter Cronkite, Chet Huntley,
         William L. Laurence. New York, NBC, March 3, 1961.
            1 reel (7 in.) 7 1/2 i. p. s. phonotape.

            L Life on other planets. L Toynbee, Arnold Joseph, 1889-
         IL Kiastiakowsky, George Bogdan. III Michaels, Donald M.
         IV. Struve, Otto, 1897-1963. V. Shapley, Harlow, 1885-1972.
         VL Cronkite, Walter Leland, 1916-   VIL Huntley, Chet,
         1911-1974. VIII. Laurence, William Leonard, 1888-

Voice Lib.
M613   Sullivan, Sir Arthur Seymour, 1842-1900.
bd.5   Preservation of sound through records.
         Source (?), 1890-1900?
            1 reel (7 in.)   7 1/2 in. per sec.
         phonotape.

            1. Phonorecords - History.

            STUDENTS - POLITICAL MOVEMENTS
Voice Lib.
M1658   FSM's sounds and songs of the
            demonstration.   Berkeley, Calif., FSM
            Records Dept., September 21, 1964.
            50 min.   phonotape (1 r.   7 1/2 i.p.s.)

            1. Free Speech Movement. 2. Students -
         Political movements.   I. Free Speech
         Movement.

Voice Lib.
M1548   Sullivan, Frank, 1892-
            Interviewed on Bob Crombie's "Book Beat"
         program.   WKAR, February 13, 1974.
            28 min.   phonotape (1 r.   7 1/2 i.p.s.)

            1. Authors - Correspondence, reminiscences,
         etc.   I. Crombie, Robert.

Voice Lib.
M1582   Sullivan, Richard Eugene, 1921-
         Pre-national Europe; excerpts.   WKAR-FM,
February 27, 1974.
         25 min.   phonotape (1 r.   7 1/2 i.p.s.)

         1. Europe - History - 476-1492.

                    Sunday, William Ashley, 1862-1935
Voice Lib.
M617   Radio in the 1920's: a series of excerpts
bd.1-   from important broadcasts of the 1920's,
bd.25   with brief prologue and epilogue; a sample
            of radio of the period.   NVL, April, 1964.
            1 reel (7 in.)   7 1/2 in. per sec.
         phonotape.
            I. Radio programs.   I. Marconi, Guglielmo, marchese, 1874-
         1937.   II. Kendall, H   G   III. Coolidge, Calvin, Pres. U.S.,
         1872-1933.   IV. Wilson, Woodrow, Pres. U.S., 1856-1924.   V.
         Roosevelt, Franklin Delano, Pres. U.S., 1882-1945.   VI. Lodge,
         Henry Cabot, 1850-1924.   VII. LaGuardia, Fiorello Henry, 1882-1947.
         VIII. The Happiness Boys (Radio program)   IX. Gallagher and Sheen.
         X. Barney Google.   XI. Vallee, Rudy, 1901-   XII. The two
                                            (Continued on next card)

C1
M34   SUMMER
         Whorf, Michael, 1933-
            In the good old summertime.
            1 tape cassette.   (The visual sounds of
         Mike Whorf. Miscellaneous, M34)
            Originally presented on his radio program, Kaleidoscope,
         WJR, Detroit.
            Duration: 37 min., 20 sec.
            It begins and ends with the strains of "In the good old
         summertime", and in between is a delightfully warm and
         sensitive description of what the season is all about.

            I. Summer.   I. Title.

Voice Lib.
M1673   Superman (radio program)
bd.2   Superman.   Golden Age Radio Records,
         1945.
            10 min.   phonotape (1 r.   7 1/2 i.p.s.)

Voice Lib.
M1615   Sunday, William Ashley, 1862-1935.
bd.6   The evils of drink.   Rare Records, Inc.,
         R1001   [19--?]
            1 min., 40 sec.   phonotape (1 r.
         7 1/2 i.p.s.)

          Surfin' bird
Voice Lib.
M762   Lieber, Jerry
bd.12   Excerpt from "The Big Beat" (Program 2);
         changes in the market for rock-and-roll
         records; including the song "Surfin' Bird".
         Westinghouse Broadcasting Corporation, 1964.
            1 reel (7 in.)   7 1/2 in. per sec.
         phonotape.   (The Music Goes Round and Round)

            I. Title: Surfin' bird.   II. Title: The
         big beat.   III. Series.

Voice Lib.
290   Sunday, William Ashley, 1862-1935.
bd.2   Regulation of liquor; statement on ideas
         regarding prohibition.   Pathe, 1925.
            1 reel (7 in.)   7 1/2 in. per sec.
         phonotape.

            1. Prohibition

Voice Lib.
1294   Susskind, David, 1920-
bd.2   Interview on Merv Griffin Show, discussing
         story of Susskind's broadcast with USSR
         Chairman Khrushchev.   CBS-TV, December 18,
         1967.
            1 reel (7 in.)   7 1/2 in. per sec.
         phonotape.

            I. Griffin, Mervyn Edward, 1925-

Voice Lib.
514   Sunday, William Ashley, 1862-1935.
bd.2   On the control of intoxicating beverages.
         Fox Movietone News, 1928.
            1 reel (7 in.)   7 1/2 in. per sec.
         phonotape.

            1. Prohibition

          SVERDLOV, ÍAKOV MIKHAÍLOVICH, 1885-1919
Voice Lib.
M1227   Lenin, Vladimir Il'ich, 1870-1924.
bd.5   Oration to the memory of Comrade Sverdlov,
         the chairman of the Central Executive
         Committee of the Communist Party of the
         USSR.   Peteler, 1919.
            1 reel (7 in.)   7 1/2 in. per sec.
         phonotape.

            1. Sverdlov, Íakov Mikhaílovich, 1885-1919.

Voice Lib.
M1692 Swainson, John Burley, 1927-
bd.1   Opening a Governor's Conference on Drug
        Dependence and Abuse, and outlining the
        scope of the problem. WKAR, December 8,
        1969.
        10 min. phonotape (1 r. 7 1/2 i.p.s.)

        1. Drug abuse.

                          Swinging on a star
Voice Lib.
591   Crosby, Bing, 1901-
bd.2   Sings sing-along version of Sammy Chan-
        Jimmy Van Heusen song "Swinging on a Star",
        prepared for use in military hospitals.
        Comments on song. V-Disc, 1943.
        1 reel (7 in.) 7 1/2 in. per sec.
        phonotape.

          I. Title: Swinging on a star.

        Swanson, Gloria, 1899?-
Voice Lib.
M669-   The legend of Cecil B. DeMille. Yul
670   Brynner, Charlton Heston, Bob Hope, Betty
        Hutton, Edward G. Robinson, Barbara Stanwyck,
        James Stewart, Gloria Swanson, Cornel
        Wilde, Samuel Goldwyn, Billy Graham, Cecil
        B. DeMille.   Recorded 1963.
        2 reels (7 in.) 7 1/2 in. per sec. phonotape.
          L. DeMille, Cecil Blount, 1881-1959. L Brynner, Yul, 1917-
        II. Heston, Charlton, 1924-   III. Hope, Bob, 1903-   IV.
        Hutton, Betty, 1921-   V. Robinson, Edward G   1893-1973.
        VI. Stanwyck, Barbara, 1907-   VII. Stewart, James Maitland,
        1908-   VIII. Swanson, Gloria, 1899?-   IX. Wilde, Cornel, 1915-
        X. Goldwyn, Samuel, 1884?-   XI. Graham, William Franklin,
        1918-   XII. DeMille, Cecil Blount, 1881-1959.

Voice Lib. Swope, Herbert Bayard, 1882-1958
M272   Biography in sound (radio program)
bd.1   Heywood Broun. NBC, date?
        1 reel (7 in.) 7 1/2 in. per sec.
        phonotape.

          L. Broun, Heywood Campbell, 1888-1939. L Broun,
        Heywood Campbell, 1888-1939. II. Swope, Herbert Bayard,
        1882-1958. III. Wilson, Mattie   IV. Jackson, Gardner
        V. Meany, Thomas   VI. Waldron, Beatrice   VII.
        Gordon, Max   VIII. Madison, Connie   IX. Gannett,
        Lewis Stiles, 1891-1966. X. Collins, Joseph, 1866-1950. XI.
        Brown, Earl Louis, 1900-   XII. Levy, Newman, 1888-
        XIII. Growth, John   XIV. Bye, George   XV.
        Roosevelt, Franklin Dela   Pres. U.S., 1882-1945. XVI.
        Reynolds, Quentin James.   2-1965.

C1   SWIFT, JONATHAN, 1667-1745
A43   Whorf, Michael, 1933-
        The unhappy genius, Jonathan Swift.
        1 tape cassette. (The visual sounds of
        Mike Whorf. Art, music and letters, A43)
          Originally presented on his radio program, Kaleidoscope,
        WJR, Detroit.
          Duration: 36 min., 40 sec.
          The creator of brilliant and biting satire, Swift gave the
        world many impressive works that reflected the political and
        social customs of his times, and yet are still relevant to ours
        today.

          L. Swift, Jonathan, 1667-1745. L. Title.

C1   Symbols of nationhood, national anthems
M6   Whorf, Michael, 1933-
        Symbols of nationhood, national anthems.
        1 tape cassette. (The visual sounds of
        Mike Whorf. Miscellaneous, M6)
          Originally presented on his radio program, Kaleidoscope,
        WJR, Detroit.
          Duration: 41 min.
          A program devoted to the national anthems of the world, with
        many musical illustrations and comments concerning the composi-
        tion, and conditions under which they were written.

          L. National songs. L. Title.

        Swigert, John L   1932-
Voice Lib.
M1423   Apollo 13 (space flight): resumé of flight
        of Apollo 13, including lift-off, mal-
        function, and splashdown, and interviews
        on future of space program. NBC TV,
        April, 1970.
        1 reel (7 in.) 7 1/2 in. per sec.
        phonotape.
          L. Project Apollo. 2. Space flight to the moon. 3. Haise,
        Fred W   1934-   4. Lovell, James Arthur, 1928-   5.
        Swigert, John L   1932-   L. Haise, Fred W   1934-
        II. Lovell, James Arthur, 1928-   III. Swigert, John L   1932-

---

Voice Lib.
M1016   Syrový, Jan, 1888-
bd.1   Radio message to Czech people explaining
        position taken by his government in sub-
        mitting to Nazi terms of conquest, following
        Munich sell-out. F. Peteler, October 30,
        1938.
        1 reel (7 in.) 7 1/2 in. per sec.
        phonotape.

        Swigert, John L   1932-
Voice Lib.
M1424   Apollo 13 (space flight): oxygen malfunction
        on Apollo 13 described by NASA, astronauts,
        and Howard K. Smith. ABC TV, April 14, 1970.
        1 reel (7 in.) 7 1/2 in. per sec.
        phonotape.

        1. Project Apollo. 2. Space flight to the
        moon. 3. Haise, Fred W   1934-   4.
        Lovell, James Arthur, 1928-   5. Swigert,
        John L   1932-   I. Haise, Fred W   1934-
        II. Lovell, James Arthur, 1928-   III. Swigert,
        John L   1932-   IV. Smith, Howard Kingsbury,
        1914-

Voice Lib.
M857   Taft, Robert Alphonso, 1889-1953.
bd.1   Interview in Pittsburgh, Pa. with Senator
        Taft, touching on current issues such as the
        national budget, taxes housing and labor
        legislation. KDKA, March 29, 1947.
        1 reel (7 in.) 7 1/2 in. per sec.
        phonotape.

Voice Lib.
M828   Taft, Robert Alphonso, 1889-1953.
bd.2   Explaining the terms and the purposes for
          the proposed enactment of the Taft-Hartley
          Labor Bill; fighting to override President
          Truman's veto. NBC, June 22, 1947.
            1 reel (7 in.)   7 1/2 in. per sec.
          phonotape.

            1. U.S. Laws, statutes, etc./Labor management
          relations act, 1947.

          Taft, Robert Alphonso, 1889-1965
Voice Lib.
M1400   Republican Party. National Convention, 25th,
bd.5   Chicago, 1952.
            Description of proceedings at Republican
          National Convention in Chicago, 1952
          (described by commentators George Hicks and
          H.V. Kaltenborn). Includes statements by
          Robert A. Taft and Dwight D. Eisenhower.
          Convention unanimously nominates Eisenhower.
          CBS Radio, 1952.
            1 reel (7 in.)   7 1/2 in. per sec.
          phonotape.

Voice Lib.
353   Taft, Robert Alphonso, 1889-1953.
bd.10   Outbreak of Korean War; time to give notice
          to Communists to stop, brought on by Pres. [sic]
          administration's bungling. NBC, July, 1950.
            1 reel (7 in.)   7 1/2 in. per sec.
          phonotape.

            Original disc off-speed.

            1. Korean War, 1950-1953 - U.S.

Voice Lib.
571   Taft, William Howard, Pres. U.S., 1857-1930.
bd.2   Abolishment of war throughout the
          world.   Victor Talking Machine Company,
          [n.d.]
            1 reel (7 in.)   7 1/2 in. per sec.
          phonotape.

          Taft, Robert Alphonso, 1889-1953
Voice Lib.
M384   I can hear it now (radio program)
bd.2   CBS, February 2, 1951.
            1 reel (7 in.)   7 1/2 in. per sec.
          phonotape.

            I. Taft, Robert Alphonso, 1889-1953. II.
          Rayburn, Samuel Taliaferro, 1882-1961. III.
          Barkley, Alban William, 1877-1956. IV. Rabaut,
          Louis Charles, 1886-1961. V. Attlee, Clement
          Richard Attlee, 1st earl, 1883-1967. VI.
          Kelly, Capt., U.S.A.

Voice Lib.
594   Taft, William Howard, Pres. U.S., 1857-1930.
bd.3   Will of the people; praises action on
          gold standard of McKinley, cites popularity
          of Theodore Roosevelt's administration.
          Thomas A. Edison, 1904.
            1 reel (7 in.)   7 1/2 in. per sec.
          phonotape.

Voice Lib.   Taft, Robert Alphonso, 1889-1953
383   I can hear it now (radio program)
            CBS, February 9, 1951.
            1 reel (7 in.)   7 1/2 in. per sec.
          phonotape.

            I. Wilson, Charles Edward, 1886-1972. II. Gabrielson, Guy
          George, 1891-   III. Taft, Robert Alphonso, 1889-1953. IV.
          Martin, Joseph William, 1884-1965. V. McCarthy, Joseph
          Raymond, 1909-1957. VI. Benton, William Burnett, 1900-1973.
          VII. Malone, George Wilson, 1890-1961. VIII. Capehart, Homer
          Earl, 1897-   IX. Eisenhower, Dwight David, Pres. U.S., 1890-
          1969. X. Lee, J   V   XI. Hodge, John Reed, 1893-
          1963. XII. Overton, Watkins   XIII. DiSalle, Michael
          Vincent, 1908-   XIV. Boyce, Eddy   XV. Conklin, Ed
          XVI. Collins, Joseph Lawton, 1896-

Voice Lib.
594   Taft, William Howard, Pres. U.S., 1857-1930.
bd.4   Rights of labor; right to unionize, limits
          on unions. Thomas A. Edison, 1906.
            1 reel (7 in.)   7 1/2 in. per sec.
          phonotape.

            1. Trade-unions.

          Taft, Robert Alphonso, 1889-1953
Voice Lib.
381-   I can hear it now (radio program)
382   CBS, April 26, 1951.
bd.1   2 reels (7 in.)   7 1/2 in. per sec.   phonotape.
            I. Radio Free Europe. 2. Strategic Air Command. I.
          Ridgway, Matthew Bunker, 1895-   II. Churchill, Winston Leonard
          Spencer, 1874-1965. III. Bevan, Aneurin, 1897-1960. IV. Nixon,
          Richard Milhous, Pres. U.S., 1913-   V. Kerr, Robert Samuel, 1896-
          1963. VI. Brewster, Ralph Owen, 1888-1962. VII. Wherry, Kenneth
          Spicer, 1892-1951. VIII. Capehart, Homer Earl, 1897-   IX.
          Lehman, Herbert Henry, 1878-1963. X. Taft, Robert Alphonso,
          1889-1953. XI. Moody, Arthur Edson Blair, 1902-1954. XII.
          Martin, Joseph William, 1884-1968. XIII. McMahon, James O'Brien,
          1903-1952. XIV. MacArthur, Douglas, 1880-1964. XVII. Wilson,
          Charles Edward, 1886-1972. XVIII. Irvine, Clarence T

Voice Lib.
M755   Taft, William Howard, Pres. U.S., 1857-
bd.4   1930.
            Democratic policy prevents restoration
          of prosperity. Comparing Republican and
          Democratic methods of regulation and
          prosecution of the trusts; upholding the high
          protective tariff. VTM, 1908.
            1 reel (7 in.)   7 1/2 in. per sec.
          phonotape.

Voice Lib.
M755   Taft, William Howard, Pres. U.S., 1857-
bd.5   1930.
            Our army and navy, stressing Republicans'
        desire and accomplishment of strong efficient
        army and navy as compared to silence on
        that subject in the Democratic platform.
        VTM, 1908.
            1 reel (7 in.)   7 1/2 in. per sec.
        phonotape.

Voice Lib.
M759   Taft, William Howard, Pres. U.S., 1857-
bd.5   1930.
            Campaign speech on the anti-trust laws.
        VTM, 1912.
            1 reel (7 in.)   7 1/2 in. per sec.
        phonotape.

Voice Lib.
M755   Taft, William Howard, Pres. U.S., 1857-
bd.3   1930.
            Rise and progress of the Negro, stressing
        the advancement of the Negro since his
        freedom from slavery and the Republican
        platform demanding justice to all men and
        enforcement of the 13th, 14th, and 15th
        amendments of the Constitution.   VTM, 1908.
            1 reel (7 in.)   7 1/2 in. per sec.
        phonotape.

Voice Lib.
M759   Taft, William Howard, Pres. U.S., 1857-
bd.4   1930.
            "Popular Unrest"; campaign speech.   VTM,
        1912.
            1 reel (7 in.)   7 1/2 in. per sec.
        phonotape.

Voice Lib.
M755   Taft, William Howard, Pres. U.S., 1857-
bd.6   1930.
            America's responsibilities in the extension
        of civilization; must help other countries
        and people; Christianity is democracy; our
        position in the Philippines.   VTM, 1909.
            1 reel (7 in.)   7 1/2 in. per sec.
        phonotape.

Voice Lib.
M759   Taft, William Howard, Pres. U.S., 1857-
bd.2   1930.
            Pres. Taft discusses labor and capital.
        VTM, 1912.
            1 reel (7 in.)   7 1/2 in. per sec.
        phonotape.

Voice Lib.
M756   Taft, William Howard, Pres. U.S., 1857-
bd.1   1930.
            Postal Savings Bank vs. Enforced Insurance
        of Deposits. The benefits of postal savings
        banks for use by the public vs. alternate
        plan sponsored by the Democratic Party.
        VTM, 1910.
            1 reel (7 in.)   7 1/2 in. per sec.
        phonotape.

Voice Lib.
653   Taft, William Howard, Pres. U.S., 1857-1930.
bd.2   Prosperity; political speech during campaign
        of 1912 stressing Republican prosperity.
        Source (?), 1912.
            1 reel (7 in.)   7 1/2 in. per sec.
        phonotape.

Voice Lib.
653   Taft, William Howard, Pres. U.S., 1857-1930.
bd.1   Irish humor; discussion of visit to
        Ireland and of Irish poetry and humor.
        Source (?), 1911.
            1 reel (7 in.)   7 1/2 in. per sec.
        phonotape.

Voice Lib.
653   Taft, William Howard, Pres. U.S., 1857-1930.
bd.3   The Protective Tariff; review of
        President Taft's administration's stand on
        Tariff legislation.   Source (?), 1912.
            1 reel (7 in.)   7 1/2 in. per sec.
        phonotape.

Voice Lib.
M759   Taft, William Howard, Pres. U.S., 1857-
bd.3   1930.
        "Who are the People?" Campaign speech.
VTM, 1912.
        1 reel (7 in.)   7 1/2 in. per sec.
phonotape.

        I. Title.

        Taft-Hartley Act
        see
U.S. Laws, statutes, etc. Labor management
        relations act, 1947.

        VOICE LIBRARY

        Taking a trip up the Hudson
Voice Lib.
649   Murray, Billy
bd.9   Singing old popular song "Taking a Trip
up the Hudson". Re-recorded from Edison
cylinder record.   Edison, 1906.
        1 reel (7 in.)   7 1/2 in. per sec.
phonotape.

        I. Title: Taking a trip up the Hudson.

C1   A tale of a tune
M20
Whorf, Michael, 1933-
        A tale of a tune, with Gerald Marks.
        1 tape cassette.   (The visual sounds of
Mike Whorf. Miscellaneous, M40)
        Originally presented on his radio program, Kaleidoscope,
WJR, Detroit.
        Duration: 52 min.
        A delightful nostalgic look at how some of our popular songs
were written, featuring composer Gerald Marks.

        L. Music, Popular (Songs, etc.) L. Marks, Gerald. II. Title.

C1   Tales of the frontier and the forty-niners
H14
Whorf, Michael, 1933-
        Tales of the frontier and the forty-niners.
        1 tape cassette.   (The visual sounds of
Mike Whorf. History and heritage, H14)
        Originally presented on his radio program, Kaleidoscope,
WJR, Detroit.
        Duration: 39 min.
        The year was 1849, and from every corner of the globe came
all types of men searching for quick wealth. "Gold," was the
cry from California and with their hopes and dreams came the
seekers. For a few months it meant adventure and excitement for
those who confronted the frontier and were called the forty-niners.

        L. California - Gold discoveries. 2. Frontier and pioneer life.
L. Title.

        The talk in Vandalia (Television program)
Voice Lib.
M1249   Huntley, Chet, 1911-
bd.1   Documentary TV program: "The Talk in
Vandalia", first capital of state of Illinois,
prompted by Joseph P. Lyford's book "What's
Wrong with Vandalia", a small American mid-
western community. Discussion covers automation
and unemployment problems, farm problems,
increasing of intellectual activities.   NBC,
April 30, 1967.
        1 reel (7 in.) 7 1/2 in. per sec. phonotape.
        L. Vandalia, Ill. 2. Lyford, Joseph P   L. The
talk in Vandalia (Television program)

        The talking machine
Voice Lib.
539   Gay Nineties Revue (Radio program)
bd.5   The talking machine; skit with Joe Howard,
Al Rinker, and Beatrice Kay concerning
Edison's talking machine. Simulated voices
of P.T. Barnum and Florence Nightingale.
CBS, 1940.
        1 reel (7 in.)   7 1/2 in. per sec.
phonotape.

        I. Howard, Joe   II. Rinker, Al
III. Kay, Beatrice

        The tall tales of America - folklore, legends
C1
H39   Whorf, Michael, 1933-
        The tall tales of America - folklore, legends.
        1 tape cassette.   (The visual sounds of
Mike Whorf. History and heritage, H39)

        Originally presented on his radio program, Kaleidoscope,
WJR, Detroit.
        Duration: 45 min., 30 sec.
        John Henry, Johnny Appleseed, Paul Bunyan, the great legends
of American folklore come to life in this amusing account of folk
tales and folk-songs about America.

        L. Folk-lore, American. 2. Folk-songs, American. L. Title.

        Talmadge, Herman Eugene, 1913-
Voice Lib.
M1800   U.S. Congress. Senate. Select Committee on Presidential
        Campaign Activities.
        Watergate gavel to gavel, phase I: May 17 - August 7, 1973.
Pacifica, May 17 - August 7, 1973.
        172 reels (5 in.)   3 3/4 i.p.s. phonotape.

        "These tapes include commentaries by Pacifica's Washington
correspondents and interviews with members of the Senate Committee
taped during recesses of the hearings."

        L. Presidents - U.S. - Elections - 1972. 2. Watergate Affair,
1972-   L. Ervin, Samuel James, 1896-   II. Talmadge,
Herman Eugene, 1913-   III. Inouye, Daniel Ken, 1924-
IV. Baker, Howard H., 1925-   V. Gurney, Edward John, 1914-
VI. Weicker, Lowell P., 19   VII. Title.

Voice Lib.
M863   Tanguay, Eva
bd.3   Performing her act and song "I Don't Care".
IRCC, 1906.
        1 reel (7 in.)   7 1/2 in. per sec.
phonotape.

Voice Lib.
M322   Taurog, Norman, 1899-
     Biography in sound (radio program)
       W.C. Fields, the magnificent rogue.
       NBC, 1955.
         1 reel (7 in.) 7 1/2 in. per sec. phonotape.
         I. Fields, W.C., 1879-1946. I. Fields, W.C., 1879-1946.
     II. Allen, Fred, 1894-1956. III. LaBaron, William   IV.
     Taylor, Robert Lewis, 1912-   V. McCarey, Thomas Leo, 1898-
     1969. VI. Harkins, James   - VII. Chevalier, Maurice,
     1889-1972. VIII. Kuromoto, Mrs. George   IX. Flynn,
     Errol Leslie, 1909-1959. X. Wynn, Ed, 1886-1966. XI. Dowling,
     Ray Dooley   XII. Sennett, Mack   XIII. Overacher,
     Ronald Leroy   XIV. Bergen, Edgar, 1903-   XV. Taurog,
     Norman, 1899-   XVI. Runnell, Ann   XVII. Cowen,
     Lester

Voice Lib.
M1579   Taylor, Judy K
bd.2   Halverson, Craig
      23 tonight; MSU controversy over curb and
     ramp cuts, with Eric Gentile and Judy K. Taylor.
     WKAR-TV, November 13, 1973.
       15 min. phonotape (1 r.   7 1/2 i.p.s.)

      1. Physically handicapped - Law and legis-
    lation. I. Gentile, Eric Anton, 1943-
    II. Taylor, Judy K

Voice Lib.
M1696   Taylor, Billy
bd.6   Columbia Broadcasting System, inc.
      Special memorial to Duke Ellington, with
    John Hart, Sonny Greer, Russell Procope,
    Billy Taylor, Stanley Dance, and Ella
    Fitzgerald. CBS-TV, May 24, 1974.
      15 min. phonotape (1 r.   7 1/2 i.p.s.)

      1. Ellington, Duke, 1899-1974. I. Hart,
    John. II. Greer, Sonny. III. Procope,
    Russell, 1908- IV. Taylor, Billy.
    V. Dance, Stanley. VI. Fitzgerald, Ella,
    1918-

Voice Lib.
M322   Taylor, Robert Lewis, 1912-
     Biography in sound (radio program)
       W.C. Fields, the magnificent rogue.
       NBC, 1955.
         1 reel (7 in.) 7 1/2 in. per sec. phonotape.
         I. Fields, W.C., 1879-1946. I. Fields, W.C., 1879-1946.
     II. Allen, Fred, 1894-1956. III. LaBaron, William   IV.
     Taylor, Robert Lewis, 1912-   V. McCarey, Thomas Leo, 1898-
     1969. VI. Harkins, James   - VII. Chevalier, Maurice,
     1889-1972. VIII. Kuromoto, Mrs. George   IX. Flynn,
     Errol Leslie, 1909-1959. X. Wynn, Ed, 1886-1966. XI. Dowling,
     Ray Dooley   XII. Sennett, Mack   XIII. Overacher,
     Ronald Leroy   XIV. Bergen, Edgar, 1903-   XV. Taurog,
     Norman, 1899-   XVI. Runnell, Ann   XVII. Cowen,
     Lester

Voice Lib.
541   Taylor, Deems, 1885-1966
bd.2   Cantor, Eddie, 1893-1964. ____
      Documentary program for U.S. Treasury
    Department. Introduction by Deems Taylor.
    WABC-NY, January 25, 1952.
      1 reel (7 in.) 7 1/2 in. per sec.
    phonotape.

      I. Taylor, Deems, 1885-1966. II. U.S.
    Treasury Dept.

Voice Lib.
385   Taylor, Telford, 1908-
     I can hear it now (radio program)
       CBS, February 2, 1951.
       1 reel (7 in.) 7 1/2 in. per sec.
    phonotape.

      I. Austin, Warren Robinson, 1877-1962. II.
    Pandit, Vijaya Lakshmi (Nehru) 1900-   III.
    Roosevelt, Eleanor (Roosevelt) 1884-1962. IV.
    Morse, Wayne Lyman, 1900-   V. Chandler,
    Albert Benjamin, 1898-   VI. Taylor, Telford,
    1908-   VII. Whi   Jack.

Voice Lib.
573   Taylor, Glen Hearst, 1904-
bd.2-   I can hear it now (radio program)
574   1945-1949. CBS, 1950?
bd.1   2 reels (7 in.) 7 1/2 in. per sec.
    phonotape.
      I. Murrow, Edward Roscoe, 1908-1965. II. Nehru, Jawaharlal,
    1889-1964. III. Philip, duke of Edinburgh, 1921- IV. Elizabeth II,
    Queen of Great Britain, 1926-   V. Ferguson, Homer, 1889- VI.
    Hughes, Howard Robard, 1905- VII. Marshall, George Catlett,
    1880- VIII. Ruth, George Herman, 1895-1948. IX. Lilienthal,
    David Eli, 1899- X. Trout, Robert, 1908- XI. Gage, Arthur.
    XII. Jackson, Robert Houghwout, 1892-1954. XIII. Gromyko, Ana-
    tolii Andreevich, 1908-   XIV. Baruch, Bernard Mannes, 1870-
    1965. XV. Churchill, Winston Leonard Spencer, 1874-1965. XVI.
    Winchell, Walter, 1897-19 XVII. Davis, Elmer Holmes, 1890-
                            (Continued on next card)

C1
H46   TAYLOR, TOM, 1817-1880
         OUR AMERICAN COUSIN
    Whorf, Michael, 1933-
      The play that Lincoln never saw.
      1 tape cassette. (The visual sounds of
    Mike Whorf. History and heritage, H46)
      Originally presented on his radio program, Kaleidoscope,
    WJR, Detroit.
      Duration: 30 min.
      "Our American cousin" was the play Abraham Lincoln attended on
    that fateful night. In the shadows awaited death and the nation went
    into shock. But what of the play - its actors and actresses?

      I. Taylor, Tom, 1817-1880. /Our American cousin.
    2. Lincoln, Abraham, Pres. U.S., 1809-1865. I. Title.

Voice Lib.
M1615   Taylor, John Francis Adams
      The social implications of the energy
    crisis. WKAR-FM, March 28, 1974.
      35 min. phonotape (1 r. 7 1/2 in. per sec.)
      Part of the "Energy and Life" symposium
    held at Michigan State University.

      1. Man - Influence on nature. 2. Power
    resources - U.S.

C1
PWM21   Tchaikovsky
     Whorf, Michael, 1933-
      Tchaikovsky.
      1 tape cassette. (The visual sounds of
    Mike Whorf. Panorama; a world of music, PWM-21)

      Originally presented on his radio program, Kaleidoscope,
    WJR, Detroit.
      Duration: 28 min., 30 sec.
      The life and times of Tchaikovsky, including excerpts of
    his music.

      I. Chaikovskii, Petr Il'ich, 1840-1893. I. Title.

C1
H83
TECUMSEH, SHAWNEE CHIEF, 1768-1813

Whorf, Michael, 1933-
Tecumseh.
1 tape cassette. (The visual sounds of Mike Whorf. History and heritage, H83)
Originally presented on his radio program, Kaleidoscope, WJR, Detroit.
Duration: 27 min., 35 sec.
A brave, noble Indian chief far ahead of his time; a rarity in an age of change and exploitation. His name was Tecumseh, an idealist who knew what the coming of the white man meant to his people.

L Tecumseh, Shawnee chief, 1768-1813. L Title.

C1
H83
Tecumseh

Whorf, Michael, 1933-
Tecumseh.
1 tape cassette. (The visual sounds of Mike Whorf. History and heritage, H83)
Originally presented on his radio program, Kaleidoscope, WJR, Detroit.
Duration: 27 min., 35 sec.
A brave, noble Indian chief far ahead of his time; a rarity in an age of change and exploitation. His name was Tecumseh, an idealist who knew what the coming of the white man meant to his people.

L Tecumseh, Shawnee chief, 1768-1813. L Title.

C1
R18
TEILHARD DE CHARDIN, PIERRE

Whorf, Michael, 1933-
Teilhard de Chardin.
1 tape cassette. (The visual sounds of Mike Whorf. Religion, R18)
Originally presented on his radio program, Kaleidoscope, WJR, Detroit.
Duration: 43 min.
A highly acclaimed religious philosopher is the subject of this critical examination of Pierre Teilhard de Chardin. Destined to pass this world without fame or reknown, today he is generally regarded as the voice of a new understanding.

L Teilhard de Chardin, e. L Title.

C1
R18
Teilhard de Chardin

Whorf, Michael, 1933-
Teilhard de Chardin.
1 tape cassette. (The visual sounds of Mike Whorf. Religion, R18)
Originally presented on his radio program, Kaleidoscope, WJR, Detroit.
Duration: 43 min.
A highly acclaimed religious philosopher is the subject of this critical examination of Pierre Teilhard de Chardin. Destined to pass this world without fame or reknown, today he is generally regarded as the voice of a new understanding.

L Teilhard de Chardin, e. L Title.

Voice Lib.
M382
bd.2
TELEPHONE

Hobart, Garett Augustus, 1844-1899.
Talking from Washington, D.C., to New York City via telephone for the first time, extolling the "electric age" (1898)
CBS, April 26, 1951.
1 reel (7 in.) 7 1/2 i.p.s. phonotape.

1. Telephone. 2. Phonorecords - History.

Voice Lib.
M957
TELEVISION BROADCASTING

The magic of broadcasting; variety TV program about radio and TV broadcasting with Arthur Godfrey, emcee, and Don Ameche, Bing Crosby, Lucille Ball, Gale Gordon, John Scott Trotter, Rod Serling, Sheldon Leonard, Dianne Sherry, Cary MacLane, and the "Wee Five". CBS-TV, May 1, 1966.
1 reel (7 in.) 7 1/2 in. per sec. phonotape.

I. Godfrey, Arthur, 1903-

Voice Lib.
M1670
TELEVISION BROADCASTING

Serling, Rod, 1924-
Speaking at the First Annual Midwest Film Festival, at Michigan State University. WKAR, May 24, 1972.
45 min. phonotape (1 r. 7 1/2 i.p.s.)

1. Television broadcasting. I. Midwest Film Festival. 1st, Michigan State University, 1972.

Voice Lib.
M1719
TELEVISION BROADCASTING

Wallace, Mike, 1918-
The press: credible or incredible? address at Michigan State University. WKAR, March 5, 1970.
36 min. phonotape (1 r. 7 1/2 i.p.s.)

1. Television broadcasting. 2. Marihuana. 3. Homosexuality - U.S.

Voice Lib.
M1473
TELEVISION BROADCASTING OF NEWS

Agnew, Spiro T 1918-
Speech on TV network newscasts delivered to Midwest Regional Republican Committee in Des Moines, Iowa. NBC, November 13, 1969.
1 reel (7 in.) 7 1/2 i.p.s. phonotape.

1. Television broadcasting of news.

Voice Lib.
M389
bd.7
Teller, Edward, 1908-
Development of nuclear weapons; describes effects atomic energy through fallout could have on future generations, on peaceful world. Hearst Metrotone News, 1963.
1 reel (7 in.) 7 1/2 in. per sec. phonotape.

1. Atomic weapons

"The Temperance Lecture"
Voice Lib.
M1359 Fields, W.C., 1879-1946.
bd.1-   "The Temperance Lecture"; "The day I drank
bd 2 a glass of water". Blue Thumb Records ₍1968?₎
1 reel (7 in.) 7 1/2 in. per sec.
phonotape.

I. Title. II. Title: The day I drank a
glass of water.

TERRITORIALITY (ZOOLOGY)
Voice Lib.
M1585 Ardrey, Robert
bd.2 Property, status, and self-respect.
WKAR-TV, February 23, 1974.
15 min. phonotape (1 r. 7 1/2 in. per sec.)

1. Territoriality (Zoology) 2. Communism.
3. Cities & towns - Planning. I. Halverson,
Craig.

Temple, Shirley, 1928-
Voice Lib.
M619 Radio in the 1930's (Part II): a series of
bd.1-   excerpts of the 1930's; a sample of radio
14   of the period. NVL, April, 1964.
1 reel (7 in.) 7 1/2 in. per sec. phonotape.
I. Allen, Fred, 1.894-1956. II. Delmar, Kenny   III. Donald,
Peter   IV. Pious, Minerva   V. Fennelly, Parker   VI.
Boyer, Charles, 1899-   VII. Dunne, Irene, 1904-   VIII.
DeMille, Cecil Blount, 1881-1959. IX. West, Mae, 1893-   X.
Dafoe, Allan Ray, 1883-1943. XI. Dionne quintuplets. XII. Ortega,
Santos   XIII. War of the worlds (radio program) XIV. Ives, Burl,
1909-   XV. Robinson, Earl, 1910-   XVI. Temple, Shirley,
1928-   XVII. Earhart, Amelia, 1898-1937. XVIII. Lawrence,
Gertrude, 1901-1952. XIX. Cohan, George Michael, 1878-1942.
XX. Shaw, George Bernard, 1856-1950. XXI. Hitler, Adolf, 1889-
1945. XXII. Chamberlain, Neville, 1869-1940. XXIII. Roosevelt,
Franklin Delano, Pres. U.S., 1882-1945.

Terry, Dame Ellen, 1848-1928
Voice Lib.
M225 Packard, Frederick
Styles in Shakespearean acting, 1890-1950.
Creative Associates, 1963?
1 reel (7 in.) 7 1/2 L.p.s. phonotape.
I. Sothern, Edward Askew, 1826-1881. II. Marlowe,
Julia, 1865-1950. III. Booth, Edwin, 1833-1893. IV. Gielgud,
John, 1904-   V. Robeson, Paul Bustill, 1898-   VI. Terry,
Dame Ellen, 1848-1928. VII. Allen, Viola. VIII. Welles,
Orson, 1915-   IX. Skinner, Otis, 1858-1942. X. Barrymore,
John, 1882-1942. XI. Olivier, Sir Laurence Kerr, 1907-
XII. Forbes-Robertson, Sir Johnston, 1853-   XIII. Evans,
Maurice, XIV. Thorndike, Dame Sybil, 1882-   XV. Robson,
Flora. XVI. LeGallienne, Eva, 1899-   XVII. Anderson,
Judith. XVIII. Duncan, Augustin. XIX. Hampden, Walter.
XX. Speaight, Robert, 1904-   XXI. Jones, Daniel.

The Ten Commandments
C1
R31 Whorf, Michael, 1933-
The Ten Commandments.
1 tape cassette. (The visual sounds of
Mike Whorf. Religion, R31)
Originally presented on his radio program, Kaleidoscope,
WJR, Detroit.
Duration: 37 min.
The graven tables which presented spiritual guidance for
millions have been passed down to us by oral tradition and the
works of the scriptures. The monumental importance of this moral
code has stood the test of time through the ages, and served as a
universal guide to mankind.
I. Commandments, Ten. I. Title.

Voice Lib.
640 Texaco Star Theater.
bd.6 Admiral Byrd skit. WABC Line, October 22,
1941.
1 reel (7 in.) 7 1/2 in. per sec.
phonotape.

1. Byrd, Richard Evelyn, 1888-1957

Voice Lib.
613 Tennyson, Alfred Tennyson, 1st baron, 1809-1892.
bd.2 "Charge of the Light Brigade"; excerpt
from poem. London, Edison, 1890.
1 reel (7 in.) 7 1/2 in. per sec.
phonotape.

Voice Lib.
M709 Texaco Star Theater.
bd.3 Radio variety show. Speaker: Fred Allen.
Melchior collection, CBS, December 10, 1943.
25 min., 50 sec. phonotape (1 r.
7 1/2 i.p.s.)

I. Allen, Fred, 1894-1956.

Voice Lib.
M975 Terriss, Ellaline, 1871-
bd.9 Singing British popular music hall selection
"Everybody Loves Me". Rococo-Can., 1909.
1 reel (7 in.) 7 1/2 in. per sec.
phonotape.

I. Title: Everybody loves me.

Thaddeus S. C. Lowe
C1
FA13 Whorf, Michael, 1933-
Thaddeus S. C. Lowe.
1 tape cassette. (The visual sounds of
Mike Whorf. The forgotten American, FA13)
Originally presented on his radio program, Kaleidoscope,
WJR, Detroit.
Duration: 12 min., 20 sec.
Aeronaut and inventor, Lowe acted as an aerial spy for the
Union in the Civil War. He was the father of cold storage and
invented water gas.
I. Lowe, Thaddeus, S.C., 1832-1913. I. Title.

C1
S42
THANKSGIVING DAY
Whorf, Michael, 1933–
    Days of thanks – about Thanksgiving.
    1 tape cassette.   (The visual sounds of
Mike Whorf. Social, S42)
        Originally presented on his radio program, Kaleidoscope,
WJR, Detroit.
        Duration: 48 min., 55 sec.
        Bradford, Brewster, Alden, Mullins, Standish – these were the
leading figures aboard the Mayflower, who would later colonize
Plymouth and play out their roles in Europe's age of exploration and
discovery. Persecuted as Puritans, they came seeking freedom and
found the beginning of a nation.

        I. Thanksgiving Day.   I. Title.

Voice Lib.
M344
bd.1
THANT, U, 1909–
Zorin, Valerian Alexandrovich, 1902–
    U.N. interpreter's translation on
temporary agreement by the Soviet Union to
accept U Thant as Secretary General.   CBS,
November 3, 1961.
    1 reel (7 in.)   7 1/2 in. per sec.
phonotape.

        1. Thant, U, 1909–   2. United Nations.

Voice Lib.
344
bd.4
Thant, U, 1909–
    News conference at the U.N. on the
future role of the United Nations.
CBS, December 1, 1961.
    1 reel (7 in.)   7 1/2 in. per sec.
phonotape.

        1. United Nations

C1
H31
Thar' she blows
Whorf, Michael, 1933–
    Thar' she blows.
    1 tape cassette.   (The visual sounds of
Mike Whorf. History and heritage, H31)
        Originally presented on his radio program, Kaleidoscope,
WJR, Detroit.
        Duration: 43 min.
        Comes the leviathan of the deep – the story of whaling as it
was lived by those who sailed the great sailing ships.

        I. Whaling.   I. Title.

Voice Lib.
M391
bd.1
Thant, U, 1909–
Apollo 11 (space flight): reception of Apollo 11 astronauts at
    United Nations Plaza. Statement by U.N. Secretary-
    General U Thant. Reply by Neil Armstrong. Presentation
    of tokens of appreciation to all three astronauts and their
    wives and Dr. Thomas Paine. Presentation of duplicate of
    plaque left on moon to U Thant. NBC TV, August 13, 1969.
    1 reel (7 in.) 7 1/2 in. per sec. phonotape.

        I. Project Apollo. 2. Space flight to the moon. 3. Aldrin,
Edwin E   1930–   4. Collins, Michael, 1930–   5.
Armstrong, Neil, 1930–   I. Aldrin, Edwin E   1930–
II. Collins, Michael, 1930–   III. Armstrong, Neil, 1930–
IV. Thant, U, 1909–   V. Paine, Thomas Otten, 1921–

Voice Lib.
375
bd.2
That Was the Week That Was (television
    program)
Meadows, Audrey, 1922–
    Excerpt from "That Was the Week That Was":
"Nobody's Mad at L.B.J." NBC, January 9,
1964.
    1 reel (7 in.)   7 1/2 in. per sec.
phonotape.

        I. That Was the Week That Was (television
program). II. Title: Nobody's mad at L.B.J.

Voice Lib.
M1255
bd.1
Thant, U, 1909–
U.N. General Assembly. Emergency Session.
    Remarks by U.N. Secretary General U Thant
replying to Israeli and U.S. criticism
regarding withdrawal of U.N. Middle East
emergency forces and defending his position.
CBS-TV, June 20, 1967.
    1 reel (7 in.)   7 1/2 in. per sec.
phonotape.

        I. Thant, U, 1909–

C1
S53
That woman in the White House
Whorf, Michael, 1933–
    That woman in the White House; wives of
Presidents.
    1 tape cassette.   (The visual sounds of Mike Whorf. Social, S53)
        Originally presented on his radio program, Kaleidoscope,
WJR, Detroit.
        Duration: 48 min., 20 sec.
        Along with the many presidents that have served our nation,
are the wives and hostesses who have served as well. From Washing-
ton to Nixon; here is a capsule comment on the vivacious,
intelligent women in the White House.

        I. Presidents – U.S. – Wives. I. Title.

Voice Lib.
M1247
Thant, U, 1909–
United Nations. Security Council.
    Morning session of U.N. Security Council,
called by its president, Hans Tabor of Denmark,
to hear about the outbreak of hostilities
between Israel and Arab countries. Main speakers:
U Thant, Secretary General, reading latest
reports, followed by delegate of Israel and
delegate of United Arab Republic.   NBC-TV,
June 5, 1967.
    1 reel (7 in.) 7 1/2 in. per sec. phonotape.
        I. Israel-Arab War, 1967– – Diplomatic history.
        I. Thant, U, 1909–

Voice Lib.
577
bd.2
THEATER – HISTORY
Frohman, Daniel, 1851-1940.
    The theater today and yesterday.   GRV,
October 20, 1937.
    1 reel (7 in.)   7 1/2 in. per sec.
phonotape.

        1. Theater – Hist.

THEATER - U.S.

Voice Lib.
M611   Janis, Elsie, 1889-
bd.8   Recalls early 20ᵗʰ century theater in song
           parodies; imitates Ethel Barrymore, George M.
           Cohan, Beatrice Lillie and Fanny Brice.
           National Vocarium, 1939.
              1 reel (7 in.)   7 1/2 i.p.s.   phonotape.

           1. Theater - U.S.

Voice Lib.
M1675   Theme songs from the Green hornet, the Lone
bd.2   Ranger, Dick Tracy, and Hop Harrigan.
           Golden Age Radio Records, 1940's.
           10 min.   phonotape (1 r.   7 1/2 i.p.s.)

           I. Green hornet (radio program) II. Lone
           Ranger (radio program) III. Dick Tracy (radio
           program) IV. Hop Harrigan (radio program)

Theorist of evolution - Charles Darwin

C1
SC28   Whorf, Michael, 1933-
           Theorist of evolution - Charles Darwin.
           1 tape cassette.   (The visual sounds of
        Mike Whorf. Science, SC28)
           Originally presented on his radio program, Kaleidoscope,
        WJR, Detroit.
           Duration: 36 min., 30 sec.
           Throughout his life controversy raged around him, yet this quiet,
        self-contained, self-assured man did not engage his detractors, but
        forged ahead with his life's work. His life's work was engaging
        Nature on Nature's terms, and the result was the storm of disagreement
        which surrounds his name.

           I. Darwin, Charles Robert, 1809-1882. I. Title.

There are some days you don't forget - Pearl
Harbor
C1
H25   Whorf, Michael, 1933-
           There are some days you don't forget - Pearl
        Harbor.
           1 tape cassette.   (The visual sounds of
        Mike Whorf. History and heritage, H25)
           Originally presented on his radio program, Kaleidoscope,
        WJR, Detroit.
           Duration: 42 min., 50 sec.
           December 7th, 1941 - from out of the skies came the enemy at
        8 o'clock Sunday morning - less than an hour later they had gone,
        leaving in their wake wreckage and death.

           I. Pearl Harbor, Attack   1941. I. Title.

There's a service flag flying at our house
Voice Lib.
M611   Shannon Four.
bd.1   World War I song "There's a service flag
        flying at our house".   Victor Talking
        Machine Co., 1917.
           1 reel (7 in.)   7 1/2 i.p.s.   phonotape.

           1. European War, 1914-1918 - Songs and
        music. I.Title: There's a service flag
        flying at our house.

There's nothing like a good old-fashioned
hymn
C1
R17   Whorf, Michael, 1933-
           There's nothing like a good old-fashioned
        hymn.
           1 tape cassette.   (The visual sounds of
        Mike Whorf. Religion, R17)
           Originally presented on his radio program, Kaleidoscope,
        WJR, Detroit.
           Duration: 54 min., 30 sec.
           A few familiar, well-loved melodies and a close appraisal of
        what makes the song is the content of this program.

           I. Hymns. I. Title.

They don't write 'em like that anymore
C1
M29   Whorf, Michael, 1933-
           They don't write 'em like that anymore.
           1 tape cassette.   (The visual sounds of
        Mike Whorf. Miscellaneous, M29)
           Originally presented on his radio program, Kaleidoscope,
        WJR, Detroit.
           Duration: 54 min., 30 sec.
           Gerald Marks tells the story of some of America's favorite
        melodies.

           I. Songs, American. 2. Music, Popular (Songs, etc.) - U.S.
        I. Marks, Gerald. II. Title.

They don't write 'em like that anymore
C1
PMW17   Whorf, Michael, 1933-
           They don't write 'em like that anymore.
           1 tape cassette.   (The visual sounds of
        Mike Whorf. Panorama; a world of music, PMW-17)
           Originally presented on his radio program, Kaleidoscope,
        WJR, Detroit.
           Duration: 25 min.
           Composer Gerald Marks relates anecdotes and stories behind
        the composing of several popular American songs.

           I. Music, Popular (Songs, etc.) - U.S. I. Marks, Gerald,
        1900-   II. Title.

They lived happily ever after
C1
A7   Whorf, Michael, 1933-
           They lived happily ever after.
           1 tape cassette.   (The visual sounds of
        Mike Whorf. Art, music, and letters, A7)
           Originally presented on his radio program, Kaleidoscope,
        WJR, Detroit.
           Duration: 41 min., 15 sec.
           From their childhood, Jacob and Wilhelm Grimm remembered
        the wonderful and magic stories of make-believe, and with their
        own special brand of inventiveness they created a heritage for
        generations to come.

           I. Grimm, Jakob Ludwig Karl, 1785-1863. 2. Grimm, Wilhelm
        Karl, 1786-1859.   I. Title.

They marched off to war to a military
quickstep
C1
H72   Whorf, Michael, 1933-
           They marched off to war to a military
        quickstep; Civil War, part 5.
           1 tape cassette.   (The visual sounds of Mike Whorf.
        History and heritage, H72)
           Originally presented on his radio program, Kaleidoscope,
        WJR, Detroit.
           Duration: 39 min., 55 sec.
           If there were any two wars which gave the world an abundance
        of music, they were World War I and the War between the States.
        This program is devoted to the lyrics and melodies of the Civil
        War and the impact they played on the North and South.

           I. U.S. - History - Civil War, 1861-1865 - Songs & music.
        I. Title.

C1
527
They was reckless mountain boys - Hatfields and Martins
Whorf, Michael, 1933-
They was reckless mountain boys - Hatfields and Martins.
1 tape cassette. (The visual sounds of Mike Whorf. Social, 527)
Originally presented on his radio program, Kaleidoscope, WJR, Detroit.
Duration: 30 min., 30 sec.
Out from the mountain regions of the Smokies . . . this tale. It involved two families, the Hatfields and McCoys, and has become a typical American legend dealing in equal shares of violence and virtue.
L. Hatfield-McCoy Feud.   L. Title.

Voice Lib.
M929
bd.1
Thomas, Norman Mattoon, 1884-1968.
Address at testimonial dinner given at the Hotel Commodore, N.Y., to Mr. Thomas. Discusses civil liberties, warning not to confuse socialism with communism; pleading for restriction of armaments; proposing the strengthening of UN peace force. Introductory remarks by John Haynes Holmes. CBS, February 4, 1950.
. 1 reel (7 in.)   7 1/2 in. per sec. phonotape.

Voice Lib.
M1579
bd.1
Third Civic Presence Group/Legislative luncheon, with Craig Halverson, Lynn Jondahl, Gary Owen, Phil Mastin, and Eric Gentile.   WKAR-TV, February 15, 1973.
10 min. phonotape (1 r.   7 1/2 i.p.s.)

1. Physically handicapped - Law and legislation. I. Halverson, Craig. II. Jondahl, R. Lynn, 1936-   III. Owen, Gary M., 1944-
IV. Mastin, Philip O., 1930-   V. Gentile, Eric Anton, 1943-

Voice Lib.
M1093-
1094
Thomas, Norman Mattoon, 1884-1968.
Address on MSU campus to students and faculty about "the garrison state".   WKAR, Bergman, April 26, 1963.
2 reels (7 in.)   7 1/2 in. per sec. phonotape.

Voice Lib.
M733-
734
This is the fiftieth year; resumé of events taking place during the first half of the twentieth century.   KLXY Radio, 1950.
2 reels (7 in.)   7 1/2 in. per sec. phonotape.

1. Twentieth century

Voice Lib.
M1095
bd.1
Thomas, Norman Mattoon, 1884-1968.
Questions and answers upon conclusion of speech by Mr. Thomas at MSU Erickson Kiva on the subject of "The garrison state".   WKAR, April 26, 1963.
1 reel (7 in.)   7 1/2 in. per sec. phonotape.

Voice Lib.
M261-
262
Thomas, Lowell Jackson, 1892-
Lowell Thomas recalls.   CBS, 1958.
2 reels (7 in.)   7 1/2 i.p.s.   phonotape.

1. U.S. - Social conditions.

C1
FA2
Thomas Fitzpatrick
Whorf, Michael, 1933-
Thomas Fitzpatrick.
1 tape cassette. (The visual sounds of Mike Whorf. The forgotten American, FA2)
Originally presented on his radio program, Kaleidoscope, WJR, Detroit.
Duration: 9 min., 50 sec.
One of the most colorful of the American mountain men, he was noted for his dealings with the Indians.
L. Fitzpatrick, Thomas, 1799-1854.   L. Title.

Voice Lib.
M620
bd.1-
bd.16
Thomas, Lowell Jackson, 1892-
Radio in the 1940's (Part I): a series of excerpts from important broadcasts of the 1940's; a sample of radio of the period. NVL, April, 1964.
1 reel (7 in.) 7 1/2 in. per sec. phonotape.
L. Radio programs. L. Thomas, Lowell Jackson, 1892-   II. Gunther, John, 1901-1970. III. Kaltenborn, Hans von, 1878-1965. IV. Delmar, Kenny. V. Those were the good old days (Radio program) VI. Elman, Dave. VII. Hall, Frederick Lee, 1916-1970. VIII. Hobby lobby (Radio program) IX. Roosevelt, Franklin Delano, Pres. U.S., 1882-1945. X. Willkie, Wendell Lewis, 1892-1944. XI. Hoover, Herbert Clark, Pres. U.S., 1874-1964. XII. Johnson, Hugh Samuel, 1882-1942. XIII. Cobb, Irvin Shrewsbury, 1876-1944. XIV. Roosevelt, Theodore, 1858-1919. XV. Nye, Gerald Prentice, 1892-1971. XVI. Lindbergh, Charles Augustus, 1902-   XVII. Toscanini, Arturo, 1867-1957.

C1
FA12
Thomas W. Gregory
Whorf, Michael, 1933-
Thomas W. Gregory.
1 tape cassette. (The visual sounds of Mike Whorf. The forgotten American, FA12)
Originally presented on his radio program, Kaleidoscope, WJR, Detroit.
Duration: 11 min., 25 sec.
Attorney-General during the administrations of Woodrow Wilson, Gregory was responsible for the internal security of the United States during World War I.
L. Gregory, Thomas Watt, 1861-1933.   L. Title.

THOREAU, HENRY DAVID, 1817-1862

C1
S18
Whorf, Michael, 1933-
I hear a different drummer.
1 tape cassette. (The visual sounds of
Mike Whorf. Social, S18)
Originally presented on his radio program, Kaleidoscope,
WJR, Detroit.
Duration: 54 min.
Henry David Thoreau, American poet and essayist, was
perhaps one of the first outspoken critics of social and economic
problems in 19th century America.

L. Thoreau, Henry David, 1817-1862. L. Title.

Voice Lib. Threlkeld, Richard
M1707
bd.
Milliken, William G   1922-
Governors Milliken, Lucey and Askew at
the Governors' Conference in Seattle on the
new financing morality. Richard Threlkeld,
reporting. CBS, June 5, 1974.
3 min. phonotape (1 r.   7 1/2 i.p.s.)

1. Watergate Affair, 1972-   I. Lucey,
Patrick Joseph, 1918-   II. Askew,
Reubin O'D. III. Threlkeld, Richard.

Voice Lib. Thorndike, Dame Sybil, 1882-
M316
bd.1
British Broadcasting Corporation.
This was the week that was; comments and
reminiscences of Kennedy by the cast of
weekly BBC show; a rebroadcast of original
live show of November 23, 1963, including
poem "To Jackie" by Dame Sybil Thorndike.
NBC, November 24, 1963.
1 reel (7 in.)   7 1/2 i.p.s.   phonotape.

1. Kennedy, John Fitzgerald, Pres. U.S.,
1917-1963 - Assassination. I. Thorndike,
Dame Sybil, 1882-

---

*"Through Jordan"
Voice Lib.
M756
bd.8
Booth, William, 1829-1912.
"Through Jordan"; an address in verse
by the late General Booth, founder of the
Salvation Army. VTM, 1910.
1 reel (7 in.)   7 1/2 in. per sec.
phonotape.

1. Salvation Army. I. Title.

Voice Lib. Thorndike, Dame Sybil, 1882-
M225
Packard, Frederick
Styles in Shakespearean acting, 1890-1950.
Creative Associates, 1963?
1 reel (7 in.) 7 1/2 i.p.s. phonotape.

L. Sothern, Edward Askew, 1826-1881. II. Marlowe,
Julia, 1865-1950. III. Booth, Edwin, 1833-1893. IV. Gielgud,
John, 1904-   V. Robeson, Paul Bustill, 1898-   VI. Terry,
Dame Ellen, 1848-1928. VII. Allen, Viola. VIII. Welles,
Orson, 1915-   IX. Skinner, Otis, 1858-1942. X. Barrymore,
John, 1882-1942. XI. Olivier, Sir Laurence Kerr, 1907-
XII. Forbes-Robertson, Sir Johnston, 1853-   XIII. Evans,
Maurice. XIV. Thorndike, Dame Sybil, 1882-   XV. Robson,
Flora. XVI. LeGallienne, Eva, 1899-   XVII. Anderson,
Judith. XVIII. Duncan, Augustin. XIX. Hampden, Walter.
XX. Speaight, Robert, 1904-   XXI. Jones, Daniel.

C1
R4
The thunderer
Whorf, Michael, 1933-
The thunderer.
1 tape cassette. (The visual sounds of
Mike Whorf. Religion, R4)
Originally presented on his radio program, Kaleidoscope,
WJR, Detroit.
Duration: 28 min., 30 sec.
Here is the narrative that deals with a prophet of God. He was
humble, yet his spirit challenged the brilliance and intelligence of
kings and priests.

L. John the Baptist. L. Title.

C1
PWM14
Those ragtime years
Whorf, Michael, 1933-
Those ragtime years.
1 tape cassette. (The visual sounds of
Mike Whorf. Panorama; a world of music, PWM-14
Originally presented on his radio program, Kaleidoscope,
WJR, Detroit.
Duration: 25 min.
Music from the decade between the turn of the century and
World War I, including some by composer Scott Joplin.

L. Ragtime music. 2. Joplin, Scott, 1868-1917. L. Title.

Tiger rag
Voice Lib.
M1100
bd.4
Dixieland (original jazz band)
Playing "Tiger Rag" in Dixieland tempo.
LaRocca, cornet; Shields, clarinet; Edwards,
trombone; Regas, piano; Shabaro, drums.
Forrest, 1918.
1 reel (7 in.)   7 1/2 in. per sec.
phonotape.

I. Title: Tiger rag.

Those were the good old days (Radio program)
Voice Lib.
M620
bd.1-
bd.16
Radio in the 1940's (Part I): a series of
excerpts from important broadcasts of the 1940's; a
sample of radio of the period. NVL, April, 1964.
1 reel (7 in.) 7 1/2 in. per sec. phonotape.
L. Radio programs. L. Thomas, Lowell Jackson, 1892-   II.
Gunther, John, 1901-1970. III. Kaltenborn, Hans von, 1878-1965.
IV. Delmar, Kenny. V. Those were the good old days (Radio
program) VI. Elman, Dave. VII. Hall, Frederick Lee, 1916-1970.
VIII. Hobby lobby (Radio program) IX. Roosevelt, Franklin Delano,
Pres. U.S., 1882-1945. X. Willkie, Wendell Lewis, 1892-1944.
XI. Hoover, Herbert Clark, Pres. U.S., 1874-1964. XII. Johnson,
Hugh Samuel, 1882-1942. XIII. Cobb, Irvin Shrewsbury, 1876-1944.
XIV. Roosevelt, Theodore, 1858-1919. XV. Nye, Gerald Prentice,
1892-1971. XVI. Lindbergh, Charles Augustus, 1902-   XVII.
Toscanini, Arturo, 1867-1957.

Time and space
Voice Lib.
M737
bd.2
Lodge, Sir Oliver Joseph, 1851-1940.
Time and space; lecture on the measurement of interstellar distances by timing
effects of New Star explosions.
8 min., 23 sec. phonotape (1 r.
7 1/2 i.p.s.)

I. Title.

Voice Lib.
M1099 Tinney, Frank, 1878-1940.
bd.3- Humorous monologue by Frank Tinney and
bd.4 Charles A. Prince with musical accompaniment,
entitled: "Frank Tinney's First Record" and
"Frank Tinney's Second Record", depicting
the making of an acoustic phonograph record.
Colonel Graph, 1917.
1 reel (7 in.) 7 1/2 in. per sec.
phonotape.

I. Prince, Charles A
1. Phonorecords - History

Tito, Josip Broz, Pres. Yugoslavia, 1892-
Voice Lib.
573 I can hear it now (radio program)
bd.2- 1945-1949. CBS, 1950?
574 2 reels (7 in.) 7 1/2 in. per sec.
bd.1 phonotape.
L. Murrow, Edward Roscoe, 1908-1965. II. Nehru, Jawaharlal,
1889-1964. III. Philip, duke of Edinburgh, 1921- IV. Elizabeth II,
Queen of Great Britain, 1926- V. Ferguson, Homer, 1889- VI.
Hughes, Howard Robard, 1905- VII. Marshall, George Catlett,
1880- VIII. Ruth, George Herman, 1895-1948. IX. Lilienthal,
David Eli, 1899- X. Trout, Robert, 1908- XI. Gage, Arthur.
XII. Jackson, Robert Houghwout, 1892-1954. XIII. Gromyko, Ana-
tolii Andreevich, 1908- XIV. Baruch, Bernard Mannes, 1870-
1965. XV. Churchill, Winn[...] Leonard Spencer, 1874-1965. XVI.
Winchell, Walter, 1897-19[...] XVII. Davis, Elmer Holmes, 1890-
(Continued on next card)

Voice Lib.
M952 Tirpitz, Alfred Peter Friedrich von, 1849-1930.
bd.14 Speaking about German U-boat warfare.
F. Peteler, 1915.
1 reel (7 in.) 7 1/2 in. per sec.
phonotape.

1. European War, 1914-1918 - Naval
operations - Submarine. 2. European War,
1914-1918 - Naval operations, German.

To live with honor, Disraeli
C1
H59 Whorf, Michael, 1933-
To live with honor, Disraeli.
1 tape cassette. (The visual sounds of
Mike Whorf. History and heritage, H59)
Originally presented on his radio program, Kaleidoscope,
WJR, Detroit.
Duration: 41 min., 15 sec.
Rising above the discrimination against his Judaic heritage,
Disraeli was an accomplished linguist, a writer of gay and brilliant
satire, possessed of a phenomenal memory, and schooled in the
social graces.
L. Beaconsfield, Benjamin Disraeli, 1st Earl of, 1804-1881.
L. Title.

TITANIC (STEAMSHIP)
C1
H21 Whorf, Michael, 1933-
The tragedy of the Titanic.
1 tape cassette. (The visual sounds of
Mike Whorf. History and heritage, H21)
Originally presented on his radio program, Kaleidoscope,
WJR, Detroit.
Duration: 37 min.
It was indeed a night to remember, on that cold April night
in the North Atlantic. The largest ship ever built was to make its
first and last voyage as she sailed into the treacherous ice fields.
Before morning came, one of the greatest tragedies on the high
seas was to unfold.
L. Titanic (Steamship) L. Title.

Voice Lib.
M761 Tobias, Charlie
bd.4 Excerpt from "Whatever happened to Tin Pan
Alley?" (Program 3); tells about his direct
method of plugging songs. Westinghouse
Broadcasting Corporation, 1964.
53 sec. phonotape (1 r. 7 1/2 i.p.s.)
(The music goes round and round)

1. Music, Popular (Songs, etc.) - U.S.

I. Title: Whatever happened to Tin Pan Alley?
II. Series.

Voice Lib.
235- Tito, Josip Broz, Pres. Yugoslavia, 1892-
237 Interview by Edward R. Murrow, with comments
bd.1 and analysis by Richard C. Hottelet, Clare
Boothe Luce, William H. Lawrence, and Hamilton
F. Armstrong, CBS, June 30, 1957.
3 reels (7 in.) 7 1/2 in. per sec.
phonotape.

I. Hottelet, Richard Curt II. Luce,
Clare (Boothe) 1903- III. Lawrence,
William H IV. Armstrong, Hamilton Fish,
1893-1973.

Voice Lib.
M1315 Today (TV program)
bd.2 Celebrating George Gershwin Week in New
York. Reminiscences of George Gershwin by
former colleagues and his sister. NBC-TV,
May 7, 1968.
1 reel (7 in.) 7 1/2 i.p.s. phonotape.

1. Gershwin, George, 1898-1937.

Voice Lib.
M738 Tito, Josip Broz, Pres. Yugoslavia, 1892-
bd.3 Speaking about co-existence with the
West. November 23, 1959.
1 reel (7 in.) 7 1/2 in. per sec.
phonotape.

Today is a good day to die
C1
S10 Whorf, Michael, 1933-
Today is a good day to die.
1 tape cassette. (The visual sounds of
Mike Whorf. Social, S10)
Originally presented on his radio program, Kaleidoscope,
WJR, Detroit.
Duration: 45 min., 30 sec.
This program relates the story of the Indian's ancestry, his
origin, his survival on the continent, the number of nations and
tribes, and their locations, his religion, customs, and the manner
in which he lived in early America.

L. Indians of North America. L. Title.

C1
SC33 Whorf, Michael, 1933-

Today, they changed the world

Today, they changed the world; inventions.
1 tape cassette. (The visual sounds of
Mike Whorf. Science, SC33)
Originally presented on his radio program, Kaleidoscope,
WJR, Detroit.
Duration: 37 min., 50 sec.
What causes the creative spark to kindle the flame of a new
idea ... a new process ... a new product? This narrative takes a
look at the march of progress in the individual efforts of the
innovators whose contributions change the course of history.

1. Inventions. I. Title.

Today with Mrs. Roosevelt

Voice Lib.
M1096 Roosevelt, Eleanor (Roosevelt) 1884-1962.
bd.1 Weekly panel of guests on live television
program entitled, "Today with Mrs. Roosevelt",
discussing the future of atomic energy and
the hydrogen bomb. NBC-TV, February 12,
1950.
1 reel (7 in.) 7 1/2 i.p.s. phonotape.

1. Atomic energy. I. Title: Today with
Mrs. Roosevelt.

Voice Lib.
345 Todd, Michael, 1909-1958.
bd.12 Last statement before his death
(interview); philosophy of life and
plans for the future. CBS, March 22,
1958.
1 reel (7 in.) 7 1/2 in. per sec.
phonotape.

1. Todd, Michael, 1909-1958

Voice Lib.
M939 Tolstaîa, Aleksandra Lvovna, grafinîa, 1884-
Lecture at Conrad Auditorium, MSU, on
the subject of Tolstoy and Russia today,
followed by answers to questions by student
audience. February 15, 1966.
1 reel (7 in.) 7 1/2 in. per sec.
phonotape.

1. Tolstoi, Lev Nikolaevich, graf, 1828-
1910.

Voice Lib.
M1040 Tolstoi, Lev Nikolaevich, graf, 1828-1910.
bd.8 Excerpt of his book "For Every Day".
TV&R, 1902.
1 reel (7 in.) 7 1/2 in. per sec.
phonotape.

TOLSTOI, LEV NIKOLAEVICH, GRAF, 1828-1910

Voice Lib.
M939 Tolstaîa, Aleksandra Lvovna, grafinîa, 1884-
Lecture at Conrad Auditorium, MSU, on
the subject of Tolstoy and Russia today,
followed by answers to questions by student
audience. February 15, 1966.
1 reel (7 in.) 7 1/2 in. per sec.
phonotape.

1. Tolstoi, Lev Nikolaevich, graf, 1828-
1910.

Voice Lib.
M1028 Toscanini, Arturo, 1867-1957.
bd.4 Excerpt from NBC Symphony Orchestra
selection. Michigan State University,
Department of Television and Radio, 1940's.
1 reel (7 in.) 7 1/2 in. per sec.
phonotape.

Voice Lib.
589 Toscanini, Arturo, 1867-1957.
bd.2 Special message to people of Italy for use
by U.S. on invasion of Italy. Conducts NBC
Symphony in famous Italian composition
"Garibaldi's Hymn", conducts group in "Stars
and Stripes Forever". V-Disc, 1944.
1 reel (7 in.) 7 1/2 in. per sec.
phonotape.

Toscanini, Arturo, 1867-1957

Voice Lib.
M620 Radio in the 1940's (Part I): a series of
bd.1- excerpts from important broadcasts of the 1940's; a
bd.16 sample of radio of the period. NVL, April, 1964.
1 reel (7 in.) 7 1/2 in. per sec. phonotape.
I. Radio programs. I. Thomas, Lowell Jackson, 1892- II.
Gunther, John, 1901-1970. III. Kaltenborn, Hans von, 1878-1965.
IV. Delmar, Kenny. V. Those were the good old days (Radio
program) VI. Elman, Dave. VII. Hall, Frederick Lee, 1916-1970.
VIII. Hobby lobby (Radio program) IX. Roosevelt, Franklin Delano,
Pres. U.S., 1882-1945. X. Willkie, Wendell Lewis, 1892-1944.
XI. Hoover, Herbert Clark, Pres. U.S., 1874-1964. XII. Johnson,
Hugh Samuel, 1882-1942. XIII. Cobb, Irvin Shrewsbury, 1876-1944.
XIV. Roosevelt, Theodore, 1858-1919. XV. Nye, Gerald Prentice,
1892-1971. XVI. Lindbergh, Charles Augustus, 1902- XVII.
Toscanini, Arturo, 1867-1957

Voice Lib.
M1074- Toscanini, Arturo, 1867-1957.
1075 "Toscanini Remembered", by members of
bd.1 his NBC symphony orchestra upon 100th
anniversary of his birth, on "Today" show.
NBC-TV, March 24, 1967.
2 reels (7 in.) 7 1/2 in. per sec.
phonotape.

I. Title. 1. Toscanini, Arturo, 1867-1957.

Toscanini remembered

Voice Lib.
M1074- Toscanini, Arturo, 1867-1957.
1075   "Toscanini Remembered", by members of
bd.1   his NBC symphony orchestra upon 100th
         anniversary of his birth, on "Today" show.
         NBC-TV, March 24, 1967.
           2 reels (7 in.)   7 1/2 in. per sec.
         phonotape.

           I. Title.

Voice Lib.
119-   A tour of the White House (Television program)
120   Tour of the White House with Mrs. John F.
         Kennedy. Narrated by Charles Collingwood.
         CBS-TV special, February, 1962.
           2 reels (7 in.)   7 1/2 in. per sec.
         phonotape.

           I. Collingwood, Charles Cummings, 1917-
           II. Kennedy, Jacqueline (Bouvier), 1929-

C1   TOWER, CHARLEMAGNE, 1809-1889
FA11   Whorf, Michael, 1933-
           Charlemagne Tower.
           1 tape cassette.   (The visual sounds of
         Mike Whorf. The forgotten American, FA11)
           Originally presented on his radio program, Kaleidoscope,
         WJR, Detroit.
           Duration: 11 min., 17 sec.
           Tower risked his name and his fortune to provide iron ore
         from the Minnesota wilderness, which made the United States
         a steel producing giant.

           I. Tower, Charlemagne, 1809-1889.   I. Title.

Tower, John Goodwin, 1925-
Voice Lib.
M1478   The Pentagon Papers; discussion of content,
         meaning. Bernard Kalb, CBS; Senator J.W.
         Fulbright; Senator John Tower; Arthur
         Schlesinger; Walt Rostow; Max Frankel,
         New York Times; Crosby Noyes, Washington
         Evening Star. CBS-TV, July 13, 1971.
           1 reel (7 in.)   7 1/2 in. per sec.
         phonotape.
           I. Kalb, Bernard   II. Fulbright, James William, 1905-
         III. Tower, John Goodwin, 1925-   IV. Schlesinger, Arthur
         Meier, 1888-   V. Rostow, Walt Whitman, 1916-   VI.
         Frankel, Max   VII. Noyes, Crosby

Tower, John Goodwin, 1925-
Voice Lib.
M1745   McIntyre, Thomas James, 1915-
           Debate with Senator John Tower on
         defense spending. WKAR, June 26, 1974.
           15 min.   phonotape (1 r.   7 1/2 i.p.s.)

           1. U.S. - Defenses.   I. Tower, John
         Goodwin, 1925-

Voice Lib.
M1223   Town meeting of the world (Television program)
bd.1   Discussion and questions by students of
         various countries from Britain about the image
         of America in the eyes of youth. Answers by
         Senator Robert F. Kennedy of New York and
         Governor Ronald Reagan of California, with
         Charles Collingwood as moderator. Principle
         items covered: Vietnam, civil rights. CBS-TV,
         May 15, 1967.
           1 reel (7 in.)   7 1/2 in. per sec.   phonotape.
           I. Kennedy, Robert Francis, 1925-1968.   II. Reagan, Ronald
         Wilson, 1911-   III. Collingwood, Charles Cummings, 1917-

---

Townsend, Dallas
Voice Lib.
M771   Gemini 4 (space flight): excerpts of announce-
bd.2   ments from NBC reporters and Gemini Control,
         regarding preparations for and the actual
         splashdown. Conversation with astronauts
         before pickup by helicopter. Dallas Townsend
         from carrier "Wasp" and David Brinkley and
         Chet Huntley for NBC. NBC TV, June 7, 1965.
           1 reel (7 in.)   7 1/2 in. per sec.   phonotape.
           1. Project Gemini.   2. McDivitt, James Alton, 1929-   3.
         White, Edward Higgins, 1930-1967.   I. McDivitt, James Alton,
         1929-   II. White, Edward Higgins, 1930-1967.   III. Townsend,
         Dallas.   IV. Brinkley, David McClure, 1920-   V. Huntley,
         Chet, 1911-1974.

Townsend, Francis Everett, 1867-1960
Voice Lib.
M618   Radio in the 1930's (Part I): a series of
bd.1-   excerpts from important broadcasts of the
14   1930's; a sample of radio of the period.
         NVL, April, 1964.
           1 reel (7 in.)   7 1/2 in. per sec.   phonotape.
           I. Shaw, George Bernard, 1856-1950.   II. Crosby, Bing, 1901-
         III. Barkley, Alban William, 1877-1956.   IV. Roosevelt, Franklin
         Delano, Pres. U.S., 1882-1945.   V. Hoover, Herbert Clark, Pres.
         U.S., 1874-1964.   VI. Long, Huey Pierce, 1893-1935.   VII. Town-
         send, Francis Everett, 1867-1960.   VIII. Coughlin, Charles Edward,
         1891-   IX. Rogers, Will, 1879-1935.   X. Pius XII, Pope, 1876-
         1958.   XI. Edward VIII, king of Great Britain, 1894-1972.   XII.
         Barrymore, John, 1882-1942.   XIII. Woollcott, Alexander, 1887-
         1943.   XIV. Allen, Fred, 1894-1956.   XV. Benchley, Robert Charles,
         1889-1945.

Voice Lib.   Toynbee, Arnold Joseph, 1889-
M1435
         Life in other worlds: exploratory discussion about life on other
         planets. Arnold J. Toynbee, Dr. G. B. Kiastiakowsky
         (professor at Harvard), Dr. Donald M. Michaels, Dr. Otto
         Struve, Dr. Harlow Shapley, Walter Cronkite, Chet Huntley,
         William L. Laurence. New York, NBC, March 3, 1961.
           1 reel (7 in.)   7 1/2 i.p.s.   phonotape.

           1. Life on other planets.   I. Toynbee, Arnold Joseph, 1889-
         II. Kiastiakowsky, George Bogdan.   III. Michaels, Donald M.
         IV. Struve, Otto, 1897-1963.   V. Shapley, Harlow, 1885-1972.
         VI. Cronkite, Walter Leland, 1916-   VII. Huntley, Chet,
         1911-1974.   VIII. Laurence, William Leonard, 1888-

Toynbee, Arnold Joseph, 1889-
Voice Lib.
M1033   Voice of America.
           Twentieth anniversary program of Voice of
         America broadcasts narrated by Henry Fonda,
         and including the voices of Carl Sandburg,
         Danny Kaye, Jawaharlal Nehru, Franklin D.
         Roosevelt, Charles Malik, Arnold Toynbee,
         William Faulkner, Harry S. Truman, Dwight D.
         Eisenhower, Helen Hayes, Dag Hammarskjöld,
         Winston Churchill, and John F. Kennedy.
         Voice of America, 1963.
           1 reel (7 in.)   7 1/2 in. per sec.
         phonotape.
                                         (Continued on next card)

Toynbee, Arnold Joseph, 1889-

Voice Lib.
M1033   Voice of America. Twentieth anniversary
          program... 1963.   (Card 2)

I. Fonda, Henry Jaynes, 1905-   II. Sandburg, Carl,
1878-1967. III. Kaye, Danny, 1913-   IV. Nehru, Jawaharlal,
1889-1964. V. Roosevelt, Franklin Delano, Pres. U.S., 1882-
1945. VI. Malik, Charles Habib, 1906-   VII. Toynbee,
Arnold Joseph, 1889-   VIII. Faulkner, William, 1897-1962.
IX. Truman, Harry S., Pres. U.S., 1884-1972. X. Eisenhower,
Dwight David, Pres. U.S., 1890-1969. XI. Hayes, Helen,
1900-   XII. Hammarskjöld, Dag, 1905-1961. XIII. Churchill,
Winston Leonard Spencer, 1874-1965. XIV. Kennedy, John
Fitzgerald, Pres. U.S., 1917-1963.

TRANSCENDENTAL MEDITATION

Voice Lib.
M1322   Mahesh Yogi, Maharishi, 1911 (?)-
bd.2   Interview of Maharishi Yogi of India
          at college seminar held at MSU about
          transcendental meditation.   MSU Information
          Service, June 18, 1968.
          1 reel (7 in.)   7 1/2 in. per sec.
          phonotape.

TRADE-UNIONS

Voice Lib.
594   Taft, William Howard, Pres. U.S., 1857-1930.
bd.4   Rights of labor; right to unionize, limits
          on unions. Thomas A. Edison, 1906.
          1 reel (7 in.)   7 1/2 in. per sec.
          phonotape.

TRANSPORTATION - U.S.

Voice Lib.
M1545   Nixon, Richard Milhous, Pres. U.S., 1913-
bd.1   Transportation message. CBS, February 9,
          1974.
          12 min.   phonotape (1 r.   7 1/2 i.p.s.)

          1. Transportation - U.S.

C1   The tragedy of the Titanic
H21   Whorf, Michael, 1933-
          The tragedy of the Titanic.
          1 tape cassette.   (The visual sounds of
          Mike Whorf. History and heritage, H21)
          Originally presented on his radio program, Kaleidoscope,
          WJR, Detroit.
          Duration: 37 min.
          It was indeed a night to remember, on that cold April night
          in the North Atlantic. The largest ship ever built was to make its
          first and last voyage as she sailed into the treacherous ice fields.
          Before morning came, one of the greatest tragedies on the high
          seas was to unfold.

          1. Titanic (Steamship)   I. Title.

C1   TRAPP, MARIA AUGUSTA
A13   Whorf, Michael, 1933-
          The wonderful world of the Trapp family.
          1 tape cassette.   (The visual sounds of
          Mike Whorf. Art, music, and letters, A13)
          Originally presented on his radio program, Kaleidoscope,
          WJR, Detroit.
          Duration: 40 min., 30 sec.
          A lovely story, set against the background of pre-World War
          II Europe, and of the bravery and courage of Maria Von Trapp
          and her family.

          I. Trapp, Maria, Augusta.   I. Title.

Voice Lib.
1720   Train, Russell Errol, 1920-
bd.2   Interview on the Today Show with Barbara
          Walters and Robert Guralski. NBC, June 11,
          1974.
          5 min.   phonotape (1 r.   7 1/2 i.p.s.)

          1. U.S. Environmental Protection Agency.
          I. Walters, Barbara, 1931-   II. Guralski,
          Robert.

Voice Lib.
M708   Traubel, Helen, 1903-1972.
bd.1   Helen Traubel sings "The Battle Hymn of
          the Republic"; excerpts from NBC's VE-day
          program. Melchior collection, May 8, 1945.
          1 reel (7 in.)   7 1/2 in. per sec.
          phonotape.

          I. Title: The battle hymn of the republic.

TRAMPS

Voice Lib.
M793   Olde, Lewis
bd.1   Hobo Lewis reads his poetry and tells
          about life on the open road; narration by
          Bernard Mayes of Pacifica Radio in Berkeley.
          KPFK, December 4, 1964.
          21 min., 10 sec.   phonotape (1 r.
          7 1/2 i.p.s.)

          1. Tramps.   I. Mayes, Bernard.

Voice Lib.
640   "A Tree Grows in Brooklyn"; comedy song sung
bd.2   by Barry Wood and Patsy Kelly. NBC, July
          15, 1944.
          1 reel (7 in.)   7 1/2 in. per sec.
          phonotape.

          I. Wood, Barry   II. Kelly, Patsy

Voice Lib.
M1092   A tribute to Eugene O'Neill; excerpt from
bd.2   his play "Anna Christie"; presented by
         the Speech Department, University of Cali-
         fornia at Berkeley. Bergman, 1963.
         1 reel (7 in.)   7 1/2 in. per sec.
         phonotape.

         1. O'Neill, Eugene Gladstone, 1888-1953
         I. O'Neill, Eugene Gladstone, 1888-1953./
         Anna Christie.

Voice Lib.
M1092   A tribute to Eugene O'Neill; excerpt from
bd.1   his play "Beyond the Horizon"; presented
         by the Speech Department, University of
         California at Berkeley. Bergman, 1963.
         1 reel (7 in.)   7 1/2 in. per sec.
         phonotape.

         I. O'Neill, Eugene Gladstone, 1888-1953./
         Beyond the horizon.

Voice Lib.
M1092   A tribute to Eugene O'Neill; excerpt from
bd.4   his play "Strange Interlude"; presented
         by the Speech Department, University of
         California at Berkeley. Bergman, 1963.
         1 reel (7 in.)   7 1/2 in. per sec.
         phonotape.

         1. O'Neill, Eugene Gladstone, 1888-1953.
         I. O'Neill, Eugene Gladstone, 1888-1953./
         Strange interlude.

Voice Lib.
M1092   A tribute to Eugene O'Neill; excerpt from
bd.3   his play "Mourning Becomes Electra";
         presented by the Speech Department, Univer-
         sity of California at Berkeley. Bergman,
         1963.
         1 reel (7 in.)   7 1/2 in. per sec.
         phonotape.
         1. O'Neill, Eugene Gladstone, 1888-1953
         I. O'Neill, Eugene Gladstone, 1888-1953./
         Mourning becomes Electra.

Voice Lib.
238   Trout, Robert, 1908-
bd.1   Description of arrival of Nikita Khrushchev
         in U.S., with welcoming address by President
         Eisenhower and response by Khrushchev.
         1 reel (7 in.)   7 1/2 in. per sec.
         phonotape.

         1. Khrushchev, Nikita Sergeevich, 1894-1971.
         I. Eisenhower, Dwight David, Pres. U.S., 1890-
         1969.

Voice Lib.
M1027   Trout, Robert, 1908-
bd.3   The world today: direct news reports from
         Belgian front; statement from SHAEF (Supreme
         Headquarters Allied Expeditionary Force);
         news of war in the Pacific discussed by CBS
         correspondents Robert Trout, Douglas Edwards,
         Richard C. Hottelet, and Ned Kalmer. CBS
         News, December 23, 1944.
         1 reel (7 in.) 7 1/2 in. per sec. phonotape.

         I. Trout, Robert, 1908-   II. Edwards, Douglas
         III. Hottelet, Richard Curt   IV. Kalmer, Ned

Voice Lib.
M740   Trout, Robert, 1908-
bd.8-D   News flash announcing termination of
         World War II and promotion of General
         MacArthur to Supreme Commander. CBS,
         1945.
         1 reel (7 in.)   7 1/2 in. per sec.
         phonotape.

         1. World War, 1939-1945. 2. MacArthur,
         Douglas, 1880-1964.

Voice Lib.
M1028   Trout, Robert, 1908-
bd.11   Excerpt of news broadcast about the
         election of Republican 80th Congress.
         November, 1946.
         1 reel (7 in.)   7 1/2 i.p.s.)   phonotape.

         1. U.S. Congress - Elections.

Voice Lib.
M724   Trout, Robert, 1908-
bd.2   On Democratic loyalty oath, including
         Senator Blair Moody of Michigan, Gov. Battle
         of Virginia, Speaker Sam Rayburn, Col. Jack
         Arvey of Chicago, Gov. Willis of Alabama and
         Jim Farley. 1952.
         8 min., 12 sec. phonotape (1 r.
         7 1/2 i.p.s.)

         1. Democratic Party. 2. Presidents - U.S.
         - Election - 1952.

Voice Lib.
M714   Trout, Robert, 1908-
bd.5   Recollecting events in preparing the
         first "Fireside chat" with Franklin D.
         Roosevelt on the banking situation, in
         March, 1933. CBS, 1963.
         2 min., 30 sec. phonotape (1 r.
         7 1/2 i.p.s.)

         1. Roosevelt, Franklin Delano, Pres. U.S.,
         1882-1945.

Trout, Robert, 1908-
Voice Lib.
M774-   Farewell to Studio Nine; historical broadcasts
775,   made by CBS correspondents at time of action
bd.1   and reflections by them in retrospect. 1964.
    2 reels (7 in.)   7 1/2 in. per sec.
    phonotape.

    I. Trout, Robert, 1908-   II. Pierpoint,
Robert   III. Murrow, Edward Roscoe,
1908-1965. IV. Kaltenborn, Hans von, 1878-
1965. V. Sevareid, Arnold Eric, 191.'-
VI. Daly, John Charles, 1914-

Trout, Robert, 1908-
Voice Lib.
M715   Cronkite, Walter Leland, 1916-
bd.1   Walter Cronkite and Robert Trout
    interpolating address by Adolf Hitler,
    wherein announcement is made of calling up
    of Reichstag; also commentary on prelude
    to and beginning of World War II. 1939.
    1 reel (7 in.)   7 1/2 in. per sec.
    phonotape.

    I. Hitler, Adolf, 1889-1945. II. Trout,
Robert, 1908-

Trout, Robert, 1908-
Voice Lib.
572-   I can hear it now (radio program)
573   1933-1946. CBS, 1948.
bd.1   2 reels (7 in.)   7 1/2 in. per sec.
    phonotape.
    L Murrow, Edward Roscoe, 1908-1965. IL LaGuardia, Fiorello
Henry, 1882-1947. III. Chamberlain, Neville, 1869-1949. IV.
Roosevelt, Franklin Delano, Pres. U.S., 1882-1945. V. Churchill,
Winston Leonard Spencer, 1874-1965. VI. Gaulle, Charles de,
Pres. France, 1890-1970. VII. Eisenhower, Dwight David, Pres. U.S.,
1890-1969. VIII. Willkie, Wendell Lewis, 1892-1944. IX. Martin,
Joseph William, 1884-1968. X. Elizabeth II, Queen of Great Britain,
1926-   XI. Margaret Rose, Princess of Gt. Brit., 1930-   XII.
Johnson, Hugh Samuel, 188?-?42. XIII. Smith, Alfred Emanuel,
1873-1944. XIV. Lindbergh, Charles Augustus, 1902-   XV. Davis,
                  (Continued on next card)

Trout, Robert, 1908-
Voice Lib.
573   I can hear it now (radio program)
bd.2-   1945-1949. CBS, 1950?
574   2 reels (7 in.)   7 1/2 in. per sec.
bd.1   phonotape.
    L Murrow, Edward Roscoe, 1908-1965. IL Nehru, Jawaharlal,
1889-1964. III. Philip, duke of Edinburgh, 1921- IV. Elizabeth II,
Queen of Great Britain, 1926- V. Ferguson, Homer, 1889-   VL
Hughes, Howard Robard, 1905-   VII. Marshall, George Catlett,
1880- VIII. Ruth, George Herman, 1895-1948. IX. Lilienthal,
David Eli, 1899- X. Trout, Robert, 1908-   XL Gage, Arthur.
XII. Jackson, Robert Houghwout, 1892-1954. XIII. Gromyko, Anatolii Andreevich, 1908-   XIV. Baruch, Bernard Mannes, 1870-
1965. XV. Churchill, Winston Leonard Spencer, 1874-1965. XVL
Winchell, Walter, 1897-1?? XVII. Davis, Elmer Holmes, 1890-
              (Continued on next card)

Trout, Robert, 1908-
Voice Lib.
242   Rayburn, Samuel Taliaferro, 1882-1961.
    A tribute to Sam Rayburn, with Stuart
    Novin and Robert Trout. CBS Radio,
    November 16, 1961.
    1 reel (7 in.)   7 1/2 in. per sec.
    phonotape.

    I. Novin, Stuart   II. Trout, Robert,
1908-

TRUJILLO MOLINA, RAFAEL LEÓNIDAS, PRES. DOMINICAN
            REPUBLIC, 1891-1961
Voice Lib.
M258   Dominican Government Radio.
bd.7   Assassination of Trujillo and announcement
    of his death. New York, CBS, May 31, 1961.
    1 reel (7 in.)   7 1/2 in. per sec.
    phonotape.

    1. Trujillo Molina, Rafael Leónidas,
Pres. Dominican Republic, 1891-1961.

Voice Lib.
652   Truman, Harry S, Pres. U.S., 1884-1972.
bd.23   Acceptance speech for Vice-presidential
    nomination. CBS, July 2, 1944.
    1 reel (7 in.)   7 1/2 in. per sec.
    phonotape.

Voice Lib.
M854   Truman, Harry S, Pres. U.S., 1884-1972.
bd.2   Announcing VE Day victory over Germany
    and reading a proclamation. NBC, May 8,
    1945.
    1 reel (7 in.)   7 1/2 in. per sec.
    phonotape.

Voice Lib.
M1427   Truman, Harry S, Pres. U.S., 1884-1972.
    Addressing U.N.C.I.O. 10th plenary
    meeting at San Francisco. U.N. Archives,
    June 25, 1945.
    1 reel (7 in.)   7 1/2 in. per sec.
    phonotape.

Voice Lib.
M846   Truman, Harry S, Pres. U.S., 1884-1972.
bd.1   Navy Day address by President Truman in
    Central Park, New York City, stating postwar
    U.S. foreign policy and the outlook for uses of
    atomic power. NBC, October 27, 1945.
    1 reel (7 in.)   7 1/2 in. per sec.
    phonotape.

    1. U.S.- Foreign policy. 2. Atomic power.

Voice Lib.
M832   Truman, Harry S, Pres. U.S., 1884-1972.
bd.2-   Army Day address in Chicago, Illinois,
833.   dealing with continued preparedness and U.S.
bd.1   aid in the reconstruction of Europe. KDKA.
        April 6, 1946.
            2 reels (7 in.)   7 1/2 in. per sec.
        phonotape.

Voice Lib.
M724   Truman, Harry S, Pres. U.S., 1884-1972.
bd.5   Excerpt of acceptance speech.   1948.
            1 reel (7 in.)   7 1/2 in. per sec.
        phonotape.

Voice Lib.
M857   Truman, Harry S, Pres. U.S., 1884-1972.
bd.2   Address made at the national palace while
        visiting Mexico City.   NBC, March 3, 1947.
            1 reel (7 in.)   7 1/2 in. per sec.
        phonotape.

Voice Lib.
M873   Truman, Harry S., Pres. U.S., 1884-1972.
bd.1   Address to joint session of Congress on
        European economic needs (Marshall Plan),
        Communist pressure on Czechoslovakia, Finland,
        Italy and Greece requiring economic help in
        order to help free nations recover; also
        requesting support for universal military
        training and temporary selective service.
        KDKA, March 17, 1948.
            1 reel (7 in.) 7 1/2 in. per sec. phonotape.

            L Economic assistance, American.

Voice Lib.
M862   Truman, Harry S, Pres. U.S. 1884-1972.
bd.1   Address to joint session of Congress
        requesting financial and economic aid to
        Greece and Turkey.   NBC, March 12, 1947.
            1 reel (7 in.)   7 1/2 in. per sec.
        phonotape.

Voice Lib.
M873   Truman, Harry S, Pres. U.S., 1884-1972.
bd.2   Address to the Friendly Sons of St. Patrick
        outlining his plan for economic aid to
        European countries and discussing universal
        military training in the U.S.   KDKA, March 17,
        1948.
            1 reel (7 in.)   7 1/2 in. per sec.
        phonotape.

Voice Lib.
M829   Truman, Harry S, Pres. U.S., 1884-1972.
bd.2   Radio address to the nation from the White
        House explaining his position on Taft-Hartley
        bill after veto of it and his opinions of
        that legislation.   KDKA, June 20, 1947.
            1 reel (7 in.)   7 1/2 in. per sec.
        phonotape.

            1. U.S. Laws, statutes, etc./ Labor
        management relations act, 1947.

Voice Lib.
M832   Truman, Harry S, Pres. U.S., 1884-1972.
bd.1   Address at Omaha, Nebraska, dealing with
        agricultural problems; delivered at a reunion
        of his former army unit, the 35th Division,
        U.S. Army.   KDKA, June 5, 1948.
            1 reel (7 in.)   7 1/2 in. per sec.
        phonotape.

Voice Lib.
137-   Truman, Harry S, Pres. U.S., 1884-1972.
138   Speaking before Joint Session of 80th
bd.1   Congress on inflationary curbs and foreign
        aid.   CBS, November 17, 1947.
            2 reels (7 in.)   7 1/2 in. per sec.
        phonotape.

Voice Lib.
M724   Truman, Harry S, Pres. U.S., 1884-1972.
bd.7   Excerpt from President's acceptance speech
        at Democratic National Convention in 1948.
        July 15, 1948.
            1 reel (7 in.)   7 1/2 in. per sec.
        phonotape.

Voice Lib.
M738   Truman, Harry S, Pres. U.S., 1884-1972.
        Truman's 1948 acceptance speech at
Democratic convention. KCMO, July 15, 1948.
        1 reel (7 in.)   7 1/2 in. per sec.
phonotape.

Voice Lib.
234   Truman, Harry S, Pres. U.S., 1884-1972.
bd.1   Point four, an address to American
Newspaper Guild. CBS, June 28, 1950.
        1 reel (7 in.)   7 1/2 in. per sec.
phonotape.

Voice Lib.
M837   Truman, Harry S, Pres. U. S., 1884-1972.
bd.1   Addressing special joint session of 80th
Congress urging precautionary measures against
inflation and asking for housing and other
legislation. NBC, August 14, 1948.
        1 reel (7 in.)   7 1/2 in. per sec.
phonotape.

Voice Lib.
M1099   Truman, Harry S, Pres. U.S., 1884-1972.
bd.1   Radio address to the nation describing
dangers to U.S. in Korea, plans for calling
up more troops, increased production,
higher taxes, decision to declare a national
emergency, and deploring the current railroad
strike. CBS, December, 1950.
        1 reel (7 in.)   7 1/2 in. per sec.
phonotape.

Voice Lib.
204   Truman, Harry S, Pres. U.S., 1884-1972.
bd.1   Campaign speech, with an introduction
by Mayor Martin H. Kennelly of Chicago.
Detroit, WJR, October 25, 1948.
        1 reel (7 in.)   7 1/2 in. per sec.
phonotape.

        I. Kennelly, Martin Henry, 1887-1961.

Voice Lib.
248   Truman, Harry S, Pres. U.S., 1884-1972.
bd.1   The Korean situation, relieving Gen.
MacArthur of duty. CBS Radio, April 11, 1951.
        1 reel (7 in.)   7 1/2 in. per sec.
phonotape.

        1. MacArthur, Douglas, 1880-1964.

Voice Lib.
M835   Truman, Harry S, Pres. U.S., 1884-1972.
        Ceremonies and speeches at the signing
of the North Atlantic Pact by 12 nations
at the Department of Labor, Washington,
D.C. 1949.
        1 reel (7 in.)   7 1/2 in. per sec.
phonotape.

Voice Lib.
241   Truman, Harry S, Pres. U.S., 1884-1972.
        Speaking on the first anniversary of
the start of the Korean War. CBS,
June 25, 1951.
        1 reel (7 in.)   7 1/2 in. per sec.
phonotape.

Voice Lib.
M855   Truman, Harry S, Pres. U.S., 1884-1972.
        Address on the State of the Union,
delivered in person to combined session of
Congress, Washington, D.C. NBC, January 5,
1949.
        1 reel (7 in.)   7 1/2 in. per sec.
phonotape.

Voice Lib.
M1235   Truman, Harry S, Pres. U.S., 1884-1972.
bd.2   Political campaign speech at the 7th
Constitutional Convention of the International
Union of Electrical, Radio and Machine Workers
in St. Louis, Mo., lambasting Republican
administration and endorsing Adlai Stevenson.
WJR, September 14, 1956.
        1 reel (7 in.)   7 1/2 in. per sec.
phonotape.

Voice Lib.
M1474   Truman, Harry S, Pres. U.S., 1884-1972.
         Informal interview. Discusses Gen.
         MacArthur, Nelson Rockefeller, Cabot Lodge,
         Congressmen as reserve officers, Sen.
         Goldwater, atomic bombs, the Democratic
         party, businessmen in government, politics,
         Eisenhower. Mutual Radio, 1960's.
            1 reel (7 in.)   7 1/2 in. per sec.
         phonotape.

                    Truman, Harry S, Pres. U.S., 1884-1972
Voice Lib.
573   I can hear it now (radio program)
bd.2-   1945-1949. CBS, 1950?
574   2 reels (7 in.)   7 1/2 in. per sec.
bd.1   phonotape.
            I. Murrow, Edward Roscoe, 1908-1965. II. Nehru, Jawaharlal,
         1889-1964. III. Philip, duke of Edinburgh, 1921-   IV. Elizabeth II,
         Queen of Great Britain, 1926- V. Ferguson, Homer, 1889- VI.
         Hughes, Howard Robard, 1905-   VII. Marshall, George Catlett,
         1880- VIII. Ruth, George Herman, 1895-1948. IX. Lilienthal,
         David Eli, 1899-   X. Trout, Robert, 1908-   XI. Gage, Arthur.
         XII. Jackson, Robert Houghwout, 1892-1954. XIII. Gromyko, Ana-
         tolii Andreevich, 1908-   XIV. Baruch, Bernard Mannes, 1870-
         1965. XV. Churchill, Winston Leonard Spencer, 1874-1965. XVI.
         Winchell, Walter, 1897-19   XVII. Davis, Elmer Holmes, 1890-
                                        (Continued on next card)

Voice Lib.
344   Truman, Harry S, Pres. U.S., 1884-1972.
bd.9   Humorous excerpts from speech in Los
         Angeles on Republican maladministration,
         role of the dissenter, reservists who
         complain about being drafted. CBS,
         December 8, 1961.
            1 reel (7 in.)   7 1/2 in. per sec.
         phonotape.

                    Truman, Harry S., Pres. U.S., 1884-1972
Voice Lib.
M1029   Kaltenborn, Hans von, 1878-1965.
bd.2   "A Tribute to Hans von Kaltenborn".
         Excerpts of various radio news broadcasts by
         Mr. Kaltenborn, and comments by his colleagues
         upon his death. Speakers: Morgan Beatty,
         narrator; Mary Margaret McBride; H. R. Baukhage;
         Harry S Truman. MSU Dept. of TV and Radio, 1965.
            1 reel (7 in.)   7 1/2 in. per sec.
         phonotape.
            I. Kaltenborn, Hans von, 1878-1965. I. Beatty, Morgan.
         II. McBride, Mary Margaret, 1899-   III. Baukhage, Hilmar
         Robert   IV. Truman, Harry S, Pres. U.S., 1884-1972.

Voice Lib.
M 311   Truman, Harry S, Pres. U.S., 1884-1972.
bd.6   Assassination: statement by Harry Truman
         and description of his mood. NBC, November
         23, 1963.
            1 reel (7 in.)   7 1/2 in. per sec.
         phonotape.

            1. Kennedy, John Fitzgerald, Pres. U.S.,
         1917-1963. - Assassination.

                    Truman, Harry S., Pres. U.S., 1884-1972
Voice Lib.
234   Marshall, George Catlett, 1880-1959.
bd.2   Distinguished Service Medal, awarded
         by Pres. Harry S. Truman. CBS, November 26,
         1945.
            1 reel (7 in.)   7 1/2 in. per sec.
         phonotape.

            I. Truman, Harry S, Pres. U.S., 1884-1972.

                    Truman, Harry S., Pres. U.S., 1884-1972
Voice Lib.
M308   Columbia Broadcasting System, inc.
bd.2   Assassination: announcement of Kennedy's
         death by CBS commentator Walter Cronkite; on
         film of assassination, search for suspect,
         future events and Johnson's oath; announcement
         of shooting of Dallas policeman and arrest
         of Oswald; comments by Eisenhower and Truman.
         CBS, November 22, 1963.
            1 reel (7 in.)   7 1/2 in. per sec.
         phonotape.
            I. Kennedy, John Fitzgerald, Pres. U.S., 1917-1963 - Assassination.
         I. Cronkite, Walter Leland, 1916-   II. Eisenhower, Dwight
         David, Pres. U.S., 1890-1969. III. Truman, Harry S, Pres. U.S.,
         1884-1972.

                    Truman, Harry S., Pres. U.S., 1884-1972
Voice Lib.
M1033   Voice of America.
           Twentieth anniversary program of Voice of
         America broadcasts narrated by Henry Fonda,
         and including the voices of Carl Sandburg,
         Danny Kaye, Jawaharlal Nehru, Franklin D.
         Roosevelt, Charles Malik, Arnold Toynbee,
         William Faulkner, Harry S.Truman, Dwight D.
         Eisenhower, Helen Hayes, Dag Hammarskjöld,
         Winston Churchill, and John F. Kennedy.
         Voice of America, 1963.
            1 reel (7 in.)   7 1/2 in. per sec.
         phonotape.
                                (Continued on next card)

                    Truman, Harry S, Pres. U.S., 1884-1972
Voice Lib.
572-   I can hear it now (radio program)
573   1933-1946. CBS, 1948.
bd.1   2 reels (7 in.)   7 1/2 in. per sec.
         phonotape.
            I. Murrow, Edward Roscoe, 1908-1965. II. LaGuardia, Fiorello
         Henry, 1882-1947. III. Chamberlain, Neville, 1869-1949. IV.
         Roosevelt, Franklin Delano, Pres. U.S., 1882-1945. V. Churchill,
         Winston Leonard Spencer, 1874-1965. VI. Gaulle, Charles de,
         Pres. France, 1890-1970. VII. Eisenhower, Dwight David, Pres. U.S.,
         1890-1969. VIII. Willkie, Wendell Lewis, 1892-1944. IX. Martin,
         Joseph William, 1884-1968. X. Elizabeth II, Queen of Great Britain,
         1926-   XI. Margaret Rose, Princess of Gt. Brit., 1930-   XII.
         Johnson, Hugh Samuel, 1882-   '42. XIII. Smith, Alfred Emanuel,
         1873-1944. XIV. Lindbergh, Charles Augustus, 1902-   XV. Davis,
                            (Continued on next card)

                    Truman, Harry S., Pres. U.S., 1884-1972
Voice Lib.
M1033   Voice of America. Twentieth anniversary
             program... 1963. (Card 2)

            I. Fonda, Henry Jaynes, 1905-   II. Sandburg, Carl,
         1878-1967. III. Kaye, Danny, 1913-   IV. Nehru, Jawaharlal,
         1889-1964. V. Roosevelt, Franklin Delano, Pres. U.S., 1882-
         1945. VI. Malik, Charles Habib, 1906-   VII. Toynbee,
         Arnold Joseph, 1889-   VIII. Faulkner, William, 1897-1962.
         IX. Truman, Harry S, Pres. U.S., 1884-1972. X. Eisenhower,
         Dwight David, Pres. U.S., 1890-1969. XI. Hayes, Helen,
         1900-   XII. Hammarskjöld, Dag, 1905-1961. XIII. Churchill,
         Winston Leonard Spencer, 1874-1965. XIV. Kennedy, John
         Fitzgerald, Pres. U.S., 1917-1963.

Voice Lib.
M1691 TRUMAN, HARRY S., PRES. U.S., 1884-1972
Bd.2   Miller, Merle, 1918-
       On Mike Douglas Show discussing his book
       on Truman. Includes Viveca Lindfors and
       David Steinberg. WILS-TV, May 23, 1974.
       5 min. phonotape (1 r. 7 1/2 i.p.s.)

       1. Truman, Harry S, Pres. U.S., 1884-1972.
       2. Miller, Merle, 1918- /Plain speaking.
       I. Douglas, Mike, 1925?- II. Lindfors,
       Viveca, 1920- III. Steinberg, David.

TRUMAN, HARRY S., PRES. U.S., 1884-1972
C1
H98   Whorf, Michael, 1933-
      Harry S Truman - American.
      1 tape cassette. (The visual sounds of
      Mike Whorf. History and heritage, H98)
      Originally presented on his radio program, Kaleidoscope,
      WJR, Detroit.
      Duration: 46 min.
      One of the most outspoken and straightforward leaders of all
      our presidents, Harry Truman was praised and cursed, revered and
      reviled.

      1. Truman, Harry S, Pres. U.S., 1884-1972. I. Title.

Trumpets in the afternoon --legend and
         sport of bullfight
C1
M51   Whorf, Michael, 1933-
      Trumpets in the afternoon --legend and
      sport of bullfight.
      1 tape cassette. (The visual sounds of
      Mike Whorf. Miscellaneous, M51)
      Originally presented on his radio program, Kaleidoscope,
      WJR, Detroit.
      Duration: 37 min.
      The unique world of the bullfight arena: the blood, the gore,
      the colorful spectacle of brave matadors and their worthy
      opponents - the ground-scraping, glaring black bulls.
      1. Bull-fights. I. Title.

Voice Lib.
M1100 Tucker, Sophie, 1884-1966.
bd.5   Singing her well-known number, "Some of
       These Days". Forrest, 1928.
       1 reel (7 in.) 7 1/2 in. per sec.
       phonotape.

       I.Title: Some of these days.

Voice Lib.
M971- Tugwell, Rexford Guy, 1891-
972,   "Memoirs of the New Deal"; informal talk
bd.1   with Dean Zelman Cowen (University of
       Melbourne) at Center for the Study of
       Democratic Institutions in Santa Barbara,
       California. CSDI, 1962.
       2 reels (7 in.) 7 1/2 i.p.s. phonotape.

       1. U.S. - Social policy. I. Cowen, Zelman.

OFFICIAL

Voice Lib.
M969   Tugwell, Rexford Guy, 1891-
       Conversation with Frank Kelly at Center
       for Study of Democratic Institutions in
       Santa Barbara, Calif., regarding F.D.R.,
       presidential power, campaigning techniques
       and Tugwell's accomplishments as Governor
       of Puerto Rico. CSDI, 1964.
       1 reel (7 in.) 7 1/2 in. per sec.
       phonotape.

       I. Kelly, Frank

Tully, Grace
Voice Lib.
M273- Biography in sound (radio program)
274   Franklin Delano Roosevelt: the friends and
bd.1   former associates of Franklin Roosevelt on
       the tenth anniversary of the President's death.
       NBC Radio, April, 1955.
       2 reels (7 in.) 7 1/2 in. per sec.
       phonotape.
       1. Roosevelt, Franklin Delano, Pres. U.S., 1882-1945. I.
       McIntire, Ross T 1889- II. Mellett, Lowell, 1884-1960.
       III. Tully, Grace IV. Henderson, Leon, 1895-
       V. Roosevelt, Eleanor (Roosevelt) 1884-1962. VI. DeGraaf, Albert
       VII. Lehman, Herbert Henry, 1878-1963. VIII. Rosenman, Samuel
       Irving, 1896- IX. Arvey, Jacob X. Moley, Raymond,
       1886- XI. Farley, James Aloysius, 1888- XII. Roosevelt,
       (Continued on next card)

Tunesmiths past and present
Voice Lib.
M761   Caesar, Irving, 1895-
bd.13 Excerpt from "Tunesmiths past and present"
       (Program 4); comments on writing songs, how
       difficult it can be at times but other times
       how easy it is. Westinghouse Broadcasting
       Corporation, 1964.
       2 min., 58 sec. phonotape (1 r. 7 1/2
       i.p.s.) (The music goes round and round)

       1. Music, Popular (Songs, etc.) - Writing
       and publishing. I. Title: Tunesmiths past
       and present. II. Series.

Tunesmiths past and present
Voice Lib.
M761   Gilbert, L Wolfe
bd.9   Excerpt from "Tunesmiths past and present"
       (Program 4); relates how he began by selling
       six parodies to Al Jolson. Westinghouse
       Broadcasting Corporation, 1964.
       2 min., 23 sec. phonotape (1 r.
       7 1/2 i.p.s.) (The music goes round and
       round)

       1. Music, Popular (Songs, etc.) - Writing
       and publishing. I. Title: Tunesmiths
       past and present II. Series.

Tunesmiths past and present
Voice Lib.
M761   Harbach, Otto Abels, 1873-1963.
bd.14 Excerpt from "Tunesmiths Past and Present"
       (Program 4); speaking about Rudolph Friml
       and his technique in composing. Westinghouse
       Broadcasting Corporation, 1964.
       1 reel (7 in.) 7 1/2 in. per sec.
       phonotape. (The Music Goes Round and Round)

       1. Friml, Rudolph, 1881- I. Title:
       Tunesmiths past and present. II. Series.

Voice Lib.
M762   Tunesmiths past and present
bd.2   Lieber, Jerry
          Excerpt from "Tunesmiths past and present"
          (Program 4); comments on success in relation
          to "song writer" vs. "record writing".
          Westinghouse Broadcasting Corporation, 1964.
          2 min., 28 sec.   phonotape (1 r.
          7 1/2 i.p.s.) (The music goes round and
          round)

              1. Music, Popular (Songs, etc.) - Publishing
          and writing.   I. Title: Tunesmiths past and
          present.   II. Series.

Voice Lib.
M761   Tunesmiths past and present
bd.15   Olman, Abe
          Excerpt from "Tunesmiths Past and Present"
          (Program 4); pessimistic outlook for present-
          day song writers. Westinghouse Broadcasting
          Corporation, 1964.
          1 reel (7 in.)   7 1/2 in. per sec.
          phonotape. (The Music Goes Round and Round)

              I. Title: Tunesmiths past and present.
          II. Series.

Voice Lib.
M761   Tunesmiths past and present
bd.10   Ruby, Harry
          Excerpt from "Tunesmiths Past and Present"
          (Program 4); tells about the big composers
          in the days before the golden era of the
          '20's and '30's. Westinghouse Broadcasting
          Corporation, 1964.
          1 reel (7 in.)   7 1/2 in. per sec.
          phonotape. (The Music Goes Round and Round)

              I. Title: Tunesmiths past and present.
          II. Series.

Voice Lib.
M762   Tunesmiths past and present
bd.3   Sholes, Steven H   1911-1968.
          Excerpt from "Tunesmiths Past and Present"
          (Program 4); comments on today's emphasis
          on youth as song writers and as the audience
          of these songs. Westinghouse Broadcasting
          Corporation, 1964.
          1 reel (7 in.)   7 1/2 in. per sec.
          phonotape. (The Music Goes Round and Round)

              I. Title: Tunesmiths past and present.
          II. Series.

Voice Lib.
M762   Tunesmiths past and present
bd.1   Spector, Phil
          Excerpt from "Tunesmiths Past and Present"
          (Program 4); explanation as to why many of
          the old writers apparently can no longer make
          the grade, also comments on his goal in the
          business; including two songs, "Be My Baby"
          and "Spanish Harlem". Westinghouse Broad-
          casting Corporation, 1964.
          1 reel (7 in.)   7 1/2 in. per sec.
          phonotape. (The Music Goes Round and Round)
              I. Title: Tunesmiths past and present. II.
          Series.

Voice Lib.
M762   Tunesmiths past and present
bd.4   Yellen, Jack
          Excerpt from "Tunesmiths Past and Present"
          (Program 4); relates his view that our
          musical future is not as black as many
          would believe. Westinghouse Broadcasting
          Corporation, 1964.
          1 reel (7 in.)   7 1/2 in. per sec.
          phonotape. (The Music Goes Round and Round)

              I. Title: Tunesmiths past and present. II.
          Series.

Voice Lib.
M1082-   Turkel, Studs
1083.   Baldwin, James, 1924-
bd.1   An interview with James Baldwin by Studs
          Turkel about "The Black man in America".
          Credo Records, 1963.
          2 reels (7 in.)   7 1/2 in. per sec.
          phonotape.

              1. Negroes - U.S.   I. Turkel, Studs.

Voice Lib.
M1052   Twelve crowded months; 1940 year-end CBS
          radio correspondents' review of the events
          of the year. CBS Radio, December 29, 1940.
          1 reel (7 in.)   7 1/2 i.p.s.   phonotape.

              1. History - Yearbooks - 1940.

Voice Lib.   TWENTIETH CENTURY
M733-   This is the fiftieth year; resumé of events
734   taking place during the first half of the
          twentieth century. KLXY Radio, 1950.
          2 reels (7 in.)   7 1/2 in. per sec.
          phonotape.

Voice Lib.
M289   Twentieth Century (Television program)
bd.2   Production on career of Alfred E. Smith.
          Various excerpts of addresses by Gov. Smith;
          recollections by Robert Moses on life of
          Gov. Smith; narration by Walter Cronkite;
          placing of Smith's name in nomination for
          President by F.D.R.   CBS, 1962.
          1 reel (7 in.)   7 1/2 in. per sec.
          phonotape.
          L. Smith, Alfred Emanuel, 1873-1944. L. Smith, Alfred
          Emanuel, 1873-1944. IL. Moses, Robert, 1888-   IIL. Cronkite,
          Walter Leland, 1916-   IV. Roosevelt, Franklin Delano, Pres. U.S.,
          1882-1945.

Voice Lib.
M655   The Twentieth Century (TV program)
bd.1   "The creative thirties", narrated by
        Walter Cronkite. CBS, 1963.
            25 min.   phonotape (1 r.   7 1/2 i.p.s.)

        L. U.S. - Civilization - 1918-1945. L. Bowen, Edward,
        1874-1946. IL. Geismar, Maxwell David, 1909-
        III. MacDonald, Dwight, 1906-   IV. Welles, Orson, 1915-
        V. Cronkite, Walter Leland, 1916-   VL. Gable, Clark, 1901-
        1960. VII. Lewis, Sinclair, 1885-1951. VIII. Houseman,
        John, 1902-   IX. Roosevelt, Franklin Delano, Pres. U.S.,
        1882-1945.

                The ugly land
CL
S37   Whorf, Michael, 1933-
            The ugly land; ecology, part 1.
            1 tape cassette.   (The visual sounds of
        Mike Whorf. Social, S37)
            Originally presented on his radio program, Kaleidoscope,
        WJR, Detroit.
            Duration: 50 min.
            This program deals with what was here on earth before and
        after man came, and how he unknowingly began the process of
        slow destruction which has caused his great dilemma of the present.

            L. Ecology. L. Title.

            Two black crows
Voice Lib.
262   Mack and Moran.
bd.2   Two Black Crows; comedy dialogue. WEAF,
        1923.
            1 reel (7 in.)   7 1/2 in. per sec.
        phonotape.

Voice Lib.
M1800   Ulasewicz, Anthony, 1919?-
WG   Testimony before the Senate Committee
0523.02 investigating the Watergate Affair.
        Pacifica, May 23, 1972.
            47 min.   phonotape (1 r.   3 3/4 i.p.s.)
        (Watergate gavel to gavel, phase 1)

            1. Watergate Affair, 1972-

            The two black crows (Radio program)
Voice Lib.
M617   Radio in the 1920's: a series of excerpts
bd.1-   from important broadcasts of the 1920's,
bd.25   with brief prologue and epilogue; a sample
        of radio of the period. NVL, April, 1964.
            1 reel (7 in.)   7 1/2 in. per sec.
        phonotape.
            L. Radio programs. L. Marconi, Guglielmo, marchese, 1874-
        1937. IL. Kendall, H   G   III. Coolidge, Calvin, Pres. U.S.,
        1872-1933. IV. Wilson, Woodrow, Pres. U.S., 1856-1924. V.
        Roosevelt, Franklin Delano, Pres. U.S., 1882-1945. VL. Lodge,
        Henry Cabot, 1850-1924. VII. LaGuardia, Fiorello Henry, 1882-1947.
        VIII. The Happiness Boys (Radio program) IX. Gallagher and Sheen.
        X. Barney Google. XL. Vallee, Rudy, 1901-   XII. The two
        (Continued on next card)

Voice Lib.
M1800   Ulasewicz, Anthony, 1919?-
WG   Testimony before the Senate Committee
0718.01- investigating the Watergate Affair.
.02   Pacifica, July 18, 1973.
            182 min.   phonotape (3 r.   3 3/4 i.p.s.)
        (Watergate gavel to gavel, phase 1)

            1. Watergate Affair, 1972-

Voice Lib.
M1720   Udall, Morris K., 1922-
bd.4   On the Today Show with Sam Steiger, debating
        their opposing bills for land-use funding.
        Includes Barbara Walters and Bill Monroe.
        NBC-TV, June 10, 1974.
            8 min.   phonotape (1 r.   7 1/2 i.p.s.)

            1. Land. 2. Man - Influence on nature.
        I. Steiger, Sam, 1929-   II. Walters,
        Barbara, 1931-   III. Monroe, Bill.

            Under the double eagle march
Voice Lib.
M1095   Sousa, John Philip, 1854-1932.
bd.3   Sousa's band playing "Under the Double
        Eagle March".   Victor, 1920.
            1 reel (7 in.)   7 1/2 in. per sec.
        phonotape.

            I. Title: Under the double eagle march.

Voice Lib.
M1697   Udall, Stewart L
bd.1   The environmental crisis, the crisis of
        survival; address at Michigan State Univer-
        sity. WKAR, April 24, 1970.
            37 min.   phonotape (1 r.   7 1/2 i.p.s.)

            1. Ecology. 2. Man - Influence on nature.

            UNDERWATER EXPLORATION
Voice Lib.
652   Anderson, William Robert, 1921-
bd.9   Voice taped aboard the "Nautilus", four
        to ten miles from the North Pole under the
        ice cap; addressed to crew on this historic
        occasion. CBS, August 8, 1958.
            1 reel (7 in.)   7 1/2 in. per sec.
        phonotape.

C1
A3

The unforgetable Isadora

Whorf, Michael, 1933-
The unforgetable Isadora.
1 tape cassette. (The visual sounds of
Mike Whorf. Art, music, and letters, A3)
Originally presented on his radio program, Kaleidoscope,
WJR, Detroit.
Duration: 29 min.
Isadora Duncan, a carefree, spirited nymph of considerable
ability, was driven by inner urges and pressures that often
possess the gifted.

L. Duncan, Isadora, 1878-1927. L. Title.

UNITED NATIONS

Voice Lib.
M555   Evatt, Herbert Vere, 1894-1965.
bd.4   Press conference on Australia's position
on current Conference procedures and charter
problems of the United Nations Organization.
GRV, 1945.
1 reel (7 in.)   7 1/2 i.p.s.   phonotape.

1. United Nations.

C1
A43

The unhappy genius, Jonathan Swift

Whorf, Michael, 1933-
The unhappy genius, Jonathan Swift.
1 tape cassette. (The visual sounds of
Mike Whorf. Art, music, and letters, A43)
Originally presented on his radio program, Kaleidoscope,
WJR, Detroit.
Duration: 36 min., 40 sec.
The creator of brilliant and biting satire, Swift gave the
world many impressive works that reflected the political and
social customs of his times, and yet are still relevant to ours
today.

L. Swift, Jonathan, 1667-1745. L. Title.

UNITED NATIONS

Voice Lib.
M715   Stevenson, Adlai Ewing, 1900-1965.
bd.16   Excerpt of statement at U.N. Security
Council meeting on U.S. position on Cuban
missile build up October 23, 1962 and his
reply to USSR Ambassador Zorin at U.N.
Security Council meeting of October 25,
1962.   October 23-25, 1962.
2 min., 24 sec.   phonotape (1 r.
7 1/2 i.p.s.)

1. United Nations.

Voice Lib.
556-   United Nations.
557   Statements at the signing of the Charter
in San Francisco. GRV, June 26, 1945.
2 reels (7 in.)   7 1/2 in. per sec.
phonotape.

UNITED NATIONS

Voice Lib.
344   Thant, U, 1909-
bd.4   News conference at the U.N. on the
future role of the United Nations.
CBS, December 1, 1961.
1 reel (7 in.)   7 1/2 in. per sec.
phonotape.

Voice Lib.
M1454   United Nations.
bd.2   Ceremonies from 25th anniversary of the
founding of UN at San Francisco, with
Pauline Frederick as MC. ABC, August,
1971.
1 reel (7 in.)   7 1/2 in. per sec.
phonotape.

I. Frederick, Pauline

UNITED NATIONS

Voice Lib.
M805   United Nations Special Tape no. 1.
U.N. Archives, various dates.
33 min., 40 sec.   phonotape (1 r.
7 1/2 i.p.s.)

CONTENTS. - bd. 1 African member of Judicial Committee
on International law (5 min., 32 sec.). -bd. 2. U.N. Indian
delegate describing Mahatma Gandhi as a "half-naked fakir"
(54 sec.). -bd. 3. Woman president of a committee adjourning
meeting because of lack of speakers, amidst laughter (1 min.,
38 sec.). -bd. 4. U.N. sound crew testing equipment: "take
your pot up there" (1 min., 22 sec.). -bd. 5. "Song of United
Nations" rehearsal (3 min., 4 sec.). -bd. 6. Address by
Minister of External Affairs of Cuba at U.N., delivered in

(Continued on next card)

UNITED NATIONS

Voice Lib.
344   Ball, George Wildman, 1909-
bd.16   Speech in Los Angeles on objectives of
U.N. in the Congo. CBS, December 19,
1961.
1 reel (7in.)   7 1/2 in. per sec.
phonotape.

1. Congo question. 2. United Nations.

UNITED NATIONS

Voice Lib.
M805   United Nations Special Tape no. 1. Various dates (Card 2)

CONTENTS (cont'd.) Spanish, starting a riot from the galleries;
warning given, then meeting adjourned (5 min., 41 sec.). -bd. 7
Khrushchev quote; arguments among U.N. Secretariat (1 min.,
50 sec.). -bd. 8. Adlai Stevenson speaking about the Congo
situation; outbreak of rioting of African visitors until session is
suspended; galleries ordered cleared (10 min., 26 sec.). -bd. 9.
U.N. delegate, Social and Economic Council, pleading "don't
send underdeveloped persons to underdeveloped areas" (1 min., 8
sec.). -bd. 10. Adlai Stevenson speaking at the U.N. and making
an error of speech, covered up by humorous remark (40 sec.). -
bd. 11. U.K. delegate enthusiastically endorsing U.S.S.R. proposal
to adjourn (1 min., 25 sec.).

1. United Nations. L. Stevenson, Adlai Ewing, 1900-1965.

Voice Lib.
M344   UNITED NATIONS
bd.1   Zorin, Valerian Alexandrovich, 1902-
       U.N. interpreter's translation on
temporary agreement by the Soviet Union to
accept U Thant as Secretary General.   CBS,
November 3, 1961.
       1 reel (7 in.)   7 1/2 in. per sec.
phonotape.

       1. Thant, U, 1909-   2. United Nations.

Voice Lib.
M1255 U.N. General Assembly. Emergency Session.
bd.1   Remarks by U.N. Secretary General U Thant
replying to Israeli and U.S. criticism
regarding withdrawal of U.N. Middle East
emergency forces and defending his position.
CBS-TV, June 20, 1967.
       1 reel (7 in.)   7 1/2 in. per sec.
phonotape.

       I. Thant, U, 1909-

Voice Lib.
M344   UNITED NATIONS - MEMBERSHIP
bd.5   Stevenson, Adlai Ewing, 1900-1965.
       Speech at the U.N. on admittance of Red
China to the United Nations.   CBS,
December 1, 1961.
       1 reel (7 in.)   7 1/2 i.p.s.   phonotape.

       1. United Nations - Membership.

Voice Lib.
M1242- United Nations. Security Council.
1243   Emergency session of U.N. Security Council
to discuss the Near East Crisis between
Israel and Arab States. Main speakers:
United States delegate; United Arab Republic
delegate; Danish delegate; and excerpt of
Israeli delegate.   NBC-TV, May 29, 1967.
       2 reels (7 in.)   7 1/2 i.p.s.   phonotape.

       1. Israel-Arab War, 1967-   - Diplomatic
history.

Voice Lib.
M344   UNITED NATIONS - MEMBERSHIP
bd.6   Zorin, Valerian Alexandrovich, 1902-
       Interpreter's translation of his
reply to Adlai Stevenson on issue of
Red China membership in U.N.   CBS,
December 1, 1961.
       1 reel (7 in.)   7 1/2 i.p.s.   phonotape.

       1. United Nations - Membership.

Voice Lib.
M1247 United Nations. Security Council.
       Morning session of U.N. Security Council,
called by its president, Hans Tabor of Denmark,
to hear about the outbreak of hostilities
between Israel and Arab countries. Main speakers:
U Thant, Secretary General, reading latest
reports, followed by delegate of Israel and
delegate of United Arab Republic.   NBC-TV,
June 5, 1967.
       1 reel (7 in.)   7 1/2 in. per sec.   phonotape.
       L Israel-Arab War, 1967-   - Diplomatic history.
       L Thant, U, 1909-

Voice Lib.
554   U.N. Conference on international organization.
bd.1   Expression of appreciation to International
Secretariat.   GRV, June 23, 1945.
       1 reel (7 in.)   7 1/2 in. per sec.
phonotape.

Voice Lib.
M1252 United Nations. Security Council.
       Meeting on Arab-Israeli conflict. Excerpt
of statement by Pres. Nasser of UAR
announcing his resignation followed by
Emergency Session of U.N. Security Council.
Speakers: Gideon Rafael, Ambassador to U.N.
from Israel reprimanding Ambassador Federenko
of U.S.S.R.; Nikolai Federenko in reply
accusing U.S.; Arthur J. Goldberg; U.N.
Ambassador from Syria; Gideon Rafael
accepting cease-fire.   Resolution for
                        (Continued on next card)

Voice Lib.
548-   U.N. Conference on international organization,
553   San Francisco, California. GRV, April, 1945.
bd.2   6 reels (7 in.)   7 1/2 in. per sec.
phonotape.

Voice Lib.
M1252 United Nations. Security Council.
       Meeting on Arab-Israeli conflict...
June 9, 1967.   (Card 2)

       Israel but point out further fighting by
Syria.   CBS-TV, June 9, 1967.
       1 reel (7 in.)   7 1/2 in. per sec.
phonotape.

Voice Lib.
M805   United Nations Special Tape no. 1.
            U. N. Archives, various dates.
            33 min., 40 sec.   phonotape (1 r.
            7 1/2 i.p.s.)

              CONTENTS. - bd. 1 African member of Judicial Committee
            on international law (5 min., 32 sec.). -bd. 2. U. N. Indian
            delegate describing Mahatma Gandhi as a "half-naked fakir"
            (54 sec.). -bd. 3. Woman president of a committee adjourning
            meeting because of lack of speakers, amidst laughter (1 min.,
            38 sec.). -bd. 4. U. N. sound crew testing equiment: "take
            your pot up there" (1 min., 22 sec.). -bd. 5. "Song of United
            Nations" rehearsal (3 min., 4 sec.). -bd. 6. Address by
            Minister of External Affairs of Cuba at U. N., delivered in

                                      (Continued on next card)

Voice Lib.
M805   United Nations Special Tape no. 1.   Various dates (Card 2)

              CONTENTS (cont'd.) Spanish, starting a riot from the galleries;
            warning given, then meeting adjourned (5 min., 41 sec.). -bd. 7
            Khrushchev quote; arguments among U. N. Secretariat (1 min.,
            50 sec.). -bd. 8. Adlai Stevenson speaking about the Congo
            situation; outbreak of rioting of African visitors until session is
            suspended; galleries ordered cleared (10 min., 26 sec.). -bd. 9.
            U. N. delegate, Social and Economic Council, pleading "don't
            send underdeveloped persons to underdeveloped areas" (1 min., 8
            sec.). -bd. 10. Adlai Stevenson speaking at the U. N. and making
            an error of speech, covered up by humorous remark (40 sec.). -
            bd. 11. U. K. delegate enthusiastically endorsing U. S. S. R. proposal
            to adjourn (1 min., 25 sec.).

              I. United Nations.   I. Stevenson, Adlai Ewing, 1900-1965.

Voice Lib.
M806   United Nations Special Tape No. 2.
            U.N. Archives (various dates)
            1 reel (7 in.)   7 1/2 in. per sec.
            phonotape.

              CONTENTS. -bd. 1. Excerpt from speech by Sen. Tom Connally
            at disarmament committee criticizing U. S. S. R. -bd. 2. U. N.
            translators in row, getting into fist fight and interrupting Pakistani
            delegate. -bd. 3. Nepal U. N. delegate at 77st Plenary Session of
            General Assembly interrupted by screaming agitator. -bd. 4. Harold
            MacMillan, honorary president of U. N. Association, welcoming Dag
            Hammarskjöld to England; interrupted by isolationist heckler conser-
            vative, but continuing speech undisturbed. -bd. 5. U. N. delegate
            from Saudi Arabia arguing with Chairman of Committee about
                                      (Continued on next card)

Voice Lib.
M806   United Nations Special Tape No. 2.   (various
            dates)   (Card 2)

              CONTENTS, cont'd. "point of order". -bd. 6. U. N. delegate
            speaking about "hamburgers with a college education" and the
            effect of advertising slogans on the masses. -bd. 7. Turkish U. N.
            delegate at U. N. replying to Greek delegate on "point of order". -
            bd. 8. U. N. delegate speaking about white slavery and high cost of
            women. -bd. 9. U. N. delegate telling anecdote about an
            incident in underdeveloped country: "A U. N. Bull". -bd. 10. U. N.
            delegate balling up anecdote about cats. -bd. 11. U. N. delegate
            speaking about lizards hindering business in Nigeria. -bd. 12. U. N.
            delegate advocating more scientific progress on old age rather than
            the progress on moon exploration. -bd. 13. U. N. delegate telling
            anecdote about co-operation. -bd. 14. South African delegate
                                      (Continued on next card)

Voice Lib.
M806   United Nations Special Tape No. 2.   (various
            dates)   (Card 3)

              CONTENTS, cont'd. telling anecdote at U. N. -bd. 15. Chairman
            opening the 714th session of the Second Committee of the 15th
            session of the U. N. General Assembly. -bd. 16. U. N. delegate
            indicating the number of seats available for various countries at the
            U. N. -bd. 17. Chairman of Committee instructing delegates how to
            indicate their vote. -bd. 18. U. N. delegate from Liberia debating
            on how to address a woman chairman.

              I. Connally, Thomas Terry, 1877-1963.   II.
            MacMillan, Harold, 1894-

                    U.S. AGENCY FOR INTERNATIONAL DEVELOPMENT
Voice Lib.
M1742   Hannah, John Alfred, 1902-
  bd.1   Address at his retirement dinner at
            Michigan State University.   Introduction
            by Duffy Daugherty.   WKAR, March 17, 1968.
            29 min.   phonotape (1 r.   7 1/2 i.p.s.)

              1. U.S. Agency for International
            Development.   I. Daugherty, Hugh.

                    U.S. ARMY - MILITARY LIFE
Voice Lib.
M260   Hargrove, Marion Lawton, 1919-
  bd.3   How to become a sergeant in less than
            twenty years; anecdotes on army life.
            G.R. Vincent, 1942.
            1 reel (7 in.)   7 1/2 i.p.s.   phonotape.

              1. U.S. Army - Military life.

                    U.S. ARMY - NEGRO TROOPS
Voice Lib.
M1290-   Same mud, same blood; a one-hour actual
1291   report on the integration of white and
  bd.1   colored troops of the 101st Airborne
            Division.   NBC, December 1, 1967.
            2 reels (7 in.)   7 1/2 in. per sec.
            phonotape.

              1. U.S. Army - Negro troops.   I. McGee,
            Frank, 1921-

Voice Lib.   U.S. ATTORNEY-GENERAL
M1602   Ervin, Samuel James, 1896-
              Summation of the proposed legislation to
            reform the office of the Attorney-General,
            as a result of the Watergate investigations.
            WKAR-AM, April 1, 1974.
            30 min.   phonotape (1 r.   7 1/2 i.p.s.)

              1. U.S. Attorney-General.

                    U.S. - BIOGRAPHY
C1
H8   Whorf, Michael, 1933-
              Of men and legends.
            1 tape cassette.   (The visual sounds of
            Mike Whorf.   History and heritage, H8)
              Originally presented on his radio program, Kaleidoscope,
            WJR, Detroit.
              Duration: 50 min., 30 sec.
              Beloved and revered, despised and dislike, they were figures
            in our history that helped to make a great land. Here are brief
            character sketches of personalities in our heritage whose contri-
            butions and efforts are gratefully acknowledged by an appreciative
            nation.

              I. U. S. - Biography.   I. Title.

C1
S12

UNITED STATES. BUREAU OF INDIAN AFFAIRS

Whorf, Michael, 1933–
  The velvet leash.
  1 tape cassette. (The visual sounds of
Mike Whorf. Social, S12)
    Originally presented on his radio program, Kaleidoscope,
WJR, Detroit.
    Duration: 49 min., 15 sec.
    This segment deals with the Indian and his involvement with
the Bureau of Indian Affairs. What is the B.I.A. and what
influence does it have on the Indian? What and where were the
forces for good and evil and how has the Indian fared?

    1. Indians of North America - Government relations.
    2. United States. Bureau of Indian Affairs. I. Title.

Voice Lib.
M1562
bd.2

U.S. - CENTENNIAL CELEBRATIONS, ETC.

Armstrong, Anne
  Speech to National Press Club, Washington,
D.C. Introduced by Sam Fogg. February 14,
1974.
  25 min. phonotape (1 r. 7 1/2 i.p.s.)

    1. U.S. - Centennial celebrations, etc.
I. Fogg, Sam.

Voice Lib.
M655
bd.1

U.S. - CIVILIZATION - 1918-1945

The Twentieth Century (TV program)
  "The creative thirties", narrated by
Walter Cronkite. CBS, 1963.
  25 min. phonotape (1 r. 7 1/2 i.p.s.)

    I. U.S. - Civilization - 1918-1945. I. Bowes, Edward,
1874-1946. II. Geismar, Maxwell David, 1909-
III. MacDonald, Dwight, 1906- IV. Welles, Orson, 1915-
V. Cronkite, Walter Leland, 1916- VI. Gable, Clark, 1901-
1960. VII. Lewis, Sinclair, 1885-1951. VIII. Houseman,
John, 1902- IX. Roosevelt, Franklin Delano, Pres. U.S.,
1882-1945.

C1
S54

U.S. - CIVILIZATION - 1918-1945

Whorf, Michael, 1933–
  Rendezvous with destiny; the 1930's.
  1 tape cassette. (The visual sounds of
Mike Whorf. Social, S54)
    Originally presented on his radio program, Kaleidoscope,
WJR, Detroit.
    Duration: 47 min.
    Apple stands on the street corners, dust bowls, the unemployed,
the dispossessed - this was the depression of the 1930's. It was the
era of Roosevelt, the NRA, the CCC, and the TVA.

    1. U.S. - Civilization - 1918-1945. 2. U.S. - History -
1933-1945. I. Title.

C1
S54

U.S. COMMISSION ON CIVIL RIGHTS

Voice Lib.
304

Hannah, John Alfred, 1902-
  Address at MSU Men's Club on the work
of the Civil Rights Commission. NVL location
recording, November 10, 1963.
  1 reel (7 in.) 7 1/2 in. per sec.
phonotape.

    1. U.S. Commission on Civil Rights.

U.S. COMMISSION ON CIVIL RIGHTS

Voice Lib.
305
bd.1

Hannah, John Alfred, 1902-
  Address at MSU Men's Club on the work
of the Civil Rights Commission. NVL
location recording, November 10, 1963.
  1 reel (7 in.) 7 1/2 in. per sec.
phonotape.

    1. U.S. Commission on Civil Rights.

Voice Lib.
M1571
bd.2

U.S. CONGRESS

Bolling, Richard, 1916-
  Speaking at the National Press Club on
the need for reorganizing Congress.
WKAR, April 18, 1974.
  20 min. phonotape (1 r. 7 1/2 i.p.s.)

    1. U.S. Congress.

Voice Lib.
M1028
bd.11

U.S. CONGRESS - ELECTIONS

Trout, Robert, 1908-
  Excerpt of news broadcast about the
election of Republican 80th Congress.
November, 1946.
  1 reel (7 in.) 7 1/2 i.p.s.; phonotape.

    1. U.S. Congress - Elections.

Voice Lib.
M1656
bd.3

U.S. Congress. House. Committee on the
  Judiciary.
  House Judiciary Committee, 1st public
meeting of impeachment hearings, with
Chairman Peter Rodino and Edward Hutchinson.
WKAR, May 9, 1974.
  15 min. phonotape (1 r. 7 1/2 i.p.s.)

    1. Nixon, Richard Milhous, Pres. U.S., 1913–
I. Rodino, Peter Wallace, 1909-
II. Hutchinson, Edward, 1914-

Voice Lib.
M746
bd.2

U.S. Congress. Senate. Committee on Government Operations.
  Permanent Subcommittee on Investigations.
  Proceedings of the [1st session] of Senate Army-McCarthy
hearings, April 22, 1954. Testimony by various witnesses
regarding pressure put on the Army to obtain a commission for
Private David Schine. Some of the people speaking are:
Griffin Bancroft, CBS announcer, describing the scenes at the
hearings; Joseph N. Welch, counsel for the Army; Ray Jenkins,
counsel for the subcommittee; Army Secretary Robert Stevens;
General Reber and Senator McClellan of Arkansas. CBS Radio,
April 22, 1954.
  1 reel (7 in.) 7 1/2 in. per sec. phonotape.

    I. McCarthy-Army controversy, 1954. I. Bancroft, Griffin
II. Welch, Joseph Nye, 1890-1960. III. Jenkins, Ray Howard,
1897- IV. Stevens, Robert Ten Broeck, 1899- V.
Reber, Miles VI. McClellan, John Little, 1896-

Voice Lib.
M747
bd.2
U.S. Congress. Senate. Committee on Government Operations.
Permanent Subcommittee on Investigations.
Proceedings of the 2nd session of Senate Army-McCarthy
hearings, April 23, 1954. Discussion of pressure put upon Army
Secretary Stevens to obtain direct commission for Private David
Schine with intimation of dropping the Fort Monmouth
investigation. CBS Radio, April 23, 1954.
1 reel (7 in.) 7 1/2 in. per sec. phonotape.

L. McCarthy-Army controversy, 1954.

Voice Lib.
M748
U.S. Congress. Senate. Committee on Government Operations.
Permanent Subcommittee on Investigations.
Proceedings of the 3rd session of Senate Army-McCarthy
hearings, April 26, 1954. Cross-examination of Secretary of
the Army Robert Stevens. CBS Radio, April 26, 1954.
1 reel (7 in.) 7 1/2 in. per sec. phonotape.

L. McCarthy-Army controversy, 1954. L. Stevens, Robert
Ten Broeck, 1899-

Voice Lib.
M749
U.S. Congress. Senate. Committee on Government Operations.
Permanent Subcommittee on Investigations.
Proceedings of the 4th session of Senate Army-McCarthy
hearings, April 27, 1954. Testimony regarding an altered
photograph submitted in evidence by McCarthy committee showing
Secretary Stevens and Private David Schine. CBS Radio,
April 27, 1954.
1 reel (7 in.) 7 1/2 in. per sec. phonotape.

L. McCarthy-Army controversy, 1954.

Voice Lib.
M750
bd.1
U.S. Congress. Senate. Committee on Government Operations.
Permanent Subcommittee on Investigations.
Proceedings of the 4th session of Senate Army-McCarthy
hearings, continued, April 27, 1954. Circumstances under
which the altered photograph was taken was questioned; examination of Sec. Stevens in his attempts to sidetrack investigation from
Army to Air Force and Navy; a cross-examination by McCarthy
of Secretary Stevens referring to his attempts to block investigation;
questioning of Stevens by Senator Mundt demanding exact charges
against Carr, Cohn and McCarthy. CBS Radio, April 27, 1954.
1 reel (7 in.) 7 1/2 in. per sec. phonotape.

L. McCarthy-Army controversy, 1954. L. Stevens, Robert
Ten Broeck, 1899- II. McCarthy, Joseph Raymond, 1909-
1957. III. Mundt, Karl Earl, 1900-

Voice Lib.
M933
U.S. Congress. Senate. Committee on Government Operations.
Permanent Subcommittee on Investigations.
Proceedings of the 5th session of Senate Army-McCarthy
hearings, April 28, 1954. Cross-examination of Army Secretary
Stevens by Senator McCarthy; Counselor Jenkins questions
Stevens and Private Schine; McCarthy denies charges of special
privileges for Schine. WJR, 10:30 p.m., April 28, 1954.
1 reel (7 in.) 7 1/2 in. per sec. phonotape.

L. McCarthy-Army controversy, 1954. L. Stevens, Robert
Ten Broeck, 1899- II. McCarthy, Joseph Raymond, 1909-1957.
III. Jenkins, Ray Howard, 1897- IV. Schine, G David,
1927-

Voice Lib.
M934
U.S. Congress. Senate. Committee on Government Operations.
Permanent Subcommittee on Investigations.
Proceedings of the 6th session of Senate Army-McCarthy
sessions, April 29, 1954. Private Schine makes first appearance;
he is cross-examined by Secretary Stevens and Counselor Jenkins;
Schine comments on circumstances of doctoring the "famous
photograph" and delivering it for publication at a Washington
restaurant. Evening session, WJR, April 29, 1954.
1 reel (7 in.) 7 1/2 in. per sec. phonotape.

L. McCarthy-Army controversy, 1954. I. Schine, G
David, 1927- II. Stevens, Robert Ten Broeck, 1899-
III. Jenkins, Ray Howard, 1897-

Voice Lib.
M938
bd.2
U.S. Congress. Senate. Committee on Government Operations.
Permanent Subcommittee on Investigations.
Proceedings of the 7th session of Congressional hearings.
Continuation of discussion regarding the controversial blow-up
of photograph of Army Secretary Stevens and Private David
Schine; discussion about the transfer of General Lawton from
command at Fort Monmouth, N.J. CBS, April 30, 1954.
1 reel (7 in.) 7 1/2 in. per sec. phonotape.

L. McCarthy-Army controversy, 1954.

Voice Lib.
M1022
bd.1
U.S. Congress. Senate. Committee on Government Operations.
Permanent Subcommittee on Investigations.
Proceedings of the [8th session] of Senate Army-McCarthy
hearings, May 3, 1954. Participants: Secretary of the Army
Stevens and Senator McCarthy discussing the case of Major
Peress; controversy between Army counsel Adams and
McCarthy; McCarthy questioning creditability of Secretary
Stevens. WJR, May 3, 1954.
1 reel (7 in.) 7 1/2 in. per sec. phonotape.

L. McCarthy-Army controversy, 1954. L. Stevens, Robert
Ten Broeck, 1899- II. McCarthy, Joseph Raymond, 1909-
1957. III. Adams, John G

Voice Lib.
M1022
bd.2-
1923
U.S. Congress. Senate. Committee on Government Operations.
Permanent Subcommittee on Investigations.
Proceedings of the 9th session of Senate Army-McCarthy
hearings, May 4, 1954. Discussion concerning the possibility
of shortening the hearings; statements by Senators Dirksen,
Mundt, McClellan, Potter, etc.; Aaron Coleman and the
stripping of Army files; discussion of FBI confidential letter
and how it was obtained by McCarthy; suggestion of night and
Saturday sessions. WJR, May 4, 1954.
2 reels (7 in.) 7 1/2 in. per sec. phonotape.

L. McCarthy-Army controversy, 1954. L. Dirksen, Everett
McKinley, 1896-1969. II. Mundt, Karl Earl, 1900- III. McClellan,
John Little, 1896- IV. Potter, Charles Edward, 1916-

Voice Lib.
M1069
U.S. Congress. Senate. Committee on Government Operations.
Permanent Subcommittee on Investigations.
Proceedings of the 10th session of Senate Army-McCarthy
hearings, May 5, 1954. Senator McCarthy on witness stand;
debate concerning letter from FBI files; verbal duel between
Counsel Welch and McCarthy; Secretary of Army Stevens
on witness stand. CBS Radio, May 5, 1954.
1 reel (7 in.) 7 1/2 in. per sec. phonotape.

L. McCarthy-Army controversy, 1954. L. McCarthy,
Joseph Raymond, 1909-1957. II. Welch, Joseph Nye, 1890-1960.
III. Stevens, Robert Ten Broeck, 1899-

Voice Lib.
M1281 U.S. Congress. Senate. Committee on Government Operations.
Permanent Subcommittee on Investigations.
Proceedings of the 11th session of Senate Army-McCarthy hearings, May 6, 1954. Sen. McCarthy on witness stand, pertaining to missing letter from J. Edgar Hoover regarding possible spies at Ft. Monmouth, N.J. Other speakers: Roy Cohn, Committee Counsel Jenkins, Robert A. Collier. Summary by CBS' Griffin Bancroft. CBS Radio, May 6, 1954.
1 reel (7 in.) 7 1/2 in. per sec. phonotape.

I. McCarthy-Army controversy, 1954. I. McCarthy, Joseph Raymond, 1909-1957. II. Cohn, Roy M 1927-
III. Jenkins, Ray Howard, 1897- IV. Collier, Robert A
V. Bancroft, Griffin

Voice Lib.
M1299 U.S. Congress. Senate. Committee on Government Operations.
bd.2 Permanent Subcommittee on Investigations.
Proceedings of the 15th session of Senate Army-McCarthy hearings, Part II, May 12, 1954. Army Counsel Adams describes luncheon with McCarthy, Cohn and himself; further abuse and pressure to station Private David Schine; Cohn's threat, "We'll wreck the army if Schine is sent overseas". CBS-TV, May 12, 1954.
1 reel (7 in.) 7 1/2 in. per sec. phonotape.

I. McCarthy-Army controversy, 1954. I. Adams, John G

Voice Lib.
M1283 U.S. Congress. Senate. Committee on Government Operations.
Permanent Subcommittee on Investigations.
Proceedings of the 12th session of Senate Army-McCarthy hearings, May 7, 1954. Secretary Stevens alleges he was threatened by Sen. McCarthy. Sen. Mundt queries Stevens. Much bantering and ribbing. Question of legality of McCarthy holding certain documents. Discussion of pressure to give Private Schine an Army commission. CBS Radio, May 7, 1954.
1 reel (7 in.) 7 1/2 in. per sec. phonotape.

I. McCarthy-Army controversy, 1954. I. Stevens, Robert Ten Broeck, 1899- II. Mundt, Karl Earl, 1900-

Voice Lib.
M1319 U.S. Congress. Senate. Committee on Government Operations.
Permanent Subcommittee on Investigations.
Proceedings of the 16th session of Senate Army-McCarthy hearings, May 13, 1954. Ray Jenkins questioning John Adams about actions of Sec. Stevens. Was Sec. Stevens afraid to ship Private Schine overseas due to pressure by Roy Cohn and Sen. McCarthy? Was discussion of Mr. Adams private law practice? CBS-TV, May 13, 1954.
1 reel (7 in.) 7 1/2 in. per sec. phonotape.

I. McCarthy-Army controversy, 1954. I. Jenkins, Ray Howard, 1897- II. Adams, John G

Voice Lib.
M1284 U.S. Congress. Senate. Committee on Government Operations.
Permanent Subcommittee on Investigations.
Proceedings of the 13th session of Senate Army-McCarthy hearings, May 10, 1954. Senator Dirksen suggests they be held privately; Secretary Stevens makes statement and Senator McCarthy and his counsel, Roy Cohn, cross-examine Stevens; discussion of alleged communists at Ft. Monmouth and pressure of favored treatment for Private Schine. CBS Radio, May 10, 1954.
1 reel (7 in.) 7 1/2 in. per sec. phonotape.

I. McCarthy-Army controversy, 1954. I. Dirksen, Everett McKinley, 1896-1969. II. Stevens, Robert Ten Broeck, 1899-
III. McCarthy, Joseph Raymond, 1909-1957. IV. Cohn, Roy M 1927-

Voice Lib.
M1320 U.S. Congress. Senate. Committee on Government Operations.
Permanent Subcommittee on Investigations.
Proceedings of the 17th session of Senate Army-McCarthy hearings, May 14, 1954. Sen. Mundt questioning Mr. Adams about high-level meeting dealing with United Nations. Exchanges between senator Mundt and Army Counsel Welch. Senator McCarthy examining Sen. Dirksen. Discussion of purgery charges against Carr. Cohn and Adams speak about private dinner party. CBS TV, May 14, 1954.
1 reel (7 in.) 7 1/2 in. per sec. phonotape.

I. McCarthy-Army controversy, 1954. I. Mundt, Karl Earl, 1900- II. Welch, Joseph Nye, 1890-1960. III. McCarthy, Joseph Raymond, 1909-1957. IV. Dirksen, Everett McKinley, 1896-1969. V. Cohn, Roy M 1927- VI. Adams, John G

Voice Lib.
M1287 U.S. Congress. Senate. Committee on Government Operations.
bd.1 Permanent Subcommittee on Investigations.
Proceedings of the 14th session of Senate Army-McCarthy hearings, May 11, 1954. Vote on Dirksen amendment to shorten hearings. Sen. Potter claims that hearings are a disgrace to America. Various motions by Sen. McCarthy and Army counsel Welch. CBS, May 11, 1954.
1 reel (7 in.), 7 1/2 in. per sec. phonotape.

I. McCarthy-Army controversy, 1954. I. Potter, Charles Edward, 1916- II. McCarthy, Joseph Raymond, 1909-1957. III. Welch, Joseph Nye, 1890-1960.

U.S. Congress. Senate. Ervin Committee.
see
U.S. Congress. Senate. Select Committee on Presidential Campaign Activities.

Voice Lib.
M1296 U.S. Congress. Senate. Committee on Government Operations.
bd.2 Permanent Subcommittee on Investigations.
Proceedings of the 15th session of Senate Army-McCarthy hearings, Part I, May 12, 1954. Army counsel Adams describes resentment of McCarthy counsel Roy Cohn at being restricted in certain areas at Ft. Monmouth, N.J. Also, complaints by Adams at being abused by Cohn regarding Private David Schine. CBS-TV, May 12, 1954.
1 reel (7 in.) 7 1/2 in. per sec. phonotape.

I. McCarthy-Army controversy, 1954. I. Adams, John G

U.S. Congress. Senate. Foreign Relations Committee
Voice Lib.
M954 McNamara, Robert S 1916-
Testimony at U.S. Senate Foreign Relations Committee hearings. NBC, April 20, 1966.
1 reel (7 in.) 7 1/2 i.p.s. phonotape.

1. U.S. - Foreign relations. I. U.S. Congress. Senate. Foreign Relations Committee.

U.S. Congress. Senate. Rackets Committee.
    see
U.S. Congress. Senate. Seclect Committee to
investigate racketeering in labor unions.

Voice Lib.
M1489   U.S. Congress. Senate. Special Committee
bd.2   to Investigate Organized Crime in
            Interstate Commerce.
        Excerpt of examinnation of racketeer Frank
    Costello by Kefauver Committee Counsel
    Rudolf Halley.   New York, WMGM Radio, March
    20, 1951.
        1 reel (7 in.)   7 1/2 in. per sec.
    phonotape.
        I. Costello, Frank   II. Halley,
    Rudolf, 1913-1956.

Voice Lib.
M1800   U.S. Congress. Senate. Select Committee on Presidential
            Campaign Activities.
        Watergate gavel to gavel, phase 1: May 17 - August 7, 1973.
    Pacifica, May 17 - August 7, 1973.
    172 reels (5 in.) 3 3/4 i.p.s. phonotape.

        "These tapes include commentaries by Pacifica's Washington
    correspondents and interviews with members of the Senate Committee
    taped during recesses of the hearings."

        1. Presidents - U.S. - Elections - 1972. 2. Watergate Affair,
    1972-   L Ervin, Samuel James, 1896-   II. Talmadge,
    Herman Eugene, 1913-   III. Inouye, Daniel Ken, 1924-
    IV. Baker, Howard H., 1925-   V. Gurney, Edward John, 1914-
    VI. Welcker, Lowell P., 1   VII. Title.

Voice Lib.
M263-   U.S. Congress. Senate. Special Committee to
265   investigate organized crime in interstate
bd.1   commerce.
        Committee anti-trust hearing on baseball;
    interrogation and testimony of Casey Stengel.
    CBS, July 9, 1958.
        3 reels (7 in.)   7 1/2 in. per sec.
    phonotape.

        1. Baseball.   I. Stengel, Casey

Voice Lib.
M1800   U.S. Congress. Senate. Select Committee
WG   on Presidential Campaign Activities.
0517.01   Opening statements at committee hearings.
        Pacifica, May 17, 1973.
        62 min.   phonotape (1 r.   3 3/4 i.p.s.)
    (Watergate gavel to gavel, phase 1)

        1. Watergate Affair, 1972-

U.S. Congress. Senate. Watergate Committee.
    see
U.S. Congress. Senate. Select Committee
on Presidential Campaign Activities.

Voice Lib.
256   U.S. Congress. Senate. Select committee
bd.5   to investigate racketeering in labor
            unions.
        Senator John Kennedy and Counsel Robert
    Kennedy questioning Faunce, Vice-President
    of Continental Baking Company. CBS News,
    October 23, 1957.
        1 reel (7 in.)   7 1/2 in. per sec.
    phonotape.
        1. Faunce, George, 1891-   II. Kennedy, John
    Fitzgerald, Pres. U.S., 1917-1963.   III. Kennedy, Robert
    Francis, 1925-1968.

                    U.S. - DEFENSES
Voice Lib.
M1745   McIntyre, Thomas James, 1915-
        Debate with Senator John Tower on
    defense spending. WKAR, June 26, 1974.
        15 min.   phonotape (1 r.   7 1/2 i.p.s.)

        1. U.S. - Defenses.   I. Tower, John
    Goodwin, 1925-

Voice Lib.
M1233- U.S. Congress. Senate. Special Committee
1235,   on Astronautics and Space Exploration.
bd.1   Discussion between various U.S. Senators
        on Space Committee and astronauts and NASA
    officials regarding their opinions and
    experiences. Voice of America, March 1,
    1962.
        3 reels (7 in.)   7 1/2 i.p.s.   phonotape.

        1. Outer space - Exploration.

                    U.S. - DEFENSES
Voice Lib.
M905   Roosevelt, Franklin Delano, Pres. U.S.,
            1882-1945.
        Fireside talk discussing necessity of
    speed-up in national defense and reviewing
    accomplishments of military and economic
    preparedness so far. CBS, May 26, 1940.
        1 reel (7 in.)   7 1/2 i.p.s.   phonotape.

        1. U.S. - Defenses. 2. U.S. - Politics and
    government - 1933-1945.

U.S. - DEFENSES

Voice Lib.
M901   Roosevelt, Franklin Delano, Pres. U.S.,
1882-1945.
Fireside chat on national defense program,
giving reasons for American aid to Britain.
CBS, December 29, 1940.
1 reel (7 in.)   7 1/2 i.p.s.   phonotape.

1. U.S. - Defenses.

Voice Lib.   U.S. - DEFENSES
M917   Roosevelt, Franklin Delano, Pres. U.S.,
bd.2-   1882-1945.
918   Fireside chat defining position of U.S. on
national defense and alliances with Pan
American republics.   May 27, 1941.
2 reels (7 in.)   7 1/2 in. per sec.
phonotape.

1. U.S. - Defenses. 2. U.S. - Foreign
relations - Latin America. 3. Latin America -
Foreign relations - U.S.

U.S.   DEPT. OF JUSTICE

Voice Lib.
M1222   Washington Reports; CBS television news. Reports by CBS
bd.1   news correspondents about President Kennedy's Civil
Rights message to Congress and interviews with Attorney
General Robert F. Kennedy pertaining to his views on
his own work in the Justice Department and his own future.
CBS-TV News, Bergman, March 3, 1963.
1 reel (7 in.)   7 1/2 i.p.s.   phonotape.

1. Civil rights. 2. U.S. Dept. of Justice. 3. Kennedy,
Robert Francis, 1925-1968. I. L. Kennedy, Robert Francis,
1925-1968.

U.S. - ECONOMIC CONDITIONS

Voice Lib.
652   Baruch, Bernard Mannes, 1870-1965.
bd.10   On recession and danger of inflation.
CBS, April 1, 1958.
1 reel (7 in.)   7 1/2 in. per sec.
phonotape.

U.S. - ECONOMIC CONDITIONS

Voice Lib.
351   Eisenhower, Dwight David, Pres. U.S., 1890-1969.
bd.4   Excerpts of speech in Los Angeles on
economy of U.S., business monopoly, legal
review of world laws.   CBS, February 1,
1962.
1 reel (7 in.)   7 1/2 in. per sec.
phonotape.

1. U.S. - Econ. condit.

U.S. - ECONOMIC CONDITIONS
Voice Lib.
M1575-   McCracken, Paul Winston, 1915-
1576,   Is American optimism at an end? Economic
bd.1   Club of Detroit address.   WKAR-FM, February
25, 1974.
60 min.   phonotape (2 r.   7 1/2 in. per
sec.)

1. U.S. - Economic conditions.

U.S. - ECONOMIC CONDITIONS
Voice Lib.
M1566   Nixon, Richard Milhous, Pres. U.S., 1913-
bd.2   Address on the energy crisis, followed by
excerpts from question and answer period with
the press.   WKAR-FM, February 24, 1974.
20 min.   phonotape. 7 1/2 in. per sec.

1. Power resources - U.S. 2. U.S. - Economic conditions.
3. Nixon, Richard Milhous, Pres. U.S., 1913-

U.S. - ECONOMIC CONDITIONS
Voice Lib.
M714   Roosevelt, Franklin Delano, Pres. U.S.,
bd.3   1882-1945.
First fireside chat, on banking situation
in the U.S. (opening and closing statements
of this broadcast).   March 12, 1933.
2 min., 9 sec.   phonotape (1 r.   7 1/2
i.p.s.)

1. U.S. - Economic conditions. 2. Banks
& banking - U.S.

U.S. - ECONOMIC CONDITIONS
Voice Lib.
M612   Shriver, Robert Sargent, 1915-
War on poverty; reviews President Lyndon
Johnson's fight against domestic poverty,
discusses his role in the fight, briefly
reviews his own career.   NET, March 30, 1964.
1 reel (7 in.)   7 1/2 i.p.s.   phonotape.

1. U.S. - Economic conditions. 2. Johnson, Lyndon
Baines, Pres. U.S., 1908-1973. 3. Shriver, Robert Sargent,
1915-

U.S. - ECONOMIC CONDITIONS
Voice Lib.
M715   Stock market slump of 1962; newscast and
bd.5   "on-the-spot" interview with customers
in brokerage firm.   May 29, 1962.
2 min., 52 sec.   phonotape (1 r.
7 1/2 i.p.s.)

1. U.S. - Economic conditions.

U.S. - ECONOMIC POLICY, 1971-
Voice Lib.
M1484, Connally, John Bowden, 1917-
bd.2-   News conference, details of Phase two of
1485   economic policy.   October 8, 1971.
        2 reels (7 in.)   7 1/2 in. per sec.
    phonotape.

U.S. - ECONOMIC POLICY, 1971-
Voice Lib.
M1482 Nixon, Richard Milhous, Pres. U.S., 1913-
bd.1   Address at joint session of Congress
    asking for implementation of the President's
    new economic policies.   CBS, September 9,
    1971.
        1 reel (7 in.)   7 1/2 in. per sec.
    phonotape.

U.S. - ECONOMIC POLICY - 1971-
Voice Lib.
M1484 Nixon, Richard Milhous, Pres. U.S., 1913-
bd.1   National broadcast describing Phase Two
    of the wage-price freeze.   CBS, October 7,
    1971.
        1 reel (7 in.)   7 1/2 in. per sec.
    phonotape.

U.S. ENVIRONMENTAL PROTECTION AGENCY
Voice Lib.
1720   Train, Russell Errol, 1920-
bd.2   Interview on the Today Show with Barbara
    Walters and Robert Guralski.   NBC, June 11,
    1974.
        5 min.   phonotape (1 r.   7 1/2 i.p.s.)

    1. U.S. Environmental Protection Agency.
    I. Walters, Barbara, 1931-   II. Guralski,
    Robert.

U.S. FEDERAL BUREAU OF INVESTIGATION
Voice Lib.
M1616   Kelly, Clarence M
    National Press Club address.   WKAR-AM,
    April 4, 1974.
        55 min.   phonotape (1 r.   7 1/2 in. per
    sec.)

    1. U.S. Federal Bureau of Investigation.

U.S. - FOREIGN POLICY
Voice Lib.
M796- Brinkley, David McClure, 1920-
799   White Paper, on U.S. foreign policy from
    post World War II period to current hostilities
    in Vietnam, with various commentators, U.S.
    government officials, foreign dignitaries,
    and actual scenes and sound.   NBC-TV,
    September 7, 1965.
        4 reels (7 in.)   7 1/2 in. per sec.   phonotape.

    Running time approximately 3 hours.

    1. U.S. - Foreign policy.   I. Huntley, Chet, 1911-1974.

U.S. - FOREIGN POLICY
Voice Lib.
M1454 Nixon, Richard Milhous, Pres. U.S., 1913-
bd.1   Discussion of U.S. foreign policy with
    network newscasters Eric Sevareid (CBS),
    John Chancellor (NBC), and Howard K. Smith
    (ABC).
        1 reel (7 in.)   7 1/2 in. per sec.
    phonotape.

    I. Sevareid, Arnold Eric, 1912-   II.
    Chancellor, John William, 1927-   III.
    Smith, Howard Kingsbury, 1914-

U.S. - FOREIGN POLICY
Voice Lib.
M846   Truman, Harry S, Pres. U.S., 1884-1972.
bd.1   Navy Day address by President Truman in
    Central Park, New York City, stating postwar
    U.S. foreign policy and the outlook for uses of
    atomic power.   NBC, October 27, 1945.
        1 reel (7 in.)   7 1/2 in. per sec.
    phonotape.

    1. U.S.- Foreign policy.   2. Atomic power.

U.S. - FOREIGN RELATIONS
Voice Lib.
M534- "America first" anti-war rally in Madison
536   Square Garden, New York City.   GRV,
    October, 1941.
        3 reels (7 in.)   7 1/2 i.p.s.   phonotape.

    1. U.S. - Foreign relations.

U.S. - FOREIGN RELATIONS
Voice Lib.
M652   Bradley, Omar Nelson, 1893-
bd.16   U.S. does not want war; our problems
    and responsibilities pertaining to this
    policy.   CBS [n.d.]
        1 reel (7 in.)   7 1/2 i.p.s.   phonotape.

    1. U.S. - Foreign relations.

U.S. - FOREIGN RELATIONS

Voice Lib.
M728
bd.5
Hoover, Herbert Clark, Pres. U.S., 1874-1964.
"Shall we send our youth to war?" Advice against involvement by the U.S. in European power politics. RCA Victor, 1938.
4 min., 8 sec.   phonotape (1 r. 7 1/2 i.p.s.)

1. U.S. - Foreign relations.

U.S. - FOREIGN RELATIONS - LATIN AMERICA

Voice Lib.
M917
bd.2-
918
Roosevelt, Franklin Delano, Pres. U.S., 1882-1945.
Fireside chat defining position of U.S. on national defense and alliances with Pan American republics.   May 27, 1941.
2 reels (7 in.)   7 1/2 in. per sec. phonotape.

1. U.S. - Defenses. 2. U.S. - Foreign relations - Latin America.   3. Latin America - Foreign relations - U.S.

U.S. - FOREIGN RELATIONS

Voice Lib.
M954
McNamara, Robert S   1916-
Testimony at U.S. Senate Foreign Relations Committee hearings.   NBC, April 20, 1966.
1 reel (7 in.)   7 1/2 i.p.s. phonotape.

1. U.S. - Foreign relations.   I. U.S. Congress. Senate. Foreign Relations Committee.

U.S. - FOREIGN RELATIONS - RUSSIA

Voice Lib.
M133
bd.2
Kennedy, John Fitzgerald, Pres. U.S., 1917-1963.
Cuba blockade, an address to the nation. NBC, October 22, 1962.
1 reel (7 in.)   7 1/2 i.p.s.   phonotape.

1. Military bases, Russian - Cuba.
2. U.S. - Foreign relations - Russia.
3. Russia - Foreign relations - U.S.

U.S. - FOREIGN RELATIONS - EGYPT

Voice Lib.
M1745
bd.4
al Sadat, Anwar.
Sadat: an exclusive interview; an extensive interview with Walter Cronkite on the changes in U.S. policy regarding Egypt.   CBS, June 21, 1974.
30 min.   phonotape (1 r.   7 1/2 i.p.s.)

1. U.S. - For. rel. - Egypt. 2. Egypt - For. rel. - U.S. 3. Egypt - Pol. & govt. - 1952-   I. Cronkite, Walter Leland, 1916-

---

U.S. - FOREIGN RELATIONS - RUSSIA

Voice Lib.
M1746
Kissinger, Henry Alfred, 1923-
Excerpts of press conference, explaining that the arms limitations talks with the Russians will serve the best interests of both nations; denying secret agreements. WKAR, June 24, 1974.
30 min.   phonotape (1 r.   7 1/2 i.p.s.)

1. U.S. - Foreign relations - Russia.
2. Russia - Foreign relations - U.S.

U.S. - FOREIGN RELATIONS - GT. BRIT.

Voice Lib.
M1583
Ramsbotham, Sir Peter Edward, 1919-
National Press Club address.   WKAR-AM, March 21, 1974.
30 min.   phonotape (1 r.   7 1/2 i.p.s.)

Includes questions and answer period.

1. Gt. Brit. - Foreign relations - U.S.
2. U.S. - Foreign relations - Gt. Brit.
3. Gt. Brit. - Economic conditions.

U.S. - FOREIGN RELATIONS - RUSSIA

Voice Lib.
M899
Marshall, George Catlett, 1880-1959.
Report on his mission to Moscow, delivered from the State Department, Washington, D.C. WJR, April 28, 1947.
1 reel (7 in.)   7 1/2 i.p.s.   phonotape.

1. U.S. - Foreign relations - Russia.
2. Russia - Foreign relations - U.S.

U.S. - FOREIGN RELATIONS - ISRAEL

Voice Lib.
M864
Silver, Abba Hillel, 1893-1963.
Portion of the principal address to the 2000 delegates of the 51st annual convention of the Zionist Organization of America, held at Syria Mosque in Pittsburgh, Pa. Dr. Silver criticizes U.S. Government for its vascillating policies on the question of Palestine partition, reviews the steps leading to the formation of Jewish homeland, culminating in a reversal of his policy by President Truman. KDKA, July 4, 1948
1 reel (7 in.)   7 1/2 i.p.s. phonotape.

1. Zionism. 2. U.S. - Foreign relations - Israel.
3. Israel - Foreign relations - U.S.

U.S. - HISTORY

C1
H41
Whorf, Michael, 1933-
Days of valor.
1 tape cassette.   (The visual sounds of Mike Whorf. History and heritage, H41)

Originally presented on his radio program, Kaleidoscope, WJR, Detroit.
Duration: 49 min.
In each of America's wars there have been given moments, certain occasions when men rise above the normal call of duty to perform at the peak of their endurance whether in victory or defeat.

1. U.S. - History.   2. War.   I. Title.

C1
H69

U.S. - HISTORY - CIVIL WAR, 1861-1865

Whorf, Michael, 1933-
    The blue and the gray; Civil War, part 2.
    1 tape cassette. (The visual sounds of
Mike Whorf. History and heritage, H69)
      Originally presented on his radio program, Kaleidoscope,
WJR, Detroit.
      Duration: 37 min., 35 sec.
      This program concerns itself with the stories of the northern
soldier and the southern yeoman, their convictions emblazoned
in history. The north and the south, the blue and the gray, brave
men fighting for ideals - not for right or wrong - but fighting for
what they believed was their sacred duty.

      L. U.S - History - Civil War, 1861-1865. L. Title.

C1
H68

U.S. - HISTORY - CIVIL WAR, 1861-1865

Whorf, Michael, 1933-
    We are coming Father Abraham; Civil War,
part 1.
    1 tape cassette. (The visual sounds of
Mike Whorf. History and heritage, H68)
      Originally presented on his radio program, Kaleidoscope,
WJR, Detroit.
      Duration: 38 min., 15 sec.
      The beginning of a six-part series on the American Civil War,
this program emphasizes the why and how it all began, and our
title comes from Lincoln's call for volunteers to combat an
aggressive and brave foe.

      L. U.S. - History -   Civil War, 1861-1865. L. Title.

C1
H72

U.S. - HISTORY - CIVIL WAR, 1861-1865 -
SONGS AND MUSIC

Whorf, Michael, 1933-
    They marched off to war to a military
quickstep; Civil War, part 5.
    1 tape cassette. (The visual sounds of Mike Whorf.
History and heritage, H72)

      Originally presented on his radio program, Kaleidoscope,
WJR, Detroit.
      Duration: 39 min., 55 sec.
      If there were any two wars which gave the world an abundance
of music, they were World War I and the War between the States.
This program is devoted to the lyrics and melodies of the Civil
War and the impact they played on the North and South.

      L. U.S. - History - Civil War, 1861-1865 - Songs & music.
L. Title.

C1
H71

U.S. - HISTORY - CIVIL WAR, 1861-1865 -
WOMEN'S WORK

Whorf, Michael, 1933-
    Women of the war [Civil War, part 4]
    1 tape cassette. (The visual sounds of
Mike Whorf. History and heritage, H71)
      Originally presented on his radio program, Kaleidoscope,
WJR, Detroit.
      Duration: 39 min.
      Part 4 of his Civil War, here is a compilation of tales which
tell of heroic deeds by women who spied, lied, nursed, and
fought in the front lines.

      L. U.S. - History - Civil War, 1861-1865 - Women's work.
L. Title.

C1
854

U.S. - HISTORY - 1933-1945

Whorf, Michael, 1933-
    Rendezvous with destiny; the 1930's.
    1 tape cassette. (The visual sounds of
Mike Whorf. Social, 854)
      Originally presented on his radio program, Kaleidoscope,
WJR, Detroit.
      Duration: 47 min.
      Apple stands on the street corners, dust bowls, the unemployed,
the dispossessed - this was the depression of the 1930's. It was the
era of Roosevelt, the NRA, the CCC, and the TVA!

      L. U.S. - Civilization - 1918-1945. 2. U.S. - History -
1933-1945. L. Title.

C1
H1

U.S. - HISTORY, MILITARY

Whorf, Michael, 1933-
    The last of the heroes.
    1 tape cassette. (The visual sounds of
Mike Whorf. History and heritage, H1)
      Originally presented on his radio program, Kaleidoscope,
WJR, Detroit.
      Duration: 45 min., 45 sec.
      A free verse ode to America's fighting men, tracing our
involvement in wars with other nations; pointing to courage and
bravery as well as the futility of armed conflict. Patriotic music
is used abundantly to create mood and a sense of heritage.

      L. U.S. - History, Military. L. Title.

U.S. LAWS, STATUTES, ETC.
LABOR MANAGEMENT RELATIONS ACT, 1947

Voice Lib.
M831
bd.2
    Green, William, 1873-1952.
    Labor Day address at Summit Beach Park,
Akron, Ohio, denouncing Taft-Hartley
Slave Labor Bill. NBC, September 6, 1948.
    1 reel (7 in.)   7 1/2 in. per sec.
phonotape.

    1. U.S. Laws, statutes, etc. Labor
management relations act, 1947.

U.S. LAWS, STATUTES, ETC.
LABOR MANAGEMENT RELATIONS ACT, 1947.

Voice Lib.
M828
bd.2
    Taft, Robert Alphonso, 1889-1953.
    Explaining the terms and the purposes for
the proposed enactment of the Taft-Hartley
Labor Bill; fighting to override President
Truman's veto. NBC, June 22, 1947.
    1 reel (7 in.)   7 1/2 in. per sec.
phonotape.

U.S. LAWS, STATUTES, ETC.
LABOR MANAGEMENT RELATIONS ACT, 1947

Voice Lib.
M829
bd.2
    Truman, Harry S, Pres. U.S., 1884-1972.
    Radio address to the nation from the White
House explaining his position on Taft-Hartley
bill after veto of it and his opinions of
that legislation. KDKA, June 20, 1947.
    1 reel (7 in.)   7 1/2 in. per sec.
phonotape.

    1. U.S. Laws, statutes, etc. Labor
management relations act, 1947.

C1·
H51

U.S. MARINE CORPS

Whorf, Michael, 1933-
    From the halls of Montezuma.
    1 tape cassette. (The visual sounds of
Mike Whorf. History and heritage, H51)

      Originally presented on his radio program, Kaleidoscope,
WJR, Detroit.
      Duration: 39 min., 60 sec.
      As America's greatness is often written in the deeds of her
fighting men, so does this moving narrative of the United States
Marine Corps illustrate the countless moments of heroism, the
personal sacrifices and the gallant battles of our country's history.

      L. U.S. Marine Corps.   L. Title.

U.S. - MILITARY POLICY

Voice Lib.
M1698   Aspin, Les, 1938-
bd.2   Interviewed on Firing Line by William
Buckley. WKAR-TV, May 28, 1974.
         15 min. phonotape (1 r. 7 1/2 i.p.s.)

         1. Industry and state - U.S. 2. U.S. -
Military policy. I. Buckley, William
Frank, 1925-

○

U.S. NATIONAL GALLERY OF ART

Voice Lib.
M903   Roosevelt, Franklin Delano, Pres. U.S.,
             1882-1945.
Dedication of National Gallery of Art in
Washington, D.C. CBS, March 17, 1941.
         1 reel (7 in.) 7 1/2 i.p.s. phonotape.

         1. U.S. National Gallery of Art.

○

U.S. - POLITICS AND GOVERNMENT

Voice Lib.
M1702   Baker, Howard H., 1925-
             On Watergate, with Clyde Lamont, of the
National Press Club. WKAR, May 30, 1974.
         50 min. phonotape (1 r. 7 1/2 i.p.s.)

         1. Watergate Affair, 1972-   2. U.S. -
Politics and government. I. Lamont, Clyde

○

Voice Lib. U.S. - POLITICS AND GOVERNMENT
M1691   Commager, Henry Steele, 1902-
bd.1   On public service and private
creativity, with Bill Moyers.
WKAR-TV, May 23, 1974.
         25 min. phonotape (1 r. 7 1/2 i.p.s.)

         1. Impeachments. 2. U.S. - Politics and
government. I. Moyers, Bill D., 1934-

○

U.S. - POLITICS AND GOVERNMENT

Voice Lib.
M1567-   Maddox, Lester Garfield, 1915-
1568,   Option; television broadcast originating
bd.1   at the University of Buffalo. WKAR-AM,
February 19, 1974.
         45 min. phonotape (2 r. 7 1/2 in. per
sec.)

         Speech delivered November 1973.

         1. U.S. - Social conditions. 2. U.S. -
Politics and government.

○

U.S. - POLITICS AND GOVERNMENT

Voice Lib.
M1724   Morse, Wayne Lyman, 1900-
bd.2   Question and answer session with Michigan
State University students. Includes Dr.
Thomas H. Greer. WKAR, January 13, 1970.
         20 min. phonotape (1 r. 7 1/2 i.p.s.)

         1. U.S. - Politics and government.
I. Greer, Thomas Hoag, 1914-

○

U.S. - POLITICS AND GOVERNMENT

Voice Lib.
M1720   O'Neill, Thomas P., 1912-
bd.1   Interview on Washington Straight Talk,
by Paul Duke. WKAR-TV, June 11, 1974.
         30 min. phonotape (1 r. 7 1/2 i.p.s.)

         1. U.S. - Politics & government.
         2. Nixon, Richard Milhous, Pres. U.S., 1913-
I. Duke, Paul.

○

U.S. - POLITICS AND GOVERNMENT

Voice Lib.
M1573-   Percy, Charles Harting, 1919-
1574,   The government's response to change;
bd.1   Eisenhower Symposium, Johns Hopkins University. WBJC, Baltimore, October 29, 1973.
         45 min. phonotape (2 r. 7 1/2 i.p.s.)

         Includes question and answer period.

         1. U.S. - Politics and government.
         2. Watergate Affair, 1972-

○

Voice Lib. U.S. - POLITICS AND GOVERNMENT
M1584   Percy, Charles Harting, 1919-
             Money - politics. WKAR-AM, February 27,
1974.
         30 min. phonotape (1 r. 7 1/2 i.p.s.)

         1. Campaign funds. 2. U.S. - Politics
and government.

○

U.S. - POLITICS AND GOVERNMENT

Voice Lib.
M1663   Powell, Adam Clayton, 1908-1972.
             Speech to Great Issues Class at MSU,
co-sponsored by ASMSU. WKAR, January 17,
1969.
         35 min., 30 sec. phonotape (1 r.
7 1/2 i.p.s.)

         1. Passive resistance to government.
         2. U.S. - Politics and government.

○

U.S. - POLITICS AND GOVERNMENT - 1933-1945

Voice Lib.
M892   Roosevelt, Franklin Delano, Pres. U.S.,
          1882-1945.
          Address to the special session of Congress
          which he called to request repeal of the
          embargo act of trading with belligerents
          in war materials. WJR, September 21, 1939.
          1 reel (7 in.)   7 1/2 i.p.s.   phonotape.

          1. U.S. - Politics and government -
          1933-1945.

U.S. - POLITICS AND GOVERNMENT - 1933-1945

Voice Lib.
M905   Roosevelt, Franklin Delano, Pres. U.S.,
          1882-1945.
          Fireside talk discussing necessity of
          speed-up in national defense and reviewing
          accomplishments of military and economic
          preparedness so far. CBS, May 26, 1940.
          1 reel (7 in.)   7 1/2 i.p.s.   phonotape.

          1. U.S. - Defenses. 2. U.S. - Politics and
          government - 1933-1945.

U.S. - POLITICS AND GOVERNMENT - 1933-1945

Voice Lib.
M1027   The World Today; CBS radio news program;
bd.1   reports concerning war situation in Europe
          and Asia; resignations from FDR cabinet;
          reorganization of the 79th Congress;
          Russian progress on Eastern front.
          CBS News, December 20, 1944.
          1 reel (7 in.)   7 1/2 i.p.s.   phonotape.

          1. World War, 1939-1945. 2. U.S. -
          Politics and government - 1933-1945.

Voice Lib. U.S. - POLITICS AND GOVERNMENT - 1945-1953
M1245   Murrow, Edward Roscoe, 1908-1965.
bd.2   News broadcast on current topics, dealing
          primarily with testimony by Attorney General
          Brownell and J. Edgar Hoover, at Un-American
          Activities Committee, condemning Truman
          administration in promoting Harry Dexter
          White, an alleged Communist spy. WJR,
          November 17, 1953.
          1 reel (7 in.)   7 1/2 i.p.s.   phonotape.

          1. U.S. - Politics and government - 1945-1953.

U.S. - POLITICS AND GOVERNMENT - 1963-1969

Voice Lib.
M1708   Johnson, Lyndon Baines, Pres. U.S., 1908-1973.
          Address to a Joint Session of Congress on
          continuation of current U. S. policies under
          his administration. NBC, November 27, 1963.
          30 min. phonotape (1 r.   7 1/2 i.p.s.)

          Transcript of the address included with
          tape.

          1. U.S. - Politics and government - 1963-
          1969.

U.S. - POLITICS AND GOVERNMENT - 1963-1969

Voice Lib.
M1680   Smith, Howard Kingsbury, 1914-
          Speaking at MSU Mass Communications
          Colloquium. WKAR, April 7, 1967.
          50 min. phonotape (1 r.   7 1/2 i.p.s.)

          1. Vietnamese Conflict, 1961-   - U.S.
          2. U.S. - Politics and government - 1963-
          1969.

U.S. - POLITICS AND GOVERNMENT, 1969-

Voice Lib.
M1611   Conyers, John, 1929-
bd.3   Discusses impeachment and opinion poll
          bias. WKAR-TV (1974?)
          8 min. phonotape (1 r.   7 1/2 i.p.s.)

          1. Nixon, Richard Milhous, Pres. U.S., 1913-
          2. U.S. - Politics and government, 1969-

U.S. - POLITICS AND GOVERNMENT - 1969-

Voice Lib.
M1568   Cranston, Alan, 1914-
bd.2   Proposing to the Ervin Committee the
          establishment of a Counsel-General, to be a
          non-Cabinet attorney for the Congress of the
          U.S. WKAR-AM, March 26, 1974.
          20 min. phonotape (1 r.   7 1/2 i.p.s.)

          1. U.S. - Politics and government - 1969-

U.S. - POLITICS AND GOVERNMENT - 1969-

Voice Lib.
M1692   Jackson, Henry Martin, 1912-
bd.3   Tells the National Press Club his
          optimistic estimate of America's economic
          future. WKAR, May 23, 1974.
          25 min. phonotape (1 r.   7 1/2 i.p.s.)

          Includes question & answer session through
          Clyde Lamont.

          1. U.S. - Politics and government - 1969-
          2. Impeachments. I. Lamont, Clyde.

U.S. - POLITICS AND GOVERNMENT - 1969-

Voice Lib.
M1657   Kennedy, Edward Moore, 1932-
          Discusses visit with Brezhnev, Watergate,
          Chappaquiddick, and 1976 politics.
          Interviewed by Paul Duke. WKAR-TV,
          May 7, 1974.
          30 min. phonotape (1 r.   7 1/2 i.p.s.)

          1. U.S. - Politics and government - 1969-
          2. Watergate Affair, 1972-   I. Duke,
          Paul.

Voice Lib.
M1720
bd.3
U.S. - POLITICS AND GOVERNMENT - 1969-
Kissinger, Henry Alfred, 1923-
Emotionally denying ordering wiretapping of his associates. NBC-TV, June 12, 1974.
1 min., 15 sec. phonotape (1 r. 7 1/2 i.p.s.)

1. U.S. - Politics and government - 1969-

Voice Lib.
M1609
U.S. - POLITICS AND GOVERNMENT - 1969-
Nixon, Richard Milhous, Pres. U.S., 1913-
Address before the Executive Club of Chicago. WKAR-AM, March 15, 1974.
40 min. phonotape (1 r. 7 1/2 i.p.s.)

Includes question & answer session.

1. U.S. - Politics and government - 1969-

Voice Lib.
M1557-
1558,
bd.1
U.S. - POLITICS AND GOVERNMENT - 1969-
Mansfield, Michael Joseph, 1903-
Reply to the State of the Union Address by President Nixon; excerpts. WJIM (CBS), February 1, 1974.
40 min. phonotape (2 r. 7 1/2 in. per sec.)

Includes question and answer period.

1. U.S. - Politics and government - 1969-

Voice Lib.
M1628-
1629,
bd.1
U.S. - POLITICS AND GOVERNMENT - 1969-
Nixon, Richard Milhous, Pres. U.S., 1913-
Address before the National Radio & Television News Directors Association and questions following from the members and from the national press. Summary and analysis by CBS newsmen Roger Mudd and Bruce Morton. CBS, March 19, 1974.
60 min. phonotape (2 r. 7 1/2 i.p.s.)

1. U.S. - Politics and government - 1969-
2. Power resources - U.S. I. Mudd, Roger. II. Morton, Bruce.

Voice Lib.
M1561
U.S. - POLITICS AND GOVERNMENT - 1969-
Muskie, Edmund S 1914-
Firing line, interviewed by William Buckley. WKAR-AM, February 15, 1974.
25 min. phonotape (1 r. 7 1/2 i.p.s.)

1. U.S. - Politics and government - 1969-
I. Buckley, William Frank, 1925-

Voice Lib.
M1634
bd.2
U.S. - POLITICS AND GOVERNMENT - 1969-
Nixon, Richard Milhous, Pres. U.S., 1913-
Speaking at Bad Axe, Michigan, in support of James Sparling, Republican candidate for Congress. MSU Dept. of Journalism, April, 1974.
10 min. phonotape (1 r. 7 1/2 i.p.s.)

1. U.S. - Politics and government - 1969-
2. Sparling, James

Voice Lib.
M1549-
1550,
bd.1
U.S. - POLITICS AND GOVERNMENT - 1969-
Nixon, Richard Milhous, Pres. U.S., 1913-
News conference recorded over CBS television network. CBS, October 26, 1973.
35 min. phonotape (2 r. 7 1/2 i.p.s.)

Includes question and answer session, including Nelson Benton.

1. U.S. - Politics and government - 1969-
2. Watergate Affair, 1972. 3. Power resources - U.S. I. Benton, Nelson

---

Voice Lib.
M1685
bd.2
U.S. - POLITICS AND GOVERNMENT - 1969-
Rodino, Peter Wallace, 1909-
Telling PBS that transcript damages Nixon. Question under investigation is how much? Interview with Paul Duke on Washington straight talk. PBS, May 21, 1974.
30 min. phonotape (1 r. 7 1/2 i.p.s.)

1. U.S. - Politics and government - 1969-
2. Nixon, Richard Milhous, Pres. U.S., 1913-
I. Duke, Paul.

Voice Lib.
M1556
U.S. - POLITICS AND GOVERNMENT - 1969-
Nixon, Richard Milhous, Pres. U.S., 1913-
State of the Union address; excerpts. WKAR-FM, January 30, 1974.
42 min. phonotape (1 r. 7 1/2 in. per sec.)

1. U.S. - Politics and government - 1969-

Voice Lib.
M1661
bd.2
U.S. - POLITICS AND GOVERNMENT - 1969-
Strauss, Robert Schwartz, 1918-
On Nixon tapes and other current political issues; interview by Jim Lehrer, on "Straight Talk". WKAR-TV, May 14, 1974.
20 min. phonotape (1 r. 7 1/2 i.p.s.)

1. U.S. - Politics and government - 1969-
I. Lehrer, Jim.

U.S. - POLITICS AND GOVERNMENT - 1969-

Voice Lib.
M1643   Vander Veen, Richard, 1922-
               Issues & answers presents Richard
           Vander Veen. CBS, April 21, 1974.
               30 min.   phonotape (1 r.   7 1/2 i.p.s.)

               1. U.S. - Politics and government -
           1969-

Voice Lib. U.S. - SOCIAL CONDITIONS
M261- Thomas, Lowell Jackson, 1892-
  262   Lowell Thomas recalls. CBS, 1958.
               2 reels (7 in.)   7 1/2 i.p.s.   phonotape.

               1. U.S. - Social conditions.

U.S. POST OFFICE DEPARTMENT

Voice Lib.
M900   Walker, Frank Comerford, 1886-1959.
  bd.3   Describes post office department's part in
           the sale of bonds and stamps; also their
           part in national defense. CBS, April 30,
           1941.
               1 reel (7 in.)   7 1/2 i.p.s.   phonotape.

               1. U.S. Post Office dept.

Voice Lib. U.S. - SOCIAL CONDITIONS
M1572   Ussery, William J
               National Press Club address, plus some
           questions and answers. WKAR-AM, February 25,
           1974.
               35 min.   phonotape (1 r.   7 1/2 i.p.s.)

               1. U.S. - Social conditions. 2. Labor and
           laboring classes - U.S.

Voice Lib. U.S. - RELATIONS (GENERAL) WITH AFRICA
M1679   Williams, G   Mennen, 1911-
               The United States and Africa. WKAR,
           May 18, 1970.
               45 min.   phonotape (1 r.   7 1/2 i.p.s.)

               1. U.S. - Relations (General) with Africa.
           2. Africa - Relations (General) with the U.S.

U.S. - SOCIAL CONDITIONS

C1
S70
           Whorf, Michael, 1933-
               The frenzied home front.
               1 tape cassette.   (The visual sounds of
           Mike Whorf. Social, S70)
               Originally presented on his radio program, Kaleidoscope,
           WJR, Detroit.
               Duration: 36 min., 50 sec.
               The period of the First World War marked a dramatic transition
           in American life. As we consider the "good old days" to be around
           the turn of the century and the end of the Victorian era, so the war
           served as a bridge to the roaring twenties to follow.

               1. European War, 1914-1918 - U.S. 2. U.S. - Social conditions.
           I. Title.

Voice Lib. U.S. - SOCIAL CONDITIONS
M1687   Abernathy, Ralph David, 1926-
               Address at Michigan State University.
           WKAR, 1972.
               50 min.   phonotape (1 r.   7 1/2 i.p.s.)

               1. Negroes. 2. U.S. - Social conditions.

U.S. - SOCIAL CONDITIONS

C1
S40
           Whorf, Michael, 1933-
               The Gibson girl.
               1 tape cassette.   (The visual sounds of
           Mike Whorf. Social, S40)
               Originally presented on his radio program, Kaleidoscope,
           WJR, Detroit.
               Duration: 29 min., 15 sec.
               A charming look at the lovely, illusive American girl. The
           drawings of Charles Gibson come to life with the romantic music
           of the period, along with an account of the love triangle of the
           century.

               1. Gibson, Charles Dana, 1867-1944. 2. U.S. - Social
           conditions. I. Title.

U.S. - SOCIAL CONDITIONS

Voice Lib.
M1567-   Maddox, Lester Garfield, 1915-
  1568,   Option; television broadcast originating
  bd.1   at the University of Buffalo. WKAR-AM,
           February 19, 1974.
               45 min.   phonotape (2 r.   7 1/2 in. per
           sec.)

               Speech delivered November 1973.

               1. U.S. - Social conditions. 2. U.S. -
           Politics and government.

C1
S45-   U.S. - SOCIAL CONDITIONS
S47   Whorf, Michael, 1933-
               The roaring twenties.
               3 tape cassettes.   (The visual sounds of
           Mike Whorf. Social, S45-S47)
               Originally presented on his radio program, Kaleidoscope,
           WJR, Detroit.
               Duration: 40 min., 30 sec.; 40 min., 30 sec.; 52 min.
               The voices of the famous and infamous relating the times as to
           what transpired and why. Part 2 has the banner stories of the decade.
           The year 1929 brought the depression, but the 20's were doomed to
           die.

               1. U.S. - Social conditions. I. Title.

U.S. - SOCIAL LIFE AND CUSTOMS

C1
820
    Whorf, Michael, 1933–
      The adolescent years.
      1 tape cassette. (The visual sounds of
    Mike Whorf. Social, S20)

      Originally presented on his radio program, Kaleidoscope,
    WJR, Detroit.
      Duration: 43 min.
      With rich harmonies of those wonderful gay-ninety songs, with
    memoires of band concerts, of tree-lined streets of which travelled
    the horseless carriage, comes this delightful musical narrative
    depicting life when the world was young.

      L. U.S. - Social life and customs. L. Title.

U.S. - SOCIAL LIFE AND CUSTOMS

C1
S7
    Whorf, Michael, 1933–
      The good old days.
      1 tape cassette. (The visual sounds of
    Mike Whorf. Social, S7)

      Originally presented on his radio program, Kaleidoscope,
    WJR, Detroit.
      Duration: 45 min., 30 sec.
      Life as it once was, unhurried, pleasant, "countrified" and
    simple. Here is a nostalgic look at ourselves in the "not so
    long ago."

      L. U.S. - Social life and customs. L. Title.

U.S. - SOCIAL LIFE AND CUSTOMS - 20TH CENTURY
Voice Lib.
M878- American mood series (Radio program)
879   Conversation on a party line: John David
bd.1 Hamilton talking to people in North Carolina,
    Connecticut, New York, Texas, Colorado, New
    Mexico, all intellectuals and numerous school
    teachers. "Little Boxes" (the conformity song);
    description of American life and its meaning;
    definition of socialism; discussing Americans'
    international ideas; discussion of Texas
    University students and attitudes; Berkeley
    professor attitudes; discussion on how to make
    money; advocating the study of medicine.
    CBC, 1963.

U.S. - SOCIAL LIFE AND CUSTOMS - 20TH CENTURY
Voice Lib.
M878- American mood series (Radio program)
879   Conversation on a party line... 1963.
bd.1   (Card 2)

      2 reels (7 in.) 7 1/2 in. per sec.
    phonotape.

      1. U.S. - Social life & customs - 20th cent.
    I. Hamilton, John David   II. Project
    '64.

U.S. - SOCIAL POLICY
Voice Lib.
M971- Tugwell, Rexford Guy, 1891–
972,   "Memoirs of the New Deal"; informal talk
bd.1 with Dean Zelman Cowen (University of
    Melbourne) at Center for the Study of
    Democratic Institutions in Santa Barbara,
    California. CSDI, 1962.
    2 reels (7 in.) 7 1/2 i.p.s. phonotape.

      1. U.S. - Social policy. I. Cowen, Zelman.

U.S. SUPREME COURT - HISTORY
Voice Lib.
M1740 Williams, Edward Bennett
bd.1   Discusses the Warren Supreme Court on Firing
    Line with William F. Buckley. WKAR, June 14,
    1974.
      20 min. phonotape (1 r. 7 1/2 i.p.s.)

      1. U. S. Supreme Court - Hist. I.
    Buckley, William Frank, 1925–

U.S. Treasury Dept.
Voice Lib.
541   Cantor, Eddie, 1893-1964. ____
bd.2   Documentary program for U.S. Treasury
    Department. Introduction by Deems Taylor.
    WABC-NY, January 25, 1952.
      1 reel (7 in.) 7 1/2 in. per sec.
    phonotape.

      I. Taylor, Deems. 1885-1966. II. U.S.
    Treasury Dept.

U.S.A.
Voice Lib.
M1467- Dos Passos, John, 1896-1970.
1469   U.S.A.; a 2 1/2 hour dramatization by
    Hollywood TV Theatre, based on the three
    Dos Passos books dealing with the first
    three decades of the 20th century. Host:
    Edward G. Robinson. WMSB-TV, May 30, 1971.
      3 reels (7 in.) 7 1/2 in. per sec.
    phonotape.
      I. Robinson, Edward G   1893-1973.
    II. Title.

University of Essex. Dept. of
VOICE LIBRARY   Sociology
D   Oral history.
16   no.1-
.07   Colchester, University of Essex, Dept. of
    Sociology, 1972–
      no. irreg.

      Journal of the Oral History Society, 1974–

      1. Oral history - Period. I. University of
    Essex. Dept. of Sociology. II. Oral History
    Society.

Unruh, Jesse Marvin, 1922–
Voice Lib.
M1323- Democratic Party. National Convention,
M1328,   Chicago, 1968.
bd.1   Hubert Humphrey, Democratic presidential nom..,
    announcing his selection of Sen. Muskie as his running mate;
    convention floor reports; interview with Mrs. Humphrey. Mayor
    Daley of Chicago defending police action. Interviews with Sen-
    ator McGovern and Jesse Unruh of California. Remote address by
    Sen. Edward Kennedy introducing a memorial motion picture on
    the late Sen. Robert F. Kennedy. Various reports on riots and
    general confusion, reluctance of delegates to come to order.
    Nominations for Vice-President; seconding speeches for Sen.
    Muskie and nominating speech by Wisconsin delegation of Julian
    Bond of Georgia. Interview with Julian Bond, who declined
    nomination of the vice-presidency. Story told by chairman of
    the New Hampshire [delegation] regarding his arrest. Interview
    (Continued on next card)

Voice Lib.
      Unruh, Jesse Marvin, 1922-
M1323- Democratic Party. National Convention,
M1328,   Chicago, 1968... (Card 2)
bd.1 with Paul O'Dwyer of the New York delegation regarding the
      nomination of Richard Daley for Vice-President. General
      confusion. Nomination of Sen. Edmund Muskie as Vice-President
      and resulting confusion with the Oregon delegation. Followed by
      Sen. Muskie's acceptance speech. NBC-TV, August 29, 1968.
      6 reels (7 in.) 7 1/2 in. per sec. phonotape.
      L. Humphrey, Hubert Horatio, 1911- II. Humphrey, Muriel Fay
      (Buck) 1912-   III. Daley, Richard J   1902-   IV. McGovern,
      George Stanley, 1922-   V. Unruh, Jesse Marvin, 1922-   VI.
      Kennedy, Edward Moore, 1932-   VII. Bond, Julian, 1940-   VIII.
      O'Dwyer, Paul, 1907-   IX. Muskie, Edmund S   1914-

Voice Lib. Urey, Harold Clayton, 1893-
353 Russia and the bomb, discussed by various
bd.19 personalities. NBC, September 25, 1949.
      1 reel (7 in.) 7 1/2 in. per sec.
      phonotape.

      Participants: Harrison Brown, Harold Urey,
      Samuel Allison, Thornton Hugness, Brien McMahon,
      Paul Douglas, John Foster Dulles, Leslie Groves,
      Winston Churchill, Dean Acheson, James Fleming.

      I. Brown, Harrison Scott, 1917-   II.
      Urey, Harold Clayton, 1893-   III. Allison,
                        (Continued on next card)

Voice Lib. Urey, Harold Clayton, 1893-
353 Russia and the bomb... 1949. (Card 2)
bd.19

      Samuel King, 1900-   IV. Hugness, Thornton.
      V. McMahon, James O'Brien, 1903-1952. VI.
      Douglas, Paul Howard, 1892-   VII. Dulles,
      John Foster, 1888-1959. VIII. Groves, Leslie
      R   1896-1970. IX. Churchill, Winston
      Leonard Spencer, 1874-1965. X. Acheson, Dean
      Gooderham, 1893-1971. XI. Fleming, James,
      1915-

Voice Lib.
M389 Urey, Harold Clayton, 1893-
bd.4 Development of nuclear weapons; calls for
      development of hydrogen bomb and winning of
      arms race. Hearst Metrotone News, 1963.
      1 reel (7 in.) 7 1/2 in. per sec.
      phonotape.

      1. Atomic weapons

Voice Lib.
M1572 Ussery, William J
      National Press Club address, plus some
      questions and answers. WKAR-AM, February 25,
      1974.
      35 min. phonotape (1 r. 7 1/2 i.p.s.)

      1. U.S. - Social conditions. 2. Labor and
      laboring classes - U.S.

Voice Lib.   Ustinov, Peter Alexander, 1921-
M1037 Biography in sound (radio program)
bd.1 "The Actor", narrated by Morgan Beatty.
      Cast includes Tallulah Bankhead, Hy Gardner,
      Rocky Graziano, Arthur Miller, Uta Hagen,
      Jackie Cooper, Sir Laurence Olivier, Gad
      Gayther, Barbara Ashley, Hortense Powdermaker,
      Peter Ustinov, Alfred Hitchcock, Leonard Lyons,
      John Guston, Helen Hayes, Dick Mayne, Ralph
      Bellamy, Lionel Barrymore, Sir Ralph Richardson,
      José Ferrer, and Walter Kerr. NBC Radio, 1950's.
      1 reel (7 in.) · 7 1/2 in. per sec.
      phonotape.
                        (Continued on next card)

C1   The Valentine's Day ironclad
H103 Whorf, Michael, 1933-
      The Valentine's Day ironclad (Galena,
      Monitor, Merrimac)
      1 tape cassette. (The visual sounds of Mike Whorf.
      History and heritage, H103)
      Originally presented on his radio program, Kaleidoscope.
      WJR, Detroit.
      Duration: 38 min., 10 sec.
      The birth of the ironclads during the Civil War was on the
      tongue of every citizen. Although the Monitor and the Merrimac
      were household words, the ship Galena was nearly unknown. Our
      story tells of the American ironclads, their rise, their fall.
      L Armored vessels. L Title.

      Valeriani, Richard
Voice Lib.
M1479 Nixon, Richard Milhous, Pres. U.S., 1913-
bd.1 President Nixon announces trip to China;
      comment by John Chancellor, Richard Valeriani.
      NBC-TV, July 15, 1971.
      1 reel (7 in.) 7 1/2 in. per sec.
      phonotape.

      I. Chancellor, John William, 1927-
      II. Valeriani, Richard

      Vallee, Rudy, 1901-
Voice Lib.
M1047 Old-time radio excerpts of the 1930's and
      1940's, including: Rudy Vallee singing
      "Linger a little longer"; Will Rogers on
      panaceas for the Depression; Bing Crosby
      singing "Sweet Georgia Brown"; Eddie Cantor;
      Jimmy Durante singing "Inka-dinka-do";
      musical skit by Clayton, Jackson and Durante;
      wit by Harry Hershfield; musical selection
      "Thinking of you" by Kay Kyser; Kate Smith
      singing theme song, "When the moon comes over
      the mountain"; W.C. Fields' temperance
                        (Continued on next card)

Voice Lib. Vallee, Rudy, 1901-
M1047 Old-time radio excerpts of the 1930's and
      1940's... (Card 2)
      lecture; Al Jolson singing "Rocka-by-your
      baby"; and George Burns and Gracie Allen
      skit. TV&R, 1930's and 1940's.
      1 reel (7 in.) 7 1/2 in. per sec.
      L Vallee, Rudy, 1901-   II. Rogers, Will, 1879-1935. III.
      Crosby, Bing, 1901- IV. Cantor, Eddie, 1893-1964. V. Durante,
      Jimmy, 1893-   VI. Clayton, Patti   VII. Jackson,
      Eddie   VIII. Hershfield, Harry, 1885-   IX. Kyser, Kay,
      1906-   X. Smith, Kate, 1909-   XI. Fields, W.C., 1879-
      1946. XII. Jolson, Al, 1886-1950. XIII. Burns, George, 1896-
      XIV. Allen, Gracie, 1906-

Voice Lib.
M1696   Vallee, Rudy, 1901-
bd.1   Reminiscing on the Mike Douglas Show.
           ABC-TV, May 27, 1974.
              10 min.   phonotape (1 r.   7 1/2 i.p.s.)

              1. Vallee, Rudy, 1901-
           I. Douglas, Mike, 1925?-

                  Vallee, Rudy, 1901-
Voice Lib.
134   Dickens, Charles, 1812-1870.
           Christmas Carol, dramatized by an all-star
         cast led by Lionel Barrymore and Rudy Vallee.
         NBC, 1941.
            1 reel (7 in.)   7 1/2 in. per sec.
         phonotape.

            I. Barrymore, Lionel, 1878-1954. II.
         Vallee, Rudy, 1901-   III. Title.

               Vallee, Rudy, 1901-
Voice Lib.
M617   Radio in the 1920's: a series of excerpts
bd.1-   from important broadcasts of the 1920's,
bd.25   with brief prologue and epilogue; a sample
           of radio of the period. NVL, April, 1964.
            1 reel (7 in.)   7 1/2 in. per sec.
         phonotape.
            I. Radio programs. L Marconi, Guglielmo, marchese, 1874-
         1937. IL Kendall, H   G   III. Coolidge, Calvin, Pres. U.S.,
         1872-1933. IV. Wilson, Woodrow, Pres. U.S., 1856-1924. V.
         Roosevelt, Franklin Delano, Pres. U.S., 1882-1945. VI. Lodge,
         Henry Cabot, 1850-1924. VII. LaGuardia, Fiorello Henry, 1882-1947.
         VIII. The Happiness Boys (Radio program) IX. Gallagher and Sheen.
         X. Barney Google. XI. Vallee, Rudy, 1901-   XII. The two
                          (Continued on next card)

Voice Lib.
611   Van and Schenck
bd.10-   Comedy team singing "Ain't You Coming
11   Out, Melinda?" and "Wang Wang Blues".
         Columbia Graphophone Company, 1920, 1922.
            1 reel (7 in.)   7 1/2 in. per sec.
         phonotape.

            I. Title: Ain't you coming out, Melinda?
         II. Title: Wang Wang blues.

               Van Arsdale, Harry, 1905-
Voice Lib.
M658-   Dialogues in depth: the LaGuardia years
659   (TV program from the New York World's Fair).
bd.1   Anecdotes and reminiscences about the late
           New York mayor, Fiorello LaGuardia.
           July 22, 1964.
            2 reels (7 in.)   7 1/2 i.p.s.   phonotape.

            L LaGuardia, Fiorello Henry, 1882-1947. L Canudo,
         Eugene R. IL Berle, Adolph Augustus, 1895-1971.
         III. Van Arsdale, Harry, 1905-   IV. Delany, Hubert T.
         V. Morris, Newbold, 1902-1966.

               VANDALIA, ILL.
Voice Lib.
M1249   Huntley, Chet, 1911-
bd.1   Documentary TV program: "The Talk in
           Vandalia", first capital of state of Illinois,
           prompted by Joseph P. Lyford's book "What's
           Wrong with Vandalia", a small American mid-
           western community. Discussion covers automation
           and unemployment problems, farm problems,
           increasing of intellectual activities.   NBC,
           April 30, 1967.
            1 reel (7 in.) 7 1/2 in. per sec. phonotape.
            L Vandalia, Ill. 2. Lyford, Joseph P   L The
         talk in Vandalia (Television program)

Voice Lib.
280   Vandenberg, Arthur Hendrick, 1884-1951.
bd.1   Address at Cleveland Forum on American
           foreign policy. From private collection
           of Representative Hébert of Louisiana;
           1947.
            1 reel (7 in.)   7 1/2 in. per sec.
         phonotape.

               Van Denny, Raymond
Voice Lib.
M1044   London after dark; on-the-spot recordings of various
           points during the London air-raid attacks: the Savoy Hotel
           kitchen, Trafalgar Square, anti-aircraft battery near London,
           air-raid shelter. With newsmen Edward R. Murrow, Robert
           Bowman, Raymond Van Denny, Larry Lesueur, Eric Sevareid,
           Vincent Sheean, J. B. Priestley, Michael Standing, and
           Winfred Von Thomas. CBS and BBC, August 24, 1940.
            1 reel (7 in.)   7 1/2 in. per sec.   phonotape.

            L Murrow, Edward Roscoe, 1908-1965. IL Bowman, Robert
         III. Van Denny, Raymond   IV. Lesueur, Laurence Edward,
         1909-   V. Sevareid, Arnold Eric, 1912-   VI. Sheean,
         Vincent, 1899-   VII. Priestley, John Boynton, 1894-
         VIII. Standing, Michael   IX. Von Thomas, Winfred

Voice Lib.
M1643   Vander Veen, Richard, 1922-
           Issues & answers presents Richard
           Vander Veen. CBS, April 21, 1974.
              30 min. phonotape (1 r.   7 1/2 i.p.s.)

              1. U.S. - Politics and government -
           1969-

Voice Lib.
599-   Van Doren, Irita, 1891-1966.
600   Book and authors luncheon, Hotel Astor,
bd.1   New York City; introduces Eleanor Ruggles,
           Maurice Herzog, Frederick Lewis Allen.
           WNYC, March 10, 1953.
            2 reels (7 in.)   7 1/2 in. per sec.
         phonotape.

Voice Lib.
597-   Van Doren, Irita, 1891-1966.
598   Book and authors luncheon, Hotel Astor,
        New York City; introduces Russel Lyons,
        Fred Allen, Alben Barkley. WNYC,
        December 2, 1954.
            2 reels (7 in.)   7 1/2 in. per sec.
        phonotape.

Van Heusen, James
Voice Lib.
590-   Cahn, Sammy, 1913-
591   "Today" show salute to Sammy Cahn and
bd.1   Jimmy Van Heusen; tells how "Three Coins in
        the Fountain" came to be written, on winning
        an Oscar on "High Hopes", talks about working
        with Jimmy Van Heusen, talks about favorite
        charity, story behind "Tender Trap", on "It's
        Magic", sale of songs in Hollywood, sings and
        describes "The Second Time Around", recalls
        selling song to Mario Lanza, sings parody on
        "Call Me Irresponsible". NBC, March 20, 1964.
            2 reels (7 in.) 7 1/2 in. per sec. phonotape.
            L Van Heusen, James

Voice Lib.
M311   Vanocur, Sander, 1928-
bd.5   Assassination: Sander Vanocur of NBC
        compares deaths of FDR and JFK. NBC,
        November 23, 1963.
            1 reel (7 in.)   7 1/2 in. per sec.
        phonotape.

            1. Roosevelt, Franklin Delano, Pres. U.S.,
        1882-1945. 2. Kennedy, John Fitzgerald, Pres.
        U.S., 1917-1963 - Assassination.

Voice Lib.
M1220   Vanocur, Sander, 1928-
          Narrating NBC-TV special documentary program:
        "The Pursuit of Pleasure", dealing with such
        topics as narcotics, sex, promiscuity, fads,
        morals of the current era. NBC-TV, May 8,
        1967.
            1 reel (7 in.)   7 1/2 in. per sec.
        phonotape.

            I. Title: The pursuit of pleasure.

Voice Lib.
M1481   Vanocur, Sander, 1928-
bd.3   Interviewed by David Frost on believing
        the government, being misled, journalistic
        responsibility. Comments from Sam Levenson.
        July, 1971.
            1 reel (7 in.)   7 1/2 i.p.s.   phonotape.

            1. Journalistic ethics. I. Frost, David
        Paradine, 1939-   II. Levenson, Samuel,
        1911-

VAUDEVILLE
Voice Lib.
352   Rooney, Pat
bd.4   On the reviving of vaudeville in the
        late 40's. NBC, 1949.
            1 reel (7 in.)   7 1/2 in. per sec.
        phonotape.

VAUDEVILLE
C1
M5   Whorf, Michael, 1933-
          When vaudeville was king.
            1 tape cassette.   (The visual sounds of
        Mike Whorf. Miscellaneous, M5)
            Originally presented on his radio program, Kaleidoscope,
        WJR, Detroit.
            Duration: 40 min.
            The Keith circuit, The Tony Pastor Music Hall, the Palace,
        the curtain would rise of this great age of show business when
        vaudeville was the rage.

            L. Vaudeville. L. Title.

Voice Lib.
M1499   Veldhuis, Zachary, 1870-
bd.1   Oldest living Michigan Agricultural College
        alumnus, aged 102, interviewed by Jim Denison
        at National Voice Library. Topic: campus life
        in the past. MSU Voice Library, May 14, 1972.
            1 reel (7 in.)   7 1/2 i.p.s.   phonotape.

            1. Michigan State University. I. Denison,
        Jim

                The velvet leash
C1
S12   Whorf, Michael, 1933-
          The velvet leash.
            1 tape cassette.   (The visual sounds of
        Mike Whorf. Social, S12)
            Originally presented on his radio program, Kaleidoscope,
        WJR, Detroit.
            Duration: 49 min., 15 sec.
            This segment deals with the Indian and his involvement with
        the Bureau of Indian Affairs. What is the B.I.A. and what
        influence does it have on the Indian? What and where were the
        forces for good and evil and how has the Indian fared?

            1. Indians of North America - Government relations.
        2. United States. Bureau of Indian Affairs. L. Title.

                Vernon, Jackie
Voice Lib.
M1263   Armstrong, Louis, 1900-1971.
          Kraft Music Hall with Herb Alpert and
        Tijuana Brass, with guest stars Jackie
        Vernon and Robin Wilson. NBC-TV,
        August 13, 1967.
            1 reel (7 in.)   7 1/2 in. per sec.
        phonotape.

            I. Alpert, Herb, 1935(?)-   II. Vernon,
        Jackie   III. Wilson, Robin

C1
A28

Verses from the heart - Henry W. Longfellow

Whorf, Michael, 1933-
Verses from the heart - Henry W. Longfellow.
1 tape cassette. (The visual sounds of
Mike Whorf. Art, music and letters, A28)
Originally presented on his radio program, Kaleidoscope,
WJR, Detroit.
Duration: 37 min., 30 sec.
He was the dean of poets and held in high esteem by his fellow
writers; he was nature's poet in the 19th century and a man who
blended words and beauty in an extraordinarily skillful manner.

I. Longfellow, Henry Wadsworth, 1807-1882. I. Title.

C1
PWM8

Victor Herbert

Whorf, Michael, 1933-
Victor Herbert.
1 tape cassette. (The visual sounds of
Mike Whorf. Panorama; a world of music, PWM-8)

Originally presented on his radio program, Kaleidoscope,
WJR, Detroit.
Duration: 25 min.
The life and times of Victor Herbert, including excerpts
of his music.

I. Herbert, Victor, 1859-1924. I. Title.

Voice Lib.
M1095
bd.2

Vesta Victoria; old time British song medley.
British Col., 1906.
1 reel (7 in.) 7 1/2 in. per sec.
phonotape.

CONTENTS.- a. Waiting at the church. b.
He calls me his own Gracie darling. c. It's
all right in the summertime. d. Now I have to
call him "father". e. Poor John. f. Daddy
wouldn't buy me a bow-wow.

I. Music, Popular (Songs, etc.) - Great Britain.

VIETNAMESE CONFLICT, 1961-
Voice Lib.
M1731

Clark, Ramsey, 1927-
Debate on amnesty for draft evaders on
"Firing Line" with William Buckley. WKAR,
June 21, 1974.
45 min. (1 r. 7 1/2 i.p.s.)

1. Military service, compulsory - U. S.
2. Vietnamese conflict, 1961- I. Buckley,
William Frank, 19

Voice Lib.
M1744
bd.1

Vestal, M S
Discussing his book Jerry Ford, up close,
on the Today Show with Bill Monroe, Barbara
Walters, and Jess Marlowe. NBC-TV, June 25,
1974.
10 min. phonotape (1 r. 7 1/2 i.p.s.)

1. Ford, Gerald R., 1913- 2. Vestal,
M.S./Jerry Ford, up close. I. Monroe, Bill.
II. Walters, Bar( ) 1931- III. Marlowe,
Jess.

VIETNAMESE CONFLICT, 1961-
Voice Lib.
M1286
bd.1

Eisenhower, Dwight David, Pres. U.S., 1890-1969.
Conversation by Harry Reasoner with General
Dwight D. Eisenhower and General Omar N.
Bradley at Eisenhower's office in Gettysburg,
Pennsylvania, about the U.S. military partici-
pation in Vietnam and the conduct of it.
CBS-TV, November 28, 1967.
1 reel (7 in.) 7 1/2 in. per sec.
phonotape.

I. Reasoner, Harry, 1923- II. Bradley,
Omar Nelson, 1893-

VESTAL, M. S.
JERRY FORD, UP CLOSE

Voice Lib.
M1744
bd.1

Vestal, M S
Discussing his book Jerry Ford, up close,
on the Today Show with Bill Monroe, Barbara
Walters, and Jess Marlowe. NBC-TV, June 25,
1974.
10 min. phonotape (1 r. 7 1/2 i.p.s.)

1. Ford, Gerald R., 1913- 2. Vestal,
M.S./Jerry Ford, up close. I. Monroe, Bill.
II. Walters, Bar( ), 1931- III. Marlowe,
Jess.

VIETNAMESE CONFLICT, 1961-
PERSONAL NARRATIVES, AMERICAN
Voice Lib.
M825

Campo, Jo Lynne, 1942-
Informal remarks pertaining to this MSU
graduate student's two-month assignment in
South Vietnam; delivered before Kiwanis
Club, Mason, Michigan. NVL location recording, October 5, 1965.
1 reel (7 in.) 7 1/2 in. per sec.
phonotape.

Voice Lib.
M844

Vey, Marvyn
LaMour, Dorothy
Radio dramatization entitled: "The Face
of an Angel", with comments by the new star,
Marvyn Vey, and Miss Dorothy LaMour.
November 9, 1947.
1 reel (7 in.) 7 1/2 in. per sec.
phonotape.

I. Vey, Marvyn. II. Title: The face of an
angel.

VIETNAMESE CONFLICT, 1961- - U.S.
Voice Lib.
M1703

Chomsky, Noam
Address at Michigan State University.
WKAR, May 9, 1972.
50 min. phonotape (1 r. 7 1/2 i.p.s.)

1. Vietnamese Conflict, 1961- - U.S.

VIETNAMESE CONFLICT, 1961-   - U.S.
Voice Lib.
M913- Collingwood, Charles Cummings, 1917-
914   "Where we stand in Vietnam"; CBS Reports pro-
bd.1   gram. Various CBS news correspondents discussing
         current situation of the war in Vietnam,
         including Peter Kalisher, Eric Sevareid, Marvin
         Kalb, Roger Mudd, Harry Reisner, and British
         correspondent James Cameron. CBS-TV,
         December 14, 1964.
            2 reels (7 in1)   7 1/2 in. per sec.
         phonotape.
            1. Vietnamese Conflict, 1961-   - U.S.
         I. Title.

VIETNAMESE CONFLICT, 1961-   - U.S.
Voice Lib.
M1478 The Pentagon Papers; discussion of content,
       meaning. Bernard Kalb, CBS; Senator J.W.
       Fulbright; Senator John Tower; Arthur
       Schlesinger; Walt Rostow; Max Frankel,
       New York Times; Crosby Noyes, Washington
       Evening Star. CBS-TV, July 13, 1971.
          1 reel (7 in.)   7 1/2 in. per sec.
       phonotape.
          I. Kalb, Bernard   II. Fulbright, James William, 1905-
       III. Tower, John Goodwin, 1925-   IV. Schlesinger, Arthur
       Meier, 1888-   V. Rostow, Walt Whitman, 1916-   VI.
       Frankel, Max   VII. Noyes, Crosby

VIETNAMESE CONFLICT, 1961-   - U.S.
Voice Lib.
M1399- A day in October; NBC-TV documentary about
1400   "Moratorium Day" throughout the United
         States in protest to our continued partici-
         pation in the war in Vietnam. Description
         of origin and growth of the moratorium and
         comments by various personalities. Statement
         by President Nixon, "Not affected." NBC-TV,
         October 15, 1969.
            2 reels (7 in.)   7 1/2 in. per sec.
         phonotape.

VIETNAMESE CONFLICT, 1961-   - U.S.
Voice Lib.
M1406 Nixon, Richard Milhous, Pres. U.S., 1913-
       President Nixon's address to nation on
       current U.S. position on the war in Vietnam.
       November 3, 1969.
          1 reel (7 in.)   7 1/2 in. per sec.
       phonotape.

VIETNAMESE CONFLICT, 1961-   - U.S.
Voice Lib.
M1612- Ellsberg, Daniel, 1931-
1614   Address at Michigan State University.
         MSU Voice Library, February 28, 1974.
         90 min.   (3 r.   7 1/2 i.p.s.)

            1.Vietnamese Conflict, 1961-   - U.S.

VIETNAMESE CONFLICT, 1961-   - U.S.
Voice Lib.
M1410 Nixon, Richard Milhous, Pres. U.S., 1913-
bd.3   Nixon's report to the nation on further
         withdrawal of troops from Vietnam. CBS-TV,
         December 15, 1969.
            1 reel (7 in.)   7 1/2 in. per sec.
         phonotape.

VIETNAMESE CONFLICT, 1961-   - U.S.
Voice Lib.
M1724 Morris, Clyde D   J
bd.1   Next steps to control the military; part
         of the MSU Moratorium against the War -
         introduces a slogan and a song, sung by
         Ruth Knapp, Doug Solomon, and Phyllis Hart.
         WKAR, October 15, 1969.
            15 min.   phonotape (1 r.   7 1/2 i.p.s.)
            1. Vietnamese Conflict, 1961-   - U.S.
         I. Knapp, Ruth. II. Solomon, Douglas S.
         III. Hart, Phyllis

VIETNAMESE CONFLICT, 1961-   - U.S.
Voice Lib.
M1460 Nixon, Richard Milhous, Pres. U.S., 1913-
bd.1   Message to the nation on new peace initiative
         in Vietnam. 1970.
            1 reel (7 in.)   7 1/2 in. per.sec.
         phonotape.

VIETNAMESE CONFLICT, 1961-   - U.S.
Voice Lib.
M1717 Morse, Wayne Lyman, 1900-
         Address at Michigan State University;
         segments. WKAR, January 21, 1970.
         50 min.   phonotape (1 r.   7 1/2 i.p.s.)

            1. Vietnamese Conflict, 1961-
         U.S.

VIETNAMESE CONFLICT, 1961-   - U.S.
Voice Lib.
M1419 Nixon, Richard Milhous, Pres. U.S., 1913-
         TV address to nation regarding troop
         withdrawals from Vietnam. CBS-TV, April 20,
         1970.
            1 reel (7 in.)   7 1/2 in. per sec.
         phonotape.

VIETNAMESE CONFLICT, 1961-   - U.S.
Voice Lib.
M1420   Nixon, Richard Milhous, Pres. U.S., 1913-
         Press conference held at White House
         regarding present status of war in Vietnam
         and regarding Cambodia.   CBS-TV, May 8,
         1970.
           1 reel (7 in.)   7 1/2 in. per sec.
         phonotape.

VIETNAMESE CONFLICT, 1961-   - U.S.
Voice Lib.
M1680   Smith, Howard Kingsbury, 1914-
         Speaking at MSU Mass Communications
         Colloquium.   WKAR, April 7, 1967.
           50 min.   phonotape (1 r.   7 1/2 i.p.s.)

           1. Vietnamese Conflict, 1961-   - U.S.
         2. U.S. - Politics and government - 1963-
         1969.

VIETNAMESE CONFLICT, 1961-   - U.S.
Voice Lib.
M1436   Nixon, Richard Milhous, Pres. U.S., 1913-
bd.1   On Vietnam troop withdrawals.   NBC-TV.
         April 7, 1971.
           1 reel (7 in.)   7 1/2 in. per sec.
         phonotape.

VIETNAMESE CONFLICT, 1961-   - U.S.
Voice Lib.
M942   Vietnam perspective (Television program)
         CBS Special Report on Senate Foreign
         Relations Committee hearings and the war
         in Vietnam.   CBS, February 18, 1966.
           1 reel (7 in.)   7 1/2 in. per sec.
         phonotape.

           1. Vietnamese conflict, 1961-   - U.S.
         I. Mudd, Roger   II. Sevareid, Arnold Eric,
         1912-   III. Reasoner, Harry, 1923-   IV.
         Kalb, Marvin L

VIETNAMESE CONFLICT, 1961-   - U.S.
Voice Lib.
M1500   Nixon, Richard Milhous, Pres. U.S., 1913-
         Special TV broadcast to the nation regarding
         start of blockade of shipping to North
         Vietnam and mining of Haiphong harbor;
         also extended bombing of North Vietnam.
         Followed by commentary of NBC and CBS
         correspondents.   NBC, May 8, 1972.
           1 reel (7 in.)   7 1/2 in. per sec.
         phonotape.

VIETNAMESE CONFLICT, 1961-   - U.S.
Voice Lib.
M1202   Westmoreland, William Childs, 1914-
bd.1   Report to joint session of U.S. Congress
         on status of war in Vietnam. Commentary by
         Robert Goralski.   NBC-TV, April 28, 1967.
           1 reel (7 in.)   7 1/2 in. per sec.
         phonotape.

           I. Goralski, Robert

VIETNAMESE CONFLICT, 1961-   - U.S.
Voice Lib.
M1475-   Rusk, Dean, 1909-
1476,   Dean Rusk, former Secretary of State,
bd.1   discusses the Pentagon Papers with Edwin
         Newman and Barbara Walters. NBC, July 2,
         1971.
           2 reels (7 in.)   7 1/2 i.p.s.   phonotape.

           1. Pentagon papers. 2. Vietnamese
         Conflict, 1961-   - U.S. I. Newman,
         Edwin Harold, 1919-   II. Walters,
         Barbara, 1931-

Voice Lib.
M942   Vietnam perspective (Television program)
         CBS Special Report on Senate Foreign
         Relations Committee hearings and the war
         in Vietnam.   CBS, February 18, 1966.
           1 reel (7 in.)   7 1/2 in. per sec.
         phonotape.

           1. Vietnamese conflict, 1961-   - U.S.
         I. Mudd, Roger   II. Sevareid, Arnold Eric,
         1912-   III. Reasoner, Harry, 1923-   IV.
         Kalb, Marvin L

VIETNAMESE CONFLICT, 1961-   - U.S.
Voice Lib.
M1546-   Rusk, Dean, 1909-
1547,   Interview on William F. Buckley's Firing
bd.1   Line show.   WKAR-FM, February 5, 1974.
           40 min.   phonotape (2 r.   7 1/2 i.p.s.)

           1. Vietnamese Conflict, 1961-   - U.S.
         I. Buckley, William Frank, 1925-

C1   The viking - Leif Ericson
H112   Whorf, Michael, 1933-
           The viking - Leif Ericson.
           1 tape cassette.   (The visual sounds of
         Mike Whorf. History and heritage, H112)
             Originally presented on his radio program, Kaleidoscope,
         WJR, Detroit.
             Duration: 37 min.
             He has been called Leif the Lucky. He was probably the first
         white man to set foot on North America. This program presents
         the story of Leif Ericson; his birth, his infamous father, Eric the
         Red, and his life as an early sea-voyager.

           I. Leifr Eiriksson, hinn Heppni, d. ca. 1021.   I. Title.

C1
H28   VIKINGS
    Whorf, Michael, 1933-
        The men before Columbus.
        1 tape cassette.   (The visual sounds of
    Mike Whorf. History and heritage, H28)
        Originally presented on his radio program, Kaleidoscope,
    WJR, Detroit.
        Duration: 40 min., 15 sec.
        1000 years before Columbus' exploration of San Salvador came
    the Vikings whose culture and life style made little impression on the
    world, but their knowledge of sailing and their spirit of adventure
    would inspire others to undertake the role of discoverer.
        1. Vikings. 2. America - Discovery and exploration - Norse.
    L. Title.

Voice Lib.
353   Villiard, Irving
bd.13   Outbreak of Korean War; Middle West
        supports Truman.   NBC, July, 1950.
        1 reel (7 in.)   7 1/2 in. per sec.
        phonotape.

        Original disc off-speed.

        1. Korean War, 1950-1953

Voice Lib.
M345   Vinall, James
bd.6   Interviews unemployed in Detroit during
        Eisenhower recession.   CBS, March 18,
        1958.
        1 reel (7 in.)   7 1/2 i.p.s.   phonotape.

Voice Lib.
298   Vincent, G   Robert
bd.3   Discussion of the National Voice Library
        on NBC's "Today" show, November 4, 1963.
        Air-check recorded in Michigan, November 4,
        1963.
        1 reel (7 in.)   7 1/2 in. per sec.
        phonotape.

Voice Lib. Vincent, G   Robert
M1048 Gilbert, L   Wolfe
bd.2   Interview with G. Robert Vincent at his
        office regarding Wolfe Gilbert's song
        "Waiting for the Robert E. Lee"; also,
        rendition of this song.   1952.
        1 reel (7 in.)   7 1/2 in. per sec.
        phonotape.

        I. Vincent, G   Robert   II. Title:
    Waiting for the Robert E. Lee.

Vincent, G. Robert
Voice Lib.
M640   Hanna, Mark
bd.5   Telephone conversation with G. Robert
        Vincent, changing date of appearance of
        Admiral Byrd on Fred Allen Show. GRV,
        October 10, 1941.
        1 reel (7 in.)   7 1/2 i.p.s.   phonotape.

        I. Vincent, G. Robert.

Vincent, G   Robert
Voice Lib.
M1098 Ripley, Robert LeRoy, 1893-1949.
bd.2   Rehearsal and discussion regarding text
        of introductory remarks to the recording
        of "The Bugler of Balaclava" with G.R. Vincent,
        followed by 1890-recording of trumpeter
        Kenneth Landfrey.   NVL location recording,
        August 7, 1939.
        1 reel (7 in.)   7 1/2 in. per sec.
        phonotape.
            I. Vincent, G   Robert. II. Landfrey, Kenneth.
        III. Title: The bugler of Balaclava.

C1   Vision of America
H111   Whorf, Michael, 1933-
        Vision of America.
        1 tape cassette.   (The visual sounds of
    Mike Whorf. History and heritage, H111)
        Originally presented on his radio program, Kaleidoscope,
    WJR, Detroit.
        Duration: 37 min.
        In this narration we are presented with cameo portraits of
    Presidents of the United States. In their speeches, philosophies
    and maxims, these past leaders bring us a stirring vision of
    America.
        L. Presidents - U.S. L. Title.

Voice Lib.
267-   Vivian, C   T
268   On segregation and freedom; Provost Lecture
        no. 5, Michigan State University.   National
        Voice Library, spring, 1963.
        2 reels (7 in.)   7 1/2 in. per sec.
        phonotape.

        1. Civil rights

Voice Lib.
M1033 Voice of America.
        Twentieth anniversary program of Voice of
    America broadcasts narrated by Henry Fonda,
    and including the voices of Carl Sandburg,
    Danny Kaye, Jawaharlal Nehru, Franklin D.
    Roosevelt, Charles Malik, Arnold Toynbee,
    William Faulkner, Harry S. Truman, Dwight D.
    Eisenhower, Helen Hayes, Dag Hammarskjöld,
    Winston Churchill, and John F. Kennedy.
    Voice of America, 1963.
        1 reel (7 in.)   7 1/2 in. per sec.
        phonotape.
                        (Continued on next card)

Voice Lib.
M1033   Voice of America. Twentieth anniversary
          program... 1963. (Card 2)

L. Fonda, Henry Jaynes, 1905-   II. Sandburg, Carl,
1878-1967. III. Kaye, Danny, 1913-   IV. Nehru, Jawaharlal,
1889-1964. V. Roosevelt, Franklin Delano, Pres. U.S., 1882-
1945. VI. Malik, Charles Habib, 1906-   VII. Toynbee,
Arnold Joseph, 1889-   VIII. Faulkner, William, 1897-1962.
IX. Truman, Harry S, Pres. U.S., 1884-1972. X. Eisenhower,
Dwight David, Pres. U.S., 1890-1969. XI. Hayes, Helen,
1900-   XII. Hammarskjöld, Dag, 1905-1961. XIII. Churchill,
Winston Leonard Spencer, 1874-1965. XIV. Kennedy, John
Fitzgerald, Pres. U.S., 1917-1963.

Voice Lib.
M302   Voice of America (Radio program)
bd.2   Jimmy Durante: Voice of America reviews
          Durante's career with the comedian; Durante's
          life and times in show business, future trends
          in American entertainment. Voice of America,
          November 8, 1961.
            1 reel (7 in.)   7 1/2 in. per sec.
          phonotape.

            1. Durante, Jimmy, 1893-   I. Durante,
          Jimmy, 1893-

Voice Lib.
353   Voice of America (radio program)
bd.15   Outbreak of Korean War; description of
          outbreak. NBC, July, 1950.
            1 reel (7 in.)   7 1/2 in. per sec.
          phonotape.

            In Russian.
            Original disc off-speed.

            1. Korean War, 1950-1953

C1   The voice of the patriot
H5   Whorf, Michael, 1933-
          The voice of the patriot.
            1 tape cassette. (The visual sounds of
          Mike Whorf. History and heritage, H5)
            Originally presented on his radio program, Kaleidoscope,
          WJR, Detroit.
            Duration: 46 min., 30 sec.
            Here are poems of devotion and love expressed by those who
          lived through perilous and difficult times, and these words are
          the living testimony of a nation's struggle.

            L. Patriotic poetry. L. Title.

          Voices from the inaudible
Voice Lib.
M746   Reik, Theodor
bd.1   Reading from his book "Voices from the
          Inaudible" and giving reminiscences of his
          association with Dr. Sigmund Freud.
          Introduced by Marie Coleman Nelson, managing
          editor of the "Psychoanalytical Review."
          Psychoanalytical Review, 1964.
            1 reel (7 in.)   7 1/2 in. per sec.
          phonotape.
            L. Freud, Sigmund, 1856-1939. L. Nelson, Marie Coleman,
          1915-   II. Title: Voices from the inaudible.

          VOLTAIRE, FRANÇOIS MARIE AROUET DE, 1694-
Voice Lib.   1778
M1464   Beyerlein, Alfred
bd.3   Narrating Victor Hugo's speech on
          Voltaire in German translation. Peteler,
          1932.
            1 reel (7 in.)   7 1/2 i.p.s.   phonotape.

            1. Voltaire, François Marie Arouet de,
          1694-1778.   I. Hugo, Victor Marie, comte,
          1802-1885.

          VOLTAIRE, FRANÇOIS MARIE AROUET DE,
C1   1694-1778
S51   Whorf, Michael, 1933-
          The enigma of genius - Voltaire.
            1 tape cassette.   (The visual sounds of
          Mike Whorf. Social, S51)
            Originally presented on his radio program, Kaleidoscope,
          WJR, Detroit.
            Duration: 37 min.
            Voltaire was considered a genius, possessing one of the
          finest minds of his day and consorting with his peers and contem-
          poraries. His life was complex to the point of being enigmatic,
          and we'll give you the right to disagree with our findings.
            L. Voltaire, François Marie Arouet de, 1694-1778.
          L. Title.

Von Bülow, Bernhard Heinrich Martin Karl,
    fürst, 1849-1929.
  see
Bülow, Bernhard Heinrich Martin Karl, Fürst
    von, 1849-1929.

VOICE LIBRARY

---

von Faulhaber, cardinal, 1869-1952.
  see
Faulhaber, Michael von, cardinal, 1869-1952.

VOICE LIBRARY

Von Hindenburg, Paul
  see
Hindenburg, Paul von, pres. Germany,
    1847-1934.

VOICE LIBRARY

Von Hötzendorf, Franz Conrad.
see
Conrad von Hötzendorf, Franz, graf, 1852-1925.

VOICE LIBRARY

Von Seyss-Inquart, Artur, 1892-1946
see
Seyss-Inquart, Artur von, 1892-1946

Von Lichberg, Heinz
see
Lichberg, Heinz von

Von Thomas, Winfred

Voice Lib.
M1044   London after dark; on-the-spot recordings of various
points during the London air-raid attacks: the Savoy Hotel
kitchen, Trafalgar Square, anti-aircraft battery near London,
air-raid shelter. With newsmen Edward R. Murrow, Robert
Bowman, Raymond Van Denny, Larry Lesueur, Eric Sevareid,
Vincent Sheean, J. B. Priestley, Michael Standing, and
Winfred Von Thomas. CBS and BBC, August 24, 1940.
1 reel (7 in.)   7 1/2 in. per sec.   phonotape.

L. Murrow, Edward Roscoe, 1908-1965. IL. Bowman, Robert
III. Van Denny, Raymond   IV. Lesueur, Laurence Edward,
1909-   V. Sevareid, Arnold Eric, 1912-   VI. Sheean,
Vincent, 1899-   VII. Priestley, John Boynton, 1894-
VIII. Standing, Michael   IX. Von Thomas, Winfred

Von Papen, Franz, 1879-1969.
see
Papen, Franz von, 1879-1969.

VOICE LIBRARY

Von Tirpitz, Alfred Peter Friedrich.
see
Tirpitz, Alfred Peter Friedrich von, 1849-1930.

VOICE LIBRARY

Von Ribbentrop, Joachim, 1893-1946.
see
Ribbentrop, Joachim von, 1893-1946.

Von Zeppelin, Ferdinand Adolf August
Heinrich
see
Zeppelin, Ferdinand Adolf August Heinrich,
graf von, 1838-1917.

VOICE LIBRARY

Von Schirach, Baldur, 1907-
see
Schirach, Baldur von, 1907-

VOICE LIBRARY

Voice Lib.
M1206   Vorposten an der italienischen Grenze;
bd.3   German descriptive war scene of life in
trenches and in the field.   Victor, 1916.
1 reel (7 in.)   7 1/2 in. per sec.
phonotape.

Vorwärts
Voice Lib.
M1004   Hitler youth fight song, entitled "Vorwärts".
bd.2   Peteler, 1935.
     1 reel (7 in.)   7 1/2 in. per sec.
     phonotape.

     1. Songs, German.   I. Title: Vorwärts.

C1   WJR (RADIO STATION) DETROIT
M9
     Whorf, Michael, 1933-
       We don't make much money--but.
       1 tape cassette.   (The visual sounds of
     Mike Whorf. Miscellaneous, M9)

       Originally presented on his radio program, Kaleidoscope,
     WJR, Detroit.
       Duration: 36 min.
       A hilarious account of the indiscretions and faux pas of radio
     station WJR's personalities.

       L. WJR (Radio station) Detroit.   L. Title.

Voss, John
Voice Lib.
M1739   Smith, Dianna
bd.4   Interviews with John Voss and Derwood Boyd,
     county commissioners, who proposed cutting
     their salaries.   WKAR, June 14, 1974.
     5 min. phonotape (1 r.   7 1/2 i.p.s.)

     1. County government. 2. County officials
     and employees - Salaries, allowance, etc.
     I. Voss, John. II. Boyd, Derwood.

C1   WJR - our time
M28
     Whorf, Michael, 1933-
       WJR - our time; 50 eventful years in
     broadcasting.
       1 tape cassette.   (The visual sounds of
     Mike Whorf. Miscellaneous, M28)

       Originally presented on his radb program, Kaleidoscope,
     WJR, Detroit.
       Duration: 57 min., 45 sec.
       A nostalgic look at the development of radio through the
     history of Radio Station WJR.

       L. WJR (Radio station) Detroit.   L. Title.

Vyshinskiĭ, Andreĭ Ianuar'evich, 1883-1954
Voice Lib.
573   I can hear it now (radio program)
bd.2-   1945-1949.   CBS, 1950?
574   2 reels (7 in.)   7 1/2 in. per sec.
bd.1   phonotape.
     L. Murrow, Edward Roscoe, 1908-1965. IL. Nehru, Jawaharlal,
     1889-1964. III. Philip, duke of Edinburgh, 1921- IV. Elizabeth II,
     Queen of Great Britain, 1926- V. Ferguson, Homer, 1889- VL
     Hughes, Howard Robard, 1905- VII. Marshall, George Catlett,
     1880- VIII. Ruth, George Herman, 1895-1948. IX. Lilienthal,
     David Eli, 1899- X. Trout, Robert, 1908- XL. Gage, Arthur.
     XII. Jackson, Robert Houghwout, 1892-1954. XIII. Gromyko, Ana-
     toilii Andreevich, 1908- XIV. Baruch, Bernard Mannes, 1870-
     1965. XV. Churchill, Win- Leonard Spencer, 1874-1965. XVL
     Winchell, Walter, 1897-19   XVII. Davis, Elmer Holmes, 1890-
          (Continued on next card)

Voice Lib.   Wade, Al
M630   Ober, Norman
bd.2   Interviews Roy Fitzsimons and Dr. Wade
     upon their return from the Second Antarctic
     Expedition, sponsored by Admiral Richard E.
     Byrd.   GRV, 1941.
     1 reel (7 in.)   7 1/2 i.p.s.   phonotape.

     1. Byrd Antarctic Expedition, 2d,
     1933-1935.   I. Wade, Al. II. Fitzsimons,
     Roy.

Voice Lib.
M741   WJR (radio station) Detroit.
bd.1   Memorial program for the late Brace
     Beemer, including former members of Lone
     Ranger radio cast and Mr. Beemer himself
     in reminiscences.   WJR, March 4, 1965.
     37 min.   phonotape (1 r.   7 1/2 i.p.s.)

     1. Beemer, Brace, 1903-1965.   I. Beemer,
     Brace, 1903-1965.

Voice Lib.
M315   Wade, Henry M
bd.5   Report of District Attorney Henry Wade
     of Dallas County; Wade's statement at news
     conference on Oswald case.   NBC, November
     24, 1963.
     1 reel (7 in.)   7 1/2 in. per sec.
     phonotape.

     1. Kennedy, John Fitzgerald, Pres. U.S.,
     1917-1963 - Assassination. 2. Oswald, Lee
     Harvey, 1939-1963.

C1   WJR (RADIO STATION) DETROIT
M28
     Whorf, Michael, 1933-
       WJR - our time; 50 eventful years in
     broadcasting.
       1 tape cassette.   (The visual sounds of
     Mike Whorf. Miscellaneous, M28)

       Originally presented on his radb program, Kaleidoscope,
     WJR, Detroit.
       Duration: 57 min., 45 sec.
       A nostalgic look at the development of radio through the
     history of Radio Station WJR.

       L. WJR (Radio station) Detroit.   L. Title.

Voice Lib.
M1357   Wagner, Adolf
bd.7-   Speaking to the old comrades of the Nazi
1358   Party and Stormtroopers from the Munich
bd.1   Beer Cellar. Concluded by instrumental
     version of "Deutschland erwache".   Peteler,
     November 8, 1944.
     2 reels (7 in.)   7 1/2 in. per sec.
     phonotape.

Wagner, Linda Wershimer
Voice Lib.
M1652   Wakoski, Diane, 1937-
         In a rap session with MSU students and
         Prof. Linda Wagner; excerpts. Private
         taping, February, 1974.
         50 min.   phonotape (1 r.   7 1/2 i.p.s.)

         I. Wagner, Linda Wershimer.

Voice Lib.
M1652   Wakoski, Diane, 1937-
         In a rap session with MSU students and
         Prof. Linda Wagner; excerpts. Private
         taping, February, 1974.
         50 min.   phonotape (1 r.   7 1/2 i.p.s.)

         I. Wagner, Linda Wershimer.

Voice Lib.
M751   Wagner, Robert Ferdinand, 1877-1953.
bd.1   Address at testimonial dinner in his honor
         at Lotos Club. Reminiscences. WNYC,
         December 26, 1954.
         1 reel (7 in.)   7 1/2 in. per sec.
         phonotape.

Voice Lib.
M1686   Wald, George
         Address at Michigan State University.
         WKAR, March 4, 1970.
         50 min.   phonotape (1 r.   7 1/2 i.p.s.)

         1. Science - Addresses, essays, lectures.
         2. Abortion.

Voice Lib.
M523   Wainwright, Jonathan Mayhew, 1883-1953.
bd.1   World War II; surrender of U.S. and
         Philippine troops to Japanese. Manila,
         KZRX, 1942.
         1 reel (7 in.)   7 1/2 in. per sec.
         phonotape.

         1. World War, 1939-1945 - Campaigns -
         Philippine Islands.

Waldron, Beatrice
Voice Lib.
M272   Biography in sound (radio program)
bd.1   Heywood Broun. NBC, date?
         1 reel (7 in.)   7 1/2 in. per sec.
         phonotape.

         I. Broun, Heywood Campbell, 1888-1939. I. Broun,
         Heywood Campbell, 1888-1939. II. Swope, Herbert Bayard,
         1882-1958. III. Wilson, Mattie   IV. Jackson, Gardner
         V. Meany, Thomas   VI. Waldron, Beatrice   VII.
         Gordon, Max   VIII. Madison, Connie   IX. Gannett,
         Lewis Stiles, 1891-1966. X. Collins, Joseph, 1866-1950. XI.
         Brown, Earl Louis, 1900-   XII. Levy, Newman, 1888-
         XIII. Growth, John   XIV. Bye, George   XV.
         Roosevelt, Franklin Delano, Pres. U.S., 1882-1945. XVI.
         Reynolds, Quentin James   2-1965.

Wainwright, Jonathan Mayhew, 1883-1953
Voice Lib.
M621   Radio in the 1940's (Part II): a series of
bd.1-   excerpts from important broadcasts of the
12   1940's; a sample of radio of the period.
         NVL, April, 1964.
         1 reel (7 in.)   7 1/2 in. per sec. phonotape.
         I. Daly, John Charles, 1914-   II. Hall, Josef Washington,
         1894-   III. Shirer, William Lawrence, 1904-   IV. Roosevelt,
         Eleanor (Roosevelt) 1884-1962. V. Roosevelt, Franklin Delano,
         Pres. U.S., 1882-1945. VI. Churchill, Winston Leonard Spencer,
         1874-1965. VII. Wainwright, Jonathan Mayhew, 1883-1953. VIII.
         Cantor, Eddie, 1893-1964. IX. Sinatra, Francis Albert, 1917-
         X. Hope, Bob, 1903-   XI. Crosby, Bing, 1901-   XII. Shore,
         Dinah, 1917(?)-   XIII. Bergen, Edgar, 1903-   XIV. Armstrong,
         Louis, 1900-1971. XV. Eldridge, Roy, 1911-

Waldrop, Oliver
Voice Lib.
379   Sitwell, Edith, 1887-1964.
bd.1   Talks to Oliver Waldrop and Neil Schumaker
         on becoming a poet, creation of poetry,
         technique for reading poetry. WQED (NET),
         1959.
         1 reel (7 in.)   7 1/2 in. per sec.
         phonotape.

         I. Waldrop, Oliver   II. Schumaker,
         Neil

Waiting for the Robert E. Lee
Voice Lib.
M1048   Gilbert, L   Wolfe
bd.2   Interview with G. Robert Vincent at his
         office regarding Wolfe Gilbert's song
         "Waiting for the Robert E. Lee"; also,
         rendition of this song. 1952.
         1 reel (7 in.)   7 1/2 in. per sec.
         phonotape.

         I. Vincent, G   Robert   II. Title:
         Waiting for the Robert E. Lee.

Walker, Danton
Voice Lib.
M275-   Biography in sound (radio program)
276   Alexander Woollcott. N.B.C., date?
bd.1   2 reels (7 in.)   7 1/2 in. per sec.
         phonotape.
         I. Woollcott, Alexander, 1887-1943. I. Woollcott, Alexander,
         1887-1943. II. Banghardt, Kenneth   III. Hecht, Ben, 1893-
         1964. IV. Roosevelt, Eleanor (Roosevelt) 1884-1962. V. Walker,
         Danton   VI. Brackett, Charles, 1892-1969. VII. Grant,
         Jane   VIII. Rude, Robert Barnes   IX. West,
         Rebecca, pseud. X. Henessy, Joseph   XI. Letterer,
         Charles   XII. Welles, Orson, 1915-

Voice Lib.
M1741   Walker, Ed
 bd.3   The blindness of the sighted. WKAR,
         June 17, 1994.
            25 min.   phonotape (1 r.   7 1/2 i.p.w.)

            1. Blind.

Voice Lib.
M900   Walker, Frank Comerford, 1886-1959.
 bd.3   Describes post office department's part in
         the sale of bonds and stamps; also their
         part in national defense. CBS, April 30,
         1941.
            1 reel (7 in.)   7 1/2 i.p.s.   phonotape.

            1. U.S. Post Office dept.

Voice Lib.
M1064   Walker, James John Joseph, 1881-1946.
 bd.5   Excerpt of welcoming remarks by Mayor
         Walker of New York at City Hall to golfer
         Bobby Jones; reply to Mayor Walker by
         Bobby Jones. Fox Movietone News, 1929.
            1 reel (7 in.)   7 1/2 in. per sec.
         phonotape.

            I. Jones, Robert Tyre, 1902-

Voice Lib.
577   Walker, James John Joseph, 1881-1946.
 bd.5   Plymouth World Tour farewell speech;
         assesses importance of world tour, wishes
         the tourists best of luck, peace of the
         world. New York, WOR Radio, 1929.
            1 reel (7 in.)   7 1/2 in. per sec.
         phonotape.

Voice Lib.
540   Walker, James John Joseph, 1881-1946.
 bd.6   Welcomed to Chicago by Mayor Anton Cermak.
         Fox Movietone, 1931.
            1 reel (7 in.)   7 1/2 in. per sec.
         phonotape.

            I. Cermak, Anton Joseph, 1873-1933.

Voice Lib.
540   Walker, James John Joseph, 1881-1946.
 bd.19   Address to Grand Street Boys' Club;
         reviews his record and denies misdeeds.
         Fox Movietone, 1932.
            1 reel (7 in.)   7 1/2 in. per sec.
         phonotape.

Voice Lib.
M1064   Walker, James John Joseph, 1881-1946.
 bd.11   Excerpt from address to the Grand Street
         Boys' Club in New York in defense of his
         city administration by Mayor James J. Walker.
         Fox Movietone, 1932.

            Walker, James John Joseph, 1881-1946
Voice Lib.
M1064   Cermak, Anton Joseph, 1873-1933.
 bd.6   Welcoming address by Mayor Cermak of Chicago
         to visiting Mayor James J. Walker of New York
         City; Mayor Walker's reply. Fox Movietone,
         1931.
            1 reel (7 in.)   7 1/2 in. per sec.
         phonotape.

            I. Walker, James John Joseph, 1881-1946.

            Walker, James John Joseph, 1881-1946
Voice Lib.
540   Jones, Robert Tyre, 1902-
 bd.5   Welcoming in New York City by Mayor Jimmy
         Walker; replies. Fox Movietone, 1930.
            1 reel (7 in.)   7 1/2 in. per sec.
         phonotape.

            I. Walker, James John Joseph, 1881-1946.

            WALKER, JAMES JOHN JOSEPH, 1881-1946
Voice Lib.
629   The Jimmy Walker Story, from "Twentieth
 bd.1   Century" TV series. On removing of
         railway tracks from 8th Avenue, welcomes
         Mayor of Berlin to New York, speech before
         Grand Street Boys' Club, says "hello" to
         New York from Europe, in Cannes, France,
         comments on his tax problems while in
         England, on his return to New York in 1935.
         CBS, April 17, 1964.
            1 reel (7 in.)   7 1/2 in. per sec.
         phonotape.
            1. Walker, James John Joseph, 1881-1946.

C1
A38
WALLACE, DEWITT, 1889-

Whorf, Michael, 1933-
The original big-little book.
1 tape cassette.   (The visual sounds of
Mike Whorf. Art, music and letters, A38)
Originally presented on his radio program, Kaleidoscope,
WJR, Detroit.
Duration: 40 min.
Here is the story of the Reader's digest, the people who write it,
why they write it and how this popular magazine is compiled.

1. The Reader's digest. 2. Wallace, DeWitt, 1889-
I. Title.

Voice Lib.
M724   Wallace, Henry Agard, 1888-1965.
bd.1   Repudiating the Truman doctrine,
            followed by Wallace campaign song.   1948.
            51 sec.   phonotape (1 r.   7 1/2 i.p.s.)

1. Presidents - U.S. - Election - 1948.

Voice Lib.
M840   Wallace, Edgar, 1875-1932.
bd.11   Telling his mystery thriller "The Man in
            the Ditch". HMV. 1929.
            1 reel (7 in.)   7 1/2 in. per sec.
            phonotape.

I. Title: The man in the ditch.

Wallace, Henry Agard, 1886-1965
Voice Lib.
M273-   Biography in sound (radio program)
274   Franklin Delano Roosevelt: the friends and
bd.1   former associates of Franklin Roosevelt on
            the tenth anniversary of the President's death.
            NBC Radio, April, 1955.
            2 reels (7 in.)   7 1/2 in. per sec.
            phonotape.
    I. Roosevelt, Franklin Delano, Pres. U.S., 1882-1945. I.
McIntire, Ross T   1889-   II. Mellett, Lowell, 1884-1960.
III. Tully, Grace   IV. Henderson, Leon, 1895-
V. Roosevelt, Eleanor (Roosevelt) 1884-1962. VI. DeGraaf, Albert
VII. Lehman, Herbert Henry, 1878-1963. VIII. Rosenman, Samuel
Irving, 1896-   IX. Arvey, Jacob   X. Moley, Raymond,
1886-   XI. Farley, Jar Aloysius, 1888-   XII. Roosevelt,
                              (Continued on next card)

Voice Lib.   Wallace, George Corley, 1919-
M1346   Nixon, Richard Milhous, Pres. U.S., 1913-
bd.2   Post-1968 election news described by
            Huntley, Brinkley and other NBC staff men.
            Statements of victory by Nixon and of defeat
            by Humphrey; also by Wallace and LeMay.
            Comments from countries overseas. Report of
            Congressional elections.   NBC-TV, November 6,
            1968.
            1 reel (7 in.)   7 1/2 in. per sec.
    I. Huntley, Chet, 1911-   II. Brinkley, David McClure, 1920-
III. Humphrey, Hubert Horatio, 1911-   IV. Wallace, George
Corley, 1919-   V. LeMay, Curtis Emerson, 1906-

Wallace, Henry Agard, 1888-1965
Voice Lib.
573   I can hear it now (radio program)
bd.2-   1945-1949.   CBS, 1950?
574   2 reels (7 in.)   7 1/2 in. per sec.
bd.1   phonotape.
    I. Murrow, Edward Roscoe, 1908-1965. II. Nehru, Jawaharlal,
1889-1964. III. Philip, duke of Edinburgh, 1921-   IV. Elizabeth II,
Queen of Great Britain, 1926-   V. Ferguson, Homer, 1889-   VI
Hughes, Howard Robard, 1905-   VII. Marshall, George Catlett,
1880-   VIII. Ruth, George Herman, 1895-1948. IX. Lilienthal,
David Eli, 1899-   X. Trout, Robert, 1908-   XI. Gage, Arthur.
XII. Jackson, Robert Houghwout, 1892-1954. XIII. Gromyko, Anatolii Andreevich, 1908-   XIV. Baruch, Bernard Mannes, 1870-
1965. XV. Churchill, Wi   Leonard Spencer, 1874-1965. XVI.
Winchell, Walter, 1897-   XVII. Davis, Elmer Holmes, 1890-
                              (Continued on next card)

Voice Lib.
272   Wallace, Henry Agard, 1888-1965.
bd.2   The future outlook.   G. Robert
            Vincent (private recording). 1938.
            1 reel (7 in.)   7 1/2 in. per sec.
            phonotape.

Wallace, Mike, 1918-
Voice Lib.
M1386   Apollo 11 (space flight): excerpts of old
bd.3   Mercury Theatre "War of the Worlds" of
            1938; an interview with Orson Welles by
            Mike Wallace.   CBS TV, July 20, 1969.
            1 reel (7 in.)   7 1/2 in. per sec.
            phonotape.
    I. Project Apollo. 2. Space flight to the moon. 3. Aldrin,
Edwin E   1930-   4. Collins, Michael, 1930-
5. Armstrong, Neil, 1930-   I. Aldrin, Edwin E   1930-
II. Collins, Michael, 1930-   III. Armstrong, Neil, 1930-
IV. Welles, Orson, 1915-   V. Wallace, Mike, 1918-

Voice Lib.
131   Wallace, Henry Agard, 1888-1965.
bd.2   Address at Michigan State University,
            with introduction by President John A.
            Hannah. WKAR, 1961.
            1 reel (7 in.)   7 1/2 in. per sec.
            phonotape.

I. Hannah, John Alfred, 1902-

Voice Lib.
M1719   Wallace, Mike, 1918-
            The press: credible or incredible?
            address at Michigan State University.
            WKAR, March 5, 1970.
            36 min.   phonotape (1 r.   7 1/2 i.p.s.)

1. Television broadcasting. 2. Marihuana.
3. Homosexuality - U.S.

Voice Lib.
M1491   Wallace, Mike, 1918-
bd.2   Segment on alleged Howard Hughes auto-
        biography on CBS "60 Minutes" program,
        describing the controversy, picturing present
        physical appearance of Hughes and bringing
        up loan by Hughes to President Nixon's
        brother of $205,000. Speakers: Mike Wallace
        and Clifford Irving.   CBS-TV, January 16,
        1972.
            1 reel (7 in.)   7 1/2 in. per sec.
        phonotape.
                            (Continued on next card)

Voice Lib.
M1491   Wallace, Mike, 1918-   Segment on
bd.2   alleged Howard Hughes autobiography...
        January 16, 1972.   (Card 2)

            1. Hughes, Howard Robard, 1905-
        I. Irving, Clifford, Michael, 1930-

Voice Lib.
M1491   Wallace, Mike, 1918-
bd.3   Segment on sequel to the mystery of Howard
        Hughes' alleged autobiography on CBS' "Sixty
        Minutes".   Mystery woman cashes $650,000
        check in Switzerland and description of
        procedures in Swiss banks.   CBS-TV, January 23,
        1972.
            1 reel (7 in.)   7 1/2 in. per sec.
        phonotape.

            1. Hughes, Howard Robard, 1905-

Voice Lib.
M1491   Wallace, Mike, 1918-
bd.4   New developments in the mystery case of
        Howard Hughes and Clifford Irving, described
        by Mike Wallace on CBS "60 Minutes".   CBS-TV,
        January 30, 1972.
            1 reel (7 in.)   7 1/2 in. per sec.
        phonotape.

            I. Hughes, Howard Robard, 1905-   II.
        Irving, Clifford Michael, 1930-

                Wallace, Mike, 1918-
Voice Lib.
M1498   Beard, Dita Davis, 1918-
bd.1   Interview with Mrs. Dita Beard, ITT
        lobbyist, with Mike Wallace on CBS "60
        Minutes" regarding the famous memo about a
        $400,000 contribution to the Republican
        convention of 1972, and Mrs. Beard's personal
        association with Attorney General Mitchell
        pertaining to the Hartford Fire Insurance
        anti-trust case.   CBS-TV, April 2, 1972.
            1 reel (7 in.)   7 1/2 in. per sec.
        phonotape.
            I. Wallace, Mike, 1918-

                Wallach, John
Voice Lib.
M1744   Allende Gossens, Salvador, 1908-1973.
bd.4   Interview with John Wallach.   WKAR,
        August, 1973.
            2 min., 40 sec.   phonotape (1 r.   7 1/2
        i.p.s.)

            Wallach in turn was interviewed by Rich Adams.

            1. Chile - Pol & govt.   2. Socialism in
        Chile.   3. Allende Gossens, Salvador, 1908-
        1973.   I. Wallach, John.   II. Adams, Rich.

Voice Lib.
M1087   Waller, Fats, 1904-1943.
bd.2   Commenting, singing, and playing piano
        at V-Disc recording session.   V-Discs,
        April, 1944.
            1 reel (7 in.)   7 1/2 in. per sec.
        phonotape.
            CONTENTS.-a."That's what the bird sang to
        me".-b."The reefer song".-c."Slightly less
        than wonderful" and "The gal in my life".-d.
        "This is so nice, it must be illegal" and
        "There's 'yes' in the air in Martinique".

                Walter Reed, M.D.
C1
SC9   Whorf, Michael, 1933-
            Walter Reed, M.D.   (The visual sounds of
        1 tape cassette.   Mike Whorf.   Science, SC9)

            Originally presented on his radio program, Kaleidoscope,
        WJR, Detroit.
            Duration: 28 min.
            The story of the man who fought and conquered the dreaded
        mosquito and yellow fever.

            I. Reed, Walter, 1851-1902.   I. Title.

                Walters, Barbara, 1931-
Voice Lib.
M1706   Andrews, Julie, 1935-
bd.2   Discusses her career and her two books
        and her family on the Today Show with
        Barbara Walters.   NBC, June 5, 1974.
            10 min.   phonotape (1 r.   7 1/2 i.p.s.)

            1. Andrews, Julie, 1935-   I. Walters,
        Barbara, 1931-

                Walters, Barbara, 1931-
Voice Lib.
M1298   Capote, Truman, 1924-
bd.2   Excerpt of interview with Barbara Walters
        of "Today" show, on contemporary music,
        hippies, drugs and being visible.   NBC-TV,
        January 3, 1968.
            1 reel (7 in.)   7 1/2 in. per sec.
        phonotape.

            I. Walters, Barbara, 1931-

Walters, Barbara, 1931-
Voice Lib.
M1402   Capote, Truman, 1924-
bd.1   Discussion with Barbara Walters on the
         Today Show about his book and movie
         "Trilogy".   NBC, November 11,1969.
            1 reel (7 in.)   7 1/2 in. per sec.
         phonotape.

            I. Walters, Barbara, 1931-

Walters, Barbara, 1931-
Voice Lib.
M1726   Coppola, Francis Ford, 1939-
Bd.2   Interviewed on Today Show by Barbara
         Walters and Gene Shalitt. NBC, June 18,
         1974.
            12 min.   phonotape (1 r.   7 1/2 i.p.s.)

            1. Moving-pictures.   I. Shalitt, Gene.
         II. Walters, Barbara, 1931-

Voice Lib.   Walters, Barbara, 1931-
M1681   Fonda, Henry Jaynes, 1905-
bd.2   Interviewed on the Today show by Barbara
         Walters. NBC-TV, May 10, 1974.
            5 min.   phonotape (1 r.   7 1/2 i.p.s.)

            1. Fonda, Henry Jaynes, 1905-
         I. Walters, Barbara, 1931-

Walters, Barbara, 1931-
Voice Lib.
M1727   Magruder, Jeb Stuart, 1934-
Bd.1   Interviewed by Barbara Walters on the
         Today Show. NBC, June 14, 1974.
            20 min.   phonotape (1 r.   7 1/2 i.p.s.)

            1. Watergate Affair, 1972-
         I. Walters, Barbara, 1931-

Walters, Barbara, 1931-
Voice Lib.
M1475-   Rusk, Dean, 1909-
1476,   Dean Rusk, former Secretary of State,
bd.1   discusses the Pentagon Papers with Edwin
         Newman and Barbara Walters. NBC, July 2,
         1971.
            2 reels (7 in.)   7 1/2 i.p.s.   phonotape.

            1. Pentagon papers. 2. Vietnamese
         Conflict, 1961-   - U.S.   I. Newman,
         Edwin Harold, 1919-   II. Walters,
         Barbara, 1931-

Walters, Barbara, 1931-
Voice Lib.
M1741   Sayegh, Fayez Abdullah, 1922-
bd.1   In an emotional debate with Jess Marlowe
         and Barbara Walters on the Today Show.
         NBC-TV, June 24, 1974.
            15 min.   phonotape (1 r.   7 1/2 i.p.s.)

            1. Refugee, Arab.   I. Marlowe, Jess.
         II. Walters, Barbara, 1931-

Walters, Barbara, 1931-
Voice Lib.
1720   Train, Russell Errol, 1920-
bd.2   Interview on the Today Show with Barbara
         Walters and Robert Guralski. NBC, June 11,
         1974.
            5 min.   phonotape (1 r.   7 1/2 i.p.s.)

            1. U.S. Environmental Protection Agency.
         I. Walters, Barbara, 1931-   II. Guralski,
         Robert.

Walters, Barbara, 1931-
Voice Lib.
M1720   Udall, Morris K., 1922-
bd.4   On the Today Show with Sam Steiger, debating
         their opposing bills for land-use funding.
         Includes Barbara Walters and Bill Monroe.
         NBC-TV, June 10, 1974.
            8 min.   phonotape (1 r.   7 1/2 i.p.s.)

            1. Land. 2. Man - Influence on nature.
         I. Steiger, Sam, 1929-   II. Walters,
         Barbara, 1931-   III. Monroe, Bill.

Walters, Barbara, 1931-
Voice Lib.
M1744   Vestal, M   S
bd.1   Discussing his book Jerry Ford, up close,
         on the Today Show with Bill Monroe, Barbara
         Walters, and Jess Marlowe. NBC-TV, June 25,
         1974.
            10 min.   phonotape (1 r.   7 1/2 i.p.s.)

            1. Ford, Gerald R., 1913-   2. Vestal,
         M.S./Jerry Ford, up close.   I. Monroe, Bill.
         II. Walters, Barbara, 1931-   III. Marlowe,
         Jess.

Voice Lib.
M1800   Walters, Vernon
WG   Testimony before the Senate Committee
0803.01 investigating the Watergate Affair.
         Pacifica, August 3, 1973.
            175 min.   phonotape (2 r.   3 3/4 i.p.s.)
            (Watergate gavel to gavel, phase 1)

            1. Watergate Affair, 1972-

Waltzing Matilda
Voice Lib.
589   White, Josh, 1908-1969.
bd.3   Sings Australian war song "Waltzing
        Matilda". V-Disc, 1944.
         1 reel (7 in.)   7 1/2 in. per sec.
        phonotape.

         I. Title: Waltzing Matilda.

Voice Lib.
M1362 War Crimes Trials - Nuremberg, 1945-1949.
bd.2   Defendants plead "not guilty". November 20,
        1945.
         1 reel (7 in.)   7 1/2 in. per sec.
        phonotape.

Wang Wang blues
Voice Lib.
611   Van and Schenck
bd.10-   Comedy team singing "Ain't You Coming
11   Out, Melinda?" and "Wang Wang Blues".
        Columbia Graphophone Company, 1920, 1922.
         1 reel (7 in.)   7 1/2 in. per sec.
        phonotape.

         I. Title: Ain't you coming out, Melinda?
        II. Title: Wang Wang blues.

Voice Lib.   War of the worlds (radio program)
M619   Radio in the 1930's (Part II): a series of
bd.1-   excerpts of the 1930's; a sample of radio
14   of the period. NVL, April, 1964.
        1 reel (7 in.) 7 1/2 in. per sec. phonotape.
        I. Allen, Fred, 1.894-1956. II. Delmar, Kenny   III. Donald,
        Peter   IV. Pious, Minerva   V. Fennelly, Parker   VI.
        Boyer, Charles, 1899-   VII. Dunne, Irene, 1904-   VIII.
        DeMille, Cecil Blount, 1881-1959. IX. West, Mae, 1893-   X.
        Dafoe, Allan Ray, 1883-1943. XI. Dionne quintuplets. XII. Ortega,
        Santos   XIII. War of the worlds (radio program) XIV. Ives, Burl,
        1909-   XV. Robinson, Earl, 1910-   XVI. Temple, Shirley,
        1928-   XVII. Earhart, Amelia, 1898-1937. XVIII. Lawrence,
        Gertrude, 1901-1952. XIX. Cohan, George Michael, 1878-1942.
        XX. Shaw, George Bernard, 1856-1950. XXI. Hitler, Adolf, 1889-
        1945. XXII. Chamberlain, Neville, 1869-1940. XXIII. Roosevelt,
        Franklin Delano, Pres. U.S., 1882-1945.

WAR
Voice Lib.
654   Cox, James Middleton, 1870-1957.
bd.8   Prevention of war: campaign speech
        stressing preventive measures against war.
        Nation's Forum, 1920.
         1 reel (7 in.)   7 1/2 in. per sec.
        phonotape.

WAR OF THE WORLDS (RADIO PROGRAM)
Voice Lib.
M1024- Murrow, Edward Roscoe, 1908-1965.
1025,   Television network dramatization "Studio
bd.1   One" entitled "The night America trembled",
        pertaining to the CBS Mercury Theater Show
        "War of the worlds". Westinghouse, 1958.
         2 reels (7 in.)   7 1/2 i.p.s.   phonotape.

         1. War of the worlds (radio program.)
         I. Title: The night America trembled.

C1   WAR
H41   Whorf, Michael, 1933-
        Days of valor.
         1 tape cassette.   (The visual sounds of
        Mike Whorf. History and heritage, H41)

        Originally presented on his radio program, Kaleidoscope,
        WJR, Detroit.
        Duration: 49 min.
        In each of America's wars there have been given moments,
        certain occasions when men rise above the normal call of duty
        to perform at the peak of their endurance whether in victory or
        defeat.

        1. U.S. - History.   2. War.   I. Title.

War of the worlds
Voice Lib.
568-   Welles, Orson, 1915-
569   Mercury Theater on the Air: "War of
        the Worlds". CBS, October 30, 1938.
         2 reels (7 in.)   7 1/2 in. per sec.
        phonotape.

         I. Title: War of the worlds.

Voice Lib.
M354- War Crimes Trials - Nuremberg, 1945-1949.
361   Pleas of defendants, opening address.
        Official Government Recording, November 21,
        1945.
         8 reels (7 in.)   7 1/2 i.p.s.   phonotape.

         1. Nuremberg Trial of Major German War
        Criminals, 1945-1946.

Voice Lib.
M1032 The war relived; documentary television
        program about World War II, Adolf Hitler
        and his dream of world domination,
        beginning with German preparations in the
        summer of 1939 through D-Day, 1944. NET,
        January 29, 1967.
         1 reel (7 in.)   7 1/2 in. per sec.
        phonotape.

         1. World War, 1939-1945

WAR-SONGS, GERMAN

Voice Lib.
M1300   Musical ceremonies and bugle calls of
bd.5   German Wehrmacht; also military marches
            and orchestral rendering of "Deutschland-
            lied". Peteler, n.d.
            1 reel (7 in.)   7 1/2 i.p.s.   phonotape.

            1. War-songs, German.   I. Title:
        Deutschlandlied.

WAR-SONGS, GERMAN

Voice Lib.
M953   Nationalsozialistische Deutsche Arbeiter-Partei.
bd.3   War songs of the Nazi Party: a. Wir sind das
            Heer von Hakenkreuz; b. Brüder in Zeehen und
            Gruben; c. Es pfeift von allen Dächern; d. Zum
            Kampfe wollen wir marschieren; e. Als die
            gold'ne Abendsonne; f. Durch Berlin marschieren
            wir; g. Deutschland, du Land der treue; h. Wenn
            die SS und die SA aufmarschiert. Peteler, 1930's.
            1 reel (7 in.)   7 1/2 in. per sec.
        phonotape.

            1. War-songs, German.

Voice Lib. WAR SONGS, GERMAN
M980   Nazi martial music: "Die Fahne hoch", war
bd.1   song of the NSDAP (Nazi Party); 3 stanzas.
            Peteler, 1938.
            1 reel (7 in.)   7 1/2 in. per sec.
        phonotape.

WAR SONGS, GERMAN
Voice Lib.
M1361   Nazi war songs; stormtroopers singing Nazi
bd.3   war song, "Heil unserem Führer".
            Peteler, 1945.
            1 reel (7 in.)   7 1/2 i.p.s.   phonotape.

            1. War songs, German.

WAR-SONGS, GERMAN
Voice Lib.
M1304   Nazi war songs: three stanzas of "We're
bd.5   on our way to conquer England" ("Wir
            fahren gegen England"). Peteler, n.d.
            1 reel (7 in.)   7 1/2 i.p.s.   phonotape.

            1. War-songs, German.   2. World War, 1939-
        1945 - Songs and music.

WAR SONGS, RUSSIAN
Voice Lib.
M1073   Russian marching song; song of the Russian
bd.11   army guardsmen (vocal). Peteler, 1941.
            1 reel (7 in.)   7 1/2 in. per sec.
        phonotape.

WAR-SONGS, RUSSIAN
Voice Lib.
M1073   Russian marching song; song of the USSR
bd.18   artillery (vocal and instrumental).
            Peteler, 1941.
            1 reel (7 in.)   7 1/2 in. per sec.
        phonotape.

Voice Lib.   Ward, Russ
M1558   Nixon, Richard Milhous, Pres. U.S., 1913-
bd.2   Comments on invasion of privacy; radio
            address. Followup to State of the Union
            Address. With commentary by Russ Ward.
            NBC, February 23, 1974.
            22 min.   phonotape (1 r.   7 1/2 in. per
        sec.)

            1. Privacy, Right of.   I. Ward, Russ.

Voice Lib.
M1470   Warlimont, Walter, 1895-
bd.18   a) Interview with General Warlimont regard-
            ing Hitler's aims in Czechoslovakia and
            his build-up for war in 1938. b) Regarding
            Hitler's military strategy in 1930. Peteler,
            1964.
            1 reel (7 in.)   7 1/2 in. per sec.
        phonotape.

            1. Germany - History - 1933-1945

Voice Lib.   Warner, Albert, 1884-1967
M1045   The world today; radio broadcast with
bd.1   discussions of George Bernard Shaw by
            Alexander Woollcott; John Daly regarding
            offensive on Moscow; Edward R. Murrow
            from London; Albert Warner concerning
            coal miners' strike.   CBS Radio, October
            30, 1941.
            1 reel (7 in.)   7 1/2 in. per sec.
        phonotape.
            I. Shaw, George Bernard, 1856-1950. I. Woollcott, Alexander,
        1887-1943. II. Daly, John Charles, 1914-   III. Murrow, Edward
        Roscoe, 1908-1965. IV. Warner, Albert, 1884-1967.

Voice Lib.
M1739   Warner, Dale, 1941-
Bd.2   Appearance after mistrial declared on
        narcotics charge. WJIM-TV, June 16, 1974.
        3 min. phonotape (1 r. 7 1/2 i.p.s.)

            1. Warner, Dale, 1941-

                                        WARREN, JOSEPH, 1741-1775
C1
H101   Whorf, Michael, 1933-
            An American story, as we have forgotten it -
        Joseph Warren.
            1 tape cassette. (The visual sounds of Mike Whorf. History
        and heritage, H101)

            Originally presented on his radio program, Kaleidoscope,
        WJR, Detroit.
            Duration: 35 min., 10 sec.
            A young American doctor, active in Revolutionary politics,
        Joseph Warren eagerly participated in many rebel militia activities.
        Constantly fighting for the American cause Dr. Warren helped
        create independence.

            I. Warren, Joseph,   1741-1775. I. Title.

Voice Lib.
M592   Warnow, Mark
bd.4   Allied marching songs, with orchestra
        and Lyn Murray chorus. V-Disc, 1943.
            1 reel (7 in.) 7 1/2 i.p.s. phonotape.

            CONTENTS.-Meadowland (Russian).-Che Li
        (Chinese); I've got sixpence (English);
        When the Yanks go marching in (American)

            1. World War, 1939-1945 - Songs and
        Music.

Voice Lib.
M539   Washington, Booker Taliaferro, 1859?-1915.
bd.4   The American Negro (Atlanta Exposition
        address); improvement of race relations,
        conditions in the South. Columbia Gramophone
        Company, 1906.
            1 reel (7 in.) 7 1/2 i.p.s. phonotape.

            1. Race problems - Addresses, essays,
        lectures.

Voice Lib.
M314   Warren, Earl, 1891-
bd.3   Remarks at bier of President Kennedy,
        lying in state at Capitol Rotunda. Also
        remarks by Speaker of the House McCormack;
        beginning of line of dignitaries to pass
        the bier. ABC, November 24, 1963.
            1 reel (7 in.) 7 1/2 in. per sec.
        phonotape.
            1. Kennedy, John Fitzgerald, Pres. U.S.,
        1917-1963 - Assassination. I. McCormack,
        John William, 1891-

                                        WASHINGTON, BOOKER TALIAFERRO, 1859?-1915
C1
S5   Whorf, Michael, 1933-
            The interracial statesman.
            1 tape cassette. (The visual sounds of
        Mike Whorf. Social, S5)

            Originally presented on his radio program, Kaleidoscope,
        WJR, Detroit.
            Duration: 34 min.
            Booker T. Washington was one of the first of American Black
        men to discover that he must accept the world on its terms. He was
        a leader who saw prejudice and bigotry, yet prevailed to become
        accepted as an individual, a man deserving of his fellow man's
        respect.
            I. Washington, Booker Taliaferro, 1859?-1915. I. Title.

Voice Lib.
M718   Warren, Earl, 1891-
bd.1   At presidential inaugural ceremonies.
        January 20, 1965.
            1 reel (7 in.) 7 1/2 in. per sec.
        phonotape.

                                        WASHINGTON, GEORGE, PRES. U.S., 1732-1799
C1
H23   Whorf, Michael, 1933-
            First in the heart of his countrymen.
            1 tape cassette. (The visual sounds of
        Mike Whorf. History and heritage, H23)
            Originally presented on his radio program, Kaleidoscope,
        WJR, Detroit.
            A dauntless and fearless commander-in-chief, who led his
        ragged army to victory in war and guided his young nation to
        victory in peace.

            I. Washington, George, Pres. U.S., 1732-1799.
        I. Title.

            Warren, Earl, 1891-
Voice Lib.
206   Kennedy, John Fitzgerald, Pres. U.S., 1917-1963.
bd.1   Inaugural speech and swearing in
        ceremony by Earl Warren. Detroit,
        WJR, January 20, 1961.
            1 reel (7 in.) 7 1/2 in. per sec.
        phonotape.

            I. Warren, Earl, 1891-

                                        WASHINGTON, GEORGE, PRES. U.S., 1732-1799
C1
H106   Whorf, Michael, 1933-
            The perfect legend - George Washington.
            1 tape cassette. (The visual sounds of
        Mike Whorf. History and heritage, H106)
            Originally presented on his radio program, Kaleidoscope,
        WJR, Detroit.
            Duration: 37 min., 30 sec.
            As commander of a new country, General George Washington
        watched his soldiers falter. His faith, trust and heroics led his
        men to a nearly impossible victory.

            I. Washington, George, Pres. U.S., 1732-1799. I. Title.

Washington, D.C. National Gallery of Art.
see
U.S. National Gallery of Art.

VOICE LIBRARY

WATERGATE AFFAIR, 1972

Voice Lib.
M1586   Baker, Howard H., 1925-
The lessons of Watergate. WKAR,
February 28, 1974.
30 min. phonotape (1 r. 7 1/2 in. per
sec.)

1. Watergate Affair, 1972. 2. Campaign
funds.

Voice Lib.
M1222   Washington Reports; CBS television news. Reports by CBS
bd. 1   news correspondents about President Kennedy's Civil
Rights message to Congress and interviews with Attorney
General Robert F. Kennedy pertaining to his views on
his own work in the Justice Department and his own future.
CBS-TV News, Bergman, March 3, 1963.
1 reel (7 in.) 7 1/2 i.p.s. phonotape.

1. Civil rights. 2. U.S. Dept. of Justice. 3. Kennedy,
Robert Francis, 1925-1968. ': I. Kennedy, Robert Francis,
1925-1968.

WATERGATE AFFAIR, 1972-

Voice Lib.
M1702   Baker, Howard H., 1925-
On Watergate, with Clyde Lamont, of the
National Press Club. WKAR, May 30, 1974.
50 min. phonotape (1 r. 7 1/2 i.p.s.)

1. Watergate Affair, 1972-   2. U.S. -
Politics and government. I. Lamont, Clyde

Voice Lib.   WATER - POLLUTION
M1689   Nelson, Gaylord, 1916-
Man, the endangered species; address at
Michigan State University. Introduction by
President Wharton. WKAR, January 19, 1970.
41 min. phonotape (1 r. 7 1/2 i.p.s.)

1. Water - Pollution. 2. Ecology.
I. Wharton, Clifton Reginald, 1926-

WATERGATE AFFAIR, 1972-

Voice Lib.
M1800   Baldwin, Alfred
WG   Testimony before the Senate Committee
0524.03 investigating the Watergate Affair.
Pacifica, May 24, 1973.
84 min. phonotape (1 r. 3 3/4 i.p.s.)
(Watergate gavel to gavel, phase 1)

1. Watergate Affair, 1972-

WATERGATE AFFAIR, 1972-

Voice Lib.
M1800   Alch, Gerald
WG   Testimony before the Senate Committee
0523.03 investigating the Watergate Affair.
Pacifica, May 23, 1973.
109 min. phonotape (2 r. 3 3/4 i.p.s.)
(Watergate gavel to gavel, phase 1)

1. Watergate Affair, 1972-

WATERGATE AFFAIR, 1972-

Voice Lib.
M1800   Barker, Bernard, 1917?-
WG   Testimony before the Senate Committee
0524.02 investigating the Watergate Affair.
Pacifica, May 24, 1973.
117 min. phonotape (2 r. 3 3/4 i.p.s.)
(Watergate gavel to gavel, phase 1)

1. Watergate Affair, 1972-

WATERGATE AFFAIR, 1972-

Voice Lib.
M1800   Alch, Gerald
WG   Testimony before the Senate Committee
0524.01 investigating the Watergate Affair.
Pacifica, May 24, 1973.
188 min. phonotape (3 r. 3 3/4 i.p.s.)
(Watergate gavel to gavel, phase 1)

1. Watergate Affair, 1972-

WATERGATE AFFAIR, 1972-

Voice Lib.
M1800   Butterfield, Alexander Porter, 1926-
WG   Testimony before the Senate Committee
0716.02 investigating the Watergate Affair.
Pacifica, July 16, 1973.
86 min. phonotape (5 in. 3 3/4 i.p.s.)
(Watergate gavel to gavel, phase 1)

1. Watergate Affair, 1972-

WATERGATE AFFAIR, 1972-

Voice Lib.
M1800 Caulfield, John, 1929?
WG Testimony before the Senate Committee
0522.03 investigating the Watergate Affair.
Pacifica, May 22, 1973.
89 min. phonotape (1 r. 3 3/4 i.p.s.)
(Watergate gavel to gavel, phase 1)

1. Watergate Affair, 1972-

WATERGATE AFFAIR, 1972-

Voice Lib.
M1800 Dean, John Wesley, 1938-
WG Testimony before the Senate Committee
0627 investigating the Watergate Affair.
Pacifica, June 27, 1973.
375 min. phonotape (5 r. 3 3/4 i.p.s.)
(Watergate gavel to gavel, phase 1)

1. Watergate Affair, 1972-

WATERGATE AFFAIR, 1972-

Voice Lib.
M1800 Caulfield, John, 1929?-
WG Testimony before the Senate Committee
0523.01 investigating the Watergate Affair.
Pacifica, May 23, 1973.
80 min. phonotape (1 r. 3 3/4 i.p.s.)
(Watergate gavel to gavel, phase 1)

1. Watergate Affair, 1972-

WATERGATE AFFAIR, 1972-

Voice Lib.
M1800 Dean, John Wesley, 1938-
WG Testimony before the Senate Committee
0628 investigating the Watergate Affair.
Pacifica, June 28, 1973.
353 min. phonotape (5 r. 3 3/4 i.p.s.)
(Watergate gavel to gavel, phase 1)

1. Watergate Affair, 1972-

WATERGATE AFFAIR, 1972-

Voice Lib.
M1800 Cushman, Robert Everton, 1914-
WG Testimony before the Senate Committee
0802.03 investigating the Watergate Affair.
Pacifica, August 2, 1973.
96 min. phonotape (2 r. 3 3/4 i.p.s.)
(Watergate gavel to gavel, phase 1)

1. Watergate Affair, 1972-

WATERGATE AFFAIR, 1972-

Voice Lib.
M1800 Dean, John Wesley, 1938-
WG Testimony before the Senate Committee
0629 investigating the Watergate Affair.
Pacifica, June 29, 1973.
349 min. phonotape (5 r. 3 3/4 i.p.s.)
(Watergate gavel to gavel, phase 1)

1. Watergate Affair, 1972-

WATERGATE AFFAIR, 1972-

Voice Lib.
M1800 Dean, John Wesley, 1938-
WG Statement made before the Senate Committee
0625 investigating the Watergate Affair.
Pacifica, June 25, 1973.
400 min. phonotape (5 r. 3 3/4 i.p.s.)
(Watergate gavel to gavel, phase 1)

1. Watergate Affair, 1972-

WATERGATE AFFAIR, 1972-

Voice Lib.
M1800 Ehrlichman, John Daniel, 1925-
WG Testimony before the Senate Committee
0724 investigating the Watergate Affair.
Pacifica, July 24, 1973.
292 min. phonotape (4 r. 3 3/4 i.p.s.)
(Watergate gavel to gavel, phase 1)

1. Watergate Affair, 1972-

WATERGATE AFFAIR, 1972-

Voice Lib.
M1800 Dean, John Wesley, 1938-
WG Testimony before the Senate Committee
0626 investigating the Watergate Affair.
Pacifica, June 26, 1973.
343 min. phonotape (5 r. 3 3/4 i.p.s.)
(Watergate gavel to gavel, phase 1)

1. Watergate Affair, 1972-

WATERGATE AFFAIR, 1972-

Voice Lib.
M1800 Ehrlichman, John Daniel, 1925-
WG Testimony before the Senate Committee
0725 investigating the Watergate Affair.
Pacifica, July 24, 1973.
291 min. phonotape (4 r. 3 3/4 i.p.s.)
(Watergate gavel to gavel, phase 1)

1. Watergate Affair, 1972-

WATERGATE AFFAIR, 1972-

Voice Lib.
M1800   Ehrlichman, John Daniel, 1925-
WG   Testimony before the Senate Committee
0726   investigating the Watergate Affair.
             Pacifica, July 26, 1973.
               317 min.   phonotape (4 r.   3 3/4 i.p.s.)
             (Watergate gavel to gavel, phase 1)

             1. Watergate Affair, 1972-

WATERGATE AFFAIR, 1972-

Voice Lib.
M1800   Gray, Louis Patrick, 1916-
WG   Testimony before the Senate Committee
0806   investigating the Watergate Affair.
             Pacifica, August 6, 1973.
               325 min.   phonotape (4 r.   3 3/4 i.p.s.)
             (Watergate gavel to gavel, phase 1)

             1. Watergate Affair, 1972-

WATERGATE AFFAIR, 1972-

Voice Lib.
M1800   Ehrlichman, John Daniel, 1926-
WG   Testimony before the Senate Committee
0727   investigating the Watergate Affair.
             Pacifica, July 27, 1973.
               296 min.   phonotape (4 r.   3 3/4 i.p.s.)
             (Watergate gavel to gavel, phase 1)

             1. Watergate Affair, 1972-

WATERGATE AFFAIR, 1972-

Voice Lib.
M1800   Haldeman, Harry R., 1926-
WG   Testimony before the Senate Committee
0730.03   investigating the Watergate affair.
             Pacifica, July 30, 1973.
               160 min.   phonotape (2 r.   3 3/4 i.p.s.)
             (Watergate gavel to gavel, phase 1)

             1. Watergate Affair, 1972-

WATERGATE AFFAIR, 1972-

Voice Lib.
M1800   Ehrlichman, John Daniel, 1925-
WG   Testimony before the Senate Committee
0730.01-   investigating the Watergate Affair.
.02   Pacifica, July 30, 1973.
               258 min.   phonotape (4 r.   3 3/4 i.p.s.)
             (Watergate gavel to gavel, phase 1)

             1. Watergate Affair, 1972-

WATERGATE AFFAIR, 1972-

Voice Lib.
M1800   Haldeman, Harry R., 1926-
WG   Testimony before the Senate Committee
0731   investigating the Watergate Affair.
             Pacifica, July 31, 1973.
               418 min.   phonotape (5 r.   3 3/4 i.p.s.)
             (Watergate gavel to gavel, phase 1)

             1. Watergate Affair, 1972-

WATERGATE AFFAIR, 1972-

Voice Lib.
M1633   Graham, Katherine (Meyer) 1917-
                Speaking on Watergate and the press.
             WKAR-FM, April 15, 1974.
               45 min.   phonotape (1 r.   7 1/2 i.p.s.)

             1. Watergate Affair, 1972-

WATERGATE AFFAIR, 1972-

Voice Lib.
M1800   Haldeman, Harry R., 1926-
WG   Testimony before the Senate Committee
0801   investigating the Watergate Affair.
             Pacifica, August 1, 1973.
               357 min.   phonotape (5 r.   3 3/4 i.p.s.)
             (Watergate gavel to gavel, phase 1)

             1. Watergate Affair, 1972-

WATERGATE AFFAIR, 1972-

Voice Lib.
M1800   Gray, Louis Patrick, 1916-
WG   Testimony before the Senate Committee
0802.02   investigating the Watergate Affair.
             Pacifica, August 3, 1973.
               112 min.   phonotape (2 r.   3 3/4 i.p.s.)
             (Watergate gavel to gavel, phase 1)

             1. Watergate Affair, 1972-

WATERGATE AFFAIR, 1972-

Voice Lib.
M1800   Harmony, Sally J
WG   Testimony before the Senate Committee
0605.01   investigating the Watergate Affair.
             Pacifica, June 5, 1973.
               121 min.   phonotape (1 r.   3 3/4 i.p.s.)
             (Watergate gavel to gavel, phase 1)

             1. Watergate Affair, 1972-

WATERGATE AFFAIR, 1972-

Voice Lib.
M1800   Helms, Richard, 1913-
WG   Testimony before the Senate Committee
0802.01- investigating the Watergate Affair.
.02   Pacifica, August 2, 1973.
             225 min.   phonotape (4 r.   3 3/4 i.p.s.)
          (Watergate gavel to gavel, phase 1)

          1. Watergate Affair, 1972-

WATERGATE AFFAIR, 1972-

Voice Lib.
M1657   Kennedy, Edward Moore, 1932-
             Discusses visit with Brezhnev, Watergate,
          Chappaquiddick, and 1976 politics.
          Interviewed by Paul Duke.   WKAR-TV,
          May 7, 1974.
             30 min.   phonotape (1 r.   7 1/2 i.p.s.)

          1. U.S. - Politics and government - 1969-
          2. Watergate Affair, 1972-   I. Duke,
          Paul.

WATERGATE AFFAIR, 1972-

Voice Lib.
M1665   Hunt, Everette Howard, 1918-
             On "Firing line" about Watergate payments,
          with William Buckley, Ralph Fine, John Owen,
          and Miss Bernstein.   WKAR-TV, May 14, 1974.
             50 min.   phonotape (1 r.   7 1/2 i.p.s.)

          1. Watergate Affair, 1972-   I.
          Buckley, William Frank, 1925-   II. Fine,
          Ralph Adam, 1941-   III. Owen, John

WATERGATE AFFAIR, 1972-

Voice Lib.
M1800   Kleindienst, Richard Gordon, 1923-
WG   Testimony before the Senate Committee
0807.01 investigating the Watergate Affair.
          Pacifica, August 7, 1973.
             204 min.   phonotape (3 r.   3 3/4 i.p.s.)
          (Watergate gavel to gavel, phase 1)

          1. Watergate Affair, 1972-

WATERGATE AFFAIR, 1972-

Voice Lib.
M1800   Kalmbach, Herbert Warren, 1921-
WG   Testimony before the Senate Committee
0716.03 investigating the Watergate Affair.
          Pacifica, July 16, 1973.
             105 min.   phonotape (2 r.   3 3/4 i.p.s.)
          (Watergate gavel to gavel, phase 1)

          1. Watergate Affair, 1972-

WATERGATE AFFAIR, 1972-

Voice Lib.
M1800   LaRue, Frederick C., 1928?-
WG   Testimony before the Senate Committee
0718.03 investigating the Watergate Affair.
          Pacifica, July 18, 1973.
             156 min.   phonotape (2 r.   3 3/4 i.p.s.)
          (Watergate gavel to gavel, phase 1)

          1. Watergate Affair, 1972-

WATERGATE AFFAIR, 1972-

Voice Lib.
M1800   Kalmbach, Herbert Warren, 1921-
WG   Testimony before the Senate Committee
0717   investigating the Watergate Affair.
          Pacifica, July 17, 1973.
             289 min.   phonotape (4 r.   3 3/4 i.p.s.)
          (Watergate gavel to gavel, phase 1)

          .1. Watergate Affair, 1972-

WATERGATE AFFAIR, 1972-

Voice Lib.
M1800   LaRue, Frederick C., 1928?-
WG   Testimony before the Senate Committee
0719.01 investigating the Watergate Affair.
          Pacifica, July 19, 1973.
             101 min.   phonotape (2 r.   3 3/4 i.p.s.)
          (Watergate gavel to gavel, phase 1)

          1. Watergate Affair, 1972-

WATERGATE AFFAIR, 1972-

Voice Lib.
M1800   Kehrli, Bruce
WG   Testimony before the Senate Committee
0517.04 investigating the Watergate Affair.
          Pacifica, May 17, 1973.
             57 min.   phonotape (1 r.   3 3/4 i.p.s.)
          (Watergate gavel to gavel, phase 1)

          1. Watergate Affair, 1972-

WATERGATE AFFAIR, 1972-

Voice Lib.
M1800   Leeper, Barrett
WG   Testimony before the Senate Committee
0517.05 investigating the Watergate Affair.
          Pacifica, May 17, 1973.
             67 min.   phonotape (1 r.   3 3/4 i.p.s.)
          (Watergate gavel to gavel, phase 1)

          1. Watergate Affair, 1972-

WATERGATE AFFAIR, 1972-

Voice Lib.
M1800   McCord, James Walter, 1918?-
WG   Testimony before the Senate Committee
0518.02- investigating the Watergate Affair.
.03   Pacifica, May 18, 1973.
               238 min.   phonotape (4 r.   3 3/4 i.p.s.)
            (Watergate gavel to gavel, phase 1)

               1. Watergate Affair, 1972-

WATERGATE AFFAIR, 1972-

Voice Lib.
M1800   Mardian, Robert Charles, 1923-
WG   Testimony before the Senate Committee
0720.01- investigating the Watergate Affair.
.02   Pacifica, July 20, 1973.
               205 min.   phonotape (3 r.   3 3/4 i.p.s.)
            (Watergate gavel to gavel, phase 1)

               1. Watergate Affair, 1972-

WATERGATE AFFAIR, 1972-

Voice Lib.
M1800   McCord, James Walter, 1918?-
WG   Testimony before the Senate Committee
0522.01 investigating the Watergate Affair.
.02   Pacifica, May 22, 1973.
               264 min.   phonotape (4 r.   3 3/4 i.p.s.)
            (Watergate gavel to gavel, phase 1)

               1. Watergate Affair, 1972-

WATERGATE AFFAIR, 1972-

Voice Lib.
M1707   Milliken, William G   1922-
bd.   Governors Milliken, Lucey and Askew at
            the Governors' Conference in Seattle on the
            new financing morality. Richard Threlkeld,
            reporting.   CBS, June 5, 1974.
               3 min.   phonotape (1 r.   7 1/2 i.p.s.)

               1. Watergate Affair, 1972-   I. Lucey,
            Patrick Joseph, 1918-   II. Askew,
            Reubin O'D.   III. Threlkeld, Richard.

WATERGATE AFFAIR, 1972-

Voice Lib.
M1727   Magruder, Jeb Stuart, 1934-
Bd.1   Interviewed by Barbara Walters on the
            Today Show.   NBC, June 14, 1974.
               20 min.   phonotape (1 r.   7 1/2 i.p.s.)

               1. Watergate Affair, 1972-
            I. Walters, Barbara, 1931-

WATERGATE AFFAIR, 1972-

Voice Lib.
M1800   Mitchell, John Newton, 1913-
WG   Testimony before the Senate Committee
0710   investigating the Watergate Affair.
            Pacifica, July 10, 1973.
               312 min.   phonotape (4 r.   3 3/4 i.p.s.)
            (Watergate gavel to gavel, phase 1)

               1. Watergate Affair, 1972-

WATERGATE AFFAIR, 1972-

Voice Lib.
M1800   Magruder, Jeb Stuart, 1934-
WG   Testimony before the Senate Committee
0614   investigating the Watergate Affair.
               361 min.   phonotape (5 r.   3 3/4 i.p.s.)
            (Watergate gavel to gavel, phase 1)

               1. Watergate Affair, 1972-

WATERGATE AFFAIR, 1972-

Voice Lib.
M1800   Mitchell, John Newton, 1913-
WG   Testimony before the Senate Committee
0711   investigating the Watergate Affair.
            Pacifica, July 11, 1973.
               325 min.   phonotape (4 r.   3 3/4 i.p.s.)
            (Watergate gavel to gavel, phase 1)

               1. Watergate Affair, 1972-

WATERGATE AFFAIR, 1972-

Voice Lib.
M1800   Mardian, Robert Charles, 1923-
WG   Testimony before the Senate Committee
0719.02- investigating the Watergate Affair.
.03   Pacifica, July 19, 1973.
               213 min.   phonotape (3 r.   3 3/4 i.p.s.)
            (Watergate gavel to gavel, phase 1)

               1. Watergate Affair, 1972-

WATERGATE AFFAIR, 1972-

Voice Lib.
M1800   Mitchell, John Newton, 1913-
WG   Testimony before the Senate Committee
0712.01- investigating the Watergate Affair.
.02   Pacifica, July 12, 1973.
               201 min.   phonotape (3 r.   3 3/4 i.p.s.)
            (Watergate gavel to gavel, phase 1)

               1. Watergate Affair, 1972-

WATERGATE AFFAIR, 1972-

Voice Lib.
M1800   Moore, Richard Arthur, 1914-
WG   Testimony before the Senate Committee
0712.03 investigating the Watergate Affair.
         Pacifica, July 12, 1973.
            98 min.   phonotape (2 r.   3 3/4 i.p.s.)
         (Watergate gavel to gavel; phase 1)

            1. Watergate Affair, 1972-

WATERGATE AFFAIR, 1972

Voice Lib.
M1549-   Nixon, Richard Milhous, Pres. U.S., 1913-
1550,   News conference recorded over CBS
bd.1   television network.   CBS, October 26, 1973.
            35 min.   phonotape (2 r.   7 1/2 i.p.s.)

            Includes question and answer session, including Nelson
         Benton.

            1. U.S. - Politics and government - 1969-
            2. Watergate Affair, 1972. 3. Power resources - U.S.
            I. Benton, Nelson

WATERGATE AFFAIR, 1972-

Voice Lib.
M1800   Moore, Richard Arthur, 1914-
WG   Testimony before the Senate Committee
0713   investigating the Watergate Affair.
         Pacifica, July 13, 1973.
            360 min.   phonotape (5 r.   3 3/4 i.p.s.)
         (Watergate gavel to gavel, phase 1)

            1. Watergate Affair, 1972-

WATERGATE AFFAIR, 1972-

Voice Lib.
M1800   Odle, Robert C., 1944?-
WG   Testimony before the Senate Committee
0517.02- investigating the Watergate Affair.
.03   Pacifica, May 17, 1973.
            218 min.   phonotape (2 r.   3 3/4 i.p.s.)
         (Watergate gavel to gavel, phase 1)

            1. Watergate Affair, 1972-

WATERGATE AFFAIR, 1972-

Voice Lib.
M1800   Moore, Richard Arthur, 1914-
WG   Testimony before the Senate Committee
0716.01 investigating the Watergate Affair.
         Pacifica, July 16, 1973.
            119 min.   phonotape (2 r.   3 3/4 i.p.s.)
         (Watergate gavel to gavel, phase 1)

            1. Watergate Affair, 1972-

WATERGATE AFFAIR, 1972-

Voice Lib.
M1573-   Percy, Charles Harting, 1919-
1574,   The government's response to change;
bd.1   Eisenhower Symposium, Johns Hopkins Univer-
         sity.   WBJC, Baltimore, October 29, 1973.
            45 min.   phonotape (2 r.   7 1/2 i.p.s.)

            Includes question and answer period.

            1. U.S. - Politics and government.
            2. Watergate Affair, 1972-

WATERGATE AFFAIR, 1972-

Voice Lib.
M1654-   National Public Radio.
1655   Transcript of conversation between Nixon,
         Dean and Haldeman, read by Linda Wertheimer,
         Bob Edwards, and Mike Waters.   NPR, May 1,
         1974.
            1 hr., 40 min.   phonotape (2 r.   7 1/2
         i.p.s.)

            1. Watergate Affair, 1972-
         I. Wertheimer, Linda. II. Edwards, Bob.
         III. Waters, Mike.

WATERGATE AFFAIR, 1972-

Voice Lib.
M1800   Peterson, Henry E
WG   Testimony before the Senate Committee
0807.02 investigating the Watergate Affair.
         Pacifica, August 7, 1973.
            173 min.   phonotape (2 r.   3 3/4 i.p.s.)
         (Watergate gavel to gavel, phase 1)

            1. Watergate Affair, 1972-

WATERGATE AFFAIR, 1972

Voice Lib.
M1559   Nixon, Richard Milhous, Pres. U.S., 1913-
             The Watergate Affair; address to the nation,
         with instant analysis by Roger Mudd and
         Daniel Schorr.   CBS, April 30, 1973.
            30 min.   phonotape (1 r.   7 1/2 i.p.s.)

            1. Watergate affair, 1972. I. Mudd,
         Roger. II. Schorr, Daniel Louis, 1916-

WATERGATE AFFAIR, 1972-

Voice Lib.
M1800   Porter, Herbert L., 1938?-
WG   Testimony before the Senate Committee
0607.02 investigating the Watergate Affair.
         Pacifica, June, 7, 1973.
            168 min.   phonotape (2 r.   3 3/4 i.p.s.)
         (Watergate gavel to gavel, phase 1)

            1. Watergate Affair, 1972-

WATERGATE AFFAIR, 1972-

Voice Lib.
M1800   Porter, Herbert L., 1938?-
WG   Testimony before the Senate Committee
0612.01   investigating the Watergate Affair.
           Pacifica, June 12, 1973.
               87 min.   phonotape (1 r.   3 3/4 i.p.s.)
           (Watergate gavel to gavel, phase 1)

               1. Watergate Affair, 1972-

WATERGATE AFFAIR, 1972-

Voice Lib.
M1800   Reisner, Robert Alan Fernon, 1946-
WG   Testimony before the Senate Committee
0605.02   investigating the Watergate Affair.
           Pacifica, June 5, 1973.
               158 min.   phonotape (2 r.   3 3/4 i.p.s.)
           (Watergate gavel to gavel, phase 1)

               1. Watergate Affair, 1972-

WATERGATE AFFAIR, 1972-

Voice Lib.
M1800   Shoffler, Carl
WG   Testimony before the Senate Committee
0518.01   investigating the Watergate Affair.
           Pacifica, May 18, 1973.
               34 min.   phonotape (1 r.   3 3/4 i.p.s.)
           (Watergate gavel to gavel, phase 1)

               1. Watergate Affair, 1972-

WATERGATE AFFAIR, 1972-

Voice Lib.
M1800   Sloan, Hugh W., 1941?-
WG   Testimony before the Senate Committee
0606   investigating the Watergate Affair.
           Pacifica, June 6, 1973.
               261 min.   phonotape (4 r.   3 3/4 i.p.s.)
           (Watergate gavel to gavel, phase 1)

               1. Watergate Affair, 1972-

WATERGATE AFFAIR, 1972-

Voice Lib.
M1800   Sloan, Hugh W., 1941?-
WG   Testimony before the Senate Committee
0607.01   investigating the Watergate Affair.
           Pacifica, June 7, 1973.
               130 min.   phonotape (2 r.   3 3/4 i.p.s.)
           (Watergate gavel to gavel, phase 1)

               1. Watergate Affair, 1972-

WATERGATE AFFAIR, 1972-

Voice Lib.
M1800   Stans, Maurice Hubert, 1908-
WG   Testimony before the Senate Committee
0612.02   investigating the Watergate Affair.
           Includes statement by Robert W. Barker,
           counsel. Pacifica, June 12, 1973.
               46 min.   phonotape (1 r.   3 3/4 i.p.s.)
           (Watergate gavel to gavel, phase 1)

               1. Watergate Affair, 1972-
           I. Barker, Robert

WATERGATE AFFAIR, 1972-

Voice Lib.
M1800   Stans, Maurice Hubert, 1908-
WG   Testimony before the Senate Committee
0612.03   investigating the Watergate Affair.
           Pacifica, June 12, 1973.
               161 min.   phonotape (2 r.   3 3/4 i.p.s.)
           (Watergate gavel to gavel, phase 1)

               1. Watergate Affair, 1972-

WATERGATE AFFAIR, 1972-

Voice Lib.
M1800   Stans, Maurice Hubert, 1908-
WG   Testimony before the Senate Committee
0613   investigating the Watergate Affair.
           Pacifica, June 13, 1973.
               299 min.   phonotape (4 r.   3 3/4 i.p.s.)
           (Watergate gavel to gavel, phase 1)

               1. Watergate Affair, 1972-

WATERGATE AFFAIR, 1972-

Voice Lib.
M1619   Stone, Chuck
bd.2   Perspectives in Black, with Roz Abrahms,
           Cheri Mazingo, and J. Markisha Johnson.
           WKAR, 1974.
               27 min.   phonotape (1 r.   7 1/2 i.p.s.)

               1. Race discrimination - U.S. 2. Watergate
           Affair, 1972-   I. Abrahms, Roz.
           II. Mazingo, Cheri. III. Johnson, J.
           Markisha.

WATERGATE AFFAIR, 1972-

Voice Lib.
M1800   Strachan, Gordon Creighton, 1943-
WG   Testimony before the Senate Committee
0720.03   investigating the Watergate Affair.
               27 min.   phonotape (1 r.   3 3/4 i.p.s.)
           (Watergate gavel to gavel, phase 1)

               1. Watergate Affair, 1972-

WATERGATE AFFAIR, 1972–

Voice Lib.
M1800
WG
0723
Strachan, Gordon Creighton, 1943–
Testimony before the Senate Committee
investigating the Watergate Affair.
Pacifica, July 23, 1973.
274 min.   phonotape (4 r.   3 3/4 i.p.s.)
(Watergate gavel to gavel, phase 1)

1. Watergate Affair, 1972–

WATERGATE AFFAIR, 1972–

Voice Lib.
M1800
WG
0803.01
Walters, Vernon
Testimony before the Senate Committee
investigating the Watergate Affair.
Pacifica, August 3, 1973.
175 min.   phonotape (2 r.   3 3/4 i.p.s.)
(Watergate gavel to gavel, phase 1)

1. Watergate Affair, 1972–

WATERGATE AFFAIR, 1972–

Voice Lib.
M1800
WG
0523.02
Ulasewicz, Anthony, 1919?–
Testimony before the Senate Committee
investigating the Watergate Affair.
Pacifica, May 23, 1972.
47 min.   phonotape (1 r.   3 3/4 i.p.s.)
(Watergate gavel to gavel, phase 1)

1. Watergate Affair, 1972–

WATERGATE AFFAIR, 1972–

Voice Lib.
M1741
bd.2
Wills, Frank
Interview with Bill Monroe.   NBC, June
17, 1974.
10 min.   phonotape (1 r.   7 1/2 i.p.s.)

1. Watergate affair, 1972–   I. Monroe,
Bill.

WATERGATE AFFAIR, 1972–

Voice Lib.
M1800
WG
0718.01–
.02
Ulasewicz, Anthony, 1919?–
Testimony before the Senate Committee
investigating the Watergate Affair.
Pacifica, July 18, 1973.
182 min.   phonotape (3 r.   3 3/4 i.p.s.)
(Watergate gavel to gavel, phase 1)

1. Watergate Affair, 1972–

WATERGATE AFFAIR, 1972–

Voice Lib.
M1704
Woodward, Robert
Woodward and Bernstein, exposers of
Watergate, at the National Press Club,
talking to other reporters.   Includes
Clark Mollenhoff.   WKAR, June 6, 1974.
50 min.   phonotape (1 r.   7 1/2 i.p.s.)

1. Watergate Affair, 1972–
I. Bernstein, Carl.   II. Mollenhoff, Clark
Raymond, 1921–

WATERGATE AFFAIR, 1972–

Voice Lib.
M1800
U.S. Congress. Senate. Select Committee on Presidential
Campaign Activities.
Watergate gavel to gavel, phase 1: May 17 – August 7, 1973.
Pacifica, May 17 – August 7, 1973.
172 reels (5 in.)   3 3/4 i.p.s.   phonotape.

"These tapes include commentaries by Pacifica's Washington
correspondents and interviews with members of the Senate Committee
taped during recesses of the hearings."

1. Presidents – U.S. – Elections – 1972.   2. Watergate Affair,
1972–   I. Ervin, Samuel James, 1896–   II. Talmadge,
Herman Eugene, 1913–   III. Inouye, Daniel Ken, 1924–
IV. Baker, Howard H., 1925–   V. Gurney, Edward John, 1914–
VI. Weicker, Lowell P., 19   VII. Title.

Watergate Committee.
see
U.S. Congress. Senate. Select Committee
on Presidential Campaign Activities.

WATERGATE AFFAIR, 1972–

Voice Lib.
M1800
WG
0517.01
U.S. Congress. Senate. Select Committee
on Presidential Campaign Activities.
Opening statements at committee hearings.
Pacifica, May 17, 1973.
62 min.   phonotape (1 r.   3 3/4 i.p.s.)
(Watergate gavel to gavel, phase 1)

1. Watergate Affair, 1972–

Watergate gavel to gavel, phase 1: May 17 –
August 7, 1973

Voice Lib.
M1800
U.S. Congress. Senate. Select Committee on Presidential
Campaign Activities.
Watergate gavel to gavel, phase 1: May 17 – August 7, 1973.
Pacifica, May 17 – August 7, 1973.
172 reels (5 in.)   3 3/4 i.p.s.   phonotape.

"These tapes include commentaries by Pacifica's Washington
correspondents and interviews with members of the Senate Committee
taped during recesses of the hearings."

1. Presidents – U.S. – Elections – 1972.   2. Watergate Affair,
1972–   I. Ervin, Samuel James, 1896–   II. Talmadge,
Herman Eugene, 1913–   III. Inouye, Daniel Ken, 1924–
IV. Baker, Howard H., 1925–   V. Gurney, Edward John, 1914–
VI. Weicker, Lowell P., 19   VII. Title.

Waters, Mike
Voice Lib.
M1654-   National Public Radio.
1655   Transcript of conversation between Nixon,
          Dean and Haldeman, read by Linda Wertheimer,
          Bob Edwards, and Mike Waters. NPR, May 1,
          1974.
              1 hr., 40 min. phonotape (2 r.   7 1/2
          i.p.s.)

              1. Watergate Affair, 1972-
          I. Wertheimer, Linda. II. Edwards, Bob.
          III. Waters, Mike.

Voice Lib.
M994   Watrous, Richard B
bd.2   Talks about the National Vocarium, tells
          of his feelings of the past coming to life,
          of his relations with T. R. Roosevelt, P.T.
          Barnum. G.R. Vincent, May 12, 1939.
              1 reel (7 in.)   7 1/2 i.p.s. phonotape.

              1. National Vocarium.

Voice Lib.
M765   Wax, Morty
bd.3   Excerpt from "The anatomy of a hit"
          (Program 9); comments on his role as an
          independent record promoter; also answers
          question whether or not the songs we are
          hearing day after day are being given to us
          against our will. Westinghouse Broadcasting
          Corporation, 1964.
              2 min., 55 sec. phonotape (1 r.   7 1/2 i.p.s.)
          (The music goes round and round)

              1. Music, Popular (Songs, etc.) - Writing & publishing.
          2. Phonorecords.   I. Title: The anatomy of a hit.
          II. Series.

Voice Lib.
M764   Waxman, Frank
bd.4   Excerpt from "Sound Track" (Program 7);
          comments on where the new group of composers
          came from besides Broadway. Westinghouse
          Broadcasting Corporation, 1964.
              1 min., 5 sec. phonotape (1 r.
          7 1/2 i.p.s.) (The music goes round and round)

              1. Music, Popular (Songs, etc.) -
          Writing and publishing. I. Title: Sound
          track. II. Series.

Voice Lib.
M1472   The way it was and the way it is. Fiftieth
          anniversary of radio broadcasting in U.S.
          Voice of America, 1970.
              1 reel (7 in.)   7 1/2 in. per sec.
          phonotape.

              CONTENTS.-Lee De Forest describes Hughes-
          Wilson election; KDKA Harding-Cox election
          broadcast; Harold Arlend, first radio announcer;
          Lowell Thomas reports Lindbergh landing; Herb
          Morrison reports "Hindenberg" crash; H. V. Kalten-
          born, Spanish Civil War broadcast; East Coast
          (Continued on next card)

Voice Lib.
M1472   The way it was and the way it is...   1970.
          (Card 2)

              CONTENTS, cont'd.-power failure bulletins;
          miscellaneous station calls, program excerpts,
          jingles.

              1. Radio.

C1   The way of life - the Mormon story
R16   Whorf, Michael, 1933-
              The way of life - the Mormon story.
              1 tape cassette. (The visual sounds of
          Mike Whorf. Religion, R16)
              Originally presented on his radio program, Kaleidoscope,
          WJR, Detroit.
              Duration: 30 min., 40 sec.
              In the 19th century, Joseph Smith was assassinated in Nauvoo,
          Ill. His successor was Brigham Young, a man who would lead those
          who professed the Mormon faith across hundreds of miles to the
          state of Utah to a religious haven.

              L. Mormons and Mormonism.   L. Title.

C1   We are coming Father Abraham
H68   Whorf, Michael, 1933-
              We are coming Father Abraham; Civil War,
          part 1.
              1 tape cassette. (The visual sounds of
          Mike Whorf. History and heritage, H68)
              Originally presented on his radio program, Kaleidoscope,
          WJR, Detroit.
              Duration: 38 min., 15 sec.
              The beginning of a six-part series on the American Civil War,
          this program emphasizes the why and how it all began, and our
          title comes from Lincoln's call for volunteers to combat an
          aggressive and brave foe.

              L. U.S. - History -   Civil War, 1861-1865.   L. Title.

C1   We don't make much money--but
M9   Whorf, Michael, 1933-
              We don't make much money--but.
              1 tape cassette. (The visual sounds of
          Mike Whorf. Miscellaneous, M9)
              Originally presented on his radio program, Kaleidoscope,
          WJR, Detroit.
              Duration: 35 min.
              A hilarious account of the indiscretions and faux pas of radio
          station WJR's personalities.

              L. WJR (Radio station) Detroit.   L. Title.

C1   We who are about to die
S3   Whorf, Michael, 1933-
              We who are about to die.
              1 tape cassette. (The visual sounds of
          Mike Whorf. Social, S3)

              Originally presented on his radio program, Kaleidoscope,
          WJR, Detroit.
              Duration: 39 min., 30 sec.
              Caught at Stalingrad, 300,000 German soldiers question their
          fathers, wives, mothers, sweethearts, friends and relations as
          they prepare to die, and in their final moments see the utter
          futility of conflict.

              L. Stalingrad, Battle of,   1942-1943.   L. Title.

We'll march to Hell and back again - for
Ulysses Simpson Grant

C1
H110 Whorf, Michael, 1933-
We'll march to Hell and back again - for
Ulysses Simpson Grant.
1 tape cassette. (The visual sounds of
Mike Whorf. History and heritage, H110)
Originally presented on his radio program, Kaleidoscope,
WJR, Detroit.
Duration: 37 min., 30 sec.
This program follows Grant from his humble beginnings in Ohio,
through his education at West Point to the time of his emergence into
greatness as commander of the Union Army.

L. Grant, Ulysses Simpson, Pres. U.S., 1822-1885. L. Title.

WEBSTER, DANIEL, 1782-1852

C1
H74 Whorf, Michael, 1933-
The brilliant orator - Black Dan; Daniel
Webster.
1 tape cassette. (The visual sounds of
Mike Whorf. History and heritage, H74)
Originally presented on his radio program, Kaleidoscope,
WJR, Detroit.
Duration: 37 min., 45 sec.
Here is the life and times of America's brilliant orator,
Daniel Webster, with the emphasis on his deeds and thoughts -
but primarily on his words.

L. Webster, Daniel, 1782-1852. L. Title.

Voice Lib.
544 "We shall overcome: a lyric affirmation of
freedom"; a montage of actual sounds:
speeches, statements, songs. WRVR,
August 28, 1963.
1 reel (7 in.) 7 1/2 in. per sec.
phonotape.

1. Negroes - Civil rights

Voice Lib.
W975 Wedgwood, Josiah Clement Wedgwood, baron,
bd.4   1872-1943.
Speech on land and labour. Rococo-
Can., 1910.
1 reel (7 in.) 7 1/2 in. per sec.
phonotape.

Voice Lib.
545 We shall overcome: a lyric affirmation
bd.1   of freedom.
King, Martin Luther, 1929-1968.
Address at Lincoln Memorial at march on
Washington ceremonies: "I have a dream..."
WRVR, August 28, 1963.
1 reel (7 in.) 7 1/2 in. per sec.
phonotape.

I. We shall overcome: a lyric affirmation
of freedom.

Voice Lib.
M1630 Weidman, Jerome, 1912-
bd.1   Discussing Benny Kramer, his autobiographical
hero of his series of Bronx ghetto novels.
WKAR, April 17, 1974.
30 min. phonotape (1 r. 7 1/2 i.p.s.)

1. Weidman, Jerome, 1913-

Voice Lib.
M1063 Weaver, Robert Clifton, 1907-
bd.2   Address at Symposium of Race Relations
in Chicago under the auspices of the Center
for the Study of Democratic Institutions
entitled, "The Negro as an American".
CSDI, 1963.
1 reel (7 in.) 7 1/2 in. per sec.
phonotape.

1. Negroes.

Weicker, Lowell P., 1931-
Voice Lib.
M1800 U.S. Congress. Senate. Select Committee on Presidential
Campaign Activities.
Watergate gavel to gavel, phase I: May 17 - August 7, 1973.
Pacifica, May 17 - August 7, 1973.
172 reels (5 in.) 3 3/4 i.p.s. phonotape.

"These tapes include commentaries by Pacifica's Washington
correspondents and interviews with members of the Senate Committee
taped during recesses of the hearings."

L. Presidents - U.S. - Elections - 1972. 2. Watergate Affair,
1972-   L. Ervin, Samuel James, 1896-   II. Talmadge,
Herman Eugene, 1913-   III. Inouye, Daniel Ken, 1924-
IV. Baker, Howard H., 1925-   V. Gurney, Edward John, 1914-
VI. Weicker, Lowell P., 19   VII. Title.

Voice Lib.
649 Weber, Joe, 1867-
bd.11- Weber and Fields; two scenes from
12   vaudeville skit by the comedians. VTM,
1906.
1 reel (7 in.) 7 1/2 in. per sec.
phonotape.

CONTENTS.-bd.11. Hypnotic scene.-bd.12.
Mike and Meyer's drinking scene.

I. Fields, Lew, 1897-1941.

Voice Lib.
128 Weill, Kurt, 1900-1950.
bd.1-3 On his own works. Private recording [n.d.]
1 reel (7 in.) 7 1/2 in. per sec.
phonotape.

CONTENTS.-Bd.1. Speak low; bd.2. The Jersey
plunk, and The trouble with women; bd.3. Vary,
very, very, and Wooden wedding.

Weill, Kurt, 1900-1950
Voice Lib.
M955 Lawrence, Gertrude, 1901-1952.
bd.11- Singing selections from album of
14   Ira Gershwin-Kurt Weill musical comedy
"Lady in the dark". RCA, 1938.
    1 reel (7 in.) 7 1/2 in. per sec.
phonotape.

    CONTENTS.-bd.11. "My ship".-bd.12. "Jenny".-
bd.13. "This is new".-bd. 14. "One life to live".

    I. Gershwin, Ira, 1896- II. Weill, Kurt,
1900-1950.

Voice Lib.
M1304 Weinert, Erich, 1890-1953.
bd.12 Poetic reading to Nazi soldiers by
German revolutionary poet Erich Weinert.
Peteler, 1942.
    1 reel (7 in.) 7 1/2 in. per sec.
phonotape.

Weisenfeld, Paul
Voice Lib.
M1607 Brennan, Thomas E., 1929-
bd.2 Off the record. Interviewed by Tim
Skubick, Tom Green, Gary Schuster, and
Paul Weisenfeld. WKAR-TV, January 25, 1974.
    15 min. phonotape (1 r. 7 1/2 in. per
sec.)

    1. Courts - Michigan. I. Skubick, Tim.
II. Green, Tom. III. Schuster, Gary. IV.
Weisenfeld, Paul

Welch, Joseph Nye, 1890-1960
Voice Lib.
M746 U.S. Congress. Senate. Committee on Government Operations.
bd.2   Permanent Subcommittee on Investigations.
    Proceedings of the [1st session] of Senate Army-McCarthy
hearings, April 22, 1954. Testimony by various witnesses
regarding pressure put on the Army to obtain a commission for
Private David Schine. Some of the people speaking are:
Griffin Bancroft, CBS announcer, describing the scenes at the
hearings; Joseph N. Welch, counsel for the Army; Ray Jenkins,
counsel for the subcommittee; Army Secretary Robert Stevens;
General Reber and Senator McClellan of Arkansas. CBS Radio,
April 22, 1954.
    1 reel (7 in.) 7 1/2 in. per sec. phonotape.

    L McCarthy-Army controversy, 1954. L Bancroft, Griffin
II. Welch, Joseph Nye, 1890-1960. III. Jenkins, Ray Howard,
1897-   IV. Stevens, Robert Ten Broeck, 1899-   V.
Reber, Miles   VL McClellan, John Little, 1896-

Welch, Joseph Nye, 1890-1960
Voice Lib.
M1069 U.S. Congress. Senate. Committee on Government Operations.
    Permanent Subcommittee on Investigations.
    Proceedings of the 10th session of Senate Army-McCarthy
hearings, May 5, 1954. Senator McCarthy on witness stand;
debate concerning letter from FBI files; verbal duel between
Counsel Welch and McCarthy; Secretary of Army Stevens
on witness stand. CBS Radio, May 5, 1954.
    1 reel (7 in.) 7 1/2 in. per sec. phonotape.

    L McCarthy-Army controversy, 1954. L McCarthy,
Joseph Raymond, 1909-1957. II. Welch, Joseph Nye, 1890-1960.
III. Stevens, Robert Ten Broeck, 1899-

Welch, Joseph Nye, 1890-1960
Voice Lib.
M1320 U.S. Congress. Senate. Committee on Government Operations.
    Permanent Sub committee on Investigations.
    Proceedings of the 17th session of Senate Army-McCarthy
hearings, May 14, 1954. Sen. Mundt questioning Mr. Adams
about high-level meeting dealing with United Nations. Exchanges
between Senator Mundt and Army Counsel Welch. Senator
McCarthy examining Sen. Dirksen. Discussion of purgery charges
against Carr. Cohn and Adams speak about private dinner party.
CBS TV, May 14, 1954.
    1 reel (7 in.) 7 1/2 in. per sec. phonotape.

    L McCarthy-Army controversy, 1954. L Mundt, Karl Earl,
1900-   II. Welch, Joseph Nye, 1890-1960. III. McCarthy,
Joseph Raymond, 1909-1957. IV. Dirksen, Everett McKinley, 1896-
1969. V. Cohn, Roy M   1927-   VL Adams, John G

Voice Lib.
568- Welles, Orson, 1915-
569   Mercury Theater on the Air: "War of
the Worlds". CBS, October 30, 1938.
    2 reels (7 in.) 7 1/2 in. per sec.
phonotape.

    I. Title: War of the worlds.

Welles, Orson, 1915-
Voice Lib.
M1386 Apollo 11 (space flight): excerpts of old
bd.3 Mercury Theatre "War of the Worlds" of
1938; an interview with Orson Welles by
Mike Wallace. CBS TV, July 20, 1969.
    1 reel (7 in.) 7 1/2 in. per sec.
phonotape.

    L Project Apollo. 2. Space flight to the moon. 3. Aldrin,
Edwin E   1930-   4. Collins, Michael, 1930-
5. Armstrong, Neil, 1930-   L Aldrin, Edwin E   1930-
II. Collins, Michael, 1930-   III. Armstrong, Neil, 1930-
IV. Welles, Orson, 1915-   V. Wallace, Mike, 1918-

Welles, Orson, 1915-
Voice Lib.
M622 Radio in the 1940's (Part III): a series of
bd.1-   excerpts from important broadcasts of the 1940's; a sample
bd.15 of radio of the period. NVL, April, 1964.
    1 reel (7 in.) 7 1/2 in. per sec. phonotape.

    L Radio programs. L Miller, Alton Glenn, 1909(?)-1944. IL
Diles, Ken   III. Wilson, Donald Harlow, 1900-   IV.
Livingstone, Mary   V. Benny, Jack, 1894-   VL Harris,
Phil   VII. Merman, Ethel, 1909-   VIII. Smith, "Wonderful"
IX. Bennett, Richard Dyer   X. Louis, Joe, 1914-   XL
Eisenhower, Dwight David, Pres. U.S., 1890-1969. XIL MacArthur,
Douglas, 1880-1964. XIII. Romulo, Carlos Pena, 1899-   XIV.
Welles, Orson, 1915-   XV. Jackson, Robert Houghwout, 1892-1954.
XVL LaGuardia, Fiorello Henry, 1882-1945. XVII. Nehru, Jawa-
harlal, 1889-1964. XVIII. Gandhi, Mohandas Karamchand, 1869-1948.

Welles, Orson, 1915-
Voice Lib.
M275- Biography in sound (radio program)
276   Alexander Woollcott. N.B.C., date?
bd.1   2 reels (7 in.) 7 1/2 in. per sec.
phonotape.

    L Woollcott, Alexander, 1887-1943. L Woollcott, Alexander,
1887-1943. IL Banghardt, Kenneth   III. Hecht, Ben, 1893-
1964. IV. Roosevelt, Eleanor (Roosevelt) 1884-1962. V. Walker,
Danton   VL Brackett, Charles, 1892-1969. VII. Grant,
Jane   VIII. Rude, Robert Barnes   IX. West,
Rebecca, pseud.   X. Henessy, Joseph   XL Letterer,
Charles   XIL Welles, Orson, 1915-

Welles, Orson, 1915–

Voice Lib.
110   Doyle, Sir Arthur Conan, 1859–1930.
bd.2   The Final Problem, an episode read by
         John Gielgud, Ralph Richardson, and Orson
         Welles. His Master's Voice, 1947.
            1 reel (7 in.)   7 1/2 in. per sec.
         phonotape.

            I. Gielgud, John, 1904–   II. Richardson,
         Ralph David, 1902–   III. Welles, Orson,
         1915–   IV. Title.

Welles, Orson, 1915–

Voice Lib.
M1677   Dracula (radio program)
            Mercury Theatre production of Dracula
         with Orson Welles, George Colouris, and
         Martin Gabel. Ferris State College, 1937.
            55 min.   phonotape (1 r.   7 1/2 i.p.s.)

            I. Welles, Orson, 1915–   II. Colouris,
         George. III. Gabel, Martin, 1912–

Welles, Orson, 1915–

Voice Lib.
M225   Packard, Frederick
            Styles in Shakespearean acting, 1890–1950.
         Creative Associates, 1963?
            1 reel (7 in.)   71/2 i.p.s.   phonotape.

            I. Sothern, Edward Askew, 1826–1881. II. Marlowe,
         Julia, 1865–1950. III. Booth, Edwin, 1833–1893. IV. Gielgud,
         John, 1904–   V. Robeson, Paul Bustill, 1898–   VI. Terry,
         Dame Ellen, 1848–1928. VII. Allen, Viola. VIII. Welles,
         Orson, 1915–   IX. Skinner, Otis, 1858–1942. X. Barrymore,
         John, 1882–1942. XI. Olivier, Sir Laurence Kerr, 1907–
         XII. Forbes-Robertson, Sir Johnston, 1853–   XIII. Evans,
         Maurice. XIV. Thorndike, Dame Sybil, 1882–   XV. Robson,
         Flora. XVI. LeGallienne, Eva, 1899–   XVII. Anderson,
         Judith. XVIII. Duncan, Augustin. XIX. Hampden, Walter.
         XX. Speaight, Robert, 1904–   XXI. Jones, Daniel.

Welles, Orson, 1915–

Voice Lib.
M655   The Twentieth Century (TV program)
bd.1   "The creative thirties", narrated by
         Walter Cronkite. CBS, 1963.
            25 min.   phonotape (1 r.   7 1/2 i.p.s.)

            I. U.S. - Civilization - 1918–1945. I. Bowes, Edward,
         1874–1946. II. Geisman, Maxwell David, 1909–
         III. MacDonald, Dwight, 1906–   IV. Welles, Orson, 1915–
         V. Cronkite, Walter Leland, 1916–   VI. Gable, Clark, 1901–
         1960. VII. Lewis, Sinclair, 1885–1951. VIII. Houseman,
         John, 1902–   IX. Roosevelt, Franklin Delano, Pres. U.S.,
         1882–1945.

WELLINGTON, ARTHUR WELLESLEY, 1st DUKE OF,
            1769–1852

C1
H62   Whorf, Michael, 1933–
            The iron duke - Wellington.
            1 tape cassette.   (The visual sounds of
         Mike Whorf. History and heritage, H62)

            Originally presented on his radio program, Kaleidoscope,
         WJR, Detroit.
            Duration: 38 min., 50 sec.
            His military genius, the ability to persevere with his raw and
         untrained recruits, and his unquestioned courage in adversity
         turned the tide against the Corsican, and earned Wellington his
         place as one of England's foremost national heroes.

            I. Wellington, Arthur Wellesley, 1st duke of, 1769–1852.
         I. Title.

C1
H24   The Wells Fargo

         Whorf, Michael, 1933–
            The Wells Fargo.
            1 tape cassette.   (The visual sounds of
         Mike Whorf. History and heritage, H24)
            Originally presented on his radio program, Kaleidoscope,
         WJR, Detroit.
            Duration: 27 min., 30 sec.
            The long, lonely rides across a continent, bringing news and
         passengers to the frontier and over the wilderness to California.
         This was the job of Wells Fargo, facing Indians, desperadoes and
         the elements; this narrative strives to describe life in the old west.

            I. Wells, Fargo and Company. I. Title.

C1
H24   WELLS, FARGO AND COMPANY

         Whorf, Michael, 1933–
            The Wells Fargo.
            1 tape cassette.   (The visual sounds of
         Mike Whorf. History and heritage, H24)
            Originally presented on his radio program, Kaleidoscope,
         WJR, Detroit.
            Duration: 27 min., 30 sec.
            The long, lonely rides across a continent, bringing news and
         passengers to the frontier and over the wilderness to California.
         This was the job of Wells Fargo, facing Indians, desperadoes and
         the elements; this narrative strives to describe life in the old west.

            I. Wells, Fargo and Company. I. Title.

Wertheimer, Linda

Voice Lib.
M1654–   National Public Radio.
1655   Transcript of conversation between Nixon,
         Dean and Haldeman, read by Linda Wertheimer,
         Bob Edwards, and Mike Waters. NPR, May 1,
         1974.
            1 hr., 40 min.   phonotape (2 r.   7 1/2
         i.p.s.)

            1. Watergate Affair, 1972–
         I. Wertheimer, Linda. II. Edwards, Bob.
         III. Waters, Mike.

WESLEY, CHARLES, 1707–1788

C1
R19   Whorf, Michael, 1933–
            Founder of Methodism
            1 tape cassette.   (The visual sounds of
         Mike Whorf. Religion, R19)

            Originally presented on his radio program, Kaleidoscope,
         WJR, Detroit.
            Duration: 42 min., 30 sec.
            The founders of a new Christian denomination, beset upon by
         turmoil and frustration, yet John and Charles Wesley lived to see
         a new age in spirituality.

            I. Wesley, John, 1703–   2. Wesley, Charles, 1707–1788.
         I. Title.

WESLEY, JOHN, 1703–1791

C1
R19   Whorf, Michael, 1933–
            Founder of Methodism
            1 tape cassette.   (The visual sounds of
         Mike Whorf. Religion, R19)

            Originally presented on his radio program, Kaleidoscope,
         WJR, Detroit.
            Duration: 42 min., 30 sec.
            The founders of a new Christian denomination, beset upon by
         turmoil and frustration, yet John and Charles Wesley lived to see
         a new age in spirituality.

            I. Wesley, John, 1703–   2. Wesley, Charles, 1707–1788.
         I. Title.

Voice Lib.
664 West, Austin
bd.2   Reading his own poetry: poem dedicated
to Irene Harvey, widow of the Commander of
the U.S.S."Thresher". Author's contribution,
1964.
1 reel (7 in.)   7 1/2 in. per sec.
phonotape.

Voice Lib.   West, Mae, 1893-
M619 Radio in the 1930's (Part II): a series of
bd.1-   excerpts of the 1930's; a sample of radio
14   of the period. NVL, April, 1964.
1 reel (7 in.)   7 1/2 in. per sec.   phonotape.
L. Allen, Fred, 1.894-1956. II. Delmar, Kenny   III. Donald,
Peter   IV. Pious, Minerva   V. Fennelly, Parker   VI.
Boyer, Charles, 1899-   VII. Dunne, Irene, 1904-   VIII.
DeMille, Cecil Blount, 1881-1959. IX. West, Mae, 1893-   X.
Dafoe, Allan Ray, 1883-1943. XI. Dionne quintuplets.   XII. Ortega,
Santos   XIII. War of the worlds (radio program)   XIV. Ives, Burl,
1909-   XV. Robinson, Earl, 1910-   XVI. Temple, Shirley,
1928-   XVII. Earhart, Amelia, 1898-1937. XVIII. Lawrence,
Gertrude, 1901-1952. XIX. Cohan, George Michael, 1878-1942.
XX. Shaw, George Bernard, 1856-1950. XXI. Hitler, Adolf, 1889-
1945. XXII. Chamberlain, Neville, 1869-1940. XXIII. Roosevelt,
Franklin Delano, Pres. U.S., 1882-1945.

Voice Lib.
608 West, James Edward, 1876-
bd.2   Boy Scouts of America; comments during
27th Boy Scout Anniversary Week, describes
Boy Scout Jamboree in Washington, D.C., what
scouting stands for, future accomplishments,
presents Boy Scout statue to Fred Waring.
New York City, WABC (CBS), February 11, 1937.
1 reel (7 in.)   7 1/2 in. per sec.
phonotape.

1. Boy Scouts of America.

WEST, MAE, 1893-
Voice Lib.
M1743 Raft, George
bd.2   Reminisce on the Mike Douglas Show.
WILX-TV, June 27, 1974.
10 min.   phonotape (1 r.   7 1/2 i.p.s.)

L. Raft, George.   2. O'Brien, Pat, 1899-   3. Muni,
Paul, 1895-1967. 4. Crawford, Joan, 1908-   5. West, Mae,
1893-   6. Richman, Harry. 7. Entertainers - U. S.   L.
Douglas, Mike, 1925-

Voice Lib.
M1026 West, Mae, 1893-
bd.2   "Adam and Eve"; skit written by Arch
Oboler, from Charlie McCarthy radio program.
NBC, December 12, 1937.
1 reel (7 in.)   7 1/2 in. per sec.
phonotape.

I. Oboler, Arch, 1907-

West, Rebecca, pseud.
Voice Lib.
M275- Biography in sound (radio program)
276   Alexander Woollcott. N.B.C., date?
bd.1   2 reels (7 in.)   7 1/2 in. per sec.
phonotape.
L. Woollcott, Alexander, 1887-1943. L. Woollcott, Alexander,
1887-1943. II. Banghardt, Kenneth   III. Hecht, Ben, 1893-
1964. IV. Roosevelt, Eleanor (Roosevelt) 1884-1962. V. Walker,
Danton   VI. Brackett, Charles, 1892-1969. VII. Grant,
Jane   VIII. Rude, Robert Barnes   IX. West,
Rebecca, pseud.   X. Henessy, Joseph   XI. Letterer,
Charles   XII. Welles, Orson, 1915-

Voice Lib.
M937 West, Mae, 1893-
bd.2-   Singing various specialty musical selections.
938   Proscenium Records, 1940.
bd.1   2 reels (7 in.)   7 1/2 in. per sec.
phonotape.

CONTENTS.-"Frankie and Johnny", "My Man
Friday", "Page 54", "That's All, Brother",
"Pardon Me for Loving and Running", "Put
It Off Until Tomorrow", "Slow Down", "Come
Up and See Me Sometime".

Voice Lib.
M1202 Westmoreland, William Childs, 1914-
bd.1   Report to joint session of U.S. Congress
on status of war in Vietnam. Commentary by
Robert Goralski. NBC-TV, April 28, 1967.
1 reel (7 in.)   7 1/2 in. per sec.
phonotape.

1. Vietnamese Conflict, 1961-   - U.S.
I. Goralski, Robert

Voice Lib.
352 West, Mae, 1893-
bd.10   On her return to Broadway in the
recreation of "Diamond Lil;" her
favorite kind of man. NBC, 1949.
1 reel (7 in.)   7 1/2 in. per sec.
phonotape.

Voice Lib.
M293 Whalen, Grover Aloysius, 1886-1962.
First ticket sale to 1939 World's Fair,
Flushing Meadows, Long Island, New York.
Mr. Whalen, president of New York World's
Fair Committee and New York's official
welcomer, sells first ticket book to F. H.
LaGuardia, Mayor of New York. WNYC Radio,
February 23, 1939.
1 reel (7 in.)   7 1/2 i.p.s.   phonotape.

L. New York. World's Fair, 1939-1940. I. LaGuardia,
Fiorello Henry, 1882-1947

WHALING

C1
H31   Whorf, Michael, 1933-
          Thar' she blows.
          1 tape cassette. (The visual sounds of
        Mike Whorf. History and heritage, H31)

          Originally presented on his radio program, Kaleidoscope,
        WJR, Detroit.
          Duration: 43 min.
          Comes the leviathan of the deep - the story of whaling as it
        was lived by those who sailed the great sailing ships.

          I. Whaling. I. Title.

Voice Lib.
M1433   Wharton, Clifton Reginald, 1926-
bd.2   Press conference after being appointed
        President of Michigan State University.
        October 24, 1969.
          1 reel (7 in.)   7 1/2 in. per sec.
        phonotape.

Voice Lib.
M1565- Wharton, Clifton Reginald, 1926-
1566,   The perspectives of four major constituen-
bd.1   cies: faculty, student, administrative, and
        legislative perspectives; state of the
        university address. WKAR, February 14, 1974.
          40 min. phonotape (2 r.   7 1/2 in. per
        sec.)

          I. Title.

        Wharton, Clifton Reginald, 1926-
Voice Lib.
M1700   Borlaug, Norman Ernst, 1914-
            The green revolution; its genesis, impact,
        dangers & hope. Includes awarding of
        honorary D.Sc. degree from Michigan State
        University and introduction by President
        Wharton. WKAR, May 12, 1971.
          50 min. phonotape (1 r.   7 1/2 i.p.s.)

          1. Population. I. Muelder, Milton E.
        II. Wharton, Clifton Reginald, 1926-

        Wharton, Clifton Reginald, 1926-
Voice Lib.
M1590   Fleming, Robben Wright, 1916-
            Who am I; commencement address, Michigan
        State University winter term 1974.
        Introduction by President Clifton Wharton.
        WKAR-AM, March 10, 1974.
          20 min.   phonotape (1 r.   7 1/2 i.p.s.)

          I. Wharton, Clifton Reginald, 1926-

Voice Lib. Wharton, Clifton Reginald, 1926-
M1689   Nelson, Gaylord, 1916-
            Man, the endangered species; address at
        Michigan State University. Introduction by
        President Wharton. WKAR, January 19, 1970.
          41 min. phonotape (1 r.   7 1/2 i.p.s.)

          1. Water - Pollution. 2. Ecology.
        I. Wharton, Clifton Reginald, 1926-

        What all the screaming's about
Voice Lib.
M760   Aberbach, Jean
bd.7   Excerpt from "What All the Screaming's
        About" (Program 1); the real reason for the
        success of Elvis Presley and the Beatles.
        Westinghouse Broadcasting Corporation, 1964.
          1 min. phonotape (1 r.   7 1/2 i.p.s.)
        (The music goes round and round)

          1. Music, Popular (Songs, etc.) - U.S.
        2. Presley, Elvis Aron, 1935- 3. The
        Beatles. I. Title: What all the screaming's
        about. II. Series.

        What all the screaming's about
Voice Lib.
M760   Goldmark, Goldie
bd.2   Excerpt from "What All the Screaming's
        About" (Program 1); Beatle music is actually
        nothing new. Westinghouse Broadcasting
        Corporation, 1964.
          23 sec. phonotape (1 r.   7 1/2 i.p.s.)
        (The music goes round and round)

          1. Music, Popular (Songs, etc.) I. Title:
        What all the screaming's about. II. Series.

        What all the screaming's about
Voice Lib.
M760   Kellem, Manny
bd.4   Excerpt from "What All the Screaming's
        About" (Program 1); promotion of the Beatles,
        including remarks by teenaged girls of their
        feelings toward the new singing group called
        the Beatles. Westinghouse Broadcasting
        Corporation, 1964.
          1 reel (7 in.)   7 1/2 in. per sec.
        phonotape. (The Music Goes Round and Round)

          I. Title: What all the screaming's about.
        II. Series.

        What all the screaming's about
Voice Lib.
M760   Levy, Leonard
bd.1   Excerpt from "What All the Screaming's
        About" (Program 1); discusses the effect
        of Beatle music on adolescents. Westing-
        house Broadcasting Corporation, 1964.
          1 reel (7 in.)   7 1/2 in. per sec.
        phonotape. (The Music Goes Round and Round)

          I. Title: What all the screaming's about.
        II. Series.

What all the screaming's about

Voice Lib.
M760   Mann, Arthur
bd.3   Excerpt from "What All The Screaming's
        About" (Program 1); English-based music
        of Beatles; what serious musicians find
        interesting about the music of the Beatles.
        Westinghouse Broadcasting Corporation, 1964.
            1 reel (7 in.)   7 1/2 in. per sec.
        phonotape.   (The Music Goes Round and Round)

            1. The Beatles.   I. Title: What all the
        screaming's about.   II. Series.

What all the screaming's about

Voice Lib.
M760   Schimmel, John L
bd.5   Excerpt from "What All the Screaming's
        About" (Program 1); psychiatrist's approach
        to Beatlemania and its effects on teenage
        girls.   Westinghouse Broadcasting Corporation,
        1964.
            1 reel (7 in.)   7 1/2 in. per sec.
        phonotape.   (The Music Goes Round and Round)

            I. Title: What all the screaming's about.
        II. Series.

What all the screaming's about

Voice Lib.
M760   Sholes, Steven H   1911-1968.
bd.6   Excerpt from "What all the screaming's
        about (Program 1); Elvis' progress to fame
        and fortune, including one of his first hits,
        "That's all right"; a comparison is made
        between Elvis and the Beatles.   Westinghouse
        Broadcasting Corporation, 1964.
            8 min., 6 sec.   phonotape (1 r.   7 1/2 i. p. s.)   (The
        music goes round and round)

            1. Presley, Elvis Aron, 1935-   2. Music, Popular (Songs,
        etc.) - U. S.   1. Title: What all the screaming's about.   II.
        Series.

What all the screaming's about

Voice Lib.
M760   Stoller, Mike
bd.8   Excerpt from "What all the screaming's
        about" (Program 1); anything Elvis had sung
        at the peak of his career would have been
        popular.   Westinghouse Broadcasting
        Corporation, 1964.
            9 sec.   phonotape (1 r.   7 1/2 i.p.s.)
        (The music goes round and round)

            1. Presley, Elvis Aron, 1935-   2. Music, Popular (Songs,
        etc.) - U. S.   1. Title: What all the screaming's about.
        II. Series.

What are you going to do to help the
                                boys?

Voice Lib.
M1206   Popular American patriotic song of World War I
bd.5   entitled "What are you going to do to help
        the boys?" (Gus Kahn-Egbert Van Alstyne)
        Sung by Charles Hart.   Victor, 1917.
            1 reel (7 in.)   7 1/2 in. per sec.
        phonotape.

            I. Hart, Charles   II. Title:
        What are you going to do to help the boys?

What is it like to be crippled?

Voice Lib.
M1592   Stigma I.
            What is it like to be crippled?
        Center for Independent Living, University
        of California at Berkeley, 1973.
            25 min.   phonotape (1 r.   7 1/2 i.n.s.)

            1. Physically handicapped.   I. Title.

What makes you laugh

C1
S4   Whorf, Michael, 1933-
            What makes you laugh.
            1 tape cassette.   (The visual sounds of
        Mike Whorf.   Social, S4)

            Originally presented on his radio program, Kaleidoscope,
        WJR, Detroit.
            Duration: 34 min.
            Philosophers have stated that laughter is the fireworks of the
        soul, yet laughter is peculiar, for man is the only creature who
        laughs.

            1. Laughter.   1. Title.

Whatever happened to Tin Pan Alley?

Voice Lib.
M761   Gorney, Jay
bd.6   Excerpt from "Whatever happened to Tin Pan
        Alley" (Program 3); comments on methods of
        Max Dreyfus to get great artists to sing his
        songs; also the publisher's degradation from
        a play of creativity to merely a messenger boy.
        Westinghouse Broadcasting Corporation, 1964.
            3 min., 54 sec.   phonotape (1 r.   7 1/2 i. p. s.)
        (The music goes round and round)

            1. Music, Popular (Songs, etc.) - Writing and publishing.
        1. Title: Whatever happened to Tin Pan Alley?   II. Series.

Whatever happened to Tin Pan Alley?

Voice Lib.
M761   Marks, Herbert E
bd.1   Excerpt from "Whatever Happened to Tin Pan
        Alley?" (Program 3); comments on rise of
        Tin Pan Alley and the popularity of records.
        Westinghouse Broadcasting Corporation, 1964.
            1 reel (7 in.)   7 1/2 in. per sec.
        phonotape.   (The Music Goes Round and Round)

            I. Title: Whatever happened to Tin Pan Alley?
        II. Series.

Whatever happened to Tin Pan Alley?

Voice Lib.
M761   Meyer, Joseph
bd.7   Excerpt from "Whatever happened to Tin Pan
        Alley?" (Program 3); relates how he got Al Jolson to introduce
        his song "California here I come", including Al Jolson singing
        this song.   Westinghouse Broadcasting Corporation, 1964.
            1 reel (7 in.)   7 1/2 in. per sec.   phonotape.   (The music
        goes round and round)

            1. Music, Popular (Songs, etc.) - U.S.   1. Jolson, Al, 1886-
        1950.   II. Title: Whatever happened to Tin Pan Alley?
        III. Series.

Voice Lib.   Whatever happened to Tin Pan Alley?
M761   Olman, Abe
bd.3   Excerpt from "Whatever Happened to Tin Pan Alley?" (Program 3); composed "Down Among the Sheltering Palms" and "Oh, Johnny, Oh"; comments on how he went about plugging songs. Westinghouse Broadcasting Corporation, 1964.
    1 reel (7 in.)   7 1/2 in. per sec. phonotape. (The Music Goes Round and Round)

    I. Title: Whatever happened to Tin Pan Alley? II. Series.

Voice Lib.   Whatever happened to Tin Pan Alley?
M761   Ruby, Harry
bd.2   Excerpt from "Whatever Happened to Tin Pan Alley?" (Program 3); comments on how he plugged his songs and others. Westinghouse Broadcasting Corporation, 1964.
    1 reel (7 in.)   7 1/2 in. per sec. phonotape. (The Music Goes Round and Round)

    I. Title: Whatever happened to Tin Pan Alley? II. Series.

Whatever happened to Tin Pan Alley?
Voice Lib.
M761   Spaeth, Sigmund, 1885-1965.
bd.8   Excerpt from "Whatever Happened to Tin Pan Alley?" (Program 3); comments on the replacement of pianos with records. Westinghouse Broadcasting Corporation, 1964.
    1 reel (7 in.)   7 1/2 in. per sec. phonotape. (The Music Goes Round and Round)

    I. Title: Whatever happened to Tin Pan Alley? II. Series.

Whatever happened to Tin Pan Alley?
Voice Lib.
M761   Tobias, Charlie
bd.4   Excerpt from "Whatever happened to Tin Pan Alley?" (Program 3); tells about his direct method of plugging songs. Westinghouse Broadcasting Corporation, 1964.
    53 sec. phonotape (1 r. 7 1/2 i.p.s.) (The music goes round and round)

    1. Music, Popular (Songs, etc.) - U.S.
I. Title: Whatever happened to Tin Pan Alley? II. Series.

Whatever happened to Tin Pan Alley?
Voice Lib.
M761   Whitmark, Julius
bd.5   Excerpt from "Whatever happened to Tin Pan Alley?" (Program 3); comments on importance of vaudeville artist in popularizing songs in the days before radio. Westinghouse Broadcasting Corporation, 1964.
    1 min., 35 sec. phonotape (1 r. 7 1/2 i.p.s.) (The music goes round and round)

    1. Music, Popular (Songs, etc.) - U.S.
I. Title: Whatever happened to Tin Pan Alley? II. Series.

WHEAT
C1
S25   Whorf, Michael, 1933-
    The staff of life.
    1 tape cassette. (The visual sounds of Mike Whorf. Social, S25)
    Originally presented on his radio program, Kaleidoscope, WJR, Detroit.
    Duration: 41 min.
    This is the story of wheat, of bread, its impact on mankind, where and how it is processed and utilized.

    1. Wheat. 2. Bread. L. Title.

WHEATLEY, PHILLIS, AFTERWARDS PHILLIS PETERS, 1753?-1784
C1
S32   Whorf, Michael, 1933-
    Heroes come in many colors, part 2; the life of Phyllis Wheatly.
    1 tape cassette. (The visual sounds of Mike Whorf. Social, S32)
    Originally presented on his radio program, Kaleidoscope, WJR, Detroit.
    Duration: 31 min., 20 sec.
    A gentle, frail, quiet girl who grew up in a Caucasion world and from the love she was given, expressed her inner feelings in the form of poetry. She was one of the first of her race to bring to the western world a genuine, artistic talent.

    1. Wheatley, Phillis, afterwards Phillis Peters, 1753?-1784. L. Title.

When the grown-up ladies act like babies
Voice Lib.
M946   Jolson, Al, 1886-1950.
bd.4   Singing "When the Grown-Up Ladies Act Like Babies" (novelty pop song). Col. Phono., 1920.
    1 reel (7 in.)   7 1/2 in. per sec. phonotape.

    I. Title: When the grown-up ladies act like babies.

When the moon comes over the mountain
Voice Lib.
M160   Smith, Kate, 1909-
bd.4   Singing her theme song "When the Moon Comes Over the Mountain", and remarks by Kate Smith at Carnegie Hall, New York. RCA, November 2, 1963.
    1 reel (7 in.)   7 1/2 in. per sec. phonotape.

    I. Title: When the moon comes over the mountain.

When vaudeville was king
C1
M5   Whorf, Michael, 1933-
    When vaudeville was king.
    1 tape cassette. (The visual sounds of Mike Whorf. Miscellaneous, M5)
    Originally presented on his radio program, Kaleidoscope, WJR, Detroit.
    Duration: 40 min.
    The Keith circuit, The Tony Pastor Music Hall, the Palace; the curtain would rise of this great age of show business when vaudeville was the rage.

    1. Vaudeville. L. Title.

"Where we stand in Vietnam"
Voice Lib.
M913-   Collingwood, Charles Cummings, 1917-
914   "Where we stand in Vietnam"; CBS Reports pro-
bd.1   gram. Various CBS news correspondents discussing
        current situation of the war in Vietnam,
        including Peter Kalisher, Eric Sevareid, Marvin
        Kalb, Roger Mudd, Harry Reasner, and British
        correspondent James Cameron.   CBS-TV,
        December 14, 1964.
            2 reels (7 in1)   7 1/2 in. per sec.
        phonotape.
            1. Vietnamese Conflict, 1961-   - U.S.
        I. Title.

Voice Lib.
M773   White, Edward Higgins, 1930-1967.
bd.1   Ceremonies at University of Michigan
        presenting McDivitt and himself with Doctorate
        degrees, presentation to Colonel White of
        Doctor of Astronomical Science and remarks
        by Colonel White.   Ann Arbor, WUOM, June 15,
        1965.
            1 reel (7 in.)   7 1/2 in. per sec.
        phonotape.

Wherry, Kenneth Spicer, 1892-1951
Voice Lib.
381-   I can hear it now (radio program)
382   CBS, April 26, 1951.
bd.1   2 reels (7 in.) 7 1/2 in. per sec. phonotape.
            1. Radio Free Europe. 2. Strategic Air Command. L
        Ridgway, Matthew Bunker, 1895-   IL Churchill, Winston Leonard
        Spencer, 1874-1965. IIL Bevan, Aneurin, 1897-1960. IV. Nixon,
        Richard Milhous, Pres. U. S., 1913-   V. Kerr, Robert Samuel, 1896-
        1963. VL Brewster, Ralph Owen, 1888-1962. VIL Wherry, Kenneth
        Spicer, 1892-195L VIIL Capehart, Homer Earl, 1897-   IX.
        Lehman, Herbert Henry, 1878-1963. X. Taft, Robert Alphonso,
        1889-1953. XL Moody, Arthur Edson Blair, 1902-1954. XIL
        Martin, Joseph William, 1884-1968. XIII. McMahon, James O'Brien,
        1903-1952. XIV. MacArthur, Douglas, 1880-1964. XVII. Wilson,
        Charles Edward, 1886-197?.   IIL Irvine, Clarence T

WHITE, EDWARD HIGGINS, 1930-1967
Voice Lib.
M1030   Huntley, Chet, 1911-1974.
bd.1   Description by Chet Huntley of funeral
        services at burial of astronauts Virgil
        Grissom and Roger Chaffee at Arlington
        Cemetery and of Edward White at West Point,
        New York.   NBC-TV, January 31, 1967.
            1 reel (7 in.)   7 1/2 in. per sec. phonotape.
            L Grissom, Virgil Ivan, 1926-1967. 2. White, Edward
        Higgins, 1930-1967. 3. Chaffee, Roger B., 1936-1967.

White, Edward Higgins, 1930-1967
Voice Lib.
M771   Gemini 4 (space flight): excerpts of descrip-
bd.1   tion of take-off; Gemini 4 and Gemini Control
        announcements.   June 3, 1965.
            1 reel (7 in.)   7 1/2 in. per sec.
        phonotape.

            1. Project Gemini. 2. McDivitt, James Alton,
        1929-   3. White, Edward Higgins, 1930-1967.
        I. McDivitt, James Alton, 1929-   II. White,
        Edward Higgins, 1930-1967.

Voice Lib.
M955   White, Francis
bd.15-   Singing selections from Raymond Hitchcock's
bd.16   show "Hitchy-Koo."   V.T.M., 1922.
            1 reel (7 in.)   7 1/2 in. per sec.
        phonotape.

            CONTENTS.-bd.15. "Six times six is thirty-
        six."-bd.16. "M.I.S.S.I.S.S.I.P.P.I."

White, Edward Higgins, 1930-1967
Voice Lib.
M771   Gemini 4 (space flight): excerpts of announce-
bd.2   ments from NBC reporters and Gemini Control,
        regarding preparations for and the actual
        splashdown. Conversation with astronauts
        before pickup by helicopter. Dallas Townsend
        from carrier "Wasp" and David Brinkley and
        Chet Huntley for NBC.   NBC TV, June 7, 1965.
            1 reel (7 in.)   7 1/2 in. per sec. phonotape.
            L Project Gemini. 2. McDivitt, James Alton, 1929-   3.
        White, Edward Higgins, 1930-1967. L McDivitt, James Alton,
        1929-   II. White, Edward Higgins, 1930-1967. IIL Townsend,
        Dallas. IV. Brinkley, David McClure, 1920-   V. Huntley,
        Chet, 1911-1974.

White, Jack
Voice Lib.
385   I can hear it now (radio program)
        CBS, February 2, 1951.
            1 reel (7 in.)   7 1/2 in. per sec.
        phonotape.

            I. Austin, Warren Robinson, 1877-1962.   II.
        Pandit, Vijaya Lakshmi (Nehru) 1900-   III.
        Roosevelt, Eleanor (Roosevelt) 1884-1962. IV.
        Morse, Wayne Lyman, 1900-   V. Chandler,
        Albert Benjamin, 1898-   VI. Taylor, Telford,
        1908-   VII. Wh , Jack.

Voice Lib.   **White, Edward Higgins, 1930-1967**
M772   Gemini 4 (space flight): pickup of astronauts
bd.1   McDivitt and White and the capsule, described
        by Chet Huntley and David Brinkley. NBC TV,
        June 7, 1965.
            1 reel (7 in.)   7 1/2 in. per sec.
        phonotape.

            1. Project Gemini. 2. McDivitt, James Alton,
        1929-   3. White, Edward Higgins, 1930-1967.
        I. McDivitt, James Alton, 1929-   II. White,
        Edward Higgins, 1930-1967. III. Huntley, Chet,
        1911-1974 IV. Brinkley, David McClure, 1920-

Voice Lib.
589   White, Josh, 1908-1969.
bd.3   Sings Australian war song "Waltzing
        Matilda". V-Disc, 1944.
            1 reel (7 in.)   7 1/2 in. per sec.
        phonotape.

            I. Title: Waltzing Matilda.

Voice Lib.
M258   White, Lincoln
bd.16   Press conference at the White House on the
recall of the chief U.S. negotiator from
the test ban talks in Geneva. New York,
CBS, June 20, 1961.
1 reel (7 in.)   7 1/2 in. per sec.
phonotape.

1. Atomic power - International control.

Voice Lib.   White, Paul Welrose, 1902-1955
M1041   Behind the scenes in the CBS newsroom; CBS
bd.2   radio news with Elmer Davis, Edward R.
Murrow and Paul White, describing the
operations of radio news broadcasting.
CBS Radio, June 1, 1941.
1 reel (7 in.)   7 1/2 i.p.s.   phonotape.

1. Radio journalism.   I. Davis, Elmer
Holmes, 1890-1958. II. Murrow, Edward
Roscoe, 1908-1965. III. White, Paul Welrose,
1902-1955.

White, Theodore Harold, 1915-
The making of the president, 1964
Voice Lib.
M846   The Making of the President, 1964 (TV program)
bd.2   Excerpts of political speeches and statements by presidential candidates Lyndon
Johnson and Barry Goldwater, from TV dramatization of Theodore H. White's book "The
making of the president, 1964".
6 min.   phonotape (1 r.   7 1/2 i.p.s.)

1. Johnson, Lyndon Baines, Pres. U.S., 1908-1973.
II. Goldwater, Barry Morris, 1909-   III. White, Theodore
Harold, 1915- /The making of the president, 1964.

Voice Lib.   White, William Allen, 1868-1944
M574   I can hear it now (radio program)
bd.2-   1919-1933.   CBS, 1953.
575   2 reels (7 in.)   7 1/2 in. per sec.
phonotape.

I. Murrow, Edward Roscoe, 1908-1965. II.
Rogers, Will, 1879-1935. III. White, William
Allen, 1868-1944. IV. Hoover, Herbert Clarke,
Pres. U.S., 1874-1964. V. Roosevelt, Franklin
Delano, Pres. U.S., 1882-1945. VI. Rice,
Grantland, 1880-1954. VII. McNamee, Graham,
1888-1942.

Voice Lib.
M763   Whiteman, Paul, 1890-1967.
bd.5   Excerpt from "The Scope of Jazz" (Program
6); comments on Bing Crosby at the beginning
of his career, including song by Crosby,
"Pennies from Heaven." Westinghouse
Broadcasting Corporation, 1964.
1 reel (7 in.)   7 1/2 in. per sec.
phonotape.   (The Music Goes Round and Round)

1. Crosby, Bing, 1901-   I. Title: The
scope of jazz. II. Series.   2. Jazz music.

Voice Lib.
M764   Whiteman, Paul, 1890-1967.
bd.8   Excerpt from "The World of Wax" (Program 8);
comments on how the recording was accomplished;
including music "Whispering". Westinghouse
Broadcasting Corporation, 1964.
1 reel (7 in.)   7 1/2 in. per sec.
phonotape.   (The Music Goes Round and Round)

1. Phonorecords
I. Title: The world of wax. II. Series.

C1
FA8   WHITMAN, MARCUS, 1802-1847
Whorf, Michael, 1933-
The Whitmans.
1 tape cassette.   (The visual sounds of
Mike Whorf. The forgotten American, FA8)
Originally presented on his radio program, Kaleidoscope,
WJR, Detroit.
Duration: 14 min., 20 sec.
Leaving their homes in the East, the Whitmans built a
mission in the Oregon country. Their deaths at the hands of
the Indians gave impetus to the creation of the Oregon Territory.
1. Whitman, Marcus, 1802-1847. 2. Whitman, Narcissa
(Prentiss) 1808-1847. I. Title.

C1
FA8   WHITMAN, NARCISSA (PRENTISS) 1808-1847
Whorf, Michael, 1933-
The Whitmans.
1 tape cassette.   (The visual sounds of
Mike Whorf. The forgotten American, FA8)
Originally presented on his radio program, Kaleidoscope,
WJR, Detroit.
Duration: 14 min., 20 sec.
Leaving their homes in the East, the Whitmans built a
mission in the Oregon country. Their deaths at the hands of
the Indians gave impetus to the creation of the Oregon Territory.
1. Whitman, Marcus, 1802-1847. 2. Whitman, Narcissa
(Prentiss) 1808-1847. I. Title.

Whitman, Walt, 1819-1892.
When lilacs last in the door-yard bloom'd
Voice Lib.
M310   American Broadcasting Company.
Tribute to President John Fitzgerald Kennedy
from the arts. Fredric March emcees; Jerome
Hines sings "Worship of God and Nature" by
Beethoven; Florence Eldridge recites "When
lilacs last in the door-yard bloom'd" by Walt
Whitman; Marian Anderson in two songs. Include:
Charlton Heston, Sidney Blackmer, Isaac Stern,
Nathan Milstein, Christopher Plummer, Albert
Finney. ABC, November 24, 1963.
55 min.   phonotape (7 in.   7 1/2 i.p.s.)

 (Continued on next card)

C1
A44   WHITMAN, WALT, 1819-1892
Whorf, Michael, 1933-
The poet of democracy - Walt Whitman.
1 tape cassette.   (The visual sounds of
Mike Whorf. Art, music and letters, A44)
Originally presented on his radio program, Kaleidoscope,
WJR, Detroit.
Duration: 37 min.
The likeable, candid Whitman has become the poet of
America. During his life he strived for freedom; for the
country, for his poetry.
1. Whitman, Walt, 1819-1892. I. Title.

C1
FA8
    The Whitmans
Whorf, Michael, 1933–
        The Whitmans.
    1 tape cassette. (The visual sounds of
Mike Whorf. The forgotten American, FA8)
        Originally presented on his radio program, Kaleidoscope,
WJR, Detroit.
        Duration: 18 min., 20 sec.
        Leaving their homes in the East, the Whitmans built a
mission in the Oregon country. Their deaths at the hands of
the Indians gave impetus to the creation of the Oregon Territory.

        1. Whitman, Marcus, 1802–1847. 2. Whitman, Narcissa
(Prentiss) 1808–1847. I. Title.

C1
H36
Whorf, Michael, 1933–
        The admiral – John Paul Jones.
    1 tape cassette. (The visual sounds of
Mike Whorf. History and heritage, H36)
        Originally presented on his radio program, Kaleidoscope,
WJR, Detroit.
        Duration: 38 min., 30 sec.
        He was a revolutionary – from his trials and hardships as a
young Scotsman to his days as the admiral of a brave, young,
inexperienced navy.

        1. Jones, John Paul, 1747–1792. I. Title.

                                        OFFICIAL

Voice Lib.
N761
bd.5   Whitmark, Julius
        Excerpt from "Whatever happened to Tin Pan
Alley?" (Program 3); comments on importance
of vaudeville artist in popularizing songs
in the days before radio. Westinghouse
Broadcasting Corporation, 1964.
        1 min., 35 sec. phonotape (1 r. 7 1/2
i.p.s.) (The music goes round and round)

        1. Music, Popular (Songs, etc.) – U.S.
I. Title: Whatever happened to Tin Pan Alley?
II. Series.

C1
S20
Whorf, Michael, 1933–
        The adolescent years.
    1 tape cassette. (The visual sounds of
Mike Whorf. Social, S20)
        Originally presented on his radio program, Kaleidoscope,
WJR, Detroit.
        Duration: 43 min.
        With rich harmonies of those wonderful gay-ninety songs, with
memoires of band concerts, of tree-lined streets of which travelled
the horseless carriage, comes this delightful musical narrative
depicting life when the world was young.

        1. U.S. – Social life and customs. I. Title.

        "Who are the People?"
Voice Lib.
M759
bd.3   Taft, William Howard, Pres. U.S., 1857–
            1930.
        "Who are the People?" Campaign speech.
VTM, 1912.
        1 reel (7 in.) 7 1/2 in. per sec.
phonotape.

        I. Title.

C1
PWM13
Whorf, Michael, 1933–
        The adolescent years.
    1 tape cassette. (The visual sounds of
Mike Whorf. Panorama; a world of music, PWM-13)
        Originally presented on his radio program, Kaleidoscope,
WJR, Detroit.
        Duration: 23 min.
        A discussion with examples of the music of the gay
nineties.

        1. Music, Popular (Songs, etc.) – U.S. I. Title.

C1
S74
Whorf, Michael, 1933–
        Abracadabra.
    1 tape cassette. (The visual sounds of
Mike Whorf. Social, S74)
        Originally presented on his radio program, Kaleidoscope,
WJR, Detroit.
        Duration: 37 min.
        Magic! Throughout civilization magic has brought men's
curiosity to a head. Every culture has had its superstitions, its
sorcerers. Throughout mankind's history magic has been studied,
has been practiced.

        1. Magic. I. Title.

                                        OFFICIAL

C1
S8
Whorf, Michael, 1933–
        Age of anxiety.
    1 tape cassette. (The visual sounds of
Mike Whorf. Social, S8)
        Originally presented on his radio program, Kaleidoscope,
WJR, Detroit.
        Duration: 48 min., 45 sec.
        A man standing up for an ideal, acting to improve the lot
of others, striking out against injustice; such was the life of
Robert F. Kennedy.

        1. Kennedy, Robert Francis, 1925–1968. I. Title.

                                        OFFICIAL

C1
R25
Whorf, Michael, 1933–
        The accusative – John Calvin.
    1 tape cassette. (The visual sounds of
Mike Whorf. Religion, R25)
        Originally presented on his radio program, Kaleidoscope,
WJR, Detroit.
        Duration: 36 min.
        Born of an affluent family in France, John Calvin turned from the
study of law to the scriptures as his religious convictions deepened.
His work and his life illustrate the burning fires of reformation which
raged through Europe.

        1. Calvin, Jean, 1509–1564. I. Title.

C1
A22
Whorf, Michael, 1933–
        All the world's a stage, Shakespeare.
    1 tape cassette. (The visual sounds of
Mike Whorf. Art, music, and letters, A22)
        Originally presented on his radio program, Kaleidoscope,
WJR, Detroit.
        Duration: 44 min., 10 sec.
        William Shakespeare is considered the father of literature, for
this prolific author composed plays, stories, sonnets and poems that
are as popular today as when he first wrote them.

        1. Shakespeare, William, 1564–1616. I. Title.

C1
A19   Whorf, Michael, 1933–
            The amazing Mr. Frost.
            1 tape cassette. (The visual sounds of
       Mike Whorf. Art, music, and letters, A19)

            Originally presented on his radio program, Kaleidoscope,
       WJR, Detroit.
            Duration: 43 min., 45 sec.
            Actual recordings of Frost reading his own works make up the
       body of this program, yet the narrator brings in important aspects
       of his life that made Robert Frost the man he was.

            L Frost, Robert, 1874–1963. L Frost, Robert, 1874–1963.
       II. Title.

C1
M21   Whorf, Michael, 1933–
            The American troubador.
            1 tape cassette. (The visual sounds of
       Mike Whorf. Miscellaneous, M21)

            Originally presented on his radio program, Kaleidoscope,
       WJR, Detroit.
            Duration: 40 min.
            This narrative deals with the life and trials of the gifted, but
       melancholy Stephen Foster.

            L Foster, Stephen Collins, 1826–1864. L Title.

C1
S38   Whorf, Michael, 1933–
            America the beautiful; pollution, part 2.
            1 tape cassette. (The visual sounds of
       Mike Whorf. Social, S38)
            Originally presented on his radio program, Kaleidoscope,
       WJR, Detroit.
            Duration: 54 min.
            This second narration looks at the types of pollution which have
       engulfed the globe. Here are the acts of water and air poisoning
       which man has slowly but deliberately committed, and the results
       of his carelessness and negligence.

            L Pollution. 2. Nature – influence of man on. L Title.

C1
H82   Whorf, Michael, 1933–
            America's first citizen, the President.
            1 tape cassette. (The visual sounds of
       Mike Whorf. History and heritage, H82)

            Originally presented on his radio program, Kaleidoscope,
       WJR, Detroit.
            Duration: 37 min., 30 sec.
            Here are the ins and outs, the political aspects and
       attributes of the election of a president.

            L Presidents – U.S. – Election. L Title.

C1
M53   Whorf, Michael, 1933–
            The American dance craze.
            1 tape cassette. (The visual sounds of
       Mike Whorf. Miscellaneous, M53)

            Originally presented on his radio program, Kaleidoscope,
       WJR, Detroit.
            Duration:
            For those that are musically inclined here is a program
       concerning the famous dances of the American people.
       Along with the music are capsule anecdotes about the life and
       times of those who are swept up in the American dance craze.

            L Dancing – U.S.   L Title.

C1
H19   Whorf, Michael, 1933–
            America's first modern.
            1 tape cassette. (The visual sounds of
       Mike Whorf. History and heritage, H19)
            Originally presented on his radio program, Kaleidoscope,
       WJR, Detroit.
            Duration: 40 min., 15 sec.
            The leader whose ideas shocked, alienated, and eventually
       reformed the early Pilgrim settlements, Roger Williams turned
       his back on the intolerance of the Puritans in Massachusetts
       and his face toward true freedom in his own colony.

            L Williams, Roger, 1604?–1683.   L Title.

                                                              OFFICIAL

C1
PWM16 Whorf, Michael, 1933–
            The American dance craze.
            1 tape cassette. (The visual sounds of
       Mike Whorf. Panorama; a world of music,
       PWM–16)

            Originally presented on his radio program, Kaleidoscope,
       WJR, Detroit.
            Duration: 25 min.
            A discussion of dancing in the United States, with examples
       of dance music.

            L Dancing. 2. Dance music, American. L Title.

C1
H100   Whorf, Michael, 1933–
            America's grand old man – Benjamin Franklin.
            1 tape cassette. (The visual sounds of
       Mike Whorf. History and heritage, H100)
            Originally presented on his radio program, Kaleidoscope,
       WJR, Detroit.
            Duration: 36 min.
            The wise man of America has become one of the most quoted,
       most remembered men of the American Revolution. His life revolved
       around his country, his countrymen. His books, his studies, and his
       maxims echo to us throughout history.

            L Franklin, Benjamin, 1706–1790.   L Title.

                                                              OFFICIAL

C1
H101   Whorf, Michael, 1933–
            An American story, as we have forgotten it –
       Joseph Warren.
            1 tape cassette. (The visual sounds of Mike Whorf. History
       and heritage, H101)

            Originally presented on his radio program, Kaleidoscope,
       WJR, Detroit.
            Duration: 35 min., 10 sec.
            A young American doctor, active in Revolutionary politics,
       Joseph Warren eagerly participated in many rebel militia activities.
       Constantly fighting for the American cause Dr. Warren helped
       create independence.

            L Warren, Joseph,   1741–1775. L Title.

C1
S77   Whorf, Michael, 1933–
            America's tarnished Robinhood – John Dillinger.
            1 tape cassette. (The visual sounds of
       Mike Whorf. Social, S77)
            Originally presented on his radio program, Kaleidoscope,
       WJR, Detroit.
            Duration: 37 min.
            1934, with the country climbing out of depression, John
       Dillinger arrived upon the scene. The clever criminal's
       escapades are fully described as we learn about the tarnished
       Robin Hood.

            L Dillinger, John, 1903–1934. L Title.

                                                              OFFICIAL

C1
M25
Whorf, Michael, 1933–
   And the band played on.
   1 tape cassette.   (The visual sounds of
Mike Whorf. Miscellaneous, M25)
   Originally presented on his radio program, Kaleidoscope,
WJR, Detroit.
   Duration: 55 min., 30 sec.
   A highly successful and original work, depicting musically
what the instruments are, what they do and sound like.

   L Bands (Music) L Title.

OFFICIAL

C1
H77
Whorf, Michael, 1933–
   The apostle of the strenuous life, Theodore
Roosevelt.
   1 tape cassette.   (The visual sounds of
Mike Whorf. History and heritage, H77)
   Originally presented on his radio program, Kaleidoscope,
WJR, Detroit.
   Duration: 38 min., 45 sec.
   America's favorite hero is the underdog, the frail, ninety-
seven pound weakling who rises to accept no threat from any
adversary. One such man was Theodore Roosevelt, a weak and
frail youth who builds his body and character, and one day reaches
the highest office in the land.
   L Roosevelt, Theodore, Pres., U.S., 1858-1919. L Title.

C1
M40
Whorf, Michael, 1933–
   And the days grow short when you reach
September.
   1 tape cassette.   (The visual sounds of
Mike Whorf. Miscellaneous, M40)
   Originally presented on his radio program, Kaleidoscope,
WJR, Detroit.
   Duration: 36 min., 25 sec.
   Here in an evocative word-portrait of autumn, is brought to life
the bittersweet qualities of this special season. As the leaves turn
to brilliant scarlets, yellows and oranges and the nip of frost steals
into the evenings, your mind's eye will conjure up visions and
memories.
   L Autumn. L Title.

OFFICIAL

C1
H65
Whorf, Michael, 1933–
   Apostles of destruction; Caesar, Alexander,
Ghenghis Khan, Hitler.
   1 tape cassette.. (The visual sounds of Mike Whorf.
History and heritage, H65)

   Originally presented on his radio program, Kaleidoscope,
WJR, Detroit.
   Duration: 39 min
   Here are graphically related the tales of the despots of the ages –
for though many would strive for goodness and the best in man – a
few were blindly corrupt and evil, and in their time attempted to
bring the world to ruin.
   L Caesar, C. Julius. 2. Alexander the Great, 356-323 B. C.
3. Jenghis Khan, 1162-1227.   4. Hitler, Adolf, 1889-1945.
L Title.

C1
SC27
Whorf, Michael, 1933–
   And then came the light – Copernicus, Galileo.
   1 tape cassette.   (The visual sounds of
Mike Whorf. Science, SC27)
   Originally presented on his radio program, Kaleidoscope,
WJR, Detroit.
   Duration: 39 min., 15 sec.
   For the true stargazer here is an accurate account of the great
astronomers. Included are brief accounts of the lives of Copernicus,
Galileo, and others who have contributed to the science of
astronomy.

   L Copernicus, Nicolaus, 1473-1543. 2. Galilei, Galileo,
1564-1642. L Title.

OFFICIAL

C1
R28
Whorf, Michael, 1933–
   The Arabian prophet – Mahomet.
   1 tape cassette.   (The visual sounds of
Mike Whorf. Religion, R28)
   Originally presented on his radio program, Kaleidoscope,
WJR, Detroit.
   Duration: 38 min., 15 sec.
   He was the founder of Islam and became its prophet. Today
millions of people the world over revere his teachings, and follow
the precepts which he ordained.

   L Muhammad, the prophet. L Title.

OFFICIAL

C1
H50
Whorf, Michael, 1933–
   Another day in June – D-Day.
   1 tape cassette.   (The visual sounds of
Mike Whorf. History and heritage, H50)

   Originally presented on his radio program, Kaleidoscope,
WJR, Detroit.
   Duration: 42 min.. 30 sec.
   June 6, 1944 – D-Day. Here is an unusual account of the
greatest armada to ever set sail in the Allies' attempt to turn
the tide of battle in their favor.

   L World War, 1939-1945 – Campaigns – Normandy.
L Title.

C1
S64
Whorf, Michael, 1933–
   As big as all outdoors; the story of Canada.
   1 tape cassette.   (The visual sounds of
Mike Whorf. Social, S64)
   Originally presented on his radio program, Kaleidoscope,
WJR, Detroit.
   Duration: 37 min., 30 sec.
   As big as all outdoors is the story of America's great neighbor
to the north – Canada. A country of riches – wealthy in people,
land, beauty, and raw material, yet a country that has not
reached its destiny.

   L Canada. L Title.

OFFICIAL

C1
R3
Whorf, Michael, 1933–
   The apostle.
   1 tape cassette.   (The visual sounds of
Mike Whorf. Religion, R3)

   Originally presented on his radio program, Kaleidoscope,
WJR, Detroit.
   Duration: 36 min., 30 sec.
   Paul of Tarsus was a man who persecuted and tormented the early
believers of the Christian following. Yet he would one day become
one of them and bring organization and firmness to the early church.

   L Paul, Saint, apostle. L Title.

C1
H16
Whorf, Michael, 1933–
   The assassin.
   1 tape cassette.   (The visual sounds of
Mike Whorf. History and heritage, H16)
   Originally presented on his radio program, Kaleidoscope,
WJR, Detroit.
   Duration: 37 min.
   Violence stalked the land in the person of John Wilkes Booth,
a bitter man, a resentful man, a man full of hate whose deed was
the ultimate act of tragedy.

   L Booth, John Wilkes, 1838-1865. L Title.

OFFICIAL

C1
S28
Whorf, Michael, 1933–
Astrology.
1 tape cassette. (The visual sounds of
Mike Whorf. Social, S28)
Originally presented on his radio program, Kaleidoscope,
WJR, Detroit.
Duration: 56 min., 45 sec.
Here are a few pro and con observations on one of mankind's
oldest interests, astrology.

I. Astrology. I. Title.

C1
A10
Whorf, Michael, 1933–
Beethoven, the incredible.
1 tape cassette. (The visual sounds of
Mike Whorf. Art, music, and letters, A10)
Originally presented on his radio program, Kaleidoscope,
WJR, Detroit.
Duration: 37 min., 30 sec.
Dealing not with symphonies and serenades, but rather with
emotions and feelings, this is the story of perhaps the greatest
musical genius who ever lived, Beethoven.

I. Beethoven, Ludwig van, 1770–1827. I. Title.

C1
R30
Whorf, Michael, 1933–
Augustine, the saint.
1 tape cassette. (The visual sounds of
Mike Whorf. Religion, R30)
Originally presented on his radio program, Kaleidoscope,
WJR, Detroit.
Duration: 36 min., 30 sec.
In the history of the Christian Church, few stories are as
inspiring as that of Saint Augustine. Here is presented the
account of his life and of his devotion to God.

I. Augustinus, Aurelius, Saint, bp. of Hippo. I. Title.

OFFICIAL

C1
S16
Whorf, Michael, 1933–
The beginning of man.
1 tape cassette. (The visual sounds of
Mike Whorf. Social, S16)
Originally presented on his radio program, Kaleidoscope,
WJR, Detroit.
Duration: 40 min., 36 sec.
This program takes an open-minded look in a narrative
which concerns itself with the possibility of evolution and
how man began.

I. Evolution. 2. Man - Origin. I. Title.

C1
A40
Whorf, Michael, 1933–
Autocrat of the breakfast table - O. W. Holmes,
Sr.
1 tape cassette. (The visual sounds of
Mike Whorf. Art, music and letters, A40)
Originally presented on his radio program, Kaleidoscope,
WJR, Detroit.
Duration: 36 min., 30 sec.
Oliver Wendell Holmes, Sr., was a poet and philosopher, and
here mixed with his works is the story of his life.

I. Holmes, Oliver Wendell, 1809–1894. I. Title.

OFFICIAL

C1
R29
Whorf, Michael, 1933–
The best that is in me - William Bradford.
1 tape cassette. (The visual sounds of
Mike Whorf. Religion, R29)
Originally presented on his radio program, Kaleidoscope,
WJR, Detroit.
Duration: 35 min., 45 sec.
In the story of the hardships and the struggles of the Pilgrims'
journey to the New World, William Bradford stands out as a pillar
of strength. Instrumental in the success of the venture, at all
times he gave his best.

I. Bradford, William, 1588–1657. I. Title.

OFFICIAL

C1
S11
Whorf, Michael, 1933–
Back to the blankets.
1 tape cassette. (The visual sounds of
Mike Whorf. Social, S11)
Originally presented on his radio program, Kaleidoscope,
WJR, Detroit.
Duration: 52 min., 45 sec.
The Indian's world for the past 100 years has been on the
reservation, yet he has frequently been induced to compete in the
outside world. What have been and what are the results?

I. Indians of North America. I. Title.

C1
M19
Whorf, Michael, 1933–
The big broadcast.
1 tape cassette. (The visual sounds of
Mike Whorf. Miscellaneous, M19)
Originally presented on his radio program, Kaleidoscope,
WJR, Detroit.
Duration: 53 min.
The history and the personalities who made the radio a
fixture in the household.

I. Radio broadcasting. I. Title.

C1
PWM1
Whorf, Michael, 1933–
Beethoven.
1 tape cassette. (The visual sounds of
Mike Whorf. Panorama; a world of music, PWM-1)
Originally presented on his radio program, Kaleidoscope,
WJR, Detroit.
Duration: 25 min.
The life and times of Beethoven, including excerpts of
his music.

I. Beethoven, Ludwig van, 1770–1827. I. Title.

C1
M7
Whorf, Michael, 1933–
The big top.
1 tape cassette. (The visual sounds of Mike Whorf.
Miscellaneous, M7)
Originally presented on his radio program, Kaleidoscope,
WJR, Detroit.
Duration: 40 min., 45 sec.
Here is a fascinating look at the three-ringed world wherein
lies the greatest show on earth, the animals, the clowns, the
aerialist, the animal trainer, the marvelous magic of Barnum,
Bailey and Ringling North.

I. Circus - U.S. 2. Barnum, Bailey and Ringling North.
I. Title.

OFFICIAL

C1
H22
Whorf, Michael, 1933-
Birth of a nation; Columbus, the adventurer.
1 tape cassette. (The visual sounds of
Mike Whorf. History and heritage, H22)
Originally presented on his radio program, Kaleidoscope,
WJR, Detroit.
Duration: 38 min., 10 sec.
A generous mixture of poetry and seldom-presented historical fact is blended to tell this greatest of all nautical tales. Aboard three ships, they sailed into the unknown. "Sail on, sail on and on," commanded the admiral and sail they did, into high adventure, the like of which the world had never known.

L. Colombo, Cristoforo   L. Title.

OFFICIAL

C1
PWM20
Whorf, Michael, 1933-
Blare of bugles, ruffle of drums.
1 tape cassette. (The visual sounds of
Mike Whorf. Panorama; a world of music,
PWM-20)
Originally presented on his radio program, Kaleidoscope,
WJR, Detroit.
Duration: 26 min.
The life and times of John Philip Sousa, with excerpts of his music.

L. Sousa, John Philip, 1854-1932.   L. Title.

C1
S73
Whorf, Michael, 1933-
The birth of the Boy Scouts.
1 tape cassette. (The visual sounds of
Mike Whorf. Social, S73)
Originally presented on his radio program, Kaleidoscope,
WJR, Detroit.
Duration: 36 min., 35 sec.
A historic narration of Lord Baden-Powell's life work of creating boys into young adults. The history of the Boy Scouts from its initiation to the present day world-wide organization is presented.

L. Boy Scouts. 2. Baden-Powell, Sir Robert Stephenson Smyth- Baden-Powell, 1857-1944. L. Title.

C1
H69
Whorf, Michael, 1933-
The blue and the gray; Civil War, part 2.
1 tape cassette. (The visual sounds of
Mike Whorf. History and heritage, H69)
Originally presented on his radio program, Kaleidoscope,
WJR, Detroit.
Duration: 37 min., 35 sec.
This program concerns itself with the stories of the northern soldier and the southern yeoman, their convictions emblazoned in history. The north and the south, the blue and the gray, brave men fighting for ideals – not for right or wrong – but fighting for what they believed was their sacred duty.

L. U.S. - History - Civil War, 1861-1865. L. Title.

C1
S14
Whorf, Michael, 1933-
The black cowboy.
1 tape cassette. (The visual sounds of
Mike Whorf. Social, S14)
Originally presented on his radio program, Kaleidoscope,
WJR, Detroit.
Duration: 30 min.
Along with the rustlers, wranglers, badmen and heroes, were Black men who rode the same trails and equalled the exploits of Earp, Bass, Bonney and Hickok.

L. Negroes as cowboys. L. Title.

OFFICIAL

C1
H32
Whorf, Michael, 1933-
The bold buccaneers - Kidd, Teach, Lafitte.
1 tape cassette. (The visual sounds of
Mike Whorf. History and heritage, H32)
Originally presented on his radio program, Kaleidoscope,
WJR, Detroit.
Duration: 55 min., 20 sec.
William Kidd, Edward Teach, Jean Lafitte were bold captains who sailed the bounding main in search of rich prizes. Who were they and why did they sail under the Jolly Roger? Here is the picturesque account of the bold buccaneers.

L. Pirates. L. Title.

C1
M12
Whorf, Michael, 1933-
Black magic.
1 tape cassette. (The visual sounds of
Mike Whorf. Miscellaneous, M12)
Originally presented on his radio program, Kaleidoscope,
WJR, Detroit.
Duration: 30 min.
Considered by many to be one of the greatest comics who ever lived, Bert Williams was idolized by millions and adored by those who knew him.

L. Williams, Bert. L. Title.

OFFICIAL

C1
M42
Whorf, Michael, 1933-
The bonny land of Scotland.
1 tape cassette. (The visual sounds of
Mike Whorf. Miscellaneous, M42)
Originally presented on his radio program, Kaleidoscope,
WJR, Detroit.
Duration: 36 min., 10 sec.
An ancient land with a proud people, Scotland is a heritage for its descendants, and a state of mind for all.

L. Scotland. L. Title.

C1
M22
Whorf, Michael, 1933-
A blare of bugles and a ruffle of drums.
1 tape cassette. (The visual sounds of
Mike Whorf. Miscellaneous, M22)
Originally presented on his radio program, Kaleidoscope,
WJR, Detroit.
Duration: 39 min., 30 sec.
He was called the "march king" and indeed he was, for John Philip Sousa gave the world hundreds of stirring melodies.

L. Sousa, John Philip, 1854-1932. L. Title.

C1
H79
Whorf, Michael, 1933-
Bound to be rich, John D. Rockefeller.
1 tape cassette. (The visual sounds of
Mike Whorf. History and heritage, H79)
Originally presented on his radio program, Kaleidoscope,
WJR, Detroit.
Duration: 36 min., 30 sec.
John D. Rockefeller had learned the value of money from his father and ever since he collected a bit of interest on a loan, he thought of nothing but money until the day he died.

L. Rockefeller, John Davison, 1839-1937. L. Title.

C1
H9
    Whorf, Michael, 1933-
      Brave, bold and bad.
      1 tape cassette. (The visual sounds of
Mike Whorf. History and heritage, H9)

      Originally presented on his radio program, Kaleidoscope,
WJR, Detroit.
      Duration: 41 min.
      The gunslinger, the desperado, the hero, the villain. Was the
gunman a legend, or was he a paranoid psychopath? They
were men who included William Bonny, Sam Bass, Wyatt Earp
and Bill Hickock - about 250 men in all who were bad, bold
and brave - or were they?
      1. Frontier and pioneer life - The West. 2. Crime and
criminals - The West.   1. Title.

C1
FA19
    Whorf, Michael, 1933-
      Captain James B. Eads.
      1 tape cassette. (The visual sounds of
Mike Whorf. The forgotten American, FA19)

      Originally presented on his radio program, Kaleidoscope,
WJR, Detroit.
      Duration: 11 min., 5 sec.
      Eads challenged and tamed the Mississippi river. He
pioneered in salvaging in the river, designed, and built boats
used to clear the river during the Civil War, and built the
first bridge across the river at St. Louis.

      1. Eads, James Buchanan, 1820-1887. 1. Title.

C1
H74
    Whorf, Michael, 1933-
      The brilliant orator - Black Dan; Daniel
Webster.
      1 tape cassette. (The visual sounds of
Mike Whorf. History and heritage, H74)
      Originally presented on his radio program, Kaleidoscope,
WJR, Detroit.
      Duration: 37 min., 45 sec.
      Here is the life and times of America's brilliant orator,
Daniel Webster, with the emphasis on his deeds and thoughts -
but primarily on his words.

      1. Webster, Daniel, 1782-1852. 1. Title.

C1
R34
    Whorf, Michael, 1933-
      The carpenters from Nazareth; Jesus and
Joseph.
      1 tape cassette. (The visual sounds of
Mike Whorf. Religion, R34)
      Originally presented on his radio program, Kaleidoscope,
WJR, Detroit.
      Duration: 37 min.
      Jesus emerges from the shadows to walk in a world peopled
by simple hard-working men in a town named Nazareth.

      1. Jesus Christ. 2. Joseph, Saint. 1. Title.

C1
FA22
    Whorf, Michael, 1933-
      Brooks Adams.
      1 tape cassette. (The visual sounds of
Mike Whorf. The forgotten America, FA22)

      Originally presented on his radio program, Kaleidoscope,
WJR, Detroit.
      Duration: 12 min., 47 sec.
      A philosopher of history, he stood alone preaching simplicity,
responsibility, honor, and service.

      1. Adams, Brooks, 1848-1927. 1. Title.

C1
SC25
    Whorf, Michael, 1933-
      The case of the vanishing monsters.
      1 tape cassette. (The visual sounds of
Mike Whorf. Science, SC25)
      Originally presented on his radio program, Kaleidoscope,
WJR, Detroit.
      Duration: 30 min.
      Here are the great beasts that roamed the earth long before
the coming of man. The huge dinosaurs prevailed for centuries and
then suddenly, they disappeared. Here are some of the answers, the
questions, the conjectures in a half-hour of gripping scientific fact.

      1. Dinosauria. 1. Title.

C1
H55
    Whorf, Michael, 1933-
      Buffalo Bill.
      1 tape cassette. (The visual sounds of
Mike Whorf. History and heritage, H55)

      Originally presented on his radio program, Kaleidoscope,
WJR, Detroit.
      Duration: 41 min.
      Scout, soldier, Indian fighter, impressario, entrepreneur;
he was all of these, yet above all, William Frederick Cody was
a legend.

      1. Cody, William Frederick, 1846-1917. 1. Title.

C1
S6
    Whorf, Michael, 1933-
      The celluloid queen.
      1 tape cassette. (The visual sounds of
Mike Whorf. Social, S6)

      Originally presented on his radio program, Kaleidoscope,
WJR, Detroit.
      Duration: 40 min., 30 sec.
      The story of the rise and fall of these glamorous stars who
were legends of their times, Theda Bara, Clara Bow, Gloria
Swanson, Colleen Moore, Lana Turner, Marilyn Monroe, is
outlined here.

      1. Moving-pictures -U.S. 1. Title.

OFFICIAL

C1
H33
    Whorf, Michael, 1933-
      By the dawn's early light - Francis Scott Key.
      1 tape cassette. (The visual sounds of
Mike Whorf. History and heritage, H33)

      Originally presented on his radio program, Kaleidoscope,
WJR, Detroit.
      Duration: 37 min., 30 sec.
      It was during the War of 1812 when Francis Scott Key wrote of
the momentous Battle of Fort McHenry. This is the story of the
life and times of the man who wrote our national anthem.

      1. Key, Francis Scott, 1779-1843. 1. Title.

C1
S22
    Whorf, Michael, 1922-
      Champion of the working man.
      1 tape cassette. (The visual sounds of
Mike Whorf. Social, S22)

      Originally presented on his radio program, Kaleidoscope,
WJR, Detroit.
      Duration: 27 min.
      Amidst the tumult of labor's early struggle to unionize,
Walter Reuther stood as a pillar of strength in the movement.

      1. Reuther, Walter Philip, 1907-1970. 1. Title.

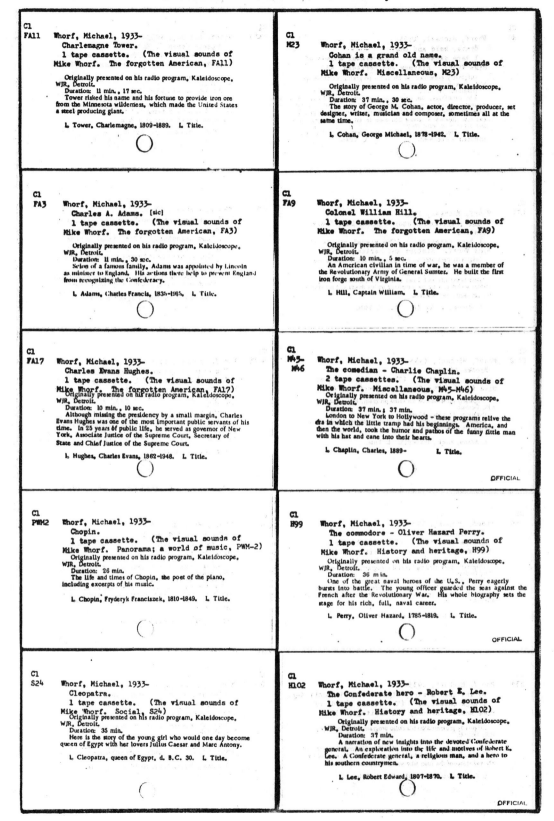

C1
FA11
Whorf, Michael, 1933–
 Charlemagne Tower.
 1 tape cassette. (The visual sounds of
Mike Whorf. The forgotten American, FA11)

 Originally presented on his radio program, Kaleidoscope,
WJR, Detroit.
 Duration: 11 min., 17 sec.
 Tower risked his name and his fortune to provide iron ore
from the Minnesota wilderness, which made the United States
a steel producing giant.

 L. Tower, Charlemagne, 1809–1889. L. Title.

C1
M23
Whorf, Michael, 1933–
 Cohan is a grand old name.
 1 tape cassette. (The visual sounds of
Mike Whorf. Miscellaneous, M23)

 Originally presented on his radio program, Kaleidoscope,
WJR, Detroit.
 Duration: 37 min., 30 sec.
 The story of George M. Cohan, actor, director, producer, set
designer, writer, musician and composer, sometimes all at the
same time.

 L. Cohan, George Michael, 1878–1942. L. Title.

C1
FA3
Whorf, Michael, 1933–
 Charles A. Adams. [sic]
 1 tape cassette. (The visual sounds of
Mike Whorf. The forgotten American, FA3)

 Originally presented on his radio program, Kaleidoscope,
WJR, Detroit.
 Duration: 11 min., 30 sec.
 Scion of a famous family, Adams was appointed by Lincoln
as minister to England. His actions there help to prevent England
from recognizing the Confederacy.

 L. Adams, Charles Francis, 1835–1915. L. Title.

C1
FA9
Whorf, Michael, 1933–
 Colonel William Hill.
 1 tape cassette. (The visual sounds of
Mike Whorf. The forgotten American, FA9)

 Originally presented on his radio program, Kaleidoscope,
WJR, Detroit.
 Duration: 10 min., 5 sec.
 An American civilian in time of war, he was a member of
the Revolutionary Army of General Sumter. He built the first
iron forge south of Virginia.

 L. Hill, Captain William. L. Title.

C1
M45–
M46
Whorf, Michael, 1933–
 The comedian – Charlie Chaplin.
 2 tape cassettes. (The visual sounds of
Mike Whorf. Miscellaneous, M45–M46)
 Originally presented on his radio program, Kaleidoscope,
WJR, Detroit.
 Duration: 37 min.; 37 min.
 London to New York to Hollywood – these programs relive the
era in which the little tramp had his beginnings. America, and
then the world, took the humor and pathos of the funny little man
with his hat and cane into their hearts.

 L. Chaplin, Charles, 1889– L. Title.

OFFICIAL

C1
FA17
Whorf, Michael, 1933–
 Charles Evans Hughes.
 1 tape cassette. (The visual sounds of
Mike Whorf. The forgotten American, FA17)
 Originally presented on his radio program, Kaleidoscope,
WJR, Detroit.
 Duration: 10 min., 10 sec.
 Although missing the presidency by a small margin, Charles
Evans Hughes was one of the most important public servants of his
time. In 25 years of public life, he served as governor of New
York, Associate Justice of the Supreme Court, Secretary of
State and Chief Justice of the Supreme Court.

 L. Hughes, Charles Evans, 1862–1948. L. Title.

C1
PWM2
Whorf, Michael, 1933–
 Chopin.
 1 tape cassette. (The visual sounds of
Mike Whorf. Panorama; a world of music, PWM-2)
 Originally presented on his radio program, Kaleidoscope,
WJR, Detroit.
 Duration: 26 min.
 The life and times of Chopin, the poet of the piano,
including excerpts of his music.

 L. Chopin, Fryderyk Franciszek, 1810–1849. L. Title.

C1
H99
Whorf, Michael, 1933–
 The commodore – Oliver Hazard Perry.
 1 tape cassette. (The visual sounds of
Mike Whorf. History and heritage, H99)
 Originally presented on his radio program, Kaleidoscope,
WJR, Detroit.
 Duration: 36 min.
 One of the great naval heroes of the U.S., Perry eagerly
bursts into battle. The young officer guarded the seas against the
French after the Revolutionary War. His whole biography sets the
stage for his rich, full, naval career.

 L. Perry, Oliver Hazard, 1785–1819. L. Title.

OFFICIAL

C1
S24
Whorf, Michael, 1933–
 Cleopatra.
 1 tape cassette. (The visual sounds of
Mike Whorf. Social, S24)
 Originally presented on his radio program, Kaleidoscope,
WJR, Detroit.
 Duration: 35 min.
 Here is the story of the young girl who would one day become
queen of Egypt with her lovers Julius Caesar and Marc Antony.

 L. Cleopatra, queen of Egypt, d. B.C. 30. L. Title.

C1
H102
Whorf, Michael, 1933–
 The Confederate hero – Robert E. Lee.
 1 tape cassette. (The visual sounds of
Mike Whorf. History and heritage, H102)
 Originally presented on his radio program, Kaleidoscope,
WJR, Detroit.
 Duration: 37 min.
 A narration of new insights into the devoted Confederate
general. An exploration into the life and motives of Robert E.
Lee. A Confederate general, a religious man, and a hero to
his southern countrymen.

 L. Lee, Robert Edward, 1807–1870. L. Title.

OFFICIAL

C1
H64

Whorf, Michael, 1933–
    Conquer or be conquered, David Farragut.
    1 tape cassette.   (The visual sounds of
Mike Whorf. History and heritage, H64)
    Originally presented on his radio program, Kaleidoscope,
WJR, Detroit.
    Duration: 40 min.
    David Farragut was dauntless, brave, courageous – having all
the attributes of the typical warrior. Yet, with all the notoriety
that comes with heroism, he was a lonely, much misunderstood
man.

    L Farragut, David Glasgow 1801–1870.

C1
A23

Whorf, Michael, 1933–
    The creator of immortal characters.
    1 tape cassette.   (The visual sounds of
Mike Whorf. Art, music, and letters, A23)
    Originally presented on his radio program, Kaleidoscope,
WJR, Detroit.
    Duration: 42 min., 30 sec.
    What he was and what he was to the world is forthrightly
told in the story of Dickens, the writer and the man.

    L Dickens, Charles, 1812–1870. L Title.

C1
H48

Whorf, Michael, 1933–
    The conquistadors.
    1 tape cassette. (The visual sounds of
Mike Whorf. History and heritage, H48)
    Originally presented on his radio program, Kaleidoscope,
WJR, Detroit.
    Duration: 44 min., 15 sec.
    Sent from Spain to settle and civilize the new world, they
plundered, killed, stole, and vanquished the Indian nations of the
Southwest, Central America, and Mexico.

    L America – Discovery and exploration – Spanish. L Title.

C1
H49

Whorf, Michael, 1933–
    The crusaders.
    1 tape cassette.   (The visual sounds of
Mike Whorf. History and heritage, H49)

    Originally presented on his radio program, Kaleidoscope,
WJR, Detroit.
    Duration: 39 min., 15 sec.
    The religious wars were led by men who engaged in savage
encounters with the infidels as they attempted to recapture the
cities where Christ once lived. Out of this period came many great
men – none greater than Richard the Lion-Hearted.
    L Richard I, King of England, 1157–1199. 2. Crusades. L Title.

C1
H35

Whorf, Michael, 1933–
    The Corsican conqueror.
    1 tape cassette. (The visual sounds of
Mike Whorf. History and heritage, H35)
    Originally presented on his radio program, Kaleidoscope,
WJR, Detroit.
    Duration: 38 min., 30 sec.
    He was born a Corsican, but would one day serve and command
the French armies and wage combat against the great armies of
Europe. He was a brilliant military strategist, often a cruel
emperor, but always a man of noble spirit.

    L Napoléon I, Emperor of the French, 1769–1821. L Title.

C1
S61

Whorf, Michael, 1933–
    Customs of marriage.
    1 tape cassette.   (The visual sounds of
Mike Whorf. Social, S61)
    Originally presented on his radio program, Kaleidoscope,
WJR, Detroit.
    Duration: 37 min., 40 sec.
    The great institution is described with music, prose, and
poetry which delves into the lore, myth, and legend behind
marriage customs.

    L Marriage. L Title.

C1
FA18

Whorf, Michael, 1933–
    Cotten Mather.
    1 tape cassette.   (The visual sounds of
Mike Whorf. The forgotten American, FA18)
    Originally presented on his radio program, Kaleidoscope,
WJR, Detroit.
    Duration: 12 min., 20 sec.
    The most distinguished American of his generation, he made
contributions in many fields, unrivaled by anyone of his time.
No other American writer ever exceeded him in volume.

    L Mather, Cotten, 1663–1728. L Title.

C1
SC20

Whorf, Michael, 1933–
    Daughter of mercy – Clara Barton.
    1 tape cassette.   (The visual sounds of
Mike Whorf. Science, SC20)
    Originally presented on his radio program, Kaleidoscope,
WJR, Detroit.
    Duration: 48 min., 55 sec.
    This narrative concerns the crusading Clara Barton, the "angel
of the battlefield," and the founder of the Red Cross in America.

    L Barton, Clara Harlowe, 1821–1912. L Title.

OFFICIA

C1
H47

Whorf, Michael, 1933–
    The cowboy.
    1 tape cassette. (The visual sounds of
Mike Whorf. History and heritage, H47)

    Originally presented on his radio program, Kaleidoscope,
WJR, Detroit.
    Duration: 40 min., 30 sec.
    This program depicts the cowhand as he was, not as the novel,
the movie and television has made him but rather as a tough breed
of man.

    L Cowboys. L Title.

C1
S42

Whorf, Michael, 1933–
    Days of thanks – about Thanksgiving.
    1 tape cassette. (The visual sounds of
Mike Whorf. Social, S42)
    Originally presented on his radio program, Kaleidoscope,
WJR, Detroit.
    Duration: 48 min., 55 sec.
    Bradford, Brewster, Alden, Mullins, Standish – these were the
leading figures aboard the Mayflower, who would later colonize
Plymouth and play out their roles in Europe's age of exploration and
discovery. Persecuted as Puritans, they came seeking freedom and
found the beginning of a nation.

    L Thanksgiving Day. L Title.

OFFICIAL

C1
SC13   Whorf, Michael, 1933–
    The days of the iron horse.
    1 tape cassette.   (The visual sounds of
Mike Whorf. Science, SC13)
    Originally presented on his radio program, Kaleidoscope,
WJR, Detroit.
    Duration: 30 min. , 50 sec.
    It was a boon to mankind, an invention which would cut
continents in half. The great iron horse, the trains that would
fly over nations, serving the millions of people of the world.
Today its roar of engines and shrill whistles are but dim echoes
filtering down from the past.

    L Railroads. L Title.

C1
H63   Whorf, Michael, 1933–
    Down to the sea in ships.
    1 tape cassette.   (The visual sounds of
Mike Whorf. History and heritage, H63)
    Originally presented on his radio program, Kaleidoscope,
WJR, Detroit.
    Duration: 38 min. , 50 sec.
    What is the lure of the sea that calls men to their destiny?
In this narrative the great tragedies of the ocean are recounted.

    L Shipwrecks. L Title.

C1
H41   Whorf, Michael, 1933–
    Days of valor.
    1 tape cassette.   (The visual sounds of
Mike Whorf. History and heritage, H41)

    Originally presented on his radio program, Kaleidoscope,
WJR, Detroit.
    Duration: 49 min.
    In each of America's wars there have been given moments,
certain occasions when men rise above the normal call of duty
to perform at the peak of their endurance whether in victory or
defeat.

    L U.S. - History.   2. War. L Title.

C1
S1   Whorf, Michael, 1933–
    A dream of freedom.
    1 tape cassette.   (The visual sounds of
Mike Whorf. Social, S1)

    Originally presented on his radio program, Kaleidoscope,
WJR, Detroit.
    Duration: 40 min. , 45 sec.
    Utilizing many of his famous speeches and delving into his
biography, the narrator gives continuity to this story of the life
and times of Martin Luther King.

    L King, Martin Luther, 1929–1968. L Title.

C1
R27   Whorf, Michael, 1933–
    David, King of Israel.
    1 tape cassette.   (The visual sounds of
Mike Whorf. Religion, R27)

    Originally presented on his radio program, Kaleidoscope,
WJR, Detroit.
    Duration: 37 min. , 50 sec.
    The warrior, the poet, the leader of his people, David was a
bulwark of strength to the Jews.

    L David, king of Israel. L Title.

C1
PWM22   Whorf, Michael, 1933–
    Edvard Grieg.
    1 tape cassette.   (The visual sounds of
Mike Whorf. Panorama; a world of music, PWM-22)
    Originally presented on his radio program, Kaleidoscope,
WJR, Detroit.
    Duration: 25 min.
    The life and times of Edvard Grieg, including excerpts.
of his music.

    L Grieg, Edvard Hagerup, 1843–1907. L Title.

C1
M52   Whorf, Michael, 1933–
    The dependables; firemen and firefighting.
    1 tape cassette.   (The visual sounds of
Mike Whorf. Miscellaneous, M52)
    Originally presented on his radio program, Kaleidoscope,
WJR, Detroit.
    Duration: 37 min.
    The exciting, dangerous world of some of our country's most
important citizens, the firemen, is told in this visual narrative.
Beginning with their simple origin as volunteers as the neighbor's
fire, to the story of the modern day fire brigades - it's all here.

    L Firemen. L Title.

                                        OFFICIAL

C1
S51   Whorf, Michael, 1933–
    The enigma of genius - Voltaire.
    1 tape cassette.   (The visual sounds of
Mike Whorf. Social, S51)
    Originally presented on his radio program, Kaleidoscope,
WJR, Detroit.
    Duration: 37 min.
    Voltaire was considered a genius, possessing one of the
finest minds of his day and consorting with his peers and contemporaries. His life was complex to the point of being enigmatic,
and we'll give you the right to disagree with our findings.

    L Voltaire, François Marie Arouet de, 1694–1778.
L Title.

C1
M24   Whorf, Michael, 1933–
    The detective.
    1 tape cassette.   (The visual sounds of
Mike Whorf. Miscellaneous, M24)
    Originally presented on his radio program, Kaleidoscope,
WJR, Detroit.
    Duration: 46 min.
    The adventures of Alan Pinkerton - his rise from obscurity to
fame as head of the world's foremost detective agency.

    L Pinkerton, Allan, 1819–1884. L Title.

                                        OFFICIAL

C1
A35   Whorf, Michael, 1933–
    England's first poet. - Geoffrey Chaucer.
    1 tape cassette.   (The visual sounds of
Mike Whorf. Art, music and letters, A35)

    Originally presented on his radio program, Kaleidoscope,
WJR, Detroit.
    Duration: 40 min.
    His works preceded those that were synonymous with the English
contribution to the literary world. Chaucer was poet and author,
and his commentary on life, philosophy, mores, and social aware-
ness was brought to its zenith with a collection of works entitled
Canterbury Tales.

    L Chaucer, Geoffrey,   d. 1400. L Title.

C1
E76

Whorf, Michael, 1933–
 The English patriot, Edmund Burke.
 1 tape cassette. (The visual sounds of
Mike Whorf. History and heritage, H76)
  Originally presented on his radio program, Kaleidoscope,
WJR, Detroit.
  Duration: 36 min.
  This story not only details Edmund Burke's endeavors in
America's cause, but also relates his own world.

  L. Burke, Edmund, 1729?–1797.   L. Title.

C1
M13

Whorf, Michael, 1933–
 Father of the blues.
 1 tape cassette. (The visual sounds of
Mike Whorf. Miscellaneous, M13)
  Originally presented on his radio program, Kaleidoscope,
WJR, Detroit.
  Duration: 54 min.
  The creator of "St. Louis blues" and a dozen other great
blues songs was W. C. Handy. This is the story of a troubled
spirit who finally found his life in music. As they said when
he died, "The mold is now broken."

  L. Handy, William Christopher, 1873–1958.   L. Title.

C1
FA15

Whorf, Michael, 1933–
 Enoch H. Crowder.
 1 tape cassette. (The visual sounds of
Mike Whorf. The forgotten American, FA15)
  Originally presented on his radio program, Kaleidoscope,
WJR, Detroit.
  Duration: 10 min.
  Crowder was a U. S. army officer who administered the
Selective service act during World War I and later served as
Ambassador to Cuba.

  L. Crowder, Enoch Herbert, 1859–1932.   L. Title.

C1
H80

Whorf, Michael, 1933–
 Fight for liberty and equality – French
Revolution.
 1 tape cassette. (The visual sounds of
Mike Whorf. History and heritage, H80)
  Originally presented on his radio program, Kaleidoscope,
WJR, Detroit.
  Duration: 38 min.
  The story of the French Revolution is one of the greatest sagas of
the western world. "Liberty, equality and fraternity" was the hue
and cry of the Frenchmen and the strains of the "Marseillaise" were
heard everywhere.
  L. France – History – Revolution.   L. Title.

C1
S66

Whorf, Michael, 1933–
 The eternal people – Jews.
 1 tape cassette. (The visual sounds of
Mike Whorf. Social, S66)
  Originally presented on his radio program, Kaleidoscope,
WJR, Detroit.
  Duration: 37 min., 30 sec.
  They gave the Western World a philosophy, a culture, and a
religion, yet in many instances they were rejected and despised.
They were the Jews – professing and embracing the Judaic faith –
yet, it was more than a faith. They have been searching for the
promised land, and modern day Israel is but part of it.

  L. Jews.   L. Title.

OFFICIAL

C1
H23

Whorf, Michael, 1933–
 First in the heart of his countrymen.
 1 tape cassette. (The visual sounds of
Mike Whorf. History and heritage, H23)
  Originally presented on his radio program, Kaleidoscope,
WJR, Detroit.
  A dauntless and fearless commander-in-chief, who led his
ragged army to victory in war and guided his young nation to
victory in peace.

  L. Washington, George, Pres. U.S., 1732–1799.
L. Title.

OFFICIAL

C1
A12

Whorf, Michael, 1933–
 The eternal Romance.
 1 tape cassette. (The visual sounds of
Mike Whorf. Art, music, and letters, A12)
  Originally presented on his radio program, Kaleidoscope,
WJR, Detroit.
  Duration: 37 min.
  The tender romance of Elizabeth Barrett and Robert Browning,
a story of a sickly young woman and her love for the tempestuous
Browning.

  L. Browning, Elizabeth (Barrett) 1806–1861. 2. Browning,
Robert, 1812–1889.   L. Title.

C1
R2

Whorf, Michael, 1933–
 The fisher of men.
 1 tape cassette. (The visual sounds of
Mike Whorf. Religion, R2)
  Originally presented on his radio program, Kaleidoscope,
WJR, Detroit.
  Duration: 29 min., 30 sec.
  The story of Peter, a man of rough-hewn manner, who became
the leader of the disciples once the Christ had been crucified.

  L. Peter, Saint, Apostle.   L. Title.

C1
M3

Whorf, Michael, 1933–
 Fanny.
 1 tape cassette. (The visual sounds of
Mike Whorf. Miscellaneous, M3)
  Originally presented on his radio program, Kaleidoscope,
WJR, Detroit.
  Duration: 30 min.
  Fanny Brice – songstress, comedienne, star of stage and broad-
casting, and girl who brought tears and laughter, who was able to
express on stage those qualities which were found in her own life.

  L. Brice, Fanny, 1891–   L. Title.

C1
H27

Whorf, Michael, 1933–
 The flag is passing by.
 1 tape cassette. (The visual sounds of
Mike Whorf. History and heritage, H27)
  Originally presented on his radio program, Kaleidoscope,
WJR, Detroit.
  Duration: 38 min.
  A stirring, patriotic splash of red, white, and blue as the
Visual Sounds takes a look at the story of Old Glory.

  L. Flags – U.S.   L. Title.

OFFICIAL

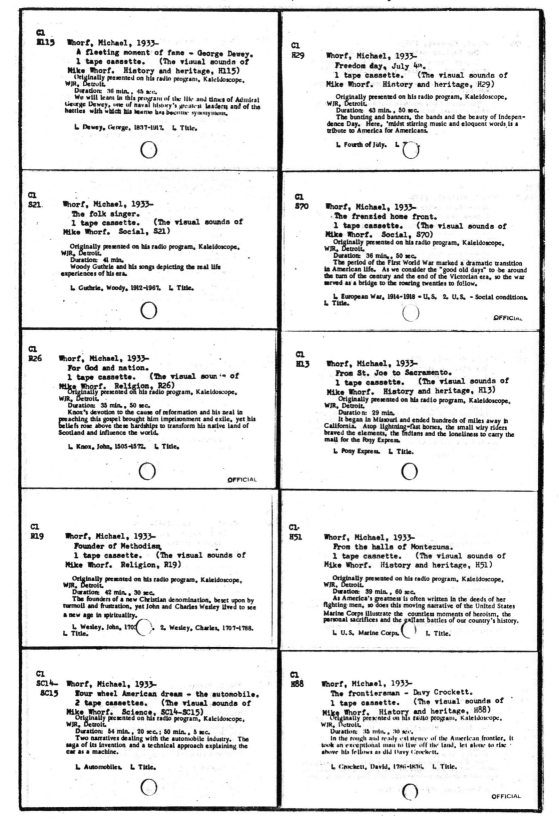

C1
H115
Whorf, Michael, 1933-
    A fleeting moment of fame - George Dewey.
    1 tape cassette.   (The visual sounds of
Mike Whorf. History and heritage, H115)
    Originally presented on his radio program, Kaleidoscope,
WJR, Detroit.
    Duration: 36 min., 45 sec.
    We will learn in this program of the life and times of Admiral
George Dewey, one of naval history's greatest leaders and of the
battles with which his name has become synonymous.

    L Dewey, George, 1837-1917. L Title.

C1
H29
Whorf, Michael, 1933-
    Freedom day, July 4th.
    1 tape cassette.   (The visual sounds of
Mike Whorf. History and heritage, H29)

    Originally presented on his radio program, Kaleidoscope,
WJR, Detroit.
    Duration: 43 min., 50 sec.
    The bunting and banners, the bands and the beauty of Indepen-
dence Day. Here, 'midst stirring music and eloquent words is a
tribute to America for Americans.

    L Fourth of July. L Title.

C1
S21
Whorf, Michael, 1933-
    The folk singer.
    1 tape cassette.   (The visual sounds of
Mike Whorf. Social, S21)

    Originally presented on his radio program, Kaleidoscope,
WJR, Detroit.
    Duration: 41 min.
    Woody Guthrie and his songs depicting the real life
experiences of his era.

    L Guthrie, Woody, 1912-1967. L Title.

C1
S70
Whorf, Michael, 1933-
    The frenzied home front.
    1 tape cassette.   (The visual sounds of
Mike Whorf. Social, S70)
    Originally presented on his radio program, Kaleidoscope,
WJR, Detroit.
    Duration: 36 min., 50 sec.
    The period of the First World War marked a dramatic transition
in American life. As we consider the "good old days" to be around
the turn of the century and the end of the Victorian era, so the war
served as a bridge to the roaring twenties to follow.

    L European War, 1914-1918 - U.S. 2. U.S. - Social conditions.
L Title.
                                    OFFICIAL

C1
R26
Whorf, Michael, 1933-
    For God and nation.
    1 tape cassette.   (The visual sounds of
Mike Whorf. Religion, R26)
    Originally presented on his radio program, Kaleidoscope,
WJR, Detroit.
    Duration: 35 min., 50 sec.
    Knox's devotion to the cause of reformation and his zeal in
preaching this gospel brought him imprisonment and exile, yet his
beliefs rose above these hardships to transform his native land of
Scotland and influence the world.

    L Knox, John, 1505-1572. L Title.
                                    OFFICIAL

C1
H13
Whorf, Michael, 1933-
    From St. Joe to Sacramento.
    1 tape cassette.   (The visual sounds of
Mike Whorf. History and heritage, H13)
    Originally presented on his radio program, Kaleidoscope,
WJR, Detroit.
    Duration: 29 min.
    It began in Missouri and ended hundreds of miles away in
California. Atop lightning-fast horses, the small wiry riders
braved the elements, the Indians and the loneliness to carry the
mail for the Pony Express.

    L Pony Express. L Title.

C1
R19
Whorf, Michael, 1933-
    Founder of Methodism.
    1 tape cassette.   (The visual sounds of
Mike Whorf. Religion, R19)

    Originally presented on his radio program, Kaleidoscope,
WJR, Detroit.
    Duration: 42 min., 30 sec.
    The founders of a new Christian denomination, beset upon by
turmoil and frustration, yet John and Charles Wesley lived to see
a new age in spirituality.

    L Wesley, John, 1703-   . 2. Wesley, Charles, 1707-1788.
L Title.

C1
H51
Whorf, Michael, 1933-
    From the halls of Montezuma.
    1 tape cassette.   (The visual sounds of
Mike Whorf. History and heritage, H51)

    Originally presented on his radio program, Kaleidoscope,
WJR, Detroit.
    Duration: 39 min., 60 sec.
    As America's greatness is often written in the deeds of her
fighting men, so does this moving narrative of the United States
Marine Corps illustrate the countless moments of heroism, the
personal sacrifices and the gallant battles of our country's history.

    L U.S. Marine Corps.   L Title.

C1
SC14-
SC15
Whorf, Michael, 1933-
    Four wheel American dream - the automobile.
    2 tape cassettes.   (The visual sounds of
Mike Whorf. Science, SC14-SC15)
    Originally presented on his radio program, Kaleidoscope,
WJR, Detroit.
    Duration: 54 min., 20 sec.; 50 min., 5 sec.
    Two narratives dealing with the automobile industry. The
saga of its invention and a technical approach explaining the
car as a machine.

    L Automobiles. L Title.

C1
H88
Whorf, Michael, 1933-
    The frontiersman - Davy Crockett.
    1 tape cassette.   (The visual sounds of
Mike Whorf. History and heritage, H88)
    Originally presented on his radio program, Kaleidoscope,
WJR, Detroit.
    Duration: 35 min., 30 sec.
    In the rough and ready existence of the American frontier, it
took an exceptional man to live off the land, let alone to rise
above his fellows as did Davy Crockett.

    L Crockett, David, 1786-1836. L Title.
                                    OFFICIAL

C1
H78
Whorf, Michael, 1933–
   The fur trader - John Jacob Astor.
   1 tape cassette. (The visual sounds of
Mike Whorf. History and heritage, H78)
     Originally presented on his radio program, Kaleidoscope,
WJR, Detroit.
     Duration: 37 min., 50 sec.
     This depicts the life and style of John Jacob Astor, a German
immigrant who literally turned the sidewalks into gold and paved
the streets with silver.

     L. Astor, John Jacob, 1763-1848. L. Title.

C1
H20
Whorf, Michael, 1933–
   The gentleman from Virginia.
   1 tape cassette. (The visual sounds of
Mike Whorf. History and heritage, H20)
     Originally presented on his radio program, Kaleidoscope,
WJR, Detroit.
     Duration: 49 min.
     Gentleman and General was Lee; Lee of the Confederacy; Lee
of Virginia - a man as noble as his ancestors, as brave as his
contemporaries. Lee was a patriot, a figure emerging from
history who would loom as large as anyone on the American scene.

     L. Lee, Robert Edward, 1807-1870. L. Title.

OFFICIAL

C1
M35
Whorf, Michael, 1933–
   Games people play.
   1 tape cassette. (The visual sounds of
Mike Whorf. Miscellaneous, M35)

     Originally presented on his radio program, Kaleidoscope,
WJR, Detroit.
     Duration: 37 min.
     Not only is this a session on the history of game playing, but also
some instruction as to how and why some games are played. There's
also a brief look into the sociocultural aspect of the games that
people play.

     L. Games. L. Title.

C1
FA5
Whorf, Michael, 1933–
   George W. Perkins.
   1 tape cassette. (The visual sounds of
Mike Whorf. The forgotten American, FA5)
     Originally presented on his radio program, Kaleidoscope,
WJR, Detroit.
     Duration: 11 min., 30 sec.

     Perkins rose from obscurity to a position of wealth and
power. He used his energies and money to promote the welfare
of his fellow man.

     L. Perkins, George W. L. Title.

C1
H2
Whorf, Michael, 1933–
   The general.
   1 tape cassette. (The visual sounds of
Mike Whorf. History and heritage, H2)

     Originally presented on his radio program, Kaleidoscope,
WJR, Detroit.
     Duration: 30 min., 30 sec.
     The life and times of Dwight Eisenhower, from his boyhood to
his nomination as president.

     L. Eisenhower, Dwight David, Pres. U.S., 1890-1969.
L. Title.

C1
A41
Whorf, Michael, 1933–
   Ghost story.
   1 tape cassette. (The visual sounds of
Mike Whorf. Art, music and letters, A41)
     Originally presented on his radio program, Kaleidoscope,
WJR, Detroit.
     Duration: 37 min., 45 sec.
     With stories of the real and the unreal the listener is transported
to a realm in which the dead walk, voices call from the grave,
and ghostly arms reach out for good or ill.

     L. Ghost stories. L. Title.

C1
H38
Whorf, Michael, 1933–
   General George Armstrong Custer.
   1 tape cassette. (The visual sounds of
Mike Whorf. History and heritage, H38)

     Originally presented on his radio program, Kaleidoscope,
WJR, Detroit.
     Duration: 49 min., 15 sec.
     Yellow Hair, General of the Long Knives, George Armstrong
Custer, was he the terror of the plains, the egotist, the bombastic,
or was he a general who followed his orders with flare and dash?

     L. Custer, George Armstrong, 1839-1876. L. Title.

C1
A20
Whorf, Michael, 1933–
   Giant of the age, Michelangelo.
   1 tape cassette. (The visual sounds of
Mike Whorf. Art, music, and letters, A20)

     Originally published on his radio program, Kaleidoscope,
WJR, Detroit.
     Duration: 28 min., 50 sec.
     His life and the story of his works unfolds in this narrative
dealing with the world of Michelangelo.

     L. Buonarroti, Michel Angelo, 1475-1564. L. Title.

C1
M43
Whorf, Michael, 1933–
   Genius.
   1 tape cassette. (The visual sounds of
Mike Whorf. Miscellaneous, M43)

     Originally presented on his radio program, Kaleidoscope,
WJR, Detroit.
     Duration: 36 min., 15 sec.
     What are the attributes of the giants of the ages that brings
them their label of genius?

     L. Genius. L. Title.

C1
S40
Whorf, Michael, 1933–
   The Gibson girl.
   1 tape cassette. (The visual sounds of
Mike Whorf. Social, S40)
     Originally presented on his radio program, Kaleidoscope,
WJR, Detroit.
     Duration: 29 min., 15 sec.
     A charming look at the lovely, illusive American girl. The
drawings of Charles Gibson come to life with the romantic music
of the period, along with an account of the love triangle of the
century.

     L. Gibson, Charles Dana, 1867-1944. 2. U.S. - Social
conditions. L. Title.

OFFICIAL

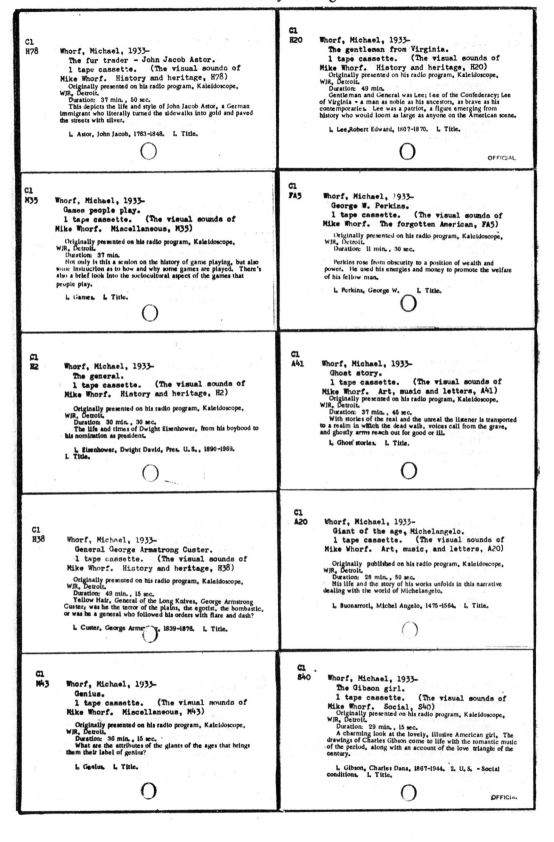

The G. Robert Vincent Voice Library

638

C1
M37
Whorf, Michael, 1933–
The glory of the Grecian games.
1 tape cassette. (The visual sounds of
Mike Whorf. Miscellaneous, M37)

Originally presented on his radio program, Kaleidoscope,
WJR, Detroit.
Duration: 36 min.
From antiquity comes this tale of gods and goddesses, of
athletes who saluted the reigning deities and participated in
peace coexistence. Since a Frenchman revived the games in the
the 1800's, the contests have provided the world with fascinating
spectacle.
L. Olympic games.   L. Title.

C1
SC30
Whorf, Michael, 1933–
Great balls of fire; unidentified flying
saucers.
1 tape cassette. (The visual sounds of
Mike Whorf. Science, SC30)
Originally presented on his radio program, Kaleidoscope,
WJR, Detroit.
Duration: 38 min.
Of course no one believes in flying saucers. No one believes
in interplanetary space travel. No one believes in life on distant
planets. But ... if no one believes in any of this, what's all
this talk about "great balls of fire"?
L. Flying saucers.   L. Title.

OFFICIAL

C1
PWM12
Whorf, Michael, 1933–
Gonna sing all over God's Heaven.
1 tape cassette. (The visual sounds of
Mike Whorf. Panorama; a world of music, PWM-12)

Originally presented on his radio program, Kaleidoscope,
WJR, Detroit.
Duration: 25 min.
The story of the music in the religious experience of the
American Negro.

L. Negro spirituals.   L. Title.

C1
H54
Whorf, Michael, 1933–
The great dissenter – Justice Oliver Wendell
Holmes.
1 tape cassette. (The visual sounds of
Mike Whorf. History and heritage, H54)

Originally presented on his radio program, Kaleidoscope,
WJR, Detroit.
Duration: 41 min.
A heart warming and tender story of Oliver Wendell Holmes,
who was a lawyer, professor and justice of the Supreme Court,
equally adept at each, an inspiration to all who listened to him.

L. Holmes, Oliver   Wendell, 1841-1935.   L. Title.

C1
S7
Whorf, Michael, 1933–
The good old days.
1 tape cassette. (The visual sounds of
Mike Whorf. Social, S7)

Originally presented on his radio program, Kaleidoscope,
WJR, Detroit.
Duration: 45 min., 30 sec.
Life as it once was, unhurried, pleasant, "countrified" and
simple. Here is a nostalgic look at ourselves in the "not so
long ago."

L. U.S. - Social life and customs.   L. Title.

C1
SC8
Whorf, Michael, 1933–
The great Dr. Einstein.
1 tape cassette. (The visual sounds of
Mike Whorf. Science, SC8)

Originally presented on his radio program, Kaleidoscope,
WJR, Detroit.
Duration: 29 min., 30 sec.
His life in Europe, his coming to America and the theory
that changed the world is told in this biography of Albert Einstein.

L. Einstein, Albert, 1879-1955.   L. Title.

C1
H42
Whorf, Michael, 1933–
The great American buffalo.
1 tape cassette. (The visual sounds of
Mike Whorf. History and heritage, H42)

Originally presented on his radio program, Kaleidoscope,
WJR, Detroit.
Duration: 40 min., 45 sec.
The bison supplied every need for the sustenance of the Indian;
yet, later he would be wantonly slain for the rugs and coats of the
American Caucasian. He was a beautiful, gigantic beast, who
nearly became extinct, but today survives in ever-growing numbers.

L. Bison, American.   L. Title.

C1
SC12
Whorf, Michael, 1933–
The great mysteries of science.
1 tape cassette. (The visual sounds of
Mike Whorf. Science, SC12)
Originally presented on his radio program, Kaleidoscope,
WJR, Detroit.
Duration: 31 min.
What is photosynthesis? What caused the ice age? What
causes the common cold? What mysteries do the stars, the sun,
and the sea hold? This program presents a look at some of those
great questions which since the beginning of creation have puzzled
mankind.
L. Natural history.   L. Title.

C1
M31
Whorf, Michael, 1933–
The great American pastime - baseball.
1 tape cassette. (The visual sounds of
Mike Whorf. Miscellaneous, M31)
Originally presented on his radio program, Kaleidoscope,
WJR, Detroit.
Duration: 39 min.
"Whoever would understand the heart and mind of America had
better learn the game of baseball ..." As this quotation sums up
our attitude toward the national pastime, so our program illuminates
the origin and the history of the great game of baseball.

L. Baseball.   L. Title.

C1
R24
Whorf, Michael, 1933–
The greatest book ever written.
1 tape cassette. (The visual sounds of
Mike Whorf. Religion, R24)
Originally presented on his radio program, Kaleidoscope,
WJR, Detroit.
Duration: 38 min.
Few stories shed such fascinating sidelights on the history
of man as the heritage of the body of literature which we now
know as the Bible.

L. Bible.   L. Title.

OFFICIAL

C1
S62
Whorf, Michael, 1933–
The greatest privilege of mankind – the family.
1 tape cassette. (The visual sounds of
Mike Whorf. Social, S62)
Originally presented on his radio program, Kaleidoscope,
WJR, Detroit.
Duration: 39 min., 30 sec.
For a thousand centuries man has received an abundance of
blessings – but none so rewarding as the family. The family of
"names" is also encountered with a study of the origin of the
head of the family.

L. Family. L. Title.

OFFICIAL

C1
H67
Whorf, Michael, 1933–
Heart of oak, Alexander Hamilton.
1 tape cassette. (The visual sounds of
Mike Whorf. History and heritage, H67)
Originally presented on his radio program, Kaleidoscope,
WJR, Detroit.
Duration: 43 min., 10 sec.
His gifts of intelligence and wisdom had a dramatic impact
on the young nation. Alexander Hamilton was a man of conviction and
ideals, and his perseverance led to his being referred to as the
man with a heart of oak.

L. Hamilton, Alexander, 1757–1804. L. Title.

C1
M32
Whorf, Michael, 1933–
The greatest woman in the world, mother.
1 tape cassette. (The visual sounds of
Mike Whorf. Miscellaneous, M32)
Originally presented on his radio program, Kaleidoscope,
WJR, Detroit.
The selections are those that contain some very basic truths
and sentiments about mothers, yet the presentation is not overly
saccharine in upholding the truth, wisdom, and virtue of the
world's prime example of the unsung heroine.

L. Mothers. 2. Mother's Day. L. Title.

C1
SC18
Whorf, Michael, 1933–
The heart of the matter.
1 tape cassette. (The visual sounds of
Mike Whorf. Science, SC18)
Originally presented on his radio program, Kaleidoscope,
WJR, Detroit.
Duration: 45 min.
Here unfolds the amazing story of the heart, its functions, its
disease, its recuperative powers – of transplants and of the men who
devote their hearts, minds and courage in this tremendous endeavor.

L. Heart – Surgery. L. Title.

OFFICIAL

C1
S67
Whorf, Michael, 1933–
The gypsies.
1 tape cassette. (The visual sounds of
Mike Whorf. Social, S67)
Originally presented on his radio program, Kaleidoscope,
WJR, Detroit.
Duration: 37 min., 45 sec.
Like the wayward winds, the gypsies are constantly in motion,
living for today in a nomadic existence which almost defies
description.

L. Gypsies L. Title.

OFFICIAL

C1
H66
Whorf, Michael, 1933–
Hero of the old west, Kit Carson.
1 tape cassette. (The visual sounds of
Mike Whorf. History and heritage, H66)
Originally presented on his radio program, Kaleidoscope,
WJR, Detroit.
Duration: 37 min., 30 sec.
Here, set against the background of the American southwest,
are the exploits of Kit Carson, a two-fisted hard-living frontiers-
man, who was as much at home in the peaceful hills and mountains
of the west as he was skulking and scouting for the U. S. Cavalry.

L. Carson, Christopher, 1809–1868. L. Title.

C1
H98
Whorf, Michael, 1933–
Harry S Truman – American.
1 tape cassette. (The visual sounds of
Mike Whorf. History and heritage, H98)
Originally presented on his radio program, Kaleidoscope,
WJR, Detroit.
Duration: 46 min.
One of the most outspoken and straightforward leaders of all
our presidents, Harry Truman was praised and cursed, revered and
reviled.

L. Truman, Harry S, Pres. U. S., 1884–1972. L. Title.

OFFICIAL

C1
S32
Whorf, Michael, 1933–
Heroes come in many colors, part 2; the life
of Phyllis Wheatly.
1 tape cassette. (The visual sounds of Mike Whorf. Social, S32)
Originally presented on his radio program, Kaleidoscope,
WJR, Detroit.
Duration: 31 min., 20 sec.
A gentle, frail, quiet girl who grew up in a Caucasion world
and from the love she was given, expressed her inner feelings in the
form of poetry. She was one of the first of her race to bring to the
western world a genuine, artistic talent.

L. Wheatley, Phillis, afterwards Phillis Peters, 1753?–1784.
L. Title.

OFFICIAL

C1
H18
Whorf, Michael, 1933–
He loved her truly.
1 tape cassette. (The visual sounds of Mike Whorf. History
and heritage, H18)
Originally presented on his radio program, Kaleidoscope,
WJR, Detroit.
Duration: 36 min., 30 sec.
Much has been written about the life, times and experiences of
Abraham Lincoln, but perhaps the nicest part of the truth is the
story of Lincoln and his stepmother, Sarah. Here was the motivation
behind Lincoln's quest for greatness.

L. Lincoln, Sarah Bush Johnston, 1788–1869. 2. Lincoln,
Abraham, Pres. U. S., 1809–1865. L. Title.

OFFICIAL

C1
S33
Whorf, Michael, 1933–
Heroes come in many colors; part 3 – The life
of Frederick Douglas.
1 tape cassette. (The visual sounds of Mike Whorf. Social, S33)
Originally presented on his radio program, Kaleidoscope,
WJR, Detroit.
Duration: 36 min., 45 sec.
From the heartaches and agonies of slavery came Frederick
Douglass, a giant of a man in mind and spirit, who would express
himself in a manner that no black man had done before.

L. Douglass, Frederick, 1817?–1895. L. Title.

C1
S34
Whorf, Michael, 1933–
   Heroes come in many colors, part 4 - The life
of Matthew Henson.
   1 tape cassette. (The visual sounds of Mike Whorf. Social, S34)
   Originally presented on his radio program, Kaleidoscope, WJR, Detroit.
   Duration: 39 min.
   The story of the man who accompanied Peary the explorer to the Pole, and whose adventures and exploits are excitingly and dramatically related in this documentary on the life and times of Matthew Henson.

   L. Henson, Matthew Alexander, 1866–1955. L. Title.
                                        OFFICIAL

C1
S35
Whorf, Michael, 1933–
   Heroes come in many colors, part 5 - The
life of Dr. Daniel Williams.
   1 tape cassette. (The visual sounds of Mike Whorf. Social, S35)
   Originally presented on his radio program, Kaleidoscope, WJR, Detroit.
   Duration: 29 min., 30 sec.
   Years before open heart surgery and names like Barnard and DeBakey were household words, the name of Daniel Williams was prominent in the theatre of medicine.

   L. Williams, Daniel Hale, 1856–1931. L. Title.

C1
SC5
Whorf, Michael, 1933–
   History's first modern.
   1 tape cassette. (The visual sounds of Mike Whorf. Science, SC5)
   Originally presented of his radio program, Kaleidoscope, WJR, Detroit.
   Duration: 37 min., 5 sec.
   His world in Italy, his life as a boy and young man, his exploits and endeavors as a mature man are given generous attention in this account of Leonardo da Vinci.

   L. Leonardo da Vinci, 1452–1519. L. Title.

C1
H73
Whorf, Michael, 1933–
   A house united; Civil War, part 6.
   1 tape cassette. (The visual sounds of Mike Whorf. History and heritage, H73)
   Originally presented on his radio program, Kaleidoscope, WJR, Detroit.
   Duration: 39 min.
   After the Civil War in the South there is the scorched earth, the burnt plantation and the carpetbagger, and yet the word throughout the land is reconstruction.

   L. Reconstruction. L. Title.

C1
M27
Whorf, Michael, 1933–
   How simple a tune.
   1 tape cassette. (The visual sounds of Mike Whorf. Miscellaneous, M27)
   Originally presented on his radio program, Kaleidoscope, WJR, Detroit.
   Duration: 43 min., 40 sec.
   A heart-warming look at some of the stories that lie behind the composition of America's most familiar old tunes.

   L. Music, Popular (Songs, etc.) - U.S. L. Title.

C1
S18
Whorf, Michael, 1933–
   I hear a different drummer.
   1 tape cassette. (The visual sounds of Mike Whorf. Social, S18)
   Originally presented on his radio program, Kaleidoscope, WJR, Detroit.
   Duration: 54 min.
   Henry David Thoreau, American poet and essayist, was perhaps one of the first outspoken critics of social and economic problems in 19th century America.

   L. Thoreau, Henry David, 1817–1862. L. Title.
                                        OFFICIAL

C1
H81
Whorf, Michael, 1933–
   Hitler's inferno.
   1 tape cassette. (The visual sounds of Mike Whorf. History and heritage, H81)
   Originally presented on his radio program, Kaleidoscope, WJR, Detroit.
   Duration: 39 min., 50 sec.
   Tyrant, dictator, despot, madman - all aptly describe the Austrian-born paperhanger who rose from obscurity to become the devil in human form. With the sound of storm troopers' boots, and the clank of panzer divisions comes this tale of the world's most despised man.
   L. Hitler, Adolf, 1889–1945. L. Title.

C1
A27
Whorf, Michael, 1933–
   The Homer of painters - Peter Rubens.
   1 tape cassette. (The visual sounds of Mike Whorf. Art, music and letters, A27)
   Originally presented on his radio program, Kaleidoscope, WJR, Detroit.
   Duration: 40 min.
   Peter Paul Rubens was diplomat, courtier, and raconteur, but most of all a brilliant artist. His brilliant technique led to influencing others of his day and those that were to follow; his works today are beyond price.

   L. Rubens, Sir Peter Paul, 1577–1640. L. Title.
                                        OFFICIAL

C1
M10
Whorf, Michael, 1933–
   I hear America singing.
   1 tape cassette. (The visual sounds of Mike Whorf. Miscellaneous, M10)
   Originally presented on his radio program, Kaleidoscope, WJR, Detroit.
   Duration: 56 min., 30 sec.
   The great traditional music of America with authentic, descriptive notes on the background of the writing of these songs. With each story is a musical example and with each example a familiar song.

   L. Music, American. L. Title.
                                        OFFICIAL

C1
PWM11
Whorf, Michael, 1933–
   I hear America singing.
   1 tape cassette. (The visual sounds of Mike Whorf. Panorama; a world of music, PWM-11)
   Originally presented on his radio program, Kaleidoscope, WJR, Detroit.
   Duration: 25 min.
   A presentation of songs popular in the U. S., including Barbara Allen, Yankee Doodle, Auld Lang Syne, Oh Susanna, Pop goes the weasel, Carry me back to old Virginny, The man on the flying trapeze, and I've been working on the railroad.

   L. Music, Popular (Songs, etc.) - U.S. L. Title.

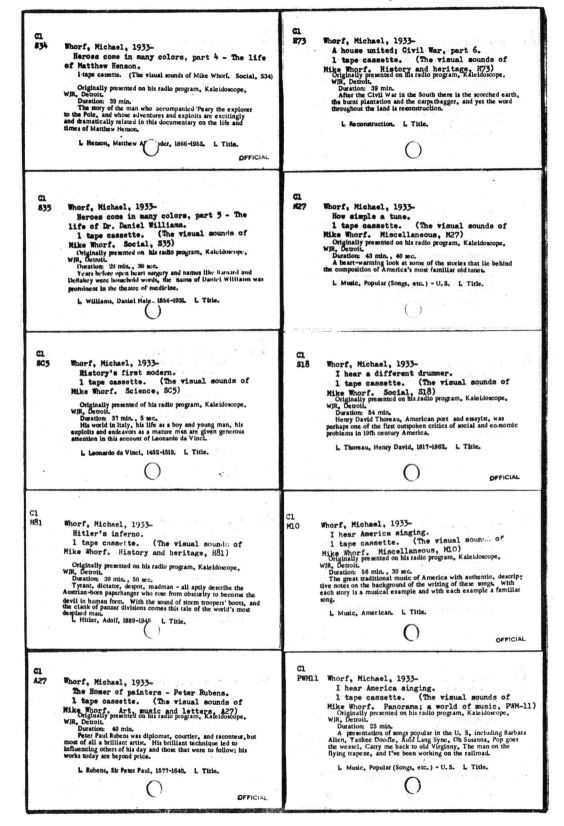

C1
M8

Whorf, Michael, 1933-
　I love to hear a military band.
　1 tape cassette.　(The visual sounds of
Mike Whorf.　Miscellaneous, M8)
　　Originally presented on his radio program, Kaleidoscope,
WJR, Detroit.
　　Duration: 50 min., 30 sec.
　　With guest, Frederick Fennell, the tempos are 4/4 and the
music is vibrant and varied, as through narrative and melody, the
story of the march is related.

　　L. Marches.　L. Fennell, Frederick.　II. Title.

C1
M34

Whorf, Michael, 1933-
　In the good old summertime.
　1 tape cassette.　(The visual sounds of
Mike Whorf.　Miscellaneous, M34)
　　Originally presented on his radio program, Kaleidoscope,
WJR, Detroit.
　　Duration: 37 min., 20 sec.
　　It begins and ends with the strains of 'In the good old
summertime', and in between is a delightfully warm and
sensitive description of what the season is all about.

　　L. Summer.　L. Title.

C1
SC7

Whorf, Michael, 1933-
　I wouldn't have believed it.
　1 tape cassette.　(The visual sounds of
Mike Whorf.　Science, SC7)
　　Originally presented on his radio program, Kaleidoscope,
WJR, Detroit.
　　Duration: 43 min., 45 sec.
　　Many believe that the fourth dimension is a world of ghosts,
poltergeists, of spirits and ghouls - others do not.　Can a person
see things if he or she wants to?　Turn down the lights and listen.

　　L. Fourth dimension.　L. Title.

OFFICIAL

C1
H53

Whorf, Michael, 1933-
　In the shadow of tragedy - Edwin Booth.
　1 tape cassette.　(The visual sounds of
Mike Whorf.　History and heritage, H53)
　　Originally presented on his radio program, Kaleidoscope,
WJR, Detroit.
　　Duration: 37 min., 45 sec.
　　A splendid tragedian, fate would deal with him cruelly.
Despite talent, creative genius and a warm friendly personality,
Edwin Booth would never overcome the blows that destiny dealt him.

　　L. Booth, Edwin, 1833-1893.　L. Title.

C1
A45

Whorf, Michael, 1933-
　The immortal poet - Robert Burns.
　1 tape cassette.　(The visual sounds of
Mike Whorf.　Art, music and letters, A45)
　　Originally presented on his radio program, Kaleidoscope,
WJR, Detroit.
　　Duration: 37 min., 15 sec.
　　Romantic, poetic Robert Burns comes to life as his rhythmic
verses are set to music.　Much of his poetry is read, intimately
revealing his various moods throughout his life.

　　L. Burns, Robert, 1759-1796.　L. Title.

C1
H75

Whorf, Michael, 1933-
　The incomparable emperor, Frederick the Great.
　1 tape cassette.　(The visual sounds of
Mike Whorf.　History and heritage, H75)
　　Originally presented on his radio program, Kaleidoscope,
WJR, Detroit.
　　Duration: 37 min., 10 sec.
　　Frederick the Great was a hero to the Germans - a king, an
emperor - who ruled as majestically, and at times as oppressively,
as any of his contemporaries, and this is a story rich in pageantry,
intrigue and tyranny.

　　L. Friedrich II, der Grosse, King of Prussia, 1712-1786.
L. Title.

C1
A36

Whorf, Michael, 1933-
　An imposing symposium.
　1 tape cassette.　(The visual sounds of Mike Whorf.
Art, music and letters, A36)
　　Originally presented on his radio program, Kaleidoscope,
WJR, Detroit.
　　Duration: 38 min., 30 sec.
　　Longfellow, Agassiz, Emerson, Dana, these were the kings of
the world of literature in the nineteenth century.　Every Saturday
night they met at a private club to discuss the current events of
their day.
　　L. Longfellow, Henry Wadsworth, 1807-1882.　2. Agassiz,
Louis, 1807-1873.　3. Emerson, Ralph Waldo, 1803-1882-
4. Dana, Richard Henry, 1815-1882.　L. Title.

OFFICIAL

C1
H58

Whorf, Michael, 1933-
　The incredible adventurer, Marco Polo.
　1 tape cassette.　(The visual sounds of
Mike Whorf.　History and heritage, H58)
　　Originally published on his radio program, Kaleidoscope,
WJR, Detroit.
　　Duration: 41 min., 30 sec.
　　So arduous were the journeys to the ends of the globe, and so
alien was the culture and society of the East, that Marco Polo's
achievements reveal his herculean drive and the audacity of his
vision.

　　L. Polo, Marco.　　　　　　1254-1323?　L. Title.

C1
H85

Whorf, Michael, 1933-
　In days of old when knights were bold -
knighthood.
　1 tape cassette.　(The visual sounds of
Mike Whorf.　History and heritage, H85)
　　Originally presented on his radio program, Kaleidoscope,
WJR, Detroit.
　　Duration: 36 min., 30 sec.
　　The romance and the glories of knighthood are a heritage of
chivalry, but with a misty background in the Arthurian legends.

　　L. Knights and knighthood.　2. Arthur, King.　L. Title.

C1
A5

Whorf, Michael, 1933-
　The incredible Grandma Moses.
　1 tape cassette.　(The visual sounds of
Mike Whorf.　Art, music, and letters, A5)
　　Originally presented on his radio program, Kaleidoscope,
WJR, Detroit.
　　Duration: 24 min.
　　At the tender young age of 80 she painted quaint pictures
of the America she knew and loved, as a legacy for future
generations.

　　L. Moses, Anna Mary (Robertson) 1860-1961.　L. Title.

C1
M14

Whorf, Michael, 1933-
  The incredible Houdini.
  1 tape cassette. (The visual sounds of
Mike Whorf. Miscellaneous, M14)
    Originally presented on his radio program, Kaleidoscope,
WJR, Detroit.
    Duration: 48 min., 10 sec.
    Trickster, magician, seer and scientist - what was it that
made Harry Houdini the most outstanding slight-of-hand artist,
the most original prestidigitator of his time? A look behind the
scenes as one of the world's most incredible performers.

    L. Houdini, Harry, 1874-1926. L. Title.

C1
H62

Whorf, Michael, 1933-
  The iron duke - Wellington.
  1 tape cassette. (The visual sounds of
Mike Whorf. History and heritage, H62)

    Originally presented on his radio program, Kaleidoscope,
WJR, Detroit.
    Duration: 38 min., 50 sec.
    His military genius, the ability to persevere with his raw and
untrained recruits, and his unquestioned courage in adversity
turned the tide against the Corsican, and earned Wellington his
place as one of England's foremost national heroes.

    L. Wellington, Arthur Wellesley, 1st duke of, 1769-1852.
L. Title.

C1
H4

Whorf, Michael, 1933-
  The indispensable, Jim Bridger.
  1 tape cassette. (The visual sounds of
Mike Whorf. History and heritage, H4)
    Originally presented on his radio program, Kaleidoscope,
WJR, Detroit.
    Duration: 37 min., 30 sec.
    The country was unsettled and few men had gone beyond the
Mississippi; yet one man among the few would venture forth, to
trap, hunt, fight, explore, and to discover the marvels of the
frontier.

    L. Bridger, James, 1804-1881. L. Title.

OFFICIAL

C1
PWM19

Whorf, Michael, 1933-
  It's a grand old flag.
  1 tape cassette. (The visual sounds of
Mike Whorf. Panorama; a world of music,
PWM-19)

    Originally presented on his radio program, Kaleidoscope,
WJR, Detroit.
    Duration: 25 min.
    The story of the American flag, with selected patriotic
music.

    L. Flags. 2. Patriotic music, American. L. Title.

C1
S5

Whorf, Michael, 1933-
  The interracial statesman.
  1 tape cassette. (The visual sounds of
Mike Whorf. Social, S5)

    Originally presented on his radio program, Kaleidoscope,
WJR, Detroit.
    Duration: 34 min.
    Booker T. Washington was one of the first of American Black
men to discover that he must accept the world on its terms. He was
a leader who saw prejudice and bigotry, yet prevailed to become
accepted as an individual, a man deserving of his fellow man's
respect.
    L. Washington, Booker Taliaferro, 1859?-1915. L. Title.

C1
FA4

Whorf, Michael, 1933-
  Joel Barlow.
  1 tape cassette. (The visual sounds of
Mike Whorf. The forgotten American, FA4)

    Originally presented on his radio program, Kaleidoscope,
WJR, Detroit.
    Duration: 13 min., 50 sec.
    Appointed minister to France by President Madison during the
time of the War of 1812, Barlow worked for a trade treaty with
Napoleon.

    L. Barlow, Joel, 1754-1812. L. Title.

C1
SC10

Whorf, Michael, 1933-
  Inventions in medicine.
  1 tape cassette. (The visual sounds of
Mike Whorf. Science, SC10)
    Originally presented on his radio program, Kaleidoscope,
WJR, Detroit.
    Duration: 53 min., 40 sec.
    A fast moving account of some of the noblest inventions and
discoveries of medicine and science. Pasteur, Harvey and many
more highlight this adventure of men pitted against disease and
sickness.

    L. Medicine - History.   L. Title.

OFFICIAL

C1
H17

Whorf, Michael, 1933-
  John Smith's great lady.
  1 tape cassette. (The visual sounds of
Mike Whorf. History and heritage, H17)
    Originally presented on his radio program, Kaleidoscope,
WJR, Detroit.
    Duration: 29 min., 30 sec.
    It is one of America's first romantic histories, fired by an
adventurous spirit of a man and the inner courage of a woman.

    L. Pocahontas, d. 1617. 2. Smith, John, 1580-1631.
L. Title.

OFFICIAL

C1
R33

Whorf, Michael, 1933-
  The Irish saint, St. Patrick.
  1 tape cassette. (The visual sounds of
Mike Whorf. Religion, R33)
    Originally presented on his radio program, Kaleidoscope,
WJR, Detroit.
    Duration: 37 min.
    From a life shrouded in myth and legend, emerges the
story of the patron saint of Ireland, Saint Patrick.

    L. Patrick, Saint, 373?-463? L. Title.

C1
SC32

Whorf, Michael, 1933-
  John Glenn's day of miracles.
  1 tape cassette. (The visual sounds of
Mike Whorf. Science, SC32)
    Originally presented on his radio program, Kaleidoscope,
WJR, Detroit.
    Duration: 37 min., 15 sec.
    From his days as pilot, to the day he climbed aboard
Friendship Seven, here is the story of the Ohio-born airman who
took the first giant step that led to mankind's gigantic leap.

    L. Glenn, John Herschel, 1921-   L. Title.

OFFICIAL

C1
FA21
Whorf, Michael, 1933–
Jonathan Edwards.
1 tape cassette. (The visual sounds of
Mike Whorf. The forgotten American, FA21)

Originally presented on his radio program, Kaleidoscope,
WJR, Detroit.
Duration: 12 min., 33 sec.
Puritan clergyman and theologian, he exerted a permanent
influence on our American heritage.

L. Edwards, Jonathan, 1703-1758. L. Title.

C1
A30
Whorf, Michael, 1933–
The king of the storytellers – Rudyard Kipling.
1 tape cassette. (The visual sounds of
Mike Whorf. Art, music and letters, A30)

Originally presented on his radio program, Kaleidoscope,
WJR, Detroit.
Duration: 37 min., 45 sec.
Rudyard Kipling was king of the storytellers. From England to
India he wrote of the strange, the fascinating, and became an
international author.

L. Kipling, Rudyard, 1865-1936. L. Title.

OFFICIAL

C1
FA10
Whorf, Michael, 1933–
Joseph Lane.
1 tape cassette. (The visual sounds of
Mike Whorf. The forgotten American, FA10)

Originally presented on his radio program, Kaleidoscope,
WJR, Detroit.
Duration: 10 min., 24 sec.
Soldier, politician, and pioneer, Lane was one of the
first senators from Oregon. He was the Vice Presidential
candidate on the breakaway Democratic ticket with John C.
Breckinridge in 1860.

L. Lane, Joseph, 1801-1881. L. Title.

C1
H52
Whorf, Michael, 1933–
Known but to God – Armistice Day.
1 tape cassette. (The visual sounds of
Mike Whorf. History and heritage, H52)

Originally presented on his radio program, Kaleidoscope,
WJR, Detroit.
Duration: 38 min., 45 sec.
A solemn approach to America's fallen – a tribute to the
unknown soldier – a brief biographical sketch of Sergeant Alvin
York is the content of this Armistice Day program.

L. Armistice Day. 2. York, Alvin Cullum, 1887–
L. Title.

C1
M47-
49
Whorf, Michael, 1933–
Journey into jazz.
3 tape cassettes. (The visual sounds of
Mike Whorf. Miscellaneous, M47-M49)
Originally presented on his radio program, Kaleidoscope,
WJR, Detroit.
Duration: 36 min., 30 sec.; 37 min.; 37 min.
A three part series on the unique style of music called
jazz. The movement of jazz is followed from its origin in
New Orleans to its rollicking acceptance in the wide open city of
Chicago. The third part deals with jazz grown-up. That is the
music form adopted by such greats as Goodman, James and Miller.

L. Jazz music. L. Title.

OFFICIAL

C1
H2
Whorf, Michael, 1933–
The Lafayette Escadrille.
1 tape cassette. (The visual sounds of
Mike Whorf. History and heritage, H2)
Originally presented on his radio program, Kaleidoscope,
WJR, Detroit.
Duration: 28 min., 30 sec.
A group of daring young American aviators went to France at
the out-set of World War I to fly and fight for the Allies. Here is
the unlikely adventure of a group of young flyers who were at war
long before their own country entered the conflict.

L. France. Armée. Escadrille Lafayette. L. Title.

C1
PWM15
Whorf, Michael, 1933–
A journey into jazz.
1 tape cassette. (The visual sounds of
Mike Whorf. Panorama; a world of music,
PWM-15)

Originally presented on his radio program, Kaleidoscope,
WJR, Detroit.
Duration: 35 min.
The capsule story of the development of jazz and
performances by key contributors to jazz.

L. Jazz music. L. Title.

C1
A8
Whorf, Michael, 1933–
The land of Runyon.
1 tape cassette. (The visual sounds of
Mike Whorf. Art, music, and letters, A8)

Originally presented on his radio program, Kaleidoscope,
WJR, Detroit.
Duration: 28 min., 35 sec.
Damon Runyon travelled with mugs and molls, gamblers and
their gals, and gave the world humor and human interest.

L. Runyon, Damon, 1880-1946. L. Title.

OFFICIAL

C1
S75
Whorf, Michael, 1933–
Kidnap of the century – Lindbergh.
1 tape cassette. (The visual sounds of
Mike Whorf. Social, S75)
Originally presented on his radio program, Kaleidoscope,
WJR, Detroit.
Duration: 37 min., 30 sec.
A vivid, exciting account of the notorious Lindbergh kidnapping.
The evening of March 1, 1932, was the scene of the most publicized
abduction of the century. The kidnapping, and the ensuing manhunt
are narrated in this anxious, fearful report.

L. Lindbergh, Charles Augustus, 1930-1932. 2. Hauptmann,
Bruno Richard, 1899-1936. L. Title.

C1
H113
Whorf, Michael, 1933–
The last flight; Amelia Earhart.
1 tape cassette. (The visual sounds of
Mike Whorf. History and heritage, H113)
Originally presented on his radio program, Kaleidoscope,
WJR, Detroit.
Duration: 35 min., 45 sec.
The search for the world's most famous aviatrix has been
kept alive through the years since her disappearance – kept
alive by rumors, half-truths and wild speculations.

L. Earhart, Amelia, 1898-1937. L. Title.

C1
S19
Whorf, Michael, 1933–
  The last full measure.
  1 tape cassette. (The visual sounds of
Mike Whorf. Social, S19)

  Originally presented on his radio program, Kaleidoscope,
WJR, Detroit.
  Duration: 47 min., 20 sec.
  John F. Kennedy, his life as a young, wealthy, charming man,
a Navy Lieutenant, a Senator and finally President is outlined
in this narrative of a dedicated American.

  L. Kennedy, John Fitzgerald, Pres. U.S., 1917-1963.
  L. Title.

                                         OFFICIAL

C1
R8
Whorf, Michael, 1933–
  Left hand of God.
  1 tape cassette. (The visual sounds of
Mike Whorf. Religion, R8)

  Originally presented on his radio program, Kaleidoscope,
WJR, Detroit.
  Duration: 46 min., 30 sec.
  In every conflict in which this country has ever been involved,
the chaplain has stood beside the fighting man. They are the
soldiers of God.

  L. Chaplains, Military. L. Title.

C1
H84
Whorf, Michael, 1933–
  The last of the great explorers – James Cook.
  1 tape cassette. (The visual sounds of
Mike Whorf. History and heritage, H84)
  Originally presented on his radio program, Kaleidoscope,
WJR, Detroit.
  Duration: 37 min., 30 sec.
  James Cook was an extraordinary seaman and an intelligent
and far-seeing individual who realized that the way to make
England stronger was to claim for her the lands that lay beyond.

  L. Cook, James, 1728-1779. L. Title.

                                         OFFICIAL

C1
A32
Whorf, Michael, 1933–
  The legend called Leatherstocking – James
Fenimore Cooper.
  1 tape cassette. (The visual sounds of Mike Whorf.
Art, music and letters, A32)

  Originally presented on his radio program, Kaleidoscope,
WJR, Detroit.
  Duration: 27 min., 40 sec.
  In a time of adventure, discovery, and exploration comes the
man to tell the story of frontier days, of savages both red and white,
of wilderness and beauty.

  L. Cooper, James Fenimore, 1789-1851. L. Title.

                                         OFFICIAL

C1
H1
Whorf, Michael, 1933–
  The last of the heroes.
  1 tape cassette. (The visual sounds of
Mike Whorf. History and heritage, H1)
  Originally presented on his radio program, Kaleidoscope,
WJR, Detroit.
  Duration: 45 min., 45 sec.
  A free verse ode to America's fighting men, tracing our
involvement in wars with other nations; pointing to courage and
bravery as well as the futility of armed conflict. Patriotic music
is used abundantly to create mood and a sense of heritage.

  L. U.S. – History, Military. L. Title.

C1
SC11
Whorf, Michael, 1933–
  The legend of Stonehenge.
  1 tape cassette. (The visual sounds of
Mike Whorf. Science, SC11)
  Originally presented on his radio program, Kaleidoscope,
WJR, Detroit.
  Duration: 30 min., 30 sec.
  What were the strange rock formations which had dotted the
English countryside for centuries? What purpose did these great
stones serve and where did they come from?

  L. Stonehenge. L. Title.

C1
S17
Whorf, Michael, 1933–
  The last of the Queen of Scots.
  1 tape cassette. (The visual sounds of
Mike Whorf. Social, S17)

  Originally presented on his radio program, Kaleidoscope,
WJR, Detroit.
  Duration: 42 min.
  Against the pageantry of royalty and majesty of kings and queens
of English nobility, comes the story of the last of the queens of
Scotland.

  L. Mary Stuart, queen of the Scots, 1542-1587. L. Title.

C1
R1
Whorf, Michael, 1933–
  The lesson never learned.
  1 tape cassette. (The visual sounds of
Mike Whorf. Religion, R1)

  Originally presented on his radio program, Kaleidoscope,
WJR, Detroit.
  Duration: 46 min., 15 sec.
  This is the story of Jesus from His birth, through His ministry and
teaching, to His death. It is based on the Bible, the stories which
unfold in the Gospels, and is ecumenical in approach.

  L. Jesus Christ. 2. Christianity. L. Title.

C1
H45
Whorf, Michael, 1933–
  Lawrence of Arabia – T. E. Lawrence.
  1 tape cassette. (The visual sounds of
Mike Whorf. History and heritage, H45)

  Originally presented on his radio program, Kaleidoscope,
WJR, Detroit.
  Duration: 42 min., 30 sec.
  He was an enigma, a perplexing figure; yet an intellectual,
archaeologist, brilliant warrior, and still a man much misunder-
stood for his depth.

  L. Lawrence, Thomas Edward, 1888-1935. L. Title.

C1
H86
Whorf, Michael, 1933–
  The liberator – Simon Bolivar.
  1 tape cassette. (The visual sounds of
Mike Whorf. History and heritage, H86)

  Originally presented on his radio program, Kaleidoscope,
WJR, Detroit.
  Duration: 34 min., 15 sec.
  He was called the Washington of South America and it was a
title richly deserved. Bolivar struck a blow for freedom against the
misrule of Spain, and led his countrymen in the battles that changed
the map of a continent and the future of a people.

  L. Bolivar, Simon, 1783-1830. L. Title.

                                         OFFICIA

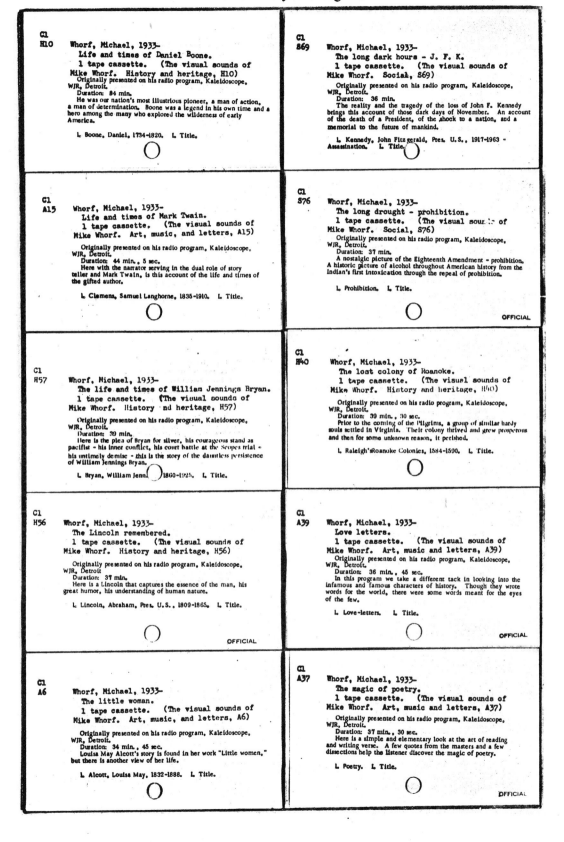

C1
H10
Whorf, Michael, 1933–
   Life and times of Daniel Boone.
   1 tape cassette. (The visual sounds of
Mike Whorf. History and heritage, H10)
    Originally presented on his radio program, Kaleidoscope,
WJR, Detroit.
    Duration: 84 min.
    He was our nation's most illustrious pioneer, a man of action,
a man of determination. Boone was a legend in his own time and a
hero among the many who explored the wilderness of early
America.

    l. Boone, Daniel, 1734-1820. l. Title.

C1
869
Whorf, Michael, 1933–
   The long dark hours - J. F. K.
   1 tape cassette. (The visual sounds of
Mike Whorf. Social, 869)
    Originally presented on his radio program, Kaleidoscope,
WJR, Detroit.
    Duration: 36 min.
    The reality and the tragedy of the loss of John F. Kennedy
brings this account of those dark days of November. An account
of the death of a President, of the shock to a nation, and a
memorial to the future of mankind.

    l. Kennedy, John Fitzgerald, Pres. U.S., 1917-1963 -
Assassination. l. Title.

C1
A15
Whorf, Michael, 1933–
   Life and times of Mark Twain.
   1 tape cassette. (The visual sounds of
Mike Whorf. Art, music, and letters, A15)
    Originally presented on his radio program, Kaleidoscope,
WJR, Detroit.
    Duration: 44 min., 5 sec.
    Here with the narrator serving in the dual role of story
teller and Mark Twain, is this account of the life and times of
the gifted author.

    l. Clemens, Samuel Langhorne, 1835-1910. l. Title.

C1
S76
Whorf, Michael, 1933–
   The long drought - prohibition.
   1 tape cassette. (The visual sounds of
Mike Whorf. Social, S76)
    Originally presented on his radio program, Kaleidoscope,
WJR, Detroit.
    Duration: 37 min.
    A nostalgic picture of the Eighteenth Amendment - prohibition.
A historic picture of alcohol throughout American history from the
Indian's first intoxication through the repeal of prohibition.

    l. Prohibition. l. Title.

OFFICIAL

C1
H57
Whorf, Michael, 1933–
   The life and times of William Jennings Bryan.
   1 tape cassette. (The visual sounds of
Mike Whorf. History and heritage, H57)
    Originally presented on his radio program, Kaleidoscope,
WJR, Detroit.
    Duration: 39 min.
    Here is the plea of Bryan for silver, his courageous stand as
pacifist - his inner conflict, his court battle at the Scopes trial -
his untimely demise - this is the story of the dauntless persistence
of William Jennings Bryan.

    l. Bryan, William Jenn... 1860-1925. l. Title.

C1
H40
Whorf, Michael, 1933–
   The lost colony of Roanoke.
   1 tape cassette. (The visual sounds of
Mike Whorf. History and heritage, H40)
    Originally presented on his radio program, Kaleidoscope,
WJR, Detroit.
    Duration: 39 min., 30 sec.
    Prior to the coming of the Pilgrims, a group of similar hardy
souls settled in Virginia. Their colony thrived and grew prosperous
and then for some unknown reason, it perished.

    l. Raleigh's Roanoke Colonies, 1584-1590. l. Title.

C1
H56
Whorf, Michael, 1933–
   The Lincoln remembered.
   1 tape cassette. (The visual sounds of
Mike Whorf. History and heritage, H56)
    Originally presented on his radio program, Kaleidoscope,
WJR, Detroit.
    Duration: 37 min.
    Here is a Lincoln that captures the essence of the man, his
great humor, his understanding of human nature.

    l. Lincoln, Abraham, Pres. U.S., 1809-1865. l. Title.

OFFICIAL

C1
A39
Whorf, Michael, 1933–
   Love letters.
   1 tape cassette. (The visual sounds of
Mike Whorf. Art, music and letters, A39)
    Originally presented on his radio program, Kaleidoscope,
WJR, Detroit.
    Duration: 36 min., 45 sec.
    In this program we take a different tack in looking into the
infamous and famous characters of history. Though they wrote
words for the world, there were some words meant for the eyes
of the few.

    l. Love-letters. l. Title.

OFFICIAL

C1
A6
Whorf, Michael, 1933–
   The little woman.
   1 tape cassette. (The visual sounds of
Mike Whorf. Art, music, and letters, A6)
    Originally presented on his radio program, Kaleidoscope,
WJR, Detroit.
    Duration: 34 min., 45 sec.
    Louisa May Alcott's story is found in her work "Little women,"
but there is another view of her life.

    l. Alcott, Louisa May, 1832-1888. l. Title.

C1
A37
Whorf, Michael, 1933–
   The magic of poetry.
   1 tape cassette. (The visual sounds of
Mike Whorf. Art, music and letters, A37)
    Originally presented on his radio program, Kaleidoscope,
WJR, Detroit.
    Duration: 37 min., 30 sec.
    Here is a simple and elementary look at the art of reading
and writing verse. A few quotes from the masters and a few
dissections help the listener discover the magic of poetry.

    l. Poetry. l. Title.

OFFICIAL

C1
SC2
Whorf, Michael, 1933–
    The man called healer.
    1 tape cassette. (The visual sounds of
Mike Whorf. Science, Sc2)
    Originally presented on his radio program, Kaleidoscope,
WJR, Detroit.
    Duration: 39 min.
    Actual recordings are used to relate the story of medicine -
its history and progress under difficult conditions.

    I. Physicians. 2. Medicine. I. Title.

C1
M11
Whorf, Michael, 1933–
    The man in the iron mask.
    1 tape cassette. (The visual sounds of
Mike Whorf. Miscellaneous, M11)
    Originally presented on his radio program, Kaleidoscope,
WJR, Detroit.
    Duration: 42 min., 10 sec.
    An account of the thoughts and ideas of a big league catcher.
The emphasis is on baseball, but a ball player thinks of other
things as well.

    I. Freehan, Bill, 1941– 2. Baseball. I. Title.

C1
A26
Whorf, Michael, 1933–
    A man for all ages - Dante.
    1 tape cassette. (The visual sounds of
Mike Whorf. Art, music and letters, A26)
    Originally presented on his radio program, Kaleidoscope,
WJR, Detroit.
    Duration: 38 min.
    To many critics the world over Dante's "Divine comedy" is the
finest piece of writing mankind has ever accomplished. Here is a
look at the writing and at the man.

    I. Dante Alighieri, 1265–1321. I. Title.

C1
S2
Whorf, Michael, 1933–
    A man named Ghandi.
    1 tape cassette. (The visual sounds of
Mike Whorf. Social, S2)
    Originally presented on his radio program, Kaleidoscope,
WJR, Detroit.
    Duration: 29 min.
    Gandhi was counselor, advisor, and spiritual guide to a nation
which upheld the caste system and he alone was able to break
through to open the eyes of the world.

    I. Gandhi, Mohandas Karamchand, 1869–1948. I. Title.

OFFICIAL

C1
M4
Whorf, Michael, 1933–
    Man from Oklahoma.
    1 tape cassette. (The visual sounds of
Mike Whorf. Miscellaneous, M4)
    Originally presented on his radio program, Kaleidoscope,
WJR, Detroit.
    Duration: 40 min.
    The dry, brilliant humor of Will Rogers comes through in this
narrative concerning the cowboy philosopher.

    I. Rogers, Will, 1879–1935. I. Title.

C1
H7
Whorf, Michael, 1933–
    The man of steel and velvet.
    1 tape cassette. (The visual sounds of
Mike Whorf. History and heritage, H7)
    Originally presented on his radio program, Kaleidoscope,
WJR, Detroit.
    Duration: 55 min.
    A historical account of the young Lincoln, his days as a
struggling young lawyer, his political aspirations, his arduous
years as a president, his tragic death.

    I. Lincoln, Abraham, Pres. U.S., 1809–1865. I. Title.

OFFICIAL

C1
H26
Whorf, Michael, 1933–
    The man from Osawattmie - John Brown's story.
    1 tape cassette. (The visual sounds of
Mike Whorf. History and heritage, H26)
    Originally presented on his radio program, Kaleidoscope,
WJR, Detroit.
    Duration: 30 min.
    Fanatic or hero, prophet or fool; here is the life and times
of old John Brown.

    I. Brown, John, 1800–1859. I. Title.

C1
A25
Whorf, Michael, 1933–
    The man who wrote Moby Dick - Herman Melville.
    1 tape cassette. (The visual sounds of
Mike Whorf. Art, music and letters, A25)
    Originally presented on his radio program, Kaleidoscope,
WJR, Detroit.
    Duration: 42 min.
    Herman Melville, like his characters, lived a life of adventure
aboard ship. He knew the seas and islands and he drew from his
experiences to write what critics believe is one of the ten best books
ever written.

    I. Melville, Herman, 1819–1891. I. Title.

C1
SC3–
SC4
Whorf, Michael, 1933–
    The man in the glass box.
    2 tape cassettes. (The visual sounds of
Mike Whorf. Science, SC3–SC4)
    Originally presented on his radio program, Kaleidoscope,
WJR, Detroit.
    Duration: 39 min., 46 min.
    Two documentary programs on one of today's greatest
medical and social problems ... alcoholism.

    I. Alcoholics. I. Title.

C1
H114
Whorf, Michael, 1933–
    The march to the sea - Sherman.
    1 tape cassette. (The visual sounds of
Mike Whorf. History and heritage, H114)
    Originally presented on his radio program, Kaleidoscope,
WJR, Detroit.
    Duration: 36 min., 15 sec.
    Was he ruthless or merely a genius at the art of warfare?
Was William Tecumseh Sherman's March to the sea across
Georgia one of fiery retaliation against the South, or the
necessary means to an end?

    I. Sherman, William Tecumseh, 1820–1891. I. Title.

C1
S15
Whorf, Michael, 1933–
Marching as to war.
1 tape cassette. (The visual sounds of
Mike Whorf. Social, S15)
Originally presented on his radio program, Kaleidoscope,
WJR, Detroit.
Duration: 42 min.
Outlined against the background of the 19th century in
England, is the story of William Booth and the Salvation Army.

L Booth, William, 1829–1912. 2. Salvation Army.
L Title.

C2
R7
Whorf, Michael, 1933–
The miracle of Saint Joan.
1 tape cassette. (The visual sounds of
Mike Whorf. Religion, R7)
Originally presented on his radio program, Kaleidoscope,
WJR, Detroit.
Duration: 40 min., 30 sec.
Her immolation at the stake was the beginning of a legend rather
than the end of a life, and amidst the splendor and pageantry her
story is told.

L Jeanne d'Arc, Saint, 1412–1431. L Title.

C1
PWM23–
24
Whorf, Michael, 1933–
The masters.
1 tape cassette. (The visual sounds of
Mike Whorf. Panorama; a world of music,
PWM-23-PWM-24)
Originally presented on his radio program, Kaleidoscope,
WJR, Detroit.
Duration: 29 min.; 21 min., 45 sec.
The great melodies of classical music are set forth here
under various themes.

L Music - History and criticism. L Title.

C1
R5
Whorf, Michael, 1933–
Miracle of the twelve.
1 tape cassette. (The visual sounds of
Mike Whorf. Religion, R5)
Originally presented on his radio program, Kaleidoscope,
WJR, Detroit.
Duration: 35 min., 40 sec.
Grouped together as a determined force carrying the word of the
Messiah, were twelve men selected by the Christ to bring to the
world a philosophy which mankind has never improved on.

L Apostles. L Title.

C1
H97
Whorf, Michael, 1933–
The Mayflower story.
1 tape cassette. (The visual sounds of
Mike Whorf. History and heritage, H97)
Originally presented on his radio program, Kaleidoscope,
WJR, Detroit.
Duration: 36 min., 30 sec.
With the determination born out of persecution and the
struggle to retain their religious beliefs, the Pilgrims strove to
establish a new order. This account follows their journey from
England to the New World, tracing their travels and recounting
the hardships that accompanied their quest.

L Mayflower (Ship) L Title.

OFFICIAL

C1
M39
Whorf, Michael, 1933–
Mr. Hohner's amazing harmonica.
1 tape cassette. (The visual sounds of
Mike Whorf. Miscellaneous, M39)
Originally presented on his radio program, Kaleidoscope,
WJR, Detroit.
Duration: 38 min.
Never underestimate the power of this six-inch instrument,
the harmonica. Its history is rich and long, dating from
ancient China to the twentieth century.

L Mouth-organ. L Title.

C1
H28
Whorf, Michael, 1933–
The men before Columbus.
1 tape cassette. (The visual sounds of
Mike Whorf. History and heritage, H28)
Originally presented on his radio program, Kaleidoscope,
WJR, Detroit.
Duration: 40 min., 15 sec.
1000 years before Columbus' exploration of San Salvador came
the Vikings whose culture and life style made little impression on the
world, but their knowledge of sailing and their spirit of adventure
would inspire others to undertake the role of discoverer.

L Vikings. 2. America - Discovery and exploration - Norse.
L Title.

OFFICIAL

C1
S48
Whorf, Michael, 1933–
The Molly Maguires.
1 tape cassette. (The visual sounds of
Mike Whorf. Social, S48)
Originally presented on his radio program, Kaleidoscope,
WJR, Detroit.
Duration: 37 min.
From the green hills of Ireland they came to work in the black
hills of Pennsylvania. Because of hardship, ill housing, poor food,
and intolerable working conditions, they formed themselves into a
band of marauding vigilantes called the Molly Maguires.

L Molly Maguires. L Title.

OFFICIAL

C1
R32
Whorf, Michael, 1933–
Minister to millions - Norman Vincent Peale.
1 tape cassette. (The visual sounds of
Mike Whorf. Religion, R32)
Originally presented on his radio program, Kaleidoscope,
WJR, Detroit.
Duration: 57 min., 30 sec.
Norman Vincent Peale, remembered as the author of The
power of positive thinking, is a man of varied accomplishments,
some well-known, others which go almost unnoticed.

L Peale, Norman Vincent, 1898– L Title.

OFFICIAL

C1
S65
Whorf, Michael, 1933–
Mother Russia - from 1900 to the present.
1 tape cassette. (The visual sounds of
Mike Whorf. Social, S65)
Originally presented on his radio program, Kaleidoscope,
WJR, Detroit.
Duration: 39 min., 25 sec.
From the age of Czar Nicholas to the present, here is the bigger
than life story of the great "Mother Russia".

L Russia. L Title.

C1
PWM3
Whorf, Michael, 1933–
Mozart.
1 tape cassette. (The visual sounds of
Mike Whorf. Panorama; a world of music, PWM-3)

Originally presented on his radio program, Kaleidoscope,
WJR, Detroit.
Duration: 25 min.
The life and times of Mozart, including excerpts of his
music.

L. Mozart, Johann Chrysostom Wolfgang Amadeus, 1756–
1791. L. Title.

C1
A11
Whorf, Michael, 1933–
Music for the heavens.
1 tape cassette. (The visual sounds of
Mike Whorf. Art, music, and letters, A11)

Originally presented on his radio program, Kaleidoscope,
WJR, Detroit.
Duration: 36 min., 45 sec.
Was Johann Sebastian Bach the most creative and brilliant
musician artist on the European scene? Those aspects and attitudes
can conceivably be confirmed as one delves into his life and times.

L. Bach, Johann Sebastian, 1685–1750. L. Title.

C1
A14
Whorf, Michael, 1933–
My love is like a red, red rose.
1 tape cassette. (The visual sounds of
Mike Whorf. Art, music, and letters, A14)

Originally presented on his radio program, Kaleidoscope,
WJR, Detroit.
Duration: 35 min.
The Scottish highlands, the swift of tartans, the pipes, the
smell of heather, is the setting for the heart-warming story of
Robert Burns.

L. Burns, Robert, 1759–1796. L. Title.

C1
M44
Whorf, Michael, 1933–
The mystery of the Mary Celeste.
1 tape cassette. (The visual sounds of
Mike Whorf. Miscellaneous, M44)
Originally presented on his radio program, Kaleidoscope,
WJR, Detroit.
Duration: 36 min.
The strange story of a ship and its missing crew. What
happened? Who was involved? Over the years since the
derelict ship's reappearance, many theories have been
expounded.

L. Mary Celeste (Brig) L. Title.

OFFICIAL

C1
A46
Whorf, Michael, 1933–
The mystery of William Porter – O. Henry.
1 tape cassette. (The visual sounds of
Mike Whorf. Art, music and letters, A46)

Originally presented on his radio program, Kaleidoscope,
WJR, Detroit.
Duration: 36 min., 30 sec.
The man spent many of his years behind bars, movements
inhibited, freedom gone. But his mind was free, free to imagine,
then to put down on paper his short stories.

L. Porter, William Sydney, 1862–1910. L. Title.

OFFICIAL

C1
H108
Whorf, Michael, 1933–
The navigator – Vasco de Gama.
1 tape cassette. (The visual sounds of
Mike Whorf. History and heritage, H108)

Originally presented on his radio program, Kaleidoscope,
WJR, Detroit.
Duration: 38 min.
Hundreds of years ago when the race to expand the world made
rivals of the world's great powers, Portugal sent forth its greatest
soldier and mariner, Vasco de Gama.

L. Gama, Vasco da, 1469–1524. L. Title.

OFFICIAL

C1
H60
Whorf, Michael, 1933–
Never strike the colors – Stephen Decatur.
1 tape cassette. (The visual sounds of
Mike Whorf. History and heritage, H60)

Originally presented on his radio program, Kaleidoscope,
WJR, Detroit.
Duration: 43 min.
Handsome, brave, and honorable, Stephen Decatur was one of
America's most daring naval officers.

L. Decatur, Stephen, 1779–1820. L. Title.

C1
M16
Whorf, Michael, 1933–
Now batting for the New York Yankees.
1 tape cassette. (The visual sounds of
Mike Whorf. Miscellaneous, M16)

Originally presented on his radio program, Kaleidoscope,
WJR, Detroit.
Duration: 40 min., 30 sec.
This is the story of Babe Ruth, the orphan boy of Baltimore who
would one day become the great New York Yankee slugger.

L. Ruth, George Herman, 1894–1948. L. Title.

C1
H8
Whorf, Michael, 1933–
Of men and legends.
1 tape cassette. (The visual sounds of
Mike Whorf. History and heritage, H8)
Originally presented on his radio program, Kaleidoscope,
WJR, Detroit.
Duration: 50 min., 30 sec.
Beloved and revered, despised and dislike, they were figures
in our history that helped to make a great land. Here are brief
character sketches of personalities in our heritage whose contri-
butions and efforts are gratefully acknowledged by an appreciative
nation.

L. U. S. – Biography. L. Title.

C1
R22
Whorf, Michael, 1933–
Of myths and gods.
1 tape cassette. (The visual sounds of
Mike Whorf. Religion, R22)

Originally presented on his radio program, Kaleidoscope,
WJR, Detroit.
Duration: 48 min., 30 sec.
From antiquity comes the history of gods and legends. Who were
the great Egyptian, Greek and Roman gods – and what part did man
play in their world and they in his?

L. Mythology. L. Title.

C1
S26

Whorf, Michael, 1933–
Oh, to be a kid again.
1 tape cassette. (The visual sounds of
Mike Whorf. Social, S26)
Originally presented on his radio program, Kaleidoscope,
WJR, Detroit.
Duration: 28 min., 30 sec.
An ode to the school, the childи and the teacher in this
narrative which deals with a nostalgic look at some of our
experiences.

1. Education. L Title.

C1
A38

Whorf, Michael, 1933–
The original big-little book.
1 tape cassette. (The visual sounds of
Mike Whorf. Art, music and letters, A38)
Originally presented on his radio program, Kaleidoscope,
WJR, Detroit.
Duration: 40 min.
Here is the story of the Reader's Digest, the people who write it,
why they write it and how this popular magazine is compiled.

1. The Reader's digest. 2. Wallace, DeWitt, 1889–
L Title.

OFFICIAL

C1
H30

Whorf, Michael, 1933–
Old Hickory, Andrew Jackson.
1 tape cassette. (The visual sounds of
Mike Whorf. History and heritage, H30)

Originally presented on his radio program, Kaleidoscope,
WJR, Detroit.
Duration: 30 min., 10 sec.
The life of Andrew Jackson from his backwoods beginnings,
through his battles with Indians and British, to his service as
president.

1. Jackson, Andrew, Pres. U.S., 1767-1845. L Title.

C1
H11

Whorf, Michael, 1933–
Our legacy from Mr. Jefferson.
1 tape cassette. (The visual sounds of
Mike Whorf. History and heritage, H11)
Originally presented on his radio program, Kaleidoscope,
WJR, Detroit.
Duration: 38 min.
This historical account follows him through his years as a young
Virginia scholar influenced by Patrick Henry to his days as a patriot
who left a legacy to each and every American.

1. Jefferson, Thomas, Pres. U.S., 1743-1826. L Title.

C1
H104–
H105

Whorf, Michael, 1933–
Old soldiers never die – General Douglas
MacArthur.
2 tape cassettes. (The visual sounds of
Mike Whorf. History and heritage, H104–H105)

Originally presented on his radio program, Kaleidoscope,
WJR, Detroit.
Duration: 37 min.; 37 min.
Who was General MacArthur? This questions and others are
explored, and frequently answered in his own words in this two-part
series on one of our country's great military leaders.

1. MacArthur, Douglas, 1880-1964. L Title.

OFFICIAL

C1
A4

Whorf, Michael, 1933–
Painter of the plains.
1 tape cassette. (The visual sounds of
Mike Whorf. Art, music, and letters, A4)

Originally presented on his radio program, Kaleidoscope,
WJR, Detroit.
Duration: 30 min.
Those who never saw the American West in its greatness can
thank the creativeness of Frederic Remington, who seemed to know
that a way of life, a people, and a time would quickly vanish,
and so he captured it on canvas.

1. Remington, Frederic, 1861-1909. L Title.

C1
PWM6

Whorf, Michael, 1933–
The old sweet songs.
1 tape cassette. (The visual sounds of
Mike Whorf. Panorama; a world of music, PWM-6)

Originally presented on his radio program, Kaleidoscope,
WJR, Detroit.
Duration: 26 min.
The story and instrumental renditions of Greensleeves,
My Old Kentucky home, After the ball, and Mighty lak' a
rose.

1. Music, Popular (Songs, etc.) – U.S. L Title.

C1
H3

Whorf, Michael, 1933–
The patriot, Patrick Henry.
1 tape cassette. (The visual sounds of
Mike Whorf. History and heritage, H3)
Originally presented on his radio program, Kaleidoscope,
WJR, Detroit.
Duration: 28 min.
From his humble beginnings - to his days as barrister - to
his appointment in Virginia's House of Burgesses, there was about
him the qualities of the patriot.

1. Henry, Patrick, 1736-1799. L Title.

C1
PWM5

Whorf, Michael, 1933–
Operetta memories.
1 tape cassette. (The visual sounds of
Mike Whorf. Panorama; a world of music, PWM-5
Originally presented on his radio program, Kaleidoscope,
WJR, Detroit.
Duration: 27 min., 45 sec.
A history of operettas including excerpts from The merry
widow and The chocolate soldier.

1. Musical revues, comedies, etc. L Title.

C1
H34

Whorf, Michael, 1933–
Patton.
1 tape cassette. (The visual sounds of
Mike Whorf. History and heritage, H34)

Originally presented on his radio program, Kaleidoscope,
WJR, Detroit.
Duration: 54 min.
A cavalry officer in W.W. I, a tank commander in the
second global holocaust, here is the story of the brilliant bold
general who led his armament against Rommel in Africa, and
fought one of the great campaigns shortly before the end of W.W. II.

1. Patton, George Smith, 1885-1945. L Title.

C1
H106
Whorf, Michael, 1933–
    The perfect legend – George Washington.
    1 tape cassette.   (The visual sounds of
Mike Whorf. History and heritage, H106)
    Originally presented on his radio program, Kaleidoscope,
WJR, Detroit.
    Duration: 37 min., 30 sec.
    As commander of a new country, General George Washington
watched his soldiers falter. His faith, trust and heroics led his
men to a nearly impossible victory.

    L Washington, George, Pres. U.S., 1732–1799.   L Title.

OFFICIAL

C1
A17
Whorf, Michael, 1933–
    Poe, evermore.
    1 tape cassette.   (The visual sounds of
Mike Whorf. Art, music, and letters, A17)
    Originally presented on his radio program, Kaleidoscope,
WJR, Detroit.
    Duration: 47 min., 40 sec.
    Works of Poe are featured, as well as a close look at the
man who was an enigma to his friends as well as himself.

    L Poe, Edgar Allan, 1809–1849.   L Title.

C1
FA20
Whorf, Michael, 1933–
    Peter Cooper.
    1 tape cassette.   (The visual sounds of
Mike Whorf. The forgotten American, FA20)
    Originally presented on his radio program, Kaleidoscope,
WJR, Detroit.
    Duration: 10 min., 40 sec.
    Cooper made and piloted the first steam engine on the
Baltimore and Ohio railroad. He participated in the laying
of the Atlantic Cable. Founder of the Cooper Union, he was
also Greenback candidate for President of the United States.

    L Cooper, Peter, 1791–1883.   L Title.

C1
A44
Whorf, Michael, 1933–
    The poet of democracy – Walt Whitman.
    1 tape cassette.   (The visual sounds of
Mike Whorf. Art, music and letters, A44)
    Originally presented on his radio program, Kaleidoscope,
WJR, Detroit.
    Duration: 37 min.
    The likeable, candid Whitman has become the poet of
America. During his life he strived for freedom; for the
country, for his poetry.

    L Whitman, Walt, 1819–1892.   L Title.

C1
R21
Whorf, Michael, 1933–
    The phenomenal Billy Graham.
    1 tape cassette.   (The visual sounds of
Mike Whorf. Religion, R21)
    Originally presented on his radio program, Kaleidoscope,
WJR, Detroit.
    Duration: 41 min., 30 sec.
    Here are the thoughts and ideas, aspirations and inspirations
of Billy Graham, a leading personality of our age bent on bringing
man to God.

    L Graham, William Franklin, 1918–   L Title.

C1
A9
Whorf, Michael, 1933–
    Poet of the piano.
    1 tape cassette.   (The visual sounds of
Mike Whorf. Art, music, and letters, A9)
    Originally published on his radio program, Kaleidoscope,
WJR, Detroit.
    Duration: 27 min., 30 sec.
    With aspects of his career known only to the devotee, this
narrative is a portrait of one of the masters, Chopin.

    L Chopin, Fryderyk Franciszek, 1810–1849.   L Title.

C1
R15
Whorf, Michael, 1933–
    The plain people; the Amish story.
    1 tape cassette.   (The visual sounds of
Mike Whorf. Religion, R15)
    Originally presented on his radio program, Kaleidoscope,
WJR, Detroit.
    Duration: 45 min.
    The life style, traditions, habits, customs and heritage of
the Amish folk of Pennsylvania.

    L Mennonites.   L Title.

C1
H61
Whorf, Michael, 1933–
    Portrait of a patriot – Ethan Allen.
    1 tape cassette.   (The visual sounds of
Mike Whorf. History and heritage, H61)
    Originally presented on his radio program, Kaleidoscope,
WJR, Detroit.
    Duration: 40 min.
    Ethan Allen's small band of Green Mountain boys captured the
heavily-fortified garrison at Fort Ticonderoga in a daring attack
at dawn, and gave the struggling Continental Congress a much-
needed victory.

    L Allen, Ethan, 1738–1789.   L Title.

C1
H46
Whorf, Michael, 1933–
    The play that Lincoln never saw.
    1 tape cassette.   (The visual sounds of
Mike Whorf. History and heritage, H46)
    Originally presented on his radio program, Kaleidoscope,
WJR, Detroit.
    Duration: 30 min.
    "Our American cousin" was the play Abraham Lincoln attended on
that fateful night. In the shadows awaited death and the nation went
into shock. But what of the play – its actors and actresses?

    L Taylor, Tom, 1817–1880. /Our American cousin.
    2. Lincoln, Abraham, Pres. U.S., 1809–1865.   L Title.

OFFICIAL

C1
SC26
Whorf, Michael, 1933–
    The practical genius – Thomas Edison.
    1 tape cassette.   (The visual sounds of
Mike Whorf. Science, SC26)
    Originally presented on his radio program, Kaleidoscope,
WJR, Detroit.
    Duration: 42 min.
    Regarded as a failure in early life, Edison's personal strength and
dogged perseverance bore him above the hardships of life, and
established him as one of the world's greatest and most inventive
minds.

    L Edison, Thomas Alva, 1847–1931.   L Title.

OFFICIAL

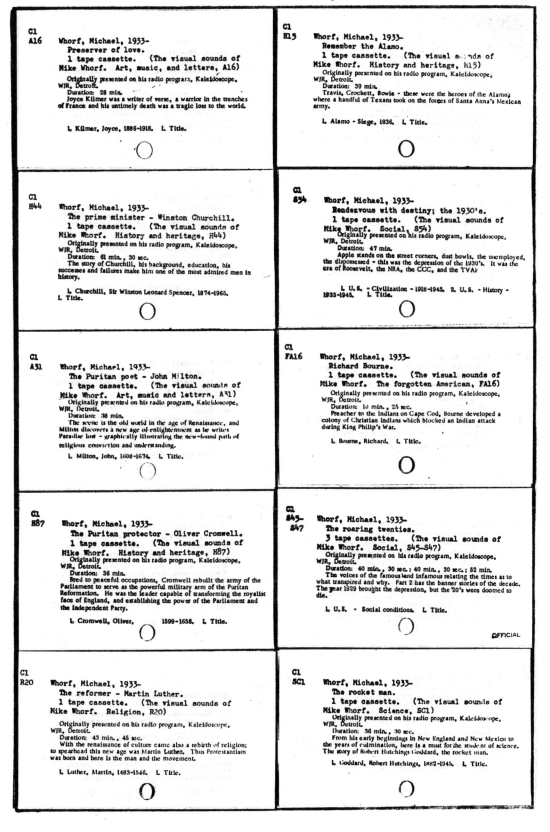

C1
A16

Whorf, Michael, 1933–
   Preserver of love.
   1 tape cassette.   (The visual sounds of
Mike Whorf. Art, music, and letters, A16)
   Originally presented on his radio program, Kaleidoscope,
WJR, Detroit.
   Duration: 28 min.
   Joyce Kilmer was a writer of verse, a warrior in the trenches
of France and his untimely death was a tragic loss to the world.

   I. Kilmer, Joyce, 1886–1918. I. Title.

C1
H15

Whorf, Michael, 1933–
   Remember the Alamo.
   1 tape cassette.   (The visual sounds of
Mike Whorf. History and heritage, H15)
   Originally presented on his radio program, Kaleidoscope,
WJR, Detroit.
   Duration: 39 min.
   Travis, Crockett, Bowie - these were the heroes of the Alamo,
where a handful of Texans took on the forces of Santa Anna's Mexican
army.

   I. Alamo - Siege, 1836. I. Title.

C1
H44

Whorf, Michael, 1933–
   The prime minister - Winston Churchill.
   1 tape cassette.   (The visual sounds of
Mike Whorf. History and heritage, H44)
   Originally presented on his radio program, Kaleidoscope,
WJR, Detroit.
   Duration: 61 min., 30 sec.
   The story of Churchill, his background, education, his
successes and failures make him one of the most admired men in
history.

   I. Churchill, Sir Winston Leonard Spencer, 1874–1965.
I. Title.

C1
S54

Whorf, Michael, 1933–
   Rendezvous with destiny; the 1930's.
   1 tape cassette.   (The visual sounds of
Mike Whorf. Social, S54)
   Originally presented on his radio program, Kaleidoscope,
WJR, Detroit.
   Duration: 47 min.
   Apple stands on the street corners, dust bowls, the unemployed,
the dispossessed - this was the depression of the 1930's. It was the
era of Roosevelt, the NRA, the CCC, and the TVA.

   I. U. S. - Civilization - 1918-1945. 2. U. S. - History -
1933-1945. I. Title.

C1
A31

Whorf, Michael, 1933–
   The Puritan poet - John Milton.
   1 tape cassette.   (The visual sounds of
Mike Whorf. Art, music and letters, A31)
   Originally presented on his radio program, Kaleidoscope,
WJR, Detroit.
   Duration: 38 min.
   The scene is the old world in the age of Renaissance, and
Milton discovers a new age of enlightenment as he writes
Paradise lost - graphically illustrating the new-found path of
religious conviction and understanding.

   I. Milton, John, 1608–1674. I. Title.

C1
FA16

Whorf, Michael, 1933–
   Richard Bourne.
   1 tape cassette.   (The visual sounds of
Mike Whorf. The forgotten American, FA16)
   Originally presented on his radio program, Kaleidoscope,
WJR, Detroit.
   Duration: 10 min., 25 sec.
   Preacher to the Indians on Cape Cod, Bourne developed a
colony of Christian Indians which blocked an Indian attack
during King Philip's War.

   I. Bourne, Richard. I. Title.

C1
H87

Whorf, Michael, 1933–
   The Puritan protector - Oliver Cromwell.
   1 tape cassette.   (The visual sounds of
Mike Whorf. History and heritage, H87)
   Originally presented on his radio program, Kaleidoscope,
WJR, Detroit.
   Duration: 36 min.
   Bred to peaceful occupations, Cromwell rebuilt the army of the
Parliament to serve as the powerful military arm of the Puritan
Reformation. He was the leader capable of transforming the royalist
face of England, and establishing the power of the Parliament and
the Independent Party.

   I. Cromwell, Oliver,   1599–1658. I. Title.

C1
S45-
S47

Whorf, Michael, 1933–
   The roaring twenties.
   3 tape cassettes.   (The visual sounds of
Mike Whorf. Social, S45-S47)
   Originally presented on his radio program, Kaleidoscope,
WJR, Detroit.
   Duration: 40 min., 30 sec.; 40 min., 30 sec.; 52 min.
   The voices of the famous and infamous relating the times as to
what transpired and why. Part 2 has the banner stories of the decade.
The year 1929 brought the depression, but the 20's were doomed to
die.

   I. U. S. - Social conditions. I. Title.

OFFICIAL

C1
R20

Whorf, Michael, 1933–
   The reformer - Martin Luther.
   1 tape cassette.   (The visual sounds of
Mike Whorf. Religion, R20)
   Originally presented on his radio program, Kaleidoscope,
WJR, Detroit.
   Duration: 43 min., 45 sec.
   With the renaissance of culture came also a rebirth of religion;
to spearhead this new age was Martin Luther. Thus Protestantism
was born and here is the man and the movement.

   I. Luther, Martin, 1483–1546. I. Title.

C1
SC1

Whorf, Michael, 1933–
   The rocket man.
   1 tape cassette.   (The visual sounds of
Mike Whorf. Science, SC1)
   Originally presented on his radio program, Kaleidoscope,
WJR, Detroit.
   Duration: 36 min., 30 sec.
   From his early beginnings in New England and New Mexico to
the years of culmination, here is a must for the student of science.
The story of Robert Hutchings Goddard, the rocket man.

   I. Goddard, Robert Hutchings, 1882–1945. I. Title.

C1
A24
Whorf, Michael, 1933–
    Romance of the Audubons--John and Lucy.
    1 tape cassette.   (The visual sounds of
Mike Whorf. Art, music, and letters, A24)
        Originally presented on his radio program, Kaleidoscope,
    WJR, Detroit.
        Duration: 46 min.
        From the reaches of time is drawn this story of romance, of
    the love of John Audubon and his wife, Lucy, who survived the
    struggles and hardships of the wilderness so that her gifted husband
    would achieve his ambition and dreams.

        1. Audubon, John James, 1788–1851. 2. Audubon, Lucy
    (Bakewell) 1. Title.

                                                    OFFICIAL

C1
A34
Whorf, Michael, 1933–
    The romantic poet – Victor Hugo.
    1 tape cassette.   (The visual sounds of
Mike Whorf. Art, music and letters, A34)
        Originally presented on his radio program, Kaleidoscope,
    WJR, Detroit.
        Duration: 36 min., 45 sec.
        He was a gifted author, and a product of the elite French
    literary circle, but though his prose and poetry was voluminous
    and varied, there was but one novel which insured his
    immortality.

        1. Hugo, Victor Marie, comte, 1802–1885.

                                                    OFFICIAL

C1
M36
Whorf, Michael, 1933–
    The sad, strange saga of the Great Eastern.
    1 tape cassette.   (The visual sounds of
Mike Whorf. Miscellaneous, M36)
        Originally presented on his radio program, Kaleidoscope,
    WJR, Detroit.
        Duration: 38 min., 15 sec.
        Many great ships have sailed the seven seas. Why couldn't
    this splendid vessel surmount superstition, obstacle, and nature?
    This is the plot of the sad strange saga of the Great Eastern.

        1. Great Eastern (Ship) 1. Title.

C1
A29
Whorf, Michael, 1933–
    The sage of Concord – Ralph Waldo Emerson.
    1 tape cassette.   (The visual sounds of
Mike Whorf. Art, music and letters, A29)
        Originally presented on his radio program, Kaleidoscope,
    WJR, Detroit.
        Duration: 38 min., 45 sec.
        Ralph Waldo Emerson was a witness of his times, able to
    exert influence on the manners and mores of the public. His
    poetry is laced with wisdom and depth, and its meanings are
    as vital today and when first read.

        1. Emerson, Ralph Waldo, 1803–1882.   1. Title.

                                                    OFFICIAL

C1
R6
Whorf, Michael, 1933–
    The saint from Assisi.
    1 tape cassette.   (The visual sounds of
Mike Whorf. Religion, R6)
        Originally presented on his radio program, Kaleidoscope,
    WJR, Detroit.
        Duration: 39 min., 30 sec.
        This is the tale of Francis of Assisi, who would form the Franciscan
    order, would be friend to man and animal, and would teach mankind
    the meaning of true humility.

        1. Francis of Assisi, Saint, 1182–1226. 1. Title.

C1
H37
Whorf, Michael, 1933–
    Sam Houston.
    1 tape cassette.   (The visual sounds of
Mike Whorf. History and heritage, H37)
        Originally presented on his radio program, Kaleidoscope,
    WJR, Detroit.
        Duration: 40 min.
        In the days of the young Texas territory many men would ennoble
    themselves for the cause of independence. One man much
    criticized, and yet admired was Sam Houston.

        1. Houston, Samuel, 17?? 1863. 1. Title.

C1
PWM4
Whorf, Michael, 1933–
    Schumann.
    1 tape cassette.   (The visual sounds of
Mike Whorf. Panorama; a world of music,
PWM-4)
        Originally presented on his radio program, Kaleidoscope,
    WJR, Detroit.
        Duration: 25 min., 50 sec.
        The life and times of Robert Schumann, including excerpts
    of his music.

        1. Schumann, Robert Alexander, 1810–1856. 1. Title.

C1
S30
Whorf, Michael, 1933–
    Seeing things at night – Halloween.
    1 tape cassette.   (The visual sounds of
Mike Whorf. Social, S30)
        Originally presented on his radio program, Kaleidoscope,
    WJR, Detroit.
        Duration: 49 min., 15 sec.
        "Seein' things at night," "The goblins will getcha" and the
    terrifying tale of Sawney Beane and his family are tales appropriate
    for this Halloween special.

        1. Halloween. 1. Title.

C1
H116
Whorf, Michael, 1933–
    Seward's big deal – purchase of Alaska.
    1 tape cassette.   (The visual sounds of
Mike Whorf. History and heritage, H116)
        Originally presented on his radio program, Kaleidoscope,
    WJR, Detroit.
        Duration: 36 min., 10 sec.
        They called it Seward's ice box or Seward's folly – this big deal
    made by William Seward. This program tells the story of Seward,
    the men, the man responsible for the purchase of Alaska.

        1. Seward, William henry, 1801–1872. 2. Alaska – History :
    To 1867. 1. Title.

                                                    OFFICIAL

C1
M1
Whorf, Michael, 1933–
    The silent screen.
    1 tape cassette.   (The visual sounds of
Mike Whorf. Miscellaneous, M1)
        Originally presented on his radio program, Kaleidoscope,
    WJR, Detroit.
        Duration: 41 min.
        It was a history-making event when Edison came forward with
    his moving-picture machine. Mary Pickford, Douglas Fairbanks,
    Valentino, Clara Bow – the story of their era would unfold with
    stories and stars coming alive on the silent screen.

        1. Moving-pictures,   Silent. 1. Title.

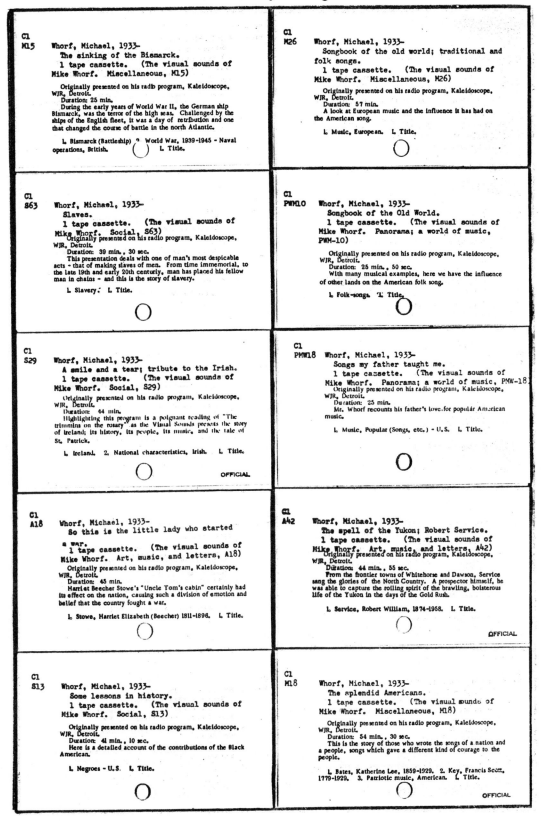

C1
M15
Whorf, Michael, 1933–
    The sinking of the Bismarck.
    1 tape cassette.   (The visual sounds of
Mike Whorf. Miscellaneous, M15)

    Originally presented on his radio program, Kaleidoscope,
WJR, Detroit.
    Duration: 25 min.
    During the early years of World War II, the German ship
Bismarck, was the terror of the high seas. Challenged by the
ships of the English fleet, it was a day of retribution and one
that changed the course of battle in the north Atlantic.

    L. Bismarck (Battleship) 2. World War, 1939-1945 - Naval
operations, British.   L. Title.

C1
M26
Whorf, Michael, 1933–
    Songbook of the old world; traditional and
folk songs.
    1 tape cassette.   (The visual sounds of
Mike Whorf. Miscellaneous, M26)

    Originally presented on his radio program, Kaleidoscope,
WJR, Detroit.
    Duration: 57 min.
    A look at European music and the influence it has had on
the American song.

    L. Music, European. L. Title.

C1
S63
Whorf, Michael, 1933–
    Slaves.
    1 tape cassette.   (The visual sounds of
Mike Whorf. Social, S63)
    Originally presented on his radio program, Kaleidoscope,
WJR, Detroit.
    Duration: 39 min., 30 sec.
    This presentation deals with one of man's most despicable
acts - that of making slaves of men. From time immemorial, to
the late 19th and early 20th century, man has placed his fellow
man in chains - and this is the story of slavery.

    L. Slavery. L. Title.

C1
PWM10
Whorf, Michael, 1933–
    Songbook of the Old World.
    1 tape cassette.   (The visual sounds of
Mike Whorf. Panorama; a world of music,
PWM-10)

    Originally presented on his radio program, Kaleidoscope,
WJR, Detroit.
    Duration: 25 min., 50 sec.
    With many musical examples, here we have the influence
of other lands on the American folk song.

    L. Folk-songs. L. Title.

C1
S29
Whorf, Michael, 1933–
    A smile and a tear; tribute to the Irish.
    1 tape cassette.   (The visual sounds of
Mike Whorf. Social, S29)

    Originally presented on his radio program, Kaleidoscope,
WJR, Detroit.
    Duration: 44 min.
    Highlighting this program is a poignant reading of "The
trimmins on the rosary" as the Visual Sounds presents the story
of Ireland; its history, its people, its music, and the tale of
St. Patrick.

    L. Ireland. 2. National characteristics, Irish. L. Title.

                                        OFFICIAL

C1
PMW18
Whorf, Michael, 1933–
    Songs my father taught me.
    1 tape cassette.   (The visual sounds of
Mike Whorf. Panorama; a world of music, PMW-18)
    Originally presented on his radio program, Kaleidoscope,
WJR, Detroit.
    Duration: 25 min.
    Mr. Whorf recounts his father's love for popular American
music.

    L. Music, Popular (Songs, etc.) - U.S. L. Title.

C1
A18
Whorf, Michael, 1933–
    So this is the little lady who started
a war.
    1 tape cassette.   (The visual sounds of
Mike Whorf. Art, music, and letters, A18)
    Originally presented on his radio program, Kaleidoscope,
WJR, Detroit.
    Duration: 45 min.
    Harriet Beecher Stowe's "Uncle Tom's cabin" certainly had
its effect on the nation, causing such a division of emotion and
belief that the country fought a war.

    L. Stowe, Harriet Elizabeth (Beecher) 1811-1896. L. Title.

C1
A42
Whorf, Michael, 1933–
    The spell of the Yukon; Robert Service.
    1 tape cassette.   (The visual sounds of
Mike Whorf. Art, music, and letters, A42)
    Originally presented on his radio program, Kaleidoscope,
WJR, Detroit.
    Duration: 44 min., 55 sec.
    From the frontier towns of Whitehorse and Dawson, Service
sang the glories of the North Country. A prospector himself, he
was able to capture the rolling spirit of the brawling, boisterous
life of the Yukon in the days of the Gold Rush.

    L. Service, Robert William, 1874-1958. L. Title.

                                        OFFICIAL

C1
S13
Whorf, Michael, 1933–
    Some lessons in history.
    1 tape cassette.   (The visual sounds of
Mike Whorf. Social, S13)

    Originally presented on his radio program, Kaleidoscope,
WJR, Detroit.
    Duration: 41 min., 10 sec.
    Here is a detailed account of the contributions of the Black
American.

    L. Negroes - U.S. L. Title.

C1
M18
Whorf, Michael, 1933–
    The splendid Americans.
    1 tape cassette.   (The visual sounds of
Mike Whorf. Miscellaneous, M18)

    Originally presented on his radio program, Kaleidoscope,
WJR, Detroit.
    Duration: 54 min., 30 sec.
    This is the story of those who wrote the songs of a nation and
a people, songs which gave a different kind of courage to the
people.

    L. Bates, Katherine Lee, 1859-1929. 2. Key, Francis Scott,
1779-1929. 3. Patriotic music, American. L. Title.

                                        OFFICIAL

C1
M30

Whorf, Michael, 1933–
    Spring.
    1 tape cassette.   (The visual sounds of
Mike Whorf. Miscellaneous, M30)

    Originally presented on his radio program, Kaleidoscope,
WJR, Detroit.
    Duration: 36 min., 15 sec.
    For the nature lover - for the poetry enthusiast - for those
who love the season of promise, here is a delightful and
refreshing episode devoted to spring.

    I. Spring. I. Title.

C1
H107

Whorf, Michael, 1933–
    Stonewall - Thomas Jonathan Jackson.
    1 tape cassette.   (The visual sounds of
Mike Whorf. History and heritage, H107)
    Originally presented on his radio program, Kaleidoscope,
WJR, Detroit.
    Duration: 38 min.
    This program tells the exciting story of the life of one of the
Confederacy's most colorful leaders. The humanness of the man is
stressed as the narrator weaves his tale with equal amounts of
pathos and tender humor.

    I. Jackson, Thomas Jonathan, 1824-1863. I. Title.

C1
H43

Whorf, Michael, 1933–
    Squanto.
    1 tape cassette.   (The visual sounds of
Mike Whorf. History and heritage, H43)

    Originally presented on his radio program, Kaleidoscope,
WJR, Detroit.
    Duration: 45 min., 40 sec.
    He was guide, interpreter, agricultural agent and comrade,
yet his life was as strange and as bizarre as the tale of the white
man he would greet on the shores of Cape Cod.

    I. Squanto. I. Title.

C1
A1

Whorf, Michael, 1933–
    The strange life of Paul Gauguin.
    1 tape cassette.   (The visual sounds of
Mike Whorf. Art, music and letters, A1)

    Originally presented on his radio program, Kaleidoscope,
WJR, Detroit.
    Duration: 26 min., 15 sec.
    Gauguin forsook the comforts of his world to wander half
way around the globe as a painter.

    I. Gauguin, Paul, 1848-1903. I. Title.

C1
S25

Whorf, Michael, 1933–
    The staff of life.
    1 tape cassette.   (The visual sounds of
Mike Whorf. Social, S25)

    Originally presented on his radio program, Kaleidoscope,
WJR, Detroit.
    Duration: 41 min.
    This is the story of wheat, of bread, its impact on mankind,
where and how it is processed and utilized.

    I. Wheat. 2. Bread. I. Title.

C1
S9

Whorf, Michael, 1933–
    The stranger.
    1 tape cassette.   (The visual sounds of
Mike Whorf. Social, S9)
    Originally presented on his radio program, Kaleidoscope,
WJR, Detroit.
    Duration: 46 min., 30 sec.
    Dealing with the American Indian, it relates the saga of the
warrior from boyhood to manhood, how and why he fought, the
ritual of his ceremony, and the explanation of his way of life.

    I. Indians of North America. I. Title.

OFFICIAL

C1
S68

Whorf, Michael, 1933–
    Statesmen and sages; Demosthenes, Aristotle,
Socrates, Cicero.
    1 tape cassette. (The visual sounds of Mike Whorf. Social, S68)

    Originally presented on his radio program, Kaleidoscope,
WJR, Detroit.
    Duration: 36 min.
    As ancient Greece and Rome served as the cradle of our modern
democracy, so do their citizens serve as shining examples of wisdom
and statecraft for us today.

    I. Demosthenes. 2. Aristoteles. 3. Socrates. 4. Cicero,
Marcus Tullius. I. Title.

OFFICIAL

C1
S23

Whorf, Michael, 1933–
    Stranger, no more.
    1 tape cassette.   (The visual sounds of
Mike Whorf. Social, S23)
    Originally presented on his radio program, Kaleidoscope,
WJR, Detroit.
    Duration: 42 min., 15 sec.
    This is the conclusion to the American Indian series. The
story concerns the redman today. It speaks, as does the Indian,
of his needs, aspirations and hopes.

    I. Indians of North America. I. Title.

OFFICIAL

C1
PWM7

Whorf, Michael, 1933–
    Stephen Foster.
    1 tape cassette.   (The visual sounds of
Mike Whorf. Panorama; a world of music, PWM-7)

    Originally presented on his radio program, Kaleidoscope,
WJR, Detroit.
    Duration: 25 min.
    The life and times of Stephen Foster, including excerpts
of his music.

    I. Foster, Stephen Collins, 1826-1864. I. Title.

C1
M50

Whorf, Michael, 1933–
    Stranger then fiction.
    1 tape cassette.   (The visual sounds of
Mike Whorf. Miscellaneous, M50)

    Originally presented on his radio program, Kaleidoscope,
WJR, Detroit.
    Duration: 36 min., 30 sec.
    Are these short stories fact or fiction, which elements are
true, which untrue?

    I. Title.

C1
PWM9
Whorf, Michael, 1933-
  Strauss.
  1 tape cassette. (The visual sounds of
Mike Whorf. Panorama; a world of music,
PWM-9)

  Originally presented on his radio program, Kaleidoscope,
WJR, Detroit.
  Duration: 25 min.
  The life and times of Johann Strauss, the younger, the
waltz king, including excerpts of his music.

  L Strauss, Johann, 1825-1899.   L Title.

C1
H39
Whorf, Michael, 1933-
  The tall tales of America - folklore, legends.
  1 tape cassette. (The visual sounds of
Mike Whorf. History and heritage, H39)

  Originally presented on his radio program, Kaleidoscope,
WJR, Detroit.
  Duration: 45 min., 30 sec.
  John Henry, Johnny Appleseed, Paul Bunyan, the great legends
of American folklore come to life in this amusing account of folk
tales and folk-songs about America.

  L Folk-lore, American. 2. Folk-songs, American.   L Title.

C1
SC6
Whorf, Michael, 1933-
  A study in prophecy.
  1 tape cassette. (The visual sounds of
Mike Whorf. Science, SC6)

  Originally presented on his radio program, Kaleidoscope,
WJR, Detroit.
  Duration: 55 min.
  Jeane Dixon expounds of her faith, tells why she has been
able to see glimpses of another world, and tells of her predictions,
some of which have come true and others which have not.

  L Dixon, Jeane.   L Title.

C1
PWM21
Whorf, Michael, 1933-
  Tchaikovsky.
  1 tape cassette. (The visual sounds of
Mike Whorf. Panorama; a world of music, PWM-21)

  Originally presented on his radio program, Kaleidoscope,
WJR, Detroit.
  Duration: 28 min., 30 sec.
  The life and times of Tchaikovsky, including excerpts of
his music.

  L Chaǐkovskiǐ, Petr Il'ich, 1840-1893.   L Title.

C1
M6
Whorf, Michael, 1933-
  Symbols of nationhood, national anthems.
  1 tape cassette. (The visual sounds of
Mike Whorf. Miscellaneous, M6)

  Originally presented on his radio program, Kaleidoscope,
WJR, Detroit.
  Duration: 41 min.
  A program devoted to the national anthems of the world, with
many musical Illustrations and comments concerning the composi-
tion, and conditions under which they were written.

  L National songs. L Title.

C1
H83
Whorf, Michael, 1933-
  Tecumseh.
  1 tape cassette. (The visual sounds of
Mike Whorf. History and heritage, H83)
  Originally presented on his radio program, Kaleidoscope,
WJR, Detroit.
  Duration: 27 min., 35 sec.
  A brave, noble Indian chief far ahead of his time; a rarity
in an age of change and exploitation. His name was Tecumseh,
an idealist who knew what the coming of the white man meant to
his people.

  L Tecumseh, Shawnee chief, 1768-1813. L Title.

C1
M20
Whorf, Michael, 1933-
  A tale of a tune, with Gerald Marks.
  1 tape cassette. (The visual sounds of
Mike Whorf. Miscellaneous, M40)
  Originally presented on his radio program, Kaleidoscope,
WJR, Detroit.
  Duration: 52 min.
  A delightful nostalgic look at how some of our popular songs
were written, featuring composer Gerald Marks.

  L Music, Popular (Songs, etc.) L Marks, Gerald. IL Title.

                                                    OFFICIAL

C1
R31
Whorf, Michael, 1933-
  The Ten Commandments.
  1 tape cassette. (The visual sounds of
Mike Whorf. Religion, R31)
  Originally presented on his radio program, Kaleidoscope,
WJR, Detroit.
  Duration: 37 min.
  The graven tables which presented spiritual guidance for
millions have been passed down to us by oral tradition and the
works of the scriptures. The monumental importance of this moral
code has stood the test of time through the ages, and served as a
universal guide to mankind.
  L Commandments, Ten. L Title.

C1
H14
Whorf, Michael, 1933-
  Tales of the frontier and the forty-niners.
  1 tape cassette. (The visual sounds of
Mike Whorf. History and heritage, H14)
  Originally presented on his radio program, Kaleidoscope,
WJR, Detroit.
  Duration: 39 min.
  The year was 1849, and from every corner of the globe came
all types of men searching for quick wealth. "Gold," was the
cry from California and with their hopes and dreams came the
seekers. For a few months it meant adventure and excitement for
those who confronted the frontier and were called the forty-niners.

  L California - Gold discoveries. 2. Frontier and pioneer life.
L Title.

C1
FA13
Whorf, Michael, 1933-
  Thaddeus S. C. Lowe.
  1 tape cassette. (The visual sounds of
Mike Whorf. The forgotten American, FA13)

  Originally presented on his radio program, Kaleidoscope,
WJR, Detroit.
  Duration: 12 min., 20 sec.
  Aeronaut and inventor, Lowe acted as an aerial spy for the
Union in the Civil War. He was the father of cold storage and
invented water gas.

  L Lowe, Thaddeus, S. C., 1832-1913. L Title.

C1
H31
Whorf, Michael, 1933–
Thar' she blows.
1 tape cassette. (The visual sounds of Mike Whorf. History and heritage, H31)

Originally presented on his radio program, Kaleidoscope, WJR, Detroit.
Duration: 43 min.
Comes the leviathan of the deep - the story of whaling as it was lived by those who sailed the great sailing ships.

L. Whaling. L. Title.

C1
A7
Whorf, Michael, 1933–
They lived happily ever after.
1 tape cassette. (The visual sounds of Mike Whorf. Art, music, and letters, A7)

Originally presented on his radio program, Kaleidoscope, WJR, Detroit.
Duration: 41 min., 15 sec.
From their childhood, Jacob and Wilhelm Grimm remembered the wonderful and magic stories of make-believe, and with their own special brand of inventiveness they created a heritage for generations to come.

1. Grimm, Jakob Ludwig, 1785-1863. 2. Grimm, Wilhelm Karl, 1786-1859. L. Title.

C1
S53
Whorf, Michael, 1933–
That woman in the White House; wives of Presidents.
1 tape cassette. (The visual sounds of Mike Whorf. Social, S53)

Originally presented on his radio program, Kaleidoscope, WJR, Detroit.
Duration: 88 min., 20 sec.
Along with the many presidents that have served our nation, are the wives and hostesses who have served as well. From Washington to Nixon, here is a capsule comment on the vivacious, intelligent women in the White House.

L. Presidents - U.S. - Wives. L. Title.

C1
H72
Whorf, Michael, 1933–
They marched off to war to a military quickstep; Civil War, part 5.
1 tape cassette. (The visual sounds of Mike Whorf. History and heritage, H72)

Originally presented on his radio program, Kaleidoscope, WJR, Detroit.
Duration: 39 min., 55 sec.
If there were any two wars which gave the world an abundance of music, they were World War I and the War between the States. This program is devoted to the lyrics and melodies of the Civil War and the impact they played on the North and South.

L. U.S. - History - Civil War, 1861-1865 - Songs & music. L. Title.

C1
SC28
Whorf, Michael, 1933–
Theorist of evolution - Charles Darwin.
1 tape cassette. (The visual sounds of Mike Whorf. Science, SC28)
Originally presented on his radio program, Kaleidoscope, WJR, Detroit.
Duration: 36 min., 30 sec.
Throughout his life controversy raged around him, yet this quiet, self-contained, self-assured man did not engage his detractors, but forged ahead with his life's work. His life's work was engaging Nature on Nature's terms, and the result was the storm of disagreement which surrounds his name.

L. Darwin, Charles Robert, 1809-1882. L. Title.

OFFICIAL

C1
S27
Whorf, Michael, 1933–
They was reckless mountain boys - Hatfields and Martins.
1 tape cassette. (The visual sounds of Mike Whorf. Social, S27)
Originally presented on his radio program, Kaleidoscope, WJR, Detroit.
Duration: 35 min., 30 sec.
Out from the mountain regions of the Smokies comes this tale. It involved two families, the Hatfields and McCoys, and has become a typical American legend dealing in equal shares of violence and virtue.

L. Hatfield-McCoy Feud. L. Title.

C1
M29
Whorf, Michael, 1933–
They don't write 'em like that anymore.
1 tape cassette. (The visual sounds of Mike Whorf. Miscellaneous, M29)

Originally presented on his radio program, Kaleidoscope, WJR, Detroit.
Duration: 54 min., 30 sec.
Gerald Marks tells the story of some of America's favorite melodies.

1. Songs, American. 2. Music, Popular (Songs, etc.) - U.S. L. Marks, Gerald. II. Title.

C1
FA2
Whorf, Michael, 1933–
Thomas Fitzpatrick.
1 tape cassette. (The visual sounds of Mike Whorf. The forgotten American, FA2)

Originally presented on his radio program, Kaleidoscope, WJR, Detroit.
Duration: 9 min., 50 sec.
One of the most colorful of the American mountain men, he was noted for his dealings with the Indians.

L. Fitzpatrick, Thomas, 1799-1854. L. Title.

C1
PMW17
Whorf, Michael, 1933–
They don't write 'em like that anymore.
1 tape cassette. (The visual sounds of Mike Whorf. Panorama; a world of music, PMW-17)
Originally presented on his radio program, Kaleidoscope, WJR, Detroit.
Duration: 25 min.
Composer Gerald Marks relates anecdotes and stories behind the composing of several popular American songs.

1. Music, Popular (Songs, etc.) - U.S. L. Marks, Gerald, 1900– II. Title.

C1
FA12
Whorf, Michael, 1933–
Thomas W. Gregory.
1 tape cassette. (The visual sounds of Mike Whorf. The forgotten American, FA12)
Originally presented on his radio program, Kaleidoscope, WJR, Detroit.
Duration: 11 min., 25 sec.
Attorney-General during the administrations of Woodrow Wilson, Gregory was responsible for the internal security of the United States during World War I.

L. Gregory, Thomas Watt, 1861-1933. L. Title.

C1
PWM14   Whorf, Michael, 1933-
        Those ragtime years.
        1 tape cassette.   (The visual sounds of
Mike Whorf. Panorama; a world of music, PWM-14

      Originally presented on his radio program, Kaleidoscope,
WJR, Detroit.
     Duration: 25 min.
     Music from the decade between the turn of the century and
World War I, including some by composer Scott Joplin.

      1. Ragtime music. 2. Joplin, Scott, 1868-1917. I. Title.

C1
H59   Whorf, Michael, 1933-
        To live with honor, Disraeli.
        1 tape cassette.   (The visual sounds of
Mike Whorf. History and heritage, H59)
      Originally presented on his radio program, Kaleidoscope,
WJR, Detroit.
     Duration: 41 min., 15 sec.
     Rising above the discrimination against his Judaic heritage,
Disraeli was an accomplished linguist, a writer of gay and brilliant
satire, possessed of a phenomenal memory, and schooled in the
social graces.

      1. Beaconsfield, Benjamin Disraeli, 1st Earl of, 1804-1881.
I. Title.

C1
R4   Whorf, Michael, 1933-
        The thunderer.
        1 tape cassette.   (The visual sounds of
Mike Whorf. Religion, R4)

      Originally presented on his radio program, Kaleidoscope,
WJR, Detroit.
     Duration: 28 min., 30 sec.
     Here is the narrative that deals with a prophet of God. He was
humble, yet his spirit challenged the brilliance and intelligence of
kings and priests.

      1. John the Baptist. I. Title.

C1
S10   Whorf, Michael, 1933-
        Today is a good day to die.
        1 tape cassette.   (The visual sounds of
Mike Whorf. Social, S10)
      Originally presented on his radio program, Kaleidoscope,
WJR, Detroit.
     Duration: 45 min., 30 sec.
     This program relates ... story of the Indian's ancestry, his
origin, his survival on the continent, the number of nations and
tribes, and their locations, his religion, customs, and the manner
in which he lived in early America.

      1. Indians of North America. I. Title.

C1
R18   Whorf, Michael, 1933-
        Teilhard de Chardin.
        1 tape cassette.   (The visual sounds of
Mike Whorf. Religion, R18)

      Originally presented on his radio program, Kaleidoscope,
WJR, Detroit.
     Duration: 43 min.
     A highly acclaimed religious philosopher is the subject of this
critical examination of Pierre Teilhard de Chardin. Destined to
pass this world without fame or reknown, today he is generally
regarded as the voice of a new understanding.

      1. Teilhard de Chardin, ... e. I. Title.

C1
SC33   Whorf, Michael, 1933-
        Today, they changed the world; inventions.
        1 tape cassette.   (The visual sounds of
Mike Whorf. Science, SC33)
      Originally presented on his radio program, Kaleidoscope,
WJR, Detroit.
     Duration: 37 min., 50 sec.
     What causes the creative spark to kindle the flame of a new
idea ... a new process ... a new product? This narrative takes a
look at the march of progress in the individual efforts of the
innovators whose contributions change the course of history.

      1. Inventions. I. Title.

C1
H25   Whorf, Michael, 1933-
        There are some days you don't forget - Pearl
Harbor.
        1 tape cassette.   (The visual sounds of
Mike Whorf. History and heritage, H25)
      Originally presented on his radio program, Kaleidoscope,
WJR, Detroit.
     Duration: 42 min., 50 sec.
     December 7th, 1941 - from out of the skies came the enemy at
8 o'clock Sunday morning - less than an hour later they had gone,
leaving in their wake wreckage and death.

      1. Pearl Harbor, Attack on, 1941. I. Title.

C1
H21   Whorf, Michael, 1933-
        The tragedy of the Titanic.
        1 tape cassette.   (The visual sounds of
Mike Whorf. History and heritage, H21)
      Originally presented on his radio program, Kaleidoscope,
WJR, Detroit.
     Duration: 37 min.
     It was indeed a night to remember, on that cold April night
in the North Atlantic. The largest ship ever built was to make its
first and last voyage as she sailed into the treacherous ice fields.
Before morning came, one of the greatest tragedies on the high
seas was to unfold.

      1. Titanic (Steamship) I. Title.

C1
R17   Whorf, Michael, 1933-
        There's nothing like a good old-fashioned
hymn.
        1 tape cassette.   (The visual sounds of
Mike Whorf. Religion, R17)

      Originally presented on his radio program, Kaleidoscope,
WJR, Detroit.
     Duration: 54 min., 30 sec.
     A few familiar, well-loved melodies and a close appraisal of
what makes the song is the content of this program.

      1. Hymns. I. Title.

C1
M51   Whorf, Michael, 1933-
        Trumpets in the afternoon --legend and
sport of bullfight.
        1 tape cassette.   (The visual sounds of
Mike Whorf. Miscellaneous, M51)

      Originally presented on his radio program, Kaleidoscope,
WJR, Detroit.
     Duration: 37 min.
     The unique world of the bullfight arena: the blood, the gore,
the colorful spectacle of brave matadors and their worthy
opponents - the ground-scraping, glaring black bull.
      1. Bull-fights. I. Title.

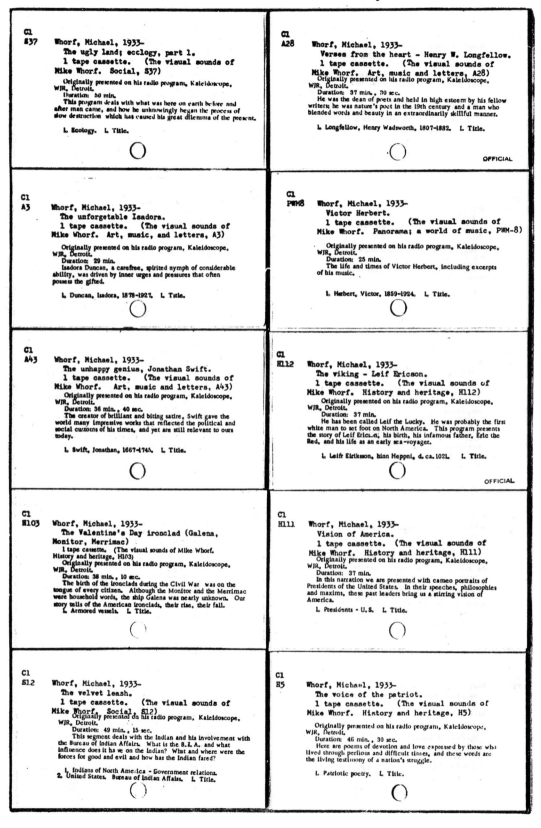

C1
S37

Whorf, Michael, 1933-
    The ugly land; ecology, part 1.
    1 tape cassette. (The visual sounds of Mike Whorf. Social, S37)
    Originally presented on his radio program, Kaleidoscope, WJR, Detroit.
    Duration: 50 min.
    This program deals with what was here on earth before and after man came, and how he unknowingly began the process of slow destruction which has caused his great dilemma of the present.

    1. Ecology. L. Title.

C1
A28

Whorf, Michael, 1933-
    Verses from the heart - Henry W. Longfellow.
    1 tape cassette. (The visual sounds of Mike Whorf. Art, music and letters, A28)
    Originally presented on his radio program, Kaleidoscope, WJR, Detroit.
    Duration: 37 min., 30 sec.
    He was the dean of poets and held in high esteem by his fellow writers; he was nature's poet in the 19th century and a man who blended words and beauty in an extraordinarily skillful manner.

    1. Longfellow, Henry Wadsworth, 1807-1882. L. Title.

OFFICIAL

C1
A3

Whorf, Michael, 1933-
    The unforgetable Isadora.
    1 tape cassette. (The visual sounds of Mike Whorf. Art, music, and letters, A3)
    Originally presented on his radio program, Kaleidoscope, WJR, Detroit.
    Duration: 29 min.
    Isadora Duncan, a carefree, spirited nymph of considerable ability, was driven by inner urges and pressures that often possess the gifted.

    1. Duncan, Isadora, 1878-1927. L. Title.

C1
PWM8

Whorf, Michael, 1933-
    Victor Herbert.
    1 tape cassette. (The visual sounds of Mike Whorf. Panorama; a world of music, PWM-8)
    Originally presented on his radio program, Kaleidoscope, WJR, Detroit.
    Duration: 25 min.
    The life and times of Victor Herbert, including excerpts of his music.

    1. Herbert, Victor, 1859-1924. L. Title.

C1
A43

Whorf, Michael, 1933-
    The unhappy genius, Jonathan Swift.
    1 tape cassette. (The visual sounds of Mike Whorf. Art, music and letters, A43)
    Originally presented on his radio program, Kaleidoscope, WJR, Detroit.
    Duration: 36 min., 40 sec.
    The creator of brilliant and biting satire, Swift gave the world many impressive works that reflected the political and social customs of his times, and yet are still relevant to ours today.

    1. Swift, Jonathan, 1667-1745. L. Title.

C1
H112

Whorf, Michael, 1933-
    The viking - Leif Ericson.
    1 tape cassette. (The visual sounds of Mike Whorf. History and heritage, H112)
    Originally presented on his radio program, Kaleidoscope, WJR, Detroit.
    Duration: 37 min.
    He has been called Leif the Lucky. He was probably the first white man to set foot on North America. This program presents the story of Leif Ericson; his birth, his infamous father, Eric the Red, and his life as an early sea-voyager.

    1. Leifr Eiriksson, hinn Heppni, d. ca. 1021. L. Title.

OFFICIAL

C1
H103

Whorf, Michael, 1933-
    The Valentine's Day ironclad (Galena, Monitor, Merrimac)
    1 tape cassette. (The visual sounds of Mike Whorf. History and heritage, H103)
    Originally presented on his radio program, Kaleidoscope, WJR, Detroit.
    Duration: 38 min., 10 sec.
    The birth of the ironclads during the Civil War was on the tongue of every citizen. Although the Monitor and the Merrimac were household words, the ship Galena was nearly unknown. Our story tells of the American ironclads, their rise, their fall.
    1. Armored vessels. L. Title.

C1
H111

Whorf, Michael, 1933-
    Vision of America.
    1 tape cassette. (The visual sounds of Mike Whorf. History and heritage, H111)
    Originally presented on his radio program, Kaleidoscope, WJR, Detroit.
    Duration: 37 min.
    In this narration we are presented with cameo portraits of Presidents of the United States. In their speeches, philosophies and maxims, these past leaders bring us a stirring vision of America.

    1. Presidents - U.S. L. Title.

C1
S12

Whorf, Michael, 1933-
    The velvet leash.
    1 tape cassette. (The visual sounds of Mike Whorf. Social, S12)
    Originally presented on his radio program, Kaleidoscope, WJR, Detroit.
    Duration: 49 min., 15 sec.
    This segment deals with the Indian and his involvement with the Bureau of Indian Affairs. What is the B.I.A. and what influence does it have on the Indian? What and where were the forces for good and evil and how has the Indian fared?

    1. Indians of North America - Government relations.
    2. United States. Bureau of Indian Affairs. L. Title.

C1
H5

Whorf, Michael, 1933-
    The voice of the patriot.
    1 tape cassette. (The visual sounds of Mike Whorf. History and heritage, H5)
    Originally presented on his radio program, Kaleidoscope, WJR, Detroit.
    Duration: 46 min., 30 sec.
    Here are poems of devotion and love expressed by those who lived through perilous and difficult times, and these words are the living testimony of a nation's struggle.

    1. Patriotic poetry. L. Title.

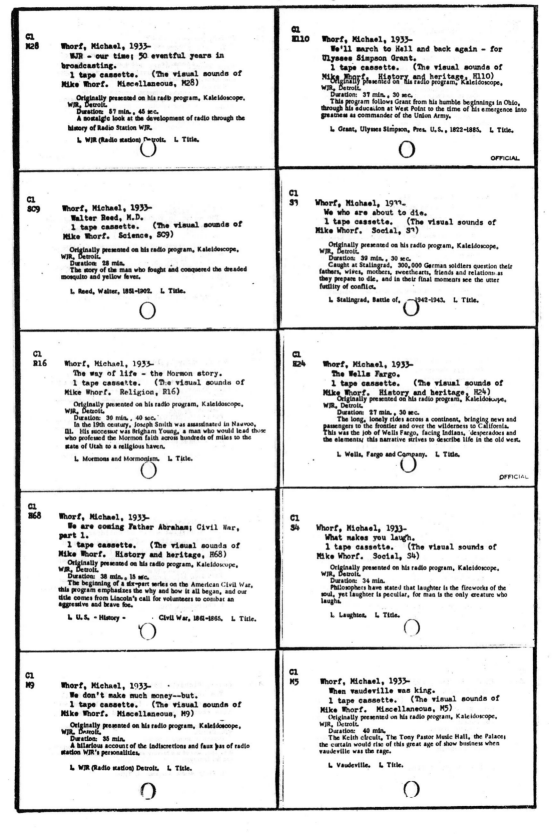

C1
M28
Whorf, Michael, 1933-
WJR - our time; 50 eventful years in broadcasting.
1 tape cassette. (The visual sounds of Mike Whorf. Miscellaneous, M28)

Originally presented on his radio program, Kaleidoscope, WJR, Detroit.
Duration: 57 min., 45 sec.
A nostalgic look at the development of radio through the history of Radio Station WJR.

L. WJR (Radio station) Detroit. L. Title.

C1
H110
Whorf, Michael, 1933-
We'll march to Hell and back again - for Ulysses Simpson Grant.
1 tape cassette. (The visual sounds of Mike Whorf. History and heritage, H110)
Originally presented on his radio program, Kaleidoscope, WJR, Detroit.
Duration: 37 min., 30 sec.
This program follows Grant from his humble beginnings in Ohio, through his education at West Point to the time of his emergence into greatness as commander of the Union Army.

L. Grant, Ulysses Simpson, Pres. U.S., 1822-1885. L. Title.

OFFICIAL

C1
SC9
Whorf, Michael, 1933-
Walter Reed, M.D.
1 tape cassette. (The visual sounds of Mike Whorf. Science, SC9)

Originally presented on his radio program, Kaleidoscope, WJR, Detroit.
Duration: 28 min.
The story of the man who fought and conquered the dreaded mosquito and yellow fever.

L. Reed, Walter, 1851-1902. L. Title.

C1
S7
Whorf, Michael, 1933-
We who are about to die.
1 tape cassette. (The visual sounds of Mike Whorf. Social, S7)

Originally presented on his radio program, Kaleidoscope, WJR, Detroit.
Duration: 39 min., 30 sec.
Caught at Stalingrad, 300,000 German soldiers question their fathers, wives, mothers, sweethearts, friends and relations as they prepare to die, and in their final moments see the utter futility of conflict.

L. Stalingrad, Battle of, 1942-1943. L. Title.

C1
R16
Whorf, Michael, 1933-
The way of life - the Mormon story.
1 tape cassette. (The visual sounds of Mike Whorf. Religion, R16)

Originally presented on his radio program, Kaleidoscope, WJR, Detroit.
Duration: 30 min., 40 sec.
In the 19th century, Joseph Smith was assassinated in Nauvoo, Ill. His successor was Brigham Young, a man who would lead those who professed the Mormon faith across hundreds of miles to the state of Utah to a religious haven.

L. Mormons and Mormonism. L. Title.

C1
H24
Whorf, Michael, 1933-
The Wells Fargo.
1 tape cassette. (The visual sounds of Mike Whorf. History and heritage, H24)
Originally presented on his radio program, Kaleidoscope, WJR, Detroit.
Duration: 27 min., 30 sec.
The long, lonely rides across a continent, bringing news and passengers to the frontier and over the wilderness to California. This was the job of Wells Fargo, facing Indians, desperadoes and the elements; this narrative strives to describe life in the old west.

L. Wells, Fargo and Company. L. Title.

OFFICIAL

C1
H68
Whorf, Michael, 1933-
We are coming Father Abraham; Civil War, part 1.
1 tape cassette. (The visual sounds of Mike Whorf. History and heritage, H68)
Originally presented on his radio program, Kaleidoscope, WJR, Detroit.
Duration: 38 min., 15 sec.
The beginning of a six-part series on the American Civil War, this program emphasizes the why and how it all began, and our title comes from Lincoln's call for volunteers to combat an aggressive and brave foe.

L. U.S. - History - Civil War, 1861-1865. L. Title.

C1
S4
Whorf, Michael, 1933-
What makes you laugh.
1 tape cassette. (The visual sounds of Mike Whorf. Social, S4)

Originally presented on his radio program, Kaleidoscope, WJR, Detroit.
Duration: 34 min.
Philosophers have stated that laughter is the fireworks of the soul, yet laughter is peculiar, for man is the only creature who laughs.

L. Laughter. L. Title.

C1
M9
Whorf, Michael, 1933-
We don't make much money--but.
1 tape cassette. (The visual sounds of Mike Whorf. Miscellaneous, M9)

Originally presented on his radio program, Kaleidoscope, WJR, Detroit.
Duration: 35 min.
A hilarious account of the indiscretions and faux pas of radio station WJR's personalities.

L. WJR (Radio station) Detroit. L. Title.

C1
M5
Whorf, Michael, 1933-
When vaudeville was king.
1 tape cassette. (The visual sounds of Mike Whorf. Miscellaneous, M5)
Originally presented on his radio program, Kaleidoscope, WJR, Detroit.
Duration: 40 min.
The Keith circuit, The Tony Pastor Music Hall, the Palace; the curtain would rise of this great age of show business when vaudeville was the rage.

L. Vaudeville. L. Title.

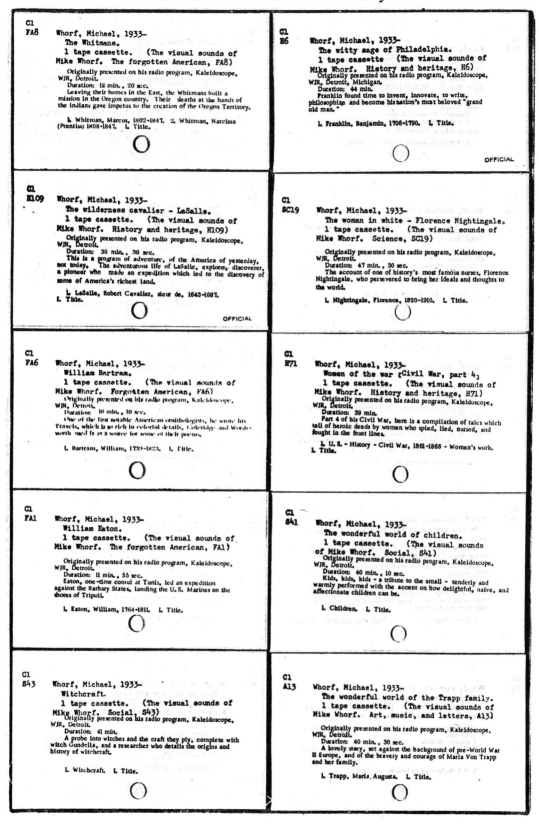

C1
FA8

Whorf, Michael, 1933–
  The Whitmans.
  1 tape cassette. (The visual sounds of
Mike Whorf. The forgotten American, FA8)
    Originally presented on his radio program, Kaleidoscope,
WJR, Detroit.
    Duration: 18 min., 20 sec.
    Leaving their homes in the East, the Whitmans built a
mission in the Oregon country. Their deaths at the hands of
the Indians gave impetus to the creation of the Oregon Territory.

    1. Whitman, Marcus, 1802-1847. 2. Whitman, Narcissa
(Prentiss) 1808-1847. I. Title.

C1
H6

Whorf, Michael, 1933–
  The witty sage of Philadelphia.
  1 tape cassette. (The visual sounds of
Mike Whorf. History and heritage, H6)
    Originally presented on his radio program, Kaleidoscope,
WJR, Detroit, Michigan.
    Duration: 44 min.
    Franklin found time to invent, innovate, to write,
philosophize and become his nation's most beloved "grand
old man."

    1. Franklin, Benjamin, 1706-1790. I. Title.

OFFICIAL

C1
H109

Whorf, Michael, 1933–
  The wilderness cavalier – LaSalle.
  1 tape cassette. (The visual sounds of
Mike Whorf. History and heritage, H109)
    Originally presented on his radio program, Kaleidoscope,
WJR, Detroit.
    Duration: 36 min., 30 sec.
    This is a program of adventure, of the America of yesterday,
not today. The adventurous life of LaSalle, explorer, discoverer,
a pioneer who made an expedition which led to the discovery of
some of America's richest land.

    1. LaSalle, Robert Cavalier, sieur de, 1643-1687.
I. Title.

OFFICIAL

C1
SC19

Whorf, Michael, 1933–
  The woman in white – Florence Nightingale.
  1 tape cassette. (The visual sounds of
Mike Whorf. Science, SC19)
    Originally presented on his radio program, Kaleidoscope,
WJR, Detroit.
    Duration: 47 min., 30 sec.
    The account of one of history's most famous nurses, Florence
Nightingale, who persevered to bring her ideals and thoughts to
the world.

    1. Nightingale, Florence, 1820-1910. I. Title.

C1
FA6

Whorf, Michael, 1933–
  William Bartram.
  1 tape cassette. (The visual sounds of
Mike Whorf. Forgotten American, FA6)
    Originally presented on his radio program, Kaleidoscope,
WJR, Detroit.
    Duration: 10 min., 10 sec.
    One of the first notable American ornithologists, he wrote his
Travels, which is so rich in colorful details, Coleridge and Words-
worth used is as a source for some of their poems.

    1. Bartram, William, 1739-1823. I. Title.

C1
H71

Whorf, Michael, 1933–
  Women of the war [Civil War, part 4]
  1 tape cassette. (The visual sounds of
Mike Whorf. History and heritage, H71)
    Originally presented on his radio program, Kaleidoscope,
WJR, Detroit.
    Duration: 39 min.
    Part 4 of his Civil War, here is a compilation of tales which
tell of heroic deeds by women who spied, lied, nursed, and
fought in the front lines.

    1. U.S. – History – Civil War, 1861-1865 – Women's work.
I. Title.

C1
FA1

Whorf, Michael, 1933–
  William Eaton.
  1 tape cassette. (The visual sounds of
Mike Whorf. The forgotten American, FA1)

    Originally presented on his radio program, Kaleidoscope,
WJR, Detroit.
    Duration: 11 min., 55 sec.
    Eaton, one-time consul at Tunis, led an expedition
against the Barbary States, landing the U.S. Marines on the
shores of Tripoli.

    1. Eaton, William, 1764-1811. I. Title.

C1
S41

Whorf, Michael, 1933–
  The wonderful world of children.
  1 tape cassette. (The visual sounds
of Mike Whorf. Social, S41)
    Originally presented on his radio program, Kaleidoscope,
WJR, Detroit.
    Duration: 40 min., 10 sec.
    Kids, kids, kids – a tribute to the small – tenderly and
warmly performed with the accent on how delightful, naive, and
affectionate children can be.

    1. Children. I. Title.

C1
S43

Whorf, Michael, 1933–
  Witchcraft.
  1 tape cassette. (The visual sounds of
Mike Whorf. Social, S43)
    Originally presented on his radio program, Kaleidoscope,
WJR, Detroit.
    Duration: 41 min.
    A probe into witches and the craft they ply, complete with
witch Gundella, and a researcher who details the origins and
history of witchcraft.

    1. Witchcraft. I. Title.

C1
A13

Whorf, Michael, 1933–
  The wonderful world of the Trapp family.
  1 tape cassette. (The visual sounds of
Mike Whorf. Art, music, and letters, A13)

    Originally presented on his radio program, Kaleidoscope,
WJR, Detroit.
    Duration: 40 min., 30 sec.
    A lovely story, set against the background of pre-World War
II Europe, and of the bravery and courage of Maria Von Trapp
and her family.

    1. Trapp, Maria, Augusta. I. Title.

C1
A21   Whorf, Michael, 1933-
The world of Jack London.
1 tape cassette. (The visual sounds of
Mike Whorf. Art, music, and letters, A21)
Originally presented on his radio program, Kaleidoscope,
WJR, Detroit.
Duration: 30 min., 30 sec.
Adventures in the north, of roustabouts, rogues, sailors, and
longshoremen, this was the world of Jack London, which he brought
to the readers of the world in his exciting narratives.
L. London, Jack, 1876-19   L. Title.

Voice Lib.
131   Wickard, Claude Raymond, 1893-1967.
bd.3   Address at Michigan State University.
with introduction by President John A.
Hannah. WKAR, 1961.
1 reel (7 in.)   7 1/2 in. per sec.
phonotape.

I. Hannah, John Alfred, 1902-

Voice Lib.
M1501 Wigner, Eugene Paul, 1902-
Lecture on social responsibility of the
scientist, and other topics, visiting the
campus of MSU at Wells Hall. Location
recording, May 23, 1972.
1 reel (7 in.)   7 1/2 in. per sec.
phonotape.

1. Science - Social aspects.

Voice Lib.   Wilde, Cornel, 1915-
M669- The legend of Cecil B. Demille. Yul
670   Brynner, Charlton Heston, Bob Hope, Betty
Hutton, Edward G. Robinson, Barbara Stanwyck,
James Stewart, Gloria Swanson, Cornel
Wilde, Samuel Goldwyn, Billy Graham, Cecil
B. DeMille.   Recorded 1963.
2 reels (7 in.)   7 1/2 in. per sec. phonotape.
L. DeMille, Cecil Blount, 1881-1959. L. Brynner, Yul, 1917-
II. Heston, Charlton, 1924-   III. Hope, Bob, 1903-   IV.
Hutton, Betty, 1921-   V. Robinson, Edward G   1893-1973.
VI. Stanwyck, Barbara, 1907-   VII. Stewart, James Maitland,
1908- VIII. Swanson, Gloria, 1899?-   IX. Wilde, Corn l, 1915-
X. Goldwyn, Samuel, 1884?-   XI. Graham, William Franklin,
1918-   XII. DeMille, Cecil Blount, 1881-1959.

The wilderness cavalier - LaSalle
C1
H109   Whorf, Michael, 1933-
The wilderness cavalier - LaSalle.
1 tape cassette. (The visual sounds of
Mike Whorf. History and heritage, H109)
Originally presented on his radio program, Kaleidoscope,
WJR, Detroit.
Duration: 30 min., 30 sec.
This is a program of adventure, of the America of yesterday,
not today. The adventurous life of LaSalle, explorer, discoverer,
a pioneer who made an expedition which led to the discovery of
some of America's richest land.
L. LaSalle, Robert Cavalier, sieur de, 1643-1687.
I. Title.

Voice Lib.
M952   Wilhelm II, German emperor, 1859-1941.
bd.5   Statement of his personal beliefs on
world understanding. H.E. Scholz,
January 24, 1904.
1 reel (7 in.)   7 1/2 in. per sec.
phonotape.

Voice Lib.
M1466 Wilhelm II, German emperor, 1859-1941.
bd.1   Call-up of the German people upon entering
World War I. Peteler, August 8, 1914.
1 reel (7 in.)   7 1/2 i.p.s.   phonotape.

1. European war, 1914-1918.

Voice Lib.
M952   Wilhelm II, German emperor, 1859-1941.
bd.12 Calling up the German people for service
to their country. F. Peteler, April 8,
1914.
1 reel (7 in.)   7 1/2 in. per sec.
phonotape.

Voice Lib.
M894   Wilhelmina, Queen of the Netherlands, 1880-
bd.3   1962.
Speaking from London, England, in exile.
CHS, May 15, 1940.
1 reel (7 in.)   7 1/2 in. per sec.
phonotape.

Voice Lib.
M1088 Wilkins, Roy, 1901-
bd.3   Interview on Barry Gray Show with Roy
Wilkins, Executive Secretary of NAACP,
pertaining to social and economic problems
of Negroes in America and equal rights for
all minority groups. WMCA, 1962.
1 reel (7 in.)   7 1/2 in. per sec.
phonotape.

1. Race discrimination - U.S.

Voice Lib.
M1085 Wilkins, Roy, 1901-
Radio interview with Roy Wilkins by
Elizabeth Morgan about methods to attain
civil rights for Negroes. Bergman, May 9,
1962.
1 reel (7 in.) 7 1/2 in. per sec.
phonotape;

1. Negroes - Civil rights. I. Morgan,
Elizabeth.

Voice Lib. Wilkins, Roy, 1901-
M1083 Analysis and criticism of President Kennedy's
bd.2 administration after a year and a half of
its incumbency, by Howard K. Smith, Leon
Keyserling, Roy Wilkins, Theodore Sorensen,
and various economists, mostly adverse
opinions; comparison to Wilson and FDR
administrations. Bergman, July 25, 1962.
1 reel (7 in.) 7 1/2 in. per sec. phonotape.
I. Kennedy, John Fitzgerald, Pres. U.S., 1917-1963. I.
Smith, Howard Kingsbury, 1914- II. Keyserling, Leon Hersch,
1908- III. Wilkins, Roy, 1901- IV. Sorensen, Theodore
Chaikin, 1928-

Voice Lib.
M315 Wilkins, Roy, 1901-
bd.4 Statement by Roy Wilkins to NBC newsman
Frank McGee, at the assassination of President
Kennedy, his ideas about the future of civil
rights. NBC, November 24, 1963.
1 reel (7 in.) 7 1/2 in. per sec.
phonotape.

1. Kennedy, John Fitzgerald, Pres. U.S.,
1917-1963 - Assassination. I. McGee, Frank,
1921-1974.

C1
FA6
William Bartram
Whorf, Michael, 1933-
William Bartram.
1 tape cassette. (The visual sounds of
Mike Whorf. Forgotten American, FA6)
Originally presented on his radio program, Kaleidoscope,
WJR, Detroit.
Duration: 10 min., 10 sec.
One of the first notable American ornithologists, he wrote his
Travels, which is so rich in colorful details, Coleridge and Words-
worth used is as a source for some of their poems.

I. Bartram, William, 1739-1823. I. Title.

C1
FA1
William Eaton
Whorf, Michael, 1933-
William Eaton.
1 tape cassette. (The visual sounds of
Mike Whorf. The forgotten American, FA1)

Originally presented on his radio program, Kaleidoscope,
WJR, Detroit.
Duration: 11 min., 55 sec.
Eaton, one-time consul at Tunis, led an expedition
against the Barbary States, landing the U.S. Marines on the
shores of Tripoli.

I. Eaton, William, 1764-1811. I. Title.

WILLIAMS, BERT
C1
M12
Whorf, Michael, 1933-
Black magic.
1 tape cassette. (The visual sounds of
Mike Whorf. Miscellaneous, M12)
Originally presented on his radio program, Kaleidoscope,
WJR, Detroit.
Duration: 30 min.
Considered by many to be one of the greatest comics who
ever lived, Bert Williams was idolized by millions and adored
by those who knew him.

I. Williams, Bert. I. Title.

WILLIAMS, DANIEL HALE, 1856-1931
C1
S35
Whorf, Michael, 1933-
Heroes come in many colors, part 5 - The
life of Dr. Daniel Williams.
1 tape cassette. (The visual sounds of
Mike Whorf. Social, S35)
Originally presented on his radio program, Kaleidoscope,
WJR, Detroit.
Duration: 29 min., 30 sec.
Years before open heart surgery and names like Barnard and
DeBakey were household words, the name of Daniel Williams was
prominent in the theatre of medicine.

I. Williams, Daniel Hale, 1856-1931. I. Title.

Voice Lib.
M1740 Williams, Edward Bennett
bd.1 Discusses the Warren Supreme Court on Firing
Line with William F. Buckley. WKAR, June 14,
1974.
20 min. phonotape (1 r. 7 1/2 i.p.s.)

1. U. S. Supreme Court - Hist. I.
Buckley, William Frank, 1925-

Voice Lib.
M1679 Williams, G Mennen, 1911-
The United States and Africa. WKAR,
May 18, 1970.
45 min. phonotape (1 r. 7 1/2 i.p.s.)

1. U.S. - Relations (General) with Africa.
2. Africa - Relations (General) with the U.S.

WILLIAMS, ROGER, 1604?-1683
C1
H19
Whorf, Michael, 1933-
America's first modern.
1 tape cassette. (The visual sounds of
Mike Whorf. History and heritage, H19)
Originally presented on his radio program, Kaleidoscope,
WJR, Detroit.
Duration: 40 min., 15 sec.
The leader whose ideas shocked, alienated, and eventually
reformed the early Pilgrim settlements, Roger Williams turned
his back on the intolerance of the Puritans in Massachusetts
and his face toward true freedom in his own colony.

I. Williams, Roger, 1604?-1683. I. Title.

Voice Lib.
M540   Willingdon, Freeman Freeman-Thomas, 1st earl
bd.13   of, 1866-1941.
        Swearing-in ceremonies as Viceroy of India.
        Fox Movietone, 1932.
        1 reel (7 in.)   7 1/2 in. per sec.
        phonotape.

Willkie, Wendell Lewis, 1892-1944
Voice Lib.
572-   I can hear it now (radio program)
573   1933-1946.   CBS, 1948.
bd.1   2 reels (7 in.)   7 1/2 in. per sec.
        phonotape.
        I. Murrow, Edward Roscoe, 1908-1965. II. LaGuardia, Fiorello
        Henry, 1882-1947. III. Chamberlain, Neville, 1869-1949. IV.
        Roosevelt, Franklin Delano, Pres. U. S., 1882-1945. V. Churchill,
        Winston Leonard Spencer, 1874-1965. VI. Gaulle, Charles de,
        Pres. France, 1890-1970. VII. Eisenhower, Dwight David, Pres. U.S.,
        1890-1969. VIII. Willkie, Wendell Lewis, 1892-1944. IX. Martin,
        Joseph William, 1884-1968. X. Elizabeth II, Queen of Great Britain,
        1926-   XI. Margaret Rose, Princess of Gt. Brit., 1930-   XII.
        Johnson, Hugh Samuel, 188_ _ _42. XIII. Smith, Alfred Emanuel,
        1873-1944. XIV. Lindberg_ harles Augustus, 1902-   XV. Davis,
                                    —(Continued on next card)

Voice Lib.
378   Willkie, Wendell Lewis, 1892-1944.
bd.2   Future of America (excerpt); campaign
        speech, 1940 Presidential campaign; attacks
        recovery of U.S. from depression.   Private
        recording (air check), May 15, 1940.
        1 reel (7 in.)   7 1/2 in. per sec.
        phonotape.

WILLKIE, WENDELL LEWIS, 1892-1944
Voice Lib.
633   LaGuardia, Fiorello Henry, 1882-1947.
        Willkie vs. Willkie; offers his views on
        the campaign speeches of the Republican
        presidential candidate, Wendell Willkie.
        Sponsored by the National Independent
        Committee for Roosevelt and Wallace.   CBS,
        October 24, 1940.
        1 reel (7 in.)   7 1/2 in. per sec.
        phonotape.

        1. Willkie, Wendell Lewis, 1892-1944.

Voice Lib.
M231   Willkie, Wendell Lewis, 1892-1944.
bd.1   Americans for Defense address at Freedom
        Rally, with introduction by Fiorello
        LaGuardia.   Source (?), April 7, 1941.
        1 reel (7 in.)   7 1/2 i.p.s.   phonotape.

Voice Lib.
M741   Wills, Frank
bd.2   Interview with Bill Monroe.   NBC, June
        17, 1974.
        10 min.   phonotape (1 r.   7 1/2 i.p.s.)

        1. Watergate affair, 1972-   I. Monroe,
        Bill.

Voice Lib.
M982   Willkie, Wendell Lewis, 1892-1944.
bd.9   Excerpt of address about peace and one-
        world unity, after his trip abroad.   N.V.,
        1943.
        1 reel (7 in.)   7 1/2 in. per sec.
        phonotape.

Voice Lib.
611   Wills, Nat M
bd.9   Comedy monologue "No news, or, what killed
        the dog?"   Victor Talking Machine Co., 1917.
        1 reel (7 in.)   7 1/2 in. per sec.
        phonotape.

        I. Title: No news, or, what killed the
        dog?

Willkie, Wendell Lewis, 1892-1944
Voice Lib.
M620   Radio in the 1940's (Part I): a series of
bd.1-   excerpts from important broadcasts of the 1940's; a
bd.16   sample of radio of the period.   NVL, April, 1964.
        1 reel (7 in.)   7 1/2 in. per sec.   phonotape.
        I. Radio programs.   I. Thomas, Lowell Jackson, 1892-   II.
        Gunther, John, 1901-1970. III. Kaltenborn, Hans von, 1878-1965.
        IV. Delmar, Kenny. V. Those were the good old days (Radio
        program) VI. Elman, Dave. VII. Hall, Frederick Lee, 1916-1970.
        VIII. Hobby lobby (Radio program) IX. Roosevelt, Franklin Delano,
        Pres. U.S., 1882-1945. X. Willkie, Wendell Lewis, 1892-1944.
        XI. Hoover, Herbert Clark, Pres. U.S., 1874-1964. XII. Johnson,
        Hugh Samuel, 1882-1942. XIII. Cobb, Irvin Shrewsbury, 1876-1944.
        XIV. Roosevelt, Theodore, 1858-1919. XV. Nye, Gerald Prentice,
        1892-197 . XVI. Lindbergh, Charles Augustus, 1902-   XVII.
        Toscanini, Arturo, 1867-195 .

Wilson, Charles Edward, 1886-1972
Voice Lib.
383   I can hear it now (radio program)
        CBS, February 9, 1951.
        1 reel (7 in.)   7 1/2 in. per sec.
        phonotape.
        I. Wilson, Charles Edward, 1886-1972. II. Gabrielson, Guy
        George, 1891-   III. Taft, Robert Alphonso, 1889-1953. IV.
        Martin, Joseph William, 1884-1968. V. McCarthy, Joseph
        Raymond, 1909-1957. VI. Benton, William Burnett, 1900-1973.
        VII. Malone, George Wilson, 1890-1961. VIII. Capehart, Homer
        Earl, 1897-   IX. Eisenhower, Dwight David, Pres. U.S., 1890-
        1969. X. Lee, J   V   XI. Hodge, John Reed, 1893-
        1963. XII. Overton, Watkins   XIII. DiSalle, Michael
        Vincent, 1908-   XIV. Boyce, Eddy   XV. Conklin, Ed
        XVI. Collins, Joseph Lawton, 1896-

Wilson, Charles Edward, 1886-1972

Voice Lib.
381-　　I can hear it now (radio program)
382　　　CBS, April 26, 1951.
bd.1　　　2 reels (7 in.)　7 1/2 in. per sec.　phonotape.
　　　L. Radio Free Europe.　2. Strategic Air Command.　L.
Ridgway, Matthew Bunker, 1895-　　IL. Churchill, Winston Leonard
Spencer, 1874-1965.　IIL. Bevan, Aneurin, 1897-1960.　IV. Nixon,
Richard Milhous, Pres. U.S., 1913-　V. Kerr, Robert Samuel, 1896-
1963.　VL. Brewster, Ralph Owen, 1888-1962.　VII. Wherry, Kenneth
Spicer, 1892-195L.　VIII. Capehart, Homer Earl, 1897-　IX.
Lehman, Herbert Henry, 1878-1963.　X. Taft, Robert Alphonso,
1889-1953.　XL. Moody, Arthur Edson Blair, 1902-1954.　XII.
Martin, Joseph William, 1884-1968.　XIII. McMahon, James O'Brien,
1903-1952.　XIV. MacArthur, Douglas, 1880-1964.　XVII. Wilson,
Charles Edward, 1886-1972.　XVIII. Irvine, Clarence T

Wilson, Donald Harlow, 1900-

Voice Lib.
M622　　Radio in the 1940's (Part III): a series of
bd.1-　　　excerpts from important broadcasts of the 1940's; a sample
bd.15　　　of radio of the period.　NVL, April, 1964.
　　　1 reel (7 in.)　7 1/2 in. per sec.　phonotape.
　　　L. Radio programs.　L. Miller, Alton Glenn, 1909(?)-1944.　IL.
Diles, Ken　　III. Wilson, Donald Harlow, 1900-　IV.
Livingstone, Mary　　V. Benny, Jack, 1894-　VL. Harris,
Phil　　VII. Merman, Ethel, 1909-　VIII. Smith, "Wonderful"
IX. Bennett, Richard Dyer　　X. Louis, Joe, 1914-　　XL.
Eisenhower, Dwight David, Pres. U.S., 1890-1969.　XII. MacArthur,
Douglas, 1880-1964.　XIII. Romulo, Carlos Pena, 1899-　　XIV.
Welles, Orson, 1915-　　XV. Jackson, Robert Houghwout, 1892-1954.
XVL. LaGuardia, Fiorello Henry, 1882-1945.　XVII. Nehru, Jawa-
harial, 1889-1964.　XVIII. Gandhi, Mohandas Karamchand, 1869-1948.

Voice Lib.
M1666　　Wilson, John Anthony Burgess, 1917-
　　　　Autobiographical anecdotes.　WKAR,
　　　April 5, 1971.
　　　　50 min.　phonotape (1 r.　7 1/2 i.p.s.)

　　　1. Wilson, John Anthony Burgess, 1917-

Voice Lib.　Wilson, Mattie
M272　　Biography in sound (radio program)
bd.1　　　Heywood Broun.　NBC, date?
　　　　1 reel (7 in.)　7 1/2 in. per sec.
　　　phonotape.

　　　L. Broun, Heywood Campbell, 1888-1939.　L. Broun,
Heywood Campbell, 1888-1939.　IL. Swope, Herbert Bayard,
1882-1958.　III. Wilson, Mattie　　IV. Jackson, Gardner
V. Meany, Thomas　　VL. Waldron, Beatrice　　VIL.
Gordon, Max　　VIII. Madison, Connie　　IX. Gannett,
Lewis Stiles, 1891-1966.　X. Collins, Joseph, 1866-1950.　XL.
Brown, Earl Louis, 1900-　　XII. Levy, Newman, 1888-
XIII. Growth, John　　XIV. Bye, George　　XV.
Roosevelt, Franklin Delano, Pres. U.S., 1882-1945.　XVL.
Reynolds, Quentin James　　2-1965.

Wilson, Robin

Voice Lib.
M1263　Armstrong, Louis, 1900-1971.
　　　　Kraft Music Hall with Herb Alpert and
　　　Tijuana Brass, with guest stars Jackie
　　　Vernon and Robin Wilson.　NBC-TV,
　　　August 13, 1967.
　　　　1 reel (7 in.)　7 1/2 in. per sec.
　　　phonotape.

　　　I. Alpert, Herb, 1935(?)-　　II. Vernon,
Jackie　　III. Wilson, Robin

Voice Lib.
M1615　　Wilson, Woodrow, Pres., 1856-1924.
bd.3　　　Democratic principles.　Rare Records,
　　　Inc., P707 (19--?)
　　　　3 min., 30 sec.　phonotape (1 r.
　　　7 1/2 i.p.s.)

Voice Lib.
M757　Wilson, Woodrow, Pres. U.S., 1856-1924.
bd.9　　Campaign speech about the tariff and the
　　　regulation of trusts; partnership of all
　　　people with the federal government.　VTM,
　　　1912.
　　　　1 reel (7 in.)　7 1/2 in. per sec.
　　　phonotape.

Voice Lib.
M757　Wilson, Woodrow, Pres. U.S., 1856-1924.
bd.8　　Mr. Wilson talks about the interests of
　　　labor and compares his views with those of
　　　the third party in a campaign speech.
　　　VTM, 1912.
　　　　1 reel (7 in.)　7 1/2 in. per sec.
　　　phonotape.

Voice Lib.
M770　Wilson, Woodrow, Pres. U.S., 1856-1924.
bd.3　　The New Freedom, defining the nation's
　　　awakening.　VTM, 1912.
　　　　1 reel (7 in.)　7 1/2 in. per sec.
　　　phonotape.

Voice Lib.
M276　Wilson, Woodrow, Pres. U.S., 1856-1924.
bd.2　　On democratic principles.　Camden,
　　　New Jersey, Victor Talking Machine Co.,
　　　1912.
　　　　1 reel (7 in.)　7 1/2 in. per sec.
　　　phonotape.

Voice Lib.
M1250   Wilson, Woodrow, Pres. U.S., 1856-1924.
bd.5   Political address made during campaign
         of 1912 entitled "The New Freedom".
         VTM, 1912.
             1 reel (7 in.)   7 1/2 in. per sec.
         phonotape.

Voice Lib. WILSON, WOODROW, PRES. U.S., 1856-1924
M654   Cummings, Homer Stillé, 1870-
bd.6   Address as temporary chairman of
         Democratic Convention of 1920, eulogizing
         President Wilson and condemning his
         opponents.   Nation's Forum, 1920.
             1 reel (7 in.)   7 1/2 in. per sec.
         phonotape.

Voice Lib.
653   Wilson, Woodrow, Pres. U.S., 1856-1924.
bd.10   The tariff question; tariff as a
         political and economic issue.   Victor
         Talking Machine, 1912.
             1 reel (7 in.)   7 1/2 in. per sec.
         phonotape.

Voice Lib.
M1028   Winchell, Walter, 1897-1972.
bd.10   Excerpt of news broadcast about cold war
         of "Big Three".   1946.
             1 reel (7 in.)   7 1/2 in. per sec.
         phonotape.

Voice Lib.
653   Wilson, Woodrow, Pres. U.S.,1856-1924.
bd.9   The third party; talking about the new
         Progressive Party; criticizing Theodore
         Roosevelt and his methods of supporting
         the small business man.   Victor Talking
         Machine, 1912.
             1 reel (7 in.)   7 1/2 in. per sec.
         phonotape.

Voice Lib.
M1231   Winchell, Walter, 1897-1972.
bd.2   Gruen Watch Radio News broadcast on current
         gossip and suspected communists in government.
         ABC Radio, November 15, 1953.
             1 reel (7 in.)   7 1/2 in. per sec.
         phonotape.

Voice Lib.
M982   Wilson, Woodrow, Pres. U.S., 1856-1924.
bd.11   Address from his home on S Street,
         Washington, D.C., on November 10, 1923,
         to a gathering of admirers on Armistice
         Day.   Frank L. Capp, 1923.
             1 reel (7 in.)   7 1/2 in. per sec.
         phonotape.

                 Winchell, Walter, 1897-1972
Voice Lib.
573   I can hear it now (radio program)
bd.2-   1945-1949.   CBS, 1950?
574   2 reels (7 in.)   7 1/2 in. per sec.
bd.1   phonotape.
         I. Murrow, Edward Roscoe, 1908-1965. II. Nehru, Jawaharlal,
         1889-1964. III. Philip, duke of Edinburgh, 1921-   IV. Elizabeth II,
         Queen of Great Britain, 1926-   V. Ferguson, Homer, 1889-   VI.
         Hughes, Howard Robard, 1905-   VII. Marshall, George Catlett,
         1880-   VIII. Ruth, George Herman, 1895-1948. IX. Lilienthal,
         David Eli, 1899-   X. Trout, Robert, 1908-   XI. Gage, Arthur.
         XII. Jackson, Robert Houghwout, 1892-1954. XIII. Gromyko, Ana-
         tolii Andreevich, 1908-   XIV. Baruch, Bernard Mannes, 1870-
         1965. XV. Churchill, Winston Leonard Spencer, 1874-1965. XVI.
         Winchell, Walter, 1897-1   XVII. Davis, Elmer Holmes, 1890-
                                    (Continued on next card)

         Wilson, Woodrow, Pres. U.S., 1856-1924
Voice Lib.
M617   Radio in the 1920's: a series of excerpts
bd.1-   from important broadcasts of the 1920's,
bd.25   with brief prologue and epilogue; a sample
         of radio of the period.   NVL, April, 1964.
             1 reel (7 in.)   7 1/2 in. per sec.
         phonotape.
         I. Radio programs. I. Marconi, Guglielmo, marchese, 1874-
         1937. II. Kendall, H   G   III. Coolidge, Calvin, Pres. U.S.,
         1872-1933. IV. Wilson, Woodrow, Pres. U.S., 1856-1924. V.
         Roosevelt, Franklin Delano, Pres. U.S., 1882-1945. VI. Lodge,
         Henry Cabot, 1850-1924. VII. LaGuardia, Fiorello Henry, 1882-1947.
         VIII. The Happiness Boys (Radio program) IX. Gallagher and Sheen.
         X. Barney Google. XI. Vallee, Rudy, 1901-   XII. The two
                                    (Continued on next card)

Voice Lib.
M739   Windsor, Wallis (Warfield) duchess of,
bd.2   1896-
             Talking about cooking.   CBS, 1953.
             30 sec.   phonotape (1 r.   7 1/2 i.p.s.)

Voice Lib.
M1605   Winograd, Morley
bd.2   Off the record. With Tim Skubick, Tom
        Greene, Gary Schuster, and Hugh Morgan.
        WKAR-TV, February 15, 1974.
            17 min.   phonotape (1 r.   7 1/2 in. per sec.)

            1. Democratic Party. Michigan. 2. Elections -
        Michigan. 3. Youngblood, Charles N., 1932-
        I. Skubick, Tim. II. Greene, Tom. III. Schuster,
        Gary. IV. Morgan, Hugh.

            Wir glauben an die neue Zeit
Voice Lib.
M1004   Nazi May Day ceremonies. Male choir singing
bd.3-B   (3 stanzas) of song "Wir glauben an die
        neue Zeit". Peteler, May 1, 1935.
            1 reel (7 in.)   7 1/2 i.p.s.   phonotape.

            1. Songs, German.   I. Title: Wir glauben
        an die neue Zeit.

Voice Lib.
M654   Wise, Stephen Samuel, 1874-1949.
bd.3   "League of Nations"; urging the U.S.
        to participate and uphold the policies of
        Woodrow Wilson.   Nation's Forum, 1920.
            1 reel (7 in.)   7 1/2 in. per sec.
        phonotape.

            1. League of Nations

Voice Lib.
154   Wise, Stephen Samuel, 1874-1949.
bd.4   New Year's Day prayer.   WNYC,
        January 1, 1943.
            1 reel (7 in.)   7 1/2 in. per sec.
        phonotape.

            Witchcraft
C1
S43   Whorf, Michael, 1933-
            Witchcraft.
            1 tape cassette.   (The visual sounds of
        Mike Whorf. Social, S43)
            Originally presented on his radio program, Kaleidoscope,
        WJR, Detroit.
            Duration: 41 min.
            A probe into witches and the craft they ply, complete with
        witch Gundella, and a researcher who details the origins and
        history of witchcraft.

            1. Witchcraft. 1. Title.

            The witty sage of Philadelphia
C1
H6   Whorf, Michael, 1933-
            The witty sage of Philadelphia.
            1 tape cassette   (The visual sounds of
        Mike Whorf. History and heritage, H6)
            Originally presented on his radio program, Kaleidoscope,
        WJR, Detroit, Michigan.
            Duration: 44 min.
            Franklin found time to invent, innovate, to write,
        philosophize and become his nation's most beloved "grand
        old man."

            1. Franklin, Benjamin, 1706-1790. 1. Title.

Voice Lib.
M1003   Witzleben, Erwin von,   -1944.
bd.5   Administering oath of loyalty to German
        3rd Army troops pledging allegiance to Adolf
        Hitler as supreme commander.   Peteler,
        August 4, 1934.
            1 reel (7 in.)   7 1/2 in. per sec.
        phonotape.

Voice Lib.
M1751   Wodehouse, Pelham Grenville, 1881-
bd.1   Reminiscences about his early career,
        favorite authors, the British sense of
        humor, the market for comedy, on Book Beat
        with Robert Cromie.   WKAR-TV, June 26, 1974.
            10 min.   phonotape (1 r.   7 1/2 i.p.s.)

            1. Wodehouse, Pelham Grenville, 1881-
        I. Cromie, Robert.

            WOMAN - RIGHTS OF WOMEN
Voice Lib.
656   Kennedy, John Fitzgerald, Pres. U.S., 1917-1963.
bd.3   Press conference excerpt: Mrs. Craig
        questioning President on equal rights for
        women.   CRI, 1962.
            1 reel (7 in.)   7 1/2 in. per sec.
        phonotape.

            1. Woman - Rights of women.   I. Craig,
        Elisabeth May.

            The woman in white - Florence Nightingale
C1
SC19   Whorf, Michael, 1933-
            The woman in white - Florence Nightingale.
            1 tape cassette.   (The visual sounds of
        Mike Whorf. Science, SC19)

            Originally presented on his radio program, Kaleidoscope,
        WJR, Detroit.
            Duration: 47 min., 30 sec.
            The account of one of history's most famous nurses, Florence
        Nightingale, who persevered to bring her ideals and thoughts to
        the world.

            1. Nightingale, Florence, 1820-1910. 1. Title.

Women of the war

C1
H71 Whorf, Michael, 1933–
  Women of the war [Civil War, part 4]
  1 tape cassette. (The visual sounds of
  Mike Whorf. History and heritage, H71)
   Originally presented on his radio program, Kaleidoscope,
  WJR, Detroit.
   Duration: 39 min.
   Part 4 of his Civil War, here is a compilation of tales which
  tell of heroic deeds by women who spied, lied, nursed, and
  fought in the front lines.

   L. U.S. – History – Civil War, 1861–1865 – Women's work.
  L. Title.

Wood, Barry

Voice Lib.
640 "A Tree Grows in Brooklyn"; comedy song sung
bd.2 by Barry Wood and Patsy Kelly. NBC, July
  15, 1944.
  1 reel (7 in.) 7 1/2 in. per sec.
  phonotape.

   I. Wood, Barry   II. Kelly, Patsy

WOMEN'S LIBERATION MOVEMENT

Voice Lib.
M1667 Friedan, Betty
  Revolution in the consciousness of women;
  speech at Albion College. WKAR, March 5,
  1971.
   47 min. phonotape (1 r. 7 1/2 i.p.s.)

  1. Women's liberation movement.

Voice Lib.
380 Wood, Leonard, 1860–1927.
bd.2 On Americanism: action the nation must
  take following World War I, the role of
  labor in the U.S.. Columbia, 1919.
   1 reel (7 in.) 7 1/2 in. per sec.
  phonotape.

WOMEN'S LIBERATION MOVEMENT

Voice Lib.
M1693 Spock, Benjamin McLane, 1903–
bd.2 On the younger generation and his own
  pro-peace activities, anti-obscenity
  activities, etc., on Merv Griffin Show.
   25 min. phonotape (1 r. 7 1/2 i.p.s.)

  1. Women's Liberation Movement.
  2. Children – Care & hygiene. 3. Johnson,
  Lyndon Baines, Pres. U.S., 1908–
  I. Griffin, Mervyn Edward, 1925–

Voice Lib.
653 Wood, Leonard, 1860–1927.
bd.5 Tribute to Theodore Roosevelt. Analysis
  of Teddy Roosevelt's character. Nation's
  Forum, 1929.
   1 reel (7 in.) 7 1/2 in. per sec.
  phonotape.

  1. Roosevelt, Theodore, Pres. U.S., 1858–
  1919.

The wonderful world of children

C1
S41 Whorf, Michael, 1933–
  The wonderful world of children.
  1 tape cassette. (The visual sounds
  of Mike Whorf. Social, S41)
   Originally presented on his radio program, Kaleidoscope,
  WJR, Detroit.
   Duration: 40 min., 10 sec.
   Kids, kids, kids – a tribute to the small – tenderly and
  warmly performed with the accent on how delightful, naive, and
  affectionate children can be.

   L. Children. L. Title.

Voice Lib.
M1704 Woodward, Robert
  Woodward and Bernstein, exposers of
  Watergate, at the National Press Club,
  talking to other reporters. Includes
  Clark Mollenhoff. WKAR, June 6, 1974.
   50 min. phonotape (1 r. 7 1/2 i.p.s.)

  1. Watergate Affair, 1972–
  I. Bernstein, Carl. II. Mollenhoff, Clark
  Raymond, 1921–

The wonderful world of the Trapp family

C1
A13 Whorf, Michael, 1933–
  The wonderful world of the Trapp family.
  1 tape cassette. (The visual sounds of
  Mike Whorf. Art, music, and letters, A13)

   Originally presented on his radio program, Kaleidoscope,
  WJR, Detroit.
   Duration: 40 min., 30 sec.
   A lovely story, set against the background of pre-World War
  II Europe, and of the bravery and courage of Maria Von Trapp
  and her family.

   L. Trapp, Maria, Augusta. L. Title.

Voice Lib.
290 Woollcott, Alexander, 1887–1943.
bd.1 "Town Crier" radio program; reminiscences
  of American life in 1913. Gotham
  Recording, October 6, 1933.
   1 reel (7 in.) 7 1/2 in. per sec.
  phonotape.

Voice Lib.
112   Woollcott, Alexander, 1887-1943.
bd.1   For us, the living: a commentary on
the Gettysburg Address. Linguaphone,
1941.
    1 reel (7 in.)   7 1/2 in. per sec.
phonotape.

Woollcott, Alexander, 1887-1943
Voice Lib.
M1045   The world today; radio broadcast with
bd.1   discussions of George Bernard Shaw by
Alexander Woollcott; John Daly regarding
offensive on Moscow; Edward R. Murrow
from London; Albert Warner concerning
coal miners' strike.   CBS Radio, October
30, 1941.
    1 reel (7 in.)   7 1/2 in. per sec.
phonotape.
    L. Shaw, George Bernard, 1856-1950. L. Woollcott, Alexander,
1887-1943. IL Daly, John Charles, 1914-   III. Murrow, Edward
Roscoe, 1908-1965. IV. Warner, Albert, 1884-1967.

Woollcott, Alexander, 1887-1943
Voice Lib.
M618   Radio in the 1930's (Part I): a series of
bd.1-   excerpts from important broadcasts of the
14   1930's; a sample of radio of the period.
NVL, April, 1964.
    1 reel (7 in.)   7 1/2 in. per sec.   phonotape.
    L. Shaw, George Bernard, 1856-1950. IL Crosby, Bing, 1901-
III. Barkley, Alban William, 1877-1956. IV. Roosevelt, Franklin
Delano, Pres. U.S., 1882-1945. V. Hoover, Herbert Clark, Pres.
U.S., 1874-1964. VL Long, Huey Pierce, 1893-1935. VII. Town-
mand, Francis Everett, 1867-1960. VIII. Coughlin, Charles Edward,
1891-   IX. Rogers, Will, 1879-1935. X. Pius XII, Pope, 1876-
1958. XL Edward VIII, king of Great Britain, 1894-1972. XII.
Barrymore, John, 1882-1942. XIII. Woollcott, Alexander, 1887-
1943. XIV. Allen, Fred, 1894-1956. XV. Benchley, Robert Charles,
1889-1945.

Woollcott, Alexander, 1887-1943
Voice Lib.
M275-   Biography in sound (radio program)
276   Alexander Woollcott. N.B.C., date?
bd.1   2 reels (7 in.)   7 1/2 in. per sec.
phonotape.
    L. Woollcott, Alexander, 1887-1943. I. Woollcott, Alexander,
1887-1943. IL Banghardt, Kenneth   III. Hecht, Ben, 1893-
1964. IV. Roosevelt, Eleanor (Roosevelt) 1884-1962. V. Walker,
Danton   VL Brackett, Charles, 1892-1969. VII. Grant,
Jane   VIII. Rude, Robert Barnes   IX. West,
Rebecca, pseud. X. Henessy, Joseph   XL Letterer,
Charles   XII. Welles, Orson, 1915-

Voice Lib.   Worden, Alfred M   1930-
M1480   Apollo 15 (space flight): lift-off.
bd.1   CBS TV, July 26, 1971.
    1 reel (7 in.)   7 1/2 in. per sec.
phonotape.

    1. Project Apollo. 2. Space flight to the
moon. 3. Scott, David Randolph, 1932-   4.
Irwin, James B   1932-   5. Worden, Alfred
M   1930-   I. Scott, David Randolph,
1932-   II. Irwin, James B   1932-   III.
Worden, Alfred M   1930-

         Worden, Alfred M   1930-
Voice Lib.
M1480   Apollo 15 (space flight): beginning of power
bd.2   descent to moon. NBC TV, July 31, 1971.
    1 reel (7 in.)   7 1/2 in. per sec.
phonotape.

    1. Project Apollo. 2. Space flight to the
moon. 3. Scott, David Randolph, 1932-   4.
Irwin, James B   1932-   5. Worden, Alfred
M   1930-   I. Scott, David Randolph,
1932-   II. Irwin, James B   1932-   III.
Worden, Alfred M   1930-

       Worden, Alfred M   1930-
Voice Lib.
M1480   Apollo 15 (space flight): walk in deep space
bd.3   by Al Worden to retrieve film packages.
Commentary of Gene Cernan, who walked in
space during Gemini 9 flight. NBC TV,
August, 1971.
    1 reel (7 in.)   7 1/2 in. per sec.
phonotape.
    L. Project Apollo. 2. Space flight to the moon. 3. Scott,
David Randolph, 1932-   4. Irwin, James B   1932-   5.
Worden, Alfred M   1930-   L. Scott, David Randolph, 1932-
IL Irwin, James B   1932-   III. Worden, Alfred M   1930-
IV. Cernan, Eugene Andrew, 1934-

       Worden, Alfred M   1930-
Voice Lib.
M1480   Apollo 15 (space flight): splashdown,
bd.4   commentary, speeches. NBC TV, August 7,
1971.
    1 reel (7 in.)   7 1/2 in. per sec.
phonotape.

    1. Project Apollo. 2. Space flight to the
moon. 3. Scott, David Randolph, 1932-   4.
Irwin, James B   1932-   5. Worden, Alfred
M   1930-   I. Scott, David Randolph,
1932-   II. Irwin, James B   1932-   III.
Worden, Alfred M   1930-

Voice Lib.
M1046   World news tonight; radio news commentary.
bd.2   CBS Radio news broadcast from Honolulu,
London, New York and Washington; including
William Ewing, Norman Corwin, Albert Leitch
and Harry Marble. CBS, September 12, 1942.
    1 reel (7 in.)   7 1/2 in. per sec.
phonotape.

    I. Ewing, William   II. Corwin, Norman
Lewis, 1910-   III. Leitch, Albert
    IV. Marble, Harry

       The world of Jack London
C1
A21   Whorf, Michael, 1933-
      The world of Jack London.
      1 tape cassette. (The visual sounds of
Mike Whorf. Art, music, and letters, A21)
    Originally presented on his radio program, Kaleidoscope,
WJR, Detroit.
    Duration: 30 min., 30 sec.
    Adventures in the north, of roustabouts, rogues, sailors, and
longshoremen, this was the world of Jack London, which he brought
to the readers of the world in his exciting narratives.

    L. London, Jack, 1876-19   L. Title.

The world of wax

Voice Lib.
M764   Goldmark, Goldie
bd.11   Excerpt from "The world of wax" (Program 8); comments on the production of another phenomenon which has had a profound effect on the recording industry, the disc jockey. Also comments on the dissatisfaction of a large segment of the record industry with the radio-record relationship. Westinghouse Broadcasting Corporation, 1964.
    7 min., 58 sec.   phonotape (1 r.   7 1/2 i.p.s.)   (The music goes round and round)

    I. Disc jockeys.   I. Title: The world of wax.   II. Series.

The world of wax

Voice Lib.
M764   Goodman, Benny, 1909-
bd.10   Excerpt from "The World of Wax" (Program 8); comments on recording with the use of electricity. Including music "Blue Skies". Westinghouse Broadcasting Corporation, 1964.
    1 reel (7 in.)   7 1/2 in. per sec. phonotape.   (The Music Goes Round and Round)

    I. Title: The world of wax.   II. Series.

The world of wax

Voice Lib.
M764   Higgins, Joe
bd.7   Excerpt from "The World of Wax" (Program 8); comments on what the record store was like in the early days as compared to today. Westinghouse Broadcasting Corporation, 1964.
    1 reel (7 in.)   7 1/2 in. per sec. phonotape.   (The Music Goes Round and Round)

    I. Title: The world of wax.   II. Series.

The world of wax

Voice Lib.
M764   Kapp, David
bd.6   Excerpt from "The World of Wax" (Program 8); discusses his father when he sold phonographs door to door. Westinghouse Broadcasting Corporation, 1964.
    1 reel (7 in.)   7 1/2 in. per sec. phonotape.   (The Music Goes Round and Round)

    I. Title: The world of wax.   II. Series.

The world of wax

Voice Lib.
M764   Kapp, Mickey
bd.13   Excerpt from "The World of Wax" (Program 8); comments on how a small label survives against the giants. Westinghouse Broadcasting Corporation, 1964.
    1 reel (7 in.)   7 1/2 in. per sec. phonotape.   (The Music Goes Round and Round)

    I. Title: The world of wax.   II. Series.

The world of wax

Voice Lib.
M764   Sholes, Steven H   1911-1968.
bd.9   Excerpt from "The World of Wax" (Program 8); discusses why radio almost killed the record business, and the biggest change in the record business. Westinghouse Broadcasting Corporation, 1964.
    1 reel (7 in.)   7 1/2 in. per sec. phonotape.   (The Music Goes Round and Round)

    I. Title: The world of wax.   II. Series.

The world of wax

Voice Lib.
M764   Spector, Phil
bd.12   Excerpt from "The World of Wax" (Program 8); discusses the effect of all the factors on the quality of the records being produced, after the advent of rock-and-roll. Westinghouse Broadcasting Corporation, 1964.
    1 reel (7 in.)   7 1/2 in. per sec. phonotape.   (The Music Goes Round and Round)

    I. Title: The world of wax.   II. Series.

The world of wax

Voice Lib.
M764   Whiteman, Paul, 1890-1967.
bd.8   Excerpt from "The World of Wax" (Program 8); comments on how the recording was accomplished; including music "Whispering". Westinghouse Broadcasting Corporation, 1964.
    1 reel (7 in.)   7 1/2 in. per sec. phonotape.   (The Music Goes Round and Round)

    I. Title: The world of wax.   II. Series.

Voice Lib.
M1045   The world today; radio broadcast with
bd.1   discussions of George Bernard Shaw by Alexander Woollcott; John Daly regarding offensive on Moscow; Edward R. Murrow from London; Albert Warner concerning coal miners' strike. CBS Radio, October 30, 1941.
    1 reel (7 in.)   7 1/2 in. per sec. phonotape.
    I. Shaw, George Bernard, 1856-1950.   I. Woollcott, Alexander, 1887-1943.   II. Daly, John Charles, 1914-   III. Murrow, Edward Roscoe, 1908-1965.   IV. Warner, Albert, 1884-1967.

Voice Lib.
M1027   The World Today; CBS radio news program;
bd.1   reports concerning war situation in Europe and Asia; resignations from FDR cabinet; reorganization of the 79th Congress; Russian progress on Eastern front. CBS News, December 20, 1944.
    1 reel (7 in.)   7 1/2 i.p.s.   phonotape.

    1. World War, 1939-1945.   2. U.S. - Politics and government - 1933-1945.

Voice Lib.
M1027 The World Today; CBS News correspondent
bd.2 Joseph C. Harsch discusses the meaning of
the news of the new German offensive in
Belgium and Prime Minister Churchill's
policy in Greece. CBS News, December 20,
1944.
1 reel (7 in.) 7 1/2 i.p.s. phonotape.

1. World War, 1939-1945. I. Harsch,
Joseph Close, 1905-

Voice Lib.
M1027 The world today: direct news reports from
bd.3 Belgian front; statement from SHAEF (Supreme
Headquarters Allied Expeditionary Force);
news of war in the Pacific discussed by CBS
correspondents Robert Trout, Douglas Edwards,
Richard C. Hottelet, and Ned Kalmer. CBS
News, December 23, 1944.
1 reel (7 in.) 7 1/2 in. per sec. phonotape.

I. Trout, Robert, 1908- II. Edwards, Douglas
III. Hottelet, Richard Curt IV. Kalmer, Ned
1. World War, 1939-1945.

Voice Lib. WORLD WAR, 1939-1945
576, Blitzkrieg; report on beginning of World War
bd.2- II, with voices of the actual participants.
577, Columbia Records, Inc., 1953.
bd.1 2 reels (7 in.) 7 1/2 in. per sec.
phonotape.

WORLD WAR, 1939-1945
Voice Lib.
M829 Churchill, Sir Winston Leonard Spencer,
bd.1 1874-1965.
Shortwave broadcast to the world reviewing
past and current war situation, Russian
military progress, Japan's conquests in the
East; cautioning against discouragement on
the loss of Singapore and Malayan Peninsula.
KDKA, February 14, 1942.
22 min., 30 sec. phonotape (1 r.
7 1/2 i.p.s.)
1. World War, 1939-1945.

WORLD WAR, 1939-1945
Voice Lib.
M1050- Corwin, Norman Lewis, 1910-
1051, CBS Radio Workshop program "On a note of
bd.1 triumph", written and directed by Norman
Corwin to celebrate Allied war victory in
Europe. CBS, May 13, 1945.
2 reels (7 in.) 7 1/2 i.p.s. phonotape.

1. World War, 1939-1945. I. Title: On
a note of triumph.

WORLD WAR, 1939-1945
Voice Lib.
M529 Daladier, Edouard, 1884-1970.
bd.2 Announcement of war with Germany.
Shortwave, Paris Mondial, September 3, 1939.
1 reel (7 in.) 7 1/2 in. per sec.
phonotape.

In French.

WORLD WAR, 1939-1945
Voice Lib.
M587 Daly, John Charles, 1914-
bd.2 Hosts program "The World Today" on war
status, reports on Russian fighting,
rumored resignation of Pétain, possibility
of German invasion of Spain, surprise
offensive in Mediterranean. CBS,
December 23, 1941.
1 reel (7 in.) 7 1/2 i.p.s. phonotape.

1. World War, 1939-1945.

Voice Lib. WORLD WAR, 1939-1945
M1071 Goebbels, Joseph, 1897-1945.
Radio report from Ministry of Propaganda,
read by Goebbels, stating Hitler's decision
to end amicable relations with Yugoslavia and
to occupy it militarily. Peteler, April 6,
1941.
1 reel (7 in.) 7 1/2 in. per sec.
phonotape.

1. Germany - Foreign relations - Yugoslavia. 2. Yugoslavia -
Foreign relations - Germany. 3. World War, 1939-1945.

WORLD WAR, 1939-1945
Voice Lib.
M871 Kaltenborn, Hans von, 1878-1965.
bd.2 Broadcasting news of cessation of
hostilities ending World War II; announcing
acceptance of terms of unconditional surrender
of Japan and the proclamation of a 2-day
holiday for government workers of Great
Britain and U.S.; speculation on zones of
occupation. NBC, August 14, 1945.
1 reel (7 in.) 7 1/2 in. per sec.
phonotape.

WORLD WAR, 1939-1945
Voice Lib.
M1285 King, Ernest Joseph, 1878-1956.
bd.2 Statement on current military situation
by Admiral King on the occasion of VE-Day,
in the form of a report. AFRS, May 8,
1945.
1 reel (7 in.) 7 1/2 in. per sec.
phonotape.

WORLD WAR, 1939-1945
Voice Lib.
M736   Montgomery of Alamein, Bernard Law Montgomery,
bd.5   1st viscount, 1887-
           Announcing the terms of local German
       surrender in Holland and various islands.
       CBS, May 4, 1945.
           1 reel (7 in.)   7 1/2 in. per sec.
       phonotape.

WORLD WAR, 1939-1945
Voice Lib.
M1027 The World Today; CBS radio news program;
bd.1   reports concerning war situation in Europe
       and Asia; resignations from FDR cabinet;
       reorganization of the 79th Congress;
       Russian progress on Eastern front.
       CBS News, December 20, 1944.
           1 reel (7 in.)   7 1/2 i.p.s.   phonotape.

           1. World War, 1939-1945. 2. U.S. -
       Politics and government - 1933-1945.

Voice Lib. WORLD WAR, 1939-1945
M524
           National Broadcasting Company, inc.
           Special NBC program on first anniversary
       of the war, featuring NBC news commentators.
       September 3, 1940.
           1 reel (7 in.)   7 1/2 in. per sec.
       phonotape.

WORLD WAR, 1939-1945
Voice Lib.
M1027 The World Today; CBS News correspondent
bd.2   Joseph C. Harsch discusses the meaning of
       the news of the new German offensive in
       Belgium and Prime Minister Churchill's
       policy in Greece.   CBS News, December 20,
       1944.
           1 reel (7 in.)   7 1/2 i.p.s.   phonotape.

           1. World War, 1939-1945. I. Harsch,
       Joseph Close, 1905-

Voice Lib. WORLD WAR, 1939-1945
M1025 Radio news reports concerning U.S. and Allied
bd.3   landings on North Africa, November 7, 1942;
       followed by military analysis by Major George
       Fielding Eliot.   CBS Radio, November 7, 1942.
           1 reel (7 in.)   7 1/2 in. per sec.
       phonotape.

           1. World War, 1939-1945. I. Eliot, George
       Fielding, 1894-1971.

Voice Lib. WORLD WAR, 1939-1945
M1027 The world today: direct news reports from
bd.3   Belgian front; statement from SHAEF (Supreme
       Headquarters Allied Expeditionary Force);
       news of war in the Pacific discussed by CBS
       correspondents Robert Trout, Douglas Edwards,
       Richard C. Hottelet, and Ned Kalmer.   CBS
       News, December 23, 1944.
           1 reel (7 in.) 7 1/2 in. per sec. phonotape.
       I. Trout, Robert, 1908-   II. Edwards, Douglas
       III. Hottelet, Richard Curt   IV. Kalmer, Ned

WORLD WAR, 1939-1945
Voice Lib.
M740   Trout, Robert, 1908-
bd.8-D   News flash announcing termination of
       World War II and promotion of General
       MacArthur to Supreme Commander.   CBS,
       1945.
           1 reel (7 in.)   7 1/2 in. per sec.
       phonotape.

           1. World War, 1939-1945. 2. MacArthur,
       Douglas, 1880-1964.

WORLD WAR, 1939-1945 - AUSTRIA
Voice Lib.
M1010 Schuschnigg, Kurt, 1897-
bd.4   Announcement of Hitler's ultimatum to
       Austria, his resignation as Chancellor, and
       recommending non-resistance to Nazi troops
       by Austrian armed forces.   Peteler,
       March 11, 1938.
           1 reel (7 in.)   7 1/2 i.p.s.   phonotape.

           1. World War, 1939-1945 - Austria.

WORLD WAR, 1939-1945
Voice Lib.
M1032 The war relived; documentary television
       program about World War II, Adolf Hitler
       and his dream of world domination,
       beginning with German preparations in the
       summer of 1939 through D-Day, 1944.   NET,
       January 29, 1967.
           1 reel (7 in.)   7 1/2 in. per sec.
       phonotape.

WORLD WAR, 1939-1945 - CAMPAIGNS - NORMANDY
Voice Lib.
M1439 Baruch, Andre
bd.3   Narrated description of General Patton's
       speech to U.S. troops in England before
       invasion of Europe (D-Day), by Major Andre
       Baruch.   AFRS, 1944.
           1 reel (7 in.)   7 1/2 in. per sec.
       phonotape..

WORLD WAR, 1939-1945 - CAMPAIGNS - NORMANDY

Voice Lib.
205   British Broadcasting Corporation
            D-Day, 1944; being views expressed by
        combatants and reporters.   BBC, June 6,
        1944.
            1 reel (7 in.)   7 1/2 in. per sec.
        phonotape.

WORLD WAR, 1939-1945 - CAMPAIGNS - NORMANDY

C1
H50   Whorf, Michael, 1933-
            Another day in June - D-Day.
            1 tape cassette.   (The visual sounds of
        Mike Whorf. History and heritage, H50)

            Originally presented on his radio program, Kaleidoscope,
        WJR, Detroit.
            Duration: 42 min. 30 sec.
            June 6, 1944 - D-Day. Here is an unusual account of the
        greatest armada to ever set sail in the Allies' attempt to turn
        the tide of battle in their favor.

            1. World War, 1939-1945 - Campaigns - Normandy.
            1. Title.

WORLD WAR, 1939-1945 - CAMPAIGNS - NORMANDY

Voice Lib.
M739   Collingwood, Charles Cummings, 1917-
bd.8   Recording he made on the beach during
        D-Day in France, describing activities of the
        invasion, including short interview with a
        sailor. CBS, June 6, 1944.
            1 reel (7 in.)   7 1/2 in. per sec.
        phonotape.

WORLD WAR, 1939-1945 - CAMPAIGNS -
        PHILIPPINE ISLANDS
Voice Lib.
M740   MacArthur, Douglas, 1880-1964.
bd.8-A   Excerpts of remarks made in Australia
        pledging to liberate Philippines, using
        famous quote, "I shall return". CBS,
        1944.
            1 reel (7 in.)   7 1/2 in. per sec.
        phonotape.

WORLD WAR, 1939-1945 - CAMPAIGNS -
        NORMANDY
Voice Lib.
M872   Description of and actual sounds from
bd.2   battle action during D-Day invasion of
        French Coast. NBC shortwave, June 7,
        1944.
            1 reel (7 in.)   7 1/2 in. per sec.
        phonotape.

            1. World War, 1939-1945 - Campaigns -
        Normandy.

WORLD WAR, 1939-1945 - CAMPAIGNS -
        PHILIPPINE ISLANDS
Voice Lib.
M523   Wainwright, Jonathan Mayhew, 1883-1953.
bd.1   World War II; surrender of U.S. and
        Philippine troops to Japanese. Manila,
        KZRX, 1942.
            1 reel (7 in.)   7 1/2 in. per sec.
        phonotape.

            1. World War, 1939-1945 - Campaigns -
        Philippine Islands.

WORLD WAR, 1939-1945 - CAMPAIGNS - NORMANDY

Voice Lib.
350   Eisenhower, Dwight David, Pres. U.S., 1890-1969.
bd.5   Message to people of Western Europe
        on D-Day Invasion (incomplete).   CBS,
        June 6, 1944.
            1 reel (7 in.)   7 1/2 in. per sec.
        phonotape.

WORLD WAR, 1939-1945 - CRETE

Voice Lib.
M1071   Nazi actual on-the-spot reports of paratroop
bd.20- invasion on the island of Crete, given by
1073   correspondents; also narration of exper-
bd.1   iences of captured Nazi soldier. Peteler,
        May 20-27, 1941.
            3 reels (7 in.)   7 1/2 in. per sec.
        phonotape.

            1. World War, 1939-1945 - Crete.

WORLD WAR, 1939-1945 - CAMPAIGNS - NORMANDY

Voice Lib.
650-   Eisenhower, Dwight David, Pres. U.S., 1890-1969.
651   D-Day plus 20 years (CBS Reports); discussion
        of strategy and procedures and preparation for
        invasion of Nazi-occupied France on June 6, 1944
        by former Commander of Allied Expeditionary
        Forces with Walter Cronkite. CBS, June 6, 1964.
            2 reels (7 in.)   7 1/2 in. per sec.
        phonotape.

            I. Cronkite, Walter Leland, 1916-

WORLD WAR, 1939-1945 - CZECHOSLOVAK
        REPUBLIC
Voice Lib.
M1016   Ribbentrop, Joachim von, 1893-1946.
            Reading the official Nazi terms of
        administering the protectorate of Bohemia
        and Maehren in Czechoslovakia. Peteler,
        March 16, 1939.
            1 reel (7 in.)   7 1/2 i.p.s.   phonotape.

            1. World War, 1939-1945 - Czechoslovak
        Republic.

WORLD WAR, 1939-1945 - FRANCE

Voice Lib.
M736   Keitel, Wilhelm, 1882-1946.
bd.8   Announcing the armistice required by
France. CBS, June 22, 1940.
25 sec.   phonotape (1 r.   7 1/2 i.p.s.)

1. World War, 1939-1945 - France.

WORLD WAR, 1939-1945 - FRANCE

Voice Lib.
M607   Shirer, William Lawrence, 1904-
bd.3   Fall of France; reports on fall of France
in special shortwave report from Berlin,
reviews states falling to Germany to date.
CBS, June 17, 1940.
1 reel (7 in.)   7 1/2 i.p.s.   phonotape.

1. World War, 1939-1945 - France.

WORLD WAR, 1939-1945 - FRANCE

Voice Lib.
M714   Churchill, Sir Winston Leonard Spencer,
bd.9   1874-1965.
Speaking about France's surrender in
World War II. June 16-22, 1940.
7 min., 1 sec.   phonotape (1 r.
7 1/2 i.p.s.)

1. World War, 1939-1945 - France.

WORLD WAR, 1939-1945 - GT. BRIT.

Voice Lib.
M738   Air raid sirens and bombing over London
bd.4   during Blitzkrieg. CBS, 1940.
55 sec.   phonotape (1 r.   7 1/2 i.p.s.)

1. World War, 1939-1945 - Gt. Brit.

WORLD WAR, 1939-1945 - ITALY

Voice Lib.
M714   Mussolini, Benito, 1883-1945.
bd.8   Speaking in broadcast from Rome, Italy
announcing Italy's entrance into World War
II on the side of the Axis. July 10, 1940.
1 min., 1 sec.   phonotape (1 r.
7 1/2 i.p.s.)

1. World War, 1939-1945 - Italy.

WORLD WAR, 1939-1945 - JAPAN

Voice Lib.
M871   Jordan, Max
bd.3   Japan's acceptance of Potsdam Declaration.
NBC, August 14, 1945.
1 reel (7 in.)   7 1/2 i.p.s.   phonotape.

1. World War, 1939-1945 - Japan.

WORLD WAR, 1939-1945 - JAPAN

Voice Lib.
M740   MacArthur, Douglas, 1880-1964.
bd.8-E   Excerpt of ceremonies on U.S. Battleship
Missouri, accepting unconditional surrender
of Japan. CBS, September 1, 1945.
1 reel (7 in.)   7 1/2 in. per sec.
phonotape.

1. World War, 1939-1945 - Japan.

WORLD WAR, 1939-1945 - NAVAL OPERATIONS,
                                      BRITISH

C1
M15   Whorf, Michael, 1933-
The sinking of the Bismarck.
1 tape cassette. (The visual sounds of
Mike Whorf. Miscellaneous, M15)

Originally presented on his radio program, Kaleidoscope,
WJR, Detroit.
Duration: 25 min.
During the early years of World War II, the German ship
Bismarck, was the terror of the high seas. Challenged by the
ships of the English fleet, it was a day of retribution and one
that changed the course of battle in the north Atlantic.

1. Bismarck (Battleship) 2. World War, 1939-1945 - Naval
operations, British.   L. Title.

WORLD WAR, 1939-1945 - NORWAY

Voice Lib.
M526   Haakon VII, King of Norway, 1872-1957.
bd.3   Refusal to abdicate Norwegian throne on
grounds that his people do not desire him
to, justifies exile government. Speaks from
his exile headquarters in London; reviews
early years in Norway. CBS, 1940.
1 reel (7 in.)   7 1/2 i.p.s.   phonotape.

1. World War, 1939-1945 - Norway.
2. Norway - Politics and government - 1940-
1945.

WORLD WAR, 1939-1945 - PACIFIC OCEAN

Voice Lib.
M982   Stilwell, Joseph Warren, 1883-1946.
bd.10   Excerpt of short-wave radio message
about conditions and the welfare of American
troops in the Pacific during World War II.
N.V., 1944.
1 reel (7 in.)   7 1/2 in. per sec.
phonotape.

WORLD WAR, 1939-1945 - PEACE

Voice Lib.
M851-   Roosevelt, Franklin Delano, Pres. U.S., 1882-1945.
852   Report to joint session of Congress about Yalta conference of
the Big Three. Explaining purpose of conference, describing
devastation of Russia, plans for a peace organization in San Francisco to start April 25, 1945, touching on the free elections for
conquered countries; objectives for Poland; France's role in the
future; delays caused by "primadonnas" meeting with King Farouk,
King Ibn Saud and Emperor Haile Selassie; the current Japanese
situation; hopes for United Nations organization. NBC, March 1,
1945.
     59 min., 30 sec.   phonotape (2 r. 7 1/2 i.p.s.)

     1. World War, 1939-1945 - Peace. 2. Crimea Conference,
Yalta, 1945.

WORLD WAR, 1939-1945 - PRISONS AND
PRISONERS

Voice Lib.
M1471   Red Cross. International Committee, Geneva.
bd.3-B   Report by a German journalist about his
experiences as an allied prisoner-of-war.
May 5, 1965.
     1 reel (7 in.)   7 1/2 i.p.s.   phonotape.

     1. World War, 1939-1945 - Prisons and
prisoners.

WORLD WAR, 1939-1945 - SONGS AND MUSIC

Voice Lib.
M1463   British Broadcasting Corporation.
bd.15   BBC beaming songs with German lyrics to
Nazi troops: "Lili Marlene" parody and "Lady
in the dark" parody. Peteler, 1944.
     1 reel (7 in.)   7 1/2 i.p.s.   phonotape.

     1. World War, 1939-1945 - Songs and music.

WORLD WAR, 1939-1945 - SONGS AND MUSIC

Voice Lib.
M375   German songs of World War II. Private
bd.3-   collection (German radio transcriptions)
6   1942.
     1 reel (7 in.)   7 1/2 in. per sec.
phonotape.
     In German.
     CONTENTS.-bd.3. "Lili Marlene", Lale Andersen.
bd.4. "Horst Wessel" song, Stormtroopers SA 33.-
bd.5."Heil Hitler Dir", Stormtroopers SA 33.-
bd.6. "Die Jugend marschiert", boys of the
Berlin Mittelschule.
     1. World War, 1939-1945 - Songs and music.

WORLD WAR, 1939-1945 - SONGS AND MUSIC

Voice Lib.
M1018   Nazi parody song on "We're gonna hang our
bd.7   washing on the Siegfried line". Peteler.
     1 reel (7 in.)   7 1/2 i.p.s.   phonotape.

     1. World War, 1939-1945 - Songs and music.

Voice Lib.
M1304   Nazi war songs: three stanzas of "We're
bd.5   on our way to conquer England" ("Wir
fahren gegen England"). Peteler, n.d.
     1 reel (7 in.)   7 1/2 i.p.s.   phonotape.

     1. War-songs, German. 2. World War, 1939-
1945 - Songs and music.

WORLD WAR, 1939-1945 - SONGS AND MUSIC

Voice Lib.
M592   Warnow, Mark
bd.4   Allied marching songs, with orchestra
and Lyn Murray chorus. V-Disc, 1943.
     1 reel (7 in.)   7 1/2 i.p.s.   phonotape.

     CONTENTS.-Meadowland (Russian).-Che Li
(Chinese); I've got sixpence (English);
When the Yanks go marching in (American)

     1. World War, 1939-1945 - Songs and
Music.

WORLD WAR, 1939-1945 - U.S.

Voice Lib.
M872   Grauer, Benjamin Franklin, 1908-
bd.1   Describing pre-VJ Day celebration in
Times Square, N.Y. NBC, August 14, 1945.
     1 reel (7 in.)   7 i.p.s.   phonotape.

     1.World War, 1939-1945 - U.S.

WORLD WAR, 1939-1945 - U.S.

Voice Lib.
M830   Roosevelt, Franklin Delano, Pres. U.S., 1882-1945.
     Description of proceedings at Joint Session of Congress on
December 8, 1941, prior to President's address asking for
declaration of war; including news flashes by NBC correspondents
Carlton Smith, Morgan Beatty, and Baukhage. NBC, December 8,
1941.
     32 min.   phonotape (1 r. 7 1/2 i.p.s.)

     1. World War, 1939-1945 - U.S. I. Smith, Carlton.
II. Beatty, Morgan. III. Baukhage, Hilmar Robert.

World's Fair, 1939-1940, New York city
see
New York. World's Fair, 1939-1940.

Voice Lib.
M1681
bd.4

WRIGHT, RICHARD, 1908-1960

Allen, Samuel W
Richard Wright and Black America.
WKAR, December 3, 1968.
25 min.   phonotape (1 r.   7 1/2 i.p.s.)

1. Wright, Richard, 1908-1960.

O

"Years of Lightning, Day of Drums"
Voice Lib.
M671
bd.2

Kennedy, John Fitzgerald, Pres. U.S., 1917-1963.
"Years of Lightning, Day of Drums";
excerpts of comments by JFK on Peace Corps,
Alliance for Progress, space race, Civil
Rights. Narrated by Gregory Peck.   Voice
of America, 1964.
1 reel (7 in.)   7 1/2 in. per sec.
phonotape.

I. Peck, Gregory, 1916-   II. Title.

O

Voice Lib.
M322

Wynn, Ed, 1886-1966

Biography in sound (radio program)
W.C. Fields, the magnificent rogue.
NBC, 1955.
1 reel (7 in.)   7 1/2 in. per sec.   phonotape.
L. Fields, W.C., 1879-1946. L. Fields, W.C., 1879-1946.
II. Allen, Fred, 1894-1956. III. LaBaron, William   IV.
Taylor, Robert Lewis, 1912-   V. McCarey, Thomas Leo, 1898-
1969. VI. Harkins, James   - VII. Chevalier, Maurice,
1889-1972. VIII. Kuromoto, Mrs. George   IX. Flynn,
Errol Leslie, 1909-1959. X. Wynn, Ed, 1886-1966. XI. Dowling,
Ray Dooley   XII. Sennett, Mack   XIII. Overacher,
Ronald Leroy   XIV. Bergen, Edgar, 1903-   XV. Taurog,
Norman, 1899-   XVI. Runnell, Ann   XVII. Cowen,
Lester

O

Voice Lib.
M762
bd.4

Yellen, Jack
Excerpt from "Tunesmiths Past and Present"
(Program 4); relates his view that our
musical future is not as black as many
would believe.   Westinghouse Broadcasting
Corporation, 1964.
1 reel (7 in.)   7 1/2 in. per sec.
phonotape.   (The Music Goes Round and Round)

1. Music, Popular (Songs, etc.) - U.S.
I. Title: Tunesmiths past and present. II.
Series.

O

X, Malcolm
see
Little, Malcolm, 1925-1965

VOICE LIBRARY

O

C1
H52

YORK, ALVIN CULLUM, 1887-

Whorf, Michael, 1933-
Known but to God - Armistice Day.
1 tape cassette.   (The visual sounds of
Mike Whorf. History and heritage, H52)

Originally presented on his radio program, Kaleidoscope,
WJR, Detroit.
Duration: 38 min., 45 sec.
A solemn approach to America's fallen - a tribute to the
unknown soldier - a brief biographical sketch of Sergeant Alvin
York is the content of this Armistice Day program.

L. Armistice Day. 2. York, Alvin Cullum, 1887-
L. Title.

O

YALTA CONFERENCE, 1945.
see
CRIMEA CONFERENCE, YALTA, 1945.

VOICE LIBRARY

O

Voice Lib.
M1742
bd.3

York, Herbert Frank, 1921-

Kaul, Triloki Nath
Discussion on capacity for nuclear war
in Egypt and Israel, by Triloki Nath Kaul and
Herbert F. York on the "Today Show". WKAR,
June 21, 1974.
10 min.   phonotape (1 r.   7 1/2 i.p.s.)

1. Atomic energy. 2. Jewish-Arab relations.
I. York, Herbert Frank, 1921-

O

Voice Lib.
M740
bd.2

Yankee Go Home; a musical jingle. Excerpt
from shortwave broadcast of jingle in
Spanish, praising Cuban revolution.
CBS, April 28, 1960.
1 min., 16 sec.   phonotape (1 r.
7 1/2 i.p.2.)

O

Voice Lib.
M1332-
1333
bd.1

Yorty, Samuel William, 1909-

Kennedy, Robert Francis, 1925-1968.
Comments and news regarding condition of
Senator Robert F. Kennedy after assassination
attempt in Los Angeles. Statement by Mayor
Yorty and Los Angeles police chief. Statement by Jordanian ambassador regarding
assassin Sirhan; also Mr. and Mrs. Wagner,
former employers. Flashback to scene of
assassination. Views from Washington on
gun legislation. NBC-TV, June 6, 1968.
2 reels (7 in.)   7 1/2 in. per sec.
phonotape.

O   (Continued on next card)

Yorty, Samuel William, 1909-
Voice Lib.
M910-
911,   Stout, Bill
bd.1   Resumé of the Watts riots in Los Angeles
          County, during the most violent riots in Los
          Angeles history; including actual sounds and
          voices of Police Chief William H. Parker,
          Mayor Yorty, etc. CBS, August, 1965.
             2 reels (7 in.) 7 1/2 i.p.s. phonotape.

             1. Los Angeles - Riots, 1965. I. Parker,
          William H., 1902-   II. Yorty, Samuel
          William, 1909-

Voice Lib.
M1611   Young, Andrew, 1932-
bd.4   Discusses Vice President Gerald Ford.
          WKAR-TV [1974?]
             4 min. phonotape (1 r.   7 1/2 i.p.s.)

             1. Ford, Gerald R., 1913-

Voice Lib.
M1551-
1552   Young, Andrew, 1932-
             A lecture series by the College of Urban
          Affairs, Michigan State University, with
          Prof. Robert Green and Asst. Prof. Barnes
          McConnell. MSU Dept. of Information
          Services, January 17, 1974.
             90 min. phonotape (2 r.   7 1/2 i.p.s.)

             1. Local transit. 2. Atlanta. I. Green,
          Robert Lee. II. McConnell, Barnes.

Voice Lib.
M1597   Young, Coleman A., 1918-
             Address at the Urban Forum luncheon,
          Michigan State University. MSU Information
          Services, March 7, 1974.
             40 min. phonotape (1 r.   7 1/2 in. per
          sec.)

             1. Detroit. 2. Michigan State University.
          College of Urban Development.

Young, John Watts, 1930-
Voice Lib.
M1377   Apollo 10 (space flight): lift-off. Commentary
bd.1   by NBC TV news; countdown, lift-off. Astro-
          nauts Tom Stafford, John Young. Eugene Cernan.
          NBC TV, May 18, 1969.
             1 reel (7 in.) 7 1/2 in. per sec.
          phonotape.
             1. Project Apollo. 2. Space flight to the
          moon. 3. Stafford, Thomas F 1931- 4.
          Young, John Watts, 1930- 5. Cernan, Eugene
          Andrew, 1934- I. Stafford, Thomas F 1931-
          II. Young, John Watts, 1930-   III. Cernan,
          Eugene Andrew, 1934-

Young, John Watts, 1930-
Voice Lib.
M1377   Apollo 10 (space flight): television pictures.
bd.2   Commentary from astronauts, NBC TV, on
          initial separation and docking of Lunar
          Landing Module, first live color television
          pictures from space, and pictures of the
          earth from 6,500 nautical miles out. NBC
          TV, May, 1969.
             1 reel (7 in.) 7 1/2 in. per sec. phonotape.
             1. Project Apollo. 2. Space flight to the moon. 3. Stafford,
          Thomas P 1931- 4. Young, John Watts, 1930- 5.
          Cernan, Eugene Andrew, 1934-   I. Stafford, Thomas P
          1931- II. Young, John Watts, 1930-   III. Cernan, Eugene
          Andrew, 1934-

Young, John Watts, 1930-
Voice Lib.
M1377   Apollo 10 (space flight): splashdown and
bd.3   recovery of Apollo 10; astronauts' first
          words after returning to earth; from the
          recovery ship U.S.S. "Princeton".   CBS TV,
          May 26, 1969.
             1 reel (7 in.) 7 1/2 in. per sec.
          phonotape.
             1. Project Apollo. 2. Space flight to the moon. 3. Stafford,
          Thomas P 1931- 4. Young, John Watts, 1930- 5.
          Cernan, Eugene Andrew, 1934-   I. Stafford, Thomas P
          1931- II. Young, John Watts, 1930-   III. Cernan, Eugene
          Andrew, 1934-

Voice Lib.
M1056   Young, Owen D   1874-1962.
bd.3   Remarks at dedication of new studio at
          radio station WGY at Schenectady, New York.
          Audio Scriptions, July 9, 1938.
             1 reel (7 in.) 7 1/2 in. per sec.
          phonotape.

             Incomplete.

YOUNGBLOOD, CHARLES N., 1932-
Voice Lib.
M1605   Winograd, Morley
bd.2   Off the record. With Tim Skubick, Tom
          Greene, Gary Schuster, and Hugh Morgan.
          WKAR-TV, February 15, 1974.
             17 min. phonotape (1 r.   7 1/2 in. per sec.)

             1. Democratic Party. Michigan. 2. Elections -
          Michigan. 3. Youngblood, Charles N., 1932-
          I. Skubick, Tim. II. Greene, Tom. III. Schuster,
          Gary. IV. Morgan, Hugh.

You're a grand old flag
Voice Lib.
M611   American Quartet.
bd.7   World War I song "You're a grand old flag".
          Victor Talking Machine Co., 1918.
             1 reel (7 in.) 7 1/2 i.p.s.   phonotape.

             1. European War, 1914-1918 - Songs and
          music. I. Title: You're a grand old flag.

Voice Lib.
M1071 YUGOSLAVIA - FOREIGN RELATIONS - GERMANY
    Goebbels, Joseph, 1897-1945.
        Radio report from Ministry of Propaganda,
    read by Goebbels, stating Hitler's decision
    to end amicable relations with Yugoslavia and
    to occupy it militarily. Peteler, April 6,
    1941.
        1 reel (7 in.)   7 1/2 in. per sec.
    phonotape.
            1. Germany - Foreign relations - Yugoslavia. 2. Yugoslavia -
        Foreign relations - Germany. 3. World War, 1939-1945.

Voice Lib.
h1470 Zetkin, Klara, 1857-1933.
bd.9   Opening the first session of the 6th
    election period in the German Reichstag.
    Peteler, August 30, 1932.
        1 reel (7 in.)   7 1/2 in. per sec.
    phonotape.

            1. Germany - Politics and government -
        1918-1933.

Voice Lib.
M1071 YUGOSLAVIA - FOREIGN RELATIONS - GERMANY
bd.7   Ribbentrop, Joachim von, 1893-1946.
        Excerpt of note to Yugoslavia justifying
    German military intervention because of
    unfriendly policies. Peteler, April 6,
    1941.
        1 reel (7 in.)   7 1/2 i.p.s.   phonotape.

            1. Germany - Foreign relations - Yugoslavia.
        2. Yugoslavia - Foreign relations - Germany.

Voice Lib.   ZIONISM
M864   Silver, Abba Hillel, 1893-1963.
        Portion of the principal address to the 2000 delegates of the
    51st annual convention of the Zionist Organization of America,
    held at Syria Mosque in Pittsburgh, Pa. Dr. Silver criticizes
    U. S. Government for its vascillating policies on the question
    of Palestine partition. Reviews the steps leading to the formation
    of Jewish homeland, culminating in a reversal of his policy by
    President Truman. KDKA, July 4, 1948
        1 reel (7 in.)   7 1/2 i.p.s.   phonotape.

            1. Zionism. 2. U. S. - Foreign relations - Israel.
        3. Israel - Foreign relations - U. S.

Voice Lib.
M1257 Ysaye, Lisa
bd.3   Various German poems narrated by the author.
    Reeves SS, 1937.
        1 reel (7 in.)   7 1/2 in. per sec.
    phonotape.

        CONTENTS.-Mein Prinz aus Traumland; 2.
    Er schrieb ihr einst; 3. Andante; 4. Ich
    bin eine junge Koenigin; 5. Es war die
    Koenigin von Brabane; 6. Lisette.

        1. German poetry (Collections)

Voice Lib.
M344   Zorin, Valerian Alexandrovich, 1902-
bd.6   Interpreter's translation of his
    reply to Adlai Stevenson on issue of
    Red China membership in U.N.   CBS,
    December 1, 1961.
        1 reel (7 in.)   7 1/2 i.p.s.   phonotape.

        1. United Nations - Membership.

Voice Lib.
M805   ZAIRE - POLITICS AND GOVERNMENT
bd.8   Stevenson, Adlai Ewing, 1900-1965.
        Speaking about the Congo situation;
    outbreak of rioting of African visitors
    until session is suspended; galleries
    ordered cleared.   U.N. Archives [n.d.]
        10 min., 26 sec.   phonotape (1 r.
    7 1/2 i.p.s.)

        On United Nations Special Tape no. 1.

        1. Zaire - Politics and government.

Voice Lib.
M344   Zorin, Valerian Alexandrovich, 1902-
bd.1   U.N. interpreter's translation on
    temporary agreement by the Soviet Union to
    accept U Thant as Secretary General.   CBS,
    November 3, 1961.
        1 reel (7 in.)   7 1/2 in. per sec.
    phonotape.

        1. Thant, U, 1909-   2. United Nations.

Voice Lib.
M952   Zeppelin, Ferdinand Adolf August Heinrich,
bd.6   graf von, 1838-1917.
        Statement by Count von Zeppelin.
    H.E. Scholz, 1908.
        1 reel (7 in.)   7 1/2 in. per sec.
    phonotape.